Nineteenth-Century Literature Criticism

Guide to Gale Literary Criticism Series

For criticism on	Consult these Gale series
Authors now living or who died after December 31, 1999	*CONTEMPORARY LITERARY CRITICISM (CLC)*
Authors who died between 1900 and 1999	*TWENTIETH-CENTURY LITERARY CRITICISM (TCLC)*
Authors who died between 1800 and 1899	*NINETEENTH-CENTURY LITERATURE CRITICISM (NCLC)*
Authors who died between 1400 and 1799	*LITERATURE CRITICISM FROM 1400 TO 1800 (LC)* *SHAKESPEAREAN CRITICISM (SC)*
Authors who died before 1400	*CLASSICAL AND MEDIEVAL LITERATURE CRITICISM (CMLC)*
Authors of books for children and young adults	*CHILDREN'S LITERATURE REVIEW (CLR)*
Dramatists	*DRAMA CRITICISM (DC)*
Poets	*POETRY CRITICISM (PC)*
Short story writers	*SHORT STORY CRITICISM (SSC)*
Literary topics and movements	*HARLEM RENAISSANCE: A GALE CRITICAL COMPANION (HR)* *THE BEAT GENERATION: A GALE CRITICAL COMPANION (BG)*
Asian American writers of the last two hundred years	*ASIAN AMERICAN LITERATURE (AAL)*
Black writers of the past two hundred years	*BLACK LITERATURE CRITICISM (BLC)* *BLACK LITERATURE CRITICISM SUPPLEMENT (BLCS)*
Hispanic writers of the late nineteenth and twentieth centuries	*HISPANIC LITERATURE CRITICISM (HLC)* *HISPANIC LITERATURE CRITICISM SUPPLEMENT (HLCS)*
Native North American writers and orators of the eighteenth, nineteenth, and twentieth centuries	*NATIVE NORTH AMERICAN LITERATURE (NNAL)*
Major authors from the Renaissance to the present	*WORLD LITERATURE CRITICISM, 1500 TO THE PRESENT (WLC)* *WORLD LITERATURE CRITICISM SUPPLEMENT (WLCS)*

ISSN 0732-1864

Volume 145

Nineteenth-Century Literature Criticism

Criticism of the
Works of Novelists, Philosophers, and Other
Creative Writers Who Died between 1800
and 1899, from the First Published Critical
Appraisals to Current Evaluations

Russel Whitaker
Project Editor

THOMSON

GALE

Detroit • New York • San Francisco • San Diego • New Haven, Conn. • Waterville, Maine • London • Munich

Nineteenth-Century Literature Criticism, Vol. 145

Project Editor
Russel Whitaker

Editorial
Jessica Bomarito, Kathy D. Darrow, Jeffrey W. Hunter, Jelena O. Krstović, Michelle Lee, Ellen McGeagh, Joseph Palmisano, Linda Pavlovski, Thomas J. Schoenberg, Lawrence J. Trudeau

Data Capture
Francis Monroe, Gwen Tucker

Indexing Services
Sue Kelsch

Rights and Acquisitions
Margaret Abendroth, Margaret Chamberlain, Lori Hines

Imaging and Multimedia
Dean Dauphinais, Robert Duncan, Leitha Etheridge-Sims, Lezlie Light, Michael Logusz, Dan Newell, Kelly A. Quin, Denay Wilding

Composition and Electronic Capture
Kathy Sauer

Manufacturing
Rhonda Williams

Product Manager
Janet Witalec

LIBRARY OF CONGRESS CATALOG CARD NUMBER 84-643008

ISBN 0-7876-8629-8
ISSN 0732-1864

Printed in the United States of America
10 9 8 7 6 5 4 3 2 1

Contents

Preface vii

Acknowledgments xi

Literary Criticism Series Advisory Board xiii

Preface

Since its inception in 1981, *Nineteeth-Century Literature Criticism* (*NCLC*) has been a valuable resource for students and librarians seeking critical commentary on writers of this transitional period in world history. Designated an "Outstanding Reference Source" by the American Library Association with the publication of is first volume, *NCLC* has since been purchased by over 6,000 school, public, and university libraries. The series has covered more than 450 authors representing 33 nationalities and over 17,000 titles. No other reference source has surveyed the critical reaction to nineteenth-century authors and literature as thoroughly as *NCLC*.

Scope of the Series

NCLC is designed to introduce students and advanced readers to the authors of the nineteenth century and to the most significant interpretations of these authors' works. The great poets, novelists, short story writers, playwrights, and philosophers of this period are frequently studied in high school and college literature courses. By organizing and reprinting commentary written on these authors, *NCLC* helps students develop valuable insight into literary history, promotes a better understanding of the texts, and sparks ideas for papers and assignments. Each entry in *NCLC* presents a comprehensive survey of an author's career or an individual work of literature and provides the user with a multiplicity of interpretations and assessments. Such variety allows students to pursue their own interests; furthermore, it fosters an awareness that literature is dynamic and responsive to many different opinions.

Every fourth volume of *NCLC* is devoted to literary topics that cannot be covered under the author approach used in the rest of the series. Such topics include literary movements, prominent themes in nineteenth-century literature, literary reaction to political and historical events, significant eras in literary history, prominent literary anniversaries, and the literatures of cultures that are often overlooked by English-speaking readers.

NCLC continues the survey of criticism of world literature begun by Thomson Gale's *Contemporary Literary Criticism* (*CLC*) and *Twentieth-Century Literary Criticism* (*TCLC*).

Organization of the Book

An *NCLC* entry consists of the following elements:

- The **Author Heading** cites the name under which the author most commonly wrote, followed by birth and death dates. Also located here are any name variations under which an author wrote, including transliterated forms for authors whose native languages use nonroman alphabets. If the author wrote consistently under a pseudonym, the pseudonym will be listed in the author heading and the author's actual name given in parenthesis on the first line of the biographical and critical information. Uncertain birth or death dates are indicated by question marks. Single-work entries are preceded by a heading that consists of the most common form of the title in English translation (if applicable) and the original date of composition.

- The **Introduction** contains background information that introduces the reader to the author, work, or topic that is the subject of the entry.

- A **Portrait of the Author** is included when available.

- The list of **Principal Works** is ordered chronologically by date of first publication and lists the most important works by the author. The genre and publication date of each work is given. In the case of foreign authors whose works have been translated into English, the list will focus primarily on twentieth-century translations, selecting those works most commonly considered the best by critics. Unless otherwise indicated, dramas are dated by first performance, not first publication. Lists of **Representative Works** by different authors appear with topic entries.

- Reprinted **Criticism** is arranged chronologically in each entry to provide a useful perspective on changes in critical evaluation over time. The critic's name and the date of composition or publication of the critical work are given at the beginning of each piece of criticism. Unsigned criticism is preceded by the title of the source in which it appeared. All titles by the author featured in the text are printed in boldface type. Footnotes are reprinted at the end of each essay or excerpt. In the case of excerpted criticism, only those footnotes that pertain to the excerpted texts are included. Criticism in topic entries is arranged chronologically under a variety of subheadings to facilitate the study of different aspects of the topic.

- A complete **Bibliographical Citation** of the original essay or book precedes each piece of criticism.

- Critical essays are prefaced by brief **Annotations** explicating each piece.

- An annotated bibliography of **Further Reading** appears at the end of each entry and suggests resources for additional study. In some cases, significant essays for which the editors could not obtain reprint rights are included here. Boxed material following the further reading list provides references to other biographical and critical sources on the author in series published by Thomson Gale.

Indexes

Each volume of *NCLC* contains a **Cumulative Author Index** listing all authors who have appeared in a wide variety of reference sources published by Thomson Gale, including *NCLC*. A complete list of these sources is found facing the first page of the Author Index. The index also includes birth and death dates and cross references between pseudonyms and actual names.

A **Cumulative Nationality Index** lists all authors featured in *NCLC* by nationality, followed by the number of the *NCLC* volume in which their entry appears.

A **Cumulative Topic Index** lists the literary themes and topics treated in the series as well as in *Classical and Medieval Literature Criticism, Literature Criticism from 1400 to 1800, Twentieth-Century Literary Criticism,* and the *Contemporary Literary Criticism* Yearbook, which was discontinued in 1998.

An alphabetical **Title Index** accompanies each volume of *NCLC*, with the exception of the Topics volumes. Listings of titles by authors covered in the given volume are followed by the author's name and the corresponding page numbers where the titles are discussed. English translations of foreign titles and variations of titles are cross-referenced to the title under which a work was originally published. Titles of novels, dramas, nonfiction books, and poetry, short story, or essay collections are printed in italics, while individual poems, short stories, and essays are printed in roman type within quotation marks.

In response to numerous suggestions from librarians, Thomson Gale also produces an annual paperbound edition of the *NCLC* cumulative title index. This annual cumulation, which alphabetically lists all titles reviewed in the series, is available to all customers. Additional copies of this index are available upon request. Librarians and patrons will welcome this separate index; it saves shelf space, is easy to use, and is recyclable upon receipt of the next edition.

Citing *Nineteenth-Century Literature Criticism*

When citing criticism reprinted in the Literary Criticism Series, students should provide complete bibliographic information so that the cited essay can be located in the original print or electronic source. Students who quote directly from reprinted criticism may use any accepted bibliographic format, such as University of Chicago Press style or Modern Language Association style.

The examples below follow recommendations for preparing a bibliography set forth in *The Chicago Manual of Style,* 14th ed. (Chicago: The University of Chicago Press, 1993); the first example pertains to material drawn from periodicals, the second to material reprinted from books:

Guerard, Albert J. "On the Composition of Dostoevsky's *The Idiot.*" *Mosaic: A Journal for the Interdisciplinary Study of Literature* 8, no. 1 (fall 1974): 201-15. Reprinted in *Nineteenth-Century Literature Criticism.* Vol. 119, edited by Lynn M. Zott, 81-104. Detroit: Gale, 2003.

Berstein, Carol L. "Subjectivity as Critique and the Critique of Subjectivity in Keats's *Hyperion.*" In *After the Future: Postmodern Times and Places,* edited by Gary Shapiro, 41-52. Albany, N. Y.: State University of New York Press, 1990. Reprinted in *Nineteenth-Century Literature Criticism.* Vol. 121, edited by Lynn M. Zott, 155-60. Detroit: Gale, 2003.

The examples below follow recommendations for preparing a works cited list set forth in the *MLA Handbook for Writers of Research Papers,* 5th ed. (New York: The Modern Language Association of America, 1999); the first example pertains to material drawn from periodicals, the second to material reprinted from books:

Guerard, Albert J. "On the Composition of Dostoevsky's *The Idiot.*" *Mosaic: A Journal for the Interdisciplinary Study of Literature* 8. 1 (fall 1974): 201-15. Reprinted in *Nineteenth-Century Literature Criticism.* Ed. Lynn M. Zott. Vol. 119. Detroit: Gale, 2003. 81-104.

Berstein, Carol L. "Subjectivity as Critique and the Critique of Subjectivity in Keats's *Hyperion.*" *After the Future: Postmodern Times and Places.* Ed. Gary Shapiro. Albany, N. Y.: State University of New York Press, 1990. 41-52. Reprinted in *Nineteeth-Century Literature Criticism.* Ed. Lynn M. Zott. Vol. 121. Detroit: Gale, 2003. 155-60.

Suggestions are Welcome

Readers who wish to suggest new features, topics, or authors to appear in future volumes, or who have other suggestions or comments are cordially invited to call, write, or fax the Product Manager:

Product Manager, Literary Criticism Series
Thomson Gale
27500 Drake Road
Farmington Hills, MI 48331-3535
1-800-347-4253 (GALE)
Fax: 248-699-8054

Acknowledgments

The editors wish to thank the copyright holders of the criticism included in this volume and the permissions managers of many book and magazine publishing companies for assisting us in securing reproduction rights. We are also grateful to the staffs of the Detroit Public Library, the Library of Congress, the University of Detroit Mercy Library, Wayne State University Purdy/Kresge Library Complex, and the University of Michigan Libraries for making their resources available to us. Following is a list of the copyright holders who have granted us permission to reproduce material in this volume of *NCLC*. Every effort has been made to trace copyright, but if omissions have been made, please let us know.

COPYRIGHTED MATERIAL IN *NCLC*, VOLUME 145, WAS REPRODUCED FROM THE FOLLOWING PERIODICALS:

COPYRIGHTED MATERIAL IN *NCLC*, VOLUME 145, WAS REPRODUCED FROM THE FOLLOWING BOOKS:

Thomson Gale Literature Product Advisory Board

The members of the Thomson Gale Literature Product Advisory Board—reference librarians from public and academic library systems—represent a cross-section of our customer base and offer a variety of informed perspectives on both the presentation and content of our literature products. Advisory board members assess and define such quality issues as the relevance, currency, and usefulness of the author coverage, critical content, and literary topics included in our series; evaluate the layout, presentation, and general quality of our printed volumes; provide feedback on the criteria used for selecting authors and topics covered in our series; provide suggestions for potential enhancements to our series; identify any gaps in our coverage of authors or literary topics, recommending authors or topics for inclusion; analyze the appropriateness of our content and presentation for various user audiences, such as high school students, undergraduates, graduate students, librarians, and educators; and offer feedback on any proposed changes/enhancements to our series. We wish to thank the following advisors for their advice throughout the year.

William Bartram
1739-1823

American naturalist, essayist, and travel writer.

INTRODUCTION

Bartram was an eighteenth-century American naturalist and explorer who spent four years classifying the flora and fauna and chronicling his adventures in the uncharted wilderness of the southeastern region of the United States. This region now comprises North and South Carolina, Georgia, Florida, Alabama, Mississippi, Louisiana, and Tennessee. Collected in Bartram's *Travels* (1791), these insights present a unique combination of scientific inquiry, exotic travelogue, and religious fervor. Written in a florid, exuberant prose style, the work fired the imagination of countless European readers who had a romantic notion of life on the American frontier and influenced the pastoral imagery employed by such Romantic poets as Samuel Taylor Coleridge, William Wordsworth, and Robert Southey. The *Travels* is now recognized as an important historical and cultural work which documents an untrammeled American landscape prior to its settlement and development.

BIOGRAPHICAL INFORMATION

Bartram was born February 9, 1739, near Philadelphia, Pennsylvania. He was the son of the celebrated botanist, John Bartram, who had cultivated the first Botanic Garden in North America and who had established a thriving commercial business selling rare and exotic plants and seeds to horticulturists in Europe. Early on, William demonstrated an interest similar to his father's in botany and scientific discovery. He accompanied his father on several horticultural expeditions into the frontier region where he nurtured his skill at sketching images of the plants and animals that they discovered in the region. Despite his skill at drawing natural objects and his interest in botany, Bartram did not distinguish himself in his formal education at the Philadelphia Academy. By 1756, the elder Bartram had removed William from school and placed him in the apprenticeship of a Philadelphia merchant. Demonstrating a growing restlessness, Bartram did not remain an apprentice for long, nor did he accept the offer of family friend, Benjamin Franklin, to become an apprentice in his engraving business. In 1761, with the financial backing of his uncle, Colonel William Bartram, Bartram opened up

a trading depot at Cape Fear, North Carolina. This venture lasted a few years before failing. To ameliorate Bartram's losses, his father offered him a position on his imminent scientific expedition to the Florida territory which recently had been acquired by the British in the Peace of Paris of 1763. After the expedition, Bartram decided to remain in Florida and start an indigo and rice plantation. Like the Cape Fear venture, this enterprise failed, leaving him in desperate financial straits. In these years of uncertainty, Bartram worked on the family farm and considered other business ventures in North Carolina and Florida.

In 1772, Bartram received a commission from English botanist and family friend, Dr. John Fothergill, to explore southeastern American territories and produce specimens, seeds, and drawings of the rare and exotic plants of the region. This expedition, which lasted from 1773 until 1777, formed the basis for Bartram's *Travels*. Despite the scientific success of Bartram's wilderness adventure, the onset of the Revolutionary War interrupted the exchange of horticultural specimens for his financial backing. Further, Bartram had contracted a fever in Alabama which permanently impaired his eyesight. In 1777, he returned to Philadelphia where he convalesced and helped maintain the family gardens. Largely due to his extended foray into the Florida wilderness, Bartram had established a reputation akin to his father's as one of America's foremost botanists. In 1782, he was offered a position as professor of botany at the University of Pennsylvania, but he declined due to his poor health. Four years later, he was elected to the American Philosophical Society, an organization which had been founded by his father and Franklin, among others. In 1791, after some fifteen years of collection and revision, Bartram published his *Travels.* The work extended his fame from America to Europe where it became an immediate success in England before being translated into German, Dutch, and French. Bartram spent his later years corresponding and consulting with other scientists in the botanical community. In the early nineteenth century, President Thomas Jefferson offered him a position on the Lewis and Clark expedition to explore the Louisiana territory, but once again poor health forced Bartram to decline. Instead, he stayed home and helped to cultivate the family Botanical Garden. Bartram died while walking in his garden on July 22, 1823.

MAJOR WORKS

Bartram's *Travels* has been viewed as a product of the confluence of the eighteenth-century Enlightenment pursuit of rational, scientific order, and the imminent nineteenth-century Romantic concept of the sublime beauty of nature. While it was Bartram's objective to catalogue and classify all manner of flora, fauna, and terrain with an eye toward the future exploitation and agricultural utilization of the land, nevertheless he was repeatedly overcome by a wondrous joy at each new discovery in the uncharted wilderness. Further, Bartram's passion was underscored by his Pennsylvania Quaker upbringing in which one identifies the omniscient role of God the Creator in all that occurs in the natural world. As a result, Bartram's rational observations about such natural phenomena as the complex symmetric shapes of plants and the instinctive habits of animals are always tempered by the reminder that God's hand in the natural order is an act which can only elicit incomprehensible wonder in humans. But such an abject faith in God's work also reveals an ominous undercurrent which runs throughout the *Travels.* The book abounds with images of hunting and warfare which characterize the wilderness as an environment of incessant conflict. Whether he is documenting his struggle for survival against Florida alligators, the eating habits of spiders, or the hostile relations between white settlers and native Indians, Bartram's idealistic descriptions of the wilderness as an Edenic paradise are leavened by the fact that a closer examination of nature reveals it to be a violent, inhospitable place.

CRITICAL RECEPTION

Although it was initially intended to be a scientific report to Bartram's patron, Dr. Fothergill, the *Travels* quickly became a classic in the burgeoning literary traditions of American naturalism and travel literature. Bartram's graphic and eloquent descriptions of the unspoiled and forbidding American wilderness excited countless leisure readers across Europe. Physical scientists were drawn to his detailed identification and classification of theretofore unknown plants and animals. Indeed, Bartram's compilation of some 215 native birds was at that time the most comprehensive documentation of the species. In the centuries since its publication, the *Travels* has endured as an important scientific, literary, and historical record of the southeastern United States prior to its settlement and development. N. Bryllion Fagin has focused on Bartram's artistic approach to writing the *Travels,* maintaining that the author's rhapsodic literary style and exuberant enthusiasm vitalizes his descriptions with a painter's eye for graphic detail. Robert D. Arner has identified several dichotomies in the thematic structure of the work—such as poetry and science, wilderness and civilization, cultivated land and pristine nature—which reveal Bartram's ambivalence about his project. Bruce Silver has discussed Bartram's careful examination of nature without the modern limitation of imposing a strict level of impartiality on his observations, concluding that the author's insights—suffused with religious, aesthetic, and utilitarian convictions—give his descriptions a compelling philosophical dimension. Several commentators have analyzed the influence of prominent eighteenth-century concepts in Bartram's *Travels.* While Hugh Moore has noted the remarkable fusion of Romantic and Rationalist ideas in the work, John Seelye has pointed out the author's wholehearted belief in the divine providence of nature. In recent years, scholars have underscored these philosophical and religious sentiments in the *Travels.* Pamela Regis has demonstrated how Bartram employed two distinct descriptive techniques—the identification of natural history and the presentation of sublime beauty—to reveal two complementary aspects of creation. In addition, Charles H. Adams has interpreted Bartram as an ironist who recognizes in his natural discoveries the transience and insignificance of humankind in the long history of the planet. Further, Thomas P. Slaughter has asserted that Bartram adopts the persona of "philosophical pilgrim" who has a revelation that all of nature is collectively infused with God's spirit. According to the critic, this realization creates a tension in Bartram between his utilitarian desire to see the cultivation of nature and his teleological belief that God's creation should remain unspoiled.

PRINCIPAL WORKS

Travels through North & South Carolina, Georgia, East & West Florida, the Cherokee country, the extensive territories of the Muscogulges, or Creek Confederacy, and the country of the Chactaws (prose) 1791; also published as *Travels of William Bartram: Naturalist's Edition* [enlarged edition] 1958

"Observations on the Creek and Cherokee Indians, 1789" (essay) 1853

*Travels in Georgia and Florida, 1773-74: A Report to Dr. John Fothergill (prose) 1943

*This is an official report on the expedition that also produced Bartram's prose work *Travels.*

CRITICISM

N. Bryllion Fagin (essay date 1933)

SOURCE: Fagin, N. Bryllion. "The Art of Bartram." In *William Bartram: Interpreter of the American Landscape,* pp. 101-123. Baltimore: The Johns Hopkins Press, 1933.

[*In the following excerpt, Fagin provides an important reassessment of Bartram's* Travels, *noting unique stylistic techniques and describing underpinnings of his philosophy. Fagin also briefly notes the influences on Bartram as well as the effect he had on later writers.*]

Throughout this study Bartram's "style" has received incidental mention. This has been inevitable because of the amount of attention it has attracted from both literary and scientific commentators. English reviewers noted his "luxuriant and poetical" language; Carlyle enjoyed his "wondrous kind of floundering eloquence"; Zimmermann, in translating the *Travels,* corrected his "poetischen Floskeln";[1] Squier insisted on retaining "the antiquated and somewhat quaint phraseology and style of the author"[2] of the **"Observations"**; Miss Dondore was impressed by his "luxuriant detail";[3] a modern American reviewer has been pleased by his "lush descriptions";[4] and Tracy has found his language "rhetorical," not, however, without at the same time being aware of the prime virtue of Bartram's art, his "genuine sensitiveness" to all the aspects of nature.[5]

It is this sensitiveness that nourishes Bartram's art and stamps his reactions to nature with originality. His style may derive partly from the conventional nature notations of his time, but his senses are acute and his sensations genuine. His love of nature transcends the occasionally stilted diction in which it is expressed and infuses his writings with an infectious enthusiasm. Imperceptibly, what begins by sounding as bombast, soon establishes itself as native exuberance. Alexander Wilson acknowledged that he had caught this enthusiasm from Bartram, when he wrote:

> I confess that I was always an enthusiast in my admiration of the rural scenery of nature; but since your example and encouragement have set me to attempt to imitate her productions, I see new beauties in every bird, plant, or flower I contemplate.[6]

And we today must acknowledge that it is Bartram's enthusiasm, exuberance, or gusto which vitalizes his landscape and compels us to sense it is an immediate experience. The record of his sense impressions is not only genuine, accurate, and varied, but it is shot through with poetic coloring, which, while it never distorts, adds a touch of the glamorous to his descriptions.

One form of the glamorous, imparted by his enthusiasm, is a frequent lapse into sheer rhapsody. As a consequence, his visual impressions, which are for the most part carefully and temperately expressed, occasionally become fervent and exclamatory. A sunrise inspires him to such a passage as the following:

> Behold how gracious and beneficent smiles the roseate morn! now the sun arises and fills the plains with light, his glories appear on the forests, encompassing the meadows, and gild the top of the terebinthine Pine and exalted Palms, now gently rustling by the pressure of the waking breezes: the music of the seraphic crane resounds in the skies, in separate squadrons they sail, encircling their precincts, slowly descend beating the dense air, and alight on the green dewy verge of the expansive lake; its surface yet smoking with the grey ascending mists, which, condensed aloft in clouds of vapour, are born away by the morning breezes and at last gradually vanish on the distant horizon.
>
> (pp. 245-246)

A forest scene makes him exclaim:

> Behold yon promontory, projecting far into the great river, beyond the still lagoon, half a mile distance from me, what a magnificent grove arises, on its banks! how glorious the Palm! how majestically stands the Laurel, its head forming a perfect cone! its dark green foliage, seems silvered over with milkwhite flowers. They are so large, as to be distinctly visible at the distance of a mile or more.
>
> (p. 85)

The rhapsodist is, of course, never entirely separated from the scientist, and frequently his style is a combination of botany and poetry:

> What sylvan scene is here! the pompous Magnolia, reigns sovereign of the forests; how sweet the aromatic Illisium groves? how gaily flutters the radiated wings of the Magnolia auriculata? each branch supporting an

expanded umbrella superbly crested with a sliver plume, fragrant blossom, or crimson studded strobile and fruits! I recline on the verdant bank, and view the beauties of the groves, Aesculus pavia, Prunus memoralis, floribus racemosis, ...

(pp. 407-408)

Nor are his reactions to sound, on occasion, less ecstatic. This is his notation of evening sounds:

How harmonious and soothing is this native sylvan music now at still evening! inexpressibly tender are the responsive cooings of the innocent dove, in the fragrant Zanthoxilon groves, and the variable and tuneful warblings of the nonpareil; with the more sprightly and elevated strains of the blue linnet and golden icterus; this is indeed harmony even amidst the incessant croaking of the frogs; the shades of silent night are made more chearful, with the shrill voice of the whip-poor-will and active mock-bird. . . .

(p. 154)

And this of running water:

How harmonious and sweetly murmur the purling rills and fleeting brooks, roving along the shadowy vales, passing through the dark, subterranean caverns, or dashing over steep rocky precipices, ...

(p. 322)

But Bartram's descriptions of sound need special emphasis. They are set down with such skill that their impression upon the Romantic poets of his time is not surprising. They are varied enough to include the gentle cooing of doves and the violent roaring of tempests. He hears the lapping of the surf; "the heavy tread of some animal" at night, "the dry limbs of trees upon the ground" cracking "under his feet" (p. 158); the "social prattling coot" and "the squeeling water-hen" (p. 159); the "languishing softness and melancholy air in the Indian convivial songs" (p. 245); "the whooping of owls, screaming bitterns . . . the wood-rats running amongst the leaves" (p. 124); the "various languages, cries, and fluttering" of birds. He hears the different noises of frogs: that of "the largest frog known in Florida," which resembles "the grunting of a swine"; that of the bell frog, which "seems clamorous and disgusting"; that of the green frog, which "exactly resembles the barking of little dogs, or the yelping of puppies," that of "a less green frog," whose notes are remarkably like that of young chickens"; and that of the shad frog, from whose noise "at some distance one would be almost persuaded that there were assemblies of men in serious debate" (pp. 276-78). And, of course, there is the noise of the alligators. He hears them "plunging and roaring" (p. 88); he hears "the horrid noise of their closing jaws" (p. 123), a "surprising" noise, "like that which is made by forcing a heavy plank with violence upon the ground" (p. 129). It is not at all surprising to find that Coleridge copied into his Note Book the climax of Bartram's description of "the incredible loud and terrifying roar," which

resembles very heavy distant thunder, not only shaking the air and waters, but causing the earth to tremble; and when hundreds and thousands are roaring at the same time, you can scarcely be persuaded, but that the whole globe is violently and dangerously agitated.

(p. 129)

Bartram, as will soon be shown, saw nature principally as a painter, and his writings are consequently rich in visual descriptions. Yet his sensitiveness to sound—which has just been indicated—was only slightly less remarkable, and any extensive study of his art cannot ignore his notation of gustatory, tactile, and olfactory sensations. He notes the "aromatic flavour" and bitter taste of the palmetto royal tree (p. 72); the "sweet and agreeable" taste of the live oak acorn, from which "the Indians obtain . . . a sweet oil, which they use in the cooking of hommony, rice, & c. . . ." (p. 85); the "most disagreeable taste . . . brassy and vitriolic" of a hot spring (p. 145); the "gratifying" taste of oranges (p. 200); the "sweet and pleasant eating . . . like chesnuts" of the *Nymphaea Nelumbo* (p. 409). To be sure, some of these taste descriptions are the observations of a scientist, exact statements of the properties of plants such as one finds in a botanical dictionary. Yet such adjectives as "agreeable," "gratifying," and "pleasant" are purely subjective and add an emotional coloring to Bartram's scientific notations. Tactile sensations are suggested by the "silky hair" of a spider (p. xxix); the "fine . . . downy pubescence of a *rhododendron* (p. 336); the "hard . . . couch" on which he reclined at night (p. 50); the "tepid" water of a spring (p. 145); the "sandy beach, hard and firm by the beating surf" (p. 157); "humid rocks" and "smooth pebbles"; the sting of burning flies, "no less ocute than a prick from a red-hot needle, or a spark of fire on the skin" (p. 385). He records the smell of "sweet scented flowers" (p. xxviii); of vegetation "breathing fragrance every where" (p. 34); the breeze "perfumed by the fragrant breath of the superb . . . White Lily" (p. 59); the "offensive smell" of a geyser (p. 145); "odoriferous Illisium [Illicium?] groves" (p. 160); the "fragrant red strawberry" (p. 344). Sometimes he notes several sensations at the same time: thus the orange groves are "loaded with both green and ripe fruit and embellished with their fragrant bloom, gratifying the taste, the sight, and the smell at the same instant" (p. 200), and "the pericarpium and berries [of the laurel magnolia] possess an agreeable spicy scent, and an aromatic bitter taste. The wood when seasoned is of straw colour, compact, and harder and firmer, than that of the Poplar . . ." (p. 86).

To Bartram's notations of sight, sound, smell, taste, and touch reactions, must be added his perception of mass and motion. For Bartram's descriptions are seldom static. He is constantly on the move, hence the woods and fields and promontories are perceived as passing by. He speaks of the "alternate appearance and recess of the coast, whilst the far distant blue hills slowly retreat and disappear; or, as we approach the coast, the capes and promontories first strike our sight, emerging from the water expanse, and like mighty giants, elevating their crests towards the skies . . ." (p. 3). He speaks of "squadrons" of birds and "nations" of birds and "tribes" of birds, of "flocks" of turkeys and "communities" of cranes, of "squadrons" and "troops" and "parties" of horses, of "droves" of cattle, of "herds" of deer, of "bands" and "armies" of fish, of "companies" of traders and "companies of young innocent Cherokee virgins," of "masses" and "groups" of rocks, of "extensive" forests and "extensive" savannas. And these masses are usually dynamic, in motion: the birds are in flight, the horses frolic in the fields or are being driven to market, the cattle graze, the deer take fright and scamper away into the woods, the fish swim, the traders go to town, the Cherokee virgins prick strawberries, and even the rocks and the forests approach or recede as Bartram travels from or toward them. His rivulets "glide in serpentine mazes," his creeks are "brisk-flowing" and his rivers run "with foaming rapidity." There is perpetual change and flux in his landscape. The flowers are in the very act of "painting the coves with a rich and cheerful scenery, continually unfolding new prospects as I traverse the shores; the towering mountains seem continually in motion as I pass along, pompously rising their superb crests towards the lofty skies, traversing the far distant horizon" (p. 346).

The rhapsodic element which Bartram's record of his sense impressions often contains is mingled with an emotion deeper than mere aesthetic enthusiasm, a sensation of awe and sublimity. The vastness of the landscape evokes a feeling of grandeur, of magnitude, of majesty, so that the air of exuberance which pervades his descriptions is not merely a physical quality but is a more subtle and spiritual emotion. He discerns "few objects out at sea . . . but what are sublime, awful, and majestic . . ." (p. 2). Standing on the shore he notes "how awfully great and sublime is the majestic scene . . . !" (p. 61). A forest of pine trees continuing for five or six miles is "sublime." A tempest exhibits "a very awful scene." In high, projecting promontories he sees "grandeur and sublimity." He approaches a vale and observes that it is situated "amidst sublimely high forests" and "awful shades!" (p. 343). He is struck "with a kind of awe, at beholding the stateliness of the trunk" of the *Cupressus disticha* tree (p. 96).

Bartram was no theorist in aesthetics, yet in regarding sublimity as a vital element in landscape he shows his kinship with the aestheticians of his time. "The Sublime," Hussey tells us, had been noted by Shaftesbury as "the highest order of scenery," but it was Edmund Burke who was "the first to recognize it as a category co-ordinate with the Beautiful."[7] Hussey could, of course, have gone back all the way to Longinus but it is true nevertheless that the eighteenth century saw the development of the idea of the Sublime as an element of beauty to a degree which previous centuries had not dreamed of. "Vastness," Hussey continues, "became on of the sublime qualities" in Burke's categories.[8] And vastness, it will be noted, is one of the qualities that strikes Bartram as "sublime," "awful," or "majestic." Thus he finds that an "ancient sublime forest . . . intersected with extensive savannas and far distant Rice plantations, captivates" his "senses by scenes of magnificence and grandeur" (*Travels*, p. 309). In fact, he is capable of losing himself in vastness, to the neglect of his business as a scientific observer, which requires minute and close attention to specific objects. Once, he confesses, standing on the top of a mountain whence he enjoyed "a view inexpressible magnificent and comprehensive," he became "wholly engaged in the contemplation of this magnificent landscape, infinitely varied, and without bound," until he realized that he was "insensible or regardless of the charming objects more within . . . reach: a new species of . . ." (pp. 335-6).

It has already been stated that aesthetically William Bartram saw nature with the eyes of a painter. It is important to note to what extent this is true and how this quality influenced his descriptions. He had an accurate eye for line and color; he copied nature: turtles, vines, flowers, birds. It was therefore logical enough that when he came to describe nature, using words instead of paints as his medium, the methods and habits of the painter should still persist. Always he sees his landscape with the painter's eye, and always he translates his visual impressions in terms of color, of lights and shades, using the concentrated impressionism and the economy of means of an artist painting a canvas. Moreover, it is quite clear that he knew paintings, had observed them not only with pleasure, but with a retentive memory. Speaking of the Snake Birds which he saw in the waters of Florida, he remarks, "I think I have seen paintings of them on the Chinese screens and other India pictures" (p. 132). Or, again, watching fish and crocodiles in a fountain he comments: "This amazing and delightful scene, though real, appears at first but as a piece of excellent painting; there seems no medium." Besides the language of the painter in this description, there is apparent his knowledge of perspective in the finishing touches of this scene: "You imagine the picture to be within a few inches of your eyes, and that you may without the least difficulty touch any one of the fish, or put your fingers upon the crocodile's eye, when it really is twenty or thirty feet under water" (p. 167).

Even more definite is his knowledge of painting and his use of painter's terms as disclosed by his writings on the Indians. An answer to one of the *Queries about Indians* contains the following remarks:

Like Egyptian mystical hieroglyphics—extremely caricature & picturesque. No chiaro scuro, yet bold outlines, natural. Most beautiful painting on bodies.[9]

A fuller answer to this or a similar query appears in the
"Observations," in which, among other things, he says:

I am sensible that these specimens of their paintings
will, to us, who have made such incomparable progress
and refinement in the arts and sciences, appear trifling
and ludicrous. . . . Most beautiful painting now to be
found among the Muscogulges is on the bodies of their
ancient chiefs or *micos,* breast, trunk, arms, thighs. . . .
Commonly the sun, moon, and planets occupy the
breast; zones or belts, or beautiful fanciful scrolls, wind
round the trunk of the body, thighs, arms, and legs, dividing the body into many fields or tablets, which are
ornamented or filled up with innumerable figures, as
representations of animals of the chase,—a sketch of a
landscape. . . . These paintings are admirably well executed and seem like *mezzotinto.* . . .[10]

To these comments must be added a passage from the
Travels:

The pillars and walls of the houses of the square are
decorated with various paintings and sculptures; which
I suppose to be hieroglyphic, and as an historic legendary of political and sacerdotal affairs: but they are extremely picturesque or caricature, as men in variety of
attitudes, some ludicrous enough, others having the
head of some kind of animal, as those of a duck, tur-
key, bear, fox, wolf, buck, &c. and again those kind of
creatures are represented having the human head. These
designs were not ill executed; the outlines bold, free,
and well proportioned.

(*Travels,* 455)

Seeing nature, then as Bartram often did, from the point
of view of a painter, his style has the linear and colorful
flow of pictorial art. He has the ability to vivify a scene
by means of a stroke here and a touch there. His descriptions abound in complete pictures—brilliant
flashes, crisp miniatures, and, once in a while, a sprawl-
ing canvas:

The little gold-fish instantly fled from every side, darting through the transparent waters like streams of lightning . . . .

(pp. 43-44)

The ultimate angle of the branchiostega [of the red-
belly fish] extends backwards with a long spatula, ending with a round, or oval particoloured spot, representing the eye in the long feathers of a peacock's train,
verged round with a thin flame-coloured membrane,
and appears like a brilliant ruby fixed on the side of the
fish. . . .

(p. 12)

They [the Snake Birds] delight to sit in little peaceable
communities, on the dry limbs of trees, hanging over
the still waters, with their wings and tails expanded, I

suppose to cool and air themselves, when at the same
time they behold their images in the watery mirror: at
such times, when we approach them, they drop off the
limbs into the water as if dead, and for a minute or two
are not to be seen; when on a sudden at a vast distance,
their long slender head and neck only appear, and have
very much the appearance of a snake, and no other part
of them is to be seen when swimming in the water, except sometimes the tip end of their tail. In the heat of
the day they are seen in great numbers, sailing very
high in the air, over lakes and rivers.

(p. 133)

The last passage is really a group of pictures, unmistakably of the type one is accustomed to call Japanese and
Chinese, and those Bartram, by his own admission, saw
"on the Chinese screens and other Indian pictures." An
even more representative example of Bartram's Chinese-
screen pictorial ability is his description of the wood
pelican. He devotes two paragraphs to this bird, and,
among other things, paints this sketch:

he stands alone on the topmost limb of tall dead Cypress trees, his neck contracted or drawn in upon his
shoulders, and beak resting like a long scythe upon his
breast: in this pensive posture and solitary situation,
they look extremely grave, sorrowful and melancholy,
as if in the deepest thought.[11]

(p. 150)

But the vividness of his art is not confined to descriptions of birds, fishes, or flowers. Phenomena of nature
receive the same bold treatment. Little of the grandeur
and power of the subtropical gales he observed fails to
be translated, as in the following description:

now the earth trembles under the peals of incessant distant thunder, the hurricane comes on roaring,[12] and I
am shocked again to life: I raise my head and rub open
my eyes, painted with gleams and flashes of lightning;
when just attempting to wake my afflicted brethren and
companions, almost overwhelmed with floods of rain,
the dark cloud opens over my head, developing a vast
river of the etherial fire;[12] I am instantly struck dumb,
inactive and benumbed; . . . .

(p. 386)

A quality in Bartram's artistry which deserves special
mention is his happy faculty of seizing upon the dominant trait of a particular scene or object and making it
impressive and memorable. This descriptive method can
best be designated by the French word "raccourci." By
means of it Bartram often reduces a long, diffuse passage into a single unforgettable sentence or phrase and
even when he begins his description with secondary aspects he can sum up its dominant impression, its distinctive character, in a "raccourci." The selective quality which such a method involves is of the highest
artistic order, as only essentials must be seized upon.
The frequency and ease with which Bartram employs
this method are ample proof that he was never at a loss

to detect the essence of a scene. Thus after describing an old champion alligator and his attitude toward the other alligators in the lake, Bartram writes: "He acts his part like an Indian chief when rehearsing his feats of war" (p. 130). Again, he compresses a long paragraph describing the sun fish into this vivid phrase: "a warrior in a gilded coat of mail" (p. 154). Or he finishes a description of the noise of frogs "uttered in chorus" with the striking comparison to "the rushing noise made by a vast quantity of gravel and pebbles together, at one precipitated from a height" (p. 278).

The diction of Bartram presents an interesting problem. It is a peculiar mixture. At times it is simple and straightforward, at other times it is stilted and florid. In the same paragraph, even in the same sentence, it may vary from austere clearness to overlush vagueness, from bare exposition to imagistic rhapsody. So that both the commentators who, like Carlyle have praised his style and those who, like Zimmermann, have condemned it can be said to have been justified according to their respective points of view; Carlyle liked Bartram's "eloquence," which he found in abundance, and Zimmermann, being a scientist, would have preferred Bartram's accurate observations without his rhapsodic overtones. The key to an understanding of Bartram's diction is, however, simple; it lies in a knowledge of his education, his reading, his Quaker upbringing, his scientific absorption, and his own personality, for, if ever style adequately expressed the man, Bartram's style surely and completely expressed Bartram. It is this complete self-expression of an interesting personality, of a man who could be "by turn enthusiastic, sober; dramatic, Idyllic; reflective, naive; diffusive, firm; redundant, precise,"[13] and, above all, natural, to which the vitality of his writings is due.

Bartram, as has been shown, was not highly educated. There is evidence that he attended the old college in Philadelphia and that for time Charles Thomson was his tutor. The value of this education of whether he received any other is not known. It may reasonably be assumed that most of what real knowledge Bartram possessed came to him through his own efforts, picked up in a desultory way. At any rate, he never quite mastered the English language for literary purposes. His grammar is often shaky and his construction sometimes beyond his abilities, defect which account for the numerous minor "improvements" made in the London and subsequent editions of the *Travels*. And even in the editions where his English has been corrected such sentences as the following are still to be found:

> indeed the musquitoes alone would have been abundantly sufficient to keep any creature awake that possessed their perfect senses.[14]

> his eyes red as burning coals, and his brandishing forked tongue of the colour of the hottest flame, con-

tinually menaces death and destruction, yet never strikes unless sure of his mark.[15]

> the sooty songs of Afric forgetting their bondage, in chorus sung. . . .[16]

Nor was Bartram's reading without its influence on his literary style. The poetic diction of his purple passages is the same as that commonly found in eighteenth-century English poetry. Echoes of Pope have already been noted; it is reasonable to suppose that Bartram read other eighteenth-century English poets and that they left their impress upon his mind. At any rate, his diction frequently is reminiscent of the worst of Thomson, Gray, Collins, Akenside. It has what Professor Havens has called the "elegant pseudo-classic" note and the "vicious 'poetic diction' which blighted English poetry for a century, worming its way into the work even of the best and most natural poets of the time, and giving to many excellent productions an affected and artificial tone."[17] Bartram speaks of "cool eve's approach," of "feathered songsters," and "of leafy coverts" (*Travels*, pp. 81-2); of "solitary groves and peaceful shades" (p. 140); of resuming his "sylvan pilgrimage" (p. 153); of "the glorious sovereign of day, calling in his bright emanations" and leaving "in his absence . . . the milder government . . . of the silver queen of night, attended by millions of brilliant luminaries" (p. 190); of "winged emigrants" celebrating their nuptials (p. 287); of "those moral virtues which grace and ornament the most approved and admired characters in civil society" (p. 310). His tendency towards periphrases is obvious. Zimmermann, who was interested in Bartram's scientific facts and not his style, found this tendency irksome and in his translation trimmed down many passages to simple statements. "Schade," he wrote of Bartram, "das er mit allen diesen Vorzügen nicht auch einen guten Style verbinded. . . . Das Publikum wird mir daher hoffentlich Dank wissen, dass ich ihm in der Uebersetzung lesbarer zu machen gesucht, und won dem Ueberflüssigen vieles weggestrichen, oder es doch sehr zusammen gezogen habe."[18] As an example of Zimmermann's attempt to make Bartram "lesbarer," a comparison of the following passage from the *Travels* with Zimmermann's translation of it is instructive:

> The glorious sovereign of day, cloathed in light refulgent, rolling on his gilded chariot, speeds to revisit the western realms. Grey pensive eve now admonishes us of gloomy night's hasty approach: I am roused by care to seek a place of secure repose, ere darkness comes on.
>
> (*Travels*, 50)

> Itzt kam der Abend heran, und erinnerte mich, einen sicheren Ruheort zu suchen.
>
> (*Reisen*, 53)

Along with the echoes of eighteenth-century poetic diction Bartram's style carries a coloring of biblical expression. He was brought up in an atmosphere of simple piety and reverence for God, in a home where the Bible was read regularly and religiously. To the very end of his life John Bartram exhorted his children to "Love God & one another; extend charity to the necessitous and mercy to the distressed."[19] William Bartram's writings echo these sentiments in almost identical terms. In his letter to his nephew, Dr. James Bartram, he urges him to "Fear and adore the Divinity" and to "be charitable . . . to the poor and distressed." In his petition on Negro slavery he admonishes his fellow citizens to "do justice," to show "mercy" and to "fear God." And throughout his *Travels* he speaks of the "glorious display of the Almighty hand," "the most acceptable incense we offer to the Almighty," ". . . our God, who in due time will shine forth in brightness," "universal Father . . . with an eye of pity and compassion," "the wisdom and power of the Supreme Creator," "thanksgiving to the Supreme Creator and preserver," "celestial endowments," "great altars and temples similar to the high places and sacred groves anciently amongst the Canaanites and other nations of Palestine and Judea." Some of his rhapsodic passages read like the spontaneous evocation of Quaker prayer, such, for instance, as the following:

> How glorious the powerful sun, minister of the Most High, in the rule and government of this earth, leaves our hemisphere, retiring from our sight beyond the western forests! I behold with gratitude his departing smiles, tinging the fleecy roseate clouds, now riding far away on the Eastern horizon; behold they vanish from sight in the azure skies!
>
> (*Travels,* 158)

It is in Bartram's scientific diction that the greatest measure of his originality is to be found. Tracy's statement that "The nature men have not given us new word-sets" but have only "used words in a new way"[20] is eminently true of Bartram. He has the faculty of welding together the most commonplace scientific nomenclature with the most gorgeous poetic imagery, so that ordinary vegetables and weeds and birds and snakes become glamorous objects of nature. Analyzed coldly this mixture of botany, ornithology, zoology, and poetry sometimes strikes one as somewhat ludicrous, even pathetic, as when he writes that "the vegetables smile in their blooming decorations and sparkling crystalline dew-drop" (*Travels,* 387), but read without any intent to dismember, Bartram's style soon begins to exert an effect which is far from unpleasant. Scientific term and poetic image merge perfectly, support and mellow each other, and create a mode of expression characteristic of the author-naturalist. Other botanical observers may have catalogued the following trees in the forest: "Fraxinus, Ulmus, Acer rubrum, Laurus Barbonia, Quercu dentata, Ilex aquafolium, Olea Americana, Morus, Gleditsia traicanthus, and . . . a species of Sapindus," but it is only Bartram who could add that the last species mentioned "spreads his brawny arms" and that the

Live Oaks "strive while young to be upon an equality with their neighbors . . . but the others at last prevail, and their proud heads are seen at a great distance . . ." (p. 84). The touch of imagination changes a dull catalogue into a vivid reality. Sometimes the artistic transformation is accomplished by the phrase which introduces the catalogue, as when he states that "At this rural retirement were assembled a charming circle of mountain vegetable beauties, Magnolia auriculata, Rhododendron ferruginium, Kalmia latifolia, . . ." (p. 342). The effect of this style upon the non-scientific reader can perhaps best be studied in the following comment of a modern reviewer of his *Travels*:

> To a common reader like myself who am a lover of plants and flowers rather than a botanist, the recurring scientific nomenclature of the volume proves at first disconcerting, forbidding. I am shocked and chagrined to find how few of my familiar friends I am able to recognize in this guise. I stumble over such technical terms as "cordated appendage" and "incarnate lobes" and wonder whether to continue. However, I can and do appreciate "sportive vegetables" and am encouraged to go on. For there is much that I would see in this long-desired book.
>
> Others have enjoyed it in spite of the obtruding nomenclature and so shall I. There is, I find, less of the technical than at first appears; or it may be that I become accustomed to it and learn that it does not matter. Names neither make nor mar the beauty of such a passage as. . . .
>
> . . . Did none of the volume's treasures escape the indefatigable Coleridge and Wordsworth? I seek in vain for such an omission—unless it be the "splendid fields of golden Oenothera" which I recognize as my friend the primrose.[21]

That Bartram's style is a perfect expression of his personality has already been suggested. Nature to Bartram was not cold and impersonal, but an object of love and reverence. All its manifestations partook of the miraculous. Nature was a vast unknown region for him to explore, but he did not stop with the accumulation of impersonal knowledge. His imagination played upon what he observed and drew personal meanings; it found beneath the surfaces a confirmation of the immanence of God and it delighted in the beauty of God's world. His exaltation carried him to rhapsodic exclamations and hyperbolic diction, but it also animated nature-description and imparted to it an imaginative glow. He abounds in such subjective epithets as "beautiful," "hideous," "disagreeable," "pleasant," "excellent," and in such superlatives as "incredible," "prodigious," "amazing," "magnificent," "intolerable," "extraordinary," "unparalleled," "exceedingly," and "irresistibly." The effect he is thus able to transmit is precisely what the effect of his travels was upon himself. It makes a reader in 1928 exclaim that "To be young was heaven for a naturalist in eighteenth-century America" and that "This is what the New World was like to a loving spirit, thrilled by nature, and conscious of beauty."[22] His "poetic diction," objectionable as it may be in the Classicist poets he read, is tolerable and at times not ineffectual in him, for it is not, in his case, "due to lack of imagination" or "to a lack of close observation of nature."[23] Bartram added both imagination and careful observation to nature description, and, above all, he is emotionally genuine and sincere. The fact is that while he was born and reared in the neo-classic period he came to maturity and did his writing in the period when Romantic tendencies were beginning to dominate. "Reason" and "rational" frequently appear in his pages, but also "imagination," "sublime," "sensibility." His very enthusiasm, his unrestrained enjoyment of nature, is what has come to be termed Romantic. Even his periphrases are not always the objectionable neo-classic circumlocution, "vague, unnatural, and mechanical . . . attempts to be elegant and poetical in an artificial way."[24] On the contrary, they are often imaginative and original attempts to convey an emotional response to the scene he describes. They are figurative evocations which transcribe not only the objects he saw but the mood which they engendered within him. Thus, to take a representative example, he translates his vision of the beating surf into a personification: "the dashing of yon liquid mountains, like mighty giants, in vain assail the skies; they are beaten back, and fall prostrate upon the shores of the trembling island" (*Travels*, 61). This is periphrastic description, to be sure, but it is founded upon accurate observation and effectively conveys the dramatic quality of the scene. Incidentally, the quotation at the same time indicates Bartram's sense of prose rhythm and his use of onomatopaeia and even alliteration—stylistic devices that come naturally to one whose sight is clear and whose emotion is genuine and spontaneous.

One other element in Bartram's art needs consideration, his narrative ability. The dynamic nature of his description has already been indicated, its movement and animation, but Bartram's gifts as a story-teller are largely responsible for this liveliness of his landscape. His *Travels* is primarily a narrative and Bartram never permits it to drag. His description is woven, in comparatively small increments, into the account of his movements and experiences. The very first three pages of his book take us from Philadelphia to South Carolina, and the rest of his account bristles with incidents, strange encounters, dramatic episodes, Indian legends, and complete short stories. His landscape ceases to be merely a colorful canvas spread before the eyes of a painter and becomes the background against which the heated spectacle of life is enacted. In spite of the apparent discursiveness of his narrative, Bartram has a directness of communication which springs from an instinctive perception of the dramatic elements of a situation. He selects his materials skillfully, knowing what to exclude, when to linger and when to move on.

In the course of his travels into the Indian territory he met many planters and traders. Their life is depicted not by long descriptions and speculations, but by sketching these men as he came in contact with them. He does not give a complete list of all his experiences and observations, but singles out a few of the numerous white people he has met and recounts a few episodes of their lives. Thus he tells us of the hospitality of the planters by recounting his reception at the plantation of Mr. McIntosh, who greeted him with the words: "Welcome, stranger; come in, and rest; the air is now very sultry; it is a very hot day," and of Mr. Bailey, who treated him "very civilly" (pp. 13, 15). Or he tells us of a friendly planter who housed him for three days while a storm raged outside, working "almost irreparable damages" everywhere in the neighborhood (p. 143). The life of the white traders among the Indians is pictured in a number of short stories. One of these tells of an unhappy trader "who had for a companion a very handsome Siminole young woman" who "dishonestly distributes amongst her savage relations . . . all his possessions," so that "he now endeavors to drown and forget his sorrows in deep draughts of brandy" (pp. 111-2). There is the incident of Mr. M'Latche who presumed to refuse credit to the proud Long Warrior, who thereupon threatened to command "the terrible thunder now rolling in the skies above, to descend upon your head, in rapid fiery shafts, and lay you prostrate at my feet" (pp. 258-59). And there is the story, already referred to, of the trader who had had an affair with the wife of an Indian chief and was threatened with having his ears cut off (pp. 447-8).

There are numerous incidents of encounters with Indians and in telling of these Bartram is able to arouse and maintain a suspense which indicates no mean narrative skill. His first description of meeting with an Indian alone in the forest is an apt illustration of his instinctive mastery of the narrative technique. Deftly he sketches in the setting: "It was drawing on towards the close of day, the skies serene and calm, the air temperately cool . . . the prospect around enchantingly varied and beautiful. . . ." Then comes the directness of his vision: ". . . on a sudden, an Indian appeared . . . armed with a rifle." Bartram's reaction to this threatening apparition, his endeavor to elude the Indian's sight by stopping and "keeping large trees between" them, at once sets the stage for a looming conflict. The antagonists take each other's measure, then the Indian "sat spurs to his horse, and came up on full gallop." The sentences that follow heighten the suspense, so that there is a genuine relief at the dénouement,

> I never before this was afraid at the sight of an Indian, but at this time I must own that my spirits were very much agitated: I saw at once, that being unarmed, I was in his power, and having now but a few moments to prepare, I resigned myself entirely to the will of the Almighty. . . . The intrepid Siminole stopped sud-

denly, three or four yards before me, and silently viewed me, his countenance angry and fierce, shifting his rifle from shoulder to shoulder and looking about instantly on all sides. I advanced towards him, and with an air of confidence offered him my hand, hailing him, brother; at this he hastily jerked back his arm, with a look of malice, rage, and disdain, seeming every way disconcerted;[25] when again looking at me more attentively, he instantly spurred up to me, and, with dignity in his look and action, gave me his hand.

The tenseness and compression of this incident is not diminished by the construction Bartram places upon the Indian's action in the unspoken words and Romantic sentiments he ascribes to him:

> Possibly the silent language of his soul, during the moment of suspense (for I believe his design was to kill me when he first came up) was after this manner: "White man, thou art my enemy, and thou and thy brethren may have killed mine; yet it may not be so, and even were that the case, thou art now alone; and in my power. Live; the Great Spirit forbids me to touch thy life; go to thy brethren, tell them thou sawest an Indian in the forests, who knew how to be humane and compassionate.
>
> (pp. 20-21)

Not all of his Indian encounters are of this threatening nature, but they are interesting none the less. Trifling as they may turn out to be they are presented in a way which, for the moment, quickens the pulse with anticipations.

> I had not left sight of my encampment, following a winding path through a grove of Live Oak, Laurel (Magn. grandiflora) and Sapindus, before an Indian stepped out of a thicket, and crossed the path just before me, having a large turkey cock, slung across his shoulders, he saw me stepping up and smiling, spoke to me in English, bidding me good morning. I saluted him with "It's well brother," led him to my camp, and treated him with a dram.
>
> (p. 75)

One other illustration will serve to emphasize the directness with which Bartram relates these encounters:

> I took out of my wallet some biscuit and cheese, and a piece of neat's tongue, composing myself to ease and refreshment; when suddenly appeared within a few yards, advancing towards me from behind the point, a stout likely Indian fellow, armed with a rifle gun, and two dogs attending, upon sight of me stood, and seemed a little surprised, as I was very much; but instantly recollecting himself and assuming a countenance of benignity and cheerfulness, he came briskly to me and shook hands heartily; and smiling enquired from whence I came, and whither going, but speaking only in the Cherokee tongue, our conversation was not continued for a great length.
>
> (pp. 361-62)

However, it is in encounters which contain the element of danger that Bartram is at his best. In such cases he builds up, by subtle little touches, an atmosphere of real suspense. The antagonist need not always be an Indian. The limitless savannas and virgin forests are fraught with all sorts of dire possibilities, and one feels in reading Bartram that at any minute something may happen. To cite another example:

> Observed a number of persons coming up a head which I soon perceived to be a party of Negroes: I had every reason to dread the consequence; for this being a desolate place, I was by this time several miles from any house or plantation, and had reason to apprehend this to be a predatory band of Negroes: people being frequently attacked, robbed, and sometimes murdered by them at this place; I was unarmed, alone, and my horse tired; thus situated every way in their power, I had no alternative but to be resigned and prepare to meet them, as soon as I saw them distinctly a mile or two off, I immediately alighted to rest, and give breath to my horse, intending to attempt my safety by flight, if upon near approach they should betray hostile designs, thus prepared, when we drew near to each other, I mounted and rode briskly up; and though armed with clubs, axes and hoes, they opened to right and left, and let me pass peaceably . . . .
>
> (pp. 471-72)

The same ability to portray a situation full of suspense is discernible in Bartram's encounters with animals. The element of conflict, so essential in any narrative, is never absent from his descriptions of these adventurous incidents. His fight with the alligators, a part of his book which has proved most memorable, is actually thrilling. First he describes a battle among the alligators themselves, which he has witnessed, a sort of prelude which causes his "apprehensions" to become "highly alarmed." To add to the atmosphere of danger, he sets down, with truly Poesque sensitiveness to the shadings of a situation, that "the sun was near setting." Then the battle begins. His canoe is "attacked on all sides" and his plight becomes "precarious to the last degree." The realism of the struggle is most meticulous and highly effective. His diction becomes precise and dramatic. Nouns become concrete and specific; verbs spring alive with action. "Two very large ones attacked me closely, at the same instant, rushing up with their heads and part of their bodies above the water, roaring terribly and belching floods of water over me. They struck their jaws together so close to my ears, as almost to stun me, and I expected every moment to be dragged out of the boat and instantly devoured" (pp. 118-19).

Equally thrilling are other scenes, in which Bartram himself was not an antagonist, often not even a participant, but merely a spectator. Such are the numerous hunting episodes or battles between animals which he describes. These are seldom purely objective descriptions but are colored either by pity or by a sense of the dramatic. There is the account, in the Introduction, of the killing of a mother bear and her cub, which "fell to weeping and . . . cried out like a child" (p. xxvi). There is the description of Indians hunting deer, which moves with the tempo of the genuine story-teller:

> The red warrior, whose plumed head flashes lightning, whoops in vain; his proud, ambitious horse strains and pants; the earth glides from under his feet, his flowing mane whistles in the wind, as he comes up full of vain hopes. The bounding roe views his rapid approaches, rises up, lifts aloft his antled head, erects the white flag, and fetching a shrill whistle, says to his fleet and free associates, "follow;" he bounds off, and in a few minutes distances his foe a mile; suddenly he stops, turns about, and laughing says "how vain, go chase meteors in the azure plains above, or hunt butterflies in the fields about your towns."

(p. 188)

And there is the account of a battle between a hawk and a snake "that had wreathed himself several times round the hawks body." The two, he tells us, finally "mutually agreed to separate themselves, each one seeking his own safety, probably considering me as their common enemy" (pp. 218-19).

Besides these stories of encounters between man and man, man and animals, and animals and animals, Bartram also relates many Indian stories. He picks up historical episodes and tribal legends and relates them with his usual gusto and charm, with especial care to their dramatic values. To these belong his account of the Indian's disagreement with the Georgians's determination of the land boundaries (pp. 39-40); his account of the origin of the Creek Confederacy (pp. 54-55); and the beautiful legend of the mythical island in Lake Ouaquaphenogaw,

> a most blissful spot of the earth . . . inhabited by a peculiar race of Indians, whose women are incomparably beautiful; . . . this terrestrial paradise has been seen by some . . . enterprising hunters, when in pursuit of game, who being lost in inextricable swamps and bogs, and on the point of perishing, were unexpectedly relieved by a company of beautiful women, whom they call daughters of the sun, who kindly gave them such provisions as they had with them, which were chiefly fruit, oranges, dates, &c. and some corn cakes, and then enjoined them to fly for safety to their own country; for that their husbands were fierce men, and cruel to strangers. . . .

(pp. 24-26)

The importance of Bartram's narrative ability becomes heightened if a comparison is made between his art and that of the other travel writers who preceded him. There is neither vividness nor particularization in Catesby, Lawson, Byrd, or Carver. Lawson, for instance, frequently deals with situations similar to those described by Bartram, but they are neither dramatic nor memorable. He too mentions the hospitality of the planters, but in vague, general, and colorless terms. "About noon," he says, "we reached another island . . . ; there lived an honest Scot who gave us the best protection his Dwelling afforded. . . ."[26] Not the slightest attempt at individualization of dialogue. He also records encounters with Indians, but his record has no element of possible conflict and hence no suspense. "The next day about noon we accidentally met with a Southward Indian, amongst those that us'd to trade backward and forward, and spoke a little English, whom we hir'd. . . ."[27] One must conclude that it was not a mere accident that Bartram's *Travels* has remained a memorable book, a work of art in many respects, while the accounts of Lawson and his contemporaries have today but a mild historical interest.

Writing, one feels, was a pleasant art for Bartram. There is an ease about his style, a sense of effortlessness; he was a traveler with creative ability, a combination not often found among earlier travelers and seldom found among later travelers. His father, for example, "seems always to have handled the pen with a certain stiffness . . . he evidently does not feel at liberty with his inkhorn. It was this fact, doubtless, that tended to lose in the dust of the past a name that otherwise would have held its place with the greatest."[28] William Bartram's name, instead of being lost in the dust, is becoming more widely known. His art is alive. He saw the American landscape clearly, hugely enjoyed what he saw, and had the ability to dramatize it in words. One wonders what Bartram would have done with the Natural Bridge in Virginia. Thomas Jefferson spent a page and a half in his *Notes* and succeeded in conveying merely a few expository details. He talked about the fissure being 270 feet deep, 45 feet wide, 90 feet at the top; he talked about his looking down from the top and getting a violent headache; and when he became emotional he gave up describing altogether, exclaiming that "the rapture of the spectator is really indescribable."[29] The magnificence, the colors, the lights and shades, that Bartram would have seen and painted for us!

Bartram capture not only the aesthetic surfaces of nature, but the spirit of distance, solitude, and the unknown. Into the romantic remote he traveled and his days and nights pass before our eyes, the succession of morning, noon, and night, of sunrise and sunset and moonlight; we meet strange objects of nature, people, silence and solitude and song, and sunrise again, "the roseate moon."

Notes

1. *Reisen* [Bartram, William], p. 50.

2. *Op. cit.,* Prefatory Note [Squier, E. G. Prefatory and Supplementary Notes to "Observations on the Creek and Cherokee Indians. By William Bar-

tram." *Transactions of the American Ethnological Society,*], pg. 6.

3. Dorothy Anne Dondore, *The Prairie and the Making of Middle America: Four Centuries of Description.* Cedar Rapids, Iowa, p. 133.

4. "Notes of a Rapid Reader," *The Saturday Review of Literature,* April 21, 1928.

5. *Op. cit.* [Tracy, Henry C. *American Naturalists*], pg. 38.

6. *Ibid.,* p. 38.

7. Christopher Hussey, *The Picturesque.* London, 1927, p.55.

8. *Ibid.,* p. 55.

9. Answer to Question 7 in John Howard Payne's *Commonplace Book.*

10. *Transactions of the Am. Ethnological Society,* III, Part I, 18-19.

11. For the use that Wordsworth made of this passage see the next chapter.

12. For the use which Coleridge made of the last phrase see next chapter.

13. Review of *The Travels* in *The Nation,* CXXVI (1928), 328.

14. *Travels,* Van Doren ed., p. 128.

15. *Ibid.,* p. 222.

16. *Ibid.,* p. 257.

17. Raymond Dexter Havens, "The Poetic Diction of the English Classicists," *Anniversary Papers by Colleagues and Pupils of George Lyman Kittredge,* Boston, 1913, pp. 437-38.

18. E. A. W. Zimmermann, *Reisen,* pp. ix-x.

19. MS. of eighteen pages in the *Bartram Papers,* in handwriting of John Bartram, but unsigned and undated.

20. Henry Chester Tracy, *op. cit.,* p. 8.

21. "Browsing through Bartram," by F. H. *The Christian Science Monitor.*

22. "Notes of a Rapid Reader," *The Saturday Review of Literature,* April 21, 1928.

23. R. D. Havens, *op. cit.,* p. 440.

24. *Ibid.,* p. 442.

25. The Van Doren edition substitutes "discontented" (p. 45), an emendation taken over from the London edition (p. 21).

25. John Lawson, *op. cit.,* p. 2.

27. *Ibid.,* p. 20.

28. *Harper's Magazine,* LX, 322. Also see *Popular Science Monthly,* XL, 834: "His observations are minute and sagacious, and his language is simple, but his sentences are loosely strung out, and the record is the barest statement of facts." However, Middleton has indicated that John Bartram "on occasion displayed an excellent command of English and an almost poetic finish in description" (*The Scientific Monthly,* XXI, 210), which merely, if granted, proves that William Bartram's descriptive talent is a flowering of a hereditary proclivity.

29. Thomas Jefferson, *Notes on Virginia,* pp. 34-35.

Works Cited

Anonymous. "Notes of a Rapid Reader." *The Saturday Review of Literature,* IV (1928).

———. "The Travels of William Bartram." *The Nation,* CXXXVI (1928).

Bartram, John. *Bartram Papers.* The Simon Gratz Collection, Manuscript Division, Pennsylvania Historical Society, Philadelphia.

Bartram, William. "Answers to Queries about Indians." In John Howard Payne's *Commonplace Book.* Manuscript Division, Pennsylvania Historical Society, Philadelphia.

———. "Observations on the Creek and Cherokee Indians, 1789." *Transactions of the American Ethnological Society,* III. New York, 1853.

———. *The Travels of William Bartram,* edited by Mark Van Doren. New York, 1928.

———. *Reisen durch Nord- und Sud- Karolina, Georgien, Ost- and West- Florida, das Gebiet der Tskerokesen, Krihks und Tschaktahs.* Aus dem Englischen mit Anmerkungen von E. A. W. Zimmermann. Berlin, 1793.

Dondore, Dorothy A. *The Prairie and the Making of Middle America: Four Centuries of Description.* Cedar Rapids, Iowa, 1926.

H., F. "Browsing through Bartram." *The Christian Science Monitor,* May 2, 1929.

Havens, Raymond Dexter. "The Poetic Diction of the English Classicists." *Anniversary Papers by Colleagues and Pupils of George Lyman Kittredge.* Boston, 1913.

Hussey, Christopher. *The Picturesque.* London, 1927.

Jefferson, Thomas. *Notes on the State of Virginia with Appendix.* (A few copies printed in Paris, 1784. Written, 1782.) Second American edition, Philadelphia, 1794.

Lawson, John. *The History of Carolina: Containing the Exact Description and Natural History of the Country:*

Together with the Present State thereof And a Journal of a Thousand Miles, Travel'd thro' Several Nations of Indians. Giving a particular Account of their Customs, Manners, &c. London, 1714. Reprint of copy in the North Carolina State Library at Raleigh. Charlotte, 1903.

Middleton, William S. "John Bartram, Botanist." *The Scientific Monthly,* XXI (1925).

Payne, John Howard. *Commonplace Book.* Manuscript Division, Pennsylvania Historical Society, Philadelphia.

Squier, E. G. Prefatory and Supplementary Notes to "Observations on the Creek and Cherokee Indians. By William Bartram." *Transactions of the American Ethnological Society,* III, part I (1853). New York.

Tracy, Henry C. *American Naturists.* New York, 1930.

Zimmermann, E. A. W. "Vorrede des Ubersetzers." In *Reisen durch Nord- und Sud- Karolina,* etc. Berlin, 1793.

Robert D. Arner (essay date 1973)

SOURCE: Arner, Robert D. "Pastoral Patterns in William Bartram's *Travels." Tennessee Studies in Literature* 18 (1973): 133-45.

[*In the following essay, Arner explores Bartram's account of his travels in terms of his personal discoveries and the impact the work had on future American literature.*]

Like many of the classic works of American literature, William Bartram's *Travels* is structured around a three-part pastoral pattern that begins with the naturalist's withdrawal from society, focuses upon an encounter with nature, usually intensely personal and fraught with ambiguities, and ends either with the explorer's return to civilization or with some ironic qualification of pastoral idyllicism. In its broadest sense, the book is enclosed by this thematic and narrative pattern, starting with Bartram's departure from Philadelphia in April of 1773 and concluding in the final sentence of Part III with his return to that city and to his father's house on the banks of the Schuylkill River in January 1778; the fourth part is totally devoted to the Indians Bartram encountered on his journeys, and while it is thus loosely related to the main body of the *Travels,* its separate title page suggests that he thought of it as a separate composition. At the heart of the book, of course, are the explorations of Georgia, the Carolinas, and East and West Florida which supplied so much raw material for the imaginations of Coleridge and Wordsworth, among others.[1] Bartram's emotionally and philosophically complex experiences with nature are registered by the dis-

parity of styles employed in the book, now mundanely scientific and purely factual, now soaringly poetic and highly figurative. The tension between the styles enforces the tension in Bartram's mind between cultivated and untrammeled nature, productive and merely picturesque or sublime landscapes, garden and wilderness.[2] The style, in other words, dramatizes a rhythm of consciousness[3] which underlies the whole of the *Travels* and which in various ways provides the work with unity and meaning.

In the first two sections of the *Travels,* Bartram's ambivalent feelings toward the wilderness are most strikingly evident in a number of brief, largely self-contained episodes which can be isolated from the body of the text for convenience in discussion. The two landscapes, garden and wilderness, are juxtaposed in his lament for a "venerable grove"[4] on the shores of Lake George which he had visited fifteen years earlier in the company of his father. At that time, he says, "in that uncultivated state it possessed an almost inexpressible air of grandeur" (99). Now, however,

> all has been cleared away and planted with indigo, corn, and cotton, but since deserted: there was now scarcely five acres of ground under fence. It appeared like a desart to a great extent, and terminated, on the land side, by frightful thickets, and open pine forests.
>
> (100)

There appears to be a contradiction here, for Bartram alternately praises one "uncultivated state" and characterizes another as a "desart" bounded by "frightful thickets." A closer look at the "uncultivated" countryside reveals, however, that Bartram's appreciation of the earlier scene had depended upon his perception of unity and order in the landscape. As he describes it,

> what greatly contributed towards completing the magnificence of the scene, was a noble Indian highway, which led from the great mount, on a straight line, three quarters of a mile, first through a point or wing of the orange grove, and continuing thence through an awful forest of live oaks, it was terminated by palms and laurel magnolias, on the verge of an oblong artificial lake, which was on the edge of an extensive green level savanna. This grand highway was about fifty yards wide, sunk a little below the common level, and the earth thrown up on each side, making a bank about two feet high. Neither nature nor art could any where present a more striking contrast, as you approached this savanna.
>
> (99)

Bartram's style in this passage becomes almost a metaphor for the idea of order which he sees underlying "untamed" nature. The elements of his sentences, particularly of the first sentence, are neatly parceled into separate clauses and phrases, their relationship to each other defined by grammatical rules of modification and their boundaries firmly established by commas. In the same way, Bartram's eye perceives each feature of the landscape separately, then in juxtaposition one to the other, and finally as part of a vista into which all elements are integrated by means of the implicitly metaphoric "striking contrast," a phrase that suggests the rules of formal landscape painting.[5] Providing linear visual unity for the entire composition are the Indian highway and the geographical and mathematical lines of demarcation associated with it. The eye travels along the *straight* road, which is *three quarters of a mile long,* about *fifty yards wide,* and *lined* with embankments about *two feet high*; the road passes a *point* of the orange grove and ends at a stand of palms and laurel magnolias, which is on the *verge* of an *artificial* lake, which is on the *edge* of the *level* savanna (my emphasis). Demonstrably, Bartram's aesthetic appreciation of the uncultivated depends upon man-made refinements, the remnants of an ancient civilization which create geometrical designs on the landscape, not upon wilderness. The artificially defined spatial relationships, which imply chronological sequences as well, are precisely what he misses in the "desarts" and "frightful thickets."[6]

In the animal kingdom, Bartram seeks (and most often is able to convince himself that he has found) a moral order corresponding to the physical order which he values in the landscape. Thus he argues the basic benevolence of the rattlesnake (267-73) and the wolf (158-59). So, too, when his life is threatened and then spared by a Seminole renegade, he offers the reader this profitable speculation:

> Can it be denied, but that the moral principle, which directs the savages to virtuous and praiseworthy actions, is natural or innate? It is certain they have not the assistance of letters, or those means of education in the schools of philosophy, where the virtuous sentiments and actions of the most illustrious characters are recorded, and carefully laid before the youth of civilized nations: therefore this moral principle must be innate, or they must be under the immediate influence and guidance of a more divine and powerful preceptor, who, on these occasions, instantly inspires them, and as with a ray of divine light, points out to them at once the dignity, propriety, and beauty of virtue.
>
> (22-23)

When Bartram cannot detect evidence of this underlying moral principle and cannot ground his pastoral idyllicism firmly in the ideas of order and benevolence, the result is often a version of the pastoral which admits reality and thus brings subtle irony to bear against the idea of retreat into nature. At times, Bartram seems to be aware of the pastoral design he is creating, though not of all its implications, as when he extols the rural hospitality he received on the island of St. Simon. "Our rural table," he writes, "was spread under the shadow of Oaks, Palms, and Sweet Bays, fanned by the lively salubrious breezes wafted from the spicy groves" (61). For music, he and his host, who seems a character fitted for residence in Oliver Goldsmith's Auburn in its happier days, enjoy the

> responsive love-lays of the painted nonpareil, and the alert gay mock-bird; whilst the brilliant humming-bird darted through the flowery groves, suspended in air, and drank nectar from the flowers of yellow Jasmine, Lonicera, Andromeda, and sweet Azalea.
>
> (61)

Altogether, he paints a scene of beauty, innocence, and ease to rival Eden before the Fall.

In the very next paragraph, however, he apparently wishes to remind us that there is another side to nature, a destructive and anarchic one, and so he contrasts the birds' singing with the roar of the ocean to the east: "the solemn sound of the beating surf strikes our ears; the dashing of yon liquid mountains, like mighty giants, in vain assail the skies; they are beaten back, and fall prostrate upon the shores of the trembling island" (61).[7] The defeat of the assaulting waves signals a victory for order and for the ideal pastoral environment, but the threatening power of the ocean functions to contain Bartram's rhetorical flight within a vision of reality that is markedly different from the one represented by his insistence upon underlying order and harmony.

A similar tension between ideal and actual is generated in the following episode, which makes use of the tripartite pastoral pattern of withdrawal, encounter, and return identified at the outset of this paper:

> Whilst my fellow travellers were employing themselves in collecting fire-wood, and fixing our camp, I improved the opportunity in reconnoitring our ground; and taking my fusee with me, I penetrated the grove, and afterwards entered some almost unlimited savannas and plains, which were absolutely enchanting. . . .
>
> How happily situated is this retired spot of earth! What an elysium it is! where the wandering Siminole, the naked red warrior, roams at large, and after the vigorous chase retires from the scorching heat of the meridian sun. Here he reclines, and reposes under the odoriferous shades of Zanthoxylon, his verdant couch guarded by the Deity; Liberty, and the Muses, inspiring him with wisdom and valour, whilst the balmy zephyrs fan him to sleep.
>
> Seduced by these sublime enchanting scenes of primitive nature, and these visions of terrestrial happiness, I had roved far away from Cedar Point, but awakening to my cares, I turned about, and in the evening regained our camp.
>
> (107-108)

The key words in this passage are to be found in the last paragraph: "seduced," "enchanting," and "visions." The "visions" are explicitly contrasted to the geographical reality represented by Cedar Point, mention of which ties Bartram firmly to the actual physical universe. Both "seduced" and "enchanting" suggest unreality and an excess of fantasy, as if Bartram were always conscious that the imagined life of his "naked red warrior" is more fairy tale than fact, a poetic rather than a possible existence. The very luxuriance and richness of nature seem to indicate danger, and the traveler awakens to his cares with something of the sense of relief experienced by the speaker of Frost's "Stopping by Woods on a Snowy Evening," turning his back on the dark and deep forests to return to the routine of work in the world of the village. On the one hand, the woods offer an aesthetic experience that provides a necessary psychological release from the spiritually deadening duties of normal daily life; on the other hand, it is precisely this routine which keeps man from going out too far and in too deep, from becoming totally a creature of natural instincts who does nothing but sleep while balmy zephyrs fan him. Bartram here appears to reject his own vision of terrestrial happiness in favor of the organized white man's world of work.

Nor is this the only paradise which Bartram discovers to be an illusion. Observing the "innumerable bands of fish" (166) in the "Elysian springs" (168) near Lake George, one of the scenes that helped to inspire the crystal fountains and subterranean rivers of Coleridge's "Kubla Khan," he calls attention to the peaceful behavior of the inhabitants of the deep. Here alligators, gar, trout, bream, catfish, spotted bass, and other fish swim around each other "with free and unsuspicious intercourse. . . ." There are "no signs of enmity, no attempt to devour each other . . ." (167). But this, Bartram warns us, is no peaceful kingdom, no piscatorial Garden of Eden. Although this "paradise of fish" seems to exhibit the "happy state of nature which existed before the fall," it is all deception.

> For the nature of the fish is the same as if they were in Lake George or the river; but here the water or element in which they live and move, is so perfectly clear and transparent, it places them all on an equality with regard to their ability to injure or escape from one another . . .
>
> (168)

The central tension in this passage is generated between pre- and post-lapsarian states of nature, between innocence and corrupt aggressiveness. It is significant that Bartram identifies post-lapsarian nature as reality, for this identification implicitly suggests that hostility and violence lie at the heart of the natural world, not benevolence and moral order as he had earlier asserted in his account of the generous Indian who spared his life. His view of nature in the "paradise of fish" episode reminds us of Ishmael's perception that the beautiful undulating surface of the ocean is also a mask for voracious sharks. The more thoroughly one becomes acquainted with nature, the more he learns of her subtleties and deceits.

Thus it is that in the third part of the *Travels* Bartram pays increased attention to the unpleasant and sinister sides of nature. The general conformity of the book to the pastoral pattern of withdrawal, encounter, and return is, of course, largely accidental, since any narrative of exploration necessarily follows the same development. But it is a fortunate accident nevertheless, for it underlines a change in attitudes which the text reveals from Parts I and II to Part III, the excursions into the land of the Cherokees and thence into West Florida. If the first two sections are characterized by many encomiums to wilderness, or at least to Bartram's personal version of uncultivated nature, the third section reverses the emphasis. Bartram now experiences more depressing and frightening moments than exhilarating ones. He begins with a zest for discovery, and on several occasions, driven by the "restless spirit of curiosity" (73), he braves the wrath of Indians and the elements to venture into undiscovered country. His sense of mission is explicitly stated:

> My chief happiness consisted in tracing and admiring the infinite power, majesty, and perfection of the great Almighty Creator, and in the contemplation, that through divine aid and permission, I might be instrumental in discovering, and introducing into my native country, some original productions of nature, which might become useful to society.
>
> (73-74)

There is never any serious doubt about his fulfilling the second part of his goal, and his conviction that God operates benevolently through nature can survive even the challenge of the rattlesnake. But as his travels continue, evidence begins to accumulate that the wilderness is not, in fact, under the guidance of moral law, but that it is hostile or at best indifferent to man. Like Thoreau climbing "Ktaadn," Bartram becomes aware of the threatening and chaotic attributes of nature.

At first, the sinister side of the natural world shows itself in the broad sweep of a landscape which is inhospitable to travelers. Journeying from Fort James in the Carolinas, Bartram gazes upon

> chains of hills whose gravelly, dry, barren summits present detached piles of rocks, which delude and flatter the hopes and expectations of the solitary traveller, full sure of hospitable habitations; heaps of white, gnawed bones of ancient buffalo, elk and deer, indiscriminately mixed with those of men, half grown over with moss, [which] altogether, exhibit scenes of uncultivated nature, on reflection, perhaps, rather disagreeable to a mind of delicate feelings and sensibility, since some of these objects recognize past transactions and events, perhaps not altogether reconcileable to justice and humanity.
>
> (322)

In a book characterized by eighteenth-century circumlocution and indirection, this passage is remarkable for its equivocation, as if Bartram sensed that the implications of this scene of "uncultivated nature" would eventually lead him to a point where to continue exploration would be to challenge and perhaps to disprove the idea of natural benevolence. The barren summits testify to nature's deceitfulness, her power to thwart the hopes and expectations of man. Then, says Bartram, *perhaps* the sight of human bones scattered in this wasteland is *rather disagreeable* to some people because *perhaps* the bones are evidence of actions *not altogether reconcileable* to justice and humanity (my emphasis). So many qualifications and evasive negatives indicate, I think, a mind seriously engaged in debate with itself and genuinely uncertain as to the outcome.

Emerging from this valley of dry bones, Bartram continues his journey to the Cherokee town of Sinica and travels the next day to Fort Prince George Keowe in the Vale of Keowe. The valley is surrounded by "lofty, superb, misty and blue mountains" and is "at this season enamelled with the incarnate fragrant strawberries and blooming plants, through which the beautiful river meanders" (330). Bartram greets the prospect as ample recompense for the hardships of his journey, yet his passage in praise of the vista curiously devotes more attention to his remote situation and to his difficulties than it does to a description of the valley itself.

> Abandoned as my situation now was, yet thank heaven many objects met together at this time, and conspired to conciliate, and in some degree compose my mind, heretofore somewhat dejected and unharmonized: all alone in a wild Indian country, a thousand miles from my native land, and a vast distance from any settlements of white people. It is true, here were some of my own colour, but they were strangers; and though friendly and hospitable, their manners and customs of living so different from what I had been accustomed to, administered but little to my consolation: some hundred miles yet to travel; the savage vindictive inhabitants lately ill-treated by the frontier Virginians; blood being spilt between them, and the injury not yet wiped away by formal treaty: the Cherokees extremely jealous of white people travelling about their mountains, especially if they should be seen peeping in amongst the rocks, or digging up their earth.
>
> (331)

From dark thoughts such as these, the Vale of Keowe offers a temporary sanctuary, and Bartram becomes a sojourner in Elysium. He compares the valley to the "Fields of Pharsalia or the Vale of Tempe" (354). It is, in short, a terrestrial paradise, and about it hangs the rich odor of ripe strawberries. Here he and his companion, a young trader, come upon a band of Cherokee virgins "collecting strawberries, or wantonly chasing their companions, tantalizing them, staining their lips and cheeks with the rich fruit." The "sylvan scene of primi-

tive innocence" proves too great a temptation and, "nature prevailing over reason," the two men approach the "joyous scene of action." There follows a passage charged with sexual innuendo which ends with the maidens whom Bartram and his friend have cornered in a grove "half unveiling their blooming faces, incarnated with the modest maiden blush, and with native innocence and cheerfulness, . . . [presenting] their little baskets, merrily telling us their fruit was ripe and sound." Had it not been for the watchfulness of the Indian matrons, Bartram confesses, there is no telling "to what lengths our passions might have hurried us, thus warmed and excited . . ." (357). Even in this apparently idyllic interlude, then, two concepts of nature are juxtaposed and contend for supremacy: natural innocence, as represented by the young Indian virgins, and instinctual nature, particularly sexual aggressiveness, on the part of the two white men. The contextual ambiguity of the maidens' offering their "ripe and sound" fruit suggests that Bartram may again be bringing a gentle irony to bear against the ideal of innocence in a garden setting.[8]

Two days after this event, Bartram sets out from the Vale of Keowe for the territory of the Overhill Indians, who are presently "in an ill humour with the whites, in consequence of some late skirmishes between them and the frontier Virginians . . ." (359). His determination to explore their country in spite of their hostility reminds the reader of his earlier decision to go to St. John's Island in East Florida in spite of the Indian trouble that had recently developed. Then he had persevered, but now the outcome is far different. When the old trader, Mr. Galahan, parts company with him, he feels the depressing weight of the solitude and oppressiveness of the wilderness descend:

> I was left again wandering alone in the dreary mountains, not indeed totally pathless, nor in my present situation entirely agreeable, although such scenes of primitive unmodified nature always pleased me.
>
> May we suppose that mankind feel in their hearts a predilection for the society of each other; or are we delighted with scenes of human arts and cultivation, where the passions are flattered and entertained with variety of objects for gratification?
>
> I found myself unable, notwithstanding the attentive admonitions and persuasive arguments of reason, entirely to erase from my mind those impressions which I had received from the society of the amiable and polite inhabitants of Charleston; and I could not help comparing my present situation in some degree to Nebuchadnezzar's, when expelled from the society of men, and constrained to roam in the mountains and wildernesses, there to herd and feed with the wild beasts of the forests.
>
> (360)

So far as any single moment in so rich and diverse a book can be identified as crucial without exaggerating its importance, this dark moment when Bartram discovers God's curse on Nebuchadnezzar rather than the evidence of benevolence he had anticipated finding marks the psychological turning point of his travels. In his Introduction, he had advised the traveler to search out God's endless abundance in nature and had, in fact, made natural variety the underlying theme of his prefatory remarks. When he employs the term nature, he includes, of course, men and manners, but the bulk of his Introduction he devotes to a celebration of the variety of wild nature. Now, however, he thinks only of the "variety of objects for gratification" that may be found in "scenes of human arts and cultivation." The awesome solitude of the wilderness appears at last to have overcome his psychological resources and left him defenseless to despair.

In this context, the allusion to Nebuchadnezzar is especially enlightening, since it associates madness with the wilderness. Perhaps unwittingly and certainly without full awareness of all he was implying, Bartram casts himself in the role of one who has been stricken by God, an outcast from humanity by divine decree, and thus the passage stands in stark contrast to his earlier proclamation of his sense of mission. The rational mind proves ineffectual in combating the despair engendered by the wilderness and by the loneliness of Bartram's surroundings, for the wilderness inspires emotions far more powerful than rational thought. In terms of the biblical allusion and of Bartram's primitive psychological analysis of his state of mind, the wilderness is both the cause and the symbolic setting of man's degeneration into a bestial or semi-bestial condition in which the irrational dominates the rational. At this moment in his travels, Bartram has arrived at a point as close to the divine and natural heart of darkness as he will ever go. Two days later, still pushing on slowly towards the Overhill Indians' territory, he abruptly decides that the "slow progress of the vegetation in this mountainous, high country" (366) makes the journey scarcely worth the effort. "I suddenly came to a resolution to defer these researches at this time" (366), he tells us, though we have seen this resolution forming for some time. In a few days he has returned to the Indian town and the company of Mr. Galahan. Thus his "lonesome pilgrimage," as he aptly termed his trip through Cherokee country, comes to an unsuccessful conclusion.

We might pause here to speculate why the Carolina wildernesses should have proved so frightening and depressing to Bartram when even his battles with the alligators in East Florida did not seem to dampen his enthusiasm for exploration. Three reasons can be advanced. The first is that he had by this time been three years absent from Philadelphia, most of which he spent in wilderness environments. Long exposure may have helped to intensify whatever negative reactions earlier experiences might have begun. Second, Bartram spends much of his time alone in this aborted expedition, and,

as some of the passages already quoted show, the loneliness he felt greatly affected his response to his surroundings. The third reason, and probably the decisive one, is that the wilderness of the Carolinas is a very different country from East Florida. As the abundant references to mountains, cascades, and waterfalls establish, it is a mountainous area where forests are tall and dense, emphasizing the darkness and the gloom, and where hills slope down to narrow valleys which do not provide the visual relief of the savannas. For the most part, it is a wilderness which surrounds and contains the human figure. That Bartram responded to this difference and that sweeping vistas were necessary parts of his psychological landscape are revealed in his account of his passage through a forest in which he saw "vast heaps of . . . stones, Indian graves undoubtedly."

> After I left the graves, the ample vale soon offered on my right hand, through the tall forest trees, charming views, which exhibited a pleasing contrast, immediately out of the gloomy shades and scenes of death, into expansive, lucid, green, flowery fields, expanding between retiring hills, and tufty eminences. . . .⁹

(348)

After Bartram returns from the wilderness area of the Carolinas, he immediately begins preparations for the journey into West Florida. In this expedition, he never ventures into the wilderness alone, but always has human company, even if, as he says, it is only three slaves. He spends almost as much time describing the plants that flourish in cultivated gardens on plantation estates as in discussing the wild vegetation (429, 436, and 469, for example). This is not accidental, since he does not stray far from settlements of some sort, Indian or white, and consequently this section of the book is the least interesting to read. Admittedly, the region was more inhabited than other areas he had explored, excluding his early excursions into Georgia, and possibly there were simply fewer natural wonders to relate. But even his first glimpse of the storied Mississippi River does not seem able to inspire the old enthusiasm or stimulate his imagination. When we recall his poetic flights in praise of the Altamaha and compare them with his attempt to portray the Father of Waters as "a prospect of the grand sublime" (428), chiefly in terms of depths and distances, who does not feel that Bartram's ardor for the wilderness and for scenes of wild magnificence, even if only for the carefully controlled wilderness of his mind, has cooled considerably?

Moreover, the few encounters with wild nature that Bartram does experience in West Florida carry forward the established theme of nature's hostility to man, to human enterprise, and to rational modes of consciousness. Bartram devotes more space to an account of the extreme heat and tormenting flies of Florida than he gives to the Mississippi, and when he describes the insects as "evil spirits," "persecuting spirits," and "demons" (385-86), he employs a metaphor that, perhaps unintentionally but nevertheless significantly, links the Florida wildernesses to the demon-haunted woodlands of medieval legend and fable. Nor does he attempt to argue the benevolence of these insects as he might have done earlier. The heat and flies combine to sap the energy of the entire company with which he is traveling. "The animal spirits sink under the conflict," he writes, "and we fall into a kind of mortal torpor rather than refreshing repose; and startled or terrified at each others [sic] plaintive murmurs and groans" (386). Almost literally, the wilderness seems to have extinguished all human faculties and to have reduced the travelers to the level of beasts, communicating with each other in inarticulate groans.

One misery succeeds another, as Bartram and his companions are drenched by a heavy thunderstorm which, however, temporarily revives them. For a brief moment, they contemplate the familiar smiling face of nature: "The birds sung merrily in the groves, and the alert roebuck whistled and bounded over the ample meads and green turfy hills" (387). Yet even now the implicitly metaphoric "meads" suggests that Bartram is describing more a landscape of the mind than of actuality. The sinister side of nature reappears when he develops the symptoms of a fever, which quickly grows worse and threatens his sight and his life. Though he recovers, vision in his left eye is seriously impaired (418, 436). Mosquitoes plague the travelers, swollen rivers confront them with nearly impassable barriers, and Indians once again pose a problem that necessitates a change in the proposed route of travel. In the end, his ill health causes Bartram to cut short his trip into West Florida, but the reader is left with the distinct impression from the brief four chapters recounting these final experiences with the wilderness that the traveler was not disappointed to be forced to end his explorations.

This reading of the last part of the *Travels* depends, of course, upon emphasis, not upon any absolute shift in attitude. Ambivalence characterizes Bartram's responses to nature throughout the book, but in Part III his reactions seem to be more negative than positive, a reversal of Parts I and II. There is one important piece of biographical evidence in support of this interpretation, which is that Bartram did not undertake another expedition, even though he was later offered the chance to head a group of naturalists who were to explore the identical territory of the Overhill Indians which he had wished to visit in his travels. His attendant spirit, curiosity, seems to have deserted him in this instance, and perhaps we need look no further than the last hundred pages of the *Travels* to discover sufficient explanation.

Although it is not an attempt at fiction, Bartram's account of his travels, in its concentration upon man's confrontation with nature and in its use of the central device of the journey of withdrawal, can be recognized as an important piece of American literature related to such works as Poe's *Narrative of Arthur Gordon Pym*, Cooper's *Prairie*, Melville's *Moby-Dick*, Faulkner's *The Bear*, Dickey's *Deliverance*, and to the non-fiction essays *Nature* and *Walden*. Like these later writers, Bartram can reconcile garden to wilderness, order to chaos, benevolence to hostility, and beauty to terror only through the force of imaginative metaphors or transcendent vision, and for him, as for them, the psychological tension is reflected in the style and form of his narrative. If the line of descent from the *Travels* to these and other works of later American literature is not direct, there is nevertheless sufficient family resemblance to establish the authenticity of the lineage beyond dispute.

Notes

1. The indebtedness of English romantics, and of certain American romantics as well, is discussed in John Livingston Lowes' *The Road to Xanadu* (Boston: Houghton, 1927), Ernest Earnest's *John and William Bartram: Botanists and Explorers* (Philadelphia: Univ. of Pennsylvania Press, 1940), Nathan Fagin's *William Bartram: Interpreter of the American Landscape* (Baltimore: Johns Hopkins Univ. Press, 1933), and Josephine Herbst's *New Green World* (New York: Hastings House, 1954). Of these, Fagin's offers the most comprehensive treatment of Bartram's influence on later literature.

2. Roderick Nash, *Wilderness and the American Mind* (New Haven: Yale Univ. Press, 1967), 54-55, briefly notes Bartram's negative responses to the wilderness.

3. The phrase is Leo Marx's in "Pastoral Ideals and City Troubles," *JGE* [*Journal of General Education*] 20 (1969), 251-71. See also his *The Machine in the Garden* (New York: Oxford Univ. Press, 1967) for a discussion of some of the tensions of the American pastoral.

4. William Bartram, *Travels Through North & South Carolina, Georgia, East & West Florida . . .* (Philadelphia: James & Johnson, 1791), 100. Further references to the *Travels* are to this edition and will be noted in the text by page number only.

5. Elsewhere in the *Travels,* Bartram shows the artist's sensitivity to tones of color, especially to shades of green (335-36, for example), and to perspective and line (esp. 102, 179-80, and 187-88).

6. This reading of Bartram's passage differs widely from that of Josephine Herbst, who is inclined to accept his "uncultivated nature" at face value. See *New Green World*, 256.

7. Note Bartram's use of alliteration, particularly of sibilant *s*'s as counterpoints to the weightier consonants, to convey the sound of the sea.

8. Bartram most often romanticized the noble savage he encountered in the American wilderness, but, as his tale of the unfortunate trader with the conniving Seminole wife (111-12) demonstrates, he was not totally blinded by the appearance of virtue and innocence; he could also see to moral realities lying under the appearances.

9. Additionally, we might note that mountainous scenery was not much appreciated by any traveler during the first half of the eighteenth century and for a good while thereafter. See Ola Elizabeth Winslow, "Seventeenth-Century Prologue," *Essays on American Literature in Honor of Jay B. Hubbell,* ed. Clarence Gohdes (Durham, N. C.: Duke Univ. Press, 1967), 27, and Samuel Holt Monk, "The Sublime in Natural Scenery," *The Sublime* (Ann Arbor: Univ. of Michigan Press, 1960), 203-32.

Bruce Silver (essay date 1978)

SOURCE: Silver, Bruce. "William Bartram's and Other Eighteenth-Century Accounts of Nature." *Journal of the History of Ideas* 39, no. 4 (1978): 597-614.

[*In the following essay, Silver argues that critics have overlooked the contribution of Bartram to the naturalist literary tradition. Also investigated is how the* Travels *characterize the natural world.*]

Despite the intellectual productivity of our Bicentennial year, too little was said about colonial Americans whose contributions to our culture were not tied to the decision and struggle for independence. William Bartram (1739-1823), the apolitical son of the Quaker botanist John Bartram (1699-1777), is among those who have been neglected.[1] Bartram's significance as a naturalist and amateur scientist is a matter of record.[2] He learned about plants from his father and from working with him in their garden on the banks of the Schuylkill river. The combination of William Bartram's botanical knowledge, his talents as an artist - naturalist, and the influence of his name among European horticulturists enabled him to travel throughout the southeastern American wilderness under the patronage of Dr. John Fothergill, the wealthy English gardener and botanist.[3] Bartram set out to collect plants and seeds in April 1773 and did not return to Philadelphia until January 1778, after he had explored substantial portions of the Carolinas, Florida, Alabama, Georgia, Mississippi, and Louisiana.[4]

Bartram published the record of his five years of wandering as the *Travels through North and South Carolina, Georgia, East and West Florida . . .* (1791). His book—probably the "first genuine and artistic interpretation of the American landscape"—influenced the romantic poets of England and France, presented a lucid and compassionate account of the Cherokees and other Indians of the Southeast,[5] secured his own election into the American Philosophical Society,[6] and induced Thomas Jefferson to ask that Bartram accompany an expedition into the newly acquired Louisiana territory.[7]

My concern is not with Bartram's place in history, art or literature, nor with the details and examples of his contributions to our strictly scientific knowledge. I am rather impressed by Bartram's *Travels* as a blend of careful observation and moral prepossessions about the goodness of nature, a blend so complete that a description of American plant and animal life becomes a celebration of nature's design and worth. Bartram's world, as the product of a benevolent God, is full of value and goodness.[8] His descriptions of nature are equivalent to scientific descriptions suffused with aesthetic, utilitarian, and religious values which do not affect his objectivity. The notion that a description should be neutral, i.e., that facts and values ought to be distinguished and separated for purposes of scientific inquiry, never occurred to him. In this respect Bartram is one with the Jeffersonians whom Daniel Boorstin discusses in *The Lost World of Thomas Jefferson*:

> By admiring the universe as the complete and perfected work of divine artifice . . . , the Jeffersonian was insisting that the values by which the universe was to be assessed were somehow implicit in nature. All facts were endowed with an ambiguous quality: they became normative as well as descriptive.[9]

In an important sense, however, Bartram was different from the Jeffersonian *virtuosi* and from the natural theologians of his day. Unlike the former, he did not allow his convictions to dominate or to cloud what he observed.[10] He was traveling through the American wilderness to discover and to collect its products. He was not out to confirm a theory about the goodness of the universe. Unlike the typical natural theologians of the eighteenth century, Bartram was not arguing from nature's goodness to God's. As a consequence, he neither narrowed his view to include only those phenomena and organisms that seemed most easily to point to God's benevolence nor did he involve himself in unconvincing vindications of God's beneficence where the harsh efficiency of nature sometimes called it into question.

Bartram believed passionately that nature was good, and he believed that much of what he found in his travels mirrored the power and goodness of its architect. But he was also a tough-minded naturalist whose mission was one of science and discovery. He was not interested in gathering evidence for a belief that, in his own estimation, needed no argument. Instead, he described what he saw with a scope and objectivity unequalled by others who traveled and wrote about the frontiers of eighteenth-century America.

I. Nature and Design—The prominence of the design argument for the existence and goodness of God is a commonplace in the history of speculative thought. That the existence of a benevolent deity could be established by appealing to order and contrivance in nature was a conviction shared by Thomas Aquinas, Isaac Newton, Robert Boyle, William Paley, and many others.[11] Philosophers, naturalists, and scientists of the Enlightenment looked to the variety of plant and animal life, to the adaptation of organisms to their environments, and to the structure and mechanics of organs like the heart or the eye. All of this was seen as incontrovertible evidence for the existence, providence, and skill of a creator.

Philosophically, the argument from design, after Spinoza's critique of it (*Ethics,* Appendix to Part I), suffered its deathblow with the publication of Hume's *Dialogues concerning Natural Religion* (1779).[12] Developments in nineteenth-century science were no friend to this argument either. Darwin's *The Origin of Species* (1859) could account for all instances of apparent design and purposeful contrivance in nature in terms of the purely mechanical ingredients of natural selection.[13] There was no reason to appeal to any transcendent and unverifiable theological hypothesis.

Bartram's book appeared nearly seventy years before Darwin's, and there is no evidence that the *Travels* was influenced by the proto-evolutionary theories of the European Enlightenment.[14] If Bartram read any Hume, it was the *History of England* (1763) and not the unsettling *Dialogues,* a work published only a year after Bartram's return to Philadelphia.[15] Immune to or unaware of these new currents in science and philosophy, Bartram wrote lyrically of nature as God's great product:

> We admire the mechanism of a watch and the fabric of a piece of brocade as being the production of art; these merit our admiration, and must excite our esteem for the ingenious artist or modifier; but nature is the work of God omnipotent.[16]

Wherever we look we are likely to be struck by the beauty and variety of what God has made:

> This world, as a glorious apartment of the boundless palace of the sovereign Creator, is furnished with an infinite variety of animated scenes, inexplicably beautiful and pleasing, equally free to the inspection and enjoyment of all his creatures.[17]

Even among living things that cannot be praised for their beauty, e.g., plants and trees that fall short of the splendid "pompous Palms of Florida," the "glorious Magnolia," or the "umbrageous Live Oak," the traces of God's skill and workmanship are patent. Species lacking aesthetic quality inevitably possess something of equal or greater value. Bartram mentions as examples

the medicinal properties of thyme and the nutritive importance of *Oryza sativa* (rice) or *Pyrus augustifolia* (crab apple).[18] Thus utility, not less than beauty, reminds us of the wisdom of the author of nature:

> Though none of these most useful tribes are conspicuous for stateliness, figure, or splendour, yet their valuable qualities and virtues excite love, gratitude, and adoration to the great Creator, who was pleased to endow them with such eminent qualities, and reveal them to us for our sustenance, amusement, and delight.[19]

Taken together, the beauty, usefulness, and variety of nature are marks or vestiges that point to the wisdom and providence of their transcendent cause. Bartram sees the natural order—even as Saint Francis and others in the Middle Ages had seen it—as a *speculum Dei* in which plants and animal life show us how "the great Author has impartially distributed his favours to his creatures, so that the attributes of each one seem to be of sufficient importance to manifest the divine and inimitable workmanship."[20]

The study of nature has clear intrinsic, instrumental, and didactic value for Bartram. Its intrinsic value, i.e., what satisfies disinterested inquiry, was of undeniable importance to him. He kept accurate and extensive records of the migration of various birds despite the fact that many considered such a study productive of nothing that had any practical application.[21]

There is no question that Bartram believed that the investigations of a naturalist are instrumentally valuable. He was persuaded, as were others involved in the work of the American Philosophical Society, that expanding our knowledge of the world helps to increase the happiness and comfort of mankind.[22] His own travels and observations satisfied his desire to know, expressed his veneration for God and his creation, and worked to the benefit of society:

> I, continually impelled by a restless spirit of curiosity, in pursuit of new productions of nature, my chief happiness consisted in tracing and admiring the infinite power, majesty, and perfection of the great Almighty Creator, and in the contemplation, that through divine aid and permission, I might be instrumental in discovering, and introducing into my native country, some original productions of nature, which might become useful to society.[23]

The didactic value of natural history for Bartram arises from the discovery of nature's order and richness, together with the awareness that these are impressed upon it by God. The steadiness and regularity that characterize and account for the balance of the living world should serve as a model for our own conduct:[24]

> Let us rely on Providence, and by studying and contemplating the works and power of the Creator, learn wisdom and understanding in the economy of nature, and be seriously attentive to the divine monitor within.[25]

Even being caught in a severe storm near the banks of Georgia's Alatamaha river is instructive for Bartram. A generally peaceful river, swollen by a severe storm, once again becomes placid as the wind and rain abate. Despite occasional storms and other disturbances, calm and balance in nature are always restored. From this one can learn, according to Bartram, that balance and temperance can be restored to our own behavior following those instances in which it is excessive, immoderate, and clouded.[26]

It is true, of course, that much of what Bartram says about the instructive value of nature, design, and the clockwork of the created order is conventional for the age in which he wrote. Robert Boyle and Leibniz are two among many in the seventeenth century who had stressed the analogy between creation and the intricate mechanism of a watch or clock. The most familiar statement of this analogy, after the publication of Bartram's *Travels,* was that of William Paley in his influential *Natural Theology* (1802).[27]

Others, e.g., George Berkeley, Jonathan Edwards, and the English poet Thomas Traherne, had written before Bartram of nature as a kind of theophany which points beyond itself to its wise creator. This is clearly the notion Paley had in mind when he suggested that the principal reason for attending to the beauty, variety, and splendid adjustment of the living world is that we come to know and to appreciate its spiritual underpinnings for the first time. Nature becomes a

> temple, and life itself one continued act of adoration . . . Whereas formerly God was seldom in our thoughts, we can now scarcely look upon anything without perceiving its relation to him. Every organized natural body, in the provisions which it contains for its sustentation and propagation, testifies a care, on the part of the Creator, expressly directed to these purposes.[28]

The belief that nature is a guide or teacher is also a theme that precedes Bartram. Thomas More's Utopians insisted that virtuous conduct is the consequence of following nature and that improper conduct is the result of deviating from it. Joseph Butler made the same point in his *Fifteen Sermons* (1726) as did Rousseau in the *Origins of Inequality among Men* (1755).[29]

It comes as no surprise, then, that Bartram's *Travels* (1791) should have themes and elements in common with important contemporaneous works in philosophy, morals, and natural religion; neither is it a revelation to find that a work written during the period of the American Enlightenment was touched by the thought of the European Enlightenment. It would have been more remarkable if the content of his book bore no resemblance to the science, theology, and literature of the period in which it was written.

More interesting than these similarities, however, is the extent to which the *Travels* is different from the general scientific and theoretical tradition of which it is, nonetheless, a part. Bartram did more than repeat the claims and propositions already familiar to a literate eighteenth-century audience. There are features that make the *Travels* unique and important among theologically oriented natural histories, and a few of these are worth examining.

II. Design without Argument in the *Travels.*—Besides the regional character of its scientific material, it is the absence of a deliberate argument for the existence and goodness of God that helps to distinguish Bartram's *Travels* from the mixtures of natural history and theology common to the Enlightenment.[30] Strictly speaking, Bartram is not arguing at all. He writes as a moralist and as a naturalist who sees the American wilderness as the product of a benevolent creator.[31] The goodness of God is axiomatic; and the goodness, beauty, and utility of creation are apparent to all who will look around them.[32]

Freed from any need to argue from the goodness of nature to the existence of God as its beneficent cause, Bartram could devote his energies to the real business of the *Travels,* i.e., natural science. As a scientist, he was concerned to describe and to classify a part of the animate world. Bartram's insistence that this world, insofar as it was fashioned by a benevolent maker, is a realm of values as well as facts does not interfere with his role and responsibilities as an objective scientist. Indeed, his antecedent belief in God's goodness and the inherent value of nature made it unnecessary for him to burden the *Travels* with theological proofs which might reduce or dilute the scientific content of his work. Bartram gives us penetrating descriptions of plant and animal life in the wilderness, not unpersuasive arguments for God's benevolence or *a priori* principles of cosmic harmony intended to explain away apparent evil or maladjustment in nature.[33]

By contrast, Paley's *Natural Theology* is one among many works that employ the kind of arguments Bartram was able to avoid. Paley argues, for example, that the happiness of beasts is itself a proof that the world is the product of wise and beneficent design.[34] He describes the greedy joy of aphids as they rob plants of their vital juices. He writes enthusiastically about clouds of young shrimp.

> in the act of bounding into the air from the shallow margin of the water or from wet sand. If any motion of a mute animal could express delight, it was this. . . . Suppose, then, what I have no doubt of, each individual of this number be in a state of positive enjoyment; what a sum, collectively, of gratification and pleasure have we here before our view![35]

A trained naturalist would have darker, well-founded suspicions about Paley's account. Far from regarding the leaping of shrimp as evidence that God is interested in sustaining the uninterrupted happiness of all his creatures, he would see it for what it is, i.e., their frantic effort to escape the fish that constantly prey upon them.

Bartram says very little about shrimp, but his description of bounding fish helps to illustrate the difference between his own careful science and Paley's casual hedonism. To be sure, Bartram is given over to personification when he writes about the marine life of lakes and sink-holes in northeastern Florida. Schools of fish, "after encountering various obstacles, and beholding new and unthought-of scenes of pleasure and disgust, after many days absence from the surface of the world, emerge again from the dreary vaults, and appear exulting in gladness, and sporting in the transparent waters of some far distant lake."[36]

It may seem at first that Bartram and Paley are saying about the same thing and that each is guilty of unscientific excess, but this is not the case. Paley is persuaded that the shrimp are truly delighted and that their happiness proves the pervasiveness of God's goodness. He is silent about the animals which feed upon them. He has either missed or suppressed a fact critical to a complete and accurate scientific account of the jumping of shrimp.

On the other hand, Bartram's fish merely "appear exulting in gladness." His description is not intended to prove God's providence and goodness. His report begins with poetic imagery, but poetry quickly yields to an exhaustive list of the outward characteristics of these fish and to a statement of their fate. The spotted garr, "accoutred in an impenetrable coat of mail," is cannibalistic. The mud fish is large, thick, and round; and the yellow beam is actually multicolored.[37] All of them fall victim to the great soft-shelled tortoise.[38] Their happiness is merely apparent. This is a fact, and there is neither joy nor delight in it.

Even in a rich and romantic word-picture of a small spring-fed lake a few miles from Florida's Lake George, Bartram suggests but then resists the opportunity to speculate about nature in the language of theology and morals. The water of this basin is so clear and so full of life that it looks to him "at first but as a piece of excellent painting." The scene is quite real, but we are warned against jumping to erroneous conclusions about the moral harmony of this microcosm. Among the assorted fish and crocodiles Bartram finds in this spring, there seems to be "no sign of enmity, no attempt to devour each other; the different bands seem peaceably and complaisantly to move a little aside, as if it were to make room for others to pass."[39] How are we to explain this atypical and seemingly benevolent community of predators?

Paley might have insisted, as he had with the shrimp, that such happiness and tranquility are the basis for arguing that divine benevolence extends to every living creature. Bartram prefers a naturalistic explanation of the phenomenon and does not rest the case for God's or nature's goodness on this kind of observation. Hence he writes that while

> this paradise of fish may seem to exhibit a just representation of the peaceable and happy state of nature which existed before the fall, yet in reality it is a mere representation; for the nature of the fish is the same as if they were in Lake George or the river; but here the water or element in which they live and move, is so perfectly clear and transparent, it places them all on an equality with regard to their ability to injure or escape from one another.[40]

It is almost as though these words were meant as a caution both to the reader of the *Travels* and to the unwitting naturalist who misreads the book of nature. Where they are in conflict, sentiment must yield to fact. Apparent benevolence is not true benevolence. Properly understood, the situation in this clear lake is more like Thomas Hobbes' state of nature than it is a prelapsarian, liquid Arcadia.[41] These fish forbear attacking each other only because an antagonism of equals, without the advantage of murky hiding places from which to attack and into which to retreat, produces an unproductive standoff.

Bartram did not question that the natural order, taken as a whole, manifests its maker's benevolence. If, however, one approaches nature as many natural theologians of the Enlightenment did—as a system in which every part and detail *can be shown* to be good—the yield is little more than unsound arguments and *non sequiturs*. N. B. Fagin seems to have missed this point in his usually perceptive analysis of Bartram and his works. Discussing Bartram's view of nature as the revelation of God's goodness, he writes:

> The objective scientist in Bartram occasionally observes a phenomenon in nature which clashes with the concept of benevolence; his description, for instance, of a spider pouncing upon a bee, inflicting wounds like a *butcher,* and finally devouring it, is quite horribly realistic. But such disquieting moments are rare in Bartram. Nourished upon the ideals of the mid-eighteenth century, Bartram accepts the physical world of God as wholly good. . . .[42]

The case is not quite what Fagin suggests. Neither Bartram's description of the predatory spider nor, to cite another example, his account of the warlike behavior of alligators is at odds with his belief in the general goodness of nature.[43] It is important to notice that Bartram's conclusion to his description of the spider's hunt is a reminder that the spider became probably that same day "the delicious evening repast of a bird or lizard."[44] This is but one example of the balance, economy, and control maintained by nature itself. Those who pick out a spider's hunting practices as evidence for indifference or disharmony in nature do no better than those who look to leaping shrimp or sporting bream to argue for its goodness. For Bartram it is the entire scheme, the clockwork of nature, that testifies to a principle of benevolence. Separated from the general system into which it fits, a particular phenomenon is inconclusive as a basis for arguing for or against nature's goodness or that of its creator.

In Bartram's vivid description of troublesome insects, one can see clearly the extent to which his views as a working naturalist differ from those of the closet naturalists of the seventeenth and eighteenth centuries. Once again, a comparison between Paley and Bartram is useful.

Bartram refused to glorify insect pests merely to demonstrate that everything which exists is, in itself and in its actions, good. Paley, on the other hand, felt the need to reconcile God's benevolence, especially towards man, with the existence of insects. What place can venomous and stinging insects have in nature? By appealing to the principle of plentitude, Paley could argue that their presence does not mar an inherently good world. His own second-hand knowledge of the New World was well-suited to his defense:

> We complain of what we call the exorbitant multiplication of some troublesome insects, not reflecting that large portions of nature might be left void without it. If the accounts of travelers may be depended upon, immense tracts of forest in North America would be nearly lost to sensitive existence, if it were not for gnats. . . . Thus it is that, where we looked for solitude and death-like silence, we meet with animation, activity, enjoyment—with a busy, a happy, and a peopled world.[45]

Bartram too is stirred by the exuberance of the American wilderness; and in prose no less lyrical than Paley's, he chants a litany to life and light:

> At the return of morning, by the powerful influence of light, the pulse of nature becomes more active, and the universal vibration of life insensibly and irresistibly moves the wondrous machine. How cheerful and gay all nature appears![46]

Indeed, Bartram went further than Paley. He believed that what Paley later called "sensitive existence" belonged to certain native American plants.[47] It was, however, unthinkable to Bartram, as he made his way in June through the wilderness of Georgia, that he could celebrate the existence of stinging flies and gnats. No argument for the goodness of God or his world arises from his unforgettable description of these insects and the pain they inflict. He there finds no joy in the fullness of nature:

> Biting flies are of several species, and their numbers incredible. . . . They are armed with a strong sharp beak or proboscis, shaped like a lancet, and sheathed in flexible thin valves; with this beak they instantly pierce the veins of the creatures, making a large orifice from whence the blood springs in large drops, rolling down as tears, causing a fierce pain or aching for a considerable time after the wound is made. . . . Whenever we approach the cool shades near creeks, impatient for repose and relief, almost sinking under the persecutions from evil spirits . . . , we are surprised and quickly invested with dark clouds of these persecuting demons, besides musquitoes [sic] and gnats.[48]

Encounters with annoying insects do not, of course, induce Bartram to question nature's design or goodness. Creation as a whole always excites his "admiration, and equally manifests the almighty power, wisdom, and beneficence of the Supreme Creator and Sovereign Lord of the universe."[49] It is not, however, his function as a naturalist to justify his admiration in the face of discomfort and impediments to his work. To believe that stinging flies, mosquitoes, and gnats somehow contribute to the fullness and goodness of nature is one thing, and to offer arguments supporting that belief is another. Bartram chose not to argue the case. He gives us instead a vivid, descriptively accurate account of these flies (*hippobosca* and *asilus*) and their debilitating effects on mammals. We do not get a tortured theodicy intended to prove, in the absence of acceptable evidence, that such beasts fill a niche in the scale of nature and are, therefore, an element essential to the perfection of the whole.

III. Scientific and Normative Description: Mayflies and Snakes.—Up to now I have been concerned to point out some representative examples of the claim that Bartram's science is unencumbered by his theological conviction that nature is the handiwork of a benevolent deity. It is also clear that his descriptions of the animal inhabitants of this value-laden world are unaffected by his moralizing or by his normative evaluations of their behavior. Even among those few instances in which Bartram appears to be less interested in natural history than in viewing the natural order as an exemplification of some virtue or value, his observations remain sound and ring true. His descriptions of (a) ephemerae (short-lived Mayflies) and of (b) benevolent rattlesnakes help to illustrate and to support this claim.

(a) Bartram's discussion of the "incredible numbers of small flying insects, of the genus termed by naturalists Ephemera," is one of the most detailed in the *Travels.* He sees these flies among the shores of the St. John's river in the spring of 1774. His remarks end in reflection, but a description takes precedence. He first describes the mature flies' emergence, after having spent almost a year in the larval stage, from the shallow waters of the river. Their initial instinct is to mate and to deposit their eggs; thus their life cycle is both complete and continuous:

> This resurrection from the deep . . . commences early in the morning, and ceases after the sun is up. At

evening they are seen in clouds of innumerable millions, swarming and wantoning in the still air, gradually drawing near the river. They descend upon its surface, and there quickly end their day, after communicating their eggs to the deep; which being for a little while tossed about, enveloped in a viscid scum, are hatched, and the little Larva descend into their secure and dark habitation . . . where they remain gradually increasing in size, until the returning spring: they then change to a Nymph, when the genial heat brings them, as it were, into existence, and they again rise into the world.[50]

This is, however, only part of the story. A full description also includes some remarks on the place of these insects in the food chain of the river and its environs; for most of them become "delicious food for birds, frogs, and fish." Here Bartram the scientist and Bartram the romantic converge. Not content merely to describe the swarming of these flies and the feeding of fish upon them, he continues:

> How awful the procession! innumerable millions of winged beings, voluntarily verging on to destruction, to the brink of the grave, where they behold bands of their enemies with wide open jaws, ready to receive them. But as if insensible of their danger, gay and tranquil each meets his beloved mate in the still air, inimitably bedecked in their nuptial robes. . . . With what peace, love, and joy do they end the last moments of their existence![51]

Bartram speculates that there are annually more of 'these beautiful winged beings, which rise into existence, and for a few moments take a transient view of the glory of the Creator's works" than there have been men since creation itself.[52] The brevity of their being—only a few days of which are spent in adulthood—quickens his own reflections on the shortness of human life. This is followed by a long and detailed concluding paragraph on the existence of ephemerae during their subaqueous phase:

> Their whole existence in this world is but one complete year: and at least three hundred and sixty days of that time they are in the form of an ugly grub, buried in mud, eighteen inches under water, and in this condition scarcely locomotive, as each larva or grub has but its own narrow solitary cell, from which it never travels or moves, but in a perpendicular progression of a few inches, up and down, from the bottom to the surface of the mud, in order to intercept the passing atoms for its food, and get a momentary respiration of fresh air; and even here it must be perpetually on its guard, in order to escape the troops of fish and shrimps watching to catch it. . . . One would be apt almost to imagine them created merely for the food of fish and other animals.[53]

There can be little doubt that the life cycle of these Mayflies appeals to Bartram's reflective nature. Some might prefer to see natural history and all other scientific literature free of contemplation and musing. Others may wish that Bartram, perhaps following the model of Newton's *Principia,* had confined his philosophical and theological ruminations to a series of separate, well-defined notes. But unless it can be shown that Bartram's reflections interfere with his science, these preferences do not signal a fundamental weakness in his description or procedure.

The important question is, therefore, whether Bartram's moralizing distorts or diminishes his account of the ephemerae. The answer is that it does not. Neither the sentiment of the moralist nor the metaphorical excesses of the poet weaken or deflect the eye of Bartram the naturalist. "In fact only one sentence in three pages suggests a turning away from the very short period of that stage of existence (as mature flies), which we may reasonably suppose to be the only space of their life that admits of pleasure and enjoyment, what a lesson doth it not afford us of the vanity of our pursuits!"[54]

If this sentence offends a scientist's or positivist's sense of what counts, nothing else that Bartram says about the ephemerae should; for the rest is verifiable fact. What finally matters is the accuracy and completeness of his account of the life span, reproductive cycle, and environment of these Mayflies. Here his precision and comprehensiveness have enabled entymologists to make a probable identification, out of hundreds of varieties, of the species of flies he describes.[55]

(b) Bartram's insistence that rattlesnakes are generally benevolent seems both to transcend his purely scientific interests and to be descriptively less rigorous than what he says about Mayflies or about any other animals and plants in America's wilderness. Here, more than anywhere else in the *Travels,* critics write of his surprising credulity, i.e., of his suggestion that rattlesnakes hypnotize their prey.[56] But a careful reading of the text does not make it clear that Bartram believes in the fascinating power of these snakes. He writes merely that "they are supposed to have the power of fascination in an eminent degree" and that it is "generally believed that they charm birds, rabbits, squirrels, and other animals."[57] This is neither a testimony nor an argument for a rattlesnake's hypnotic capacities: and it falls short of the exaggerated, often absurd claims of others in America who accepted, without question or suspicion, the reptilian folklore of the eighteenth century.[58] Bartram simply includes the prevailing view of a facet of the rattlesnake's behavior. He does not, as Crèvecoeur does in the *Letters from an American Farmer* (1782), lead his readers to believe that he has himself witnessed instances of predatory fascination.[59] One might, of course, criticize Bartram for not rejecting this piece of rural mythology even as he had rejected a variety of extravagant theories of bird migration.[60] Nonetheless, the unwillingness to dismiss a claim is not, in the sciences, equivalent to accepting it; and Bartram does not, in the only passage in which he mentions it, defend or embrace the position that rattlesnakes infatuate their victims.

Bartram discusses the rattlesnakes of the Southeast ("where they are the largest, most numerous and supposed to be the most venomous and vindictive") largely to justify his claim that they have benevolent and peaceful dispositions. He might also have reasoned that it is a straightforward illustration of the general goodness of nature that some of its creatures have the power to do harm but forbear doing it. He insists that there is ample evidence for the benevolence of the dreaded rattlesnake; and while in this case he is more interested in the moral economy of the natural world than in descriptive herpetology, his appeal is empirically grounded:

> Since, within the circle of my acquaintance, I am known to be an advocate or vindicator of the benevolent and peaceable disposition of animal creation in general, not only towards mankind . . . , but always towards one another, except where hunger or the rational and necessary provocations of the sensual appetite interfere, I shall mention a few instances, amongst many, which I have had an opportunity of remarking during my travels, particularly with regard to the animal I have been treating of [the rattlesnake]. I shall confine myself to facts.[61]

He mentions "the dignified nature of the generous though terrible" rattlesnake which harmed neither him nor his friends as they camped for the evening on a small island near the mouth of the Altamaha river. Without knowing it, everyone had passed by and perhaps even disturbed the snake.[62] Bartram writes with compassion and regret that as a boy he killed a rattlesnake while traveling with his father near St. Augustine. He had stopped only a few inches short of the huge snake:

> Another step forward would have put my life in his power, as I must have touched if not stumbled over him. The fright and perturbation of my spirits at once excited resentment; at that time I was entirely insensible to gratitude or mercy. I instantly cut off a little sapling, and soon dispatched him. . . . I, however, was sorry after killing the serpent, when coolly recollecting every circumstance. He certainly had it in his power to kill me almost instantly, and I make no doubt that he was conscious of it.[63]

There are also praises for the moccasin and objections to those who malign or confuse it with its pernicious cousins. It is, Bartram says, "a very beautiful creature, and I believe not of a destructive or vindictive nature."[64] Bartram was himself unable to substantiate any claim that one had ever killed or seriously injured a human being. He concludes, on the basis of his own numerous observations and in the absence of any reliable contrary evidence, that the moccasin is "an innocent creature with respect to mankind."

These accounts and anecdotes do not, of course, constitute the best and most insightful science in the ***Travels.***

Other American travelers had reported, years before the publication of Bartram's work, that rattlesnakes were not aggressive.[65] Bartram was less concerned to reveal new truths about snakes than he was in confuting the spurious hearsay surrounding their behavior toward men. This hearsay was more insidious than the bites of these reptiles; for in Bartram's estimation it wrongly portrayed certain residents of the living world as indiscriminately cruel. He wanted to set the record straight; and backed by his own experience, he argued for what approaches common knowledge today, *viz.,* that snakes, like most other undomesticated animals, are shy and passive. They are predators only when their survival demands that they be.[66]

Bartram overstates the case when he ascribes benevolent motives to snakes. As the debate between ethical altruists and egoists proves, it is difficult enough to determine what motives and intentions underpin human conduct. It is just as difficult to say, with justifiable confidence, that reptiles act out of conscious benevolence.[67]

That Bartram's view of the motivation of snakes is unlikely or untenable is not in itself a sufficient reason to dismiss what he says of their observable behavior. His remarks about their behavior arise not from a normative theory of intentions but from his own frequent encounters with southeastern vipers. He wants his readers to know that some species of poisonous snakes, especially those native to the New World, are benevolent; and though a strange claim, it is not one that colors what he observes. For whatever reasons, rattlesnakes try to avoid, rather than to conflict with, human beings. The same is true of moccasins. Bartram sees their behavior towards humans as a manifestation of their beneficence. Someone else may see it as evidence that snakes are shy or secretive. The interpretations vary, but the behavior or trait to which each appeals is public and verifiable. We should not, in this instance, discount Bartram's observations on the grounds that his interpretation of them is idiosyncratic.

It is equally important to notice that Bartram's report is more than an encomium to reptiles. He lists and discusses about a dozen kinds of snakes, and some of them offend even his generous sensibilities. If, for example, he believes that most snakes are innocent of their unfortunate reputations, he does not believe it of the ground rattlesnake; he first describes it and then states why that creature deserves neither a defense nor sympathy:

> This little viper is in form and colour much like the rattle snake, but not so bright and uniformly marked: their head is broader and shorter in proportion to the other parts of their body: their nose prominent and turned upwards: their tail becomes suddenly small from vent to extremity, which terminates with three minute articulations resembling rattles. . . . This dangerous viper is from eight to ten inches in length, and of pro-

portional thickness. They are spiteful, snappish creatures. . . . They seem destitute of the pacific disposition and magnanimity of the rattlesnake, and are
unworthy of alliance with him.[68]

The detail in this passage is impressive. Anyone who
reads it should recognize a ground rattlesnake if he has
the misfortune to meet one. We can identify this snake
and be careful of it. Bartram has done his job as a descriptive naturalist. The fact that he dislikes the snake
and resents its being called a rattlesnake is incidental to
his description.

The remainder of Bartram's account of southeastern
snakes is, apart from its detail, unexceptional. He identifies the coach-whip snake, the ribband or coral snake,
the chicken and bull snake. He mentions in passing the
water snake, the black snake, and the garter snake.[69]

Bartram is not a herpetologist of the highest rank. He
is, nonetheless, among the first to make responsible and
enduring contributions, both in his *Travels* and in his
drawings, to the study of American reptiles. His
achievements in this area are acknowledged by contemporary zoologists and by historians of the biological
sciences,[70] and these achievements are undiminished by
such comparatively minor sins as the failure to reject
snake fascination or his too zealous defense of the benevolence of rattlesnakes and moccasins.

IV. Conclusion.—Because much has been written—
though not very recently—about Bartram and his influence, I have here dealt with a question that others seem
generally to have neglected, i.e., that of the relationship
between Bartram's normative view of the world, on the
one hand, and his capacities as an objective naturalist,
on the other. He makes no attempt to separate facts
from values nor does he see nature in terms of this
separation. I have tried to show that in spite of his firm
belief in the inherent worth of creation and the goodness of its architect, his science is not distorted by his
sentimentalism nor are his observations diminished by
his moralizing.

I agree with Fagin that what "Bartram has depicted is
the result of the observation of a scientist, poet, and
philosopher, a combination which was unique in his
day and which has kept his work alive in our own day."[71]
There is, however, more to it than that. This combination sustains the *Travels* as a classic in science and literature not only because it is a blend of interests but
also because Bartram does not allow one kind of observation to frustrate another. He wrote about nature as a
poet and sometimes thought about it as a philosopher;
yet his metaphors and morals never overpower the scientific aims of his odyssey. He went in order to explore
the American wilderness, to collect specimens from it,
and to learn all that he could about its animals, plants,

rivers, and terrain. These things ought, as he says in the
opening of his book, to be the chief concern of the
naturalist. The significance of the *Travels* is that its author took his own imperative seriously and did so well
what he set out to do.

Notes

1. For a sketch of John Bartram's life and attainments, see N. B. Fagin's *William Bartram: Interpreter of the American Landscape* (Baltimore,
1933), 2-7; hereafter cited as *Bartram*. John Bartram helped Benjamin Franklin to establish the
American Philosophical Society, cultivated America's first botanical garden, belonged to the Royal
Society of London, and served as the king's botanist. Carl Linnaeus, the celebrated Swedish taxonomist, called Bartram the "greatest natural botanist of the world."

2. Bartram's contributions to botany and natural history include, among many others, the first known
drawing of the Venus Flytrap, his descriptions and
drawings of alligators, turtles, and other southeastern reptiles and amphibians, and, above all else,
his and his father's joint discovery of the Franklin
Tree (*Franklinia alatamaha*). This rare plant,
named for Franklin and found near Fort Barrington, Georgia, has not been seen in the wild
since 1803. See J. Ewan's *William Bartram: Botanical and Zoological Drawings, 1756-1788*
(Philadelphia, 1968), 60, 62, 78; hereafter cited as
Bartram's Drawings.

3. Ewan discusses the connection between Fothergill
and the Bartrams. At the time Fothergill decided
to support Bartram's excursion, he himself maintained England's largest botanical garden. *Bartram's Drawings,* 6-7.

4. Bartram's exact itinerary is difficult to trace because of his backtracking and because some of the
place names have been changed over the years. H.
G. Cruikshank, in her *John and William Bartram's
America* (New York, 1957), 379f., has reconstructed his route.

5. Fagin, *Bartram,* 10. Fagin has a chapter on Bartram's Indians, 56-68; and Ewan discusses his anthropology briefly in *Bartram's Drawings,* 29-30.
For some notes documenting the influence of Bartram's *Travels* on Chateaubriand's *Atala,* see
Atala/René, trans. I Putter (Berkeley, 1952),
115-18 *passim*. J. L. Lowes, in his *Road to Xanadu* (Boston, 1927), 365-70, has established the
unquestionable influence of Bartram on Coleridge.

6. *Ibid, Bartram,* 11, 128f.

7. Cruikshank, *John and William Bartram's America,*
372-73. Writing to Jefferson, Bartram declined the

invitation because of his "advanced age and consequent infirmities."

8. Fagin, *Bartram,* 37-55 *passim.*

9. *The Lost World of Thomas Jefferson* (New York, 1948), 54.

10. *Ibid.,* 55

11. Two instructive discussions of the design argument and its problems are M. H. Carré's "Physicotheology" in *The Encyclopedia of Philosophy,* ed. Paul Edwards (New York, 1967), VI, 300-05, and F. Ferré's "The Design Argument" in *The Dictionary of the History of Ideas,* ed. Philip P. Wiener (New York, 1973), I, 670-77.

12. There are some useful comments on Hume's criticism of the design argument in Ferré's introduction to William Paley's *Natural Theology: Selections* (Indianapolis, 1963), xxi-xxvii; hereafter cited as *Natural Theology.*

13. *Ibid.,* xxi.

14. For an account of the theory of evolution and its forerunners, see L. Eiseley's *Darwin's Century: Evolution and the Men Who Discovered It* (New York, 1958). For a discussion of the impact of evolutionary theory and of the theologically biased background against which it emerged, see Philip P. Wiener's *Evolution and the Founders of Pragmatism* (Cambridge, Mass., 1949), ch. 1.

15. Hume's *History of England* was part of Bartram's private library. Fagin, *Bartram,* 20.

16. *The Travels of William Bartram,* ed. M. Van Doren (New York, 1928), 21; hereafter cited as *Travels.* This is an unabridged edition of the *Travels* published in Philadelphia in 1791. Van Doren brings the spelling and punctuation up to date.

17. *Ibid.,* 15.

18. *Ibid.,* 17.

19. *Ibid.*

20. *Ibid.* See E. A. Armstrong's discussion of natural symbolism in *Saint Francis: Nature Mystic* (Berkeley, 1973).

21. *Travels,* 234.

22. *Ibid.,* 15

23. *Ibid.,* 82.

24. Fagin, *Bartram,* 48.

25. Bartram, *Travels,* 70

26. *Ibid.,* 66-67.

27. *Natural Theology,* 3-12.

28. *Ibid.,* 84. For some discussion of others, from Saint Augustine to the New England Transcendentalists, who thought of the natural world as a sacramental realm that everywhere testifies to God's goodness and providence, see A. H. Armstrong's "St. Augustine and Christian Platonism" in *Augustine: a Collection of Critical Essays,* ed. R. A. Markus (New York, 1972), 14, 32-33.

29. The admonition to follow nature is itself ambiguous. Butler and More had in mind behaving under the direction of the highest faculty of our nature, *viz.,* reason. The forest primitive of Rousseau's *Origins of Inequality* follows nature by acting out of instinct and natural compassion, not out of the conceits and sophisms of reason. The Stoics, who placed following nature or living in accordance with it at the center of their ethical doctrine, intended the recognition of Nature's universal purpose and the conforming of our conduct to it. See Marcus Aurelius' *Meditations,* ed. and trans. G. M. A. Grube (Indianapolis, 1963), xi-xii.

30. In his *John Ray: Naturalist* (Cambridge, England, 1950), 452-478, C. E. Raven discusses amalgams of natural theology and natural history in seventeenth-century thinkers like Henry More, John Ray, and William Derham. What he says about Ray is, as one would expect, especially informative.

31. Bartram, *Travels* (Philadelphia, 1791), 21.

32. Fagin, *Bartram,* 38.

33. See, for example, Paley's *Natural Theology,* 61, 74-77, and George Berkeley's *Principles of Human Knowledge* (1710), sections 152-54, in *Berkeley's Philosophical Writings,* ed. D. M. Armstrong (New York, 1965), 126-127.

34. *Natural Theology,* 54.

35. *Ibid.,* 55.

36. Bartram, *Travels,* 157.

37. *Ibid.,* 157-58.

38. *Ibid.,* 158-59.

39. *Ibid.,* 150.

40. *Ibid.,* 151.

41. Hobbes, in his description of competitive equals in the natural state, characterizes life as "solitary, poor, nasty, brutish, and short." *Leviathan* (1651), Pt. I, ch. xiii.

42. Fagin, *Bartram,* 38.

43. Bartram, *Travels,* 115f.

44. *Ibid.,* 25.

45. Paley, *Natural Theology,* 65-66.

46. Bartram, *Travels,* 159.

47. *Ibid.,* 19-20.

48. *Ibid.,* 310-11.

49. *Ibid.,* 20-21.

50. *Ibid.,* 87-88.

51. *Ibid.,* 88. Paley also refers to the "sportive motions" and the "joy and exultation" of Mayflies (*Natural Theology,* 54). Perhaps Bartram goes too far when he writes of the joy and tranquility of primitive insects; but he, unlike Paley, draws no unscientific conclusions from his own remarks. He does not translate the joy of newborn flies into a proof of God's benevolent intentions toward his creatures.

52. *Ibid.*

53. *Ibid.,* 89.

54. *Ibid.*

55. See Ewan, *Bartram's Drawings,* 27.

56. Boorstin is one of those surprised at Bartram's comments on the hypnotic powers of snakes. *The Lost World of Thomas Jefferson,* 27.

57. *Travels,* 222.

58. D. Hawke gives examples of this extreme lore in *The Colonial Experience* (Indianapolis, 1966), 299, 300.

59. J. Hector St. John de Crèvecoeur, *Letters from an American Farmer,* ed. W. B. Blake (New York, 1967), 172-73. Less well-known than Crèvecoeur's book is John Lawson's *History of North Carolina* (London, 1714). Lawson writes that rattlesnakes "have the power or art (I know not which to call it) to charm squirrels, hares, partridges, or any such thing, in such manner that they run directly into their mouths," 133.

60. *Travels,* 234-35.

61. *Ibid.,* 222.

62. *Ibid,* 223.

63. *Ibid.,* 225. The snake that Bartram killed was an Eastern Diamondback, the largest poisonous snake in America. Ewan, *Bartram's Drawings,* 79.

64. *Ibid.,* 226.

65. See, for example, Robert Beverley's *The History and Present State of Virginia* (London, 1705), 300-01.

66. See S. and M. Minton, *Venomous Reptiles* (New York, 1969), 119-20.

67. Paley does not speculate on the higher motives of venomous snakes, but he does insist that a rattlesnake's bite is not so deadly as most believe and that men are themselves indictable for disturbing snakes on their own ground. "We invade the territories of wild beasts and venomous reptiles and then complain that we are infested by their bites and stings." *Natural Theology,* 63.

68. *Travels,* 227.

69. *Ibid.,* 187-88. Bartram's skills in the visual arts are obvious in his drawings of the snakes he describes in the *Travels.* These drawings are not, however, included in the *Travels* and are not my concern here. They are reproduced in *Bartram's Drawings,* plts. 29, 50, 53, 58.

70. See Ewan's comments and references in *Bartram's Drawings,* 23, 169.

71. *Bartram,* 80.

Hugh Moore (essay date 1981)

SOURCE: Moore, Hugh. "The Southern Landscape of William Bartram: A Terrible Beauty." *Essays in Arts and Sciences* 10, no. 1 (1981): 41-50.

[*In the following essay, Moore argues that Bartram's* Travels *is powerful and effective because of the writer's ability "to write as a Romantic poet with a sense of wonder, feeling, and imagination and as a scientific Rationalist like his father."*]

William Bartram's **Travels** (1791) is perhaps the most comprehensive work from early America. It is a pioneering and inclusive natural history of the new world—its botany, zoology, geology, ethnology—with observations on agricultural, industrial, and commercial development. It is a history and a sociological study of the South. It is a philosophical and religious quest attempting to relate man, nature, and God. It is a practical handbook on gardening and the use of plants for food and medicine. It is literature that in its narratives of wilderness adventures and exuberant descriptions of the terrible beauty of the virgin Southern landscape captures the excitement of discovery. But his **Travels** is also comprehensive in its record of Bartram's remarkable achievement in forming his own ideas and attitudes from a creative fusion of ideas and traditions that impinged upon him. His achievement in consolidating and harmonizing often seemingly contradictory impulses provides an unexpected intellectual tension and depth to his writing just as the range of his interests gives it fullness and diversity.

The effectiveness of his style and technique in this work results from his double vision, an ability to write as a Romantic poet with a sense of wonder, feeling, and imagination and as a scientific Rationalist like his father. So he produced that rarity, in the words of Elsa Allen, "literary prose of true scientific substance."[1] Poetry and science blend in his descriptions: "I was struck with surprise and delight when beholding its gayity (of the Pinckneya Bracteata) so very singular in its bloom. But that which gives the tree its chiefest gayity is the large Papery Bracteae intersperst among the Thyrsis . . ."[2] His exuberant tale of the abundance and ferocity of alligators seemed until recently to be more allied to traveler's stories of exotic strangeness similar to Josselyn's *Rareties* than to natural history. Yet every detail has since been verified; his study of their life cycle is as valid as his narrative is thrilling.

The informing tension of the *Travels* derives from Bartram's dream of man and nature in harmony, his attempt to find or create a Utopia in which wilderness and civilization, appreciation and use, the practical and the aesthetic, are balanced so that man could be at home in the natural environment. His philosophy of nature, then, stresses the value of nature in itself and for what it can provide man. Familiar tenets of both Rationalism and Romanticism provide his axioms, but his ideas are an original and well considered fusion. Nature to Bartram meant the out-of-doors, the world of plants, animals—even Indians and other primitives—geological structures, all of which manifest the wisdom, goodness, harmony, and unity of the divinity. Studying nature, he united religion and science: ". . . my chief happiness consisted in tracing and admiring the infinite power, majesty, and perfection of the great almighty Creator. . . ."[3] Natural Law was the order, morality, and justice he found in nature, which should undergird the conduct of men and the laws of society. "Let us," he says, "rely on Providence, and by studying and contemplating the works and power of the Creator, learn wisdom and understanding in the economy of nature . . ." (p. 55).

Abstract theorizing, however, is rare in Bartram's works. His generalizations derive from observation. Such is the case in his radical, exalted view of plants and animals. Their behavior has the same causes as man's whose claim to preeminence results from pride and deficiency of direct observation. As a Rationalist he calls this cause divine or universal intellect, and as a Romanticist he sees this power diffused throughout all the creator's works. Man dominates not by intellect but by power, not a Quaker virtue. At a time when most held to one or the other, Bartram reconciled instinct and intuition with reason by proving with myriad examples that they are identical. "Can any man of sense and candour, who has the use of his eyes, Rational faculty, doubt that animals are rational creatures?"[4] Accordingly he devotes much space to marvelous accounts of animal behavior to show that they, too, exhibit premeditation, perseverance, resolution, and artifice. Bird migration

and song (which he calls language) and the cunning of the butcher spider lead him to conclude that instinct is "not a mere mechanical impulse" and is in no way inferior to reason (xvii).

The mental faculties of man and animals are identical, but the uncorrupted simplicity of animals provides moral guidance. Man is "not alone imbued with knowledge of the Creator and in expressing love, gratitude, and homage to the Great Author of Being."[5] They are not as likely as man to transgress the natural law of moderation and decency. And their loves and faithfulness—proved by the grief of a bear lamenting its dead mate—are exemplary. Even the rattler is superior in generosity and magnanimity to men. Pushing primitivism further, he finds the same divine reason in plants, likewise animated by sense and instinct. Any sensitive plant, any carnivorous one, was certain to attract Bartram's fascinated attention. Possessing motion and volition, plants, too, are directed by divine impulse. "Can we after viewing this object (the Dionea Muscipula), hesitate a moment to confess that vegetable beings are endued with some sensible faculties or attributes, similar to those that dignify animal nature?" (xiii).

Ignoring neither pole of the conflicts that inform his works, Bartram searched for a resolution that comprehended both. This he achieves in his perception of the terrible beauty of nature. He was able to strengthen his belief in the benevolence of the Creator and his works in the midst of the rapacity he met with on his Southern travels. All creation was a source of wonder and reverence not classifiable as simply fair or foul. He does not ignore unpleasant aspects: rivers exhibit "eternal war or rather slaughter," rattlers are "dreadful," winds "furious," mosquitoes "rapacious," Indians "fearsome." Not often does he engage in the typical mental gymnastics of explaining the fearsome away. (He does, however, come close when he thanks Providence for an infestation of mosquitoes because they caused him a tedious, wakeful night, thus preventing roaming alligators from catching him napping.) Nature was wild, savage, awful, grand, even horrible and ferocious—qualities that appealed to his romantic sensibility—but never evil. All was there to be studied and reconciled as part of the mysterious but ultimately beneficent whole. In the tropics amid alligators and hurricanes he forged a Wordsworthian view of nature.

Typically, Bartram presents his reconciliation of horror and beneficence, not by philosophical discourse, but rather by the literary technique of juxtaposing the two, thus giving perspective to both. He follows a depiction of fierce alligators churning the waters into a maelstrom with an idyllic scene of "towering" magnolias and "exalted" palms, described with words like "magnificence," "elegance," "gracefulness," "delicacy," and "delightful" (p. 129), thus providing counterpoint to the ravenous beasts.

Since nature is on balance beneficent and since man, plants, and animals share the same divine faculties, Bartram constantly implores his readers to recognize this affinity by lovingly protecting all living things. Quaker compassion for suffering—to Bartram cruelty was the worst of sins—and Romantic appreciation of the wild and primitive combine with natural law and rights theories applied not just, as was usually the case, to men, but to all of nature. "Let us," he writes, "be obedient to the ruling powers . . . in our duties to each other and to all creatures and concerns that are submitted to our care and control" (p. 55).

The fundamental tension, then, for Bartram, was how man could balance aesthetic and religious appreciation of nature with the practical need to use it. Where does man fit into the environment? Although this conflict remained imperfectly resolved in Bartram's life and work, the evidence suggests that his own predilection was for the Romantic over the practical. The savannah crane provided him a delicious and nourishing meal; "nevertheless as long as I can get any other necessary food I shall prefer their seraphic music in the ethereal skies, and my eyes and understanding gratified in observing their economy and social communities in the expansive green savannas of Florida" (p. 219). Dr. Fothergill had desired William to go north to search out hardy plants useful for English agriculture and gardening, but Bartram insisted on exploration in the romantic, mysterious South, where, he argued, not altogether convincingly, he could find useful productions of nature. Although throughout the **Travels** Bartram carefully nurtures the impression that he was constantly inconvenienced and endangered from collecting, in actuality, unlike his father, he sent few specimens to England. Fothergill, who had introduced bamboo and cinnamon to the West Indies, was disappointed, for his commission to Bartram was to collect ornamental plants, those scientifically curious, and those useful in the arts or for medicine and food. A practical man, Dr. Fothergill shared the prevailing view that the creator had provided a natural remedy for all the maladies and inconveniences of a region. So plant hunters like Bartram could serve to open up a region for agricultural and commercial development.

Romantic primitivism, a preference for divine simplicity, philosophically unsuited Bartram from wholeheartedly serving purely practical ends. He distrusted luxury and wealth and the intensive agriculture and industry that produced them. Governments wrongly encourage mechanic arts, manufactures, trade, commerce, large scale agriculture, for these lend not to the good of mankind but to an increase of riches, luxury, and effeminacy, all pernicious ends that result in "avarice, contention, and in the end perhaps war. . . ."[6] Thus, adjectives like "noble," "exalted," "elegant," "showy," and "gracious" greatly outnumber ones like "serviceable," "ornamental," and "useful."

Yet on his travels he by no means ignores the useful, the other pole of his study of nature. Custard apples could provide agreeable, innocent food for settlers; other plants yield dye; still others insecticide, and cypress abundant lumber. He duly records lands favorable for cotton, indigo, tobacco, rice, potatoes and notes their proximity to navigable rivers. Like less poetic travelers he could tote up mercantile advantages: the "productive manure" of the South Carolina Islands could be mined and exported (p. 10); the savannas of Capola are abundant with "that most useful metal," iron ore (p. 221); the white clay of the Jore Mountains could be shipped to England for the manufacture of porcelain (p. 361), and on and on. And he was genuinely impressed with the resourcefulness of the Irish entrepreneur with his grandiose plans for agriculture and industry: the production of wine, raisins, silk, and citrus in Georgia, all enterprises that have had since then a long history of unrelieved failure.

"To promote the happiness and convenience of mankind" (p. viii) is Bartram's stated purpose for his exploration of the South, but his ideas on what this entails is more inclusive than most of his day, including his father, Peter Collinson, and Dr. Fothergill. His definition of what exactly constitutes happiness and convenience partakes of the ideas both of Franklin and of Thoreau. The practical, it is clear, has second priority:

> . . . My chief happiness consisted in tracing and admiring the infinite power, majesty, and perfection of the great Almighty Creator, and in the contemplation, that through divine aid and permission, I might be instrumental in discovering and introducing into my native country, some original products of nature, which might be useful to society.
>
> (pp. 71-72).

Typically, he awards first place in the vegetable kingdom to a plant with no practical uses, the mimosa strigilossa, because of its beauty, delicacy, and "extreme sensibility."[7]

The terrible beauty of Bartram's Southern landscape thus arises from a combination of his love of untamed nature with his more qualified appreciation of the values of civilization. They seemed mutually exclusive, for destruction inevitably followed progress. His Southern Utopia could not last. This sense of doom gives urgency to his fears of the extinction of species, his imprecations against impious and wanton destruction by the settlers, and his praise of primitive, unmodified nature. He beheld with "rapture and astonishment" (p. 360) this Edenic world which possessed "an almost inexpressible air of grandeur" (p. 97). The devastation wrought at Mt. Royal by intensive, careless agriculture produces an inferno-like landscape with "a mournful, sallow countenance." The few remaining trees seem "violated, defaced, and torn to pieces by the bleak winds, scorched by the burning sun beams in summer and chilled by the winter frosts" (pp. 251-2).

Yet Bartram's praise for the civilization that produced such a scene can at times be enthusiastic. Commercial zeal could lead him to write like a projector as in this passage on the Alachua region:

> . . . the exuberant green meadows, with the fertile fields which immediately encircle it, would if peopled and cultivated after the manner of the civilized countries of Europe without crowding or incommoding families, at a reasonable estimation, accomodate in the happiest manner above one hundred thousand human inhabitants, besides millions of domestic animals, and I make no doubt that this place will at some future day be one of the most populous and delightful seats on earth.
>
> (p. 249).

One is hard pressed to explain statements like this: "by the arts of agriculture and commerce, almost every desirable thing in life might be produced and made plentiful here . . ." (p. 232). Rational practicality can thus occasionally overwhelm the naturalist-poet.

Not for long does Bartram forget the glory of snakes, Indian simplicity, and untamed lands. Characteristically he forges a resolution, fragile though it may be, that for him reconciles civilization with wilderness, man with his environment. This reconciliation, however, is only implied, never discussed, and may be one of which Bartram was not completely aware, a subconscious fusion of opposing forces. In the majority of the passages praising agricultural development the Indian use of the land rather than the European provided the model. Indians, lacking greed, used the native orange groves, cultivated vegetables rather than cash crops, and disturbed little the awful and sublime forests, which, perceptively, Bartram saw as ameliorating the climate thus serving practical as well as aesthetic ends.

The agricultural practices of the Marshall Plantation, for example, he deems exemplary for their cultivation of corn and indigo left intact "groves of floriferous and fragrant trees and shrubs" (p. 10). Similarly, plantations in the Charleston area admirably combined the wild with the tame.

> This ancient sublime forest, frequently intersected with extensive avenues, vistas, and green lawns, opening to extensive savannas and far distant rice plantations, agreeably employs the imagination, and captures the senses by scenes of magnificence and grandeur.
>
> (p. 307).

Once again Bartram travels the perilous middle course between conflicting values as he implies a resolution that denies the validity of neither side. Wilderness and civilization both have their beauty and their terror, and, he implies, these could perhaps coexist. Early in his travels he observes, a bit wistfully, "birds are not numerous in desert forests; they draw near to the habitations of men . . ." (p. 20).

Indians, too, were an important part of Bartram's Southern landscape, the terrible beauty of the wilderness. His conflicting traditions and ideas find a nearly perfect synthesis in his passionate championing of humane treatment for Indians, an attitude at odds with his father's hatred of savages and with the prevailing opinion of the time. Repelled at the cruelty of their persecution, Bartram based his support on the rationalistic argument of fundamental principles of equality and natural rights, on a romantic appreciation of innocence and simplicity, and on Fox's doctrine that heathens also possessed the inward light of innate moral principles. As a scientist he studied Indian cultures systematically and described them accurately, always distinguishing observed fact from hearsay, so that his observations have scientific merit. He was, for instance, among the first to differentiate the customs and languages of various tribes. His theory of a vanished race of mound builders was formed from a weight of evidence and was accepted for over one hundred years. Taking Indian knowledge of nature seriously, he included Indian lore as part of his botanical descriptions.

His purpose in studying the Indians, he explains, was to ascertain if they would adopt white civilization, and if integration would benefit them. From the evidence he meticulously gathered, he concluded that persecution is unmerited and that Indians desired a closer association with whites as long as their culture could be preserved. Bartram proposed a reasonable and humane plan. The government should study Indian customs and manners prior to forming a policy. Again he reconciles both polarities.

Indians further merit study for the moral guidance that their conduct provides whites. In Indian simplicity he found a happy reconciliation of reason and intuition that stands as a corrective to greed, luxury, vice, and cruelty. Savages possess an innate "moral principle" that directs individual conduct to virtuous actions and wisdom (p. 21) and their government to peace, love, equality, and happiness (p. 111). "Divine wisdom dictates and they obey" (p. 493). Their bold ferocity is reasonable, for it stems from a virtuous tenacity in holding to the "liberties and natural rights of man" (p. 483).

Just as he dreaded the consequences of the taming of the wilderness, Bartram feared the corrupting effect of the white man upon the Indian. The primitive state, "Peacable, contented, and sociable" (p. 109), can be fearsomely altered by the onslaught of civilization. "Foreign superfluities" (p. 212) and "artificial refinements" (p. 351) can so bedazzle their "divine simplicity" (p. 351) that Indians, too, plunder the land. And worse, the tyranny, cruelty, and licentiousness of the traders can turn the Indian respect for his natural rights into fierce savagery. Indian society and customs provided the human part of Bartram's Southern Utopia, and like the wilderness, they, too, possessed a terrible beauty. Bartram's inclusive vision could encompass both his own culture and that of the Indian.

William Bartram reconciled and balanced opposing forces in his own life even more effectively than he did in the *Travels.* To many his life has appeared disjointed, drifting, even inexplicable, yet it derives directly form his creative fusion of seemingly contradictory tensions. More than most men, he lived his philosophy. Self-effacing and modest, he minutely describes and classifies plants, animals, Indians, landscapes, but tells his audience little of himself, nothing at all about his reasons for often puzzling choices. Even so, a consistent, integrated, and forceful identity emerges from his writing and from the facts of his biography.

What to do about talented young Billy and his prospects in life was a constant worry to his father and his friends Peter Collinson and Benjamin Franklin. Apprenticeship to a Philadelphia merchant failed to bring success or fulfillment. Nor was his management, with relatives, of a trading store at Cape Fear, North Carolina, from 1761-1765, more than a dutiful attempt to placate his father. In 1765-66, William accompanied his father, serving as artist and botanical apprentice on a pioneering exploration of St. John's River.

This trip through the Southern wilderness shaped the rest of his life. Here, freed from commercial drudgery, he found his Utopia. His attempt to live there, from 1766-1767, at a time when Dennis Rolle and others were trying, grandly but futilely, the same thing, seems neither surprising nor desperate. His stated purpose—to produce cotton and indigo—was obviously little more than a practical pretext to calm his father's fears. If Henry Laurens, who twice visited him, can be trusted, William clearly was seeking values other than commercial ones. The site twenty-four miles from St. Augustine was, Laurens wrote John, the least agreeable, most unhealthy one he had ever encountered, consisting of swampy, stagnant back waters and pine barrens. In Laurens's view, William seemed to lack the energy for the prodigious labor needed to turn such unpromising land into a profitable plantation. William managed to clear but one acre for rice, and his garden was drowned out. Laurens was effective, for John called his son home from his "forlorn state."[8]

This venture, called disapprovingly, "Billy's frolic" by Collinson, in reality was a serious and pragmatic working out of the tensions that inform Bartram's writings.

He was, by attempting to live in the wilderness, trying to find how man fit into the divine economy. He was empirically testing his faith that man could, after the Indian fashion, live in the wilderness without destroying it. His reluctance to clear and plant thus owes more to his philosophy than to any lack of energy and drive. Whether or not he regarded his experiment as successful, he obeyed his father's summons and returned to Philadelphia, where, for the next five years, he worked as a farm hand and developed his artistic skills by drawing shells and turtles for Dr. Fothergill.

Eagerly accepting his patron's commission to search for plants, for the next four years, 1773-1777, he achieved integration of the practical with the scientist and poet in the Southern wilderness. From this time on his life was settled, his identity secure. He remained, from the age of 38 until his death in 1823, managing and developing his father's farm and garden which had been inherited by his brother. Living a simple and retired life he refused all inducements to leave. In 1782 he declined the Chair of Botany at the University of Pennsylvania; in 1805 he refused Jefferson's invitation to accompany Lewis and Clark; and in 1806 Alexander Wilson's request to explore the Ohio. In his garden he permanently achieved the harmony and wholeness that had eluded him even in Florida. Here he systematically ordered and studied plants, observed animal behavior, wrote his *Travels* and studies of Indians, as well as an essay attacking slavery which he was preparing at the end of his life. Here he could live as a poet, a natural scientist, a defender of nature as of Indians and Blacks, as well as a farmer and nurseryman. His found Utopia, to which he returned only in memory, was in the Southern wilderness, but his created one, the one he could live in, was in Philadelphia.

The Bartram garden was unique. John had created the country's first real botanical garden, the world's largest collection of species from the wilderness. William developed, arranged, enlarged, and nurtured the collection. So renowned did the garden become that a steady stream of luminaries—Governor Martin, Manasseh Cutler, Dr. Clarkson, James Madison, Hamilton, Washington, and Jefferson—visited there. All were invariably impressed with William's knowledge of plants, his simplicity and modesty, and with the large collection of rare species. But most judged that the garden lacked design and order. Too natural for some, it was too much a plant museum to others. Accurately perceiving Bartram's intention, however, Alexander Wilson called it not a garden, but "Bartram's woods," "a little Paradise."[9]

William Bartram's most congenial life's work became not taming wild nature, but redeeming an area already civilized and returning it to nature in order to preserve and study endangered species. Anticipating trends in garden design, Bartram was obviously not trying to achieve the formality of European gardens, admired by Washington, Hamilton, and even Jefferson, but was rather trying to recreate and preserve a natural habitat. Plan and order were there, but not rigidly so. The wild beauty of his garden could at least suggest the terror of the Southern wilderness.

Notes

1. Quoted in Joseph Ewan ed., *William Bartram: Botanical and Zoological Drawings, 1756-1788.* (Philadelphia, American Philosophical Society, 1968), p. 26.

2. Ewan, p. 152.

3. William Bartram, *Travels, Through North and South Carolina, Georgia, East and West Florida.* (Savannah, Georgia, the Beehive Press). p. 11. All references are to this facsimile of the 1792 London edition.

4. Manuscript letter to Benjamin Barton, December 29, 1792. American Philosophical Society, Philadelphia.

5. *Ibid.*

6. *Bartram Papers.* Manuscript Division. Philadelphia Historical Society.

7. Ewan, p. 156.

8. Josephine Herbst, *New Green World.* (New York, Hastings House Publishers, 1954), pp. 218-220.

9. Robert Cantwell, *Alexander Wilson.* (Philadelphia and New York, J. B. Lippincott & Co., 1961) p. 120.

John Seelye (essay date 1981)

SOURCE: Seelye, John. "Beauty Bare: William Bartram and His Triangulated Wilderness." *Prospects: The Annual of American Cultural Studies* 6 (1981): 37-54.

[*In the following essay, Seelye claims that* Travels *was originally intended as a record of scientific observations, but a closer look reveals a humanistic tone that is based on the divine providence of nature.*]

In September 1753 the American botanist John Bartram set out with his young son Billy from their farm on the banks of the Schuylkill for the Catskill Mountains for the purpose of gathering seeds and plant samples. The journey ended at the Hudson Valley home of Cadwallader Colden, surveyor-general of New York and himself a botanist of note, where the Bartrams made the acquaintance of yet another botanist, Alexander Garden of Charleston, South Carolina. The elder Bartram encour-

aged Garden to open correspondence with Linnaeus, the Swedish naturalist to whom Bartram had been writing for years, correspondence that gives particular point to this triangular meeting on the banks of the Hudson. For the Bartrams' journey and their visit with the other two botanists may be said to epitomize the scientific Enlightenment in colonial America, an intellectual voluntarism that had as its political counterpart a formal gathering of regional representatives in nearby Albany the year following. That convention, necessitated by the hostilities soon to erupt as the French and Indian War, produced a prototype of the Constitution, and the impromptu congress that met at "Coldenhamia" in 1753, though animated by pacific purposes, was likewise a manifestation of federated and protonational design.

Bringing together three men (and a boy) who represented Eastern, middle, and Southern centers of colonial culture, it lacked only a native New Englander to complete the symbolic representation, and in a sense one such was present at the meeting, for gatherings of this sort at mid-century were the work, often directly, of Ben Franklin, the Boston-born *philosophe* who was rapidly becoming the chief citizen of a nascent republic and whose fame reached even to Europe. In that same year of 1753, Franklin was awarded honorary degrees from Harvard and Yale and had received a medal from the Royal Society for his experiments with electricity. Equally important, in 1753 also Ben Franklin was made postmaster-general of British North America, an appointment that required him ("enabled" would be a better word) to travel widely throughout the colonies, thereby increasing his already wide circle of friends and acquaintances. His work improving channels of colonial communication was as much a symbolic as a political task, for Franklin was even before he assumed office the mailman of America, his letter file a veritable pocket congress of the most notable personages in the colonies.

Patron of Bartram and friend to Colden, Franklin would soon make the acquaintance of Garden, and he corresponded with Linnaeus, as well as with other men of science in Europe. He was literally a medium of exchange, and when John Bartram left Philadelphia on his Catskill journey, Franklin sent along "some meteorological conjectures" for Cadwallader Colden's "amusement."[1] Because Franklin, as the publisher of *Poor Richard's Almanac* and the inventor of the lightning rod (a description of which was printed in his almanac for 1753), was also the Weather Man of America, Bartram's specific errand was doubly significant. And the correspondence of the meeting at Coldenhamia with the Albany Congress bears further witness to Franklin's pervasive influence, for it was he who was the chief author of the embryonic Constitution presented there. Although the document failed of adoption by the colonial legislatures, it attests to Franklin's many-sidedness—a diamond-like interfacedness that made him not only a generic Yankee but something of a cosmic American. An Enlightenment equivalent of the Renaissance man, Ben Franklin in 1753 was a colonial and protonational counterpart to Uncle Sam.

Among other symbolic forces on the move in 1753 must be listed the young George Washington, who set out late in the year with Christopher Gist to carry a message from Governor Dinwiddie of Virginia to the commander of the French forces in the Ohio Valley, a heroic mountain crossing that prefigured his return in 1754 with a considerably enlarged company of men. That martial expedition ended with an exchange of shots which started the French and Indian War, a conflict generally agreed upon as having made possible the Revolution, which began some twenty years later with gunfire on the banks of a stream much farther to the east. Washington would be the champion of the War for Independence, a struggle that he in a very real sense initiated by his wilderness voyage to Ohio in 1753. Thus Washington's wintry trek across the Alleghenies can be seen as not only a personal but a national rite of passage, the epical sweep of which is dramatically demonstrated by yet another journey undertaken in 1753: A typical New England hegira from Boston "by way of Litchfield" to Portsmouth on the Piscataqua and back, it was a summertime vacation jaunt that got young John Adams back to Harvard in time for the start of classes. As always, Adams provides something by way of comic contrast as cosmic events unfold.

But more meaningful counterpoint to Washington's trans-Allegheny adventure is provided by Billy Bartram, for whom the Catskill journey with his father was his own rite of passage, an apprenticeship to the craft of gathering seeds and plant samples for shipment abroad. And no more stark antithesis to George Washington could be imagined than Billy Bartram. John Bartram was a rural version of Ben Franklin, being a Quaker farmer of humble origins whose garden brought him international fame but who seldom transcended his utilitarian view of botany. His son, by contrast, was less able at business but had considerable artistic talents, and would in time become a traveler of a transcendent sort, a naturalist with an errand far beyond the collecting and identifying of North American flora. Father and son are virtual personifications of the developing Enlightenment spirit in America, at one end a persistent but pedestrian gathering of information, at the other a sunburst of rising glory merging with the nimbus of revolutionary romanticism.

For John Bartram nature was a storehouse of useful commodities created by a beneficent Diety for man, but for William the natural world was irradiated with an almost mystical aura, a divine light that gave a religious meaning to Linnaean order. As a rustic Franklin, John

Bartram in his writing spoke directly and helpfully to his contemporaries, but William's most appreciative audience was a newer generation than even his own. His writings were criticized upon publication for containing less science than poetry, but they were praised later on for their imaginative qualities by Coleridge, Wordsworth, and Carlyle. Based upon journeys undertaken even as the opening battles of the Revolution were being waged, Bartram's writings evince a creative counterpart to that martial Enlightenment epic, an unselfconscious expression of the spirit that matches Washington's heroic élan and succeeds where the intended bardic exercises of republican poets like Joel Barlow and Timothy Dwight do not. Those celebrations of Independence wore chains of heroic couplets, linking the American muse to British modes, but William Bartram's *Travels* evinces a freshness of creation, recommending itself to English poets who were seeking to throw off the Augustan yoke.

And yet in terms of neoclassical and romantic, Enlightenment and Revolutionary, William Bartram remains less easy to classify than the unusual plants he collected. Hovering between generations and generalities, he is of the Enlightenment yet beyond it, while not quite within the Romantic zone. He is perhaps best described as the American Blake—though his graphic skills were considerably less—for his vision is both private and eccentric, an expression of the reclusive muse. For to compare his *Travels* with that classic of contemporary British naturalist writing, Gilbert White's *Selborne* (1789), is to detect definitive American (and protoromantic) differences, a cosmic as opposed to a microcosmic perspective and a love of an exotic instead of a local milieu. Where White wrote of his native haunts, Bartram was haunted by visions of faraway Florida, where he first went in 1765, accompanying his father on another plant-gathering expedition.

Enthralled by the tropic scene, William stayed on for a year, much to his father's irritation, setting up in a quixotic venture involving an indigo plantation. This having failed, he returned home in 1767, but when the opportunity presented itself in 1773 to go back to Florida, he did so, undertaking the first of the journeys that make up his *Travels.* For the prosaic John Bartram Florida was just another, if exceptionally interesting, place from which to harvest plant samples and information, but for William it had a powerful fascination, drawing on something deep within his psyche, a hunger for the unknown and mysterious that transcended an urge to gather and classify the "curiosities" of nature. John Bartram was never more than an enlightened farmer, scientific counterpart to those who fired the shots at Concord Bridge, but William was closer in spirit to that other seedsman, Thoreau, who planted beans that reached to the sky.

Something further of the difference between John and William Bartram may be gathered by comparing the son's *Travels* with the record of a journey his father took in 1743, just thirty years before William set out for the wilds of Florida.[2] Taken in company with Conrad Weiser and Lewis Evans, John Bartram's trip to the sources of the Susquehanna was an epochal event, a prelude of several sorts to the epical collision of geopolitical forces soon to take place. It was nominally a diplomatic mission by Weiser, who was traveling to an Iroquois council at Onandaga in the hope of securing a treaty of peace with the Six Nations, another in a series of ambassadorial visits by Weiser that would eventually secure Iroquois loyalty in the subsequent war with France. And Lewis Evans came along to gather data for his great map of 1749, an early draft of his even greater map of 1755, which would serve to guide Braddock over the Allegheny Mountains and into the ambush set by the French and Indians. Against these geopolitical errands, Bartram's quest seems small enough, yet his observations concerning "curious plants, shrubs, and trees" was matched by remarks relevant to sites for future settlements, an imperial perspective that is given further point by Bartram's attitude toward the region's Indians, for unlike Weiser he had little admiration for the red man, whom he regarded as not worth his notice, save for wary glances.

Given an epic élan by the gathering tensions of impending war, John Bartram's 1743 journey is a logical extension of earlier travels of colonial exploration, and may be seen as a continuation of Captain John Smith's voyage as far as the falls of the Susquehanna in 1608. As such, it is counterpart to George Washington's trans-Allegheny trip in 1753, which was another diplomatic mission in the interests of securing Anglo-American empire. All three were imperial journeys, undertaken by men acting under instructions from colonial powers, and, most important, all three were harbingers of civilized order, whether in the shape of exploration bringing settlement in its wake or as scientific discovery for the benefit of mankind. All three likewise took their way largely by means of river valleys, whether those of the Susquehanna or Potomac or the westward-flowing Monongahela, for running water in the seventeenth and eighteenth centuries determined the flow chart of empire, being essential both for initial exploration and for the commercial exchange that inevitably followed. Voyages of discovery were for both centuries matters of imperial fact, but for Americans during the height of the Enlightenment they gained the power of metaphor, as dramatic actions extending the borders of both knowledge and civilization, and when Joel Barlow set out to write his Enlightenment epic, it was only natural that he chose Columbus for his visionary hero and likewise that he provided his nationalistic poem long catalogues of major American streams.

By contrast, William Bartram's *Travels* shares in common with these imperial errands and epics only the necessity of traveling mostly by rivers. His was not a national but a highly individualistic exercise, a personal and subjective errand into the wilderness, nor was he a likely figure for a heroic action: "Town-eater" was what the Indians called Washington, while Bartram was dubbed "Flower-hunter" by the Seminoles. As a label it was accurate enough, for his Florida mission was to gather plant specimens for his patron, Dr. John Fothergill of England, and in other respects also William was the son of his father even though the kind of child that is father to the man. He differed most, perhaps, in his regard toward Indians, an attitude bordering on a Rousseauistic appreciation of noble savagery, and this is a substantial difference especially in America, where direct contact with the red man tended to rid travelers of (among other things) a misplaced primitivism. William's fond regard for Indians, moreover, was a manifestation of his love of nature in its wildest forms—a quality of religious adoration that recommended him to Wordsworth but most certainly distinguished him from his rationalistic, Deist father. That William traveled in 1773-74 the same route he had earlier taken with his father, and that he freely borrowed from his father's own journal of that previous voyage, may be an eighteenth-century Oedipal (or Telemachean) manifestation, but we have only to lay one journal next to the other to measure the generational gap.

Moreover, the better to comprehend the purpose and nature of John Bartram's Florida journal, it must be put within the frame of the book with which it was published in 1766, William Storck's *Description of East-Florida*. Storck's contribution, somewhat larger than Bartram's, had appeared independently earlier the same year and was written to encourage the settlement and economic exploitation of the region recently ceded to Great Britain by Spain, part of the massive geopolitical realignment of North American territories occasioned by the Treaty of Paris in 1763. "The importance of East-Florida, in a national view," wrote Storck in the introduction to his work, "depends upon two grounds; first, its fertility in producing such articles of commerce as will be beneficial to Great Britain; secondly, upon its convenience, from its situation and other circumstances, to carry on a beneficial commerce with the Spanish settlements in time of peace; and to intercept the trade, and cut off their communication with Europe in time of war" (p. ii).[3] Storck's point of view was unabashedly imperial, and gave point to his conviction that "the southern colonies, though the latest settled . . . yield more valuable articles of trade and (the number of inhabitants considered) greatly surpass the northern in the amount of their exports" (p. iv). In the manner of most colonial propagandists, Dr. Storck "in estimating the value of East-Florida . . . accounted upon what it will be when settled, rather than upon what it now is" (p.

vii). And John Bartram's appended journal is likewise emphatic on matters of potential value, what *is* being assessed chiefly for what it *might be.*

Dr. Storck supplied a brief introduction to Bartram's journal, in which he recommended the author "as an able Naturalist," whose reputation "in the learned world" was attested to by his recently becoming "Botanist to his Majesty for both the Floridas." "The usefulness of his Journal," observed Storck, "in making early known to the world what are the natural productions of the country to which it relates, is a sufficient proof of the usefulness of his appointment" (p. i). This lends a utilitarian handle to the whole, while Storck's general observation, "that intelligent men, whose knowledge is extended over the whole globe, will endeavour to multiply the articles of commerce in his Majesty's dominions," provides an Enlightenment candle (p. ii). Such multiplication, moreover, will be affected "by transferring the useful trees, plants, and grains, from countries where they are cultivated to those where they are not, but may be cultivated equally well." For the introduction of a single grain of rice in Carolina has "totally changed the face and condition of the country." Thus His Majesty's American plantations will become literally trans-plantations, "a field in which the naturalist may make his science peculiarly useful."

The union of Enlightenment ideals and colonial exploitation was a mid-eighteenth-century equivalent to the missionary impulse that graced the entry of England into the imperial games of the late sixteenth century. The chief motive remained the acquisition of profit and the great need was for investment capital, but there is no denying the zeal for knowledge that dignified commercial enterprise, a synergetic combination epitomized by Storck's pronouncement that "a country unknown, must, if a paradise, still continue a desart" (p. xi). "It is," he wrote, "the happiness of the present age, that an active spirit is seen every where; and that all means of acquiring wealth and bettering the private condition of life are sought after, and examined to the bottom, so that nothing which deserves attention, remains long unknown, after the means of information are to be come at" (p. xi). No better personification of that "active spirit" could be found in America than John Bartram (unless it was his city cousin-german Ben Franklin), whose "enlarged and active mind" (Storck's phrase) had taken in the length and breadth of the colonies, traveling in quest of knowledge not so much for its own sake as for the material well-being of himself and others. John Bartram was the kind of naturalist for whom the "nature . . . of any country" was intimate to its potential "value."

Bartram's Florida journal is a record of his "search for the head of the river St. John's," that unusual stream that runs due north, parallel to the eastern coast. But as with his journey to the sources of the Susquehannah, the occasion was chiefly a catalogue of those aspects of the landscape that "may be improved by culture" (pp. 1-2). Like Thoreau, John Bartram had a fondness for "choice swamps," but as places in which to plant rice, not himself, and he lists also the high ground in between marshes that would be "rich for corn" and enumerates the plentiful (and edible) wildlife. If Bartram's journal differs from the usual imperial survey, it is in its reflection of abundance and sheer size that is characteristic of tropic places, aspects of natural plenitude that first stagger then baffle man's capacity for measurement,

> . . . the monstrous grapevines, 8 inches in diameter, running up the oaks 6 foot in diameter, swamp-magnolias 70 foot high strait, and a foot diameter, the great magnolia very large, liquid amber, white swamp and live oaks, chinquapines and cluster-cherry, all of an uncommon size, mixed with orange-trees, either full of fruit or scattered on the ground, where the sun can hardly shine for the green leaves at Christmas [this entry was for December 27], and in a mass of white or yellow soil 16 foot more or less above the surface of the river.
>
> [p. 5]

This breathless run of prose is like a man floundering through a jungle marsh, where rational mensuration soon ceases and sinks below the surface of plenty with one last desperate "more or less" calculation.

John Bartram's emphasis on sheer size extends to the great fountains, which his son would make famous among the poets of England, but the sources from which flowed Coleridge's emblem for the imagination were for the father reckoned chiefly in terms of utility, being "big enough to turn a mill" (p. 12). John Bartram was not without his capacity for wonder, but here again it takes the form of dimension: "What a surprising fountain must it be, to furnish such a stream, and what a great space of ground must be taken up in the pinelands, pines, savannahs, and swamps, to support and maintain so constant a fountain, continually boiling right up from under the deep rocks, which undoubtedly continue under most part of the country at uncertain depths" (p. 12). His delight likewise in experiencing December in Florida takes on the look of a Christmas in Cockayne, as when he records on the nineteenth day of the season a "fine warm morning, birds singing, fish jumping, and turkies gobbling" (p. 21). Still, Bartram's desire to please King and country was not so great as to cause him to elide the less pleasant facts about the abundant life along the Saint John's, which included "the very troublesome muskitoe," as well as "the ticks creeping and lizards running about our tent" (p. 19). Moreover, if the fountains were of all things large and beautiful, they also had "a loathsome taste" (p. 19).

As for the region Indians, they are conspicuous by their monumental absence from John Bartram's journal, as in the great "tumulus" that provides the chief feature and name for "Mount Royal," an Indian mound "nearly 100 yards in diameter, nearly round, and near 20 foot high," which had some "bones scattered on it," and which Bartram reckoned as "very ancient, as live-oaks are growing upon it three foot in diameter" (p. 25). Though he devotes considerable space to pondering how primitive men could have raised such a mound, Bartram leaves the general impression that such activities have long since ceased, the "tumulus" itself being the "burying-place or sepulchre" of those who built it (p. 26). Like "the remains of an old Spanish entrenchment" found on the bank of the Saint John's, the Indian mound is evidence of prior, not present, tenancy (p. 27). Bartram calls the southwest shore of the river "the Indian side," but nothing is seen of the inhabitants there.

John Bartram's perspective is epitomized by the view he obtains from "a fine rich low dry bluff," which provided "a very extensive prospect to the Indian side over marshes and large swamps; this is the finest piece of rich dry ground I observed since we left the head of the river; it produced very good rich grass, palms, and live oaks," and cutting down one of the cabbage palms, Bartram and his party dined on its "top bud, the white tender part. . . . I never eat half so much cabbage at a time, and it agreed the best with me of any sauce I ever eat, either alone or with meat" (p. 20). This place, like the palm cabbage, so agreed with the naturalist that he named it "Bartram's Bluff," which was, in a sense, called when his son attempted to farm the "excellent swamps" in the neighborhood, for Billy seems to have taken his father at his written word, even though he had accompanied him on the voyage. In John Bartram's opinion, Billy was so much more the fool for taking his propaganda literally: "Nothing will do with him now," he wrote to a friend in June 1766, "but he will be a planter upon St. John's River," a venture John called "this frolic of his."[4]

And yet, once again, Billy was very much his father's boy, for if John's "enlarged and active mind" was symbolic of the utilitarian bent of the Enlightenment in England and America, then William's equally capacious and active soul expanded into idealistic spheres, evincing a Rousseauistic quality of optimism and philanthropy that was characteristic of the Enlightenment at its farthest end. His fling at farming the rich swamps of the Saint John's ended in near tragedy, yet he was able, a few years later, to return to the very same region and record the scene in terms which make his father's praises very pale prose by comparison. William Bartram's account of his Florida travels belongs next to Crèvecoeur's *Letters From an American Farmer,* which is another example of the hyperpastoral mode engendered by the American experience. Written at about the same time, Crèvecoeur's semifictional account of life in the New World had such an air of truth to it that the

book inspired Coleridge to make plans for a Pantisocracy on the banks of the Susquehanna, which had they materialized would have gained America a very poor farmer and lost England a great poet.

Coleridge instead made immortal poetry out of Bartram's book, a wise choice and one that testifies to the common bond linking the Enlightenment to the Romantic period, which followed. Coleridge's use of Bartram's fountain was perhaps more symbolic than he realized, the one a welling up of cosmic optimism that became further irradiated (even to the extent of producing a few ominous shadows) by the poet's Romantic lamp. At the center of Hector St. John's book is John Bartram, cousin-german to his autobiographical Farmer James (who is given an English father, like Bartram's, while Crèvecoeur's Bartram, like himself, is of French extraction), a pastoral and georgic ideal of Enlightenment rationality. At the center of William's book are the marvelous fountains of the Saint John's, which inspired one of the most mystical, mysterious, and intensely lyrical poems of the English Romantic period.

Yet both William Bartram and Crèvecoeur are Enlightenment men, and the comparison often made between both men and Thoreau is of more shadow than substance. Each evinces certain of Thoreau's characteristics—his pastoralism verging on primitivism, his abhorrence of slavery, his intense engagement with the natural world—but they do so in distinctly Enlightenment terms. Crèvecoeur, for all his praise of the New Man, remains in his *Letters* a loyal subject to the English Crown, an advocate of law and order subsumed to higher authority, and he evinces no love of wilderness raw, preferring his land cleared and his woodchuck roasted. Bartram is perhaps closer to Thoreau in his intensity of rapport with wildness, including Indians, but if we look closely at his *Travels* we find the marks of Enlightenment order all along the lush banks of the Saint John's River, and a quality of wonder that yields to an impulse to explain.

In assessing the form and purpose of Bartram's *Travels,* we must at the start state the obvious—because it has not always been obvious—that the book is in large part a work of science. The poetic aspects of Bartram's book were early seen to be in conflict with his scientific intention, and their use by the romantic poets has acted subsequently to throw a weight of attention on those parts at the cost of neglecting the voluminous catalogues and classifications that make up a large percentage of the total bulk. Modern readers clearly prefer the live aspects of Bartram's garden to his *hortus siccus,* and a number of recent editions have excised the scientific material in order to salvage the rest. When it was restored to the text by Francis Harper, the editor felt compelled to warn away casual readers by calling his work a "Naturalist's Edition." Harper is certainly right in maintaining, as he does, that there is nothing less interesting than yesterday's data. Science is of the essence of progress, and its findings are, like the clouds of ephemera observed by Bartram along the Saint John's, sufficient unto the day. Today's giant step forward is tomorrow's dusty pile of moon rocks. Thus Bartram's observations on bird migration, innovative for his time, serve little purpose today other than to demonstrate his acumen, and a number of his descriptions of Floridian wildlife remain useless because they are, in Harper's word, unidentifiable. We cannot even be assured that Bartram was describing species now extinct, because his descriptive abilities were limited by the rudimentary technical language of his day. Thus, as science, Bartram's *Travels* is not of much value today.

Yet it was intended originally as a record of scientific observations, and to edit out the now useless data is to distort the true shape of the work. When Bartram, in defending his observations of bird migration against the anticipated charge of uselessness, as being an "enquiry not to be productive of any real benefit to mankind" because "merely speculative, and only fit to amuse and entertain the idle virtuouso," his response was akin to Ben Franklin's retort to a similar charge: "Of what use is a newborn baby?" Appealing at first to the example of the ancients, Bartram suggested that a "calendar" of bird migrations "might be useful to the husbandman and gardener" (p. 178).[5] It would be difficult to find a neater paradigm of Enlightenment attitudes, for in defending himself, Bartram in effect admits that "speculation" *is* "mere" unless it has utilitarian value. So also Franklin, for if a baby is useless, the adult it will become is not. Thus Bartram's defense of his observations on bird migration is essential to an understanding of the basis of modern scientific inquiry: If data are not useful in themselves, they will be of use at a future point. Thus one is better off piling up information indiscriminately than dismissing certain observations out of hand, for one never knows which may prove to be the right baby.

There is, moreover, a second Enlightenment dimension to Bartram's lengthy catalogues of flora and fauna: As his periodic apostrophes to the "supreme author" suggest, nature's plenty is divine in its origins and has been dispersed over the earth for the good of God's favorite creature, man (cf. p. 121). Thus it is man's sacred duty to determine the proper use of God's plenty, for to neglect divine intention would be sinful (cf. p. 65). Moreover, by piling up knowledge we get closer and closer to the source of things, which is the wellhead also of truth, for as the outlines of God's plan become clearer, the beauty and fitness of His design become more apparent, which makes Him all the more to be worshiped. William Bartram was especially fond of a line from Pope's *Essay on Man*—"Hills peep o'er Hills, and Alps on Alps arise"—which changes its

meaning when removed from its proper context. Pope intended to suggest the futility of learning, which serves only to reveal how much more there is to know, but Bartram was exhilarated not discouraged by the prospect, and as in his and his father's wanderings through the mountains of eastern North America, Bartram's urge was to discover what lay on the other side. "Continually impelled by a restless spirit of curiosity" is how he describes his quest, a constant "pursuit of new productions of nature," and his "chief happiness consisted in tracing and admiring the infinite power, majesty and perfection of the great Almighty Creator, and in the contemplation, that through divine aid and permission, I might be instrumental in discovering, and introducing into my native country, some original productions of nature, which might become useful to society" (p. 48). Though hardly of the essence of poetry, Bartram's assiduous accumulation of data is intimately connected with his frequent apostrophes to natural beauty and his hymns to divine creation, at once religious in essence and scientific in spirit.

Most authorities recognize the second part of Bartram's *Travels,* his voyages on the Saint John's River, as the most interesting in terms of science, and it has been that part also which has proved most productive of poetry. There is moreover a natural order imposed on any narrative of a river voyage, an upward and downward movement essential to those actions we call plots. And the particular and unique characteristics of the Saint John's serve to enhance that inherent formal dimension, exotic local color further accented by exciting events and sudden discoveries. How much of Bartram's narrative is a genuine record, how much manipulated and exaggerated fact, we shall never know, but there are numerous indications that he compressed, expanded, and rearranged his material at will. Whether consciously imposed or purely coincidental, there is an order to be found in Bartram's account of his voyage up and down the Saint John's that encompasses and transcends his catalogues of Linnean classifications.

The river, first of all, plays a geopolitical role, serving, as Bartram Senior observed, to separate the lands claimed by the English from Indian country, and this natural boundary is expanded in William's account to something very like a symbolic line, equivalent to the frontier. Thus the Indian terrain lies to the west, the settled portion to the east, and throughout the narrative the big, two-sided river presents contrasting vistas:

> The Eastern coast of the river now opens, and presents to view ample plains, consisting of grassy marshes and green meadows, and affords a prospect almost unlimited and extremely pleasing. The opposite shore presents to view a sublime contrast, a high bluff bearing magnificent forests of grand Magnolii, glorious Palms, fruitful Orange groves, Live Oaks, Bays, and others.

[pp. 88-89]

At other times the west side of the river is all "swamps and marshes," or one "endless wild desert" with "adjoining wild plains, forests, and savanas" (pp. 99. 103-4). The east side by contrast opens to "the beautiful appearance of green meadows," an "Elysium" that bids the observer to pay a visit (p. 93).

Over this paradise wheel flocks of savanna cranes, a virtual emblem of order in nature, "all rising and falling as one bird: now they mount aloft, gradually wheeling about, each squadron performing its evolution, incircling the expansive plains, observing each one their [*sic*] own orbit . . . ascending aloft in spiral circles, bound on interesting discoveries, [they] wheel round and double the promontory, in the silvery regions of the clouded skies" (p. 93). And it is on the eastern side of the river, likewise, that Bartram discovers the marvelous fountain containing a "paradise of fish":

> Behold . . . a vast circular expanse before you, the waters of which are so extremely clear as to be absolutely diaphanous or transparent as the ether; the margin of the bason ornamented with a great variety of fruitful and floriferous trees, shrubs, and plants, the pendant Orange dancing on the surface of the pellucid waters, the balmy air vibrates [with] the melody of the merry birds, tenants of the encircling aromatic grove.

> At the same instant innumerable bands of fish are seen, some cloathed in the most brilliant colours; the voracious crocodile stretched along at full length, as the great trunk of a tree in size, the devouring garfish, inimical trout, and all the varieties of gilded painted bream, the barbed catfish, dreaded sting-ray, skate and flounder, spotted bass, sheeps head and ominous drum; all in their separate bands and communities, with free and unsuspicious intercourse performing their evolutions: there are no signs of enmity, no attempt to devour each other; the different bands seem peaceably and complaisantly to move a little aside, as it were to make room for others to pass by.

> [p. 105]

"This amazing and delightful scene," observes Bartram, "appears at first but as a piece of excellent painting . . . a just representation of the peaceable and happy state of nature which existed before the fall." But Bartram as a rural Quaker was no Hicks: "In reality it is a mere representation, for the nature of the fish is the same as if they were in lake George or the river; but here the water or element in which they live and move, is so perfectly clear and transparent, it places them all on an equality with regard to their ability to injure or escape from one another," for "here is no covert, no ambush, here the trout freely passes by the very nose of the alligator and laughs in his face, and the bream by the trout" (p. 106). At a later point Bartram discusses the effect of different environments on the "Upper" and "Lower" nations of Creeks, the first a stern culture of adversity, the other a happy one of plenty, and here a similar influence is operating. Thus what appears to be

a work of art is a natural manifestation, and what seems to be a miracle is merely the result of special circumstances. The nature of the predator remains constant and is only temporarily changed by the environment within the enchanted circle of the fountain. So miracles yield their secrets to reason while reinforcing the harmonies of the eastern side of the river.

The contrast between the eastern and western shore is borne out by Bartram's discovery, while traveling westward with Indian traders, of another marvelous fountain in the great Alachua Savanna, an "infundibuliform cavity . . . exactly circular, as if struck with a compass, sloping gradually inwards to a point at the bottom, forming an inverted cone, or like the upper wide part of a funnel" (p. 130). Within this water-filled funnel or "Great Sink" are to be found "incredible numbers of crocodiles, some of which are of enormous size," all gorging themselves on the legions of fish that crowd into the sink "from the rivers and creeks, draining from the savanna." Populated by an apparent "league or confederacy . . . of warlike voracious creatures," the Great Sink is styled by Bartram a "fatal fountain," and as an "extraordinary place and very wonderful work of nature," it provides a counterpart to the paradise of fish on the other side of the Saint John's.

At the center, metaphysically if not metaphorically, is the zone through which Bartram and his companions passed on their way west, the "Sand Hills," with an ocean-like appearance and

> . . . sparkling ponds and lakes, which at the same time gleam through the open forests, before us and on every side, retaining them on the eye, until we come up with them; and at last the imagination remains flattered and dubious, by their uniformity, being mostly circular or elliptical, and most always surrounded with expansive green meadows; and always a picturesque dark grove of Live Oak, Magnolia, Gordonia, and the fragrant Orange, encircling a rocky shaded grotto, of transparent water, on some border of the pond or lake; which, without the aid of any poetic fable, one might naturally suppose to be the sacred abode or temporary residence of the guardian spirit, but is actually the possession of a thundering absolute crocodile.

> [p. 110]

Here again is the quality of illusion, reinforced by natural symmetry and allusions to literature, but which gives way to reality. Yet these midpoint grottos, like those of Halfway Pond, where Bartram and his party spent the first night of their westward trek, do indeed contain the resident "genius of the place," though such a guardian spirit as was never dreamed of by Alexander Pope.

For John Bartram the alligator was just another example of large Floridian life, but as his son's drawings and extended descriptions suggest, William was both fascinated and terrified by the great reptiles he encountered along the Saint John's. Akin to the apocalyptic beast, the alligator is for Bartram a tropical version of Leviathan:

> Behold him rushing forth from the flags and reeds. His enormous body swells. His plaited tail brandished high, floats upon the lake. The waters like a cataract descend from his opening jaws. Clouds of smoke issue from his dilated nostrils. The earth trembles with his thunder. When immediately from the opposite coast of the lagoon, emerges from the deep his rival champion. They suddenly dart upon each other. The boiling surface of the lake marks their rapid course, and a terrific conflict commences. They now sink to the bottom folded together in horrid wreaths. The water becomes thick and discoloured. Again they rise, their jaws clap together, re-echoing through the deep surrounding forests. Again they sink, when the contest ends at the muddy bottom of the lake, and the vanquished makes a hazardous escape, hiding himself in the muddy turbulent waters and sedge on a distant shore. The proud victor exulting returns to the place of action. The shores and forests resound his dreadful roar, together with the triumphing shouts of the plaited tribes around, witnesses of the horrid combat.
>
> [pp. 75-76]

Something other than detached scientific observation, Bartram's description is designed to evoke both an epic battle and nature in its most sublime aspects, for if the scenery along the Saint John's is characterized by abundance, whether figured in groves of great trees or multitudinous swarms of ephemera, so also is it a gigantic terrain, a field of force in which fountains suddenly erupt with the sound of "a mighty hurricane," tearing the earth asunder (p. 151). The alligator is a fit, even symbolic, denizen of such a titanic arena, swamp-dwelling equivalent to the ocean's whale or the Rocky Mountain's grizzly bear.

At the farthest reach of his upriver voyage, Bartram encountered the most terrifying tropical creature of all, a hurricane, which began with "extremely sultry" weather, "not a breath of wind stirring, hazy or cloudy, and very heavy distant thunder, which answered by the crocodiles, sure presage of a storm!" (p. 89). Appalled by "the approaching tempest, the terrific appearance of which now at once confounded me," Bartram flees like Adam in paradise, as "the skies appeared streaked with blood or purple flame overhead, the flaming lightning streaming and darting about in every direction around, seems to fill the world with fire, whilst the heavy thunder keeps the earth in a constant tremor" (pp. 89-90). Taking shelter in his boat "under the high reedy bank of the lake," Bartram was drenched by the rain that soon fell, "with such rapidity and . . . in such quantities, that every object was totally obscured, excepting the continual streams or rivers of lightning, pouring from the clouds; all seemed a frightful chaos. When the wind

and rain abated, I was overjoyed to see the face of nature again appear" (p. 90). This last figure of speech implicitly establishes a disjunctive dualism: the storm, having hidden the face of nature from sight, is therefore not part of nature, but distinct. Yet like the alligator, it is not only of but in terms of the voyage at the very center of the natural world, an eruption like that of the great fountain, whose sound is compared to a hurricane. Its might, unlike the fertile swamps and placid glades, acts against man's best interests, and Bartram soon after views its devastating effect on the plantation toward which he was heading when the storm broke.

Where evidences of natural order are apt to inspire a rhapsodic hymn to the supreme wisdom of the best of all possible deities, Bartram remains silent on divine purposes when confronting the alligator or witnessing the terrific force of tropical hurricanes. These silences provide a metaphysical adjunct to his occasional logical slips of a minor sort, as in the following passage, in which Bartram reveals the inherent fallacy of his dualistic quest:

> We gently descend again over sand ridges, cross a rapid brook, rippling over the gravelly bed, hurrying the transparent waters into a vast and beautiful lake, through a fine fruitful Orange grove; which magnificently adorns the banks of the lake to a great distance on each side of the capes of the creek. This is a fine situation for a capital town. These waters are tributary to St. John's.
>
> We alighted to refresh ourselves, and adjust our packs. Here are evident signs and traces of a powerful settlement of the ancients.
>
> Set off again, and continued traveling over a magnificent Pine forest, the ridges low, but their bases extensive, with proportionable plains. The steady breezes gently and continually rising and falling, fill the high lonesome forests with an awful reverential harmony, inexpressibly sublime, and not to be enjoyed anywhere, but in these native wild Indian regions.
>
> [p. 115]

This region, as the last sentence reveals, is found on the west side of the Saint John's, in Indian country, and Bartram's confused observations, his selecting a site for a future town while admiring the wildness of the scene, reveals both his paternity and the inherent flaw in Enlightenment thinking when confronted by "native wild Indian regions." It also reveals the considerable chasm between Bartram's thinking and Thoreau's.

In his longest hymn of "anthem" to the "great Creator," Bartram prays that "the universal sovereign" will "grant that universal peace and love, may prevail in the earth, even that divine harmony, which fills the heavens, thy glorious habitation" (p. 65). This expression is intrinsic not only to Bartram's Quaker religion but to his own pacific, benevolent spirit. He declares himself "an advo-

cate or vindicator of the benevolent and peaceable disposition of animal creation in general," and in particular is willing to ascribe natural virtue to a rattlesnake
and a renegade Indian. Throughout his *Travels,* Bartram
entertains a primitivistic vision of nature and natural
man, depicting "sublime enchanting scenes" against
which are enacted "visions of terrestrial happiness," a
natural "elisium" in which the "wandering Seminole,
the naked red warrior, roams at large, and after the vigorous chase retires from the scorching heat of the meridian sun. Here he reclines, and reposes under the odoriferous shades of Zanthoxilon, his verdant couch
guarded by the Deity, Liberty, and the Muses, inspiring
him with wisdom and valour, whilst the balmy zephyrs
fan him to sleep" (p. 69). But as the mixture of pagan
and Enlightenment gods attending the Indian in his
sleep suggests, Bartram's is not Emerson's naked eye-
ball but is covered by a cluttered as well as a rose-
tinted lens.

His picture of the noble red man likewise differs from
Thoreau's, for Bartram had the disadvantage of first-
hand contact, and against his sketches of savagery at its
most noble must be placed the Conradian anecdote of
the white trader ruined by his Indian wife, a "little
charmer" who exemplifies "the power of beauty in a
savage, and their art and finess in improving it to their
private ends" (pp. 71-72). Bartram goes on to assure his
reader that the woman was "condemned and detested
by her own people," who have a "delicate sense of the
honour and reputation of their tribes and families . . .
the divine principle which influences their moral conduct, and solely preserves their constitution and civil
government in that purity in which they are found to
prevail amongst them." But one vivid anecdote is worth
several dozen like abstractions.

Bartram is at his most Thoreauvian when he compares
the life he led while with the Indian traders to "that of
the primitive state of man, peaceable, contented, and
sociable. The simple and necessary calls of nature, being satisfied, [men live] together as brethren of one
family, strangers to envy, malice, and rapine" (p. 71).
But he also describes the Seminole in terms other than
natural harmony: Having depicted the Alachua Savanna
as a peaceable kingdom, in which "herds of sprightly
deer, squadrons of the beautiful, fleet Seminole horse,
flocks of turkeys, civilized communities of the sono-
rous, watchful crane, mix together, appearing happy and
contented in the enjoyment of peace," he next conjures
up a disturbing image of "warrior man": "Behold, yon-
der, coming upon them through the darkened groves,
sneakingly and unawares, the naked red warrior, invad-
ing the Elysian fields and green plains of Alachua. At
the terrible appearance of the painted, fearless, uncon-
trolled and free Seminole, the peaceful, innocent nations are at once thrown into disorder and dismay" (p.
120). The imagery is much too close to that of an alli-

gator loose in a fountain filled with fish to ignore its
implication: There is a crocodile smile set in the red
face of man.

Keepers of slaves, the Seminoles "wage eternal war
against deer and bear" and "make war against, kill and
destroy their own species, and their motives spring from
the same erroneous source as it does in all other nations
of mankind; that is the ambition of exhibiting to their
fellows, a superior character of personal and national
valour . . . or in revenge of their enemy, for publich or
personal insults, or lastly, to extend the borders and
boundaries of their territories" (p. 135). As with the
hurricane, the Indian must be distinguished from the
paradise in which he lives. And though Bartram observes of that paradise that "such a natural landscape,
such a rural scene, is not to be imitated by the united
ingenuity and labour of man," his is a neoclassical and
orderly consciousness that accommodates natural chaos
by ignoring it and wildness by civilizing it: "This vast
plain," he remarks as he contemplates a rich vista, "together with the forests contiguous to it, if permitted (by
the Seminoles who are sovereigns of these realms) to
be in possession and under the culture of industrious
planters and mechanicks, would in a little time exhibit
other scenes than it does at present, delightful as it is;
for by the arts of agriculture and commerce, almost every desirable thing in life might be produced and made
plentiful here, and thereby establish a rich, populous,
and delightful region" (p. 148). In fairness to due proportion, such observations occupy a very small place in
Bartram's book, yet they are consistent with the whole
and are not mere token gestures, made in the hope of
recommending his *Travels* to the widest possible audience. Young George Washington, in traversing the Ohio
region in 1753-54, recorded in his journal similar if less
ornate thoughts concerning the future sites of settlements and forts, and so did John Bartram as he followed the course of the Susquehanna ten years earlier.
William's travels on the Saint John's in 1773-74 most
certainly invest his father's observations with a great
deal of poetry, but the filial effulgent branch is sustained by the paternal utilitarian root.

Like his father (and like George Washington), William
Bartram is an instrument of empire as well as of the
Enlightenment as he explores the rich Floridian savannas. With Euclidean eyes he sees cones and pyramids
everywhere, from the symmetrical sinks and magnificent magnolia to the nests of alligators, rats, and crayfish, evincing an orderly neoclassic aesthetic by imposing triangular and mathematical precision on the
abundance of a teeming nature. Dominating this orderly
landscape are the "pyramidal" or "cone-like" Indian
mounds, truncated monuments of buried empire, whose
meaning to his narrative is best provided by the name
of the mound described in most detail by both himself
and his father: "Mount Royal," a name with several

layers of implication. Like his father before him, William Bartram set out in 1773 as an agent of British empire, but when he returned to Philadelphia, in 1777, it was like Rip Van Winkle to a new nation, and the royal Indian mound in Florida would soon provide a national not a colonial perspective. Lake George, that beautiful "dilation" of the Saint John's, was named for the English king, but like its counterpart in Upstate New York and the inn in Irving's story, it would soon echo the name of the first President of the United States. On the Great Seal of that imperial republic is imprinted an Enlightenment icon, a truncated but royal pyramid topped like the magnolia with a glory, symbol of a rising nation shaped by divine authorship.

Like John Denham's *Cooper's Hill,* a poem celebrating the river Thames, Bartram's prose account of his travels along the Saint John's is in the topographical mode, being filled with the spirit of place, and though reflecting a much more enlightened sensibility than the poem by the seventeenth-century Royalist, it reflects also an equivalent love of order—in both natural and artificial terms. Transforming his father's Florida errand into a rhapsody, William Bartram still retains a utilitarian touch, and beyond the glory with which he endows the landscape we can see technological terms. William's view of nature contains a kind of "expans'd hieroglyphics," to use Denham's phrase, a secret language written large along the river's bank. Expressing a message in triangular characters of fire, an optimism so intense as to suggest a millennial gleam, it casts shadows also, in which may be seen lurking an apocalyptic beast. Fountains of light, the sources of the Saint John's are also basins of darkness, evoking the revelations of the wilderness saint for whom the river was named.

Notes

1. *The Papers of Benjamin Franklin,* ed. Leonard W. Labaree, Vol. 5 (New Haven, Conn., 1962), 81.

2. *Observations on the Inhabitants* [etc.] *Made by Mr. John Bartram, In his Travels from Pensilvania to Onondago, Oswego and the Lake Ontario . . .* (London, 1751).

3. *A Description of East-Florida, with a Journal Kept by John Bartram of Philadelphia, Botanist to His Majesty for the Floridas . . . The Third Edition, much enlarged and improved* (London, 1769), p. ii. (The pagination of Bartram's *Journal* begins after p. 39 of Storck's *Description.*) All subsequent references to the *Journal* are to pages of this edition and are given parenthetically as here.

4. Ernest Earnest, *John and William Bartram: Botanists and Explorers* (Philadelphia, 1940), p. 104.

5. *The Travels of William Bartram: Naturalists's Edition,* ed. Francis Harper (New Haven, Conn.,

1967), p. 178. All subsequent references are to pages of this edition of Bartram's *Travels* and are given parenthetically as here.

L. Hugh Moore (essay date 1983)

SOURCE: Moore, L. Hugh. "The Aesthetic Theory of William Bartram." *Essays in Arts and Sciences* 12, no. 1 (March 1983): 17-35.

[*In the following essay, Moore argues that Bartram is a prime example of a writer trying to describe nature within the context of eighteenth-century aesthetic theory.*]

From its publication in 1791, William Bartram's *Travels through North and South Carolina, Georgia, East and West Florida* has been praised for its scientific and literary merit. Francis Harper and Joseph Ewan, among others, have demonstrated the value of Bartram's contributions to zoology, botany, and ethnology, the precision of his observations, and the logic of his speculations. Harper, for example, verified the combat and bellowing of alligators from his own observations.[1] Bartram's list of birds is the most complete prior to Alexander Wilson's, whom he tutored. The *Travels,* according to Witmer Stone, is "The first ornithological contribution worthy of the name written by a native American."[2] John R. Swanton called his observations of Southern Indians "one of the best early works" and used the facts in the *Travels* to refute Bartram's theory of an ancient race of mound builders.[3] Elliott Coues praised his nomenclature as effectively binomial and found that he was the first to relate animal size to environment.[4] Even the lush descriptions have been validated. John R. Small rediscovered the Ixia coelestina in North Florida thus verifying Bartram's "azure fields of cerulean Ixia."[5] Finally, Joseph Ewan called Bartram "the one indigenous colonial artist of merit for natural history."[6]

Commentators have long responded to the charm of Bartram's descriptions and the excitement of his narrative and have noted the value of the *Travels* in the tradition of the literature of travel and discovery. Early reviewers judged it as a worthy natural history, but many deplored its "rather too luxuriant and florid" style.[7] That Wordsworth, Coleridge, Chateaubriand, and other poets were impressed by both style and content has been abundantly demonstrated by John Livingston Lowes, Lane Cooper, and N. Bryillon Fagin in their studies of the influence of the *Travels* on their work. Coleridge called it "a work of high merit in every way."[8] Thomas Carlyle recommended the *Travels* to Emerson as having "a wondrous kind of floundering eloquence in it. All American libraries ought to provide themselves with that kind of book, and keep them as a kind of *biblical* article."[9]

Literary scholarship has focused on Bartram's life, his themes, and, to a lesser extent, his style. Ernest Earnest has studied the influence of classicism and romanticism in his work,[10] and Fagin has written a general study of his personality, themes, and techniques.[11] Richard Gummere has studied his classicisms,[12] and William Sullivan his romanticism.[13] And, in the most detailed literary study yet, Frieder Busch has analyzed the devices Bartram used to achieve a sense of movement.[14] For the most part, however, literary analysis of the *Travels* has lagged behind scientific study. Few have investigated the ways in which Bartram achieved his much admired literary effectiveness or analyzed the book as a conscious work of art.

The major literary influence on Bartram was eighteenth century aesthetic theory of the beautiful, sublime, and picturesque, an aesthetic tradition comprehensive enough to enable him to present his diverse Southern landscape effectively. That he was thoroughly familiar with this theory is obvious from the frequency with which the terminology appears in his works and the books he owned or had available to him. As a member of the Library Company, a founder of the Derby Library, and a recipient of books from his British correspondents, especially Peter Collison, John Bartram had a wide selection of books beyond those on natural history that William would have had access to: John Woolman's *Journal*, Ramsey's *Travels of Cyrus*, Franklin's *Essays*, Pope's *Moral Essays*, and *Windsor Forest*, the latter quoted in William's letters and echoed in the *Travels*, Thompson's *The Seasons*, Sir John Hawkins' *The Life of Samuel Johnson*, William Hayley's *Life of William Cowper*, and Addison's *Tatler* and *The Spectator* essays. Additionally, his four years (1752-1756) at the Academy of Philadelphia brought him into contact with contemporary English literature as well as the classics, especially through his tutor, Charles Thompson. No doubt, too, he read the essays and poetry in *The American Magazine and Monthly Chronicle of the British Colonies* published by the provost William Smith. Contemporary aesthetic theory could also have reached him through the influence of poets like Thomas Godfrey, Jr., whose *Prince of Parthia* he subscribed to, and the works of his fellow students, Francis Hopkinson and Nathaniel Evans. Further, the influence of English poets working within this tradition was pervasive in the intellectual climate of Philadelphia. Benjamin Smith Barton, for example, for whom Bartram did the drawings in *Elements of Botany*, prefaced this text book with lines 79-97 on the joys of botanical research from Mark Akinside's *The Pleasures of Imagination*, a compendium on the beautiful and sublime in nature.

An analysis of the *Travels* reveals that Bartram structured his work around current theory of the beautiful, the sublime, and the picturesque. Bartram is the best example we have of a writer who could present nature and develop a theory of its benefits by writing within eighteenth century literary theory. Taking ideas from theorists like Addison, Burke, Hutcheson, and many others, he developed his original aesthetic theory. This vast body of theory represents attempts to explain the different types of aesthetic pleasure that inhere in very different objects, to classify the qualities that elicit such reactions, and to analyze the emotional, mental, and spiritual responses of the individual to objects within the environment. Whether grounded in sensational, faculty, or associational psychology, all saw the aesthetic response to nature as a way of relating man to the universe, to God, or to both. The *Travels* reveals that Bartram was fully aware of the subtleties of current aesthetic theory, that this tradition colored his perception of the Southern landscape and his scientific observations, and that he used it to structure his work and present his observations and philosophy.

Further, the *Travels,* viewed in the context of eighteenth century aesthetic theory, contributes importantly to the speculation on the categories of aesthetic pleasure from nature and the way in which the beautiful, the sublime, and the picturesque yield psychological, moral, philosophical, and religious values. Like other aestheticians—Hutcheson, Richardson, Burke, Stewart, Price, and Knight for instance—Bartram inherited concepts which he modified and explained in original ways. Bartram's is certainly the most impressive, complete, and consistent aesthetic theory produced in America up to his day. Because of the influence the *Travels* exerted on American travellers, naturalists, and explorers it influenced the way later observers saw American nature. Naturalists like William Baldwin, Humphrey Marshall, Benjamin Smith Barton, Alexander Wilson, Francis André Michaux, William H. Keating, John LeConte, and Thomas Say went to Bartram for zoological and botanical information, but they received his aesthetic theory as well. They tended to see the natural world as Bartram directed. Through these and many others such as Thoreau, Muir, and Burroughs Bartram's aesthetic reaches into the present informing perception of the wilderness.

Bartram subtly set up the three categories of beauty, sublimity, and picturesqueness in the philosophical essay with which he introduces his *Travels,* a speculation on the meaning of his experience that he did not allow himself in the objective presentation of his Florida trip in *The Report to Fothergill.* Here he states ". . . I attempt only to exhibit to your notice, the outward forms of Nature, or the productions of the surface of the earth; without troubling you with any notions of their particular causes or design by Providence, such attempts I leave for the amusement of Men of letters and superior genius."[15] The introductory essay gives notice that the *Travels* is to be philosophical as well as a "true and natural account." The qualities of plants all of which "manifest the divine and inimitable workmanship" of "the Great Author" are precisely the qualities of the sublime, the beautiful, and the picturesque. Beginning with sublimity he mentions "pompous Palms," "glorious Magnolias," which "struck us with the senses of dignity and magnificence" and lead to "an awful veneration." Next comes beauty: "the harmony and gracefulness" of the Carica papaya, the "mirth and gaiety" of the Kalmias, the fragrance of the Ilisium. Then comes the picturesque, the only category into which Bartram allowed utility: the Triticium amd Zea, for food, Linium for clothes, Hyssops for "medical virtues," "none stately or splendid" (qualities of sublimity and beauty respectively), but all "excite love, gratitude and admiration for the great Creator" who provided them for "our sustenance, amusement and delight" (pp. lii-liii). In the *Travels,* Bartram, by implication, provides his full definition of these aesthetic categories in his original combination and modification of the ideas of the major eighteenth century aestheticians.

Theorists of the Eighteenth Century separated the aesthetic response into the categories of beauty and sublimity with several later adding the picturesque. All agreed that beauty was of the emotions not the understanding, a distinction basic to their theories. Joseph Addison said, "But there is nothing that makes its way more directly to the Soul than Beauty which immediately diffuses a secret Satisfaction and complacency through the Imagination. . . . It gives gaiety . . . it strikes the mind with an inward Joy, and spreads a Cheerfulness and Delight through all its faculties."[16] In a statement that would have appealed to Bartram's primitivistic views, Francis Hutcheson stated that a "sense of beauty" was "independent of all customs, education, or examples," for it is inherent.[17] To Edmund Burke, beauty was "that quality or those qualities in bodies, by which they cause love or some passion similar to it."[18] Consequently, proportion and symmetry have no role. Addision, deploring the mathematical regularity of parterres and topiary, recommended naturalness for the garden. In Burke's view, "mathematical ideas are not the measure of beauty."[19] For the same reason, they rejected utility as a characteristic of beauty as being of the mind not the emotions. For Hucheson, a sense of beauty was independent of pratical considerations, a gratuitous gift of God for our happiness not our welfare.[20]

A consideration of the specific emotional effects of beauty is the logical next step in developing a theory. Addison found it soothing, especially the beauty of a garden, "It is naturally apt to fill the mind with Calmness and Tranquility, and to lay all its turbulent Passions at Rest."[21] Beauty in Burke's theory produces ". . . that sinking, that melting, that langour which is the characteristic effect of the beautiful as it regards every sense."[22] For Thomas Reid, the emotional effects of beauty had social and psychological value: "the emotion produced by beautiful objects is gay and pleasant. It sweetens and harmonizes the temper, is friendly to every benevolent affection, and tends to allay sullen and angry passions."[23] Reid's concept became a common idea throughout the century.

But the ultimate justification of beauty was moral and spiritual. To Hutcheson, aesthetic pleasure is identical with moral pleasure and reinforces it. He located absolute beauty only in nature where it is diffused throughout, giving evidence of a benevolent creator.[24] Goodness, he continues, determined "the Great Architecht to adorn the stupendous theater [a frequent term in the *Travels*] in a manner agreeable to the spectators . . . so that he designed to discover himself to them as wise and good, as well as powerful; for thus he has given them greater evidence through the whole earth of his art, wisdom, design, and beauty."[25] Similarly, to Burke, beauty is the first means by which the Creator allows us to "discover the adorable wisdom of God in his works."[26] Finally, for Reid, it is "the signature of His divine wisdom, power, and benignity. . . ."[27]

The next step in designing an aesthetic theory was to determine what qualities elicit the emotional and spiritual effects of the beautiful. Some variation of the doctrine of unity within variety became the most usual explanation of the origin of beauty. "The figures which excite in us the ideas of beauty," Hutcheson states, "seem to be those in which there is unity within variety."[28] This principle is what charms the botanist: "In the almost infinite multitude of leaves, fruit, seed, flowers of any species we often see a very great uniformity in the structure and situation of the smallest flowers."[29] From the animal world he finds another example in their adaptive structure, "from the mechanisms apparently adapted to the necessities and advantages of any animal which pleases us though there may be no advantage to ourselves ensuing from it. . . ."[30] Hugh Blair saw this principle as the basis for pleasing landscapes; "perhaps the most beautiful objects that can anywhere be found is presented by a rich, natural landscape, where there is a sufficient variety of objects."[31] Burke, too, like Bartram, stressed variety more than unity in his high valuation of novelty.[32] His list of the qualities of beauty consists of smallness, smoothness, gradual variation with no angularity (Hogarth's line of beauty), and clear, bright colors.[33] Archibald Alison added soothing sounds to the list, and Blair the sentimental beauty of compassion, mildness, friendship, and generosity.[34]

Bartram reveals his concept of beauty in his description of the South, descriptions which reveal and understanding and modification of the aesthetic theory of his day. The beautiful for Bartram is associated with the idyllic part of his natural landscape, far removed from "the seats of strife" (p. 71). Only in the context of idyllic beauty does he notice small plants such as "the fair lily of the valley" near the blissful strawberry fields of the Vale of Cowe (p. 224). Amid sublimity as at Flat Rock he passed over the small, even unusual plants like Diamorpha which occur there. Burke's smoothness also contributes to beauty. The Carica papaya, "the most beauteous of any vegetable production" is "smooth and polished" giving it a "charming appearance" (p. 83). In idyllic scenes his lakes became smooth and his savannas "lawns." "What a beautiful retreat is here," he said of the Isle of Palms with its "limpid waters" and "blooming lawns" (p. 99). Bartram as a painter achieved some of his most notable effects with color, and his are as bright and clear as Burke called for. The lupin is a "celestial blue" (p. 14), a pond is "sparkling" (p. 127), the St. John's has an "unparalleled transparency," "a crystal flood" (pp. 142-144). On the Ocone he finds "illumined green fields" and "glittering rills" (pp. 243-244). Color abounds in his idyllic regions from the soil strata to the brilliant azure and gold of fish sporting in Florida springs.

Bartram's aesthetic of beauty permits more geometric regularity than does those of Addison and Burke. An impressive magnolia has a "perfectly erect trunk in the form of a beautiful column "with a head like an obtuse cone" (p. 55). For the most part, however, his idyllic landscapes exhibit Hogarth's line of beauty. His "serpentine" rivers (p. 28) "meander" through fields of gently "waving" grass and "swelling hills" (p. 242). Vines such as Ipomea twist into "hanging garlands" (p. 87). Blending science and aesthetics he describes "the elegantly sinuated" Convolvulus (p. 67).

Odors in the *Travels* never evoke sublimity, but they were to Bartram a major source of beauty. He thus expands aesthetic theory, for most limited beauty to the visual, merely giving passing notice to the pleasures of smell and sound. Fragrances greatly contribute to the idyllic charm of the Isle of Palms: "A fascinating atmosphere surrounds this blissful garden; the balmy Lantana, ambrosial citra, perfumed Crinium, perspiring their mingled odours, wafted through Zanthoxilon groves" (p. 99). Even in scientific descriptions he adds odor as an identifying characteristic to a far greater degree than did his contemporary botanists like Humphrey Marshall and William Baldwin. Collinsonia has "a lively aromatic scent partaking of lemon and aniseed" (p. 261).

Sounds, too, contribute to the beauty of his idyllic scenes, and to the scientific authenticity of the works. Elliot Coues found his ability to render bird songs one of his most impressive achievements.[35] Bartram's major purpose, it seems clear, however, was aesthetic: "the songs of the nonpareil are remarkably low, soft and warbling, exceedingly tender and soothing" (p. 169). Even frogs afford "a pleasing kind of music" (p. 174).

The qualities of beauty listed by Burke and other literary theorists thus contributed to the scientific as well as the literary value of the *Travels.*

Variety becomes in Bartram's theory the most important single quality of beauty. At times, he, like Addison, seems to make variety or novelty a separate category rather than subsuming it as a quality. A species of Silphium, for example, is "most conspicuous both for beauty and novelty" (p. 253). Any beautiful landscape has more variety than unity. The land near Wrightsborough is agreeable for its "variety of objects and views" (p. 204). Near Chata Uche the "variable sylvan scene" forms a "delightful territory" with the "chains of low hills," "expansive savannah," and lawns watered with rivulets and glittering brooks (p. 245).

Beauty affects Bartram first emotionally, then spiritually. The "native sylvan music" of birds has a "soothing" effect, and he is "cheerful and invigorated" when "nature presents her cheerful countenance" (p. 244). The Seminoles who live in such a world possess sentimental or moral beauty. Their visage and deportment bespeak "joyous simplicity" "like the grey eve of a serene and calm day . . ." (p. 135). Such natural beauty leads him to praise the beneficence of its Creator. Birds raise an anthem of praise. "My heart and voice unite with yours in sincere homage to the great Creator, the universal sovereign" (p. 68).

Bartram uses the idyllic beauty he finds everywhere in nature to balance the horrors of nature, a reconciliation by subtle balance rather than by statement. After the turmoil of the alligator battle and the danger it represents to himself he immediately presents a peaceful scene of "delightful shades" dominated by the Carica papaya unexcelled "in elegance, delicacy and gracefulness" (pp. 83-84). After traversing a "burning sandy desert," he is revived by the harmonious music of nature (p. 115). His aesthetic theory, at least in part, helps lead him to a reconciliation of the two polarities of nature. It further provides him with a means of pointing up the ecological horrors of exploitive British agriculture. He intensifies the scene of the land "nakedly exposed and destitute" with trees "violated, defaced and torn to pieces" by contrast with the wondrous beauty of undisturbed nature and of Indian agriculture (p. 100).

The sublime, to eighteenth century theorists, was the most intense aesthetic experience possible, one that for most operated on principles distinct from beauty. It overpowers the senses, the reason, and the imagination. The imagination, Addison said, "loves to be filled with an Object, or to grasp at any thing that is too big for its capacity," and "we are flung into a pleasing Astonishment at such unbounded views, and feel a delightful Stillness and Amazement in the Soul at the Apprehension of them."[36] To Burke it is "the strongest emotion which the mind is capable of feeling,"[37] producing "a sort of swelling and triumph, that is extremely grateful to the human mind."[38] Hugh Blair details the overwhelming nature of the experience:

> It produces a sort of internal elevation and expansion; it raises the mind much above the ordinary state and fills it with a degree of wonder and astonishment, which it cannot well express. The emotion is certainly delightful, but it is altogether of a serious kind; a degree of awfulness and solemnity . . . very distinguishable from the more gay and brisk emotion raised by beautiful objects.[39]

The major theorists saw sublimity as ennobling the perceiver and leading him to religious devotion. The mind, said Burke, always claims to itself "some part of the dignity and importance of the things which it contemplates," and this glory reflects divine strength and wisdom by admitting us "unto the counsels of the Almighty by a consideration of his works."[40] It is, as Mark Akinside said, "Heaven's image in the hearts of man."[41] The sublime experience, to Alexander Gerard, gives "a striking indication of the omnipotence of its author."[42] Reid took this idea further into the realm of morality when he stated the sublimity leads to "a serious recollected temper, which inspires magnanimity and disposes it to the most heroic acts of virtue."[43]

The qualities that produce sublimity derive from the irregularity and wildness of nature. Addison's list of scenes which exhibit the "rude magnificence which appears in many of the stupendous works of Nature" echoes throughout the century: "the prospectus of an open champion country, a vast uncultivated Desert, of high Heaps of Mountains, high Rocks and precipices, or a wide Expance of Waters."[44] Similarly, Akinside located it in the "vast majestic pomp" of nature.[45] In Burke's influential theory, the idea of terror was essential to sublimity. "Whatever is fitted in any sort to excite the ideas of pain and danger, that is to say, what ever is in any sort terrible is a source of the sublime."[46]

Burke's list of sublime qualities reappears in one form or another in theories of most eighteenth century theorists. It is the one closest to the practice of Bartram. The qualities productive of sublimity are: terror, obscurity, power, privation, vastness, infinity, succession, difficulty, light, color, sound, suddenness, and the idea of pain. Obscurity is a powerful cause because "It is our ignorance of things that causes all our admiration and chiefly excites our passions." Privation includes "vacuity, Darkness, Solitude, and Silence." Vastness of any kind confounds us by suggesting infinity. Light produces the experience if it is sudden or if dark and gloomy and color if sad and fuscous. Loudness—"the noise of vast cataracts, raging storms, thunder, or artillery"—can produce the awful experience of sublimity.[47] From such ideas, Bartram developed his own theory of

sublimity, a theory which gives form to his observations and structure to his *Travels.*

Bartram wrote a natural history travel book, not a speculative aesthetic philosophy; but the way he describes his Southern landscape, what he notices and fails to notice, and his ideas on the religious, moral, and philosophical effects of his wilderness pilgrimage all are in accord with a well thought out aesthetic theory. Sublimity to Bartram was to be found only in wild nature. In "the high lonesome forest" he finds "an awful reverential harmony, inexpressibly sublime and not to be enjoyed anywhere but in these wild Indian regions" (p. 115). As "inexpressible" and the frequently used "incredible" indicate, sublimity goes beyond the intellect.

It is so pleasurable, fascinating, and enchanting that it carries him far from practical considerations. "Seduced by these enchanting scenes of primitive nature . . . I had roved far away from Cedar Point, but awakening to my cares, I turned about, and in the evening regained our camp" (p. 69). Sublimity produces intense pleasure—the "sublime and pleasing" Mount Hope and the "enchanting prospect" of Lake George (p. 64). It produces astonishment and wonder—the Dionea is an "astonishing production" and the Indian mounds are "wonderful remains of the power and grandeur of the ancients" (p. 241). It vexes the mind; at the Alachua Savannah he is "agitated and bewildered" at the astonishing wild scene" (p. 120). It stimulates the imagination—the high forest at Three Sisters Ferry "agreeably employs the imagination and captivates the senses by their magnificence and grandeur" (p. 196). It invigorates: "A magnificent grove of stately Pines succeeding to the expansive wild plains we had a long time traversed, had a pleasing effect, rousing the faculties of the mind, awakening the imagination by its sublimity, and awakening every active, inquisitive idea by the variety of the scenery and the solemn symphony of the steady Western breezes, playing incessantly, rising and falling through the thick and waxy foliage" (p. 110). Finally, the sublime experience excites awe. Of the river cypress he says, "we are struck with a kind of awe, at beholding the stateliness of the trunk, lifting its cumbrous top towards the skies . . ." (p. 58).

The effect of nature's sublimity for Bartram results in both a love of nature and of God but in a more complex way than does beauty. The "terror and devastation" of the storm at sea which begins his journey points up "how vain and uncertain are human expectation" (1). And a hurricane which sweeps the Altamaha illustrates how "finite and circumscribed is human power" (p. 33). The plains of Alachua manifest God's sublimity. "On the first view of such an amazing display of the wisdom and power of the supreme author of nature, the mind for a moment seems suspended and impressed with awe" (p. 121).

If for Bartram the sublime humbles man's pride, it also exalts him with a feeling of preeminence as he identifies with the power of nature. The grandeur of Mount Hope leads him to pay homage to "the universal sovereign" and to pray for "pity and compassion" to be worthy of the power entrusted to mankind by manifesting "a due sense of charity that we may be enabled to do thy will, and perform our duty towards those submitted to our service and protection" (p. 65). Later, on the St. John's, his "terror and astonishment" at the "innumerable band" of tropical fish rushing into the fountain leads to love and concern for and a brotherhood with them. Bartram's concept of sublimity thus reinforces his Quaker love and compassion for all living creatures.

Bartram's enumeration of qualities that elicit the sublime response is more inclusive than any of the eighteenth century aestheticians. Vastness, magnitude, and power played a crucial role. The objects in his sublime landscape as, for instance, the one at Wrightsborough have "vast" savannas, "gigantic" oaks and magnolias with "mighty trunks" (p. 25). Huge trees and enormous vines seemingly shade out the bluets and spring beauties. He never observes mosses despite the fact that his father had made an extensive study of them and was honored by having a genus named for him. He describes few insects and these only in swarms. His fullest description is of the ephemera which ascend "in clouds of innumerable millions" (p. 52). His small tropical fish arrest his attention primarily because they occur in "unspeakable numbers" (p. 131). His "stupendous" Indian mounds on the Little River he believes to be the work of a powerful nation whose "period of grandeur perhaps long preceded the discovery of this continent" (p. 25). Here and elsewhere Bartram introduces the vastness of time, which David Hume thought one of the most effective causes of the sublime. Since Francis Harper could find no trace of these mounds, they may be more literary than actual. Evidence from J. R. Swanton and others indicates, further, that Bartram greatly overestimated the antiquity of such mounds.

Significantly, in spite of his scientific accuracy, he characteristically appears to use measurements for the literary effect of magnitude. His account of alligator behavior has been verified except for his estimate of the number of eggs and the size of the adults. He reports two hundred eggs per nest, whereas forty is the usual number. The twenty foot alligator also strains credulity. He is likewise undependable in his estimate of the sizes of plains, rivers, and trees, invariably overestimating. He doubles the actual size of his magnificent Alachua Savannah. His practice of writing "yards" for "feet" may be mere carelessness, but it contributes to the vastness of his landscape by a factor of three. That he changed his field record for literary effect becomes obvious on comparing the *Report to Fothergill* with the *Travels.* He compressed two trips up the St. John's—

one in May and June, another in August—into one June trip, a time when he could not have seen nests, eggs, and young. This technique allows him to heighten the incredible numbers, but it falsifies his zoological observations.

Sounds, colors, light, and movement play an important role in Bartram's sublimity. The "incredible loud and terrifying roar" of the bellowing alligators "resembles very heavy distant thunder" that causes "the earth to tremble" (p. 82). On a less terrifying note the "solemn symphony of the steady Western breezes, playing incessantly, rising and falling through the thick and waxy foliage" (p. 110), suggests succession and infinity. Bartram expands Burke's ideas on colors. His sublime landscape has the dark sombreness of dense shades and storms, but he also has the "fiery azalea, flaming on the ascending hills"—"the color of red lead, orange and bright gold"—seen in "incredible profusion" through dark shades. "We are alarmed with the apprehension of the hills being set on fire" (pp. 204-5). The light and movement that call forth the sublime experience are brilliant and rapid. There are the frequently described flashes of lightnings, but he also mentions "the sudden transition from darkness to light" from the forest to the plains (p. 119). The "rapidity of its motion" which "appears like a vapour" of the rattler's tail (p. 167), and the writhing alligators contribute to the grandeur of these adventures.

Variety in Bartram's aesthetic becomes a major component of sublimity, a quality related to the complexity and ultimate mystery of nature. His aesthetic theory thus explains and justifies the inclusiveness of the *Travels.* Here he departs from the more unified sublimity of Addison, Burke, and Hutcheson which is more dependent upon one grand and overwhelming impression. Any scene which Bartram labels sublime includes great diversity. The prospect from the high bluff at Hawkinsville encompasses unlimited marshes and meadows, "magnificent forests of "grand Magnolias, glorious Palms, fruitful Orange groves, Live Oaks," a "grand elevation" above the curving river "ornamented by a sublime grove of Palms consisting of many hundreds of trees together," dark swamps, "glittering ponds," high hommocks, "solitary groves," "capacious coves," and "floating fields of Pistia" (pp. 88-89). Perhaps the same impulse that led him to ignore the mundane and the simple found expression in the unusual importance he attached to variety.

Similarly, a complexity that is beyond human understanding contributes to the sublime mystery of Bartram's South. He often applies the terms "singular" and "curious" to plants and animals whose structure and adaptation defy understanding and suggest a spirit moving through nature. The pelican's pouch, the Dionea's predation, the Pistia's life cycle, the wood rat's "conical pyramids," the mimosa's sensitivity manifest "that in-expressibly more essential principle, which operates within" (p. lvi). Along with the diversity and complexity of nature Bartram emphasizes the mysterious. His theory of a vanished ancient race of mound builders, a theory which Swanton has refuted, relates to his tendency to heighten the mysterious. So too does his picturing in his imagination "the secret labyrinths" and "subterranean lakes" (p. 143, of the Florida springs, the unseen world that so impressed Coleridge.)

Terror for Bartram was not merely a literary concept; it was an essential aspect of nature, one that his aesthetic theory helped him to reconcile. Burning deserts, dreary swamps, somber mountains, solitary wastes contribute to the fearsome spectacle of the wilderness. In the famous scenes depicting the horrid combat of alligators Bartram used visual, auditory, and tactile imagery and diction to achieve a memorable scene of sheer terror:

> Behold him rushing forth from the flags and reeds. His enormous body swells, His plaited tail brandished high, floats upon the lake. The waters like a cataract descend from his opening jaws. Clouds of smoke issue from his dilated nostrils. The earth trembles with his thunder. When immediately from the opposite coast of the lagoon, emerges from the deep his rival champion. They suddenly dart upon each other. The boiling surface of the lake marks their rapid course, and a terrific conflict commences. They now sink to the bottom folded together in horrid wreaths.

> (p. 75)

In all such episodes, in keeping with Burke's idea that danger that presses too closely is not sublime, Bartram never terms the actual event sublime. Only in retrospect, when he is out of physical danger, does it contribute to the sublimity of the landscape. After his encounter with the alligator Bartram finds "peaceful repose" in "a magnificent forest" that provides a "sublime contrast" with the "dreary swamp" (pp. 88-89).

His literary theory prompted Bartram to underscore the terror in his wilderness adventure with animals and Indians, an emphasis that he must then reconcile with his philosophy of "the benevolent and peaceable disposition of animal creation" and his primitivistic view of Indian character. He does this by precariously balancing polarities. The fearsome rattlesnakes are, in the end, "generous" and "magnanimous" for none struck him (p. 169) and he counters the fierceness of Indians with their magnanimity and mercy (p. 308).

Solitude was to Bartram the most difficult aspect of the terror of sublimity to bear, the one that he had the most difficulty in reconciling. It became increasingly burdensome toward the end of his travels when he was no longer praising God as his protector and preserver. In the "solitary waste and gloomy wilderness" (p. 209) of

Georgia, he laments" . . . I could not help comparing my present situation in some degree to Nebuchdadnezzar's when expelled from the society of men, and constrained to roam in the mountains and wilderness, there to herd and feed with the wild beasts of the forest" (p. 228). Yet in the immediately preceding paragraph he had stated that "scenes of primitive unmodifield nature always pleased me" (p. 227). Bartram's painful resolution of this conflict, as well as the process of the working of sublime horror, are suggested allegorically in the life cycle of the ephemera. The eggs are deposited in the deep where the larvae exist in "a viscid scum" of their dark "oozy bed." But the "genial heat" effects their "resurrection from the deep" and they "arise into the world in "clouds" (p. 52). In the solitary wilderness Bartram confronted one of the major aesthetic problems of eighteenth century literary theory: an explanation of the way in which the unpleasant, the painful, and the tragic can give pleasure. The aesthetic tradition in which Bartram was writing aided him in placing his painful desert solitude into the context of the sublime Alachua Savannah and Vale of Cowe. The concept of the sublime, at least in part, reconciled the opposing forces in Bartram's *Travels.*

The picturesque arose as a separate category in British aesthetic theory in the latter part of the Eighteenth Century, partially in response to an increasing interest in travel to rural areas and in landscape gardening and painting. After all, travel into the sublime grandeur of the Alps was difficult, and gardeners despaired of achieving sublime effects in their restricted space. Addison had to a limited degree anticipated the picturesque in his view that an imitation of what is "Little, Common, or Deformed" could be acceptable to the imagination though not as delightful as the imitation of "the Great, Surprising, or Beautiful."[48] To William Gilpin, the prolific author of books of picturesque tours, the picturesque was "any quality of being illustrated in a painting."[49] Goats and cart horses were to Gilpin more picturesque than sleek race horses, ruins more than well maintained buildings. "Is there a greater ornament of a landscape, than the ruins of a castle?"[50] Sir Uvedale Price justified in theory the addition of the picturesque to beauty and sublimity. It was a convenient way to account for objects that please but yet are not beautiful or grand: ". . . the picturesque fills up a vacancy between the sublime and the beautiful, and accounts for the pleasure we receive from many objects on principles distinct from them both. . . ."[51] Further, "it corrects the languor of beauty and the tension of sublimity."[52]

The picturesque became the aesthetic category connected with rural life, agriculture, and with an old, pastoral landscape not vast enough for sublimity nor gentle enough for beauty. As Humphrey Repton, the most influential landscape gardener of his day, put it, "the scenery of nature, called landscape, and that of a garden, are as different as their uses; one is to please the eye, the other is for the comfort and occupation of man: one is wild while the other is appropriate to man in the highest state of refinement."[53] The picturesque became a most useful concept for Bartram and helped him reconcile the polarities of a major tension in his life and art: his love of wild primitive nature versus his appreciation of agricultural development and civilization. His futile attempt to support himself in the sublimity of Florida forests and swamps had been his effort to reconcile these forces in his life. For the remainder of his life after his attempt to become a farmer near St. Augustine and after his travels he chose Repton's Middle Distance at his garden at Kingsessing, revisiting the beautiful and sublime South only in dreams and memory. Eighteenth Century aesthetic theory gave him a metaphor for the conduct of his life as well as literary concepts and techniques that influenced his scientific discoveries and poetic descriptions.

In the *Travels* it is the idyllic beauty and sublime grandeur of the wilderness that Bartram stressed. He could, however, occasionally see nature as well as inhabited regions as picturesque. Some of his drawings and paintings could serve as illustrations for the books of William Gilpin, Thomas West, or the host of travellers who, with sketch pad and camera obscura, were searching England and America for picturesque prospects. Plate three in Joseph Ewan's *The Drawings of William Bartram,* for example, depicts a purple finch poised on a blasted, cracked stump of star anise which sprouts a single, twisted flower. In plate 14 stems and tendrils of the African cucumber twist about the page, in the center of which are the large, gnarled seed pods. In prose, too, he could see picturesquely, as in his descriptions of the wood ibis which Audubon thought more fanciful than accurate:

> . . . he stands alone in the topmost limbs of tall dead Cypress trees, his neck contracted or drawn in upon his sholders, and beak resting like a long scythe upon his breast: in this pensive posture and solitary situation, they look extremely grave, sorrowful and melancholy, as if in the deepest thought.
>
> (p. 95)

The concept of the picturesque becomes Bartram's aesthetic justification for agricultural development which he occasionally advocates. Early in the *Travels* he claimed his chief joy consisted "in discovering, and introducing into my native country, some original productions of nature, which might become useful to society" (p. 48). He could even find the site of Augusta "the most delightful and eligible of any in Georgia for a city," for he described it in picturesque, not sublime, terms: it was a "fertile hilly country" with a navigable river (p. 200). Twice in the *Travels* he described a white plantation with approval. One at Medway had forested

canals and avenues, "floriferous and fragrant trees and shrubs," and "Pyramidal laurels" with a distant view of "extensive plantations of rice and corn" from "the humble but elegant and neat habitation of the happy proprietor." This "charming and animating" scene fills the traveller with joy. Such farms seen a part of the wild grandeur of nature. The "delightful habitation" at St. Simons looked over the "awfully great and sublime" sea (p. 39).

The Indian, more successful at living in natural beauty and sublimity, adapted himself and his pursuits to it. This adaptation becomes the major reason for Bartram's view of the moral and spiritual superiority of his natives, a superiority that David Taitt did not find in his extensive travels in the region.[54] Such a surrender to nature seems a chief motive for Bartram's trip. "I resigned my bark to the friendly current. . . . ," he states, as he descends the St. John's which "unfolded fresh scenes of grandeur and sublimity" (pp. 31-32).

Indian agriculture did not destroy nature's beauty or sublimity. They lived in a rural picturesque landscape in harmony with natural beauty and sublimity quite distant from the "destruction and devastation" wrought by the British (160). At the Alachua capital of Cuscowilla, small garden plots on the verge of an "infinite green plain," seemed to unite with skies and waters of the lakes (p. 123). "Such a landscape," he concludes, "such a rural scene is not be imitated by the united ingenuity and labour of man" (p. 123). Obviously he is referring to the white man. The Indians live in their landscape "blithe and free as birds of the air"—"the most striking picture of happiness in this life" (p. 134). This scene provides Bartram's most striking picture of man and nature in harmony.

William Bartram's knowledge of eighteenth century aesthetic theory on the beautiful, the sublime, and the picturesque accounts for the inclusiveness of his observations, the multiplicity of his themes, and the structure of his book. He found, within this rich, aesthetic tradition, a means to incorporate into his *Travels* his love of the wilderness, his religious views, his primitivistic attitude towards Indians, animals, and plants, his scientific curiosity, and even a practicality that led him to observe rich soil, useful plants, and navigable rivers.

Notes

1. Francis Harper, ed., *The Travels of William Bartram.* Naturalist's Edition (New Haven, 1958), p. 355. All references to the *Travels* are to this edition.

2. "Work of William Son of John Bartram," *Bartonia* 12 (Supplement) (1932), p. 20.

3. "The Interpretation of Aboriginal Indian Mounds by Means of Creek and Indian Customs," *Report of the Smithsonian Institute* (1927), p. 495.

4. "Fasti Ornithologiae Redivivi—No. I Bartram's *Travels*," *Proceedings of the Philadelphia Academy of Natural Science,* XXIV (1875), pp. 338-358.

5. "Bartram's Ixia coelestina rediscovered," *Journal of the New York Botanical Garden,* XXXII (1931), pp. 155-161.

6. Joseph Ewan, *William Bartram. Botanical and Zoological Drawings, 1756-1788* (Philadelphia, 1968), p. 4.

7. Anon. "Monthly Review of New American Books." "Travels through North and South Carolina, East and West Florida, etc., etc.," *Massachusetts Magazine or Monthly Museum,* IV (November, 1792), p. 687.

8. *Specimens of Table Talks of Samuel Taylor Coleridge,* 2nd ed. (London, 1836), p. 33.

9. *The Correspondence of Thomas Carlyle and Ralph Waldo Emerson 1834-1872,* vol. II (Boston, 1884), p. 198.

10. *John and William Bartram Botanists and Explorers* (Philadelphia, 1940).

11. *William Bartram Interpreter of the American Landscape* (Baltimore, 1933).

12. "William Bartram, A Classical Scientist," *Classical Journal,* L (January, 1955), pp. 167-170.

13. "Towards Romanticism: A Study of William Bartram." Ph.D. Dissertation, University of Utah, 1969.

14. "William Bartram's Bewegter Stil." In *Litteratur and Sprache der Vereinigten Straaten* ed. by Hans Helmche (Heidelberg, Germany, 1969), pp. 47-61.

15. *Travels in Georgia and Florida, 1773-1774. A Report to Dr. John Fothergill.* Annotated by Francis Harper. *Transactions of the American Philosophical Society.* New Series. XXXIII (November, 1943), p. 138.

16. *The Spectator* ed. by G. Gregory Smith. 8 vols. (London, 1897-98). VI, Section 412, p. 61.

17. *An Inquiry Concerning Beauty, Order, Harmony, Design.* 1725 ed. by Peter King (The Hague, 1973), p. 82.

18. *On Taste, On the Sublime and Beautiful.* 2nd ed. (New York, 1937), p. 74.

19. Burke, p. 83.

20. Hutcheson, p. 37.

21. Addison, VI, p. 17.

22. Burke, p. 100.

23. *The Works* (New York, 1822), p. 416.

24. Hutcheson, p. 9.

25. Hutcheson, p. 93.

26. Burke, p. 88.

27. Reid, p. 424.

28. Hutcheson, p. 41.

29. Hutcheson, p. 43.

30. Hutcheson, p. 45.

31. *Lecture on Rhetoric and Belles Lettres,* 4th ed. 3 vols. (London, 1790), vol. I, pp. 108-9.

32. Burke, pp. 29-30.

33. Burke, pp. 92-96.

34. Blair, Vol. I, p. 101.

35. *Key to North American Birds* (Boston, 1885), p. xviii.

36. Addison, VI, p. 57.

37. Burke, p. 35.

38. Burke, p. 46.

39. Blair, Vol. I, p. 15.

40. Burke, pp. 46-47.

41. *The Pleasure of Imagination,* Book I, line 437 in *The Works of Mark Akinside, M. D.* (New Brunswick, N.J. 1808), p. 24.

42. *An Essay on Taste* 1759 (Gainesville, Fla., 1963), p. 18.

43. Reid, p. 407.

44. Addison, VI, p. 59.

45. *The Pleasure of Imagination,* Book I, line 440, p. 24.

46. Burke, p. 35.

47. Burke, pp. 52-71.

48. Addison, VI, p. 81.

49. *Essay on Picturesque Beauty* (London, 1792), p. i.

50. Gilpin, p. 27.

51. *Essays on the Picturesque as Compared with the Sublime and the Beautiful and on the Use of Pictures, for the Purpose of Informing Real Landscape.* (London, 1810), p. 114.

52. Price, pp. 88-89.

53. *The Landscape Gardening and Landscape Architecture of the Late Humphrey Repton, Esq.* (London, 1840), p. 530.

54. *Journal of David Taitt's Travels from Pensacola, West Florida, to and through the country of the Upper and Lower Creeks,* 1772. In *Travels in the American Colonies,* ed. by Newton D. Mereness (New York, 1916), p. 501.

Christopher Looby (essay date 1987)

SOURCE: Looby, Christopher. "The Constitution of Nature: Taxonomy as Politics in Jefferson, Peale, and Bartram." *Early American Literature* 22, no. 3 (1987): 252-73.

[*In the following essay, Looby discusses the writings of Thomas Jefferson, Charles Willson Peale, and Bartram in relation to their views on the relationship between the natural order and the social order.*]

Natural history," Benjamin Rush wrote, "is the foundation of all useful and practical knowledge." He made this remark in 1791, in the context of designing the proper education for the citizens of the new American republic. "By making natural history the first study of a boy, we imitate the conduct of the first teacher of man," Rush continued. "The first lesson that Adam received from his Maker in Paradise, was upon natural history. It is probable that the dominion of our great progenitor over the brute creation, and every other living creature, was founded upon a perfect knowledge of their names and qualities" (47-48). What Rush did not explicitly say—but what was implicit in his discussion, and in similar discussions of taxonomic natural history by other leading writers of early republican America—was that knowledge of the names and qualities of the beings in nature was not only the basis of the American's control over his environment, but might also be, in some sense, the foundation of the collective life of the new nation of which he was a member. Not only could it serve to make the elements of the new world familiar to him and render them useful for his purposes, but it could also help him to imagine the shape of the new society that he was then in the midst of making. Like the biblical Adam, whose precedent they commonly invoked, and who (Genesis 2:18-20) immediately upon naming the creatures became aware of his need of a companion—that is, commenced his life as a social being—so too did Americans in the early years of the republic engage in taxonomic construction as a rehearsal, so to speak, of social and political construction.[1] "In designating a thing I designate it *to the Other,*" as Emmanuel Levinas has written; the act of designation precedes *and founds* the social relation (209; emphasis added). This relation between the natural and the social—the grounding of social order in a posited natural order—is distinctly present in such early national writers as Thomas Jefferson, Charles Willson Peale, and William Bartram.

In the thought of cultural leaders of the early national period, there is a kind of automatic metaphorical exchange between images of natural order and ideas of social and political order.[2] The period is one of cultural "constitution" in a broad sense, and it is important to place the making of the written instrument of government—the Constitution—within the context of larger constitutive cultural processes. Certainly it was evident to an individual like Madison, for instance, that the logical problems affecting the construction of legitimate natural taxonomies were essentially the same as those affecting the delineation of legitimate political institutions. In the *Federalist* No. 37, Madison treated the construction of political forms—e.g., "marking the proper line of partition, between the authority of the general, and that of the State Governments"—as a version of the general epistemological effort "to contemplate and discriminate objects, extensive and complicated in their nature" (234-35). "The boundaries between the great kingdoms of nature, and still more, between the various provinces, and lesser portions, into which they are subdivided, afford another illustration of the same important truth," he continued.

> The most sagacious and laborious naturalists have never yet succeeded, in tracing with certainty, the line which separates the district of vegetable life from the neighboring region of unorganized matter, or which marks the termination of the former and the commencement of the animal empire. A still greater obscurity lies in the distinctive characters, by which the objects in each of the great departments of nature, have been arranged and sorted. When we pass from the works of nature, in which all delineations are perfectly accurate, and appear to be otherwise only from the imperfection of the eye which surveys them, to the institutions of man, in which the obscurity arises as well from the object itself, as from the organ by which it is contemplated; we must perceive the necessity of moderating still farther our expectations and hopes from the efforts of human sagacity. Experience has instructed us that no skill in the science of Government has yet been able to discriminate and define, with sufficient certainty, its three great provinces, the Legislative, Executive and Judiciary; or even the privileges and powers of the different Legislative branches.
>
> (235)

Madison's expressed pessimism as to the probability of successful political delineations on the model of those of natural scientific taxonomy should not obscure for us, however, the ease and satisfaction with which he entertains such a possibility. *Kingdom, province, district, neighbouring region,* and *empire* are the terms—all of them borrowed from the political register—that he instinctively employs to characterize natural taxonomic differences. They enable his mind to pass smoothly from one realm to another, and they indicate a desire to constitute, despite the difficulty of such a project, a political order in which "all delineations" would be as "perfectly accurate," as "natural" and as certain, as those inherent in the order of nature itself. To observe that such a project seeks to claim for the "institutions of man" an authority transcending the human is to recognize a familiar ideological device, one that has a particular power in the early American republic.

I

"A Society," Durkheim wrote, "is not made up merely of the mass of individuals who compose it, the ground which they occupy, the things which they use and the movements which they perform, but above all is the idea which it forms of itself" (470). This observation—that a society needs to represent itself to itself in order to certify its existence and its legitimacy—is illustrated by the American republic in the immediate post-revolutionary period. As the heroic excitements of the Revolution receded into the past and were replaced by the domestic convulsions of the succeeding decades, it became apparent to observers that America lacked a compelling idea of its own coherence, a self-conception that would make it a genuine society—a nation—rather than a mere mass of individuals. Diversity characterized the American population, and instability characterized the state that had been formed to govern it. Operating after 1776 under a bad constitution that was not even adopted until 1781, and then replaced by 1789, the viability of the republic was very much in question for several decades following independence. The threat of monarchical counter-revolution or military putsch, local insurrections like Shays' Rebellion and the Whiskey Rebellion, several secessionist movements, a series of treasonous plots against the state, and regular eruptions of mob violence were the conspicuous features of political life in the early republic. And there were, of course, even among the leaders who had joined to prosecute the Revolution, fundamental differences as to the proper form the state should take—differences that are sufficiently indicated by invoking the names of Jefferson on the one hand, and Hamilton on the other; Paine on one side, Adams on the other.

These differences of political conviction, which were articulated with increasing insistence as the memory of the Revolution faded, were probably less threatening in the short run than the incidents of actual violence, but they were potentially at least as dangerous to the future of the republic. The linguistic violence of the 1780s and '90s—the "wordy battle, and paper war" that Irving satirized so effectively in *Salmagundi* (144)—was the audible evidence of the Americans' lack of a common idea of the kind of society they wanted. Dissensus then was as deep, as general, and as powerful as it has been at any other time in American history. The American republic was as yet a factitious entity, a concocted political framework that gathered together people whose primordial loyalties were attached to local, ethnic, sectarian, and linguistic communities, rather than to the vaguely conceived national society. Having established a new state, the revolutionary leaders discovered to their dismay that they had not succeeded in creating a new nation.

It occurred to some of them, in this situation, that nature might aid them in constituting the nation. A society that is in need of a collective self-conception will ordinarily find some ready-made structure close at hand that can provide a model of coherence—a *form* that, when apprehended, can be transferred to society itself. I want to claim that after the American Revolution, men like Jefferson, Peale, and Bartram found such a structure in nature; or, to be more precise, they found it in the taxonomic order that they represented nature as exhibiting: the visible order of identities and alterities that they believed nature displayed to the eye. The search for a total conceptual order is common to several of the well-known texts of post-revolutionary America. Let me begin with a characteristic exclamation from William Bartram's *Travels,* a passage that typifies not only his usual attitude toward nature, but that of many of his compatriots. "We admire the mechanism of a watch, and the fabric of a piece of brocade, as being the production of art," he wrote, because they show the obvious presence of *design*: all parts in them appear to conspire toward a single end or effect. A similar kind of inner intentionality, he believed, was plainly to be seen in nature. "The animal creation also, excites our admiration. . . . [H]ow wonderful is the mechanism of these finely formed, self-moving beings, how complicated their system, yet what unerring uniformity prevails throughout every tribe and particular species!" (xliv). The evidence of design was written on the face of nature, Bartram believed; in this he anticipated the view that Emerson would later take in his address on "The Method of Nature," where he claimed that "the spirit and peculiarity of that impression nature makes on us, is this, that there is in it no private will, no rebel leaf or limb, but the whole is oppressed with one superincumbent tendency" (121). What is striking about such a claim, I think, is that it assumes that this singleness of purpose is spontaneously presented to the eye and to the mind by nature in its ordinary appearance. There is very little in our everyday experience, I would say, to suggest that nature in all its parts is involved in a single task, that it is moving as a whole toward some goal; there is, on the contrary, everything to suggest otherwise. And the testimony of numerous others who recorded their impressions of American nature was that the appearance it presented was that of "the incredible, the immeasurable, the unpredictable, and the horrifying," to quote the apt summary of Howard Mumford Jones (61). Indeed, Bartram frequently found it so too; but here, at the beginning of his book, he assumed and claimed, nevertheless, that nature's surface was beautifully ordered. And he went on with utter confidence to draw inferences from his *a priori* assumption:

> If then the visible, the mechanical part of the animal creation, the mere material part is so admirably beautiful, harmonious and incomprehensible, what must be the intellectual system? that inexpressibly more essential principle, which secretly operates within?
>
> (xliv)

This is an *a priori* assumption because, despite the determination with which he asserts it, Bartram nevertheless, in those places where he seems to have transcribed most faithfully (or unselfconsciously) in his prose the impressions nature made on him, described not a harmonious order of things, but a nearly random set of motions, a concatenation of fortuitous processes, an intersection of unpredictable transformations. That is, he observed a world of things that moved, a world of change and becoming, rather than one of static being.

This is not to say that the world appeared to Bartram in fact as a total flux of colored spots, strange noises, and sensations of warmth and cold—a world that would resist all logical formulation. But it appeared to him as something like the world John Dewey described as the "colored, resounding, fragrant, lovable, attractive, beautiful" world of objects as they are disclosed to the prescientific consciousness (98). That is, it appeared to him as it appears to us before science and philosophy abstract, simplify, reduce, quantify, control and possess it. I make a point of emphasizing here that the world is never present to us as a sheer chaos of shifting impressions; even in the "natural attitude," as the phenomenologists call it, we perceive a world composed of somewhat coherent arrangements of relatively well-circumscribed objects having more or less determinate properties. We are born into a world already largely preconceived: all perceptions, as William James said, are *acquired* perceptions (2:78). Perceptual chaos, when it is invoked—and here I anticipate my argument a little—is not a report of what the senses detect in the world, but is rather a *figure* for social anarchy—a trope of perception, as it were—and it is employed as such for particular rhetorical purposes. Likewise, a hard-set and fixed conceptual system is a figure for social order. The stiff and immutable world that men like Jefferson, Peale, and Bartram constructed was their rhetorical invention: it was a figure for social stability and—as I wish to claim—for an intensely desired end to the flux of revolutionary social-historical change.

But if the world as we know it is composed of objects that are relatively stable, those objects do, however, despite our best intellectual preventions, tend to change over time and even vanish. They do not form a reality fixed and complete, rigidly categorized and statically

exhibited to the eye of the mind. They form a world of some uncertainty, for a world in motion is a world about which people may hold conflicting opinions. A world that changes is one that invites different individuals to form different and perhaps incompatible judgments, and it invites even the same individual to form different, perhaps incompatible judgments at different times. In such a world, we are liable to lose faith in the unity of truth: as Melville asks in *Clarel,* "That stable proof which man would fold, / How may it be derived from things / Subject to change and vanishings?" (112). And if a more or less uncontroversial stock of knowledge is a necessary social resource—the foundation of basic agreement among men—then the transformations in nature, which inhibit the acquisition of uncontroversial knowledge, constitute a threat to social well-being. The scientifically formulated world, however, is essentially inert and is therefore a world about which there can be certain knowledge and about which there ought to be no disagreement. At least this is what the enlightened eighteenth-century philosopher believed: refusing to be distracted by the mutability of natural objects, he held that the Linnæan intellectual system represented the one true world, the fixed order of nature as it objectively subsisted. He was, we may say, mistaking the unchangeability of his concepts for the invariance of nature: we find him, in the person, for instance, of Bartram, in what may seem the rather comical act of strolling through the wilderness of Georgia, reciting to himself the scientific nomenclature of the animals and plants he finds, not interested in them in their contingent and mutable specificity, but only in their conceptual universality: "Magnolia glauca, Itea, Clethra, Chionanthus, Gordonia lasianthus, Ilex angustifolium, Olea Americana, Hopea tinctoria," and so on (24).[3] This incantation, this ritual prophylaxis, invoked the complete and consistent set of categories that the eighteenth century employed to describe and construct nature. As such, it united Bartram, alone there in the wilderness, with the minds of other men, whom he met, as it were, in the integrated world of stable ideas that the Linnæan classifications constituted. As Durkheim said, the crucial fact about such a total intellectual system is that the world it describes is a world that no individual knowing subject, with his limited perspective on things, can contemplate; only society as a whole, the putative collective subject, can regard it. The Linnæan system, since it represents the whole natural world, necessarily exceeds the experience of any single knowing subject, since such an individual subject, no matter how extensive his acquaintance with the plants and animals of the earth, could still know only some of them. The natural world *in toto,* then, according to Durkheim, is "an object [that] can be embraced only by a subject which contains all the individual subjects within it." It is, we might say, an imaginary object, only visible to an imaginary subject—the collective subject. Durkheim, of course, in this connection concluded with a famous dictum: "The concept of totality is only the abstract form of the concept of society" (490).

It is taxonomy in this respect—as a total system of concepts exhaustively representing the world of natural things, and corresponding to the total form of society—that was particularly important to post-revolutionary America. Collective unity in the social moment of the synthesis of thought was what Bartram, along with Jefferson and Peale, aimed to stimulate. It might be possible to study certain particular parallels between specific social classes and specific natural categories, such as many cultures draw; such correspondences seem, however, to be severely attenuated in developed Western cultures. (They survive vestigially in such totems as the donkey and the elephant, representing the two established political parties in the United States.) It seems, rather, that the compelling feature of the Linnæan taxonomy was its comprehensive unity, and that in the modern West the expressive relation between nature and society operates almost exclusively at the level of the whole. This is where men like Jefferson, Peale, and Bartram focused their attention, anyway: they felt deeply the lack of social unanimity in late eighteenth-century America, and they imagined that in nature—prearranged nature—they saw a powerful totality that might be of use in constructing the collective American subject. This was the natural world that Bartram went to Georgia, the Carolinas and the Floridas to find, and he found it; this world promised to be the unifier of minds. Implicitly present in Bartram's perception of nature, *actively determining* it, was the whole of society; or, since my argument is that we can't properly speak of a coherent society in America at the time, but only of a set of communities that cultural leaders were trying to tie together as a single society, I should say that what was present in Bartram's perception of nature was an *idea* of the whole of society, a *wish* for social unity that found its expression vicariously in his determination to see *in* nature the taxonomic scheme he brought *to* it.

In this connection, Bartram's obsessive habit of describing groups of animals and even plants as social groups is relevant: flowers "associate in separate communities" (14), fish comprise "nations" (101) and "bands and communities" (105), butterflies rally to their "kindred tribes" (106). Sometimes the metaphors are those of specifically military societies: "armies" of fish (111), "well disciplined squadrons" of cranes (121), a "company" of wolves (126).[4] And Bartram never hears the lowing of cows and fails to comment on their "cheerful, social voices" (120). He goes so far as to imagine that "different tribes and bands"—deer, wild horses, turkeys, cranes—will, upon the appearance of a predator, "draw towards each other . . . as it were deliberating upon the general good" (120). That verbal hedge—"as it were"—barely disguises the wish, dis-

creetly present here, that diverse human groups may also find it possible, in America, to agree upon a general good or a common interest. But Bartram only imagines that the animals do so when confronted with the danger of an attack; and this circumstance recalls, without examining, the political problem American leaders faced in the period in question. For Americans—like Bartram's several species—*had* united when faced with a threat from outside; but when that threat was eliminated, their unanimity had dissolved. It is the restoration of that unanimity that Bartram seeks as he gazes at nature, subsuming its objects under his conceptual scheme, executing an act of consciousness on behalf of the society that he intended thereby to call into being, the society that alone could complete the act of total cognitive synthesis he was proposing. Bartram's contemplation of nature was the self-contemplation of the American nation at the moment of its creation.

II

In the first, formative stages of American nationality, as I have said, cultural leaders had to confront the threat of social disintegration that was posed by the conflicting racial, ethnic, religious, linguistic, sectional, local, and ideological categories of self-definition and social loyalty that were inhibiting the formation of a genuinely national identity. As Jefferson wrote, "During the war of Independance . . . the pressure of an external enemy hooped us together. . . . The spirit of the people, excited by danger," produced a unanimity that "was a supplement to the Confederation," which was otherwise an inadequate political instrument (*Writings* 70-71). It was this inadequacy that the Constitution was intended to remedy, but the decades of reciprocal violence that followed the ratification of the Constitution showed that it was not the deficiency of the particular instrument of government that was the real problem, but rather a deficient "spirit of the people." There was no collective identity, no collective subject whose will the state could be considered to be expressing. In traditional societies, the existence of such a collective subject is a product of history and custom. All kinds of primordial attachments—blood ties (real or presumed), common racial characteristics, linguistic community, geographical concentration, religious orthodoxy, shared usages and practices—all of these enable spokesmen for historically-grounded, organically-evolved nations to use the first person plural with confidence: "We" do this or do that, are this or are that, believe this or believe that.[5] However, for Americans after the Revolution, too many kinds of cultural heterogeneity stood in the way of establishing an integral national self. Despite the grandiloquent gesture of the Constitution's opening—"We the People"—there was no "People" of whom "We" could speak.

It is in this context of threatened social disintegration that we must consider the meaning of the Jeffersonian generation's special affinity for natural history. Men like Jefferson, Peale, and Bartram saw in nature—nature as Linnæus constructed it—a promise of social unanimity that held a profound fascination for them. More often than not, ethnologists tell us, societies in search of images of ideal order will have recourse to zoological and botanical taxonomies, which are presumed to be objectively given in nature and which seem to provide man with what Lévi-Strauss has called "the most intuitive picture at his disposal" of a permanent order of things (137). We should not, then, be surprised to find that in the post-revolutionary period, Americans had such recourse. In so doing, it may be, they were acting in obedience to an essential human impulse that seeks to organize society as a reflection or projection of the natural world; and while we don't usually treat the Linnæan taxonomy of nature as the equivalent of the so-called "ethno-taxonomies" of other (presumably less "enlightened") cultures, it served much the same purpose. Like other collective representations or worldviews, it was directed not only against cognitive dissonance, but against social disintegration as well. In so functioning, it realized a particular late eighteenth-century conviction, part of the myth of enlightenment: the conviction that institutionalized science, as the organized discovery of truth, could serve as a model for the organization of state and society (Habermas 146). The advantage of science as a social model was its established procedures for reaching understanding, its methods for overcoming disagreements. Scientific societies were "always in peace," as Jefferson said, "however their nations may be at war. Like the republic of letters, they form a great fraternity spreading over the whole earth" (*Writings* 1201). In the 1780s and '90s, as it happened, classificatory natural science exemplified for Americans the ideal of scientific inquiry.[6] Jefferson remarked that while it was "impossible for a man who takes a survey of what is already known, not to see what an immensity in every branch of science yet remains to be discovered" (*Writings* 1064), natural science had the advantage over other branches of inquiry of having in the Linnæan scheme a "Catholic system," a "universal language" that had obtained "the general consent," thus "rallying all to the same names for the same objects, so that they could communicate understandingly on them" (*Writings* 1330-33). That is, while other sciences were as yet plagued by fundamental disagreements as to their proper objects and proper methods, natural history had what we might today call a paradigm or research program—what Jefferson called a "universal language"—that united its practitioners in an effective community of inquiry. Although he would eventually come to admit, with Buffon, that "Nature has, in truth, produced units only through all her works," and that "classes, genera, species, are not of her work" but are constructions of human intelligence that "fix arbitrarily on such characteristic resemblances

and differences as seem to us most prominent and invariable in the several subjects," he nevertheless believed that to abandon the "received, understood, and conventionally settled" system of Linnæus would mean that we could "no longer communicate intelligibly with one another" (*Writings* 1329-31). And although his recognition of the arbitrary status of the Linnæan categories led him to confess that it was not "intrinsically preferable" to any other classification,[7] he definitely preferred it to what he derisively called "the no-system of Buffon, the great advocate of individualism in opposition to classification" (*Writings* 1331-33). This reference to *individualism* tells us something, for Jefferson began the letter from which I have been quoting by expressing his reluctance to discuss the "comparative merits of the different methods of classification adopted by different writers on Natural History," since (as he said) his had been "a life of continued occupation in civil concerns," which had taken him away from natural science (*Writings* 1329). Relenting, however, he expressed himself on the subject anyway, and, when doing so, those "civil concerns" were still clearly present to his mind. Having concluded that "classes, genera, species" are human institutions, the simple basis upon which he decided the "comparative merits" of the different taxonomic systems was therefore necessarily a social one. "I adhere to the Linnæan because it is sufficient as a ground-work, admits of supplementary insertions as new productions are discovered, and mainly because it has got into so general use that it will not be easy to displace it, and still less to find another which shall have the same singular good fortune of obtaining the general consent" (*Writings* 1332-33). An attempt to replace it would lead, he said, "directly to the confusion of tongues of Babel" and to "schism" (*Writings* 1330-33). The one substantive merit of the Linnæan scheme that Jefferson was willing to specify was that it dwelt more consistently upon the surface appearances of things: it assigned particular things to particular categories according to outward features. This choice of "such exterior and visible characteristics as every traveller is competent to observe, to ascertain and to relate" (*Writings* 1331) made it that much easier for the principles and procedures of scientific cooperation to become the principles and practices of social intercourse in general, since the orthodox Common Sense epistemology of the Jeffersonian generation held that the act of knowing was analogous to the act of seeing.[8] Hence if a science that would yield certainty, and yield it to everyone, was needed, natural history of the Linnæan sort would be the best choice.

This preference for natural history, based on political considerations, was also present in the Reverend Nicholas Collin's *Essay on those inquiries in Natural Philosophy, which at present are most beneficial to the* UNITED STATES OF NORTH AMERICA, in which Collin, a Swede, posed as an appointed messenger of "the great

Linnæus" himself: "I often heard [him] wish that he could have explored the continent of North America," Collin attested; "[M]ay this wish animate American philosophers" (xv). "Patriotic affections" were behind the privilege Collin granted to taxonomic investigations; he thought it relevant to refer to the "convulsion of public affairs, for a considerable time past, which occasioned many and great domestic distresses: the natural events of the late war are universally known" (vi). The inner relation between natural and political history emerged, as if automatically, within Collin's language: the "events of the late war" are called "natural," and when he goes on to remark that "numbers of virtuous citizens have also felt the dire effects of the succeeding anarchy, especially in the loss of property," he is preparing a set of political connotations that will be in place when, turning to nature proper, he stigmatizes the "apparent disorders" that are observed in nature. He insists that they are merely that—*apparent*—and that nature in fact obeys "fixed principles," so strongly fixed that "there can be *no chance* in it" (vi-xxvii). We encounter, once again, the strong prejudice in favor of the identical, the persisting, the solid—as opposed to the self-differing, and changeable, the chaotic—that operated nearly everywhere in American science at the time, a prejudice that is regularly reinforced by the ritual repetition of moments of transformation, turbulence, and sheer motion, moments which place the conceptual scheme (and the social order) at risk, but which provide the opportunity for its reassertion. I want to refer to some of these moments presently, but let me prepare my remarks by quoting again from Durkheim, who illustrates his thesis on the social reference in all natural classifications by means of imagery that uncannily repeats some of Bartram's most vivid imagery. Durkheim is concerned to characterize the *concept* by defining it in opposition to sensual representations—sensations, perceptions, images—as basically *stable*:

> Sensual representations are in perpetual flux; they come after each other like the waves of a river, and even during the time that they last, they do not remain the same thing. Each of them is an integral part of the precise instant when it takes place. We are never sure of again finding a perception such as we experienced it the first time; for if the thing perceived has not changed, it is we who are no longer the same. On the contrary, the concept is, as it were, outside of time and change; it is in the depths below all this agitation; it might be said that it is in a different portion of the mind, which is serener and calmer. It does not move of itself, by an internal and spontaneous evolution, but, on the contrary, it resists change. It is a manner of thinking that, at every moment of time, is fixed and crystallized. In so far as it is what it ought to be, it is immutable.
>
> (481)

Durkheim's diction is very precise: "In so far as it is what it *ought* to be, it is immutable." That is, in the permanence of the concept is invested a measure of so-

ciety's conviction that its ways are morally right. And Durkheim's water imagery—the "flux," "agitation" and "waves" versus the "depths" which are "serener and calmer"—jibes nicely with a typical feature of Bartram's writing, for Bartram also characteristically uses imagery of watery flow and agitation (on the one hand) and glassy stillness (on the other) to represent, respectively, the intrinsic changeability of sensual experience and the relative permanence of conceptual order. Many times in the course of his travels he finds himself admiring the "polished surface" of a "peaceful stream," looking through its "pellucid" waters at the objects below (49). But almost without fail, the smooth surface then becomes "ruffled," and its "wavy surface disfigures every object, presenting them obscurely to the sight, and they at length totally disappear" (51). Inevitably, however, the "waters are purified" once again, "the waves subside, and the beautiful river regains its native calmness." And "so it is with the varied and mutable scenes of human events on the stream of life," Bartram adds, perhaps too explicitly. The "well contrived system at once becomes a chaos . . . every pleasing object is defaced, all is deranged . . . a gloomy cloud pervades the understanding" (52). At another place in the text it is not the ruffled surface of a stream but a heavy rain that interferes with Bartram's comfortable and secure relation to the world of objects: "such floods of rain fell . . . that every object was totally obscured . . . all seemed a frightful chaos. When the wind and rain abated, I was overjoyed to see the face of nature again appear" (142). Instances could be multiplied, but the essential point is, I trust, clear: in a book devoted to establishing the authority of a conceptual scheme, occasional ritual moments of perceptual disorientation are produced, then quickly followed by the restoration of conceptual security, which is an affirmation of the social structure to which the concepts belong.

III

A similar affirmation can be seen in Jefferson's *Notes on the State of Virginia*. The book's ostensible motive is to record and promulgate a certain organized body of knowledge respecting the flora, fauna, geography, and human and social institutions of Virginia. It illustrates the standard anthropological dictum that "Any culture is a series of related structures which comprise social forms, cosmology, the whole of knowledge and through which all experience is mediated" (Douglas 128). There is a relation between the concepts of nature that are so prominent in the book and the ideas of historical self-understanding that Jefferson adhered to. We know that the dynamics of social change often aroused in Jefferson a reactionary anxiety. Despite a few well-known expressions of a contrary opinion, he could scarcely conceive of social process—the movement of a nation through time—except in negative terms, that is, as decay, corruption, and degeneration (McCoy 13-47). The only kind of society that had any chance to forestall the process of corruption was one that was conflict-free: a homogeneous, egalitarian, agricultural republic. "It is for the happiness of those united in society to harmonize as much as possible in matters which they must of necessity transact together. Civil government being the sole object of forming societies, its administration must be conducted by common consent" (*Notes* 84). It was therefore crucial that the American population not be "a heterogeneous, incoherent, distracted mass," as it might very well become if emigrants, who "will bring with them the principles of the governments they leave," were allowed to "warp and bias its direction" (*Notes* 85). In order that the republic might be "more homogeneous, more peaceable, more durable," it was necessary that precautions be taken to insure uniformity of sentiments and conceptions among the people.

It is this uniformity that the overwhelmingly static, synchronic presentation of knowledge in the *Notes on Virginia* was intended to foster. The predominant manner of presentation was in the form of charts, diagrams, tables, and lists—that is, in graphic, two-dimensional formats—all of which explicitly exclude the possibility of change or development. Indeed, we know that Jefferson, in his one scientific paper, on the megalonyx or great-claw (an animal known only from its fossilized remains), could not bring himself to believe that this particular species was no longer in existence. Having discussed its bones, one by one; having classified it with "the unguiculated quadrupeds"; having estimated its size, and given it a name, he finally had to face the "difficult question" that he conceded "now presents itself. What is become of the great-claw?" ("Memoir" 251). His conclusion: "In fine, the bones exist; therefore the animal has existed," and since the only motions present in nature are movements "in a never ending circle," it followed that "if this animal has once existed, it is probable on this general view of the movements of nature that he still exists" ("Memoir" 255). Jefferson reasoned along the same lines with respect to the mammoth, when he discussed it in *Notes on Virginia*: "It may be asked," he wrote to justify his having included the mammoth in the table that exhibited the hierarchy of species of quadrupeds, "why I insert the Mammoth, as if it still existed? I ask in return, why I should omit it, as if it did not exist? Such is the economy of nature, that no instance can be produced of her having permitted any one race of animals to become extinct; of her having formed any link in her great work so weak as to be broken" (*Notes* 53-54). The same taboo on change in the order of nature informed Jefferson's refusal to countenance Buffon's theory that the species degenerated in America. Although it is usually thought that Jefferson's response to Buffon was a simple expression of resentment at the suggestion that nature in America was smaller and weaker than nature in Europe, I think, instead, that it is best interpreted as a rejection of the possibility of change or evolution *per se,* since such change would imply that the supposed invariability of nature, and hence the stability of its conceptualization, were in error. And what was at stake in such a matter was not only the validity of the intellectual system, but also that of the social regime of which the intellectual system was the abstract equivalent.

In addition to this general theme running through the *Notes on Virginia,* there is a specific occasion when Jefferson allows the world of natural objects to appear in its changeability, a moment when the adequacy of his concepts is at risk. The moment comes under the head of Query VII, which asks for "A notice of all what can increase the progress of human knowledge?" (*Notes* 73). "Under the latitude of this query," Jefferson wrote, "I will presume it not improper nor unacceptable to furnish some data for estimating the climate of Virginia" (*Notes* 73). This may seem a peculiar choice; why should information about the climate contribute especially to the total of human knowledge? The chapter is perhaps the most curious in the book, since it calls into question the validity of assertions that are made prominently in the rest of the work. That is, in this chapter, ostensibly devoted to increasing knowledge, Jefferson instead, perversely, includes a passage that calls the very possibility of certain knowledge into question. He describes the strange optical phenomenon of "*looming,*" a familiar phenomenon at sea, but one that is unaccountable, Jefferson says, in the present case. Standing upon the elevation of Monticello—which, in this passage, and, indeed, in Jefferson's life in general, represents for him the neutral, disinterested standpoint posited by the specular rationality of the Enlightenment—he finds that "in opposition to the general law of vision" that makes distant objects diminish in apparent size, looming makes them appear larger, and it makes them change their shapes:

> There is a solitary mountain about 40 miles off, in the South, whose natural shape, as presented to view here, is a regular cone; but by the effect of looming, it sometimes subsides almost totally into the horizon; sometimes it rises more acute and more elevated; sometimes it is hemispherical; and sometimes its sides are perpendicular, its top flat, and as broad as its base. In short it assumes at times the most whimsical shapes, and all these perhaps successively in the same morning.
>
> (*Notes* 80-81)

Philosophy has not accounted for this phenomenon, Jefferson says; it is behind the seamen, no less, for philosophy has not even *named* this phenomenon officially. And despite having introduced this discussion under the rubric of climate, he says he can "remark no particular state, either in the weight, moisture, or heat of the atmosphere, necessary to produce this. . . . Refraction will not account for this metamorphosis. That only changes the proportions of length and breadth, base and altitude, preserving the general outlines," while in this case it is the very shape itself that appears to change (*Notes* 80-81). So not only is this a phenomenon that tends to defeat the project of knowledge-acquisition, it is also a phenomenon that it is, evidently, impossible to know in itself. It interferes with the relation of mind to object, and it is itself also an obscure object. Jefferson is present in this passage as the ideal knowing subject, whose effort is directed toward taking what is presented to sight and assimilating it to several ideal categories of objects—in this case, certain geometrical forms (cone, hemisphere, square). That is what knowledge consists in, for him; and it is a view of knowledge that the book as a whole tries to promote: to know is to overrule the sensibly intuited bodies in nature by means of a universally-available, all-encompassing conceptual system that, not incidentally, makes time stand still.

Charles Willson Peale is the taxonomist par excellence. And his natural history museum, installed in the Pennsylvania State House, made most explicit the relation between taxonomic natural science and political order. He hoped, in fact, that his museum would serve as an effective apparatus of the national state, and he was bitterly disappointed when its efficacy went unrecognized by the government. The specimens he mounted and displayed were arranged, in the museum's rooms, in the perfect visual order of the Linnæan pattern. And at the top of the hierarchy—in two rows along the ceiling above the cabinets—were displayed the portraits Peale had painted of the heroes of the Revolution, presiding over the rational order of things, of which they were the superior extension. The portraits recalled the lost unanimity of the Revolutionary moment, but Peale seems actually to have believed that the majestic taxonomy of his exhibit would have the effect of restoring that unanimity if people came to see it and allowed it to impress its message upon their minds.

> One very important effect may be produced,—persons having different sentiments in politicks, being drawn together for the purpose of studying the beauties of nature, while conversing on those agreeable subjects, may find a concordance of sentiments, and most probably from a slight acquaintance, would think better of each other, than while totally estranged.
>
> (*Discourse* 39)

But this was not mere conjecture on his part, as he attested:

> An instance of this is in the memory of my hearers. The chiefs of several nations of Indians, who had an historical enmity to each other, happened to meet unexpectedly in the Museum in 1796 . . . surrounded by a scene calculated to inspire the most perfect harmony, the first suggestion was,—that as men of the same species they were not enemies by nature; but ought forever to bury the hatchet of war.
>
> (*Discourse* 39-40)

The political design of the museum is clear: it was "calculated to inspire the most perfect harmony." And within the museum, as within the texts of Bartram and Jefferson, there were produced certain ritual dissolutions and restorations of its conceptual order. In Peale's case, he devised a magic lantern show—an "Exhibition of Perspective Views, With Changeable Effects; or, Nature Delineated, and in Motion"—which represented a series of scenes (both natural and social) involving perceptual transformations. By means of painted transparencies illuminated from behind, and shifted in a coordinated manner, illusions were created involving the coming of dawn, the arrival of dusk and the lighting of street lamps, a storm gathering over a view of architectural forms, a rushing stream turning a water-wheel, a battle between ships at sea, and, tellingly, the raising of Pandemonium as described by Milton (*Descriptive Catalogue*). Each sequence of images delineated a movement, but ended (when the final image was resolved) in stasis; a stasis that returned the viewers, when the show was ended, to the ordered environment of the museum itself. The museum, of course, was a display of certainties: it was a world free of ambiguities, obscurities, and difficulties, and hence a world about which there was no reason ever to disagree: a world of perfect consensus. "Facts, and not theories, are the foundation on which the whole superstructure is built," Peale claimed. "Not on theoretical, speculative things, but on the objects of our sight and feelings" (*Discourse* 41). But even Peale—otherwise the least likely individual to entertain nominalistic doubts—wondered, perhaps unconsciously, whether his assured, static view of the world wasn't, in fact, an illusion. When the trustees of the museum commissioned him, late in his life, to paint a self-portrait that would then form part of the museum's exhibit, he complied by producing the painting known as "The Artist in His Museum," which depicted him, full-length, standing before the main room of the museum, raising a curtain with his right hand to reveal, at his back, the ordered realm of knowledge it had been his long effort to construct. The portrait is dramatically lighted, and the attitude in which Peale placed himself is less that of a scientist than that of a showman; the whole composition, in fact, is governed by a theatrical metaphor that insinuates a terrible doubt of appearances into what is meant to be a reassuring picture of the world as it really, indubitably exists. And this again raises the question of whether all these attempts to present something as reconciled that actually is not—whether it be the heterogeneous elements of nature, or the social diversity and conflict that natural disorder represented for the authors I have treated—isn't one of the standard ideological reflexes of the period. For each of the writers I have considered, classificatory schemes are figures for social order, and while the pragmatic status of those schemes is here and there conceded—more willingly by Jefferson than by either Bartram or Peale—they are nevertheless held to be necessary, and whatever would falsify them is held to be dangerous. The watery dissolutions of perceived objects in Bartram, the looming in Jefferson, and the unwitting confession of the artificiality of classification in the theatricality of Peale's representation of his museum—these moments operate to reinforce the mind's attachment to the images of order they temporarily put at risk.

The obsession with natural harmony that marks this period in America would seem to mask an anxiety about the political dissonance that also marks the period. The power of the cultural presence of natural classification as a representation of social order may be best appreciated when we observe that it makes possible the elaborate humor of Hugh Henry Brackenridge, when, in *Modern Chivalry,* he has Teague O'Regan, the "bog-trotting Irishman" who is his figure of social transgression, be mistaken for "a monster in creation, or at least a new species of animal, never before known in these woods" (317) when he is found, tarred and feathered, by two hunters who see him in a tree. He is captured, caged, and exhibited as a natural curiosity; the Philosophical Society hears of him, and sends two representatives to examine him scientifically and make a report to be published in their transactions; in a preliminary determination of his genus, they offer the opinion that "it is an animal of a species wholly new, and of a middle nature between a bird and a beast," and that it "would seem to form the link between the brutal and the human species" (320). He is shipped to France to be exhibited to the learned societies, but upon coming ashore the tar and feathers have worn off his backside; he is mistaken for a sans-culotte, and the mob rises and frees him. The narrator concludes the episode by remarking of this unclassifiable creature that it is not certain "whether he joined the army of the patriots, or is on his way home again to this country" (324). But evidently a being that disrupts the ordered categories of nature is bound to make political trouble somewhere.

Notes

1. The myth of Adamic naming is a familiar and persistent one in American culture and in studies of American culture. It is usually identified, of course, with writers of the American Renaissance like Emerson, Thoreau, and Whitman; but it is present even in less obviously imaginative writers—like those under discussion here. It survives even in recent academic studies. In his otherwise quite prosaic narrative of American scientific developments in the early republic, Greene opens his chapter on "Natural History in a New World: Botany" with these words: "Like Adam in the garden of Eden, the naturalists of the infant American republic faced the exhilarating task of naming, classifying, and describing the plants and animals of a new world" (253). Needless to say, this sort of wholesale appropriation of the Adamic myth is intellectually suspect, for it perpetuates several fallacies: that there were no human subjects on the scene before European settlers arrived; that the objects of the natural world were therefore unnamed until those settlers arrived; that the scientific project of those settlers—their taxonomic construction—was undertaken *de novo.* Of course there were human subjects on the scene, and they had their own names for things; and the scientific project of the later settlers consisted mostly in reconciling new objects to old categories.

2. Since writing this essay, I have found that a recent historian of the early republic has reached similar conclusions. Robert H. Wiebe characterizes the mental habits of the cultural leaders of the early republic in these terms: "The gentry reasoned by formulating broad categories, sorting information into them, then explaining the information through the rules governing their categories. . . . Nothing better exemplified their ideal than the magnificently arching branches of biological classification: phylum down to genus to species to subspecies, ordering all of life in one grand pattern. . . . Whatever rules governed the natural sciences covered politics and the arts as well. . . . Just as categories of knowledge molded their data, so in the end structures of government would mold their people" (7-11).

3. As Prigogine and Stengers have maintained, the trajectory of modern physical science has been away from the "rather naive assumption of a direct connection between our description of the world and the world itself" (54-55), which had been the assumption of classical science, and toward a recognition that "randomness, complexity, and irreversibility" (54)—that is, temporality—are proper objects of natural scientific knowledge, not just illusions of a phenomenal order that distract us from true knowledge of substances. Classical science, they say, is "the mythical science of a simple, passive world" (55), while modern science is "rediscovering time" (xxviii) and studying a world that is intrinsically active. On the importance of the concept of temporality for the transition to modern scientific inquiry, see also Collingwood.

4. As John Arthos shows, the conventional diction of eighteenth-century English poetry includes countless such figures; poets of the time "exploited a stable language because they believed that the design of the world was stable" (vii), and, since the "sure constancy of things was the charm of nature" (viii), political and social terms could both

lend and borrow connotations of stability from the natural objects they were made to represent. See his Appendix A for instances of the use of such words as *Band* (106), *Citizen* (114-15), *Empire* (156-57), *Kingdom* (232-34), *Nation* (255-56), *People* (271-73), *Race* (281-82), *Reign* (294-95), *Tribe* (332-34), and *Troop* (334), among other terms.

5. See Geertz, "After the Revolution," for an illuminating analysis of the cultural politics of post-revolutionary nationalism. I have found this essay, and also his study of the "Integrative Revolution," particularly suggestive and helpful for the present study.

6. Boorstin *passim*; Sheehan ch. 1.

7. Taxonomic realism—the view that there is one unambiguously correct taxonomic theory, which could successfully distinguish "real essences" or "natural kinds"—has been largely given up by scientists, in favor of an attitude that recognizes the pragmatic value of a commonly-accepted system of classification while granting the arbitrary status of its terms and their extensions. This pragmatic-relativistic position was the result, obviously, of the competition between taxonomic representations that commenced in the late eighteenth century. The secondary literature on this development is extensive but fragmentary.

8. The reign of Common Sense philosophy in eighteenth-century America has been extensively documented in recent works by White, Wills, and others. The privilege enjoyed by the faculty of sight—its status as a figure for certain knowledge—is perhaps most unambiguously stated in Thomas Reid's *An Inquiry into the Human Mind,* where it is claimed that sight is "without doubt the noblest" of the senses. But "it is looked upon, not only as more noble than the other senses, but as having something in it of a nature superior to sensation." Reasoning from ordinary language, Reid goes on to notice that the "evidence of reason is called *seeing,* not *feeling, smelling,* or *tasting*" (145, 147-48). A general study of "the domination of the mind of the West by ocular metaphors" (13) is Rorty, *Philosophy and the Mirror of Nature.*

Works Cited

Adorno, T. W. *Aesthetic theory.* Trans. C. Lenhardt. London: Routledge & Kegan Paul, 1984.

Arthos, John. *The Language of Natural Description in Eighteenth-Century Poetry.* Ann Arbor: Univ. of Michigan Press, 1949.

Bartram, William. *Travels through North & South Carolina, Georgia, East & West Florida . . .* Philadelphia, 1791.

Brackenridge, Hugh Henry. *Modern Chivalry.* New York: Hafner, 1962.

Collin, Nicholas. *An Essay on those inquiries in Natural Philosophy, which at present are most beneficial to the* UNITED STATES OF NORTH AMERICA. *Transactions of the American Philosophical Society.* Vol. III. Philadelphia, 1793. iii-xxvii.

Collingwood, R. G. *The Idea of Nature.* London: Oxford Univ. Press, 1960.

Dewey, John. *The Quest for Certainty: A Study of the Relation of Knowledge and Action.* New York: Paragon, 1979.

Douglas, Mary. *Purity and Danger: An analysis of the concepts of pollution and taboo.* London: Routledge & Kegan Paul, 1966.

Durkheim, Emile. *The Elementary Forms of the Religious Life.* Trans. Joseph Ward Swain. New York: Free Press, 1965.

Emerson, Ralph Waldo. *Essays and Lectures.* New York: Library of America, 1983.

The Federalist. Ed. Jacob E. Cooke. Middletown, Conn.: Wesleyan Univ. Press, 1961.

Geertz, Clifford. "After the Revolution: The Fate of Nationalism in the New States." *The Interpretation of Cultures.* New York: Basic Books, 1973. 234-54.

———. "The Integrative Revolution: Primordial Sentiments and Civil Politics in the New States." *The Interpretation of Cultures.* 255-310.

Greene, John C. *American Science in the Age of Jefferson.* Ames, Iowa: Iowa State Univ. Press, 1984.

Habermas, Jürgen. *The Theory of Communicative Action.* Vol. 1, *Reason and the Rationalization of Society.* Trans. Thomas McCarthy. Boston: Beacon, 1984.

Irving, Washington. *History, Tales and Sketches.* New York: Library of America, 1983.

James, William. *The Principles of Psychology.* 2 vols. New York: Dover, 1950.

Jefferson, Thomas. "A Memoir on the Discovery of certain Bones of a Quadruped of the Clawed Kind in the Western Parts of Virginia." *Transactions of the American Philosophical Society.* Vol. IV. Philadelphia, 1799. 246-60.

———. *Notes on the State of Virginia.* Ed. William Peden. New York: Norton, 1972.

———. *Writings.* Ed. Merrill D. Peterson. New York: Library of America, 1984.

Jones, Howard Mumford. *O Strange New World: American Culture: The Formative Years.* New York: Viking, 1964.

Levinas, Emmanuel. *Totality and Infinity: An Essay on Exteriority.* Trans. Alphonso Lingis. Pittsburgh: Duquesne Univ. Press, 1969.

Lévi-Strauss, Claude. *The Savage Mind.* Chicago: Univ. of Chicago Press, 1966.

McCoy, Drew R. *The Elusive Republic: Political Economy in Jeffersonian America.* New York: Norton, 1982.

Melville, Herman. *Clarel: A Poem and Pilgrimage in the Holy Land.* Ed. Walter E. Bezanson. New York: Hendricks House, 1960.

Peale, Charles Willson. *A Descriptive Catalogue of Mr. Peale's Exhibition of Perspective Views, With Changeable Effects; or, Nature Delineated, and in Motion.* Philadelphia, 1786.

———. *Discourse Introductory to a Course of Lectures on the Science of Nature.* Philadelphia, 1800.

Prigogine, Ilya, and Isabelle Stengers. *Order out of Chaos: Man's New Dialogue with Nature.* New York: Bantam, 1984.

Reid, Thomas. *An Inquiry into the Human Mind.* 6th ed. Glasgow, 1804.

Rorty, Richard. *Philosophy and the Mirror of Nature.* Princeton: Princeton Univ. Press, 1979.

Rush, Benjamin. "Observations upon the study of the Latin and Greek languages; as a branch of liberal Education, with hints of a plan of liberal Instruction, without them, accomodated to the present state of society, manners and government in the United States" [Aug. 24, 1791]. *Essays, Literary, Moral, and Philosophical.* Philadelphia, 1798. 21-56.

Sheehan, Bernard. *Seeds of Extinction: Jeffersonian Philanthropy and the American Indian.* New York: Norton, 1974.

White, Morton. *The Philosophy of the American Revolution.* New York: Oxford Univ. Press, 1978.

Wiebe, Robert H. *The Opening of American Society: From the Adoption of the Constitution to the Eve of Disunion.* New York: Knopf, 1984.

Wills, Garry. *Inventing America: Jefferson's Declaration of Independence.* Garden City, N.Y.: Doubleday, 1978.

Douglas Anderson (essay date 1990)

SOURCE: Anderson, Douglas. "Bartman's *Travels* and the Politics of Nature." *Early American Literature* 25, no. 1, (1990): 3-17.

[*In the following essay, Anderson examines the lessons Bartram attempts to teach his reader in* Travels, *lessons that nature can teach society about its social and political organization.*]

William Bartram's *Travels* (1791), like so many of the most interesting products of the Anglo-American sensibility in the eighteenth century, challenges the reader's capacities of adjustment. It presents itself at various times as a travel journal, a naturalist's notebook, a moral and religious effusion, an ethnographic essay, and a polemic on behalf of the cultural institutions and the rights of American Indians—a range of modes and interests that has led William Hedges to describe the *Travels* as "the most astounding verbal artifact of the early republic."[1] This mixture of discourses is already sufficiently rich to invite the quite different critical approaches brought to Bartram's work in recent years by Roderick Nash, Robert Arner, Richard Slotkin, Patricia Medeiros, and Bruce Silver, among others.[2] But invariably readers of the *Travels* have insisted upon, or assumed, Bartram's nearly complete physical and imaginative isolation within the southeastern wilderness that he explored.[3] Francis Harper's careful edition of the *Travels* for the Yale University Press more than thirty years ago calls attention to Bartram's curious confusion of dates at crucial points in his narrative, but neither Harper nor any reader since has pursued the chronological parallel that Bartram himself quietly draws between his botanical expeditions and the most volatile years of the American Revolution.[4]

Bartram's *Travels* has in common with the more celebrated voyages of Lemuel Gulliver an interest in the wider social and political context within which they take place. Swift's work, of course, is wholly fabulous, whereas Bartram is primarily a scientist even when his science and his natural piety collide.[5] But in addition to describing and cataloguing the natural phenomena of the American wilderness, Bartram sought to comment as well on the political turmoil within which he worked and wrote.

Bartram shares this double focus with his two distinguished contemporaries, Thomas Jefferson and J. Hector St. John de Crèvecoeur, both of whom produced books during the revolutionary period that comment directly and indirectly on their political setting. Jefferson's *Notes on the State of Virginia* is both a dispassionate reply to the inquiries of a "Foreigner of Distinction" and an act of revolutionary self-defense against the invidious, Eurocentric naturalism of the Comte de Buffon and the loyalist opposition to American independence within the colonies themselves. Jefferson's superbly pointed definition of "tory"—"a traitor in thought but not in deed"—begins the short chapter that falls between otherwise even-tempered descriptions of Virginia's colleges, roads, public buildings, and different religions (Jefferson 281-82). Crèvecoeur's *Letters from an American Farmer* addresses the violence and disruption of the revolution most directly and passionately in his last chapter, "Distresses of a Frontier Man," which records the farmer James's near hysterical lament for the destruction of what he had perceived as his idyllic rural way of life by border warfare and his determination to unite his family with a tribe of neutral Indians and wait for peace (Crèvecoeur 200-227).

Compared with these two prominent figures, William Bartram often seems to be writing about a different continent altogether. His botanical excursions through the American southeast took place during some of the most troubled years of the revolutionary period, yet the only open acknowledgment Bartram makes of the civil crisis within which his *Travels* takes place is the few dates he allows to appear in the text: his departure from Philadelphia in the spring of 1773 a few months prior to the Boston Tea Party; a collecting trip begun in April 1776, as the Second Continental Congress prepared to convene; an excursion by boat from Mobile in November 1777; and the return to his father's farm near Philadelphia, which Bartram reports as taking place in January 1778, when Washington's army was wintering not many miles away and the future of American independence was very much in doubt. Francis Harper's examination of Bartram's itinerary and correspondence has led him to the discovery that Bartram actually returned to Philadelphia in January 1777, a year earlier than Bartram claims he did and at a much less symbolically fateful time.[6] This uncharacteristic misstatement of fact Harper attributes to Bartram's "blind spot" for dates, but in light of the nature of the *Travels* as a whole Bartram's fictive return at such a critical moment in the Revolution underscores a narrative pattern that he had been at some pains to establish as he reworked his field notes for publication. By the time Bartram published the *Travels* in 1791, the contrast between his own distinctly pacific activity of thirteen years earlier and that of his politically active contemporaries must have seemed even more pronounced as the events of the Revolution began to cohere into a triumphant mythology, with Valley Forge serving as the point of moral and spiritual crisis, the dark night of the soul before salvation.

Instead of political engagement, Bartram offers the reader long paragraphs composed of the Linnaean names for the plants he finds covering the savannahs of Georgia, South Carolina, and Florida. In dramatic contrast to Crèvecoeur's interest in human beings and human institutions, or to Jefferson's sharply partisan sentiments, Bartram apparently turns his attention, with equal singlemindedness, to birds, fish, trees, or soil. The one exception to this focus upon nonhuman nature is the interest Bartram shows in the Indians he meets and visits in the course of his journeys. But even the Indians recognize the peculiar nature of Bartram's errand, honoring him with the oddly amusing name of Puc Puggy, the Flower Hunter, a designation that sharpens

still further the subtle but distinct line that Bartram maintains between himself and his historical context: a hunter of flowers, not of deer, or bear, or men.[7]

William Bartram was serious about his botany and serious about the piety that nature's spectacle nourished in him—"O thou Creator supreme, almighty! how infinite and incomprehensible thy works! most perfect, and every way astonishing" (72)—but he also recognized the value of his vocation, even in its apparent detachment from social turmoil, as a political gesture and as a pretext for addressing the painful problems of nation building. Scientific detachment itself is a posture as well as a professional attribute. From the comparative wilderness of west Florida, the sounds of revolution are inaudible—fainter even than the sounds of the Concord militia carried on the breeze to Walden Pond. But that very remoteness permits Bartram to consider the broader implications of social transformation. Nature does not speak with the immediacy of one of Benjamin Franklin's political tracts, but to a surprising degree the wilderness enables Bartram to place his own eventful times in a context wide enough to provide a basis for measured skepticism as a corrective for patriotic fervor.

The most direct appeal that Bartram makes to his reader's political conscience involves his advocacy for the Indians. He is not blind to their vices. Indians slaughter animals, keep slaves, make war, get drunk, and fornicate, much as the white man does (183-84). But Bartram also finds much to admire in Indian character and institutions. Unlike Crèvecoeur's James, who joins a tribe of neutral Indians only as a last resort and in spite of his fears of their barbarizing influence on his children, Bartram clearly sees the Indians in the context of national debates on the stability and the dangers of democracy. At the end of his introduction to the *Travels,* he suggests a tentative plan for bringing the Indian tribes into "civilization and union" with the United States, and he concludes his book with a brief, largely admiring appendix on Indian customs and government in which his sole reservation about Indian manners has to do with the "extravagantly libidinous" songs they sometimes sing at their dances (396)—a complaint perfectly consistent with the apprehensions many Federalists and moderate Republicans felt about the democratic "extravagance" unleashed by the Revolution. The unruly nature of American democracy as a whole was already amply evident to Bartram and many other observers of the first years of national existence under the Articles of Confederation. The debates over the new Constitution were taking place during the months that Bartram was preparing his manuscript for publication. The challenges of "civilization and union" that Bartram addresses with respect to communities of Indians, in other words, were general ones that he introduces into his *Travels* in such a way as to suggest quite early in the book that the management of nature and of native populations is no different from the management of ourselves.

The Indian tribes themselves are most significant for Bartram as parts of a pattern of growth and decay, death and life, in which all of existence participates. It would be well, in his view, if white traders ceased corrupting the Indians with rum, but even under the most ideal circumstances imaginable, no civilization or people can expect to endure forever. The world that Bartram describes during his journeys is haunted by an unstable balance of appetites, by violence, by false paradises, irrecoverable utopias, and by ruin. Nature in all its manifestations is unfailingly beautiful, but it tells, at the same time, a sobering story of endless mutability. The "universal vibration of life insensibly and irresistibly moves the wondrous machine," Bartram exults at one point, mingling his pre- and postenlightenment metaphors, but the direction in which the machine of nature moves, as often as not, is toward death (159).[8]

The natural world, even in the experience of a devout optimist like Bartram, is constantly at war. On one botanically inspired stroll about a campsite, Bartram notes "a number of little gravelly pyramidal hills" in a streambed that proved to be the defensive stronghold of a community of crayfish, "their citadel, or place of retreat for their young against the attacks and ravages of their enemy, the goldfish" (61). The beautiful yellow bream is a spectacular creature, with fins that are decorated (according to Bartram) like the eyes in a peacock's tail, but the bream is also fierce, "a warrior in a gilded coat of mail" giving "no rest or quarter to small fish, which he preys upon" (141). Vultures and ravens lurk about Bartram's campsites, "sharpening their beaks, in low debate" and waiting for the men to depart. Alligators and gar, equally "warlike" predators, seem to Bartram to form a "confederacy . . . to enslave and devour the numerous defenceless tribes" of smaller fishes (178).

Contemporary political and military metaphors are a natural language for describing the kind of systematic hostility with which Bartram finds himself surrounded in the wilderness and of which he is himself nearly a victim. On an early excursion up the San Juan River in east Florida, Bartram is set upon by great numbers of alligators that seem to oppose the progress of his journey with a disturbing degree of concerted action, surrounding his canoe, blockading his landing sites, closing off the mouths of lagoons as if consciously preparing traps for unwary naturalists. Only by great good luck does Bartram escape becoming a meal. The fish that later try to run the alligator blockade are less fortunate:

> What expressions can sufficiently declare the shocking scene that for some minutes continued, whilst this mighty army of fish were forcing the pass? During this

TRAVELS

THROUGH

NORTH & SOUTH CAROLINA,

GEORGIA,

EAST & WEST FLORIDA,

THE CHEROKEE COUNTRY, THE EXTENSIVE TERRITORIES OF THE MUSCOGULGES, OR CREEK CONFEDERACY, AND THE COUNTRY OF THE CHACTAWS;

CONTAINING

AN ACCOUNT OF THE SOIL AND NATURAL PRODUCTIONS OF THOSE REGIONS, TOGETHER WITH OBSERVATIONS ON THE MANNERS OF THE INDIANS.

EMBELLISHED WITH COPPER-PLATES.

By WILLIAM BARTRAM.

PHILADELPHIA:

PRINTED BY JAMES & JOHNSON.

M,DCC,XCI.

Title page for the 1791 first edition of Bartram's Travels.

attempt, thousands, I may say hundreds of thousands, of them were caught and swallowed by the devouring alligators. I have seen an alligator take up out of the water several great fish at a time, and just squeeze them betwixt his jaws, while the tails of the great trout flapped about his eyes and lips, ere he had swallowed them. The horrid noise of their closing jaws, their plunging amidst the broken banks of fish, and rising with their prey some feet upright above the water, the floods of water and blood rushing out of their mouths, and the clouds of vapour issuing from their wide nostrils, were truly frightful.

(118-19)

Bartram himself is a bit reassured to discover that the alligators' strategy is directed at these fish rather than at him. But his description has much of the animation and atmosphere of an eighteenth-century sea battle and he refers to this place hereafter in the *Travels* as "Battle Lagoon."

Even without the metaphors from human conflict to emphasize the parallel, Bartram makes it clear that in moving quite deliberately away from the center of revolutionary violence, he has placed himself in the midst of the still more fundamental violence of nature. Crève-coeur too had employed violent images from the natural "world" to dramatize the essential political and social violence of American life in *Letters from an American Farmer*: wasps and birds that feed on a dying slave who is caged and suspended from a tree, hummingbirds that embody both natural beauty and a natural "lacerating" ferocity, snakes whose insidious venom suggests the poison of slavery that is latent in the northern as well as overt in the southern states.[9] But Crèvecoeur's focus in the *Letters* is on the temperamental transformation of his narrator from euphoric celebrant of American promise to hysterical refugee from American ambiguity. The consciousness of James, in Henry May's helpful terminology, leaps from that of the moderate to that of the radical enlightenment in the space of a few pages.[10] Bartram, though much more remote from scenes of revolutionary violence than Crèvecoeur's narrator, is much less in flight from them. Because his vision of nature is never so idyllic as that of Crèvecoeur's James, his disappointments are never so apocalyptic. But this moderation of response derives less from optimism than from a sense on Bartram's part that the sobering lessons of the natural world are pervasive.

This fact is clear from the celebrated moment in his introduction when Bartram describes a particularly formidable spider ("his body was about the size of a pigeon's egg") stalking a bumblebee that eventually succumbs to "the repeated wounds of the butcher" (24). Bartram elsewhere characterizes himself as a "vindicator of the benevolent and peaceable disposition of animal creation in general," but among the inhabitants of creation in general something is nearly always particularly hungry, and even as he recounts the "extraordinary deliverance" that saved him from a wolf that stole some of his fish, Bartram's language unavoidably suggests that this instance of natural mercy is among the rare exceptions that prove the grim rule:

> How much easier and more eligible might it have been for him to have leaped upon my breast in the dead of sleep, and torn my throat, which would have instantly deprived me of life, and then glutted his stomach for the present with my warm blood, and dragged off my body, which would have made a feast afterwards for him and his howling associates! I say, would not this have been a wiser step, than to have made protracted and circular approaches, and then after, by chance, espying the fish over my head, with the greatest caution and silence rear up, and take them off the snags one by one, then make off with them, and that so cunningly as not to waken me until he had fairly accomplished his purpose?
>
> (145)

The animal in this passage, of course, is merely deft at gaining a meal and justifiably wary of man. As Bartram himself dramatically illustrates, it is the human imagination and the human community, with its capacity for calculating foresight, that is bloody.

In a world where alligators feed on their own young, where mud turtles devour "any animal they can seize" (159), where even the beautiful and harmless ephemera fly seems to be created simply to be eaten (89), the expectation of slaughter is only natural. Indeed it is noteworthy but not particularly shocking to Bartram on one wilderness ride to pass by "heaps of white, gnawed bones of ancient buffalo, elk, and deer, indiscriminately mixed with those of men, half grown over with moss" (263). A mind of "delicate feelings" might be appalled at such sights, Bartram admits, and he himself prefers a nature more amenable to his endless fund of trite euphemisms: "the glorious sovereign of the day," "the finny inhabitants" of "the pellucid floods," "the feathered songsters of the grove." But predatory violence is a fact of life so inescapable that when he encounters an apparent exception to the rule, Bartram is careful to explain it away. In an unusually deep and clear sinkhole, or spring, Bartram notes a "paradise" of fish and alligators where all the creatures seem to sail "like butterflies in the cerulean ether" with "no signs of enmity, no attempt to devour each other" despite the mutual hostility he had seen them display in other settings. The solution to the mystery is that the water is "so perfectly clear and transparent, it places them all on an equality with regard to their ability to injure or escape from one another" (151). The wisdom of the Creator expresses itself here not in an Edenic peace—which Bartram dismisses as a "mere representation"—but in a balance of terror that Bartram presents as a kind of dark parody of Madison's argument in Federalist 10 that republican "representation" functions as a restraint upon the bitterness of faction (Madison 127-28). It is not surprising to Bartram, in such a natural context, that human communities show an equal vulnerability to predatory violence, but Bartram is less willing than Madison to express his "pleasure and pride" in a system of restraint founded upon a competition of brute instincts.

Bartram in fact discovers that the American Revolution is taking place on a continent accustomed to revolution, to the succession of one form of civilization and the disappearance of another. Men are quite capable of the same acts of cruelty and destruction that Bartram finds so prevalent among animals, and white men are, perhaps, more culpable in this regard than Indians. But it is a difference of degree only, not a difference in basic nature. Of greater significance, particularly to Bartram's nation-building contemporaries, is the fact that the political and natural turmoil of the present occurs, quite literally, on the ruins of "ancient" civilizations, both Indian and European. The course of his travels takes Bartram through ancient Indian burial grounds, over the sites of old and bloody battles, past ruined plantations, abandoned colonies, decayed forts. On occasion the Indians even build their villages on top of the pyramid-shaped monuments of some earlier people whose history and fate are completely unknown. When William Cullen Bryant makes a similar sense of American antiquity and the succession of civilizations part of his subject in "The Prairies" (1834), his own skepticism is less perceptible amid the romantically poignant sentiments with which he views the past and the faith with which he envisions the "advancing multitudes / Which soon shall fill these deserts."[11] By contrast, in the context of Bartram's experience, whole cultures seem as easily produced as generations of the ephemera fly and just as easily replaced. The process of revolution, Bartram suggests, like its cousin the process of predation, is ongoing, scientifically impersonal, and no respecter of human monuments, human sentiments, or human aspirations to permanence.

As if to give this discovery an unmistakably contemporary pertinence, Bartram describes the current ascendancy of the Creek Indians over their Indian neighbors in such a way that the parallel to contemporary American events would be clear. He had already hinted at this parallel in the pun on Madison's hopeful view of "representation" with which he described the uneasy balance of natural "interests" he found in the paradisal, transparent spring. The parallel with the Creeks is more elaborately drawn. The Creeks, Bartram notes, were recent emigrants to the southeast from "their original native country" west of the Mississippi (68). Having arrived at their current place of residence on the banks of the Oakmulge River, "they were obliged to make a stand, and fortify themselves . . . as their only remaining hope, being to the last degree persecuted and weakened by their surrounding foes" (68). This last stand proved so successful that the Creeks "recovered their spirits" and conquered their enemies "in a memorable and decisive battle" before forming their own "confederacy" with the vanquished tribes and establishing their rule.

The elements of the correspondence between Creek and American experience would have been particularly clear to Bartram's contemporaries. The Creeks, also an emigrant people, had their own Valley Forge and Yorktown to endure and to celebrate before they, in turn, began to feel the pressure of encroaching Europeans—a pressure that Bartram also documents in the accounts he gives of treaty negotiations which he observed involving the Creeks, their Indian neighbors, and the white governments of the new American states. The parallel is too closely drawn to be accidental, and its implications for the permanence of the American "emigrant" political community were, perhaps, too obvious or too disturbing to bear direct statement. Bartram at least does not state them directly, but he makes it apparent here and elsewhere in the *Travels* that he means to chasten the exuberance of political life in the postrevolutionary United States with a vision of life's limits and of its obligations.

A recurring rhetorical set piece in the *Travels* with which Bartram underscores his perception of those limits is the series of descriptions he provides of the sudden, nearly apocalyptic thunderstorms of the southeast that strike without warning, "spread terror and devastation," and serve to remind mankind of "how vain and uncertain are human expectations" (29). In some ways these resemble the "Tremendous thunders" of the hurricane that temporarily devastates the groves of Philip Freneau's tropical retreat in "The Beauties of Santa Cruz" (1779). Freneau's poem is nearly contemporary with Bartram's *Travels* and establishes a similar relationship between natural and political turbulence. But Freneau's storm, though a "Daughter of chaos and eternal night," has little of the biblical gravity of Bartram's, just as Freneau's nature never quite provides him with the sort of admonitory, providential text that Bartram's Quaker sensibility was prepared to find side by side with the nomenclature of Linnaeus.[12] According to Bartram, the skies in one memorable cloudburst that he witnessed "appeared streaked with blood" while lightning "seemed to fill the world with fire" (132), and in another he writes in deliberate evocation of the Eighteenth Psalm, "the mountains tremble" and the "ancient hills" are "shaken to their foundations" (279).

Bartram's most lengthy account of a storm makes explicit a connection between the moral world of mankind and the grand disturbances of nature that is in some respects traditional and in others surprising. The storm itself becomes both a familiar means of chastening human pride and an emblem of human psychology. It is both an inner and an outer phenomenon, an instrument of God and an intrinsic weakness in the "chain" of reasoning in which men too readily come to place their trust. In this inward-looking sense it has a specific bearing upon American experience:

> The tempest now relaxed, its impetus being spent, and a calm serenity gradually took place . . . the steady western wind resumed his peaceful reign. . . . So it is with the varied and mutable scenes of human events on the stream of life. The higher powers and affections of the soul are so blended and connected with the inferior passions, that the most painful feelings are excited in the mind when the latter are crossed: thus in the moral system, which we have planned for our conduct, as a ladder whereby to mount to the summit of terrestrial glory and happiness, and from whence we perhaps meditated our flight to heaven itself at the very moment when we vainly imagine ourselves to have attained its point, some unforeseen accident intervenes, and surprises us; the chain is violently shaken, we quit our hold and fall: the well-contrived system at once becomes a chaos . . . and the flattering scene passes quite away. . . . But let us wait and rely on our God, who

in due time will shine forth in brightness, dissipate the envious cloud, and reveal to us how finite and circumscribed is human power, when assuming to itself independent wisdom.

(66-67)

The lesson that Bartram draws from these storms, like those he draws from the predatory wars of animal life and the pervasive presence of ruins even in a "new" world, suggests that the American community faces, in Bartram's view, a choice between a deceptive faith in its own "independent wisdom" and a chastened submission to Providence. The pun on American independence, like Bartram's punning allusion to the "mere representation" of harmony among predators in the paradisal spring, makes it clear that the "moral system" about which he is speculating in this passage is both generically vague and at the same time quite specific in its reference to the system that Americans had in 1791 only recently "planned for our conduct" and from which they too hoped to date their national "terrestrial glory." All well-contrived systems tend to chaos. The natural world that Bartram describes in his *Travels* offers little hope that the cycle of life and death will make an exception in favor of any "constitution," civil or biological. But there is still a kind of covenant available to men that offers a promise of deliverance, provided that human beings and human governments have the humility and the breadth of vision to seize it:

> And, O sovereign Lord! since it has pleased thee to endue man with power and pre-eminence here on earth, and establish his dominion over all creatures, may we look up to thee, that our understanding may be so illuminated with wisdom, and our hearts warmed and animated with a due sense of charity, that we may be enabled to do thy will, and perform our duty towards those submitted to our service and protection, and be merciful to them, even as we hope for mercy.
>
> Thus may we be worthy of the dignity and superiority of the high and distinguished station in which thou hast placed us here on earth.

(103)

The "due sense of charity" that Bartram invokes here is every bit as central to the meaning of his *Travels* as John Winthrop's evocation of Christian charity had been to his earlier vision of a community facing perilous choices and temptations. Like Winthrop, Bartram, too, felt the implicit predicament in his ideal, the conviction that a society without mercy itself could expect none from its judges.

It was by no means clear to William Bartram in 1791 that Americans would embrace this covenant. The reiterative wars, ruins, and apocalyptic storms of his book reflect Bartram's personal attempt to make the dangers of national life clear to his contemporaries. Richard Poirier has observed that "the most interesting Ameri-

can books are an image of the creation of America itself" (Poirier 6). William Bartram dealt in such national images directly, often in remarkably compact form, and on one occasion at least with a sense of literary tradition that identifies his work with one of the most complex pastorals in English poetry, Andrew Marvell's "The Garden." A similar sense of kinship with seventeenth-century poets had led Freneau to echo Milton and allude to Waller in his praise of the pleasures of retirement on Santa Cruz.[13] Bartram's use of Marvell's haunting lines underscores his sense of the ethical and spiritual uncertainties of American life. In his account of a tour of Saint Simons Island off the Georgia coast in March of 1774—the month that Parliament passed the Boston Port Act—Bartram reports that he came upon a "delightful habitation" situated in an "excellent bay or cove on the south end of the island," distinguished by a "spacious avenue" leading inland, lined with beehives that "exhibited a lively image of a colony that has attained to a state of power and affluence, by the practice of virtue and industry" (72). This scale-model America—an imaginative reconstruction of the Port of Boston—is inhabited solely by an enlightened farmer, "reclining on a bear-skin," enjoying his pipe.

The welcoming words of Bartram's rustic host are a caricature of eighteenth-century secular culture—"Welcome, stranger; I am indulging the rational dictates of nature, taking a little rest, having just come in from the chace and fishing"—but at this point the anecdote ceases to be a portrait of ideal colonial simplicity. A few pages earlier Bartram had already alluded to the moments "when we vainly imagine ourselves" on the point of heavenly triumphs only to be thwarted by unforeseen accidents. Now in the shadow of "Oaks, Palms, and Sweet Bays," those vain imaginings recur as Bartram and this genial colonist reenact the circumstances of Andrew Marvell's cryptic and disturbing poem, from which Bartram's triad of sheltering trees derives:

> How vainly men themselves amaze
> To win the Palm, the Oke, or Bayes;
> And their uncessant Labours see
> Crown'd from some single Herb or Tree
> Whose short and narrow verged Shade
> Does prudently their Toyles upbraid;
> While all Flow'rs and all Trees do close
> To weave the Garlands of repose.
> Fair quiet, have I found thee here,
> And Innocence thy Sister dear!
> Mistaken long, I sought you then
> In busie Companies of Men.
> Your sacred Plants, if here below,
> Only among the Plants will grow
> Society is all but rude,
> To this delicious Solitude.

(Gardner 255-56)

Like Marvell's lines, Bartram's *Travels* evokes the society from which they appear to have retreated, the "busie Companies of Men" whose turbulence and passion Marvell's speaker, like William Bartram, seems to repudiate in favor of the world of plants. Even the amorous atmosphere of Marvell's refuge, its improbable fertility, and the music of the Soul that preens and sings like a bird, waving "in its Plumes the various Light," have wonderfully precise equivalents in the splendid "rural table" with which Bartram's host regales him, to the accompaniment of "the responsive love-lays of the painted nonpareil, and the alert and gay mock-bird; whilst the brilliant humming-bird darted through the flowery groves, suspended in air, and drank nectar from the flowers" (73).

But just as Marvell's vision is chastened by loneliness and by intimations of death, so Bartram's experience with his insistent host is troubled both by a desperation for companionship that drives this instance of wilderness hospitality and by the "solemn sound" of the ocean, beating on the shores of the "trembling island" in a futile attempt to "assail the skies." The annihilating "Ocean" of the mind in Marvell's poem becomes an annihilating ocean in fact in Bartram's *Travels,* an image that, for Bartram, proclaims both the durability of the colonies in the face of assaults by "mighty giants" from the sea and the vulnerability of even the most perfectly regulated republic to inner and outer enemies.

There is greater cause for optimism than for despair in this short interlude, for as Bartram returns from the home of his "sylvan friend" he notes the ruins of a once extensive English colony and fortress on Saint Simons Island that are slowly being replaced by a "few neat houses" which owe their prosperity to the mercantile vigor of the island's "president." This is a scale-model revolution that sustains and vivifies the miniature America Bartram had discovered on Saint Simons, incorporating the new Constitution into the pattern of significances. But the same ocean that represents England's imperial futility represents as well the inescapable empire of death, always at war with life, even in the most captivating and apparently inexhaustible of national gardens.[14]

Notes

1. Hedges's comment is from his brief introductory essay, "Toward a National Literature" in the *Columbia Literary History.*

2. The essays of Silver and Arner are the most substantial treatments of Bartram in recent years. Robert Lawson-Peebles's book on landscape rhetoric during the revolutionary period offers a suggestive intellectual context for reading the *Travels* but he does not touch directly on Bartram's work.

3. See Silver's essay for a representative view of Bartram's "apolitical" character (597).

4. Harper's detailed examination of the chronology of Bartram's trips is contained in the textual commentary to the Yale edition, though Harper does profess surprise at Bartram's apparent indifference to the Revolution in his report to the American Philosophical Society: "One of [Bartram's] amazing achievements was to have published an account of travels extending all the way from Pennsylvania to Florida and the Mississippi, and including nearly two years of the Revolution, without once referring to that momentous conflict" (Harper, *Proceedings* 574).

5. This is the thrust of Silver's argument.

6. Harper's blind spot is the more interesting here because his own careful scholarship suggests the likelihood that Bartram had enlisted in a detachment of revolutionary soldiers on a mission during one of his trips into Georgia in 1776. Harper discusses the bases for his conclusion in *Proceedings* 572-73.

7. Richard Slotkin discusses Bartram's chance meeting with one Indian in particular as an example of his unusually humane attitude toward Indians and as part of an emerging tradition of American frontier consciousness. The discussion of Bartram's work in particular, however, is quite brief. See Slotkin 320-34.

8. Arner's view of the pastoral pattern in the *Travels* involves this sense on Bartram's part of nature's ambiguity, but Arner presents the pattern as part of a psychological development within Bartram himself, not as a rhetorical tactic that Bartram might employ (Arner 140-44).

9. Philbrick discusses Crèvecoeur's use of natural imagery as a psychological vocabulary in the *Letters.*

10. May's categories are distinguished in many respects by their chief literary spokesmen: Pope and Locke for the Moderate Enlightenment, Rousseau and Paine for the Radical. Crèvecoeur quotes two lines from the "Essay on Man" inscribed above a barn door as emblems of the benign morality of the Bartrams, whose farm is the topic of one of the last optimistic chapters in the *Letters.*

11. Bryant does, it is true, lose this heartening glimpse of the future to a "fresher wind" that passes and leaves him alone "in the wilderness," troubled by the vision of imperial violence that his own lines have evoked. But the sense of Bryant's text remains distinctly anticipatory. Bartram on the other hand is much closer to the sensibility of "Ozymandias."

12. Emory Elliott argues that Freneau follows "Lycidas" in returning to the poet's moral calling in the

world, but I do not think a reading of any version of Freneau's poem can resolve the question of the speaker's status and commitment to public responsibility, particularly the earliest untitled version of the text (Freneau 41-47). The final version, with the title "The Beauties of Santa Cruz," is more troubled by the presence of slavery in the poet's refuge, but even this version has little of the moral urgency of Bartram's prose. See Eberwein 206-21. In her article on the poem, Eberwein makes a persuasive case for the complexity of Freneau's lines, though there too she recognized their fundamentally descriptive nature.

13. Emory Elliott notes the echoes of Milton. Freneau compares his own blissful condition on Santa Cruz to the less blessed exile of Waller.

14. Both Emory Elliott and William Hedges argue for the contradictions confronted by writers in the postrevolutionary decades. Bartram in fact expresses perfectly in this passage one of the "biformities" that Michael Kammen finds endemic in the cultural life of America in the last third of the eighteenth century: that of optimistic pessimism (Kammen 157-68).

Works Cited

Arner, Robert D. "Pastoral Patterns in William Bartram's *Travels.*" *Tennessee Studies in Literature* 18 (1973): 133-45.

Bartram, William. *Travels of William Bartram.* Ed. Mark Van Doren. New York: Dover, 1955.

Bryant, William Cullen. "The Prairies." *The Norton Anthology of American Literature.* Ed. Gottesman et al. Vol. I. New York: Norton, 1979.

Crèvecoeur, J. Hector St. John de. *Letters from an American Farmer and Sketches of Eighteenth-Century America.* Ed. Albert E. Stone. Middlesex, England: Penguin, 1981.

Eberwein, Jane Donahue, ed. *Early American Poetry.* Madison: Univ. of Wisconsin Press, 1978.

———. "Freneau's 'Beauties of Santa Cruz.'" *Early American Literature* 12 (Winter 1977/78): 271-76.

Elliott, Emory. *Revolutionary Writers: Literature and Authority in the New Republic.* New York: Oxford Univ. Press, 1982.

Freneau, Philip. *The Newspaper Verse of Philip Freneau.* Ed. Judith R. Hiltner. Troy, N.Y.: Whitston, 1986.

Gardner, Helen, ed. *The Metaphysical Poets.* Middlesex, England: Penguin, 1957.

Harper, Francis. "William Bartram and the American Revolution." *Proceedings of the American Philosophical Society* 97 (1953): 571-77.

———, ed. *The Travels of William Bartram.* New Haven: Yale Univ. Press, 1958.

Hedges, William. "Toward a National Literature." *Columbia Literary History of the United States.* Ed. Emory Elliott. New York: Columbia Univ. Press, 1988.

———. "Charles Brockden Brown and the Culture of Contradictions." *Early American Literature* 9 (1974): 107-42.

Jefferson, Thomas. *Writings.* New York: Library of America, 1984.

Kammen, Michael. *People of Paradox.* New York: Knopf, 1972.

Lawson-Peebles, Robert. *Landscape and Written Expression in Revolutionary America.* Cambridge: Cambridge Univ. Press, 1988.

Madison, James; Hamilton, Alexander; Jay, John. *The Federalist Papers.* Ed. Isaac Kramnick. New York: Viking Penguin, 1987.

May, Henry F. *The Enlightenment in America.* New York: Oxford Univ. Press, 1976.

Medeiros, Patricia M. "Three Travelers: Carver, Bartram, and Woolman." *American Literature, 1764-1789, The Revolutionary Years.* Ed. Everett Emerson. Madison: Univ. of Wisconsin Press, 1977.

Nash, Roderick. *Wilderness and the American Mind.* New Haven: Yale Univ. Press, 1967.

Philbrick, Thomas. *St. John de Crèvecoeur.* New York: Twayne, 1970.

Poirier, Richard. *A World Elsewhere: The Place of Style in American Literature.* New York: Oxford Univ. Press, 1966.

Silver, Bruce. "William Bartram's and Other Eighteenth-Century Accounts of Nature." *Journal of the History of Ideas* 39 (1978): 597-614.

Slotkin, Richard. *Regeneration through Violence.* Middletown: Wesleyan Univ. Press, 1973.

Pamela Regis (essay date 1992)

SOURCE: Regis, Pamela. "Description and Narration in Bartram's *Travels.*" In *Describing Early America: Bartram, Jefferson, Crèvecoeur, and the Rhetoric of Natural History,* pp. 40-78. Northern Illinois University Press, 1992.

[In the following essay, Regis examines Bartram's use of narrative as a mode for employing two different description techniques for the external world.]

As an instance of the literature of place, William Bartram's *Travels* represents large portions of the territories of North and South Carolina, Georgia, and Florida to readers eager for images of the New World they had never seen. Using the rhetoric and method of natural history, Bartram details "the furniture of the earth" to be found in these regions—the minerals and animals and, in particular, the plants. Using Edmund Burke's theory of the sublime and the beautiful, he describes the scenes through which he sailed, paddled, rode, and walked during his three-and-a-half-year journey through the Southeast. The two methods, natural history and the sublime, complement each other. Each compels notice of a different selection of the creation. The natural historical practitioner described individual items. The Burkean practitioner described entire scenes. For Bartram, both methods were objective. The natural historical method, as we have seen, relied on observation conducted according to exact procedures. Burke's theory, relying as it did on the observer's accurate reporting of his emotional responses, provided Bartram with a scientific way of representing his reactions to the scenes he saw.

The frame for both kinds of description is narrative, the defining characteristic of the travel genre. Travel books include interruptions of the forward progress of narrative to accommodate extended descriptions of countryside or city. Narrative and description are counterpoints to each other, narrative propelling the narrator forward through time and space, description halting him to detail the scene before him.

Narrative is for Bartram a potentially mediating form of discourse between the two modes of description that he employs. He describes both the things of the external world, represented in *Travels* through natural historical description, and his internal responses to the external world, represented through Burkean description of the land and the sea. Individual action, represented in *Travels* through narrative, is both external, as Bartram moves through the world, and internal, as he experiences his own action. Bartram reports his movements as he travels, but this narrative remains a mere frame for the description. It fails to provide a middle ground between the impersonal facts of natural history and the psychologically immediate sensations of Burkean aesthetics.

This failure of narrative in *Travels* is most clearly illustrated by Bartram's representations of the American Indians. When narrative fails him, he ultimately resorts to natural historical description. Natural history, the means to knowledge of a place and the provider of a universal frame for the contents of that place, is, in Bartram's hands, inadequate when it is turned upon native people. Bartram's own response to the native Americans is often given as fear or awe, the two establishing emotions of the sublime, and this leads him into perorations on the American Indians' heroic, "noble savage" natures. A representational mediate ground between the discrete facts of the manners-and-customs account and the soaring moralizing of the Burkean description is available to Bartram. Narrative would permit Bartram's reader to see American Indians in action, and might vouchsafe him and his readers a glimpse into an individual native's experience. Bartram makes a few tentative narrative forays in the first three parts of *Travels.* Then, in part 4, he resorts to a manners-and-customs description as the rhetoric and method of natural history provide him with the most available means to represent America's original inhabitants.

Bartram was born in 1739 near Philadelphia, where his father, one of the first botanists in America, had founded a botanical garden on the banks of the Schuylkill. He traveled from 1773 to 1778 through the American Southeast under the patronage of Dr. John Fothergill of London, returned to his family's garden, and wrote an account of his journey, *Travels through North & South Carolina, Georgia, East & West Florida, The Cherokee Country, the Extensive Territories of the Muscogulges, or Creek Confederacy, and the Country of the Chactaws; containing An Account of the Soil and Natural Productions of those Regions, together with Observations on the Manners of the Indians.*[1] During Bartram's lifetime, *Travels* was published in Philadelphia (1791), London (1791), Dublin (1793), Berlin (1793), Haarlem (1794-97), and Paris (1799).[2] This book, Bartram's only major publication, found an audience in England and on the Continent, eventually entering the canon of American literature through the auspices of readers such as Wordsworth, Coleridge, Emerson, and Thoreau.

Commentators on *Travels* have established a tradition of ignoring the natural history in the book. The early literary-source hunters did not have to concern themselves with Bartram's scientific accomplishments. Lane Cooper and later John Livingston Lowes simply followed the echoes of Bartram's text in the poetry of Wordsworth and Coleridge. Although N. Bryllion Fagin included in his book a consideration of Bartram's life, philosophy (including his science), and landscape, he too concentrated on an assessment of Bartram's influence on other writers.[3]

More recently, Robert Arner and Wayne Franklin have examined only the narrative portions of the text (parts 1 through 3) to discover the pastoral and chivalric elements of *Travels.* Thomas Vance Barnett extends this appropriation of the text to narrowly literary uses. He declares, after a demonstration that William Bartram was "a mediocre scientist" that, in fact, "William Bartram's *Travels* is . . . a literary work."[4] Efforts to limit the text before interpreting it bespeak these critics' discomfort in dealing with science, or with those elements of a text that are scientific.

Critics may simply be following Bartram's contemporary reputation as a "difficult" son to his father, a judgment that is first recorded in the letters the patron Fothergill wrote to John Bartram about his most gifted child.[5] William Bartram's relationship with Fothergill determined his relationship with the entire natural history community. That is, it determined his pre-*Travels* reputation.

William Bartram was first brought to the notice of Dr. John Fothergill (1712-80) by Peter Collinson, who showed Bartram's drawings of butterflies and plants to many members of the natural history circle.[6] Fothergill was a physician, and owner of the largest private garden in England. Adjoining a sitting room at his Upton home was a 260-foot greenhouse.[7] He owned more than 3,000 different species of exotic plants.[8] He prized botanical illustrations, employing artists to draw new items as they were added to his collection. In 1770 he agreed to buy any drawing that Bartram might send; in 1773, he agreed to sponsor Bartram on a trip to the Southeast.[9]

As we have seen in chapter 1, patrons could be self-interested purchasers of a service. Fothergill, like Collinson, was not motivated solely by the pure spirit of science. For patrons of plant hunters, their gardens "proved to be the most conspicuous means of enjoying the natural riches of the far corners of the earth." Much is often made of Fothergill's generosity in thinking of and supporting William Bartram.[10] Less is made of the advantages he reaped—the possession of curiosities from the New World to show his botanizing friends and to help him maintain his status in the British collectors' community.

In his letter to John offering to pay William's expenses on his trip to the Southeast, Fothergill made one thing clear: "I would not have it understood that I mean to support him." Indeed, Fothergill was not happy about Bartram's destination:

> He proposes to go to Florida. It is a country abounding with great variety of plants, and many of them unknown. To search for these, will be of use to science in general; but I am a little selfish. I wish to introduce into this country the more hardy American plants, such as will bear our winters without much shelter. However, I shall endeavour to assist his inclination for a tour through Florida; and if he succeeds, shall, perhaps, wish him to see the back parts of Canada.[11]

Two years later Fothergill was complaining about William to John:

> I have received from him about one hundred dried specimens of plants, and some of them very curious; a very few drawings, but neither a seed nor a plant.
>
> I am sensible of the difficulty he is at in travelling through those inhospitable countries; but I think he should have sent me some few things as he went along.

> I have paid the bills he drew upon me; but must be greatly out of pocket, if he does not take some opportunity of doing what I expressly directed, which was, to send me seeds or roots of such plants, as wither by their beauty, fragrance, or other properties, might claim attention.[12]

A dried specimen is what a botanist puts in an herbarium, a library of plants. When an unknown specimen comes to light, the botanist compares it to the specimens that are already in the herbarium to determine the new plant's classification. A seed or root, once planted and growing in the possessor's garden, can always produce cuttings, blossoms, and fruit to dry and mount for an herbarium specimen. Thus, seeds and roots yield more glory for the collector, and a better return on his investment. This acquisitiveness is reflected in Fothergill's charge to William when he agreed to sponsor a plant-gathering trip: "I am not so far a systematic botanist, as to wish to have in my garden all the grasses, or other less observable, humble plants, that nature produces. The useful, the beautiful, the singular, or the fragrant, are to us the most material."[13]

When Fothergill complains that William has not sent him seeds or roots, only dried plants and drawings, he is neatly reflecting the division between the pure hunt for knowledge about plants and his desire to have the best garden he can manage. Clearly, he thought of Bartram primarily as a plant hunter. Despite this limiting characterization, Fothergill did carry Bartram's name into the natural history circle both in England and on the Continent. When Fothergill died in 1780, three years after Bartram's return from the Southeast, the American botanist was deprived of this access. Bartram had probably begun writing *Travels* by then.[14] But the war and his patron's death must have made its completion more urgent. At the time it was his single remaining opportunity for receiving the recognition he knew he deserved.

Despite his subordinate relationship to Fothergill, Bartram transcended the role of plant hunter to become a respected and accomplished botanist. He never took a university degree, but studied botany and natural history with an acknowledged master—his father, John.[15] He was paid for his work as a plant collector.[16] He had read the revolutionizing work of Linnaeus and was aware, as we shall see, of the current concerns of an eighteenth-century botanist.[17] Bartram appears in contemporary lists of scientists. One F. A. A. Meyer, commentator on *Travels* in its German edition, included Bartram in a 1794 list of all living zoologists; Bartram was the only American thus honored.[18] In the preface to the first American botanical publication, Henry Muhlenberg lists Bartram simply as "William Bartram, Botanist."[19] The University of Pennsylvania offered him a professorship in botany, but he refused it, citing his poor health.[20] Despite Bartram's lack of a formal post, students eagerly sought him out, then went on to illustrious careers of their own, most notably Alexander Wilson, author of *The American Ornithology*.[21] One account of Bartram's influence on botany links him with thirty-three investigators and fourteen texts.[22] His scientific achievements were recognized by his election to the American Philosophical Society.[23]

A cursory glance at *Travels* itself shows Bartram to be a natural historian with a wide range of interests—geology; botany; zoology in all of its forms, including entomology, ornithology, herpetology, and malacology; as well as anthropology. Botany was his strongest interest and the area of most of his lasting contributions. Had his drawings and verbal descriptions been published promptly, he would have claimed credit for the discovery of twenty-three American species. He was an illustrator of great talent, and his work has been favorably compared to that of Georg Ehret, the leading contemporary botanical illustrator on the Continent.[24]

The methods of eighteenth-century natural history little resemble those of natural history's modern-day descendants, the life sciences. Thomas S. Kuhn reminds us of the "unhistorical stereotype drawn from science texts" that mistakenly urges us to hold early practitioners of a given science to a modern standard of what constitutes doing that particular science.[25] One popular definition holds that an enterprise is a science if information that counts as knowledge in that field is discovered through duplicatable experiments. By this criterion, natural history is not a science at all. "Scientist" is not even a term that Bartram would have applied to himself. It was coined in 1840. "Scientific," employed in the modern sense, was not widespread until after the turn of the nineteenth century. "Science" had a long history predating Bartram, but at the time he wrote it was still being used to mean any knowledge of natural phenomena. Although Bartram did not perform experiments, he would have known about experimentation—his father was one of the first botanists in America to experiment with "mule" (hybrid) plants.[26] Bartram did, however, make observations of the most painstaking sort. He classified the specimens he observed using the Linnaean system, and he communicated these results to others in his scholarly community.

If the lack of experiments makes Bartam's science hard to recognize, so does the nature of his arguments in the introduction to *Travels,* the primary repository of his theoretical pronouncements on botany. In the introduction he writes a long essay on natural history that is organized hierarchically, covering first the vegetable and then the animal kingdom. The resulting overview establishes his metaphysical stance, and his scientific one as well. He invokes ideas of design and plenitude in the form of the Great Chain. He introduces the opposing activities of contemplation and use, opposites that re-

main unreconciled in the entire book as they become translated into description (which, like contemplation, is passive) and narrative (which by its nature is active, like use). To an eye alert to the signs, Bartram's introduction is a catalogue of the concerns of an eighteenth-century botanist. Such a catalogue reveals the still-close association of botany and teleology, and teleology of a grand sort—the use of design or purpose to explain events in nature.

The scope of the introduction is nothing less than the entire animate world. Bartram divides it into distinct sections whose subjects are located on progressively higher links of the Great Chain of Being: an eleven-paragraph section on the vegetable world with teleological as well as physiological speculations on several of the problems then current in botany; an eight-paragraph section on the animals with anecdotes carefully chosen to illustrate their moral system; and a four-paragraph section on American Indians that constitutes a plea for considering them to be more civilized than the usual European believed them. The general movement is toward elevation—the plants Bartram mentions are animal-like; the animals are humanlike; the savages are not savage at all. For Bartram, all creatures, plants, and inanimate things yearn upward; for those who can understand its hidden reality, everything in creation has more to recommend it than was commonly thought. Bartram reads the universe as more exalted, more able, more accomplished than it was usually seen to be. In addition to this improvement plan for the universe, he uses a mode of thought characteristic of eighteenth-century botany: analogy.

The first two sentences embody the hierarchical thinking with which Bartram's prose is suffused:

> The attention of the traveller should be particularly turned, in the first place, to the various works of Nature, to mark the distinctions of the climates he may explore, and to offer such useful observations on the different productions as may occur. Men and manners undoubtedly hold the first rank—whatever may contribute to our existence is also of equal importance, whether it be found in the animal or vegetable kingdom; neither are the various articles, which tend to promote the happiness and convenience of mankind, to be disregarded.[27]

Here Bartram states his immediate end in writing: use. (Ultimately, his end was to glorify God.) "Men and manners" are at the top of the chain, then that part of creation lesser than man but living—animals and plants—then inanimate creation (the last-mentioned "various articles") at the bottom of the chain. Lovejoy reminds us of the common place that this hierarchy occupied in Bartram's era: "It was in the eighteenth century that the conception of the universe as a Chain of Being, and the principles which underlay this conception—plenitude, continuity, gradation—attained their widest diffusion and acceptance."[28] Bartram authorizes the enterprise to his British audience first by mentioning his father, botanist to King George III; then his Father: "This world, as a glorious apartment of the boundless palace of the sovereign Creator, is furnished with an infinite variety of animated scenes, inexpressibly beautiful and pleasing, equally free to the inspection and enjoyment of all his creatures."[29] This invocation of the Creator, with its reference to plenitude ("infinite variety"), at once authorizes the enterprise and determines its ultimate end. In addition to use, Bartram states a more immediate end for his enterprise—inspection and enjoyment. Throughout *Travels* Bartram claims his reason for writing is to be of use, but the text represents and invites "inspection and enjoyment," as does his practice in the field.

The second section, which begins the long discourse on the vegetables, continues this teleological bent: "There is not any part of creation, within reach of our observations, which exhibits a more glorious display of the Almighty hand, than the vegetable world." Having once again framed his remarks with mention of the universe and its creator, Bartram narrows his scope, confining himself merely to the earth: "It is difficult to pronounce which division of the earth, between the polar circles, produces greatest variety." He provides a Linnaean catalogue of tropical plants that seem intended for "luxurious scenes of splendour."[30] The temperate zone "exhibits scenes of infinitely greater variety, magnificence, and consequence, with respect to human economy, in regard to the various uses of vegetables."[31] He follows with another long list of plants of the temperate zone, which provides evidence of plenitude, one of the principles of the Great Chain of Being. The fulsome list evokes the brimming creation.

This section has another aim as well. Bartram has divided the globe into zones—a common practice today. But traveling in the colonies in 1749, Peter Kalm, a Linnaean disciple, records in his diary this conversation with William's father: "[John Bartram] reiterated what he had often told me before, namely that all plants and trees have a special latitude where they thrive best, and that the further they grow from this region, whether to the north or south, the smaller and more delicate they become, until finally they disappear entirely."[32] In 1749 this observation was noteworthy. As a topic of conversation it recurred in Kalm's talks with John Bartram. It was not simply a settled matter. The rest of their conversation that day involved instances of plants at the extreme limits of what we now call their range, including an aloe growing in Virginia.

In a section of the introduction devoted to plants that seem to straddle the boundary between plants and animals, William Bartram discusses the function of parts of the pitcher plants (*Sarracenia*), of the apparently volitional motion of both the Venus flytrap (*Dionea muscipula*), and of the tendrils of certain climbing plants, such as the cucumber (*Curcurbita*). He speculates on the little "lid" of the pitcher plant, the "cordated appendage," which nature has provided to guard against the vessel's filling with water and breaking. The plant's leaves, shaped like pitchers, cannot support a "sudden and copious supply of water from heavy showers of rain, which would bend down the leaves, never to rise again because their straight parallel nerves which extend and support them are so rigid and fragile, the leaf would inevitably break when bent down to a right angle."[33] This is our first evidence of Bartram's link to branches of natural history other than taxonomy. Bartram is speculating as to the function of certain structures he observed and sketched.[34] The prominent "nerve"—the supporting rib and its branches—is featured in each of several renderings he made of the plant. The mode of discourse here, rather than the catalogue, is analysis; the mechanism of explanation, the analogy. Parts of plants are compared to parts of animals.

In employing analogies, Bartram weaves into his work one of the dominant threads of eighteenth-century botanical discourse. For many historians of botany, the analogic method of investigation marks Bartram as, at the very least, one who would be left by the wayside when the histories of botany were finally written. In one such history Philip C. Ritterbush has recovered the place that analogy held in eighteenth-century botanical reasoning. Naturalists believed, and based arguments on the proposition, that "plants were analogous to animals because of their close proximity in the scheme of nature." His disapproval of such analogizing is plain: "Although the authority of science was invoked on [its] behalf the concept reflected an improper understanding of organic nature, far exceeded the evidence given for [it], and too often led naturalists to neglect observations and experiment in favor of abstract conceptions."[35]

A second historian of botany, François Delaporte, sets himself against historians like Ritterbush who vilify the analogists and champion the experimentalists:

> The analogical method was a hindrance, it is argued, because it was a procedure the eighteenth century presumably inherited from the Renaissance or even Antiquity. The identification of the various parts of the vegetable organism with the known parts of the animal was, we are told, a source of error. In contrast, the work done by experimentalists and observers was supposedly a prefiguration of the nineteenth century.

This separation of the botanists into two camps—the successful observers and the misguided analogists—is problematic, says Delaporte.

> That the discipline has had to be divided up in this way is one indication that something has gone wrong. For one thing, the logical connections among certain state-

ments are obscured, because botanists numbered among the analogists happen to have become involved in observation or experiment. For another, the use of analogy by those described as observers and experimentalists is disguised.[36]

Ritterbush discovers the relationship between the Great Chain, the usual eighteenth-century way of visualizing the Creator's plan, and analogy: "There was a reciprocal relationship between analogies and imputed proximity of place on the scale. The discovery of certain properties which plants shared with animals lent encouragement to the belief that they were close to animals upon the scale of beings and that consequently any number of analogies might pertain between them."[37] Analysis—what Bartram calls *analysis* moderns would likely call *observation and description*—went hand in hand with reasoning from analogy. And since there was a plan, one could reason not only from the Creation to the blueprint for it, but from the blueprint back to the Creation. This is much more consequential than the accidentally heuristic models that twentieth-century scientists construct. This same correspondence, this same path to truth, was also possible with the parts of the Creation—plants were believed to be like animals because they shared with them certain functions such as nourishing themselves, reproducing themselves, and moving volitionally. One could reason from the better-known animals to the lesser-known plants just as one could reason from the blueprint to the Creation. Analogy was not simply a way to explain a lesser-known thing in terms of a better-known thing—a one-way flow of knowledge; instead, it was a way to know both things in terms of each other—a two-way flow.

This speculative reasoning in the introduction is quite different from the taxonomy that is the focus of parts 1-4 of Bartram's *Travels*. It places Bartram's thought in a broader context. The Great Chain of Being figures not only as the overarching scheme for the taxonomic work that Bartram did but also as a sort of metaphysical abacus. A plant's essence, like a counter on an abacus rod, could be moved higher, toward the animals, or lower, toward inanimate matter, through this analogical thinking. By choosing certain difficult cases, such as an animal-like "carnivorous vegetable" (the Venus flytrap) and arguing from observable characteristics to metaphysical states, Bartram could slide enough counters toward a higher state of being to shift the whole nature of the Creation. Analogy between plants and animals had led Linnaeus to his "sexual system" of taxonomy. (Reproduction in animals was understood before reproduction in plants.) Bartram, in his speculations here, was in tune with the scientific methods of his day, however odd it now seems to us that he would try to demonstrate the animality of certain plants.

This elevation of the things in the "glorious apartment of the Creator" is carried through to his observations of

certain animals. Bears seem humanlike in their "parental and filial affections."[38] Spiders are "cunning" and "intrepid" in their hunting; birds, "social and benevolent creatures."[39] But if one consequence of his analogizing is his exaltation and sentimentalization of animals, another is his willingness to look at American Indians in a spirit of equality. The final paragraphs of the introduction are Bartram's plea to European settlers to send visitors to the American Indians "to learn perfectly their languages, and by a liberal and friendly intimacy become acquainted with their customs and usages, religious and civil; their system of legislation and police, as well as their most ancient and present traditions and history." This is quite a program. Its goal might be assimilation: "[The Indians] were desirous of becoming united with us, in civil and religious society," but it is assimilation based on thorough knowledge.[40] He does not suggest a missionary excursion where European visitors would teach the native Americans an imported language, traditions, and history; rather, he suggests exactly the kind of visit that he himself makes in *Travels*—to "learn perfectly" and to return "to make true and just reports." He suggests, in short, an expedition whose methodology is scientific within the broad compass of natural history.

Bartram's introduction, written after his return from the Southeast, puts into motion the elements of his science and of his thinking, and offers us a way to understand where many of his more-commented-upon ideas came from. The universe is a hierarchy, traditionally divided into three kingdoms—minerals, plants, and animals—with man at the top of animal creation. But science shows Bartram a way of blurring these categories, or employing them to redefine them: plants are like animals, animals are like men, and American Indians are like Europeans. More particularly, certain characteristics that we ascribe to animals, such as volitional movement, are also present in plants, and this blurring of the boundaries between plants and animals is grounds for reevaluating creation wholesale—and for promoting its constituents upward in our estimation of them. So animals display humanlike characteristics, and since in humans the source of these characteristics is a refined and reasoning intellect, animals must have one, too. So, too, do American Indians display European-like characteristics. They must also have similar sources for such beliefs and will benefit from the same sort of treatment that Europeans might expect under similar circumstances.

Within this universal teleology is a program for man's relationship with the natural world. There are two choices: observation and use. In Bartram's text, the corollary of observation is description; the corollary of use, narration. For Bartram traveling through the Southeast, observation and use define his possibilities for interacting with the territories through which he passes.

For Bartram writing *Travels,* the two associated modes of discourse define the possibilities for representing that country in the text. *Travels* contains both modes: description on the Linnaean and Burkean models, and narrative.

Bartram was trained in the Linnaean system. His father had received a copy of Linnaeus's *Systema Naturae* in 1736, three years before William's birth, and had been tutored in its use by James Logan, an accomplished colonial botanist who demonstrated, experimentally, the mechanism by which pollen fertilized corn.[41] Bartram's mastery of the Linnaean system is best demonstrated by his account of his most famous discovery, *Franklinia alatamaha.*

> It is a flowering tree, of the first order for beauty and fragrance of blossoms: the tree grows fifteen or twenty feet high, branching alternately; the leaves are oblong, broadest towards their extremities, and terminate with an acute point, which is generally a little reflexed; they are lightly serrated, attenuate downwards, and sessile, or have very short petioles; they are placed in alternate order, and towards the extremities of the twigs are very large, expand themselves perfectly, are of a snow white colour, and ornamented with a crown or tassel of gold coloured refulgent staminae in the centre, the inferiour petal or segment of the corolla is hollow, formed like a cap or helmet, and entirely includes the other four, until the moment of expansion; its exterior surface is covered with a short silky hair; the borders of the petals are sessile in the bosom of the leaves, and being near together towards the extremities of the twigs, and usually many expanded at the same time, make a gay appearance: the fruit is a large, round, dry woody apple or pericarp, opening at each end oppositely by five alternate fissures, containing ten cells, each replete with dry woody cuneiform seed.[42]

The concentration on the flower and the fruit is the hallmark of Linnaeus's sexual system of classification.[43] Other characteristics are not ignored, but these are the most closely scrutinized. Hence Bartram's remark about his first look at the shrub: "This very curious tree was first taken notice of about ten or twelve years ago, at this place, when I attended my father (John Bartram) on a botanical excursion; but it being then late in the autumn, we could form no opinion to what class or tribe it belonged." *Franklinia* blooms in the spring. He adds this footnote:

> On first observing the fructification and habit of this tree, I was inclined to believe it a species of *Gordonia*; but afterwards, upon stricter examination, and comparing its flowers and fruit with those of the *Gordonia lasianthus,* I presently found striking characteristics abundantly sufficient to separate it from that genus, and to establish it the head of a new tribe, which we have honoured with the name of the illustrious Dr. Benjamin Franklin.

Bartram was obviously more than a simple Quaker boy who rode through the American Southeast gathering new-looking plants and sending them back to England.

The comparison of the flowers and fruit of one plant with those of another—the most essential procedure in naming a plant using the Linnaean method of classification—also marks him as more than a literary-minded pilgrim on a pastoral retreat.[44]

The rhetoric imposed by the Linnaean method resulted in a series of descriptions, all of them static or, as in the case of *Franklinia,* atemporal, where blossom and fruit are represented in the same description. Even as they suspend or transcend time they establish the physical reality of the country. To represent the Southeast's natural history, Bartram had at his disposal three different forms of natural historical description: an entry describing a single item, a list of like items, and an essay encompassing the range of natural history in a given locale.

In the third chapter of the first volume of *Travels,* Bartram offers the reader a description of "a new species of Anona." This is an instance of an entry describing a single item. The passage serves as an "exploded" version of an entry in a work like the *Species Plantarum.* It also serves as a verbal gloss on the engraving that appears on the facing page of the London 1792 edition.[45] The text-and-illustration combination permits the reader to experience the method of natural history—to look at the specimen and at the same time to read the description that Bartram has produced.

"It is very dwarf, the stems seldom extending from the earth more than a foot or eighteen inches." With this scale in mind the reader then learns, "The leaves are long, extremely narrow, almost lineal." A glance at the picture confirms this. "However, small as they are, they retain the figure common to the species, that is, lanceolate, broadest at the upper end and attenuating down to the petiole [leaf stalk] which is very short." This is especially clear in the largest, centermost leaf. "Their leaves stand alternately, nearly erect, forming two series, or wings, on the arcuated [bow-shaped] stems." The drawing clearly shows the alternating leaves, the bowed stem. "The flowers, both in size and colour, resemble those of the Antrilove"—this was beyond his technical means to show in the drawing—"and are single from the axillae of the leaves [the upper angle between a leaf or petiole and the stem from which it springs] on incurved pedunculi [stems bearing single flowers], nodding downwards." The uppermost flower best shows this relationship between stem and leaf, the nontechnical "nodding" mirroring the "incurved pedunculi" that produce this downward-looking attitude.

This careful description and the equally careful drawing teach the reader how to look at all of the drawings and read all of the descriptions in the volume. The details of leaf shape, attachment, and flower position are precise. The verbal description enables a nonbotanical reader to understand much of the information, particularly with the aid of the drawing. Foucault explains this close association of the verbal and the visual. He notes that "the blind man in the eighteenth century can perfectly well be a geometrician, but he cannot be a naturalist." In natural history, sight has "an almost exclusive privilege, being the sense by which we perceive extent and establish proof." But sight itself has been narrowed, refined, reduced to the most certain of its elements. It is "a visibility freed from all other sensory burdens and restricted, moreover, to black and white." Bartram's illustrations for this edition of *Travels* were black-and-white line drawings. Visibility determines natural history: "This area, much more than the receptivity and attention at last being granted to things themselves, defines natural history's condition of possibility, and the appearance of its screened objects: lines, surfaces, forms, reliefs."[46] Foucault notes that the natural historian's sight operates within four variables: "The form of the elements, the quality of those elements, the manner in which they are distributed in space in relation to each other, and the relative magnitude of each element." Variations in form, quality, distribution, and magnitude of five parts of the plant—"roots, stem, leaves, flowers, fruits"—become the keys to the plant's identification. He asserts that the relationship between the name and that which it denotes, between language and things, "can . . . be established in a manner that excludes all uncertainty."[47] Furthermore, "the plant is thus engraved in the material of the language into which it has been transposed, and recomposes its pure form before the reader's very eyes. The book becomes the herbarium of living structures."[48]

In Bartram's description of the Anona we have the apotheosis of the Linnaean form of natural historical inquiry. A single plant is reconstituted in the mind of the reader by a verbal description. Bartram's volume included seven illustrations of natural historical specimens, yet it contained more than fifty verbal descriptions of the flora and fauna of America. He relied on the shared language of natural historical description to represent the contents of the American Southeast to the reader. The specimens and the book are made one by the rhetoric of the Linnaean method. Samples of American plants and animals are included in every copy of the book.

As we saw in chapter 1, every Linnaean binomial is backed by a description similar to the one that Bartram offered of his "new species of Anona." When Bartram includes a Linnaean name in *Travels,* he invokes the entire intellectual scheme upon which the Linnaean system was built—the unique description of a single plant as well as that plant's place in the Great Chain. If the invocation of this context made the name an unambiguous representation of a part of America, it also abstracted the thing represented out of its American con-

text. Bartram's lists compensate for this deficiency in the rhetoric that grew out of the method.

In describing an island off the coast of Sunbury, Georgia, Bartram includes lists of all of "the natural produce of these testaceous ridges"—the plants and animals.[49]

> The general surface of the island being low, and generally level, produces a very great variety of trees, shrubs, and herbaceous plants; particularly the great long-leaved Pitch-Pine, or Broom-Pine, *Pinus palustris, Pinus squamosa, Pinus lutea, Gordonia Lasianthus,* Liquid ambar *(Styraciflua) Acer rubrum, Fraxinus excelcior; Fraxinus aquatica, Quercus aquatica, Quercus phillos, Quercus dentata, Quercus humila varietas, Vaccinium varietas, Andromeda varietas, Prinos varietas, Ilex varietas, Viburnum prunifolium, V. dentatum, Cornus florida, C. alba, C. sanguinea, Carpinus betula, C. Ostrya, Itea Clethra alnifolia, Halesia tetraptera, H. diptera, Iva, Rhamnus frangula, Callicarpa, Morus rubra, Sapindus, Cassine,* and of such as grow near watercourses, round about ponds and savannas, *Fothergilla gardini, Myrica cerifera, Olea Americana, Cyrilla recemiflora, Magnolia glauca, Magnolia pyramidata, Cercis, Kalmia angustifolia, Kalmia ciliata, Chionanthus, Cephalanthos, Aesculus parva.*[50]

These names would appear in a work like Linnaeus's *Species Plantarum* or Gronovius's *Flora Virginica* separated from each other by many pages of text. *Fraxinius excelcior,* for example, appears in the first edition of the *Species Plantarum* grouped with the *Polygamia Dioecia* on page 1057. There it is listed with the other *Fraxinia,* which follow the *Gleditsia* and are followed by the *Diospyros.* It occupies its niche both in the *Species Plantarum* and in the Great Chain, with gradations on one side or another duly listed. The *Magnolias* are listed with the *Polyandria Polygynia,* on page 536. Yet in Bartram's book, the two are listed in the same paragraph at the same place in the text, and so are located for the reader on the island. They are entries in the 1200-page Linnaean table of plants, where they appear with their near neighbors on the Great Chain. They are also entries in Bartram's text, where they appear with their actual neighbors in the world. Bartram's list counters the abstracting influence of the Linnaean name. It provides a local habitation or context to accompany the universal name and location on the Chain. The list represents to the reader an American scene.

Taken together, Bartram's lists of the natural productions of Georgia's Atlantic islands represent to the reader an American territory, located (off the coast of Sunbury), bounded (the islands themselves), and furnished with the items in the lists. When he made the survey on which he based his description in *Travels,* Bartram was revisiting the islands. They merited a second look because he knew they would "exhibit a comprehensive epitome of the history of all the sea-coast Islands."[51] In his *Report* to Fothergill, prepared from his field notes and sent to England while Bartram was still traveling, he wrote for his patron a four-sentence account of the islands. On them he had "discover'd nothing new, or much worth your notice."[52] In *Travels,* the description of the islands is ten times longer. Clearly, Bartram was interested in showing the reader of *Travels* not just what was new on the islands, but whatever was there. The essay describing the natural history of an entire area represented for the reader a definitely bounded piece of American territory, a country in the geographical sense of the word.

The natural historical entry, list, and essay define space at the expense of time: they suspend narrative. Bartram's visit to the islands begins in narrative: "Next day, being desirous of visiting the islands, I forded a narrow shoal, part of the sound, and landed on one of them, which employed me the whole day to explore." Curiously, it ends in the same bit of action: "The sight of this delightful and productive island, placed in front of the rising city of Sunbury, quickly induced me to explore it; which I apprehended, from former visits to this coast, would exhibit a comprehensive epitome of the history of all the sea-coast Islands of Carolina and Georgia, as likewise in general of the coast of the main."[53] The opening statement is truly narrative, containing the details of Bartram's path from the mainland to the island. But the closing passage takes us back to a moment before the opening passage, to Bartram's seeing the island and the city of Sunbury, and to knowledge that he had from a prior visit ("former visits to this coast"). In between the parenthetical narrative statements we read about the island's soil, artifacts (fragments of earthen vessels), plants, and animals. In these passages, particularly in the lists of plants with their Linnaean names, the temporal element present in the narrative drops out, and we are presented with a list located in space, but no longer in time. As an observer moving through time, Bartram disappears. He reappears as the describer who is not in time ("throughout the seasons"). Time suspends before the calling of the eternal Linnaean names. The static, curiously still descriptions partake of the verbless nature of the Linnaean names themselves. The reader reconstitutes the scene, but does so in the historyless "now" that is a consequence of the Linnaean rhetoric.

The other descriptive method used in *Travels* is Edmund Burke's. "Romantic" passages conveying Bartram's awe and terror at the vistas he encountered have received more critical attention than the natural historical description.[54] Critics assume that aesthetics and science must be warring points of view. If a writer is romantic, he must not be scientific. If a writer is scientific, he cannot truly be said to be romantic. These divisions are modern, imposed from a perspective in which science is looked upon as positivism and art as extrarational. But in Bartram's day, and in Bartram's text, science and art are not at war with each other.

The sublime makes its appearance early in *Travels,* and is invoked throughout to convey the immensity of the objects and the magnitude of the experience that Bartram faced. Edmund Burke is the most important eighteenth-century theorist of the sublime, and there is evidence that Bartram saw his work. A survey of treatises on art and aesthetics available in America shows among its forty-seven entries for Burke's *Philosophical Enquiry into the Origin of Our Ideas of the Sublime and Beautiful* that as early as 1760 a copy was offered for sale in a Philadelphia bookseller's catalogue. At some point before 1807 a French translation of the work was donated to the Library Company of Philadelphia, an institution where Bartram would have had privileges. And in 1771, in a letter recommending books appropriate for a gentleman's library, Thomas Jefferson included Burke.[55] Bartram lived within a morning's ride of Philadelphia, a city that certainly knew of Burke's theory and that contained copies of Burke's *Enquiry.* He had the opportunity to know Burke's book, as his own text demonstrates.

In the early pages of *Travels,* when Bartram introduces the reader to the ideas that will be needed to navigate the book itself, he includes an account of a storm that lasted for the second and third days of his voyage from Philadelphia to Charleston:

> The powerful winds, now rushing forth from their secret abodes, suddenly spread terror and· devastation; and the wide ocean, which, a few moments past, was gentle and placid, is now thrown into disorder, and heaped into mountains, whose white curling crests seem to sweep the skies!
>
> This furious gale continued near two days and nights, and not a little damaged our sails, cabin furniture, and state-rooms, besides retarding our passage.[56]

Contrast this account with Bartram's interpretation of ocean travel, offered just one paragraph later:

> There are few objects out at sea to attract the notice of the traveller, but what are sublime, awful, and majestic: the seas themselves, in a tempest, exhibit a tremendous scene, where the winds assert their power, and, in furious conflict, seem to set the ocean on fire. On the other hand, nothing can be more sublime than the view of the encircling horizon, after the turbulent winds have taken their flight, and the lately agitated bosom of the deep has again become calm and pacific; the gentle moon rising in dignity from the east, attended by thousands of glittering orbs; the luminous appearance of the seas at night, when all the waters seem transmuted into liquid silver; the prodigious bands of porpoises foreboding tempest, that appear to cover the ocean; the mighty whale, sovereign of the watery realms, who cleaves the seas in his course; the sudden appearance

of land from the sea, the strand stretching each way, beyond the utmost reach of sight; the alternate appearance and recess of the coast, whilst the far distant blue hills slowly retreat and disappear; or, as we approach the coast, the capes and promontories first strike our sight, emerging from the watery expanse, and, like mighty giants, elevating their crests towards the skies; the water suddenly alive with its scaly inhabitants; squadrons of sea-fowl sweeping through the air, impregnated with the breath of fragrant aromatic trees and flowers; the amplitude and magnificence of these scenes are great indeed, and may present to the imagination, an idea of the first appearance of the earth to man at the creation.[57]

This is not so much a description of a storm—the earlier, four-sentence account is such a description—as it is a theory of what looking at the ocean is like, of the contrast between stormy seas and quiet ones, generalized to apply to almost any ocean voyage, to any view at sea. The ocean, in other words, causes certain effects in the viewer, who is generalized along with Bartram ("we approach") until both fade into the perceiving imagination of Adam himself.

This account of the effects of the ocean on the viewer, indeed on the first viewer, is put forth in Burke's *Enquiry* as productive of the sublime: "A level plain of a vast extent on land, is certainly no mean idea; the prospect of such a plain may be as extensive as a prospect of the ocean; but can it ever fill the mind with any thing so great as the ocean itself? This is owing to several causes, but it is owing to none more than this, that the ocean is an object of no small terror."[58] Burke's textbook example of sublimity is also Bartram's. And although it appears in a book about a particular man traveling a particular route, Bartram couches his explanation in the broadest terms. This is partly because he seems self-conscious, in those opening pages, of introducing the reader to the kind of analysis he will be doing in the book itself—interested, that is, in giving the reader the essential frameworks from which he will be operating.

But Bartram's explanation goes beyond Burke's, which had been offered in the section entitled "Terror," to provide an example of the terrible producing the sublime.[59] Bartram, instead, provides us in this first instance of sublimity in *Travels* with a sort of compendium of the sublime. He adds details that support most of the elements that Burke notes as productive of the sublime. In the shorter, specific description Bartram offers us terror and devastation; then, in the more generalized lecture on the sublime, he includes the "encircling horizon" (vastness), the moon with its "thousands of glittering orbs" (vastness and intensity of light), the "luminous appearance of the seas . . . transmuted into liquid silver" (intensity of light, vastness), "prodigious bands of porpoises foreboding tempest" (the threat of danger), "the mighty whale" (magnificence), "who cleaves the

seas in his course" (power), "the sudden appearance of land from the sea" (suddenness), "the alternate appearance and recess of the coast" (intermittence), "promontories . . . like mighty giants" (vastness), "the water suddenly alive" (suddenness), and finally, what seems to be Bartram's own contribution to the idea of the sublime, "the air impregnated with the breath of fragrant aromatic trees and flowers (the opposite of Burke's intolerable stenches). Before he has even gotten off of the boat that took him south, Bartram's retrospective narrator has offered the reader a compendium of the sublime. All of these elements reappear in the narrative, over and over, as Bartram beholds still another prospect whose awesome or terrible appearance compels him to convey his reactions.

Both the American traveler and the British aesthetician trace the source of these reactions to the same emotions. Bartram nominates "curiosity" as the "attendant spirit" of his travels. Burke, in the first sentence of part 1 of the *Enquiry*, says, "The first and the simplest emotion which we discover in the human mind, is Curiosity." Bartram traveled in search of new plants for Fothergill, and new scenes to gratify his own curiosity. Burke's theory also recognizes the importance of the new: "Some degree of novelty must be one of the materials in every instrument which works upon the mind; and curiosity blends itself more or less with all our passions." The sources, then, of passion and information, for Bartram and for Burke, were the same—novelty and its motivating spirit, curiosity.[60]

Both men also shared a belief in the importance of direct observation. In defending the limitations of his theory Burke noted, "A theory founded on experiment and not assumed, is always good for so much as it explains."[61] Burke's departure from previous aesthetic practice was to examine his own reactions rather than to simply convey the findings of the rhetoricians who had preceded him.[62] Bartram's entire method was one of seeing and observing. The very enterprise of traveling to observe attests to that. Indeed, this similarity in aims—from the beginning, Bartram speaks of "observations" and the importance of the visual (Burke's theory is a visual one)—is everywhere apparent in *Travels*. Burke's theory is also an unusually democratic one: "The true standard of the arts is in every man's power; and an easy observation of the most common, sometimes of the meanest things in nature, will give the truest lights, where the greatest sagacity and industry that slights such observation, must leave us in the dark, or what is worse, amuse and mislead us by false lights."[63]

Yet Burke is not claiming that each observer makes up his own mind independent of other observers. Having made the reactions of one person the basis of his theory, he goes on to assert that all men have similar reactions—"the standard both of reason and Taste is the

becomes a treatise on natural (or national) order: "each nation, though subdivided into many different tribes, retain[s] its general form or structure, a similarity of customs, and a sort of dialect or language, particular to that nation or genus from which those tribes seem to have descended or separated" (25). This pristine order has its human complement, as is evident in Bartram's reflections on Creek national character:

> Their country having a vast frontier, naturally accessible and open to the incursions of their enemies on all sides, they find themselves under the necessity of associating in large populous towns. . . . This consequently occasions deer and bear to be scarce and difficult to procure, which obliges them to be vigilant and industrious; this naturally begets care and serious attention, which we may suppose in some degree forms their natural disposition and manners. . . .
>
> (181)

The Seminole, by contrast, "enjoy a superabundance of the necessaries and conveniences of life," and thus "appear as blithe and free as the birds of the air, and like them as volatile and active, tuneful and vociferous" (182). As Regis writes, such environmentalism has a tendency to "cast the American Indians . . . into the timeless 'now' of the historical present" (37); as I have said, moreover, the collapsing of Indians with "Nature" works against an awareness of native cultures *as* cultures, as products of human labor and ingenuity.[13]

Then, too, one should not divorce Bartram's naturalism from expansionism. A failed planter himself, he is clearly invested in promoting white settlement: "This vast plain, together with the forests contiguous to it, if permitted (by the Siminoles who are sovereigns of these realms) to be in possession and under the culture of industrious planters and mechanics, would in a little time exhibit other scenes than it does at present, delightful as it is . . ." (199). As Mary Louise Pratt has written, the naturalist occupies a peculiarly invulnerable position among apologists for expansion. Though naturalism "extracts all the things of the world and redeploys them into a new knowledge formation," claiming the world by naming it, this process is veiled by its seeming innocence: "In comparison with the navigator or the conquistador, the naturalist-collector is a benign, often homely figure, whose transformative powers do their work in the domestic contexts of the garden or the collection room" (*Imperial Eyes* 33). One need only recall Bartram as "Puc Puggy, or the Flower hunter" (163), a harmless man-child whom the Indians permit to roam at will, to understand the rhetoric of "anti-conquest," by which explorers "secure their innocence in the same moment as they assert European hegemony" (*Imperial Eyes* 7).

These are important considerations, revealing the extent to which Bartram's text operates within discursive limitations. Yet Regis erects limitations of her own when she concludes that Bartram "is led to record only what the rhetoric [of naturalism] has devised formulas to represent" (76). Bartram's naturalism, far from removing him from the cultural conflicts of his time, is his point of entrance into those conflicts; as a naturalist, he is perhaps more able than most to trace racial conflict to the very soil of the continent, and to use the language of naturalism to question imperial truisms. Bartram is not seeking, nor is he able, to discard his own people's ways; rather, his contact with Indians alerts him to the inadequacy of these ways of viewing the natives and their relationships to the land. His writing, then, reveals the strain of conveying with a conventional language new and unconventional insights. In the following passage, contrasting himself with a traveling companion, Bartram complicates the partnership of naturalism and expansionism, as he attempts to reconcile opposing attitudes toward the land:

> Our views were probably totally opposite; he, a young mechanic on his adventures, seemed to be actuated by no other motives, than either to establish himself in some well-inhabited part of the country, where, by following his occupation, he might be enabled to procure, without much toil and danger, the necessaries and conveniences of life; or by industry and frugality, perhaps establish his fortune. Whilst I, continually impelled by a restless spirit of curiosity, in pursuit of new productions of nature, my chief happiness consisted in tracing and admiring the infinite power, majesty, and perfection of the great Almighty Creator, and in the contemplation, that through divine aid and permission, I might be instrumental in discovering, and introducing into my native country, some original productions of nature, which might become useful to society. Each of our pursuits was perhaps equally laudable; and, upon this supposition, I was quite willing to part with him upon amicable terms.
>
> (82-83)

The "probably" in the first sentence, and the "perhaps" in the last, are singularly ambivalent, revealing Bartram's troubles in harmonizing what he sees as his duty as naturalist with his countrymen's proprietary desires. Bartram cannot escape the terms of acquisitive individualism ("instrumental," "useful"), but he cannot help seeing that, while those terms illuminate, they also travesty his role. Hence this passage—one of many in which what could have been a hostile confrontation ends "amicably"—dramatizes Bartram's nagging sense of the inadequacy of single, absolute claims to the land.

Most significant of these passages is his meeting with a Seminole renegade, whom he encounters beyond "the utmost frontier of the white settlements" (44). Having entered the Indian's world, Bartram realizes that "I was in his power" (44). But he determines to make a bold show: "I advanced towards him, and with an air of confidence offered him my hand, hailing him, brother; at this he hastily jerked back his arm . . . when again looking at me more attentively, he instantly spurred up to me, and with dignity in his look and action, gave me his hand" (45). Bartram imagines what the "silent language of his soul" might be striving to communicate: "Live; the Great Spirit forbids me to touch thy life; go to thy brethren, tell them thou sawest an Indian in the forests, who knew how to be humane and compassionate'" (45). Later, Bartram discovers that this man had been beaten at a trading post and had vowed to kill the first white he saw.

This highly-charged moment, clearly a plea for racial brotherhood, is, perhaps, a fantasy. Richard Slotkin reads it as such, a progenitor of the communion of Natty and Chingachgook: "Bartram descends into the wilderness, finds a kindred spirit in an Indian, and emerges with moral wisdom" (326). What is striking about this encounter, however, is not Bartram's kinship with the Indian, but his distance. Though he seeks to domesticate the Seminole with quakerisms, the motives of the Indian who "knew how to be humane and compassionate" remain beyond the writer's ken; shopworn pieties appear inadequate. In the space past "the utmost frontier," roles have reversed and distinctions collapsed. The disempowered Indian holds power; the savage is civil. That this Indian is a renegade, and a Seminole—a splinter group of the Creeks who, mingling with escaped slaves, were considered particularly miscreant—heightens the significance of the encounter, as Bartram begins to suspect that conventional categories may fail to take into account the anomalies he has witnessed, just as they have failed to specify his own anomalous role.

It is customary to treat this aspect of Bartram's thought as proof of his membership in the cult of the Noble Savage.[14] Surely, Bartram was influenced by such notions; he speculates that the Seminole's behavior might be attributable to "the immediate influence and guidance of a more divine and powerful preceptor, who, on those occasions, instantly inspires them, and as with a ray of divine light, points out to them at once the dignity, propriety, and beauty of virtue" (46). But we must distinguish between a primitivism such as Beverley's—calculated to reinscribe the line between idle Indian and industrious white—and a primitivism such as Bartram's, which is of a potentially radical nature. Contemporary odes to the "vanishing Indian," such as Sarah Wentworth Morton's *Ouâbi, or the Virtues of Nature* (1790), were motivated by a fantasy of Indian impotence; their praise of the vanished Noble Savage masked a desire that the savages would hurry up and vanish. Thus Morton on Indian purity:

> *Native reason's* piercing eye,
> *Melting pity's* tender sigh,
> *Changeless virtue's* living flame,
> *Meek contentment,* free from blame,

> *Open friendship's* gen'rous care,
> EV'RY BOON OF LIFE IS HERE!

(27)

Morton's Indians are weak, accommodating; they disappear without the briefest mention that they would prefer not to. Bartram's primitivism, on the other hand, is activated by his encounters with peoples who protest the fate that whites have decided for them, peoples ready to sacrifice "their blood, and life itself, to defend their territory and maintain their rights" (381). These Indians are not silent, and what they say has an effect on what others say about them. Consider the following passage:

> Such is the virtue of these untutored savages; but I am afraid this is a common-phrase epithet, having no meaning, or at least improperly applied; for these people are both well-tutored and civil; and it is apparent to an impartial observer, who resides but a little time amongst them, that it is from the most delicate sense of the honour and reputation of their tribes and families, that their laws and customs receive their force and energy.

(111)

Bartram's dismantling of the "common-phrase epithet" is remarkable for its avoidance of bathos. He does not indulge in panegyrics on native virtue; rather, he points out that the terms—"untutored" and "savage"—are meaningless in this alien context. By contrast, we might point to the purported speech of Opay Mico, a Creek chief who visited New York in 1790, as reported by Philip Freneau: "Happy in what nature had voluntarily bestowed upon them, [my people] put her not to the torture to gratify fancied wants—She was their mother, and she fed them plentifully, without being forced to shed the tear of anguish in contributing to their fantastical support" (n. pag). Here the Indians' relationship to the earth is purely natural, and their supplanting equally so:

> the seeds of the different kind of grass brought from the ancient countries of the white men, when sowed among the wild vegetation of the plains and meadows of America do not long subsist in a state of good neighbourhood . . . and many years do not elapse till we perceive the one kind entirely displaced by the other, and not a single blade left as a token that it once existed.

(n. pag)

Bartram, on the other hand, denies that the distinction is between nature and culture; rather, it is between different cultures. All humans have their "laws and customs," and to apply one's own labels to people with unique ideas of training and civility is to do violence to sense. Bartram retreats, to be sure, from his pronouncement that the terms "have no meaning"; then, too, his incipient relativism is compromised by his need to employ the very language he deems inadequate—civil, honor, reputation. Yet he attempts to point out the limitations of the words he uses, as in his 1789 response to Benjamin Smith Barton's queries: "*If* adopting or imitating the manners and customs of the white people is *to be termed* civilization, *perhaps* the Cherokees have made the greatest advance" (20, my emphasis). Bartram approaches what Michael Fischer calls the "bifocality that has always been part of the anthropological rationale: seeing others against a background of ourselves, and ourselves against a background of others" (199). Bartram's critique destabilizes what his fellows saw as an absolute—inalienable—distinction, incapable of becoming alien to itself by being filtered through the self of the alien.

Thus, though his work was well-received, critics on both sides of the Atlantic were quick to detect an unseemly relativism. A reviewer for the *Universal Asylum* confessed that "We cannot help thinking that he magnifies the virtues of the Indians, and views their vices through too friendly a medium," and continued with unintended irony, "A proof this, if our suspicion be well founded, that not even observation can always overcome the force of preconceived opinion, however erroneous" (266). And a writer for the London *Monthly Review* was nettled by Bartram's apparent stand on the wrong side of the cultural divide: "Mr. Bartram is indeed so enthusiastically attached to rude nature, that he deplores the intrusions of civilization. . . . The savage alone might be expected to lament the loss of his hunting grounds; and if he be thus driven to betake himself to any kind of agriculture, he is made a more sociable and useful being by the alteration" (131-32).

This reviewer, like so many of his contemporaries, could not tolerate even the suggestion of an existing Indian agriculture and social structure—for Bartram provides ample evidence of both:

> In the spring, the ground being already prepared on one and the same day, early in the morning, the whole town is summoned, by the sound of a conch shell, from the mouth of the overseer, to meet at the public square, whither the people repair with their hoes and axes; and from thence proceed to their plantation, where they begin to plant, not every one in his own little district, assigned and laid out, but the whole community united begins on one certain part of the field, where they plant on until finished, and when their rising crops are ready for dressing and cleansing they proceed after the same order, and so on day after day, until the crop is laid by for ripening.
>
> (400-01)

This exemplary portrait of order, it must be said, resembles primitivist paeans to the Indians' harmony with nature. But where such writers as Beverley and Freneau saw unconscious Arcadianism as the extent of Indian capabilities, Bartram sees a community capable both of grasping diurnal and seasonal rhythms and of converting them to human productivity. In the process, he complicates the very distinction—natural versus cultural—upon which primitivism (and its negation, appropriation to the cultural sphere of private ownership) was based. Aware of the uses to which other writers had put the Indians' practices, Bartram attacks the terms themselves: "It has been said . . . that [the Indians] have every thing in common, and no private property; which are terms in my opinion too vague and general, when applied to these people" (400). The Indians practice something for which there is, in Bartram's view, no English equivalent: "This is their common plantation, and the whole town plant in one vast field together; but yet the part or share of every individual family or habitation, is separated from the next adjoining . . ." (400). Discovering the Indians to be industrious *in their own terms,* Bartram discovers that land usage is itself determined by usage; that "civilization" is an option, not an absolute.

But Bartram does not make this discovery on his own. The Indians were not the silent phantoms of Euro-American desires; they were participants in a debate over the meaning and use of the land. Thus I would argue that it is their presence in Bartram's world that forces upon him an understanding of their claims. I would like to examine, then, two myths that structure Bartram's *Travels,* two views of the land and of its possible use.

The first is Bartram's myth. In the company of a young trader, Bartram happens upon a "most enchanting" vision (288):

> a vast expanse of green meadows and strawberry fields . . . companies of young, innocent Cherokee virgins, some busy gathering the rich fragrant fruit, others . . . lay reclined under the shade of floriferous and fragrant native bowers . . . disclosing their beauties to the fluttering breeze, and bathing their limbs in the cool fleeting streams; whilst other parties, more gay and libertine, were yet collecting strawberries, or wantonly chasing their companions, tantalising them, staining their lips and cheeks with the rich fruit.
>
> (288-89)

This "sylvan scene of primitive innocence," an erotic paradise anticipating *Typee,* is "perhaps too enticing for hearty young men long to continue idle spectators" (289). Accepting the basket the maidens offer, Bartram and his companion "regal[e] ourselves on the delicious fruit, encircled by the whole assembly of the innocent jocose sylvan nymphs" (289-90). Sated, the interlopers depart "these Elysian fields" and return to town (290).

Bartram would not, perhaps, label this mythic interlude as such, though it is flagged by its dreamy intensity, sportive tone, and mock-chivalric gestures. A self-parody, perhaps, or a swipe at the fantasies of Beverley and company, it is nonetheless closely allied with those fantasies. Bartram indulges in what Annette Kolodny has termed the "lay of the land." A feminized wilderness, both innocent and lascivious, tempts the white man's desire for mastery; the fruits of the earth are offered willingly, in a soothing ritual which disguises or obviates the reality of violent conquest.[15] Here Bartram falls back on the primitivist association of native with nature, both equally helpless—and equally accommodating—before the white man. This is the America of the conqueror's fondest dreams, a yielding land that silently surrenders to its rightful owner.

But there is another myth in Bartram's *Travels,* a myth qualifying the wishful vision of undisputed conquest. It is a Creek myth of the proper human relationship to the land:

> This vast accumulation of waters . . . contains some large islands or knolls, of rich high land; one of which the present generation of the Creeks represent to be a most blissful spot of the earth: they say it is inhabited by a peculiar race of Indians, whose women are incomparably beautiful; they also tell you that this terrestrial paradise has been seen by some of their enterprising hunters, when in pursuit of game, who being lost in inextricable swamps and bogs, and on the point of perishing, were unexpectedly relieved by a company of beautiful women, whom they call daughters of the sun, who kindly gave them such provisions as they had with them, which were chiefly fruit, oranges, dates, & c. and some corn cakes, and then enjoined them to fly for safety to their own country; for that their husbands were fierce men, and cruel to strangers; they further say, that these hunters had a view of their settlements, situated on the elevated banks of an island, or promontory, in a beautiful lake; but that in their endeavours to approach it, they were involved in perpetual labyrinths, and, like enchanted land, still as they imagined they had just gained it, it seemed to fly before them, alternately appearing and disappearing. They resolved at length, to leave the delusive pursuit, and to return; which, after a number of inexpressible difficulties, they effected. When they reported their adventures to their countrymen, their young warriors were enflamed with an irresistible desire to invade, and make a conquest of, so charming a country; but all their attempts hitherto have proved abortive, never having been able again to find that enchanting spot. . . .
>
> (47-48)

This myth resembles Bartram's myth of conquest, yet marks conquest as delusory. The daughters of the sun, who give the hunters corn cakes, freely offer the knowledge of agriculture; but the land is not to be possessed. This is a myth of non-conquest, a myth that pays tribute to the fruitfulness of the earth but denies its possession. Indeed, one might speculate that this myth arose, or was modified, by the arrival of Europeans; the fierce husbands who are cruel to strangers, and who refuse to allow these intruders to possess their wives, may repre-

sent the Indians' response to the fantasies and actualities of European possession. As a warning to the white invaders, this myth gives the lie to Bartram's dream of peaceful conquest; as an alternative reading of human being in nature, it problematizes the myth of individual mastery, revealing it to be but one possible relationship to the land.[16]

One could argue that Bartram is guilty of casting European and Indian as rival monoliths: no people possesses a single model for existence and enterprise in the natural world. Then, too, the hunters' vain pursuit of the terrestrial paradise might easily be offered as evidence of the Indians' inability to possess the land. Indeed, since we "know" this myth only through Bartram, we must grant the possibility that he altered it—or, perhaps, created it from whole cloth—to suit his agenda. Yet if—and this is also a possibility—the Creek myth *does* represent beliefs held by the peoples among whom Bartram traveled, then one might argue that the myth—a translated myth, to be sure—itself translates the Euro-American myth of dominance. By recording the Creek beliefs along with the European, that is, Bartram's account dialogizes itself, and both myths emerge *as* myths: imaginative constructs rather than facts, each a possibility, and neither necessary nor absolute.[17] Refusing to subordinate one myth to another, Bartram questions not only Euro-American notions of dominance but also the dominance of those notions: neither a fantasized negation of white ideals nor an infallible measure of how far the Indians are from attaining some absolute standard of civilization, Indian practices emerge as self-generating cultural possibilities, as alternative systems of belief. Whether Bartram imagines the Creek myth as an alternative for him is thus less important than his imagining it at all: in his account, perhaps, the Indians retain the power to be their own mythologizers.

Toward this end, one of the most remarkable things about the *Travels* is what it does *not* contain. It was customary to conclude such works with a plan for the amelioration, assimilation, or conversion of the Indians; Bartram does not do so. In his introduction, to be sure, he writes that the Indians are "desirous of becoming united with us, in civil and religious society" (26), but this single sentence strikes one as pro forma, a nod to convention which the rest of the work does its best to undermine, not least by complicating the terms "civil" and "religious." For the Indians are religious; in place of the expected disquisition on Indian conversion, Bartram provides a lively description of the Creek "busk" or Green Corn ceremony. In this passage, important to Thoreau in *Walden,*[18] Bartram details the Indians' annual earth-renewal rites:

> When a town celebrates the busk, having previously provided themselves with new cloaths, new pots, pans, and other household utensils and furniture, they collect

all their worn-out cloaths and other despicable things, sweep and cleanse their houses, squares, and the whole town, of their filth, which with all the remaining grain and other old provisions, they cast together into one common heap, and consume it with fire. After having taken medicine, and fasted for three days, all the fire in the town is extinguished. . . . On the fourth morning, the high priest, by rubbing wood together, produces new fire in the public square, from whence every habitation in the town is supplied with the new and pure flame. Then the women go forth to the harvest field, and bring from thence new corn and fruits. . . .

(399)

The Creek ceremony, like the myth, transcends its status as ethnographic artifact. A ritual of relinquishing, the busk is a powerful enactment of communal nonpossession. As such, it provides an ironic gloss on the terms meant to contain it, proclaiming its distance from the language of consumerism in which it is conveyed. (It is the town fire which "consumes") Similarly, though Bartram attempts to translate the busk into paradigms of Christian conversion—a rebirth into purity, signaled by the forsaking of earthly goods—these are no Christians; these are savages worshiping corn. The busk problematizes European notions of ownership; indeed, it problematizes European language's self-possession, employing its own terms (worn-out, despicable, filth) to provide alternatives to itself. In Bartram's description of the busk, capitalist conceptions are translated, alienated from themselves, no longer their own property.[19] If, as Arnold Krupat writes, the relatively more flexible model of native identity encourages "*dialogic* models of the self," in which "the self most typically is not constituted by the achievement of a distinctive, special voice that separates it from others, but, rather, by the achievement of a particular placement in relation to the many voices without which it could not exist" (*Voice* 133), then we might even say that this alienation of the language of capitalism from itself is, in some sense, due to Bartram's contacts with the Indians' discourses. In capitalism, that is, the central concern is *ownership,* the absoluteness of a single claim to a single space; whereas in communalism, the central concern is *relation,* the need for a continuously generated multiplicity in determining the nature of any space. Communalism, of course, possesses no sole claim to dialogue; aside from being a logical contradiction, this is the sort of opposition one does well to avoid. But Bartram's exercises in relational identity—whatever their source—relativize a discourse of capitalist individualism which cannot allow relativism, which refuses to accept itself as being merely one option in a heterogeneous array. In Bartram's description of the busk, we are left with no stable ground, and must contend with the anomalous: ownership through disencumbering, piety as heathenism. As such, the Green Corn ceremony—embracing the religious use (which may be neither religion nor use as he knows it) of agricultural products (which may not be agriculture

as he knows it)—forces Bartram to ask whether any claim, literal or linguistic, can be wholly self-evident, the sole possessor of value.

Thus Bartram falls silent, leaving the Indians to create their own values, renew their own covenant with their own land. The Indians' language does not survive in Bartram's account, but one can perceive their voices in the words he says, or has trouble saying, the words he cannot say, or the words newly inflected by alien accents. One should not exaggerate the significance of Bartram's travels; the history of Indian-white relations was (and is) too little influenced by alternatives, and even Bartram's commitment to alternatives, like the enchanted land of the Creeks, alternately appears and disappears. His text, far from ushering in an era of racial enlightenment, stands at the gateway of spiraling land cessions, tribal dislocation, and human disaster. Nonetheless, we are mistaken when we consider Indian-white history only a record of what the latter did to the former. This position replicates the rhetoric I have been discussing: Indians drop out of the picture early on, their distinctive productions and influences robbed of lasting value. Hence, I do not wish to leave the impression that Bartram was a token voice of sympathy redeeming a history of ugliness. Such a representation would fail on all counts. Though a member of a distinct minority, he was not a token; though sympathetic, he was only intermittently so; and though it may be remembered, a history of ugliness cannot be redeemed. My point is that we acknowledge, even in the texts which record their dispossession, the ability of the Indians to engage their dispossessors in debate over the celebration and use of the land.

Notes

1. Searcy notes the significance of this treaty: "For many years to come, these areas would be called the 'Ceded Lands'" (10).

2. Discussions of post-war cessions include Cotterill 57-165; Downes; and Prucha 43-61.

3. On the legal and scriptural arguments whites used in claiming native lands, see Washburn.

4. A general discussion of Indian agriculture may be found in Hurt 27-41. For the South, see Herndon, and Wright 21-27.

5. For the impact of capitalism on native economies, see White. The effects of white contact on the southern tribes are treated by Goodwin, Hudson, and Wright 101-53.

6. The literature on Indian conceptions of land usage is vast, reflecting the fact that "communalism" manifested itself in an array of regional varieties. In most cases, though land itself was not alien-

able, separate plots were worked by kinship networks, while the distribution of tools, seeds, and produce might be administered by other bodies. Among the Creeks, for example, surplus produce was under the control of local chiefs, who employed this store for ceremonial or diplomatic purposes. Among the Iroquois, on the other hand, seeds, agricultural implements, and food distribution were controlled by clan matrons. Though "communalism" is a helpful abstraction—it does point to a conceptual difference between native and European economies—it should not be taken as an absolute, unalloyed by local variants and historical transformations. Useful discussions of Indian land-holding appear in Cheyfitz 41-58, Cronon 54-81, and Synderman.

7. On the contrary, as Hurt writes, "the Indians were skilled agriculturalists who not only raised a substantial portion of their annual food but also provided a surplus for times of crop failure or for trade among themselves and white settlers" (39).

8. I take the concept of relational identity from Cheyfitz 54. See also Krupat, *For Those Who Come After* 28-35, and *Ethnocriticism* 201-31, for discussions of "Indian autobiography," a problematic form which forces us to reconsider the construction of selfhood.

9. The trivialization of Indians while putatively exalting them persists in the modern tendency to elevate native peoples to "environmental sainthood" (White xiii). For an attempt to avoid this pitfall, see the balanced account of Vecsey, who speculates that Indians may have experienced difficulty in reconciling an ideology of respect for nature with a need to exploit it.

10. See Horsman for government Indian policies during the Confederation and early national periods.

11. On McGillivray's role in the southern conflicts, see Green.

12. An exception is Terrie, who writes that "The possibility that an Indian war is about to occur lurks on nearly every page" of Bartram's text (27). Articles by Anderson and by Looby represent recent attempts to relate Bartram's naturalism to the political conflicts and uncertainties of the early national period.

13. See Pratt, "Scratches," for a critique of the "ethnographic present," in travel writing and anthropological discourse.

14. Bissell is perhaps the most extreme proponent of this view—"Sentimental exoticism seems to reach its height in William Bartram" (46)—but other writers concur. Medeiros, for example, writes that

"Bartram clearly conceives of the Indian as the 'noble savage'" (205). For Fagin, Bartram's Indian is "the favorite child of nature" (53). Ziff writes that, to Bartram and his fellows, the Indian was "either an outgrown version of modern man's primitive self or an idealized model of modern man's irrecoverably lost self" (158). And Pearce believes that "Bartram himself wanted soft, luxuriant, primitive wisdom, and he thought civilized men needed it. . . . So he went to the noble savage, who, of course, was there waiting for him" (143). Though I disagree with his assessment of Bartram, Pearce (136-50, 169-95) remains an excellent resource on the Noble Savage theme.

15. See Kolodny, *Lay* 10-70, for a discussion of this image in exploration and settlement narratives of the sixteenth through eighteenth centuries.

16. Swanton, in his collection of southeastern Indian myths, includes Bartram's myth "by way of supplement" (83); and, indeed, Bartram's telling resembles other Creek myths of the origin of corn (9-17). Mooney's Cherokee myths (321-23, 431-42) also share features with Bartram's, such as the enchanted lake and the lost settlement. Since these tales of the inaccessible homeland were recorded in the late nineteenth and early twentieth centuries, however, they surely reflect the impact of the removals of the 1830s.

17. My understanding of "dialogism" is, of course, informed by Bakhtin. See Krupat, *Voice,* for a consideration of how Bakhtinian dialogism might be applied to Native American texts.

18. Thoreau writes: "The customs of some savage nations might, perchance, be profitably imitated by us, for they at least go through the semblance of casting their slough annually. . . ." After quoting from Bartram, Thoreau concludes: "I have scarcely heard of a truer sacrament . . . and I have no doubt that they were originally inspired directly from Heaven to do thus . . ." (51). It is intriguing that Thoreau, who similarly examines capitalist discourses in *Walden,* should have been so powerfully—and ambiguously—affected by Bartram; like the earlier writer, he is at a loss to determine whether the busk is truly a "sacrament," or merely a "semblance."

19. Bakhtin's thoughts on dialogism are peculiarly appropriate here: "language, for the individual consciousness, lies on the borderline between oneself and the other. The word in language is half someone else's. It becomes 'one's own' only when the speaker populates it with his own intention, his own accent, when he appropriates the word. . . . And not all words for just anyone submit equally easily to this appropriation, to this seizure and

transformation into private property; many words stubbornly resist, others remain alien, sound foreign in the mouth of the one who appropriated them and who now speaks them; they cannot be assimilated into his context and fall out of it; it is as if they put themselves in quotation marks against the will of the speaker" (293-94).

Works Cited

Adair, James. *Adair's History of the American Indians.* Ed. Samuel Cole Williams. Johnson City, Tenn.: Watauga, 1930.

American State Papers: Indian Affairs. Vol. 1. Washington, D.C.: Gales and Seaton, 1832. 2 vols.

Anderson, Douglas. "Bartram's *Travels* and the Politics of Nature." *Early American Literature* 25 (1990): 3-17.

Bakhtin, M. M. *The Dialogic Imagination: Four Essays.* Trans. Caryl Emerson and Michael Holquist. Austin: University of Texas Press, 1981.

Balibar, Etienne. "The Nation Form: History and Ideology." *Review* 13 (1990): 329-61.

Bartram, William. "Observations on the Creek and Cherokee Indians, 1789." *Transactions of the American Ethnological Society* 3 (1853): 3-81.

———. *Travels of William Bartram.* Ed. Mark Van Doren. New York: Dover, 1955.

"Bartram's Travels." *The Monthly Review, or, Literary Journal* 2nd ser. 10 (Jan., Feb. 1793): 13-22, 130-38.

"Bartram's Travels." *Universal Asylum, and Columbian Magazine* 8 (Mar., Apr. 1792): 195-97, 255-67.

Beverley, Robert. *The History and Present State of Virginia.* Ed. Louis B. Wright. Chapel Hill: University of North Carolina Press, 1947.

Bissell, Benjamin. *The American Indian in English Literature of the Eighteenth Century.* New Haven: Yale University Press, 1925.

Cheyfitz, Eric. *The Poetics of Imperialism: Translation and Colonization from* The Tempest *to* Tarzan. New York: Oxford University Press, 1991.

Cotterill, R. S. *The Southern Indians: The Story of the Civilized Tribes Before Removal.* Norman: University of Oklahoma Press, 1954.

Cronon, William. *Changes in the Land: Indians, Colonists, and the Ecology of New England.* New York: Hill and Wang, 1983.

Downes, Randolph C. "Creek-American Relations, 1782-1790." *Georgia Historical Quarterly* 21 (1937): 142-84.

Esarey, Logan, ed. *Government Messages and Letters: Messages and Letters of William Henry Harrison.* Vol 1. Indianapolis: Indiana Historical Commission, 1922. 2 vols.

Fagin, N. Bryllion. *William Bartram: Interpreter of the American Landscape.* Baltimore: Johns Hopkins University Press, 1933.

Fischer, Michael M. J. "Ethnicity and the Post-Modern Arts of Memory." *Writing Culture: The Poetics and Politics of Ethnography.* Eds. James Clifford and George E. Marcus. Berkeley: University of California Press, 1986. 194-233.

Freneau, Philip. "Reflections on My Journey from the Tullassee Towns to the Settlements on the River Hudson. By Opay Mico." *New York Daily Advertiser* 8 Sept. 1790. N. pag.

Goodwin, Gary C. *Cherokees in Transition: A Study of Changing Culture and Environment Prior to 1775.* University of Chicago Department of Geography, Research Paper No. 181. Chicago: University of Chicago Press, 1977.

Green, Michael D. "Alexander McGillivray." *American Indian Leaders: Studies in Diversity.* Ed. R. David Edmunds. Lincoln: University of Nebraska Press, 1980. 41-63.

Herndon, G. Melvin. "Indian Agriculture in the Southern Colonies." *North Carolina Historical Review* 44 (1967): 283-97.

Horsman, Reginald. *Expansion and American Indian Policy, 1783-1812.* East Lansing: Michigan State University Press, 1967.

Hudson, Charles M., Jr. "Why the Southeastern Indians Slaughtered Deer." *Indians, Animals, and the Fur Trade: A Critique of* Keepers of the Game. Ed. Shepard Krech III. Athens: University of Georgia Press, 1981. 155-76.

Hurt, R. Douglas. *Indian Agriculture in America, Prehistory to the Present.* Lawrence: University Press of Kansas, 1987.

Kolodny, Annette. *The Lay of the Land: Metaphor as Experience and History in American Life and Letters.* Chapel Hill: University of North Carolina Press, 1975.

———. "Letting Go Our Grand Obsessions: Notes Toward a New Literary History of the American Frontiers." *American Literature* 64 (1992): 1-18.

Krupat, Arnold. *Ethnocriticism: Ethnography, History, Literature.* Berkeley: University of California Press, 1992.

———. *For Those Who Come After: A Study of Native American Autobiography.* Berkeley: University of California Press, 1985.

————. *The Voice in the Margin: Native American Literature and the Canon.* Berkeley: University of California Press, 1989.

Lawson, John. *A New Voyage to Carolina.* Ed. Hugh Talmage Lefler. Chapel Hill: University of North Carolina Press, 1967.

Looby, Christopher. "The Constitution of Nature: Taxonomy as Politics in Jefferson, Peale, and Bartram." *Early American Literature* 22 (1987): 252-73.

Medeiros, Patricia M. "Three Travelers: Carver, Bartram, and Woolman." *American Literature, 1764-1789: The Revolutionary Years.* Ed. Everett Emerson. Madison: University of Wisconsin Press, 1977. 195-211.

Mooney, James. *Myths of the Cherokee.* Washington, D.C.: U.S. Government Printing Office, 1900. St. Clair Shores, Mich.: Scholarly, 1970.

Morton, Sarah Wentworth. *Ouâbi: or the Virtues of Nature.* Boston: I. Thomas, 1790.

Pearce, Roy Harvey. *Savagism and Civilization: A Study of the Indian and the American Mind.* Berkeley: University of California Press, 1988.

Pratt, Mary Louise. *Imperial Eyes: Travel Writing and Transculturation.* London: Routledge, 1992.

————. "Scratches on the Face of the Country; Or, What Mr. Barrow Saw in the Land of the Bushmen." *"Race," Writing, and Difference.* Ed. Henry Louis Gates, Jr. Chicago: University of Chicago Press, 1986. 138-62.

Prucha, Francis Paul. *The Sword of the Republic: The United States Army on the Frontier, 1783-1846.* London: Macmillan, 1969.

Regis, Pamela. *Describing Early America: Bartram, Jefferson, Crèvecoeur, and the Rhetoric of Natural History.* DeKalb: Northern Illinois University Press, 1992.

Richardson, James D., comp. *A Compilation of the Messages and Papers of the Presidents.* Vol. 1. New York: Bureau of National Literature, 1897. 20 vols.

Searcy, Martha Condray. *The Georgia-Florida Contest in the American Revolution, 1776-1778.* University: University of Alabama Press, 1985.

Slotkin, Richard. *Regeneration Through Violence: The Mythology of the American Frontier, 1600-1860.* Middletown, Conn.: Wesleyan University Press, 1973.

Snyderman, George S. "Concepts of Land Ownership Among the Iroquois and Their Neighbors." *Symposium on Local Diversity in Iroquois Culture.* Ed. William N. Fenton. Smithsonian Institution Bureau of American Ethnology, Bulletin 149. Washington, D.C.: U.S. Government Printing Office, 1951. 13-34.

Swanton, John R. *Myths and Tales of the Southeastern Indians.* Washington, D.C.: U.S. Government Printing Office, 1929.

Terrie, Philip G. "Tempests and Alligators: The Ambiguous Wilderness of William Bartram." *North Dakota Quarterly* 59.2 (Spring 1991): 17-32.

Thoreau, Henry David. *Walden or, Life in the Woods.* New York: New American Library, 1960.

Vecsey, Christopher. "American Indian Environmental Religions." *American Indian Environments: Ecological Issues in Native American History.* Ed. Christopher Vecsey and Robert W. Venables. Syracuse: Syracuse University Press, 1980. 1-37.

Washburn, Wilcomb E. *Red Man's Land/White Man's Law: A Study of the Past and Present Status of the American Indian.* New York: Scribner's, 1971.

White, Richard. *The Roots of Dependency: Subsistence, Environment, and Social Change among the Choctaws, Pawnees, and Navajos.* Lincoln: University of Nebraska Press, 1983.

Wright, J. Leitch, Jr. *Creeks and Seminoles: The Destruction and Regeneration of the Muscogulge People.* Lincoln: University of Nebraska Press, 1986.

Ziff, Larzer. *Writing in the New Nation: Prose, Print, and Politics in the Early United States.* New Haven: Yale University Press, 1991.

Gregory A. Waselkov (essay date 1995)

SOURCE: Waselkov, Gregory A. *"Travels through North & South Carolina, Georgia, East & West Florida. . . ."* In *William Bartram on the Southeastern Indians,* edited by Gregory A. Waselkov and Kathryn E. Holland Braund, pp. 25-32. Lincoln: University of Nebraska Press, 1995.

[*In the following essay, Waselkov examines the evolution of the manuscript of Bartram's* Travels *and its general reception.*]

William Bartram's **Travels** has been dubbed "the most astounding verbal artifact of the early republic."[1] Indeed, Bartram's work, which "presents itself at various times as a travel journal, a naturalist's notebook, a moral and religious effusion, an ethnographic essay, and a polemic on behalf of the cultural institutions and the rights of American Indians," is a true classic of American literature.[2] **Travels** is based on Bartram's field notes, journals, and remembrances that accrued during his tour of the southern backcountry, from 1773 to 1777. The time when Bartram decided to polish his diaries and produce a publishable account of his journey is not known—perhaps he conceived the notion very early, while still in the South. In any case, he must have begun editing his rough notes soon after his return to Philadelphia, in early 1777. By 1783 he had produced a manuscript, which he showed to several interested visitors.[3] In 1786, a Philadelphia publisher, Enoch Story, attempted to raise subscribers for the work and even went so far as to notify Benjamin Franklin that Bartram wished to dedicate the proposed volume to him.[4] But Story did not publish Bartram's book.

The failure of this first publishing attempt appears to be at least partially attributable to the interference of Benjamin Smith Barton, a young Philadelphian who recognized Bartram's genius and befriended the older man, while continually exploiting him for information on the natural world and the American Indians. Bartram's publisher charged Barton, who was about to leave America for study in Scotland, with plotting to have Bartram's manuscript published abroad, to the detriment of his profit. Barton denied any such intent and, through deft persuasion, he managed to salvage his relationship with Bartram as the proposed venture with Story foundered. Barton was bold enough to write to Bartram from Edinburgh, in August 1787, that he had mentioned the manuscript to "many other learned and worthy men: they *all* seem anxious to see it *in print*; and I am very certain the work, especially if illustrated with plates, would sell *very well.*" Further, he proposed that Bartram allow him to edit the journal, add material of his own, and have it printed under both their names at his own expense.[5]

Barton wrote to Bartram again on February 19, 1788, urging him to proceed with publication of his journal. Again, he maintained that his interest arose "almost wholly from a desire to rescue from obscurity (you will pardon the phrase)" a valuable contribution to science. Barton reassured Bartram there was a market for the work: "I need hardly inform you again that *Natural History and Botany* are the fashionable and the favourite studies of the polite as well as of the learned parts of Europe."[6] Bartram tactually deflected Barton's offer to publish jointly, and the two men remained on good terms. In the years that followed, Barton incorporated Bartram's expertise on natural history into his own books, and usually gave Bartram proper credit for his contributions. Though historians have sometimes castigated Barton for "pilfering" Bartram's work, the younger man's enthusiasm and encouragement doubtless served as a catalyst, prompting the more retiring older man to proceed with the publication of his manuscript.[7]

Many scholars have puzzled over the fact that Bartram's book did not appear until fourteen years after his return from the South. Although Story had advertised the proposed book in 1786, Bartram was still polishing the manuscript and adding material at that time. In a 1787 letter, in answer to Barton's inquiries from Edinburgh, Bartram wrote that he had still not decided on publication and that his manuscript "remains yet in improper Embryo." Moreover, Bartram suffered from nagging doubts as to the value of his own work: "I am doubtful of its consiquence in respect to publick benefit[.] The Narative might afford some amusement & serve to kill time with the Inquisitive of all Denominations." Bartram further noted that he had given some thoughts to retracing his southern tour and thereby gaining additional material, but was prevented by his long convalescence following his fall from a cypress tree.[8]

Another reason for the delay in publication was that Bartram was awaiting species identifications from the trained botanists in England whom Fothergill had charged with classifying the botanical specimens Bartram sent to London. Unfortunately, those who had been entrusted with overseeing the task were soon diverted from their job by the even more spectacular specimens then coming from Australia and the tropical Pacific.[9] Perhaps the arrival of a trunk of his sent to him from Charleston in the summer of 1786 by Mary Lamboll Thomas facilitated Bartram's efforts to complete his manuscript. Mrs. Thomas, the daughter of Thomas Lamboll, had received Bartram into her home during his time in Charleston. Bartram had left his trunk in her care when he left Charleston in late 1776. The war, and the consequent disruption of shipping, had prevented its return until ten years later. Bartram was surprised to find that the books, papers, and botanical specimens stored for a decade in the trunk looked "nearly as well" as they had when he had consigned them to her care in 1776.[10] Their unexpected resurrection may have inspired renewed activity on the manuscript.

In time, the manuscript was finally finished, and in 1790, the Philadelphia publishing firm of James and Johnson began soliciting subscribers for *Travels*. Robert Parrish, a fellow Quaker, directed the subscription efforts and traveled to New York, the temporary seat of the U.S. government under the recently adopted Constitution, to promote the forthcoming work. In June, he wrote to Bartram: "I find the disposition of the Inhabitants of this City much more favourable to the work than I heretofore apprehended, they not being that unenlightened set of People which they are frequently represented to be." Moreover, Parrish urged Bartram to provide more illustrations to enhance the book's marketability. According to Parrish, while the sketches of birds that Bartram had provided were "very much admired," he believed that if Bartram would send him "the head of the Indian Chief & Some other drawings I think it would be of still greater advantage, nay Numbers of Persons wish to have the Indian in full stature & dress. If thee could recollect clear enough to draw him I am inclined to believe that I could procure a number of Subscribers from the St. Tamminy's Society here who are extremely fond of anything that resembles an Indian—at any rate I think it best to forward me his Head as soon as possible."[11]

Parrish was correct in his assessment of the St. Tammany's Society. When a Creek treaty delegation visited New York City later in the year, the society invited the entire delegation, as well as many prominent members of the government, to a banquet. The timely journey of the Creeks from their homeland to New York undoubtedly inspired many subscriptions to Bartram's work. Advertisements for *Travels* appeared that summer in the *Pennsylvania Packet and Daily Advertiser,* usually accompanied by extracts from the text relating to the Seminole village of Cuscowilla.[12] In the summer of 1791, the book finally appeared.[13]

One of Bartram's main goals was to describe the new plants he had discovered during his journey, but in *Travels* he accomplished much more. Far more than a catalog of plants and their habitats, the book included graphic accounts of the landscapes, animals, and peoples he had encountered. Thus, to credit Bartram merely with the discovery of a few new plant species is not sufficient, for he presented to his contemporaries a well-rounded picture of relatively unknown lands, and he preserved for posterity a picture of the eighteenth-century southeastern environment prior to extensive change and disruption by white settlement.

The book consists of four major parts. Part 1, which contains five chapters, covers the first stage of Bartram's journey. It details the author's first exploration of the Georgia coast, his attendance at the New Purchase Cession with the Creeks and Cherokees, held in Augusta, Georgia, and his participation in the survey of the ceded Indian lands. Part 1 concludes with an account of a trip up the Altamaha River, including Bartram's account of Indian mounds and the Creek migration legend. Events in the first four chapters of part 1 occurred principally in 1773, but the last chapter, judging from internal evidence, is placed out of sequence. Francis Harper speculated that this Altamaha voyage actually took place in 1776.[14]

Part 2 describes Bartram's travels through East Florida and the Seminole towns, which mostly occurred in 1774, including his famous account of the Alachua savanna and the Indian town of Cuscowilla, although here, too, Bartram rearranged the sequence of his various excursions.[15] Part 3 presents his travels among the Cherokee villages, his momentous journeys on horseback through the Creek country, and boat trips in West Florida and on the Mississippi River. It ends with descriptions of his last months in Georgia and his return to Philadelphia.

Part 4, which contains six chapters and carries its own title page, may have been intended for separate publication. With this section, entitled "An Account of the Persons, Manners, Customs and Government of the Muscogulges or Creeks, Cherokees, Chactaws, & c.,

Aborigines of the Continent of North America," Bartram provided us with one of the finest ethnographic accounts of the southeastern Indians written in the eighteenth century.

Whatever else may be said of Bartram's work, it is certainly not a precisely dated travel diary. Indeed, scarcely a date can be trusted in the entire volume. Francis Harper, who devoted much of his professional career to studying Bartram's writings and retracing Bartram's route, noted that the traveler "suffered either from a faulty memory or from an indifference to dates—if not from both!"[16] Part of Bartram's problem was the very nature of his adventure, for he, like the Indians and the traders who lived among them, was relatively free from the constraints of the Western world's rigid calendar. Thus, Bartram recorded the passage of time, as did the Indians, by the rhythms of nature. He found no need to be precise: he stays a week or two at one location, travels several days to reach another. Bartram was more intent on describing the wonders he encountered and enjoying his sojourn to the fullest extent possible than on achieving exactitude with dates. It was simply not his priority. The modern reader must be indulgent, and most will forgive the writer for literally "losing track of time."

But more troubling than Bartram's failure to record precise dates consistently is his apparent carelessness when he did supply dates. In the first report sent to his English patron, Dr. Fothergill, he began by stating that he departed Philadelphia on March 20, 1774—one year later than he actually left that city. One may surmise that Bartram substituted, for the year he left Philadelphia, the year in which he was actually writing the report, but other errors are harder to understand. For instance, a letter to Lachlan McIntosh, in which he described his journey to the Alachua savanna, was dated July 15, 1775. However, the contents of the letter and other known facts about Bartram's journey seem to indicate that the letter must have been written in 1774, not 1775.[17] Such errors, some of even greater magnitude, occur frequently in the *Travels.* Many of these are printers' errors, not Bartram's, but taken together, such mistakes make it nearly impossible to reconstruct an accurately dated itinerary for Bartram, though many have tried.[18] There is evidence to suggest that Bartram did not see the proofs of the completed work, which may explain the many typographical errors and some of the incorrect dates.

Following publication of *Travels,* the *Universal Asylum and Columbia Magazine* ran excerpts from the work, including much of part 4 and parts of the Cuscowilla journey narrative. While the magazine's reviewer generally credited Bartram with providing much useful information regarding the natural sciences, he disapproved "of the garb in which they appear," calling Bartram's "rhapsodical effusions . . . [and] style so very incorrect and disgustingly pompous." The reviewer also could not "help thinking that he magnifies the virtues of the Indians, and views their vices through too friendly a medium."[19] Other magazines were likewise critical of Bartram's melodramatic prose but were generally complimentary of his contribution to natural history. The reviewer for the *Massachusetts Magazine* believed that Bartram's "botanical researches are more copious than any other writers" and noted that even "the Aboriginals . . . [have not] escaped the minutiae of attention." The reviewer found Bartram's descriptions "rather too luxuriant and florid," but declared "a thousand of these trivia faults, the effect of a poetical imagination, are amply compensated for, by a rich vein of piety, blended with the purest morality."[20]

However, many doubted the validity of Bartram's most original observations, particularly his vivid account of alligator behavior. Later observers proved his observations, almost without exception, to have been correct, but Bartram must have been mortified to see his veracity questioned so publicly. Considering the overall lack of praise the work received, Francis Harper concluded: "The generally indifferent reception accorded his maximum effort must have been vastly discouraging. . . . Is it any wonder that the contributions from his pen during the next 31 years were so meager?"[21]

Apart from a few brief articles, Bartram wrote little during the remainder of his life. In addition to lingering memories of reviewers' disparagements, Bartram's failing eyesight and generally poor health, and the fact that he never traveled again, contributed to his lack of interest in writing for the public. Though he published little, he remained active, observing nature in his garden, collaborating with and serving as a mentor for numerous young scientists, as well as undertaking illustrative work for his friend Barton.

The book fared well abroad, and several editions promptly appeared in England, Ireland, Germany, Austria, and France.[22] There, the unrestrained classical imagery in Bartram's writings, and what Thomas Carlyle labeled his "wondrous kind of floundering eloquence," inspired a generation of European romantic writers.[23] Samuel Taylor Coleridge drew on Bartram's dreamlike descriptions of the lush Florida landscape for his own works, notably "The Rime of the Ancient Mariner" and "Kubla Khan." *Travels* provided inspiration for William Wordsworth, who fancifully envisioned Bartram, in his poem "Ruth," as "a youth from Georgia's shore" who attempts to win a young woman's affection. Likewise, the French writer François René de Chateaubriand drew on Bartram's images in his "Atala."[24] For these writers, Bartram's Indians were symbols of humanity untarnished by the hypocrisy of Western civilization. In America itself, Henry David Thoreau, in his classic essay *Walden,* cited Bartram's description of the Creek "busk," or annual renewal ceremony, in which the Indians destroyed wornout domestic articles and clothing, as an appropriate remedy for American materialism.[25] The wide popularity of Bartram's work continues to the present, and the book has seen numerous reprintings, including the authoritative *Naturalist's Edition* by Francis Harper, published in 1958.

While the Indian references in *Travels,* excerpted here, are a critical and voluminous segment of Bartram's Indian writings, and must, therefore, be included in a volume that claims to be comprehensive in its coverage of that subject, we are also acutely aware that presenting extracts from that book distorts the author's holistic portrayal of the American South. We recognize Bartram's *Travels* as a masterpiece of literature and natural history, and we vigorously encourage everyone with an interest in the region to read his book in its entirety, preferably Francis Harper's ably annotated version, which faithfully reproduces the original Philadelphia edition of 1791.

Notes

1. William Hedges, "Toward a National Literature," [*Columbia Literary History of the United States,* edited by Emory Elliott, 1988,] p. 190.

2. Douglas Anderson, "Bartram's *Travels* and the Politics of Nature," [*Early American Literature,* 25, no. 1, 1990,] p. 3.

3. In 1783, Johann David Schoepf saw an "unprinted manuscript" in Bartram's possession "on the nations and products" of Florida. Schoepf, *Travels in the Confederation,* 1:91.

4. [Francis] Harper, ed., *Travels of William Bartram,* [1998,] p. xxi.

5. Benjamin Smith Barton to William Bartram, August 26, 1787, BP, HSP, vol. 1, folder 3.

6. Benjamin Smith Barton to William Bartram, February 19, 1788, BP, HSP, vol. 1, p. 4. In the letter, Barton mentioned the forthcoming work by Joseph Banks.

7. Ewan, ed., *William Bartram: Drawings,* p. 29.

8. William Bartram to Benjamin Smith Barton, undated draft of letter [1787], Jane Gray's Autograph Collection, item 104a, Gray Herbarium, Harvard University.

9. See Ewan, ed., *William Bartram: Drawings,* for a full discussion of the fate of the botanical specimens. Peck, "William Bartram and His Travels," pp. 40-42.

10. William Bartram to Mrs. M. L. Thomas, July 15, 1786, Misc. W. Bartram Collection, New York

Historical Society. Previously, Mary Lamboll Thomas had shipped Bartram several plants native to the South, at Bartram's request. Mary Lamboll Thomas to William Bartram, May 11, 1785, BP, HSP, vol. 4, folder 111.

11. Robert Parrish to William Bartram, New York, 6 month 1790, Misc. Darlington Collection, New York Historical Society.

12. *Pennsylvania Packet and Daily Advertiser,* July 24, 1790. For advertisements of *Travels,* see the issues for July 30, 1790, and August 2, 1790. The St. Tammany's Society, or the Society of the Sons of Saint Tammany, also called the Columbian Order, was one of many social-political organizations that originated during the Federal period. That the Sons of Saint Tammany found Bartram's work interesting is not surprising, for they dressed like Indians, referred to their leader as the "Grand Sachem," and called their meeting hall a "Wigwam." Donald A. Grinde and Bruce E. Johansen, *Exemplar of Liberty,* pp. 169-89.

13. Francis Harper could find "no conclusive evidence" that *Travels* was published in 1791, but he accepted the date on the verso of the title page—August 26, 1791. Harper, ed., *Travels of William Bartram,* p. xxiii.

14. Bartram evidently returned to Savannah from his excursion with the New Purchase survey team sometime in December. He stated in his report to Dr. Fothergill, "Soon after my return from the Tugilo journey to Savanah the country was alarmed by an express from Augusta, that the Indians were for war, & had actually murdered Several Families not far from Augusta. . . ." (Bartram, "Travels in Georgia and Florida," p. 144). Harper incorrectly dated this part of Bartram's journey to the fall of 1773. However, Bartram was referring to the White-Sherrill murders, which occurred in late December 1773. Bartram's description of the Altamaha is not that of the winter months. Harper assigns that part of the journey to 1776, which he dates by an eclipse of the moon described by Bartram. See Harper, ed., *Travels of William Bartram,* pp. 346, 417. Further confusing the issue, Bartram sent "one trunk and one box" of goods to East Florida in August 1773, in anticipation of a "Tour of the St. John's River." According to James Spalding, who made sure that Bartram's luggage reached East Florida, Bartram himself was expected in the area "about the month of October." Perhaps Bartram consigned the material to Spalding prior to leaving for Augusta (James Spalding to Charles McLatchy, August 15, 1773, BP, HSP, vol. 4, folder 103). At any rate, it is generally believed, as Bartram himself states in

Travels (p. 57), that he left Savannah in March 1774 for East Florida.

15. This is documented by Bartram's letters to his father and to Lachlan McIntosh. Harper, ed., *Travels of William Bartram,* pp. 353, 361.

16. Harper, ed., *Travels of William Bartram,* p. 346. The extent of Bartram's travels between April 1773 and January 1777 is shown on the endpapers map in this volume and in figures 6-8. These maps are based on Lester J. Cappon, *Atlas of American History,* pp. 108-9; Harper, ed., "Travels in Georgia and Florida," maps 1 and 4; and Robert M. Peck, ed., *Bartram Heritage.*

17. William Bartram to Lachlan McIntosh, July 15, 1775 [1774], Dreer Collection, Scientists, Historical Society of Pennsylvania.

18. Francis Harper set the standard by which all scholars evaluate Bartram's chronology. See also Lester J. Cappon, "Retracing and Mapping the Bartrams' Southern Travels [Proceedings of the American Philosophical Society, 118, no. 6 (1974): 507-513]." The routes of both John and William Bartram are detailed in Cappon, *Atlas of American History,* pp. 108-9.

19. *Universal Asylum and Columbia Magazine,* vol. 1 (1792). The quotes are from the April issue, p. 267 (first quotation) and p. 266 (second quotation). Other excerpts appeared in January (pp. 8, 22), February (pp. 91-97), March (pp. 195-97), and April (pp. 255-67). Modern zoologists have since confirmed the accuracy of Bartram's alligator account, as well as most of his other observations.

20. Quoted in Harper, ed., *Travels of William Bartram,* p. xxiv. As William Hedges has noted, Bartram's prose is characterized by "Latinate poeticisms and elaborate syntactical sonority." Hedges, "Toward a National Literature," p. 191.

21. Harper, ed., *Travels of William Bartram,* p. xxviii.

22. Harper, ed., *Travels of William Bartram,* p. xxvii. Harper thought there may have been a Dutch edition as well.

23. In a letter to Ralph Waldo Emerson, written in 1851, Thomas Carlyle recommended Bartram's work. "Do you know *Bartram's Travels*? This is one of the Seventies (1770) or so; treats of *Florida* chiefly; has a wondrous kind of floundering eloquence in it; and has also grown immeasurably *old.*" Charles Eliot Norton, ed., *Correspondence of Thomas Carlyle and Ralph Waldo Emerson, 1834-1872,* 2:198.

24. The best study of Bartram's influence on literature is Fagin, *William Bartram,* pp. 128-200. More re-

cent examinations of Bartram's influence on literature and philosophy include Thomas V. Barnett, "William Bartram and the Age of Sensibility" [Ph.D. dissertation]; Mary S. Mattfield, "Journey to the Wilderness"; Bruce Silver, "William Bartram's and Other Eighteenth-Century Accounts of Nature" [*Journal of the History of Ideas,* 39, no. 4 (1978): 597-614]; L. Hugh Moore, "Aesthetic Theory of William Bartram" [*Essays in Arts and Sciences,* 12, no. 1, (March, 1983): 17-35] and "Southern Landscape of William Bartram" [*Essays in Arts and Sciences,* 10, no. 1 (1981): 41-50]; and John Seelye, "Beauty Bare [*Prospects: The Annual of American Cultural Studies,* 6 (1981): 37-54]."

25. Henry David Thoreau, *A Week on the Concord and Merrimack Rivers; Walden, or Life in the Woods,* pp. 376-77.

Thomas P. Slaughter (essay date 1996)

SOURCE: Slaughter, Thomas P. "Perspectives." In *The Natures of John and William Bartram,* pp. 177-96. New York: Alfred A. Knopf, 1996.

[*In the following essay, Slaughter claims that, while* Travels *is a complicated work that has many facets, there is one message that Bartram wanted to voice more than any other: "all of nature is one . . . and infused with the spirit of its creator."*]

Is William Bartram's *Travels* poetry, readers have asked, fiction, or science? Are the author and the "philosophical pilgrim" the same person or different ones sharing the same name? Is the story true, readers have always wanted to know, or did the author alter the record and transfigure time—create, transform, embellish, recall things that never happened, and forget some that did? The answer to all these questions is yes; the book is all these things and more.

The *Travels* is a complicated story told by a person who wanted to tell the truth, but who didn't always know what it was; it was written by a man who didn't let smaller truths obscure larger ones that he wanted to share. William Bartram was a persona, a character in a book whom the author imagined back in his plantation swamp and whom he became over the course of his travels, in writing his *Travels,* in the garden after his traveling was done. The personal transformation was a self-conscious act, but the creation of the pilgrim's persona was not, so the book is richly autobiographical in ways that William never intended, didn't recognize, would never know, and would have denied.

Is the author of the *Travels* an Enlightenment figure, a Romantic, or a pre-Romantic writer? other readers have asked. Does the book bear structural resemblances to the novels, natural histories, or travel accounts of William's day? Again, the answer is that William and the book are all those things. Since the principal character in the *Travels* isn't a literal rendering of the author, since his story is an idealization of nature and self, the book should be approached cautiously as a biographical source, with attention to contextual materials and internal evidence that suggest it isn't always what it appears to be. The ancillary sources include William's life, the drawings he made on his journey, the three surviving manuscript chapters written and corrected in his hand, and the *Report* that he wrote for his patron, Dr. Fothergill, which parallels events in the *Travels,* but offers a strikingly different account of William's journey from April 1773 to January 1777.

In all these revelations about nature and self, William had but one message that he consciously shared, and he voiced it with a clarity and simplicity that defined who he became as he entered his forties and continued becoming for the last forty years of his life. All of nature is one, he believed, and infused with the spirit of its creator; this common soul reveals God and is an active spiritual presence in the natural world, an essence that connects all nature and makes the characteristics shared by animals and plants more significant than the differences among us. If such ideas sound familiar, it may be because they were inspired by John's strikingly similar philosophy. William's message was a distinctive combination of traditional notions, lessons learned at his father's knee, and visionary ideals of his own, a view of the natural world that had a greater kinship with both seventeenth-century spiritualism and nineteenth-century Transcendentalism than did the nature writings of such contemporaries as Crèvecoeur, Kalm, and Jefferson.[1]

William accepted nature on its own terms—on God's terms, he would say. Wilderness was just as God intended without any improvement by man, without the clearing, tilling, and fencing that others, including his father, saw as natural beauty. No American of his day waxed so romantic about wilderness settings. The *Travels* is, among other things, an ode to unspoiled natural beauty. Inhale William's reverie on the Altamaha River:

> How gently flow thy peaceful floods, O Altamaha! How sublimely rise to view, on thy elevated shores, yon magnolian groves, from whose tops the surrounding expanse is perfumed, by clouds of incense, blended with the exhaling balm of the liquidambar, and odours continually arising from circumambient aromatic groves of illicium, myrica, laurus and bignonia. . . . Thus secure and tranquil, and meditating on the marvellous scenes of primitive nature, as yet unmodified by the hand of man, I gently descended the peaceful stream, on whose polished surface were depicted the mutable shadows from its pensile banks; whilst myriads of finny inhabitants sported in its pellucid floods.[2]

Hear William's drawing of Florida's Alachua Savanna. Everything wondrous he has to say about the shared nature of all creation echoes there, too. The picture is really a series of mirror images that display the connections among animal and plant life. The central focus of the drawing is the lowland feature that begins with the sinkhole in the top center. The swamp is shaped like the leaf of a tree, with the streams running out of the sinkhole taking on the characteristics of both the veins of the large leaf and of branches leading to interior leaf-shaped lowlands and ponds. The cranes flying through the top right of the picture are reflected in two terrestrial features below them.[3]

The drawing evokes classical imagery, with the columnlike tree framing the foreground and left side of the scene. The elevated perspective of the viewer is also traditional in European landscape art, and is often interpreted as an expression of dominance, a declaration of control over nature by artists steeped in Western cultural conventions, who see with imperial eyes. As always for William, though, dominance and control are deeply troubling prospects, implying responsibilities that he's not prepared to accept, a confidence that he doesn't really have, and a hierarchical configuration of nature to which he isn't emotionally attached. He undermines these messages within his own portrayal by representing humans as less significant in the savanna than animals and plants.

If he had simply left out mankind altogether, implying our presence as the elevated viewers of the scene, our dominance would be clear; but he muddies the story by including at least some of us on his landscape. Humans are represented by the building in the lower central part of the drawing. We know from a key to William's map of the savanna that this structure stands for the Seminole village of Cuscowilla. Typical of William, where humans are visible in his scenes, our place is modest in scale and scope, not a dominating presence, more Eastern than Western in the way he situates mankind in nature. We saw this as well in the sketch of his father's house, in which William included a man dwarfed by his trees (page 36).

His drawing of the *arethusa divaricata* also portrays a tiny figure in a canoe and a town on the opposite bank. The lone paddler may again be the artist, as the fisherman may be in the sketch of John's house. Plants dominate; birds are an interior focus, detailed enough to discern species and their graceful ease gliding across the landscape. Humans are more remote, but we are part of the natural habitat, nonetheless. The meticulously drawn frame defines the portrait as a pose that freezes the subjects in place.

By representing Indians in the Alachua Savanna, the artist has left open the interpretive possibility that a European "we," who exist above and outside the image field, rule this domain, thereby "othering" nature in

ways typical of Western conventions of seeing dating back to the "discovery" of the Americas in the late fifteenth century. Since the drawing subverts such conventions, though, challenging the very perspectives it takes, this is a reading to which we shouldn't leap. Indeed, the fisherman and the paddler show that William sees the Cuscowilla Seminoles in nature just as he views the rest of us, including himself.

In William's landscape, there are flowers larger than the trees that surround them, which suggests that foreground and background don't have the relationship traditional in Western pictorial art. Animal size doesn't shrink as we move toward the top of the picture; the scene does not recede into either a distant horizon or a dim past. Our view takes in the whole savanna with the same focus and depth. Such novel perspectives imply a timelessness or, at least, that change comes slowly here.

As in William's description of the Altamaha, the wilderness present is "primitive," "as yet unmodified by the hand of man," still "peaceful." The drawing stops time, as all pictures do, and constructs an unnatural view that bounds reality in ways our eyes and the terrain never could. It freezes a view into a scene; vision becomes a bounded field with a central focus and clearly defined edges that exist only in the artist's mind, telling us his story rather than reporting visual "facts" that anyone else would behold. The picture is true to William's feelings and to the sensations that others might experience at the savanna, thereby discerning a different "Truth" than his father perceived in the same place. In another subversion of the expected, the viewer looks *backward* in time from an imagined perspective beside the classical tree. This feature, which at its base so resembles the column William may have helped John build on his house, stands for the present, civilization, and the structures of man—including the artificial frame constructed by the artist—rather than simply evoking an idealized European past. The column is imposed to give shape, to define an edge of the image field, to hide from our eyes what exists beyond the lined borders that William draws.

As viewers, we are much closer to the column than we are to the savanna below. The idealized savanna is a memory, not just of the place that William saw, but of one that we must struggle inside our hearts to reach. It's an attempt to escape from the past through a back door, to a world that existed before the failures of William's life, before Europeans disturbed the savanna's tranquility, which is why he leaves out the roads that transect the "map" he sent to Fothergill.

The presence of commercial highways on this map would alter the story, dampen the emotional fires of sublimity that William is trying to stoke for the reader, and introduce change. This drawing not only stops time;

it captures a moment now past. It's unclear whether this reflects an antidevelopmental prejudice, because like his father William can both admire nature on its own terms *and* imagine fences and fields as pleasant prospects. A letter that he wrote to Lachlan McIntosh about the savanna captures William's wilderness idyll and a developmental dream in the same paragraph.

> The wide and almost unlimited prospect of this verdant plain varied with glittering pieces of water and jetting points of the hammocks forms a scene inchangingly beautiful. . . . The land about it very good and extremely proper for indigo, would grow good corn & c., the whole savanna in the summer and fall a meadow of very good kind of grass. . . . In short would those Indians part with this land, it would admit of a very valuable settlement and would be a very considerable acquisition.[4]

In the *Travels* as well, there are odes to wilderness beauty juxtaposed with developmental proposals. This isn't surprising in light of John's easy blending of these two ways of seeing one place. There are reasons to believe, though, that William experienced a tension between these two visions closer in some ways to those a modern advocate for unspoiled nature would feel than to what his father ever revealed. The adverb "inchangingly" from the letter provides a clue that William may have felt conflicted about developing this particular plot of land, perhaps more than he did about others that he witnessed in his travels. The invented word conflates "unchanging" and "inchantingly," to use William's usual spelling, which implies that the savanna's beauty, its enchantment, would be shattered by change. A passage in his *Report* likewise contemplates

> the wonderful harmony and perfection in the lovely simplicity of Nature tho naked yet unviolated by the rude touch of the human hand. Tho admitting that human inventions, arts and sciences to be a part in the progress of Nature, yet [they] are perpetually productive of innovations, and events, that show the defects of human policy; What a beautiful scenery is Vegetable Nature![5]

What we see here are the opening eyes of a man who has a greater fear of the future, less confidence in science, commerce, and man, and a greater love of unspoiled nature than John had. Compared to his father, William was a more romantic, less constrained, celebrant of wild nature. William also had mixed feelings about civilization as a consequence of his inability to find a place where he fit. Whether he realized the complex, sometimes conflicted, nature of his thinking, he didn't edit the *Travels* for a false consistency. That's why some readers have pegged him—based on their reading of this one writing of his—as a natural, who favored the wild over civilized life, while others have seen him—again based solely on a reading of the *Travels*—as another European exploiter of virgin lands and native peoples. William was to some extent torn between the lure of the natural and the culture that was imbedded in him, but we tend to exaggerate the conflict that we feel more than he did, because we know that development will not end with farms, because of our own guilt, perhaps, our own sense of consumptive complicity in a culture that overdeveloped the land, drove the manatees out, and bulldozed Indian burial mounds for road-paving materials.[6]

What William did in his 1774 letter to Lachlan McIntosh and the *Report to Fothergill* was reverse the reportorial style of his father, using the more private genre of personal correspondence for his discussion of productive potential and reserving his most romantic prose for the public audience of the *Travels.* Where John presented a scientific persona in public writings, waxing romantic about nature only in letters to a close friend, William's public agenda was emotional and aesthetic, not advocacy for development and use. *The Report to Fothergill* is stylistically the closest of William's writings to John's published journals, adopting the tone of the philosophical reporter of size, distances, terrain, and "useful" plant life. The differences between William's *Report* and John's journals are also instructive, because William is a more active, visible presence even in his most philosophical pose than John ever was in his.

The Report covers the first two years of William's journey, 1773 and 1774, and was composed in two volumes, which are numbered separately and were apparently sent to Fothergill at different times. William corrected the spelling of only the second volume, suggesting that the first came wild from the field and the second was domesticated back in Charleston with a dictionary in hand. *The Report*'s twentieth-century editor values it as "a far fresher document than the *Travels,* and . . . almost wholly free from the disturbing discrepancies that the discriminating student finds in the published work."[7] As a scientist himself, the editor sees William's reportage as "careless," his memory as "faulty," and his frequent inaccuracies as a "blind spot in his mental vision." He's disturbed that William's lunar eclipse of 1773 actually occurred three years later, that his chronology is "sadly confused," and that chapters of the *Travels* are shuffled out of the order in which events took place. The editor offers illness, damaged eyesight, and scandalous editing by the *Travels*'s publisher as excuses for William. *The Report* is better "science" by modern lights and by the standards of John's published journals as well.[8]

The Report gets its starting date wrong, hardly an auspicious beginning for a "scientist," revealing that William lost track of years early on. The opening is similar in structure to that of the *Travels*'s first chapter, but there is no identity of language; some passages have more information, others less. He leaves out many of the philosophical flights of fancy that so richly adorn the book. Such phrases as "the face of the angry ocean" reveal William's authorial voice. He tells us in the *Report* that two horses washed overboard in his ocean journey and that he heard a good sermon in Georgia, delivered to a "respectable and genteel congregation," which is the sort of detail that the reader of the *Travels* doesn't learn, but he leaves out any mention of a long visit with McIntosh upon his arrival and provides fewer particulars here than in the *Travels* about a clay urn that he found.

Like his father's journals, William's *Report* includes practical information about "the soil being very rich" and "very good mills." Even such "useful" details, though, are cast in a less restrained prose: "the land flat, the soil sandy, but the country everywhere clad with green grass in the forests and beautiful savannas, richly painted over with various colored flowers." There's no restraining the poet, no repressing the artist who sees color as paint—viewing landscape as "pictures from the surrounding painted hills." Also differently from John, William sees abundant animal life—wolves, vultures, eagles, cranes, alligators, snakes, panthers, buffalo, scorpions, spiders, possums, fish, weasels, vast "herds and flocks of deer and turkeys bounding and tripping over the hills and savannas"—and witnesses signs of an animal presence even when fauna hide from his sight. Nor does he often dig beneath the surface, feel and taste nature as John did, "as I attempt only to exhibit to your notice the outward furniture of Nature, or the productions of the surface of the earth."[9]

William smells nature, but he is irrepressibly visual in his *Report*. Where he digs, it isn't to explore rocks or determine the fitness of soil for crops; it's into the human past that he tunnels, through the burial mounds of "ancient civilizations" about which he wants to know more. The scariness of wilderness travel is more visible in William's account. Whether he's "enveloped in an almost endless savage wilderness" that damps his spirits "with a kind of gloomy horror" or finds a kind of sublime "terror" in the flight of a bald eagle, his *Report* is more emotionally accessible than John wanted his journals to be.[10]

Why did William retrace the trip that he took with his father in 1765, write a *Report* about the same places they "discovered" together, and botanize the same ground that he and John had already searched? John's journal was already published in multiple editions; why didn't William seek out a spot of his own? What had he lost the last time; what did he hope to find; what was he trying to say to his father, to others, and to himself? William tells much that John didn't, records things that John couldn't see, finds plants that they had both overlooked. Was he competing, revising his father; had he a need to better his father's courage, competence, science, and art? Perhaps he imagined a book about the emotional experience of travel in this wilderness as virgin literary ground. Maybe he wanted to see the "enchanted" Alachua Savanna again.

William's personal failures as a merchant, from which he fled in both 1765 and 1773, have a bright side in the story that he tells about the Alachua Savanna, for he won't be one of those harbingers of civilization who brings his wares here or who, like his father, shows others the way. By leaving the roads out of his picture, romanticizing the savanna in his *Report,* and mythologizing it in the *Travels,* he indicts the dominant culture that he represents, but from which he wants to distance himself, hide himself, find himself in a newer self than the one who sold pots, bought rice, accompanied his father, and owned slaves. William's view of the savanna as a refuge from time, trouble, and want also explains why he rotates the map's eastern features by ninety degrees, subverting any effort to find this special place in the world. A traveler can't reach William's savanna by walking down the roads that he draws on the map, making the idealized portrait and "Romantic" *Travels* more reliable guides to the terrain than the "scientific" *Report* and "objective" map. The scientist/editor of the *Report* got the story wrong, mistaking facts for truth, as perhaps William thought that John did, not realizing that William was a philosopher of the emotions, an even higher calling in his eyes than the philosopher of birds and flowers he also was.

William was not the same explorer for empire that his father became; it wasn't his intent to help Europeans master this place, to write a guide for locating, clearing, plowing, and fencing the scene that he drew. The map's artifices also imply that the Alachua Savanna is more a state of mind than a feature on the face of the earth. To see what William saw the viewer and reader must change as William was changing, as he wanted to believe, wanted us to believe, that he already had. He began writing while he was still in the woods, sketching a primitive outline for a section of the *Travels* on a scrap of paper from one of Fothergill's letters, drafting the manuscript chapter about the savanna while he was still in Florida, then correcting it back in Charleston, when he had a dictionary and a copy of Linnaeus's *Systema Naturae* close at hand.[11] The bracketed deletions and insertions in the manuscript conform exactly with the published version. Both the *Travels* and the draft have a much more extensive discussion of the savanna than the *Report to Fothergill,* which doesn't seem drawn from the manuscript any more than the *Travels* was drawn from the *Report* in any obvious sense.

William wrote the manuscript before he sent the second of the *Report*'s two parts to Fothergill, where he corrected spelling and substituted scientific names for more general descriptions. Given this relationship among the three written texts, it makes sense to call the manuscript a field journal, even though it doesn't conform to botanists' expectations for what the genre looks like, even though scientists still lament that William's field notes are "lost." Again, as in his drawings and published writings, William challenged form and convention in the way that he worked. His "notes" were more reveries, explications of states of mind, evocations of God in nature, and explorations of themes developed through the *Travels,* than they were dates, distances, and lists of flora and fauna that he saw as he crossed the landscape.

William added the lists of Latin names to his book for credibility's sake, to recover authority from a dead Roman past. They are now the passages that seem most antique, giving the *Travels* a clear border in time, just as the columnlike tree bounds his drawing of the Alachua Savanna in culture and place. The lists also add beauty, to some readers' eyes, even as they provide "facts" that the scientist craves. The poet James Dickey experiences the lists as

> a kind of shade, and because the names themselves are strange, special and beautiful, and taken together with Bartram's descriptions of the creatures and plants they designate, call up an entire flora and fauna that hover with Edenic colors in the reader's uninformed—that is, still virgin—mind. A state of innocence not unlike Bartram's is possible for him, too.[12]

Although that is not an effect the author anticipated—a way that he calculated his writing—it is a cogent insight into why the book still lives long after science, literature, and art have adopted other fashions, when the authority of Latin has died yet again, when our innocence is a product of ignorance, as Dickey remarks. The reader is still with William under the trees, struggling with the same torments of alienation and self, and trying to find the redemption in nature that the sylvan pilgrim sought, that he found, that he promises us.

As the text written the nearest in time to William's visit and the one least recalculated for an audience of others, the manuscript chapter on the Alachua Savanna is a place to continue exploring nature's meaning for him. All other versions were revisions of this original story. Since the published section is the one he chose to represent the whole book when his editor produced a sample for recruiting subscribers in 1791, there is good reason to believe that it's the one that pleased him most and that he anticipated would appeal best to an audience of like-minded readers.[13]

Because William calculated the descriptions in the *Report* and the map so differently from the other depictions, the contrasting accounts provide access to the ways that William told his stories with different audiences in mind. With two drawings and three written accounts, William's literary encounters with the Alachua

Savanna reveal the process of his personal transformation and desire to recast his tale for an audience of others in whose eyes he hoped to redeem himself as he refashioned who he really was. The revisions to this and the other two surviving manuscript chapters provide clues to the ways in which the transformation was incomplete, where he struggled to delete his "old" self from the text, and where he couldn't see that "Billy" was still part of him.

The principal variations from the manuscript chapters to the book are an editing for style, grammar, spelling, syntax, and tone, a shortening of the most rhapsodic commentaries about landscape, and deletion of some prayerful references to God. The revisions are toward a more secular, less romantic text that he hoped would be a more authoritative one. The changes consistently aim for scientific credibility, greater precision in naming, measuring, and counting than his methods of observation actually supplied. Since the "facts" are consistently erroneous, the changes are a ploy, but a psychologically complicated one, because at a conscious level William wanted to get the story right and was deeply hurt when people challenged his objectivity as a scientist. He doubles the acreage of the Alachua Savanna, overstates the magnitude of plains, rivers, and trees, writes "yards" when "feet" would be the accurate measure, and reports such phenomena as a 200-egg average for alligator nests when 40 is the real norm and a twenty-foot alligator, which is unlikely at best.[14]

These errors consistently exaggerate size, number, and distance, which suggests that William's "science" was calculated for literary effect. His numbers reported the true feelings of the sylvan pilgrim and are thus better considered guides to emotionality than lies, bad science, or failed efforts at literal counts. As such they reflect an eighteenth-century rhetorical revolution that also affected art. As Jay Fliegelman describes the philosophy behind this search for "natural" expression, it was a "new model of representation that defines truth as truthfulness to feelings rather than to facts," in which "the misrepresentation of . . . [an] event serves to make possible the accurate representation of an emotion or emotions that otherwise could not be represented."[15] That is what William wanted—to share how he felt and elicit the same feelings in those who read his book or witnessed his art.

The emotion that William sought in these exaggerated counts was the sublime, which could be a product of size, number, variety, height, sound, beauty, or fear. Willing, indeed eager, to sacrifice mere numbers for emotional truth, he drew on the aesthetic theory that he'd been exposed to in school, of Joseph Addison, Lord Kames, William Hogarth, and Edmund Burke. He saw the same emotionality in the poetry of Mark Akenside, and he would have found it also in Jefferson's

Declaration and Paine's *Common Sense* had he not been off in the woods when they first appeared. He would have plenty of time later, though, in the serenity of his family's garden, to read about the sublime in the writings of Immanuel Kant, Archibald Alison, William Smellie, and Gilbert White.[16]

Addison's *Spectator* essays on "The Pleasures of the Imagination" articulated a vision of nature as God's creation for improving men's souls. Since imagination is the vehicle for receiving God's lessons inscribed in nature, the imaginative faculty is elevated to new heights that are seized by artists, poets, novelists, and natural historians as the focal point of their work. In the latter part of the century, theories of the sublime, Deism, and Romanticism merge with classical traditions furthering this process of emotionalizing nature. So, for example, John's generation venerated Virgil's *Georgics* as both a poem and a didactic work on scientific agriculture, one that proclaimed a gospel of work and idealized rural life. William's contemporaries would find greater appeal in Virgil's *Eclogues,* which portrayed an Arcadian myth about an imaginary existence far removed from real life. The two pastoral visions aren't so much conflicting ones as celebrations of "natural" life in different forms. Emphasizing, as they do, alternative visions of nature, the poems appealed to the different tastes, different sensibilities, and different values of William and John. It was the concept of the sublime that fomented this process of change.[17]

Cultural transformations illustrated by the natural sublime redefined "imagination" even as it was becoming more highly esteemed. The more traditional role of the imaginative faculty, as defined by Samuel Johnson, saw poetry as the "art of uniting pleasure with truth by calling the imagination to the help of reason." Others, more affected by the new sensibilities than Johnson, proclaimed that only by divorcing the poetic imagination from reason can poetry achieve the highest accomplishment.[18] This, to be sure, was contested terrain, and William was not an exemplar of the most extreme advocacy of imagination over and apart from reason. However, he was affected by this revolution in artistic consciousness in ways that John, and many of William's readers, never appreciated.

Just as Thomas Burnet's *The Sacred Theory of the Earth* gave John a theoretical focus and *The Morals of Confucius* supported what he already believed, so there were books that either influenced William or reinforced his existing views. Mark Akenside's *Pleasures of Imagination,* for example, illustrates one of the fissures between the writings of William and John. The poem and its didactic introduction endorse the powers and pleasures of the imagination, elevating subjective over objective perception. Theoretically indebted to Addison's essays on the sublime, Akenside seeks the emotional effects of nature on humanity.

> With what attractive charms this goodly frame of nature touches the consenting hearts of mortal men

Having set the frame thus in the first line, Akenside celebrates "indulgent fancy," and proclaims "Let FICTION come," which, he predicts, will result in a liberating "Majestic TRUTH" superior to other claims to mere lower-case truths derived from nature.[19]

The key biological metaphor is the heart, not the mind, but Akenside's endorsement of an imaginative approach to nature isn't a call for aesthetic or emotional chaos. Indeed, the expectation is that universal comprehension and feeling will be achieved, uniting the senses of mankind with the revelations of the natural world. As Edmund Burke explains in his *Philosophical Enquiry,* "we do and must suppose, that as the conformation of their organs are nearly, or altogether the same in all men, so the manner of perceiving external objects is in all men the same, or with little difference."[20]

The goal was quite similar in some respects to that of John's generation, but the locus of exploration had changed. From a sensory search for physically discernible phenomena, the quest was now for emotional truths discovered by a man of universal feeling. The confidence of eighteenth-century aestheticians that they could identify and classify emotions was of a piece with the botanical enterprise and no more humble than scientists' faith in objective sight. If William was a reliable witness, his sensations upon experiencing nature would be substantiated by those of other writers and artists. He would convey those emotions in a fashion that elicited the same response in his readers, thereby replicating the discoveries of other nature poets and artists in the same manner that the Royal Society directed its philosophical travelers to achieve a high degree of "probabilism" by the use of identical scientific methods. The limits on the artist's discernment of Truth were those of talent, integrity, and imagination; any doubt or disbelief by readers was a very personal assault on the man of feeling.

Sublimity can be a pleasant and/or an awful experience, but must evoke a passion comparable to horror. As Burke explained,

> whatever is fitted in any sort to excite the ideas of pain, and danger, that is to say, whatever is in any sort terrible, or is conversant about terrible objects, or operates in a manner analogous to terror, is a source of the *sublime*; that is, it is productive of the strongest emotion which the mind is capable of feeling. I say the strongest emotion, because I am satisfied the ideas of pain are much more powerful than those which enter on the part of pleasure.[21]

Such theories of the sublime led William to find terror even in the way that a bird flaps its wings.

. . . the eagle closes the points of his wings towards his body, and with collected power cleaves the elastic air and seems to rend the skies which indeed can be only equalled by the Terror of sudden and unexpected thunder.[22]

The sublime helps explain the degree of emotionality William aims for in describing great beauty, such as that of the Altamaha River, and why he takes what Burke would call "delight" from frights that he survives. What William tries to capture is the degree of sublime astonishment that, according to Burke, is a state of the soul "in which all its motions are suspended, with some degree of horror."[23]

William wants to appear credible in the same ways that John did, but some part of him with which he is not entirely in touch challenges the scientific method, thereby undermining his self-confidence and the reliability of his reporting in ways that trouble him. This leads him to edit his draft of the *Travels* by adding the sort of details, largely manufactured, that his father scrupulously noted when he traveled this same wilderness a decade before, melding the approaches of aesthetics and science, which weren't necessarily in conflict in any event. That's not to say that William got everything wrong, distorted the facts purposely, or that the book isn't "science" at all. It is the seminal source for much botanical and anthropological data, and the author intended the *Travels* to report what was true. It's simply that truth is elusive and William lacked the discipline and desire to tell what seemed to him sterile tales, to take careful notes, and to see specimens, locations, and relations in nature as John had. Even more importantly, William lacked John's confidence that Truth lay in those details rather than in the emotions with which he was more closely in touch, especially the darkness of the sublime. With the rest of his culture, but ahead of the crowd, William contemplated inner truth; state of mind assumed a greater significance for him than external "facts."[24]

In both its unedited and edited versions, William's chapter on the Alachua Savanna is the most moving passage that he ever wrote. It shows him at his greatest emotional height, inspired by the beauty of this most wondrous site and the poetry and aesthetic theories of the sublime that he read. He feared that his writing was too religious and waxed too romantical (an opinion with which reviewers agreed even about the edited, published version), but that's what the place meant to him. The first draft was emotionally honest; in the second he tried to refine the effect that it would have on his readers. He deleted descriptions of "inchanted ground," "bewitching" birds, and fireflies as the moon's "ministering agents of Light"; substituted "elevated mind" for "inraptured soul"; changed "sacred" to "grand"; and removed the prayerful phrase that ended a paragraph: "O

most bountifull & benificent Creator!" He dropped references to a flight of birds at sunset as a "solemn religious rite" and to their song as an "evening hymn." And he eliminated the bracketed phrases from the passage below.

> I am sensible that my countrymen, the refined civilised nations of white people, will conclude & say [to one another] these paradisial scenes are surely [are] nothing more than [the] mere visionary dreams [of the Sylvan Pilgrim] or [mere] phantoms of a sickly mind [or deranged imagination] [but such] Yet I speak but the truth.[25]

William's audience is precisely the "refined, civilised nations of white people" to whom he refers, a readership about which we can detect in his tone a mix of fear and disdain. He dreads rejection, having felt it before, and thinks he can anticipate civilized men's reaction to him. Perhaps the "sylvan pilgrim" apprehends some truth in the rejection that he predicts. Is he merely a dreamer, who experiences "phantoms" in his "sickly mind," a man cursed with a "deranged imagination"? No, he insists, answering himself rather than them, "I speak but the truth." He toned down the passage's indictment of himself and made it a little less personal, a little less offensive and defensive at the same time, but essentially left his resentment, fear, and response. He also dropped another self-reference describing his "apprehensions" as "bewildered," again perhaps because, although true, the depiction was too revealing, leaving him more vulnerable to a charge that he wished to deny.

William also deleted long passages that were even harder on his audience than those he left in. Having depicted nature's "rational system of social fraternal intercourse," which rejects avarice and diminishes the impact of war, he compares humans unfavorably to our animal kin.

> How unseemly it looks! How debasing to humanity to see every day and everywhere amongst what are called civilised nations such a disparity, such an inequality in the conditions and situations of men.

> It appears to me to be within the reach or ability of a man to live in this world, and even in this depraved age and Nation to a good old age without greatly injuring himself or his neighbor and if one man can continue in a state of innocence as long as he lives why not all men? If they would unite seriously in the cause of righteousness we should gain upon the common enemy every day and in time it would be as easy and natural to do right as to do wrong. Is it not in the power of every one of us to do justly, love mercy, and walk humbly before God?

William apparently drafted this passage, along with the rest of the chapter on the Alachua Savanna, during or shortly after his visit in 1774. Although the Boston Tea Party had already occurred, it was by no means certain that an actual war would ensue. Even here, though, in this natural retreat from the failings of mankind and of a man, news reached William's ears of the "depraved age and nation" in which he lived. What a strong indictment of his country and countrymen, which it makes good sense to edit out after the war, during an era that celebrated independence and resented what was seen as Quakers' closet Toryism, when he was looking for a sympathetic audience to read his book.

William also deleted another passage that casts his peace testimony in a more positive tone: "I profess myself of the Christian sect of the people called Quakers and consequently am against War and violence in any form or manner whatever." This line, too, might have narrowed his potential readership, offended others with different views and harsh feelings toward the Quakers, who were still denounced as traitors or cowards unwilling to risk themselves and their fortunes for liberty's cause. It was consistent with his pilgrim's persona, a biographical link between himself and his text, which might have seemed too personal, too preachy, and that wasn't even literally true.

William served, at least briefly, as a spy for Patriot forces in 1776 during his travels. He often said that Charles Thomson, his beloved college tutor and future secretary of the Continental Congress, had instilled "republican principles" in his mind. He also had family members who joined the "Free Quakers"—those who broke with the peace testimony to actively support the war in 1781; publicly praised some of the Revolution's leaders—dedicating his book to one (Thomas Mifflin) after another (George Washington) turned him down; rejoiced in American independence; and supported a nephew-in-law's application for an army commission later in life. No, this wasn't the real William he deleted to enhance his standing with readers. It was the Quaker pilgrim persona that he brought closer in line with the man he was and remained. Like his father, William's pacifism was contingent; there were, he believed, good reasons to fight, good causes to fight for, and bad people whom we have an obligation to kill. Such beliefs are not those of the Society of Friends, which makes no such exceptions, but a product of the Bartrams' shared view that violence was natural, however regrettable; one of nature's ways of balancing life.[26]

Notes

1. On influences, for the debate over William's poetic versus scientific visions, and for characterization of his authorial identity within the context of existing genres, see Larry R. Clarke, "The Quaker Background of William Bartram's View of Nature," *JHI,* 46 (1985): 435-448; Bruce Silver, "Clarke on the Quaker Background of William Bartram's Approach to Nature," *JHI,* 47 (1986):

507-510; Thomas Vance Barnett, "William Bartram and the Age of Sensibility," Ph.D. diss., Georgia State University, 1982; Samuel Robert Aiken, "The New-Found-Land Perceived: An Exploration of Environmental Attitudes in Colonial British America," Ph.D. diss., The Pennsylvania State University, 1971; Charlotte Porter, "Bartram's Travels and American Literature, or Why Did He Wait so Long to Publish?," The Bartram Trail Conference and Symposium, *Proceedings of the Symposium* (1991): 59-64; L. Hugh Moore, "The Aesthetic Theory of William Bartram," *Essays in Arts and Sciences,* 12 (1983): 17-35; Pamela Regis, *Describing Early America: Bartram, Jefferson, Crèvecoeur, and the Rhetoric of Natural History* (DeKalb, 1992); Robert McCracken Peck, "William Bartram and His Travels and Books from the Bartram Library," in Society for the Bibliography of Natural History, *Contributions to the History of North American Natural History* (London, 1983), 35-50; James Rosen, "William Bartram's Sketches: The Field and the Image," Bartram Trail Conference, *Proceedings of the Symposium* (1991): 41-54; William L. Hedges, "Toward a National Literature," in Emory Elliott, ed., *Columbia Literary History of the United States* (New York, 1988), 190-191; John Seelye, "Beauty Bare: William Bartram and His Triangulated Wilderness," *Prospects,* 6 (1981): 37-54; William Gummere, "William Bartram, A Classical Scientist," *Classical Journal,* 50 (1955): 167-170; Bruce Silver, "William Bartram's and Other Eighteenth-Century Accounts of Nature," *JHI,* 39 (1978): 597-614; N. Bryllion Fagin, *William Bartram: Interpreter of the American Landscape* (Baltimore, 1933); Charlotte M. Porter, "The Drawings of William Bartram (1739-1823), American Naturalist," *Archives of Natural History,* 16 (1989): 289-303; Mary S. Mattfield, "Journey to the Wilderness: Two Travelers in Florida, 1696-1774," *Florida Historical Quarterly,* 45 (1967): 327-351; Clive Bush, *The Dream of Reason: American Consciousness and Cultural Achievement from Independence to the Civil War* (London, 1977); Myra Jehlen, *American Incarnation: The Individual, the Nation, and the Continent* (Cambridge, MA, 1986); Christopher Looby, "The Constitution of Nature: Taxonomy and Politics in Jefferson, Peale, and Bartram," *EAL,* 22 (1987): 252-273; Berta Grattan Lee, "William Bartram: Naturalist or 'Poet'?" *EAL,* 7 (1972): 124-129; Edward Nygren, "From View to Vision," in Nygren, ed., *Views and Visions: American Landscape before 1830* (Washington, D.C., 1986), 3-81; Catherine L. Albanese, *Nature Religion in America: From the Algonkian Indians to the New Age* (Chicago, 1990); William Martin Smallwood, *Natural History and the American*

Mind (New York, 1941); Glacken, *Traces on the Rhodian Shore*; Roxanne M. Gentilcore, "The Classical Tradition and American Attitudes Towards Nature in the Seventeenth and Eighteenth Centuries," Ph.D. diss., Boston University, 1992; Kastner, *Species of Eternity*; Richard Slotkin, *Regeneration Through Violence: The Mythology of the American Frontier, 1600-1860* (Middletown, CT, 1973); Larzer Ziff, *Writing in the New Nation: Prose, Print, and Politics in the Early United States* (New Haven, 1991); Patricia McClintock Medeiros, "The Literature of Travel of Eighteenth-Century America," Ph.D. diss., University of Massachusetts, 1971; Amy R. Weinstein Meyers, "Sketches from the Wilderness: Changing Conceptions of Nature in American Natural History Illustration: 1680-1880," Ph.D. diss., Yale University, 1985.

2. WB, *Travels* [*Travels Through North and South Carolina, Georgia, East and West Florida, The Cherokee Country, the Extensive Territories of the Muscogulges, or Creek Confederacy, and the Country of the Chactaws* (Philadelphia, 1791; London, 1792; New York: Penguin Books, 1981)], 64-65.

3. Amy R. W. Meyers, "Imposing Order on the Wilderness: Natural History Illustration and Landscape Portrayal," in Edward J. Nygren and Bruce Robertson, eds., *Views and Visions: American Landscapes before 1830* (Washington, D.C., 1986), 105-131. I owe my initial insight into William's drawings of the Alachua Savanna to Meyers, who sees his linkage of animals and plants "through reflections of form" (121).

4. WB to Lachlan McIntosh, July 15, 1775 [*sic,* 1774], HSP, Dreer Autograph Collection. The corrected dating was made by Francis Harper, ed., WB, "Travels in Georgia and Florida, 1773-74: A Report to Dr. John Fothergill," *Transactions* of the American Philosophical Society, new series, 33 (Philadelphia, 1943), 188.

5. WB, *Report,* 140.

6. Francis Harper to Charles F. Jenkins, June 25, 1939; March 31, April 19, May 18, 1940; February 12, 1941, Academy of Natural Sciences, MSS/Archives, Coll. 15.

7. WB, *Report,* 123.

8. Ibid., 134.

9. Ibid., 136, 138.

10. Ibid., 160, 164.

11. Outline, BP, box 4, 24, identified in finding aid: "seems to be Wm. Bartram's notes re book on travels (1772)." It is unclear how the document was dated 1772, but it was certainly written before 1777.

12. James Dickey, Introduction, WB, *Travels,* viii-ix.

13. Francis Harper, "Proposals for Publishing Bartram's *Travels,*" *The American Philosophical Society Library Bulletin* (1945): 34.

14. Moore, "Aesthetic Theory of William Bartram," 27-28; WB, *Report*; Francis Harper, ed., *The Travels of William Bartram: Naturalist's Edition* (New Haven, 1958).

15. Jay Fliegelman, *Declaring Independence: Jefferson, Natural Language, and the Culture of Performance* (Stanford, 1994), 60, 76, and passim.

16. Immanuel Kant, *Observations on the Feeling of the Beautiful and Sublime,* John T. Goldthwait, trans. (1764, 1799; Berkeley, 1960); Archibald Alison, *Essays on the Nature and Principles of Taste* (Edinburgh, 1790); William Smellie, *The Philosophy of Natural History* (Edinburgh, 1790; Philadelphia, 1791); Gilbert White, *The Natural History and Antiquities of Selborne, in the County of Southampton* (London, 1789).

17. Virgil, *The Eclogues,* trans. by Guy Lee (New York, 1984); Virgil, *The Georgics,* trans. by L. P. Wilkinson (New York, 1982); Gentilcore, "The Classical Tradition"; Tuveson, "Space, Deity, and the Natural Sublime." [*Modern Language Quarterly,* 12 (1951): 28-38.]

18. Tuveson, *Imagination as a Means of Grace,* 1, 6, 26.

19. Mark Akenside, *The Pleasures of Imagination. A Poem in Three Books* (London, 1763), v, vi, 15, 16.

20. Edmund Burke, *A Philosophical Enquiry into the Origin of Our Ideas of the Sublime and Beautiful* (London, 1767), 7-8.

21. Ibid., 58.

22. WB, *Report,* 164.

23. Ibid., 95 and passim.

24. Tuveson, *Imagination as a Means of Grace,* 26.

25. WB, MS journal, "A Journey from Spaldings lower Trading House to Cuscowilla & the Great Alachua Savanna," HSP, BP, small Bartram volumes.

26. *Cabinet of Natural History and American Rural Sports,* 2 (1832), iii; Francis Harper, "William Bartram and the American Revolution," *Proceedings* of the American Philosophical Society, 97 (1953): 571-577.

Abbreviations Used in the Notes

AHR: *American Historical Review*

APS: American Philosophical Society

BP: Bartram Papers, Historical Society of Pennsylvania

cpb: William Bartram, commonplace book, privately owned

EAL: *Early American Literature*

gb: William Bartram, garden book, Academy of Natural Sciences

HSP: Historical Society of Pennsylvania

LC: Library Company of Philadelphia

JB: John Bartram

JHI: *Journal of the History of Ideas*

NEQ: *New England Quarterly*

NYHS: New-York Historical Society

PC: Peter Collinson

WB: William Bartram

WMQ: *William and Mary Quarterly*

Thomas Hallock (essay date fall 2001)

SOURCE: Hallock, Thomas. "'On the Borders of a New World': Ecology, Frontier Plots, and Imperial Elegy in William Bartram's *Travels*." *South Atlantic Review* 66, no. 4 (fall 2001): 109-33.

[*In the following essay, Hallock traces the development of Bartram's* Travels, *noting its integration of contemporary artistic modes as well as its internal contradictions, and concludes by characterizing the work as one of America's first outstanding pastoral projects.*]

> such attempts I leave for the amusement of men of Letters
>
> —William Bartram[1]

As the movement in any pastoral away from politics will draw politicized critiques, the *Travels* of William Bartram holds a characteristically ambivalent place in the canon of American pastoral literature. Viewed against the environmental writings of its day, the book provides a refreshing alternative to the usual rhetoric of expansion and usurpation, and critics can not discuss the author, it seems, without eventually broaching some form of ethical judgement. Bartram on one hand provides a specimen model of what Mary Louise Pratt calls the "anti-conquest," in that "natural history provided means for narrating inland travel and exploration aimed not at the discovery of trade routes, but at territorial surveillance, appropriation of resources, and administrative control" (39). Citing Pratt so they may dismiss her, on the other hand, sympathetic readers often argue that *Travels* marked the edges of a discourse. Joshua David Bellin writes that the book "unsettles" frontiers, registering "doubts about the absoluteness of Euro-American conceptions of, and claims to, the continent" (3). Ecological critics tend to equate veneration for the natural world with social tolerance. In the Bartram chapter from his remarkable study on the Appalachian Trail, Ian Marshall writes:

> Perhaps the insights of ecology could do more to advance the cause of multiculturalism than any amount of politically correct preaching about tolerance and respect for others. . . . To recognize the advantages of diversity and the verities of interrelationship and interdependency—that is the ecological way of knowing. And it is a habit of mind that translates to the human realm, involving a movement out of self and toward consideration of others, both other living things and other people.
>
> (45-46)

An analogy to the outside world—natural and vaguely benevolent—allows a slave-holder and accomplice to republican expansion—however guarded his positions may have been—to be cast as a lonely voice against imperialism. That these judgements enter a textual reading at all points to the slippery quality of good pastoral writing.

This essay argues that William Bartram artfully defined his status as a border figure and made his the kind of text for which scholars would want to offer apologies. Celebrated by poets but chided in reviews in the 1790s, *Travels* now stands as the first *bona fide* classic of pastoral writing in the United States.[2] Such an ambivalent reception, a position at both the margins and center of a culture, may be attributed to biography and to the book's long gestation. *Travels* in some sense began as a father-son Florida tour in 1765-66. Using a small stipend which came with the elder Bartram's appointment of Botanist to the King, the two journeyed to Carolina, down the coast of Georgia and into central Florida (Berkeley 221-35). A journal by William does not survive but John's notebook (later excerpted for William Stork's promotional tract, *An Account of East Florida*) would become the first *ur*-text of *Travels.* Most of John's *Diary,* in contrast to his often impassioned correspondence, catalogues the uses of a recently-ceded territory in flat, turgid prose—a planter outside Charleston "made surprising improvements in draining salt marshes & converting them into excelent rice fields."[3] *Travels* would unfold over the following decades through oppositional, but empowering, generational dynamics. At a time when William was floundering through a string of professional failures (including a disastrous turn as a planter), the British patron and member of the Royal Society, John Fothergill, offered fifty pounds yearly for a southern tour. Still the son-of-John-Bartram, William left Charleston in 1773, recrossed many sites that he had covered the previous decade, lost himself on new side-paths and excursions, and remained in the wilderness much longer than anyone had expected or requested (Slaughter 172-75). The book evolved quite slowly, as William found a public voice that could capture the veneration his father expressed only in private writing, and as the republic also defined itself.

The various drafts of **Travels** capture this development. An initial **Report to Dr. John Fothergill,** largely the reward for a patron, combines an itinerarium, field notebook, and botanic report in a remarkably plain style, and lacks the self-conscious drama of the later tour. As a work of science, the **Report** balks before the very questions that give shape and meaning to **Travels.** A description of Florida limesinks, for example, noticeably fails to offer commentary:

> I thought it worth your notice, & for that end have indeavourd to give a true Idea of them by a description of their natural & simple appearance: altho the cause & design of them appear evident, yet I am not capable of entering into the various dark mazes in the progress of Nature, & will detain you no longer on my notions of this subject.
>
> (**Report** 156)

Elsewhere the author promises to provide only "the outward furniture of Nature;" he does not trouble the reader with "particular causes or design by Providence, such attempts I leave for the amusement of Men of Letters & Superior genius" (**Report** 138). The scope of his work expanded only as William undertook these "attempts" himself, and by 1783 a manuscript was completed that would contain the core of **Travels.** This recently recovered version recounts lost years in the South with a more defined persona, and it uses Quaker theology to portray the wanderings as a religious quest. Long meditations on the divine operations in nature, held against a corrupt civilization, give the text its idiosyncratic feel. Although the spiritual singularity was later toned down by editors, the manuscript nonetheless shows that an organizing and thematic framework was in place.

With the publication of **Travels** in 1791, Bartram presents what began as a private journey for public consumption. Douglas Anderson, Christopher Looby, Charles H. Adams, and others note that the work provides a parallel or "small scale model" of the Revolution,[4] and revisions to the manuscript underscore those pressures by moving from near-antinomianism to national themes. The genetic text shows little interest in expansion, as its editor Nancy Hoffmann observes, and

portrays nature as a source of inspiration rather than as commodity. The Quaker influence, perhaps suspected as closet Toryism, was squelched; a typical substitution would be "Spirit" (in Native Americans) for the lower-case and theologically-neutral "principle" (Hoffmann 157). Botanic notes in the 1791 version answer the market demand for utilitarian information and the earlier persona of a "philosophical pilgrim" becomes *Puc-Puggy*—a benign hybrid character who straddles two worlds, and who epitomizes the republic's contradictory frontier and Indian policies.[5] A discursive flexibility, born from several stages of revision, qualifies **Travels** tenuously as an example of the "anti-conquest," as the natural history provided a means for surveillance and control. But that was just one mode, and Pratt's term—the "anti-conquest"—has the clear-eyed focus of a contemporary morality tale. The power of Bartram's text lies in its ability to work the in-between, colonialist setting of the early national frontier. To anticipate later conquests misses the slippery position that the post-Revolutionary years and the author's experiences afforded.

An extended textual history to **Travels** instead yields a highly ambivalent work: one that serves as both a critique of American spatial politics and an early contribution to the rhetoric of Manifest Destiny, a utilitarian natural history that was an elegy for disappearing ecologies. Bartram wavers between so many positions that the search for perspective becomes its own theme. From the opening pages, William establishes *his* nature against his father's practical reports. A difference unfolds over generations, one is left to assume, as the two men appear to embody the shift from a colonial/neo-classical to a national/romantic environmental ethos. In nature, the first paragraph opines, "Men and manners undoubtedly hold the first rank. . . ." But that prosaic note, following an upper-case reference to JOHN BARTRAM, bursts into religious euphoria by the next paragraph: "This world, as a glorious apartment of the boundless pattern of the sovereign Creator, is furnished with an infinite variety of animated scenes, inexpressibly beautiful and pleasing, equally free to the inspection and enjoyment of all his creatures" (li). The remainder of the introduction swims between the pressures that would contribute to the work's formation. A botanic catalogue leads into a geographic overview of the United States, then toward a spiritual epiphany, then through a short Florida ramble that is, in current terms, ecocentric: a flower is described, then a spider on a leaf of that plant, then insects and bumble-bees, then a bird that eats that bee, then back to the flower *via* the species that the red thrush prefers (lviii-lx). In contrast to John Bartram's *Diary,* the introduction emphasizes the interdependence of natural species—not their uses by man. A short defense of Native Americans closes the paragraph and the result, a dizzying excursion through several modes, distills the contradictions that would work themselves out over the next five hundred pages.[6]

This blend of voices and genres shows that William Bartram had defined the material that was necessary for articulating the peculiar role in which he had found himself. *Travels* resonates powerfully, both within and against an imperial discourse, because it synthesizes several layers from a long composition process. The ambivalence that results is especially rich, as critics have noted, because his position paralleled debates that lay before the new nation. On one hand, an ideology of progress across space remained prevalent throughout the early republic and would appear in any piece of geographic writing of the time. William Bartram is not above advancing such a view, and surveys border regions for future development. He would visit planters, botanize on the edges of their farms, and express the compulsion to have marshes drained into arable fields. Yet a veneration for wilderness, often read as an empathy with its inhabitants, also fuels his prose. Bartram nursed a deep biocentrism that set him at the borders of a literature, and the immersion in place would move his almost contemporary ethos beyond John's more mainstream views. This shift would render possible a response to an early national anxiety, the need to define an individual and society as American. Negotiating the tensions that Gordon Sayre identifies in contemporaneous reports of Indian mounds (243), Bartram maintains an ambivalence that softens political pressures through aesthetics. The erstwhile developer expresses astonishment over "wild scenes of landscape;" *Puc-Puggy*, meanwhile, may exclaim "how is the mind agitated and bewildered, at being thus, as it were, placed on the borders of a new world!" (120) But the cause for this exclamation would remain significantly ambiguous, and does not necessarily set the work against expansion. Was this new world, in other words, central Florida or a geographically-defined republic? And what would become of Native Americans as the nation increasingly defined itself through wilderness? A response does not require pioneering methodologies or archival research, only a clear-headed review of the text, with attention to its construction and elisions and to loose strands in the existing scholarship.

TRANSFORMATIONS, PERSONAL AND POLITICAL

Put in the simplest of terms, the lasting resonance in *Travels* comes from its ability to weave into plot what were and still are topics of national debate. Thomas Slaughter notes in a popular biography how the strained relations between a father and son would translate into cultural anxieties that persist to this day:

> Compared to his father, William was a more romantic, less constrained, celebrant of wild nature. William also had mixed feelings about civilization as a consequence

of his inability to find a place where he fit. Whether he realized the complex, sometimes conflicted, nature of his thinking, he didn't edit the *Travels* for false consistency. That's why some readers have pegged him—based on their reading of this one writing of his—as a natural, who favored the wild over civilized life, while others have seen him—again based solely on a reading of the *Travels*—as another European exploiter of virgin lands and native peoples.

(Slaughter 185)

The younger Bartram presses ethical positions by hovering between environmental ethos, thereby framing future usurpations and ecological changes against a set of open questions. A skepticism over civilization, carried over from the genetic text, would seem to anticipate present and presumably more enlightened views. (For this reason, *Travels* fits comfortably into a canon of pastoral literature that privileges later authors like Thoreau, John Muir, and Aldo Leopold while glossing earlier, and sometimes, equally uninteresting colonial writers.) The narrative operates through archetypes, in classic Adamic form, as the individual steps outside society, meets a raw nature that he cannot control then reforges a new identity through that experience (Arner 133). This well-worn plot does not define *man in wilderness*, so much as it traces a progress from familiar settlements into trackless beyonds. There could not be of course a more European motif. Leo Marx's observation that a pastoral derives from the "urge to withdraw from civilization's growing power and complexity" (9) indicates the dichotomy at the root of any classically "green" mythos. And so competing Bartrams—father and son, the exploiter and the natural, the manuscript and print personae—find commerce in a single text.

This pattern will become evident by the close of part 1, the Carolina and Georgia tour, which provides a kind of keynote to *Travels*. "At the request of Dr. Fothergill, of London," the narrator sets out, "I embarked for Charleston" (1). Having received these instructions from the metropolitan center, he follows the steps of securing a route, checking the political waters, and gathering letters of introduction. When Bartram crosses the line into "wild" country, he lets the reader know. "It may be proper to observe," he notes on the Altamaha River, "that I had now passed the utmost frontier of the white settlements on that border" (14). His entrance (in case readers miss the shift) gets punctuated by an encounter with a lone Seminole, who appears in caricature with a "countenance angry and fierce." The two shake hands, only for the narrator to learn later that the stranger had earlier resolved to kill the next man he met. This episode, while taken from experience, probably occurred in 1776. By folding the scene into the opening pages of the work (1773 in literary time), Bartram telegraphs the thematic ends of his plot. Each succeeding venture onto the frontier, following some sort of trial, would force the often solitary pilgrim to clarify an understanding of

Native Americans and their land. Richard Slotkin observes of this passage that the traveler "descends into the wilderness, finds a kindred spirit in an Indian, and emerges with moral wisdom," but this private change gets freighted with imperial politics. Before returning to the settled regions in part 1, Bartram reviews a controversial Creek cession of Cherokee claims.[7]

Part 2 develops the thematic germ into a fully-realized narrative. Like the shorter Carolina tour the Florida section follows the movement from society to wilderness, and as the solitary wanderer forges an identity for himself, he suggests a new direction for his culture. The literal route moves up the St. John's, crosses Florida twice, and after a (shortened) second upriver adventure, closes with a catalogue of southeastern fauna. Over this loosely-constructed, 250-page stretch, the pilgrim charts a psychic development that would correspond with national anxieties. Editors have noted that Bartram rearranged the order of the earlier *Report,* folding the second St. John's trip into a longer journey;[8] this reshuffling emphasizes a movement to a more organic community in the wilderness. The result would be a hybrid identity, a creative response to the disjunction between the early republic and place. Bartram suggests that, somewhere on the "middle ground" of central Florida, he had become native to the physical environment. Yet the ideological implications for this frontier narrative, at least in Bartram's hands, have come under surprisingly little scrutiny. The work rarely receives examination as a coherent whole (critics usually deal with passages in isolation), and ecological readings often focus upon the veneration of wilderness for its own sake—sometimes addressing form, but rarely addressing the role that wilderness served in light of expansion.[9] Yet a political thrust, what the eleven chapters of the Florida tour set out to do, becomes clear by the end of the section. In the penultimate chapter (chapter 10), Bartram pauses the travelogue to offer a lengthy discourse on fauna. It is a strange digression, one that includes observations from years later,[10] and the gap in chronology begs the question why such information gets disclosed here. A more conventional organization might have tucked the natural history into an appendix, creating an equivalent to the ethnography in part 4.

The intention was to destabilize lines between the personal and scientific. In keeping with an affective science, the tableau opens with Bartram at Spalding's lower store. He is "drawing some curious flowers," awaiting the schooner that would return him to Georgia, when a diamondback rattler slithers into camp. At first the naturalist tries to ignore the ruckus that follows, but a group of Seminoles call his name—it being Bartram's "pleasure," they amusingly protest, "to collect all their animals and other natural productions of their land." *Puc-Puggy* should now "collect" the "natural production" of a pit viper. He clocks the snake with one blow of a stick, cuts off its head and carries the trophy home. (Three Seminole men later try to scratch blood from the white hero to make him "more mild and tame," a gesture that may have been teasing or may have been meant to "appease the manes of the slain rattle snake" [166-67]). This wonderfully related story makes possible the shift from a narrative-experiential to descriptive-taxonomic mode, and in narrative logic, outlines the path that a particular specimen took from field to cabinet. Bartram files the snake head in his collection, draws it and sends the sketch to London. The zoological drawings would eventually work their way into the British Museum, and the episode from *Travels* provides the pretense for an overview of Southern fauna (Ewan 79).

The taxonomizing comes at the very end of the journey and notably follows a series of *criss-crossing* excursions throughout East Florida. Again, why there? The arrangement of these chapters points to a question of legitimacy; it asks the readers to ask how one comes to know. For early national writers especially, an emphasis upon gathering would signify its own kind of cultural revolution. Consider by contrast the opening of Mark Catesby's *Natural History of Carolina, Florida, and the Bahama Islands,* the standard source on American birds: with an "inclination . . . being much suppressed by my residing too far from London, the center of all science, I was deprived of all opportunities and examples to excite me to a stronger pursuit after those things to which I was naturally bent." The ornithologist then moves from the "center of all science" to a periphery. "Virginia was the place," the colonial author continues, "where I arrived the 23rd of April 1712" (137). One best describes the continent by inhabiting it, Bartram suggests, by losing one's self within its space and not just visiting. His narrative links an often directionless travelogue and the taxonomic tables because the basis of authority had been wandering. The discussion of snakes—and in fact, the entire chapter—begins with the story of how he obtained a sample upon the eve of his departure. The catalogue that follows is accordingly both authoritative and anecdotal, scientific and poetic. Herpetological notes come with an apology for the author's pacifism, his reluctance to kill a rattler in other cases, and biographical reflections on John Bartram (168-69). The table corrects several omissions by Catesby, and offers a gentle but persistent defense of what was presumably a Revolutionary method. By remaining in one place through the course of seasons, through what *Puc-Puggy* calls his "peregrinations," one discovers and better understands a wider variety of species (180).

These corrections reflect a growing sense of independence, a kind of literary analogue to Charles Willson Peale's famous raising of the curtain, that was imagined over an American border region. Yet the premium upon place would remain unique to Bartram. More than any work of its time, *Travels* defines the world ecologically, taking into account "the full diversity *and* complex unity of nature." It organizes flora and fauna around ecosystems; where a Linnaean model divided and classified, Charles Adams notes, "William Bartram remained open to the possibility of unity and complexity in all forms of life" ("Reading" 70). What the language indicates, the mixture of the technical and poetic, is a shift to recognize authority from both sides of the Atlantic. It speaks for a way of knowing that is experiential and therefore rooted in locale. The innovation in narrative strategy, I would argue, responds to an uncertainty over the republic's colonial roots. Bartram offers a corrective to imported government and culture: not so much an allegory for the past war as the product of a society's still tenuous identification with the physical terrain. His word for four years in the South, "peregrinations," uses a prefix that is strikingly non-linear. In a very different book, Timothy Dwight would distinguish the term "emigration" (to leave Europe) from "immigration" (wherein a "stream of population . . . flows *into* the United States" [Dwight 4:200]). As Dwight would monitor environmental changes wrought by the colonization of New England, the older landscapes that he documents hold less appeal. Bartram by contrast describes a tangential path; he internalizes a pre-settlement countryside by wandering the *peri*phery or *peri*meter.

The premium on place, especially when set against other republican accounts, may help explain the elegiac quality of *Travels*. For the resonance in Bartram's pastoral impulse comes from his continual effort to graft the conventional narrative of progress onto a more ecological form of writing. In the midst of his catalogue, the naturalist apologizes by emphasizing the commercial value of his work. *Puc-Puggy* describes how he figured out a puzzle; he cites the advantage of inhabiting a region and (in a semantic equation between himself and his subject) notes that ornithology is best practiced by "residing a whole year at least in the various climates from north to south to the full extent of their peregrinations." Behind the haphazard process of discovery lurks a need for the son of John Bartram to redeem himself:

> There may be perhaps some persons who consider this enquiry not to be productive of any real benefit to mankind, and pronounce such attention to natural history merely speculative, and only fit to amuse and entertain the idle virtuoso; however, the ancients thought otherwise, for with them, the knowledge of the passage of birds was the study of their priests and philosophers, and was considered a matter of real and indispensible use to the state, next to astronomy, as we find their system and practice of agriculture was in a great degree regulated by the arrival and disappearance of birds of passage, and perhaps a calender under such a regulation at this time, might be useful to the husbandman and the gardener.
>
> (178)

The conflicting personae of *Travels* here find a textual venue. William manages to negotiate, even if only for a moment, between the utilitarian basis of republican natural histories and a pilgrim soul. And this commerce between the two worlds may just be the real destination of *Travels*. The book offers an appreciation of wilderness against a backdrop of rapid change; it establishes an identity that is fully attached to neither Anglo nor Native American societies but somehow capable of embodying them both.

What brought the narrative to this moment? The account of migration suggests a kind of imaginative claim to the continent, but it does so through partly biographical tensions. Caught between pragmaticism and a veneration that his father felt but did not publicly express, William invariably would have to contradict himself, and an unsteady pastoralism saves the work from committing too deeply to any one side. *Travels* presents the classic instance of a machine in the garden, but as remains the case always in the American pastoral, an elegy comes at the face of changes that the author does not completely reject. This is not to say, as with most "green" writers, that *Puc-Puggy* was ready to turn back the dumptrucks of civilization. For his romanticism reflects an awareness of incipient change that came with expansion, nor does a categorized wilderness ever move the work beyond the expediencies of an Anglo-European natural history. Even by establishing himself on the borders of print culture, William apparently would remain within the discursive boundaries of his genre. That part 2 closes between a biocentric and anthrocentric stance, therefore, should come as no surprise. He had been working the narrative to that ambivalence over the previous nine chapters. A review of the unit will show how the highly personal transformation, from son of John Bartram to *Puc-Puggy*, could supply the fabric for national myth.

Following the plot that part 1 had established, the Florida tour begins with a farewell to the more settled regions. The narrator again collects letters of introduction and cannot view the Atlantic barriers islands without suggesting why they have remained undeveloped (37-43). A route up the St. John's from the abandoned Fort Picolata (near St. Augustine) carries the author across a difficult psychological landscape. He had visited the post in 1765, and further upriver was the site of his old plantation—a stinging reminder of his past lack of focus. These memories being what a traveler struggles to leave behind, the path—or the literary one at least—delivers him to an increasingly solitary state. Settlements have a way of disappearing from the text (the *Report to Fothergill* reads more like an agricultural report), and the narrator makes no mention of the former homestead when he approaches it. Any repressed doubts surface only as meditations on a new identity. When a companion quits the "hardships and dangers" of exploration, the philosophical pilgrim declares his purpose:

> continually impelled by a restless spirit of curiosity . . . my chief happiness consisted in tracing and admiring the infinite power, majesty and perfection of the great Almighty Creator, and in the contemplation, that through divine aid and permission, I might be instrumental in discovering, and introducing into my native country, some original productions of nature, which might become useful to society.
>
> (48)

The statement poises William Bartram, the son of the Botanist to King George III, on the verge of becoming *Puc-Puggy,* a complete individual who could serve an American republic on his own terms.

Biographical pressures and a larger historical geography would provide the grist for plot. Following the traveler into the wilderness and toward a more complete realization of self, chapter 4 closes with a scene of primitive fellowship outside corrupt society. In a passage that editors would tone down from the genetic manuscript, Bartram joins a backwoods feast: "The simple and necessary calls of nature, being satisfied," he joyously notes, "[w]e were together as brethren of one family, strangers to envy, malice and rapine."[11] Companions disappear from the narrative and leave the hero bare before nature. The beginning of a solitude is painted with an appropriately flamboyant brush. "At the upper end of this bluff is a fine Orange grove," the text explains:

> Here my Indian companion requested me to set him on shore, being already tired of rowing under a fervid sun, and having for some time intimated a dislike of his situation, I readily complied with his desire, knowing the impossibility of compelling an Indian against his own inclinations . . . when labour is in the question; before my vessel reached the shore, he sprang out of her and landed, when uttering a shrill and terrible whoop, he bounded off like a roebuck, and I lost sight of him.
>
> (74)

A trader actually accompanied the "solitary traveler" to Spalding's upper store (**Report** 151-54); what the account sacrifices in accuracy, however, it gains in dramatic effect, as the scene—punctuated by the "shrill and terrible whoop"—foreshadows an extended immersion in the natural sublime. What better cauldron for psychological change, after all, than a lonely wanderer in a hostile wilderness? After this scene, the narrator experiences nature in its most terrifying forms—the alligators and the hurricane (not then in season) that usually appear in anthologies. These encounters are followed by a series of highly-charged effusions, where nearly every paragraph starts with an exclamation:

"What a most beautiful creature is this fish before me! (97)"; "What a beautiful display of vegetation is here before me!" (98); "Behold . . . a vast circular expanse before you" (105). The border experience works through a standard plot (one that is every bit as Anglo-European as the unreliable Indian who abandons Bartram). These familiar chapters require little commentary, except to note how the sublime jars the unproductive son toward a new self. The allegorized journey would allow the author to articulate the polarities that he embodied. By casting observations from two ascents of the river as one tour, the author sets up the christening of *Puc-Puggy,* and the theme shifts from the classic man-in-wilderness to a white-man-among-Native-Americans. After exploring the St. John's, William joins a trading company to the Alachua Savanna, then crosses the isthmus again *en route* to Talahasochte, a Seminole town on the Suwannee. Textual evidence suggests that these lateral journeys represented the core of ***Travels*,**[12] and the bio-historical tensions of the introduction would converge by the latter half of part 2. The setting would provide a medium within which one could contrast utilitarian reportage and a proto-romantic ecological sense, balancing the pressures of an expanding nation and the rights of Native Americans.

A psychic transformation foments a new social self, and the Alachua Savanna provides the grounds wherein a private and public William Bartram meet. It is, appropriately, where his identity as a botanist is recognized. (This identity, in turn, renders as possible the catalogue that closes chapter 10.) In Cuscowilla, a Seminole town that bordered the savanna, Cowkeeper renames the author and opens the country in one sentence:

> He received me with complaisance, giving me unlimited permission to travel over the country for the purpose of collecting flowers, medicinal plants, & c. saluting me by the name of PUC PUGGY or the Flower hunter, recommending me to the friendship and protection of his people.
>
> (118)

The apparent innocence with which *Puc-Puggy* is received, however, betrays the obvious uses of exploration. On one hand, Bartram had earned the trust of Native Americans. *Travels* (and his unpublished writings especially) show a concern for indigenous peoples that was exceptional for eighteenth-century America. But as the preface to an account by John Bartram would note, "knowledge must precede a settlement" (*Observations* iii), and plant gathering rarely served the neutral function that Cowkeeper is portrayed to assume. Just a few pages prior to the promise of "unlimited permission," *Puc-Puggy* would identify "a fine situation for a capital town" (115). William would adopt the Seminole name as his own, in other words, but he was grounded in the politics of a civilization moving across space.

Attempting to establish an identification with place on the most uncertain of terms, the author must wrestle with problems that were endemic to republican frontier politics. Through what narrative machinery, the book asks, could an Anglo-American become native to the continent? Standing on the edge of the savanna, contemplating "the unlimited, varied, and truly astonishing native wild scenes of landscape," Bartram bursts out in an unconscious quote of the *Tempest,* "how is the mind agitated and bewildered, at being thus, as it were, placed on the borders of a new world!" (120). In keeping with standard aesethic formulas, this "native wild landscape" conveys an equivalent social order. Anthropomorphic hills and groves "re-echo" the "cheerful, social voices" of the "lordly bull" and cattle; "squadrons" of horses, and "civilized communities of the sonororous crane, mix together." When a hunter appears on the scene, the "bounding roe . . . erects the white flag" as a warning to his "fleet and free associates" (119-20). Dusk finds the cranes returning to their roost as one unit:

> The sonorous savanna crane, in well disciplined squad-rons, now rising from the earth, mount aloft in spiral circles, far above the dense atmosphere of the humid plain; they again view the glorious sun, and the light of day still gleaming on their polished feathers, they sing their evening hymn, then in a strait line, majestically descend, and alight on the towering Palms or lofty Pines, their secure and peaceful lodging places.

The travelers follow suit: "All around being still and silent, we repair to rest" (121). Although a private and poetic epiphany, one that could be set on the page as verse, the scene speaks to the ideological geography of a new nation. The Alachua Savanna seems to slide between the stages of Anglo-American space, embracing both neo-classical environmentalism and a contemporary biocentrism. Cuscowilla itself straddles that temporal-spatial frontier line which presumed to split settlement from wilderness. With seemless transitions, the scenery moves from settlement to farm to wilderness. The plain will remain a border region even to the native inhabitants, while the "town stands on the most pleasant situation"; Bartram writes, "such a rural scene, is not be imitated by the united ingenuity and labour of man" (123). Alongside the savanna, villagers maintain a farm so that a portion of nature remains undeveloped—where even the deer can raise their "white flag" and escape a Seminole hunter. This sense of an historical geography explains the fascination with ruins that Gordon Sayre has elsewhere examined (239-42). "Passing through a great extent of ancient Indian fields," Bartram notes evidence of "the ancient Alachua, the capital of that famous and powerful tribe." He remarks upon "stately trees," the abandoned orange groves and "luxuriant herbage," and he explains how thousands once gathered to play ball on these "happy fields and green plains" (126). The question that has been identified in Indian monuments also informs Bartram's portrayal of the Alachua Savanna: what kind of nation could the back country nurture?[13]

But the artistry here comes from the ability to weigh the prospects of expansion versus existing uses for the land, and a commerce between a social and natural order, where cranes fly in "squadrons" and bulls bellow "socially," gets embedded so deeply into the prose that neither author nor audience need examine its implications too deeply. A remarkably slippery account results. Bartram fails either to endorse or castigate civilization as he knows it; instead, he allows the text to amble within the dichotomies that his contemporaries defined. He negotiates a still-open problem through what would become a national pastoral. On a second journey across Florida, Bartram again encounters some sandhill cranes. He provides a simple but majesterial account of the bird, describing its height and wingspan, the shape of its body, its plumage, and he makes a breathtaking analogy between the sound of quills in flight and the creak of an ocean vessel. Like Audubon who would follow him, however, Bartram revels over what has been killed. His companions dress the fowl for soup, and while *Puc-Puggy* may prefer its "seraphic music in the etherial skies" to the food in his dish, William would still eat (140). A similar if not more serious conflict surfaces at Talahasochte. The natives again give Bartram leave to wander the territory, this time equating his role of botanist with a symbolic adoption:

> The king in particular complimented me, saying that I was as one of his own children or people, and should be protected accordingly, while I remained with them, adding, 'Our whole country is before you, where you may range about at pleasure, gather physic plants and flowers, and every other production. . . .'
>
> (150)

But three pages earlier, Bartram had recommended soil for "Corn, Rice, Indigo, Sugar-cane, Flax, Cotton, Silk, Cochineal and all the varieties of esculent vegetables" (148). The frontier again is sited for future plantations. Although he had conceded in the prior passage that development would depend upon the Seminoles ("sovereigns of these realms"), the author shows an alarming ability to shift allegiances. He skirts the vague boundary between admiration and (for lack of a better word) consumption.

Although *Travels* has been described as generally formless, as not "tidy" (Irmscher 37), a movement nonetheless is visible by the close of part 2. The trust shown to *Puc-Puggy* in central Florida anticipates the coming scientific catalogue. A Seminole chief again opens the land, "Our whole country is before you," and this permission leads to the insistence that *Puc-Puggy* gather the "production" of a rattlesnake. William would define a national space after the symbolic adoption by natives.

He would describe a creolized region, one that Americans could occupy, or "peregrinate" through, and therefore catalogue on their own terms. *Travels* maps out a wilderness that moves so seemlessly across arbitrary boundaries of the frontier that readers to this day are loathe to scrutinize its historical basis—which is, of course, what pastoral writing does.

<h2 style="text-align:center">EXPANSION AND ELEGY</h2>

Ethical judgments invariably creep into readings of Bartram, and he has been approached from this angle since the 1790s. The first reviewers took *Travels* as a critique, chafing in particular against the author's erstwhile sympathy for native ties to the land. "The savage alone," an early commentator would gripe,

> might be expected to lament the loss of his hunting grounds; and if he be thus driven to betake himself to any kind of agriculture, he is made a more sociable and useful being by the alteration. On such a continent, there will always be groves enough for the botanist. . . . Swamps, crocodiles, wild beasts of prey, snakes, lizards, musquitoes, rank grass, weeds, and all their putridity, are unfriendly to man, and the enumeration of them is not very inviting to adventurers.

> (qtd. Slaughter 244-45)

These reviews strengthen the claim that Bartram should be read as a liminal figure, a lead that recent critics are wont to follow. Seemingly in sync with a contemporary ecological conscience, his portrayals of both wilderness and its inhabitants pushed the limits of republican expectations. As some scholars note, *Travels* gives as much voice to Native Americans as was then possible; Bellin argues that one should "acknowledge, even in the texts which regard their dispossession, the ability of the Indians to engage their dispossessors in debates over the celebration and use of the land" (19). He means, I think rightly, that Bartram allows at least the *traces* of conflict to surface in his narrative. Ian Marshall uses *Puc-Puggy* as a morality tale.

Yet the compulsion to implicate or absolve an author from an imperial context fails to address what a work like *Travels* manages to accomplish as narrative; that is, to imagine an alternative set of relations without endangering the culture that it purportedly critiques. Bartram would remain always a republican writer, if not a marginal one, and the castigations—especially when read against his more conventional turns—indicate the pressures that framed his book. The counter-narrative that he provides, after all, would depend upon the very ideological geography that he purportedly "unsettles." Herein lie the vagaries—and the suggestive power—of a frontier myth. As settlement must precede a wilderness, the tension between conquest and anti-conquest gets woven into the fabric of plot. My point may seem tendentious, since Bartram held enormously progressive

views toward both nature and Native Americans, but even his most impassioned pleas on their behalf (the equation between land and people being his, not mine) invariably returned to the usual thinking of an empire across space. In a manuscript from the late 1780s, **"Some Hints & Observations concerning the civilization of the Indians, or Aborigenes of America,"** Bartram makes two puzzling assertions. He first argues that the "Muscoges or Cricks" were "strongly inclined to our modes of civilization," willing to adopt Anglo-European agriculture, when in fact they were not (Waselkov and Braund 197-98). Second, he stakes a claim on the basis of conscience that equates the continent's future with the republic. "Let us my Brethren convince the world," Bartram writes,

> that the Citizens of the United States are Men in every Sense. Let us support our dignity in all things. Let our actions, in this memorable *age of our establishment, as a nation or People,* be as a Mirror to succeeding Generations. Let us leave to our Children, a monument inscribed with Lessons of Virtue, which may remain from age to age, as approved examples for their Posterity: that they, in similar cases may say to one another; see how benevolently, how gratefully[,] how nobly, our forefathers acted!

> (Waselkov and Braund 198)

With its address to the future, this vexing document parallels the pastoral strategy that governs *Travels*. Bartram argues for fair treatment on the basis of Native Americans' capacity to adopt a largely white economy, then puts its persuasive thrust behind the anticipated legacies of the Revolution. The manuscript is elegiac before the fact and organized around apology.

Regardless of sincere hopes for peace, Bartram would always provide a way around the brute pressures of expansion. An appeal to later generations—oppositional on the surface only—strengthens the identification of a self in republican community, and like *Travels,* "Short Hints" anticipates future usurpations. The author in this way registers the prospects of loss without confronting their causes; he regrets expansion while paradoxically contributing to the literature of expansion. An elegy for the lost garden, Leo Marx noted decades ago, was rendered possible by the inescapable truth of the machine. Pastoralism accordingly operates in *Travels* against a backdrop of incipient land development. Even the most cherished passages, where the author is rapt within an entirely contemporary view, can revert to the level of a utilitarian report. On his return from Talahasochte, Bartram would re-visit the site of his prior transformation, the Alachua Savanna. His second portrayal of the plain reveals a developer's side, not *Puc-Puggy's.* "Next day we passed over part of the great and beautiful Savanna," the narrator explains,

> whose exuberant green meadows, with the fertile hills which immediately encircle it, would if peopled and cultivated after the manner of the civilized countries of

Europe, without crouding or incommoding families, at a moderate estimation, accomodate in the happiest manner, above one hundred thousand human inhabitants, besides millions of domestic animals; and I make no doubt this place will at some future day be one of the most populous and delightful seats on earth.

(158)

One might discount this nod to utilitarian literature as *pro forma,* but no amount of qualification ("without crouding," "accomodate in the happiest manner") can palliate the blunt language of usurpation here—what Pratt calls the "anti-conquest." An awareness of change lurks behind or, better put, defines an identification with the back country in its then-current state. In this case, Bartram was aware of designs by the planter Joseph Bryan (whom he visited in 1776) to secure a 99-year lease for the savanna.[14] That the Seminoles did not agree does not change the mood of this passage.

As a desire to evade lies at the crux of *Travels,* narrative and counternarrative together provide a governing structure. The discovery of a new social identity may drive the plot of part 2, but a central vantage point remains the republican plan; the author's aesthetics are tied to the prospects of change, even if oppositionally. Border regions are portrayed as anterior to civilization, and a politics of progress across space—while softened by symbolic adoptions—would inform Bartram's representations of both the wilderness and its inhabitants. Although elsewhere in the book and in manuscripts especially, the author would provide fair and accurate descriptions of southeast peoples, the private author must define his voice in a print community. The faith that an Other would join the march of progress allowed him to accept the name *Puc-Puggy* while being aware of plans to develop lands that were clearly being used. The outcome of the southern territories would become its own story, as the close of the Jeffersonian plan led to removal and new configurations in frontier narratives, but this moment of irresolution for the time being would yield rich results in *Travels.* The story of a personal transformation bridges eighteenth-century and romantic attitudes toward nature and natives, and the resulting pastoralism (bolstered by pleas for fairness) creates a wilderness that is at once European and local. The evolution of a persona would provide the solution for a work that sought to incorporate the spatial geography of the new republic, a growing identification with place, and an inclination to be indigenous to the continent. A literary natural history, an early masterpiece of environmental writing in the United States, materializes from the open conflicts of that specific moment. A measure of the work's genius, a *coup* for its plot, is the continued compulsion of readers to echo an apology that was made over two hundred years ago.

Notes

1. William Bartram, *Report* (156). This quotation has relevance as well for the author: my thanks to

Nancy Hoffmann, John Hiers, Gary E. Cooper, Julie Armstrong, and to the anonymous reviewers of this journal for their help with this article.

2. On literary significance, see N. Bryllion Fagin; reception is discussed in *The Travels of William Bartram: Naturalist Edition,* ed. Francis Harper (xviii-xxviii); a standard geneology that places Bartram at the beginning of a tradition is Thomas J. Lyon (276-81).

3. John Bartram *Diary of a Tour* (13); In John Seelye's words, "we have only to lay one journal next to the other to measure the generational gap" (41).

4. See Douglas Anderson (13), Christopher Looby (260-61), Charles H. Adams, "William Bartram's *Travels.* A Natural History of the South" (114). Edward J. Cashin, by contrast, explores the absence of a political context (663-72).

5. On the genetic text, see Nancy Hoffmann (51-68); on Quaker politics and voice, see Slaughter (195-96).

6. Critics describe *Travels* as anything from "polyphonic" to a "ragbag": on the various rhetoric modes, see Larry R. Clarke (435); Charles H. Adams, "William Bartram's *Travels.* A Social History of the South" (119); James Dickey (ix); N. Brillion Fagin (102); Christoph Irmscher (37).

7. Slotkin (326); for discussions of the New Purchase, see Eve Kornfield (300) and Joshua David Bellin (1-3); on Bartram and the lone Seminole, see Waselkov and Braund (35, 231).

8. See Francis Harper's notes in *Travels* (353), *A Report to Dr. John Fothergill* (130).

9. Ian Marshall mines *Travels* for a contemporary, multicultural allegory in "Puc Puggy in the Nantahalas: The Turning Point of William Bartram's *Travels*" (35-50).

10. Bartram confesses that "I have never travelled the continent south of New Orleans," when to this point he had not been West of Florida (*Travels* 179).

11. *Travels* (71). The draft reads, "we contemplated no other pleasure than what naturally arises from the rational and moderate gratification of the Passions & Appetite given to us by the Great and bountiful Deity" (Hoffman 153).

12. Bartram began to describe the Florida plain while still in the woods and he folded this draft, with corrections, almost verbatim into the later manuscript. A 1786 broadside later used this scene to promote the work (Slaughter 188).

13. On Bartram's stylized response to the environmental politics of the American Revolution, see

also Adams, "William Bartram's *Travels*. "A Natural History of the South" (115), Anderson (14).

14. Alan Gallay (94, 145-46), Waselkov and Braund (202, 243).

Works Cited

Adams, Charles H. "Reading Ecologically: Language and Play in Bartram's *Travels*." *The Southern Quarterly* 32.4 (1994): 65-74.

———. "William Bartram's *Travels*: A Natural History of the South." *Rewriting the South: History and Fiction*. Ed. Lothar Hönninghausen and Valeria Gennaro Lerda. Tübingen: Francke, 1993.

Anderson, Douglas. "Bartram's *Travels* and the Politics of Nature." *Early American Literature* 25.1 (1990): 3-17.

Arner, Robert D. "Pastoral Patterns in William Bartram's *Travels*." *Tennessee Studies in Literature* 18 (1973): 133-45.

Bartram, John. *Diary of a Tour through the Carolinas, Georgia, and Florida from July 1, 1765 to April 10, 1766*. *Transactions of the American Philosophical Society* 33.1. Ed. Francis Harper. Philadelphia: American Philosophical Society, 1942.

———. *Observations on the inhabitants, climate, soil, rivers, productions animals, and other matters worthy of notice . . . by Mr. John Bartram, in his travels from Pensilvania to Onondago, Oswego and the lake Ontario in Canada*. London: 1751.

Bartram, William. *The Travels of William Bartram: Naturalist's Edition* [*Travels through North & South Carolina, Georgia, East & West Florida, the Cherokee Country, the Extensive Territories of the Muscogulges, or Creek Confederacy, and the Country of the Chactaws*]. Ed. Francis Harper. Athens: U of Georgia P, 1998.

———. *Travels Through North & South Carolina, Georgia, East & West Florida, the Cherokee Country, the Extensive Territories of the Muscolgulges, or Creek Confederacy, and the Country of the Chactaws*. Intro. James Dickey. New York: Penguin, 1988.

———. *Travels in Georgia and Florida, 1773-74: A Report to Dr. John Fothergill*. *Transactions of the American Philosophical Society* 33.2. Ed. Francis Harper. Philadelphia: American Philosophical Society, 1943.

———. *William Bartram: Botanical and Zoological Drawings, 1756-1788*. *Memoirs of the American Philosophical Society* 74. Ed. Joseph Ewan. Philadelphia: American Philosophical Society, 1968.

Bellin, Joshua David. "Wicked Instruments: William Bartram and the Dispossession of the Southern Indians." *Arizona Quarterly* 52.3 (1995): 1-23.

Berkeley, Edmund & Dorothy Smith Berkeley. *The Life and Travels of John Bartram: From Lake Ontario to the River St. John*. Tallahassee: U Press of Florida, 1982.

Cashin, Edward J. "A 'Philosophical Pilgrim' on the Southern Frontier: New Approaches to William Bartram." *The Georgia Historical Quarterly* 81.3 (1997): 663-72.

Catesby, Mark. *Catesby's Birds of Colonial America*. Ed. Alan Feduccia. Chapel Hill: U of North Carolina P, 1985.

Clarke, Larry R. "The Quaker Background of William Bartram's View of Nature." *Journal of the History of Ideas* 46.3 (1985): 435-48.

Dwight, Timothy. *Travels in New England and New York*. Ed. Barbara Miller Solomon. Cambridge: Harvard UP, 1969.

Earnest, Ernest P. *John and William Bartram: Botanists and Explorers*. Philadelphia: U of Pennsylvania P, 1940.

Fagin, N. Bryllion. *William Bartram: Interpreter of the American Landscape*. Baltimore: Johns Hopkins UP, 1933.

Gallay, Allan. *The Formation of a Planter Elite: Jonathan Bryan and the Colonial Southern Frontier*. Athens: U of Georgia P, 1989.

Hoffmann, Nancy E. *The Construction of William Bartram's Narrative Natural History: A Genetic Text of the Draft Manuscript for "Travels through North and South Carolina, Georgia, East and West Florida."* Dissertation: University of Pennsylvania, 1996.

Irmscher, Christoph. *The Poetics of Natural History: From John Bartram to William James*. New Brunswick: Rutgers UP, 1999.

Jefferson, Thomas. *Notes on the State of Virginia*. Ed. William Peden. Chapel Hill: U of North Carolina P, 1954.

Kornfield, Eve. "Encountering 'the Other': American Intellectuals and Indians in the 1790s." *William and Mary Quarterly* Third Series, 52.10 (1995): 286-314.

Looby, Christopher. "The Constitution of Nature: Taxonomy and Politics in Jefferson, Peale, and Bartram." *Early American Literature* 22 (1987): 252-73.

Lyon, Thomas J. "A Taxonomy of Nature Writing." *The Ecocriticism Reader: Landmarks in Literary Ecology*. Ed. Cheryll Glotfelty and Harold Fromm. Athens: U of Georgia P, 1995.

Marshall, Ian. *Story Line: Exploring the Literature of the Appalachian Trail*. Charlottesville: U of Virginia P, 1998.

Marx, Leo. *The Machine in the Garden: Technology and the Pastoral Ideal in America*. New York: Oxford UP, 1964.

Pratt, Mary Louise. *Imperial Eyes: Travel Writing and Transculturation.* London: Routledge, 1992.

Sayre, Gordon M. "The Mound Builders and the Imagination of American Antiquity in Jefferson, Bartram, and Chateaubriand." *Early American Literature* 33.3 (1998): 225-49.

Seelye, John. "Beauty Bare: William Bartram and His Triangulated Wilderness." *Prospects: The Annual of American Cultural Studies* 6 (1981): 37-54.

Slaughter, Thomas P. *The Natures of John and William Bartram.* New York: Knopf, 1996.

Slotkin, Richard. *Regeneration through Violence: The Mythology of the American Frontier, 1600-1860.* Middletown: Wesleyan UP, 1973.

Waselkov, Gregory A. and Kathryn E. Holland Braund. *William Bartram on the Southeastern Indians.* Lincoln: U of Nebraska P, 1995.

FURTHER READING

Biography

Lowes, John Livingston. "Introduction." In *The Travels of William Bartram,* edited by Francis Harper, pp. xvii-xxxv. New Haven: Yale University Press, 1958.

Provides an overview of Bartram's life and career.

Criticism

Branch, Michael. "Indexing American Possibilities: The Natural History Writing of Bartram, Wilson, and Audubon." In *The Ecocriticism Reader,* edited by Cheryll Glotfelty and Harold Fromm, pp. 282-97. Athens: The University of Georgia Press, 1996.

Compares early romantic ideas about nature in the New World.

Curtis, S. E. G. "A Comparison between Gilbert White's *Selborne* and William Bartram's *Travels.*" In *Proceedings of the 7th Congress of the International Comparative Literature Association,* edited by Milan V. Dimic and Juan Ferrate, pp. 137-41. Stuttgart: Kunst Und Wissen, 1979.

Compares and contrasts two works considered works of natural science as well as minor literary classics.

Lee, Berta Grattan. "William Bartram: Naturalist or 'Poet'?" *Early American Literature* 7 (1972): 124-129.

Surveys the tone and substance of Bartram's *Travels* in an attempt to classify the varied literary techniques contained in the work.

Medeiros, Patricia M. "Three Travelers: Carver, Bartram, and Woolman." In *American Literature: 1764-1789 The Revolutionary Years,* edited by Everett Emerson, pp. 195-211. Madison: University of Wisconsin Press, 1977.

Discusses the importance of travel writers such as Bartram to Americans who knew little of the land they were settling.

Sayre, Gordon M. "The Mound Builders and the Imagination of American Antiquity in Jefferson, Bartram, and Chateaubriand." *Early American Literature* 33, no. 3 (1998): 225-49.

Examines the varying perspectives of Bartram and other writers as to the existence and meaning of native American burial mounds.

Silver, Bruce. "Clarke on the Quaker Background of William Bartram's Approach to Nature." *Journal of the History of Ideas* 47, no. 3 (July-Sept. 1986): 507-10.

Examines the issue of Bartram's Quakerism and argues that it was not as great an influence on his writings as some have claimed.

Sullivan, Bill. "Bartram's Romantic Trail." In *Essays on the Literature of Mountaineering,* edited by Armand E. Singer, pp. 26-34. Morgantown, W.Va.: West Virginia University Press, 1982.

Discusses the movement of Bartram toward the romantic perspective exhibited in his *Travels.*

Wurth, Kiene Brillenburg. "Burke, Bartram, and the Sublime: The Spectacle of Death and the Limits of Representation." In *Revolutions and Watersheds: Transatlantic Dialogues 1775-1815,* edited by W. M. Verhoeven and Beth Dolan Kautz, pp. 27-37. Atlanta: Rodopi, 1999.

Examines how Bartram uses the eighteenth-century conception of the sublime to describe and evaluate the instances of death he encountered.

Additional coverage of Bartram's life and career is contained in the following sources published by Thomson Gale: *American Nature Writers*; *Dictionary of Literary Biography,* Vol. 37; and *Literature Resource Center.*

Robert Bloomfield
1766-1823

English poet.

INTRODUCTION

Bloomfield is considered by some critics to have been influential as a forerunner to Romantic poets such as William Wordsworth and Samuel Taylor Coleridge. Raised in the countryside and almost entirely self-taught, Bloomfield was at odds with city life though he lived in London for much of his adulthood. His nostalgia for rural life resulted in a sizeable collection of poems. His first success, *The Farmer's Boy* (1800), earned him considerable popularity with both fellow poets and his reading public. However, neither that poem nor any from his five ensuing collections earned him either wealth or enduring recognition.

BIOGRAPHICAL INFORMATION

Born in 1766 to George, a tailor, and Elizabeth, a school mistress, Bloomfield received an education in his mother's home, briefly supplemented by several months of tutoring paid for by friends. After four years of laboring on his uncle's farm, work for which he was particularly ill-suited due to his slight frame and small stature, he moved to London to work as a shoemaker with his brother George. He was not particularly well-suited to that career either, which resulted in his being assigned the task of reading the newspaper to his fellow cobblers while they worked. That assignment instigated an interest in language and literature that his brother nurtured with the gift of a dictionary and Bloomfield himself cultivated with visits to public lectures and attention to the poetry and reviews published in the *London Magazine*. He began composing poetry in his head while he made shoes, constructing rhyming couplets to facilitate memorization, and eventually composed much of his most famous poem, *The Farmer's Boy,* in that manner. With his brother's help, he found an important patron in the figure of Capel Lofft, a barrister and writer who gave *The Farmer's Boy* to publisher Vernor and Hood. Over the next twenty-three years, he published five more collections of poetry, though without the commercial success of his first. With his wife Mary-Anne Church, whom he had married in 1790, and their two daughters and one son (who struggled with various physical infirmities), he eventually moved from London

in an effort to combat the family's relative poverty. Bloomfield spent the remainder of his life working simultaneously as craftsman (he made harps as well as shoes) and wordsmith. Having had little success in either endeavor, in 1823, Bloomfield died in debt and poor spirits.

MAJOR WORKS

The Farmer's Boy was Bloomfield's greatest success, selling over twenty-six thousand copies in fourteen separate editions. He also published five other collections of poetry, each a scrutiny of some aspect of rural life, as well as a small assortment of prose. Variously labeled a peasant or rural poet, self-taught or unlearned, Bloomfield made his subjects the laboring poor of the countryside. The relationship of country people to their land, their values, and their joys and pains, remained his primary thematic focus throughout his writing career. John Lucas describes him as "the English Theocritus because he writes about a *first world* of rural circumstance, one now gone," and critics frequently note both the influence of and similarities to James Thomson's *The Seasons*. As with the other peasant poets—Stephen Duck, George Crabbe, John Clare, William Cobbett, and James Hogg, among others—his poetry foregrounds experience and sensory perception. *Rural Tales, Ballads, and Songs* (1802), which he wrote while waiting for the publication of *The Farmer's Boy*, succeeded in accurately depicting rural life for some readers, like John Clare, despite Clare's admonition of its "elevated" style. *Good Tidings* (1804), a poem about smallpox vaccination, shifted Bloomfield's subject matter from the rural to the scientific. A children's tale, *The History of Little Davy's New Hat* (1815) was meant to teach rural values, and *Wild Flowers* (1806), pursued similar themes, including a celebration of the harvest festival and country courtships. *The Banks of the Wye* (1811), converts a travel journal to verse, and *May Day with the Muses* (1819), takes as its subject the rural poet himself. In the last year of Bloomfield's life, he produced a dramatic sketch, *Hazelwood Hall* (1823), and one year later, in an effort to raise some funds for Bloomfield's surviving family, Joseph Weston edited and issued *The Remains of Robert Bloomfield* (1824), which includes correspondence as well as "The Bird and Insect Post Office," a natural history for children.

CRITICAL RECEPTION

His contemporaneous critics, in such journals as the *Monthly Review, Critical Review,* and *British Critic,* consistently appreciated Bloomfield's work for its originality and lack of pretension. They celebrated, too, his humanity, his humility, and what many found to be a simple and beautiful use of language, as well as wit in his characterizations and a refreshing absence of either idealization or moral judgment. Though accused of having "a poor mind" by Charles Lamb, Bloomfield found influential supporters in his fellow poets William Wordsworth and John Clare, and critics Robert Southey and William Hazlitt. In the twentieth century, Bloomfield has been both limited and liberated by being primarily considered in the context of the peasant poet. Edmund Blunden, for example, faults Bloomfield for never extending in his work beyond the world he knew, even while he acknowledges *The Farmer's Boy* as "a phenomenal piece of work" in its "tenacious contentment in the bosom of the earth." In *The Rural Muse,* Rayner Unwin finds Bloomfield's poetry exemplary and excellent within the genre of peasant poetry. John Lucas considers the social and political implications of Bloomfield using poetry to redefine himself as a self-taught poet. Bloomfield's most active late-twentieth-century defender, Jonathan Lawson, endorses Bloomfield's modesty and sees a marked moral conviction evident in his characters' values.

PRINCIPAL WORKS

The Farmer's Boy; A Rural Poem [*Le Valet du Fermier*] (poetry) 1800
Rural Tales, Ballads, and Songs (poetry) 1802
Good Tidings; or, News from the Farm (poetry) 1804
Wild Flowers; or, Pastoral and Local Poetry (poetry) 1806
The Banks of the Wye; A Poem (poetry) 1811
The History of Little Davy's New Hat (prose) 1815
May Day with the Muses (poetry) 1822
Hazelwood Hall: A Village Drama (play) 1823
The Remains of Robert Bloomfield (poetry, prose, and letters) 1824
Selections from the Correspondence of Robert Bloomfield, The Suffolk Poet (letters) 1870
Collected Poems, 1800-1822 (poetry) 1971

CRITICISM

Monthly Review, or Literary Journal (review date September 1800)

SOURCE: Review of *The Farmer's Boy,* by Robert Bloomfield. *Monthly Review, or Literary Journal* 32 (September 1800): 50-56.

[*In the following excerpt, the reviewer notes Bloomfield's elevation of his rustic subject through unaffected and eloquent poetry.*]

This poem [**The Farmer's Boy**] is ushered into the world under the obstetric auspices of the ingenious Mr. Capel Lofft, but it is the production of a journeyman shoemaker, who was himself originally destined to be a **Farmer's Boy.** The preface contains some particulars of his life, communicated by his brother to Mr. Lofft; whence it appears that the only literary instructions which he ever had he received from his mother in reading, and from a country schoolmaster in writing, for the space of two or three months. He was afterward sent to London, to his brother, in order to learn to make shoes; and there he continued till, in consequence of the dispute between the journeymen and master shoemakers, in 1784, he returned into the country to his old master, Mr. Austin: who, as the brother says,

> "Kindly bade him take his house for his home till he could return to me. And here, with his mind glowing with the fine Descriptions of rural scenery which he found in THOMSON'S SEASONS, he again retraced the very fields where first he began to think. Here, free from the smoke, the noise, and the contention of the City, he im-

bibed that Love of rural Simplicity and rural Innocence, which fitted him, in a great degree, to be the writer of such a thing as *[T]he Farmer's Boy.*"

"Here he lived two Months: . . . at length, as the dispute in the trade still remained undecided, Mr. DUD-BRIDGE offered to take *Robert* Apprentice, to secure him, at all events, from any consequences of the Litigation."

'He was bound by Mr. *Ingram,* of *Bell-alley,* to Mr. *John Dudbridge.* His Brother *George* paid five shillings for *Robert,* by way of form, as a premium. Dudbridge was their Landlord, and a *Freeman* of the *City of London.* He acted most honourably, and took no advantage of the power which the Indentures gave him. *George Bloomfield* staid with *Robert* till he found he could work as expertly as his self.

'Mr. GEORGE BLOOMFIELD adds, "When I left *London* he was turned of eighteen; and much of my happiness since has arisen from a constant correspondence which I have held with him."

"After I left him, he studied *Music,* and was a good player on the *Violin.*"

"But as my Brother *Nat* had married a *Woolwich* woman, it happened that *Robert* took a fancy to a comely young woman of that Town, whose father is a boat-builder in the Government yard there. His name is CHURCH."

"Soon after he married, *Robert* told me, in a Letter, that 'he had sold his Fiddle and got a Wife.' Like most poor men, he got a wife first, and had to get household stuff afterward. It took him some years to get out of ready furnished Lodgings. At length, by hard working, & c. he acquired a Bed of his own, and hired the room up one pair of stairs at 14, *Bell-alley, Coleman-street.* The Landlord kindly gave him leave to sit and work in the light *Garret,* two pair of stairs higher."

"In *this* Garret, amid six or seven other workmen, his active Mind employed itself in composing ***The Farmer's Boy.***"

"In my correspondence I have seen several *poetical* effusions of his; all of them of a good moral tendency; but which he very likely would think do him little credit: on that account I have not preserved them."

"ROBERT is a *Ladies Shoemaker,* and works for DAVIES, *Lombard street.* He is of a slender make; of about 5 *F.* 4 *I.* high; very *dark* complexion. . . . His MOTHER, who is a very religious member of the *Church of England,* took all the pains she could in his infancy to make him pious: and as his Reason expanded, his love of God and Man increased with it. I never knew his fellow for mildness of temper and Goodness of Disposition. And since I left him, universally is he praised by those who know him best, for the best of Husbands, an indulgent Father, and quiet Neighbour. He is about thirty-two years old, and has three Children."

To describe the various occupations of a farmer's boy, in the four seasons of the year, is the main design of the poem; and however humble these employments may appear as objects of poetical attention, the very ingenious writer has contrived to embellish their rusticity and meanness with a harmony of numbers, which could not be expected from an uncultivated mind; to soften the harshness of minute detail, by blending apt and picturesque descriptions; and to enliven the whole by strokes of poetic imagery, and unaffected sentiment. . . .

Mr. Lofft remarks in the preface, that, on first seeing this poem in MS. and observing that it was divided into the *Four Seasons,* he apprehended that the writer had been vainly endeavouring to follow (in verse) the steps of the admirable Thomson: but that he was soon relieved from that apprehension, on discovering that, 'although the RURAL SCENERY naturally branches itself into these divisions, there was little else except the general qualities of a musical ear; flowing numbers, feeling, pioty, poetic imagery and animation, a taste for the picturesque, a true sense of the natural and pathetic, force of thought, and liveliness of imagination, which were in common between Thomson and this Author.'

The poem certainly discovers very clearly the powers of natural unassisted genius; and we hope that the friends of Robert Bloomfield will take warning from the injudicious treatment of preceding poets in humble stations, (Stephen Duck, Robert Burns, & c.) and not suffer the inconsistency of his turn of mind and his situation in life to prove his ruin, through the baneful influence of flattery, and by *misguided* attempts to befriend merit in obscurity.

British Critic (review date April 1802)

SOURCE: Review of *Rural Tales and Poems,* by Robert Bloomfield. *British Critic* 19 (April 1802): 338-43.

[*In the following excerpt, the author finds Bloomfield's second book an extension of the virtuosity of his first.*]

We are pleasingly called away from our abstruser studies, by these productions of a genuine Child of Nature. In Bloomfield's first Poem, the ***Farmer's Boy,*** we saw and commended the evidence of an original genius, well deserving of encouragement and cultivation[1]. The public has agreed with us, and five editions of that work exhibit the most unequivocal attestation of general favour. Of the author's history, as detailed in the Preface, by Mr. C. Lofft, we gave a sketch in the article referred to in the margin, and we are happy now to add to it, in the words of the author himself:

> "The consequence has been such as my true friends will rejoice to hear; it has procured me many essential blessings: and I feel peculiarly gratified in finding that a poor man in England may assert the dignity of Virtue, and speak of the imperishable beauties of Nature, and be heard; and heard, perhaps, with greater attention for his being poor."

With the *Farmer's Boy* we were highly pleased, because it showed, in the most striking manner, the natural movements of an ingenious mind; and evinced how perfectly new a subject, apparently preoccupied, may be made by taking it in a different view. But we hesitate not to declare ourselves still more satisfied with the present volume. The author here relates Tales, in themselves pleasing, in the language of beautiful simplicity, and natural poetry; or pours forth pastoral Songs, full of pleasing ideas, in a style exactly suited to their expression. Such is the general texture of this volume of Poems; but the intelligence of Peace has tempted the author, at the close of his Preface, to venture into a new line; his success in which, sufficiently demonstrates that his mind has all the versatility of real genius. We much doubt, whether the return of Peace will receive any gratulation more truly poetical than the following Ode. Nor must we omit, in justice to the good heart of the author, the introduction he has prefixed to it.

> Since affixing the above date (Sep. 29, 1801) an event of much greater importance than any to which I have been witness, has taken place, to the universal joy (it is to be hoped) of every inhabitant of Europe. My portion of joy shall be expressed while it is yet warm. And the reader will do sufficient justice, if he only believes it to be sincere.
>
> —Oct. 10.

More than that justice will probably be done by every reader of taste, who will allow it to be animated and poetical.

"Peace."

I.

> "Halt! ye Legions, sheathe your steel:
> Blood grows precious; shed no more:
> Cease your toils; your wounds to heal
> Lo! beams of Mercy reach the shore!
> From realms of everlasting light
> The favour'd guest of Heaven is come:
> Prostrate your banners at the sight,
> And bear the glorious tidings home.

II.

> The plunging corpse with half-clos'd eyes,
> No more shall stain th' unconscious brine;
> Yon pendant gay, that streaming flies,
> Around its idle staff shall twine.
> Behold! along th' etherial sky
> Her beams o'er conquering navies spread;
> Peace! Peace! the leaping sailors cry,
> With shouts that might arouse the dead.

III.

> Then forth Britannia's thunder pours;
> A vast reiterated sound!
> From line to line the cannon roars,
> And spreads the blazing joy around.

> Return, ye brave! your country calls;
> Return; return, your task is done:
> While here the tear of transport falls,
> To grace your laurels nobly won.

IV.

> Albion Cliffs—from age to age,
> That bear the roaring storms of Heav'n,
> Did ever fiercer warfare rage,
> Was ever peace more timely given?
> Wake! sounds of joy: rouse, generous isle;
> Let every patriot bosom glow.
> Beauty, resume thy wonted smile,
> And, Poverty, thy cheerful brow.

V.

> Boast, Britain, of thy glorious guests;
> Peace, Wealth, and Commerce, all thine own:
> Still on contented labour rests
> The basis of a lasting throne.
> Shout, Poverty! 'tis Heaven that saves;
> Protected Wealth, the chorus raise,
> Ruler of War, of Winds, and Waves,
> Accept a prostrate nation's praise."

P. vii.

The four concluding lines of this spirited and feeling Ode rise to sublimity, by their connection with devotion, the expression of which is apposite and solemn. Under such auspices opens this volume; the contents of which we shall now briefly recite.

The first poem is a Ballad, entitled **"Richard and Kate,"** full of the simple beauties which result from the plain and true expression of the best natural feelings. A slight mixture of provincial terms gives it the peculiar cast, which is so pleasing in many poems of Burns. **"Walter and Jane,"** the second poem, is an artless tale of two lovers, related with a simplicity by no means inelegant, in couplet verse; and in a manner calculated to remind the reader of the narrative style of our best English poets. **"The Miller's Maid"** is still more interesting and affecting. The circumstances are novel, and many of the situations new to poetry. The following passage will not perhaps easily be surpassed, for originality and truth. A boy and girl, early exposed to hardships, meet at length in better circumstances.

> "Past deeds now from each tongue alternate fell;
> For news of dearest import both could tell.
> Fondly, from childhood's tears to youth's full prime,
> They match'd the incidents of jogging time;
> And prov'd that when with tyranny oppress'd,
> Poor *Phœbe* groan'd with wounds and broken rest,
> *George* felt no less; was harass'd and forlorn
> A rope's-end followed him both night and morn.
> And in that very storm when *Phœbe* fled,
> When the rain drench'd her yet unshelter'd head;
> That very storm he on the Ocean brav'd,
> The vessel founder'd, and the boy was sav'd!
> Mysterious Heav'n! and O with what delight

She told the happy issue of her flight:
To his charm'd heart a living picture drew,
And gave to Hospitality its due."

P. 46.

The Ballads that follow are all pleasing, and original. **"The Widow and her Hour-Glass,"** is natural and poetical; **"The Fakenham Ghost,"** full of unaffected humour and good moral; **"The French Mariner,"** pathetic; and, **"Dolly,"** pastoral and interesting. But that entitled **"Market Night,"** contains so natural and pleasing a picture of conjugal tenderness, drawn with so much genuine feeling and animation, that no other proof of the author's singular merit can be required by those who read it. . . .

The remaining Poems are few. The Ode occasioned by a visit to Whittlebury Forest, is in a higher strain than the rest; but the author rises with security, because he never loses sight of nature. The Song for **"A Highland Drover,"** has much tenderness and ease; and the remaining small Poems all confirm the claim of Robert Bloomfield to the genuine inspiration of a mind, whose thoughts and feelings naturally turn to poetry.

We are well convinced, that the patronage of the public will attend this little volume, in the same degree as it has the *Farmer's Boy.* Among other favourable testimonies of the author's disposition, we remark his lively gratitude to Mr. Lofft, who had the merit of drawing him from obscurity, and still continues his encomiast, at the close of each Poem. Those observations are certainly dictated by the same laudable zeal which led the writer first to protect and assist Bloomfield; but they are superfluous; and it is rather irksome to readers who can judge for themselves, to be told in every instance, what they ought to think, and how much they should admire. Bloomfield's poetry does not require this aid; and it is hardly fair for the critic to jump up and ride behind him, wherever he may turn his Pegasus. Mr. Lofft is not so often querulous as in some of his other effusions, otherwise we should say,

Post equitem sedet atra cura.

Note

1. See *Brit. Crit.* vol. xv. p. 601.

Critical Review (review date May 1802)

SOURCE: Review of *Rural Tales and Poems,* by Robert Bloomfield. *Critical Review* 35 (May 1802): 67-75.

[*In the following excerpt, the critic asserts that Bloomfield's second work,* Rural Tales, *equals the brilliance of his well-known* The Farmer's Boy.]

This volume cannot be better introduced than by the author's preface—a manly and modest performance, highly honourable to his feelings and his abilities.

'The poems here offered to the public were chiefly written during the interval between the concluding, and the publishing of *The Farmer's Boy,* an interval of nearly two years. The pieces of a later date are, **"The Widow to her Hour-Glass," "The Fakenham Ghost," "Walter and Jane,"** & c. At the time of publishing *The Farmer's Boy,* circumstances occurred which rendered it necessary to submit these poems to the perusal of my friends: under whose approbation I now give them, with some confidence as to their moral merit, to the judgement of the public. And as they treat of village manners, and rural scenes, it appears to me not ill-timed to avow, that I have hopes of meeting in some degree the approbation of my country. I was not prepared for the decided, and I may surely say extraordinary attention which the public has shown towards *The Farmer's Boy*: the consequence has been such as my true friends will rejoice to hear; it has produced me many essential blessings. And I feel peculiarly gratified in finding that a poor man in England may assert the dignity of Virtue, and speak of the imperishable beauties of Nature, and be heard—and heard, perhaps, with greater attention for his being poor.

'Whoever thinks of me or my concerns, must necessarily indulge the pleasing idea of gratitude, and join a thought of my first great friend Mr. Lofft. And on this head, I believe every reader, who has himself any feeling, will judge rightly of mine: if otherwise, I would much rather he would lay down this volume, and grasp hold of such fleeting pleasures as the world's business may afford him. I speak not of that gentleman as a public character, or as a scholar. Of the former I know but little, and of the latter nothing. But I know from experience, and I glory in this fair opportunity of saying it, that his private life is a lesson of morality; his manners gentle, his heart sincere: and I regard it as one of the most fortunate circumstances of my life; that my introduction to public notice fell to so zealous and unwearied a friend.

'I have received many honourable testimonies of esteem from strangers; letters without a name, but filled with the most cordial advice, and almost a parental anxiety, for my safety under so great a share of public applause. I beg to refer such friends to the great teacher Time: and hope that he will hereafter give me my deserts, and no more.'

p. iii.

When we took up *The Farmer's Boy,* no popular opinion had been pronounced upon its merit. Robert Bloomfield was a name unknown to us and to the world; and amid the volumes of insipidity which it is our lot to examine, we were delighted to meet with excellence that we had not expected. The present volume appears with less advantage; it has a more difficult test to encounter. To acquire reputation has ever been easier than to preserve it. Mr. Bloomfield's poems will now be compared with what he formerly produced; and the *Farmer's Boy* is his most dangerous rival.

The first piece in the volume is entitled **"Richard and Kate, or Fair-Day; a Suffolk Ballad."** The opening is uncommonly spirited.

> "Come, Goody, stop your humdrum wheel,
> Sweep up your orts, and get your hat;
> Old joys reviv'd once more I feel,
> Tis Fair-day;—ay, *and more than that.*
>
> "Have you forgot, Kate, prithee say,
> How many seasons here we've tarry'd?
> 'Tis *forty* years, this very day,
> Since you and I, old girl, were *married!*
>
> "Look out;—the sun shines warm and bright,
> The stiles are low, the paths all dry;
> I know you cut your corns last night:
> Come; be as free from care as I."
>
> P. 1.

Mr. Lofft has bestowed no exaggerated praise upon this poem ["**Walter and Jane, or the Poor Blacksmith**"] in saying that it exhibits 'much of the clear, animated, easy narrative, the familiar but graceful diction, and the change of numbers so interesting in Dryden.'

"The Miller's Maid."—This poem has the same power of versification as the foregoing; but the story is improbable. The discovery too nearly resembles the trick of novel-mongers.

The next piece we must quote at length.—

"The Widow to her Hour-Glass."

> 'Come, friend, I'll turn thee up again:
> Companion of the lonely hour!
> Spring thirty times hath fed with rain
> And cloath'd with leaves my humble bower,
>   Since thou hast stood
>   In frame of wood,
> On chest or window by my side:
> At every birth still thou wert near,
> Still spoke thine admonitions clear.—
>   And, when my husband died,
>
> 'Iv'e often watch'd thy streaming sand
> And seen the growing mountain rise,
> And often found Life's hopes to stand
> On props as weak in Wisdom's eyes:
>   Its conic crown
>   Still sliding down,
> Again heap'd up, then down again;
> The sand above more hollow grew,
> Like days and years still filt'ring through,
>   And mingling joy and pain.
> 'While thus I spin and sometimes sing,
> (For now and then my heart will glow)
> Thou measur'st Time's expanding wing:
> By thee the noontide hour I know:
>   Though silent thou,
>   Still shalt thou flow,
> And jog along thy destin'd way:
> But when I glean the sultry fields,

> When Earth her yellow harvest yields,
>   Thou get'st a holiday.
>
> 'Steady as Truth, on either end
> Thy daily task performing well,
> Thou'rt Meditation's constant friend,
> And strik'st the heart without a bell:
>   Come, lovely May!
>   Thy lengthen'd day
> Shall gild once more my native plain:
> Curl inward here, sweet woodbine flow'r;—
> "Companion of the lonely hour,
>   I'll turn thee up again."
>
> P. 59.

"Market-Night."—Mr. Bloomfield sometimes deviates in this poem from his usual truth. A farmer's wife does not apostrophise the winds and the echo,—nor call upon the guardian spirits—

> '——————————————that dwell
> Where woods, and pits, and hollow ways,
> The lone night-trav'ler's fancy swell
> With fearful tales, of older days—.'
>
> P. 64.

Every-day rhymers can write thus: but it is in such passages as the following we discover that the poet is delineating feelings which he understands.

> 'Where have you stay'd? put down your load.
> How have you borne the storm, the cold?
> What horrors did I not forbode———
> *That beast is worth his weight in gold.'*
>
> P. 68.

"The Fakenham Ghost."—A spirited little tale. A woman is followed by an ass's foal in the dark, and mistakes it for a spirit. The circumstance actually happened.

The next poem is the complaint of an old **"French Mariner,"** whose children have all been slain in the war.—Dolly, which follows, commences beautifully.

> 'The bat began with giddy wing
> His circuit round the shed, the tree;
> And clouds of dancing gnats to sing
> A summer-night's serenity.
> 'Darkness crept slowly o'er the east!
> Upon the barn-roof watch'd the cat;
> Sweet breath'd the ruminating beast
> At rest where Dolly musing sat.'
>
> P. 83.

"Lines, occasioned by a Visit to Whittlebury Forest; addressed to my Children."—This is a fine poem.

> 'Thy dells by wint'ry currents worn,
> Secluded haunts, how dear to me!
> From all but Nature's converse borne,
> No ear to hear, no eye to see.

Their honour'd leaves the green oaks rear'd,
And crown'd the upland's graceful swell;
While answering through the vale was heard
Each distant heifer's tinkling bell.

'Hail, greenwood shades, that stretching far,
Defy e'en Summer's noontide pow'r,
When August in his burning car
Withholds the cloud, withholds the show'r.
The deep-ton'd low from either hill,
Down hazel aisles and arches green;
(The herd's rude tracks from rill to rill)
Roar'd echoing through the solemn scene.

'From my charm'd heart the numbers sprung,
Though birds had ceas'd the choral lay:
I pour'd wild raptures from my tongue,
And gave delicious tears their way.
Then, darker shadows seeking still,
Where human foot had seldom stray'd,
I read aloud to every hill
Sweet Emma's love, "the Nut-brown Maid."

'Shaking his matted mane on high
The gazing colt would raise his head;
Or, tim'rous doe would rushing fly,
And leave to me her grassy bed.'

P. 91.

The remaining poems are only not so good as those
which we have noticed, because they are not so long.
The Epigram upon the Translation of the Farmer's Boy
into Latin is well pointed. We quote the concluding
poem: its spirit and freedom are truly original.

"The Winter Song."

'Dear Boy, throw that icicle down,
And sweep this deep snow from the door:
Old Winter comes on with a frown;
A terrible frown for the poor.
In a season so rude and forlorn
How can age, how can infancy bear
The silent neglect and the scorn
Of those who have plenty to spare?

'Fresh broach'd is my cask of old ale,
Well-tim'd now the frost is set in;
Here's Job come to tell us a tale,
We'll make him at home to a pin.
While my wife and I bask o'er the fire,
The roll of the seasons will prove,
That Time may diminish desire,
But cannot extinguish true love.

'O the pleasures of neighbourly chat,
If you can but keep scandal away,
To learn what the world has been at,
And what the great orators say;
Though the wind through the crevices sing,
And hail down the chimney rebound;
I'm happier than many a king
While the bellows blow bass to the sound.

'Abundance was never my lot:
But out of the trifle that's given,

That no curse may alight on my cot,
I'll distribute the bounty of heaven;
The fool and the slave gather wealth:
But if I add nought to my store,
Yet while I keep conscience in health,
I've a mine that will never grow poor.'

P. 117.

We hope, and believe, that the success of this volume
will equal that of **The Farmer's Boy**; as we are sure
that its merits are not inferior. The manner in which
that poem has been received is honourable to the public
taste and to the public feeling. Neglected genius has too
long been the reproach of England. To enumerate the
dead would be useless; but it is not yet too late to mention the living, whose merits have in vain appealed to
the public. We allude to a self-taught man, as humble in
his situation as 'the Farmer's Boy,' whose genius has
been admitted, and whose profound learning in the antiquities of his own country will be acknowledged and
regretted when it is too late—Edward Williams, the
Welsh bard.

Robert Bloomfield (essay date 1806)

SOURCE: Bloomfield, Robert. Preface to *Wild Flow-
ers; or, Pastoral and Local Poetry,* pp. vii-x. London:
Vernor, Hood, and Sharpe, Poultry; and Longman,
Hurst, Rees, and Orme, Paternoster-Row, 1806.

[*In the following essay, Bloomfield's preface to* Wild
Flowers; or, Pastoral and Local Poetry, *the author offers
insight into his subject matter.*]

A man of the first eminence, in whose day (fortunately
perhaps for me) I was not destined to appear before the
public, or to abide the Herculean crab-tree of his criticism, Dr. Johnson, has said, in his preface to Shakespeare, that—"Nothing can please many, and please long,
but just representations of general nature." My representations of nature, whatever may be said of their *just-
ness,* are not *general,* unless we admit, what I suspect
to be the case, that nature in a village is very much like
nature every where else. It will be observed that all my
pictures are from humble life, and most of my heroines
servant maids. Such I would have them: being fully
persuaded that, in no other way would my endeavours,
either to please or to instruct, have an equal chance of
success.

The path I have thus taken, from necessity, as well as
from choice, is well understood and approved by hundreds, who are capable of ranging in the higher walks
of literature.—But with due deference to their superior
claim, I confess, that no recompense has been half so
grateful or half so agreeable to me as female approbation. To be readily and generally understood, to have

my simple Tales almost instinctively relished by those who have so decided an influence over the lives, hearts, and manners of us all, is the utmost stretch of my ambition.

I here venture, before the public eye, a selection from the various pieces which have been the source of much pleasure, and the solace of my leisure hours during the last four years, and since the publication of the **Rural Tales.** Perhaps, in some of them, more of mirth is intermingled than many who know me would expect, or than the severe will be inclined to approve. But surely what I can say, or can be expected to say, on subjects of country life, would gain little by the seriousness of a preacher, or by exhibiting fallacious representations of what has long been termed *Rural Innocence.*

The Poem of **Good Tidings** is partially known to the world, but, as it was originally intended to assume its present appearance and size, I have gladly availed myself of an endeavour to improve it; and, from its present extended circulation, I trust it will be new to thousands.

I anticipate some approbation from such readers as have been pleased with the **Rural Tales**; yet, though I will not falsify my own feelings by assuming a diffidence which I do not conceive to be either manly or becoming, the conviction that some reputation is hazarded in "a third attempt," is impressed deeply on my mind.

With such sentiments, and with a lively sense of the high honour, and a hope of the bright recompense, of applause from the good, when heightened by the self-approving voice of my own conscience, I commit the book to its fate.

Literary Journal, a Review (review date July 1806)

SOURCE: Review of *Wild Flowers; or, Pastoral and Local Poetry*, by Robert Bloomfield. *Literary Journal, a Review* 2, no. 2 (July 1806): 61-65.

[*In the following excerpted review, the author values Bloomfield for his lack of pretension and for his generosity toward his subjects.*]

Mr. Bloomfield's poetry, when connected with the remarkable particulars of his story, possessed irresistible attractions for the public curiosity; but even had he possessed every opportunity which the young poet can require to awake his fancy and improve his taste, his poetry would have acquired him a just reputation. His writings, with very few exceptions, have nothing in them which could disparage the scholar and the man of taste: his poetry is easy, natural, and perfectly free from affectation; and he has the good sense to employ him-

self in describing those scenes and manners which have fallen particularly under his own observation. Instead, therefore, of being a mere copyist of others, as is too frequently the case with modern poets, he has a manner and a character of his own; and acquires the praise of originality without degenerating into extravagance.

The present small collection bears the same character as his former publications. Some of the pieces are of a more playful and humorous cast, and in these we think he particularly excels, as they are descriptive of those scenes which place the manners of the common villagers in the most pleasing and entertaining point of view. The first piece, which paints the courtship of Abner and the Widow Jones, contains many natural traits of simple manners. The friendship of Abner for the old horse, the companion of his toils, affects us the more that it is related without any of that high flown sentiment which unskilful writers have of late put so liberally into the mouths of our clowns.

The address **"To My Old Oak Table"** is well imagined and interesting. The author, after bringing to his recollection the joys and sorrows of his humbler days which this old companion witnessed, proceeds to describe the commencement of his better fortune:

"In that gay season, honest friend of mine,
I marked the brilliant sun upon thee shine;
Imagination took her flights so free,
Home was delicious with my book and thee,
The purchas'd nosegay, or brown ears of corn,
Were thy gay plumes upon a summer's morn,
Awakening memory, that disdains control,
They spoke the darling language of my soul:
They whisper'd tales of joy, of peace, of truth,
And conjur'd back the sunshine of my youth:
Fancy presided at the joyful birth,
I pour'd the torrent of my feelings forth;
Conscious of *truth* in Nature's humble track,
And wrote 'The Farmer's Boy' upon thy back!
Enough, old friend:—thou'rt mine; and shalt partake,
While I have pen to write, or tongue to speak,
Whatever fortune deals me.—Part with thee!
No, not till death shall set my spirit free;
For know, should plenty crown my life's decline,
A most important duty may be thine:
Then, guard me from Temptation's base control,
From apathy and littleness of soul.
The sight of thy old frame, so rough, so rude,
Shall twitch the sleeve of nodding Gratitude;
Shall teach me but to venerate the more
Honest Oak Tables and their guests—the poor:
Teach me unjust distinctions to deride,
And falshoods gender'd in the brain of Pride;
Shall give to Fancy still the cheerful hour,
To Intellect, its freedom and its power;
To Hospitality's enchanting ring-
A charm, which nothing but thyself can bring.
The man who would not look with honest pride
On the tight bark that stemm'd the roaring tide,
And bore him, when he bow'd the trembling knee,

Home, through the mighty perils of the sea,
I love him not.—He ne'er shall be my guest;
Nor sip my cup, nor witness how I'm blest;
Nor lean, to bring my honest friend to shame,
A sacrilegious elbow on thy frame;
But thou through life a monitor shalt prove,
Sacred to Truth, to Poetry, and Love."

"The Horkey," a provincial ballad, describes the fun which takes place in Suffolk at the Harvest-home, or Horkey feast, as it is called there. Some of the provincial expressions of Suffolk are retained with good effect; and upon the whole it is not unworthy to be classed with some of the compositions of Ramsey and Burns of a similar sort. It particularly resembles Christ's "Kirk on the Green," in its story and structure. . . .

The **"Broken Crutch"** is a very pretty poem of a serious cast. It relates the love of a rich farmer for a young maid, whom he was too honourable to seduce or desert although she was poor and in the station of a servant. The moral of the poem is good, and the poetry is pleasing. The style very much resembles those poems of Mr. Bloomfield which are already in the hands of the public, and will we doubt not be equally admired.

"Shooter's Hill" is a pleasing little lyric. The author repaired to this charming spot to recover his lost health, and this circumstance diffuses a tenderness and melancholy over the poem. The following extract proves how well the author deserves his better fortune, from his piety and the reflections he bestows on such as have been less successful than himself:

"I love to mark the flow'ret's eye,
　To rest where pebbles form my bed,
Where shapes and colours scatter'd lie
　In varying millions round my head.
The soul rejoices when alone,
　And feels her glorious empire free;
Sees GOD in every shining stone,
　And revels in variety.

"Ah me! perhaps within my sight,
　Deep in the smiling dales below,
Gigantic talents, Heav'n's pure light,
　And all the rays of genius glow
In some lone soul, whom no one sees
　With *power* and *will* to say 'Arise,'
Or chase away the slow disease,
　And Want's foul picture from his eyes.

"A worthier man by far than I,
　With more of industry and fire,
Shall see fair Virtue's meed pass by,
　Without one spark of fame expire!
Bleed not my heart, it will be so,
　The throb of care was thine full long;
Rise, like the Psalmist from his woe
　And pour abroad the joyful song."

"Love of the Country" and **"Barnham Water"** are pieces of a similar cast; the **"Woodland Hallo"** is a very pretty little song. The **"Visit to Ranelagh"** conveys a very good idea of the sameness and insipidity of that place of fashionable resort, which has at length been abandoned. The volume concludes with **"Good Tidings from the Farm,"** a poem already in the hands of the public, and which was reviewed in the *Literary Journal* for June, 1804. It is now improved and enlarged.

Were not the merits of this little volume sufficient to recommend it to public notice, we should still heartily wish it success. In the dedication, which is addressed to his only son, the author gives us to understand that this poor boy has an unfortunate lameness, which may prevent him from procuring for himself those comforts and advantages which might otherwise have fallen to his share, and which he can now only expect from the success of his father's writings.

Blackwood's Edinburgh Magazine (review date January-June 1822)

SOURCE: Review of *May Day with the Muses* by Robert Bloomfield. *Blackwood's Edinburgh Magazine* 11 (January-June 1822): 722-31.

[*In the following excerpt, the author satirically meditates on "humble" poets before turning to extol Bloomfield as among the best of the uneducated poets, quoting extensively from his work as evidence.*]

A great many ploughmen—shepherds—ditchers—and shoemakers—nay, even tailors—have in this free and happy country of ours wooed the Muses. Apollo, on the other hand, has been made love to, (and in some instances very nearly ravished, as, for example, by that vigorous milk-woman, Ann Yearsley,) by vast flocks of young women in the lower walks of life, dairy-maids, nurses, house-keepers, knitters in the sun, and Cinderellas. A very droll volume or two might be made up of their productions. One thing we observe in the POETRY of them all—male and female—a strong bias to the indulgence of the tender passion. They are all most excessively amorous, and every volume is a perfect dovecote, sounding with a continual coo. Roger, the ploughman, makes love in a bold, vigorous, straightforward fashion, as if he were "in glory and in joy," "following his plough upon the mountain-side." Jamie, the shepherd, the yellow-haired laddie—is more figurative and circumlocutory; but just let him alone for a few minutes, and he is sure to get upon his subject at last, and to acquit himself in a truly pastoral and patriarchal manner. Hobbinol, the ditcher, goes to work, as if he were paid by the piece. The shoemaker melts like his own wax, and shews himself to be a most active understrapper; while the tailor, forgetting that he is but a fraction, declares,

"I dare do all that may become a man;
Who dares do more, is none."

In short, the professions of the man and the lover go hand in hand; and it would be as impossible to mistake "an amatory effusion" of a genuine Roger for one of Sammy Snip, as to mistake such an erection as the London Monument for the handle of a milk-churn.

The same remark holds good with the Poetesses of lowly life. With them all alike "love is heaven, and heaven is love." Maids, wives, or widows, they all describe themselves as—burning. The Dairy-maid writes like a young woman of strong red arms, a sanguine temperament, rude health, and good wages. She is an excellent creature to Roger, and lays on flattery like butter. She calls a kiss by its proper name—a smack; and the ploughman of her most impassioned poetry is a man who, if he could be realized, might be exhibited in a booth as a very passable giant. The Nursery-maid strikes a loftier key, and prattles about chaste desires, and a little baby with a face like its papa's. She imitates Moore's Melodies, and affects to like Thomas Do-Little. She is a sort of sweet Fanny of Timmoul; and her verses, like the lips of that much-injured young woman, "keep eternally kissing and biting each other." The love poems of the House-keeper are in general fat and pursy. They are full of the "windy suspiration of forced breath;" good eating and drinking are promised liberally to her heart's Darling; and her imagination, even in its fondest and most enamoured moments, dwells on the comforts, rather than the raptures of love. As for Cinderellas in general, and not to make any invidious exceptions, it may be said of them, "with their clipsome waists," that they belong to the Cockney school—are too often almost as grossly indelicate as Leigh Hunt himself, who, in one of his love poems, describes a lady's limb above the knee, "as quivering with tremulous mass internally;" and that they study Tom Moore and Fanny of Timmoul less devoutly than the "Ranting, roaring Irishman," and "Molly, cut and come again." They despise any man either Little by name or Little by nature. That system of everlasting slobbering, recommended and expounded by "the first lyrical poet of the age," in a volume by which he cannot but be made proud while living, happy when dying, and honoured when dead, is almost wholly discarded by these maids of all work, who eschew such thin and unsubstantial diet, and like to have a good lump of English beef in the pot. From the poetry of such poetesses, a selection would require to be made with much circumspection; but perhaps Mr Bath Bowdler might be prevailed upon to undertake it; and certainly, after what Mr Jeffrey has so judiciously praised as a *"castrated edition"* of Shakespeare, this gentleman may extend his shears to the fair sex, *"sans peur et sans reproche,"* and contrive to render the somewhat luxuriant display made by these viragoes more fit for a family party, with their feet on the fender, or half asleep on a sofa. But of this hereafter.

To be serious after this little flight—of all the motley group of humble verse-men and verse-women, we think that in our days the only names worth mentioning, are Burns, Dermody, (whom Mr Jeffrey, in the Edinburgh Review, with great Christian charity, the most amiable sweetness of nature, and the most polite and gentlemanly dislike of all personality, called shortly and emphatically, "Dermody the Drunkard,") Hogg,[1] Allan Cunninghame, Clare, and——Robert Bloomfield. All these are men of genius, more or less—at least we think so—let the word genius mean what it will. They have all done some good things; how good it may not be so easy to say, but good enough to give delight, and therefore to deserve remembrance. Of Hogg and Cunninghame we have frequently spoken with high praise; and, indeed, it was an article in this Magazine, written by a gentleman distinguished by his genius and his generosity, that first directed the public attention to the latter of these two poets, and pointed out, if with somewhat of the exaggeration of free-hearted partiality, certainly with inimitable grace, and a fine spirit of truth, the peculiar bent of his poetical character, and the field in which it was calculated chiefly to succeed. But of Bloomfield we have hitherto scarcely said one word, having only quoted, in one of our early Numbers, his exquisite picture of a Blind Boy, to be found in a little poem, called **"News from the Farm."** We mean, therefore, to say a few words now about this very pleasing, and also original poet, no long-winded blast of critical cant, but merely two or three kind and enlightened paragraphs—and we shall very soon do the same of Clare— the "Northamptonshire peasant," as he is somewhat slangishly called, just as Sampson the pugilist is called "The Birmingham Youth." Their patronage of Clare has been highly honourable to Messrs Taylor and Hessey, and proves them to be persons of amiable and intelligent minds; although, with that inconsistency that has often marked the conduct of wiser and better men, they have lately degraded themselves, and their respectable periodical work, by an example of the most pitiable and stingless slander of a Tale of universally felt and acknowledged genius and pathos, and that, too, manifestly to the eyes of the blindest bat that flits about the murky recesses of the Fleet or the Row, from poor spite towards the publisher, whose name is on the title-page, and some vague and indefinite malignity towards the possible author of the volume. From an expression, by the way, in the precious article alluded to, we should suspect the critic to be a pawnbroker. The writer reviewed had applied the common expression, "Pledges of Affection," to a family of children, all of whom having died but one, that one is facetiously and piously called by the critic, *"the only unredeemed pledge!!!"*

This is the stupidest piece of blasphemy we ever recollect to have seen; and if, as we have heard, it was written by *********, (which surely is impossible,) the editors would do well never again to admit such a miserable spoon into the concern.

Mr Bloomfield, on the publication of **"The Farmer's Boy,"** was looked on as a poetical prodigy, and not without reason. For he shewed in that poem a very fine feeling for the beauties and the occupations of the country. He had had few or no advantages of training, but he had treasured up, in an innocent, and happy, and thoughtful mind, many youthful remembrances of a rural life; and immediately on hitting upon a good subject, he seems to have put them easily and naturally, and often very elegantly, into verse. Having read but little, and thought and felt much, and having no ambition of equalling or surpassing any particular model, he wrote away, from his own mind and his own heart, and the public were justly delighted with his fervour and simplicity. It is most agreeable to read his unlaboured descriptions of ploughing, and sowing, and reaping, and sheave-binding, and compunctious shooting of rooks. And every now and then he deals out, with a sort of unostentatious profusion, feelings and sentiments awakened by the contemplation of lowly life—its sufferings, and its virtues. His hero, young Giles, is really an exceedingly pleasant and interesting lad; and the situations in which he is often placed are affecting, by their solitariness, and the unconscious independence of the harmless and happy being, in his labour and his poverty. Now and then single lines occur that are quite exquisite; and his picture of Poor Polly, the ruined and insane maiden, is equal to Cowper's Crazy Jane, if not, indeed, superior to it; and there cannot be higher praise. England is justly proud of Bloomfield, on account of his genius, and of that simple and pure tone of morality which breathes over all this his first, and, of course, best Poem. Besides all these its merits, which we have just slightly glanced at, **"The Farmer's Boy"** is by far the best written, as to style and composition, of any work of our uneducated poets. The melody of the versification is often exceedingly beautiful; and there are fewer faults of coarse and vulgar taste in it, though some there undoubtedly are, than in any book of any man similarly situated, with which we are acquainted. All this shews a mind delicately formed by nature; and accordingly, **"The Farmer's Boy,"** now that the mere wonder and astonishment are passed by, continues to hold its place, and can never be perused by any candid and cultivated reader, without the highest pleasure and approbation.

His **"Rural Tales,"** which we have not looked at for a long time, were many of them very good. In these he went somewhat deeper into the human heart; but, trying more difficult things, more frequently fell into failures. But on the whole, this second volume was not a falling off, though it wanted the concentrated interest of his first Poem. There was considerable ingenuity shewn in the conception of his little domestic stories; and always much true pathos in his delineations of feeling and character. He put his heart into every thing he did, however trivial; and many of his situations were striking, original, and impressive. He writes many poor—even bad passages, but never two pages at a time utterly worthless, like some others we could name; so that his most indifferent tales leave behind them a most pleasing impression, both of his understanding and his heart. We believe this to be truth, without exaggeration, and without seeking to say any thing wisely critical about Mr Bloomfield or his writings.

The **"News from the Farm,"** is a little poem on the Vaccine Inoculation; and it is wonderful how much pathos he throws into a theme so very unpromising. The passage alluded to above—that description of the Blind Boy, is worthy of being inserted among the Flowers of English poetry;—graceful, elegant, and most deeply affecting—even to tears.

We believe there are other poems of Mr Bloomfield, but we have rather forgotten a little what they are, except a long copy of verses about the River Wye, which we did not greatly delight in at the time we endeavoured to give them a reading, and the composition of which must, we suspect, have been a kind of voluntarily self-imposed task-work.—We may be mistaken, but this is our impression.

Now, when so interesting a man as Mr Bloomfield reappears before the Public, after a retirement so long and deep as finally to have given rise (he tells us so, in his preface to **"May-day with the Muses"**) to a report of his death, it cannot but be gratifying to all lovers of good poetry—be it high or low—to hear him once more tuning his rustic reed. And it gives us pleasure to be able to say conscientiously, that his new little volume is one of the most agreeable he has ever written, and one that shews that his powers are noways impaired. The idea of the poem is really a very pretty and ingenious extravaganza; and its improbability in a world so selfish as ours, is by no means against it. Mr Bloomfield has a pleasant smile upon his own face, at the notion of a worthy old landholder accepting of rhymes from his tenants in lieu of rents; and therefore we hope that no stupid and sour critic will put a frown upon his, especially during these times of agricultural distress, when many an English farmer that formerly weighed twenty stone, is now a mere shadow, and reduced to seventeen.

Sir Ambrose Higham, being somewhere about fourscore, and having got sick of his annual Spring visit to London, resolves to give a grand fête champetre to his tenantry, and to demand payment in poetry instead of pounds. A number of big tables are set out upon a lawn near the hall; and after bolting bacon and bowzing beer, one bard after another rises up, makes a leg, and pays his poem. And this Mr Bloomfield very prettily calls **"May-day with the Muses."** Now, we think that this is just as good a plan to get into possession a few unconnected poems, as any other; and why may not Mr Bloomfield be allowed the same privilege of genius as Chaucer, Boccaccio, the Misses Lee, James Hogg, and the authors of "The Tent"? Perhaps the last inimitable production, which was erected in the shape of a round-robin, was the model which our poet had chiefly in his eye; and we are confirmed in this idea, by the first little wood-engraving in the volume, where old Sir Ambrose Higham occupies the very same place of honour which Christopher North did in "The Tent,"—with this exception, that the Baronet has his ancient wife at his side, whereas Mrs M'Whirter, *alias* Odoherty, *alias* Oglethorpe, sat on the Adjutant's knee. But the two carousals, as given on copper and wood, resemble each other in many of their great features,—the one being a "Light and Shadow" of Scottish, and the other a "Passage" of English life.

Note

1. Hogg and Hazlitt are decidedly the best prose writers of the same class. By the bye, we are delighted to see the pretty style in which Messrs Constable have got up the collected edition of Hogg's Poems. The volumes are elegant—the price moderate—the whole affair as it should be.

Edmund Blunden (essay date 1929)

SOURCE: Blunden, Edmund. "The Farmer's Boy: Duck, Bloomfield." In *Nature in English Literature*, pp. 106-131. London: The Hogarth Press, 1929.

[*In the following excerpt, Blunden examines Bloomfield's contribution to the genre of "earth-born poetry."*]

The conversation of the men who work on the land, when their topic is their life and experience, is full of translated colour and significant sound; it is with little difficulty that I have sometimes fancied, as I listened to three or four hearty haymakers, that there grew the true poem of Nature. Their whole sense seemed peculiarly trained to answer all that Nature in this country has to say or do, from the grasshopper's rustle to the assembly of the thunderstorm; their verbs seemed of the earth earthy, of the flowers flowery, and their illustrations of meaning simply added other depths of weather-beaten stoicism. We may define poetry as we will, but in the plain, shrewd, and curious eclogues which a subject like thrashing-tackle will set going in the country inn, there is an actuality of impression and a secret glory of soul which may scarcely be called anything but poetry. . . .

I now turn [from Stephen Duck] to the more celebrated though not more remarkable Farmer's Boy of the early nineteenth century, in whom we may read something of the same ultimate error after similar indications of a genuine earth-born poetry. Robert Bloomfield is not a name to conjure with to-day. Once, however, he was as popular as Hardy; of his first poem, 26,000 copies are said to have been sold within three years. But he fails, in a severe examination, as his predecessor had done, through being lured out of his own world and speech into another where he met a host of superiors. Robert Bloomfield was son of the village tailor at Honington in Suffolk, and from about 1776 to 1781, when he was fifteen years old, was employed as a handy lad at Mr Austin's farm in the next parish. Whoever goes to those places will readily find the system of life and the spirit of the countryside little altered from what they were in Bloomfield's time. The stream, the mill, the ponderous horses and rambling geese and pigs, above all the soft brightness of the scene, may be recognised. Not promising to be hard enough for the full life of a farm-labourer, Bloomfield was sent up to London and his brother made a shoemaker of him. Both brothers developed a taste for reading, and writing; Robert borrowed Thomson's "Seasons." "I never heard him give so much praise to any book as to that," observes George. A dispute about apprenticeships compelled the youth to go back to Suffolk for a time, which was passed at Mr Austin's farm; then he returned to London and settled down or rather up in a garret with other shoemakers, working on ladies' shoes and composing in his mind a long poem called *The Farmer's Boy.* When it had been written it was sent to that gallant gentleman and pleasant bookman Capel Lofft, who had a farm at Troston, near Bloomfield's home, and he finally obtained its publication in 1800. Instantly the work became the rage. By 1815 the 13th edition was required; there were translations in French (*Le Valet du Fermier*), Latin, Italian; Bloomfield had to meet the whims and advice of patrons. In spite of this whirl of luck, he did not prosper greatly; his subsequent books of verse were not very well received, and we find him making not ladies' shoes but Æolian harps for a living. He died in 1823, in a state of melancholy and weakened mind.

Lamb thought that at the best of times Bloomfield had "a poor mind," but this was hardly the point. What Bloomfield might have been was the spirit of the farm in our poetry, the prime of that delightful rustic commentary on work and weather, legend and character, which can so hardly be preserved in books. It may be that without Thomson's "Seasons" to show him the method of poetry, and the range of observation and discussion already explored, Bloomfield would never have written *The Farmer's Boy*; but it is also probable that the thinness and platitude and external polish which are the poem's defects, and which are so far removed from the expressed enthusiasms of a farm-labourer in his own surroundings, are due to an exaggerated respect for the literary model. At any rate, with all its demerits, Bloomfield's picture of the farm and its figures year in and year out must be regarded as a phenomenal piece of work, and the little sheepish stumbling boy who went about Mr Austin's fields with so fresh a sensibility and emerged into a public of tens of thousands deserves our affectionate reconsideration. I shall pay him a tribute unusual in this hurried age by taking up his poem and making a note and an extract here and there.

It begins in Thomsonian tone, Goldsmithian measure:

> O come, blest Spirit! whatsoe'er thou art,
> Thou kindling warmth that hover'st round my heart,
> Sweet inmate, hail!

That is in feeling genuine, in utterance borrowed; but presently we come to the better and more homely style, introducing Giles. Mr Austin's kindness is at once acknowledged; the campaign before us will not be so harsh at all corners as that of poor Duck.

> No stripes, no tyranny his steps pursu'd;
> His life was constant, cheerful servitude:
> Strange to the world, he wore a bashful look,
> The fields his study, Nature was his book.

The farm is small but doing well; and the time is Spring. Giles has many jobs, but among them he has to look after the scarecrows, and this brings him from bed first thing; then he joins like a young bird in the chorus along the sandy sunk lane—all is delicacy, variety, regeneration:

> Stopt in her song perchance the starting Thrush
> Shook a white shower from the black-thorn bush,
> Where dew-drops thick as early blossoms hung,
> And trembled as the minstrel sweetly sung.

With the budding and the gleaming all round, Giles sets his scarecrows dangling, and gets back to the house; there through the noise of pigs and ducks and turkeys he hears the dairymaid's bawl "Go fetch the Cows." Off he goes to the meadow and halloos them into the yard, in their usual precedency; then under the morning sun he has to help in the milking beside singing Mary:

> And crouching Giles beneath a neighbouring tree
> Tugs o'er his pail, and chants with equal glee;
> Whose hat with tattered brim, of nap so bare,
> From the cow's side purloins a coat of hair,
> An unambitious, peaceable cockade.

This ended, he is

> A *Gibeonite,* that serves them all by turns:
> He drains the pump, from him the faggot burns;
> From him the noisy Hogs demand their food,
> While at his heels run many a chirping brood,
> Or down his path in expectation stand
> With equal claims upon his strewing hand.

How gentle and how powerful is this kind of harmony with Nature! As one reads, one almost demands nothing more complete and enigmatic. Meanwhile, the boy becomes a shepherd, as the year grows serene and leafage darkens; he has to see to it that the pasture fences are whole, but even in that there is a rapture:

> High fences, proud to charm the gazing eye,
> Where many a nestling first essays to fly;
> Where blows the woodbine, faintly streak'd with red,
> And rests on every bough its tender head;
> Round the young ash its twining branches meet,
> Or crown the hawthorn with its odour sweet.

The boy turns from this fairy-piece to his young lambs at play, and all his young impulses are with them:

> A bird, a leaf will set them off again,
> Or, if a gale with strength unusual blow,
> Scattering the wild-briar roses into snow,
> Their little limbs increasing efforts try;
> Like the torn flower the fair assemblage fly.

While he sees the blown petals, and the petal-like lambs, he is struck by another parallel and a painful one; for here comes "the murdering Butcher with his cart." Poor Giles is to see his "gay companions" huddled off to the knife and block.

Summer now enters, and, from the poetical point of view, not at all well:

> The Farmer's life displays in every part
> A moral lesson to the sensual heart . . .

But we need not emphasise those errors of education which dull and cramp the youthful image of Giles, with whom we go off to turnip-sowing after a night of light rain; that task of faith accomplished, it is the boy's duty to hunt the sparrows out of the corn which they invade with a gay impudence, under "the leafy thorn." And here, after giving them a fright, he loiters, for he loves the place, and Wisdom loves him for loving it. Now for something like pecking with the sparrow, and more permissible:

> Just where the parting bough's light shadows play,
> Scarce in the shade, nor in the scorching day,
> Stretcht on the turf he lies, a peopled bed,
> Where swarming insects creep around his head.
> The small dust-colour'd beetle climbs with pain
> O'er the smooth plantain-leaf, a spacious plain!
> Thence higher still, by countless steps convey'd,
> He gains the summit of a shivering blade,
> And flirts his filmy wings, and looks around,
> Exulting in his distance from the ground.
> The tender speckled moth here dancing seen,
> The vaulting grasshopper of glossy green . . .

Giles longs to have a sharper sense of these little lives, but is called up by the skylark, starting from the corn, and soon in and out of the light cloud, and higher in the blue,

His form, his motion, undistinguish'd quite,
Save when he wheels direct from shade to light:
E'en then the songster a mere speck became
Gliding like fancy's bubbles in a dream—

for the child-farmer falls asleep. The year goes on with bounty; the reapers, gleaners come, and Giles now has to work like a slave at carting the corn. He still has feelings for the troubles of others, and laments the cruelty which has docked "poor patient Ball" of his tail, and left him there in the blaze while the flies freely suck his blood. A small thing in this great world, not so small in that farmyard; where then the poor cow, already tormented by the gadfly, is assailed by the spiteful gander and tyrannised. Humour, however, is there too. "The strolling swine" engages this braggart bird;

Whose nibbling warfare on the grunter's side
Is welcome pleasure to his bristly hide;
Gently he stoops, or stretcht at ease along,
Enjoys the insults of the gabbling throng . . .

From this serio-comedy of the strawyard the boy raises his face to the setting sun and fantasied "fiery treasures" of clouds in the west; gets to bed, but at midnight wakes to the onset of thunder, and the rising wind in the full-leafed elms, and the whimpering mastiff. Then the cool, and music of the easy rain, and harvest's last morning, and harvest-home.

But woods turn yellow, and the year declines. Giles lets out the cleanly pigs among the oaks, and sometimes knows where they are, and watches their pleasures and alarms; the wild duck's eye like a gem meets his as she sits alone, and then she springs up in fear, and they in fear

decamp with more than swinish speed,
And snorting dash through sedge and rush and reed:
Through tangling thickets headlong on they go,
Then stop and listen for their fancied foe;

Giles loses them when they herd under the roosting-bough of the pheasant, and cannot with "his piercing call" bring them in. It is a time of wild shades and excitements; of labour too, such is the mysterious wheel ever revolving with this world of farms, and swine, and boys—the plough and tumbril are out on the clogging mould, and leisure only comes when

the distant chime
Of Sabbath bells is heard at sermon-time
That down the brook sound sweetly in the gale,
Or strike the rising hill, or skim the dale.

Even the church is part of the farms; straw-roofed, broken-windowed, its stones tufted with mallows and nettles, its tower usurped by grey-capped daws, it is all an outhouse and a hovel of the earth-life. Now, as the days grow dangerous, Giles would wish to be at the fireside, warming the farmyard weaklings as himself is warmed; but fate is against him. He is sent with a shot-less gun to drive off the rooks from the sprouting wheat, dawn to dusk; and all alone in the lee of the thinned hedge he shivers, until he has a boyish inspiration. A little hut of turf and thatch, a fire of sticks, and sloe and hip to roast at the fire; he sets about the work, and finishes it. And now he obtains the promise of his junior urchins at the green to come and play "the Crusoe of the lonely fields" with him. He makes up the seats for "the coming guests"; the branches of berries sputter over the flame; "he sweeps his hearth." The guests fail him, and he stares over the solitude in vain.

The fourth season and last canto of *The Farmer's Boy* opens according to foolish plan with some unlucid moralisation, from which we are pleased to be rescued even by the lowing of cattle in frozen pastures, and the thud of swedes tumbled out of the cart by poor Giles in the sleet. Not that the moral itself was a bad one; but the humanitarian gospel according to our Suffolk labourer is best presented in picture and anecdote. The winter farm described in that way is indeed a home of equality, and all ranks—two-legged, four-legged, winged or woolly—appear in kindly mutual comprehension. The ewe and heifer must wait on Giles to break the ice and let them begin on their turnips, and when night falls there is often an innocent trick played on him by the hungriest:

From him, with bed and nightly food supplied,
Throughout the yard, hous'd round on every side,
Deep-plunging Cows their rustling feast enjoy,
And snatch sweet mouthfuls from the passing Boy,
Who moves unseen beneath his trailing load,
Fills the tall racks, and leaves a scatter'd road;
Where oft the swine from ambush warm and dry
Bolt out, and scamper headlong to the sty,
When *Giles* with well-known voice, already there,
Deigns them a portion of his evening care.

This done he creeps in among the farmer's family and servants by the hearth, for which he has helped bring the faggots and logs; and even here, if he lacks anything in natural community of feeling with his animals, he must listen to his master "mild as the vernal shower" on the subject, and his spirit must range the farm to be assured that he has failed in nothing. The horsekeeper, who has heard all this before, drops to sleep in his corner, but presently starts, and calls Giles to take a walk with him:

Ever thoughtful of his team,
Along the glittering snow a feeble gleam
Shoots from his lantern, as he yawning goes
To add fresh comfort to their night's repose;
Diffusing fragrance as their food he moves,
And pats the jolly sides of those he loves.

Besides this Giles must make sure of his sheep, in fear of some mastiff or cur that has found a taste for murder; and this duty, unpleasantly dragging him from the fireside, may sometimes have a touch of wonder in it, "if the full-orbed Moon salute his eyes." A universalising fancy occurs to him, which not the deepest mystic would be ashamed to share, as he looks at the silvered stillness above, and the ranges of clouds

> Spotless as snow, and countless as they're fair;
> Scatter'd immensely wide from east to west,
> The beauteous semblance of a *Flock* at rest.
> These to the raptur'd mind, aloud proclaim
> Their MIGHTY SHEPHERD's everlasting Name.

But, with the rural mind, idea does not preside long at a stretch, and Giles is brought "from plains of light to earth" in another fancy. "A grisley SPECTRE, cloth'd in silver-gray" stands along the lane among waving shadows, and the owl flies with terrifying invisibility and cry above him. He stands to arms, and is not unrewarded; the ghost vanishes, and all that is there is an old friendly ash—

> Slowly, as his noiseless feet draw near,
> Its perfect lineaments at once appear;
> Its crown of shivering ivy whispering peace
> And its white bark that fronts the moon's pale face.

Thus on he goes again with kind angels through the winter nights, and winter cannot last for ever; the primrose will not be daunted, the lambs come, and at the dawn beside their ewes

> Those milk-white strangers bow the trembling knee.

To find them out sheltered sunshine and promising valleys will now carry his heart on into the spring; to be praised for his cares and vigils

> By gazing neighbours, when along the road,
> Or village green, his curly-coated throng
> Suspends the chorus of the Spinner's song

will reward him wholly and complete his course. Yet never must that completion be an ending—all is in advance,

> "*Another* Spring!" his heart exulting cries,
> "*Another* Year!"

Deep and happy riddle, solved by him with painful work, and trials and fears, and something like the vision which sends the new sap into the hedge and gold into the sky.

Such is the principal poem of Bloomfield, and while it often suffers from the imposition of a literary language and philosophical convention alien to his old usages, and never completely mastered by his "poor mind," while it might have been more incisive and indeed imaginatively adequate if it had been voiced in a series of lyrical ballads, yet altogether it is the Farmer's Boy

speaking. Of him this country should be proud. He will be in heaven before the majority of us, even authors and lecturers, and will be in his element with the verification of Isaiah's pastoral; he is our Melampus, and when (through Bloomfield) I have heard the story of his heart, I do not know that any union with Nature could be more desirable than his. If civilisation kills him, so much the worse for civilisation. Of Bloomfield's subsequent poems of Nature, I shall not at present speak; many of them illuminate this actual idyll, but none can rival its tenacious contentment in the bosom of the earth and the silken or woolly or feathered sides of her children committed to the charge of human children.

Rayner Unwin (essay date 1954)

SOURCE: Unwin, Rayner. "Robert Bloomfield." In *The Rural Muse: Studies in the Peasant Poetry of England*, pp. 87-109. London: Goerge Allen and Unwin Ltd., 1954.

[*In the following excerpt, the author reviews the critical response of Bloomfield's contemporaries to his poetry as well as some of the salient features of the poet's biography. A close reading of* The Farmer's Boy *yields a discussion of Bloomfield's restraint from moralizing and of his conservative intellectual approach.*]

> First made a Farmer's Boy, and then a snob,
> A poet he became, and here lies Bob.
>
> ROBERT BLOOMFIELD: MS. scribble, April 1823

In 1781 Robert Bloomfield, a fourteen-year-old farm boy, threw his old hat in the horse-pond, sold his smock for a shilling, and set off to London to turn shoemaker. It was not without regret that he left the East-Anglian farm where he had been employed for the past three years, but his employer, Mr. Austin, declared that he was too slightly built to be of much use on the land, and in consequence it had been decided to send him to London where he could join his two brothers, George and Nat, who were already established as journeymen shoemakers in that city. "I am glad to find you are well and that you are willing to cum to London," wrote George. "Pack your Old Cloths up as clos as you can, don't waite, till Shoes or Shirts bee Mended. . . ." Robert took the stage-coach from Bury St. Edmunds and was met by his brother. He arrived "dressed just as he came from keeping sheep, hogs etc.—his shoes filled full of stumps in the heels. He, looking about him, slipt up—his nails were unused to a flat pavement. I remember viewing him as he scampered up:—how small he was."

There was little that would have attracted the attention of anyone outside his own family to the arrival in London of this young lad. He hated the city, but countrymen like himself were being drawn to the towns in increasing numbers at the turn of the century. Robert Bloomfield was seemingly destined to be absorbed by the

> Dependent, huge metropolis! where Art
> Her poring thousands stows in breathless rooms,
> Midst pois'nous smokes and steams, and rattling
>   looms.

The countryside was far from him in his lodgings in Coleman Street, and for most youths the remembrance would quickly have been blurred and forgotten. His own thoughts, Robert recollected in a letter to his mother many years later, perpetually returned to the country around Honington, where he was born, and Sapiston, where he worked. His affection for Suffolk was never dimmed by city life, and he could always "see in imagination my old neighbours and things just as they were." The intensity and accuracy of Bloomfield's memories of Suffolk life, and the detachment with which he was able to record them as an anodyne to his tedious employment won him fame and admiration in his time. The emotions that he recollected in tranquillity were destined to be acclaimed when Wordsworth's were ignored.

Robert Bloomfield was one of six children, and his father, a tailor, had died when he was still an infant. In consequence there was little money that could be spared for Robert's education. His mother, who was the schoolmistress at Honington, taught him herself, and for a short while he went to the nearby village of Ixworth where he learnt to write a laborious copperplate but failed to learn, like the rest of his family, how to spell. After the unsuccessful attempt to make him a farmer it was decided, at his mother's request, that he should join his brothers in London; but even there he was of little real use. There were five men working in the garret with Robert, and the boy was employed on errands and odd jobs. It is from his brother George that we get a picture of the life he led during these first years in London.

> We were all single men, lodgers at a shilling per week each, our beds were coarse, and all things far from being clean and snug, like what Robert had left at Sapiston. Robert was our man to fetch all things to hand. At noon he fetched our dinners from the cook's shop: and any one of our fellow-workmen that wanted to have anything fetched in, would send him, and assist in his work and teach him, for a recompense for his trouble.

> Every day when the boy from the public-house came for the pewter pots, and to hear what porter was wanted, he always brought the yesterday's newspaper. The reading of the paper we had been used to take by turns; but after Robert came, he mostly read for us,—because his time was of least value.

> He frequently met with words that he was unacquainted with: of this he often complained. I one day happened, at a book-stall, to see a small dictionary, which had

been very ill used. I bought it for him for fourpence. By the help of this he in a little time could read and comprehend the long and beautiful speeches of Burke, Fox, or North.

Reading was more of a duty than a pleasure for him, but his interest was quickened by the review section of *The London Magazine* which contained a "Poet's Corner." He was stirred to emulation, and it was here that his first attempts at verse appeared. Making verses was an innocent pastime, and for some years he occasionally indulged in such compositions, encouraged by his sympathetic and watchful brother George. When his half-brother Isaac died at the age of sixteen George, who had gone home for the funeral, wrote to Robert asking him to compose an epitaph. "I have not braine Enough to make A Verse that will please my self," he admitted, "I think there is A Dificulty in A verse of this sorte for such A youth as Isaac, for he cannot be said to have any Charicter. . . ." Robert was not daunted by the subject, and in due course a verse was forthcoming.

Before young Isaac's death the brothers had changed their lodgings. The move was occasioned by an epileptic that lived with them whose fits had horrified Robert. In their new garret they lived with one James Kay, a furious Calvinist Scot, amongst whose library of books, and held in little esteem, were those two inevitably influential books, *The Seasons* and *Paradise Lost*. Robert borrowed them, read them, and a new poetic prospect opened before him. As surely as Wordsworth at Hawkshead, Bloomfield after his discovery of these poems became a dedicated spirit. Of *The Seasons* George said, "I never heard him give so much praise to any book as to that."

Three years after his first arrival in London an apprentice dispute caused Robert to return to the country for two months. He went to Sapiston where he stayed with his old employer, Mr. Austin. These months, which confirmed his memories of past joys and were heightened by the poetic awareness he had so recently received from Thomson, were probably the happiest, and certainly the most vivid, of his life. It was a return from exile to come again to the Suffolk fields he knew so well. He saw them at the age of seventeen with a more mature eye and an increased sensitivity. The holiday was short, but its influence was enormous.

On his return to London Robert was apprenticed to a ladies' shoemaker, and while learning his trade many years slipped by. When he was twenty-one he invited the sons of his friend Mr. Austin for a visit to London. His letter to them, the earliest of his correspondence that is preserved, does not display any precocity, nor even the confidence of a man of the world. Although he had been seven years in London his life had been sheltered and unadventurous. "We must be very particular and not be out late of night," he warned his companions, "nor frequent any low lived places, and so long as we do so, there is no danger to be feared." Needless to add it was to be a cheap visit for Bloomfield was still desperately poor.

Two years later he found a comely young woman in Woolwich and married her, but his financial position had in no way improved. George describes his brother's difficulties:

> Soon after he married, Robert told me, in a letter, that he had sold his fiddle, and got a wife. Like most poor men, he got a wife first, and had to get household stuff afterward. It took him some time to get out of ready-furnished lodgings. At length, by hard working, & c. he acquired a bed of his own, and hired the room up one pair of stairs, at 14, Bell-alley, Coleman-street. The landlord kindly gave him leave to sit and work in the light garret, two pair of stairs higher.
>
> In this garret, amid six or seven other workmen, his active mind employed itself in composing *The Farmer's Boy.*

Although his surroundings were far from restful or conducive to thought, Robert committed whole sections of his poem to memory before he had a chance to write them down. The whole of **"Winter"** and most of **"Autumn"** were finished before he had put a single line on paper. It could not have been in the hope of fame or profit that he undertook this task. His ambitions were limited to the desire to present his mother with a printed copy of his poem, and before it had even been accepted for publication he assured his brother that he would not slacken off shoemaking on the chance of making five pounds out of *The Farmer's Boy.*

There was an urgency that made him write this poem which he never recaptured in his later work. It was a labour of love, a *credo,* and in a sense a gesture of defiance. He was proud of being, in his own words, a clod-bred poet, and his poem was an act of disassociation from the urban world into which he had been forced. In spirit he was never a Londoner, though he spent more than half his life in that city, "When I said that I felt myself at home," he reflected in 1810 when his fame was assured and he was already contemplating returning to the land he loved, "I ought to have said that I wish'd the Country my home; and that radical first-planted principle in my composition can never be blotted out by London and all it can produce." The great city can have made singularly little impression on this preoccupied shoemaker. He was not gifted with imagination, but his memory shielded him from uncongenial surroundings, and enabled him to transfer his mental life to those fields and woodlands where he had been most happy. "I have no leisure for any thing but thinking," he wrote at about this time. Memory was the only palliative to present misery.

The booksellers were not eager to print *The Farmer's Boy.* Bloomfield's manuscript was returned with a variety of excuses, and at last in despair of seeing it in print he gave it to his brother. In November 1798 George forwarded the poem to Capel Lofft, a gentleman of letters, eclectic and liberal in his tastes, whose benevolence not only to Bloomfield but to Kirke White earned him from Byron the stricture of being "the Maecenas of Shoemakers and preface-writer general to distressed versemen; a kind of gratis *accoucheur* to those who wish to be delivered of rhyme, but do not know how to bring forth."

Capel Lofft immediately realized the merit of *The Farmer's Boy,* and with enormous enthusiasm prepared the book for publication. He corrected the orthography and grammar, and, most important of all, found a bookseller who would produce it. "I have no doubt of its reception with the public," he said, "I have none of its going down to posterity with honour: which is not always the fate of productions which are popular in their day." Robert was content to leave the arrangements to Capel Lofft. He himself continued to make shoes, whistling and singing as he worked, and although he experienced at times the first pangs of the dejection and pain that were to haunt his later years he was tolerably content. To support a family on a journeyman's wage was no easy matter, but "there are times," he told his mother, "when the fire burns clear, and we all well, and our beer drawn good, and the candle fresh snuff'd, that I feel myself quite happy."

The publication of *The Farmer's Boy* in 1800 was an immediate success. Within three years 26,000 copies had been printed: a greater number of a new poem than had ever before been sold in so short a time. Like Duck, Bloomfield became a familiar name overnight, and he was sought out by the rich and the curious. Robert was able to send his mother a copy of the medium-sized edition of his poem, and reported to her that the Duke of Grafton, at the instigation of Capel Lofft, had invited him round and "gave me five guineas screwed up in a little bit of paper, and asked a thousand questions." The Duke was as enthusiastic as Lofft had been in the discovery of "a real untaught genius starting from our neighbourhood." He settled a small annuity of £15 on Bloomfield and obtained for him a job at the Seal Office.

At the end of the poet's first visit he was asked what books he would like. His reply was immediate: the poems of Burns. One of the ladies in the company added those of Mrs. Barbauld; but Bloomfield's choice was instinctively right. Burns was as fine a model as he could wish for, and although Robert knew himself to lack the intensity and inspiration of the Scottish poet, he clave to him rather than to the fashionable insipidities of Mrs. Barbauld. Both the success of Burns's genius and the wreckage of his life were constantly in Bloomfield's mind. Writing to the Earl of Buchan in 1802 he said: "'Remember Burns' has been the watchword of my friends. *I do remember Burns*; but I am not Burns, neither have I his fire to fan, nor to quench, nor his passions to controul." But the example of Burns held fatal fascinations for the young poet. The self-identifications of Clare were only different in degree from the parallels that Bloomfield drew between Burns's condition and his own. Contemplating the worries that surrounded him he would reflect, "perhaps Bob Burns had some such cross-grain'd vexations as these, and strove to cure them by drinking." It is probable that Bloomfield did much the same.

Robert accepted his new position as the centre of London literary interest with great calmness and without becoming conceited. Although Charles Lamb considered him to be "a damn'd stupid hound in company," he was on the whole well received, and secured both patrons and friends amongst a wide circle of society. His letters show him to have been singularly unmoved by lionization. To his brother he reported in August 1801, without adding further comment, "my Book affairs go on tolarably. I am getting acquainted with another Barronett. . . ."

Not everyone, however, was content to leave him to advance his own fame. His work was constantly interrupted by callers, and by post he received "many honourable testimonies of esteem from Strangers: Letters without a name, but filld with the most cordial advice, and allmost a parental anxiety for my safety under so great a share of publick applause." Pleasant as such interest might be to a man whom the world had hitherto always ignored, it was not helpful to his straitened financial position. To enter into society added fresh responsibilities and expenses, and Bloomfield was forced by the demands of his family to continue working when interruptions permitted. "My regular ernings are deminish'd," he complained to his brother,

> in proportion to my corispondence and calling friends, my rent is a guinea pr. Month, which you know well cannot be supported by Journyman Shoemaking, under these circumstances I must either secure a regular income, or devour the produce of my litterary fame: This last I dont like to do, neither do I like mastering. I am very well off at present, but as the World is staring at me had not I better be seen bury??

On the whole the world stared at Bloomfield and was gratified. Southey wrote enthusiastically about *The Farmer's Boy* in *The Critical Review*. Hazlitt, Rogers, Dyer, and a host of others added their praise. Lamb's was one of the few dissentient voices. Vernor and Hood, Bloomfield's publishers, pointed out that the merit of the poem was "contested pro & con by the Literary world," but despite this professional caution there were few who did not unreservedly acclaim, in Bernard Barton's words, "our own more chaste Theocritus."

In view of the unanimity of favourable opinion in 1800 and the little recognition it receives today, it will be useful at this juncture to examine in more detail the poem by which Bloomfield's poetic merits must be judged, *The Farmer's Boy.*

"I was determined that what I said on Farming should be EXPERIMENTALLY true," wrote Bloomfield to explain the principle on which he had written *The Farmer's Boy.* Truth to events within his own experience is the most distinctive feature of the poem, and the accuracy with which he describes the minutiae of agricultural procedure and natural events is all the more astonishing when one considers the circumstances under which Bloomfield wrote. Thomson's *Seasons* was never far from him, but the debt was so immediately obvious (the structural plan of the two poems being identical) that he took pains to disassociate himself in treatment of subject from the manner of his great master. "No Alpine wonders thunder through my verse," he declared in the opening lines of "Spring," obliquely referring to Thomson's love of florid, foreign descriptions. Although he is more homely in his seasonal pageant, and although verisimilitude is a poor substitute for vision, Bloomfield does succeed in capturing the spirit of the farm without being purely trivial. It is true that he lacks the flashes of genius that irradiate Thomson's turbid poem, but his average standard is surprisingly high. The couplet is handled with more freedom than in Duck's day; end-stopping is less inevitable, and there is a flexibility of diction and expression for which the credit must go not only to the poet but to the relaxing of poetic conventions during the later years of the eighteenth century.

The Farmer's Boy was not written autobiographically. It was well known that Giles was, in fact, a portrait of the poet in his youth, but none the less the lack of an insistent first person singular was conducive to better workmanship and less special pleading. Duck, in describing the arduous life of a tasker, could not detach himself from his work to view his whole surroundings with a proportionate vision. A thresher was not the mouthpiece for a composite picture of the countryside. No more was a farmer's boy; but Bloomfield used Giles only as a focal point to a larger background, much as Constable used figures in his farm-landscapes. Between Thomson and Bloomfield the difference in treatment, even of events common to both their poems, was so great that although many reviewers of *The Farmer's Boy* suggested the likelihood of parallelism, no specific accusations were lodged. Hazlitt, in a brilliant analysis of Bloomfield's poem in his *Lectures on the English Poets,* illustrates this.

> Bloomfield very beautifully describes the lambs in springtime as racing round the hillocks of green turf: Thomson, in describing the same image, makes the

mound of earth the remains of an old Roman encampment. Bloomfield never gets beyond his own experience; and that is somewhat confined. He gives the simple appearance of nature, but he gives it naked, shivering, and unclothed with the drapery of a moral imagination.

Despite his assertion that

> The Farmer's life displays in every part
> A moral lesson to the sensual heart,

Bloomfield was not a moral artist; Thomson, on the other hand, was intensely didactic. Hazlitt found a nakedness in Bloomfield's poem; certainly it is sparsely clad, but one must be grateful that he did not furbish his account with too much moral sentence. The infrequent instances of such additions are a salutary warning of weaknesses to which later he became sadly prone.

A peasant-poet is usually a humble man writing well within the orbit of his equally humble capacities. He is restricted in range, but not in excellence. *The Farmer's Boy* never attempts to strut or soar—indeed, Hazlitt considered that Bloomfield's Muse was not only rustic but menial in her aspect. This is not a condemnation so long as prosaism is avoided, and Bloomfield generally succeeded in retaining a thoroughly plain, but poetic, style. Towards the end of his life, in 1821, he wrote down what he considered to be bad ingredients in composition. These ingredients, when omitted, led to a form of writing in the language of ordinary life. Compound epithets, inversion, triplets, weak closing lines and archaic expressions he eschewed. Long passages in *The Farmer's Boy* contain no poetic diction, and sentences are linked together in so natural a way that "tills" and "ands" become tediously apparent.

The discipline of the couplet kept Bloomfield from straying far into the new, Wordsworthian theories of poetry. He had not the power of thought or invention to arrive at, or even to support, such controversial issues, and his popularity would certainly have waned if he had. In poetic technique Bloomfield was conservative but an individualist. Just as he prided himself on never meddling with politics or religion, so he refused to be associated with any school or style of literature. Wisely he desired to be known and judged as a farmer's boy: he sought no better name.

The association of Bloomfield with Wordsworth was not purely fortuitous. Although the Lake poet cannot be said to have influenced the poetry of the farmer's boy, Bloomfield's taste for simplicity of expression and accuracy of rural description made him amongst the first wholehearted admirers of Wordsworth's poetry outside the Lakers themselves. In 1801 Bloomfield was a far more esteemed and established poet than Wordsworth, and his opinions were not without influence. A hitherto unpublished letter to his brother George, dated April 19th, contains as a postscript, "I will soon send you Wordsworth's poems, if there is no poetry in them I will give up my pretention to feeling and Nature. I can trust you I think to be struck with them, first with their extreem simplicity, and then for what I before mention'd, *Nature*." Instinctive, natural taste has been claimed by a number of enthusiasts for a multitude of untaught geniuses. In this instance Bloomfield does seem to have immediately appreciated the merits of a poet who for many years laboured against fashion and prejudice. But he discovered in Wordsworth only what he had been striving to achieve himself.

Life on the farm has altered surprisingly little over the centuries. There is a universality of image in the language of nature that is the most constant and cohesive element in the flux of art and society. Giles, the farmer's boy in Bloomfield's poem, may in detail be performing different tasks from those that might fall upon him nowadays, but in general they are the same. Around him—and Giles is particularly conscious of external nature—nothing alters. The early morning chorus of birds still sings for those that rise as early as Giles, and if disturbed,

> Stopp'd in her song perchance the starting thrush
> Shook a white shower from the blackthorn bush.

With a delicate, Clare-like observation one can still watch how

> The small dust-colour'd beetle climbs with pain,
> O'er the smooth plantain-leaf, a spacious plain!
> Thence higher still, by countless steps convey'd,
> He gains the summit of a shiv'ring blade,
> And flirts his filmy wings, and looks around,
> Exulting in his distance from the ground.

Such minutely observed details are typical of Bloomfield's art. He possessed neither the scientific spirit of Erasmus Darwin, nor Thomson's flair for generalizing in his record of the natural world around him. Visual detail and precision were dear to him, but when first-hand experience failed he was timid of using his imagination. A year before *The Farmer's Boy* was published, Robert wrote to his brother, "I have read Gay's 'Trivia'; it descends to minute descriptions of London, more minute than mine do of the country; his minutiae must be more subject to change than mine, less dependent on nature." Even at the end of the century in which it was written the art of walking the streets of London had changed. Bloomfield, leaning on the immutability of the natural scene, hoped that his details would not suffer a similar fate to Gay's.

The cycle of the farming year opens with "Spring," and the reader is quickly introduced to Giles, a boy not yet grown up into the cares of the world. Hard work did not bring with it the shades of the prisonhouse because it did not bring responsibility. There is something of the unconscious, primal freshness of the child of nature in Giles, which Duck's thresher, absorbed with the duties of the labouring round, never reflected.

> 'Twas thus with Giles: meek, fatherless, and poor:
> Labour his portion, but he felt no more;
> No stripes, no tyranny his steps pursued;
> His life was constant, cheerful servitude:
> Strange to the world, he wore a bashful look,
> The fields his study, Nature was his book.

The farmer, Giles's master, kept the young lad fully occupied. But the tasks were various and performed with good will—though not always efficiently. Giles was never so hard-pressed that he could not bend his hat into a telescope to watch the ascending lark, or fall asleep in the summer sun when he should have been bird-scaring. Duck, the day-labourer, analyses the tribulations of his work. Giles is not so introspective: he accepts the task and describes the scene resulting from it. His vision is far less confined than the thresher's, but no less accurate.

Spring ploughing offers Bloomfield an opportunity for the word-painting at which he excels.

> With smiling brow the ploughman cleaves his way,
> Draws his fresh parallels, and, wid'ning still,
> Treads slow the heavy dale, or climbs the hill:
> Strong on the wing his busy followers play,
> Where writhing earth-worms meet th'unwelcome day;
> Till all is changed, and hill and level down
> Assume a livery of a sober brown;
> Again disturb'd, when Giles with wearying strides
> From ridge to ridge the ponderous harrow guides;
> His heels deep sinking every step he goes,
> Till dirt adhesive loads his clouted shoes.

There is a refreshing directness in such a passage that is seldom to be found so long-sustained even in Thomson's poem, and although there is no visionary quality in the verse there is a pictorial clarity that is entirely satisfying.

Mingled with such writing is a didactic element. Bloomfield overrides Giles to discourse on a variety of topics. The correct method of using scarecrows, the docking of horses' tails, and the new refinement that was fast imposing a caste system on rural society, all come up for discussion and judgment. On these matters Bloomfield had strong opinions and argues convincingly, but not in the manner of a farmer's boy. At times his appeal is purely pathetic: a description of lambs at play is followed by an indignant attack on the "murd'ring Butcher" whose abattoir is their destination.

> Like the fond dove from fearful prison freed,
> Each seems to say, "Come, let us try our speed;"
> Away they scour, impetuous, ardent, strong,

> The green turf trembling as they bound along;
> Adown the slope, then up the hillock climb,
> Where every molehill is a bed of thyme;
> There panting stop; yet scarcely can refrain:
> A bird, a leaf, will set them off again;
> Or, if a gale with strength unusual blow,
> Scatt'ring the wild-brier roses into snow,
> Their little limbs increasing efforts try,
> Like the torn flower the fair assemblage fly.
> Ah, fallen rose! sad emblem of their doom;
> Frail as thyself, they perish as they bloom!

Bloomfield's freedom from poetic diction has already been commented upon. Usually this was nothing but an advantage, but in technical descriptions, such as that of butter-making, he is perhaps too exact. Facts are only one of the ingredients of poetry, and although Bloomfield was adept in handling material that the Augustans would have considered unsuitable for verse, he did not always load any of the rifts of his subject with ore. On occasions he deliberately wrote colloquially, and even humorously; his lines on Mary, the village beauty, stripped to the stays in the heat of harvesting, or the gander tyrannizing over the animals in the farmyard, show an ability to laugh that only Burns amongst peasant-poets possessed to the full.

Although the farmer himself is often unwilling to leave

> his elbow-chair
> His cool, brick floor, his pitcher and his ease,

Giles is at everybody's beck and call. He has only to pass the door of the dairy and

> The chatt'ring dairy-maid immersed in steam,
> Singing and scrubbing midst her milk and cream,
> Bawls out, "Go fetch the Cows."

Even so simple a task does not pass without comment. The reluctance of the cattle to leave their pasture is noted, and the fact that one cow invariably leads the rest. Each season is filled with a succession of such precise observations, and Bloomfield's verses are packed with country lore. Nor are his interests confined to the world of nature. He tells of a young mad girl in the village with a Wordsworthian curiosity in the subject, he visits the village church, which displays "the rude inelegance of Poverty," and discusses the deterioration of master and man relationships during the recent years. "Let labour have its due," he pleads, and tells how the spirit that prevails at harvest-home, when Distinction is in abeyance, was once common for more than one day in the year.

The seasonal labours naturally occupy the greater part of the poem. In early summer the hard-clodded ground is harrowed, and Giles is sent bird-scaring. Cobbett as a youth performed a similar task, and so, early in the new century, did Joseph Arch, the founder of the Agricultural Labourers' Union. The latter did not have such pleasant memories as Giles. At the age of nine, he recollected, he used to stand for twelve hours a day "in a new-sown field shivering on an empty stomach, while the cold wind blew and the chill rain poured down in torrents." Giles's easy, sleep-interspersed vigil is in strange contrast to Arch's; but Bloomfield was fortunate in having an humane employer. Both accounts are doubtless true, but at the time it was Bloomfield's that people wanted to hear about.

Hay-making receives only a short mention, and this omission prompted an uneducated farmer at Croydon, in Surrey, to write *An Appendix to the Season of Spring, in the Rural Poem, "The Farmer's Boy."* Joseph Holland, the author, published this poem locally in 1806, and, in contrast to Duck, it was the only book of acknowledged imitation that Bloomfield inspired.

The harvest is the principal event in "Summer," and the gaiety and enjoyment with which everyone participates is more in the spirit of Thomson than Duck. But it is not an idyll, and "the sov'reign cordial, home-brew'd ale" quenches thirsts that have been raised by hard and unsparing work.

Giles's occupations during the autumn are equally various. The pigs are sent out to forage for acorns in the unenclosed woodlands, and winter wheat is sown. Once again Giles becomes a bird-scarer; he diverts himself this time by building a hut—very much as Bevis, or any country child might do—and cooks sloes and rose-hips over a little fire.

> o'er the flame the sputt'ring fruit he rests,
> Placing green sods to seat the coming guests;
> His guests by promise; playmates young and gay:—
> But ah! fresh pastimes lure their steps away!
> He sweeps his hearth, and homeward looks in vain,
> Till feeling Disappointment's cruel pain,
> His fairy revels are exchanged for rage,
> His banquet marr'd, grown dull his hermitage.

During the winter fodder must be provided for the cattle, and Giles is employed carting turnips, a newly-introduced root crop, to the beasts in the frozen fields. For those in the stalls hay needed to be carried;

> Deep-plunging cows their rustling feast enjoy,
> And snatch sweet mouthfuls from the passing boy,
> Who moves unseen beneath his trailing load,
> Fills the tall racks, and leaves a scatter'd road.

Giles himself was too young for the most arduous task of the winter season, but it is a job that Duck had fully described before him—threshing. Well into the evening the threshing-floor resounds with noise.

> Though night approaching bids for rest prepare,
> Still the flail echoes through the frosty air,

> Nor stops till deepest shades of darkness come,
> Sending at length the weary labourer home.

Daylight does not last long in winter-time; after dark there are more sinister happenings. The shepherd is on guard against the roaming dog that has been worrying his sheep, and Giles, walking down a narrow lane, is terrified by the sight of

> A grisly Spectre, clothed in silver-grey,
> Around whose feet the waving shadows play,

—an apparition that is happily discovered to be an old ash-tree.

The seasons again change, and the first lambs herald a new spring. Although the poem ends here, the theme can never end, and Bloomfield more than any other cyclical poet recognizes the recurrence of the fundamental natural force that presses the sap through the hedgerows and the flowers from the earth. Giles, perceiving the new year "returning as the wheel returns," views it with joy.

> Another Spring! His heart exulting cries,
> Another Year.

"The public taste hangs like a millstone round the neck of all original genius that does not conform to established and exclusive models," declared Hazlitt. It was Thomson who had paved the way for Bloomfield's success, and it is in connection with his study of *The Seasons* that Hazlitt took the opportunity of including **The Farmer's Boy** amongst the greater poems in his *Lectures on the English Poets*. In Hazlitt's eyes the association was not invidious. He admired the "delicacy, faithfulness and *naïveté*" of Bloomfield's poem, and bestowed on it the shrewdest criticism that it was to obtain. "We cannot expect from original genius alone," he continued, "without education, in modern and more artificial periods, the same bold and independent results as in former periods." Whether those "former periods" lay in the romantic imagination, or whether Hazlitt is referring to writers such as Langland, whose poems have come to us unburdened by biography, is not clear; but the reasons Hazlitt gives for his statement are interesting.

Although the original genius was free from the trammels of custom and other men's ideas, he tended to be oppressed by his situation. Advantages that he did not possess and glory that he did not share made him conscious and imitative of his more fortunate, but often less talented, brothers in verse; whereas his natural inclination should have led him to reap the rich harvest of his own original inspiration—a harvest the more precious for being hitherto untouched. Another reason that Hazlitt advanced to explain the ultimate failure of original genius was that such genius needed to be supported by "a corresponding state of manners, passions, and religious belief." Against such a judgment Bloomfield cannot stand; nor for that matter could any English untutored poet. Only Burns and Iolo Morganwg might be defended by these critical standards.

The tenor of Hazlitt's criticism was nevertheless highly favourable, though he realized the weakness inherent in Bloomfield's poem. Not so did Dr. Nathan Drake, who did not consider "any production can be put in competition with it since the days of Theocritus." Dr. Drake's was not an isolated opinion, and it is, therefore, refreshing to find Lamb downright in his condemnation. Writing to his friend Manning on November 3, 1800, he adds in a postscript,

> You ask me about the *Farmer's Boy*. Don't you think the fellow who wrote it (who is a shoemaker) has a poor mind? Don't you find he is always silly about *poor Giles*, and those abject kind of phrases, which mark a man that looks up to wealth? None of Burns's poet dignity. What do you think? I have just opened him; but he makes me sick.

Lamb's views have, perhaps, been vindicated by the steady decline of Bloomfield's verse in public regard; but it is too hot-blooded a criticism to be accepted without reserve. It contains an immediate perception of weaknesses that Hazlitt was later to generalize in his lecture on Thomson and Crabbe, but it is blind to many undeniable merits that the poem possesses.

The opinion of most of Bloomfield's distinguished contemporaries must have been exceedingly gratifying to him. Capel Lofft was energetic in promoting interest in a book that cast not a little reflected glory on himself. George Dyer, to whom Lofft had sent a copy, wrote back at some length in praise of the poem.

> Yes Sir, I have read *The Farmer's Boy,* and intend to read it over and over again some time hence. *The Farmer's Boy* appears to me a truly original and beautiful poem. It recalled to my mind those ages and those countries in which the poet and the shepherd were more naturally united, and under those circumstances some of the earliest Scotch Ballads were written, and they please us because they breathe the language of nature and speak to the heart. . . . I perceive no fopperies—no meretricious ornaments, no language of bigotry and enthusiasm in Bloomfield.

Amongst the reviewers Southey, writing in *The Critical Review,* was conspicuous for his encouragement and praise. "This poem abounds with beautiful lines of accurate and minute description," he declared. Lofft himself, in a note to George Bloomfield was, at least at the time of publication, unreserved in his respect. "His want of Education (what is generally so called) has had its advantages, if he had been learned it would not have been possible that he should have produced so purely

original a poem." Like Hannah More with her milkwoman, Lofft changed his tune when Bloomfield showed the first stirrings of an independent spirit.

Fame and fortune did not make Bloomfield happy. His financial affairs worried and confused him, the expenses of his new position in society, his desire to help his relations and the constant ill-health that dogged both him and his family, all combined to depress him. "I think a man really mad is far happier than one who has this dastardly sinking of the soul, and retains his reason seemingly for no other purpose than to prove its weakness," he confessed to his brother in August 1801; and again, "O Lord! what a poor creature is Man! and of Men what a poor creature is a Bloomfield." As the years passed his letters become less and less concerned with affairs of the spirit. His eagerness in the discovery of poetry, and the critical opinions that he exchanged with his brother die away. Instead there are recurrent accounts of the pain in his loins, his rheumatism and his migraine. Hypochondria and a morbid interest in his own health dominate his correspondence.

Bloomfield's wife, who might have lifted his spirits, had become an ardent disciple of Joanna Southcott. He himself hated his new employment at the Seal Office, and the insinuations he overheard that his job was a poet's sinecure. He wanted to write, but had neither the inspiration nor the time. His days were filled with callers, visits to the printers and other worries. "I have no time to write down my Rhimes," he told his brother, "I have enough on my mind to craze a saint."

To add to his distress a quarrel developed with Capel Lofft. Bloomfield was unwilling to enter into it, but was caught between his printer and his patron. Certain eulogistic notes, by Lofft and others, were to have been inserted in front of the individual poems in the new edition of Bloomfield's work. Robert claimed that this prejudiced independent judgment of the poems, and was harmful to his reputation. He asked that they might be printed at the end of the book. Lofft, who was alone in being aggrieved, accused Bloomfield of trying to squeeze him out. In fact nothing could have been farther from the truth. Capel Lofft received nothing but the sincerest praise and gratitude in both the public and the private writings of Bloomfield. The quarrel made further relationships very strained, but Robert never ceased to regret the estrangement of his "first great friend Mr. Lofft."

Robert Bloomfield never held those radical principles that some of his critics ascribed to him. In his poetry he recorded facts and not opinions, except on certain humanitarian subjects such as cruelty to horses. In his life, however, he did not cease to express the opinions, and plead the causes, of the class from which he sprang. On the subject of illiteracy he put forward his views, as might be expected, with considerable force. A remark by a Mr. Windham had offended him, and on May 30, 1802 Bloomfield wrote,

> the *common people* of his native country, are a rough set no doubt, but I dislike the doctrine of keeping them in their dirt, for though it holds good as to the preservation of potatoes, it would be no grateful reflection to good minds to know that a man's natural abilities had been smother'd for want of beeing able to read and write. How can we consistently praise the inestimable blessing of letters and not wish to extend it? Or why should the Great and the Wealthy confine the probable production of intelectual excelence to their own class, and exclude, by withholding the polish, all that might amongst the poor by nature be intended to be Newton's and Locke's?

That same month he wrote to Mr. Pratt, acknowledging his poem, *Bread,* in terms that would not have pleased his patrons. "To see one class of the community grow immencely rich at the expence of another, to me allways argue'd an inefficiency in the Laws of this or any Country where it happens."

Bloomfield was not given to flattery, but neither was he by nature a reformer. Early in his career as a poet he received and followed some excellent advice from the Duke of Grafton; and two years before his death he was able to assert "that out of all my numerous friends, none have got even a Sonnet from me; flattery is a poor way of paying debts." Duck would have profited from a similar determination. It was, perhaps, Bloomfield's noticeable silence in the matter of verse tributes, and his similar reticence in acknowledging the benefits of the Government or the Church, that caused it to be widely supposed that he had "imbibed both Deistical and Republican principles." In 1821 his good friend Mr. Baker wrote imploring him to deny the rumours that were having a damaging effect on his reputation. In his reply Bloomfield remarked that the accusations were only half the story. Cobbett, far from thinking him a republican, considered that Robert had been "taken in tow" by the Government to prevent him writing in favour of the people. Radical reformers, even when they championed the rural poor, met with no support from Bloomfield. "Cobbet and Hunt are men whom I would not trust with power," he told Baker, "they are too eager to obtain it. Universal suffrage is an impracticable piece of nonsense."

At the end of 1801 Bloomfield was anxiously awaiting the publication of his second book, *Rural Tales.* "No dying Lover in a romance ever long'd for the bridal-day more sincerely or fervently than I do for the birth of my Vollm." This collection of shorter, principally narrative, poems was again kindly received by the critics. Southey considered the standard to be as high as *The Farmer's Boy,* and Clare, in a letter written in 1825, after Bloom-

field's death, was especially attracted by one of the ballads in this collection. Recollecting all that he knew of a man whom he had never met, but whose genius he admired, Clare wrote, in his usual unpunctuated fashion,

> he dyed ripe for immortality and had he written nothing else but **"Richard and Kate"** that fine picture of Rural Life were sufficient to establish his name as the English Theocritus and the first of Rural Bards in this country and as Fashion (that feeble substitute for fame) had nothing to do in his exaltation its neglect will have nothing to affect his memory it is built on a more solid foundation and time will bring its own reward to the **"Farmers Boy."**

There is little that would attract a reader today in these sentimental anecdotes of idealized rural life. Their recitation moved Bloomfield to tears, but they are undistinguished poems, and, unlike *The Farmer's Boy,* might have been written by a townsman. Like Duck, Bloomfield's limited powers made him a one-poem man. The more he attempted to recapture his lost Muse, the farther he strayed into mediocrity. Towards the end of his poetic career he wrote,

> I sometimes dream that I shall one day venture again before the public, something in my old manner, some Country tales, and spiced with love and courtship might yet please, for Rural life by the art of Cooking may be made a relishing and high flavour'd dish, whatever it may be in reality.

A clue to his inspirational failure may be seen in this confession. When he wrote *The Farmer's Boy* no "cooking" was required. Something of the visionary gleam was still with him. When he no longer found nature sufficient in herself, and had recourse to artifices to render her attractive, he ceased to be a country poet and became a hack.

Although *Rural Tales* was very far from being a failure, the attention paid to each subsequent volume was less. Bloomfield strayed from poetry to write children's stories and a play, *Hazelwood Hall,* despite an avowed ignorance of "the 'Dramatic unities,' or of what is call'd 'Stage effect.'" But his pen grew less willing as his hypochondria increased. In his letters he constantly talked of the large sums of money he was earning. At the same time he was always in a state of near-insolvency. His misfortunes were not entirely imaginary. In 1811 his publisher, Hood, died and his successor sold most of Bloomfield's copyrights before himself going bankrupt. By his own estimation Robert lost nearly £300 from this stroke of ill-fortune.

The proceeds from his poems were never the only source of Bloomfield's income. After he had abandoned his job at the Seal Office he started bookselling; but this project failed, and he returned for a while to his original trade of shoemaking. No longer was his temperament suited to a journeyman's occupation; neither, he considered, was his health. Apart from the making of verses the only trade he consistently plied was the manufacture of aeolian harps. In July 1807 he complained to his brother of the "accumulating plagues which arise from my Harp trade . . . and from the unseasonable and impudand visits of the vain, and the interested, and the curious, taking up my time, inviting me to Dinner etc. etc." Seventeen years later amongst his personal effects auctioned after his death were six unfinished aeolian harps; a testimony, perhaps, to the number of callers who had distracted him.

There were bright moments in the gloom that enveloped his years of fame. Now and then he would escape from his wife and explore the countryside. In 1803 he was astonished at the romantic prospects around Dorking: Leith Hill and Box Hill were the highest eminences he had ever seen. For some years he made a similar expedition each summer, either alone or with friends. The most memorable of these, in 1807, was to the West Country, and he published a record in verse of all that he had seen. It did not come easily. He wrote and rewrote, submitted his manuscripts to criticism and then started again. His impressions were strong enough, but he had lost the ability to record them spontaneously. The spirit of the topographer—the guide-book writer rather than the poet—fills his pages. The horizons that opened before him were too wide, too superficially seen, to yield any profitable meditation. Into a verse-letter, written in little more than an octosyllabic jingle, he attempted to compress the history, geography, and poetic impulses of the March-lands. In days when travel was still restricted there may have been a good excuse (though not a poetic one) for such a commentary, but the charm was ephemeral and the prosaism of the work is only emphasized by Bloomfield's frequent use of footnotes to explain facts otherwise too cumbersome to be included.

The later years of Bloomfield's life, and the further books of poetry that he produced in his constant efforts to flog his failing Muse, are best passed over briefly. His inspiration had been choked by success. Like Clare and Burns drink, ill-health and the deceptive dawn of untroubled days undermined the years of his fame. *Good Tidings,* a poem written to advance the cause of Jenner's then controversial vaccine, *Wild Flowers,* and *May-Day with the Muses* did nothing to advance his reputation. Sentiment drifted with little struggle into sentimentality, and rhyming became a laborious technique without the urgency of self-expression.

In 1812 the poet, impecunious and London-sick, moved out of the city to Shefford, a village in Bedfordshire. The rent of his cottage was covered by the annuity that he had begged the new Duke of Grafton to renew. But even the reduced expenses of a country life proved too great for his straitened resources. Within four years an appeal was published soliciting contributions from the friends and admirers of Robert Bloomfield. A trust fund was formed, from which before long Robert was desirous of drawing the capital. It was not only that he was improvident; his family and many of his relatives received more assistance than he was capable of giving, and Bloomfield's popularity was not enhanced amongst his benefactors by the discovery that the money they had contributed towards his welfare had been passed on to some poor dependent.

In 1817 the Duke of Grafton, after some prompting, paid Bloomfield's annuity, with a chilly regret "that Mr. B's muse should have been so long silent." That same year Crabbe met him during a visit to London. In his journal for July 3rd he remarked, "he had better rested as a shoemaker, or even a farmer's boy; for he would have been a farmer perhaps in time, and now he is an unfortunate poet. By the way, indiscretion did much." Bloomfield's fellow East Anglian was a man who had himself experienced the misery of poverty and want; it is therefore on a more charitable note that he left him: "he is, however, to be pitied and assisted." But it could have been of little consolation to Bloomfield, the sale of whose own poems had much diminished, to learn "that Murray gave parson Crabb 3 thousand pounds for his Tales."

For a few more years he struggled to keep alive. Neither his family, nor the surrounding countryside comforted him. Sickness and debt were his companions, and the first signs of blindness only served to increase his isolated, unsupported misery. He had outgrown the society of the class from which he had originated, but had not been adopted into any new social group. This would have been no misfortune to a more self-sufficient or confident genius, but Bloomfield was neither. His slight physical strength had been sapped by hardship, insobriety and mental nagging; his easy and mild disposition had been subjected to the stresses and strains of a precarious living on the fringes of fashion. The boy who had celebrated his changing fortune with the panache of flinging his hat into the horsepond, and the young man who could mirror that gay, careless pleasure in a retrospective poem about the farming year, are hardly recognizable in Bloomfield towards the end of his life. He had too long been an exile from the sources of his inspiration; and when at last he was free to return to the fields that had brought him fame, he had not the resilience to readapt himself. The moral merit that his London training had taught him to be a necessary adjunct to bucolic poetry he never doubted to accept without testing its prefabricated sentiments against the pulse of his own experience. Cobbett, no poet but a man of rugged common sense, whose early upbringing was not unlike that of his contemporary Bloomfield, advised young writers to "never write about any matter that you do not well understand. If you clearly understand all about your matter, you will never want thoughts, and thoughts instantly become words."

Robert would have done well to heed such advice, but Shefford was not to prove another Sapiston; when he arrived there he was already a prematurely broken man. At the age of fifty-six the illnesses that had increasingly oppressed him overcame his weak resistance, and on August 19, 1823, he died. The following year his meagre household goods were auctioned, his literary remains published, and his name became all but forgotten by new generations who found in the poetry of Romanticism the secret that enabled them to step through the mirror that Thomson and Bloomfield had so lovingly held out to nature, towards an understanding of the mystery of things.

Bibliography

ROBERT BLOOMFIELD

The Farmer's Boy: A Rural Poem (London, 1800).

The Poems of Robert Bloomfield (3 vols., London, 1827).

Hart, William H., ed., *Selections from the Correspondence of Robert Bloomfield* (London, 1870).

Gant, Roland, ed., *A Selection of Poems by Robert Bloomfield* (London, 1947).

A collection of unpublished letters in the British Museum.

Jonathan Lawson (essay date 1980)

SOURCE: Lawson, Jonathan. "The Later Works: Continued Awareness and Final Decline" and "Bloomfield and the Rural Tradition: Its Value and Values." In *Robert Bloomfield*, pp. 94-154. Boston: Twayne Publishers, 1980.

[*In the following excerpt, Lawson discusses some of Bloomfield's later works, including his poem on the smallpox epidemic, and evaluates the poet's rural identity and influences.*]

THE LATER WORKS: CONTINUED AWARENESS AND FINAL DECLINE

I RURAL TALES, BALLADS, AND SONGS

If there is a unified critical opinion of Bloomfield's works, it is that the first are the best. One modern critic finds that the first poetry, *The Farmer's Boy,* was surely his best;[1] another finds Bloomfield's next work, *Rural Tales, Ballads, and Songs,* full of "undistinguished poems."[2] More recently, Graham Reed observed that in his later works Bloomfield "succumbed to gentility; he allowed a stilted formalism to suffuse his verse," and that his "most ambitious works were in a characteristically eighteenth-century style."[3] In this there is just enough truth to want correcting. Even Edmund Blunden, who is indeed Bloomfield's foremost modern champion, finds *The Farmer's Boy* to be Bloomfield's greatest poem. The rest, he writes, illuminate it, "but none can rival its tenacious contentment in the bosom of earth. . . ."[4] The careful arguments for rural life and against urbanization, nevertheless, are continued in the later works, and it is evident that Bloomfield continued to be aware of the forces that were reshaping his native ground. If his arguments are less effective, it is less from want of conviction than from a lessening of his powers.

Still, as Rayner Unwin remarks, "*Rural Tales* was very far from being a failure."[5] The *Critical Review* in which Southey had so warmly reviewed *The Farmer's Boy* continued to champion the shoemaker-poet. After conceding the difficulty a poet faces in following a meritorious and successful first book and reviewing several of the pieces in the volume, the writer concludes, "We hope and believe that the success of this volume will equal *The Farmer's Boy,* as we are sure that its merits are not inferior. The manner in which that poem has been received is honorable to the public taste and to the public feeling. Neglected genius has too long been the reproach of England."[6] The *Monthly Mirror* in applauding Bloomfield's refusal to attempt to please the critics characterized the poems as "the easy, lively, and natural effusions of a truly poetical mind, abounding in just observation of village life and manners . . ." and predicted that the volume would please well the "almost innumerable admirers of the Farmer's Boy."[7] *Rural Tales* was, in part, responsible for John Clare's glowing praise of Bloomfield:

> Whatever cause his friends may have to regret the death of the Poet—Fame is not one of them for he dyed ripe for immortality & had he written nothing else but **"Richard and Kate"** [in *Rural Tales*] that fine picture of Rural Life were sufficient to establish his name as the English Theocritus & the first of Rural Bards in this country & as Fashion (that feeble substitute for Fame) had nothing to do with his exaltation its neglect will have nothing to effect his memory it is built on a more solid foundation & time [one line heavily scored out] will bring its own reward to the **"Farmer's Boy."**[8]

Since, on the one hand, history has proved Clare very wrong—Robert Bloomfield is not a name to conjure with today—and, on the other, time has not yet brought any real reward to Bloomfield's later poems, is it not possible that Clare completely missed the critical mark too? It is a fair question, but one, I think, that can be answered fairly in the negative. Clare was given to hyperbole whenever Bloomfield's name was mentioned, and he himself might be a fitter candidate to be called best of the rural bards. But there are in Bloomfield's later verse meritorious qualities which will be noted and examined here. These qualities are attached to Bloomfield's awareness of the future of English rural life and the future of her urban and rural art.

Rural Tales is a distinct departure from the conservative meter and sometimes elevated style of ***The Farmer's Boy.*** The subject is still rural life, but here Bloomfield presents a wider variety of characters, frequently in the social context of the village. Romance, rather naturally limited in his first poem which centered on a twelve-year-old, is here celebrated in several of its aspects. Women figure more prominently in the poems than in ***The Farmer's Boy.*** And Bloomfield now has a greater freedom of setting in which he can pursue the same emotional arguments presented in his first volume. Of the eighteen pieces in the collection, five are called "ballads," two "tales," and the rest either "songs" or nothing at all.

The first of the pieces, **"Richard and Kate: or *Fair-Day,*"** is called "A Suffolk Ballad" but is not in the conventional ballad meter. Instead, Bloomfield uses alternately rhymed, four-line stanzas all in iambic tetrameter with the general effect of fast movement in the verse. The meter may be one of the devices Bloomfield employs in avoiding the rank sentimentality to which the piece might have been subject. The modern reader, in fact, when apprised of the subject of the narrative, steels himself against an encounter with the maudlin, for the poem presents an old rural couple who totter to the green on fair day to watch their children and grandchildren in the festivities and who come tearfully to bless the assembled young before returning home alone. If read as a whole, however, **"Richard and Kate"** is an affirmation of rural life and the couple themselves.

Richard urges his aging wife to leave her spinning wheel and walk with him to the green. It is fair day, and more:

"Have you forgot, KATE, prithee say,
How many Seasons here we've tarry'd?
Tis *Forty* years, this very day,
Since you and I, old Girl, were married!"[9]

A humorous realism immediately appears. Their decision to make the long trek is reached because Kate cut her corns the previous night and now can walk more easily. Although theirs has been a life of cares, none intrude on this summer day. Richard even agrees to avoid long-winded tale telling and his ale at sundown so that Kate will join him.

"Aye KATE, I wool; . . . because I know,
Though time has been we both could run,

Such days are gone and over now; . . .
I only mean to see the fun."

(***R,*** 2)

Richard's statement echoes the patterned life described in ***The Farmer's Boy,*** and his quiet acceptance of the limitations of age is a natural result of that life.

So Richard in his Sunday breeches leads his wife across the countryside that Bloomfield knew so well. For the old couple, it is a quiet journey into their own past.

The day was up, the air serene,
The Firmament without a cloud;
The Bee humm'd o'er the level green;
Where knots of trembling Cowslips bow'd.

And *Richard* thus, with heart elate,
As past things rush'd across his mind,
Over his shoulder talk'd to KATE,
Who, snug tuckt up, walk'd slow behind.

(***R,*** 4)

Again we see that life where the land, the things of rural life, and the force of time could all be felt by common folk to have a natural and positive order as Richard remembers the "sly tricks" they once played on each other near a tree they pass. The tree prompts a different reaction from Kate, revealing her awareness of another part of the natural order:

"Tis true" she said; "But here behold,
And marvel at the course of Time;
Though you and I are both grown old,
This tree is only in its prime!"

(***R,*** 5)

Bloomfield, aware of the sentimental moralizing half a step beyond her statement, has Richard reply, "Well, Goody, don't stand preaching now; / Folks don't preach Sermons at a FAIR" (***R,*** 6).

Richard has predicted that their ten sons and daughters will all greet them and, when they arrive, his expectation is met in full. Sons, daughters, and grandchildren swarm around them, and the social joys of rural life which Bloomfield praised in ***The Farmer's Boy*** are again his theme.

The games, "Dicky Races," "more fam'd for laughter than for speed," and the very little ale it takes to mellow old Richard causes him to see his own past in the racers and to feel an almost foolish rejuvenation:

"I'm surely growing young again:
I feel myself so kedge and plump.
From head to foot I've not one pain;
Nay, hang me if I cou'd'nt jump."

(***R,*** 9)

His wife cuts short his fantasy by gently reminding him of his promise to return home at sunset, and tells him the children want time to talk with them. Like a youthful lover he "chuckt her by the chin" and they join the assembled family for a farewell quart of ale. There beneath a tree on the green, the old couple watch their grandchildren play.

Richard, full of a father's pride and the knowledge of his own mortality, utters a simple and emotional speech. A realistic figure capable of stumbling and foolishness yet full of a natural dignity, Richard stands opposed to the stereotype of the loutish peasant:

> "My Boys, how proud am I to have
> My name thus round the Country spread!
>
> Through all my days I've labour'd hard,
> And could of pains and Crosses tell;
> But this is Labour's great reward,
> To meet ye thus, and see ye well."

> (**R**, 11)

There is decorousness in the old man not dwelling on the vicissitudes he has known but being pleased with his humble reward. He tells of his wife's wishes which are sometimes mixed with tears, and of his own assurance to her that life moves as it will, giving man little to do but pray. Richard then pronounces a father's blessing on them all, and the poem moves to its emotional peak. The language is more natural than that which Wordsworth usually manages for his rustics:[10]

> "May you be all as old as I,
> And see your Sons to manhood grow;
> And, many a time before you die,
> Be just as pleased as I am now."
>
> Then (raising still his Mug and Voice,)
> "An Old Man's weakness don't despise!
> I love you well, my Girls and Boys
> God bless you all;" . . . so said his eyes—
>
> For, as he spoke, a big round drop
> Fell bounding on his ample sleeve;
> A witness which he could not stop,
> A witness which all hearts believe.

> (**R**, 12-13)

Only the next, stanza 37, is unfortunate, for Bloomfield slips away from simple language to poetize on filial piety. But he ends the piece simply and satisfyingly enough for the reader to grasp something of the humble fulfillment possible in the country:

> With thankful Hearts and strengthen'd Love,
> The poor old PAIR, supremely blest,
> Saw the Sun sink behind the grove,
> And gain'd once more their lowly rest.

> (**R**, 13)

Another age of rural love is the subject of **"Walter and Jane: or, The Poor Blacksmith,"** which Bloomfield further titles "A Country Tale." The vehicle for the tale is the iambic pentameter in the rhymed couplets of *The Farmer's Boy,* but, perhaps because his intent is less serious here, the couplets are less satisfying. It is here that charges of too strong an affinity with the Augustans are most telling, although Bloomfield does put the couplet to his own unique use. The whole piece, however, is less satisfying than **"Richard and Kate."**

"Walter and Jane" is the story of a young village blacksmith who falls in love with a pretty country maid just before she leaves the village to move some twelve miles away. The smith's feelings are persistent, and it is not long before he begins walking across the countryside to see her on Sundays. But Walter hesitates to tell her offering for his girl, "conscience" soon causes him to stop his visits offering for his girl, "conscious" soon causes him to stop his visits and fall into gloomy depression. Perhaps because the verse is somewhat ponderous or because there are no clear, realistic pictures to bring the characters to life, the tale, thus far, seems interminable and flat.

After a month of "sharp conflict" within himself, Walter once more sets out to visit Jane. The Sunday bells, the warm day, and the pleasant heath, however, tempt him to rest on a bed of green where his anguished thoughts about poverty again seize him:

> "Why do I go in cruel sport to say,
> 'I love thee Jane, appoint the happy day?'
> Why seek her sweet ingenious reply,
> Then grasp her hand and proffer . . . poverty?
> Why, if I love her and adore her name,
> Why act like time and sickness on her frame?
> Why should my scanty pittance nip her prime,
> And chace away the Rose before its time?
> I'm young 'tis true; the world beholds me free;
> Labour ne'er show'd a frightful face to me;
> Nature's first wants hard labour *should* supply;
> But should it fail, 'twill be too late to fly."

> (**R**, 20-21)

The very real plight of the rural laborer is here, but it is not until this point that Bloomfield himself begins to sound convinced of his subject. Walter continues to muse on his dilemma, recognizing that his love for Jane has become the source of some humor in the village:

> "Oft from my pain the mirth of others flows;
> As when a neighbor's Steed with glancing eye
> Saw his par'd hoof supported on my thigh:
> Jane pass'd that instant; mischief came of course;
> I drove that nail awry and lam'd the Horse;
> The poor beast limp'd: I bore a Master's frown,
> A thousand times I wish'd the wound my own."

> (**R**, 21-22)

The sudden appearance of Jane at the close of his meditation is a bit contrived as is the visit of the young lovers to the cottage of the Widow Hind who counsels them to marry despite the possible hardships.

The advice of the widow is based on her own past experience, but her speech lacks the quiet dignity of the farmer's husbandry lecture to Giles in *The Farmer's Boy.* Walter's reaction, based in part on not wanting to imitate his uncle who lived all his days a bachelor, is to abandon his fears while love "Silenc'd the arguments of Time and Change" (*R*, 28). Although not an unrealistic potrayal, this still wants the less cluttered handling of events and emotions in **"Richard and Kate."** The lack of simplicity and delicacy is doubly unfortunate, for not only is the artistry of the piece damaged, but the dependent argument is also weakened.

Aside from his general concern with rural poverty, Bloomfield is preparing to argue for the continuance of the positive relationship between labor and rural wealth that he described at the close of **"Summer"** in *The Farmer's Boy.* There is an example here for every country squire who might be tempted by the new sensibility that could divorce him from the people. As Walter finishes his pledge of love, an unannounced guest enters the cottage:

> Around with silent reverence they stood;
> A blameless reverence . . . the man was good.
> Wealth had he some, a match for his desires,
> First on the list of active Country 'Squires.
> Seeing the youthful pair with downcast eyes,
> Unmov'd by Summer flowers and cloudless skies,
> Pass slowly by his gate; his book resign'd,
> He watch'd their steps and follow'd far behind,
> Bearing with inward joy, and honest pride,
> A trust of WALTER's kinsman ere he died,
> A hard earn'd mite, deposited with care,
> And with a miser's spirit worshipt there.

> (*R*, 30-31)

A man who had gained an old laborer's trust, probably by just such concerned action as the squire took for Walter and Jane, is in Bloomfield's rural ethic a good man. His concerns are more with living within the natural order of rural life than with earning money. The squire presents the couple with the small purse of gold, but goes beyond that to offer "a spare Shed that fronts the public road" as a shop for Walter (*R*, 31).

Wealth held in moderation and administered with benevolence is the friend of the natural rural order. The action of the squire parallels the good husbandry of the farmer in Bloomfield's first work. Both appear to grow from a knowledge of the human and natural bonds within which rural man must live, and both cultivate those bonds with more than enlightened self-interest. Both administer to man and nature selflessly with an unspoken recognition that the meaning of rural life lies in mutual trust between man and nature, hence between

man and man. And both know that man's dignity rests on his striving, his sense of enterprise, which is far more important than any goal. A casteless concern with the human condition, then, remains a part of Bloomfield's argument even though this particular poem lacks his best hand:

> Comforts may be procur'd and want defied,
> Heav'ns! with how small a sum, when right applied!
> Give Love and honest Industry their way,
> Clear but the Sun-rise of Life's little day,
> Those we term poor shall oft that wealth obtain,
> For which th' ambitious sigh, but sigh in vain:
> Wealth that still brightens, as its stores increase;
> The calm of Conscience, and the reign of peace.

> (*R*, 32)

The poem ends with Walter in his gratitude pledging his support to the squire. It is not simply free horse-shoeing and help with harvesting that Walter offers to the squire. The offer promises more than celebrating his good fortune or avenging his wrongs. Walter pledges his friendship as one free man to another, and the offer, although humbly and respectfully made, transcends any hint of caste that would ultimately have detracted from its value.

Bloomfield followed **"Walter and Jane"** with another tale of rural love, again in iambic pentameter and again in undistinguished form. **"The Miller's Maid,"** although of scant thematic interest, does show Bloomfield to be in better control of the couplet. The tale of two foundlings taken in at different times by a kind village miller and his wife has some familiar echoes. The youngsters fall in love, are next thought to be brother and sister, and are finally freed to marry by the discovery of their true and separate parentages. As if all this is not quite enough, the benevolent miller retires, giving the mill to the newlyweds, and with an old veteran who held the key to their identities as a new addition to the family, they all prepare to live prosperously and happily for a considerable time to come. All of this Bloomfield handles at a sprightly pace and with an enthusiasm that strains to overcome the conventional plot. For the reader who has persevered, this part of *Rural Tales* still promises a bit of charm and honest rustic sentiment.

"The Widow to her Hour-Glass" which follows in the collection may have been one of Bloomfield's more popular pieces, for Hazlitt quotes it easily in his essay "On a Sun-Dial,"[11] and it is a pleasant poem. The stanza approximates the hourglass in printed shape and meter with a final "turning up" of the new stanza as one might turn the glass:

> Come, friend, I'll turn thee up again:
> Companion of the lonely hour!
> Spring thirty times hath fed with rain
> And cloath'd with leaves my humble bower,
> Since thou has stood

In frame of wood,
On Chest or Window by my side:
At every Birth still thou wert near,
Still spoke thine admonitions clear.—
And, when my husband died,

I've often watch'd thy streaming sand
And seen the growing Mountain rise,
And often found Life's hopes to stand
On props as weak in Wisdom's eyes.

(*R*, 59-60)

Perhaps because Bloomfield's own age gives him greater sympathy with his older characters, or because his great love for his own mother is captured here, or because the widow and the hourglass and the whole sad, quiet passing of time best suits his elegiac tone, the firm control and loving execution of detail are present again. His tropes and images are quite plain:

Its conic crown
Still sliding down,
Again heap'd up, then down again;
The sand above more hollow grew,
Like days and years still filt'ring through,
And mingling joy and pain.

(*R*, 60)

Simplicity need not be displeasing or unworthy. What claim to artistic merit the poem makes, in fact, comes from that sure, quiet grace of predictability. This is not the crude conventionality of plot that mars the previous tale, but a fair and fond representation of the predictable passing of time and life and things within the greater mutability of the natural order. This is a fair representation, too, of many an aging rural woman's thought and speech; many cultural primitivists in many centuries of art have sought that voice.

There is something in the hourglass, in the object itself, that is predictable and to the widow, almost hypnotic. It is not simply the passing of time that she sees, although she does see that and she does measure her morning by it. When the widow leaves her cottage to glean in the harvest fields, time or the hourglass gets a holiday. The object is idle, of course, but more important is the sense that the past and future suddenly inhabit the timeless present of rural labor. The timeless vision of the plowman in *The Farmer's Boy* suggests the stopping of time too. It is as if the object, like so many other rural tools and furnishings, is endowed with life and meaning by the seasonal turnings around it. One remembers the tools addressed in *The Farmer's Boy*. The glass is at once a tool and an object for meditation, and the widow's language mixes these functions:

Steady as Truth, on either end
Thy daily task performing well,
Thou'rt Meditation's constant friend,
And strik'st the Heart without a Bell.

(*R*, 60)

But when the object prompts the old woman to invoke the seasons which lie within it, it has sufficient power and meaning to accomplish that:

Come, lovely May!
Thy lengthen'd day
Shall gild once more my native plain;
Curl inward here, sweet Woodbine flow'r;————.

(*R*, 62)

As she pauses, the object becomes again a thing, a tool, a reality of rural life, and she can address it directly. The marvel of the old widow, of the poem, and perhaps of rural life itself is that the calm, firm tone of her address has, since the first stanza, kept our concern with the timeless present or with the future. The past does not intrude as it might if the widow grasped for it with maudlin attachment. The past is with her in the timeless present of spinning and the hourglass and the seasons, but it is to the new season that she has turned. And as if she affirms the future in the glass, she concludes: "Companion of the lonely hour, / I'll turn thee up again." That surety of vision based on the knowable life appears again. Her attitude differs from stoicism as affirmation differs from acceptance.

"Market Night" which follows in *Rural Tales* has another country woman as speaker. This time, however, the husband is alive and is simply absent one naked winter night. As the wife awaits his return from the distant marketplace, she addresses the spirits of the elements and of his steed, those forces on which his safe journey depend:

"O WINDS, howl not so long and loud;
Nor with your vengeance arm the snow:
Bear hence each heavy-loaded cloud:
And let the twinkling Star-beams glow."

Now sweeping floods rush down the slope,
Wide scattering ruin. . . . Star, shine soon!
No other light my Love can hope—

. . . . .

O blest assurance, (trusty steed,)
To thee the buried road is known;
HOME, all the spur thy footsteps need,
When loose the frozen reign is thrown."

(*R*, 63-65)

The uncertainty of the night is broken as the storm moves off to the West and the first star appears. When her husband appears "cloth'd in snow," the reunion is almost anticlimactic. Even the husband's words of counsel that end the piece sound ordinary, as if there was really little to be concerned about:

"Dear Partner of my nights and days,
That smile becomes thee! . . . Let us then
Learn, though mishap may cross our ways,
It is not ours to reckon when."

(*R*, 69)

Such homely moralizing is not unrealistic nor, considering the wife's consternation, is it uncalled for. Even the authenticity of a husband persuading his wife to be less the worrier, however, does not rescue the poem from a final flatness. When Bloomfield essays the traditional ballad stanza in **"The Fakenham Ghost,"** flatness is thankfully relieved. A key difference between these two poems is that in the second, Bloomfield returns to artistic preservation of the good in rural life and customs which marked *The Farmer's Boy.*

Founded on an actual incident that Bloomfield heard from his mother, **"The Fakenham Ghost"** is the passing humorous tale of an ancient dame who thinks that she is being pursued by a ghoul as she walks home at night through Euston Park. The setting is established well enough as she walks quickly by the wooded hillside:

> Where clam'rous Rooks, yet scarcely hush'd
> Bespoke a peopled shade;
> And many a wing the foilage brush'd
> And hov'ring circuits made.
>
> (*R*, 71)

The ghost is soon heard padding behind the poor creature, and she, glimpsing the "monster," has her fright increased:

> Regardless of whate'er she felt,
> It follow'd down the plain!
> She own'd her sins, and down she knelt,
> And said her pray'rs again.
>
> (*R*, 73)

The humor of the piece turns on the discovery that the persistent specter that follows the old dame through the park gate and to her cottage steps where she faints is nothing more than an ass's foal which has lost its dam and has affectionately followed the woman. Such innocent fun and the years of storytelling that follow such an incident are a real enough part of rural life. And the verse itself, which Bloomfield manages with several smooth, realistic touches, is certainly no worse than a hundred other clever ballads. It was, in fact, one of Bloomfield's poems which remained quite popular with children and adults throughout the nineteenth century. What may be more important, however, is the fact that Bloomfield presents yet another facet of rural life, and presents it with much the same humorous fondness that marked several of *The Farmer's Boy* episodes. Bloomfield disapproved of the rural tendency toward superstition and chastised it gently in the piece. But the country love for a good tale that could be retold many times without losing its freshness is presented as another of Bloomfield's positive values.

"The Fakenham Ghost" is followed by another ballad in the same verse form as **"Richard and Kate."** Only the verse form, however, links this poem to the others,

for **"The French Mariner"** is an antiwar address by a dying French veteran to the conquering Britons. The old man tells of the loss of his family and companions and argues for peace. It is not one of Bloomfield's better poems, for although peace and an end to "redcoat mania" were dear to him, he has wondered too far from the source of his poetic power. The reader need only turn on to **"Dolly,"** which employs the same verse form and has as its subject a young rustic couple's parting as the boy goes to war, to find sharper representations of scene and emotion.

If **"Dolly"** is not the best of Bloomfield's short rural poems, neither is it mere doggerel. Here again Bloomfield handles sentiment in an acceptable and pleasing fashion. The situation itself allows no humor to offset the sadness of the young lovers' parting; instead, Dolly is given the perspective of time and can tell her part of the tale with the quiet resolution and self-awareness possible for the "uneducated" in the knowable life within the natural order. She can know, for instance, that the first pains of parting will be the worst. Her description of her love's horse carrying him away ends in unexpected understatement that affirms her awareness:

> Then down the road his vigour tried,
> His rider gazing, gazing still;
> *"My dearest, I'll be true,"* he cried: . . .
> And, if he lives, I'm sure he will.
>
> (*R*, 89)

The poem closes with her invocation to the turning seasons and ends, for that, rather well.

"Dolly," then, is one of the poems with relative merit that saves *Rural Tales* from charges of mediocrity. The "elevated" and unsuccessful **"Lines, Occasioned by a Visit to Whittlebury Forest"** with their unhappy Thomsonian echoes, the uninspired **"Song for a Highland Drover,"** and the occasional piece, **"Word to Two Young Ladies,"** do no such service. Of Bloomfield's three addresses to young ladies, **"Nancy," "Rosy Hannah,"** and **"Lucy,"** the last two have the merits of simplicity and pleasantness and freedom from any false literary tone. Curiously, that tone which also mars **"Hunting Song"** is absent from **"The Shepherd and His Dog Rover"** and **"Winter Song,"** and the resulting failure and success of the pieces warrant examination.

Simply stated, the difference between the successful poems and the mediocre or poor ones lies in the voice that the poet chooses. Bloomfield can attempt to speak as "the poet" as he does in **"Hunting Song,"** and the result is hollow, imitative, and strained:

> Ye darksome Woods where Echo dwells
> Where every bud with freedom swells
> To meet the glorious day;
> The morning breaks; again rejoice;

And with old Ringwood's well-known voice
  Bid tuneful Echo play.

(**R,** 113)

Old Ringwood, even given the handicap of his name, is not an accessible image; he is no more a believable hound than Echo here is a believable spirit. There is no authenticity to the speaker's voice. Any passing poet could have written the lines without having seen a fox-hunt. But when in **"The Shepherd and His Dog Rover"** Bloomfield once more speaks with the voice of the peasant poet, when he is the rural artist with all his strengths and limitations, he can assume the persona of the shepherd and a real countryside and a real dog are there:

  ROVER, awake! the grey Cock crows!
  Come, shake your coat and go with me!
  High in the East the green Hill glows;
  And glory crowns our shelt'ring Tree.
  The Sheep expect us at the fold:
  My faithful Dog, let's haste away,
  And in his earliest beams behold,
  And hail, the source of cheerful day.

(**R,** 111)

Although this verse is much more exclamatory and emotional, the excitement and joy are justified by half a dozen concrete terms and the easy observation that dogs do shake themselves in the morning. When Echo appears in the second stanza to waft the dog's "gladsome voice" across the fresh fields, there is no straining for a classical spirit to compose itself before the reader at the mention of its name. It is an echo first, simple and real. If the reader wants to move from primal reality to myth, and he probably will not, the transition would be far less strained than is the tired evocation of the myth in **"Hunting Song."** Bloomfield's language in his better poems is not, of course, without elevation and intensity. It is simply intensified and elevated within the limitations of the rural speaker's voice.

"Winter Song," which closes the volume, catches the right tone and specificity. Bloomfield uses the persona of rural man. The speaker is addressing his son in a speech full of simple morals which, if they are clichés to the modern reader, are so because the kind of life they indicate is no longer enough in our possession to make them urgent and meaningful. Although winter for the poor wears a frightening frown and Bloomfield protests "The silent neglect and the scorn / Of those who have plenty to spare," there remain the simple pleasures of the poor living within the natural order:

  Fresh broach'd is my Cask of old Ale,
  Well-tim'd now the frost is set in;
  Here's Job come to tell us a tale,
  We'll make him at home to a pin.
  While my Wife and I bask o'er the fire,
  The roll of the Seasons will prove

  That Time may diminish desire,
  But cannot extinguish true love.

(**R,** 117-18)

There are neighborly chats, free from scandal, in which the happenings of the world and the recent sayings of great orators are discussed. As in **The Farmer's Boy,** rural poverty can be protested without weakening the basic appeal of the ordered, knowable life:

  Abundance was never my lot:
  But out of the trifle that's given,
  That no curse may alight on my Cot,
  I'll distribute the bounty of Heaven;
  The fool and the slave gather wealth:
  But if I add nought to my store,
  Yet while I keep conscience in health,
  I've a Mine that will never grow poor.

(**R,** 118-19)

Without the poem's acknowledgment of rural poverty, this could be a silly, easy optimism. With it, however, the speaker has the dignified voice of rural man cognizant of the freedom and independent enterprise that are his. The sound of stereotyped sentiment may be more the result of modern inapplicability than original triteness, for it is difficult to imagine the urban poor speaking from such a recognizable system of positive values arising from their way of life—from a way of life they can trust.

Rural Tales, Ballads, and Songs, then, is not so fine and even a work as **The Farmer's Boy.** It does contain several good rural poems that recommend it, and if what Claire Blunden calls the "authentic voice of the countryman"[12] is to be valued in our culture, these are worthy of our consideration. Even at his worst, Bloomfield is more pleasing than most of the other "uneducated poets." By saying this I do not mean to damn him with faint praise. If within his own limitations and the limitations of rural poetry he wrote admirably, should he not win approbation? Should criticism demand of a rural writer that he abandon his authentic voice or demand that Milton's pastoral elegy adopt it? I think not. It is more important that Bloomfield's conviction of the merit of his earlier arguments for rural life continues and that he finds at times the right voice and vehicle for those arguments. . . .

III THE SMALLPOX POEM

"Good Tidings" is an important poem for an "uneducated" rural man to be making in the early 1800s. While many supposedly more sophisticated men were indulging in unchecked and sometimes hysterical superstition, Bloomfield reveals himself to possess an understanding of at least this area of medical science and to have an enlightened concern for humanity. The poem does suffer from the sound of occasional verse, but Bloomfield's strong feelings for his topic and his good sense in using familiar material make it an interesting piece of didactic writing.

The poem does provide a glimpse of Bloomfield structuring yet another emotional argument. Again he uses a voice his readers would find both easy to sympathize with and authoritative. Using his personal knowledge and suffering he placed his discussion of the disease within the frame of "domestic incident" where his authority lay (*W*, 106). His argument is a more immediate and direct one than that in *The Farmer's Boy*, for there is a simple, obvious, and specific course of action to be advocated in the use of the vaccine.

Bloomfield begins directly with a pathetic picture of a child blinded early in life, and when the portrait is full enough to warrant some sympathy from the reader, he reveals the cause to be smallpox. In answer to a sympathetic question from the poet's persona the child's mother speaks its history. Her tale ends with a selfless wish: "God keep smallpox from your door" (*W*, 111), and the poet is freed to ask more questions of the reader. If there were a way to stop the destruction of the horrid disease, to prevent the recurrence of such misery, would the world not rejoice? The day, Bloomfield insists, is present, and he begins by describing the vaccine as another unsuspected treasure of the mean and kine of England's rural reaches. With a brief history of the discovery of the vaccine as another unsuspected treasure of the mead and kine of various cultures throughout history and finds it quite unlike the results of war:

> Twas thine, while victories claim'd th' immortal lay,
> Through private life to cut thy desperate way;
> And when full power the wondrous magnet gave
> Ambition's sons to dare the ocean wave,
> Thee, in their train of horrid ills, they drew
> Beneath the blessed sunshine of Peru.
>
> (*W*, 117)

Recognizing that this is not his strongest voice, he continues, "But why unskill'd th' historic page explore? / Why thus pursue thee to a foreign shore?" Bloomfield promptly returns to domestic incident.

At the end of the history of an English epidemic, Bloomfield reveals that the victim was his own father. It is a very personal appeal to the readers who valued rural verse. It could, after all, have been the rural bard himself who died. Those who knew and loved his other works are invited now to act on their sympathies to prevent further loss of life (*W*, 120-22). After writing of his brother Nathaniel, who even as the poem was being written lost a third child to smallpox, Bloomfield moves to more direct questions for his readers. If they love their children and their neighbors, that love can best be shown by protecting them by using the vaccine. After

appeals to self-interest and pity, Bloomfield attempts to move his readers with patriotism, for he advocates an English cure that could well be used to cure Englishmen. The strongest of these arguments, however, are those that touch upon the disruption of the rural social order by disease. The self-interest and the respect for a neighbor's safety that might prompt a man to use the vaccine are parts of the responsibility to conserve taught by rural life:

> In village paths, hence, may we never find
> Their youth on crutches, and their children blind;
> Nor, when the milk-maid, early from her bed,
> Beneath the may-bush that embow'rs her head,
> Sings like a bird, e'er grieve to meet again
> The fair cheek injur'd by the scars of pain.
>
> (*W*, 131)

As this scene is completed, the air of things as they should be returns:

> Pure, in her [the milkmaid's] morning path, whero'er
> she treads,
> Like April sunshine and the flow'rs it feeds,
> She'll boast new conquests; Love, new shafts to fling;
> And Life, an uncontaminated spring.
>
> (*W*, 132)

Although this is not Bloomfield at his best, it is the rural writer in a surprisingly good attempt at epideictic discourse on a general and scientific theme. The greatest import of the verse may be a social one, for Bloomfield in 1804 and again in 1806 was not without influence on his large London audience.

IV TRAVEL VERSE: THE BANKS OF THE WYE

The four books of *The Banks of the Wye; A Poem* close Bloomfield's most productive period. He was well aware of the fact that the subjects supplied him by "a short excursion down the Wye, and through part of South Wales" (*B*, v) would mark a change in his verse. What he was not aware of was that although he records some charming pictures and seeks variety in the changing scene and varied rhythm of the poem, his most authoritative poetic voice is replaced by that of the visitor. The sadly missing ingredient in the poem is, I think, the sense of moral urgencies that shaped the argument of *The Farmer's Boy* and inspired the loving treatment of his subjects in the better short poems. It is Bloomfield's England that he writes about in *The Banks of the Wye*, but however much he loved the experience of the excursion, it is not his in the sense that the farms and villages of Suffolk were his. His understanding of the rural life that linked him to the land and the folk could not be tapped with any regularity in such a travel piece. The images and scenes bombard him from each side, each replete with meaning, tradition, and perhaps beauty of its own. But there is not the continuity of rural life, seasonal change and timelessness, or the natural order, to bind up his experience and make it authentic.

There is a great sadness in the fact that Bloomfield, once he had found a place to stand which lends great authenticity to his point of view, could not take that ground with him and use it to order and interpret a multifarious reality. It is sad to lose any authentic voice, and the authentic voice of the countryman is no exception. Bloomfield's inability to bring with him his ordered vision, his value system, and his rooted knowledge of life does not signal the general impossibility of such an event. The poet was farther removed from his rural experience, his youthful powers, and source of joy than ever before. There are moments in *The Banks of the Wye* when his voice seems sure again—moments usually connected to a flash of passing scenery in which the poet could naturally stand.

> A troop of gleaners chang'd their shade,
> And 'twas a change by music made;
> For slowly to the brink they drew,
> To mark our joy, and share it too,
> How oft, in childhood's flow'ry days,
> I've heard the wild impassion'd lays
> Of such a group, lays strange and new,
> And thought, was ever song so true?
> When from the hazel's cool retreat,
> They watch'd the summer's trembling heat;
> And through the boughs rude urchins play'd,
> Where matrons, round the laughing maid,
> Prest the long grass beneath! And here
> They doubtless shar'd an equal cheer;
> Enjoy'd the feast with equal glee,
> And rais'd the song of revelry:
> Yet half abash'd reserv'd, and shy,
> Watch'd till the strangers glided by.
>
> (*B,* 18-19)

Even here, however, there is more distance between the artist and his subject than is usual in Bloomfield's verse. In part it is the result of Bloomfield's situation as a tourist, a visitor, and much of it is the lack of particularization that gave life to the meaner objects of rural life in his earlier verse. Unwin's observation that this much reworked poem was filled with the "spirit of the topographer—the guidebook writer rather than the poet—" is not unfair,[13] and there are not enough of the good scenes to fully redeem the work.

Bloomfield simply fails to take those flights of fancy to give his reader real visions of the past—visions that **"The Horkey"** proves he could give. A few of the historical sights—the home of "The Man of Ross"—are of interest for themselves, but few of them are made to seem at all important in the way that Bloomfield gives importance to his simple rural histories.

V FINAL LABORS, LESSENED POWERS

Eleven full years elapsed before Bloomfield published another volume of verse. They were not the totally empty and nonproductive years that some studies envi-

sion, but Bloomfield, who was past fifty-six, could no longer write at his earlier pace. *May Day with the Muses* may be a long and elaborate exercise in wish fulfillment for the aging poet, for its subject is the acceptance of verse for rent money by an aging baronet whose love of poetry and of his rural neighbors led him to give rural bards their due. From patronage of this kind Bloomfield could have benefited hundreds of times during his career. The death of the old duke of Grafton seemed to end any hope of such enthusiastic assistance.

May Day with the Muses is a poetic frame tale in which all the folk of Oakly manor gather on May Day to present the poems that the eighty-year-old baronet has announced that he will accept as payment for their property rental. The quality of the verse is, after the disappointments of *Banks of the Wye,* surprisingly high. While not so good as *The Farmer's Boy* or the best poems in *Wild Flowers,* this is not the worst of Bloomfield's verse. That the aging poet should, despite illness, poverty, partial blindness, and great depression still be capable of some rather enjoyable poetry may be explained by the simple fact that he returned to his native ground. At times the frame verse in his familiar iambic pentameter couplets exceeds the quality of the songs and ballads themselves; it is good to know that one is listening to Robert Bloomfield again and listening to him as he speaks with a sense of who he is.

The poet begins intensely and personally:

> O for the strength to paint my joy once more!
> That joy I feel when Winter's reign is o'er;
> When the dark despot lifts his hoary brow,
> And seeks his polar-realm's eternal snow.
> Though black November's fogs oppress my brain,
> Shake every nerve, and struggling fancy chain;
> Though time creeps o'er me with his palsied hand,
> And frost-like bids the stream of passion stand.[14]

Invoking spring that rejuvenates rural life, he is soon about the business of introducing Sir Ambrose Higham, the baronet who is living out his days and taking all his pleasure in the life of Oakly Hall. Bloomfield's first themes are awakened by the portrait of this reasonable old gentleman who has said a final good-bye to the strife and discord of the city to "calmly wait the hour of his decay, / The broad bright sunset of his glorious day" (*M,* 5) on his native ground. Sir Ambrose has the proper attitude toward the rural poor and the laborers; he is capable of what Bloomfield found in the duke of Grafton, condescension in its noblest aspect, bringing succour to the hunger of the children, the loneliness of the old, and the simple desires of the plowman. His announcement of the verse for rent agreement is sent to his "neighbors," as he calls everyone in the manor. The instructions limit the subjects fit for verse by excluding stupid superstition (bloody ghosts, but not harmless fairies), vulgar things, and the gothic concerns of crimes, blood, monk's retreats, magic caverns, and midnight darkness.

Such an offer would in reality meet with reactions varying from joy to incredulity, and Bloomfield portrays them all. Most important, however, is the effect on the laboring folk of the manor:

> Now shot through many a heart a secret fire,
> A new born spirit, an intense desire
> For once to catch a spark of local fame,
> And bear a poet's honourable name!
> Already some aloft began to soar,
> And some to think who never thought before.
>
> (*M*, 10)

Naturally, not all are capable of the feat: "But, O, what numbers all their strength applied, / Then threw despairingly the task aside / With feign'd contempt, and vow'd they'd never tried" (*M*, 11). And there are humorous interruptions to the flow of the rural occupations when the would-be bards lose themselves in composing. Spring does finally arrive, and the preparations for the festival of verse are happily drawn by the poet. This time, however, the things the poet values are completely of the past. He neither hesitates to emphasize that fact (*M*, 14-15), nor when lord and labor exchange toasts, does Bloomfield fail to recall part of what he blamed for the destruction of rural life:

> Avaunt, Formality! thou bloodless dame,
> With dripping besom quenching nature's flame;
> Thou cankerworm, who liv'st but to destroy,
> And eat the very heart of social joy;—
> Thou freezing mist round intellectual mirth,
> Thou spell-bound vagabond of spurious birth,
> Away! Away! and let the sun shine clear,
> And all the kindnesses of life appear.
>
> (*M*, 16)

Only in the days before the advent of the detested false refinement could this entertainment and casteless intercourse have happened.

First of the poems to be offered is written by Philip, the farmer's son. The ballad, **"The Drunken Father,"** is an undistinguished temperance poem containing most of the standard features of any temperance piece before or since: the drunken father, the long-suffering wife, the innocent children who go off to the tavern to fetch home their father, and even the miraculous character reversal in which the poor chap takes the pledge. Its most praiseworthy feature is the fact that it moves quickly.

A few lines of transition lead to the next song which has been composed by the gamekeeper of Oakly. **"The Forester"** is one of the better poems in the collection. In this meditation on the eternal face of Nature, a central feature is a fallen oak which becomes the turning point for some moralizing on the states and kingdoms of man. Before the morals are drawn, however, there are some quiet moments reminiscent of the authentic Bloomfield:

> From every lawn, and copse, and glade,
>   The timid deer in squadrons came,
> And circled round their fallen shade
>   With all of language but its name.
> Astonishment and dread withheld
>   The fawn and doe of tender years,
> But soon a triple circle swell'd,
>   With rattling horns and twinkling ears.
>
> Some in his root's deep cavern housed,
>   And seem'd to learn, and muse, and teach,
> Or on his topmost foliage browsed,
>   That had for centuries mock'd their reach.
>
> (*M*, 42-43)

That the lines on the fallen oak are a response to the young duke of Grafton's complaint that Bloomfield's muse had been too long inactive I have already noted.

"The Shepherd's Dream" which follows has little to recommend it. **"The Soldier's Home,"** however, deserves at least a moment's notice. An old veteran's tale of returning to his rural cottage gives the reader a sense of the nonlinear time that marks the knowable rural life. The force of the familiar strikes the soldier as he crosses his father's farm to call his father's name at the cottage door. When no one answers, his reaction is not the expected one of fear or grief, "But an o'erpowering sense of peace and home, / Of toils gone by, perhaps of joys to come" (*M*, 58). Once inside the hut, the present and the past are one. He can breathe the cooler air, "And take possession of my father's chair" (*M*, 58), where, perhaps too obtrusively, his initials have survived forty years' wear. The recognition of things, of the familiar ticking clock, however, is to be expected. The appearance of a robin that could not possibly have lived the twenty years of his absence but nevertheless appears to renew an old friendship does suggest the timelessness of life in which the veteran can still find a common ground between the present, his past, and his future.

Bloomfield's disgust with war appears in the old man's raging against its cost and waste. Implicit is his distrust of another system of values alien and hostile to his own. Too, war and its celebration are not within his poetic range. Even the veteran's prologue expresses that recognition:

> My untried muse shall no high tone assume,
> Nor strut in arms;—farewell my cap and plume:
> Brief be my verse, a task within my power,
> I tell my feelings in one happy hour.
>
> (*M*, 57)

The mask of the veteran through which the poet speaks imposes further limitations on songs of valor, but these limitations do not obscure the fact that Bloomfield prefers his rural muse.

One of Bloomfield's favorite images, a parade of rural maidens, follows the veteran's song. Their invitation to the dance gives a moment of youthful joy to Sir Ambrose and forms the transition to the introduction of Philip, a rural swain whose intended has been ill, delaying their wedding for a considerable time. **"Rosamond's Song of Hope"** is her offering; it lacks any of the saving graces of Bloomfield's best poetry. The ballad is followed by **"Alfred and Jennet,"** the last and in some ways the best of the selections.

In the preface to *May Day with the Muses,* Bloomfield writes, "I will plead no excuses for any thing which the reader may find in this little volume, but merely state, that I once met with a lady in London, who, though otherwise of a strong mind and good information, would maintain that 'it is impossible for a blind man to fall in love.' I always thought her wrong, and the present tale of 'Alfred and Jennet' is written to elucidate my side of the question" (*M,* vii). The romantic and sentimental tale told by a sturdy yeoman who is Jennet's father returns to the theme of the proper relationship between labor and the landed within rural society, and for a final time the social barriers are broken—broken by youthful love. Although not far beyond Bloomfield's usual apolitical approach, the blindness of Alfred who represents the gentry has almost inescapable overtones.

The youngsters who grow slowly to love each other are a surprisingly well-matched pair. Jennet is a lively, determined, and lovely girl. Poor as her family is she is not at all a rude rustic; formed by the natural order, her character has two delightful sides:

> Her lively spirit lifted her to joy;
> To distance in the race a clumsy boy
> Would raise the flush of conquest in her eye,
> And all was dance, and laugh, and liberty.
> Yet not hard-hearted, take me right, I beg.
> The veriest romp that ever wagg'd a leg
> Was Jennet; but when pity soothed her mind,
> Prompt with her tears, and delicately kind.
> The half-fledged nestling, rabbit, mouse, or dove,
> By turns engaged her cares and infant love;
> And many a one, at the last doubtful strife,
> Warm'd in her bosom, started into life.
>
> (*M,* 74)

Alfred, the blind only child of a wealthy widow, escapes the faults of character that he might have suffered in an overly indulgent or overly protective family and society:

> But Alfred was a youth of noble mind,
> With ardent passions, and with taste refined;
> All that could please still courted heart and hand,
> Music, joy, peace, and wealth, at his command.
>
> (*M,* 75)

The providence that took his sight replaced it with an inordinate fondness for all that grows in the fields around his home. His explorations of the country immediately around his home are shared by Jennet.

When winter separates the youngsters and Alfred grows gloomy, Jennet is sent for—"just for company"—and is allowed to study with Alfred's governess. The winter passes happily with Alfred at his piano and Jennet listening and talking. The charm of her singing voice, however, she hides from Alfred until he discovers its fame through her father. Finally hearing her songs, Alfred decrees that she will go home no more but remain as his constant companion. So music and poetry, Nature and conversation come to bind them more obviously in love. Alfred's jealousy of the gardener who tries to talk to Jennet convinces her father that they are in love, and he feels morally bound to reveal the fact to Alfred's mother, the proper judge of the situation.

Jennet's tearful return home seems to signal the end of the romance. Alfred's mother, however (and herein lies the moral), does not rule against love. Jennet's returning home is her own response to what she took to be the lady's discomfort. In such a tale when it seems that a character's natural sensitivity and goodness will bring unhappiness, it is customary, to say the least, to have the course of events reversed and pluck joy out of the worst possible mess:

> Down the green slope before us, glowing warm,
> Came Alfred, tugging at his mother's arm;
> Willing she seem'd, but he still led the way,
> She had not walk'd so fast for many a day;
> His hand was lifted, and his brow was bare,
> For now no clust'ring ringlets wanton'd there,
> He threw them back in anger and in spleen,
> And shouted "Jennet" o'er the daisied green.
> Boyish impatience strove with manly grace
> In ev'ry line and feature of his face.
>
> (*M,* 91)

And joy there is when Alfred claims Jennet for his bride; love foils the force of caste, and the gardener who has been quite fond of Jennet is discovered to be too old to die for love.

A touch of Bloomfield's old powers must have survived through this writing. As in many of his other poems, what sentiment is there need not be forgiven, only recognized as part of the authentic rural voice. There are defects in the work that can and should be faulted, however. Although Bloomfield attempts to recapture some of the vibrant reality of the country in the frame to his tales, he does not ultimately succeed. The pictorial quality, so delicate and persuasive in earlier works, is remembered by the artist, but twice in this single work he falls back on the unsatisfactory device of telling the reader that his pictures are as this or that artist would fashion them. The verse itself is uneven and the voice not always true. And if Bloomfield stubbornly grasps his old awarenesses, it is with an unsteady hand.

The aging poet's hope and sense of the dignity of the attempt were not gone, but even these personal qualities were shaken. It is possible that he lost strength at the end of the work or that the publisher lost faith. Several of the poems that he mentions in the closing lines of the frame were real poems that appeared in *The Remains* but which were not published as part of *May Day.* If he knew, and I suspect that he did, that these verses were not strong enough to revive his reputation, then the appeal of his preface was the proper one. "The remembrance of what is past" does include *The Farmer's Boy, Rural Tales,* and *Wild Flowers.* That recent years have found few champions for Robert Bloomfield is no indication that there is no remembrance for him, for the verse of the peasant poets, John Clare and others, does remember him. And there is a real possibility that the popularity of Wordsworth and the other romantics, with their rural tales and images drawn from the English countryside, was in part the result of a vast audience whose appetite for such things was whetted by the writings of the farmer's boy.

BLOOMFIELD AND THE RURAL TRADITION: ITS VALUE AND VALUES

I THE POET HIMSELF

From the biography and poetry of Robert Bloomfield comes a picture of the man. It is possible that we may learn from him, for he is a man whose work is our past and hence a part of our inventive possibilities. From his writings, it may be possible to deduce something of the nature of rural poetry, and from both the poetry and the man, it may be possible to gain a further understanding of the ethical values he found in rural life.

One of the first items in the traditional picture of Bloomfield is that he once charmed audiences the size of which many modern poets might covet and that he now enjoys "real 'Augustan peace' beneath the accumulated dust of the years."[15] This might be explained through the coincidence of Bloomfield's verse with Wordsworth's and by saying that the better poet survived, yet that would be to ignore much that is very good and very bad in the poetry of each. Too, recent years have seen rural poets who stand beside Bloomfield, William Bowles and John Clare, emerge in various states of rediscovery, and two of the latest editions of Bloomfield have come in 1971. This picture of a meteoric career, then, may not contain the final disposition of Bloomfield's reputation.

A gentle man, but not without passion and conviction, Bloomfield might be better remembered now had he committed himself to pursuing his convictions more actively in the noise of politics as did Cobbett or by writing of rural life more dramatically as did Crabbe in his darker verse. His acceptance of political realities and optimistic vision of the life of labor cause the modern and Marxist critic (see Raymond Williams's *The Country and the City*) to feel that excuses must be made for the poet. Bloomfield spoke in ballad, however, not broadside; he argued with celebration, however sad, not dark criticism.

The limited legend that survives Bloomfield is in other ways inaccurate. Although it has been rumored often, it is doubtful that alcohol ruined him. An entry in Crabbe's journal which was appended as a note to *The Village* asserts that Bloomfield had better remained a farmer's boy or a cobbler and not become a poor and unhappy poet. "By the way," Crabbe wrote, "indiscretion did much."[16] By reading no farther, one might guess that the drunkenness and dissipation against which Bloomfield was so often warned by his friends (usually with the "unhappy fate of Burns" as the example) were indeed his errors. But although he was fond of ale and port, a single sodden evening produced such feelings of foolishness and pain that it is difficult to imagine Bloomfield as an habitual drunkard. Crabbe, in fact, did recognize Bloomfield's true indiscretion, but few critics bother to complete the quotation from Crabbe. "It might be virtuous and affectionate in him to help his thoughtless relations; but his more liberal friends do not love to have their favours so disposed of," wrote the parson, adding, "He is, however, to be pitied and assisted." To this excess of generosity in our picture of Bloomfield might be added a final fault: a surfeit of hope for financial success.

A memoir of the poet's life affixed to an 1835 edition of his works furthers the legend of Bloomfield's melancholy disposition, indicating that in his last years, his sanity was feared for. To be sure, as Unwin has remarked, Bloomfield suffered from hypochondria, but that "a morbid interest in his own health dominate[s] his correspondence"[17] is not so sure a thing. The letters do reveal a man in pain, but the presence of just anger, light humor, and a great compassion for his family seems to balance his interest in his own health.

That quitting London for his final home in Shefford failed to renew his spirit and make him once again the farmer's boy is true. The legend and reality are one. The reasons for the unsuccessful return to rural life, however, have not been satisfactorily explicated.

An essentially rural man with rural sensibilities and values, Bloomfield's angle of vision came from his standing place within the natural order of the open-field system of agriculture. His beliefs, his value system, grew naturally from that kind of life that may be even older than the manorial system—a "communal organization of the peasantry, a village community of share-holders who cultivated the land on the open-field system and treated the other requisites of rural life as appendant to it."[18] It was the land itself that bound such a society together. That land (some set apart by tradition and law for the mutual use of all the folk of the manor) was at the heart of Bloomfield's ethical and poetic concerns. The society built on the common dependence on the land, however, had long been threatened by change, for it was seen as an obstacle to economic growth.[19]

What such a tradition and system of governance insured was the right of cottager, laborer, or squatter to obtain a living from the land. The rather complex system of rights and privileges could work to the general advantage of everyone in the manor. The advantages for labor, and it was with labor that Bloomfield's greatest sympathies lay, are succinctly described in Bovill's *English Country Life*:

> Although the open-field system closed the door to progressive agriculture and increased production, which the Napoleonic wars made a compelling need, it gave every countryman the immense advantage of a stake in the land. Nearly all cottagers had at least a strip or two in the common fields, and the rest at least enjoyed legal or customary rights in the wastes where they could graze cows, horses, sheep, geese, and goats. Thus was the labourer able to produce both cheap food for himself and a surplus to send to market. The system gave him an opportunity to rise in the world by saving and investing in more stock or more land in the common field. It also left him free to dispose of his labour as he thought fit, as best suited his interests, on his own holdings or, for wages, on that of a larger farmer.[20]

Bloomfield's boyhood on a small but successful farm allowed him to experience the best of life in the manorial system. The changes in that life that he protested in **The Farmer's Boy** were not new. The gradual process of enclosure, the revolution in agricultural techniques, and the influence of urban capitalism had for long years been eroding the nature of the village and farm. In the sixteenth century, enclosure was given a great stimulus by the new practice of farming for a market—a market that based its demands on rising prices and a growing textile industry:

> When commerce increased its profits and the classes engaged in it stepped into a more lavish style of living, the landlord found himself in a world in which he had to make drastic changes if he wished to maintain his social prestige. In feudal times the lord's pomp and state depended on the number and condition of his tenants. As domestic order became more secure, the command of men counted for less and less; as wealth grew and all classes acquired more expensive habits, the command of money counted for more and more. With a prosperous cloth trade demanding larger supplies of wool, rich profits were to be made by substituting good pasture for poor arable farming in the Midlands.[21]

The changes already embodied the acceptance of urban social values not too different from the false sensibility that Bloomfield protests in the harvest-home section of **The Farmer's Boy.**

To the lasting detriment of Bloomfield's people, the enclosure movement gained momentum and despite the efforts to protect the rights of the peasant in the ordi-

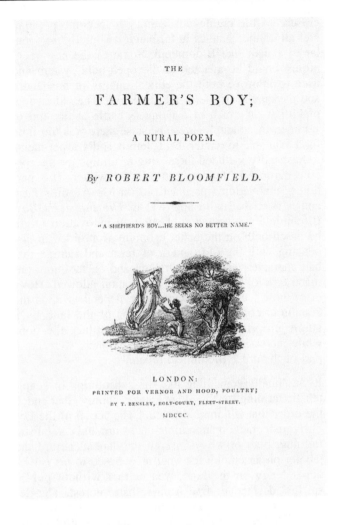

THE

FARMER'S BOY;

A RURAL POEM.

By ROBERT BLOOMFIELD.

"A SHEPHERD'S BOY....HE SEEKS NO BETTER NAME."

LONDON:
PRINTED FOR VERNOR AND HOOD, POULTRY;
BY T. BENSLEY, BOLT-COURT, FLEET-STREET.
MDCCC.

Title page for the 1800 first edition of Bloomfield's The Farmer's Boy.

nances of 1682, 1725, 1769, and 1791, the poor were usually made to suffer. When the loss of their ancient rights to the common land was compensated by awarding them small tracts of land of their own, they far too often found themselves unable to meet the legal expenses of enclosure which required surrounding the land with ditches and hedges. The small farmer or cottager was frequently without sufficient capital both to enclose and to carry on. The very poor who were awarded as little as an acre of land and a bit of cash to make up for the loss of their right to graze a cow on the commons found that a cow could not survive on such a small tract. So, like the others, they were usually forced to sell their land.[22]

Passing, then, was what Thomas Bewick called "the poor man's hermitage" where a laborer might maintain himself and his family and keep a cow, some sheep, geese, or, more commonly, a number of hives.[23] It was not, however, enclosure alone that brought this change, for new techniques of husbandry had been discovered that waited only the beginnings of the accelerated enclosure of the eighteenth century to become popular. Not all of the changes in husbandry would be unpopular to a man like Bloomfield. Some of the new techniques could be adapted to the open-field system and used to improve both the ethical quality of husbandry and the quality of life of the rural folk. The old custom of killing off much of a village's cattle at the end of summer, for example, arose because there was too little food available to winter them. Jethro Tull's experiments in husbandry included the raising of turnips for the specific purpose of feeding cattle in the winter. This particular innovation was practiced on Mr. Austin's farm and is described with approval in *The Farmer's Boy.* Bloomfield's acceptance of such an innovation might be based both on the better economy it afforded in dispensing with the old pattern of feast and famine that had characterized the country life and on the more humane type of husbandry the innovation allowed. However, those techniques, which were dependent upon the economic control of large portions of the land by a single proprietor who would then displace the poor while increasing the production of the land, were not a part of the order Bloomfield revered.

It was finally something like the substitution of "capitalistic farming for the old peasant economy" that ended the order that Bloomfield loved.[24] The action of the English aristocracy in supporting enclosure and capitalistic farming, both of which insured the dependency of the laborer on an employer-owner as opposed to his earlier dependency on the land, was neither without public spirited design nor free from selfish interest. The demand for produce made by the growing cities was resisted by the old system of cooperative control of the land, of common fields, and of widely distributed property rights. Bloomfield himself in *The Farmer's Boy* inveighed against the demands of the city while supporting the old order that gave independence to the rural laborer. At one point in 1802 Bloomfield was "dreaming with a vengence [*sic*]" of buying what was Honington Green to "throw it open" again and erect there a pedestal honoring the rural muse.[25] Writing to a Mr. Pratt who had sent him a poem on "Bread" that vindicated the cottager, the poet wrote, "To see one class of the community grow immensely rich at the expense of another, to me allways [*sic*] argue'd an inefficiency in the Laws of this or any Country where it happens. If, as Goldsmith says we are hasting to the rottenness of refinement, and if such things cannot be avoided, I see no just reason for starving and condemning the laborers of the Vinyard, or keeping from them such degrees of information as they may be capable of receiving."[26] Stephen Duck, the "Thresher poet," began his writing from a point of view not unlike Bloomfield's, arguing for the dignity of rural laborers. Unfortunately, Duck himself succumbed to the social revisions that accompanied enclosure. The authentic voice of rural labor faded from his verse when he became a tour guide in the landscape garden William Kent designed for Queen Caroline, and the artificial conventions of pastoral verse replaced his accurate rural images.[27] Prolabor opinions were not limited to minor rural poets, of course. Capel Lofft defended the rights of gleaners in the Court of Common Pleas in 1788, while Crabbe, Clare, and Wordsworth all attacked the farmers who yielded to the new, false sensibility.[28] The forces for enclosure, however, reasoned that greater production would benefit all, including the rural labor force who would have little to distract them from their loyalty to the employer.[29]

It was to a countryside changed by the dual forces of agrarian innovation and enclosure that Bloomfield returned. The changes that he had observed, sensed, and feared were accomplished facts. It was not that the rural laborer was gone or that the land was completely changed, but that the relationship in which one stood to the other was altered. If in returning to the country Bloomfield wanted to renew his place to stand (as Pope found a "place to stand, an angle of vision" in his garden and grotto)[30] Shefford did not provide it. The significant shift from present tense in his works to 1811, to the mixed tenses in *Banks of the Wye,* and finally to the past tense of *May Day with the Muses* might be a coincidental matter and not a purposeful manipulation. A similar confusion of tenses in the poetry of John Clare seems to come from viewing a scene before and after the physical changes caused by enclosure.[31] A man who has the quiet, carefully gathered, and lovingly held kind of knowledge that Bloomfield demonstrates in *The Farmer's Boy,* might instinctively change his tenses because he sensed yet another piece of knowledge: the meteoric course of his popularity and the physical and social changes in the countryside could conspire to inform the poet that his audience had not been moved by his arguments. A different kind of man, such a writer as Pope, might succeed in continuing the argument. Bloomfield could only see and sense and know that while the figurative standing place from which he argued might remain, the literal common ground on which he based his argument was gone.

The English countryside, of course, still exists, and there are prospects into which one might expect Giles to trudge. Changes that did alter the quality of rural life did not keep nature from being the material of great images in later poetry. Those same changes have not prevented the recent revival of interest in the rural poetry of such men as Clare and Bowles. But, while Bloomfield's works retained some popularity throughout the nineteenth century, the urgency they once had for their large audience is gone, and it may be that Bloomfield's major themes no longer strike us as the real or the possible. If they do not, our culture has lost something of value.

II BLOOMFIELD'S PLACE IN THE TRADITIONS: PASTORAL AND RURAL POETRY

Even if the economic possibility of the rural life Bloomfield portrayed is lost, we have not lost his record of it or his ideas of its values. As one of the earliest and best known of the nineteenth century's peasant poets, Bloomfield offers the means of identifying something of the nature of rural poetry and of both relating it to and distinguishing it from pastoral poetry. Because it is only from Bloomfield that this discussion proceeds and because other sometimes superior artists have written distinctively rural poetry, these observations can only be an explorative statement.

Hazlitt has offered one of the most important of all critical statements about Bloomfield. These early observations that place Bloomfield in "the same class of excellence" as Thomson and Cowper provide a place to begin the identification of rural poetry:

> As a painter of simple natural scenery, and of the still life of the country, few writers have more undeniable and unassuming pretension than the ingenious and self-taught poet. Among the sketches of this sort I would mention, as equally distinguished for delicacy, faithfulness, and *naivete,* his description of lambs racing, of the pigs going out acorning, of the boy sent to feed his sheep before the break of day in winter; and I might add the innocently told story of the poor bird-boy, who in vain through the live-long day expects his promised companions at his hut, to share his feast of roasted sloes with him, as an example of that humble pathos, in which this author excels. The fault indeed of his genius is that it is too humble: his Muse has something not only rustic, but menial in her aspect. He seems afraid of elevating nature, lest she would be ashamed of him. Bloomfield very beautifully describes the lambs in springtime as racing round the hillocks of green turf: Thomson in describing the same image, makes the mound of earth the remains of an old Roman encampment. Bloomfield never gets beyond his own experience; and that is somewhat confined. He gives the simple appearance of nature, but he gives it naked, shivering, and unclothed with the drapery of a moral imagination. His poetry has much the effect of the first approach of spring, "while yet the year is unconfirmed," where a few tender buds venture forth here and there, but are chilled by the early frosts and nipping breath of poverty.[32]

Although I would follow neither Hazlitt's chastisement of Bloomfield's humility nor his selection of these particular, sentimental scenes, the accuracy of his observation is marked. To the list of Bloomfield's best subjects (natural scenery and "still life" of the country) should be added the full portraits of rural folk that emerge in Bloomfield's later works. Departing again from Hazlitt who sees no "moral imagination" in Bloomfield, I would argue the existence of what is indeed moral imagination—the moral conviction of value with which Bloomfield portrays his subjects.

When Hazlitt speaks of Bloomfield's limitations, and speaks rightly of the poet's acceptance of them, the limitations appear at first to be a handicap of the first order, but in analyzing *The Farmer's Boy,* the positive possibilities of those limitations have been shown. The real service that Hazlitt performs comes when he pauses to reflect on the failure of natural genius without education to produce a new and striking literature. His two possible explanations have meaning in terms of Bloomfield and rural poetry itself:

> And one reason appears to be, that though such persons, from whom we might at first expect a restoration of the good old times of poetry, are not encumbered and enfeebled by the trammels of custom, and the dull weight of other men's ideas; yet they are oppressed by the consciousness of a want of the common advantages which others have; are looking at the tinsel finery of the age, while they neglect the rich unexplored mine in their own breasts; and instead of setting an example for the world to follow, spend their lives in aping, or in despair of aping, the hackneyed accomplishments of their inferiors.[33]

When Bloomfield did "ape" with his style or with sentiment and incident borrowed from Goldsmith or Cowper, it was most unfortunate. But he handled his conservative meter well enough and made of it, at times, something distinctively his own, and borrowed sentiments and incidents were frequently transformed by his experience and art. The best of his poetry does come from his own breast, and does, as *The Farmer's Boy* clearly demonstrates, set a moral and ethical (if not stylistic) model for the world to follow. Bloomfield's poetry is distinctively rural in its subjects and ethics, and at its best imitates the orders and forms of rural life rather than other poetry.

Hazlitt's second observation is more seriously a criticism of the society of readers than of writers like Bloomfield:

> Another cause may be, that original genius alone is not sufficient to produce the highest excellence, without a corresponding state of manners, passions, and religious belief: that no single mind can move in direct opposition to the vast machine of the world around it, that the poet can do no more than stamp the mind of his age upon his works; and that all that the ambition of the highest genius can hope to arrive at, after the lapse of one or two generations, is the perfection of that more refined and effeminate style of studied elegance and adventitious ornament, which is the result, not of nature, but of art. In fact, no other style of poetry has succeeded, or seems likely to succeed, in the present day. The public taste hangs like a millstone around the neck of all original genius that does not conform to established and exclusive models. The writer is not only without popular sympathy, but without a rich and varied mass of materials for his mind to work upon and assimilate unconsciously to itself; his attempts at originality are looked upon as affectation, and in the end,

degenerate into it from the natural spirit of contradiction, and the constant uneasy sense of disappointment and undeserved ridicule.[34]

Bloomfield, by accepting his limitations and celebrating rural life, wrote poetry that was soon in direct opposition to the "vast machine of the world around it." Because rural poetry as a rule accepts the limitations of the poet and his subject, it may always be in opposition to the world around it. If Bloomfield's audience was first moved by his limited argument in *The Farmer's Boy,* however, it may have been because they sympathized with his plea for the natural order. It is possible that the public sympathy against enclosure was fed by his argument and that the sympathy in turn made his work popular. His audience, too, would even have been in part composed of folk themselves displaced from the farms and villages. For a brief atypical moment, then, Bloomfield and his rural concerns might not have been in opposition to the spirit of the world.

His audience, however, could turn to other writers and other themes as its own concerns and life grew further removed from the natural order. Bloomfield with his vision of the ordered, natural, and knowable life could not well abandon those concerns which he thought gave life its meaning. It was inevitable, then, that he suffer "undeserved ridicule" and "the constant uneasy sense of disappointment" if he wished to remain a rural poet; however, his worst verse was written when he succumbed to the dangers of becoming "literary" and imitative. All of this is certainly not to say that rural poetry must be unpopular to be authentically rural, but it does suggest that rural poetry moves in partial opposition to the dominant urban concerns and to the urban demands for variety that would violate its natural limitations, and that Bloomfield's reputation may well have been in part a victim of that opposition.

Returning more specifically to what may be learned of rural poetry from Bloomfield, we find a more positive statement about limitations by Unwin. While discussing Bloomfield he observes, "A peasant-poet is usually a humble man writing well within the orbit of his equally humble capacities. He is restricted in range, but not in excellence."[35] Of Hazlitt's observation that the poet's muse was menial in her aspect Unwin writes, "This is not a condemnation so long as prosaism is avoided, and Bloomfield generally succeeded in retaining a thoroughly plain, but poetic style."[36] The writer of rural poetry, then, is an authentically rural man, and as such is frequently of humble station, learning, and ambition, who has chosen to write of the subjects he knows. Accepting the limitations of his capacities and subjects, the rural poet makes his poetry from the stuff of rural life—the things, the people, and the affectations of the countryside. William Empson's distinctions between proletarian literature, ballads and fairy stories, and the pastoral may be of some help. The folk literature, he asserts, is "by the people, for the people, and about the people," while most fairy stories and ballads are "by" and "for" but not "about" people. The pastoral is "about" but neither "by" nor "for" the people.[37] By extension, rural poetry is certainly "about" rural people and life, and it is "by" rural people. But while it is "for" rural people, I would count it very poor rural poetry if it were *only* for rural folk.

The rural poet such as Bloomfield is not restricted to a certain set of figures, to the use of specific verse forms, or to a particular meter, but is free to use those devices which he can best manage and which best suit his subject. Again, the limitations are those of the poet himself. That the couplet and versions of the ballad dominate Bloomfield's work should not dispel the reader's expectations of meeting a preponderance of blank verse in the canon of another rural poet. If there is too little help here in deducing something of the nature of rural poetry, a brief examination of the method of the genre may be more fruitful.

Bloomfield's poetry does exhibit the delicacy, faithfulness, and naiveté that Hazlitt observed, and if I may appropriate the second term, faithfulness, to apply to his method, it may be helpful. To say simply that he attempted a faithful portrayal of rural life is to escape at once a cluster of weighty and sometimes ambiguous critical terms and an overly literal notion of any one-to-one relationship between the things of the countryside and the representation of it in his poetry. There is no promise that because Bloomfield described a cow in Suffolk his readers could be assured of finding said cow and tugging it firmly by the teat. The faithfulness is to the real spirit of the country and to the poet's experience of it. There is a freedom, then, for the poet to treat the things of nature with gentleness or harshness, to idealize or criticize the folk of the country, or to write as mythmaker or verist all without violating the idea of faithfulness or losing his concern with the real things of the country.

Rural poets with their limited range must, as part of their method, deal carefully with the problem of finding a common ground to be shared with their audience. Bloomfield was not so unlearned as to be unaware of literary traditions, but it was not in them that he sought his common ground. He did not set about writing pastoral verse to which his readers could come with expectations of meeting certain conventions—conventions that, whether followed or varied for effect, lie outside the poet. Instead, he chose a pattern of argument in *The Farmer's Boy* that led to a common ground within the limits of the poet's experience of rural life. The method is primarily one of inviting the reader onto a ground that is first the poet's but second, that of rural men. The audience can, and did with *The Farmer's Boy,* approach with certain expectations based upon what they know of nature and the countryside and mankind. The expectations of the audience restrict somewhat the latitude of the rural poet to make the countryside too impressionistic, atypical, or surreal.

Bloomfield's primary mode, I have indicated, was celebration. The more elegiac mode of his last works is still based on the impulse to celebrate. Such an impulse on the part of the rural poet can be an indication of an ethical conviction that there is much good in the nature of rural life. The vision of that good was, for Bloomfield, a balanced one, for he does not posit the countryside as an Eden full of innocents or nature as a wholly benevolent spirit that ministers to all of man's needs. Rather, we have seen that the good lies in the relationship of rural man to nature and to his fellowman, and in the quality of rural life, and in the things of the country.

These few assertions about the nature of Bloomfield's rural poetry are amplified when the kind is seen in relation to the pastoral. Although the two share certain qualities, they are vastly different; even the history of rural verse runs counter to the tradition of the pastoral. Thomas Rosenmeyer uses the term "Hesiodic" to indicate a type of verse that is traditionally "hostile to the pastoral chant."[38] Tibullus' distinction between real agricultural scenes of labor, sweat, and pain and what Rosenmeyer calls a "pre-agriculturalist utopia" approximates that between rural and pastoral poetry. Hesiodic writing might be suggested as the tradition into which Bloomfield and the rural poets fit:

> In its origins, with Hesiod and Aristophanes, the tradition is activist, critical, and realistic. Hesiod moralizes for the benefit of his brother Perses, not concealing the burden of the labor, yet recommending it as work dear in the eyes of the gods. He takes a downright proletarian pride in the fact that he must suffer, physically and spiritually, before he can achieve success. Aristophanes, in turn, makes scornful fun of those who do not work for a living and who do not have their feet solidly on the ground. The Hesiodic code of country living is one of discipline and foresight. The farmer does not live a random life of enjoyment and self-revelation. On the contrary, he plans and saves and reins himself tightly for the sake of future gain. The Hesiodic strain demands self-imposed regimentation. One of its prominent organizing techniques is the calendar or almanac, arranging the tasks of the farmer in accordance with the seasons and the environment. . . . The calendar is didactic, and indeed didactic poetry is one branch of Hesiodic homeliness, a fact that is borne out by the many seventeenth- and eighteenth-century works modelled on Virgil's *Georgics*. The instruction is necessary, for without the expertise imparted, the harshness of the peasant's life would be overpowering.[39]

Using the term *ponos* for both labor and pain and as an indication that the philosophical stance underlying the Hesiodic demanded "that a good life furnish evidence

of effort and suffering," Rosenmeyer indicates how this impulse differs from and is basically incompatible with the pastoral. Raymond Williams, too, notes the distinction by tracing significant writing about country life "from Hesiod and the more consciously literary traditions of the pastoral from the third century B.C. landscapes of Sicily, the Greek Islands, and Egypt."[40] For a writer like Bloomfield, however, following in such a tradition could be an unconscious and unpremeditated act. As a rural poet, Bloomfield was aware of other poets whose work was similar to his own (Burns, Crabbe, and later Clare) and not deaf to the contemporary critics who inevitably related him to the pastoral tradition. But rather than identify himself as part of the pastoral tradition, Bloomfield continued to be a rural man—sometimes "the farmer's boy"—and took his poetic identity from a *personal* kinship with other rural poets. His lifelong concern with the image of Burns was a personal concern; "Brother Bard, and fellow labourer," his salutation in writing to Clare, reveals again the idea of personal kinship.

Further distinctions between the rural and the pastoral are at times matters of real difference, at times matters of degree. Rural poetry is made of the stuff of rural life and made by rural bards; the real countryside and a rural bard are not at all necessary or even usual in pastoral poetry. Both celebrate something like rural life which in rural poetry can be idealized within the confines of the possible but which, in the pastoral, need only suggest the possible and not conform to it. The traditional singing match, the love plaint, or the elegy can appear in rural poetry when it speaks of love or friendship, but the rural poet does not ground his poem in such literary conventions.

The idealizing of country life in the pastoral and in the rural differs in intent as well as in degree. Amid the voluminous critical comment on the pastoral in the eighteenth century, some of which affected those writers that Bloomfield admired, Congleton (in *Theories of Pastoral Poetry in England 1684-1798*) finds the emergence of two distinct critical approaches, both of which indicate the necessity of idealizing rural life. These schools, neoclassic and rationalistic, were by the end of the century supplanted by a romantic theory of the pastoral which in its own fashion idealized rural life.

The neoclassical school of which Pope's *A Discourse on Pastoral* seems to be the major and perhaps final eighteenth-century statement was stimulated by Rapin's *Dissertatio de Carmine Pastorali* (translated into English by Thomas Creech in his *The Idylliums of Theocritus With Rapin's Discourse of Pastorals* in 1684). The resulting English neoclassic school drew its tenets for the pastoral from the writings of the ancients, especially Virgil and the critical writings of Aristotle and Horace. These tenets are summarized neatly by the editors of the Twickenham edition of Pope's *Discourse*.

The main point on which this school agreed was that a pastoral should be an "imitation" of the action of a shepherd living in the Golden Age. From this precept stemmed certain subsequent ones: a pastoral should reflect the innocence and peace of that age and the virtues and simplicity of the shepherd who lived in it; because shepherds in this ancient past were often princes or men of affairs, the characters and language should be simple and pure rather than "clownish"; the scene should be simple and decorous, as in Virgil; the matter should reflect only the simple affairs of shepherds, that is, the loves and sorrows of a simple rural life; the fable should be simple and plain, the style neat and plain.[41]

Here the idealizing arises from the attempt to create an image of that "pre-agriculturalist utopia" or Golden Age found at the end of the path of chronological primitivism. That society of shepherd princes is not immediately in the realm of the possible, and as a cultural and literary tradition it exists in the imagination of the artist. The very creation of the image requires extensive idealizing, for the image itself is ideal. The intent is not to improve upon the nature of rural things but to create a reality in art.

Second is that school which rose from the rationalistic approach to the pastoral set forth by Fontenelle in his *Discours sur la nature de l'eglogue* (published in 1688 and translated by Motteus under the title *Of Pastorals* in 1695).[42] With a typical freedom from the authority of the ancients, Fontenelle saw the pastoral as simply "a representation of the tranquillity of rural life," a notion based on certain "psychological foundations" which, as the editors of the Twickenham text have it, holds that "the laziness of man's nature finds delight in representations of the quietness and leisure of a shepherd's life, while the passion most congenial to this laziness, love, also delights." It was also Fontenelle's contention that the pleasure of the pastoral arises from the use of "illusion," or half-truth, which "consists, in exposing to the eye only the Tranquillity of a Shepherd's Life, and in dissembling or concealing its meanness, as also in showing only its Innocence, and hiding its Miseries."[43] Even before this approach to the pastoral becomes distinctively English in the hands of Thomas Tickell and others it appears to idealize more nearly in the way that the rural poet does. The method of idealizing is the selection of scene and incident. The intent is "Illusion," however, and not a faithfulness to the spirit of rural life.

In examining Thomas Tickell's *Guardian* papers on the pastoral, Congleton observes an important development: Tickell expands on Fontenelle's explanation of the pastoral's appeal by adding something close to the natural goodness of the shepherds and the love of the natural things of the country. Most important, Tickell declares that the English countryside is a proper setting for the pastoral; the use of rural England for all save climate in the pastoral would free it from the servile following of

convention.[44] This is, in essence, cultural primitivism. Although such logic would appear to move the pastoral in many ways closer to the nature of rural poetry, the point in altering the locus of the poem was to facilitate the deception of the reader who could more easily, then, believe the pastoral creation. The essence of the countryside might creep into the pastoral without becoming the subject of the poem; the conventions and spirit of the pastoral could likewise appear in the rural without being the thing that the poet celebrates.

When in substituting cultural primitivism for chronological primitivism Joseph Warton and his romantic followers had their day with the pastoral, the two kinds become so close that the pastoral, for all practical purposes, ceased to exist. While extending the rationalist's claim that the pastoral should be made of local materials and suggesting the infusion of the more realistic portrayal with emotion, the romanticists desired a particularized representation of rural scenes and activities that made no distinction between cultural and chronological primitivism. Although for some the inhabitants of the rural world still remained idealized, John Aiken and Hugh Blair moved the portrayal of the rural society within the realms of the possible. The empirical and the concrete appear, as they do in rural poetry, hand in glove with an emotional appeal to the reader much like Bloomfield's in *The Farmer's Boy.* There may be more than ironic coincidence in the fact that the very last of the eighteenth-century's commentators on the pastoral was Dr. Nathan Drake whose warm praise of Bloomfield helped establish the poet's reputation. Drake, who thought the pastoral "based on a love of external nature and a high regard for the sentiment of primitive life," suggested that if the pastoral could not be written free from the restrictions of its conventional features and subjects, it should not be written at all.[45] An audience which demanded what the romantic critics did of the pastoral would not wish pastoral poetry to be written for them, but rather rural or peasant poetry in which a country man with the most intimate and authentic knowledge of the country wrote concretely about it.

Whatever the validity of Hazlitt's theory "that the poet can do no more than stamp the mind of his age upon his works," the idea itself provides a final possibility for differentiating between pastoral and Bloomfield's rural verse. The pastoral artist, being the more "educated" and consciously literary of the two, may have the power to make the stamp of the age a "more unique," personal, and conscious impression than can the rural artist. Those literary and philosophical impulses of Bloomfield's own age and the age preceding sometimes sit atop the fabric of his verse and at other times clash discordantly with his simple rural description. He writes only in stilted terms of "Nature," repository of natural goodness, acting as a foil to "Vanity." Underneath is the perfectly true idea that when man must rely upon the forces of nature to make seeds grow, he can take little credit for the event. But the capital letters and personified forces are not really Bloomfield's. It is probable too that the pastoral artist is generally more concerned with nature and the countryside as a medium which he neutralizes, then stamps with his moral, philosophical, and aesthetic colors than he is with real trees or real cows or (God forbid) real manure. The pastoralist may avoid real nature because his age tells him that it is evil and fallen, or because its roughness contradicts his aesthetic purpose, or because a great amount of particularized description of nature, even when the scenes are carefully selected, can be, as Dr. Johnson suggests, tedious.

The rural poet differs from the pastoralist (and, I might add, the romanticist) because his first concern is the things, folk, and events of the countryside which are important in themselves. Bloomfield may celebrate the Suffolk farm because it is familiar, comforting, a place of happy memory, but we have very little of the poet consciously interposing himself between the subject and the audience as an object to be appreciated before the reader can approach the rural subject. Bloomfield may idealize nature by selecting carefully the scenes he describes, but it is not done to sterilize and asepticize nature hence producing a characterless medium to be used for a "greater" purpose. His first purpose in portraying a scene is to celebrate the things in that scene; when he manipulates the parts of a scene and shows them to best advantage, his purpose is the greater celebration of the entire farm. The preface to **Wild Flowers** may indicate that Bloomfield thought that his celebration of specific scenes might end in the celebration of "general nature," for "nature in a village is very much like nature every where else."[46] To arrive at general nature through the particular and specific requires the cooperation of a reader willing to make associations and accept grand coincidences; general nature appears in the reader's imagination and not on the rural artist's page.

III THE THEMES AND VALUES

The natural and man-made objects of the countryside, the country folk, and country life are the stuff of Bloomfield's poetry. Because he valued his subject for itself—found it to be precious—he took his themes and values directly from it. No elaborate system of order is superimposed. If his themes and values have a relatedness of the parts, it is simply because they rise from the whole of the countryside.

It is quite important to know first some of the things that the land and man's relationship to it are not. The countryside is neither Eden, nor site of a new Golden Age, nor a new utopia. That it may become these things in the minds of writers who use it is obvious, especially when they use a neutralized landscape as both a me-

dium upon which to stamp their own order and a source from which to document the authenticity of their own order by showing parallels to the events and patterns and objects of nature. We can have the illusion of Eden, the Golden Age, or the new utopia being contained in the things of the countryside and growing naturally or organically from them when the natural patterns are mixed with the conceptual patterns of the artist; it is the same illusion that occurs when an object is cathected with erotic energy and appears to contain the energy. Although, as I have indicated, the rural poet may perforce bring ideas of his culture, ideas of benevolent nature, the natural goodness of man, perhaps pantheism and large parts of the eighteenth-century creed of sentimentalism to his poetry and give the land the illusion of a particular order, his distinction as rural artist comes in discovering the order already there in the country and in man's relationship to the land.

To reiterate, the land in Bloomfield's world was a literal and figurative common ground on which men could stand. It was literal ground from which the inhabitants of the manor took their living—a thing to which almost all had rights supported by tradition and law. Bloomfield's argument against the new refinement that marked the coming of capitalism to the farm is an argument for preserving the literal common ground between men on which they could see, for one classless moment, their mutual humanity. The literal common ground could not support the inhabitants of the manor if it was used capriciously and without a thought to good husbandry. In the mutual use of the land, the little society discovered and encouraged predictable patterns of social behavior; no one should misuse the commons by fencing them for exclusive use or destroy the arable land by turning his sheep in to pasture before the crops were removed. There are innumerable expectations for others and oneself that the mutual use of the land can produce. When there are reasonable expectations about the action of others, then trust, a necessity of ordered social life, is possible. The literal common ground becomes the figurative when the trust arising from that literal situation is transferred into the greater social sphere.

Of course a return to the open-field system of agriculture remains an impossibility. Establishing a series of commons on which urban man can learn what it is reasonable to expect from his neighbor may be an impracticable bit of dreaming. But the need for trust is real in any society intending to escape the rise of something akin to a police state in which voluntary trust is replaced by political protection of the individual. The fewer the reasonable expectations a society has for the peaceful and cooperative behavior of its members, the less trust its citizens will exhibit. A common ground, either literal or figurative, however, is not a value of the past that must remain out of reach in the limited world of Robert Bloomfield. It could be moved forward out of the past and used as a principle of discourse or argument, as a possible consideration in urban planning, or as a way of looking at human relationships.

Another of Bloomfield's themes arising from the land is that of the knowable life which may be, as I suggested in chapter 2, almost unknown to urban man. There is a natural order to life in the country. The seasons turn with predictable regularity and the rural occupations follow sensibly. The use of the land is cyclic in nature—the cycles enforced by seasonal change and the agricultural principles of rotation of use. Life on Mr. Austin's farm offered Bloomfield a structured existence in which an extensive knowledge of the past and careful observation of the present made the future predictable. The natural graduation and priority of events allows, even forces, a concern with the major over the minor. When it is time to plow, one plows; when it is time to milk, one milks. Scattered concerns align themselves within the order, and as life is structured by the passing of the seasons on the land, a sense of why one labors and when one will rest is possible despite the caprices of nature. The lessons of the past prompt preparation for the future and make life knowable as it may not be in the city. The necessity of considered actions is made apparent to everyone on the farm; and although farmers have ruined their land as surely as urban dwellers have befouled their environment, at least the structure for seeing cause and effect, past and present, is readily available in rural life. Part of the value of such a knowable life is the framework it creates around man. To see oneself reacting to the major demands of life without the insistent intrusion of the minor may be a rare experience in urban life; in fact, just being able to identify the major events and demands of life and separate them from the minor is not always easy amid our machines, our mixed media, and our talk—talk that may be our way of creating an order for the minor intrusions that we cannot control.

The folk of the countryside provide Bloomfield with another theme. His characters are, as he notes in the preface to **Wild Flowers,** almost always humble people; their relationship to the things of nature, to the land, is that of labor. Rural life demands work, labor, enterprise. The fulfillment of these demands becomes, if not a matter for pride, a moral imperative. Again and again the rural artist asserts that the yeoman who has labored his full deserves the rest of moral contentment. If no other idea gives value to the life of the poor, at least there is work by which their existence can be measured and shown to be responsible. This can, under slavery, extreme poverty, or any duress, be a horrid life from which generations of people have fled. Yet to Bloomfield the life of labor is more than one that passively and mindlessly accepted toil as the lot of man. Rural enterprise

and labor can be a cause of joy; the matching of the human body to the natural labor for which it is suited could be a harmonious experience.

Jacques Barzun, who thinks it doubtful that the labors of technologic man are those to which he is biologically and psychologically suited, describes the ironic plight of labor in the post-enclosure times when the factory's machine has replaced the farm's tool:

> The machine deprives man at once of bodily exertion and fatigue and the dramatic victory of work. Consequently man's feelings about himself during the greater part of his waking time are not joyful or single-minded. This is true not only of strictly mechanical work in the factory; it applies to all the tasks that aid and mirror industry. In them men do not exactly know what it is they do under the name of work. Beside the machine, which is so exact and tireless and perfect, man grows weary and careless and indifferent. He cannot compete with it and has no incentive to do aught else. Production no longer depends on him. When he is away from the machine, its work and its output seem self-sufficient, yet demanding: the organization of its functions is a monstrous set of remote relationships.[47]

Rural man, whose ordered, knowable life allowed him to see that his family and perhaps a good many others relied directly on the success of his labor on the land, would have a far different idea of self. The dignity in Bloomfield's portraits of the poor is, then, believable and understandable. It is made so by their position on the land and the fulfillment that is possible in their labor. Good husbandry and the pride man can take in it expand the range of labor and fulfillment.

A second value, therefore, is apparent in the theme of labor. Work-labor-enterprise, like the talk of the city, proffers a way of structuring the world and knowing oneself. It has been suggested that we talk in order to know more exactly what it is that we think or believe, and validate it. Both intellect and emotion are excited and exercised by the process. Work, as physical as is its process, occupies the intellect and emotions too. Barzun notes the absorption of the laborer in his enterprise:

> But the inner struggle goes on: wielding the tool is not the act of the hand alone; the whole man works the ax or chisel, the scythe, the plow, the oar. The breath-borne rhythm, the concert of eye and sinew, the changing purpose and the sight of it fulfilled, the assured play of muscle that we find again in physical sports, are sensations good in themselves and they betoken art. Above all, the absorption of the self in manual work is unique. Alert yet only half conscious, the craftsman knows bliss.[48]

Bloomfield's portraits of rural labor show the same bliss. It is not the escape to unessential tasks, to the minor, that Dr. Johnson describes when he speaks of Sober repairing his coal-box or amusing himself with chemistry to pass the time painlessly and avoid the major tasks,[49] although I suspect that the city tinkerer at times indulges in an imitation of labor in an attempt to satisfy the same human needs as are satisfied by work. The best of rural labor reinforces man's perception of himself, allows man to know and feel his personal harmony with the natural order, and structures his world by allowing him to select and conquer the major or primal matters of existence. Of course rural labor has not been and is not always so, but at its best it is far more joyous than the later labor amid the machines of the city where "a new and degraded slavery annihilate[s] the self."[50]

Bloomfield's poetry and rural poetry in general have at least recorded the experiences of labor. In such cultural records lie some of our inventive possibilities. More than just a way of remembering, this record of a way of being stands open to man's future should he care to learn from it or preserve its values. With no thought of returning everyone to the plow, we may still wish to invent our future with the possibility of real labor that shares the qualities of rural labor.

There is a third major theme in Bloomfield's poetry that grows naturally from the themes of land and labor. Valuing what he did, it is inevitable that the rural poet should react negatively to that which threatened his beliefs. Bloomfield sensed, correctly, that it was the growth of the city that threatened rural life as he knew it; his anti-urban stance is a result. I have demonstrated that Bloomfield's reaction was not a mindless fear of all change. He simply opposed those changes which seemed to produce less new good than the old good they destroyed. To the rural man, the city may always seem to be a perverse creation, because it has not, traditionally, fitted itself into the natural order. The smoke and fumes, the unnatural haste, the disappearance of recognizable priorities, the thoughtless waste and destruction, the impersonality and harshness, and the unnatural demands on the countryside all convinced him that the city was somehow evil. There are, of course, other, more positive ways of viewing the city, but from the vantage point of rural man, the negative is overwhelming.

Something of the same antiurban spirit appears in the pastoral and in eighteenth-century satire, too. In much of Bloomfield's poetry, the force of commentary arises from what he chooses to see in both the country and the city. When the positive qualities of the country are viewed beside the negative features of the city, the arrangement of the material is inherently critical of the latter. (The arrangement is not black and white, for he does recognize poverty and other negative features of country life.) The general picture of the country in *The*

Farmer's Boy, for example, is positive. When the city is considered at all, it appears as a structural and spiritual intrusion into rural life. The only image in Bloomfield's picture of the city that gives it any order at all is that of the whirlpool, ungoverned and ungovernable. What Bloomfield found most objectionable (and probably still would were he alive) are those things which result from poorly considered action by urban people—perhaps from actions that are not considered at all. Even in Bloomfield's day, the smoke of the city hung about it a full five miles into the country. Something about the effect of the city on our minds allowed the situation to worsen for over one hundred years before any concerned and effective action was taken. If life and labor within the natural order once taught the value and necessity of considered actions, then Bloomfield and his fellow laborers have been forgotten too soon.

It is perhaps the nature of humans to forget our past, our roots, as soon as they are no longer immediately accessible to us. It is, therefore, the foolish assumption of any generation that its age is unique. Witness our constant narrow references to "today's society" or "this modern world"—evidence that we have little contact with our own past. Had the rural folk of Bloomfield's time been isolated from their own past and the heritage of their culture, they would have continued in the most primitive fashions of husbandry. Life within the natural order, a respect for labor, and a sense of responsible purpose arising from a relationship to the land—all of these encouraged a consideration of the past not as a time to return to, but as a repository of possibilities for the present and future. Bloomfield and his poetry are not of great importance to the history of humans and their letters. Still, he had a quiet vision of rural values and wisdom that is not without meaning and possibility in a technologic age, and to ignore him and his concerns is foolish. Bloomfield's artistry was marred at times by unrefined technique, but as Edmund Blunden has recently written, "few poets could equal his sensitivity towards the meaner things in Nature."[51] It is precisely that sensitivity that man must cultivate anew if he is to continue to survive within the natural order.

Notes

1. Roland, Grant, ed., *A Selection of Poems by Robert Bloomfield* (London: Grey Wells Press, 1947), p. 14.

2. Unwin, p. 106.

3. "Bloomfield's Aeolus," *Notes and Queries,* 201 (October, 1956), 451.

4. Blunden, p. 131.

5. Unwin, p. 106.

6. Review of *Rural Tales, Ballads, and Songs,* in *The Critical Review,* 35 (May, 1802), 67-75.

7. Review of *Rural Tales, Ballads, and Songs,* in *The Monthly Mirror,* 13 (January, 1802), 24, 28.

8. *The Letters of John Clare,* p. 167.

9. *Rural Tales, Ballads, and Songs,* 1st ed. with notes by Capel Lofft (London: Vernor and Hood, 1802), p. 1; hereafter cited in the text as *R.* As line and verse numbers do not appear in each poem and are sometimes incorrectly given, page numbers will be provided.

10. Wordsworth, indeed, is sometimes incapable of fulfilling the promise of humble speech made in his poetry. In "Resolution and Independence," for example, there are five times as many lines expended in rhapsody about the old man's speech as there are lines representing it. When those lines of dialogue finally come they are rather flat and disappointing.

11. *The Complete Works of William Hazlitt,* ed. P. P. Howe, vol. 17 (London: Dent, 1933), p. 239.

12. Claire Blunden, in a letter to the author, March 24, 1970.

13. Unwin, p. 107.

14. *May Day with the Muses* (London: Baldwin, Cradock, and Joy, 1822), p. 3; hereafter cited in the text as *M.*

15. Sister Mary Eulogie Horning, *Evidences of Romantic Treatment of Religious Elements in Late Eighteenth-Century Minor Poetry (1771-1800)* (Washington: Catholic University Press, 1932), p. vii.

16. *The Poetical Works of the Rev. George Crabbe: with his Letters and Journals, and his life by his son.* (London: John Murray, 1834), I, 245.

17. Unwin, p. 104.

18. John Lawrence Hammond and Barbara Hammond, *The Village Labourer: 1760-1832, A Study in the Government of England before the Reform Bill* (1913; Reprint ed. New York: A. M. Kelley, 1967), p. 27.

19. John Lawrence Hammond and Barbara Hammond, *The Rise of Modern Industry* (London: Methuen, 1966), p. 85.

20. Bovill, p. 13.

21. Hammond, *The Rise of Modern Industry,* p. 84.

22. Bovill, p. 13.

23. As quoted in ibid., p. 14.

24. Hammond, *The Rise of Modern Industry,* p. 88.

25. British Library Add. MS. 28,268, "Letters of Robert Bloomfield principally to members of his own family, 1788-1823," fol. 111.

26. Ibid., fol. 96.

27. Raymond Williams, *The Country and the City* (New York: Oxford University Press, 1973), pp. 88-89.

28. Kenneth MacLean, *Agrarian Age: A Background for Wordsworth* (New Haven: Yale University Press, 1950), pp. 60-61.

29. Hammond, *The Rise of Modern Industry,* p. 89.

30. Maynard Mack, *The Garden and the City: Retirement and Politics in the Later Poetry of Pope, 1731-1743* (Toronto: University of Toronto Press, 1969), p. 32.

31. Barrell, pp. 96-97, 110-20.

32. "On Thomson and Cowper," in *The Complete Works of William Hazlitt,* V, 95-96.

33. Ibid., p. 96.

34. Ibid.

35. Unwin, p. 95.

36. Ibid.

37. William Empson, *Some Versions of Pastoral* (Norfolk, Conn.: New Directions, 1950), p. 6.

38. Thomas G. Rosenmeyer, *The Green Cabinet: Theocritus and the European Pastoral Lyric* (Berkeley: University of California Press, 1969), p. 20.

39. Ibid., p. 21.

40. Williams, p. 14.

41. E. Audra and Aubrey Williams, eds., *Pastoral Poetry and an Essay on Criticism,* by Alexander Pope, vol. 1 (New Haven: Yale University Press, 1961), p. 15.

42. Ibid., p. 16.

43. Ibid.

44. J. E. Congleton, *Theories of Pastoral Poetry in England: 1684-1798* (Gainesville: University of Florida Press, 1952), pp. 87-88.

45. Ibid., p. 144.

46. Robert Bloomfield, *Wild Flowers; or Pastoral and Local Poetry* (London: Vernor, Hood, & Sharpe, 1806), p. viii.

47. Jacques Barzun, *Science: The Glorious Entertainment* (New York: Harper & Row, 1964), pp. 34-35.

48. Ibid., p. 32.

49. *The Idler and The Adventurer,* ed. W. J. Bate, John M. Bullitt, and L. F. Powell, vol. 2 (New Haven: Yale University Press, 1963), pp. 97-98.

50. Barzun, p. 34.

51. Edmund Blunden, in a written statement to the author, March 24, 1970.

Selected Bibliography

PRIMARY SOURCES

1. MANUSCRIPTS.

Bloomfield's unpublished correspondence and the notes and prefaces in the handwritten volumes of poetry are the major sources for the biography as it is presented in this study.

"Letter to John Clare, 1820." British Library Egerton Manuscript 2245, fol. 186.

"Original Letters of Robert Bloomfield principally to members of his own family, 1788-32." British Library Additional Manuscript 28, 268.

"Poems and Papers of Robert Bloomfield and His Eldest Son Charles, 1791-1825." British Library Additional Manuscript 30, 809.

"Poems, etc." British Library Additional Manuscript 28, 266.

"Poems: May Day with the Muses; The Banks of the Wye; etc." British Library Additional Manuscript 26, 265.

2. PUBLISHED MATERIALS.

Bloomfield's popularity was such that his works are readily available in their original editions in research libraries. The second item is typical of several facsimile editions in which those without access to a large library are apt to encounter him. Listed here are the first editions and subsequent editions which are of bibliographical and biographical interest.

The Banks of the Wye; A Poem. London: Vernor, Hood, and Sharpe; Longman, Hurst, Rees, Orme and Brown, 1811.

Collected Poems (1800-1822). Intro. Jonathan N. Lawson. Gainesville, Florida: Scholars' Facsimiles and Reprints, 1971.

"Extract from a Poem, entitled 'Good Tidings, or News from the Farm,' by Robert Bloomfield. Recited at the Anniversary Meeting of the Royal Jennerian Society, Thursday, 17th of May, 1804." London: James Whiting, 1804.

The Farmer's Boy; A Rural Poem. 1st 8 vol. ed. London: Vernor and Hood, 1800.

The Farmer's Boy; A Rural Poem. 7th ed. Manuscript notes by the author. London: Vernor and Hood; Longman and Rees, 1803. The edition is in the British Library.

The Farmer's Boy; A Rural Poem. 9th ed. London: Vernor, Hood, and Sharpe; Longman, Hurst, Rees, and Orme, 1806.

Hazelwood Hall: A Village Drama. London: Baldwin, Cradock, and Joy, 1823.

The History of Little Davy's New Hat. London: Harvey and Darton, 1815.

May Day with the Muses. London: The Author; Baldwin, Cradock, and Joy, 1822.

The Remains of Robert Bloomfield. Edited by Joseph Weston. 2 vols. London: Baldwin, Cradock, and Joy, 1824. Includes much material between boards for the first time.

Rural Tales, Ballads and Songs. 3d ed. With notes by Capel Lofft. London: Vernor and Hood, Longman and Rees, 1802.

A Selection from the Poems of Robert Bloomfield. Edited by J. L. Carr with a foreword by Edmund Blunden. Kettering: J. L. Carr, 1966. The preface is a facsimile of Mr. Blunden's handwriting.

A Selection of Poems by Robert Bloomfield. Edited by Roland Gant. London: Grey Wells Press, 1947. Part of the Crown Classics series; has an interesting and sympathetic preface.

Selections from the Correspondence of Robert Bloomfield, The Suffolk Poet. Edited by W. H. Hart, F.S.A. London: Spottiswoode, 1870. A facsimile edition by Robert Ashby (Redhill, Surrey: Commercial Lithographic Company, 1969) is also available.

Wild Flowers; or, Pastoral and Local Poetry. 1st sm. 8vo. ed. London: Vernor, Hood, and Sharpe; Longman, Hurst, Rees, and Orme, 1806.

A Catalogue of all the Valuable Books, Household Furniture, & c. To be Sold by Auction, by W. Betts, on Friday & Saturday, the 28th & 29th of May, 1824, The Property of the Late Mr. R. Bloomfield, The Poet, on the Premises, at Shefford, Beds. Biggleswade: Jackson, 1824. Final notes to the biography of the poet can be found among the physical remains of his estate.

SECONDARY SOURCES

1. BIOGRAPHICAL.

Capel Lofft's preface and notes in the various early editions of *The Farmer's Boy* form the basis of most of the following biographies. For particulars on Lofft see his life as communicated by himself to the *Monthly Mirror,* 13 (June, 1802), 370-76; 14 (July, 1802), 9-14.

"A." "A Memoir of Robert Bloomfield." in *The Poetical Works of Robert Bloomfield and Henry Kirke White.* London: T. Nelson, 1871. This reworking of previous facts and opinions shows considerable sympathy for Bloomfield still existing in the second half of the century.

A Biographical Sketch of Robert Bloomfield, with a Portrait. N.p. [1825]. Copy in the British Library. A typical and highly derivative biography.

EVANS, JOHN. Letter to the Editors. *Metropolitan Literary Journal,* 3 (1823-1824), 424-29. Comments on some matters of biography previously discussed in the journal.

G. V. L. "A Biographical Sketch of Robert Bloomfield." *Monthly Mirror,* 10 (October, 1800), 202-5. One of the first major public notices of interest in Bloomfield.

HOLLAND, JOSEPH. *An Appendix to the Season of Spring in the Rural Poem, "The Farmer's Boy."* Croyden, Surrey: [Joseph Holland?], 1806. An interesting footnote to the career of Bloomfield.

"On the Life and Writings of Robert Bloomfield." *Metropolitan Literary Journal,* 3 (1823-1824), 208-17. See too "Additions and Corrections to the Article, 'On the Life and Writings, etc.,'" pp. 326-27 for Bloomfield's obituary notice.

RANDS, WILLIAM B., ed. *The Poetical Works of Robert Bloomfield: A New Edition with A Sketch of the Author's Life and Writings.* London: Knight, 1855. Also of interest for its description of Bloomfield's reputation by mid-century.

STORER, J[AMES], and GREIG, J[OHN], eds. *Views in Suffolk, Norfolk, and Northamptonshire; Illustrative of the Works of Robert Bloomfield; Accompanied with Descriptions: To which is Annexed, A Memoir of the Poet's Life, by Edward Wedlake Brayley.* London: Vernor, Hood, and Sharpe, 1806. Includes an interesting account by Bloomfield.

WICKETT, WILLIAM, and DUVAL, NICHOLAS. *The Farmer's Boy: The Story of a Suffolk Poet, Robert Bloomfield, His Life and Poems, 1766-1823.* Lavenham, Suffolk: Terence Dalton, 1971. Of more value for its biographical information than its criticism.

2. CRITICAL AND BIOGRAPHICAL.

BLUNDEN, EDMUND. *Nature in English Literature.* 1929; reprint ed., New York: Kennikat Press, 1970. Helpful chapter on Bloomfield. Contains a valuable chapter on Bloomfield and *The Farmer's Boy.*

HAZLITT, WILLIAM. "On Thomson and Cowper." In *The Complete Works of William Hazlitt,* edited by P. P.

Howe, V, 95ff. London: Dent, 1930. Balanced and insightful remarks on Bloomfield.

REED, GRAHAM F. "Bloomfield's Aeolus." *Notes and Queries,* 201 (October, 1956), 450-51. A generally unsympathetic view.

SOUTHEY, ROBERT. *The Lives and Works of the Uneducated Poets.* London: Humphrey Milford, 1925. Sympathetic remarks by one of Bloomfield's most generous champions.

3. MAJOR CONTEMPORARY REVIEWS.

For nearly fifteen years dozens of small, sometimes borrowed reviews of Bloomfield appeared in such publications as the *Lady's Monthly Museum,* attesting not only to his general popularity but also to his specific appeal to women. A lengthy listing of contemporary reviews is available in William S. Ward's *Literary Reviews in British Periodicals: 1789-1820* (New York: Garland, 1972). See especially reviews in the *Monthly Review,* the *Monthly Mirror,* and the *Critical Review.*

4. BACKGROUND MATERIALS AND GENERAL CRITICISM.

AUBIN, ROBERT ARNOLD. *Topographical Poetry in XVIII-Century England.* 1936; reprint ed., New York: Kraus, 1966. Study of a tradition into which much of Bloomfield's work falls.

AUDRA, E., and WILLIAMS, AUBREY, eds. *The Poems of Alexander Pope.* Vol. 1. *Pastoral Poetry and an Essay on Criticism.* New Haven: Yale University Press, 1961. Provides a useful history of the eighteenth-century pastoral.

BARRELL, JOHN. *The Idea of Landscape and the Sense of Place 1730-1840: An Approach to the Poetry of John Clare.* Cambridge: Cambridge University Press, 1972. A provocative study of the relationship of landscape painting to the poetry of the period, especially as the poetry reflects the social and economic facts of country life.

BARZUN, JACQUES. *Science: The Glorious Entertainment.* New York: Harper & Row, 1964. A fascinating examination of modern values and attitudes which in many cases are antithetical to Bloomfield's.

BISHIP, MORCHARD, ed. *Recollections of the Table-Talk of Samuel Rogers.* London: Richards Press, 1952. Bloomfield's sometimes friend and patron, Samuel Rogers, provides a full picture of the successful side of the London literary scene—a side Bloomfield only glimpsed, and then, in part, through Rogers.

BLUNDEN, EDMUND. "The Rural Tradition." In *Edmund Blunden: A Selection of His Poetry and Prose.* London: Rupert Hart-Davis, 1950. A helpful essay which details something of the history and motivation of the poetic protest against enclosure and which identifies some of the values held by the writers in the tradition.

BOVILL, E. W. *English Country Life: 1780-1830.* London: Oxford University Press, 1962. A full discussion of the background against which Bloomfield lived and wrote.

CLARE, JOHN. *The Letters of John Clare.* Edited by J[ohn] W. Tibble and Anne Tibble. London: Routledge, 1945. Of value here for numerous references to and praise of Bloomfield.

COLERIDGE, SAMUEL TAYLOR. *Collected Letters of Samuel Taylor Coleridge.* Edited by Earl Leslie Griggs. 4 vols. Oxford: Clarendon Press, 1956. Noted here for their reference to Bloomfield.

CONGLETON, J. E. *Theories of Pastoral Poetry in England: 1684-1798.* Gainesville: University of Florida Press, 1952. The neoclassic and rationalistic schools of the pastoral are thoroughly examined.

CRABBE, GEORGE. *The Poetical Works of the Rev. George Crabbe: with His Letters and Journals and His Life.* 8 vols. London: John Murray, 1834. Bloomfield's more successful contemporary deals with many of the same images and situations, but does so more successfully and more sternly.

DURLING, DWIGHT L. *Georgic Tradition in English Poetry.* 1935; reprinted., New York: Kennikat, 1963. Helpful background to pastoral and rural verse.

EMPSON, WILLIAM. *Some Versions of Pastoral.* Norfolk, Conn.: New Directions, 1950. An examination of what the pastoral is and is not which traces the spirit of the pastoral into modern poetry and novels.

HAMMOND, JOHN LAWRENCE, and HAMMOND, BARBARA. *The Rise of Modern Industry.* 1926; reprint ed., London: Methuen, 1966. The effects of industry on English country life are followed and interpreted by the authors. Their studies of the laboring classes are useful background for understanding Bloomfield in his element.

————. *The Skilled Labourer: 1760-1832.* 1936; reprint ed., New York: A. M. Kelley, 1967.

————. *The Town Labourer: 1760-1832. The New Civilization.* 1941; reprint ed., New York: A. M. Kelley, 1967.

————. *The Village Labourer: 1760-1832. A Study in the Government of England before the Reform Bill.* 1913; reprint ed., New York: A. M. Kelley, 1967.

JACK, IAN. "Poems of John Clare's Sanity." In *Some British Romantics: A Collection of Essays.* Edited by James V. Logan et al. Ohio State University Press, 1966. Reveals some of Clare's debt to Bloomfield with little sympathy for the latter.

JOHNSON, ROSSITER. *Works of the British Poets, from Chaucer to Morris with Biographical Sketches.* Vol. 2. *Rogers to Hermans.* New York: Appleton, 1876. Of interest chiefly for its prefaces dealing with such minor figures as Bloomfield.

KERMODE, FRANK, ed. *English Pastoral Poetry: From the Beginnings to Marvell.* Toronto: George C. Harrap, 1952. The introduction of value for its overview of the kind.

MACLEAN, KENNETH. *Agrarian Age: A Background for Wordsworth.* New Haven, Yale Studies in English, vol. 15. New Haven: Yale University Press, 1950. Describes in detail what is also the background for Bloomfield.

ROSENMEYER, THOMAS G. *The Green Cabinet: Theocritus and the European Pastoral Lyric.* Berkeley: University of California Press, 1969. Identifies fully the roots of the tradition of rural poetry.

SOUTHEY, ROBERT. *The Life and Correspondence of Robert Southey.* Edited by Charles Cuthburt Southey. New York: Harper, 1851. Of interest here for its chronicling of Southey's patronage of Bloomfield.

THOMSON, JAMES. *Poetical Works.* Edited by J. Logie Robertson. London: Oxford University Press, 1956. Bloomfield's chief literary source for *The Farmer's Boy.*

TIBBLE, JOHN, and TIBBLE, ANNE. *John Clare: His Life and Poetry.* London: Heinemann, 1956. Provides valuable critical background while discussing Bloomfield's "Brother Bard."

Tributary Verses to the Memory of Robert Bloomfield, The Suffolk Poet. Woodbridge, England, 1823. Some evidence is here of the limited notice that marked Bloomfield's death.

UNWIN, RAYNER. *The Rural Muse: Studies in the Peasant Poetry of England.* London: Allen and Unwin, 1954. Perhaps the best serious examination of the tradition in which Bloomfield really belongs. A generally sympathetic yet objective study.

WILLIAMS, RAYMOND. *The Country and the City.* New York: Oxford University Press, 1973. A major modern study of two metaphors that were of great importance to Bloomfield. Williams' insistent Marxism flavors his reading of such minor figures as Cuck, Clare, and Bloomfield.

WHITE, W. *History, Gazetteer, and Directory of Suffolk.* Sheffield: White, 1844. Of interest for its picture of early nineteenth-century Suffolk and for its references to Bloomfield, Lofft, and Grafton.

WORDSWORTH, WILLIAM. *The Poetical Works.* Edited by E. de Selincourt. 2d ed. 5 vols. Oxford: Clarendon Press, 1952. One can hardly read Bloomfield properly without setting him against the considerable and contrasting shadow of Wordsworth across this period.

John Lucas (essay date 1994)

SOURCE: Lucas, John. "Bloomfield and Clare." In *The Independent Spirit: John Clare and the Self-Taught Tradition,* edited by John Goodridge, pp. 55-68. Helpston: John Clare Society and the Margaret Grainger Memorial Trust, 1994.

[*In the following essay, Lucas argues that Bloomfield's "poetry was a means of securing a social identity at odds with his own origins." He also interprets Clare's praise for Bloomfield's poetry as praise for the depiction of an ideal, uncorrupted rural life.*]

[John] Clare's intense admiration for Bloomfield is well known. 'The English Theocritus & the first of the Rural Bards in this country', he called him. He also said that in his opinion Bloomfield was 'our best Pastoral poet'. Johanne Clare rather questions Clare's motives in piling up such exaggerated praise, as she thinks it to be. Clare, she says, 'must have recognized that by rallying to Bloomfield's reputation he was to some extent helping to lay the foundations for his own' (*John Clare and the Bounds of Circumstance,* p. 62). This is almost certainly unfair. True, Clare closely identified with Bloomfield, and this is hardly to be wondered at. But his warmest praise tends to occur in letters, which can hardly be thought of as a form of 'rallying', with all that implies of a *public* concern; and anyway, had he been so intent as Johanne Clare argues on using Bloomfield to help build his own reputation, he would surely have made at least some effort to write that life of Bloomfield which at one time he projected. Instead, soon after hearing of Bloomfield's death, he wrote three sonnets in his memory, one of which ends with a great line about how the fame of then fashionable poets would come to lie 'A dead wreck on the shore of dark posterity'. And he noted in his Journal that Bloomfield's 'dying neglected' is 'the common lot of genius'.

In a different essay I would want to argue that this assertion rather takes for granted the reality of a myth assiduously fed by the earlier generation of Romantic poets, for whom the death of Chatterton provided the archetypal instance of such neglect, suffering, and indeed of 'genius' itself. Here, I will note that Clare's claim that the neglect of Bloomfield was only to be expected must have a good deal to do with his conviction that he and Bloomfield both came from unprivileged circumstances; and that as Bloomfield's first and huge success with *The Farmer's Boy* was never repeated, so the heady reception given to *Poems Descriptive of Rural Life and Scenery,* followed as it was by the comparatively poor sales of *The Village Minstrel,* between them provided evidence of how 'The tide of fashion is a stream too strong / For pastoral brooks that gently flow and sing' (to quote from another of the sonnets to Bloomfield).

There is, however, a problem about all this, one unwittingly touched on by Johanne Clare when she remarks that 'Clare could hardly have been indifferent to the fact, that because of his background and because he pushed that background into the foreground of his poems, Bloomfield was seen by others as an unusual case, an exception to those genteel, educated and sophisticated men who had always been able to assume that participation in the literary life of the nation was theirs by right' (p. 63). Bloomfield was certainly an exception to the rule of cultural orthodoxy. But *in fact* in his writings he says very little about his origins, his education, his early life and work. There's more acknowledgement of rough early years in Crabbe's poetry than ever there is in Bloomfield's. (A point to make because Clare unfairly attacks Crabbe for being ignorant of the agricultural poor: 'Whats he know of the distresses of the poor musing over a coal fire in his parsonage box': answer, a great deal, as anyone who has read *The Village* and *The Borough* knows, and as Clare, who had certainly read them, chose to forget.) By comparison, very little of that suffering gets into Bloomfield's poetry, and to say this leads me to my subject.

In what follows I think I *may be* describing someone for whom poetry was a means of securing a social identity at odds with his own origins. Or perhaps it's better to say that poetry allowed Bloomfield to shift from one set of possibilities—cultural, social, political—to another, and that this shift went hand-in-hand with what I will call the poetry of reconciliation. At all events, we know that after the success of *The Farmer's Boy* Bloomfield for some years earned a reasonable living from his writing; and from the writings themselves we can see that the poet is characteristically set on producing narratives that endorse 'Amity and social love'. The phrase comes from the opening lines of 'Winter', in the fourth book of *The Farmer's Boy,* that poem which, when it was published in 1800, brought him both fame and money, and which, while it may well be based on incidents and observations of Bloomfield's own youth, was, we must note, written in the late 1790s, by which time he had been living in London for some fifteen years, earning a living as a shoemaker. I need, then, to provide a brief resumé of his life.

Bloomfield was born in 1766, in Honington, Suffolk. His father, who died in Robert's infancy, was a tailor, his mother, left to look after six small children, was, so he says in **"To A Spindle,"** his beautiful elegy to her, a village schoolmistress. She taught him to read and write, and with the help of friends found the money to give all her children some schooling. Not that this amounted to much; and Robert's in particular lasted no more than a few months. His removal from school seems to have coincided with his mother's remarriage, and when 'Robert was not above eleven years old, the late Mr W Austin, of Sapiston, took him. And though it is customary for farmers to pay such boys only 1s. 6d a week, yet he generously took him into the house. This relieved his mother of any other expense than only of finding him a few things to wear: and this was more than she knew well how to do'.[1]

Four years later—we are now at the beginning of the 1780s—Robert moved to London. According to his mother, writing to her sons Nat and George, the youth was 'so small of his age that Mr Austin said he was not likely to get his living by hard labour'. George was earning *his* living as a shoe-maker; and his younger brother, who now joined him in London, began to learn the same craft. Now comes what is surely a crucial moment. According to George's account:

> One Sunday, after a whole day's stroll in the country, we by accident went into a dissenting Meeting-house in the old Jewry, where a gentleman was lecturing. This man filled Robert with astonishment. The house was amazingly crowded with the most genteel people: though we were forced to stand in the aisle, and were much pressed, yet Robert always quickened his steps to get into the town on Sunday evening soon enough to attend this lecture. The preacher's name was Fawcet [sic].

At this point, the unidentified editor of the 1867 edition offers a footnote on Fawcett: 'Author of a justly-esteemed poem on War'. If ever a foonote was intended to mislead, this is it. Fawcett was certainly the author of the poem mentioned, but he was also, and far more importantly, one of the great voices of radical dissent of his time, although oddly E. P. Thompson doesn't include him in *The Making of the English Working Class,* nor is he thought worth a mention in Iain McCalman's *Radical Underworld: Prophets, Revolutionaries and Pornographers in London, 1795-1840.* There is, however, an illuminating discussion of Fawcett by M. Ray Adams in his neglected *Studies in the Literary Back-grounds of English Radicalism (With Special Reference to the French Revolution)* (1947). In a chapter called 'Joseph Fawcett and Wordsworth's Solitary', Adams quotes Godwin's admission that it was Fawcett who turned his attention to literature and politics. The two men first met at the very end of the 1770s, when Godwin had begun to preach as a dissenting minister at Ware, while Fawcett, who had been trained for the Unitarian ministry at the Dissenting academy at Daventry, was preaching at Walthamstow. Then, in 1783, 'Fawcett was engaged as a Sunday evening lecturer at the Old Jewry meeting-house, a position he retained for twelve years. He resigned his pastoral work in 1787'. Adams adds that 'he had evidently been more and more drawn from theology to politics', and he further notes that 'According to a contemporary record, his oratorical gifts attracted to the Old Jewry "the largest and most

genteel audience that ever assembled in a dissenting place of worship"'. Among Fawcett's audience was the young Wordsworth. And, as we have seen, so was Bloomfield.

Not for long, however. Sometime in 1784 George fell out with fellow shoe-makers and Robert, 'naturally fond of peace, and fearful for my personal safety begged to be suffered to retire from the storm'. The words are George's and he goes on to say that Robert was once again taken into Austin's house at Sapiston and that while working there he read Thomson's *The Seasons* and, 'free from the smoke, the noise, the contention of the city, he imbibed that love of rural simplicity and rural innocence, which fitted him in great degree, to be the writer of such things as *The Farmer's Boy*'. Leave aside the *non sequitur* of Robert feeling so worried for George's safety that he quits London, and what we have here is, I am certain, a statement of the greatest importance. It implies that Bloomfield the poet sets himself to be a chronicler of rural virtues, 'simplicity and innocence', against the city's 'contention'. And this will go far to explaining why *The Farmer's Boy* should have been so rapturously received in 1800. Its backward-glancing presentation of rural circumstance provides us with a vision of tranquillity, of human comfort and harmony, a kind of discreetly utopian account of the 'natural' world very far removed from the contentious actualities of the moment, in the country as well as the city, including newly energised arguments about labour's rights. From the mid 1790s onwards the most eloquent spokespeople for these were the Spencean radicals who, though they were centred on the city, had as their two main demands the Rights of Man and the insistence that the land should be held in common.[2] It will have been their predecessors with whom George Bloomfield had come into contention in 1784.

I had here better admit that I am in no position to disentangle what actually went on between the Bloomfields, their employer, a Mr Chamberlayne, of Cheapside, and those with whom they fell out, and who seem to have threatened them with physical violence. But from George's own account—which is all I have to go on—it seems that Chamberlayne and the Bloomfields decided to resist the demand that work be given only to a 'closed shop' of shoemakers who had been apprenticed to the trade. This demand appears to have been put by 'The lawful journeyman of shoemakers', who must therefore have composed a union of skilled craftsmen; and we should not find this surprising, given that shoemakers were always at the forefront of radical thought, closely identified with, and often belonging to, the Spenceans. In *The Making of the English Working Class* Thompson notes of surviving Jacobin traditions that 'as late as 1849 a shrewd Yorkshire satirist published a sketch of such a "Village Politician" which has a feel of authenticity. He is, typically, a cobbler, an old man and the sage of his industrial village'. Thompson then quotes part of the sketch:

> He has a library that he rather prides himself upon. It is a strange collection . . . There is 'The Pearl of Great Price', and Cobbett's 'Twopenny Trash': 'The Pilgrim's Progress . . .' and 'The Go-a-head Journal'. 'The Wrongs of Labour' and 'The Rights of Man'. 'The History of the French Revolution' and Bunyan's 'Holy War . . .' 'The Age of Reason', and a superannuated Bible

(pp. 183-4).

Iain McCalman also notes that shoemakers were among the most prominent of radicals in the late eighteenth century and early nineteenth century, and he mentions, *inter alia*, Robert Charles Fair, a shoemaker poet, Thomas Preston, shoemaker, Thomas Pemberton, boot-closer, and William Curry and Joseph Bacon, both of whom were shoemakers.

There is, therefore, nothing odd about shoemakers attending Joseph Fawcett's Meeting House. What *is* odd is George's decision to turn against 'The Lawful Crafts'. Perhaps his employer insisted on this, as the price for keeping his job. George says that Chamberlayne 'took an active part against the journeymen; and even went so far as to pay off every man that worked for him that had joined their clubs'. It will clearly take more work to unravel the politics and commitments of that moment as they affected George and Robert Bloomfield. Here, I can do no more than note that this is the moment when, according to his brother, Robert Bloomfield conceives the idea of *The Farmer's Boy.*

Does that mean some of the poem was written earlier than the late 1790s? Possibly. But what is certain is that when it was published Bloomfield was once again employed as a shoemaker in London. By then he was a married man and he may well have hoped that the publication of the poem, supposing it could be arranged, would bring in some useful money. (There was a tradition of shoemaker poets which stretched back at least as far as James Woodhouse and 'the cobler poet' John Lucas.) As it happened, the immediate and lasting success of *The Farmer's Boy* put sufficient money in Bloomfield's pocket for him to be able to exchange his cheap garret lodgings for a house on the City Road. There, he wrote and published at regular intervals, and although none of his publications repeated the runaway success of *The Farmer's Boy,* each sold pretty well. First, in 1802, came *Rural Tales, Ballads and Songs,* which included 'Richard and Kate: or Fair Day', the ballad poem Clare so admired. This was followed in 1804 by *Good Tidings* (about Jenner's small-pox vaccine—perhaps Bloomfield's attempt to emulate Erasmus Darwin?), then, in 1806, by *Wild Flowers* (among them the famous **'Broken Crutch'**, and such fine poems as **'The Horkey'** and **'My Old Oak Table'**), and then, in 1811, *The Banks of Wye.*

A year later Bloomfield left London for the small town of Shefford, in Bedfordshire, where he bought a pleasant house and where he wrote what was to be the final volume to appear in his lifetime, *May Day with the Muses.* But by the time that appeared, in 1822, he was in deep financial trouble and had come to hate Shefford—'this vile town' he called it. The following year he died a bankrupt. I suspect that Bloomfield's move from London was a self-conscious declaration that he now considered himself to be a country gentleman, and this would be consistent with his poetry, which typically endorses and celebrates a vision of rural circumstance as beneficent, its politics essentially feudal or at all events pre-capitalist in that relationships between master and men are based on mutual respect and acceptance of assigned function within a known structure of social and working life. We can see this if we look at the poetry itself.

The Farmer's Boy follows the procedure of the poem Clare so loved, Thomson's *The Seasons*—from Spring through to Winter—although in so doing it is inevitably drawn towards the Virgilian tradition of the Georgic rather than the Theocritean. (Bloomfield even finds room to praise 'improved' agricultural farming methods, and provides a detailed account of the making of Suffolk cheese, which is very much in the eighteenth-century Georgic tradition of exact description and advice to farmers and husbandmen as adopted by Mason, Smart, Dyer, Philips and others.) But in **'Summer'** Bloomfield reveals that all is not well with this world. He does so by contrasting past and present, the household to which Giles, his protagonist, belongs, with other, newer, more fashionable farmers' houses:

> Here once a year Distinction low'rs its crest,
> The master, servant, and the merry guest,
> Are equal all; and round the happy ring
> The reaper's eyes exulting glances fling,
> And warm'd with gratitude, he quits his place,
> With sunburnt hands, and ale-enliven'd face,
> Refills the jug his honour'd host to tend,
> To serve at once the master and the friend . . .
>
> Such were the days,—of days long past I sing,
> When pride gave place to mirth without a sting:
> Ere tyrant custom strength sufficient bore
> To violate the feelings of the poor;
> To leave them distanced in the maddening race,
> Where'er refinement shows its hated face:
> Nor causeless hated;—'tis the peasant's curse,
> That hourly makes his wretched station worse;
> Destroys life's intercourse, the social plan
> That rank to rank cements, as man to man:
> Wealth flows around him, Fashion lordly reigns;
> Yet poverty is his, and mental pains.

In my recent short monograph on Clare I have shown how in both *The Parish* and *The Shepherd's Calendar* he contrasts the old style farmers, 'who used their servants toils to share', with the newer 'refined' farmer, who will go to any length to separate himself from his workers.[3] Whether the change was as absolute as both Bloomfield and Clare declare it to have been cannot easily be decided, although I'm more inclined to believe them than those economic historians, of right *and* left, who insist that the idea of the older 'mutuality' is a sentimental delusion; but what cannot be denied is that both poets are keenly aware of the hurts and insults of the newer arrangements, which break what Alun Howkins and Ian Dyck call 'the old order', where social harmony was achieved because 'men were bound together by their "words" into a society of mutuality'.[4] Nor is it necessary to suppose that this society of mutuality was always and everywhere achieved, although there seems no reason to doubt that Bloomfield found something very like it at Sapiston. I want to suggest no more than that his eager endorsement of 'the old order' comes to him at least partly as a result of his exposure to the clash between Chamberlayne and the lawful journeymen, which he would inevitably identify with the newer, starkly divisive class-relationships of the city. It is, after all, remarkable that although he spent thirty years of his life in London he never writes about it. Instead, he always returns to the country of his upbringing or imagination: it is the great good place which, because it is identifiable as upholding the 'bond of amity and social love', by implication offers a preferable alternative to the legally-binding relations of city employer and employee. Bloomfield had been forced to earn his living in the city, but he quit London as soon as he could. (And in moving to Shefford he plays out the role of man of independent means which Clare yearned to take on when he left Helpston for Northborough; and like Clare, he finds his dream crashes about him, although in his case the crash is much longer in coming.)

Put it rather differently. Clare, I suggest, loved Bloomfield's poetry because he could find in it a pre-lapsarian rural world, one that is innocent of enclosure, that has not been laid waste by the brutal power of axe and plough. Bloomfield is therefore the English Theocritus because he writes about a *first world* of rural circumstance, one now gone. The English re-discovery of Theocritus in the latter half of the seventeenth century had been accompanied by the belief that the Greek poet was the true founder of pastoral poetry, was in that sense an original, was primitive (not that the word would have been so used), was more earthy and actual than Virgil, was, in a word, more natural. When Richard Polwhele came to add a Dissertation and Notes to his two-volume translation of the *Idyllia, Epigrams and Fragments of Theocritus, Bion and Moschus, with the Elegies of Tyrtaeus,* he remarked that 'The pieces of Theocritus are the result of his own accurate observation. He described what he saw and felt. His characters, as well as his scenes, are the immediate transcript of nature' (vol. 2, p. 6, 1692 edition). This reading of Theocritus became an accepted and lasting commonplace. And so we find

Clare, in his 'Essay on Landscape', claiming of the 'living pastorals of Rippingille' that 'Rippingille is the Theocritus of English painting—there they are as true as if nature had just left them and none of the ridiculous imaginings of fashion hung about them . . . we see nothing but natural objects not placed for effect or set off by other dictates of the painters fancys but they are just as nature placed them'. And Bloomfield, Clare says, is 'the English Theocritus'. He wants Bloomfield's poems to be the truth about rural circumstances, at all events about *past* rural circumstances.

This, I am certain, must be the reason Clare so praised **'Richard and Kate'** and **'The Broken Crutch'**, to name two of his favourite Bloomfield poems. The first, sub-titled **'A Suffolk Ballad'**, tells the story of an old couple who have been married forty years and who take the day off from their labours to go to the fair:

> 'For I'm resolved once more to see
> That place where we so often met;
> Though few have had more cares than we,
> We've none just now to make us fret.'

So says Richard, and although we hear no more of their cares, we know that he must be a hedger ('His mattock he behind the door / And hedging-gloves again replaced'), we hear snippets of Suffolk idiom ('When once a giggling mawther you'—a footnote tells us that Mawther means 'girl, in the East Anglian dialect'); and we meet their children and grandchildren, who have also gone to the fair:

> Kate viewed her blooming daughters round,
> And sons, who shook her wither'd hand;
> Her features spoke what joy she found;
> But utterance had made a stand.
>
> The children toppled on the green,
> And bowl'd their fairings down the hill;
> Richard with pride beheld the scene,
> Nor could he for his life keep still.

Richard then makes the assembled family a speech, saying how proud he is of them all, drinks their health, and the ballad ends with the old couple at close of day gaining 'once more their more lowly rest'.

'Richard and Kate' is a charming poem, but we shall not understand Clare's passionate championing of it unless we realise that what must have appealed to him about it was Bloomfield's depiction of untroubled rural harmony—the fair—and contented and fruitful family life among the rural poor. In other words, the poem is precisely an idyll. And although 'idyll' was well on the way to acquiring its newer meaning, of 'idealised description of "rustic" life', (and the use of the word rustic is itself part of the idealising) Clare would have fastened onto Bloomfield's use of dialect and his not 'looking down for a rural theme'—as Burns had famously noted in the Preface to his poems that he himself was incapable of doing—in order to endorse the poem's essential truthfulness. *That was how it used to be.* The improbability of such a claim is evident as soon as you reflect on the high incidence of infant mortality and early death among the rural poor, but such considerations are beside the point. They certainly don't offset Clare's identification with the joys of a world that for him *have* to characterise the past because they can't be thought of as typifying the present. This, then, affects his equally passionate attachment to **'The Broken Crutch'**.

Clare admired this poem enough to make mention of it in one of his own, 'Opening of the Pasture—Love & Flattery', which Robinson, Powell and Dawson date to 1823-4 (see their edition of Clare's *Cottage Tales,* Ashington and Manchester, 1993). The poem is a dialogue between two young women, Mary and Lucy, and at one point Mary tells her friend of a youth who tries to woo her by offering her 'Bloomfield's Poems', which were 'sweet indeed', she says, adding that the young man had

> . . . turned a leaf down where he bid me read
> It was a story called 'The Broken Crutch'
> Theres luck said he your face might get as much
> —I loved the poems & the story too.

Bloomfield's tale is about a young girl of humble origin whose face is her fortune. She leaves home to work for a squire, Herbert, one of the old school: he keeps a 'kitchen table, never clear of beef, / Where hunger found its solace and relief'. Herbert falls in love with the girl and the news reaches her guardian who decides that her virtue must be in danger. Off he goes to confront the squire, arriving at his house in time to discover that the young couple have just married and that a wedding feast is under way. Peggy may have come from 'the unpolished walks of humble life', Herbert tells her guardian, but his love for her is nevertheless sincere. To this her guardian replies, in words the poet italicises:

> My blessings on you: I am lame and old,
> I can't make speeches and I won't be bold;
> But from my soul I wish, and wish with pain,
> *That brave good gentlemen would not disdain*
> *The poor, because they're poor . . .*

The poem's narrative opens door after door into a receding way of life. It begins with the poet lamenting the destruction of a 'dear green valley' he'd known as a youth. The axe has cut down 'In Gain's rude service and in Pity's spite / Thy clustering alders', and has even invaded and levelled 'The last, last poplars, that compose thy shade'. Cowper's generalised lament for fallen poplars is here replaced by a specific criticism of 'gain'; and Bloomfield's poem looks not down but back

for a rural theme. (In passing I will note that a sizeable essay could be written on the theme of fallen or toppled trees as symbol or indicator of social change.) At the end of **'The Broken Crutch'** the old man, Peggy's guardian, voices his regret for a lost way of life, of the once upheld social responsibilities of 'brave good gentlemen'. Yet he himself is part of an already old tale. In a now lost past, **'The Broken Crutch'** implies, there was a world of amity characterised by the absence of social disdain and, even, by the acceptability of marriage between social unequals. You have only to think of Clare's perpetual grieving over his broken relationship with Mary Joyce and the way that came to stand for him as a particularly brutal instance of the power of class, the process of separation, to realise why he might well think **'The Broken Crutch'** a poem 'above praise', as he told Allan Cunningham. Perhaps he persuaded himself that this lost past had been Bloomfield's present. If so, it only serves to emphasise how from often stated grievances (in Clare's case) and less often stated ones (in Bloomfield's) both poets 'are borne back ceaselessly into the past' as a later writer noted of those who grieve for the lost dreams of a good society.

And what of other poems? *May Day with the Muses,* the last volume of Bloomfield's to be published in his lifetime, is his most sustained vision of 'amity and social love'. Given that at the time he was writing it he was growing increasingly disenchanted with his life as would-be man of independent means, the poem can therefore be seen as a compensatory act to set against the reality of a life beset by money difficulties and, I suspect, estrangement from the townspeople of Shefford. (For how else explain the venomous 'This vile town' than by assuming that Bloomfield felt himself spurned by neighbours and acquaintances?) There is no space here to comment at length on what is certainly a most beautiful poem, but I need to note that yet again it is set in the past. Its protagonist, the very old Sir Ambrose Higham of Oakley Hall, decides to exact payment of tithes from his tenants, not by taking their money, but by asking each of them to tell a tale in verse for the delight of the assembled company. They agree, and when they have finished Sir Ambrose's wife appears in the dress which 'sixty years before, / had sparkled on her sunshine bridal morn', to usher in the May Day evening celebrations: 'She came to grace the triumph of her Lord, / And pay him honours at his festive board'. Sir Ambrose then makes a speech in which he tells his listeners that

> Your verses shall not die as heretofore;
> Your local tales shall not be thrown away,
> Nor war remain the theme of every lay

and the poem ends with the closing of the revels: 'The owl awoke, but dared not yet complain, / And banish'd Silence reassumed her reign'.

Clare of course knew *May Day with the Muses.* In his own tale 'Valentine Eve' he names the ancient house where the story is set as Oakley Hall, which can hardly be coincidence, although 'Valentine Eve' is still closer to **'The Broken Crutch'** in that both poems deal with the marriage of social unequals. There is probably a common source at work here: Edward Drury told Clare about the 'actual circumstances of the present Marquess of Exeter's grandfather marrying a country girl of humblest life'. But 'Valentine Eve' has something of that powerful feeling for a lost past which makes *May Day with the Muses* so distinctive a performance. Early on, as Sir Ambrose's tenants gather, Bloomfield remarks that:

> Not a face was there
> But for May Day at least had banished care:
> No cringing looks, no pauper tales to tell,
> No timid glance, they knew their host too well,—
> Freedom was there, and joy in every eye:
> Such scenes were England's boast in days gone by.

Bloomfield's use of narrative couplet aligns his tale with Goldsmith's 'The Deserted Village' as well as with those numerous picturesque poems of the mid to late eighteenth century, all of which provide or imply a comparison between past and present, or which, in the case of the picturesque, underwrite, as I have argued elsewhere, the sad inevitability of change.[5] Clare would challenge such apparent inevitability. Hence, his great anti-enclosure poems. Bloomfield doesn't, although we have seen that in some lines in 'Summer' of *The Farmer's Boy,* and elsewhere for that matter, he comes close to it. But the ending of *May Day with the Muses* is haunted by a sense of irretrievable loss, a grieving for a way of life gone now into the reign of silence. So much so that in his closing couplet Bloomfield may well be intending an ironic reminder of Pope's famous consolatory vision of the goddess of Harvest overriding the folly of grand, comfortless buildings; those products of new, ostentatious wealth spreading out from London:

> Deep harvests bury all [their] pride has plann'd
> And laughing Ceres re-assume the land.

> ('Fourth Moral Essay: On the Use of Riches')

Pope foresees a future of rural peace and plenty for all, and this social vision is implicit in the generous enthusiasm of Thomson's *The Seasons,* that mid-century report on the health of the nation. But by the time Bloomfield was writing *May Day with the Muses* it was a widely-protested scandal that those who controlled the harvests withheld through their cornlaws bread from the poor. Bloomfield doesn't mention the hated cornlaws but that he should set his poem in the past and once again focus on *old* people makes it inevitable that we should read *May Day with the Muses* as an elegy for a lost way of life, a vision of mutuality long faded, one that relied on kinship, trusted relations rooted in place.

Whether he believed that a way of life in which all could rejoice in deep harvests had ever truly existed, at all events in quite the uninflected manner his poems suppose, I don't know. Probably not. But anyway this matters less than his asserting the value of 'local tales', of local language, and of those social arrangements in which there could be no room for disdain or timid glances or refinement's hated face, and in which a *shared* abundance could be taken for granted. No wonder Clare so admired him.

Notes

1. This and other quotations are taken from 'The Life of Robert Bloomfield', which introduces the 1867 edition of *The Works of Robert Bloomfield,* published by George Routledge and Sons. The 'Life' contains numerous quotations from George Bloomfield's memoir, including the above, and from Capel Lofft, Bloomfield's patron.

2. For this see David Worrall's *Radical Culture: Discourse, Resistance and Surveillance, 1795-1820* (1983).

3. John Lucas, *John Clare* (Plymouth: Northcote House, Writers and Their Work Series, 1994).

4. Alun Howkins and Ian Dyck, '"The Time's Alterations": Popular Ballads, Rural Radicals and William Cobbett', *History Workshop,* 23 (Spring 1987).

5. John Lucas, 'Wordsworth and the Anti-Picturesque', *Romantic to Modern,* 1982.

FURTHER READING

Bibliographies

Ashby, Robert F. "The First Editions of *The Farmer's Boy*." *The Book Collector* 41, no. 2 (summer 1992): 180-87.

> Describes the quality of paper, print, and illustrative engravings used in the first editions of *The Farmer's Boy.*

Bloomfield, B. C. "The Publication of *The Farmer's Boy* by Robert Bloomfield." *The Library* 15, no. 2 (June 1993): 75-94.

> Places the production and publication of Bloomfield's most famous poem in some historical context and in the context of Bloomfield's family history; also traces some of the financial transactions involved.

Cranbrook, the Earl of, and Hadfield, John. "Some Uncollected Authors XX: Robert Bloomfield, 1766-1823." *Book Collector* 8, no. 2 (summer 1959): 170-79.

    Offers a brief defense of Bloomfield's poetry and brief account of his life as a writer; then reviews the bibliographical history of his work.

Biography

Lawson, Jonathan. Introduction to *Collected Poems: 1800-1822*. Gainseville: Scholars' Facsimiles & Reprints, 1971, vii-xv.

    Surveys Bloomfield's career from his love for his craft to his ill health and poverty at the end of his life.

Criticism

Review of *Good Tidings; or, News from the Farm. A Poem. Monthly Mirror* 17 (June 1804): 385-90.

    Asserts that the *Monthly Mirror* was the first of Bloomfield's admirers before praising Bloomfield's poem "Good Tidings," a verse work about small-pox vaccinations.

Review of *The Farmer's Boy. Critical Review* 29 (1800): 66-77.

    Appreciates Bloomfield for being self-taught, and his epic poem, *The Farmer's Boy,* for its original depictions of nature's sublimity.

Review of *The Remains of Robert Bloomfield. Monthly Review* 105 (September 1824): 79-84.

    Explains the financial motive for the publishing of Bloomfield's *Remains* before discussing some of its contents.

Wickett, William and Nicholas Duval. *The Farmer's Boy: the Story of a Suffolk poet, Robert Bloomfield, His Life and Poems, 1766-1823*. Lavenham, England: T. Dalton, 1971, 144 p.

    Provides a critical overview of the poet's life and works.

Additional coverage of Bloomfield's life and career is contained in the following sources published by Thomson Gale: *Dictionary of Literary Biography,* **Vol. 93; and** *Literature Resource Center.*

Thomas Robert Malthus
1766-1834

English political economist, essayist, and travel writer.

INTRODUCTION

Considered one of the most controversial writers of the early nineteenth century, Malthus is best known for *An Essay on the Principle of Population* (1798), commonly known as the *Essay on Population*. The essay posits that population tends to increase at a faster rate than the means for sustaining the population. Unless population growth is stemmed by "Preventive" checks (such as contraception) that cause "vice," or "Positive" checks (such as famine, disease, or other form of disaster) that cause "misery," poverty levels increase. Providing relief to the poor, in the form of food, subsidized shelter, etc., encourages population growth, increasing poverty levels. The essay sparked debates on poverty for decades with Malthus's opponents claiming he was overly pessimistic and unsympathetic to the miseries of the poor, and his defenders insisting that his theory was sound and he was simply being realistic. Both Charles Darwin and Alfred Wallace credited Malthus's observations for influencing their theories on natural selection.

BIOGRAPHICAL INFORMATION

Malthus, the sixth of eight children, was born into an affluent middle-class family in Surrey, England, on February 13, 1766. His father, Daniel Malthus, had inherited sufficient money to live as a gentleman; he read literary classics as well as scientific texts and personally oversaw his son's early education. At the age of ten, Malthus was sent to Bath to study with the Reverend Richard Graves, and at the age of sixteen, he traveled to the Dissenting Academy at Warrington to study with Gilbert Wakefield, a radical Unitarian. In 1784 Malthus enrolled at Jesus College, Cambridge, Wakefield's alma mater, and graduated four years later, having distinguished himself in mathematics. He also won prizes in Latin and English although his physical disability—a cleft lip and palate—prevented him from engaging in public speaking to any great degree. He took Holy Orders and in 1789 was appointed curate at Okewood, a small chapel in an economically depressed area of Surrey. Four years later he joined Jesus College as a non-resident fellow. In 1798, at his father's urging, Malthus published *An Essay on the Principle of Population*, which challenged the views circulated by Enlightenment utopianists, and aimed to influence public policy. The essay was particularly critical of the Old Poor Law, which had been enacted in Elizabethan times, providing state-sponsored relief based on family size and food prices. Beginning in 1799, Malthus began traveling extensively, first to Scandinavia and Russia, later to France and Switzerland. In 1804 he married his cousin Harriet Eckersall; the couple had three children, two daughters and a son. He gave up his fellowship at Jesus College, which was restricted to bachelors, and in 1805 accepted a professorship at East India College in Hertfordshire. For the next several years he continued teaching, writing essays and pamphlets on political economy, and enlarging and revising the *Essay on Population*. He retired from his teaching post in 1830, by which time his reputation had declined and his theories were increasingly subject to bitter debate and criticism. Nevertheless, on August 14, 1834, a New Poor Law was passed, drastically reducing government-sponsored aid for the poor. Malthus died on December 29, 1834.

MAJOR WORKS

Malthus's *Essay on Population,* which he revised and enlarged four times between 1803 and 1826, was his most influential and most controversial work. Malthus was not the first to discuss a link between population growth and poverty, or to discuss checks to population growth, but the *Essay on Population* was distinctive in its systematic construction of theory and its aim to impact public policy. It was originally written in response to two essays—*An Inquiry into Political Justice* (1793) by William Godwin, and *Sketch for a Historical Picture of the Progress of the Human Mind* (1795) by Marie Jean Antoine Nicolas Caritat, the Marquis de Condorcet—that advanced the notion of the eventual perfection of society, which Malthus found overly optimistic. Central to Malthus's thought was his observation that, "Population, when unchecked, increases in a geometrical ratio. Subsistence increases only in an arithmetical ratio." In other words, population increases at a much faster rate than the means to support it unless population growth is checked. Checks include population growth inhibitors in the form of "vice" (such as contraception), and population reducers in the form of "misery" (such as disease or famine). The second edition of the *Essay on Population* (1806) was expanded to nearly four times the length of the original. The changes incorporated empirical evidence gleaned from Malthus's tour of Norway, Sweden, Finland, Russia, France, and Switzerland, and his study of their populations and crops. It also included a means to control population other than through misery and vice: moral restraint, or voluntary abstinence from sex. In the *Essay on Population,* Malthus maintained that alleviating some of the oppressive conditions of the poor was ultimately useless, for if conditions were made better the poor would respond by having more children, introducing the problem of sustaining them. The solution was to instill in the lower classes the desire for a higher standard of living, the achievement of which was made possible only by choosing to have a smaller family and practicing moral restraint.

Malthus's other important works include his *An Inquiry into the Nature and Progress of Rent, and the Principles by Which It Is Regulated* (1815), for which Malthus receives partial credit for discovering the law of diminishing returns. Malthus's observations concerning the import of foreign grain, in his *Observations on the Effects of the Corn Laws* (1814) and *The Grounds of an Opinion* (1815), were also influential. His *Principles of Political Economy Considered with a View to Their Practical Application* (1820) is considered the most complete expression of his views on economics. Malthus's only writing not devoted to political and economic issues was the record of his European travels, titled *The Travel Diaries of Thomas Robert Malthus,* written in 1799 but unpublished until 1966.

CRITICAL RECEPTION

Malthus's theories were highly controversial in his own time. Liberals and radicals among early Romantic writers attacked his suggestion that the problems of the poor were caused by their reproductive practices, and his belief that poor relief did more harm than good in alleviating those problems. Modern critics have been divided between those who claim Malthus's theories have been misunderstood and those who echo earlier critics in charging that his theories supported an economic system based on inequality. G. J. Cady, in his assessment of American reaction to Malthusianism, states that misperceptions of Malthusian theory abound, maintaining that he was unable to locate, within the large body of American responses, a single text "correct enough, and at the same time comprehensive enough, to provide a point of reference from which the other American comments might have been viewed." Cady reports that in general, American opinion was not favorable, but cautions that in most cases "the Americans appear to have been criticizing, not the doctrine of Malthus, but their own or, worse yet, someone else's interpretation of it." Antony Flew (see Further Reading), similarly suggests that "what Malthus himself actually advocated differs in important ways from what has become associated with his name." Flew reports that, for example, while Malthus attacked the Poor Law and rejected the utopian schemes advanced by Condorcet and Godwin, he never conceived of his theories "as providing a warrant for abandoning piecemeal and realistic efforts for improvement," as has been charged by many of his critics. Marilyn Gaull (see Further Reading) also suggests that Malthus's theories have been misunderstood and oversimplified: "It is unfortunate that the whole complex argument of the *Essay* is usually reduced to the geometrical/arithmetic ratio Malthus used to illustrate what he called a 'tendency' to reproduce at a greater rate than resources."

Representing the other side of the critical controversy is Eric B. Ross, who discusses Malthus's many revisions and expansions of the original 1798 essay in response to changing conditions in England and Europe. All of the versions, according to Ross, served the same purpose, which was to legitimize and preserve the unequal distribution of private property then in place. Malthus, in Ross's view, "not only offered the authority of natural law in defence of established property relations, but created a general explanatory framework which was to prove one of the most enduring bulwarks against any argument for the mitigation of economic or social injustice." Tim Fulford situates Malthus's theories within the context of the earlier writings of Edmund Burke; however, according to Fulford, Malthus extended Burke's arguments about poverty to the next stage. Whereas Burke claimed it was outside the provenance of government to interfere with the laws of nature and the laws of God by providing poor relief, for Malthus "poverty became not simply a calamity that laborers suffered, not simply an instance of a general human vulnerability before God, but the fault of the laborers themselves for breaking the natural and divine law." According to Ross, Malthus's influence endures to the present day, continuing to provide justification for economic inequality and discouraging efforts to reform such inequalities or alleviate the suffering of the poor.

PRINCIPAL WORKS

An Essay on the Principle of Population, As It Affects the Future Improvement of Society, with Remarks on the Speculations of Mr. Godwin, M. Condorcet, and Other Writers [anonymously] (essay) 1798; revised and enlarged as *An Essay on the Principle of Population; or, A View of Its Past and Present Effects on Human Happiness; with an Inquiry into our Prospects Respecting the Future Removal or Mitigation of the Evils Which It Occasions.* 2 vols. 1803; revised and enlarged 1806, 1807, 1809; revised and enlarged, 3 vols. 1817; revised, 2 vols. 1826, 1890

An Investigation of the Cause of the Present High Price of Provisions: Containing an Illustration of the Nature and Limits of Fair Price in Time of Scarcity; and Its Application to the Particular Circumstances of This Country [anonymously] (essay) 1800

A Letter to Samuel Whitbread, Esq., M.P. on His Proposed Bill for the Amendment of the Poor Laws (letter) 1807

A Letter to the Rt. Hon. Lord Grenville, Occasioned by Some Observations of His Lordship on the East India Company's Establishment for the Education of Their Civil Servants (letter) 1813

Observations on the Effects of the Corn Laws, and of a Rise or Fall in the Price of Corn on the Agriculture and General Wealth of the Country (essay) 1814

The Grounds of an Opinion on the Policy of Restricting the Importation of Foreign Corn, Intended as an Appendix to "Observations on the Corn Laws" (essay) 1815

An Inquiry into the Nature and Progress of Rent, and the Principles by Which It Is Regulated (essay) 1815

Statements Respecting the East-India College, with an Appeal to Facts, in Refutation of the Charges Lately Brought against It in the Court of Proprietors (essay) 1817

Principles of Political Economy Considered with a View to Their Practical Application (essay) 1820; revised and enlarged 1836

The Measure of Value Stated and Illustrated, with an Application of It to the Alterations in the Value of the English Currency since 1790 (essay) 1823

Definitions in Political Economy, Preceded by an Inquiry into the Rules Which Ought to Guide Political Economists in the Definition and Use of Their Terms; with Remarks on the Deviation from These Rules in Their Writings (essay) 1827

A Summary View of the Principle of Population (essay) 1830

The Travel Diaries of Thomas Robert Malthus (diaries) 1966

The Pamphlets of Thomas Robert Malthus (pamphlets) 1970

The Works of Thomas Robert Malthus. 8 vols. (essays, letters, diaries, pamphlets) 1986

CRITICISM

G. J. Cady (essay date October 1931)

SOURCE: Cady, G. J. "The Early American Reaction to the Theory of Malthus." In *Thomas Robert Malthus: Critical Assessments.* Vol. 4, edited by John Cunningham Wood, pp. 18-42. London: Croom Helm, 1986.

[*In the following essay, originally published in October, 1931, Cady examines pre-1840 American criticism of Malthus's theories, contending that much of it is based on misreadings.*]

That which has passed and, in fact, still passes for Malthusianism in the mind of the man in the street, the social politician, the amateur economist, and, indeed, of the professional economist, has not infrequently been a very different thing from the theory advanced more than a century ago by the distinctly atypical "country parson." In the body of literature under consideration, indeed, there was not found a single interpretation of it correct enough, and at the same time comprehensive enough, to provide a point of reference from which the other American comments might have been viewed. It has been deemed necessary, therefore, at the outset briefly to answer the perennial question: Precisely what was the doctrine of Malthus? It would not be far wrong to say that the central principle was just this: A finite earth cannot support the unchecked increase of any form of life, animal or plant, and must of necessity, therefore, prescribe such limits to the production of the means of subsistence as to prevent the full potential growth of human population.[1] The elaborate structure built up around this core, controversial in origin and for that reason argumentative in tone, consisted of three distinct yet closely related parts: first, a theory of the increase of population; second, a theory of production; and third, a theory of distribution, or, more precisely, of poverty.

Characterizing the first of these phases was Malthus' famous dictum on the rate of increase of population. This law rested on the a priori principle that at any time the potential growth was approximately a function of already existing numbers and on the assumed permanently operative biological laws bearing on human reproduction.[2] In the United States population had, for some time, doubled every twenty-five years. In the primarily controversial portions of his work Malthus was content to accept this actually observed American increase as one of the bases of his general argument. This he did, strangely enough, after having piled up evidence to prove a much more rapid growth possible. He appears to have been a debater making a concession "for the sake of argument" rather than a scientist stating the results of his investigations "for the sake of truth."[3] Of the checks which might, and, in fact, usually did, prevent the full potential geometric increase of population, some operated to decrease the birth-rate, others to increase the death-rate. In the first edition of his *Essay* Malthus placed all the checks, subjectively considered, in one or the other of the two categories, vice and misery. In later more optimistic editions he added "moral restraint."[4] Social and political institutions such as the religion of China and English poor relief might so interfere with the operation of "moral restraint" as to multiply vice and misery.[5]

The answer to the question, Must these checks operate? was supplied by Malthus' theory of production. As a critic of the institutional perfectionist doctrines of Godwin, and the social programs of Young, Pitt, and others, Malthus proposed to show that the yearly production of food, a thing assumed necessary to man, could not possibly increase rapidly enough to keep pace for very long with the potential growth of population. The task appeared easy and was, therefore, somewhat carelessly performed.

In the first edition of the *Essay* he relied on pure assertions such as this: "It will be allowing as much as any person can well demand to suppose that the yearly production of subsistence in England might be doubled in twenty-five years. It is quite impossible to suppose that the produce could be quadrupled in fifty years. It would be contrary to all our knowledge of the qualities of land."[6] Just what this knowledge and these qualities were he nowhere said. Later came an implied admission of the ineffectiveness of this demonstration. There were distinct suggestions in the second and subsequent editions that he had in mind as the thing prescribing limits to production, a principle somewhat similar to the law of diminishing returns.[7] It is a commonplace that this is merely one aspect of a more general law of diminishing productivity. Like all principles of its kind it is true only under certain assumed conditions. A correct statement of it should be preceded by the two limiting phrases, "in a given state of the arts," and "beyond a certain point in the combination of factors." Countries having populations too thin fully to utilize the available natural resources may be able, for a time, to support an increasing population at a rising standard of comfort. Eventually, however, the point will be reached. In his discussion of conditions in America Malthus impliedly recognized the necessity of making the second of the two assumptions.[8] He did not, however, see fit to abstract improvements in productive technique.[9] It appeared unnecessary. It is at this point that his European environment seems to have influenced his theory most. The changes he had observed during the industrial revolution in England had not greatly affected the production of food. As a matter of fact, progress in the arts appeared to him to be merely an evidence rather than a possible corrective of population pressure. Advances might bring on temporary plenty, but were powerless to ward off the period of scarcity bound to come as a result of the inevitable growth of population stimulated by it.[10]

Malthus' characterization of the rate of increase of food as arithmetic was another "debater's concession." He at least pretty clearly convinced himself that, in spite of improvements, the yearly production of subsistence could not be augmented even as rapidly as this.[11] As a matter of fact, the precise ratios have much less significance than is usually attributed to them. No matter at what rate production increased, the rate of population growth, being more rapid, would inevitably and inexorably lead to the necessity of the operation of one or all of the three checks.[12] The hope of eliminating vice and misery from society, of course, depended on the effectiveness of "moral restraint."

It was quite obvious that checks were not operating in the same way on all portions of the world's population. Malthus recognized the patent fact of inequality and the consequent necessity of devising a theory of distribution. There was the possibility of accounting for inequality merely by calling attention to birth-rate differentials. Malthus was aware of the limitations of such an explanation, however, and attempted in a rather unsystematic way to supplement it. It would probably not be reading too much into his distributive theory to say that he conceived of real wages as paid out of a fund comprising only a part of the total stock of subsistence goods.[13] The total, varying from year to year, was always kept within certain slowly moving limits as a result of the operation of laws just described. Malthus was not clear in his early works as to what the factors were which determined the precise proportion of the total stock of goods which would be diverted to this fund for the support of labor. He appears to have recognized the importance of competition between employers,[14] of the presence or absence of employment opportunities,[15] the bargaining power of workers as contrasted with that of the employer,[16] and, in a few instances, the institutional factors of which Godwin made so much.[17] After

1815, however, the so-called Ricardian theory of rent became an integral part of his distributive scheme and lent it a greater degree of definiteness.

As a matter of fact, the actual size of the "wage-fund" and the factors determining it were of little significance. No matter how large it was the laboring population would sooner or later so increase as to reduce all wages to a low standard of living or possibly a bare subsistence level. It was precisely because of this that all plans, such as that of Godwin, aiming toward the improvement of the condition of the poor through a modification of the institutional framework of society, were doomed to failure.[18] The permanent welfare of these unfortunates, Malthus maintained, depended to a much greater degree on the nature of the dominant population check than upon the factors determining how large a portion of the total product of society would be directed toward the support of labor. Positively pernicious were those policies, such as the poor laws, which served to stimulate the birth-rate of the poor.[19] The hope of the laborer lay in his exercise of "moral restraint."

Such was the theory of Malthus. Important in its own right, and interwoven as it was with other features of the classical theory of distribution, it was made the subject of innumerable English and Continental treatises in the early decades of the nineteenth. Most of the European writers on political economy embraced it in its entirety, or with slight modifications; some attacked it; all perforce dealt with it. Because of this fact a considerable portion of every history of economic thought has been devoted, almost of necessity, to a treatment of the European reaction to Malthusianism. Historical and critical comments on early American economic literature are, however, strangely scarce.[20] It is the purpose of this paper to tell part of the story of the classical doctrine which has never been fully told, to survey the American reaction to it prior to 1840.

European writers worked in an environment similar in its essential features to that of Malthus. The American setting was entirely different. In the United States the "short" productive factor was labor; abroad it was land. In Europe, population pressed upon the means of subsistence; in America, vast resources awaited discovery. In Europe, the problem was that of economizing productive powers; in America, the problem was that of devising the best means of exploiting them. In England, corn laws were asked for to protect the cultivators of the inferior lands drawn into use during the Napoleonic wars; in America, tariffs were demanded because of the high wage level which in turn resulted from the abundance of fertile land.[21] The dominant old world population theory to some degree reflected old world conditions; that of America reflected to some degree the buoyant confidence of a young country with almost inexhaustible natural resources.

The observer of economic literature in the United States is immediately struck by the comparatively tardy development of political economy as a systematic discipline on this side of the Atlantic. It was not until after the embargo, and the war-stimulated industrial transition of the second decade of the nineteenth century, that any formal treatises appeared. These ventures in exposition were made, for the most part, by men whose major interests were in realms other than political economy. They devoted only such time to economics as was not demanded by the academic, editorial, legal, political, and diplomatic activities which were their chief concerns. There is little wonder, therefore, that only one of their number, and he somewhat undeservedly, received international recognition. In addition to the formal works there were a number of periodical articles which form the most interesting, if not the most significant, portion of early American economic literature. The writers naturally fall into two groups, the critics and the proponents of Malthusianism.

As might be expected most of the American critics of Malthus centered their attacks on the production aspect of the English theory. Of the authors of systematic American treatises Daniel Raymond, Alexander H. Everett, Jacob N. Cardozo, Willard Phillips, William Jennison, Henry C. Carey, and George Tucker, on the basis of their knowledge of American conditions, saw little or no reason for concern over Malthus' gloomy forebodings as to scarcity of food. Four of these men, Raymond, Everett, Tucker, and Cardozo, supplemented their attacks on the principle of production with a denial of the validity of the law of the increase of population. The third aspect of Malthus' doctrine, the distributive, came in for criticism at the hands of Raymond, Tucker, Matthew Carey, S. P. Newman, Francis Wayland, A. Potter, and a number of socialists, who, like Godwin, placed the blame for poverty on pernicious institutions rather than on the laws of population and production.

Daniel Raymond, a Baltimore lawyer, was the author of the first extensive American treatise on political economy.[22] It is not without significance that in the first edition of this work there appeared a statement concerning Malthus probably unmatched for *naïveté* in all economic literature:

> Although his theory is founded upon the principles of nature, and although it is impossible to discover any flaw in his reasoning, yet the mind instinctively revolts at the conclusions to which he conducts it, and we are disposed to reject the theory, even though we could give no good reason.[23]

At this time, Raymond ventured no systematic criticism.

In later greatly modified editions, however, he attacked the doctrine of Malthus more energetically and directly in all three of its aspects. In the first place, he argued, the English economist had neglected institutional factors in his theory of poverty. With an emphasis on the legal aspects of economic problems, which was characteristic of his entire work, the American asserted that poverty in England was not traceable so much to overpopulation as to the "system of laws" which threw "all the property in the hands of a few." Raymond favored governmental provision of poor relief. Malthusianism, he believed, owed its popularity to the rich employing classes, who by the use of it were able to rationalize their neglect of the poor.[24] The law of diminishing returns held no terrors for him. In America the fertile plains of the West were effective tools demanding to be used. Raymond remarked that:

> For ought we can perceive the earth is capable of being made to yield an indefinite and almost unlimited quantity of food. We can no more fix limits to the powers of the earth to produce the necessaries of life than we can fix limits to the powers of life itself, or to the artificial wants of men. . . . The fruits of the earth are multiplied almost in proportion to the labor bestowed upon it.[25]

An increase of population would make possible a more nearly perfect division of labor and, in addition, would minimize the distance differentials, which, at the time he wrote, made the use of much of the very fertile western lands impossible.

Raymond made a rather inadvertent concession to Malthus, however, which serves to indicate how superficial his differences with the English writer really were. He asserted, in one connection, "I am far from supposing that the earth is capable of being made to increase its fruits with the same rapidity, that the unrestrained powers of pro-creation are capable of multiplying the human species."[26] There was no attempt to harmonize this statement with the patently inconsistent one quoted above. The laws of nature, according to Raymond, always regulated population in such a way that man need not concern himself about it. Godwin had previously, in his *Enquiry concerning Political Justice,* referred to the beneficent natural laws which served to limit population. Malthus had replied that, in so doing, he (Godwin) had obscured the most important features of the whole population problem, the checks to its growth.[27] He would doubtless have said the same to Raymond.

The American's criticism amounted to a denial of the principle of diminishing returns, an assertion that there were checks to population other than those mentioned by Malthus, and the contention that human institutions rather than natural laws were the cause of poverty. He overlooked two facts: first, that Malthus himself had admitted that America had not reached the stage where the difficulties in increasing production were great enough appreciably to check population; and, second, that Malthus' threefold classification of population

checks was well-nigh all inclusive. As a matter of fact, as has been suggested already, Raymond's interests were primarily in the legal aspects of problems of social policy.

Alexander H. Everett, a New England editor, had a much more lively, though misdirected, interest in abstract theory.[28] He believed that Malthus, in attacking and overthrowing the foolish theory of human perfectibility advanced by Godwin, had been carried to a state of pessimism as unwarranted as had been the latter's optimism. Everett's criticism of specific features of Malthusianism was shot through and through with misunderstanding. The significance which the English economist attached to population checks escaped him. Apparently completely unaware of the fact that Malthus had observed American population statistics only in order to determine the approximate rate at which the human race would increase if unchecked, Everett argued that the English economist was not justified in generalizing on the basis of American experience alone.[29] He went so far as to say that Malthus had disproved his own theory by bringing in the checks to population.[30] Then came the astonishing prediction that, since population had not actually grown a great deal for four thousand years, it would never increase much in the future.[31] More amazing than the prediction was the fact that Everett considered it at all pertinent. There was only scorn and ridicule for the policy of discouraging marriage by law or otherwise. Everett approached the absurdity of Raymond when he said that "any system which affirms that the universal prevalence of early marriage is adverse to the general good, and ought to be checked, is in open contradiction with the certain laws of nature; and must therefore of necessity be fatal."[32]

Everett's citation of examples in which an actual growth of population had been accompanied by a much greater proportional increase of subsistence was similarly beside the point. Besides evincing a misunderstanding of the English theory by such statements, he did just what he had criticized Malthus for doing; he generalized on the basis of observation made almost entirely in America. Everett suggested the possibility of an absurdly large rate of increase in food[33] and asserted that progress in the productive arts and better division of labor inevitably came with an increasing population.[34] For every additional mouth to feed and body to clothe there were additional hands to produce.[35] Population was not regulated by subsistence but subsistence by the extent and character of population. He apparently disregarded the necessity of recourse to worse lands, or a more intensive use of the better which ordinarily accompanied an increase in the production of human subsistence. Everett gave little indication of an understanding of either of the phases of Malthusianism he attacked.

His more famous brother, Edward, while displaying a remarkably high degree of family loyalty, gave evidence of an equally remarkable misconception of the doctrine of Malthus. Edward's complimentary discussion in the *North American Review* of the *New Ideas* is indicative of the former, and the following excerpt bears even more eloquent testimony to the latter:

> If it is one law of our nature that food must support life, and that population can increase no faster than food increases to nourish it, it is surely idle to say that population tends to increase faster than food. . . . That man can increase no faster than food, is not only true in itself, but is asserted in numerous places of Mr. Malthus' work as a law of our nature. That he should have overlooked it while urging his famous mathematical proposition, is the more astonishing when we consider the circumstances on which the increase depends.[36]

Edward Everett proceeded to call attention to the high potential rate of increase in those forms of life capable of being used for human subsistence. Like his brother, he completely overlooked both the misery involved in the adjustment of the increase of population to that of food and the limitations on the production of subsistence from the operation of the law of diminishing returns. In the same periodical, Jared Sparks spoke of the Malthusian doctrine as "curious and paradoxical" and described A. H. Everett's arguments as complete and triumphant.[37]

There is certainly little question as to the reasonableness of classifying Raymond and Everett among the critics of Malthus. Some doubt may justly arise, however, as to the propriety of so treating Jacob N. Cardozo, an editor and publisher of Charleston, and the author of an interesting volume called *Notes on Political Economy*.[38] Although he styled himself an ardent opponent of the whole Maltho-Ricardian system he was not as far from the classical theories as he professed to be.

To Cardozo the production aspect of the theory of Malthus had been "deduced from overlooking the effect of science and skill in procuring the more effectual cooperation of Nature in Agriculture as in Commerce and Manufactures."[39] Increasing rather than decreasing returns obtained, he believed, wherever

> the skill and ingenuity of cultivators with the resources of science are sufficient to overcome the failing powers of the soil. The proof that they are so is to be found in the augmentation of population whilst fresh capital is continually applied to the land.[40]

While Malthus at times looked upon improvements in the arts as being pretty largely a result of population increase, Cardozo conceived of the growth of population as impossible unless preceded by such advances. It is not strange that the American should have been more optimistic as to the possibilities of progress in productive technique than Malthus.

Their differences as to the population aspect of the English theory are not far to seek. While Malthus believed in the existence of three checks, Cardozo recognized only the one, a sort of prudential standard of living check, precisely what the English economist would have called "moral restraint." The American would probably not have admitted that the difference was slight. Cardozo maintained that general overpopulation could not possibly come for a long time because of the effective and immediate operation of this check. There appeared to him, therefore, to be an unvarying proportion between population and subsistence, the former growing quickly without friction in response to the augmented agricultural production resulting from the application of skill and science. This, he said,

> is the reverse of the new theory which connects the augmentation of population with the increased difficulty instead of the increased facility of production. This is only an extension, however, of the principle with whose wonderful results in manufacture we are familiar.[41]

From the standpoint of the development of economic thought the most significant contribution of Cardozo was a rather inarticulate suggestion as to the necessity of developing some concept of economic equilibrium. Malthus and Ricardo, Cardozo maintained, had involved themselves in a logical difficulty quite generally overlooked by their critics. They assumed an increase of population to provide a motive for the extension of cultivation and then proceeded to prove impossible the thing which they had assumed. Similarly they made the increase in the price of produce both the cause and the effect of the extension of cultivation.[42] Cardozo, and indeed Malthus and Ricardo, lacked some of the more recently developed conceptual devices which might have been used to clear up this seemingly defective logic.[43]

Like Cardozo, Willard Phillips,[44] a New England lawyer, directed his assault, for the most part, on the production aspect of Malthusianism. His suggestions as to the relativity of abstract economic principles probably constituted his most valuable contribution. Laws valid in one place might be entirely inapplicable in some other part of the world. The principle of diminishing returns, he maintained somewhat reasonably, operated only after a certain stage of national progress had been achieved. Phillips asserted that:

> Mr. Ricardo says that in the progress of a society, all things except raw produce and labor have a tendency to fall [in price]. But this will depend on the stage of national progress. In the United States, for example, the products of agriculture may be increased fourfold, and perhaps tenfold, *without requiring any additional labor in the production of a given quantity.*[45]

He was, in effect, merely commenting on the necessity of making one of the basic assumptions, to which reference has already been made, before universal validity could be imputed to the law of diminishing returns. Malthus himself had impliedly recognized this necessity.

Phillips was influenced in his views by several of the minor European critics of Malthus. He spoke of the obscure English writer, S. Gray, as having overthrown the whole classical structure. Following Gray's lead, Phillips emphasized the benefits of a large population, especially in that it provided nearby markets and lessened the significance of distance differentials.[46] The Americans also attached much significance to the progress of the productive arts. He cited with approval a statement of another English writer, Lowe, who had called attention to the fact that provisions did not cost more in labor at the time he wrote than they had formerly. Their higher money prices, Lowe had said, were merely an indication that the advancement in agriculture had not been as rapid as it had been in other productive fields. Progress, Phillips maintained following Lowe, might overcome the tendency to diminishing returns anywhere. This possibility, coupled with the fact that labor was the "short factor" in America made all forebodings as to overpopulation in the United States quite unreasonable.[47]

The fact that Phillips, Gray, and Lowe believed that statements of this kind, with nearly all of which, incidentally, Malthus himself would have agreed, constituted valid criticisms of the English theory, indicates a failure to meet the issue squarely. There was no attempt on the part of any one of them to prove that a geometric increase of human population could be supported for long anywhere on the earth's surface. Like Everett and Raymond they misunderstood the purely population aspect of the theory. The fact that Phillips accused Malthus of hailing famine as a deliverer from the evils of overpopulation and, with the air of an originator, suggested prudential restraint as the best means practicable for bettering the condition of laborers bears testimony to this misconception.[48]

Like Phillips, William Jennison,[49] presumably a Philadelphia educator, believed that there were different laws of population depending on the circumstances peculiar to them for all parts of the world. He laid emphasis on the undeveloped resources of the United States in this connection. Although admitting that population had a natural tendency to increase, he maintained that this very increase carried with it the power to supply the enlarged wants.[50] This statement implied a denial on Jennison's part of the validity of the principle of diminishing returns accompanying the extension of cultivation.

Henry C. Carey's[51] early attack on Malthus was colored by the fact that he accepted the superficial aspects of the wage-fund theory. He thought of the fund not as a store of subsistence goods, as had Malthus, but as a stock of productive factors complementary to, and creating a demand for, labor.[52] It was quite clear to this optimistic American that capital tended to increase more rapidly than population. If, Carey remarked,

> to man was granted the power of increase in a geometric ratio, there was implanted in him a principle which secures him against the effects, the desire for bettering his condition, which, if allowed time to act, would be abundantly sufficient with the increasing fruit of the land, arising out of the application of capital, to prevent the necessity of the starvation check.[53]

In answer to the objection that, no matter how rapidly capital increased, land had to remain fairly constant, he cited the positive advantages to be derived from concentration of population making possible better organization of production and a more minute division of labor.[54] His emphasis in this connection on the effects of dense population in fertilizing the soil was little less than absurd. As capital increased, Carey maintained, population tended to become more dense and even the inferior soils could be brought under cultivation with a constantly increasing return to labor.[55] He had more confidence in the prudential check to population and progress in the arts of production than had Malthus.

Two statements commenting on Carey's *Principles* appeared in the *New York Review*.[56] The earlier one spoke of his apparent unwillingness to disagree with Senior on anything. The second will be given special consideration presently. *Poulson's American Daily Advertiser* commented favorably on Carey's "refutation" of the Malthusian theory in 1835, but employed a version of the same theory two years later in condemning poor laws.[57]

George Tucker, professor of moral philosophy at the University of Virginia, directed two distinct and utterly inconsistent attacks on the doctrines of the dominant English school. In 1822, he published a volume of essays two of which dealt with the population problem.[58] In the first, "On Density of Population," he asserted that, although it was true that in the closely populated countries of Europe it seemed as though the fruits of progress had all been gathered by a small portion of society, this inequality was the consequence of "blind and unjust institutions" rather than density of population per se.[59] Tucker called attention to the fact that, in spite of such exploitation, the happiness and virtue of England had actually increased in almost direct proportion to the growth of population. Whatever might be the opinion as to the ultimate point of density which a nation might reach without lessening the chances of happiness to each individual, one had to admit, he maintained, that the United States was far from it.[60]

The other essay came to closer grips with Malthusianism. Tucker admitted that the theory had taught the legislator some valuable lessons, by indicating the limits which nature had set to numbers and the inefficacy of poor laws and charity. It had shown that the best policy lay in increasing the facility of the provision for subsistence. Tucker contended, however, as in the earlier essay, that Malthus had gone too far in attributing overpopulation, with its attendant wretchedness, to predestined natural laws instead of human habits and institutions.[61] India and China were cited as countries where tradition and religious belief had "encouraged the genitive faculties into undue activity," and prevented the benefits of progress from distributing themselves to every part of the population.[62]

There were checks, Tucker believed, other than vice and misery which were capable of holding population within the bounds prescribed by subsistence. In this connection he spoke of the growth of cities, control of the passions through training, and a desire to achieve a higher standard of life.[63] Tucker apparently failed to recognize that checks of this sort were an integral part of the theory of Malthus. He absurdly remarked that the fact that murder was odious constituted positive proof that the common sense of man disapproved of Malthusianism.[64]

Tucker, like those of his American contemporaries already considered, had great faith in the progress of the productive arts. He spoke of how the square mile which, in primitive times, "afforded a doubtful sustenance to a single human being . . . maintains now in comfort and abundance, fifty, and can easily maintain twice or thrice as many more."[65] Population, he said, increased rapidly where subsistence could be easily obtained, as in America, but with its growth checks arose and increased, independently of the greater difficulty of securing food, until they became so strong as to hold numbers stationary.[66] This was the distinctive feature of the theory set forth in his essays. He was certainly not as far from Malthus as he deemed himself to be.

A number of times, moreover, he gave some indication even of having recognized the significance which Malthus attached to prudential restraint. Like Everett, however, he believed that the English economist's admission of its efficacy in preventing a redundancy of population made his whole theory a much less effective weapon against the arguments of Godwin. Malthus' assumption, said Tucker, that the prudential check was not strong enough to prevent misery and vice, begged the only question at issue between them.[67] In fact, the American was inclined to minimize the significance of the whole doctrine. He remarked in one connection:

> To say that man is urged by his passions to excess, and that if he does not restrain them by prudence, he incurs the guilt of vice or the punishment of misery, is certainly true, but it is certainly too obvious a truth to require the principle part of a quarto volume of facts and

argument. It is but repeating those axioms of morality which are applicable to every other passion and propensity.[68]

Some fifteen years later Tucker published a more extensive and systematic treatise under the title, *The Laws of Wages, Profits, and Rent Investigated.*[69] This work should be looked upon as a rather violent, and in many respects a pedantic, attack on some of the obscure phases of the doctrine of Ricardo. Tucker was willing, in spite of the views set forth in the *Essays,* to embrace some of the features of Malthusianism if they could be made to contribute to the end of discrediting the English rent theory. He would not have admitted this because, ostensibly at least, he took issue with the whole Maltho-Ricardian scheme of distribution. His pronouncements in this work were quite inconsistent, both internally and with the views set forth in his earlier work. The final result was a population theory more pessimistic even than that of Malthus.

Wages, said Tucker, were higher where fertile lands were abundant. But when labor was rewarded with all, or nearly all, it could extract from the soil, population would increase rapidly and before long occupy all the fertile land. "As soon as this takes place," he argued, "the terms on which raw produce and labor are exchanged will begin to undergo alteration [and wages will fall]."[70] At this point Tucker made an assumption upon which the greater part of his criticism of Malthus and Ricardo rested. He supposed that the growth of population, which started under the stimulus of abundant subsistence, would not cease when the fertile lands were all intensively cultivated and food was relatively less plentiful. Assuming that the increase continued, the laborers would compete more strenuously for the limited amount of produce, and real wages would decline. This fall of wages would make recourse to less fertile lands possible. Workers would be forced to revise their aliment.[71]

This revision of aliment was not as significant to Tucker as it was to Malthus. The English theorist maintained that, under ordinary circumstances, rather than submit to it the laborers would abstain from marriage and the growth of population would be arrested. Tucker recognized this possibility, but put it aside with the statement that:

> The past history of mankind instructs us that the restraints of prudence and decent pride have never yet been sufficient to arrest the multiplying propensity, though they may check its force; and we cannot reasonably expect them to keep the population within the limit of liberal subsistence, without a more improved and enlightened state of society than has yet existed.[72]

This appears to be nothing more nor less than the theory of Malthus minus the prudential check, and is quite inconsistent, of course, with Tucker's views as advanced in the *Essays.*

The prudential check, thus so summarily dismissed, was somewhat covertly readmitted. Tucker remarked a few pages later that:

> If any particular mode of living was deemed so essential by the people of a country that they would exert self denial not to marry until they had reached this standard of comfort, population would then be stationary and so also would be the price of labor.[73]

In this connection he voiced an opinion similar to that of a number of other Americans with the words, "If the increase be supposed not greater than the improvements of husbandry, then there is no reason to suppose any change in the mode of subsistence."[74] He implied, however, that such things as the introduction of the potato culture, involving a revision of aliment, could be interpreted as improvements in the arts of husbandry. This belief pretty definitely returned him to his pessimistic position.

Tucker was the last of the formal economists of the period to direct a sustained systematic attack on the theoretical structure of Malthusian doctrine. There were numerous mild protests from others calling attention to the fact that Malthus had neglected the institutional aspects of poverty. Matthew Carey,[75] father of Henry C. Carey, often mentioned the fact that there was a natural oversupply of labor. His advocacy of nothing more fundamental to relieve the situation than the protective tariff, public poor relief, and the governmental regulation of the introduction of labor saving machinery, indicates that, in his opinion, the chief causes of overpopulation were factors other than those mentioned by Malthus. Samuel Phillips Newman,[76] combining interests in theology and economics, recognized the operation of the prudential check when he remarked that the natural price of labor was the wage sufficient to "furnish a support to the laborer and his family, according to the usual style of living in the community."[77] He accepted the wage-fund theory and the possibility of an increase of capital stimulating human reproduction, but minimized the danger of overpopulation. Newman believed that the evils usually ascribed to this condition were more often the result of abuses of civil institutions or unwise neglect of potential resources.[78]

Francis Wayland,[79] a Baptist minister, later president of Brown University, had no fear of an excess of population. Like Cardozo, he believed that the increase of numbers, limited by the prudential check, tended to follow, not to precede, the growth of capital and subsistence to support it.[80] Malthus would probably have called this statement nothing more than an overbroad generalization. The most important feature of Wayland's criticism, however, is indicated by the following excerpt:

> Nor do we need any abtruse theories of population to enable us to ascertain in what manner this excess of population [in Europe] may be prevented. Let them [the nations of Europe] reduce the unnecessary expense of government. Let them abolish those institutions which fetter and dispirit industry, by diminishing the inducements to labor. Let them foster the means by which the productiveness of labor may be increased, and the annual gifts of the Creator will so accumulate that the means will be provided for the support of all human beings that are annually brought into the world.[81]

A. Potter's work[82] was little more than a reprint of a treatise by an until recently little-known British economist, G. Poulett Scrope.[83] He spoke of the possibility of excess of population being the result not of superfecundity, as maintained by Malthus, but of "defects in the social system."[84] Following Scrope he attached much more significance to productivity than to the standard of living as a wage determinant.[85]

Similarly, the early American socialists, who were rather numerous during the decade of the thirties, went to a defective institutional system rather than to the principles of population growth and production to account for poverty. Indeed there is reason to believe that the whole organized labor movement of the period was based on an "exploitation" theory of the wage relationship.[86] William Maclure, who had been associated with Robert Owen in the New Harmony experiment, blamed land monopoly, debt-funding, primogeniture, political sinecures, monopolistic charters, and private education for the social evils associated with the unequal distribution of wealth.[87] He, like Robert Dale Owen, Frances Wright, and the Evans Brothers, had more confidence in public education than in a decrease of the birth-rate as a remedy for poverty.[88] Josiah Warren, with a labor cost theory of value proposed to modify exchange.[89] Thomas Skidmore attacked the inheritance of wealth.[90] L. Byllesby, who had come under the influence of Hodgkin and Thompson, English predecessors of Karl Marx in a theory of surplus value, was critical of the whole wage system.[91] Seth Luther blamed factories,[92] and William H. Hale, banking corporations for the suffering of the masses.[93]

Of the entire group of American critics of the institutional order, Stephen Simpson, a follower of Sismondi, was the only one specifically to mention Malthus.[94] Simpson was unwilling to ascribe human misery to the niggardliness of nature. "The excess of the bloated accumulation of the rich demonstrated the falsity of this hypothesis."[95] In America, at least, the ability of the earth to maintain a larger population could not be doubted.[96] The socially induced maldistribution of wealth was the fundamental and vicious cause of poverty. The move to limit the size of the families of the power he characterized as both dangerous and unjust.[97] Only when it is recalled that the theory of Malthus was originally a protest against an institutional exploitation theory advanced by Godwin, can the full significance of the views of these American socialists be appreciated.

A number of the critical periodical articles merit consideration. Although only a short time before he had defended Malthus and Ricardo against Cardozo, one J. Porter, writing in the *North American Review,* attacked the English doctrine rather vigorously.[98] He denied that there was any tendency for population to increase more rapidly than food. Man was capable, he said, of increasing subsistence indefinitely at will. Poverty was the result of vicious social and economic institutions rather than the "will of Providence." The prices of food were, in fact, continually going down because of improvements in the arts of agriculture.[99] An anonymous writer in the *Southern Review* exhibited a similar attitude toward European theories. A denial of the truth of the law of diminishing returns laid the foundation for an attack on the entire distributive system which had been developed by Malthus and Ricardo.[100] A year and a half later a review in the same publication of Sismondi's *Nouveaux principes* set forth the typical American attitude toward European theories in these words:

> Now as labor is the source of all capital, is capital itself, it seems to us to have been forgotten that in the very increase of population there is necessarily a proportionate increase of capital, a multiplication of the very power wanted to produce subsistence for the increasing multitudes. As long as there is land unoccupied, or unskillfully or wastefully employed, a small portion of the new progeny may produce food for the rest. When the earth shall be covered with harvests, and no room be left for industry and skill, it will be time then to inquire into the measures which ought to be pursued with the surplus of the still increasing consumers.[101]

Hezekiah Niles, who contrived to write something on nearly every subject in the columns of his *Register,* did not neglect the problem of population. He repeatedly contrasted England and American, institutionally and economically. "England," he remarked in one connection, "is overburthened with population because overburthened with taxes and monopolies—but we have room enough for the thousandth generation."[102] Again he said:

> An hundred years hence, *if* all our vacant lands shall be densely populated—*if* we shall have a public debt of four or five thousand millions of dollars, and a king and his trappings, and appurtenant nobles and others provided for out of the public taxes, . . . and a legion of locusts, in the shape of government priests, . . . we may be reduced to the same condition [England's] through the force of domestic competition for employment and wages.[103]

The contrast reappeared later in words which more definitely suggested Niles's acquaintance with the theory of Malthus:

> The want of plentiful supplies of wholesome food is among the severest checks to population; and while in England, for instance, it is thought desirable that the progress of population should be restrained—it is our great purpose to increase the numbers of our people, as being the main brace of power. In no part of our country is a large family of children thought to be an encumbrance on their parents.[104]

He was quite optimistic. The increase of capital equipment, the cause of the relative advancement of England in comparison with the rest of Europe, would, he said, go on geometrically in the United States, unless there was "too much tinkering with the currency."[105] Niles believed that immigration was unbeneficial only when it resulted in the clogging of the eastern labor market. He recognized that the country as a whole needed laborers; the problem was one of selecting and properly distributing them.[106]

An excellent analysis of the premises underlying the theories of Malthus and Ricardo appeared in the *New York Review,* in the article commenting on the third and fourth parts of Carey's *Principles* mentioned above.[107] After an attack on the theories of Malthus, McCulloch, and James Mill, the writer asserted that Carey, in developing his system of harmonies, had involved himself in absurdities almost as great as those of his European contemporaries. The American, he said, did not have to deny the premise of Malthus and Ricardo, the law of diminishing returns, in order to disprove their gloomy conclusions. Soils were certainly of differing degrees of fertility and, as population increased, recourse to inferior grades was necessary. Rent was paid for the better soils as the proof and measure of their superiority. This theory was so easily demonstrable that it was futile to deny it.[108]

Malthus' law, however, did not necessarily follow. Malthus should have demonstrated, this writer asserted, that the necessity of recourse to worse lands resulted in a decrease in per capita production sufficiently great to overcome the effects of improvements in the productive arts. This he and his followers had never done. A static theory of diminishing returns was demonstrable, and was correctly considered as sufficient basis for a theory of land rent. In a dynamic society, however, increased skill might make inferior soils more productive than the better grades previously had been. Such improvements, of course, caused a like increase in the productiveness of the better grades at the same time, and their superiority continued to provide the basis for a rent payment.[109] The ratio between food and population depended on the fertility of land and the productive efficiency of labor and capital. In the United States where there was a high degree of both, prospects were that increasing skills would be more than a match for the necessity of using poorer land for a long time to come. "Cheap bread, and plenty of it . . . [was] the law of advancing society," unless unwise governmental regulations interfered.[110]

The author of this review gave indication of a clearer insight into the assumptions underlying the Malthusian and Ricardian theories than many of his contemporaries whose works extended into volumes. In his criticism of Malthus, however, he slipped into the error of many of his countrymen when he neglected to face the problems involved in the great capacity for human increase. He seems to have assumed unconsciously that some checks operated painlessly to hold back the potential growth of population.

Several generalizations of more extended applicability may be made on the basis of this survey of the writings of the critics of Malthus. Throughout this body of literature there was a degree of misconception apparently indicative of nothing more nor less than failure carefully and understandingly to read the theories attacked. For the most part the Americans appear to have been criticizing, not the doctrine of Malthus, but their own or, worse yet, someone else's interpretation of it. Students of the present-day controversial literature on the subject of interest, for example, will probably agree that this tendency to misread, or not to read at all, is of more than merely historical and local significance. As is generally the case, these misinterpretations were largely manifestations of prejudice. During the early decades of the nineteenth century there remained, as a relic of the revolutionary days, a popular distaste in America of all things British. Theories stamped "made in England" were immediately subjected to careful and carpingly critical scrutiny. This fact may partially account for the popularity on this side of the Atlantic of the Frenchman, J. B. Say, whose optimistic views were reflected in the works of a number of the Americans just considered. The frequent statements calling attention to Malthus' neglect of cultural factors in his theory of poverty bear testimony to a similar prejudice, directed in this case toward English institutions rather than English writers and their doctrines.

Much, possibly most, of what is characterized as erroneous reasoning in the development, interpretation, and criticism of economic thought is ultimately traceable to a misuse or a misunderstanding of the device of abstraction. Theories are, in the last analysis, merely summary, tentative, hypothetical generalizations descriptive of the relationships between observed phenomena. The perceptual world is so complex that disturbing factors usually have to be abstracted before such conceptual formulas may be devised. This process involves the assumption of conditions in which these factors are inoperative. The assumptions may be expressed or implied, clearly discernible or so hidden as to require a process akin to rationalization before they can be brought to light. Theorists, especially in the social sciences, often unconsciously posit the physical environment, the institutional order, and the stage of technique which obtain in the societies of which they are members. Principles developed under such assumptions, unless due consideration is taken of their abstract character, are often clearly inapplicable to conditions existing under some other type of social organization or physical environment. Most of the American critics of Malthus failed to take this "due consideration."

The proponents of Malthus in the United States prior to 1840 were few in number. They fall into two groups which may be described, for want of better terms, as passive and active. In the first group there were a number of writers who had come under the influence of one or two of the orthodox classical economists, and who more or less uncritically accepted Malthusianism along with the other features of the European theoretical system. Strangely enough, the active proponents of Malthus were not authors of formal treatises but periodical contributors. Two of them, who as a matter of fact compose the group, produced statements which must be placed among the few really penetrating bits of early American economic analysis.

Of the passive proponents, John MacVickar,[111] a man who combined theological and pedagogical interests, was under the domination of McCulloch to so great a degree that any opposition on his part to the dominant English theories was quite impossible. Thomas Cooper,[112] an English-born president of South Carolina College, accepted the theory of Malthus without much question and held, in opposition to Raymond, Everett, and Cardozo, that there was a limit to the possible increase of productive efficiency attainable through the use of machines.[113] In the realm of social policy Cooper believed that no system of poor laws could afford more than temporary relief and that public charity was justifiable only in rare cases. "You can only decrease the competition of laborers," he remarked, "by discouraging marriages among the poor, . . . or sending them away to distant colonies. Poor laws instead of increasing capital decrease it."[114] William Beach Lawrence, a jurist and lecturer on political economy at Columbia College, in his *Two Lectures on Political Economy*[115] evinced a clear understanding and expressed a favorable opinion of the distributive theory of Ricardo and Malthus.

Henry Vethake,[116] professor of chemistry, geography, natural history, moral philosophy, and economics, at the University of Pennsylvania, was distinctly under the influence of McCulloch. His distributive theory combined his master's views on the wage-fund, Ricardo's on rent, and those of Malthus on population. Vethake clearly recognized the operation of both the preventive and positive checks to population. He did not favor the compulsory prohibition of marriage as a social policy, but advocated governmental as well as individual activities calculated to enlarge the desires of people, promote foresight, and bring about voluntary limitation of the birth-rate.[117] Thomas R. Dew,[118] true to the interests of his section, the anti-tariff South, employed his version of the theory of Malthus as a weapon against what he chose to call the restrictive system. He spoke of how Malthus, in an "able exposition of the principle of population," had shown that there was a tendency for population to increase until one or more of the so-called checks were brought into operation.[119] His argument against protection reduced itself to a recital of the advantages of territorial division of labor between new, high-wage countries, and old, low-wage countries. *Niles Register,* in commenting on Dew's *Lectures,* said in part, "The professor seems to have more credit for the zealous application with which he has studied in the school of Adam Smith, than for original enquiry on the subject."[120]

Among the periodical writers, T. Lyman, in the *North American Review,*[121] as early as 1815 set forth the subsistence theory of wages. An article, appearing in the *American Quarterly Review,* mentioned the fact that, although political economy had been established only fifty years, its chief laws, those of population and rent, had already been fully proved.[122] A few years later an anonymous writer in the same periodical employed the theory of Malthus in advocating the repeal of poor laws in the United States.[123] Another unknown, this time in the *Southern Review,*[124] used the Malthusian principle for the purpose of discrediting the "agrarian and educational system" then being advocated by the spokesmen of the labor movement in New York. He questioned the justice of allowing the idle and drunken to bring children into the world, and of compelling the honest and frugal to support and educate them on terms of equality. Such a system taxed industry to encourage idleness. It was a direct attack on the usual privileges attached to the possession of property.[125] Public schools, it was asserted, would create a vast pauper system by exonerating parents of their highest duties and cutting off the mainsprings of individual exertion.[126]

> The plan of national education, . . . by taking away the reasonable checks to early and thoughtless marriages . . . [would] inevitably multiply the competitors for employment to such a degree as to increase enormously the competition in the market of labour and all the well known evils consequent upon that competition.[127]

People who brought children into the world should be bound to support them. Education by a property tax was plunder, an entering wedge bound to lead to agrarianism.[128] At the bottom of the whole disturbing movement was universal suffrage, "a system which disregarded all honorable distinctions, all exceptional ability, and which was bound to annihilate *the whole class* of laborers."[129]

The first of the two American statements actively and constructively in support of Malthus appeared early in the decade of the twenties in the *North American Re-*

view.[130] In it the author, W. J. Spooner, characterized a reply of William Godwin to the *Essay on Population*[131] as "lame and impotent." The British perfectionist had attacked Malthus' theory as to the geometric increase of population with the criticism that the idea had arisen from his observation of only part of the world, America. In reply to this contention Spooner said in part:

> In order to ascertain whether the . . . remarks contradict Mr. Malthus' position, it is well for us to recollect precisely what is the position he assumes. His words are, that population, when unchecked, goes on doubling itself every twenty-five years. He does not affirm that such has actually been the rate of increase at all times, and throughout the world.[132]

As a matter of fact, a great part of Malthus' work, said Spooner, had been taken up with a consideration of the checks which made this theoretical increase of population actually impossible in most parts of the world. Malthus had turned to American experience merely to secure information on the potential rate of human procreation. Spooner easily showed the absurdity of Godwin's claim that the growth of population in the United States had been due chiefly to immigration and not to a surplus of births over deaths.[133] Unaware of the storm of American criticism about to break, Spooner confidently concluded:

> After the lapse of more than twenty years and when the charms of novelty must have ceased, the world has been called upon to reconsider and revise the judgment it originally pronounced upon Mr. Malthus' work. The consequence has been an entire and deliberate affirmation; and henceforth, we presume, the subject of population will be considered as at rest.[134]

A similar example of penetrating thought is to be found in an article by Louis Fitzgerald Tasistro appearing in *Hunt's Marchant's Magazine.*[135] The main burden of this rather lengthy statement was a defense of the law of population against the attacks of Nassau Senior. Tasistro stated the principle of diminishing returns in much the same way as had Malthus. He accepted the English economist's claim that population had a tendency to double every twenty-five years. It followed, necessarily, Tasistro maintained, "as the wages of labor depended upon the proportion between food and numbers, and as numbers can increase faster than food, that unless the number of laborers can be limited, the people must always be poor."[136] The truth of the Malthusian law was being demonstrated everywhere. Tasistro asserted that:

> Scarcely a year passes in which the operation of that principle is not manifest in the sufferings of one or more of the classes into which our labourers are divided—sufferings which have their immediate causes, indeed, in some casual revulsion of trade, but which are aggravated and prolonged by the habitual poverty existing among all the laboring classes, and which, it has been proved to satiety, is the consequence of the disproportion between the numbers to be employed and the means of employing them.[137]

A citation of examples of increased productive efficiency accompanying a growth of population did not, he said, constitute a valid criticism of Malthusianism. Tasistro quoted an unidentified passage written by Senior in which he (Senior) spoke of the fact that, as in the case of the American colonies, an increase of population had often been accompanied by increased per capita productiveness. In reply Tasistro called attention to the fact that in his theory Malthus had stated merely that, in the absence of checks, population tended to increase at a more rapid rate than food supply.[138] He proceeded to say that:

> What was meant to be conveyed by the proposition was, that the greater capability of increase was on the side of population; that a check must be applied there, and an impulse, if possible, applied to the production of food. And that that is the *useful* mode of stating the theory, Mr. Senior himself admits; for he tells us afterwards that, whether in the absence of disturbing causes, it be the tendency of subsistence or population, to advance with greater rapidity, is a question of slight importance, if it be acknowledged that human happiness or misery depend on their relative advance; and that there are causes, and causes within human control, by which that advance can be regulated.[139]

Tasistro displayed a better understanding of the nature and function of the device of abstraction than any of the men toward whom attention has been directed in the course of this study. He remarked that a statement that there is a tendency for population to increase at a more rapid rate than subsistence is analogous to one to the effect that there is a tendency for bodies to move in a curved path. Both are true under certain conditions but this fact disproves neither the theory of Malthus, nor the laws of Newton, in their abstract forms.[140] It is regrettable that there was not more on economics from the pen of this able thinker.

The fact that American opinion was for the most part unsympathetic to the theory of Malthus scarcely needs to be pointed out. There appears, strangely enough, to have been no distinctly American controversy on Malthusianism, however. The American writers rarely mentioned one another. They seem to have been providing a side attraction; participating at a distance in the European debate. Spooner was concerned primarily with the arguments of Godwin, Tasistro with those of Senior. Neither gave much attention to the statements of their compatriots. Of the five passive proponents of the doctrine all were teachers of economics. When this is coupled with the additional fact that the academic critics were, with the exception of the inconsistent Tucker, quite mild in their assaults on the classical structure, a generalization, possibly of present-day significance, is suggested. The purely pedagogical problems connected with instruction in economics seem to have disarmed their critical faculties. It is not difficult for a teacher to accept a teachable theoretical system, testing it for internal consistency rather than external applicability.

Although the body of literature just surveyed begins with the transcendental absurdity of Raymond and ends with the penetrating analysis of Tasistro, it is difficult to detect any definite trends in American thought on the classical theory, prior to 1840. Of the two statements which actively supported Malthus, the first appeared in 1822 and the second in 1840. Periodicals, for the most part, seem to have been affected more by the sectional and private interests their contributors represented than by efforts to pursue any definite editorial policy. Formal works designed for classroom use did not make their appearance until 1825. The attitude of passivity exhibited in them can hardly be considered evidence of any consistent development, especially in view of the fact that Tucker's later work was published in 1837. The socialistic writings were largely confined to the period from 1826 to 1833, and did not appreciably affect subsequent thought. The detection and tracing of evolutionary movements, if such there were, must, then, await the study of the post-1840 literature.

Notes

1. Cf. J. Bonar, *Malthus and His Work* (New York and London, 1885), pp. 41 ff. See also the most easily available edition of the Malthus *Essay*, the *Parallel Chapters from the First and Second Editions of an Essay on the Principle of Population by T. R. Malthus* (Ashley ed., New York & London, 1895), pp. 45, 78-79, 96.

2. Malthus, *op. cit.,* pp. 6, 82.

3. *Ibid.,* pp. 10, 52, 80-82.

4. *Ibid.,* pp. 38, 70, 90, 97 ff. The criticism of M. Gide in C. Gide and C. Rist, *History of Economic Doctrines* (Richards trans.: New York, 1923), p. 182, relative to Malthus' confusion of the reproductive and sexual "instincts," is of significance at this point. Certainly it must be admitted, with M. Gide, that the two are different, but it is vice which has made them so in the case of some individuals, and it is *moral restraint* which has made the reproductive "instinct" less irresistible in that of others.

5. Malthus, *op. cit.,* pp. 30 ff., 41 ff., 102 ff, 111.

6. Adapted from *ibid.,* pp. 10, 11. See also p. 53.

7. *Ibid.,* pp. 82, 84. Professor Edwin Cannan maintains that Malthus did not have this principle in mind at all in this connection; see his *Theories of Production and Distribution* (London, 1903), p. 144. Bonar interprets Malthus differently (*op. cit.,* pp. 35 ff. M. Gide (Gide and Rist, *op. cit.,* p. 126) asserts that the law of diminishing returns was the real basis of Malthusianism.

8. Malthus, *op. cit.,* pp. 10, 41, 81.

9. *Ibid.,* pp. 10, 12, 15, 16, 36, 53, 83, 84, 86.

10. *Ibid.,* pp. 14 ff., 91 ff.

11. *Ibid.,* pp. 11, 53, 84-85.

12. *Ibid.,* pp. 45, 86, 96, 110.

13. *Ibid.,* pp. 27, 28, 29, 36, 41, 42, 61, 62, 107. Cf. F. W. Taussig, *Wages and Capital* (New York, 1896), pp. 159-63, 203-4.

14. Malthus, *op. cit.,* pp. 17, 92, 95, 106.

15. *Ibid.,* pp. 15, 17, 36, 95, 104.

16. *Ibid.,* pp. 17, 95, 100, 105, 106.

17. *Ibid.,* pp. 17, 36, 43, 52, 111, 112, 117, 120.

18. *Ibid.,* pp. 2, 8, 14, 41, 42, 46, 57, 102-7, 121.

19. *Ibid.,* pp. 30, 34, 35, 37, 51, 102-7, 118, 120.

20. E. R. A. Seligman's "Economics in the United States," *Essays in Economics* (New York, 1925), p. 122, purports to be little more than an enumeration. Other publications dealing with American economists are H. J. Furber, *Geschichte und kritische Studien zur Entwicklung der ökonomischen Theorien in Amerika* (Halle, 1891); C. F. Dunbar, "Economic Science in America, 1776-1876," *Economic Essays* (1904); S. Sherwood, *Tendencies in American Economic Thought* (1897); T. E. C. Leslie, "Political Economy in the United States," *Essays in Political Economy* (1888); and, of special significance, J. R. Turner, *The Ricardian Rent Theory in American Economics* (New York, 1921). See also C. A. Beard, *The Economic Origins of Jeffersonian Democracy* (New York, 1915); and V. L. Parrington, *The Romantic Revolution in America* (New York, 1927).

21. See Turner, *op. cit.,* pp. 23-24, 194-201, for further treatment of this contrast.

22. The first edition was called *Thoughts on Political Economy* (Baltimore, 1820). Later editions appeared in 1823, 1836, and 1840, under the title *Elements of Political Economy*. See C. P. Neill, *Daniel Raymond: An Early Chapter in the History of Economic Theory in the United States,* "Johns Hopkins University Studies in Historical and Political Science," 15th ser., No. 6 (Baltimore, 1897).

23. Raymond, *Thoughts on Political Economy,* p. 273.

24. Raymond, *Elements* (1823), II, 67-80.

25. *Ibid.,* p. 111.

26. *Ibid.,* p. 112.

27. Malthus, *op. cit.,* p. 47.

28. In addition to his major work, *New Ideas on Population* (Boston, 1823), Everett wrote a number of short articles which appeared in the *North American Review.*

29. *New Ideas,* pp. 53-54. Everett probably drew from William Godwin's lame rejoinder to Malthus, *An Inquiry concerning the Power of Increase in the Numbers of Mankind* (London, 1820), at this point.

30. *North American Review,* XXV (July, 1827), 135-36.

31. *Ibid.,* p. 118.

32. *New Ideas,* p. 101.

33. *Ibid.,* pp. 26-27.

34. *North American Review,* XXV, 138, 139, 143; XXXIII (July, 1831). I. A similar theory had been advanced by an Englishman, S. Gray, in his *Happiness of the States* (London, 1815).

35. *New Ideas,* p. 65.

36. *North American Review,* XVII (March, 1823), 292.

37. *Ibid.,* XXIV (January, 1827), 118.

38. Published in Charleston, 1826.

39. *Notes,* p. 15. See also p. 43.

40. *Ibid.,* p. 17. See also pp. 16, 36, and 41.

41. *Ibid.,* p. 35. See also pp. 35, 36, 41, 51, 109.

42. *Ibid.,* pp. 16-17, and 24-25.

43. A short contemporary comment on Cardozo's *Notes,* written by J. Porter, appeared in the *North American Review,* XXIV (January, 1827), 170 ff.

44. Phillips was the author of *A Manual of Political Economy* (Boston, 1828).

45. *Ibid.,* p. 39. Italics my own.

46. *Ibid.,* p. 106.

47. *Ibid.,* pp. 40-41.

48. *Ibid.,* pp. 76, and 132-40.

49. Jennison wrote a brief catechism on political economy, *An Outline of Political Economy* (Philadelphia, 1828).

50. *Ibid.,* p. 48.

51. Prior to 1840, the chronological limit set for the present study, Carey wrote an *Essay on the Rate of Wages* (Philadelphia, 1835), and *Principles of Political Economy* (Philadelphia, 1837-40). His celebrated criticism of Ricardo, involving a denial of the classical principle that the cultivation of land proceeded from the better to the poorer grades, was not definitely formulated until 1848. This attack on Ricardo, it may be said in passing, reflected the environment in which he wrote and his own failure to acquaint himself thoroughly with the assumptions underlying the English

theory. See Marshall's *Principles* (8th ed.), pp. 158-60; also Bonar, *op. cit.*, pp. 38-39.

52. *Essay,* pp. 30-35.

53. *Ibid.,* p. 243.

54. *Principles,* Part I, p. 339; Part II, p. 462.

55. *Ibid.,* Part I, p. 341.

56. III (July, 1838), I; VII (October, 1840), 311.

57. See the issues of October, 16, 1836, and February 8, 1837; also that of July 3, 1835.

58. *Essays on Various Subjects of Taste, Morals and National Policy, by a Citizen of Virginia* (Georgetown, 1822).

59. *Ibid.,* pp. 80-81.

60. *Ibid.,* p. 84.

61. *Ibid.,* p. 305.

62. *Ibid.,* p. 311.

63. *Ibid.,* p. 310; also pp. 322-23.

64. *Ibid.,* p. 309.

65. *Ibid.,* p. 322.

66. *Ibid.,* p. 329.

67. *Ibid.,* p. 336.

68. *Ibid.,* p. 330.

69. Published in Philadelphia, 1837.

70. *The Laws,* pp. 19-20.

71. *Ibid.,* pp. 20-21.

72. *Ibid.,* p. 23.

73. *Ibid.,* p. 25. See also pp. 29-30.

74. *Ibid.,* p. 25.

75. His chief works on economics were an *Essay on Political Economy* (Philadelphia, 1822), and an *Appeal to the Wealthy of the Land* (Philadelphia, 1833).

76. Newman wrote *Elements of Political Economy* (Andover, 1835).

77. *Ibid.,* p. 242.

78. *Ibid.,* pp. 243-54.

79. Wayland wrote *Elements of Political Economy* (Boston, 1837). This work was the most popular American textbook in economics for several decades.

80. *Ibid.,* p. 305.

81. *Ibid.,* p. 307.

82. Indexed as Potter, *Political Economy: Its Objects, Uses, and Principles* (New York, 1840).

83. See R. Opie, "Neglected English Economist; G. Poulett Scrope," *Quarterly Journal of Economics,* XLIV (November, 1929), 101.

84. Potter, *Political Economy,* p. 45.

85. *Ibid.,* chap. v.

86. See S. Perlman, *A Theory of the Labor Movement* (New York, 1928).

87. These views were expressed in his *Opinions on Various Subjects, Dedicated to the Industrious Workers* (New Harmony, 1822), pp. 27-33. See also pp. 40-42, 149.

88. *Ibid.,* pp. 72, 121-23. Consult W. R. Waterman, *Frances Wright,* "Columbia University Studies in History, Economics, and Public Law," CXV (New York, 1924); J. H. Noyes, *History of American Socialisms* (Philadelphia, 1870), pp. 21-23; M. Hillquit, *History of Socialism in the United States* (New York, 1903), p. 59; and J. R. Commons and Others, *Documentary History of American Industrial Society,* V (Cleveland, 1910).

89. Consult W. Bailie, *Josiah Warren, The First American Anarchist* (Boston, 1906).

90. Skidmore wrote *The Rights of Man to Property* (New York, 1829).

91. Byllesby wrote *Observations on the Sources and Effects of Unequal Wealth* (New York, 1826).

92. Luther wrote *An Address to the Working Men of New England* (Boston, 1832).

93. Hale wrote *Useful Knowledge for the Producers of Wealth* (New York, 1833).

94. In his *The Workingman's Manual, A New Theory of Political Economy* (Philadelphia, 1831).

95. *Ibid.,* p. 48.

96. *Ibid.,* p. 224.

97. *Ibid.,* p. 226.

98. XXV (October, 1827), 415. The earlier statement appeared in Vol. XXIV (January, 1827). In it, Potter presented an excellent discussion of the intensive margin of cultivation, and came close to a marginal utility concept. See pp. 171-80.

99. *Ibid.,* pp. 415-23.

100. I (February, 1828), 192, 215.

101. IV (November, 1829), 283. See also p. 280, and VIII (February, 1832), 492, 496-97.

102. *Niles Weekly Register,* XXXII, 114 (April 14, 1827). See also *ibid.,* p. 372 (August 4, 1827).

103. XLII, 124 (April 21, 1832).

104. XLV, 2 (August 31, 1833).

105. L, 115 (April 16, 1836).

106. See XXII, 290 (July 6, 1822); XXIV, 393 (August 23, 1823); XLIII, 391 (February 9, 1833); XLV, 377 (February 1, 1834); XLVII, 89-90 (October 4, 1834); p. 101 (October 18, 1834); p. 132 (November, 1, 1834); p. 180 (November 22, 1834); XLIX, 69 (October 3, 1835). See also *Poulson's American Daily Advertiser,* June 22, 1837.

107. VII (October, 1840), 311 ff.

108. *Ibid.,* p. 311.

109. *Ibid.,* p. 312-13.

110. *Ibid.,* p. 314.

111. MacVickar edited and published an encyclopedia article by McCulloch entitled *Outlines of Political Economy* (New York, 1825).

112. Cooper wrote *Lectures on the Elements of Political Economy* (Columbia, 1826), and a *Manual of Political Economy* (Washington, 1834).

113. *Lectures,* pp. 18, 232-33.

114. *Manual,* pp. 22, 95.

115. Published in New York, 1832.

116. Vethake wrote *Principles of Political Economy* (Philadelphia, 1838).

117. *Ibid.,* p. 114.

118. Dew wrote *Lectures on the Restrictive System* (Richmond, 1829).

119. *Ibid.,* p. 26.

120. XXXVII, 113 (October 17, 1829).

121. I (July, 1815), 214.

122. II (September, 1827), p. 47. Robert Walsh was the editor of this publication at the time.

123. XIV (September, 1833), 66, 100; see also XII (December, 1832), 303, and *American Monthly Review,* IX, 313.

124. VI (August, 1830), I. Hugh Legaré was editor of this publication at the time.

125. *Ibid.,* p. 8.

126. *Ibid.,* p. 10.

127. *Ibid.,* p. 15.

128. *Ibid.,* pp. 17, 22, 31.

129. *Ibid.,* p. 27. Slightly more than a year later an article in the same periodical (VIII [November, 1831], p. 191), under the same editor, pointed out the great evils of concentrated riches and argued for compulsory free public education.

130. XV (October, 1822), 289.

131. *An Inquiry concerning the Power of Increase in the Numbers of Mankind* (London, 1820).

132. *Op. cit.,* p. 292.

133. *Ibid.,* pp. 293 ff., 301 ff.

134. *Ibid.,* p. 318.

135. II (January, 1840), 36. The identity of the author of this statement has remained a mystery even after careful inquiry. It is possible that Tasistro was a pen name.

136. *Ibid.,* p. 39.

137. *Ibid.,* p. 39.

138. *Ibid.,* p. 40.

139. *Ibid.,* p. 41.

140. *Ibid.,* p. 41. The disproof of the laws of Newton has come in another way.

Frederick L. Beaty (essay date 1969)

SOURCE: Beaty, Frederick L. "Byron on Malthus and the Population Problem." *Keats-Shelley Journal* 18 (1969): 17-26.

[*In the following essay, Beaty investigates the references to Malthus in Lord Byron's correspondence and poetry.*]

Both the letters and poetry of Byron contain references to Thomas Robert Malthus that were immediately clear and meaningful to early nineteenth-century readers. Malthus's concisely phrased hypothesis about the relationship of population growth to the means of subsistence and his incisive theories on political economy made him so famous in his own day that thoughtful contemporaries were obliged to read his work. If for no other reason, idealists such as Wordsworth, Southey, Coleridge, Scott, Hazlitt, and Shelley acquainted themselves with his *Essay on the Principle of Population*—his rebuttal to Godwin's and Condorcet's views on human perfectibility—in order to refute it as the prophecy of necessitarian despair. Many attackers denounced him, quite unjustly, as the spokesman of an Establishment trying to abrogate its responsibility toward the poor. Under almost constant fire, Malthus in revised subsequent editions ameliorated his original position of 1798 chiefly with the hope that "moral restraint" under the guidance of reason might save humanity from impending disaster. Specifically he suggested that if everyone were able to remain celibate by means of self-imposed chastity until such time as he and his beloved could properly support the fruits of their passion (Alfred Tennyson would have been a superb illustration), then the world might avoid the prophesied dilemma. Whether or not Malthus's enemies were placated by his emphasis on rational control—Shelley, for example, evidently thought this concession made the *Essay* almost innocuous[1]—they could neither ignore him nor dispel the fear that some grains of truth might underlie his Delphic utterances.

In the present day many literary allusions to Malthus have lost their original zest because his works are now rarely studied except by economic historians, and then largely because of the Keynesian endorsement of them.[2] As a result of having his theses frequently quoted but seldom read, he has suffered much the same fate as Charles Darwin. The passage of time, as well as the gradual absorption of his once-revolutionary doctrines into a more advanced intellectual milieu, has further obscured the clarity of Byron's remarks about him, reducing their charged topical significance to antiquarian status. A reëxamination in the light of early nineteenth-century environment is therefore necessary to revive the satire, excitement, and sense of immediacy that they must have provided for the first readers of Byron. More than the other literary men of his time, Byron (if we may pass over Keats's "hungry generations" in "Ode to a Nightingale" as a rather questionable allusion) was receptive to Malthusian concepts, though not without serious theological and psychological misgivings.

He had no doubt read Malthus's *Essay* before writing on August 21, 1811, to his half-sister Augusta in reply to her condolences for his mother's death. Casualties produced by the Napoleonic war, combined with the sudden loss of both his mother and "two most particular friends," may account for his superimposing a macabre phrase from the Book of Common Prayer upon a Malthusian postulate. Acknowledging Augusta's steady familial increment, he wrote: "Notwithstanding Malthus tells us that, were it not for Battle, Murder, and Sudden death, we should be overstocked, I think we have latterly had a redundance of these national benefits, and therefore I give you all credit for your matronly behaviour."[3] Though the trio of disasters to which he refers was appropriate in a response to Augusta's consolatory letter, the three calamities immediately preceding them in the Anglican litany—plague, pestilence, and famine—would have been far more cogent to Malthus's argument. Byron's comments indicate that he was aware of the discrepancy between acceptance of human suffering as biologically necessary and the theological endorsement of it as providential. He could not, like Wordsworth (in stanza iv of "Ode, 1815"), see pestilence and martial slaughter as the instrumentality for working out a divine intent.[4]

Scarcely three weeks later in a letter of September 13, 1811, to Francis Hodgson, Byron made similar remarks that show an obvious delight in jolting his intimate friend (who was about to be ordained a deacon) with skeptical views on religion. In the preceding letter to Hodgson he had flaunted a cavalier bachelor's attitude toward "the folly of begetting children," and now he claimed that his friend was degrading the Creator "by making Him a begetter of children" (*LJ*, II, 33, 35). What relates this concept to later observations on Malthus in the letter is not only the idea of population growth but Byron's inability to believe that a benevolent deity would permit injustice to flourish. Malthus himself in his revised edition of 1803 conceded that one of the main reasons preventing his contemporaries from acknowledging the demographic problem he had outlined was "a great unwillingness to believe, that the Deity would, by the laws of nature, bring beings into existence, which by the laws of nature, could not be supported in that existence."[5] To this contention he replied that mankind's awareness of the problem, as well as the dire consequences of ignoring the moral restraints instilled by rational powers and revelation, must remove "all apparent imputation on the goodness of the Deity." In fact, the competitive "struggle for existence," which Darwin would later reinterpret scientifically without the blessing of religion, was defended in the *Essay* as the divinely ordained impetus to human advancement. Byron, conspicuously unmoved by Malthus's justification of brutal competition, concluded his letter to Hodgson by asking: "Did you ever read 'Malthus on Population'? If he be right, war and pestilence are our best friends, to save us from being eaten alive, in this 'best of all possible Worlds'" (*LJ*, II, 36). Obviously in Byron's mind the Malthusian observation of reality was from the beginning associated with an amazing ability to deceive oneself about its true theological implications. Like Voltaire, Byron apparently assumed that if the Creator were truly benevolent He lacked the power to rid the world of misery, or if He were omnipotent then His motives were not completely beneficent. Malthus, with his unconscionable checks and balances, gave Byron an interesting argument for a "clockmaker" divinity.

Personal contact (probably in late 1813) with the author of the famous *Essay* no doubt heightened Byron's interest in the controversial theorist; yet it was not until the composition of *Don Juan* in Italy that he utilized Malthusian doctrines poetically.[6] In this context he associated them not only with delusion but also with America, which had always exercised a remarkable spell over the idealistic, pantisocratically oriented, imagination. After the eulogy to first love which follows the narrator's comments on the self-deception responsible for Donna Julia's fall, Byron added five accretive stanzas beginning:

> Man's a strange animal, and makes strange use
> Of his own nature, and the various arts,
> And likes particularly to produce
> Some new experiment to show his parts.

> (I, 128: 1-4)[7]

Though the train of thought is not immediately obvious, he is paraphrasing Malthus, who began his first *Essay* and concluded all enlarged redactions with variations on a highly provocative question: Can man with the aid of startling scientific advancement alter his own nature and society in such a way as to achieve happiness rather than misery on earth? Though Malthus's formulas for population and food growth may have been discredited as inexact, this vital question remains applicable today. During the early nineteenth century, while botanists (particularly in Germany) were first demonstrating radically improved methods of agriculture and while vast new lands were being introduced to the plow, the answer generally appeared to be a resounding affirmative. Not until the twentieth century, when there was growing disillusionment in the ability of science to cure all social ills, could Byron's passage be comprehended in the full depth of its poignancy. His implied answer is even more ominous than that of Malthus, for the narrator fills in concrete illustrations of miraculous inventions ("opposite discoveries") only to show how one cancels out the other. These examples constitute a variation on Malthus, who asserted that since smallpox was one of nature's best ways of keeping population in check, elimination of the disease through inoculation of cowpox would just increase mortality from other maladies.[8] The sequence of ideas then leads Byron to comment (I, 130-131) on the great pox, syphilis, not only an effective biological check on population but also a moral inhibitor to promiscuous sexual relations. Thus Byron carries the principle of population to a conclusion that the professorial parson, who maintained a modest reticence on such topics, did not expound—namely, that passion has its own natural restraints. Since Malthus repeatedly declared that in British America, where the food supply was as yet unlimited and people married young, population doubled every twenty-five years, Byron concludes that perhaps syphilis will return to its place of origin, the New World, and serve the same function that "war, or plague, or famine" perform in thinning population among the "civilized" nations of Europe.

The other famous blessing of Columbus's discovery was an edible tuber cultivated so extensively in Ireland that it had already become known as the "Irish" potato. And among other inventions, Byron lists a bread made (with indifferent success) from this vegetable (I, 130:1).

Malthus himself observed that the potato had made it possible for married Irishmen to obtain plots of ground sufficient to grow food for their burgeoning families.[9] However, he cautioned that, even though more nourishment could be produced by potato culture than by any other, there was a limited amount of land adaptable to cultivation and that potatoes were, after all, a perishable crop. By supplanting grain as the staff of life in Ireland, this vegetable had enabled the population to grow twice as rapidly as in England—indeed more rapidly than in any country outside America. But since Malthus realized that population soon adjusts to an increased food supply, he uttered portentous warnings about the impasse in which Ireland would soon find herself. That he should have credited the potato with effecting the population explosion, which until recently historians have attributed chiefly to the Industrial Revolution, declining death rate, increasing birth rate, and unwise administration of the Poor Laws, may seem startling.[10] But as early as his first *Essay* he cited Adam Smith's contention that if the common folk of England would adopt the potato as their favorite food many more people could be sustained than were capable of being fed by grain culture.[11]

Since Malthus blamed man's inability to achieve a Godwinian utopia less on food limitations than on the sex drive, it was inevitable that Byron should return to Malthusian doctrines in the English cantos, where love is shown to be as perishable and as marketable as potatoes. The first English women aware of Juan's arrival in London are "those pedestrian Paphians, who abound / In decent London when the daylight's o'er" (XI, 30:4-5). Without elaborating upon his analogy, Byron states that these "commodious but immoral" streetwalkers are, like Malthus, useful in promoting marriage. The poet may be recalling the passage in which Malthus staunchly averred that "the law of chastity cannot be violated without producing evil."[12] Promiscuous intercourse weakens the pure affections of the heart and degrades womanhood. Furthermore, illicit relations, "without improper arts" (the Malthusian euphemism for contraception), would produce just as many children, most of whom would likely become burdens on society. Thus prostitution, which the *Essay* acknowledged as a vicious check on population, is in a rather vague negative way said to be an incentive to virtuous marriage.

Society matrons seeking eligible husbands for their daughters in the London marriage market are also Malthusians without knowing it, for they are determined to see their nubile daughters not just married but wedded to economically sound husbands. When Byron asserts that Malthus opposed taking a bride unless one had ample cash (*Don Juan*, XII, 14:4), he adheres to the dictum advocated by all "pious" mothers. Hence, he sardonically concludes, poking fun at Scott's sentimental optimism (XII, 13:1-2), that love, the supposed ruler of the human heart and all man's aspirations, is governed ultimately by mammon. Instead of equating love with heaven, he argues that heaven is actually matrimony. In our society gratified love can be achieved only through marriage (though the two terms are by no means synonymous), and those who indulge in illicit affairs are excluded from the socially desirable state. After other digressive joking, the narrator "in this twelfth Canto" proposes being as serious as though the somber reformers Wilberforce and Malthus were his mentors, in spite of the discrepancy between their precepts and their effects. By asserting that Malthus "does the thing 'gainst which he writes" (XII, 20:8), Byron presumably alludes to apocryphal tales, which even the biographer James Bonar felt obliged to refute—namely, that Malthus sired eleven daughters (all future breeders) though in fact he had only three children. In the next stanzas Byron ironically jests about sages who

> write against all procreation,
> Unless a man can calculate his means
> Of feeding brats the moment his wife weans.
>
> (XII, 21: 6-8)

Then in true earnestness, he suggests that "Philogenitiveness" ought to meet with greater forgiveness among men, and only politeness constrains him from using the commoner short word for that very human pleasure leading to offspring.

By the time the last cantos of *Don Juan* were written, the reputation of Malthus was firmly established in at least one field of endeavor, for his strikingly original inquiries had actually revolutionized political economy. For example, *Blackwood's* review of David Ricardo's *On the Principles of Political Economy* in May of 1817 (I, 175-178) pointed out the widespread impact of Malthusian concepts.[13] An article entitled "Reflections on the Theory of Population" in *Blackwood's* for November of 1818 (IV, 207-211) defended the good intentions of the much-reviled Malthus and recommended that his precepts, having been established beyond question, be systematically applied to political economy for the benefit of the general welfare. It was commonly assumed that utilitarianism, with its goal of providing the greatest good for the greatest number, had assimilated the valid lessons of Malthus into its social, economic, and political philosophy. This amalgamation was certainly evident in a novel Byron very much admired, Peacock's *Melincourt,* in which a righteous Mr. Fax (usually taken as a combination of Malthus and Bentham) solved the problems of humanity with *reductio ad mathematicam* arguments, all based on irrefutable facts.[14] The extent of popular interest in prevailing economic theories was further reflected in the lead article of *Blackwood's* for November of 1822 (XII, 523-530), entitled simply "Political Economy." It pretended to be an abridged foretaste of a German work on the

subject of philosophical "save-all-ism"—a system founded on Bentham's variety of utilitarianism. In many ways a forerunner of Carlyle's mixture of profundity and absurdity in *Sartor Resartus,* this essay, claiming to be a combination of translation and editorial comment upon seemingly preposterous recommendations by German scientists with comical names, heralded the technological advancements in productivity that would help forestall overpopulation throughout the nineteenth century. According to the article, one Professor Gunthred Bumgroschen claimed to have discovered a solution to the Malthusian dilemma. Since people were the root of the problem, why not utilize the dead to produce more food? "All theories, as well as dogs, have their day," he claimed, "and the time may come when we shall be compelled to attend more to the calls of the stomach, then to the 'nimble caperings in a lady's chamber'" (XII, 523). Apart from the learned Professor's ludicrous treatment of the two basic Malthusian postulates, this article would have been of special interest to Byron because it contained two unquestionable allusions to him. Whether or not he would ultimately have carried out his threat to turn his best canto of *Don Juan,* "save one on Astronomy" (XII, 88:7-8), upon political economy is problematic. The fact remains, nevertheless, that it was a subject of consuming topical interest. In view of all that Harriet Martineau succeeded in writing to popularize the subject, we may regard Byron's unfulfilled promise with some feeling of relief.

In the last portion of *Don Juan,* when Lady Adeline Amundeville indulges in a favorite feminine sport of matchmaking, the ideas of Malthus recur, this time associated with interesting travel accounts of America, the land of chimerical dreams fulfilled or exploded. Byron's footnote on George Rapp in the manuscript of Canto XV included the name Cobbett, which was corrected in print to read Hulme.[15] The immediately following quotation about Harmonists' children arriving "in a little flock like those of a farmer's lambs, all within the same month perhaps" is taken verbatim from William Cobbett's book *A Year's Residence in the United States of America,* the third part of which consists of Thomas Hulme's *Journal.*[16] Having been unable to visit the *"Western Countries"* of the Republic, Cobbett was nevertheless determined to include a first-hand description of the region between the Great Lakes and the Ohio lest Englishmen with investment capital be deceptively lured to emigrate (as indeed George Keats was) by Morris Birkbeck's glowing advertisement of the area in *Notes on a Journey in America* (1818) and *Letters from Illinois* (1818).[17] The first part of Byron's note on "Rapp the Harmonist," however, could not have come from Hulme's information but echoes Birkbeck's explanation of how the Harmonists restricted population less stringently than the "Shakers."[18] Yet Byron may also have read that fascinating passage in the account of Birkbeck's *Notes* in the *Edinburgh Review* for June of

1818. It is immediately apparent that Birkbeck himself had assimilated Malthus, for he observed that the eastern centers of population sent their superfluous inhabitants westward and that western settlements in turn became the *"officina gentium"* of further westward migration. Like a dedicated Malthusian, Birkbeck noted that the followers of George Rapp in New Harmony, Indiana, would because of material plenty amidst rich farmlands along the Wabash soon have unmanageable population unless they imposed some "artificial restraint." It was precisely this "abstinence from sexual intercourse" that prompted Cobbett to denounce Birkbeck for his admiration of the Harmonists, asking: "Where else shall we look for a Society composed of persons willing and able to forego the gratification of the most powerful propensity of nature, for the sake of getting money together?"[19] Hulme was moreover amazed by a religious creed that included, as a Chancery lawyer might term it, such a *"restraining clause"* against "propagation of the species."[20] He could not refrain from sneering at the preposterousness of such unnatural prohibitions, underlining the discrepancy between profession and practice by adding that Rapp had children "as well as Parson Malthus."

Thus Byron found ideal material for satire on marriage and the absurdity of sexual restraint in accounts of contemporary backwoods America, where misapplied theories of Malthus had indeed been put to the test. One must add "misapplied" because Malthus had to defend himself, in all editions after the first *Essay,* against the imputed charge that he had ever recommended artificial restraints after the wedding. Though Byron is ready to concede that matrimony and harmony are incongruous, he is mystified by how the Harmonist's "ritual . . . grew habitual" (XV, 36:7-8). Noting the parallel between Rapp and Malthus, Byron contrasts them with the "zealous matrons" who encourage the propagation of redundant population, which can only temporarily be alleviated by that much-recommended exhaust valve, emigration. He returns to the Malthusian doctrine that the sex drive ("passions") and a growing food supply ("potatoes") are responsible for too many people (XV, 37). The last line referring to these two causes as "weeds which pose our economic Catos" has hitherto never been properly explained. What Byron alludes to is the deplorable practice of Cato the Censor in selling off his slaves after they became too old to be remunerative and, presumably, replacing them with others—a practice for which Plutarch in his *Lives,* took him severely to task.[21] Contrary to the recommendations of many political economists, Malthus declared that emigration provided only a temporary alleviation of demographic ills because the places left by departing groups were soon filled with new individuals; in fact, statistics demonstrated that areas theoretically depleted by migration to other lands actually continued to increase in population.[22] Thus Byron sees emigration in the same cold light as Cato's disposition of elderly retainers—a heartless and ultimately futile measure in what Carlyle termed "the dismal science."

Whether or not Lady Adeline had read Malthus the narrator claims not to know, but certainly she flourishes in a materialistic society that endorses what Byron calls "the eleventh commandment"—"'thou shalt not marry,' unless *well*" (XV, 38:2-3). He associates this injunction with the decalogue because Malthus asserted that to marry without being able to support a family was "clearly an immoral act," though not one that society could justly prevent or discipline since "the punishment provided for it by the laws of nature falls directly and most severely upon the individual who commits the act."[23] However much Byron respected Malthusian contributions to economic theory, he obviously regarded "moral restraint" as a potentially dangerous self-delusion, for in his view sex was the temptation man could least likely resist, even when starving. Cloaking himself in feigned naïveté, Byron's narrator pretends not to understand Malthus. Instead he claims (XV, 38:7-8), in keeping with the popular misinterpretation, that the parson's philosophy leads to ascetic conduct or the conversion of marital relations into an arithmetic problem. Upon this flippant note he concludes his treatment of a serious, highly controversial subject—in typically Byronic fashion.

Notes

1. See Shelley's note in his preface to *Laon and Cythna* (1818), *The Complete Works of Percy Bysshe Shelley,* ed. Roger Ingpen and Walter E. Peck (London and New York, 1926-30), I, 242n.

2. For the importance of Malthus in the development of modern economic theory, see John Maynard Keynes, *Essays in Biography* (London, 1933), pp. 95-149.

3. *The Works of Lord Byron: Letters and Journals,* ed. Rowland E. Prothero (London, 1898-1901), I, 332-33—hereafter cited as *LJ.*

4. Both Byron (*Don Juan,* VIII, 9: 6-8) and Shelley ("Peter Bell the Third," Part VI, xxxvi-xxxvii) burlesqued Wordsworth's original text, composed after the victory at Waterloo, asserting that Carnage was the daughter of God. Malthus would have approved of Wordsworth's original version, softened in the 1845 revision.

5. *An Essay on the Principle of Population* (London, 1803), p. 494.

6. In his Ravenna journal of "Detached Thoughts" (1821), Byron noted that one of his cleverest puns had been made at a dinner party of Sir James Mackintosh, at which Madame de Staël and

Malthus were also guests (*LJ,* V, 420). Malthus, an intimate friend of Mackintosh, had since 1805 been Professor of Modern History and Political Economy at the East India College, Haileybury.

7. All citations of this work refer to *Byron's "Don Juan": A Variorum Edition,* ed. Truman Guy Steffan and Willis W. Pratt (Austin and Edinburgh, 1957).

8. *Essay* (London, 1817), III, 136-37.

9. The same, II, 388-89.

10. For a modern historian's correlation of potato culture and European population growth, see William L. Langer, "Europe's Initial Population Explosion," *American Historical Review,* LXIX (1963), 1-17.

11. *Essay* (London, 1798), pp. 136-37. Smith had made this assertion in his *Inquiry into the Nature and Causes of the Wealth of Nations* (1776).

12. *Essay* (London, 1817), III, 87-88.

13. At this time Ricardo, Malthus, and Byron all had the same publisher, John Murray, who in August of 1818 bought half interest in *Blackwood's Edinburgh Magazine.*

14. For an elaboration of the similarities between Peacock's *Melincourt* (1817) and Byron's English cantos, see Elizabeth French Boyd, *Byron's Don Juan: A Critical Study* (New York, 1958), pp. 155-57.

15. See *Byron's "Don Juan": A Variorum Edition,* IV, 272.

16. Second ed. (London, 1819), p. 488.

17. On January 15, 1820, John Keats wrote his sister-in-law: "Gertrude of Wyoming and Birkbeck's book [*Notes*] should be bound up together like a Brace of Decoy Ducks" (*The Letters of John Keats,* ed. Hyder E. Rollins [Cambridge, Mass., 1958], II, 243). Shelley, who read both Birkbeck volumes in Italy, wrote Peacock in June of 1819 that the *Notes* interested him exceedingly though he thought the *Letters* "stupid" (*The Letters of Percy Bysshe Shelley,* ed. Frederick L. Jones [Oxford, 1964], II, 99).

18. *Notes on a Journey in America* (London, 1818), pp. 122-23.

19. *A Year's Residence,* p. 531.

20. See pages 487-89.

21. Plutarch wrote of Marcus Cato: "When his slaves became too old for work, he considered it right to sell them, instead of maintaining them in idleness. . . . For my own part, I consider that his practice of dismissing and selling, in their old age, those servants, whom in their vigour he had used like beasts of burden, shows a heart too hard, too prone to think that there is no stronger bond between man and man than mere utility" (*Plutarch's Lives,* tr. W. R. Frazer [London and New York, 1906-07], II, 41).

22. See especially the chapter "Of Emigration," II, 287-305 of the 1817 *Essay.*

23. *Essay* (London, 1817), III, 180. Godwin, in his rather feeble reply, *Of Population* (London, 1820), especially condemned Malthus for this seemingly inhuman view (pp. 18-19).

D. L. LeMahieu (essay date July-September 1979)

SOURCE: LeMahieu, D. L. "Malthus and the Theology of Scarcity." *Journal of the History of Ideas* 40, no. 3 (July-September 1979): 467-74.

[*In the following essay, LeMahieu discusses Malthus's attempt, in the last two chapters of his* Essay on Population, *to provide theological justification for his theories.*]

In the final two chapters of his first **Essay on Population,** T. R. Malthus tried to reconcile the chilling implications of his population theory with the goodness and benevolence of God. This theodicy further antagonized the critics of the **Essay,** who found it sanctimonious and hypocritical; and it tagged the author with the acrimonious title "Parson Malthus."[1] Although in later editions Malthus answered some of his critics' more specific objections, he largely abandoned his early intention to develop a thoroughgoing religious justification for his theory, leaving that task for others.[2] Malthus preferred to weather the storm of abuse provoked by his ideas behind the shelter of census statistics rather than on the exposed ground of religious speculation.

It was a wise choice. Malthus's theological ruminations have not found a place in the anthologies of religious thought. Yet, the last two chapters of his first **Essay** made explicit a dimension of his thought which is of more than casual interest to the historian of ideas. My essay is not an attempt to vindicate the ways of Malthus to man. Rather, it attempts to understand why he felt compelled to include a theodicy in his polemic; to inquire into the nature of his theodicy and its relation to more orthodox Christianity; and to explore the ethics which his theology sanctioned.

When Malthus pondered the final cause of his law of population, he was engaged in a procedure familiar to British intellectuals of the seventeenth and eighteenth centuries. To some of the practitioners of the "new science" the argument from design at the center of natural religion provided a legitimacy for their work which they exploited without reluctance or apology. Even Newton, whose physics could easily be detached from his religious speculations, believed his system contributed to the study of final causes ". . . after Descartes and others endeavored to banish them."[3] In biology, naturalists such as John Ray and William Derham embraced teleological categories eagerly, asking questions that would have embarrassed Bacon and Galileo who warned against the dangers of Peripatetic reasoning.[4]

Yet, by stipulating the final cause of his central principle, Malthus was not simply following the "new science" but was also aligning himself with the traditions of the Scottish Enlightenment. With the obvious exception of Hume, Scottish moralists constantly invoked the categories of teleological reasoning in their treatises. Indeed, the Aristotelian distinction between efficient and final cause helped shape one of the Scots' most characteristic notions: the idea of unintended consequences. "The natural course of things cannot be entirely controlled by the impotent endeavors of man," Adam Smith wrote in his *Theory of Moral Sentiments*; "the current is too rapid and too strong for him to stop it, and tho' the rules which direct it appear to have been established for the wisest and best purposes, they sometimes produce effects which shock the natural sentiments."[5] To Smith, as to other Scottish theorists, men's capacity to determine their own destiny was severely circumscribed. Reason and self-interest were deceptive guides to the complexities of human society. Ends did not always correspond with means, nor intentions with results. History was often an ironic tale.[6]

Among Malthus's complaints against Godwin and Condorcet was their inability to distinguish between the intentions of men and the often radically different social outcomes. Like the Scots, Malthus was acutely sensitive to the unpredictable in human affairs, a sensitivity no doubt heightened by the excesses of the French Revolution. He was not pessimistic about the prospects of human improvement, but he was disturbed by the misleading interpretations of the idea.[7] The inherent desire of men to procreate, which Malthus condemned, resulted in evils which demanded careful explanation. His theodicy was consequently not tacked on as a dubious means of legitimizing his conclusions. It was as integral to the method of social analysis established by the Scottish Enlightenment as, say, a watch for telling the time.

Like many of his eighteenth-century predecessors, Malthus distinguished between physical and moral evil, devoting a separate chapter to each problem. In neither case did he ever doubt that evil fulfilled a significant function in God's universe. Men suffered; some starved, but overall there was an economy of evil as just and compensatory as the law of supply and demand. Malthus predicted demographic obstacles to human perfection, but he never grasped the essence of tragedy since he refused to accept evil as an end in itself, a finality which might crush men without ennobling them. Such tidiness violates modern sensibility, if not our credulity. But it was the cornerstone of a natural religion whose deepest faith lay in God's rationality.

Malthus began his theodicy with a critical analysis of human nature. As in Aristotle's theory of motion, the natural state of humanity was rest. Men were "inert, sluggish, and averse from labour;"[8] it was movement that needed explaining. Some impetus was required "to awaken inert, chaotic matter, into spirit; to sublimate the dust of earth into soul; to elicit an aethereal spark from the clod of clay."[9] This impetus was the physical and moral evils occasioned by the law of population. To avoid pain, men awakened themselves into activity.

> To avoid evil, and to pursue good, seems to be the great duty and business of man; and this world appears to be peculiarly calculated to afford opportunity of the most unremitted exertion of this kind: and it is by this exertion, by these stimulants, that mind is formed.[10]

Men were by nature passive; the discomforts of life prompted motion. Evil was the Prime Mover of the human realm. It was consequently the force behind civilization. Malthus confronted the potentially embarrassing problem of evil by transforming it into a theory of incentive. At the lowest level, the "cravings of hunger, or the pinchings of cold" obliged men to seek food and form a society based on cultivation. At the highest level, "some of the noblest exertions of the human mind have been set in motion by the necessity of satisfying the wants of the body."[11] Malthus argued that the physical evils arising from the law of population accounted for the "imagination of the poet; . . . the flowing periods of the historian, . . . the researches of the philosopher," and "the immortal mind of a Newton."[12] This explanation was both reductionist and prophetic, since it anticipated the numerous philosophic systems of the nineteenth century which sought a single and coherent explanation for all forms of human activity. To evoke Isaiah Berlin's famous distinction, Malthus was a "hedgehog" who related everything to a central vision which he stumbled upon while arguing with his father.[13]

Moral evil was also an incentive to useful activity. "The heart that has never known sorrow itself, will seldom be feelingly alive, to the pains and pleasures, the wants and wishes, of its fellow beings."[14] Borrowing freely from a number of eighteenth-century moralists, Malthus claimed that benevolence originated in distress, that men remembered their own pain and thereby became alert to similar feelings in others. Moreover, man's imperfections contributed to the diversity and variety of the species, which in turn offered an "extensive . . . field for investigation and research."[15] God allowed moral and physical flaws in his Universe because "the constant effort to dispel this darkness, even it fail of success, invigorates and improves the mind."[16] To Malthus, the development of intelligence was central to human dignity. Moral evil assisted this development by offering a persistent, intractable problem which men's reason could neither solve nor ignore. Perfection was not only impossible; it was dangerous.

Two aspects of this approach merit comment. First, Malthus's explanation of evil eschewed traditional Christian dogma in a number of key areas. By claiming that the "original sin of man, is the torpor and corruption of the chaotic matter, in which he may be said to be born," he altered the usual notion of man's sinfulness.[17] Malthus was ambiguous about Original Sin. At one point, he specifically repudiated the concept; at another, he hinted at acquiescence.[18] In any case, sluggishness is not depravity. Moreover, it is significant that Malthus constructed a theodicy without even mentioning Jesus, perhaps because Christ saved men from sin, not laziness. Finally, Malthus denied the existence of Hell. "It is perfectly impossible to conceive," he wrote, "that any of these creatures of God's hand could be condemned to eternal suffering." Damnation contradicted God's goodness, and consequently, although virtuous men would be rewarded with immortality, "misshapen" creatures would "perish" and "mix again with their original clay."[19] Parson Malthus thus espoused a Christianity which equivocated on Original Sin, neglected Jesus, and denied Hell.

Some of these opinions were no doubt the legacy of his early education. Malthus studied at Warrington Academy, a dissenting school, where his tutor had been Gilbert Wakefield, a Unitarian who had published arguments against the eternity of Hell's torments.[20] At Cambridge, Malthus selected as his tutor William Frend, also a Unitarian. Both Wakefield and Frend were committed political radicals who later suffered for their outspoken support of the French Revolution.[21] It is reasonable to assume that Malthus learned from his teachers the elements of religious dissent and the price of political opposition. He remained within the Church of England; he condemned Jacobinism.

Malthus's rationale for moral evil also clearly prefigured the "additional check" of moral restraint which was included in the second edition of the *Essay* and which according to Gertrude Himmelfarb, drastically qualified the "pessimism" of the earlier statement.[22] In 1798, Malthus declared that "moral evil is absolutely necessary for the production of moral excellence."[23] Five years later he argued in the same vein that "natural and moral evil seem to be instruments employed by the Deity in admonishing us to avoid any mode of conduct, which . . . injures our happiness." Just as eating to excess resulted in stomach disorders, so also the immoderate bearing of children led to misery and death.[24] The analogy of nature strongly suggested that sexual passion must be regulated and directed. 'These considerations show that the virtue of chastity is not . . . a forced product of artificial society; but that it has the most real and solid foundation in nature and reason; being apparently the only virtuous means of avoiding the vice and misery which results from the principle of population."[25] Sexual restraint was a form of "moral excellence" developed by man in response to "moral evil." This new check of moral restraint was not an arbitrary and inconsistent addition to the second *Essay,* as Himmelfarb maintains, but the logical elaboration of an earlier, more fragmentary analysis.

Thus, though Malthus did not omit his theology from later editions, he channeled it into new and more pragmatic directions. "Moral restraint" was yet another manifestation of the beneficial economy of evil: the struggle for existence disciplined sexual passions, thereby mitigating the worst fears of an unchecked population. Evil thus challenged men to shape their own destiny. Malthus's blueprint for genuine social progress was founded upon an ethic which was radically individual, and yet wholly determined by a benevolent Deity. The nature of this ethic can be easily misunderstood.

In an important chapter of his *Politics and Vision,* Sheldon Wolin attempted to show that liberalism was a "philosophy of sobriety, born in fear, nourished by disenchantment, and prone to believe that the human condition was and was likely to remain one of pain and anxiety."[26] To Wolin, Malthus's theory of population marked "a crisis in the whole liberal outlook on history" since it exacerbated the fear of a stationary state by emphasizing the limits of growth. Now, more than before, it was "anxiety which drove men to unrelenting activity" and transformed happiness into an "unstable and elusive" pursuit.[27] Acquisitiveness took precedence over inner moral values; "social norms" replaced individual conscience. For Malthus, as for other liberals, the road to happiness was paved with the repression of the natural instincts.

Wolin's brilliant revaluation remains an important antidote to naive assessments of liberal "optimism." But in the case of Malthus at least, it stresses far too emphatically the despairing implications of the law of population. The theology of Malthus quickly foreclosed the pessimism of his disturbing law. He recognized that adversity was integral to human fulfillment. For Malthus, God did not condemn men to work; he bestowed its necessity upon them as an heroic opportunity for individual self-realization.

Thus, if Malthus believed that physical evil aroused men from their innate "torpor," this alienation carried with it scant sense of grievous loss. "The partial pain . . . that is inflicted by the Supreme Creator," he wrote, "is but as the dust of the balance in comparison of the happiness that is communicated."[28] The Malthusian notion of alienation differed from either the Christian or Freudian concepts. Men did not fall from Grace; they rose from the living death of inaction. Alienation brought men to, not away from, their authentic selves. The evils that stirred men to activity provided them with an identity, direction, and purpose wholly missing in the "natural" state.

Rest and leisure were the touchstones of dissatisfaction and unhappiness. Malthus repeated the litany, common to many eighteenth-century moralists, that leisure eroded men's moral fiber and robbed them of their creative gifts. Throughout the *Essay,* he served notice on the complacency of a ruling elite in a revolutionary era. For a civilized society to thrive and prosper, he argued, there must be an aristocracy of talent, not leisure. "The general tendency of an uniform course of prosperity," he warned, "is, rather to degrade, than exalt the character."[29] Malthus thus condemned laziness in the upper as well as the lower orders of society.

By equating happiness with labor toward a meaningful goal, Malthus followed the prescription of William Paley in his *Principles of Moral and Political Philosophy,* a book Malthus was required to read as a Cambridge undergraduate.[30] For Paley, happiness consisted in living by a standard which was self-imposed and self-realized. Though goals varied between individuals, it was the process of striving which counted most. "The great principle of human satisfaction is *engagement,*" Paley wrote,[31] and Malthus underscored this principle whenever he insisted upon the dignity of labor, as well as its necessity.

Malthus believed that the benefits of work could only be maintained, however, in an open, unregulated marketplace.

> We tell the common people, that if they will submit to a code of tyrannical regulations, they shall never be in want. They do submit to these regulations. They perform their part of the contract: but we do not, nay cannot, perform ours: and thus the poor sacrifice the valuable blessing of liberty, and receive nothing that can be called an equivalent in return.[32]

If these words ring hollow today, it is because we have learned with Tawney that freedom for the pike means death for the minnow. But Malthus again invoked the doctrine of unintended consequences to argue that the freedom to succeed was an essential characteristic of a dynamic, mobile society. "If no man could hope to rise, or fear to fall, . . . the middle parts would not cer-

tainly be what they now are."[33] Despite its unsavory implications, this desire to increase the size of the middle class by repealing paternalistic legislation for the poor marked a departure from the conventional thinking of the 1790s. To Hannah More, William Wilberforce, and Paley himself, social stability depended upon everyone accepting their station in life. To Malthus, on the other hand, hard work carried with it the promise of upward social mobility for at least some members of society.

To what degree this limited hope of social advancement involved a fierce "struggle for existence" has been a topic of some controversy. For example, in a recent article Robert M. Young argued that ". . . Malthus legitimized the idea of a law of struggle, impressed Darwin with the intensity of struggle, and provided a convenient natural mechanism for the changes which Darwin was studying in the selection of domesticated varieties."[34] In a thoughtful reply to Young, Peter J. Bowler found "a real conceptual gulf" between Darwin's notion of struggle and that of Malthus. Bowler discovered not one but two types of "struggle for existence" and contended that "what was central to Darwin's argument was only incidental to Malthus's."[35]

My analysis supports Bowler's claim that Malthus derived his view of competition from the Scottish Enlightenment and that consequently he placed the "struggle for existence" within the larger context of a beneficent natural harmony. Yet, to support Bowler on this point is not to reject the argument of Young. What Malthus said and what others thought he said were frequently at odds, particularly since he often changed his mind in response to the misinterpretations of his critics. Moreover, though he was a lucid stylist, Malthus was often an ambiguous thinker, especially in the first essay when he was composing a polemic rather than a formal philosophic tract. Bowler excels when he unravels some of these complexities, but he perhaps overstates his case when he contends that "competition . . . occurred within the different classes and was not seen as a means by which an individual could rise to a higher station."[36] Certainly Malthus emphasized "the mass of mankind" in his thinking, and he also knew there were limits to the size of the middle class, but his theology of scarcity, and in a sense his entire first essay, was a plea for ". . . a mode of government, by which, the numbers in the extreme region would be lessened, and the numbers in the middle regions increased."[37]

For, to Malthus, life was a moral drama. The action of this drama centered on the struggle of men to overcome the forces of evil occasioned by an expanding population. The heroes were the builders of civilization, the men who rose from their innate torpor and constructed a disciplined society based upon industriousness, frugality, and moral restraint. The stage director was a benevolent God who allowed "no more evil in the world, than what is absolutely necessary as one of the ingredients in the mighty process."[38] The victims of the play were the men who refused to participate in the struggle and who suffered for their indifference offstage, out of view. Finally, the entire drama bore a striking resemblance to the aesthetic experience which Edmund Burke characterized as the "Sublime"—the overcoming of terrible difficulties in the creation of something vast, magnificent, and astonishing.[39] To Malthus, civilization itself was the sublime justification of natural and moral evil.

Malthus believed that man was a self-defining creature, and although this process involved pain, apprehension, and anxiety—the feelings emphasized by Wolin in his analysis of liberalism—it encompassed to a far greater degree a sense of power and exhilaration. To Malthus, men need not warp their lives in response to the threat of eternal damnation. "Life [is] a blessing independent of a future state."[40] This freedom was bestowed upon man by a God who, in allowing evil, induced men to realize their full potential. Evil was the efficient cause of human creativity and this creativity was the final cause of men's happiness, freedom, and greatness. Malthus's theology of scarcity buttressed a morality only vaguely suggested by Calvin. Here at last was the Protestant ethic and the spirit of capitalism.

Notes

1. James Bonar, *Malthus and His Work*, 2nd ed. (London, 1924), 396. Though Bonar's work remains useful, a new and comprehensive intellectual biography of Malthus is much needed.

2. See, for example, John Bird Sumner, *A Treatise on the Records of Creation, and On the Moral Attributes of the Creator . . .*, 2 vols. (London, 1816). For a discussion of Sumner's relation to Malthus, see R. A. Soloway, *Prelates and People: Ecclesiastical Social Thought in England, 1783-1852* (London and Toronto, 1969), 95-106.

3. Quoted in Colin Maclaurin, *An Account of Sir Isaac Newton's Philosophical Discourses* [1748], 3rd ed. (London, 1775), 33. See also Isaac Newton, *Four Letters from Sir Isaac Newton to Dr. Bentley Containing Some Arguments in Proof of a Deity* (London, 1756), 1.

4. See John Ray, *The Wisdom of God Manifested in the Works of Creation* (London, 1704), and William Derham's *Physico-Theology* . . . (London, 1713) and *Astro-Theology* . . . (London, 1715). For Bacon and Galileo's criticisms, see Francis Bacon, *The Advancement of Learning* [1605] (London, 1951), 113; Galileo Galilei, *Dialogue on the Great World Systems* [1632], ed. Georgio de Santillana (Chicago, 1953), 121-26.

5. Adam Smith, *The Theory of Moral Sentiments* (London, 1759), 291.

6. Two of the best discussions of this theme are found in Duncan Forbes, "'Scientific' Whiggism: Adam Smith and John Millar," *The Cambridge Journal*, 7 (1954): 643-70; and Louis Schneider, ed., *The Scottish Moralists on Human Nature and Society* (Chicago and London, 1967), xxxix-lv.

7. See Samuel M. Levin, "Malthus and the Idea of Progress," *JHI* [*Journal of the History of Ideas*], 27 (1966), 92-108.

8. [T. R. Malthus], *An Essay on the Principle of Population, As It Affects the Future Improvement of Society, With Remarks on the Speculations of Mr. Godwin, Mr. Condorcet, and Other Writers* (London, 1798), 363.

9. *Ibid.*, 353.

10. *Ibid.*, 359-60.

11. *Ibid.*, 357, 358.

12. *Ibid.*, 358, 363.

13. Isaiah Berlin, *The Hedgehog and the Fox: An Essay on Tolstoy's View of History* (New York, 1970), 1-4.

14. Malthus, *Essay,* 17.

15. *Ibid.*, 378.

16. *Ibid.*, 380.

17. *Ibid.*, 354.

18. *Ibid.*, 207, 271.

19. *Ibid.*, 388-90.

20. See Gilbert Wakefield, *The Spirit of Christianity Compared with the Spirit of the Times in Great Britain* (London, 1794). For Malthus' portrait of Wakefield, see his anonymous "Remarks" in *Memoirs of the Life of Gilbert Wakefield, B. A.,* (London, 1804), 454-63. On Wakefield as a tutor, see Franklyn Kimmel Prochaska, "The Life and Thought of Gilbert Wakefield, 1756-1801" (Ph.D. diss., Northwestern Univ., 1972), 42-64.

21. On Frend's career, see Frida Knight, *University Rebel: The Life of William Frend, 1757-1841* (London, 1971).

22. Gertrude Himmelfarb, *Victorian Minds* (New York, 1970), 101-08.

23. Malthus, *Essay,* 375.

24. T. R. Malthus, *An Essay on the Principle of Population; or, A View of Its Past and Present Effects on Happiness; With an Inquiry into our Prospects Respecting the Future Removal or Mitigation of the Evils Which It Occasions* (London, 1803) 484, 488-90.

25. *Ibid.*, 496.

26. Sheldon S. Wolin, *Politics and Vision: Continuity and Innovation in Western Political Thought* (Boston and Toronto, 1960), 293-94.

27. *Ibid.*, 324, 343.

28. Malthus, *Essay* [1798], 391.

29. *Ibid.*, 372-73.

30. Paley's *Principles* became an integral part of the Cambridge curriculum in the late 1780s, only a few years after its publication in 1785. See M. L. Clarke, *Paley: Evidences for the Man* (London and Toronto, 1974), 126-27. On Paley's ethics and politics, see D. L. LeMahieu, *The Mind of William Paley: A Philosopher and His Age* (Lincoln and London, 1976), 115-52.

31. William Paley, *The Works of William Paley, D. D.*, ed. Edmund Paley, 7 Vols. (London, 1825), V, 349.

32. Malthus, *Essay* [1798], 98-99.

33. *Ibid.*, 369.

34. Robert Young, "Malthus and the Evolutionists: The Common Context of Biological and Social Theory," *Past and Present*, 43 (1969): 130.

35. Peter M. Bowler, "Malthus, Darwin, and the Concept of Struggle," *JHI*, 37 (1976), 636.

36. *Ibid.*, 639.

37. Malthus, *Essay* [1798], 368-69.

38. *Ibid.*, 391.

39. See Edmund Burke, *A Philosophical Enquiry into the Origin of our Ideas of the Sublime and Beautiful*, 2nd ed. (London, 1759), 254-58.

40. Malthus, *Essay* [1798], 391.

Geoffrey Gilbert (essay date spring 1980)

SOURCE: Gilbert, Geoffrey. "Economic Growth and the Poor in Malthus' *Essay on Population*." *History of Political Economy* 12, no. 1 (spring 1980): 83-96.

[*In the following essay, Gilbert explains Malthus's changing views on the effects of economic growth on the working poor in the 1798 and succeeding editions of the* Essay on Population.]

I

Historians of economic thought have given short shrift to Malthus' treatment of economic growth as it affects the welfare of the working classes, although the issue commands a full chapter in every edition of the *Essay on Population.* The gist of the argument, as formulated in 1798, is that growth in the national output will be harmful to the working poor if it consists only of manufactured goods, which the working man does not consume, and at the same time entails a transfer of labor from agricultural to "unhealthy" and insecure industrial employment. Edwin Cannan barely mentions the Malthusian case against growth in discussing Malthus' views on the supply and demand for food.[1] Joseph Spengler incorporates a few of the Malthusian ideas on growth and the poor into his lengthy synthesis of Malthus' "total population theory," but does not analyze them in any detail. Only in a footnote does he hint that Malthus' views on this subject underwent a substantial change over time.[2] Wesley Mitchell gives the chapter in question only passing notice.[3] And G. F. McCleary, though he finds this "one of the most interesting chapters" of the *Essay,* leaves the logic of Malthus' argument unexamined.[4]

A careful reading of the growth-and-welfare chapter in successive editions of the *Essay* yields insights into some central themes of Malthusian thought: the relative value of industry and agriculture in promoting national welfare, the role of custom and habit in determining the long-term welfare of the lower classes, and the effective constraints on population. The chapter is of interest not only for the light it throws on these issues but for its methodology, the logic and structure of its argument. In the bold, direct spirit of the first edition, Malthus builds an abstract case against industrial-biased growth,[5] then uses it to assail the trend of the British economy over the preceding century. In later editions, however, he takes a more ambiguous stand. The broad indictment of British economic experience is withheld. Specific instances of industrial abuse are cited but undercut by reports of improved conditions. On the abstract level as well, Malthus introduces notable changes in the original presentation of the case against growth. Over a twenty-year period the simple analysis of a special type of growth inimical to the welfare of the poor is gradually qualified and at the same time purged of its anti-manufacturing overtones. Indeed by the fifth edition (1817), Malthus can marshal both fact and theory behind a relatively *hopeful* view of the benefits the working poor might derive from a growing national output.

II

With the diffidence characteristic of all the British classical economists when taking issue with "Dr. Adam Smith," Malthus sets out in Chapter XVI of the first *Essay* to correct an "error" he detects in the *Wealth of Nations.* Smith has included both the "produce of land" (agricultural output) and the "produce of labour" (manufactures) in his definition of national "wealth" (to us, national product).[6] He has also asserted: "The demand for those who live by wages . . . necessarily increases with the increase of the revenue and stock [i.e., the 'wealth' or output] of every country, and cannot possibly increase without it."[7] As the rise in national product swells the revenue of employers and augments their funds for hiring labor, the demand for labor increases. Pending an increase in population, real wages rise and workers are better off. Hence Malthus sees Smith as giving his unqualified approval to growth in national output as "tending always to ameliorate the condition of the poor."[8]

From this position Malthus dissents, on both analytical and historical grounds. The analysis takes the form of a counterexample or "instance."[9] Suppose capital was accumulated in the manufacturing sector only and the result was an increase in manufactured output Smithian "wealth" would have increased, but workers would have gained nothing, because they consume only "provisions," or *non*-manufactured products. In fact this purely industrial variety of economic growth might have, to import a Marxian term, "immiserizing" effects on the poor by shifting labor away from agriculture into industry and thereby causing a decline in the per capita quantity of provisions available for workers' consumption. Though technological advance might forestall an actual reduction in agricultural output, on the whole the working poor would still have "no greater command over the necessaries and conveniences of life" than before.[10]

With respect to *health,* a non-pecuniary but "essential ingredient of happiness,"[11] the working poor would certainly be injured by industrial-biased growth. Moving from the farm to the factory, more workers would be exposed to crowding in "close and unwholesome rooms."[12] They would also experience more uncertain employment on account of "the capricious taste of man, the accidents of war, and other causes."[13]

Crucial to this negative appraisal of the effect on workers' welfare of growth in manufactured output is the implicit assumption that manufactures do not enter the consumption of workers. Malthus reveals in more than one place that he conceives of manufactures as "ornamental luxuries."[14] These "silks, laces, trinkets, and expensive furniture" are "the revenue only of the rich, and not of the society in general."[15] An increase in the output of such goods, therefore, cannot have "the same importance as an increase of food, which forms the principal revenue of the great mass of the people."[16]

One can find both an empirical and an *a priori* basis for Malthus' views on the expenditures of the working poor. Although it is unclear whether he had access to Eden's monumental *State of the Poor* (1797) in writing the *Essay* of 1798, Malthus would have found there abundant statistical evidence on workers' spending patterns. Eden's selected budgets of agricultural laborers from all over England demonstrated that most working families spent over half their income on food. Additional expenses included rent and fuel, leaving little room for discretionary purchases of "manufactures."[17]

Even if they could afford to buy non-subsistence goods, the working poor of Malthus' first *Essay* would not be expected to do so. In the counterexample to Smith, the demand for labor in the manufacturing sector increases, causing money wages to rise; workers then spend the entire increase on *food.*[18] Elsewhere in the *Essay,* Malthus analyzes the effects of private and public income transfers to the poor solely in terms of their effect on the price and distribution of *provisions.*[19] Again the implication is that the poor will spend any additional income on necessities, especially food. This is entirely consistent with the behavioral assumptions about man which lie at the core of the first *Essay.* The human race suffers from a "perpetual tendency . . . to increase beyond the means of subsistence."[20] It is always pressing against available food supplies. "Happiness" is achieved only when those supplies are abundant and increasing.[21] The working poor, who "seem always to live from hand to mouth,"[22] would be expected to use any increase in income to widen their margin of subsistence rather than indulge in manufactured goods.

Malthus rounds out the analytical case against industrial-biased growth by parrying two possible objections. First, might not the national food supply actually *increase* if higher food prices (caused by workers spending their higher money wages on food) attracted "some additional capital into the channel of agriculture"?[23] Perhaps, but this would happen only "very slowly," according to Malthus. Thus the price elasticity of supply for food is judged to be quite low. Second, might not the national food supply be augmentable by exporting some of the additional manufactured output and importing food? For a "small country with a large navy, and great inland accommodations for carriage," a country like Holland, this might be feasible, but not for countries "less advantageously circumstanced in this respect,"[24] such as England.

III

Having made the case that immiserizing growth is theoretically possible—that the poor may be made worse off even as a Smithian measure of "wealth" rises—Malthus now turns to the real world for evidence that what is abstractly possible is at the same time empirically *plausible.* He does not have to look far. Since the Revolution, England herself has followed a course of economic development which "affords a very striking elucidation of the argument in question."[25]

Consider first population. Between the views of Richard Price, who found England's population to be declining since the Revolution, and the Reverend John Howlett, who saw it increasing, Malthus takes the compromise view that population has grown either slowly or not at all.[26] Next he infers from the relative stability of population that the subsistence funds to support labor have remained constant also. For if they had increased, population would likewise have increased; if they had declined, so too population. To complete the deductive chain, Malthus argues from the unchanged volume of "funds for the maintenance of labor" to an unchanged output of food in England.[27]

That many will doubt the stagnation of subsistence output over a century-long period, Malthus fully anticipates. But such doubts must arise from an exclusive attention to the most positive aspect of Enclosure, namely, the enclosing of "waste lands." Against the undisputed gains in food production from this practice must be set the losses resulting from the widespread conversion of grain fields to pasturage.[28] Balancing the gains and losses from Enclosure, Malthus argues (in effect) for the likelihood of no net change in Britain's food production.

By contrast, British commerce and industry have been "rapidly advancing during the last century."[29] And since there are many reasons to suppose that the number of laborers employed in agriculture has declined since the Revolution,[30] it does appear that a long-term occupational shift from agriculture to industry has been occurring in England.

Manufacturing growth, agricultural stagnation, stable population, and a "much greater proportion [of British workers] employed in large manufactories, unfavourable both to health and virtue"[31]—in all these respects British historical experience proves out the empirical possibility of immiserizing growth. The ineluctable conclusion for Malthus is that "the increase of wealth of late years has had no tendency to increase the happiness of the labouring poor."[32]

Although *formally* the reference to British experience simply provides Malthus with an example of immiserizing growth, we can safely assume that the underlying intent of Chapter XVI from the outset has been to protest the long-term direction of the British economy. Bernard Semmel has argued, in *The Rise of Free Trade Imperialism,* that Malthus was an "agrarian economist," intellectually indebted to the physiocrats, profoundly at odds with the emerging commercial and industrial order in Great Britain, and determined to prove that "a trade empire based upon an industrial predominance was not viable."[33] In the chapter here examined, Malthus addresses a limited but important issue arising from Britain's industrial advance, namely, whether growth has tended to enhance the welfare of "the most numerous class" in society, the working poor.[34] His answer is a clear and forceful No.

IV

In the second, third, and fifth editions of the *Essay,* Malthus revises the chapter—which now bears a title, **"Of Increasing Wealth, as it Affects the Condition of the Poor"**—in substantial and even surprising ways. Superficially, the most obvious changes involve his handling of "empirical" evidence, whether of an historical or a contemporary nature. In this respect there are wholesale deletions and additions, as well as "rereadings" of the facts, to be noted below. But more fundamentally, Malthus retreats from the unambiguous anti-manufacturing stand of 1798, comes to see the possibility and even desirability of the poor consuming manufactures, and is at least partially reconciled to the course of British economic development.

A striking difference between Chapter XVI in the first *Essay* and the corresponding chapter of the second, which came out in 1803, is the absence of the sweeping indictment of British economic progress, Malthus omits it entirely from the second and all later editions without a word of explanation. Apparently in 1803 he no longer believed that Britain's long-term growth experience conformed to the immiserizing pattern outlined in 1798. We can only conjecture as to the reasons why. A changed perception of British population trends may offer the best explanation. The population of England and Wales, put at five and a half million by Gregory King in 1690, was found to be almost nine million in the census of 1801. Thus it must have seemed to Malthus inappropriate to maintain a parallel between his abstract case, in which the labor force is assumed *constant,* and Britain's secular experience of growing population.

To continue to assert that British agricultural output had remained stagnant since 1688 was now impossible. By the Malthusian logic, a growing population virtually proved a growing rate of provision output. And the implied rise in British agricultural production would in turn suggest a positive rate of capital formation in the agricultural sector. This, however, would violate yet another premise of the simple theoretical "instance," that capital is accumulated only in the manufacturing sector. (We may be certain Malthus had noticed the ongoing flow of capital into a prospering British agriculture long before he drew attention to it in print in 1814-15.[35])

For whatever reasons, Malthus drops from the second edition his only historical "example" of immiserizing growth. The confident assertion of 1798 that "instances nearly approximating to [immiserizing growth] may be found without any very laborious search"[36] also disappears. No claim is staked in 1803 for the empirical relevance or verifiability of the contra-Smithian "instance."

Another change in 1803 is the more detailed examination of the health and employment effects of industrial growth. There is an extended quotation from John

Aikin's *Description of the Country from Thirty to Forty Miles Round Manchester,* in which the deleterious effects on children from working in the textile mills are vividly portrayed. Aikin draws a general contrast—which Malthus is pleased to quote—between the condition of working families in agriculture and those in manufacturing. "In the former we meet with neatness, cleanliness and comfort; in the latter, with filth, rags, and poverty."[37] The vulnerability of manufacturing workers to changes in fashion and to circumstances of war and peace is also briefly documented, not merely asserted, by Malthus in this edition.[38]

Equally significant, if more subtle, are the changes in Malthus' treatment of the "abstract" issues relating to growth and the welfare of the poor. The whole contra-Smithian growth sequence, in which the national output of manufactures increases and labor shifts from agriculture into industry, is reproduced almost verbatim. "The question," posed once again by Malthus, "is how far wealth, increasing in this way, has a tendency to better the condition of the poor."[39] They will still be losers from the occupational shift. But while in 1798 industrial-biased growth brought them no greater command over the "necessaries and conveniences of life," in 1803 it merely brings them no *"permanent"* increase in command over the *"necessaries"* of life.[40] A greater command over *"conveniences"* thus is not explicitly ruled out. That the poor may now be considered (at least in theory) potential purchasers of manufactured conveniences is tacitly conceded in the following statement, new to the second edition:

> Under such circumstances of situation [i.e., given adverse effects on health and employment], unless the increase of the riches of a country from manufactures give the lower classes of the society, on an average, a decidedly greater command over the necessaries *and conveniences* of life, it will not appear that their condition is improved.[41]

These hints that manufactures may properly be considered purchasable by the poor are consistent with the new emphasis on "preventive" checks to population in the second edition.[42] The possibility is now more seriously entertained that means other than "misery" and "vice"—the "positive" checks of the first edition—may hold population within the bounds of the food supply. When men are seen exercising a free choice not to marry at the first opportunity, it becomes more difficult to view them crudely as mere food-consumers and children-producers. The range of consumption possibilities open to the working poor, therefore, must be extended beyond subsistence to include alternative, luxury-type goods. Not all of this is worked out explicitly in 1803, nor does Malthus express any opinion yet as to the social utility of luxury consumption by the poor.

Finally, one notes in the growth-and-welfare chapter of 1803 a much expanded discussion of food imports. These are no longer dismissed as an option only for a small country with a large navy. But Malthus warns that a large, landed country does well not to become too dependent on such imports because in years of poor domestic harvests, its foreign suppliers will be unprepared to meet the unexpectedly heavy demand.[43] Then, following Sir James Steuart (whom he credits in a footnote), Malthus introduces the idea that a country which, "in the progress of wealth," shifts its labor out of agricultural employment will reach the point where additional food imports are unobtainable at an acceptable price. This raises the same possibility as in the basic contra-Smithian scenario, that "no further increase of riches [i.e., no further manufacturing growth] will have any tendency to give the labourer a greater command over the necessaries of life."[44] Interestingly, Malthus does *not* assert that continued growth under these circumstances will *lower* the overall well-being of the poor—again implying that they may share in the increasing manufactured output. He does assert, with Steuart, that the point of inelasticity in the import food supply sets "the natural limit to the population of all commercial states."[45]

V

In the third edition of the *Essay* (1806), Malthus renders additional changes in the growth-and-welfare analysis. After again producing the "instance" of immiserizing growth which proves the error of Adam Smith, Malthus, in a footnote, explicitly recognizes the benefits that might accrue to the working poor from growth, even of an industrial-biased kind:

> On the supposition of a physical impossibility of increasing the food of a country, it is evident that by improvements in machinery it might grow yearly richer in the exchangeable value of its manufactured produce, but the labourer, though he might be *better clothed and lodged,* could not be better fed.[46]

We shall see the clothing-and-lodging aspect of welfare developed further in 1817.

It has come to be regarded as basic to Malthus' post-1798 thinking on the poor and the improvement of their well-being that the only real hope lies in changing their self-defeating "habits." In another important footnote to the 1806 growth-and-welfare chapter, Malthus asserts in this connection:

> The condition of the labouring poor, supposing their habits to remain the same, cannot be very essentially improved but by giving them a greater command over the means of subsistence. But any advantage of this kind must from its nature be temporary, and is therefore really of less value to them than any permanent change in their habits. But *manufactures, by inspiring a*

*taste for comforts, tend to promote a favourable change
in these habits,* and in this way perhaps counterbalance
all their disadvantages.[47]

Here is a recognition not only that manufactures may
properly be considered consumable by the poor but that
such consumption may be socially *useful* as a means of
instilling better habits in them. Though this is a line of
thought we tend to associate with economists other than
Malthus, it is one he takes more than once in the 1806
Essay. In the chapter extolling the benefits of state-
supported education, for example, Malthus includes "a
taste for the conveniences and comforts of life" among
the forces helping to raise the "standard of wretchedness"—what we might term the minimum acceptable
standard of living—among the lower classes.[48]

Minor additions are made in 1806 to the discussion of
food and population constraints. All of the "great landed
nations of Europe" are said currently to be at a safe distance from the point of inelasticity in food import supply, though the "progress of wealth" will find them all
eventually approaching it.[49] But a country can experience the pinch of limited food relative to population
whenever "the march of commerce and manufactures is
more rapid than that of agriculture."[50] Such had been
the case in England in the past ten or twelve years, in
Malthus' opinion. Thus "the nominal wages of labour
have greatly increased," but the "real recompense of the
labourer"—the subsistence he can command—has increased more slowly,[51] limiting the pace of population
growth.

VI

The mature expression of Malthus' views on economic
growth and the welfare of the working poor is to be
found in the fifth edition of the *Essay,* published in
1817.[52] In its real-world assumptions and observations,
its analytical structure, and its general tone of compla-
cent optimism, it could hardly be more dissimilar to the
version of 1798. Most of the key revisions in Malthus'
treatment of the subject are adumbrated in the 1803 and
1806 editions, as detailed above. What Malthus offers
in the 1817 chapter, "Of Increasing Wealth . . . ," is a
careful and comprehensive reformulation of earlier
ideas.

A noteworthy departure from earlier editions is the new
emphasis on the "natural progress of wealth" and the
corresponding de-emphasis of the narrower concept of
industrial-biased growth. As early as 1806 Malthus had
introduced (or borrowed from James Steuart) the idea
that "in the progress of wealth" a nation would "naturally" reach a point where food supplies could not be
increased and further growth in "wealth" must take the
form of manufactures. Not until 1817, though, does he
adopt the secular evolution of the economy as his cen-

tral perspective in discussing growth and the poor. There
are gains from this. First, it is no longer necessary, in
raising the issue of industrial-biased growth, that
Malthus make arbitrary assumptions about an abstract
economy where one "supposes . . . for a course of
years" that capital is accumulated only in the manufacturing sector, etc. It is less arbitrary and more direct to
deal with industrial-biased growth as the condition toward which a normally evolving economy moves over
time. Hence, Malthus omits the formulaic, abstract "instance" from this edition. Second, the importance of
industrial-biased growth as something more than a theoretical construct is now firmly re-established. After the
withdrawal of the British historical analogy in the second edition (cf. § IV above), it may have struck some
readers (even Malthus himself) that industrial-biased
growth did not merit the space it continued to claim in
the *Essay.* Making such growth a normal and predictable end product of long-term economic processes obviously restores its "relevance."

As to *why* industrial-biased growth should be regarded
as characteristic of the later stages of economic development, Malthus is not entirely clear. It appears to be a
simple matter of absolute limits to land, diminishing returns in agriculture, and an "increasing taste for conveniences and luxuries," all of which will tend to "direct
the greatest part of . . . new capital to commerce and
manufactures"—presumably because of higher relative
returns there.[53] Industrial-biased growth is not a phenomenon only to be anticipated in the dim future, however. Malthus indicates that it may occur whenever societies reach the limits to food and population consistent
with their institutional and technological constraints.[54]

The dominant message of 1817 is that the poor need
not experience losses of welfare when growth becomes
industrial-biased, that is, limited to manufactured output. True, the funds for the maintenance of labor, which
are the "means of marrying early and supporting a family,"[55] will then have reached their maximum. Malthus
does regard the necessity of family limitation as, in itself, a "considerable disadvantage."[56] But he holds out
to the laborer the prospect that "with a small family he
may be better lodged and clothed, and better able to
command the decencies and comforts of life."[57]

A full and explicit recognition of manufactures consumption by the poor marks the fifth edition. Malthus
announces here that the "comforts of the lower classes
of society do not depend solely upon food, nor even
upon strict necessaries."[58] In fact they "cannot be considered as in a good state unless they have the command of some conveniences and even luxuries."[59] Such
goods not only "gratify a natural or acquired want" but
"tend unquestionably to improve the mind and elevate
the character."[60] What a far cry from the Malthus of
1798, who would have barred "the introduction of

manufactures and luxuries" into America so as to keep the lower classes in their happy state of innocence![61]

Strong confirmation of Malthus' new, more positive attitude toward growth, especially the type (industrial-biased) that originally had seemed to threaten the poor, comes in his treatment of China in 1817. In every edition Malthus presents a hypothetical example in which he supposes industrial-biased growth to occur in China. In the first four editions, these are the predicted effects of such growth: a larger output of manufactures, their exchange abroad for "luxuries," an unchanged or diminished output of "produce" in China, and stable or declining real funds for the maintenance of labor. Despite the "increasing wealth" of the country, the overall condition of the working poor is "depressed" by the shift of some into unhealthy industrial occupations and the absence of any compensating increase in purchasing power. The China example of 1817 is far less damning of industrial growth.[62] The increased quantity of manufactures produced could *either* be exported for luxuries *or* "consumed at home"—by poor as well as rich? Also, any shortfall of agricultural output, due to the shift of labor into manufacturing, "would be made up, and indeed more than made up, by the beneficial effects of improved skill and economy of labour" in agriculture. There is no reference here, as previously, to the unhealthful aspects of the industrial work that would now engage more Chinese. The worst Malthus can say, or *will* say in 1817, is that under this type of economic growth workers will not be able to consume more *food* than before.

VII

It is no part of our purpose here to suggest the evolution of Thomas Malthus from an apologist for *agricultural* interests to an apologist for *industrial* interests. Neither in the chapter examined here nor in any other of Malthus' writings does one see anything like the pro-industrial bias or sympathy so transparent in Ricardo and other "mainstream" British classicists. It would be closer to the mark to suggest the emergence in Malthus' thinking of a more balanced view of industrial and agricultural growth as potential contributors to working class welfare. Item: in 1817 Malthus finally drops the invidious comparison, present in all earlier editions, between two nations which achieve equal increases of "wealth" but by different routes, one devoting itself to "commerce," the other to agriculture. No longer is Malthus willing to contend that in the former, "the poor would be comparatively but little benefited."[63] Now his position is that growth, "whether it consists principally in additions to the means of subsistence or to the stock of conveniences and comforts, will always, *ceteris paribus,* have a favourable effect on the poor."[64]

Of course industrial labor can never be as conducive to workers' health and virtue as labor in the field—this sort of bias is life-long in Malthus. But the Malthus of 1817 is able to gloss over Aikin's account of cotton-mill working conditions by reporting, in a footnote, that the situation of the children employed there "has been . . . very essentially improved, partly by the interference of the legislature, and partly by the humane and liberal exertions of individuals."[65]

It is perhaps unfair in view of the obvious analytical refinements and historical-empirical reassessments worked out through successive editions of the *Essay* to speculate that the line between what Malthus believed and what he wanted to believe in all of this is a very thin one. He seems genuinely convinced in 1817 that the direction of a normally developing economy is toward industrial-biased growth. The evidence indicates to him that manufactured output has been growing much more rapidly than population (hence, food output) in Great Britain since the Revolution.[66] With Britain moving unmistakably down the industrial path, one suspects Malthus wanted to believe the poor could reap benefits along the way, and wanted them to believe the same. But only if they could be persuaded to substitute "comforts" for children would the long-range outlook be hopeful.

Notes

1. *A History of the Theories of Production and Distribution . . .* , 3d ed. (London, 1917), pp. 188-89.

2. Joseph J. Spengler, "Malthus' Total Population Theory: A Restatement and Reappraisal," *Canadian Journal of Economics and Political Science* 11, Feb., May 1945, reprinted in Spengler and William R. Allen, eds., *Essays in Economic Thought: Aristotle to Marshall* (Chicago, 1960), pp. 361-62, 396, n. 79.

3. *Types of Economic Theory, from Mercantilism to Institutionalism,* ed. Joseph Dorfman (New York, 1967), 1:249.

4. *The Malthusian Population Theory* (London, 1953), pp. 69-70.

5. This term is used throughout the present article to denote an increase in national output consisting solely of manufactured goods.

6. *An Essay on the Principle of Population . . .* (London, 1798; reprinted, New York, 1965), p. 306.

7. Adam Smith, *An Inquiry into the Nature and Causes of the Wealth of Nations.* Modern Library ed. (New York, 1937), Book I, ch. 8, p. 69.

8. *Essay,* 1798, pp. 328-29.

9. Ibid., pp. 306-10.

10. Ibid., p. 309.

11. Ibid., p. 310.

12. Ibid., p. 313.

13. Ibid., p. 310.

14. Ibid., p. 329.

15. Ibid., pp. 335-36. See also p. 332, where manu-factures are seen as tending only "to gratify the vanity of a few rich people."

16. Ibid., p. 336.

17. Sir Frederick M. Eden, *The State of the Poor: or, An History of the Labouring Classes in England . . .*, 3 vols. (London, 1797), vol. 3, App. xii: 339-50.

18. *Essay,* 1798, p. 309.

19. Ibid., ch. 5, esp. pp. 75-84.

20. Ibid., p. 346.

21. Ibid., pp. 136-37. Such a condition is most nearly achieved in new colonies, "where the knowledge and industry of an old state operate on the fertile unappropriated land of a new one."

22. Ibid., p. 86. Note, too, Malthus' rather disdainful assumption that the poor will spend any spare time or money at the "ale-house" (pp. 87, 278), though this must be blamed, at least in part, on the poor-law system, which Malthus thoroughly deplores.

23. Ibid., p. 310.

24. Ibid., p. 311.

25. Ibid., pp. 311-12.

26. Ibid., pp. 313-15. See James Bonar, *Theories of Population from Raleigh to Arthur Young* (London, 1931), ch. 7. For background on the great popula-tion debate, see D. V. Glass, "The Population Con-troversy in Eighteenth-Century England," *Popula-tion Studies* 6, no. 1 (1952): 69-91. An excellent short summary of the economic implications of the population controversy is provided in Paul Mantoux, *The Industrial Revolution in the Eigh-teenth Century,* rev. ed. (London, 1962), pp. 341-48.

27. *Essay,* 1798, p. 315. These "deductions" are more implicit than explicit in Malthus, but capture well the sense of his argument.

28. Ibid., pp. 315-16.

29. Ibid., p. 312.

30. Ibid., pp. 319-20.

31. Ibid., p. 321.

32. Ibid.

33. *The Rise of Free Trade Imperialism: Classical Political Economy and the Empire of Free Trade and Imperialism, 1750-1850* (Cambridge, 1970), p. 48 and passim.

34. *Essay,* 1798, p. 303.

35. See both "Observations on the Effects of the Corn Laws . . ." (1814), pp. 102-3 and "An Inquiry into the Nature and Progress of Rent" (1815), pp. 198-99, in *The Pamphlets of Thomas Robert Malthus* (New York, 1970).

36. *Essay,* 1798, p. 311.

37. *Essay,* 1803, p. 423. Aikin's work was published in London in 1795.

38. Ibid., p. 424.

39. Ibid., p. 422.

40. Ibid.; italics added.

41. Ibid., pp. 424-25; italics added.

42. F. A. Fetter pointed out in 1898 ("The Essay of Malthus: A Centennial Review," *Yale Review,* p. 161) what some commentators continue to over-look, that "preventive checks" were not *introduced* in the second edition (except in name), but simply received more emphasis there than they had in 1798.

43. *Essay,* 1803, pp. 425-26.

44. Ibid., p. 427. The Steuart work is *An Inquiry into the Principles of Political Economy: Being an Es-say on the Science of Domestic Policy in Free Na-tions . . .* (London, 1767), 1:118-19.

45. *Essay,* 1803, p. 427.

46. *Essay,* 1806, p. 192; italics added.

47. Ibid., p. 206; italics added.

48. Ibid., pp. 422-23.

49. Ibid., pp. 201-2 and 202n.

50. Ibid., p. 202.

51. Ibid.

52. The fourth edition, published in 1807, is a re-issue of the third.

53. *Essay,* 1817, 3:6, 22.

54. Ibid., 3:4-6, and the "China example," described below.

55. Ibid., 3:20.

56. Ibid.

57. Ibid., 3:22-23.

58. Ibid., 3:10-11. Cf. also the new assertion, made twice in the chapter, that "the condition of the lower classes of society does not depend exclusively upon the increase of the funds for the maintenance of labour, or the power of supporting a greater number of labourers" (3:2-3, 10).

59. Ibid., 3:11.

60. Ibid., 3:25.

61. *Essay,* 1798, p. 343.

62. *Essay,* 1817, 3:7-9.

63. Ibid., 3:205-6.

64. Ibid., 3:25-26.

65. Ibid. 3:16 n.

66. Ibid., 3:6.

Arthur E. Walzer (essay date February 1987)

SOURCE: Walzer, Arthur E. "Logic and Rhetoric in Malthus's *Essay on the Principle of Population,* 1798." *Quarterly Journal of Speech* 73, no. 1 (February 1987): 1-17.

[*In the following essay, Walzer analyzes Malthus's* Essay *in terms of its rhetorical strategies.*]

In 1798, Thomas Robert Malthus published anonymously *An Essay on the Principle of Population, As It Affects the Future Improvement of Society, with Remarks on the Speculations of Mr. Godwin, M. Condorcet, and Other Writers.*[1] In his famous *Essay,* Malthus argues against the possibility of the utopian future predicted by such Enlightenment reformers as William Godwin and Antoine-Nicolas de Condorcet. To counter the reformers' philosophic optimism, Malthus advances his principle of population. According to Malthus, population tends to increase at a geometric rate by a factor of two every generation (or twenty-five years). Thus, in 1700, assuming a population of five million people in England and Wales, by 1725 population would be ten million; by 1750, twenty million; by 1775, forty million; by 1800, eighty million—*if* the actual rate were the rate of its theoretical tendency. Of course, the actual rate did not increase at a geometric (or exponential) rate. There were not eighty million people in England and Wales in 1800; there were about nine million, so it should be clear to all, and is clear to Malthus, that population is prevented from increasing at the rate to which it tends. What prevents it Malthus calls "checks," chief among which are death and dis-

ease caused by malnutrition that results from the inability of the food supply to keep pace with the increase in population. Food supply, Malthus estimates, increases at an arithmetic rate every twenty-five years: one million bushels in 1700, for example, two million in 1725, three million in 1750, four million in 1775, resulting in lower *per capita* supply of grain even as the total amount of grain increases. The discrepancy between the geometric rate of population increase and the arithmetic rate of increase for the food supply: this is the principle of population. Since the reforms proposed by Condorcet and Godwin would, if anything, increase the actual population by lessening the checks and decrease the incentive to increase food production, their utopias would either never come to pass or, if realized, soon self-destruct. In the *Essay,* Malthus summarizes his principle in Chapters I and II, traces its operation from the beginnings of civilization to the present in Chapters III-VII, brings it to bear on the predictions of, principally, Condorcet and Godwin in Chapters VIII-XVII, and in Chapters XVIII-XIX explains how the principle of population fits into the divine telos.

The *Essay* generated a response that was voluminous and emotionally charged. "No contemporary volume produced so powerful an effect upon the age in which it was written as the *Essay on Population,*" commented the *Edinburgh Review* in its retrospective article on Malthus in 1838, two years after his death.[2] Even allowing for the degree of hyperbole appropriate to the occasion in the reviewer's assessment, still, no one has ever doubted the power of Malthus's *Essay* to move readers in the nineteenth century or since. Articles in response to the *Essay* filled contemporary reviews, and book-length studies variously praised and condemned what became known as "Malthusian doctrine."[3] Robert Southey enlisted John Rickman to crush Malthus, the "mischievous reptile," and, with Coleridge's help, attacked the *Essay* in the *Annual Review.*[4] Karl Marx denounced the *Essay* as a "schoolboyish, superficial plagiary," but today Malthus is praised in the People's Republic of China and the *Essay* enshrined by Robert B. Downs as one of the sixteen most important books in the history of the world.[5] The *Essay* is formidable; it has not been, and apparently cannot be, ignored. Perhaps William Hazlitt's characterization of the *Essay* and readers' response to it is best: it is, Hazlitt observed, "a facer"—a stunning blow to the face.[6]

Despite the *Essay's* evident persuasive power, no rhetorical study of it exists.[7] It may be that the attack on the politics and philosophy of the *Essay* by romantics, including Coleridge, Hazlitt, Southey, and Shelley, explains its neglect by literary and rhetorical critics; or it may be that as neither fiction nor oral address the *Essay* would not fall routinely into the ken of either group of scholars. Today, perhaps as a result of this neglect, Malthus is often presented as an early demographer or as England's first political economist and the *Essay* seen as the result of a scientific study of the forces that influence the rate of population growth.[8] But Malthus's intentions in 1798 were those of the polemicist, and the *Essay* was the product and instrument of a refutation. Thus, as I will try to show, the *Essay on Population* is pre-eminently a rhetorical achievement: its origin is in controversy; its contribution (Malthus insists) is its tracing and dramatizing, in terms meaningful to its audience, the effects of a principle long known but little understood; and it draws its power from its evocation, even conscious imitation, of Newton's *Principia*.

RHETORICAL SITUATION

The immediate occasion of the *Essay* was, as Malthus explains in its Preface, a disagreement with "a friend" (Preface, i), apparently his father, Daniel,[9] over William Godwin's essay, "Of Avarice and Profusion," from his *Enquirer* (1797). The disagreement broadened to the general question of the prospects for progress—the question that is the heart of Godwin's more famous *Political Justice* (1793)—with Malthus taking the conservative, skeptical view against his father, once an apostle of Rousseau. In what is a documented example of rhetoric's epistemic power, Malthus, referring to himself in the third person, explains that he took up his pen only with the intention of stating in a "clearer manner" thoughts he had previously expressed, but "as the subject opened upon him, some ideas occurred, which he did not recollect to have met with before" (Preface, i). Thus did Malthus arrive at his articulation of the famous principle of population.[10]

The foci of Malthus's attack were Godwin's *Political Justice* and the Marquis de Condorcet's *Sketch for a Historical Picture of the Progress of the Human Mind* (1795).[11] Both works represent extreme versions of Enlightenment optimism and rationalism. In *Political Justice,* Godwin predicts a future in which mankind will approach perfection. According to Godwin, the principal obstacles that have in the past prevented man's realization of his perfection are government, "which is, in all cases, an evil," and its instruments that promote conformity, including principally established religion, absolute property rights, and national education.[12] The "characters of men originate in their external circumstances," Godwin writes.[13] Cleanse the environment of benighted ideas perpetuated by traditional institutions and replace them with enlightened ones and man will choose equality over competition and intellectual pleasures over vanity. Man will then direct energy toward improving health and education, not acquiring and displaying luxury, and he may attain perfection. Similarly, Marquis de Condorcet's *Sketch,* first published in 1795, combines a critique of traditional institutions and an acceptance of eighteenth-century environmentalism to explain the slow pace of man's progress in the past and the possibility of his future perfectibility. The *Sketch* traces humanity's development from tribal society to the foundation of the French Republic, which Condorcet judges the culmination of our enlightenment and progress to date, and concludes with a discussion of the likelihood of humankind's future perfection.

Malthus's philosophy, which has roots in Renaissance Christian humanism, was far more conservative than Godwin's and Condorcet's. While Condorcet and Godwin advanced the probability of the perfectibility of humankind, Malthus doubts the possibility of significant moral progress. In the *Essay,* he argues that the narrative in Genesis, even if not a historical account, does relate a philosophical truth about the "torpor and corruption" of humankind (354) that makes our approximating perfection impossible. The "vices and moral weakness of mankind . . . are invincible," Malthus insists (271). Godwin and Condorcet regard humans as *exclusively* rational and, therefore, as necessarily receptive and responsive to sound reasoning; Malthus argues that humans are not "merely intellectual" but subject also to "corporal propensities" (252) that will defeat good intentions and influence actions. While Godwin and Condorcet place much confidence in the ability of institutions to shape and change humankind, Malthus regards the shaping influence of institutions as "light and superficial . . . mere feathers that float on the surface" (177). He rejects the direct circuitry that Godwin, especially, assumes by which changes in the environment or in education necessarily result in actions consistent with them. Finally, while reformers such as Condorcet and Godwin regard traditions as obstacles to the social experimentation that would contribute to progress, Malthus regards society as an organism with roots in history and "experiments" such as those that brought about the French Revolution as "the forcing manure" that has "burst the calyx of humanity" (274).

Historical and political circumstances predisposed Malthus's readers to his point of view and made his chosen targets—Condorcet and Godwin—inviting and easy to hit. In the late 1790s, the French threat—her ideas as well as her increasingly aggressive foreign policy—was prominent in the English mind. Many in England traced the origin of the disorder in France that culminated in the Reign of Terror to the earlier philosophical attack on religious and political institutions that accompanied calls for radical social and political reform. Condorcet and Godwin were seen as systematizers of these dangerous tendencies and ideas. One reviewer of Malthus's *Essay* judged Godwin and Condorcet as holding a "conspicuous place" among the apologists for ideas that in France "left not one stone on another of that edifice which it had been the labor of so many centuries to raise, to strengthen, and to embellish."[14] The fame that *Political Justice* had won Godwin among English intellectuals in 1793 had already peaked by 1798: the radical "enquirer" began to be seen as the bearer of the disorder of France to England. As one reviewer notes, "Mr. Malthus could not have obtained more credit in the eighth century for laying the devil, than he has in the eighteenth for laying Mr. Godwin."[15] Secondly, Malthus's message was certainly congenial to the bourgeoisie and landed gentry who made up much of his audience. In arguing that poverty was caused by the discrepancy in the rates of increase of population and food, Malthus made poverty seem so nearly endemic to the nature of things that efforts to alleviate it were sure to fail: "To remove the wants of the lower classes of society, is indeed an arduous task. The truth is, that the pressure of distress on this part of a community is an evil so deeply seated, that no human ingenuity can reach it" (95). Passages like this one provoked Karl Marx to rage that Malthus was "greeted with jubilance by the English oligarchy as the great destroyer of all hankerings after human development."[16] Although other passages from the *Essay* can be cited to show that Malthus intended to help the poor and that he was not a tool of the ruling classes,[17] his recommendation to eliminate gradually the Poor Laws was welcomed by many of those taxed to support their increasing costs. Many of Malthus's bourgeois readers were, unsurprisingly, most willing to embrace his call for restraints when others were to make the sacrifices and experience the pain. As one reviewer observed, "No wonder Mr. Malthus should be a fashionable philosopher. He writes advice for the poor for the rich to read."[18]

It hardly detracts from Malthus's accomplishments as a rhetorician to grant that his victory was made easier by Godwin's waning reputation, the general fear of things French, and the frustrations brought on by the rising expenditures to relieve the poor. "Mr. Malthus embarked upon the tide just at the happy moment, at the flood when it leads to fortune," a contemporary noted. Godwin, at least, was engulfed: "'Mr. Malthus appeared, and we heard no more of Mr. Godwin.'"[19]

THE RHETORIC OF THE *ESSAY*: "THE NEWTON OF POLITICAL PHILOSOPHY"

The rhetoric of the *Essay* is best illuminated when set against the backdrop of the controversy over scientific methodology in the seventeenth and eighteenth centuries. Although Malthus marshalls many arguments in an effort to refute the views of Godwin and Condorcet, central to the credibility of these arguments is Malthus's clear implication that his method meets the test of Newtonian science, while the method of Condorcet and Godwin mimics Descartes'. Descartes' theory purported to explain the movement and relative position of the planets and gravity by postulating a "primary matter"— invisible, infinitely divisible particles that filled space and carried the planets around in whirling vortices. This "vortex theory" competed with Newton's theory well

into the eighteenth century. The Newtonians dismissed the vortex theory, which they argued only *seemed* mathematical and which could not be tested mathematically because the "primary matter" on which it depended was strictly hypothetical. The Cartesians were committed to maintaining the logical consistency of the theory only, the Newtonians insisted, not in genuinely establishing its truth by subjecting it to empirical or even rigid mathematical tests. The vortex theory is nothing more than "dreams and chimeras," Roger Cotes, one of the Newtonians, insisted in language suggesting that the vortex theory was a new version of a discredited Artistotelianism.[20]

In the *Essay,* Malthus portrays Condorcet and Godwin as Cartesians, whose method is flawed by its exclusive reliance on deduction from hypotheses that are not empirically established. Malthus opposes his Newtonian (therefore, English and modern but also universal) method to Godwin's and Condorcet's Cartesian (therefore, French, scholastic, and eccentric) method. Thus Malthus's reactionary conclusions are made to rest on a modern, English methodology. The rhetoric of the *Essay* made it possible for Malthus's readers to embrace his conservatism without abandoning the basis for all Enlightenment hopes for progress—Newtonian science.

Newton never set forth a systematic description of his method or recommended that his method be applied to works, like the *Essay,* that are not concerned with science. But some eighteenth-century logics do both, and William Duncan's *Elements of Logick* (1748) is perhaps the most important of these. Wilbur Samuel Howell singles out Duncan's *Elements* as "the most challenging and most up-to-date book of its time, place, and class," in large part for its successful explanation of a method that grafted empiricism to traditional deduction in the manner of the Newtonians.[21] The *Elements* was part of the curriculum in mathematics that Malthus took up at Jesus College, Cambridge, and Malthus refers to his study of Duncan in a letter from Cambridge to his father: "The lectures begin to-morrow. . . . We begin with mechanics and Maclaurin, Newton, and Keill's *Physics.* We shall also have lectures on Mondays and Fridays in Duncan's *Logick.*"[22] The *Elements* influenced the rhetoric of the *Essay,* and the manifest traces of this important book in the opening chapters contributed to the *Essay's* persuasive impact.[23]

Duncan's *Elements* is distinguished by its effort to combine empiricism with traditional deduction to form an idealized synthesis that Duncan identifies as Newton's method. Duncan praises both the "method of science" (deduction) and the "natural method" (empiricism), but he carefully circumscribes the claims of each. For example, Duncan points out that conclusions properly deduced from self-evident premises intuitively arrived at are "eternal, necessary, and immutable Truths."[24] But such conclusions, he cautioned, do not necessarily conform to a reality outside the mind: for those who know the definition of a circle, it will always be true that the center is equidistant from any point on the circumference, but it "does not follow, because I have the Idea of a Circle in my Mind, that therefore a Figure answering to that Idea, has a real Existence in Nature. I can form to myself the Notion of a Centaur, or a golden Mountain, but never imagine on that account, that either of them exist."[25] For Duncan, the error of the Cartesians and Aristotelians—and for Malthus, the error of Condorcet and Godwin—was to assume that what has a basis in logic has a foundation in fact; such a method, Duncan writes, "opens a Way to Castles in the Air of our own building, to many chimerical and fanciful Systems, which Men of warm and lively Imaginations love to entertain themselves with; but promises little of that Knowledge which is worth a wise Man's Regard, and respects the great Ends and Purposes of Life."[26] The corrective to the limitations of deduction is the method of Newton—one that combines deduction and empiricism: "In this manner Sir *Isaac Newton,* having determined the Laws of Gravity by a Variety of Experiments, and laying it down as a Principle, that it operates according to those Laws thro' the whole System of Nature; has thence in a Way of strict Demonstration, deduced the whole Theory of heavenly Motions. For granting once this *Postulatum,* that Gravity belongs universally to all Bodies, and that it acts according to their solid Content, decreasing with the Distance in a given Ratio; what Sir *Isaac* has determined in regard to the Planetary Motions, follows from the bare Consideration of our own Ideas; that is, necessarily and *scientifically.*"[27] This method, Duncan goes on to assert, can be applied to works of politics and morality: "The same thing happens in Politicks and Morality. If we form to ourselves Ideas of such Communities, Connections, Actions, and Conjectures, as do or may subsist among Mankind; all our Reasonings and Conclusions will then respect real Life, and serve as steddy Maxims of Behaviour in the several Circumstances to which it is liable. It is not therefore enough that we set about the Consideration of any Ideas at random; we must further take care that those Ideas truly regard Things themselves: for although Knowledge is always certain when derived from the Contemplation of our own Ideas, yet is it then only useful and worthy our Regard, when it respects Ideas taken from the real Objects of Nature, and strictly related to the Concerns of human Life."[28]

In the *Essay,* Malthus explicitly follows Duncan, associating his method with Duncan's version of Newton's. His method of arrangement conforms to Duncan's recommended "Synthetick Method."[29] This method of arrangement prescribes summarizing the principles and conclusions in syllogistic form at the outset, as distinct from the "Analytick Method," which, following the

presumed actual order of discovery, prescribes presenting the conclusions after presenting the evidence and at the end of the work. Malthus first presents his "postulata": that food is necessary for man and that the passion between the sexes will remain in its present state (11). Since these are postulata, that is self-evident, applied propositions,[30] they are capable of yielding "incontrovertible truths," as Malthus later claims (38). He next summarizes his argument in syllogistic form:

> Assuming then, my postulata as granted, I say, that the power of population is indefinitely greater than the power in the earth to produce subsistence for man.
>
> [Because]
>
> Population, when unchecked, increases in a geometrical ratio. Subsistence increases only in an arithmetical ratio. A slight acquaintance with numbers will shew the immensity of the first power in comparison of the second.
>
> [But]
>
> By the law of our nature which makes food necessary to the life of man, the effects of these two unequal powers must be kept equal.
>
> [Therefore]
>
> This implies a strong and constantly operating check on population from the difficulty of subsistence. This difficulty must fall some where; and must necessarily be severely felt by a large portion of mankind.
>
> (13-14)

After applying his postulata (what Duncan and other logicians call "scholia")[31] to the animal world, Malthus concludes in the spirit of *quod erat demonstratum*: "Consequently, if the premises are just, the argument is conclusive against the perfectibility of the mass of mankind" (17).

Duncan observed, quoting Locke, that "in all sorts of Reasonings, every single Argument should be managed as a Mathematical Demonstration, the Connection and Dependence of Ideas should be followed, till the Mind is brought to the Source on which it bottoms, and can trace the Coherence through the whole Train of Proofs."[32] Malthus's "postulata," "propositions," "laws," his insistence that his theory is undeniable because his principle is "so evident that it needs no illustration" (37): this is the language of deduction from self-evident propositions—the language of geometry. Whatever contribution, if any, this "method of science" (to use Duncan's phrase) made to Malthus's discovery or validation of his theory, the rehearsal of it in the opening chapters of the *Essay* is a means of persuasion. But Duncan's recommended "synthetick method" only begins with deduction. In the manner of Newton, we must confirm these valid conclusions from self-evident truths by subjecting them to an empirical test—the "natural method." In the *Essay,* the appeal to empiricism is also a means of persuasion. Malthus insists that, if his theory is to be judged true, it must be tested against experience: "and I think it will be found," he writes in concluding the first chapter, "that experience, the true source and foundation of all knowledge, invariably confirms its truth" (17). This is a promise and a prediction he fulfills in tracing the operation of his principle of population in societies throughout the history of civilization in Chapters III-VII. Duncan's *Elements* was the most popular logic of its day—it was into its ninth English edition by 1800[33]—and Malthus's conspicuous insistence on the importance of both deduction and empiricism in the first two chapters of the *Essay* would have had considerable persuasive impact on the educated portion of his audience who would associate Duncan's synthesis with Newton's method and Newton with truth.

In Chapters IX-XV, which comprise Malthus's refutation, the analogy of the *Essay* to the *Principia* is manifest. Malthus's criticism of Condorcet and Godwin tends to move quickly from an attack on a particular policy or prediction to the mode of reasoning on which it rests—on the assumption that if the method is wrong, the details need not be argued. Malthus faults Condorcet and Godwin on two counts: first, they ignore experience, and thus their conclusions are not empirical; second, in their enthusiasm for logic, they commit the fallacy that Aristotle identifies as inferring an absolute from a particular (*Rhetoric*, 1402[a]), in this case by moving from a premise that improvement is possible to the conclusion that unlimited improvement or perfection is probable. In sum, they confuse logical consistency for empirical reality, a confusion that parallels the criticism made by the English against the Cartesians, who "insisted on phenomena which they regarded as logically necessary but for which they could bring no actual evidence."[34] In the *Essay*, Malthus casts Condorcet and Godwin as Cartesians to play opposite to his Newton.

The circumstances in which Condorcet composed his *Sketch for a Historical Picture of the Progress of the Human Mind* are for Malthus evidence that Condorcet adheres to a theory in the face of compelling evidence to its contrary. Condorcet wrote the *Sketch* lauding the establishment of the French Republic as the apex of human progress and enlightenment while in hiding, under sentence of death, from the Reign of Terror. This irony, Malthus claims, is a "singular instance of the attachment of a man to principles, which every day's experience was so fatally for himself contradicting" (144). Malthus finds such blind adherence to theory characteristic of the thinking of Condorcet and Godwin. Malthus insists that Condorcet's prediction that man's longevity will increase "to an unlimited extent" rests on a similar valuation of logical possibility over empirical reality. That man's life span will increase to an "unlimited extent" is an inference that is "in the highest degree unphilosophical, and totally unwarranted by any appearances in the laws of nature" (157). In the absence of present evidence to support Condorcet's prediction, Malthus supposes that Condorcet advances it in the hope that evidence will later appear. This method, which if adopted generally would mark "an end to all human science," is the method not of Newton but of Descartes:

> If this be the case, there is at once an end of all human science. The whole train of reasonings from effects to causes will be destroyed. We may shut our eyes to the book of nature, as it will no longer be of any use to read it. The wildest and most improbable conjectures may be advanced with as much certainty as the most just and sublime theories, founded on careful and reiterated experiments. We may return again to the old mode of philosophizing, and make facts bend to systems, instead of establishing systems upon facts. The grand and consistent theory of Newton, will be placed upon the same footing as the wild and excentric hypotheses of Descartes.
>
> (158-59)

Condorcet's method is proof that, despite its progressive veneer, his and similar theories "so far from enlarging the bounds of human science, they are contracting it . . . [and] are throwing us back again almost into the infancy of knowledge . . . by substituting wild flights and unsupported assertions, for patient investigation, and well authenticated proofs" (161-2), Malthus writes in a note.

Malthus's critique of Godwin's ideas is the literal as well as the rhetorical center of the *Essay*: it begins in the tenth of the *Essay's* nineteen chapters. The analogy of Godwin-is-to-Descartes-as-Malthus-is-to-Newton, which is implied throughout Chapters IX-XV, can be illustrated by concentrating on two related arguments of Godwin's that Malthus is at particular pains to refute: first, Godwin's prediction that man's life span can be lengthened to approach immortality on earth; and, second, Godwin's speculation that the passion between the sexes will lessen nearly to the point of extinction. This second conjecture Godwin makes to answer the objection to the predicted increased longevity from the principle of population.

Both predictions rest on Godwin's argument that the mind can control the body, that a thought can reign absolutely over an urge. As evidence of mind over body Godwin had cited examples of the influence of mood on the experience of fatigue. But concluding from these particular examples of partial influence a general and absolute conclusion is, Malthus insists, fallacious: "the argument is from a small and partial effect, to a great and general effect, which will in numberless instances be found to be a very fallacious mode of reasoning" (222). In addition to being fallacious, since in the last thousand years "no decided difference has been observed in the duration of human life from the operation of intellect" (239), it also mistakes a logical possibility for an empirical probability. If in the absence of available empirical evidence, Godwin bases his prediction on evidence which he trusts will later appear, then Godwin has left science to dwell in the realm of prophecy (232); he has rejected Newton's uniform laws and thrown us upon "a wide field of uncertainty" where "any one supposition is then just as good as another" (232): "it is just as unphilosophical to suppose that the life of man may be prolonged beyond any assignable limits, as to suppose that the attraction of the earth will gradually be changed into repulsion, and that stones will ultimately rise instead of fall, or that the earth will fly off at a certain period to some more genial and warmer sun" (239-40).

Malthus's refutation of Godwin's apparent prediction of an end of concupiscence follows similar lines. To infer from the axiom "man is rational" that humans will one day be only and always so and thus will have complete control of appetites is fallacious. Malthus presents this reasoning as analogous to the natural philosopher's or physicist's that assumes that phenomena will act in nature as they do in the laboratory:

> Mr. Godwin considers man too much in the light of a being merely intellectual. This error, at least such I conceive it to be, pervades his whole work, and mixes itself with all his reasonings. The voluntary actions of men may originate in their opinions; but these opinions will be very differently modified in creatures compounded of a rational faculty and corporal propensities, from what they would be, in beings wholly intellectual. Mr. Godwin, in proving that sound reasoning and truth, are capable of being adequately communicated, examines the proposition first practically; and then adds, "Such is the appearance which this proposition assumes, when examined in a loose and practical view. In strict consideration it will not admit of debate. Man is a rational being, etc." So far from calling this a strict consideration of the subject, I own I should call it the loosest, and most erroneous way possible, of considering it. It is the calculating the velocity of a falling body in vacuo; and persisting in it, that it would be the same through whatever resisting mediums it might fall. This was not Newton's mode of philosophizing. Very few general propositions are just in application to a particular subject. The moon is not kept in her orbit round the earth, nor the earth in her orbit round the sun, by a force that varies merely in the inverse ratio of the squares of the distances. To make the general theory just in application to the revolutions of these bodies, it was necessary to calculate accurately, the disturbing force of the sun upon the moon, and of the moon upon the earth; and till these disturbing forces were properly estimated, actual observations on the motions of these bodies, would have proved that the theory was not accurately true.
>
> (252-54)

This passage is resonant with allusions to the *Principia*. The key phrases are "resisting mediums" and "disturbing force." In the *Principia*, Book II, the title of which

is "The Motions of Bodies (In Resisting Mediums)," Newton considers the forces of motions as they would exist not in empty space (the subject of Book I), but as they exist in media that offer resistance—such as the motions of a pendulum in air or of a ship in water. In the conclusion of Book II, he brings the laws he has deduced on the effects of resisting media on motions to bear on Descartes' vortex theory in order to show the inadequacies of it, to show that Descartes' theory could not meet strict empirical or mathematical tests. Newton's approach is to accept for the purposes of argument the existence of Descartes' hypothetical primary matter—the invisible, divisible substance that carried the planets around in whirlwinds. Then, granting Descartes this premise, he shows that Descartes' conclusions do not follow from it. Newton points out, for example, that a fluid of the type required to offer sufficient resistance to carry the heavenly bodies would not form an orbit like that which Descartes' theory requires.[35] In part to contrast his own more rigorous mathematical and empirical method to Descartes' method, Newton demonstrates in Book III how even his more precise theory of gravity cannot completely account for the position of the moon unless the "disturbing influence" of the force of the sun's gravity upon the moon is figured into the equation. In Book III Newton proves with precise calculations that the apparent irregularities of the moon's motion result from the distant, and therefore relatively weak but nonetheless significant, pull of the sun's gravity on the moon.

Malthus's intention is for the reader to see Godwin's method as parallel to Descartes' and his own method as Newtonian. Specifically, Malthus insists that man's "corporal propensities" are "disturbing forces" that will prevent Godwin's rational man from behaving in life in the way that he would in the laboratory of Godwin's imagination. Malthus grants Godwin the premise that man is rational and even the inference that Godwin insists follows from it—that the voluntary actions of men originate in their opinions, which are susceptible to education. But man will not follow the course Godwin predicts when the model moves out of Godwin's imagination and into the world of resisting media and disturbing forces in which man's actions do not always follow his resolutions:

> I am willing to allow that every voluntary act is preceded by a decision of the mind; but it is strangely opposite to what I should conceive to be the just theory upon the subject, and a palpable contradiction to all experience, to say, that the corporal propensities of man do not act very powerfully, as disturbing forces, in these decisions. . . . The cravings of hunger, the love of liquor, the desire of possessing a beautiful woman, will urge men to actions, of the fatal consequences of which, to the general interests of society, they are perfectly well convinced, even at the very time they commit them. Remove their bodily cravings, and they would not hesitate a moment in determining against

such actions. . . . But . . . under all the circumstances of their situation with these bodily cravings, the decision of the compound being is different from the conviction of the rational being.

(254-55)

In a general sense, Malthus's entire critique of Godwin is best seen as an effort to do to Godwin's theoretical utopia what Newton did to Descartes' hypothetical vortex theory. Godwin's theory, Malthus insists at the outset of his refutation, lacks "the caution that sound philosophy seems to require" and "relies too much on general and abstract propositions," ignoring at its peril applications and experience (173-74). But, as Newton did with Descartes, Malthus accepts for the purposes of argument Godwin's unrealistic view of man as "merely intellectual" and assumes that Godwin's utopia, in which luxury is despised and benevolence and reason reign, came to pass. Would this society last? Let us put it to stricter tests, Malthus says. In the absence of war, unhealthy conditions and the fear of starvation, the rate of population, Malthus concludes, would equal or surpass the doubling time of twenty-five years of North America, where conditions, though conducive to rapid population growth, were not as stimulative as Godwin's society would be. Food increase could not keep up for long. What then?

> Alas! What becomes of the picture where men lived in the midst of plenty: where no man was obliged to provide with anxiety and pain for his restless wants: where the narrow principle of selfishness did not exist: where Mind was delivered from her perpetual anxiety about corporal support, and free to expatiate in the field of thought which is congenial to her. This beautiful fabric of imagination vanishes at the severe touch of truth. The spirit of benevolence, cherished and invigorated by plenty, is repressed by the chilling breath of want. The hateful passions that had vanished, reappear. The mighty law of self-preservation, expels all the softer and more exalted emotions of the soul. The temptations to evil are too strong for human nature to resist. The corn is plucked before it is ripe, or secreted in unfair proportions; and the whole black train of vices that belong to falsehood are immediately generated. Provisions no longer flow in for the support of the mother with the large family. The children are sickly from insufficient food. The rosy flush of health gives place to the pallid cheek and hollow eye of misery. Benevolence yet lingering in a few bosoms, makes some faint expiring struggles, till at length self-love resumes his wonted empire, and lords it triumphant over the world.

> No human institutions here existed, to the perverseness of which Mr. Godwin ascribes the original sin of the worst men. No opposition had been produced by them between public and private good. No monopoly had been created of those advantages which reason directs to be left in common. No man had been goaded to the breach of order by unjust laws. Benevolence had established her reign in all hearts: and yet in so short a period as within fifty years, violence, oppression, falsehood, misery, every hateful vice, and every form of

distress, which degrade and sadden the present state of society, seem to have been generated by the most imperious circumstances, by laws inherent in the nature of man, and absolutely independent of all human regulations.

(189-91)

What Newton does with numbers and mathematical formulae to Descartes, Malthus does with rhetorical devices to Godwin. For an example, focus on the phrase "chilling breath of want." The brevity of this phrase in contrast to the long first sentence, which is lengthened by anaphora, mirrors rhetorically the calculus by which a single natural imperative (the principle of population) can defeat the most ingenious and elaborate of human plans. Furthermore, in its parallelism to and latinate play off the preceding "spirit of benevolence," the phrase ("chilling breath of want") sets the concreteness of Malthus's empirically-based laws of nature as rhetorical foil to Godwin's illusionary "picture." The same oppositions are underscored rhetorically in the antitheses that contrast the "mighty law of self preservation" to "the softer or more exalted emotions of the soul," and the idealized "rosy flush of health" to the "pallid cheek and hollow eye of misery." In the next paragraph, the repetition of "no" and the listing of "violence, oppression, falsehood, misery, every hateful vice, and every form of distress" (asyndeton) extend the reader's experience of the futility of man's efforts in the face of nature's inexorable laws. Through these stylistic devices, Malthus works to assure that Godwin's predictions will fail the test of his readers' experience.

The theodicy of the *Essay's* final two chapters has troubled some commentators, but the motivation for it is clear when it is recognized that Malthus imitates the *Principia.* In Chapters XVIII and XIX, Malthus attempts to "'Vindicate the ways of God to man'" (349). The tendency of population to increase more rapidly than the production of food is here seen as "the goad of necessity" that prompts a sluggish, inert mankind to activity. Indeed, the principle of population is a divine instrument for the creation and formation of mind (354). Evil in the form of the positive checks exists "not to create despair, but activity" (395). This explanation is obviously inspired by the bleakness of the cosmology of much of the *Essay.* But its appropriateness has been questioned by commentators on the grounds that the argument of the *Essay* is compromised by Malthus's effort to hit two "targets at one time—the scientific . . . and the theistic."[36] Malthus's decision to drop the theodicy from subsequent editions of the *Essay* may be indicative of his judgment of its success as a convincing explanation of the misery he portrays as endemic to the creation of an omnipotent, loving God. But whatever the success of the theodicy, Malthus took inspiration from the *Principia.* In the concluding chapter of the *Principia,* Newton argues that the study of nature is a way of knowing the existence and attributes of God, that the divine telos is obvious from the symmetry of the world. Since we know God through his creation, Newton argues, discourse about God "does certainly belong to Natural Philosophy."[37] Newton's dictum and practice depart markedly from the Cartesians'. In his *Principles,* Descartes declares it impossible for us to know God's purposes.[38] Descartes' followers carried the implication of his work further, making independence from theology a distinction of the new science.[39] To Malthus and the English, the Cartesians' acceptance of an ethereal "primary matter" while simultaneously banishing theology from science gave credence to the characterization of them as scholastic philosophers reincarnate in a godless form. In the *Essay,* Malthus observes a similar "inconsistency" of Godwin and Condorcet, who hold to the possibility of the near immortality of the body, while denying the immortality of the soul, "an event indefinitely more probable" (248).

The rhetoric of the *Essay* is, then, characterized by Malthus's imitation and evocation of the *Principia.* Malthus hoped his readers would see that his *Essay* debates the same question that Newton addresses in the *Principia*: what constitutes valid explanation. Newton's famous formulation in the preface to the *Principia* of his achievement could serve, with changes appropriate to their different subjects, as Malthus's statement of the *Essay*'s achievement: "I offer this work as the mathematical principles of philosophy, for the whole burden of philosophy seems to consist in this—from the phenomena of motions to investigate the forces of nature, and then from these forces to demonstrate the other phenomena."[40] As set forth in the *Principia,* Newton's program is to move from the investigation of basic phenomena, for example, the laws of motion, to an understanding and mathematical expression of the laws of forces, for example, gravity. Mathus wants his readers to understand his work as analogous to the program of the *Principia.* His postulation that population when unchecked tends to increase at a geometric rate parallels Newton's First Law of motion: "*Every body continues in its state of rest, or of uniform motion in a right line, unless it is compelled to change that state by forces impressed upon it*";[41] Malthus writes, "The passion between the sexes has appeared in every age to be so nearly the same, that it may always be considered, in algebraic language, as a given quantity" (128), its momentum slowed only by the "checks" of famine, disease, and other manifestations of the misery and vice that result from the inability of the food supply to keep pace. Similarly, Newton's achievement was to show that the laws of terrestrial mechanics applied also to the heavenly bodies: the force that brought the apple to the ground was the same force that set the relative position of the moon and earth. So also Malthus can bring his principle of population to bear on a Godwinian future as remote in time as the moon is distant in space be-

cause, he claims, the principle of population, like gravity, is a universal law.

Thus the "Principle" of Malthus's title echoes Newton's "Principia" because Malthus intends his readers to understand that his refutation of Condorcet and Godwin is focused on their false understanding of what constitutes valid explanation. In his Preface to the *Principia,* Roger Cotes, with the Cartesians in mind, wrote that the "business of true philosophy is to derive the natures of things from causes truly existent, and to inquire after those laws on which the Great Creator actually chose to found this most beautiful Frame of the World, not those by which he might have done the same, had he so pleased."[42] Malthus hoped to persuade his readers that he had embraced and followed this program of the "new philosophy," that his predictions rested on fixed physical laws. As he writes in the *Essay,* these laws are "not remote, latent and mysterious; but near us, round about us, and open to investigation of every inquiring mind" (127), not the "occult," "mysterious" explanations of Godwin and Condorcet that existed in a world that hypothetically could be but never was. Malthus's effort was not lost on his contemporaries, who styled him "The Newton of political philosophy."[43]

Obviously, the power and appeal of Malthus's *Essay* transcend his time. The source of the *Essay*'s enduring appeal cannot directly be traced to its evocation of the *Principia,* however: most readers today are not likely to hear the echoes of Newton's work, and those who do are not likely to be persuaded by them.[44] Nonetheless, the *Essay*'s enduring power does indirectly derive from Malthus's imitation of Newton.

Malthus's efforts to establish his principle of population as a uniform, immutable law that parallels Newton's law of gravity is the source of the *Essay*'s powerful simplicity, a facet of the *Essay* that derives from Malthus's imitation of Newton. According to the *Essay,* want resulting from the tendency of population growth to outpace food increases caused the evolution of man from hunter, to shepherd, to farmer (45); the "struggle for room and food" gave birth to the warrior class, caused the Mongolian invasions, and makes war inevitable (48-49); practices such as exposing aging parents and infant children that, in violating "the most natural principle of the human heart," seem incomprehensible become predictable in light of the principle of population. Famine and plague, the intractability of poverty, the problem of pain: in the *Essay,* the explanation of all these is the principle of population. In short, Malthus's effort to establish for the principle of population uniformity and universality that parallels Newton's immutable, eternal laws of nature leads him to claim for his principle an influence considerably beyond what is required to refute the particulars of Condorcet's and Godwin's arguments. In the *Essay,* the principle of population is a single, centripetal cause that governs the laws of history, political economy, anthropology, and sociology. Especially for those frustrated by man's inability to solve the most basic problems and defeated by the complexities of human experience, the comprehensibility and comprehensiveness of the *Essay* make it almost irresistible. The effect results from Malthus's imitation of the *Principia*.

Similarly, Malthus's insistence on the need to subject axioms to the empirical test, in imitation of Newton, is the motivation for the descriptions that mark the *Essay* and make it vital—a lively read. Malthus moves easily (too easily from the point of view of the science he lays claim to) from Baconian exhortations on the primacy of empiricism to a method that draws on "what we daily see around us . . . actual experience . . . facts that come within the scope of every man's observation" (53) as relevant to the practice of it. Whatever the methodological validity of this procedure, the result is credible and persuasive descriptions of, for example, people at all social ranks weighing the pleasures of marriage and family against the possibility of the resulting economic hardship:

> A man of liberal education, but with an income only just sufficient to enable him to associate in the rank of gentlemen, must feel absolutely certain, that if he marries and has a family, he shall be obliged, if he mixes at all in society, to rank himself with moderate farmers, and the lower class of tradesmen. The woman that a man of education would naturally make the object of his choice, would be one brought up in the same tastes and sentiments with himself, and used to the familiar intercourse of a society totally different from that to which she must be reduced by marriage. Can a man consent to place the object of his affection in a situation so discordant, probably, to her tastes and inclinations? Two or three steps of descent in society, particularly at this round of the ladder, where education ends, and ignorance begins, will not be considered by the generality of people, as a fancied and chimerical, but a real and essential evil. . . .
>
> These considerations undoubtedly prevent a great number in this rank of life from following the bent of their inclinations in an early attachment.
>
> (64-65)

My readers might especially identify with the dilemma of this man of "liberal education," but in the *Essay* we can find the same realistic depiction of human motivation at other "rounds of the ladder":

> The labourer who earns eighteen pence a day, and lives with some degree of comfort as a single man, will hesitate a little before he divides that pittance among four or five, which seems to be just sufficient for one. Harder fare and harder labour he would submit to, for the sake of living with the woman that he loves; but he must feel conscious, if he thinks at all, that, should he have a large family, and any ill luck whatever, no degree of

frugality, no possible exertion of his manual strength, could preserve him from the heart rending sensation of seeing his children starve, or of forfeiting his independence, and being obliged to the parish for their support.

> (67)

These pictures of "man reasoning," whatever their value as empirical evidence, are more convincing than Godwin's portrait of a theoretical "Rational Man," who is capable not only of defeating acquisitiveness but also of dismissing the claims of beauty and feeling to embrace intellectual pleasures. Furthermore, while the portraits in the *Essay* are of "economic man," the economic motive is not presented in them as an end in itself but as the means to achieving a fuller humanity.

It is also Malthus's claim to the empiricist's habit of mind that is the source of his insistence in the *Essay* that we are blind to the reality before us—an insistence that often brings to the experience of reading the *Essay* the excitement of discovery. As have empiricists before him and since, Malthus claims that we are blinded by our preconceptions and prejudices. They have prevented us from seeing the operation of the principle of population. Our histories, Malthus says, are "histories only of the higher classes" (32); as a result, the cycle that begins with a food supply sufficient to support the population, that indirectly promotes an increase in population that eventually outruns the food supply, and that ends in the malnutrition of "the children of the poor" has not been "remarked by superficial observers" (31) and has been "less decidedly confirmed by experience, than might naturally be expected" (32). We are blinded, too, by stereotypes, as well as by class prejudice. Romantic notions cause us to "fix our eyes only on the warrior in the prime of life," when we consider the putative happiness of the North American Indian, and distract us from the plight of the Indian woman, who, exhausted by the tribe's constant migrations in search of food and weakened by her own hunger, frequently miscarries (42). Similarly, only those observers like Malthus who "have attended to bills of mortality" (72) see the actual reality of country life, obscured as the true picture of this life is by our stereotypic notions of the healthy, happy farm hand:

> The sons and daughters of peasants will not be found such rosy cherubs in real life, as they are described to be in romances. It cannot fail to be remarked by those who live much in the country, that the sons of labourers are very apt to be stunted in their growth, and are a long while arriving at maturity. Boys that you would guess to be fourteen or fifteen, are upon inquiry, frequently found to be eighteen or nineteen. And the lads who drive plough, which must certainly be healthy exercise, are very rarely seen with any appearance of calves to their legs.
>
> (73)

The reader is struck by the specificity of the observation—the calveless legs of the plough boy. Among the postulata and axioms, ratios, numbers, and talk of "the poor," the fleshy particularity of the phrase startles. Apparently, Malthus cares enough to notice.

The close and sympathetic observations that mark the *Essay* complicate the ethos Malthus presents. They invite the reader to see him as more than the Newtonian scientist who brings the reality of laws and numbers to destroy Godwin's lofty abstractions. Nor is he only the "hard-hearted realist" who "tells it like it is." In the sympathy suggested by their particularity, these observations lend credence to Malthus's claim that his attack on the Poor Laws was motivated by their tendency to veil the true causes of poverty, to lower the wages of labor and raise the price of food, and to cheat their recipients by not delivering the permanent relief they seem to promise in exchange for submission to bureaucratic regulation. If Malthus is to be faulted, it is for a failure in intellect—his inability to see how poverty is itself a cause of over-population, for instance—not for a failure in sympathy.

CONCLUSION

It is ironic that today Malthus is often thought of as an early social scientist—as "England's first political economist" or demographer—and the *Essay* remembered as the acknowledged catalyst for Darwin's and Wallace's theories of evolution by natural selection. The iconoclastic intentions and mechanistic view of man that we often associate with the social scientist, Malthus identified with Godwin, whose work he undertook to refute. And regardless of what Darwin and Wallace learned from the *Essay* or, more importantly, regardless of the use to which Herbert Spencer might have put it, Malthus would never have advocated seeing warrant in nature for England's political and social inequalities. Malthus should not be viewed as an incipient social scientist or a precursor of the social Darwinists, but, with Swift, Pope, Johnson, Reynolds, Gibbon, and Burke, as part of the mainstream of an English humanism that began with Colet and Erasmus, who, in the Renaissance, took inspiration from Cicero and Quintilian and reformed the curriculum of England's schools.[45] Malthus's motives are the moral ones and his method is the verbal art of the ideal of that tradition—the rhetorician. He judged the ideas and program of Condorcet and Godwin dangerous, and he undertook to refute them. In the course of his refutation, he rediscovered the principle of population:

> The most important argument that I shall adduce is certainly not new. The principles on which it depends have been explained in part by Hume, and more at large by Dr. Adam Smith. It has been advanced and applied to the present subject, though not with its proper weight, or in the most forcible point of view, by Mr. Wallace: and it may probably have been stated by many writers that I have never met with. I should certainly

therefore not think of advancing it again, though I mean to place it in a point of view in some degree different from any that I have hitherto seen, if it had ever been fairly and satisfactorily answered.

(8)

In other words, Malthus discovered the importance ("weight") of an idea (the principle of population) whose significance ("force") to a philosophical and political question important to his contemporaries had not been elucidated. By claiming that the principle was a universal, eternal law (placing it in a different "point of view"), he gave to it new meaning as a centripetal law of history. This seems to me a just statement of Malthus's achievement, and it is a distinctively rhetorical one.[46]

Notes

1. 1798; rpt. London, Royal Economic Society: Macmillan, 1926. All quotations from Malthus's *Essay on Population* in this paper are taken from this edition.

2. Review of *Principles of Political Economy considered with a View to their Practical Application*, 2nd ed., *Edinburgh Review* 64 (1837): 483.

3. See Kenneth Smith, *The Malthusian Controversy* (London: Routledge and Kegan Paul, 1951) for a discussion of this response.

4. *New Letters of Robert Southey,* ed. Kenneth Curry (New York: Columbia Univ. Press, 1965), 1: 326-27, quoted in Patricia James, *Population Malthus: His Life and Times* (London: Routledge & Kegan Paul, 1979), 103.

5. Marx, *Capital: A Critique of Political Economy,* trans. Samuel Moore and Edward Aveling and ed. Friedrich Engels (Chicago: Charles H. Kerr & Co., 1912), 1: 675; Downs, *Books That Changed the World* (New York: New American Library, 1956).

6. *The Spirit of the Age or Contemporary Portraits* (Oxford: World's Classics, 1947), 161.

7. The *Essay* has been analyzed by political scientists, economists, demographers, and historians, but, for the most part, these scholars ignore the contribution Malthus's rhetorical skill made to his success. Exceptions to this generalization are John Maynard Keynes, who notes that the first *Essay* "is bold and rhetorical in style with much *bravura* of language and sentiment" and William D. Grampp who points out that what gave the *Essay* "its arresting quality" was the way the arguments "were put forward, the way they were brought into relation with each other, and the way they were employed to reduce the work of Godwin to a

pathetic ruin. Malthus's *Essay* is a marvelous piece of rhetoric." Neither writer goes beyond the observation of the rhetorical power of the *Essay* to consider the specific causes of it, however. See Keynes, *Essays in Biography* (London: Macmillan, 1933), 117; and Grampp, "Malthus and His Contemporaries," *History of Political Economy* 6 (1974): 294.

8. It is to Malthus's credit that economists and demographers have found so much in the *Essay* (especially in the 1803 and subsequent editions) seminal to their disciplines that today "the *Essay* is regarded only as a treatise on economics," as J. M. Pullen observes with dismay. I do not intend to denigrate either Malthus's contributions or the efforts of modern scholars who have paid homage to them. Nonetheless, language such as the following from Joseph J. Spengler, "Malthus sought to fashion cybernetic systems of collective control over fertility systems, generating feedbacks which would, in his opinion, give rise to prudential behavior respecting marriage and fertility," even while it frames Malthus's place and contribution for demographers and economists, misleadingly pictures Malthus as a demographer or economist in front of a computer terminal attempting to create a model useful to a social engineer. But whatever contribution Malthus made to economics and demography was an incidental by-product of his goal, which was victory over Godwin, and his intentions, which were moral. See Pullen, "Malthus' Theological Ideas and Their Influence on his Principle of Population," *History of Political Economy* 13 (1981): 52; Spengler, "Malthus on Godwin's *Of Population*," *Demography* 8 (1971): 10.

9. James Bonar, *Malthus and His Work* (1885; rpt. London: Frank Cass, 1966), 7.

10. Malthus cannot and does not claim to have "discovered" the principle of population. In 1752, Hume pointed out the tendency of population "to more than double every generation," restrained to greater or lesser degree depending on a country's agriculture and government, and Robert Wallace noted the importance of food supply and governmental encouragements to marriage as determinants of population. Passages such as the following from Adam Smith's *The Wealth of Nations* anticipate many passages in Malthus: "Every species of animals naturally multiplies in proportion to the means of their subsistence, and no species can ever multiply beyond it. But in civilised society it is only among the inferior ranks of people that the scantiness of subsistence can set limits to the further multiplication of the human species; and it can do so in no other way than by destroying a great part of the children which their fruitful

marriages produce." (See *An Essay on the Principle of Population: Text, Sources, and Background Criticism,* ed. Philip Appleman [New York: Norton, 1976], 3-7 where the relevant passages are conveniently reproduced.) Malthus himself acknowledges the contribution of Hume, Wallace and Smith in the *Essay's* first chapter, noting that the "most important argument that I shall adduce is certainly not new" (8). Malthus's contribution is the dramatic way in which he establishes the significance of the principle—that it is fatal to the predictions of Enlightenment optimists.

11. William Godwin, *Enquiry Concerning Political Justice and Its Influence on Morals and Happiness,* ed. F. E. L. Priestley, 3 vols. (3rd ed., 1797; Toronto: Univ. of Toronto Press, 1946); Condorcet, *Sketch* trans. June Barraclough and introd. Stuart Hampshire (London: Weidenfeld and Nicolson, 1955).

12. Godwin, *Political Justice,* 2:16; see also 233-304 for Godwin's views on religion and government and 420-67 for his attack on unlimited property rights and his advocacy of a system of equality.

13. Godwin, *Political Justice,* 1: 24.

14. *The Monthly Review* 28 (Sept., 1798): 2.

15. *The Annual Review; and History of Literature* 2 (1803): 295.

16. Karl Marx, *Capital,* 1: 676.

17. Throughout the *Essay,* Malthus insists that the Poor Laws indirectly lower the wage of labor because their promise to support a needy family lessens the preventive check, promotes population, increases the supply of (child) laborers, and, thus, lowers the wage. He also accuses "farmers and capitalists" of "growing rich from the real cheapness of labour" during periods of stable wages and rising costs and of a "conspiracy" to repress wages and to keep the causes of lower real wages (population and inflation) from the laborer. Eliminating the Poor Laws will increase labor's understanding of its plight and enable workers to act on their own behalf to direct their fate. (See *Essay,* 34-36 and 85-86, for instance.)

18. *Annual Review* 2 (1803): 295.

19. *Annual Review* 2 (1803): 292 and 295.

20. The Newtonian's side in the controversy is presented in terms contemporary to Malthus in Roger Cotes's Preface to the second edition of the *Principia* (1713), a preface which was commissioned by Newton's publishers to counter the continuing influence of Descartes' theory. The Preface was

also included in the 1726 edition of the *Principia,* which Malthus owned. In this paper I quote from the standard, modern edition of the eighteenth-century translation of the *Principia,* that is, *Sir Isaac Newton's Mathematical Principles of Natural Philosophy and His System of the World,* trans. Andrew Motte, 1729; rev. Florian Cajori (Berkeley: Univ. of California Press, 1946). This edition includes Cotes's famous Preface (xx-xxxiii). For more information on Cotes's Preface and details on the controversy, see Cajori's "An Historical and Explanatory Appendix" in this edition, 629-32.

21. Wilbur Samuel Howell, *Eighteenth-Century British Logic and Rhetoric* (Princeton: Princeton Univ. Press, 1971), 360.

22. Quoted in Bonar, *Malthus and His Work,* 407-08.

23. "Nowhere," Howell notes of the eighteenth century, "is it more certain that the historical study of the logics and rhetorics used as textbooks in a given century will make rich contributions to an understanding of the literary works produced at that time," as Howell demonstrates in his study of the influence of Duncan's *Elements* on Jefferson's composition of the Declaration of Independence. See Howell, *Eighteenth-Century British Logic and Rhetoric,* 348; and Howell, "The Declaration of Independence and Eighteenth-Century Logic," *The William and Mary Quarterly,* 3rd ser., 18 (1961): 463-84.

24. *Elements of Logic,* English Linguistics 1500-1800 (A Collection of Facsimile Reprints), ed., R. C. Alson, No. 203 (1748; Menston, England: Scolar Press), 148. Malthus's copy of Duncan's *Elements* (1752) and his copy of the 1726 edition of the *Principia* are part of the Malthus Library at Jesus College, Cambridge. See *The Malthus Library Catalogue: The Personal Collection of Thomas Robert Malthus at Jesus College, Cambridge* (New York: Pergamon Press, 1983).

25. Duncan, 146.

26. Duncan, 340.

27. Duncan, 330-31.

28. Duncan, 341-42.

29. Duncan, 275.

30. Duncan, 177 and 185.

31. Duncan, 187-88.

32. Duncan, 224-25.

33. Howell, *Eighteenth-Century British Logic and Rhetoric,* 361.

34. Herbert Butterfield, *The Origins of Modern Science, 1300-1800* (New York: Macmillan, 1957), 148.

35. *Sir Isaac Newton's Mathematical Principles,* 395-96.

36. Samuel M. Levin, "Malthus and the Idea of Progress," *Journal of the History of Ideas* 27 (1966): 106.

37. *Sir Isaac Newton's Mathematical Principles,* 546.

38. *The Meditations and Selections from the Principles of Rene Descartes,* trans. John Veitch (Chicago: Open Court Publishing Co., 1903), 192.

39. Edwin Arthur Burtt, *The Metaphysical Foundations of Modern Physical Science: A Historical and Critical Essay,* rev. ed. (London: Routledge Kegan Paul, 1932), 114-16, 160-63.

40. *Sir Isaac Newton's Mathematical Principles,* Preface to the First Edition, xvii-xviii.

41. *Sir Isaac Newton's Mathematical Principles,* 13. The parallel of Newton's First Law to Malthus's law of population increase is made by Anthony Flew, "The Structure of Malthus' Population Theory," *Australasian Journal of Philosophy* 35 (1957): 16-17.

42. Cotes's Preface, xxvii.

43. *The Annual Review; and History of Literature,* 6 (1807), 351.

44. Fredrick Rosen, for example, observes that Malthus attempts "the substitution of a utopian method of inquiry for [Godwin's] utopian theory of society," "The Principle of Population as Political Theory: Godwin's *Of Population* and the Malthusian Controversy," *Journal of the History of Ideas* 31 (1970): 38.

45. Works on the ideal of the rhetorician in the Renaissance are too well known to require, and too numerous to permit, mention, but for the humanist tradition in the eighteenth century of which I think Malthus is a part, see Paul Fussell, *The Rhetorical World of Augustan Humanism: Ethics and Imagery from Swift to Burke* (Oxford: Clarendon Press, 1965).

46. I thank John A. Campbell of the University of Washington, Tom Clayton and Tom Scanlan, both of the University of Minnesota, John Harrison of the Old Library, Jesus College, Cambridge, and Eileen Dugliss Walzer for reading, correcting, and commenting thoughtfully on this paper in its earlier stage.

Samuel Hollander (essay date 1997)

SOURCE: Hollander, Samuel. "Utilitarianism in a Theological Context." In *The Economics of Thomas Robert Malthus,* pp. 917-48. Toronto: University of Toronto Press, 1997.

[*In the following excerpt, Hollander explores Malthus's version of theological utilitarianism, claiming that his roles as Christian moralist and political economist were not incompatible.*]

I INTRODUCTION

Whether Malthus was a 'Utilitarian' is still a debated issue. D. P. O'Brien, for example, maintains that 'only the two Mills, part from Bentham himself, were really Utilitarians' (1975, 25). Against this we have the view of Lord Robbins: 'The principle that the test of policy is to be its effect on human happiness . . . is common to all the English Classical Economists. We get the picture badly out of focus if we conceive that reliance on the principle of utility was confined to Bentham and his immediate circle' (1952, 177). The justice of Robbins's perspective has been demonstrated in chapter 18 with specific reference to the population problem. A related issue is considered in this chapter: the role of Malthus's theodicy in establishing him as a 'theological' utilitarian.

The final two chapters of the first edition of the *Essay on Population* (1798) treat the compatibility of the 'disheartening' outcome of the population principle with a beneficent deity. The theodicy in these chapters, it has been argued, 'though often treated as an embarrassing and detachable part of the *Essay* . . . contains essential clues to the form of theological utilitarianism which underlies Malthus's moral philosophy' (Winch, 1987, 18-19). The removal of these concluding chapters in the later editions should not be misinterpreted: 'It is a mistake to believe that Malthus abandoned the brand of theological utilitarianism contained in his earlier theodicy in order to become a more secular social theorist; there was no conflict between Malthus the Christian "moral" philosopher and Malthus the scientist. The retention of the categories of vice and virtue, alongside, indeed attached to, pain and happiness, testify to their continuing importance. Indeed, an understanding of what precisely was 'moral' about moral restraint requires constant reference to the methodological standpoint of the theological utilitarian, for whom the greatest surplus of virtue and happiness over vice and misery was the supreme criterion for judging the worth of individual actions and social outcomes' (37).[1]

I do not deny a 'moral' dimension to Malthus's utilitarianism, though the same holds true with respect to Bentham and Mill. But my analysis supports Lord Rob-

bins's position that Malthus's explanation of 'disharmonies' by reference to Divine Wisdom is 'extraneous to analysis' and without influence on the theory of policy (1952, 28n).[2] More strongly, the last two chapters in the 1798 essay turn out to be an embarrassment, and the apologia for a benevolent Deity is radically altered in later editions.

Whether Malthus envisaged a net balance of temporal good, taking into account *this* world considered across time and space, is not absolutely clear from the theological chapters. But it is clear that what temporal good is envisaged is there unrelated to the magnitude of labour's *per-capita* income; aggregate population takes centre stage. And from his universalist perspective, Malthus represented the 'distress' characterizing the specific case of 'old settled countries'—such as Britain—as a *partial* evil that is overwhelmingly outweighed when full allowance is made for the purely spiritual dimension (and possibly outweighed, one should add, even on a universalist temporal view). This may satisfy theologians, but it clashes with the first *Essay* as a whole where, when dealing with the specifics of the British case, the magnitude of labour's *per-capita* income is the central policy concern, and suggestions are made for the mitigation of poverty through social and private action.

The *Essay* closes, it is true, with a protestation that the theological message is not one of 'despair,' since the quantity of 'evil' varies with activity or indolence. This might appear to open the door for improvement in living standards. But the theme is stated at the same universalist level as the rest of the chapter rather than with any eye to the specifics of any particular case. And in any event Malthus felt constrained, as we shall see, to reiterate that evil could never 'be removed from the world' and that any variation in its weight with activity is designed Providentially to 'keep alive a constant *expectation* of throwing it off,' which seems to withdraw much of the initial allowance, unless (and this may indeed be the case) it relates specifically to *individual* instances of improvement.

There is in addition a problem emerging in the body of the *Essay* but conspicuously absent from the last two chapters—that any reduction in misery entails, in practice, vice, casting doubt on the benevolence of the Deity. It is this problem, brought to Malthus's attention by critics of the first *Essay,* that led him to introduce the matter of 'moral restraint,' though (as will be recalled from chapter 18: V) he believed it to be empirically irrelevant. A theological dimension thus certainly remains in 1803 and thereafter—the mere fact that the two concluding chapters of 1798 disappear as such is of no consequence. Indeed, it is fair to say that the defence of the Deity is reinforced—though only if limited to an ideal rather than the real world, considering the practical insignificance of restraint. Even so, its substance differs from that of 1798. First, there is no longer any emphasis on the training of mind for a *future* existence, the most characteristic feature of the 1798 theodicy;[3] indeed there is considerable evidence that Malthus (perhaps as early as 1806) abandoned his unorthodox position. Second, the case for a reduction of poverty is now formally and conspicuously represented as a 'moral' issue, so that the theological problem is no longer to explain 'distress' but to explain the need for 'painful' checks to *avoid* distress.

Malthus also addressed the moral implications of the practical trade-off between vice and misery. But he approached practical policy issues in the manner of a social reformer, basing his recommendations on 'secular' utilitarian calculations; his taking account of 'vice' and 'virtue' does not gainsay this orientation, for the central feature of the theodicy of 1798 (training of mind for a 'superior' state of happiness) no longer plays a significant role. As for specifics, he was as much opposed to Church and State pressures towards a large population regardless of the consequences for living standards as he was to 'communist schemes' threatening the same outcome.[4] J. S. Mill adopted precisely this orientation: 'This great [Malthusian] doctrine, originally brought forward as an argument against the indefinite improvability of human affairs, we [the Philosophical Radicals] took up with ardent zeal in the contrary sense, as indicating the sole means of realizing that improvability by securing full employment at high wages to the whole labouring population through a voluntary restriction of the increase of their numbers' (1873/1981, I, 108). This comment on the 'original' doctrine is fair only if said of the theological chapters since, elsewhere in the first *Essay,* Malthus had pointed to the solution. But at least Mill recognized that a positive reformist attitude had ultimately been adopted by Malthus himself: 'Few writers have done more than himself, in the subsequent editions, to promote . . . juster and more hopeful anticipations' (1848/1965, III, 753).[5]

Section II, below, is devoted to the theological chapters of the 1798 version and the tension between them and the body of the work. Section III elaborates on the implicit secular or utilitarian orientation of the first *Essay* manifested particularly in the recommendation of prudential control, despite the inevitability of 'vice.' The following section considers moral restraint within a utilitarian framework, and demonstrates Malthus's continued efforts in 1803 and thereafter—despite the omission of the formal chapters on theology—to reconcile dogma and utility, a process involving effectively the undermining of the theological foundation. Section V carries this theme further, from the perspective of prudential control *tout court* as justified in terms of a net balance of social utility, very much in line with the procedures of the secular utilitarians. The desirability of

population expansion from a utility perspective, sharply contrasting with the standard religious case, is discussed in section VI; the argument is shown to open the door even to the justification of a stationary state in some circumstances. There are, it emerges, two theological stances—one emphasizing the *ideal* solution to the danger of potential population pressure; the other taking mankind as it is in *fact,* and arriving at a different set of recommendations. The concluding section summarizes the reasons for the decision to delete the theological chapters.

II THE THEOLOGICAL CHAPTERS OF THE FIRST *ESSAY*

The last two chapters of the 1798 *Essay* are designed to 'vindicate the ways of God to man' in the light of 'the constant pressure of distress on man from the difficulty of subsistence' (1986, 1, 122).[6] Malthus proceeded, as in an earlier footnote, to make a case envisaging this world as 'a mighty process for the creation and formation of mind' from matter, in the course of which 'many vessels will necessarily come out of this great furnace in wrong shapes. These will be broken and thrown aside as useless; while those vessels whose forms are full of truth, grace, and loveliness, will be wafted into happier situations, nearer the presence of the mighty maker' (88n).[7] This conception contrasts with a view of the world as a 'state of trial, and school of virtue, preparatory to a superior state of happiness,' since that implied 'a previously formed existence, that does not agree with the appearance of man in infancy' (122-3).[8] The essential difference is between the tribulations of existence constituting a course of *training*—Malthus's position; and one of *probation* or testing or trial—Paley's view (see especially 131). Punishment is the consequence of failure on this latter view, whereas the former entails no question of future punishment, but rather 'merely condemning to their original insensibility those beings, that, by the operation of general laws, had not been formed with qualities suited to a purer state of happiness.'

There remains some doubt whether Malthus conceived a net balance of purely *temporal* good when he summarized by asserting that 'vice' and 'misery' are aspects of the 'infinite variety of nature' and 'admirably adapted to further the high purpose of the creation, and to produce the greatest possible quantity of good' (132). There is, it is true, an effect of general and constant laws of nature on mind, and thus on temporal activity of all kinds: 'the industry and foresight of the husbandman; the indefatigable ingenuity of the artificer; the skilful researches of the physician, and anatomist; and the watchful observation, and patient investigation of the natural philosopher' (126-7). But the weight of concentration is overwhelmingly on activity resulting in aggregative expansion of numbers—not increase in per-capita income; here lies the Providential design regarding population: 'As the reasons . . . for the constancy of the laws of nature, seem, even to our understandings, obvious and striking; if we return to the principle of population, and consider man as he really is, inert, sluggish, and averse from labour, unless compelled by necessity . . . we may pronounce, with certainty, that the world would not have been peopled, but for the superiority of the power of population to the means of subsistence . . . It keeps the inhabitants of the earth always fully up to the level of the means of subsistence; and is constantly acting upon man as a powerful stimulus, urging him to the further cultivation of the earth, and to enable it, consequently, to support a more extended population. But it is impossible that this law can operate, and produce the effects apparently intended by the supreme Being, without occasioning partial evil. Unless the principle of population were to be altered, according to the circumstances of each separate country . . . ; it is evident, that the same principle, which, seconded by industry, will people a fertile region in a few years, must produce distress in countries that have been long inhabited' (127). Malthus asserted at one point that 'life is generally speaking, a blessing independent of a future state' (136). But the argument of the foregoing passage—which does not specify *why* larger population size is desirable apart from a presumed Divine intention—proceeds at so general a level as to allow representation of the 'distress in countries that have been long inhabited' as nothing but a *'partial evil'* to be expected in any universalist environment subject to general laws of nature. Any temporal balance of good need not pertain to a specific region such as Great Britain. Moreover, even a universal balance of good does not incorporate the effect on happiness of high living standards.

We must also have in mind the primary concern, which is training of the mind for the *next* world. Within that broad theological frame of reference, it is easy to appreciate why *motive* matters: 'If the scriptural denunciations of eternal punishment were brought home with the same certainty to every man's mind, as that the night will follow the day, this one vast and gloomy idea would take such full possession of the human faculties, as to leave no room for any other conceptions: the external actions of men would be all nearly alike; virtuous conduct would be no indication of virtuous disposition; vice and virtue would be blended together in one common mass; and, though the all-seeing eye of God might distinguish them, they must necessarily make the same impressions on man, who can judge only from external appearances. Under such a dispensation, it is difficult to conceive how human beings could be formed to a detestation of moral evil, and a love and admiration of God, and of moral excellence' (134-5). It is thus in a world of uncertainty alone that one is justified in assuming that virtuous behaviour reflects virtuous motive,

and conversely in the case of vicious behaviour, making it possible to learn to detest 'moral evil' (an idea to be found in Paley's *Natural Theology,* as is clarified in Waterman, 1992, 131-2). And 'moral evil is absolutely necessary to the production of moral excellence' precisely because it generates abhorrence in others (131).

This orientation implies that any scope for moral improvement applies to *individuals,* not to entire national groupings. The same seems to be true of a reduction in physical misery. For 'sorrows and distresses' are said to be necessary to excite sentiments of humanity, 'social sympathy,' 'Christian virtues' and to provide opportunities for the 'ample exertion of benevolence' (130). This theme requires further attention, considering a caution given at the very close of the ***Essay***: 'Evil exists in the world, not to create despair, but activity. We are not patiently to submit to it, but to exert ourselves to avoid it' (137). The effort to overcome evil is in fact represented as a 'duty': 'It is not only the interest but the duty of every individual, to use his utmost efforts to remove evil from himself, and from as large a circle as he can influence; and the more he exercises himself in this duty, the more wisely he directs his efforts, and the more successful these efforts are; the more he will probably improve and exalt his own mind, and the more completely does he appear to fulfil the will of his Creator.' The denial that the proposed solution to the problem of evil implies an absence of scope for improvement is elaborated thus: 'The idea that the impressions and excitements of this world are the instruments with which the Supreme Being forms matter into mind; and that the necessity of constant exertion to avoid evil, and to pursue good, is the principal spring of these impressions and excitements, seems to smooth many of the difficulties that occur in a contemplation of human life; and appears to me, to give a satisfactory reason for the existence of natural and moral evil; and, consequently, for that part of both, and it certainly is not a very small part, which arises from the principle of population. But, though upon this supposition, it seems highly improbable, that evil should ever be removed from the world; yet it is evident, that this impression would not answer the apparent purpose of the Creator; it would not act so powerfully as an excitement to exertion, if the quantity of it did not diminish or increase, with the activity or the indolence of man. The continual variations in the weight, and in the distribution of this pressure, keep alive a constant expectation of throwing it off.' We again have here a universalist perspective, rendering it unclear whether Malthus intended a balance of temporal good in any *particular* country, including his own. And at the end of the passage he seems to withdraw much of the implicit allowance for improvement—unless we read him as recognizing only the possibility of *individuals* successfully rising above the mass.

To summarize the 'solution' proposed for the theological problem: On a universal level independent of time and space, there is said to be a net balance even of temporal good ('life is, generally speaking a blessing independent of a future state'). But the 'good' in question is unrelated to the level of per-capita income; and Malthus leaves open the possibility that, considering any specific region, particularly an old-settled country such as Britain, population pressure generates actual 'distress,' albeit a 'partial' evil in the broader context encompassing spiritual training for the next world. Within that broad context Malthus considered that the 'partial pain . . . inflicted by the supreme Creator, while he is forming numberless beings to a capacity of the highest enjoyments, is but as the dust of the balance in comparison of the happiness that is communicated' (136). The positive case closes with the assertion that 'we have every reason to think, that there is no more evil in the world, than what is absolutely necessary as one of the ingredients of the mighty process.'

As noted, it is in the closing paragraphs of the *Essay* that we find the warning against 'despair.' This suggests a certain unease with the substantive defence of the Deity in the light of 'the constant pressure of distress on man from the difficulty of subsistence.' The temporal improvement allowed relates to both a diminution of 'natural' and 'moral' evil, that is, of poverty and vice. But there is an unfortunate vagueness about the allowance since it is not clarified whether such improvement is applicable to Britain and how precisely it would be achieved. The problem reflects to some extent a more basic ambiguity—whether the Providential ordinance relates to a *potentially* or an *actually* excessive growth rate of population relative to that of food; only if the problem is one of potentiality can it be avoided. On balance, we have suggested, Malthus's appeal against despair seems to open the door to *individual* rather than *collective* improvement; the problem remains one of actual population pressure in old-settled states.

It is only in the body of the first *Essay* that one finds the solution to the problem of poverty at the national level in the specific British case—it amounts, of course, to prudential control. However, prudential control entails vice, so that there emerges a trade-off between misery and vice. Malthus's defence of the Deity is thus already in difficulty in 1798. Apparently Malthus did not realize this when he published his apologia, but it was immediately brought to his attention by critics. It was this newly appreciated theological difficulty that led him to introduce moral restraint as an alternative to misery and vice, as we shall see in section IV.

* * *

Before proceeding we might consider the subsequent history of Malthus's theological position. Pullen argues the case that Malthus was persuaded to omit the two theological chapters because of their unorthodoxy—the denial of life as a state of trial or testing or probation, the notion of conditional immortality and the rejection of original sin—but did not retract his original views (1981a, 48, 50).[9] Waterman, on the other hand, maintains that Malthus finally adopted Paley's (and Sumner's) position, which considers this world to be a state of 'probation' or trial, providing challenges that invite improving solutions extending to the introduction of 'moral restraint' itself (1983, 205-6; 1991, 146-7, 172; see also Harvey-Phillips, 1984). And this latter view seems convincing.[10] The significance of the abandonment of the original theodicy in favour of Paley's is, we shall find, suggestive of a more 'mundane' treatment of the benevolence of God.[11] Certainly Malthus's original position is centred on training for the *next* world.

III A UTILITY CALCULUS, 1798

We have seen from a passage in the theological chapters of the first *Essay* that, for Malthus, motive mattered in the classification of virtuous behaviour (above, p. 923). More specifically: 'Our ideas of virtue and vice are not, perhaps, very accurate and well defined; but few, I think, would call an action really virtuous, which was performed simply and solely from the dread of a very great punishment, or the expectation of a very great reward'—an allusion to 'future' punishment and reward contained in scripture (1986, I, 135). This perhaps constitutes an implicit criticism of Paley. For Paley maintained not only that 'actions are to be estimated by their tendency to promote happiness.—Whatever is expedient, is right.—It is the utility of any moral rule alone which constitutes the obligation to it' (1785, 61); but also that virtue differed from prudence only in allowing for the consequences in the next world as well as this: 'In the one case, we consider what we shall get or lose in this world; in the other case, we consider also what we shall get or lose in the world to come' (53).[12]

It is all the more interesting to encounter in the body of the first *Essay* a utilitarian perspective on moral behaviour—involving, incidentally, a version of the psychological principle of satiety—and one that seems to run in terms of temporal consequences alone: 'Intemperance in every enjoyment defeats its own purpose. A walk in the finest day, through the most beautiful country, if pursued too far, ends in pain and fatigue. The most wholesome and invigorating food, eaten with an unrestrained appetite, produces weakness, instead of strength. Even intellectual pleasures, though certainly less liable than others to satiety, pursued with too little intermission, debilitate the body, and impair the vigour of the mind. To argue against the reality of these pleasures from their abuse, seems to be hardly just. Morality, according to Mr. Godwin [1796, I, 73], is a calculation of consequences, or, as Archdeacon Paley very

AN

ESSAY

ON THE

PRINCIPLE OF POPULATION,

AS IT AFFECTS

THE FUTURE IMPROVEMENT OF SOCIETY.

WITH REMARKS

ON THE SPECULATIONS OF MR. GODWIN,

M. CONDORCET,

AND OTHER WRITERS.

LONDON:

PRINTED FOR J. JOHNSON, IN ST. PAUL'S
CHURCH-YARD.

1798.

Title page for 1798 first edition of An Essay on the the Principle of
Population *by Thomas Robert Malthus, which was published
anonymously.*

justly expresses it, the will of God, as collected from
general expediency [cf. 1785, 423]. According to either
of these definitions, a sensual pleasure, not attended
with the probability of unhappy consequences, does not
offend against the laws of morality: and if it be pursued
with such a degree of temperance, as to leave the most
ample room for intellectual attainments, it must undoubtedly add to the sum of pleasurable sensations in
life' (77). There was then nothing immoral attached to a
sensual pleasure if unattended with the probability of
unhappy consequences.

This perspective seems to govern an implicit secular
utility calculus running through the first *Essay,* one purpose of which was to define the set of institutions which
reduces the force of the population problem. That the
criterion implicitly adopted is that of utility in the sense
of a balance of *temporal* (though not necessarily
material) happiness emerges most clearly from the dual
propositions that 'prudential' population control 'almost

necessarily, though not absolutely so, produces vice'
(14), and—as we saw in chapter 18 (p. 883)—that 'vice'
itself generates unhappiness—defined in purely temporal terms: 'The effects . . . of these [preventive] restraints upon marriage are but too conspicuous in the
consequent vices that are produced in almost every part
of the world; vices, that are continually involving both
sexes in inextricable unhappiness' (28). More strongly,
a case against the outdoor poor-relief system intimates
the toleration of prudence as a necessary evil for the
sake of avoiding misery—the toleration of vice on a net
balance of consequence: 'Every obstacle in the way of
marriage must undoubtedly be considered a species of
unhappiness. But as from the laws of our nature some
check to population must exist, it is better that it should
be checked from a foresight of the difficulties attending
a family, and the fear of dependent poverty, than that it
should be encouraged, only to be repressed afterwards
by want and sickness' (35).

The implicit secular orientation of Malthus's position
requires elaboration. An anonymous critic of the first
Essay wrote that 'without intending it, however, we
think the author, in this essay, has furnished the best
apology for prostitution, that has ever been written'
(*Analytical Review* 28, 124).[13] The point is that Malthus,
by dealing with the social problem in the body of his
1798 *Essay* in terms of man 'as he is,' was adopting a
position conflicting with the theological viewpoint of
the last two chapters, where there is no hint of any
trade-off, but merely the tangential suggestion that *both*
'natural' and 'moral evil' (misery and vice) can be reduced—and this apparently, we have found, only in individual cases.

Flew remarks that the 'unnoticed moral of the *First Essay* is very similar to the notorious paradox of Mandeville's *Fable of the bees*: "private vices, public benefits"'
(1970, 48). Similar charges were made in Malthus's
lifetime (although not necessarily in our specific
context), and Malthus later denied them: 'Let me not be
supposed to give the slightest sanction to the system of
morals inculcated in the *Fable of the Bees,* a system
which I consider as absolutely false, and directly contrary to the just definition of virtue' (1806, II, 523n).
But what Malthus was here defending is only the general proposition that by the individual's pursuit 'as his
primary object, [of] his own safety and happiness, and
the safety and happiness of those immediately connected with him . . . the most ignorant are led to promote the general happiness, an end which they would
have totally failed to attain, if the moving principle of
their conduct had been benevolence' (522-3). He did
not have his implicit allowance for 'vice' in mind in
this context. That allowance does, in fact, carry the
Mandeville message, and clashes with the theological
chapters.

When Malthus became conscious of the clash is an interesting question. In a letter to the *Monthly Magazine,* dated 1 March 1799 (though dealing with war rather than sex), he strongly denied that he had ever intended to justify vice as an alternative to misery: 'In whatever light we view the situation of man, on earth, he can never be justified in recurring to vice in order to avoid misery. To bear the unavoidable evils of life with unyielding integrity is the highest test of our virtue; to attempt to escape them by vicious means is the great proof of our weakness, and of our unfitness for a superior state' (cited Rashid, 1984, 136). This particular letter reflects the theological position of the last two chapters.[14] Malthus was apparently not yet willing to face the implication of his own observations in the body of the text.[15]

Malthus pointed to the intended implications of 'moral restraint,' or postponement of marriage not followed by 'irregular gratifications,' in the Preface to the second edition (see chapter 18, p. 886). This statement, which stamped the first *Essay* as a depressing document, is unfortunate since Malthus's demonstration in the body of that version that poverty and misery are 'absolutely irremediable' held good only *in the absence of prudential behaviour.* And from the outset—again in the body of the essay rather than in the theological chapters—he had recommended delay of marriage despite the 'vicious' consequences.[16]

IV MORAL RESTRAINT AND UTILITARIANISM

Far from the theological concerns of Malthus diminishing between the first and second editions, the introduction of moral restraint evidently constitutes an attempt to reinforce the theological defence. Allusions to the training of 'mind' and character—the substance of the expunged theological chapters—re-emerge in 1803 in Book IV, on the obligation to practise the 'virtue' of moral restraint; various beneficial social effects to be expected therefrom; possible objections; and warnings against its avoidance. But the emphasis on preparation for the next world is lacking, and there other major differences between the two versions; Malthus, in 1803 and thereafter, effectively pulled the theological carpet from under his own feet.

The first chapter of Book IV sets out the issue by focusing on that proposition of 1798 implying a trade-off of vice against misery (1798/1986, I, 35; see above, p. 883). 'This idea will admit of being pursued further' (1803/1986, *3,* 465). As noted earlier, *this proposition does not appear in the original theological chapters,* which contain no hint of a trade-off (above, p. 925). Malthus evidently realized that those chapters had to be recast. That some sort of check is inevitable is represented, as in 1798, as a 'law of nature.' But the theological emphasis is now upon the *avoidance* of excess population growth 'with the least possible prejudice to the virtue and happiness of human society'; it is no longer to explain (and justify) 'the constant pressure of distress,' but rather to explain (and justify) the necessity for checks and, at one remove, the source of that necessity, namely, sexual passion—represented against Godwin to be the 'most powerful and general of our desires' after that for food (468). Alternatively stated, Malthus *qua theologian* set himself the task in 1803 of accounting for the Deity's creation of man as a being driven by a desire that necessitates (painful) control, displacing the emphasis entirely from a disheartening outcome of the population principle defined *in terms of actual poverty.*

We turn to the details of the argument regarding sexual passion—and the consequent 'tendency' for population growth to exceed that of food. This passion is represented (much as in the 1798 theological chapters) as *necessary* to the Divine purposes of assuring: (1) the 'replenishing' of the earth; and (2) 'the formation and improvement of the human mind' by counteracting 'indolence.' The potential for 'evil' resulting from *general* or *uniform* laws is also allowed—an allusion to excess population growth in conditions of land scarcity. But there is this major difference between 1803 and the 1798 theological chapters—a new, very positive solution to the problem of poverty: 'It is however, a law, exactly similar in its great features to all the other laws of nature. It is strong and general, and apparently would not admit of any very considerable diminution, without being inadequate to its object; the evils arising from it are incidental to those necessary qualities of strength and generality; and these evils are capable of being very greatly mitigated and rendered comparatively light by human energy and virtue. We cannot but conceive that it is an object of the Creator, that the earth should be replenished [at least to a considerable degree];[17] and it appears to me clear, that this could not be effected without a tendency in population to increase faster than food; and as, with the present law of increase, the peopling of the earth does not proceed very rapidly, we have undoubtedly some reason to believe, that this law is not too powerful for its apparent object . . . [We] have reason to think that it is more conducive to the formation and improvement of the human mind, that the law should be uniform, and the evils incidental to it, under certain circumstances, be left to be mitigated or removed by man himself. His duties in this case vary with his situation; he is thus kept more alive to the consequences of his actions; and his faculties have evidently greater play and opportunity of improvement, than if the evil were removed by a perpetual change of the law according to circumstances' (471-2). That misery was avoidable, and this without corresponding increase in vice, is thus the central theological theme of 1803, and often repeated: '[If], in addition to that general activity and direction of our industry put in motion by these laws [of nature], we further consider that the incidental evils arising from them are constantly directing our attention to the proper check to population, moral restraint; and if it appear that, by a strict obedience to the duties pointed out to us by the light of nature and reason, and confirmed and sanctioned by revelation, these evils may be avoided, the objection will, I trust, be removed, and all apparent imputation on the goodness of the Deity be done away' (474). 'As it appears therefore, that it is in the power of each individual to avoid all the evil consequences to himself and society resulting from the principle of population, by the practice of a virtue clearly dictated to him by the light of nature, and expressly enjoined in revealed religion; and as we have reason to think, that the exercise of this virtue to a certain degree would tend rather to increase than diminish individual happiness; we can have no reason to impeach the justice of the Deity, because his general laws make this virtue necessary, and punish our offenses against it by the evils attendant upon vice, and the pains that accompany the various forms of premature death' (480). On this view, natural and moral evil, including poverty, could be appreciated as the avoidable consequence of inadequate self-control—with an eye always to the balance of happiness: 'Natural and moral evil seem to be the instruments employed by the Deity in admonishing us to avoid any mode of conduct which is not suited to our being, and will consequently injure our happiness . . . [If] we heed not this admonition, we justly incur the penalty of our disobedience, and our sufferings operate as a warning to others' (465-6).

* * *

Malthus's defence of the Deity is intimately bound up with the notion of utility as the foundation of morals.[18] The utilitarian rule is stated thus by Malthus:

> As animals, or till we know their consequences, our only business is to follow these dictates of nature; but, as reasonable beings, we are under the strongest obligations to attend to their consequences; and if they be evil to ourselves or others, we may justly consider it as an indication, that such a mode of indulging these passions is not suited to our state or conformable to the will of God. As moral agents, therefore, it is clearly our duty to restrain their indulgence in these particular directions; and by thus carefully examining the consequences of our natural passions, and frequently bringing them to the test of utility, gradually to acquire a habit of gratifying them only in that way, which, being unattended with evil, will clearly add to the sum of human happiness and fulfil the apparent purpose of the Creator.

> Though utility, therefore, can never be the immediate excitement to the gratification of any passion, it is the test by which alone we can know [1817: independently of the revealed will of God], whether it ought or ought not to be indulged; and is therefore the surest founda-

tion of all morality [1817: the surest criterion of moral rules] which can be collected from the light of nature. All the moral codes, which have inculcated the subjection of the passions to reason, have been, as I conceive, really built upon this foundation, whether the promulgators of them were aware of it or not.

> (531; 1817, III, 214-15)[19]

There is, however, a crucial difference between Malthus and Paley to keep in mind. For Malthus, the utilitarian rule pointed to moral restraint: 'There are perhaps few actions that tend so directly to diminish the general happiness, as to marry without the means of supporting children. He who commits this act, therefore, clearly offends against the will of God; and having become a burden on the society in which he lives, and plunged himself and family into a situation, in which virtuous habits are preserved with more difficulty than in any other, he appears to have violated his duty to his neighbours and to himself, and thus to have listened to the voice of passion in opposition to his higher obligations' (479-80). 'Judging merely from the light of nature, if we feel convinced of the misery arising from a redundant population on the one hand, and of the evils and unhappiness, particularly to the female sex, arising from promiscuous intercourse, on the other, I do not see how it is possible for any person who acknowledges the principle of utility as the great foundation of morals [1817: the great criterion of moral rules], to escape the conclusion, that moral restraint, till we are in a condition to support a family, is the strict line of duty; and when revelation is taken into the question, this duty undoubtedly receives very powerful confirmation' (482; 1817, III, 102-3).[20] But *this was not the conclusion reached by Paley* (1785, 592-3), who, to Malthus's distress—somewhat exaggerated, since in fact Paley assumed the limits to be nowhere in sight (see note 37, below)—recommended state encouragement of population expansion in conditions of increasing land scarcity: 'The particular end in view in this case appears to be absolutely criminal. We wish to force people into marriage, when from the acknowledged scarcity of subsistence they will have little chance of being able to support their children. We might as well force people into the water who are unable to swim. In both cases we rashly tempt providence. Nor have we more reason to believe that a miracle will be worked to save us from the misery and mortality resulting from our conduct in the one case than in the other' (485).

Malthus also drew on Paley's later work, *Natural Theology* (1803 [1802], 344),[21] in championing from the utilitarian perspective the regulation—not the extinction—of the passions: 'Our virtue . . . as reasonable beings, evidently consists in educing from the general materials, which the Creator has placed under our guidance, the greatest sum of human happiness; and as all our the natural impulses are abstractly considered good, and only to be distinguished by their consequences, a strict attention to these consequences, and the regulation of our conduct conformably to them, must be considered as our principal duty' (1803/1986, *3, 471*). It is precisely because the passions 'could not be generally weakened or diminished, without injuring our happiness' that their control rather than their extinction was required (467). In this context too we find *utility represented as the source of morality* (and law) in the course of an analogy drawn with hunger: 'The act of the hungry man who satisfies his appetite by taking a loaf from the shelf of another, is in no respect to be distinguished from the act of him who does the same thing with a loaf of his own, but by its consequences. From the consideration of these consequences, we feel the most perfect conviction, that, if people were not prevented from gratifying their natural desires with the loaves in the possession of others, that the number of loaves would universally diminish. This experience is the foundation of the laws relating to property, and of the distinctions of virtue and vice, in the gratification of desires otherwise perfectly the same. If the pleasure arising from the gratification of these propensities were universally diminished in vividness, violations of property would become less frequent; but this advantage would be greatly overbalanced by the narrowing of the sources of enjoyment. The diminution in the quantity of all those productions, which contribute to human gratification, would be much greater in proportion than the diminution of thefts; and the loss of general happiness on the one side would be beyond comparison greater than the gain to happiness on the other' (467-8). This same concept of a net balance of happiness is generalized to sex and all the passions: 'Few or none of them will admit of being greatly diminished, without narrowing the sources of good, more powerfully than the sources of evil. And the reason seems to be obvious. They are, in fact, the materials of all our pleasures, as well as of all our pains; of all our happiness, as well as of all our misery; of all our virtues, as well as of all our vices. It must therefore be regulation and direction that are wanted, not diminution or extinction' (470).

As for sexual passion, Malthus goes out of his way to list the sources of positive happiness flowing therefrom when 'taken in an enlarged sense' (468).[22] Thus 'the formation and steady pursuit of some plan of life involving the prospect of companionship and children is represented as 'one of the most permanent sources of happiness' (469); the 'bond of conjugal affection' had a 'most powerful tendency to soften and meliorate the human character, and keep it more alive to all the kindlier emotions of benevolence and pity'; and, furthermore, when the passion faces 'obstacles . . . in the way of very early and universal gratification,' there is a resultant positive effect on 'gentleness, kindness, and suavity of manners,' that is, on 'the formation and improvement of character' (469-70). All in all, though

some evil results from the passion between the sexes—or rather from its 'irregular gratification'—on a *balance* of considerations, the net advantage was overwhelming.

Adding in the widespread practice of moral restraint, the outlook becomes bright indeed, both from the perspective of living standards and from that of 'the female character':

> If, for the sake of illustration, we might be permitted to draw a picture of society, in which each individual endeavoured to attain happiness by the strict fulfilment of those duties, which the most enlightened of the ancient philosophers deduced from the laws of nature, and which have been directly taught, and received such powerful sanctions in the moral code of Christianity, it would present a very different scene from that which we now contemplate. Every act, which was prompted by the desire of immediate gratification, but which threatened an ultimate overbalance of pain, would be considered as a breach of duty; and consequently no man, whose earnings were only sufficient to maintain two children, would put himself in a situation in which he might have to maintain four or five, however he might be prompted to it by the passion of love . . .

> The interval between the age of puberty and the period at which each individual might venture on marriage must, according to the supposition, be passed in strict chastity; because the law of chastity cannot be violated without producing evil. The effect of anything like a promiscuous intercourse, which prevents the birth of children, is evidently to weaken the best affections of the heart, and in a very marked manner to degrade the female character. And any other intercourse would, without improper arts, bring as many children into the society as marriage, with a much greater probability of their becoming a burden to it.

> (474-5)

Sexual continence before marriage was thus the ideal, and this because promiscuity produced evil, including a weakening of 'affection' and a degradation of 'the female character.' This would be so, assuming the practice of birth control or 'improper arts'—though in its absence there would be the same problems, and worse, which flow from early marriage and poverty. As expressed a little later, 'moral restraint' was 'the strict line of duty,' since promiscuity generated 'evils and unhappiness, particularly to the female sex' (482), that is, some form or other of character degeneration, and probably also sexually transmitted diseases. This is further confirmed by various amplifications regarding 'the vice of promiscuous intercourse' resulting from mere prudence, which includes both 'moral' and 'physical' evils (495; see chapter 18, pp. 888-9).

* * *

The formal defence of the Deity in 1803 thus extends far beyond 1798. But there is reason to doubt whether Malthus continued to draw upon the *original* theological chapters of 1798 in defining his brand of utilitarianism. For one thing, it is characteristic of the later editions that training of the mind for the 'future state' or 'state of superior enjoyment,' though mentioned, does not receive anything like the same attention it is accorded in 1798; while the source of virtue in a calculation of consequences is said to be common to 'heathen' as well as Christian moralists: 'The difficulty of moral restraint will perhaps be objected to this doctrine. To him who does not acknowledge the authority of the Christian religion, I have only to say that, after the more careful investigation, this virtue appears to be absolutely necessary, in order to avoid certain evils which would otherwise result from the general laws of nature. According to his own principles, it is his duty to pursue the greatest good consistent with these laws; and not to fail in this important end, and produce an overbalance of misery by a partial obedience to some of the dictates of nature, while he neglects others. The path of virtue, though it be the only path which leads to permanent happiness, has always been represented by the heathen moralists as of difficult ascent' (477-8). Appeal to the Scriptures regarding the nature of the individual's 'duty' is secondary to the main argument for pre-marital continence—the net balance of social good (including moral tone or character) resulting therefrom.[23]

At the same time it would be misleading to pretend that Malthus's utilitarianism as applied to moral restraint is wholly plain sailing. An explanatory note attached to the term 'moral restraint' in 1806 suggests appeal to some absolute code: 'It will be observed, that I here use the term *moral* in its most confined sense. By moral restraint I would be understood to mean a restraint from marriage, from prudential motives, with a conduct strictly moral during the period of this restraint; and I have never intentionally deviated from this sense. When I have wished to consider the restraint from marriage unconnected with its consequences, I have either called it prudential restraint, or a part of the preventive check, of which indeed it forms the principal branch' (1806, I, 19-20n).[24] As Sir Leslie Stephen observed, the term 'vice' is occasionally used in the *Essay* not as 'productive' of misery, but as 'an alternative to misery; and yet something bad in itself. Is this consistent with [Malthus's] Utilitarianism?' (1900, II, 158).[25]

This problem is best approached directly by reference to Malthus's unwillingness to categorize illicit sex as 'misery' rather than 'vice.' 'Misery' was an inappropriate term for actions which in individual cases generated a balance even of long-run happiness (with an eye to *this,* not the next, life in contrast to the perspective of 1798). The 'viciousness' of promiscuity was defined relative to its *'general tendency'* to reduce individual happiness, and thus the happiness of society: 'As the general consequence of vice is misery, and as this consequence is the precise reason why an action is termed

vicious, it may appear that the term misery alone would be here sufficient, and that it is superfluous to use both. But the rejection of the term vice would introduce a considerable confusion into our language and ideas. We want it particularly to distinguish that class of action, the general tendency of which is to produce misery, but which, in their immediate or individual effects, may produce perhaps exactly the contrary. The gratification of all our passions in its immediate effect is happiness, not misery; and, in individual instances, even the remote consequences (at least in this life) come under the same denomination. I have little doubt that there have been some irregular connexions with women, which have added to the happiness of both parties, and have injured no one. These individual actions, therefore, cannot come under the head of misery. But they are still evidently vicious, because an action is so denominated, the general tendency of which is to produce misery, whatever may be its individual effect; and no person can doubt the general tendency of an illicit intercourse between the sexes, to injure the happiness of society' (1803/1986, 2, 16-17n).[26]

Malthus failed to make explicit that no stigma attaches to the behaviour of individual couples engaged in 'irregular connexions' where a net balance of happiness could be expected for that couple without injury to other parties.[27] And the fact is that he stepped back from that conclusion. For in 1817 he altered the third sentence justifying the term 'vice' to read: 'We want it particularly to distinguish those actions, the general tendency of which is to produce misery, and which are therefore prohibited by the commands of the Creator, and the precepts of the moralist, although, in their immediate or individual effects, they may produce perhaps exactly the contrary' (1817, I, 23-4n). Here then we find an appeal to biblical injunction. Similarly: 'There are perhaps few actions that tend so directly to diminish the general happiness, as to marry without the means of supporting children. He who commits this act, therefore, clearly offends against the will of God . . .' (above, p. 993). However, it is noteworthy that such injunctions are not represented as *independent*; rather, the Creator condemns certain acts *because* they tend to generate net social disutility. This perspective is implicit in Paley's dictum, approved by Malthus, that the 'method of coming at the will of God . . . by the light of nature, is to enquire into the tendency of the action to promote or diminish the general happiness' (see above, note 18). To this extent dogma and utility can proceed hand in hand, and Stephen's problem is avoided.[28]

In other contexts, too, this gloss seems to be intended, as in the reference to 'a strict obedience to the duties pointed out to us by the light of nature and reason, and confirmed and sanctioned by revelation,' or to 'the practice of a virtue clearly dictated . . . by the light of nature, and expressly enjoined in revealed religion' (cited above, p. 931). And we find the proposition that those private acts 'the general tendency of which is to produce misery' are to be classed as *vicious,* deliberately altered in 1817 to incorporate this perspective: 'An action is so denominated, which violates an express precept, founded upon its general tendency to produce misery' (24n).[29]

V PRUDENTIAL CONTROL AND UTILITARIANISM

As we emphasized in chapter 18: V, Malthus did not believe that the premarital period could be spent chastely. Yet the small likelihood of any extensive adoption of the ideal solution ('moral restraint'), Malthus insisted, did not detract from the theological defence of the Deity: 'He who publishes a moral code, or system of duties, however firmly he may be convinced of the strong obligation on each individual strictly to conform to it, has never the folly to imagine that it will be universally or even generally practised . . . I allowed myself to suppose the universal prevalence of this virtue . . . that I might endeavour to remove any imputation on the goodness of the Deity, by showing, that the evils arising from the principle of population were exactly of the same nature as the generality of other evils which excite fewer complaints; that they were increased by human ignorance and indolence, and diminished by human knowledge and virtue; and on the supposition that each individual strictly fulfilled his duty, would be almost totally removed; and this without any general diminution of those sources of pleasure, arising from the regulated indulgence of the passions, which have been justly considered as the principal ingredients of human happiness' (1803/1986, *3,* 482-3). In the Appendix of 1817, Malthus insisted again that he was doing his duty by introducing the *ideal* solution, 'whether the remedy be . . . adequate or inadequate' (see below, note 32).

Here it is illuminating to consider a charge by Robert Torrens (1815, viii-x) against Malthus of a blatant inconsistency in introducing moral restraint, despite his criticisms of Godwin and Condorcet. This criticism is, in one major respect, unjustified. Torrens failed to note Malthus's own defence in 1803 against such complaints—that his position differed in principle from that of the idealists by its emphasis on *self-interest* (subject to appropriate institutions) rather than on *benevolence*: 'It is not required of us to act from motives to which we are unaccustomed; to pursue a general good, which we may not distinctly comprehend, or the effect of which may be weakened by distance and diffusion. The happiness of the whole is to be the result of the happiness of individuals, and to begin first with them. No co-operation is required. Every step tells. He who performs his duty faithfully will reap the full fruits of it, whatever may be the number of others who fail. This duty is

express, and intelligible to the humblest capacity. It is merely, that he is not to bring beings into the world, for whom he cannot find the means of support' (1803/1986, *3,* 483).

Malthus could, however, be held to account had he proposed a solution to the population problem which he realized would not be widely adopted. He himself admitted as much when he pointed a finger at 'visionary' writers: 'If it will answer any purpose of illustration, I see no harm in drawing the picture of a society, in which each individual is supposed strictly to fulfil his duties; nor does a writer appear to be justly liable to the imputation of being visionary, unless he make such universal or general obedience necessary to the practical utility of his system, and to that degree of moderate and partial improvement, which is all that can rationally be expected from the most complete knowledge of our duties.' If, however, people see their self-interest to lie not in moral restraint but in mere 'prudence,' we are left with the practical choice between 'vice,' or premarital sexual activity, with its unwelcome social consequences (see above, pp. 935-6), and 'misery.' Malthus, to his credit, recognized this and, taking the world as it is, carried on to justify prudential population control on effectively *neutral* utilitarian grounds—notwithstanding that this line clashes with the theological defence of the Deity turning upon ideal behaviour. We have already elaborated on the net balance of social utility deriving from population control with an eye to *reality* (chapter 18: V),[30] a calculus, it will be recalled, taking account of the 'vices' attached to poverty, and including theft and murder—and their punishment envisaged as a 'painful' act or disutility—and the degradation of young persons (490-2).[31] A consequence of excessive population growth is thus an inevitable degradation of character, unless one has recourse to prudential control, *albeit involving premarital sex,* since the damage (even to character) is thereby lessened (489). It is pertinent, too, that the reduction of the misery attached to poverty is itself defined as a moral problem: 'And, with regard to the necessity of this celibacy in countries that have been long peopled, or our obligation not to marry till we have a fair prospect of being able to support our children it will appear to deserve the attention of the moralist, if it can be proved that an attention to this obligation is of more effect in the prevention of misery, than all the other virtues combined' (473). Similarly: 'Can any man of reflection,' Malthus asked in 1817, 'venture to state that there is no moral reason for repressing the inclination to early marriages; when it cannot be denied that the alternative of not repressing it must necessarily and unavoidably be premature mortality from excessive poverty?' (1817, III, 411).

To claim, as Malthus does at one point (see above, p. 937), that illicit intercourse is to be classed as 'vicious' because (viewed as a tendency, not necessarily in individual cases) it injures 'the happiness of society,' loses all substance once it is allowed that such behaviour generates a *net* balance of social happiness via its reduction of poverty and the vicious consequences of poverty. Malthus went yet further in 1806 by his insistence that he had 'taken man as he is' in arriving at 'practical applications' of his principle of population, that his was no visionary concept of man: 'Thus viewing him and knowing that some checks to populations must exist, I have not the slightest hesitation in saying, that the prudential check to marriage is better than premature mortality' (1806, II, 537-8).[32]

Malthus recognized that the elements allowed into the utility calculus is always a matter of personal judgment (1803/1986, *2,* iii, cited chapter 18, p. 886).[33] Doubtless the precise constituents of 'morality' differ somewhat between Malthus and Mill or Bentham (as they do between the latter two).[34] But the characteristic theodicy of 1798—its concept of 'the mighty process for the creation and formation of mind' to fit it for 'happier situation, nearer the presence of the mighty maker'—is played down even within the course of the defence of the Deity; and moreover is wholly irrelevant to the utilitarian calculus adopted in the actual treatment of particular social issues, which eschews the ideal. In fact, we go further. Malthus introduced a purely secular orientation by the two allowances discussed above. First, the concession that, in individual cases, 'irregular' sexual relationships might generate 'happiness' to both parties with injury to nobody (above, p. 937); such behaviour is termed 'vicious' only because of its *general* tendency to individual, and thus social unhappiness. This is far from a theological perspective, though Malthus struggled to avoid the implication. And yet more important, is the balancing of moral costs and benefits which led Malthus to countenance simple prudence as the lesser evil. This attitude is a direct invitation to abandon entirely the 'ideal' solution posited for the existence of evil.[35]

Although Malthus had introduced 'moral restraint' in response to critics of the first *Essay* (above, p. 925), the alteration did not have a mollifying effect, as is clear from the savage criticism to which he was subjected after the second and later editions (e.g., Jarrold, 1806; Hazlitt, 1807; Weyland, 1816; Ravenstone, 1821). This is particularly understandable when we keep in mind Malthus's effective rejection of moral restraint as a *practical* solution. (See on this issue Levy 1996; also on reactions to the second and later essays, James, 1979, 109-115, 116-26; Waterman, 1991, ch. 4; Bonar, 1924, Book IV.)

There are then two theological Malthuses at work, one proposing the ideal solution to the problem of the threat of poverty created by potential population pressure;[36] and the other taking the world, warts and all, and arriving at a wholly different set of recommendations. In the latter guise, there is nothing to distinguish Malthus from the secular utilitarians. It remains only to note a revealing disclaimer of any right to interfere in the event of an increase in vice with increased prudential control: 'If, on contemplating the increase of vice which might contingently follow an attempt to inculcate the duty of moral restraint, and the increase of misery that must necessarily follow the attempts to encourage marriage and population, we come to the conclusion, not to interfere in any respect, but to leave every man to his own free choice, and responsible only to God for the evil which he does in either way; this is all I contend for; I would on no account do more; but I contend, that at present we are very far from doing this' (1803/1986, *3,* 497-8).

VI More on the Desirability of Population Expansion

Paley interpreted the 'greatest happiness' rule as implying a case for large numbers: 'The happiness of a people is made up of the happiness of single persons; and the quantity of it can only be augmented by increasing the number of the percipients, or the pleasures of their perceptions' (1785, 587-8).[37] An early objection by Malthus (along typically Smithian lines) appears in the unprinted pamphlet *The Crisis,* written in 1796: 'On the subject of population I cannot agree with Archdeacon Paley, who says, that the quantity of happiness in any country is best measured by the number of people. Increasing population is the most certain possible sign of the happiness and prosperity of the state; but the actual population may be only a sign of the happiness that is past' (cited by Empson, 1837, in Semmel, 1963, 244).[38] As we have seen in chapter 18: II, increasing population—not a large population as such—was desirable, although only in so far as such increase implied a response to good standards, and would not dictate reduced standards at higher absolute population sizes.[39] In the third edition of 1806, Malthus protested strongly against misrepresentations of his position (1806, II, 507-8). His program of checks to the birth rate was consistent with population expansion, and critics had erroneously supposed his object was to check population, 'as if anything could be more desirable than the most rapid increase of population unaccompanied by vice and misery' (515-16). The consistency of the *desiderata* of 'high' wages and population growth turns, it will be recalled, on the greater potential for productivity increase in the case of a population with a high proportion of healthy adults, Malthus expecting that the initial restriction of population growth, by altering the age distribution, would 'create fresh resources, and consequently . . . encourage a continued increase of efficient population' under relatively favourable circumstances (550).

Malthus's concern with an expanded population reflects in part the notion that God intended the replenishment of the earth.[40] But this must be read with the Malthusian gloss, which deviates radically from the standard religious argument in favour of a high population by way of early marriage and large families: 'I believe that it is the intention of the Creator that the earth should be replenished; but certainly with a healthy, virtuous, and happy population, not an unhealthy, vicious, and miserable one. And if in endeavouring to obey the command to increase and multiply, we people it only with beings of this latter description, and suffer accordingly, we have no right to impeach the justice of the command, but our irrational mode of executing it' (509). But once we allow for a reduced population growth rate with an eye to the living standards of the masses, the door is wide open to justify *slow* population growth, albeit *formally* satisfying the biblical injunction, the degree of rapidity to be recommended—and the amount of 'vice' that is acceptable—entirely a matter of circumstance and subjective judgment as to appropriate living standards. As for circumstance we need only take the extreme case to see how far the theological component is diluted. J. S. Mill, unlike Malthus, formally championed stationariness, even when expanding population is not at the cost of reduced wages, on grounds of women's interests (letter dated 8 April 1852; 1972, XIV, 88-9) and amenity (1848/1965, III, 756);[41] but Malthus did allow in 1817 that, in limiting circumstances, stationariness would be *essential* (1817, III, 12-13; cited chapter 5, pp. 187-8). Evidently, the absolute magnitude of population corresponding to a stationary state will be lower with than without prudential control, and the injunction to 'replenish' the earth is to that degree lessened; yet notwithstanding this fact, Malthus championed prudence. Since for him (as well as such followers as Thomas Chalmers) population growth in certain conditions was undesirable, we cannot accept the argument for the continued significance of the original theological dimension (above, pp. 917-18).

* * *

These themes lead us back to the birth-control issue (see above, p. 935). Allowing 'promiscuity' as an alternative to the misery and the vice of poverty, as Malthus did, is inconsistent with a *global* rejection of mechanical contraception. It is, one deduces, the practice of birth control by married couples that Malthus had largely in mind by his celebrated denunciation of mechanical contraception as 'immoral.' This conclusion is reinforced in 1817 by reference to the disincentive effects supposedly attached to the practice: 'I have never adverted to the check suggested by Condorcet without the most marked disapprobation. Indeed I should always particularly reprobate any artificial and unnatural modes of checking population, both on account of their immorality and their tendency to remove a necessary

stimulus to industry. If it were possible *for each married couple* to limit by a wish the number of their children, there is certainly reason to fear that the indolence of the human race would be very greatly increased; and that neither the population of individual countries, nor of the whole earth, would ever reach its natural and proper extent. But the restraints which I have recommended are quite of a different character. They are not only pointed out by reason and sanctioned by religion, but tend in the most marked manner to stimulate industry. It is not easy to conceive a more powerful encouragement to exertion and good conduct than the looking forward to marriage as a state peculiarly desirable: but only to be enjoyed in comfort, by the acquisition of habits of industry, economy and prudence' (1817, III, 393-4; emphasis added).[42] It is clear that Malthus continued to reason as if the child-bearing decision is, *and should be,* entailed by the marriage decision, and this in part on grounds of 'morality' in some absolute sense, independently of the social consequences. There were, therefore, limits to his reformist utilitarian perspective. Yet the *logic* of his own allowances pointed directly to the obvious conclusion—that drawn by the Philosophical Radicals; for once it is allowed: (1) that 'vice' can be justified on a utilitarian balance; and (2) that there are circumstances where even stationariness of population is required, it is impossible to rule out generalized birth control as one means to achieve the end, especially since—as Francis Place pointed out—birth control would permit both early marriage and good standards, and a reduction in prostitution (Place, 1822/1930, 176-7).[43] Social utility would then dictate such practices by married couples, as (Malthus himself allowed) it did for the unmarried.

VII Summary and Conclusion

We have confirmed that the theological chapters of 1798 are—as Lord Robbins insisted—extraneous to policy. This is so even in the first edition, and *a fortiori* so in later editions. That these chapters proved an embarrassment is in fact apparent from the Senior-Malthus correspondence of 1829. As we saw in chapter 18, p. 915, Malthus rejected Senior's original attribution to him of the view that reform was to no purpose; he had intended only to convey that the solution to low wages, or the permanent maintenance of improved wages, lay in population control, since 'population was always ready, and inclined, to increase faster than food, if the checks which repressed it were removed'—whereupon Senior pointed out that 'many, perhaps the majority of your readers, adopt the proposition without the qualification,' believing 'that the expansive power of population is a source of evil incapable not only of being subdued, but even of being mitigated.' Writing two chapters expressly designed to 'vindicate the ways of God to Man,' having in mind the 'constant pressure of distress' could only have misled readers in just the manner Senior complained of. In sum: The theological chapters worked on a presumption of *actual* population pressure, whereas Malthus had in mind elsewhere in his first edition, and throughout the later editions, *potential* population pressure.

There is a further issue not taken up formally in this chapter but of high relevance—the fact that comparison of the 1798 and later editions reveals a completely changed 'vision' of the population problem (see chapter 16). The empirical issue originally, as far as concerns contemporary Britain, was a supposedly low population growth rate accounted for proximately by low wages, in turn attributable to sluggish agricultural progress.[44] In 1803 and thereafter, the picture was transformed in the light of information revealed by the censuses of 1801, 1811, and 1821. Now the problem was to explain accelerating population growth at steady (and even rising) real wages. The explanation offered turned on reductions in mortality rates—not increases in marriage and birth rates—in conditions of, and in part attributable to, rapid growth of national income and capital accumulation. The 'vision' was a *bright* not a *dismal* one, for 'the evils resulting from the principle of population have rather diminished than increased, even under the disadvantage of an almost total ignorance of their real cause' (1803/1986, *3*, 575).[45] The original theological problem had thus been entirely superannuated by events; and the revised theological problem of the need for the 'painful' check of chastity before marriage was merely *theoretical,* considering the ongoing acceleration of national product, or, at worst, a problem for some distant future.

The empirical dimension alone would account for the removal of the theological chapters. But there may be other reasons, including the abandonment of the theodicy there outlined, reflected in the contrast between God's grand spiritual end or purpose of 1798 extending *beyond* this world, and thus assuring an overwhelming net balance of good, and the *mundane* ends of material existence—namely, the replenishment of the earth and the cultivation of the soil (Harvey-Phillips, 1984, 603).[46] Our study has also confirmed that, in so far as concerns actual demographic policy in the ***Essay on Population,*** Malthus effectively eschewed theological considerations. His utilitarianism in these contexts is almost entirely earthbound.

Rashid, too, maintains that Malthus changed to Paley's view of life as a 'state of trial'; and he attempts to rationalize the adoption thus: 'As the inescapably sombre implications of his population theory sank into his daily thought, Malthus felt increasingly more comfortable with a theology that emphasized life on earth as a state of trial; for according to Malthus's early beliefs 'there was no penalty in the hereafter for failing to improve oneself. One simply returned to dust. Orthodoxy, on the

other hand, promised positive pain to those who failed to adhere; as such, orthodoxy provided more incentive to accept the moral restraint . . . [It] was Malthus the utilitarian population theorist that determined the beliefs of Malthus the theologian' (1984, 138). For my part, I dispute the notion of 'inescapably sombre implications' flowing from the population theory—the evidence is to the contrary. Malthus may have changed his theological view, but Rashid's rationalization is not convincing.[47]

As for the continued defence of the Deity in 1803 and thereafter, we have shown how, to the extent he based himself on *ideal* behaviour involving abstinence before marriage, Malthus the pure theologian clashes with Malthus the theologian-social scientist, taking account of *actual* human behaviour. In may be said that the two perspectives might be reconciled by an education program inculcating the desirability of moral restraint. But this is not Malthus's approach. Education for him was to convey the significance of prudential population control; there is no emphasis upon the inculcation, via a state-funded program, of the obligation of single people to practise continence on 'moral' grounds, except in so far as such behaviour is favourable to individual, and therefore (it is implied) social utility. To the extent that premarital sexual activity could be shown to generate a lesser net balance of social unhappiness than poverty, he tolerated such activity—and this *on moral grounds.*

Our analysis points to the proximity in practice between Malthus and J. S. Mill in their applications of the utilitarian rule. There are certainly differences of detail, but so too are there differences between Malthus and Paley. As social reformers Malthus and Mill stand side by side. In fact they are close to an extraordinary degree. Thus Malthus's insistence, in the light of increasing land scarcity, on a deceleration of population growth with an eye to the maintenance of real wages points the way to the notion, usually identified with Mill, of stationariness at high standards, and this despite formal obeisance to the biblical injunction regarding population expansion.

The one area where Malthus lags behind Mill is that of birth control by married couples—though Mill, too, was hesitant to make his position public in the *Principles*—and here it is, we have found, that a certain inconsistency emerges. There is also the problem that Malthus did not adequately attend to the social implications of irresponsible private behaviour. But all in all, the perspective on utilitarianism for Malthus as well as Mill reflects hostility to the upper-class, military, and Church ideology that rejected population control. That Malthus, unlike Mill, presumed the likely permanence of a class-based society is less significant than it appears at first glance, since his case was not based on natural law or any such appeal, but on a utilitarian calculus of the greatest happiness order, with labour's interests rated

equate, the proposal itself, and the stress which I have laid upon it, is an incontrovertible proof that I never can have considered vice and misery as themselves remedies' (1817, III, 391-2).

33. As J. S. Mill was to point out, the greatest happiness principle did not in itself yield rules of just behaviour, especially if allowance is made for the consequences of actions for character, that is, the effects of action 'upon [an individual's] susceptibilities of pleasures or pain, upon the general direction of his thoughts, feelings, and imagination . . .' (1835/1969, X, 56). All in all, there was 'as much difference in the moral judgements of different persons, as there is in their views of human nature, and of the formation of character' (67), so that 'clear and comprehensive views of education and human culture must . . . precede, and form the basis of, a philosophy of morals' (56). Thus a utilitarian perspective necessarily turns on some conception or other of 'morality' drawn from an external source defining 'right' or 'true human feeling.' This had been Bentham's position as well, and one which Mill had in his early reaction from Bentham originally disputed (cf. Hollander, 1985, 617f.).

34. As will also be recalled from chapter 18, VIII, the fact that Malthus's utilitarianism drew on Paley must not cloud their differences on the constituents of the greatest-good formula.

35. Our conclusion may be contrasted with that of Eversley, 1959, 248-9: The preventive checks which reduce fertility 'may be divided into good, bad, and indifferent checks. The good one is moral restraint, i.e. restraint from marriage with virtuous conduct, and out of regard for the well-being of society, as well as one's own advantage. The bad one is self-seeking prudential restraint from marriage with loose sexual conduct. The indifferent one is prudential restraint mostly for selfish reasons, with an occasional human lapse presumably permitted.'

36. Malthus often reverted to the ideal. Thus moral restraint is represented in 1824 (and repeated 1830) as 'the only mode of keeping population on a level with the means of subsistence, which is perfectly consistent with virtue and happiness' (1986, *4*, 203).

37. Paley in fact wrote in somewhat qualified fashion: 'within certain limits . . . it may be affirmed, I think, with certainty, that the quantity of happiness produced in any given district (the object of which all the endeavours of public wisdom should be directed,) *so far* depends upon the number of inhabitants, that, in comparing adjoining periods in the same country, the collective happiness will

be nearly in the exact proportion of the numbers, that is, twice the number of inhabitants will produce double the quantity of happiness.' Land scarcity, however, was not a practical issue for Paley: 'The fertility of the ground, in temperate regions, is capable of being improved by cultivation to an extent which is unknown' (590).

Bentham was also to qualify his utility-based case for population increase: 'Increase of population is desirable, as being an increase of—1. The beings susceptible of *enjoyment*; 2. The beings capable of being employed as *instruments of defence*. It results of course from the encrease of the means of subsistence, and *cannot be carried beyond them*' (1801-4/1954, III, 361).

38. Empson reported that Malthus subsequently regarded Paley and Pitt as 'the two converts of whom he was most proud.' For Paley's apparent 'conversion,' see chapter 18, note 35.

39. Malthus's famous statement that, without Poor Laws, 'though there might have been a few more instances of very severe distress, the aggregate mass of happiness among the common people would have been much greater than it is at present' (1803/1986, *3*, 368), implies that a *smaller* population at good average wages is preferable on utility grounds to a larger population at poor average wages. Thus it is not apparent that he countenanced growth of population (and therefore higher population at any time) when accompanied by *reduced* standards. Bonar's evaluation (1924, 333) therefore goes too far: 'Malthus desired the great numbers as well as the great happiness, and was indeed quite naturally led by his theological views to prefer a little happiness for each of many individuals to a great deal for each of a few.'

40. See Pullen, 1981, 42; Spengler, 1960, 379, 385.

41. Mill did, however, recognize the case for a large population relative to that of neighbours from the perspective of defence (755). How far Mill's case for a 'stationary state' was a matter of daydreaming is discussed in Hollander, 1994a.

42. Cf. the earlier proposition that the desire for marriage and procreation acts as stimulus to effort (chapter 18, p. 881). On this 'paradox' in the context of Malthus's optimistic theology, see Pullen, 1981, 51-2; Grampp, 1974, 298; Winch, 1993, 250.

43. Place acknowledged the connection with Malthus and gave him a sympathetic reading: 'Mr. Malthus seems to shrink from discussing the propriety of preventing conception, not so much it may be supposed from the abhorrence which he or any reasonable man can have to the practice, as from the

possible fear of encountering the prejudices of others . . .' (173).

44. This, it will be recalled from chapter 1, pp. 38-9, 41-2, by no means reflects unimpressive technology but the diversion of resources from agriculture under pressure of high luxury consumption and government interference.

45. Even in 1798, the empirical problem in Britain is *not* represented as one of excess population growth. Rather, low real wages reflected remediable impediments to agricultural growth. Strictly, then, the theological chapters were unnecessary, even in 1798.

46. This 'mundane' perspective Harvey-Phillips represents as Paley's view. This is fair enough, for Paley seems to aver to a balance of happiness in *this* world (cf. 1785, Book II, ch. V: 'The Divine Benevolence'). Yet we must not forget that, for Paley, moral behaviour allows for fear of punishment and hope of reward after death (above, section II).

47. For further evidence pointing to this conclusion, see Pullen, 1987b.

48. Mill's hostile comments on Paley's use of the utility rule in defence of 'accredited doctrines' is pertinent here (1852/1969, X,173).

References

WORKS BY THOMAS ROBERT MALTHUS

BOOKS AND PAMPHLETS

Works = The Works of Thomas Robert Malthus. Ed. E. A. Wrigley and D. Souden (8 vols.). London 1986

1798. *An Essay on the Principle of Population.* 1st ed., London; Facsimile ed., London 1926. Also in *Works, 1*

1803. *An Essay on the Principle of Population.* 2d ed. London. In *Works, 2-3*

1806. *An Essay on the Principle of Population.* 3d ed. (2 vols.). London

1807a. *An Essay on the Principle of Population.* 4th ed. (2 vols.). London

1814. *Observations on the Effects of the Corn Laws.* 1st ed., London. In *Works, 7, 87-109*

1815b. *An Inquiry into the Nature and Progress of Rent.* 1st ed., London. In *Works, 7, 115-45*

1817. *An Essay on the Principle of Population.* 5th ed. (3 vols.). London

1820. *Principles of Political Economy.* 1st ed., London. Ed. J. Pullen (2 vols.). Cambridge 1989

1826. *An Essay on the Principle of Population.* 6th ed. (2 vols.). London. In *Works, 2-3*

1989. *An Essay on the Principle of Population.* Ed. P. James (2 vols.). Cambridge

OTHER PRIMARY WORKS

[Anon]. 1798. Review of Malthus, 1798. *Analytical Review* 28/2 (August), 119-25

Bentham, Jeremy. 1801-4. ['Method and Leading Features of an Institute of Political Economy.'] In *Jeremy Bentham's Economic Writings,* ed. W. Stark, III, 305-80. London 1954

[Empson, William]. 1837. 'Life, Writings and Character of Mr. Malthus.' *Edinburgh Review* 64/130, Article IX (January) 469-506. In *Occasional Papers of T. R. Malthus,* ed. B. Semmel, 231-68. New York 1963

Godwin, William. 1796. *Enquiry Concerning Political Justice.* 2d. ed. (2 vols.). London

[Hazlitt, William]. 1807. *A Reply to the 'Essay on Population' by the Rev. T. R. Malthus.* London

Jarrold, Thomas. 1806. *Dissertations on Man, Philosophical, Physiological and Political, in Answer to Mr. Malthus's Essay.* London

Mill, J. S. 1835. 'Sedgwick's Discourse.' *London Review* 1 (July), 341-71. In *Collected Works,* X, 31-74. Toronto 1969

——— 1848. *Principles of Political Economy.* 1st ed., London; 7th ed., London, 1871. In *Collected Works,* II-III. Toronto 1965

——— 1852. 'Whewell on Moral Philosophy.' *Westminster and Foreign Quarterly Review* 58 (October), 349-85. In *Collected Works,* X, 175-201. Toronto 1969

——— 1865. *An Examination of Sir William Hamilton's Philosophy.* 1st ed., London; 4th ed., London, 1872. In *Collected Works,* IX, Toronto 1979

——— 1873. *Autobiography.* 1st ed., London. In *Collected Works,* I, 1-290. Toronto 1981

——— 1879. 'Chapters on Socialism.' *Forthnightly Review,* n.s. 25 (February), 217-37; (March), 373-82; (April), 513-30 (posthumously published). In *Collected Works,* V, 705-53. Toronto 1967

——— 1972. *The Later Letters, 1849-1873.* Collected Works, XIV-XVII, Toronto

Paley, William. 1785. *The Principles of Moral and Political Philosophy.* 1st ed., London

——— 1802. *Natural Theology, or Evidences of the Existence and Attributes of the Deity.* 1st ed., London; 2d ed., London 1803

—— 1850. 'Sermons on Several Subjects,' No. XXXIII, *The Works of William Paley D.D.* (posthumously published). 599-601. Philadelphia

Place, F. 1822. *Illustrations and Proofs of the Principle of Population.* London 1822; London 1930; New York 1967

Ravenstone, Piercy [Richard Puller]. 1821. *A Few Doubts . . . on the Subjects of Population and Political Economy.* London

Senior, Nassau. 1829. *Two Lectures on population . . . to which is added, a Correspondence Between the Author and the Rev. T. R. Malthus.* London

—— 1830. *Three Lectures on the Cost of Obtaining Money, and on Some Effects of Private and Government Paper Money.* London

Torrens, Robert. 1815. *An Essay on the External Corn Trade.* 1st ed., London; 3d ed., London 1826

Tucker, Abraham. 1763-78. *Light of Nature Pursued.* (5 vols.). London

Weyland, John. 1816. *The Principles of Population and Production.* London

SECONDARY WORKS RELATING TO MALTHUS

Bonar, J. 1924. *Malthus and His Work.* 2d ed. London

Flew, A. 1970. 'Introduction.' In Malthus, *Essay on the Principle of Population,* 7-56. Harmondsworth

Grampp, W. D. 1974. 'Malthus and His Contemporaries.' *History of Political Economy* 6/3 (Fall), 278-304

Harvey-Phillips, M. B. 1984. 'Malthus's Theodicy: The Intellectual Background to his Contribution to Political Economy.' *History of Political Economy* 16/4 (Winter), 591-608

Hollander, Samuel. 1969. 'Malthus and the Post-Napoleonic Depression.' *History of Political Economy* 1/2 (Fall), 306-35

—— 1986. 'On Malthus's Population Principle and Social Reform.' *History of Political Economy* 18/2 (Summer), 187-235

—— 1992a. 'Malthus's Abandonment of Agricultural Protectionism: A Discovery in the History of Economic Thought. *American Economic Review* 82/3 (June), 650-9

—— 1992b. 'On Malthus's Physiocratic References.' *History of Political Economy* 24/2 (Spring), 369-80

—— 1995a. 'More on Malthus and Agricultural Protection.' *History of Political Economy* 27/3 (Fall), 531-8

James, Patricia. 1979. *Population Malthus: His Life and Times.* London

Levy, D. 1996. 'Malthusian vs. Christianity: The Moral Challenge to God's Existence.' Ms.

Pullen, John M. 1981a. 'Malthus's Theological Ideas and Their Influence on His Principle of Population.' *History of Political Economy* 13/1 (Spring), 39-54

—— 1981b. 'Notes from Malthus: The Inverarity Manuscript.' *History of Political Economy* 13/4 (Winter), 794-811

—— 1987b. 'Some New Information on the Rev. T. R. Malthus,' *History of Political Economy* 19/1 (Spring), 127-40

Rashid, S. 1984. 'Malthus' Theology: An Overlooked Letter and Some Comments.' *History of Political Economy* 16/1 (Spring), 135-8

Semmel, B. 1963. 'Introductory Essay: Malthus and the Reviews.' In *Occasional Papers of T. R. Malthus,* ed. B. Semmel, 3-29. New York

Sowell, T. 1962. 'Malthus and the Utilitarians.' *Canadian Journal of Economics and Political Science* 28/2 (May), 268-74

Spengler, J. J. 1960 [1945]. 'Malthus's Total Population Theory: A Restatement and Reappraisal.' In *Essays in Economic Thought: Aristotle to Marshall,* ed. J. J. Spengler and W. R. Allen, 349-406. Chicago 1960

Waterman, A. M. C. 1983. 'Malthus as a Theologian: The First Essay and the Relation between Political Economy and Christian Theology.' In *Malthus Past and Present,* ed. J. Dupâquier, A. Fauve-Chamoux, and E. Grebenik, 198-209. London and New York

—— 1991. *Revolution, Economics, and Religion: Christian Political Economy, 1798-1833.* Cambridge

—— 1992. 'Analysis and ideology in Malthus's *Essay on Population.' Australian Economic Papers* 31 (June), 203-17

Winch, D. 1983. 'Higher Maxims: Happiness versus Wealth in Malthus and Ricardo.' In *That Nobele Science of Politics,* ed. S. Collini, D. Winch, and J. Burrow, 63-90. Cambridge

—— 1993. 'Robert Malthus: Christian Moral Scientist, Arch-Demoralizer, or Implicit Secular Utilitarian?' *Utilitas* 5/2 (November), 239-54

OTHER SECONDARY WORKS

Hollander, Samuel. 1994a. 'Economic Theory and Policy: An Introduction to John Stuart Mill's Political Economy. In *Economic Thought and Political Theory,* ed. D. Reisman, 63-101. Boston

O'Brien, D. P. 1975. *The Classical Economists.* Oxford

Robbins, L. C. 1952. *The Theory of Economic Policy in English Classical Political Economy.* London

Sowell, T. 1974. *Classical Economics Reconsidered.* Princeton, NJ

GENERAL ECONOMIC THEORY AND ITS HISTORY

Taylor, O. H. 1960. *A History of Economic Thought.* New York

WORKS ON ECONOMIC, POLITICAL, AND SOCIAL HISTORY

Eversley, D. E. C. 1959. *Social Theories of Fertility and the Malthusian Debate.* Oxford

Stephen, L. 1900. *The English Utilitarians* (3 vols). London

Viner, J. 1972. *The Role of Providence in the Social Order.* Philadelphia

Eric B. Ross (essay date 1998)

SOURCE: Ross, Eric B. "Politics and Paradigms: The Origins of Malthusian Theory." In *The Malthus Factor: Population, Poverty and Politics in Capitalist Development,* pp. 8-30. London: Zed Books, 1998.

[*In the following essay, Ross discusses the historical, political, and economic factors behind Malthus's theory of population which, Ross claims, provide justification for the system of private property as it existed in the late eighteenth and early nineteenth centuries.*]

> It is clearly the duty of each individual not to marry till he has a prospect of supporting his children; but it is at the same time to be wished that he should retain undiminished his desire of marriage in order that he may exert himself to realize this prospect, and be stimulated to make provisions for the support of greater numbers.
>
> Thomas Malthus

When Malthus's first *Essay* was published, England was in the midst of an agricultural revolution which was transforming long-standing agrarian relations between landlords and tenants; it was on the verge of an industrial revolution which would soon make it the paramount manufacturing nation in Europe; and it was five years into a counter-revolutionary war with its growing commercial rival, Napoleonic France.

It is hardly surprising that landlords, mercantilists and industrialists were all preoccupied with the question of property relations. Not only were new social and economic pressures pushing old institutional frameworks to their limits, but the French Revolution, which "destroyed the landmarks of the old established order in politics, economics, social life and thought" (Thomson

1966: 49), had unleashed many threatening ideas about the fundamental legitimacy of private property. Malthus's work emerged as a response to the anxieties which these produced in England.

Historian Carl Becker once called attention to the fact that the Jacobin spirit produced much the same response politically among the English that Bolshevism did in America over a century later (Becker 1932). As he wrote, long before the advent of Senator McCarthy and the rise of Henry Kissinger:

> To the Castlereaghs and Metternichs of our day the word "Bolshevism" is the symbol of all that is horrendously antisocial, just as the word "Jacobinism" was to the Castlereaghs and Metternichs of 1815; and the words "soviet" and "communism" have for the beneficiaries of modern democracy the same ominous import that the word "republicanism" formerly had for the beneficiaries of the age of kings and nobles.
>
> (1932: 166)

One of the earliest important English expressions of this attitude, appearing in 1790, was Edmund Burke's *Reflections on the Revolution in France.* This book was especially notable for provoking two immediate and important rejoinders. One was Mary Wollstonecraft's *A Vindication of the Rights of Men* (in 1790);[1] the other was Thomas Paine's *Rights of Man* (in 1791) (Wollstonecraft 1994; Paine 1969).

The former explicitly accused Burke of championing property and of narrowly equating the defence of liberty with the maintenance of a system of unequal property ownership. But it was Paine's work which achieved the greatest distribution and notoriety (Claeys 1989: 67-82, 112). The pamphlet became a catalyst for the organisation of local branches of what was known as the London Corresponding Society (LCS). But this development was itself a symptom of the state of the country and it justified the government's fears of the turmoil that lay on the horizon, not only at home but in Ireland as well, where The United Irishmen had formed in 1790 and took as their main objective "to form a Republic, independent from England or France; to form a constitution upon the French model" (quoted in Claeys 1989: 118).

The seeming threat of widespread insurrection (Wells 1983) led the government to take repressive measures. Noted radicals were put on trial, the Habeas Corpus Act was suspended, the Treason Act was widened (Claeys 1989: 141). One of the government's targets was Mary Wollstonecraft's husband, William Godwin, whose *Enquiry Concerning Political Justice* was published in 1793 and who barely escaped standing trial for treason. All this was obviously made easier by the onset of war with France, which provided an admirable rationale for a crack-down on radicals. It also helped to blame the state of unrest on an imported ideology, at a time when the English working class had ample reasons of its own for protest.

By the time Malthus published his *Essay* in 1798, the very year that the United Irishmen actually attempted an uprising, the dangers represented by the French Revolution seemed quite real. Malthus, who had no intention of letting his readers misunderstand his aims and allegiances, grandly entitled his pamphlet *An Essay on the Principle of Population as It Affects the Future Improvement of Society, with Remarks on the Speculations of Mr. Godwin, M. Condorcet, and Other Writers.* Godwin, of course, was an easy and logical target. Condorcet was a more esoteric reference. But it is easy to see why Malthus singled him out: a mathematician and biographer of Voltaire, Condorcet represented revolutionary Paris in the new Legislative Assembly, in which he was one of the first members to call for a republic. Unlike Malthus, who regarded material want as essential to goad the poor into serious effort, Condorcet believed that government should actually ensure that people were not "exposed to misery, to humiliation, to oppression"; for him, it was a duty of government to guarantee "That all members of society should have an assured subsistence each season, each year, and wherever they live; that those who live on their wages, above all, should be able to buy the subsistence they need" (quoted in Rothschild 1996: 341).

Over the following decades, as the character of the European social landscape changed dramatically, Malthus was encouraged to expand and embellish his essay, to adapt it to emerging conditions. As the radical impulses of the French Revolution began to wane and the Napoleonic state emerged, the ensuing struggle between France and England, which lasted over twenty years, did much to unleash the productive forces of industrial capitalism, especially in England. As antagonisms between capital and the working class intensified, the threat from French republicanism began to seem far less important than that from the advocates of socialism. Malthus's theory of population became less and less a critique of Godwin's ideas of progress and was adapted to the debates that arose out of the process of English capitalist development.

But what never changed was the role of Malthusian theory in the legitimisation of private property arrangements. It remained committed to the view that Godwin's idea of progress, which was associated with the abolition of private property, was wholly negated by the dismal consequences of population increase pressing on the available means of subsistence. It thereby absolved such a system of responsibility for human misery by describing the latter as a natural effect of irrepressible biological urges on the part of a class that, innately or

otherwise, was viewed as having little capacity for rational control. And, finally, it argued that any public obligation to mitigate that misery was fundamentally incompatible with the ultimate rights of property, since any form of social welfare was bound to be little more than a way of subsidising the fertility of the poor at the expense of the well-to-do and therefore of creating further misery. (This studiously ignored the question of how the well-to-do managed to maintain themselves, if not at the expense of the poor.) In this way, Malthus not only offered the authority of natural law in defence of established property relations, but created a general explanatory framework which was to prove one of the most enduring bulwarks against any argument for the mitigation of economic or social injustice. That it has retained this role over two centuries underscores how little fundamentally has changed between his time and our own.

TOWARD AN END OF THE OLD POOR LAWS

. . . the Poor Law discussion formed the minds of Bentham and Burke, Godwin and Malthus, Ricardo and Marx, Robert Owen and John Stuart Mill, Darwin and Spencer.

Karl Polanyi

The debates which Malthus joined reflected the concerns of English capitalists, industrial and gentry alike (since the distinction was not always a clear one; cf. Ward and Wilson 1971), who felt constrained by many of the institutional arrangements, inherited from preceding centuries, which now seemed to them to restrict opportunities for investment and profit. A major focus of their opposition was the old Elizabethan poor laws which provided for parish relief, paid for by local taxation. It is important to underscore that these laws had not originated as a form of charity. Far from it. Both in England and on the continent, such legislation had been promulgated in the sixteenth century as a form of social control, directed especially against the great numbers of poor who had been displaced by enclosures and driven to seek a living wherever and however they could (Jordan 1959). After decades of ineffectual measures, in 1597 the English Parliament passed what was called "An act for the relief of the poor", which created the system of parish relief which Malthus and others would seek to abolish two hundred years later. This law

remained, with numerous reaffirmations and quite minor amendments, the central law of the land relating to poor relief for very nearly two and one-half centuries. It fixed the parish as the unit of ultimate responsibility not only because the facts regarding poverty were best known there, but probably more importantly, because the whole scheme of poor relief rested on the assumption that a stable society, a non-migratory society, offered fewer social perils to the state.

(Jordan 1959: 97)

By the late eighteenth century, however, the Tudor poor laws were regarded by employers as an unnecessary drain on private income and the principal impediment to the creation of the free and mobile labour reserve which emergent industrial capitalism required. It was not to be until 1834, the year of Malthus's death, that the Poor Law Reform Act, passed by a new Whig government dominated by merchants and industrialists, finally "set the seal on unfettered free trade in the labour market" (Dobb 1963: 275). Until then, less brutal mechanisms were devised. Polanyi (1944) regarded 1795 as a watershed because, in that year, the magistrates who administered the poor law in the county of Berkshire met in the village of Speenhamland to revise the system of local relief. The result, which was soon emulated in many other parts of England, was imperfect and contradictory; but it highlighted the widespread discontent among the landed gentry with the nature of relief, even while it reflected their interest in maintaining a system which guaranteed the local reserves of cheap, casual labour that English agriculture, not yet mechanised, still required.

Speenhamland reflected arguments against the poor laws that had been mounting for some time. Twelve years before Malthus's *Essay,* another English cleric, Joseph Townsend, had published a pamphlet (1786), entitled *Dissertation on the Poor Laws,* which had not only argued for their abolition but had suggested, as Malthus would, that such corrective efforts were in vain, since "wretchedness has increased in proportion to the efforts made to relieve it" (quoted in Chase 1982: 55). Townsend's writings contain many of the essential features, as well as the spirit, of Malthusianism. Neither man really believed, for example, that a disparity between population growth and food production—the essence of the latter's law of population—was entirely natural or preordained. After all, both wrote in a period of unprecedented agricultural productivity. Between 1750 and 1840, when the population of England and Wales almost doubled, cereal production did as well (Hobsbawm and Rudé 1969: 27-9). This partly reflected the fact that, after 1801, Irish grain harvests counted as British; and it owed a great deal as well to the stimulus to grain production provided by the Napoleonic Wars and the Corn Laws. Under any circumstances, it meant, as Townsend observed, that it was "indeed possible to banish hunger". The problem, he emphasised, was that this would only have undesirable effects. More food would encourage the poor to breed more recklessly, whereas hunger and disease would curb the numbers of those he described as the "unworthy" (thus demonstrating why Malthusianism would ultimately find an intellectual ally in eugenics a century later).

Equally important, Townsend also regarded hunger as a necessary incentive for people to pursue employment. Anticipating Malthus, he wrote of how

Hope and fear are the springs of industry. . . . The poor know nothing of the motives which stimulate the higher ranks to action—pride, honour, and ambition. In general it is only hunger which can spur and goad them on to labour; yet our laws [i.e., the Poor Laws] have said that they shall never hunger.

(in Snell 1985: 123)

Like Townsend, Malthus also did not wish to see the poor guaranteed such entitlements. In his first *Essay* he had called for the "abolition of all the present parish laws" (Digby 1983: 97). For a man who described a world in which the means of subsistence were said to be continuously under threat from rising population, he was, as we have seen, remarkably judgemental and restrictive in his view of how that threat might be reduced by practical efforts. Yet perhaps to some extent this was because the spectre of over-population was too important and necessary as a rationale for the policies he wanted to prescribe. If it was the chief cause of human misery, he could plausibly argue against the poor laws on the grounds that they artificially subsidised the fertility of the poor. He could therefore say that it was as much in the interests of the poor as of the rich that they should be abolished, as did Malthus's friend, the economist David Ricardo. Ricardo observed that the rising costs of relief "make the rich poor" (there was little evidence for this, but this is how the rich always feel), while "every friend to the poor must ardently wish for their abolition" (Ricardo 1988: 345). (Again, it is common to hear how such entitlements degrade the poor, even more than poverty itself.)

In private, however, Malthus acknowledged that this was a theoretical assumption for which there was no real evidence, a view which has been sustained by recent research (Huzel 1969). But for the landed and commercial interests, whose arguments against the poor laws were fuelled by their disdain for the rising costs of parish relief, the Malthusian frame of reference offered the compelling line of argument that the fertility of the poor was being stimulated by the security which poor relief seemingly offered. It made the reproductive habits of the poor accountable for their poverty, for the process of proletarianisation which was a predominant feature of this period, especially in the rural areas, and for the burdens which the poor laws increasingly placed on people of property. But, in fact, neither the rise of a proletariat nor the rising cost of poor relief was really due to increasing population *per se.* It owed far more to the intense commercialisation of agriculture, especially during the Napoleonic Wars, which forced the enclosure of common lands across England during this period (Hammond and Hammond 1987; Hobsbawm and Rudé 1969: 27) and of which Malthus took remarkably little account.

ENCLOSURES, CORN LAWS AND THE DEFENCE OF PROPERTY

The enclosure process was not only the hallmark of the increasing pressure of commercial agriculture in these years. It represented the privatisation of the last vestiges of communal rights and property. As Blum writes:

> Enclosure and consolidation transformed land in which an entire community had rights of use into land in which only the individual occupant had the right of use.
>
> (1978: 263)

Between 1750 and 1850, about a quarter of England's cultivated acreage was transformed from open field, common land or waste into private property. Most of this occurred between 1760 and 1815 (Hobsbawm and Rudé 1968: 27). Many of the dispossessed could find no secure alternative employment either in the countryside or in the towns and, in the face of rising food prices, they were driven to depend on poor relief. As a result of the increasing number of claimants and the Speenhamland formula, the cost of relief nationally rose steadily during this period.

We are now told that the commons leads to tragedy (cf. Hardin 1968). But in reality it was the loss of the commons which was the tragedy, as it destroyed the economic viability of households. Even Arthur Young, the prominent agricultural writer and secretary of the Board of Agriculture, who initially regarded enclosure as part of a necessary process of modernisation, came to view it as destroying the basis of rural self-sufficiency. From first-hand experience, he had come to see how "before the enclosures, the despised commons had enabled the cottager to keep a cow, and this, so far from bringing ruin, had meant in very many cases all the difference between independence and pauperism" (in Hammond and Hammond 1987: 83).

And while enclosure proceeded, alternative rural opportunities were also shrinking, as landlords pushed their advantage, reflecting the undemocratic temper of the period. One of the few means by which the rural poor could enhance their depleted diet (Hobsbawm 1964) was by poaching, but the penalties for poaching were becoming increasingly harsh. According to Morton,

> In 1800 poachers became liable to hard labour and to two years' imprisonment for a second offence. In 1803, it was enacted that any poacher who pointed a gun or attempted to cut or stab while resisting arrest should be hanged as a felon. In 1817 any person not belonging to the class entitled to pursue game who might be found in any park or wood with a gun or any other weapon became liable to transportation.
>
> (1979: 371)

All that remained of the idea that the poor had any right to subsistence was the old poor laws, and these were plainly in the sights of the proponents of Malthusian theory.

Under such circumstances, it was natural that part of the defence against enclosure rested on an almost Arcadian ideal of rural England. If anyone ever represented this ideal and used it as effective polemic against the tide of commercialisation sweeping over rural England in the early nineteenth century, it was William Cobbett. Cobbett was a man of robust contradictions. He had first made his reputation as a Tory pamphleteer, but sometime early in the nineteenth century, after living in the United States, probably due to the influence of Paine, he emerged as the greatest radical writer of his era (Williams 1983: 23ff.). For Cobbett, the enclosures were just part of a wholesale transformation of rural England which had created a new system that had

> drawn the real property of the nation into fewer . . . hands . . . made land and agriculture objects of speculation . . . in every part of the kingdom, moulded farms into one . . . almost entirely extinguished the race of small farmers.
>
> (in Williams 1983: 12)

But even without the potato, the rural populace was being squeezed by the strategy of enclosure, initiated for landlords by a legislature run by landlords.

It has been argued that, despite this, enclosure was as necessary as the abolition of the poor laws, to modernise the economy. In the late eighteenth century, Young had been one of the most notable champions of this view. But reexamination of the data he collected suggests that he greatly overdramatised the positive impact of enclosure, that they

> do not support the conclusion that enclosures or capitalist farming caused the growth in English grain yields. This was just landlord ideology in the eighteenth century.
>
> (Allen and Ó Gráda 1988: 116)

And if productivity increased during the Napoleonic Wars, it was as much in response to the boom market for grain as anything else.

Moreover, as with the Green Revolution in our own time (Lindenbaum 1987; Franke 1987), increased food production did not necessarily correspond to greater purchasing capacity for the poor. It was actually the opposite after the war, when the Corn Laws kept an artificial floor under grain prices and pushed up the price of bread. The cost of a 4 lb loaf in London doubled between 1790-94 and 1810-14 (Mathias 1969: 474), making the issue of the price of bread one of the central focal points of working-class protest after 1815 (Thompson 1963).

Meanwhile, the enclosures, by forcing new cohorts of landless rural families to seek wage labour, were also intended to bring more workers within the orbit of English employers and to accustom them to the new realities of the market economy (Snell 1985: 120)—to the discipline and other supposed moral virtues that it required—and to moderate the level of wages. But new opportunities for wage employment did not often materialise (Snell 1985: 183). As a result, poor relief expenditures tended to rise in the wake of enclosures (Snell 1985: 195ff.). Because the process of enclosure was irreversible, landowners and employers then sought to dismantle the whole edifice of poor relief. Speenhamland was a relatively modest step in that direction, although by pegging relief to the price of bread, it had created a new set of problems. (Under the system which they devised, the working poor were to obtain a wage pegged to the price of bread; when and if their wages were insufficient, relief would raise their income to the appropriate threshold [Watson 1969: 9-10].)

But it was Malthus three years later who provided the most persuasive argument, which in the end finally won the day in the unremitting attack on the poor laws. It gained strength through the years from the evidence that there were, indeed, increasing numbers of dependent poor. But it obscured the fact that, to a very large degree, they had been made, not born.

In its particular focus on population, then, Malthusianism provided a way of looking at the origins of poverty—and, by extension to more recent times, to underdevelopment—which effectively mystified the central role of capitalist relations of production. Nowhere is this better illustrated than by Malthus's defence of the English Corn Laws. As a result of these laws—which were not repealed until 1846 (Morton 1979: 404)—the poor suffered nutritional stress, not because of an absolute scarcity of food, as classical Malthusian thinking would argue, but because of state policy, dictated by and operating in the interest of the landowners and large farmers who controlled Parliament up to the early 1840s.

There is no doubt that, at various times during the Napoleonic Wars, there were real food shortages in Britain and even famine—in 1794-96 and 1799-1801, for example (Wells 1988). While Malthus was undoubtedly influenced by these events, which would have lent his views a certain credibility, he must have recognised that they were the result, not of population growth, but of the dynamics of a war economy. Yet, again, the effects of the Napoleonic Wars on British economy and society seem to have been easily overlooked. Even as the war created an enormous national debt which forced up prices and reduced real wages, he published a pamphlet in 1800, called *An Investigation of the Cause of the Present High Price of Provisions,* which attributed rising prices solely to "the attempt in most parts of the kingdom to increase parish allowances in proportion to the price of corn" (Keynes 1956: 24-5). That is, he blamed the poor laws.

During much of the period during which Malthus wrote, British grain production was on the increase. Aside from the introduction of new farming methods and technologies—and access to Irish grain—this owed much to the fact that large amounts of land were being enclosed, in response to the high war-time grain prices. These enclosures were a major cause of the rural poverty that Malthus no longer wished to have assisted by parish relief. In the long run, however, many of the rural poor either left for the towns and cities or remained as a local under-class. If the latter were not highly regarded as workers (Kerr 1943: 366), with the growth of factory production, "town workers . . . were no longer making annual excursions into the country for harvest work" (Kerr 1943: 373). At crucial periods, English farmers actually faced a labour scarcity which had to be met by importing Irish workers (Collins 1969), whose availability was the direct result of the chronic underemployment with which British rule had inflicted Ireland.

The movement of rural population into new urban centres began in earnest in the last quarter of the eighteenth century. New wealth from the conquest of India (Baran 1957: 146) and lucrative profits derived from the Atlantic slave trade and the development of plantation economies in the Caribbean provided capital for investment in manufacturing (Mathias 1969: 105). The rapid technical expansion of English industry owed everything to the emergence of a new global colonialist system whose complex texture Deane describes so well:

> Weapons, hardware, spirits from Britain, and calicoes from India were shipped to West Africa and exchanged for slaves, ivory, and gold. The slaves were sold in the West Indies for sugar, dyestuffs, mahogany, logwood, tobacco, and raw cotton. The gold and ivory were shipped to the East and Near East for teas, silks, calicoes, coffee, and spices. The tropical goods were sold in Europe for Baltic timber, hemp, pitch, and tar (all essential naval stores), Swedish and Russian iron; and, in the fourth quarter of the century, they paid for the foreign grain which was vital when the harvest failed and which was regularly required in most years even when the harvest did not fail.
>
> (1979: 55)

But, above all, it was the English cotton textile industry that was transformed. It is here that we confront the obverse of the European picture of the developing world as one retarded by traditionalism in the idea that Europe developed economically because of the intrinsic genius of its people. This is belied above all by the nature of the transformations that are referred to as the "Industrial Revolution", the catalyst for which seems rather to have been the English gift for conquest, pillage and duplicity. The turning point in particular was Robert Clive's victory at Plassey in Bengal, a victory that was ensured less by Clive's tactical brilliance than by the fact he had bribed many of his opponent's soldiers not to fight. As Brooks Adams wrote:

very soon after Plassey, the Bengal plunder began to arrive in London, and the effect seems to have been instantaneous; for all the authorities agree that the "industrial revolution" . . . began with the year 1760.

(quoted in Baran 1957: 146)

Clive himself, officially an employee of the East India Company, returned to England a year later with over £300,000 in personal treasure (Bence-Jones 1974).

Of course, the riches from India were not the only new wealth which England capitalised upon. There was also the slave trade and the Atlantic "triangular trade", of which it was an integral part (Williams 1944). Liverpool especially grew rich on sugar and slaves (Aikin 1968); and, as its merchants enriched themselves, they invested their profits in textiles and other industries in the surrounding towns of Lancashire (Mathias 1969: 105).

Despite this, Wilkinson, in his book *Poverty and Progress,* which was hailed as a sophisticated reworking of Malthus (Boulding 1973), portrayed the rise of industrial Europe and England in particular as a matter of local responses to ecological depletion. He makes little reference to colonies—neither Ireland nor the Caribbean (or West Indies) is mentioned in the index—and in a brief account of the displacement of the woollen industry by cotton textile production—a process so complex that books have been written about it—he makes a reference to India that is perfunctory at best. According to Wilkinson,

> Although cotton was—like wool—a landbased resource, the fact that it depended on the exploitation of land in India and America rather than in England meant that it could provide a way out of the domestic impasse. The manufacture of clothing could be expanded without threatening the production of food.
>
> (1973: 128)

Of course, it did threaten food production, just not in England. Moreover, it was not from India that raw cotton came initially. On the contrary, India produced excellent-quality cotton textiles which dominated the English market up to the early eighteenth century (Mantoux 1961: 199-200) until Parliament decided to restrict their import and, through a long succession of acts, eventually managed to decimate Indian cotton manufacture (Morton 1979: 337; Dutt 1940: 124ff.). It was partly to compete with superior Indian cottons that English textile manufacturing had been impelled to contemplate new techniques of production.

Contrary to Wilkinson, "raw cotton came largely from the Levant, the southern States of America and the West Indies" (Deane 1979: 88); India was not a major supplier until after 1815. But what Wilkinson wholly overlooks in his compulsion to reduce such history to a

ruthlessly simple Malthusian calculus is that cotton did not supplant wool in England from the late eighteenth century onward simply because of its extra-territorial provenance, but because it was grown by slaves on Caribbean plantations. Those slaves, in turn, were fed on provisions imported from another English colony—Ireland—with catastrophic results for the diet of the Irish peasantry, as we will see in the next chapter.

The Caribbean plantations and, later, India were able to provide England with cotton in such prodigious quantities that cotton manufacturing not only displaced woollen production throughout Lancashire, but triggered the rise of new factory towns almost overnight (Chadwick 1862: 14). As the price of cotton dropped from 2 *s.* per lb in the 1780s to 1 *s.* in the 1820s (and halved again over the next twenty years) (Barrett Brown 1974: 87), imports soared from just over 4 million pounds of raw fibre in the period 1755-64, to 24.45 million pounds in 1775-84, to almost 43 million pounds in 1785-95 (Wilson and Lenman 1977: 121). The expansion of cotton textile manufacturing brought a commensurate rise in the demand for labour, which had a marked effect on fertility among workers.

While the enclosures were forcing rural labourers to seek new sources of income, the technical transformation of cotton production in the second half of the eighteenth century (Pinchbeck 1969: 115-17) created new opportunities. Initially, improvements were limited to the spinning of yarn and had the chief effect of providing greater supplies for domestic weaving. It led to what Pinchbeck called "the golden age" of the weaver (Pinchbeck 1969: 117). This was an inducement for earlier marriage and an interest in the positive nurturing of offspring in a new economic climate where their labour value was of increasing importance. Infant and early childhood mortality declined (Wrigley and Schofield 1981: 249). The result was that the annual population growth rate rose from 0.48 in 1745 to 1.35 in 1800 (Wrigley and Schofield 1981: 213).

With the shift in the early nineteenth century from domestic to factory production, the demand for the labour of children would become at times greater than that for their parents. In such circumstances, parents were not only eager to see their children employed, but often could not even obtain poor relief unless they sent their children to work (Morton 1979: 344). Moreover, as a result of demographic trends since the late eighteenth century, the English population had become extremely young. By 1826, some 40 percent was represented by children under the age of 16 (Wrigley and Schofield 1981). Under such circumstances, increased employment of children in an age of industrial expansion was inevitable.

Malthus, meanwhile, could only describe the increase in fertility among the English working class as a symptom of their irrationality. He was never able to see it as a strategic accommodation to the new relations of production that characterised the emergent factory system. And, if he showed so little sensitivity to the impact of the factory system on the reproductive strategies of the working class, he was equally oblivious of the conditions which increasingly affected childhood morbidity and mortality.

During the years when he was Professor of Political Economy at Haileybury, improvements in mechanisation steadily reduced the need for adult male labour and "widespread unemployment among them was often accompanied by the over-working and intense exploitation of women and especially of children" (Morton 1979: 344). By the 1830s, male unemployment was chronic in urban areas and all of a family's productive resources had to be mobilised to ensure survival. A survey in 1833 of 48,645 workers in various industrial firms in Lancashire and Cheshire found that 41 percent were under 18 years of age, while 22 percent were under 14 (Collier 1964: 68). Of 565 children working in calico print works in Lancashire, Cheshire and Derbyshire, who were sampled by the Children's Employment Commission in 1843, nearly two-thirds had begun work before the age of 9 (Hutchins and Harrison 1966: 124; cf. Chadwick 1862: 47).

Women—single or married—were also a major source of industrial labour (Anderson 1971: 73), and while this was imperative from the viewpoint of household economy, it had adverse consequences for child mortality. Maternal employment required early weaning. Wet nursing was not an option for the working class, cows' milk was expensive and often unhealthy anyway, and new manufactured infant foods were an impractical, unaffordable alternative. It was not until around 1870 that cheaper tinned condensed milk appeared, but it was deficient in vitamins A and D—and therefore was conducive to rickets—and was also likely, if used, to be diluted (like much infant formula in the Third World today) with unclean water (Hewitt 1958: 147-8). Thus, the factory system, which came to depend so much on child labour, also created material conditions which were fiercely prejudicial to the survival of the young. This can be seen clearly enough in mortality trends in the northern industrial towns. In Preston, Lancashire, for example, the proportion of all deaths climbed from 29.3 percent among the under-fives in 1783 to 53.4 percent in 1841 (Harris and Ross 1987: 115). For the working class, there was an irreconcilable tension between the need for their children to work and the detrimental impact on children of their fathers' insecure employment and their mothers' low-waged labour.

Poor nutrition, crowded and sunless housing, new infectious diseases such as cholera and typhoid which thrived on the insanitary conditions of urban industrial life (Rosen 1958: 201ff.), all combined to produce a high level of infant mortality that remained a feature of English working-class communities up to the eve of the Second World War. In the end, the most common working-class strategy was simply not to invest too much in children until they were past the period of highest risk and then to fatten them up as they approached an age when they could go out to work.

MALTHUS IN THE AGE OF INDUSTRIALISATION

With the end of the Napoleonic Wars, boom times for large farmers and speculators ceased. But grain prices never fell to pre-war levels because of the Corn Laws, which attempted to maintain prices, in large part by restricting grain imports (so that wheat imports were forbidden whenever the price fell below a certain level) (Morton 1979: 401). Dutifully, Malthus, who had argued that poverty was a matter of personal responsibility, published a pamphlet in 1815 which was entitled *The Grounds of an Opinion on the Policy of Restricting the Importation of Foreign Corn.* Growing rich was clearly a matter of government responsibility. So, for thirty years, while the Corn Laws stood as a prime example of market intervention, their effect on the price of bread was a significant factor in the declining living standards of the working class. Throughout the same period, the argument was made with great self-assurance, by Malthus, Ricardo and others, that poverty was the result of over-breeding on the part of the poor themselves.

During that same time, the commercialisation of English society—a society which subsidised large farmers on the one hand and took away common lands on the other—created enormous wealth, but also growing inequality. As the Hammonds wrote,

> The lives of the judges, the landlords, the parson, and the rest of the governing class were not becoming more meagre but more spacious in the last fifty years [to 1830]. During that period many of the great palaces of the English nobility had been built, noble libraries had been collected, and famous galleries had grown up, wing upon wing. [Meanwhile] the agricultural labourers whose fathers had eaten meat, bacon, cheese and vegetables were living on bread and potatoes.
>
> (1987: 241)

Potatoes, which had become an increasingly important part of the rural diet as the Corn Laws pushed up the price of bread, were, as the radical journalist William Cobbett continually noted, another means of impoverishing farm workers and enriching landlords. As early as 1770, Arthur Young had written in *A Six Months Tour Through the North of England* that

> these roots are everywhere considered as an excellent fallow crop, greatly ameliorating the soil, and preparing in every respect for wheat in particular, or for any

other grain in a very superior manner. It is extremely evident . . . that their culture is uncommonly profitable.

(1967: 12-13)

It was attractive advice for any landlord poised to enclose the local commons. Just six years later, in *The Wealth of Nations,* Adam Smith also advocated the wider use of the potato, again with the profits of large farmers in mind. Because the tuber was so productive,

the same quantity of land would maintain a much greater number of people, and the labourers being generally fed with potatoes, greater surplus would remain after replacing all the stock and maintaining all the labour employed in cultivation. A greater share of this surplus too would belong to the landlord. Population would increase, and rents would rise much beyond what they are at present.

(1947, Vol. 1: 145)

But Cobbett was aware—and we shall see this in the next chapter—that the same strategy had subverted the food security of rural Ireland. He understood how the potato would be another factor in the process of cheapening the value of workers' labour. Thus, in 1834, while he was travelling in Ireland, Cobbett wrote in his *Political Register* on the subject of the debate in the British Parliament about the New Poor Law. He suggested that, in the name of morally improving the poor, the abolition of out-door relief and the choice between poverty wages and entering the poor-house would force many people to accept the lower wages that employers would now offer. As a result, he argued, English workers would be forced to eat, not bread, but potatoes, as they were squeezed between the Corn Laws and low wages. All this, he maintained, was sanctioned by the economic philosophy of Malthusianism, which argued that the poor had no claim on society, even in the face of starvation. After all it was Malthus, in the second edition of his *Essay,* supposedly a more compassionate update of the first, who had written:

A man who is born into a world already possessed, if he cannot get subsistence from his parents on who he has a just demand, and if the society do not want his labour, has no claim of right to the smallest portion of food, and, in fact, has no business to be where he is. At nature's mighty feast there is no vacant cover for him. She tells him to be gone.

(in Meek 1971: 8)

Of course, it was not Nature which said "be gone", but Malthus, landlords and Parliament. But it was on the basis of this view, of class interest disguising itself as disinterested nature, that poor law reform was proposed.

Considerations of Malthus's work and influence have often overlooked just how much his theory of population was subservient in this way to a defence of private property relations (Harvey 1974). But it was this service that made Malthus's ideas congenial not only to the economic and political elite who encouraged the development of his ideas, but also to a whole generation of intellectuals and thinkers who laid the basis of classic Western economics. Foremost among them was David Ricardo, who, like Malthus, was firmly convinced of the immutability of the established order. His major work, *On the Principles of Political Economy and Taxation* (1817), rested securely on Malthusian foundations in its conception of the origins of poverty. In it, he observed:

It is a truth which admits not a doubt, that the comfort and well-being of the poor cannot be permanently secured without some regard on their part, or some effort on the part of the legislature, to regulate the increase of their numbers, and to render less frequent among them early and improvident marriages. The operation of the system of poor laws has been directly contrary to this. They have rendered restraint superfluous, and have invited imprudence, by offering it a portion of the wages of prudence and industry.

(1988: 345)

Thus, one of the great figures of classical economics talks about the "prudence and industry" that made individuals like himself wealthy and not wanting any of his wealth spent on the poor, who had died in battle during the war with France or gone hungry because of war-time prices or in the wake of the enclosure of common land, or who were transported to Australia for the crime of poaching, in order to feed their children. What prudent and industrious things did Ricardo do during the war? Ricardo was a stockbroker and a good friend of Malthus, with whom he maintained a continuous correspondence between 1811 and his own death in 1823. According to Keynes,

During the Napoleonic Wars, Ricardo was . . . a principal member of a Syndicate which took part in operations in Government stocks corresponding to what is now effected by "underwriting". His Syndicate would take up by tender from the Treasury a mixed bag of stocks of varying terms known as the *Omnium,* which they would gradually dispose of to the public at favourable opportunities offered. On these occasions Ricardo was in the habit of doing Malthus a friendly turn by putting him down for a small participation without requiring him to put up any money, which meant the certainty of a modest profit if Malthus did not hold on too long, since initially the Syndicate terms would always be comfortably below the current market price

(Keynes 1956: 30-31)

Not long after the end of the war, in 1817, Ricardo published his *Principles of Political Economy and Taxation.* War-time speculation had undoubtedly been quite profitable, because he was soon able to retire. He became a landed proprietor and entered Parliament in 1819, at a time when it was dominated by large landowners with a keen interest in passing bills of enclosure.

Another economist whose Malthusian sentiments have had lasting effect is the less well-known figure, William Forster Lloyd. Like Malthus an ordained minister in the Church of England, Lloyd held the Drummond Chair of Political Economy at Oxford. The author of a collection of essays entitled *Lectures on Population, Value, Poor-Laws and Rent* (1837), he is chiefly remembered, indirectly, as the inspiration for the biologist Garrett Hardin's famous essay "The Tragedy of the Commons" (1968) (see Chapter 3), and thus represents an important conceptual bridge between Malthusianism and one its most influential contemporary incarnations.

In 1833, Lloyd published his *Two Lectures on the Checks to Population,* which, in addition to expounding Malthus's central arguments, described what he regarded as the theoretical arguments against common property. There are several notable features of his argument, which would be harnessed later by Garrett Hardin to his Cold War vision of population and economy. First, it assumed that the threat to communal property came from individualism, as if this were an immutable feature of human nature, rather than a cultural and historical trait. Secondly, the whole point of Lloyd's argument was to advance Malthus's own use of the theory of population against the development of the common property regimes that he disparagingly referred to as "systems of equality". Like Hardin later, Lloyd maintained that democratic and open access to a "commons"—whether this were a pasture or the employment market—would offer little reason for people not to expand their numbers to fill it, because there would seem to be "no adequate individual benefit to be derived from abstinence" (Lloyd 1980: 484). This, he presumed, would probably occur only where a system of private property granted a limited number of people certain and guaranteed shares in a resource. Thus, for Lloyd, the "principle of population . . . furnishes a reason for the institution of private property" (1980: 496).

In addition—and here one catches intimations of the eugenicists still to come—any system of equality seemed, to Lloyd, to lead inevitably to a general lowering of standards, whereas social differentiation would ensure that people had drive and ambition. "A state of perfect equality," he wrote, "by its effect in lowering the standard of desire, and almost reducing it to the satisfaction of the natural necessities, would bring back society to ignorance and barbarism" (1980: 496). It is an old elitist argument—here, based on Malthusian precepts which were so congenial to such an argument—that democracy creates mediocrity. But it is certainly not unique to Lloyd. This anti-democratic temper (with its reference point, either explicitly or implicitly, in assumptions about biological differences) remains a central feature of Malthusian and Neo-Malthusian thinking to the present day.

Lloyd and Malthus both had clearly perceived the central issues of their time. As a result, long before Malthus's death, his theories had become the cornerstone not only of the campaign against the old poor laws, but of the increasingly bitter struggle against socialism. The means by which they fulfilled this role were varied, however. Arguments such as Lloyd's were one, which ultimately was revived by Garrett Hardin. Another was beginning to emerge as early as 1822, when what came to be called Neo-Malthusianism first began to develop. In that year, Francis Place, a disciple of Jeremy Bentham, wrote that working people, in their own interest, should curb their fertility in order to drive up wages and resolve all the problems that affected working people. As he said to them:

> Many indeed among you are compelled for a bare subsistence to labour incessantly from the moment you rise in the morning to the moment you lie down again at night, without even the hope of ever being better off.
>
> The sickness of yourselves and your children, the privation and pain and premature death of those you love but cannot cherish as you wish, need only be alluded to . . . what, you will ask is the remedy? Howe are we to avoid these miseries?
>
> The answer is short and plain: the means are easy. Do as other people do, to avoid having more children than they wish to have, and can easily maintain.
>
> (in Hardin 1969: 192-3)

The important departure here from conventional Malthusian thinking was that Place believed that this should be done not simply through moral restraint but by birth control (Thompson 1963: 777). But, of even greater strategic significance, he regarded this as more desirable than the structural transformation of society or any form of working-class militancy, even trade unionism. As Gordon has observed, he "offered contraception encapsulated in an ideology that promoted acceptance of the capitalist mode of production and distribution . . . as part of a theory that denied the concept of exploitation" (1976: 81). Place's efforts set the stage for the evolution of a birth control movement which was so divorced from sensitivity to the fate of working people that it would eventually find common cause with many of their enemies.

TOWARD A NEW POOR LAW

For the time being, however, Place's advocacy of birth control fell far short of the concrete demands of an increasingly active working class. According to Hobsbawm (1964: 30), the first "labour dispute" took place in 1831. But a year earlier, rural labourers across the south and east of England, under growing pressure from new commercial production, mechanisation, enclosures, the Corn Laws, had launched a violent, but short-lived campaign for agricultural reform, under the name of

"Captain Swing" (Hobsbawm and Rudé 1968). In its aftermath, hundreds were "transported" to Australia for real or alleged participation in the riots (Hughes 1987: 197-200) and the government put Cobbett on trial for supporting the agricultural workers (Morton 1979: 374).

The Swing riots, which were also called "The Last Labourers' Revolt", reflected the fact that the old agrarian order was generally on the wane (Blum 1978). Across Europe, the power of old landed interests was being challenged, especially by the ambitious middle class, frustrated in its efforts to forge a modern, competitive market. So, in the same year as the Swing riots, a wave of liberal revolutions also swept the continent. In France, a Bourbon king, restored after the defeat of Napoleon, was dethroned. Belgium was liberated from Holland. In England, where change was almost always more temperate, the Whigs took control of Parliament from the Tories. One of their first major legislative achievements was the passage of the 1832 Reform Bill, which widened the franchise, not radically, but enough to begin to consolidate Whig power by diminishing the influence of the old landed interests that controlled small borough constituencies (Morton 1979: 390-94). The Tories still remained a significant force, but the bill meant that "the bourgeoisie had shown its teeth" (Moore 1966: 32), and the manufacturing and commercial interests, especially in the large northern towns, at last acquired some political influence. It is also necessary, however, to see the bill as a defence against the more radical impulses of the time. It defined a voter as the owner or tenant of a property worth at least £10 a year, which was sufficient to disenfranchise virtually the entire working class.

While this may have had the general (if not enduring) effect of disillusioning the working class with the potential of parliamentary politics (Morton 1979: 393), it is perhaps ironic that even such a mild reform made it possible for a few individuals such as Cobbett to enter Parliament. Radical interests in the Lancashire cotton-manufacturing town of Oldham, who had previously learned how to put pressure on traders and merchants in the form of boycotts, repeated those tactics with great success in the parliamentary elections of 1832. As a result, Cobbett and another radical, John Fielden, "enjoyed tremendous majorities over their employer-backed Whig and Tory opponents" (Foster 1974: 54).

Although Cobbett was a singular minority within that Parliament, it was forced by outside events to pass the first really effective factory legislation to curb child labour in the textile industry. This largely resulted from the "pressure of a most violent working class agitation throughout the whole of the North of England" (Morton 1979: 378), which itself must be related to the cholera pandemic of 1831-82, which had profound political repercussions throughout much of Europe (cf. Blum 1978:

343). In general, however, the new Parliament consolidated the interests of the industrial class. While Cobbett continued to write and speak for the working class against the emergence of what he called an "unnatural system", while he attacked the spirit of Malthus and his supporters, the Whig Parliament prepared to reform the poor laws once and for all, to create the free labour market that industry demanded. The New Poor Law was passed in 1834, a final tribute to Thomas Malthus, whose "views were of central intellectual significance in shaping the debate over poor-law policy for nearly 40 years before the decisive reform" (Digby 1983: 104).

Whatever else this legislation pretended to be, this Act "and its subsequent administration . . . was perhaps the most sustained attempt to impose an ideological dogma, in defiance of the evidence of human need, in English history" (Thompson 1963: 267). At a time when the condition of the English working class was perceptibly worsening, the New Poor Law instituted a system of workhouses in which circumstances were deliberately made so bad that people would choose to take the poorest paid work rather than enter them. That was the whole idea. "Our intention", one Assistant Poor Law Commissioner said, "is to make the workhouses as like prisons as possible", while another declaimed: "our object . . . is to establish therein a discipline so severe and repulsive as to make them a terror to the poor and prevent them from entering" (in Thompson 1963: 267). It is little wonder that, within a short time, the Poor Law Commissioners and their Secretary, Edwin Chadwick, who had been one of the principal authors of the new law, had become "the most detested men in England" (Morton 1979: 397).

The irony, of course, is that, in order to create a so-called free labour market, employers had to *force* workers to compete. But, while classical economic theory said that a competitive market was optimal, workers defied both the prevailing theory and the interests of their employers by struggling to organise themselves against the brutality of a system in which unemployment and low wages were endemic. The combination of the New Poor Law, the Reform Bill and, as William Morris observed, "the simplest and most powerful of all causes—hunger" (Morris 1984: 172) politicised the English working class (Desmond and Moore 1991: 264). In 1837, while founding the London Workingmen's Association, William Lovett wrote "The Charter", whose simple demands soon became the rallying call of the working poor. Seemingly mild by today's standards, Marx and Engels, who allied themselves with the Chartist cause, acknowledged that their enactment would have been tantamount to a revolution (Morton 1979: 430ff.). The Whigs, however, had not reformed the poor laws just to concede political rights to workers, and the Chartists' demands were strenuously resisted (Moore 1966: 34).

By 1846, moreover, the repeal of the Corn Laws did much to disempower Chartism and to strengthen the position of the industrial elite. In Marx's words, it "reduced production costs, expansion of foreign trade, increase in profits, a reduction in the main source of revenue, and hence of the power, of the landed aristocracy, and the enhancement of their own political power". To be sure, the landed gentry survived, and still retain considerable political influence in Britain today. But the repeal of the Corn Laws was certainly one of the signs of the dawning of a new world order, the beginning of the thrust by the English—for that matter, the European—bourgeoisie to create a world market based on industrial production (which would eventually industrialise agriculture as well). That was finally possible in just a few years' time, after another wave of European revolutions in 1848 "had been precipitated by the last, and perhaps greatest, economic crisis of the ancient kind, belonging to a world which depended on the fortunes of harvests and seasons" (Hobsbawm 1979: 28).

There is no doubt that this "great European upheaval" (Thompson 1966: 204) was in large part a response to widespread political oppression. That this was a pivotal moment in the evolution of European political life is evidenced by the fact that 1848—exactly a half century after Malthus's first *Essay*—was also the year of the publication of *The Communist Manifesto*. But, at a deeper level, it reflected a final crisis in the nature of the agrarian systems of Europe, pushed to their limits in a time of rapid urban industrial development. When a potato blight arrived in Western Europe from the United States in 1844-45 and spread rapidly wherever the potato had become a staple crop (Blum 1978: 273-6), it revealed how insecure food production was.

Another symptom of the increasing vulnerability of the European system at mid-century was the recurrence of epidemic disease. And it is probably no coincidence that the year of revolution, 1848, saw the first great cholera pandemic since the early 1830s (R. J. Morris 1976: 13). In Ireland, where, as we shall see in the next chapter, the failure of the potato crop had its most disastrous consequences, and where cholera was just one of the diseases that accompanied it (Woodham-Smith 1962: 380-81), Malthusian theory was quickly brought into play, to attribute the ensuing famine and death, not to colonial underdevelopment, but to over-population.

Just as the potato blight was about to hit, Engels published his *Outlines of a Critique of Political Economy*. In it, although he made no specific reference to events in Ireland, he commented on the contradiction which Malthus, now dead, had sought to obscure through his principle of population. "I will not accept", wrote Engels,

> any defense of the Malthusian theory as competent which does not begin by explaining to me, on the basis

of the theory itself, how a people can die of hunger from sheer abundance, and which does not bring this explanation into harmony with reason and the facts.

> (in Meek 1971: 61-2)

The irony is that Malthus had already conceded that the disparity between population and resources was not entirely natural, that it was not separable from the system of production. He had written in an especially revealing passage:

> it is unquestionably true that the laws of private property, which are the grand stimulus to production, do themselves so limit it, as always to make the actual produce of the earth fall very considerably short of the power of production.

> (Malthus 1830: 36)[2]

This was so because, if capitalists must earn a profit, they would inevitably tend to exclude from use any land that could only be cultivated at an unacceptable cost. For Engels, this revealed the theoretical inconsistency at the heart of Malthusian thinking, and he maintained that it was actually "From [Malthus's] theory we derive the most powerful economic arguments in favor of a social reorganization" toward a system not predicated upon competition (quoted in Meek 1971: 62). But if Malthus admitted that an alternative system of common ownership might make it possible to exploit such land without regard for profits in the strict sense and so allow a far greater population to subsist, he immediately countered that greater productivity would simply engender more people. But more importantly, he regarded capitalism as the only admissible system, because private property embodied the "laws of nature" (Malthus 1830: 71-3).

By 1830, Malthus had taken his theory of population well beyond its humble beginnings, when he had first responded to the writings of Godwin and Condorcet over three decades earlier. But, in slowly adapting his work to the demands of the new market economy (Desmond and Moore 1991: 264-8), he had revealed not only the essential flaw in his own argument—that population increase was only a problem relative to the means of production—but his central and unrelenting aim: to justify and affirm the established order of inequality. In the process, he sought to prove that anything that humans might do through their own social or political efforts to redress inequalities or to mitigate suffering was counterproductive because it would only increase population and place more pressure on the means of subsistence. If anyone argued that it was possible to avoid this by changing the social nature of production, Malthusians would reply that this was an affront to the "natural" order of things. The poor would prove to have their own ideas.

Notes

1. Followed two years later by *A Vindication of the Rights of Woman* (Wollstonecraft 1975).

2. A good example is provided in William Hinton's report on China in the late 1980s after capitalist reforms had been introduced in the countryside. He writes of how

> Dams, terraces, and other collective engineering works were falling apart. We saw abandoned irrigation systems and washed-out earthworks. It was quite clear that many of them never would have been built under a private economy and that they would not now be restored short of recollectivization.

(Hinton 1990: 144)

References

Aikin, John (1968) (orig. 1795) *A Description of the Country from 30 to 40 Miles Round Manchester.* Newton Abbott: David and Charles.

Allen, Robert and Cormac Ó Gráda (1988) On the Road Again with Arthur Young: English, Irish, and French Agriculture during the Industrial Revolution. *The Journal of Economic History* 48(1): 93-116.

Baran, Paul (1957) *The Political Economy of Growth.* New York: Monthly Review Press.

Barratt Brown, Michael (1974) *The Economics of Imperialism.* Harmondsworth: Penguin.

Becker, Carl (1932) *The Heavenly City of the Eighteenth Century Philosophers.* New Haven, CT: Yale University Press.

Bence-Jones, Mark (1974) *Clive of India.* London: Constable.

Blum, Jerome (1978) *The End of the Old Order in Rural Europe.* Princeton, NJ: Princeton University Press.

Boulding, Kenneth (1973) Introduction to R. Wilkinson, *Poverty and Progress.* New York: Praeger, pp. xiii-xx.

Chadwick, Edwin (1862) *On the Social and Educational Statistics of Manchester and Salford.* Manchester: Cave and Sever.

Chase, Allan (1982) *Magic Shots.* New York: William Morrow and Company.

Claeys, Gregory (1989) *Thomas Paine: Social and Political Thought.* Boston: Unwin Hyman.

Collier, F. (1964) *The Family Economy of the Working Classes in the Cotton Industry, 1784-1833.* Manchester: Manchester University Press.

Collins, E. (1969) Harvest Technology and Labour Supply in Britain, 1790-1870. *Economic History* Review 22: 453-73.

Deane, Phyllis (1979) *The First Industrial Revolution.* Cambridge: Cambridge University Press.

Desmond, Adrian and James Moore (1991) *Darwin.* London: Michael Joseph.

Digby, A. (1983) Malthus and Reform of the Poor Laws, in J. Dupaquier and A. Vauve-Chamous (eds.) *Malthus Past and Present.* London: Academic Press, pp. 97-109.

Dobb, Maurice (1963) (orig. 1947) *Studies in the Development of Capitalism.* New York: International Publishers.

Dutt, R. Palme (1940) *India To-Day.* London: Victor Gollancz.

Foster, John (1974) *Class Struggle and the Industrial Revolution: Early Industrial Capitalism in Three English Towns.* London: Weidenfeld and Nicolson.

Franke, Richard (1987) The Effects of Colonialism and Neocolonialism on the Gastronomic Patterns of the Third World, in Marvin Harris and Eric B. Ross (eds.) *Food and Evolution: Toward a Theory of Human Food Habits.* Philadelphia: Temple University Press, pp. 455-79.

Gordon, Linda (1976) *Woman's Body, Woman's Right: A Social History of Birth Control in America.* Harmondsworth: Penguin.

Hammond, J. L. and Barbara Hammond (1987) (orig. 1911) *The Village Labourer 1760-1832: A Study of the Government of England Before the Reform Bill.* Gloucester: Alan Sutton.

Hardin, Garrett (1968) The Tragedy of the Commons. *Science* 162: 1243-8.

——— (1969) *Population, Evolution, and Birth Control: A Collage of Controversial Readings.* San Francisco, CA: W. H. Freeman.

Harris, Marvin and Eric Ross (1987) *Death, Sex and Fertility: Population Regulation in Preindustrial and Developing Societies.* New York: Columbia University Press.

Harvey, David (1974) Population, Resources, and the Ideology of Science. *Economic Geography* 50(3): 256-77.

Hewitt, Margaret (1958) *Wives and Mothers in Victorian Industry.* Rockliff: London.

Hobsbawn, Eric (1964) *Labouring Men: Studies in the History of Labour.* London: Weidenfeld and Nicolson.

——— (1979) *The Age of Capital, 1848-1875.* New York: New American Library.

——— and George Rudé (1968) *Captain Swing.* New York: W. W. Norton.

Hughes, Robert (1987) *The Fatal Shore: The Epic of Australia's Founding.* New York: Alfred A. Knopf.

Hutchins, B. and A. Harrison (1966) *A History of Factory Legislation*. London: Frank Cass.

Huzel, J. (1969) Malthus, the Poor Law, and Population in Early Nineteenth Century England. *Economic History Review* 22: 430-52.

Jordan, W. K. (1959) *Philanthropy in England 1480-1660: A Study of the Changing Pattern of English Social Aspirations*. London: George Allen and Unwin.

Kerr, B. (1943) Irish Seasonal Migration to Great Britain, 1800-38. *Irish Historical Studies* 4: 365-80.

Keynes, John Maynard (1956) *Essays and Sketches in Biography*. New York: Meridian Books.

Lindenbaum, Shirley (1987) Loaves and Fishes in Bangladesh, in M. Harris and E. Ross (eds.) *Food and Evolution: Toward a Theory of Human Food Habits*. Philadelphia: Temple University Press, pp. 427-43.

Lloyd, William (1980) W. F. Lloyd on the Checks to Population. *Population and Development Review* 6(3): 473-96.

Malthus, Thomas (1798) *An Essay on the Principle of Population*. London.

——— (1830) *A Summary View of the Principle of Population*. London: John Murray.

Mantoux, Paul (1961) *The Industrial Revolution in the Eighteenth Century*. New York: Macmillan.

Mathias, Peter (1969) *The First Industrial Nation: An Economic History of Britain, 1700-1914*. London: Methuen.

Meek, Ronald (ed.) (1971) *Marx and Engels on the Population Bomb*. Berkeley: Ramparts Press.

Moore, Barrington, Jr (1966) *Social Origins of Dictatorship and Democracy: Lord and Peasant in the Making of the Modern World*. Boston, MA: Beacon Press.

Morris, R. J. (1976) *Cholera 1832: The Social Response to an Epidemic*. London: Croom Helm.

Morris, William (1984) *Political Writings of William Morris*. A. L. Morton, ed. London: Lawrence and Wishart.

Morton, A. L. (1979) (orig. 1938) *A People's History of England*. London: Lawrence and Wishart.

Paine, Thomas (1969) (orig. 1791) *Rights of Man*. London: Dent.

Pinchbeck, Ivy (1969) (orig. 1930) *Women Workers and the Industrial Revolution, 1750-1850*. London: Virago.

Polanyi, Karl (1944) *The Great Transformation: The Political and Economic Origins of Our Time*. Boston, MA: Beacon Press.

Ricardo, David (1988) Ricardo on Population. *Population and Development Review* 14(2): 339-46.

Rosen, George (1958) *A History of Public Health*. New York: MD Publications.

Rothschild, Emma (1996) The Debate on Economic and Social Security in the Late Eighteenth Century: Lessons of a Road Not Taken. *Development and Change* 27(2): 331-51.

Smith, Adam (1947) (orig. 1778) *The Wealth of Nations*, Vol. 1. London: J. M. Dent and Sons.

Snell, K. D. M. (1985) *Annals of the Labouring Poor: Social Change and Agrarian England, 1660-1900*. Cambridge: Cambridge University Press.

Thompson, E. P. (1963) *The Making of the English Working Class*. New York: Vintage.

Thomson, D. (1966) *Europe Since Napoleon*. Harmondsworth: Penguin.

Ward, J. and R. Wilson (eds.) (1971) *Land and Industry: The Landed Estate and the Industrial Revolution. A Symposium*. Newton Abbot: David and Charles.

Watson, Roger (1969) *Edwin Chadwick, Poor Law and Public Health*. Harlow: Longman.

Wells, Roger (1983) *Insurrection: The British Experience, 1795-1803*. Gloucester: Alan Sutton.

——— (1988) *Wretched Faces: Famine in Wartime England, 1763-1803*. New York: St. Martin's Press.

Wilkinson, Richard (1973) *Poverty and Progress: An Ecological Perspective on Economic Development*. New York: Praeger.

Williams, Eric (1944) *Capitalism and Slavery*. London: Andre Deutsch.

Williams, Raymond (1983) *Cobbett*. Oxford: Oxford University Press.

Wilson, Charles and B. Lenman (1977) The British Isles, in Charles Wilson and G. Parker (eds.) *An Introduction to the Sources of European Economic History, 1500-1800. Vol 1: Western Europe*. London: Weidenfeld and Nicolson, pp. 115-54.

Wollstonecraft, Mary (1994) (orig. 1790) *Vindication of the Rights of Men*. New York: Woodstock Books.

Woodham-Smith, Cecil (1962) *The Great Hunger: Ireland 1845-1849*. New York: E. P. Dutton.

Wrigley, Eric and R. Schofield (1981) *The Population History of England, 1541-1871: A Reconstruction*. Cambridge, MA: Harvard University Press.

Young, Arthur (1967) *A Six Months Tour Through the North of England*. New York: A. M. Kelley.

Tim Fulford (essay date fall 2001)

SOURCE: Fulford, Tim. "Apocalyptic Economics and Prophetic Politics: Radical and Romantic Responses to Malthus and Burke." *Studies in Romanticism* 40, no. 3 (fall 2001): 345-68.

[In the following essay, Fulford explains the influence Malthus's writings exerted on the history of literature as well as on the history of politics and social science.]

> We will do some Michief if you don't lower the Brade for we cannot live. . . . We have give you a fair offer to do it before you don have your Town & Towns set on fire . . . we will begin on the One End and Continue to the other. Be all of one Mind we can do itt because we cannot But be killed then & we shall die as it is.[1]

At the end of the eighteenth century, poor people were hungry all over England. Rising prices, falling wages and increasing population produced many desperate threats to set towns on fire. To the comfortably-off, they seemed a menace. Real men and women became the frighteningly generalized "poor," a personified spectre haunting the imagination of the propertied. It was important not to provoke them: Jackson's *Oxford Journal* advised its readers to "give to no dog or other animal, the smallest bit of bread or meal." The King urged the rich to cut the oat rations of their pleasure horses.[2]

If the poor seemed a menace, they also felt like a burden. Under laws for their relief which dated from Elizabeth I's reign, local ratepayers were obliged to contribute to the welfare of deserving cases. As wages failed to keep pace with wartime prices, ratepayers found themselves subsidizing not only the disabled and elderly, but working men whose pay was too little to feed their families. Contributions soared from less than £2 million in 1783-85 to nearly £8 million in 1817. To the ratepaying (and voting) public, the poor were a national problem.

It was in a climate of fear and resentment that, in 1798, Thomas Robert Malthus first published *An Essay on the Principle of Population.*[3] Few books have had as immediate and as powerful an effect on social and political history. Malthus' argument that population increase, if not checked by misery, disease and famine, would necessarily exceed food supply rapidly persuaded William Pitt, the Prime Minister, to change government policy towards the poor. He had previously advocated giving laborers subsidies to support large families; after reading Malthus he abandoned the idea.[4] Later editions of the *Essay* spread Malthus' influence further still; his discussion of the Poor Laws shaped the legislation passed in 1834.[5] Malthus had made increase in population, once a government objective, into a problem that legislators tried to tackle by discouraging the poor from breeding.

Malthus shaped the political course of nineteenth century Britain; he also influenced its literary history. When the *Essay* appeared in 1798, it was read with particular attention by Samuel Taylor Coleridge, a former undergraduate at Malthus' Cambridge college. Coleridge had reason to pay attention: not only was this a book by his former tutor but it was a refutation of the theories of William Godwin, a personal friend with whose thought he had become dissatisfied. Coleridge, then, might have been expected to welcome Malthus' demonstration that Godwin's secularized millenarianism was based on a logical fallacy. He did not. Nor did the other dissenting radicals in Coleridge's circle—some of whom had known Malthus at Cambridge. In this essay I shall explore some of the reasons why they did not, examining the reception of Malthus in the context of the language of politics (not least that of Cambridge Unitarians) and of political economy. Malthus, I shall argue, was received in the wake of Burke and in the context of Burke's rhetorical attacks on radicals and dissenters. And he was received not only in the explicit critiques which the radicals made of him, but in the alternative vision of nature that they attempted to elaborate. Malthus helped shape the rhetoric of romanticism.

1. Burke in the 1790s: The Sublime Language of Politics

The most powerful political discourse in 1790s Britain was Edmund Burke's. Burke had attacked the French Revolution, and British radicals who supported it, with an apocalyptic rhetoric. To those who were, directly or indirectly, Burke's targets, his rhetoric amounted to an enthralling and awe-inspiring sublime. It destroyed his opponents because it left many who heard it—opponents included—under his sway. Using a style derived from the Bible and from Milton, a style that Burke himself had already identified as sublime and that Malthus was later to use, the orator and writer successfully stigmatized radicals as traitorous men of violence.

In 1757-59, Burke had discussed the sublime theoretically in his *A Philosophical Enquiry into the Origin of Our Ideas of the Sublime and Beautiful.*[6] He had paid particular attention to the personifications which Milton had made a feature of his adaptation of the Bible—*Paradise Lost.* I quote Burke on the figure of Death who appears with his mother/sister Sin in Book II of Milton's epic poem:

> No person seems better to have understood the secret of heightening, or of setting terrible things, if I may use the expression, in their strongest light, by the force of a judicious obscurity, than Milton. His description of Death in the second book is admirably studied; it is astonishing with what a gloomy pomp, with what a significant and expressive uncertainty of strokes and colouring, he has finished the portrait of the king of terrors:

—The other shape
If shape it might be called that shape had none
Distinguishable, in member, joint, or limb;
Or substance might be called that shadow seemed;
For each seemed either; black he stood as night:
Fierce as ten furies; terrible as hell:
And shook a deadly dart. What seemed his head
The likeness of a kingly crown had on.[7]

In this description all is dark, uncertain, confused, terrible, and sublime to the last degree.[8] Burke went on to criticize painters who made clear and certain images of Sin, Death and Satan. The obscurity of the "images raised by poetry" on the other hand, ensured "the mind is hurried out of itself" (*A Philosophical Enquiry* 62). Milton's obscure yet suggestive imagery made his personifications of Death and of Sin "sublime to the last degree."

Milton's Sin was a monster, a personification of incestuous lust who embodied male revulsion at female sexuality. She served Burke well in the 1790s, as did Death, for he began to put the personifications that he had previously analyzed to political use. He adapted Milton to depict the French Revolution and its supporters as terrible and monstrous. He imagined the tomb of the murdered monarch in France and, rising out of it, Death, personified as a "tremendous, unformed spectre . . . a hideous phantom."[9] This spectre owed much to Milton's Death: Burke's was "unformed," Milton's had no shape. But it was, Burke suggested, female. Burke had changed the gender of Death; his version of the spectre resembled the mother and sister of Milton's Death—Sin.[10] Sin, in Milton's poem, had given birth to Death after committing incest with Satan, her father. This is how Milton described her:

> The one seemed woman to the waist, and fair, / But ended foul in many a scaly fold / Voluminous and vast, a serpent armed / With mortal sting: about her middle round / A cry of hell hounds never ceasing barked / With wide Cerberian mouths full loud, and rung / A hideous peal: yet, when they list, would creep, / If aught disturbed their noise, into her womb, / And kennel there, yet there still barked and howled, / Within unseen.
>
> (*Paradise Lost* 2.650-59)

Burke used rhetoric of this kind to terrify and revolt his readers. He adapted the figures of epic poetry to make the revolution a specifically sexual monstrosity. The revolutionary women, he declared, were "obscene harpies, who deck themselves in I know not what divine attributes, but who in reality are foul and ravenous birds of prey, (both mothers and daughters)."[11] By participating in the murder of their king and queen, Frenchwomen had corrupted their proper femininity. They had perverted motherhood, so that they resembled Milton's incestuous Sin, delivering the spectre of revolution—Death—to the world. That spectre was itself a representation of the perverse misunion of male and female, man and animal. It was Burke's personification of the effects of revolutionary violence, the terrifying power of which lay precisely in its ability to pervert proper hierarchy and order. Revolution, through Burke's personification, became incestuous rape and monstrous birth.

Dissenting radicals suffered from Burke's anti-revolutionary Miltonics. With politics sexualized by Burke's figures, Coleridge was accused of deserting wife and children; Godwin was called a pander; Mary Wollstonecraft a whore. *The Reflections on the Revolution in France* (1790) had singled out Wollstonecraft's mentor, the leading Unitarian intellectual Dr. Richard Price. Price had welcomed the revolution in prophetic tones; "be encouraged, all ye friends of freedom, and writers in its defence! 'The times are auspicious.'"[12] But Burke turned Price's prophetic style against him by vilifying Price as a false prophet "viewing, from the Pisgah of his pulpit, the free, moral, happy, flourishing, and glorious state of France, as in a bird-eye landscape of a promised land" (*Writing and Speeches* 8.115). As Frans De Bruyn has observed, "the Miltonic vantage point permitted Adam and Jesus in *Paradise Lost* and *Paradise Regained* is sarcastically denied to Milton's spiritual descendant, who is derided as a footling, latter-day Moses."[13] The authority of Price's religious radicalism is undermined as Burke parodies his rhetoric. Burke dismisses his opponents' claims to the prophetic register, ridiculing "the confused jargon" of the "Babylonian pulpits" of Price and his fellow radical dissenters (*Writing and Speeches* 8.79). Yet he reserves a similar voice for himself as he predicts doom, rather than paradise, in France.

Gilbert Wakefield, a scholar of Jesus College, Cambridge, was another to suffer from Burke's use of Miltonic language to oppose the prophetic style of radical dissent. Wakefield had been Malthus' private tutor and had introduced him to Jesus College. A Unitarian, Wakefield later became a friend of Coleridge, who had himself become a Unitarian at Jesus College, where he knew Malthus. Wakefield wrote of the French Revolution in the prophetic tones of his fellow Unitarian, Price. They shared a millenarian political language, derived from the Bible and Milton:[14]

> . . . the neighbouring influence of the French republic; not her arms, but the silent and tranquil operation of her principles on our character, our manners and, our policy: an imperceptible efficacious energy! which nothing can preclude, nothing can counteract, and nothing eventually resist. I see that vast, formidable empire, descending, like the Nile, from the mountains of Æthiopia, circling with it's liquid arms the gay fabrics and the spacious deserts of monarchy, aristocracy, and ecclesiastical usurpation. I see that deluge of mighty waters gradually subside into their wonted channel: I

see them flow with a majestic tranquility to the ocean, and all the traces of their former ravages obliterated by one extensive and expanding Paradise of verdure, fertility, and beauty.[15]

Wakefield, however, found his millenarian vision overawed by Burke's anti-revolutionary prophecies. He wrote of Burke: "his exertions are in a stile of terrible sublimity, that thrills to the very marrow of the soul with a pleasing horrour." His eloquence was "a flood of fire, deep, flaming, and impetuous; involving every object within the vast embrace of it's expansion in one general conflagration" (*A Reply* 31). Once the spell of this language was broken, Wakefield argued, Burke's arguments could be seen to be untrue. But breaking the spell was difficult.

Coleridge wrestled with the problem in "Religious Musings" (1796), his anti-establishment anti-Burke poem that borrowed from Wakefield's *The Spirit of Christianity Compared with the Spirit of the Times* (1794). Coleridge attacked Burke in the poem, alluding to him for his role in stirring up the people against Joseph Priestley, the Unitarian radical forced into exile by the mob:

> Lo! Priestley there, Patriot, and Saint, and Sage,
>   . . . Him from his native land
> Statesmen blood-stain'd and Priests idolatrous
> By dark lies mad'ning the blind multitude
> Drove with vain hate: calm, pitying he retir'd,
> And mus'd expectant on these promis'd years.[16]

Having blamed Burke, Coleridge tried to outdo him at Miltonic rhetoric, throwing in lines from *Macbeth* for good measure. He prophesied the imminent coming of the apocalypse, when repression would be destroyed. And like Burke, and as Malthus was to do, he personified the forces of destruction. If the radicals couldn't beat Burke and the repressive establishment, then the "red-eyed Fiend" DESTRUCTION could:

> For who of woman born may paint the hour, / When seized in his mid course, the Sun shall wane, / Making noon ghastly! Who of woman born / May image in his wildly-working thought, / How the black-visaged, red-eyed Fiend outstretcht / Beneath th' unsteady feet of Nature groans / In feverish slumbers—destin'd then to wake, / When fiery whirlwinds thunder his dread name / And Angels shout, DESTRUCTION! How his arm / The mighty Spirit lifting high in air / Shall swear by Him, the ever-living ONE. / TIME IS NO MORE!
>
> (lines 402-13)

These apocalyptic personifications show that Coleridge, like other dissenting radicals, applied biblical prophecy to current politics.[17] They give Coleridge a certain rhetorical power. But they also show Coleridge's desperation. He pinned his hopes on divine intervention, on apocalypse, because he could no longer conceive how radicals could themselves lift the spell of Burke's "dark

lies," which made the "blind multitude" oppose revolution and reform.[18] Here Coleridge finds his prophetic style confronted by Burke's, and discovers that it is Burke's Miltonic rhetoric, and his Church and King loyalism, that wins the hearts and minds of the people. Coleridge was to devote his best poetry, in the late 1790s, to exploring how the spell cast by Burke, how public complicity with his terrifying and politically repressive sublime, could be lifted—only to find that Malthus was spelling it out again.

Wakefield, for all his prophecies of paradise, was also forced to experience the victory of his opponents. He found himself tried in a political theater in which concept of justice and truth had given way to the need to enforce submission to established power. Pitt's government, alarmed—not least by Burke—about the prospect of revolution in Britain, cracked down on political opposition. In the very year that Malthus was publishing the *Essay,* Wakefield was convicted of seditious writing. Coleridge was horrified—as the government intended radicals should be—that a gentlemanly classical scholar could be locked away in the name of the security of the constitution. He saw Wakefield fall ill of jail fever and die (in 1800). Malthus made no public comment on the treatment of his former tutor.

2. MALTHUS' *ESSAY* AND ITS RECEPTION

Malthus' *Essay* was published in the context of political repression, repression that the dissenting radicals attributed to the power of Burke's rhetoric over the body politic. Friends of Wakefield had especial reason to fear and resent the success of Burke's personifications in seizing the hearts and minds of the public. When they saw Malthus use a similar style to make his arguments about population seem authoritative, they viewed him through their experience of Burke's effect.

Burke's effect was not simply a matter of flights of apocalyptic language. He also persuaded readers by his mastery of empiricist terms. In the *Reflections on the Revolution in France,* sublimity went hand in hand with statistics, Miltonic personifications with mathematical ratios. In the papers he prepared on the question of poverty in 1795, he justified his economic arguments by analogy with observations drawn from nature: "Labour," he wrote (echoing Adam Smith) "is a commodity like every other, and rises or falls according to the demand."[19] By comparing men's work with a process all could agree from their own experience was a matter of fact, he was able to present his laissez-faire policy towards the poor as a natural law. Labor rose and fell like water; men were as subject as the inanimate world is to the will of God. Burke urged his reader "manfully to resist the very first idea, speculative or practical, that it is within the competence of Government, taken as Government, or even of the rich, as rich, to supply to the poor, those necessaries which it has pleased the Divine Providence for a while to with-hold from them. We the people, ought to be made sensible, that it is not in breaking the laws of commerce, which are the laws of nature, and consequently the laws of God, that we are to place our hope of softening the divine displeasure to remove any calamity under which we suffer, or which hangs over us" (*Thoughts and Details on Scarcity* 32). Here, by depicting calamity as an overhanging cliff or cloud, Burke effectively pictured "divine displeasure" in a natural object of the kind that, in the Enquiry, he had identified as a source of the sublime. This rhetorical move from empiricist analogy to an image of divinity gave Adam Smith's economics a disciplinary turn. Men, he implied, must feel "salutory fear" before an awesome and frightening nature-God (*A Philosophical Enquiry* 70). But in practice, although Burke's inclusive "we suffer" pretended that everyone was equally vulnerable to calamity, it was the poor, and not Burke's readers, who suffered starvation. His vision of God's universal displeasure was a rhetorical sleight-of-hand. His sublimity in fact appealed to the middle classes' self-interest since it not only justified their doing nothing to alleviate laborers' distresses but also allowed them to feel both pious and sorry for themselves.

Malthus used the same empiricist techniques as Burke. He even used the same analogy, arguing that "We cannot lower the waters of misery by pressing them down in different places which must necessarily make them rise somewhere else."[20] Malthus, however, took Burke's argument about "divine displeasure" a stage further. In the *Essay* poverty became not simply a calamity that laborers suffered, not simply an instance of a general human vulnerability before God, but the fault of the laborers themselves for breaking the natural and divine law.[21] They should be taught

> that they are themselves the cause of their own poverty; that the means of redress are in their own hands, and in the hands of no other persons whatever; that the society in which they live, and the government which presides over it, are totally without power in this respect; and that however ardently they may desire to relieve them, and whatever attempts they may make to do so, they are really and truly unable to execute what they benevolently wish, but unjustly promise; that when the wages of labour will not maintain a family, it is an incontrovertible sign that their king and country do not want more subjects, or at least that they cannot support them; that if they marry in this case, so far from fulfilling a duty to society, they are throwing a useless burden on it, at the same time that they are plunging themselves into distress; and that they are acting directly contrary to the will of God, and bringing down upon themselves various diseases, which might all, or in a great part, have been avoided, if they had attended to the repeated admonitions which he gives, by the general laws of nature, to every being capable of reason.

(James 2.107)

Malthus made birth control a matter of discipline, to be imposed upon the poor by nature if they did not repress their own sexual desires. The poor man had to avoid breeding, or he would be punished. And Malthus assumed authority to declare what the punishment would be, as if his rhetorical power made him God's and nature's judge:

> When nature will govern and punish for us, it is a very miserable ambition to wish to snatch the rod from her hands, and draw upon ourselves the odium of executioner. To the punishment, therefore, of nature he should be left, the punishment of severe want. He has erred in the face of a most clear and precise warning, and can have no just reason to complain of any person but himself when he feels the consequences of his error. All parish assistance should be most rigidly denied him: and if the hand of private charity be stretched forth in his relief, the interests of humanity imperiously require that it should be administered very sparingly. He should be taught to know that the laws of nature, which are the laws of God, had doomed him and his family to starve for disobeying their repeated admonitions.

(James 2.140)

Sex was sinful and would be punished. Or at least, sex among poor people was, for Malthus cosseted the well-off even as he conjured up the spectre of the poor man, a slave to his own lust, breeding his way to deeper poverty. The well-off had simply to observe the inevitable fact that the poor would be punished for their fertility.[22] The wealthy, Malthus seemed to show, were being cruel to be kind when they refused to help the distressed. Here Malthus played on current social anxieties, on the middle classes' fear that they would have to support, from the Poor Rates, an ever-increasing number of impoverished laborers.

Exactly why the poor would be punished for being numerous was the crux of the *Essay*. Malthus termed the reason the "principle of population," and strove to give it rhetorical power. First, he used apocalyptic personifications, making nature the arena where the rhetoric of Milton and the Book of Revelation becomes a grim reality:

> The power of population is so superior to the power in the earth to produce subsistence for man, that premature death must in some shape or other visit the human race. The vices of mankind are active and able ministers of depopulation. They are the precursors in the great army of destruction; and often finish the dreadful work themselves. But should they fail in this war of extermination, sickly seasons, epidemics, pestilence, and plague advance in terrific array, and sweep off their thousands and ten thousands. Should success be still incomplete, gigantic inevitable famine stalks in the rear, and with one mighty blow levels the population with the food of the world.[23]

Plague, Pestilence, Famine, Disease: Malthus' personified disasters were the four horsemen of his naturalized apocalypse. And they were flanked by other menacingly humanized figures including Want, whose "chilling breath" "repressed" benevolence, and Selfishness who, like Milton's Death, "resumes his wonted empire and lords it triumphant over the world" (Wrigley and Souden 69).

Malthus quite self-consciously employed the Miltonic and Burkean sublime. He quoted *Paradise Lost* frequently, and borrowed closely from the *Philosophical Enquiry* in defining man's relationship to God: "Infinite power is so vast and incomprehensible an idea that the mind of man must necessarily be bewildered in the contemplation of it" (Wrigley and Souden 123).[24] Like Burke's, Malthus' God was sublime because his power was too great to be comprehended. And like Burke's God, his immeasurability inspired awe and terror:[25]

> when our minds, unable to grasp the immeasurable conception, sink, lost and confounded, in admiration at the mighty incomprehensible power of the Creator, let us not querulously complain that all climates are not equally genial, that perpetual spring does not reign throughout the year, that all God's creatures do not possess the same advantages, that clouds and tempests sometimes darken the natural world and vice and misery the moral world.
>
> (Wrigley and Souden 132)

Here, Malthus uses God's sublimity to present human ills as parts of the ineffable system of nature rather than as social problems. This effectively makes them as irremediable as the climate. Godwin and the other political reformers, Malthus implies, are wasting their time. The world is a fearsome place in which vice, misery and inequality are as inevitable and incomprehensible as is the power of God which created them. Earlier in the *Essay* Malthus had promised (quoting Milton), to "vindicate the ways of God to man";[26] this was to do so via a particularly masochistic version of the sublime, a version, moreover, that courted danger since Malthus went on to argue that vice and misery are not the result of man's fall, but are means ordained by God to keep population in check and so prevent mass starvation (Wrigley and Souden 122):

> Must it not then be acknowledged by an attentive examiner of the histories of mankind, that in every age and in every state in which man has existed, or does now exist, that the increase of population is necessarily limited by the means of subsistence, that population does invariably increase when the means of subsistence increase; and that the superior power of population is repressed, and the actual population kept equal to the means of subsistence, by misery and vice?

Here personifications give way to an appeal to disinterested observation. In the name of an unbiased "examiner," Malthus propounds a law. His rhetoric, that is to say, conjures up an ideally "attentive" empiricist, whose imagined agreement to Malthus' proposition gives it the aura of truth. Readers are invited to identify with that examiner, or at least to accept that his role establishes the verifiability of Malthus' position (for such examination, it seems, lies within every industrious reader's power). Some readers, however, objected. William Paley and other orthodox divines had to remind Malthus that making vice and misery into necessary parts of God's plan was heretical. Malthus' grim view of nature made God not just awesome and repressive but evil.

Like Burke's, Malthus' political economy blended a naturalized version of the biblical sublime with a familiar appeal to the reader's observation. He said as much explicitly, in recommending "just and sublime theories, founded on careful and reiterated experiments" (Wrigley and Souden 59). In later editions, he introduced a battery of statistics drawn from "experiments" made on field expeditions to different countries. His aim was to exhaust the reader into accepting the accuracy, and therefore the irrefutable truth, of his argument.[27] Malthus' rhetoric, that is, invited the reader to view the *Essay* as a work of factual observation rather than wild theorizing. He explicitly distanced himself from the unfounded millenarianism of Godwin, Condorcet and other supporters of political reform. Mankind was not heading towards an earthly paradise of perfect peace and love but towards apocalyptic destruction—or would be if vice and misery did not keep sexuality, and therefore population increase, in check. Like Burke attacking Price, he portrayed himself and his readers as sober empiricists opposed to the fancy-drunk false prophets of revolutionary change. An early reviewer agreed, identifying Malthus as a reliable forecaster opposed to the mad prophets of a revolutionary millennium:

> Mr. Condorcet, Mr. Godwin, and Mr. Brothers have, indeed, been differently affected by the astonishing events which have lately occurred: but it would be difficult to say of the three which has reasoned and prophesied with most extravagance. It appears to us more probable, that Brothers is the appointed king of the jews, commissioned to collect that extraordinary people from the four winds of Heaven, and to replace them in their father's land, than that every man upon this globe shall be able to sustain himself and the helpless, who depend upon him, by the labour of half an hour in every day; that intellectual vigour shall destroy the sexual appetite; or that man shall no longer be subject to death, but live for ever.[28]

The reviewer had seen that what was at stake in the revolution debate as Malthus shaped it was the efficacy of a particular kind of language—the Miltonic and biblical sublime naturalized—to decide political issues. In other words, what was at issue was the relationship of poetic and scriptural rhetoric with empiricist prose, and of both with policy. What determined the relationship was a tradition of reading and the nature of the reading public. Malthus' success depended not just on a moral panic concerning the danger of a revolution by the poor but on a public united by their taste for the sublime (on one hand) and by respect for empiricism on the other. Burke had played to both in *Reflections,* using sublime passages and statistics. Now Malthus did so too. Godwin, Brothers and Condorcet, it was agreed, like Wakefield, Price and Coleridge, had let prophetic tones overwhelm the evidence of observation. They had failed, apparently, to understand the terms in which they needed to appeal to the readership that held power in Britain—the enfranchised middle and gentlemanly classes. Those classes, for whom the reviewer spoke, shared an education and aesthetic and philosophic values. They admired the sublime but they respected the factual. Neither discourse alone would capture their minds. Written together, however, these discourses made ready converts of them not least because their literary tastes as gentlemen made them ready to be converted.[29]

3. Dissenting Opposition to Malthus

Chief amongst Malthus' opponents were the dissenting radicals who had reason to think that Malthus had turned against the intellectual school in which he had been formed. Gilbert Wakefield did not live to record his reaction to seeing his former pupil add to the popular caricature of reformers as enthusiasts and false prophets. Other victims of this Burke-inspired view did. It was especially galling not just because dissenters believed in empiricism as much as did Malthus[30] but because Malthus was himself as reliant on prophetic personifications as they were. Behind his pose as an observer of natural law, they detected a prophet as speculative as those he criticized—a prophet of doom rather than perfectibility. In 1829 William Frend recalled trying to dissuade Malthus in 1798. He had argued that "were men guided by reason and instead of destroying each other" dedicated themselves to reducing births and increasing food production, then population "would increase with decreasing increment, so that at the conclusion it would terminate with an equality of births and burials. Each generation possessing the maximum of happiness adapted to its state that the earth can provide."[31] This argument, that rational humans, faced by a population explosion and the prospect of mass starvation, would regulate their fertility, was one Malthus later had to accept. In 1798 he did not, probably because it undermined his argument's prophetic power.

William Hazlitt proved a more vociferous opponent than Frend, one who was determined to expose Malthus as being as much of an illogical speculator as Malthus claimed reformers to be. Brought up a Unitarian by his minister father. Hazlitt had moved in the circles of radical dissent as a youth. His father was on friendly terms with Priestley and Price, and Hazlitt was schooled at

Hackney Day College, which they had helped to establish. Whilst there he was further radicalized by meeting the radical friends of his brother John—among them Godwin.

It was not Godwin but Coleridge whom Hazlitt credited with awakening his imagination and opening his mind to regions hitherto unknown. In January 1798, Hazlitt recalled, he heard Coleridge preach at his local Unitarian chapel: "the sermon was upon peace and war; upon church and state . . . on the spirit of the world and the spirit of Christianity, not as the same, but opposed to one another. He talked of those who had 'inscribed the cross of Christ on banners dripping with human gore.' He made a poetical . . . excursion." Hazlitt was put in mind of a prophet—St. John "crying in the wilderness."[32]

Spellbound by Coleridge's radical sermon, Hazlitt remained an admirer, as well as an analyst, of political language which worked through the prophetic. He admired Burke as a master of such language even as he opposed his politics. And he analyzed the sources of Burke's rhetorical power.

> Speaking of the new-fangled French Constitution, and in particular of the King (Louis XVI) as the chief power in form and appearance only, he repeated the famous lines in Milton describing Death, and concluded with particular emphasis
>
> —"What seem'd its head
> The likeness of a kingly crown had on"
>
> The person who heard him make the speech said, that, if ever a poet's language had been finely applied by an orator to express his thoughts and make out his purpose, it was in this instance.
>
> (Howe 12.268)

Hazlitt understood, then, that the politics of his day were shaped by the rhetoric of the sublime, by Miltonic and biblical personifications used by dissenting radicals and Church and King reactionaries alike. He understood too that Burke had won the battle of rhetoric: Burke's discourse was like "forked lightning" and "loud thunder" (Howe 6.101). It helped enshrine tyranny "in the very idioms of language" overawing "the imagination" and disarming "the will to resist it" (Howe 7.12).

Malthus, in Hazlitt's diagnosis, was continuing Burke's rhetorical device of applying Miltonic personifications to contemporary issues in order to terrify his readers. What Burke said of the French Revolution, Malthus, Hazlitt declared, said of population growth. "Population was, in fact, the great devil, the untamed Beelzebub that was only kept chained down by vice and misery, and that, if it were once let loose from these restraints, would go forth, and ravage the earth" (Howe 1.204).

Hazlitt argued that Malthus' Miltonic devils functioned as tricks, as means of frightening readers away from radicalism. Malthus' sublime was the reason for his popularity, for it disguised the banality of what he had to say:

> Mr. Malthus seems fully aware of the importance of the stage-maxim, To elevate and surprise. Having once heated the imaginations of his readers, he knows that he can afterwards mould them into whatever shape he pleases. All this bustle and terror, and stage-effect, and theatrical mummery was only to serve a temporary purpose, for all of a sudden the scene is shifted, and the storm subsides. Having frighted away the boldest champions of modern philosophy, this monstrous appearance, full of strange and inexplicable horrors, is suffered quietly to shrink back to its natural dimensions, and we find it to be nothing more than a common-sized tame looking animal, which however requires a chain and the whip of its keeper to prevent it from becoming mischievous.
>
> (Howe 1.204)

Hazlitt, then, saw through Malthus' sublime: the biblical figures of the *Essay* were the means by which Malthus sought "to confound . . . the laws of God and nature with the laws of man" (Howe 7.351). They were undermined by Malthus' own forced admission that celibacy and delayed marriage could prevent population growth, and that, therefore, plague, pestilence and "gigantic inevitable famine stalking in the rear" were not in fact nature's necessary and inevitable means of stopping an excess of population. Hazlitt's problem, however, was that the public remained under the influence of those very figures. He had seen through them; others, including the architects of policy towards the poor, had not. Hazlitt, therefore, tried to defeat Malthus on empiricist grounds as well as by undermining his sublimity. He collected data to refute Malthus' conclusions about increase in food supply.

Coleridge adopted similar strategies of opposition. He attempted both to lift the spell of the demographer's rhetoric and to refute him statistically. He researched Malthus' statistical theories in Germany in 1798-99. In 1803-4 his letters and annotations to the second edition of the *Essay* formed the basis of a critical review by his brother-in-law Southey, who concluded that Malthus "writes advice to the poor for the rich to read; they of course will approve his opinions."[33] Southey's conclusion, like Hazlitt's, was that Malthus attempted to terrify his readers through a rhetoric that could be undermined by mockery. Using Coleridge's suggestions, Southey declared that "such was the unnatural and unwholesome state of our moral and political atmosphere, that [Malthus] appeared like a philosopher, as he would have appeared like a giant had he walked abroad in a mirage" (Pyle 116). Malthus' rhetorical violence was a trick: "The pop-gun made a loud report in the world" (Pyle 123).

The report was indeed loud; mockery did not silence it. Malthus' opponents became even more hostile as his influence spread. Coleridge attacked him repeatedly and declared, "I do not believe all the heresies and sects and factions which the ignorance and weakness and the wickedness of man have ever given birth to, were altogether so disgraceful to man as a Christian, a philosopher, a statesman, or citizen as this abominable tenet."[34] For Coleridge, Malthus' "tenet" was disgraceful because it denied the possibility of willed reform, turning people into slaves of their bodily urges. In 1803 Coleridge noted "merciful God . . . the whole Question is this: Are Lust & Hunger both alike Passions of physical Necessity, and the one equally with the other independent of the Reason, & the Will?—Shame upon our Race, that there lives the Individual who dares even ask the Question."[35] Malthus' popularity was a testament to the paranoia of the age, of "a tendency to political Nightmares in our Countrymen."[36] Since Coleridge characterized nightmares as experiences in which reason and will were paralyzed by guilt and pain, this comment suggests that he attributed Malthus' popularity to aspects of the national psyche too deep to be argued away. Opposition to Malthus would, therefore, have to be made through a reform of the contemporary self as shaped by prevailing practices and discourses, before rational or statistical argument could begin to work. Rhetorical decontamination was essential if national complicity with the repressive "law" of Malthus was to be overturned.

4. MALTHUS AND *LYRICAL BALLADS*: THE ROMANTIC RESPONSE

With Burke dead and the *Essay* increasingly influential, Coleridge defined himself against Malthus' discourse, shaping a style in opposition to his rhetoric and arguments. This style drew on the prophetic personifications that Coleridge had, in common with other dissenting radicals, applied to political events, only to see Burke and Malthus do so too. But now Coleridge used those personifications in a less explicitly topical and political context. Nevertheless, the result was to contest the view of natural and divine law that, in the work of Burke and Malthus, had been used to justify the established political and social order. Coleridge's response was an effort to break Burke's and Malthus' hold on the contemporary imagination, an attempt to write liberation rather than repression as the awesome and inevitable law of nature and of God.

Coleridge had already begun this response when Malthus went into print. With Wordsworth, he had written *Lyrical Ballads,* many of which endorsed the language of the rural working classes, rather than that of the Church and State as Burke had done. Moreover, they did not seek to awe and terrify the reader into submission to the author's peculiar rhetoric and political stance. Rather, they presented the author as a collector and versifier of a language whose power lay in the fact that it was spoken in a rural community, the freedom and independence of which reflected that of the landscape in which it lived.

The Preface that Wordsworth composed, at Coleridge's instigation, for the second edition, was written in a Malthusian climate.[37] Burke's *Thoughts and Details on Scarcity* also appeared in 1800. The stigmatization of the poor, the argument that nothing should be done to relieve them, was topical. It was identified with the revered Burke as well as the previously unknown Malthus. Justifying his poetry in the Preface, Wordsworth found himself defending rural laborers in a new context in which it was thought natural, inevitable and even proper that they should suffer.[38] In the face of Burke's and Malthus' views, Wordsworth discovered what Wakefield did not, a sustaining fiction that the radical writer's language is supported by an actual radical community. Rather than appearing as an isolated combatant in a battle to lift the public from its supine thraldom to Burke's powerful defense of established laws, the writer emerges in the Preface as already empowered by an existing public language—that of the rural poor. If the writer has power, it is not to enthral readers to himself or to established institutions, but to a community of speech ignored by Burke, that of rural laborers whom Burke had casually dismissed as a "swinish multitude." It was this community that Malthus had, in practice, undermined by seeming to deny that the poor, in particular, could govern their own sexual urges. And this community, Wordsworth claimed, was more moral and more independent than the enfranchised and educated classes, who themselves were said to be victims of a population explosion. As Lucy Newlyn points out,[39] Wordsworth may have been revising Malthusian rhetoric when he declared that an "encreasing accumulation of men in cities" leads not to an excess of people over food supply but to an excess of desire over self-control. "Craving . . . extraordinary incident," city-dwellers become swamped by "deluges of idle and extravagant stories in verse," stories which corrupt their taste and their morals.[40] Wordsworth, it appears, turned Malthus' vision of humanity against him: it was not the rural poor but the urban middle classes (Malthus' readership), who were dangerously abandoned to an expansionary and "evil" logic of desire.

Wordsworth offered his own poetry as an aesthetic and moral replacement for Malthus' famine. Plain and simple poems, rather than natural disaster, would reduce the over-population of idle literature by restoring readers' taste. The degraded literary desires of the ever-growing urban public would be reformed by forcing it to learn from the population of the countryside (a population whose "sameness and narrow . . . intercourse" places it in balance with itself and with "the beautiful and permanent forms of nature") (*Prose Works* 1.124). The moral harmony and stable independence of the rural poor came, Wordsworth was sure, from their static interdependence with nature. It is in the city, not the country, and in affluence, not poverty, that people's desires lead them into excess.

If the Preface reverses Malthusian models, so do the poems Wordsworth wrote after 1798, when Malthus' *Essay* appeared. Attacks on opponents of the Poor Laws appear in "The Old Cumberland Beggar." The moral independence of the rural poor is written large across "Michael" (1800). It is endangered not by their tendency to breed in excess of nature's ability to supply food, but by economic systems which originate in the city. These systems threaten the balance between people and place that sustains community morality. Michael is an embodiment of the dignity that arises from this morality. It gives him self-control and self-reliance even when economic change is destroying the interdependence from which it originally stemmed. By the end of the poem it is impossible for the reader to revert to the generalizations through which Burke and Malthus spoke of the poor. These had ensured that their readers could avoid facing the effects on a flesh and blood individual of the laissez-faire policies they advocated. Michael's suffering aligns the reader with just such an individual; in dramatizing the mental and moral cost of the destruction of a family Wordsworth reveals the self-serving callousness of Malthus' argument. Michael, as a dramatized individual, is opposed in form as well as character to Malthus' generalized "poor man," who is deservedly punished for having a family that he cannot support. Wordsworth personalizes where Malthus personifies: the dignity with which Michael copes with pain forces the reader to admire not pity him, still less rebuke him as Malthus rebuked the imaginary father who applied for poor relief. Michael, moreover, is shown to suffer at the hands of economic systems that are socially, rather than naturally, determined. It is a particular kind of mortgage, and a particular relationship between rural and urban economies, that loses him his son. The suffering and death of the poor. Wordsworth shows, is humanly produced and frightening. It is not nature's—or God's—law to be complacently "observed" and reinforced by apocalyptic sermonizing.

Coleridge's poetic investigation of Malthusian territory reached its apogee, paradoxically enough, in a poem written before Malthus published the *Essay*. "The Rime of the Ancyent Marinere," as it appeared in *Lyrical Ballads,* explored suffering and moral paralysis. It also investigated the issues of complicity and victimization, the issues that Coleridge had previously discussed in relation to Burke and Priestley in "Religious Musings." The mariner's act of transgression—shooting the albatross—isolates him from the crew. They blame him and ostracize him, as the radicals had been ostracized in the

Britain dominated by Burke's rhetoric of terror. The mariner's mind then becomes subjugated to the power of monstrous figures. He loses his free-will and is forced to watch in terror as two personified figures play dice for the lives of the sailors. These figures strongly resemble Sin and Death in Milton, the Sin and Death Burke had adapted in his anti-revolutionary rhetoric. I quote the lines as they appeared when Coleridge first published the poem, that is—before he encountered Malthus' *Essay*:

> Are these her naked ribs, which fleck'd
>   The sun that did behind them peer?
> Are these two all, all the crew,
>   That woman and her fleshless Pheere?
> His bones were black with many a crack,
>   All black and bare, I ween;
> Jet-black and bare, save where with rust
> Of mouldy damps and charnel crust
>   They're patch'd with purple and green.
> Her lips are red, her looks are free,
>   Her locks are yellow as gold:
> Her skin is as white as leprosy,
> And she is far liker Death than he;
>   Her flesh makes the still air cold.
> The naked Hulk alongside came,
>   And the Twin were playing dice;
> "The game is done! I've won! I've won!"
>   Quoth she, and whistled thrice.

(lines 177-94)

Like one of the multitude enthralled by Burke's Miltonic figures, the mariner is subjugated mentally. He is fascinated as well as terrified.

The female figure is particularly interesting. She is both sexual (her looks free, her hair gold, her skin white) and monstrous (like leprosy, like Death). She is like Sin in Milton, Death's mother and sister. But why is she fascinating? The imagery suggests why. It is, it seems, the ability of the Sin/Death figure to personify both the repressed desires and the fears of the mariner (and the public) that makes her so enthralling. She embodies the cultural association of sexuality—particularly women's sexuality—with sin and monstrosity. Burke, of course, had played upon this association politically, stigmatizing reformers in Britain by linking them with the monstrous bodies of French revolutionary women. The mariner resembles one of his spellbound and guilty audience, as if Coleridge was diagnosing a national masochism produced by shame about sexual desire and about the bodies of women.

After 1798, and after reading Malthus, Coleridge changed the lines concerning the spectre-woman. He made her identity more explicit. He identified her much more closely with the personified figures of Milton—but also of Malthus. That he did so is not surprising. Malthus' figures were all forms of Death and Sin—famine, pestilence, plague, vice, excessive sexuality.

Clearly, these figures made a strong impact on Coleridge, not least because they reminded him of his own phrases in the "Ancient Mariner," as if he felt that Malthus was restaging the world of his poem in the political theater of contemporary Britain. Malthus, he declared in 1809, echoing the words of his famous ballad, made people believe that the poor should be "rotting away in disease, misery and wickedness" (*The Friend* 2.167). Coleridge's spectre-woman, herself diseased and rotten, and ruling a world where men are plagued and "the very deep did rot," seems an uncanny precursor of Malthus' powerful personifications. And if Malthus, according to Coleridge, showed "the tendency to Nightmares in our Countrymen," then the spectre-woman became, as if in reaction to this "tendency," a Nightmare creature. Here are the lines after Coleridge changed them:

> Are those her ribs through which the Sun / Did peer, as through a grate? / And is that Woman all her crew? / Is that a DEATH? and are there two? / Is DEATH that woman's mate? / Her lips were red, her looks were free, / Her locks were yellow as gold: / Her skin was as white as leprosy, / The Night-mare LIFE-IN-DEATH was she. / Who thicks man's blood with cold.

(lines 185-94)[41]

So why was the spectre-woman now identified as the Nightmare Life-In-Death? Very possibly because under that name she symbolized the nightmarish sexuality/sin complex that Coleridge felt haunted his countrymen. She embodied the guilt that left Britons enthralled by the monstrous personifications of Malthus, Burke and other writers who used their rhetoric to stigmatize radicals and reformers. Coleridge's image, that is to say, revised Milton's Sin in the light of what the success of Burke's and Malthus' Miltonic personifications had shown him about the psychology of his fellow countrymen. His Nightmare woman was a figure of the monstrous power, in contemporary Britain, of a rhetoric that made political reaction seem a sublime, divinely-ordained, law of nature.

Malthus and Milton remained linked in Coleridge's mind. In 1829, he quoted *Paradise Lost* to describe the influence of "the accumulating volumes on the horrors and perils of population":

> O Voice, once heard
> Delightfully, Increase and multiply!
> Now death to hear! For what can we increase
> Or multiply, but penury, woe and crime?[42]

In *Paradise Lost* the fallen Adam asks "for what can I increase / Or multiply, but curses on my head?" To the anguished new-fallen man, procreation offers only to multiply Death. God, however, corrects Adam: procreation will bring about man's redemption, for it will bring Christ into the world and so lead eventually to

Death's destruction and a new millennium. Here though, in Coleridge's version, Malthus has colonized Milton's text and so God's new covenant with Adam is forgotten. Procreation remains sinful, spreading the living death of penury, woe and crime. Malthus, Coleridge seems to be implying, has perverted Milton and the Bible. He has forgotten the central truth of Christianity, leading his readers back to the sinful despair of an Adam who, having betrayed his God, exists in anguish and isolation.

In "The Ancient Mariner" Coleridge sketched out a way beyond such anguish and isolation. The Mariner, finally, does not succumb to the Nightmare Life-In-Death. He escapes becoming her zombie-slave (unlike his crewmates). He escapes because—and this was crucial to Coleridge's opposition to both Malthus and Burke—he discovers in himself the capacity to give love, innocently and spontaneously. He sees the beauty of other life-forms and, free from the circuit of desire, shame and guilt that dogs his conscious relationships with figures of power, he blesses them. He makes an unconscious affirmation of community with nature which changes his relationship with it. No longer is it a place governed by the grim and retributive forces of Death, disease and famine as in Burke and Malthus. It is a place transformed by love. And the person is himself transformed by the recognition that he can give and receive love: his free-will is restored—

> Within the shadow of the ship / I watched their rich attire: / Blue, glossy green, and velvet black, / They coiled and swam; and every track / Was a flash of golden fire. / O happy living things! no tongue / Their beauty might declare: / A spring of love gushed from my heart, / And I blessed them unaware: / Sure my kind saint took pity on me. / And I blessed them unaware. / The self same moment I could pray; / And from my neck so free / The Albatross fell off, and sank / Like lead into the sea.

(1817 version, lines 277-91)

Subservience to the figures of Death and Sin is ended, as the emblem of the mariner's guilt falls off. The mariner is not totally freed by his action; he has more penance to do for his complicity with the cruel and repressive forces embodied by Life-in-Death. But he has begun, and so had Coleridge—begun, that is, to find a language capable of lifting the spell of the Malthusian and Burkean sublime.

Later, Coleridge came to believe that it was Wordsworth, and not he, who had finally lifted the spell. He made it is his role to announce Wordsworth's poetry as a new and liberating prophecy, one demonstrating that love and desire acted in conjunction with reason and will, one therefore that overturned the implications of Malthus. And Wordsworth returned the compliment, declaring Coleridge and himself to be "Prophets of Na-ture" who would "speak / A lasting inspiration" to their countrymen through their poetic vindication of imagination (*The Prelude* [1850]: 14.444-45).

It has become commonplace to view prophecy, imagination and the sublime as elements of the "Romantic Ideology," as transcendental concepts that Wordsworth and Coleridge articulated to disguise their retreat from commitment to political involvement. Reading "The Ancient Mariner" and the Preface in the context of opposition to Malthus suggests such views are only partially correct. Wordsworth and Coleridge may have aggrandized themselves and covered their political tracks, but their work did continue to challenge the rhetoric of reaction, to contest the spellbinding sublime and the discourse of natural law through which the poor were being oppressed. To put it another way, Malthus stands with Burke as one of the unwitting progenitors of a literary radicalism designed to succeed where political and dissenting radicalism had failed. It was in romantic poetry rather than in politics or economics that the Burkean and Malthusian sublime first met its match.

Notes

1. Quoted in Pamela Horn, *The Rural World 1780-1890: Social Change in the English Countryside* (London: Hutchinson, 1980) 46.

2. Jackson's *Oxford Journal*, 25 July 1795. Proclamation of George III, 3 December 1800; both quoted in Horn 40.

3. (London, 1798).

4. The influence of Malthus on the Prime Minister and parliament is discussed in Patricia James, *Population Malthus: His Life and Times* (London: Routledge and Kegan Paul, 1979) 65, 90-91.

5. Details of Malthus' influence on successive parliamentary debates and acts can be found in Anne Digby, "Malthus and Reform of the English Poor Law," in *Malthus and his Time*, ed. Michael Turner (Basingstoke: Macmillan, 1986) 164-67. See also Gertrude Himmelfarb, *The Idea of Poverty: England in the Early Industrial Age* (London: Faber, 1984) 100-141.

6. Burke had called the Bible and Milton "sublime to the last degree," had characterized the sublime as a discourse of power, awe and terror, and shown that it was used by kings and commanders to confer majesty and authority upon themselves. My references are taken from the edition edited by James T. Boulton (London: Oxford UP, 1958).

7. On these personifications and their influence see Steven Knapp, *Personification and the Sublime: Milton to Coleridge* (Cambridge, MA and London: Harvard UP, 1985).

8. *A Philosophical Enquiry* 59, quoting *Paradise Lost* 2.666-73. All quotations from *The Poems of John Milton,* ed. John Carey and Alastair (London and Harlow: Longmans, 1968).

9. *The Writing and Speeches of Edmund Burke,* gen. ed. Paul Langford, 17 vols (Oxford: Oxford UP, 1981-) 8.191. Hereafter cited as *Writings and Speeches* in the text.

10. Ronald Paulson, *Representations of Revolution, 1789-1820* (New Haven and London: Yale UP, 1983) 71-72, notes that Burke turns Death into a "she," without connecting his sexual transformation with Sin.

11. From *A Letter to a Noble Lord,* in *Writings and Speeches* 9.156. The passage goes on to quote Virgil's *Aeneid.*

12. From Price's sermon to the Revolution Society. 4 November 1789. In *A discourse on the love of our country* (1789) (Oxford and New York: Woodstock, 1992) 50.

13. Frans De Bruyn, *The Literary Genres of Edmund Burke: The Political Uses of Literary Form* (Oxford: Clarendon, 1996) 159.

14. Wakefield's language in the passage quoted resembles *Paradise Lost* 12. 157-72, Genesis:45-46 and Exodus:1.

15. Gilbert Wakefield, *A Reply to the Letter of Edmund Burke, Esq. to a Noble Lord* (London, 1796) 34.

16. Lines 387-94. Samuel Taylor Coleridge, *Poems,* ed. John Beer (London: Everyman, 1993) 90. All citations from Coleridge's poems are from this edition, hereafter cited as Beer.

17. As Morton D. Paley shows in "'These Promised Years': Coleridge's 'Religious Musings' and the Millenarianism of the 1790s," in Keith Hanley and Raman Selden, eds. *Revolution and English Romanticism: Politics and Rhetoric* (Sussex: Harvester, 1990) 44-66, and "Apocalypse and Millennium in the Poetry of Coleridge." *The Wordsworth Circle* 23 (1992): 24-34.

18. On Coleridge's version of Unitarian rhetoric as a response to Burke, see Peter J. Kitson, "The Whore of Babylon and the Woman in White: Coleridge's Radical Unitarian Language," in Tim Fulford and Morton D. Paley, eds., *Coleridge's Visionary Languages* (Cambridge: 1). S. Brewer, 1993) 1-14.

19. Published posthumously as *Thoughts and Details on Scarcity, Originally Presented to the Right Hon. William Pitt, in the Month of November 1795* (London, 1800) 6. Hereafter cited as *Thoughts and Details on Scarcity* in the text.

20. In the edition of the *Essay* of 1803, ed. Patricia James, 2 vols (Cambridge: Cambridge UP, 1989) 2.116. This edition hereafter cited as James in the text.

21. It became so by 1803, for it was in the second edition of that year that Malthus explicitly addressed the poor in this way.

22. On this aspect of his style see Clifford Siskin. *The Historicity of Romantic Discourse* (New York and Oxford: Oxford UP, 1988) 168.

23. I quote from the 1798 edition in *The Works of Thomas Robert Malthus,* 8 vols (London: Pickering and Chatto, 1986) v. *An Essay on the Principle of Population* (1798), eds. E. A. Wrigley and David Souden 51-52. Hereafter cited in the text as Wrigley and Souden. Cf. James 1.303-4.

24. Cf. Burke on the Deity: "But whilst we contemplate so vast an object, under the arm, as it were, of almighty power, and invested upon every side with omnipresence, we shrink into the minuteness of our own nature, and are, in a manner, annihilated before him" (*A Philosophical Enquiry* 68).

25. In the section of the *Philosophical Enquiry* entitled "power," Burke specifically refutes the argument that the power of God can be contemplated without awe and terror (67).

26. The quotation comes via Pope, who in *Essay on Man* 136, had changed Milton's "justify" to "vindicate."

27. Frances Ferguson, discussing Malthus briefly in *Solitude and the Sublime: Romanticism and the Aesthetics of Individuation* (New York and London: Routledge, 1992) 118-25, hints that the inexorability of his mathematical ratios constitutes "actuarial terror"—a statistical sublime.

28. *The Analytical Review* 28 (August 1798), quoted in *Population: Contemporary Responses to Thomas Malthus,* ed. Andrew Pyle (Bristol: Thoemmes P, 1994) 1. Hereafter cited as Pyle in the text.

29. On a taste for the sublime, and for discussions of it, as means by which a shared gentlemanliness was produced see Peter De Bolla, *The Discourse of the Sublime* (Oxford: Blackwell, 1989).

30. Priestley, for example, objected that Lavoisier's developments of his chemical discoveries depended on an over-theoretical nomenclature not reducible to observed data. See Jan Golinski, *Sciences as Public Culture: Chemistry and Enlight-*

enment in Britain, 1760-1820 (Cambridge: Cambridge UP, 1992) 177-84.

31. Quoted in Frida Knight, *University Rebel. The Life of William Frend* 1757-1841 (London: Gollancz, 1971) 303.

32. *The Complete Works of William Hazlitt,* ed. P. P. Howe, 21 vols (London: J. M. Dent, 1930-34) 17.108. Hereafter cited as Howe in the text.

33. Southey's review was published in the *Annual Review* (1803): 2: 292-301 (301). It is included in Pyle 116-35.

34. *The Table Talk of Samuel Taylor Coleridge,* ed. Carl Woodring, 2 vols (London: Routledge, Princeton: Princeton UP, 1990) 1.324.

35. Coleridge's marginal note on the 1803 edition of the *Essay.* In *Samuel Taylor Coleridge, Marginalia,* ed. H. J. Jackson and George Whalley, 5 vols (London: Routledge; Princeton: Princeton UP, 1980-) 3.806.

36. *The Friend,* ed. Barbara Rooke, 2 vols (London: Routledge and Kegan Paul; Princeton: Princeton UP. 1969) 2.167.

37. On this climate, and Wordsworth's reaction to it, see Marilyn Gaull, "Malthus on the Road to Excess," in *1798: The Year of the Lyrical Ballads,* ed. Richard Cronin (Houndmills: Macmillan, 1998) 93-107.

38. Duncan Wu, in *Wordsworth's Reading, 1770-1799* (Cambridge: Cambridge UP, 1993) 94, dates Wordsworth's reading of Malthus to 1798.

39. Lucy Newlyn, *Reading, Writing and Romanticism: The Anxiety of Reception* (Oxford: Oxford UP, 2000) 42.

40. The quotations from the Preface are from *The Prose Works of William Wordsworth,* ed. W. J. B. Owen and J. W. Smyser, 3 vols (Oxford: Oxford UP, 1974) 1.128.

41. This version is that first printed in *Sibylline Leaves* (1817), given in Beer. According to J. C. C. Mays, editor of Coleridge's poems in the forthcoming *Collected Coleridge* edition, it is not possible to determine exactly when the phrase Nightmare-Life-In-Death was added, though 1815 seems the most likely year.

42. *On the Constitution of Church and State,* ed. John Colmer (London: Routledge; Princeton: Princeton UP, 1976) 60. Coleridge is adapting *Paradise Lost* 10.729-32.

FURTHER READING

Criticism

Avery, John. "Malthus" and "The Iron Law." In *Progress, Poverty, and Population: Re-reading Condorcet, Godwin and Malthus,* pp. 55-93. London: Frank Cass, 1997.

Provides an overview of Malthus's writings and the controversy surrounding them.

Bowerbank, Sylvia. "The Bastille of Nature: Wollstonecraft versus Malthus in Scandinavia." *Studies on Voltaire and the Eighteenth Century* 304 (1992): 826-27.

Compares Malthus's *Scandinavian Diary* (1799) with Mary Wollstonecraft's *Letters Written During a Short Residence in Sweden, Norway, and Denmark* (1795).

Connell, Philip. "Wordsworth, Malthus, and the 1805 *Prelude.*" *Essays in Criticism* 50, no. 3 (July 2000): 242-67.

Discusses William Wordsworth's response to Malthusian population theories in Book XII of the *Prelude.*

Ferguson, Frances. "Malthus, Godwin, Wordsworth, and the Spirit of Solitude." In *Literature and the Body: Essays on Populations and Persons,* edited by Elaine Scarry, pp. 106-24. Baltimore: The Johns Hopkins University Press, 1988.

Compares Malthus's reaction to overpopulation with Wordsworth's response to the perceived psychic overcrowding caused by competing consciousnesses.

Flew, Antony. Introduction to *"An Essay on the Principle of Population"* and *"A Summary View of the Principle of Population,"* by Thomas Robert Malthus, edited by Antony Flew, pp. 7-56. Harmondsworth, England: Penguin Books, 1970.

Asserts that some of the theories associated with Malthus's work on population have been misunderstood by critics.

Gaull, Marilyn. "Malthus on the Road to Excess." In *1798: The Year of the "Lyrical Ballads,"* edited by Richard Cronin, pp. 93-107. Houndmills, England: Macmillan Press, 1998.

Discusses Malthus's 1798 *Essay* within the social and cultural contexts of its time.

Glass, D. V., ed. *Introduction to Malthus.* London: Frank Cass and Company, 1959, 205 p.

Provides an overview on the historical context and controversies surrounding Malthus's theories.

Grampp, William D. "Malthus and His Contemporaries." *History of Political Economy* 6, no. 3 (fall 1974): 278-304.

Explores Malthus's position as a moralist and as a political writer among his contemporaries in a variety of fields.

Huzel, James P. "Malthus, the Poor Law, and Population in Early Nineteenth-Century England." *The Economic History Review* n.s. 22, no. 3 (December 1969): 430-52.

Challenges Malthus's view that the Old Poor Law encouraged population growth.

———. "The Demographic Impact of the Old Poor Law: More Reflexions on Malthus." *The Economic History Review* n.s. 33, no. 3 (August 1980): 367-81.

Refutes the relationship between fertility rates and poverty posited in Malthus's *Essay on Population.*

Kinnaird, John. "'Philo' and Prudence: A New Hazlitt Criticism of Malthus." *Bulletin of the New York Public Library* 69, no. 3 (March 1965): 153-63.

Examines Hazlitt's attack on Malthus's *Essay on Population* contained in his *Political Essays* (1819).

Levy, David M. "Malthusianism or Christianity: The Invisibility of Successful Radicalism." *Historical Reflections* 25, no. 1 (spring 1999): 61-93.

Discusses contemporary Christian responses, both positive and negative, to the controversy surrounding Malthus's population theories.

Meek, Ronald L. "Malthus—Yesterday and To-Day: An Introductory Essay." In *Marx and Engels on Malthus: Selections from the Writings of Marx and Engels Dealing with the Theories of Thomas Robert Malthus,* edited by Ronald L. Meek, pp. 11-39. London: Lawrence and Wishart, 1953.

Explains Malthus's theory on population, its successful reception by members of the aristocracy, and the reaction of Karl Marx and Friedrich Engels.

Piette, Adam. "'Fear of Numbers': Wordsworth, Hazlitt, and Malthus." *Etudes de Lettres* 3 (July-September 1993): 55-68.

Studies the effect of Malthus's controversial theory of population on contemporary poetics.

Pullen, J. M. "Malthus' Theological Ideas and Their Influence on His Principle of Population." *History of Political Economy* 13, no. 1 (spring 1981): 39-54.

Examines the theological underpinnings of Malthus's theory of population.

Smith, Kenneth. "The Theory is Launched." In *The Malthusian Controversy,* pp. 33-43. London: Routledge & Kegan Paul, 1951.

Discusses the immediate success of the 1798 version of the *Essay on Population,* maintaining that despite its lack of originality, it was written with great style and simplicity.

Stapleton, B. "Malthus: The Origins of the Principle of Population." In *Malthus and His Time,* edited by Michael Turner, pp. 19-39. Houndmills, England: Macmillan, 1986.

Discusses the influences on Malthus's thought in the years preceding the publication of the *Essay on Population.*

Tuite, Clara. "*Frankenstein*'s Monster and Malthus' 'Jaundiced Eye': Population, Body Politics, and the Monstrous Sublime." *Eighteenth-Century Life* 22, no. 1 (February 1998): 141-55.

Discusses the intertextual relationship between Malthus's *Essay on Population,* William Godwin's "Of Avarice and Profusion" and *Political Justice,* and Mary Shelley's *Frankenstein.*

Additional coverage of Malthus's life and career is contained in the following sources published by Thomson Gale: *Dictionary of Literary Biography,* **Vols. 107, 158;** *Literature Resource Center;* **and** *Reference Guide to English Literature,* **Ed. 2.**

Vie de Jésus

Joseph Ernest Renan

The following entry presents criticism of Renan's biography *Vie de Jésus* [*The Life of Jesus*]. For discussion of Renan's complete career, see *NCLC*, Volume 26.

INTRODUCTION

Widely regarded as one of the most important and revolutionary books of the nineteenth century, Renan's *Vie de Jésus* (1863; *The Life of Jesus*) was the first biography of Jesus that accepted his historical existence while rejecting the Christian belief that he was the son of God. Because it argued that "miracles are things which never happen, and, therefore, things which Jesus never did," the book elicited a firestorm of criticism from church officials throughout Europe and America. It was denounced as blasphemous and, because of its popular appeal, was seen as a work that threatened to undermine the faith of Christians. Although Renan's portrayal of Jesus as an extraordinary mortal provoked the ire of Christian commentators well into the twentieth century, today *The Life of Jesus* is highly regarded by scholars, who see it as an important document that profoundly altered the tone and approach of western biblical interpretation. Renan's two main arguments—that New Testament sources were not infallible and that the formation of any religion, including Christianity, can best be understood through a study of social, linguistic, and psychological elements—have largely been accepted by modern secular academics. Praised for its intellectual courage, originality, stylistic beauty, and rationalist historicism, *The Life of Jesus* continues to be the work for which Renan is most highly regarded.

BIOGRAPHICAL INFORMATION

Renan had already gained a reputation as a scholar of distinction before he began writing *The Life of Jesus,* and was especially renowned for his work on Semitic languages and Islamic philosophy. In 1860, Renan went to Syria with a team of archaeologists to inspect and translate ancient Phoenician inscriptions. The following year, inspired by visits to Jerusalem and other sites mentioned in the Bible, he began to compile notes that he would later use in *The Life of Jesus* to describe the geographical and social milieu in which Jesus grew up. In 1862, months after his sister died of malaria while assisting him with his manuscript, Renan returned to France, where he was made professor of Hebraic, Chaldean, and Syrian languages at the Collège de France. His first lecture, however, drew the censure of church officials for its suggestion that Jesus had been no more than an "incomparable man." Renan's course was cancelled, although Renan continued to teach it from his home. Throughout 1863 he was often a guest at the literary salon of Princesse Mathilde, where he became acquainted with many of France's most liberal authors. In June 1863, Renan published *The Life of Jesus,* which, in spite of the official condemnation it received, was a popular success, selling over 60,000 copies in several European languages before the end of the year. The controversy surrounding Renan's skeptical account of Jesus' divinity resulted in the author's dismissal from the Collège de France in 1864. Refusing Napoleon III's subsequent invitation to work for the Bibliothèque Impériale, Renan returned to the Middle East, where he began work on *Les Apôtres* (1866; *The Apostles*), which would become the second volume, after *The Life of Jesus,* of his eight-volume study of the rise of Christianity from its Judaic roots to late antiquity. While every volume of this study, known collectively as *Histoire des origines du Christianisme* (1863-83; *The History of the Origins of Christianity*), has been praised for its scholarship, none appealed to popular tastes as much as *The Life of Jesus.*

PLOT AND MAJOR CHARACTERS

Renan opens his twenty-eight-chapter account of Jesus' life and ministry with prefatory comments that explain his methodological and philosophical approach to his subject. The preface argues that the possibility of miracles is discredited by common experience and that although the Gospels are full of information that can be historically verified, the miracles attributed to Jesus in the New Testament did not really take place. Jesus, Renan insists, was an uncommonly spiritual and charismatic figure who was born into a time and place that was ripe to welcome the messiah-figure predicted in the Old Testament, a role Jesus himself gradually began to embrace toward the end of his life. The chapters that follow attempt to reconstruct a plausible biography of Jesus through analysis and comparison of the four New Testament Gospels. Jesus is described not as the son of God born to a virgin but as a humble boy born under

272

normal circumstances to ordinary parents. Renan claims that Jesus probably received only the most rudimentary education and that his early livelihood was earned as a carpenter. Jesus' sermons, according to Renan, were initially concerned with messages of love, respect, and charity, usually conveyed by means of parables then commonly associated with rabbinical lessons. Jesus then became preoccupied with apocryphal images of the final days and a final judgment, probably because of the influence of John the Baptist. Renan claims that Jesus was an early disciple of John the Baptist before breaking away from him and enlisting his own followers. Jesus' disciples are usually described as simple men so "intoxicated" with their charismatic leader that they believed he was more than a mere mortal.

The plot and characters of Renan's *The Life of Jesus* would be familiar to anyone who has heard of or read the Gospels of Matthew, Mark, Luke, and John; only the interpretations Renan gives the events are unique. The raising of Lazarus from the dead, for example, is claimed as a fraud that Jesus and several of his disciples committed to elevate Jesus' status with the masses. Jesus' two trips to Jerusalem, the first ending in his rejection of orthodox Judaism and the second leading to his trial and death, are described in vivid, poetic, yet realistic detail. Renan argues that Jesus' resurrection was an hallucination by Mary Magdalene and that the disciples and early Christian writers uncritically accepted this story as true, which resulted in the mythological status of Jesus. Renan concludes *The Life of Jesus* with a postscript that reiterates his belief that although Jesus represented "the highest summit of human greatness," the reality of his life and message was distorted by New Testament writers who, for various reasons, wrote of Jesus as a worker of miracles and the son of God. The modern world, Renan implies, is not best served by uncritically accepting these improbable elements of Jesus' life; instead, the central meaning of Jesus' moral message is most realistically displayed by discovering the authentic Jesus, a mortal man of unparalleled moral and spiritual sensibilities.

MAJOR THEMES

There are two major arguments that run through *The Life of Jesus*. The first, having to do with biblical scholarship in general, attempts to separate myth from historical truth in order to come to a more realistic portrait of Jesus. A great deal of *The Life of Jesus* concerns itself with the veracity of the four Gospels. Contradictions within these texts themselves combined with study of other contemporary accounts by the writers Philo and Josephus convince Renan that the Gospels were not divinely inspired, infallible works but rather texts written by individuals with certain thematic preoccupations and limitations. The Gospels, Renan insists, should not be treated differently from any other writings; they

should be critically examined against other sources to separate factual information from literary or religiously inspired fancy. Although many of Renan's conclusions about the composition dates and veracity of the various Gospels have been supplanted in the last century, his methodological approach involving comparative literary analysis and historical objectivity has not.

The second, more central argument of *The Life of Jesus* has to do with the figure of Jesus himself. For Renan, it is inherently implausible that miracles ever took place or that Jesus was more than a mortal man. This idea in and of itself was not altogether new: the German theologian David Friedrich Strauss had concluded in his 1835 study of early Christianity, *Das Leben Jesu,* that the supernatural in general and the miracles of Jesus in particular were myths. However, whereas Strauss had concluded that Jesus himself was a figure of legend, Renan argued that study of biblical and secular sources proved that Jesus had in fact existed, had attracted a mass following for his spiritual teaching, and had been crucified for the revolutionary fervor he created. For Renan, the purpose of his *The Life of Jesus* was not to destroy belief in Jesus as a remarkable man with an important moral message, but rather to strip Jesus of the divine status that had been assigned to him by writers seduced by biblical prophesy of an expected messiah and furthered by Christianity's unquestioning attitude about scriptural authority. Throughout *The Life of Jesus,* Renan argues that belief in Jesus' divinity was due to two principal factors: Jesus' profound charisma combined with a period in Jewish history in which a frustrated people under the yoke of Roman repression yearned for a leader who would fulfill Old Testament prophesy and usher in a new age of Jewish glory and righteousness. Jesus himself, Renan believed, succumbed to his own growing religious fanaticism and began also to believe that he was the long-awaited messiah. Despite his own convictions or those of his immediate followers, Jesus, Renan concludes, was a "gentle," "charming," and "delightful" man around whom a myth of divinity was assigned to cope with social, political, and religious pressures that had been increasing for generations. A rational, skeptical detachment toward biblical sources was necessary, Renan insisted, to discover Jesus's timeless moral message and true place in history.

CRITICAL RECEPTION

The publication of *The Life of Jesus* created an immediate sensation across the European continent and in the United States, where the majority of critics, many of them church officials and Christian scholars, denounced Renan's conclusion that miracles were impossible and that Jesus was not the son of God. While a few of Renan's early opponents focused on the philosophical question of whether or not the possibility of miracles could be discounted by common experience, most were simply outraged that a book of such scholastic depth could conclude that Jesus was a self-deluded fraud on whom a myth of divinity had been superimposed. Many of the attacks on Renan were deeply personal in nature: Pope Pius IX called him the "European blasphemer"; others described him as a modern Judas Iscariot. Even those most inclined to accept Renan's biographical portrait of Jesus often complained that Renan's continued reverence for Jesus as the greatest of moral teachers meant that the author had been unable to achieve the historical and scientific detachment for which he argued. Despite the firestorm of criticism that *The Life of Jesus* sustained, and perhaps partly because of it, Renan's work had great popular appeal and sold extremely well. There were nineteenth-century critics, most notably Charles Augustin Sainte-Beuve, who praised Renan for his personal courage and intellectual insights, and friends and foes alike acknowledged Renan's superb prose that combined stylistic clarity with memorable, poetic descriptive passages. By the beginning of the twentieth century, the critical appraisal of *The Life of Jesus* had become largely positive. Although some commentators continued to attack Renan for his rejection of Jesus as Christ, and others, including Albert Schweitzer, pointed out fallacies in Renan's arguments about which Gospel sources were most reliable, most critics began to see *The Life of Jesus* as a defining work of its age, a masterpiece of scholasticism, stylistic clarity, wit, and courage that dared to apply scientific and historical principles to theological study. One critic even compared *The Life of Jesus* to Charles Darwin's *Origin of the Species* and Karl Marx's *Das Kapital*, asserting that all three are landmark books of the nineteenth century that revolutionized intellectual and popular thought. In the final decades of the twentieth century, interest in *The Life of Jesus* tapered off considerably, due less to failings of the work itself than to a growing acceptance of its central themes and methodology. Today, there is little of the controversy that sustained critical debates about the nature and value of Renan's biography of Jesus. While other works by Renan have become the subject of increased attention, *The Life of Jesus* remains the work with which his name is most commonly associated.

PRINCIPAL WORKS

De l'origine du langage (nonfiction) 1848

Averroès et l'averroïsme, essai historique (history) 1852

Histoire générale et système comparé des langues Sémitiques (history) 1855

Etudes d'histoire religieuse [Studies of Religious History and Criticism] (history) 1857

Essais de morale et de critique (philosophy) 1859

Histoire des origines du Christianisme. 8 vols. (history) 1863-83; translated and reprinted as *The History of the Origins of Christianity.* 7 vols. 1897-1904

Vie de Jésus [The Life of Jesus] (biography) 1863

Les Apôtres [The Apostles] (nonfiction) 1866

Questions contemporaines (philosophy) 1868

La Vie de Saint Paul [Saint Paul] (biography) 1869

La réforme intellectuelle et morale (philosophy) 1871

L'antechirst [The Antichrist] (history) 1873

Dialogues et fragments philosophiques [Philosophical Dialogues and Fragments] (philosophy) 1876

Prière sur L'Acropole [Prayer on the Acropolis] (prose) 1876

Les Evangiles et la seconde génération chrétienne (history) 1877

Caliban, suite de "La Tempête," drame philosophique [Caliban: A Philosophical Drama Continuing "The Tempest" of William Shakespeare] (drama) 1878

L'église chrétienne (history) 1879

L'eau de Jouvence, suite de Caliban (drama) 1881

Marc-Aurèle et la fin du monde antique [Renan's Marcus Aurelius] (history) 1882

Souvenirs d'enfance et de jeunesse [Recollections of My Youth] (memoirs) 1883

Nouvelles études d'histoire religieuse [Studies in Religious History] (history) 1884

L'abbesse de Jouarre [The Abess of Jouarre] (drama) 1886

Le prêtre de Nemi (drama) 1886

Histoire du people d'Israël. 5 vols. [*History of the People of Israel*] (history) 1887-93

Drames philosophiques (drama) 1888

†*L'avenir de la science: Pensées de 1848 [The Future of Science: Ideas of 1848]* (philosophy) 1890

Ernest Renan—Henriette Renan: Lettres intimes, 1842-1845 [Brother and Sister: A Memoir and the Letters of Ernest and Henriette Renan] (letters and memoirs) 1896

Cahiers de jeunesse, 1845-46 (memoirs) 1906

Oeuvres complètes. 10 vols. (philosophy, history, memoirs, and drama) 1947-61

*Published as part of the *Histoire des origines du Christianisme* series. The eighth volume of this series was an index.

†This work was written in 1848-49.

CRITICISM

North American Review Advertiser (review date January 1864)

SOURCE: "Renan's *Life of Jesus*." *North American Review Advertiser* (January 1864): 195-233.

[*In the following review, the critic praises* The Life of Jesus *for its vivid portrayal of Jesus while condemning the book for its rejection of Jesus' divinity.*]

When we take up a new book on any old and familiar subject, on which many books have been written, we naturally ask, first, Was there any need of a new book on this subject? and if so, then, Was its author the man to write it?—and the second of these questions there are two ways of answering: either to inform ourselves from other sources who and what the man is, or to read the book itself, and judge from that in what spirit he undertook his work, and with what success he has accomplished it.

These questions will come to one and another reader with peculiar force, when the new book is a Life of Jesus. We trust there are few readers that will be likely to say, "We have four Lives of Christ already, why do we want another?" To such one might reply: *For that very reason*; we want a fifth to reduce the four into one. But the four Gospels are far from being, or professing to be, any of them, *biographies* of their subject; they are simply *memorabilia,* more or less loose collections of his most impressive words, deeds, and sufferings, recorded not for the purpose of satisfying curiosity as to who he was and how he came to be what he was (which are prime questions with biography proper), but, as St. John says, for the spiritual and practical purpose of convincing us that he was sent by God to teach men how to live a godly life.

The many unsuccessful attempts that have been made to reproduce the life of Jesus in a regular biography suggest the inquiry, whether there may not be something in the nature of the case which makes this impossible; whether it may not be the intention of the Divine Providence, that at least around the beginning and the end of that remarkable life an impenetrable cloud of mystery should forever hang; whether, inasmuch as conscience, and not curiosity, was to be edified by the Gospel, and Jesus lived mainly as the instrument of awakening us to a knowledge of ourselves and of God, it may not have been meant that his own personal history should be left in a fragmentary state;—in fine, whether that saying of Jesus himself does not bear on this very subject, that "no man knoweth who the Son is but the Father."

If this is so, then the *need* of a new Life of Jesus seems to be out of the question, a biography of him in any proper sense of the word being impracticable. But now, admitting the alleged difficulty, does it, after all, though it may properly check any presumptuous expectation of a complete picture of the Christ's earthly manifestation, disprove the possibility or the desirableness of our forming for ourselves a more clear, consecutive, and consequently stimulative idea than has hitherto been gained, of so much of the life of our Master and Model as lies (however scattered in the Evangelic memoirs) within the daylight of history?

It seems to be a just opinion, that no one should undertake a biography without a love for the person who is the subject of it. Accordingly, the life of Christ, it would

seem, should be written by a Christian. Now to a Christian the very expression, Life of Jesus, is almost inseparably associated in the mind with something more, higher, and deeper than any series of past earthly incidents,—with something interior and eternal, a spirit and a power still living and striving in human souls, and connecting earth with heaven. This is what the Life of Jesus meant to Paul and his brethren; and the feeling of this may seem, at first, to give a little repulsiveness to the thought of writing and rewriting the life of Jesus in the book-making spirit of secular literature.

But still, giving due weight to all these considerations and cautions, we return to the question, Was there need of a new Life of Jesus? and we answer it confidently in the affirmative, for two reasons. The question may mean, either, Does the cause of truth demand any further attempts to make clear the method of Christ's life? or, Does the public good demand such? Now, certainly, no thoughtful observer of the progress of theological inquiry in the last generation, no one who has had any glimpse of the material which has been on all hands and in all lands accumulating towards a temple of rational faith in the Christ of history and of the spirit, can help having a presentiment that a Life of Jesus is yet to be written, which shall build out of all these materials a house of the soul's belief, open at once to the free air of earth and to the upper light of heaven; or, in plain speech, which shall apply with good sense to the Gospel records, not only the last conclusions of science, but also the everlasting sentiments of religion. Ingenious as have been the theories brought to bear upon the singular phenomena presented by the four Gospels, scarcely has one of their propounders approached, with reverence at all corresponding to his ability and ingenuity, the phenomena, the simple facts themselves, as they stand on the immortal pages, and asked, in the simplicity of common sense and conscience, How came they there? What do they mean? As a mere marvel of literary history, it seems astonishing that the question presented by this fourfold picture of a life which has wrought with such unexampled power on the world's life and fortunes, has so faintly and fitfully exercised the minds of literary men; but when we reflect that every man has a spiritual interest in the matter indefinitely transcending all mere intellectual interest, the amount of indifference on the subject seems unaccountable.

It may be said, however, Granting that no Life of Jesus has yet made the best use of all the ready material, that none has given so complete and just a picture of its subject as it would be interesting to have, is it important that another attempt should be made in this direction? In reply we say, it seems to us that a fresh presentation of the life of Jesus, conceived in the interests of humanity, under a sense of *his* humanity, and carried out in a careful, conscientious spirit, were, in these days especially, a thing to be welcomed. A timely and a thankful task, in our opinion, does he undertake, who, in a love of truth and goodness and man, seeks to re-call, through the clouds of tradition and from amidst the confused shadows of sectarian exaggeration, and to re-shape in the glow of an imaginative and sympathetic soul, the lineaments of that divine man after whom Christendom names itself, yet to whose word it has hitherto rendered, practically and comparatively, so little hearty homage. We hail as a good omen, and a most opportune labor of love, every sincere and single-hearted endeavor to revive in the heart of this age a sense of the *reality* of Him who embodies the ideal af-ter which the whole creation groans, and who is ever yearning to be born again into this world where his own are suffering and struggling, and to suffer and struggle and triumph with them in the strife of truth and right and liberty. He deserves the gratitude of every Christian and of every man who gives himself reli-giously to the work of so living over again in enlight-ened sympathy the life of Jesus as to add new strength and brightness to the bond which connects that life with the life we are living and the life we are called to live to-day; and to show that essentially we are tried as he was, and that he was tried and tempted just as we are; to make us feel, in short, Jesus still in the midst of hu-manity, to guard and guide the flame which he saw, and said that he had come to kindle, in the earth.

But now we come to the next question: Does the writer of the Life of Jesus before us give assurance of being qualified for the task which we have thus imperfectly indicated? Has he a true calling to the work? What gifts has he for it? The best answer to these questions, in-deed, is to be sought in his book itself; and we do not mean to prejudge that by any personal or partisan con-siderations,—a too common way of wronging both men and truth; but, as a natural and pleasant, and perhaps not unprofitable, way of approaching his book, we will say a word of the author.

Who is Ernest Renan? Of the man himself, apart from his writings, our knowledge is somewhat meagre. Of his literary and official history we know not much; of his personal history, almost nothing. He is said to be of Hebrew extraction. He was born in Brittany in 1823, but at an early age came to Paris, where he entered (we believe as a charity-scholar) the seminary of St. Sulpice, and received the tonsure, preparatory to entering upon the Romish priesthood. Before taking orders, however, when, why, and how we know not,—whether because of his predominant taste for *philology* (which, to one who understands the doctrine of the *Logos,* means as much as *philosophy*), or from whatever cause,—he re-nounced his clerical and Catholic connections, and en-tered upon the vocation of a *litterateur.* It is interesting, if not significant, that his first distinction in this new and independent field was the gaining of the *Volney* prize for a history of the Semitic languages in 1847. He now acquired a rapid notoriety, and took a prominent

place in various literary and philosophical associations and commissions. He has hitherto been best known to English readers by a number of able essays in the *Re-vue des Deux Mondes,* and by three poetic and schol-arly volumes of translation and exposition, devoted to Job, Ecclesiastes, and Solomon's Song. In this country he is also known by a remarkable paper on Channing, in which he finds fault with Channing, as well as with the so-called rational and liberal Protestants generally, for attempting to maintain a half-way ground between private reason and public authority in religious faith. In the preface to a volume called *Études et Essais,* formed of his contributions to the *Revue des Deux Mondes,* Renan disclaims all sympathy in opinion with either Strauss or Hegel, much as he respects the dispassionate tone of the one and the lofty spirit of the other. In the paper on the Critical Historians of Jesus, he contends that criticism ought to be reverent, as well as sympa-thetic and creative. Between the rationalistic theory of Eichhorn and the mythical one of Strauss, he prefers the former, but holds that "to no exclusive system will it be given to solve the difficult problem of the origin of Christianity."

In the general preface to the volume of Essays occurs one remark which we shall do well to remember in ex-amining the *Life of Jesus.* "It may be regretted," says M. Renan, "that, in advancing certain ideas contrary to the opinions generally received in France, I have not felt myself obliged to display a greater apparatus of demonstration"; and then he goes on to ascribe this to the sketchy nature of the contents of this volume, and to give notice that, *when he treats hereafter of the ori-gin of Christianity, he shall make good this defect.*

In the years 1860-61 Renan was at the head of a com-mission appointed to examine the remains of ancient Phœnicia, and it was during excursions into Galilee which that tour invited, that his *Life of Jesus* was con-ceived and chiefly composed. Soon after his return he was appointed to a chair in the College of France, then vacant, as Professor of the Hebrew, Chaldee, and Syriac Languages and Literatures. His inaugural address on the "Part of the Semitic Peoples in the History of Civiliza-tion," in which he spoke of Jesus as the reformer, re-generator, re-creator of Judaism, and the founder of "the eternal religion of humanity, the religion of the spirit, disengaged from everything sacerdotal, from all rites and observances," (p. 23,) alarmed the priests and the government, and a few days after its publication (Feb. 27, 1862) a decree suspended his functions. This was soon followed by an appeal to his colleagues,—(*La Chaire d'Hébreu au Collége de France. Explications à mes Collègues,*)—presenting, with great beauty of ex-pression and of spirit, his ideas of the way in which a teacher appointed to address at once Christians and Jews *ought* to speak of religion and of Christianity. Al-though these papers were subsequent to the conception and composition of the *Life of Jesus,* as a history, still they may be regarded as containing the germs of the idea of Christianity which that book implies. Particularly may we say this of the chapter in the *Explication* (page 27) entitled, "That it is not irreligious to try to separate Religion from the Supernatural." In one place he says that, inasmuch as he treats his subject not as a theologian, but as an historian, he cannot recognize miracles. He lays it down as an "inflexible rule, base of all criticism, that an event designated as *miraculous* is necessarily *legendary*." "The supernatural," he writes, "has become a sort of original defect, of which one is ashamed; even the most religious want no more than a *minimum* of it; one seeks to make it play as small a part as possible; one hides it in the corners of the past." Finally, he says:—

> Whether to be rejoiced in or regretted, the fact is, the supernatural is disappearing from the world. It no longer secures serious faith except in those classes which are not up to their age. Must religion crumble under the same blow? No, no! Religion is eternal. The day when it should disappear would see the drying up of the very heart of humanity. Religion is as eternal as poesy, as eternal as love; it will survive the destruction of all illusion, the death of the loved object. But what do I say? Its object also is eternal. Never will man content himself with a finite destiny; under one form or another always a cluster of beliefs expressing the transcendent value of life, and the participation of each one of us in the rights of a Son of God, will make part of the essential elements of humanity.

—p. 30.

We see, now and then, in these minor works, a predominance of sentiment over philosophy, not to say logic, which we shall also notice in his *Life of Jesus.* We can hardly help feeling, however, when we read such a statement as the following, that the way in which the defenders of miracles have urged their cause has too often shown them to have less insight into the heart of the truth than many of their opponents: "God does not reveal himself by miracle; he reveals himself through the heart, whence an unutterable yearning, as St. Paul says, rises towards him unceasingly." (p. 28.)

In regard to the supernatural, (about which, as it seems to us, so much has been said confusedly,) whether it is or is not "irreligious to try to separate religion from the supernatural," it surely is unreasonable to pronounce confidently where the line between nature and the supernatural runs. *Nature* (including, as its etymology shows, all that is *born,* in whatever world) is a great deal larger, perhaps, than most who enter warmly into these disputes reflect. There is a danger of presuming to limit God; but is there not also a danger of undertaking to limit nature?

Whether the speculations in these treatises be true or false, they certainly give one an agreeable impression of the author's temper and spirit. How fine, for instance,

is his statement of the neutrality required of a state professor in religious matters! "It does not consist," he says, "in satisfying everybody (which could not be done without warping the scientific spirit), nor in passing silently over the points that might wound any one's opinion (which would be to belittle everything): it consists in a propriety of tone, in a certain serious and sympathetic manner suitable to religious history, *and above all in that highest homage which the truth claims, in that supremely religious act which is truthfulness.*"[1]

Indeed, all that we learn of Renan, from his writings or otherwise, gives us the impression of a man who, "whatsoever things are true, whatsoever things are honest, whatsoever things are just, whatsoever things are pure, whatsoever things are lovely, whatsoever things are of good report," (among those whose good opinion is best worth having,) has *thought of these things.*

Have we not already gained some glimpses, in these preliminary studies, of a spirit well prepared, in some peculiar respects, to reproduce the life of Him who lived and died for the truth, in whom truthfulness did not shut out tenderness,—the gentle, the just, the resigned and resolute Jesus?

At the same time, while we hold (in spite of what Kingsley says in his ingenious little book called "Phaëthon") that truthfulness will finally lead a man into all needed truth, and while we therefore have no fears about the spiritual fate of any conscientious thinker, still, regarding those whom a writer may influence, and looking at the question, What is true? it seems to us a prime and fatal flaw in the very corner-stone of a theory of the life of Jesus, to begin with eliminating the supernatural element. To say nothing of revelation, the idea of a religion which does not recognize the supernatural seems to us like that of a religion without God. If by religion is loosely meant merely allegiance to what is morally good in man, it is hard to see how the life of any man (still more the highest) can be justly written without regard to the spiritual principle within him; and how can that be truly appreciated, without an acknowledgment of his connection with the One Infinite Spirit? Indeed, on what basis can any safe and sound allegiance to simple honesty rest, except on godliness? It may be said that these remarks bear not against our author's actual treatment of his theme, but only against an inaccuracy in stating his principles. Be it so. We hold accuracy to be a much more important ingredient of truthfulness than is popularly supposed.

Perhaps what M. Renan really means by the *supernatural* (and, indeed, a note in the *Études* seems to imply as much) is the *unnatural.* At all events (definition being secondary), we know what he is mainly denying is the miraculous part of the Gospel story. Nothing can well make a thoughtful person more curious, on approaching a new *Life of Jesus* by such a man, than the desire to see what will be the result of another effort to dissect the Evangelic record and tear out the miraculous fibres without drawing the life-blood,—to pull out the thread of miracle without unravelling the whole fabric of the wondrous narrative. Not only has the world never yet seen this sad achievement accomplished, but never yet has one opponent of the miraculous claims of the New Testament seriously looked the question we have indicated in the face. It has been uniformly slighted.

We have written thus far as if we had not yet *viewed* the book which we have undertaken to *review* (though all we have said has been shaped and colored by its presence in our thoughts); but now it is time to speak of it more directly and distinctly.

It may seem strange, at first thought, that so common a thing as a reproduction of the history of Jesus on the ground of naturalism should create such a *furore* as this book has done. What is there about it so peculiarly alluring or so peculiarly alarming? Is there anything here, in the negative or the positive part of the theory presented, with which we have not long been familiar in reproductions of German speculation, or in the free workings of English and American thought? We must remember, however, that was written for a French public and appeared in a Roman Catholic country.

Grant, however, that, as has been asserted by some of his opponents, the matter of M. Renan's book has little that is new even to its own public, that its negations are but weak restatements and its affirmations but loose and ill-digested, it is not so much to the matter as to the manner that we must look for an explanation of the *flutter* of excitement (as it has been called) which this work has occasioned. The matter may not have much novelty in it, but the mode of its presentation has an originality, individuality, freshness, and charm about it, which no work of its class has ever before displayed. Here is something quite apart from the Volneys and Voltaires, the Strausses and Baurs.

Nearly a generation has gone since the heavy stone called Strauss's *Life of Jesus* fell into the sea of public thought, and made a ripple which to this day has not ceased. It *was* a stone, and not the bread which the hearts of men oppressed with superstition and ceremony, grown lean with living on words and forms, craved for their true life. But now in this book of Renan's we have, combined with the freedom of the Straussian criticism, the saving grace of an intense regard and reverence for the Christ as a real man, and not a mere name for a nucleus of abstract truth in a nebula of myth. Men felt that *cold-bloodedness* was the word to be applied to Strauss's treatment of this theme. A certain instinct told them, not merely that it was not sentimental enough, but that it was not even thoroughly philosophical, that

is, inspired with the love of divine wisdom. Renan says in his Introduction, that he had himself been tempted in the same direction; but "I learned," he says, "that history is not a mere play of abstractions, that in it men are more than doctrines." In other words, he learned that biography is the life and soul of history. Here, then, we have something more than dry negation; we have something positive and palpable,—we have the very life-blood of humanity. This is what makes Renan's book so attractive to the people,—so alarming to sacerdotalism. This gives it that charm, which to some, indeed, may make it dangerous, but, in our judgment, will cause the harm it does to be far outweighed by its influence in helping the truth and life of the Gospel in the world. Bigots may say, and think they say something smart and stinging, "Have you seen the Gospel according to Renan?" To us it seems a poor fling. For the truth is, that, to every one who really believes and lives in the Gospel, and who has it living in him, it will be the Gospel *according to him*; and no man or body of men can claim, without gross presumption, to have, alone, the absolute and original Gospel itself, in fact or form. To every man the Gospel he holds is more or less shaped by his own nature.

The mere fact, then, that a writer has shaped anew the life of Jesus, is no ground of complaint. The simple question is, Has he done it with the care and reverence and full freedom which the subject demands? Has he wrought thoughtfully and consistently? M. Renan certainly brings with him to his high task many qualities and conditions which eminently fit him for it, but some also which unfit him for doing it justly. He comes to it not without a great deal of fine preparation in study and spirit, but at the same time not without some grave prejudgments (to use the mildest word for it), which, it is true, he frankly owns. "If the love of a subject," he beautifully says, in closing his Introduction,

> can help one to an understanding of it, it will be perceived, I hope, that this condition has not been wanting. To write the history of a religion, it is necessary, first of all, to have believed in it (without which one never could comprehend by what it has charmed and satisfied the human conscience); secondly, that one no longer believes in it in an absolute manner; for absolute faith is incompatible with sincere history. But love can go without faith. One may attach himself to none of the forms which captivate the adoration of men, and yet not renounce the enjoyment of what in them is good and beautiful. No transient apparition exhausts the Divinity; God had revealed himself before Jesus, God will reveal himself after him.

The love of Jesus is certainly a prime prerequisite for writing the life of Jesus. In divine things, love sees what no other spirit can. There is, however, in M. Renan's devotion to his "hero" (for this word naturally occurs to us) a certain melodramatic element; he surrounds him with a rose-colored atmosphere which disguises the natural hue of life. This characteristic per-haps belongs partly to M. Renan's French, and partly to his individual, nature; and sometimes we feel as if the glow of his eagerness to justify his ideal created a whirl in the mental atmosphere unfavorable to a steady sight of the sober truth. We shall notice presently an example or two of this.

One eminent preparation for his task M. Renan enjoyed in having visited the scene of his story, and become fa-miliar with the spirit of its landscape and society. Like him

> who on the Chian strand
> Beheld the Iliad and the Odyssey
> Rise to the swelling of the voiceful sea,

so did our author, as he tells us, while he mused by the Lake of Genesareth, see rise from its waters and its shores the form of his Galilean idyl,—his "fifth Gos-pel," as he calls it. But we will let him tell it in his own words, or rather our English of them:—

> All that history which at a distance seems to float in the clouds of an unreal world thus took a body, a solid-ity, which astonished me. The striking accordance of texts and places, the marvellous harmony of the evan-gelic ideal with the country which served as its frame, were like a revelation to me. I had before my eyes a fifth Gospel, torn, but still legible; and thenceforth, through the narrations of Matthew and of Mark, in place of an abstract being who, one would say, had never existed, I saw live and move a wondrous human form.
>
> —p. liii.

The picture Renan gives of the region which, he says, "alone made Christianity," is exceedingly beautiful. Af-ter speaking of Jerusalem as "the true home of that ob-stinate Judaism which, founded by the Pharisees and fixed by the Talmud, has traversed the Middle Ages and come down to us," he goes on to say:—

> An enchanting nature contributed to form that much less austere, less severely monotheistic spirit,—if I may venture to say so,—which impressed upon all the dreams of Galilee an idyllic and charming character. The most dreary country in the world, perhaps, is the region round about Jerusalem. Galilee, on the contrary, was a country very green, very umbrageous, very cheer-ful,—the true country of the Song of Songs and of the lays of the Well-Beloved.
>
> —p. 64.

> This pretty (*joli*) country—which has become to-day, in consequence of the enormous impoverishment produced by Islamism in human life, so sombre, so painfully gloomy, but where all that man has not been able to destroy still breathes *abandon,* sweetness, and tender-ness—overflowed in the days of Jesus with comfort and gayety.

Life there

> spiritualized itself in ethereal reveries,—in a sort of po-etic mysticism confounding heaven and earth. Let the austere John the Baptist, in his Judæan desert, preach penitence, storm incessantly, and live on locusts in company with jackals; why should the companions of the bridegroom fast while the bridegroom is with them? Joy will make part of the kingdom of God. Is she not the daughter of the lowly in heart, the men of good-will?

> The whole history of the birth of Christianity has thus become a delicious pastoral. A Messiah at wedding fes-tivals, the courtesan and the good Zaccheus bidden to its feasts, the founders of the kingdom of heaven as a troop of paranymphs,—that is what Galilee has dared to produce, what she has made the world accept. Greece has traced in sculpture and poesy charming representa-tions of human life, but always without perspective and distant horizons. Here marble, skilled workmen, a re-fined and exquisite language, are all wanting. But Gali-lee has created in the domain of the popular imagina-tion the most sublime ideal; for behind her idyl the fate of humanity is suspended, and the light which illu-mines her picture is the sun of the kingdom of God.
>
> —p. 68.

These passages (which we should have preferred to give in the French, the fit language for such sentiment) will prepare one for perceiving the beauties and the faults of M. Renan's book. In his desire to justify the romance of history as he feels that he has found it in the pure beginnings of Christianity, he overlays fact with fancy, and does not hesitate to give a roundness and a coloring to his novel, which the very authorities he refers us to not only fail to sustain, but even forbid. Thus he begins one of his paragraphs, "His sisters were *married* at Nazareth," and in a note refers us to Mark vi. 3; but when we turn to that passage all we find is the question of the people who cavilled at him: "Are not his sisters here with us?" Again, when he comes to the incident of Jesus standing up in the synagogue at Nazareth to read and teach, he says:—

> As there were few Pharisees in Galilee, the opposition to him did not take that degree of liveliness and that tone of acrimony which at Jerusalem would have stopped him short at the first step. These good Gal-ileans had never heard discourse so agreeable to their cheerful imagination. They admired, they petted him; they decided that he spoke well, and that his arguments were convincing. The most difficult objections he solved with confidence; the charm of his speech and of his person captivated these people, still youthful and not dried up by the pedantry of the doctors.
>
> —p. 139.

And there he stops. The reader of the account in Luke will be somewhat astonished to find a professor of his-tory throwing this rosy mist over the one half of a fact, which had anything but a rosy end in the document from which he derives it, where we find that, so soon as the wonderful youth began to tell disagreeable truth and offend their patriotic pride, these "good Galileans" were "filled with wrath" and "thrust him out of the city."

Our author shows an equally strange disregard to the *order* of events. Thus, in the Introduction, when he comes to speak of St. John's Gospel, he says, "The mystical tone of these discourses in no respect corresponds to the character of the eloquence of Jesus as it is represented to us by the" first three Evangelists. "A new spirit breathes in them; the *gnosis* has begun; the Galilean era of the kingdom of God has ended; the hope of a speedy coming of Christ recedes into the distance; one enters into the desert of metaphysics, the dark shadows of abstract dogma. The spirit of Jesus is not there, and *if the son of Zebedee really wrote these pages, he had certainly forgotten, in doing so, the Lake of Genesareth and the charming conversations which he had heard upon its shores.*" (p. xxxi.)

But has not our critic *forgotten* something himself? Has he not forgotten that the first ten chapters of St. John's Gospel relate to a period of his Master's ministry *preceding the Sermon on the Mount,* and those wanderings and preachings in Galilee which he (M. Renan) treats as the *earliest* and purest part of Christ's manifestation? Besides, what need had John to let us see that he remembered the "charming conversations" in Galilee, when his predecessors had given them so truly, and he had other work, namely, to dwell on deeds and discourses which he, the bosom friend of Jesus, had perhaps alone appreciated,—at all events, which he, writing in old age, and nearer the spiritual world, peculiarly recalled with a new sense of their significance?

But M. Renan, at the close of his glowing account of the Galilean period, the pure period (as he calls it) of the teachings of Jesus, seems to us not only unreasonable, but inconsistent with himself. He begins a paragraph of reflections:—

> To conceive what is good, is in truth not enough; it is necessary to give it success among men. For that less pure methods are needful. . . . If Jesus had died at the moment in his career which we have reached, there would not have been a page in his life to wound us, &c.

We say, is there not an inconsistency, when, having begun the paragraph thus, he draws toward its close in this way?

> Men of a very mediocre morality have written very good maxims. Very virtuous men, on the other hand, have done nothing to continue in the world the tradition of virtue. The palm is to him who has been mighty in word and in deed, who has felt what is good, and has insured its triumph at the cost of his blood. Jesus, in this double point of view, is without equal; his glory remains entire, and will be forever renewed.

—pp. 92, 93.

Is not this an example of that confusing influence of sentiment upon judgment to which we referred some time since as unfitting one for a just treatment of the life of Jesus? We have cited and admitted our author's claim to a love of his subject. But now, so far as the actual historical life of Jesus forms his subject, must we not confess that his love is alloyed by that partial fondness which one cherishes for a child,—in this case the child of his own brain? For such, surely, M. Renan's picture of the career and conceptions of Jesus, in a considerable degree, is. It is one thing to shape a life of Jesus "out of the air," as the Germans say, and another to discover the life of Jesus in the sources and grounds which history and reason combine to indicate. As one illustration of M. Renan's inconsistency and arbitrariness in handling his theme, we may note the fact, that, while he takes such liberty or indulges such carelessness in regard to the testimony of the very witnesses he appeals to for his historical information, yet, when it comes to the words of Jesus, familiar as he is with Oriental thought and speech, he insists upon understanding literally all the highly wrought prophecies about the day of judgment on the one hand, and, on the other, all those stringent and ascetic precepts of morality which are exemplified in the Sermon on the Mount.

This shows a certain wilfulness, an overriding of scholarly judgment and good sense by the predilections of the imagination, which, however favorable to the *effect* of a book, are not favorable to the just treatment of so grave and majestic a theme as the Gospel presents to thinking men. And when our author comes to the resurrection of Lazarus, and seriously proposes to us to believe the wise and discerning Jesus the dupe of a gross deception which that friend of Jesus lends himself to further, we recognize with pain how sad may be the fruits of a willingness to begin tampering with untruth, even in the mild form of inattention to truth's strict demands.

But it is time to speak upon a point where, after all, as we conceive, lies the chief difficulty with writers on the Gospels like M. Renan, the chief source and secret of their weaknesses and their wanderings, the original sin in their whole management of the subject.

In writing a life two things are necessary: first, to ascertain the facts, and, secondly, to interpret them,—in other words, to infer from them the idea of the man. M. Renan, justly perceiving that it is vitally important for him to build his castle, not on the clouds, but on the earth, admits that the four Gospels are the main source of information with regard to the life of Jesus, and accordingly he devotes a considerable number of preliminary pages to the question of their origin, composition, and authority. Unlike Strauss, he admits the four canonical Gospels as authentic. He traces them all to the first century, that is, in substance, and thinks them almost wholly the work of the authors to whom they are attributed, though their historic value, according to him, is very unequal;—Matthew being the most to be depended upon for the words of Jesus, and Mark for a pure and plain account of his actions; while in regard to Luke he seems to adopt in some considerable degree Strauss's notion of the original materials having been rolled about like boulders in the stream of tradition; and as to John, admitting that he had a deeper insight into the mind of Jesus than the others, and knew much of his external life which they did not, our author is of opinion that his imagination greatly co-operated with his memory, and, furthermore, that not a little of the speculative and spiritual part of the Gospel may have been added by the Ephesian school.

On the whole, we do not doubt that there is a good deal of truth mixed up with M. Renan's ideas on this subject; but one thing will strike a thoughtful reader,—that, after all, the mere acknowledgment of the right names having been prefixed to the four Gospels is comparatively little, and that they might as well be any other four names, unless you recognize the authority which these names express. Neglecting to do this, M. Renan, although theoretically admitting the value of these documents, practically makes them of very doubtful and wavering significance in many of the most interesting and important points of our Master's life. And so, when he tells us that the problem of the construction of the Gospels "has arrived at a solution which, though leaving room for many uncertainties, is fully adequate to the requirements of history," we seriously suspect his real meaning to be, *for such a history as he wishes to write.* For the looseness of his theory enables him to take just such things out of the Gospel records, and in such order as suits his purpose, and to emphasize these, or slur those, as his object requires.

But when we follow our author in the interpretation of the records of which he starts with such a loose, floating, indeterminate notion as regards authorship and authority, when we consider his manner of evoking the form of Jesus from this troubled sea of material, we find just the result we might naturally expect from a man of airy sentiment and lively genius, revolving in the kaleidoscope of his bright fancy the broken bits of colored fact, and calling us to look from moment to moment, from chapter to chapter, at an image which, though for the time regular and consistent, is liable to change at each shake of the hand.

We acknowledge and admire the charm of the narrative in which M. Renan has reproduced the events of Christ's marvellous passage across the scene of human life. His pictures of the landscapes in which Jesus walked and talked with his little band of companions, and of the simple, joyous, trusting life of the people who dwelt among them, have a touching beauty; and no

Christian, we think, can read his book in this view without thanking him for a more home-coming sense of the reality of the life of Jesus as a man among men than he ever had before. But whether the idea he gives us is as just as it is vivid, is another question. For ourselves, we cannot accept as anything more than a very partial, however pleasant and winning and (so far as it goes) impressive, representation of the life of the Son of Man, that which leaves out the recognition of his having any sense of a special revelation from God, a special responsibility, and powers corresponding, and a relation to God altogether peculiar and miraculous in its nature. M. Renan, indeed, himself recognizes a feeling or thought of this kind as having entered into the soul of Jesus; but, so far, he regards him as an enthusiast,—an idea which has been again and again proposed, and again and again overwhelmingly refuted, with external and internal argument amply sufficient to satisfy any mind that is in a state to hold steadily the scale of judgment, and weigh patiently the reasons of the case.

In a word, it seems to us that the same spirit which can treat the Gospel records so lightly as to be able to discard from them the miraculous element, or to regard it as mere legend, prepares one to take a shallow view of the meaning of Christ's teachings and doings. The writer who represents Jesus as catching Nathanael by guile, (that Israelite, as he himself called him, *in whom was no guile,*) and making believe he had a mysterious knowledge of his thoughts under the fig-tree; who questions whether John may not have exaggerated the affection his Master had for him; who represents Jesus as calming, by his *pure and sweet beauty,* the troubled, nervous organization of Mary Magdalen; who discovers a *fine irony* in the Saviour's reply to James and John, when they would have called down fire on the Samaritans; who pictures Jesus as being compelled to smile at Peter's downright ways, and compares Peter's intercourse with his Master to that of Joinville with St. Louis;—a writer who can thus deal with the simplicity of the Evangelic record tempts one to apply to his own work what he says of St. John, namely, that "he wrote concerning his Master that *bizarre* Gospel which contains such precious instructions, but in which, *according to us,* the character of Jesus is falsified upon many points." (p. 156.)

We have been struck with the fact that *bizarre* is a frequent and favorite expression of our author's in reference to words and ways of Jesus. We are disposed to think that the oddity he finds is often a reflection of his own odd state of mind. He finds in the narrative what he carries there. It is not necessary to appeal to Christian faith, it is enough to appeal to good sense and candid consideration, against his gay and *brusque* style of interpreting the meaning and motives of the Gospel incidents.

We are bound, indeed, to say that, free and easy (*jaunty*, we had almost said) as is M. Renan's way of paraphrasing (even to the extreme of parodying often) the simple matter and manner of his text, even this tone and treatment, with the absurdity into which they sometimes lead us,—even this seems to us a wholesome corrective to the old style of solemn dulness and lifeless monotony with which an ill-understood supernaturalism and superstitious sanctimony have too generally made the sacred stories to be read amongst us. It is good, we think, for this drowsy, droning mood to get occasionally even a somewhat rude shaking up, though at the same time, we conceive, it would be better and quite as practicable to bring this about without caricature. With whatever drawbacks, however, we must repeat our acknowledgments to M. Renan for the freshness he gives to many an incident and passage of the Gospel history, which he makes us feel as if it were something just happening. Indeed, to all who would have Jesus taken out of Sunday dreams and brought into the daily reality of life, these pictures of him with his Galileans, as he journeys through the country or goes up to the holy city, and especially the description of his last weeks and days and hours, are full of rare interest and instruction.

Unhappily, in undertaking to give order to the Evangelic *mémoires* (as M. Renan seems to esteem them), he only aggravates their original dislocation, and adds confusion to misplacement. It is convenient, too, for his theory, to assume three years (apparently) as the duration of Christ's ministry, whereas, as it seems to us, everything is explained far more naturally by limiting it to a little more than one.

But the worst confusion we have to charge him with respects his idea of Jesus,—his conception of Christ's purpose and plan. Here, we must say, M. Renan seems to us, equally with Strauss, to build up a Christ of his own out of the wreck of the actual history. It is true, that, while Strauss substitutes for the historical Jesus an abstraction, M. Renan supplies one who is intensely flesh and blood and soul and spirit; but we feel a painful uncertainty whether the being who lives and moves so vividly before us is always the same, or, rather, we feel a strong misgiving that he is not.

M. Renan exaggerates equally, in our opinion, in his Galilean idyl and in his Jerusalem tragedy. If in the one he looks through rose-colored glasses, in the other he sees through a medium which gives his world a lurid and fuliginous aspect, such as the sky has seen through the stained windows of our churches. The transition of the mind of Jesus from the earlier to the later moods which our author ascribes to it—what he calls the passage from his "innocent aphorisms" to his "revolutionary ardor"—seems to us presented in a very vague and vacillating manner, in defiance alike of the natural arrangement of the Evangelic accounts, and of the natural

impression they give us of their subject. In fact, M. Renan appears to be especially unsettled and inconsistent in this part of his theme. At one time he speaks as if Jesus began with one idea of the kingdom of God, and by and by was drawn or driven into another; and at another time he insists that all the three ideas of the kingdom of heaven,—namely, as existing in society, in the soul, or in the skies, as an earthly revolution, an internal conversion, a final judgment,—were simultaneously recognized and received by his hero. Now is not all this simply a reflection of the writer's own vacillating spirit? How much more simple and natural would it have been, how much more accordant with a reasonable conception of the wondrous teacher of Nazareth, the prophet of the soul, to understand him as referring in the gorgeous imagery of the Oriental style to a new kingdom of the Word and of the Spirit which was to begin at once, of which the downfall of the sacerdotal city was to be the signal, and which was to endure thenceforth through time into eternity? Is it the part of a true philosopher to make account only of the swaying of the branches of the mighty tree of life, and not also and rather to think of the root which this outward play and sweep only fixes more firmly in the earth?

As he comes to the last weeks of the life of Jesus, M. Renan's theory strides on (to use the words he applies to the career of Jesus) with a "frightful progression of enthusiasm." He says: "Jesus was no longer free; he belonged to his part, and in a sense to humanity. At times one would have said that his reason was disturbed. He had something like agonies and internal agitations. The grand vision of the kingdom of God, incessantly flaring (*flamboyant*) before his eyes, made his head swim. His disciples at some moments thought him mad. [And yet our author refers here away back to Mark iii. 21!] His enemies declared him possessed. His temperament, excessively impassioned, bore him every instant beyond the bounds of human nature. His work being no longer a work of reason, and sporting with all the classifications of the human mind, what he demanded most imperiously was *faith*." (p. 318.) And then the author justifies this by saying: "Reflection leads only to doubt, and if the authors of the French Revolution, for example, had been obliged to be convinced by meditations sufficiently long, they would all have reached old age without doing anything." Again: "His natural sweetness seemed to have abandoned him; he was sometimes rude and *bizarre*. . . . Sometimes his bad humor at any resistance drew him on to acts inexplicable and apparently absurd."

"It is not," our author concludes, "that his virtue stooped; but his struggle in the cause of the ideal against the reality became insupportable. He was hurt, and revolted at contact with the earth. Obstacles irritated him. His notion of the Son of God was disturbed and exaggerated. The fatal law which condemns an idea to decay the moment it seeks to convert men, applied to him. In touching him men brought him down to their level. The tone which he had taken could not be sustained more than a few months; it was time death should come to untie the knot of a situation strained to excess, to relieve him from the impossibilities of a road without issue, and, in delivering him from a too protracted trial, to introduce him henceforth impeccable into its celestial serenity." (p. 320.)

Could the force of invention further go? In a similar vein M. Renan says, when he comes to the alleged miracle of the raising of Lazarus: "We must call to mind that in that impure and oppressive city of Jerusalem Jesus was no more himself. *His conscience, by the fault of men and not by his own, had lost something of its primordial limpidity.*" (p. 360.) We fear the author confounds here his subject with himself. After such a treatment of the resurrection of Lazarus, we breathe more freely when we find that we are spared at present his views on the resurrection of Jesus, that "the life of Jesus for the historian ends with his last sigh"; though we have a painful presentiment of what is in store for us, when we reach the closing words, in regard to Mary Magdalen: "Sacred moments in which the passion of a woman in a state of hallucination gives to the world a resuscitated God!" (p. 434.)

There is one topic of M. Renan's book of which we have not yet expressly spoken. His chapter on Miracles seems to us the weakest (we might say *flimsiest*) of all. Is it not strange and significant, that the writer of a life of Jesus,—a life which has, through its miraculous character, produced the profoundest effect in the world these eighteen centuries,—and especially when this writer admits that Mark, his favorite authority for the facts of Christ's life, "is pre-eminently the Evangelist of miracles and exorcism," (p. 265,)—should dismiss the subject of miracles in fifteen feeble pages out of his four hundred and fifty? Perhaps, indeed, it is partly the fault of the unreflecting and unappreciative champions of the miracles, who have dwelt so exclusively on them as meant for proofs of *power,* that the advocates of nature and reason in the matter have not dwelt more on the wondrous works of Jesus in reference to their motive and spirit. At all events, is it not a rare defect in a life of Jesus which professes to follow the spirit rather than the letter, that it should find in the fact of Jesus refusing to furnish signs from heaven, or to do miracles merely to satisfy curiosity, nothing more than evidence that "the part of thaumaturgist was disagreeable to him,"—that, in fact, "his reputation as thaumaturgist was imposed upon him,"—and this in the face of what Jesus himself repeatedly and emphatically says of his miracles of mercy as evidences of his being the Son of the merciful God? How could the man of sentiment, the man of soul, or the man of science, think to give a life of Jesus to the world and yet throw so into the shade

Jesus the wonderworker of beneficence? Could he not have followed out, indeed, his own doctrine, that "these words, *superhuman* and *supernatural,* borrowed from our poor theology, had no meaning in the high religious conscience of Jesus? For him nature and the development of humanity were not limited kingdoms out of God, wretched realities, subject to the laws of a despairing empiricism. There was for him no supernatural, for there was no nature." (p. 246.)

As it is, we feel that M. Renan has written a life of Jesus with Jesus omitted. Not the less, however, has he given us suggestions and materials for forming an idea of Jesus, and living, if not writing, that majestic life ourselves, which we have never yet found in any other writer. We thank him especially for that beautiful delineation of Jesus as the Son of God, in opposition at once to a confused tritheism and to "a cold deism."

> He believes himself more than an ordinary man, but separated from God by an infinite distance. He is Son of God; but all men are or may become so, in divers degrees. All, every day, ought to call God their Father; all the children of the resurrection will be sons of God. The Divine filiation was ascribed in the Old Testament to beings whom no one pretended to make equal with God. The word *Son* has, in the Semitic languages and in the language of the New Testament, the largest sense. Besides, the idea which Jesus forms to himself of man is not that low idea a cold deism has introduced. In his poetic conception of nature, one sole breath pervades the universe; the breath of man is that of God; God dwells in man, lives by man, just as man lives in and by God. The transcendental idealism of Jesus never permitted him to have a very clear notion of his own personality. He is his Father, his Father is he. He lives in his disciples; he is everywhere with them; his disciples are one, and he and his Father are one.
>
> —p. 244.

This is one of the passages, indeed, in M. Renan's book, which may seem to illustrate the influence of Hegel of which we spoke; but, after all, notwithstanding some of the terms employed, we confess to finding in this passage more of the theistic doctrine of Paul, and even of Jesus, than of any pantheistic human school. The idea of Jesus having no clear notion of his own personality has been ridiculed, but perhaps it receives some countenance from his own saying, that *none knoweth who the Son is but the Father.*

We have not undertaken to give our readers a full account of the contents of the remarkable book we have been reviewing. We have not proposed to ourselves to rewrite it, or to rewrite the life of Jesus. We have not even ventured to show directly and positively how that should be done. We do not admit the old doctrine, that a critic must be equal to his author, in order to form a just estimate of his short-comings. We have aimed simply to indicate what seem to us the chief defects, as well as the chief merits, in the book under consideration. On the whole, we do not regard it as any considerable addition to our theological science,—or perhaps we should say *sacred* science, since theology, strictly speaking, it does not profess to treat. But in the literary history, in human history, it certainly is one of the most interesting and significant works that have ever appeared. As coming from one by birth a Roman Catholic, and by instinct a *human Catholic,* a man of no sect or school in religion, it comes to us like the cry of the human soul for that steady and sober assurance of Jesus Christ as the Son of man and the Son of God, which Peter affirmed in reply to that question of the Master: "Who do men say that I, the Son of man, am?"

We say *"sober* assurance"; and if there is any one word which would express the defect of M. Renan's idea of Jesus, may we not say that *sobriety* is the quality in which his book, as well as a great proportion of those that have been written in the interest of naturalism, most characteristically contrast with the spirit of Jesus? Without this quality, there can be no adequate respect for his character as an honest person, not to say reverence for his claim as a teacher from God. Without this quality, we mean the sobriety which is born of an evenly balanced mind, there cannot be the patience needed, amidst the prejudices and passions of humanity, for discerning and holding fast the simplicity of truth. He has not begun to understand the mind of Jesus, who does not recognize as a foremost trait in him a collected spirit, a freedom from exaggeration, a soul serenely lifted above the seductions and the provocations that beset him. It is well said by a recent critic of this book, that if, as all Christians agree, Jesus was *very man,* the life of Jesus should be written in a *very manly* way. M. Renan's ideal Jesus is too much a man of sentiment, or too little a man of principle. We regret to feel, too, that the pernicious principle of *pious fraud* so much indulged by the Church M. Renan was born in, but not by that Church alone, has tainted his treatment of his grave and majestic theme. Only a manly and a godly man is fitted to write the life of our Master,—the great Master in the art of a divine life.

And yet, is a man "far from the kingdom of God," while he pens such a paragraph as this on the word of Jesus at the well of Samaria?

The day when he pronounced that word, he was truly the Son of God. He spoke for the first time the word on which the edifice of the eternal religion shall rest forever. He founded that pure worship, without date, without country, which all exalted souls shall practise till the end of time. Not only on that day was his religion the good religion of humanity, it was the absolute religion; and if other planets have inhabitants endowed with reason and morality, their religion cannot be different from that which Jesus proclaimed at the well of Jacob. Man has not been able to hold himself to it; for

one attains the ideal but for a moment. The word of Jesus was a flash of lightning in a dark night; eighteen centuries were needed for the eyes of humanity—what do I say?—of an infinitely small part of humanity—to accustom themselves to it. But the gleam shall become the full day, and, after having run through all the circles of error, humanity will return to that word as the immortal expression of its faith and of its hopes.

—p. 234.

Since writing the foregoing pages, we have received the goodly handful of French pamphlets named at the head of our article. They are but a small part of the numerous, prompt, and piquant replies M. Renan's book has provoked. We shall give as fair and full a sketch of them as our limits will allow, simply as they afford a striking illustration of the *animus* of the predominant religion in France, scarcely one of them touching the heart of the subject, (though often probing most effectively weak points in M. Renan's argument),—never (or with scarcely an exception) seeking to discover how M. Renan may have slipped off from the right road, in order to try to lead him back, or dreaming it possible to learn anything from him, but almost throughout showing themselves as God, armed with terrifying thunders and avenging lightning,—in short, affording a melancholy comment on the low and barbarous state of French civilization as tried by one of the surest tests, that of a manly recognition of the right and duty of free thought. If he does not become notorious, it will not be for want of names pinned on his back in the pillory where his adversaries have placed him. He is called a Judas, a Pilate, an Erostratus, a Samson (in all but strength), a matricide, a Deicide. At the same time, in spite of the frequent substitution of base aspersion of his motives, and once or twice even of his person, it must be confessed that these *brochures* do make pretty thorough work of the weaker parts of M. Renan's book and system, if system it can "be called that shape has none discernible."

All these reviewers agree in calling M. Renan's book a romance, of which he, and not Jesus, is the hero; all dwell on the loose, inaccurate, unscholarly, and inconsistent character of his argument in the discussion of such grave subjects; on the slightness of the research and reasoning with which he justifies, the vagueness with which he announces, and the still greater recklessness with which through the book he practically treats his professed recognition of the Evangelic authorities, which he admits are the prime sources of information in the case. All reprobate the sentimentality of his style as unworthy the sublime simplicity of his theme, and take especial pains to analyze and expose the ill-matched work of his apparent reconstruction of the individuality and idea of Jesus. Several of them answer with great dignity, spirit, and strength M. Renan's demand that alleged miracles should have been submitted to a jury of *savans*. We have no room to do more than glance at the character and contents of these several replies.

The little books of Pioger and Lasserre are such as the Germans call "waistcoat-pocket editions." The former, regarding M. Renan's book as simply an attack upon the *Divinity* of Jesus (though he means the *Deity*), sets himself to prove that Christ was God: 1st, by prophecy; 2d, by his holy life; 3d, by his own words; 4th, by his miracles; 5th, by his sufferings and death. The latter is a fiery and somewhat fuliginous attack upon the audacious blasphemer who would rob the world of its God,—the wretched ingrate who, having in his poverty been fed both in *body* and soul by his dear old mother, the Church, now lifts his unnatural arm against her, tries to shake off the impression of her benediction from his head and her very image out of his memory. M. Renan is compared to an old duellist, who, having called out an innocent young man, and suffered him to fire the first shot without effect, drops his arm and proceeds to remind the young man of his mother and all he had to live for; and when the youth, moved by such magnanimous words, would rush into his arms, the cold-blooded hypocrite cries, "Stay! all these hopes you must bid adieu to forever! I have not fired!"—and, raising his pistol, shoots him dead. And this, says the writer, is M. Renan's way of betraying his victim with a kiss, only, unlike the duellist, *he* does not kill his real adversary. "With a profound attention, with a minute care, with infinite precautions, he aims at God,—God who is everywhere, . . . and he misses him!" Again: "The last hour of God was about to strike. At last the mountain is delivered. Universal deception!" Remarking on M. Renan's criticism of the four Gospels, this writer says:—

> What Gospel would have satisfied him? Ah, we have found it,—the Gospel according to Judas! For apostasy is the essential condition of sincerity. Judas, a prey to the demon of avarice, he too shuts his eyes to the divinity of Jesus Christ, otherwise he would not have dared to sell him. Like M. Renan, he had believed, and believed no longer; like M. Renan selling books against the religion which had been his, Judas traded with the enemies of his Master, his benefactor, and his God; and having become an unbeliever under the sway of his detestable passion, he would fain give the death-blow to his old faith. This would have been an impartial and truthful historian; this was the man that M. Renan wanted. . . . But leave him one thing,

M. Lasserre says, in a tone of mock magnanimity, "to deny him which would be stealing a sous out of a blind man's pocket,—he knows how to write!" Finally, he seizes upon M. Renan's admission that Jesus is a demigod, and cries, "Demigod or God, all one,—for God is indivisible." Logic like this can do no harm but to those who accept it as good reasoning. M. Renan is not touched by it.

M. Potrel's book is mainly a reproduction of the Gospels in a close paraphrase, and reduced to chronological order. To this is prefixed a rambling review of M. Renan's book, in which the following not less bitter than mean insinuation occurs: "Judas sold his God for thirty *écus*; O, why had he not a chair, or, in default of a chair, the sharpened pen of a rhetorician! he might have sold Jesus by making a great book; he might have delivered him to the beasts by writing, and instead of thirty *écus* for a word whispered in the ear of the mighty, he might have received, in exchange for five hundred pages, twenty thousand francs! So much for progress! Everything pays better today!"

This writer also gives a table of about three hundred instances in which M. Renan expresses uncertainty by such words as *perhaps, possibly, almost, apparently,* &c.

M. Hello begins by asserting that M. Renan's book "absolutely says nothing, and cannot become the occasion of any doctrinal discussion whatever." He accordingly gives only a short and somewhat slight collection of remarks and exclamations on several of M. Renan's principles and interpretations.

When we come to the Bishop of Algiers, we rise a little in the scale and style of argument. With something of the Algerine and archiepiscopal in his tone, he does, however, grapple somewhat manfully and ably with the grand points of the subject, the authenticity of the Gospels and the credibility of the miracles. He charges M. Renan with suppressing the capital question of inspiration. In regard to the pretence that the miracles could have been certified only before a bench of *savans*, he says, among other just things: "M. Renan, who has read the Gospels so much, does not then know that the miracles of our Divine Saviour were inspired much more by charity than by the necessity of demonstrating his power, and that, at all events, he never did a single one through ostentation, to satisfy a frivolous curiosity, or to answer impertinent challenges?" He complains that, in its multitude of digressions, this **Life of Jesus** is more occupied with anything than with the veritable life of Jesus.

M. Laurentie's grief at the book is caused chiefly by the evidence afforded of the corrupt state of the public mind, when apostasy is the road to popularity and preferment. He finds the whole falsehood of the book in the statement that Jesus was "a superior person, who, by his bold *initiative,* and by *the love he was able to inspire,* created the *object* and fixed the *point of departure* for the *future faith* of humanity!" and this position he devotes himself to overthrowing. He makes out that M. Renan asserts everything to be divine except what is of God, and says, the more he tries to make Jesus a man, only the more he makes him God.

The Reverend Father Félix writes in a somewhat declamatory style, with a mixture of priestly assumption and personal bitterness,—now accusing his adversary of wishing to tear from him his God ("Strike us," he says, "but spare our God!")—and now insinuating that M. Renan's "fine young man and little Galilean resembles *another fine young man* and a certain little *Breton* of our acquaintance,"—and anon relieving his mind by such words as these: "M. Ernest Renan and M. Michel Lévy, author, ex-abbé, and Israelite publisher, have made a good business of it. Those who have reproached them with having conspired to sell Jesus Christ will do them the justice to own that they have not sold him for thirty *denarii*; there was only one man to do it at that price; they would not have taken so little." He charges M. Renan with confiscating to himself the infallibility of Jesus. He finds the object of the book to be treachery to Jesus Christ,—the method of it, treachery to truth. He puts into the mouth of a freethinker, whom he imagines conversing with M. Renan, his charges against the latter, of *assertion without proof, doubts without reason, beggings of the question, naïvetés of criticism, and absurdities of exegesis,* and asserts that it would be some consolation, if, after taking away *Jesus the God,* he had left us the power of respecting *Jesus the man.* He thinks a Jew would say, If Jesus, being only a man, has done all M. Renan says, I find it more marvellous than if he were a God. Finally, he thinks that, while M. Renan, who is "eminently crepuscular," will do mischief to three classes, the ignorant, the prejudiced, and the unsettled, *per contra,* he will do good to honest outsiders, to sincere Christians, to the clergy, to Christ and the Church. Then, by way of farewell, he says: *What thou doest, do quickly!* You are preparing other works, you announce other blows, and you fear time will fail you: hasten, then; finish to-morrow, if possible; day after to-morrow you will be conquered; you will be buried in your books; your glory will die with you; and our Christ-God will reign forever!" All this personality is the more discreditable from the fact that M. Renan's own style never affords a justification for such attack, or for any low retort.

The three reviews by the Abbé Loyson, the Abbé Freppel, and Professor Delaporte are the most learned and elaborate in the list.

The first is entitled "A Pretended Life of Jesus, or M. Ernest Renan, Historian, Philosopher, and Poet." The writer begins by distinguishing between the success of an author and the success of his doctrine. He rejoices that M. Renan has "drawn from their distant fog-banks those phantoms [of German Antichristianity] formidable only at a distance. On our more limpid horizons they will vanish in smoke, and of those fantastic births of night and imagination, good sense, like the sun, will leave no trace." He then quotes some wholesome advice which M. Renan's former Oriental teacher at St.

Sulpice once gave his pupils, to the effect that criticism divorced from history attempts to *see with one eye* and *soar with one wing.* He feels that the sentimental and mystical dress of M. Renan's errors makes them dangerous, and hence he takes up his pen against him.

He first examines M. Renan's estimate of his Evangelic authorities, and finds (to use his own happy expression) that that author takes them as material "relatively solid, but malleable at his own pleasure," and the unhappy effect of this loose opinion of the Gospel records the reviewer shows in detail by quoting passages from various parts of the new biography which illustrate the practical working of the theory it starts with.

Next, the reviewer suggests the probable motive which led M. Renan to make so light of the Gospels, namely, that they are so full of the miraculous. And on this subject he dwells at some length. He charges M. Renan with reasoning in a circle, when he says that the Gospel stories are legendary in so far as they are miraculous. Then, in regard to the *scientific conditions* alleged necessary to prove a miracle, the reviewer says:—

> If the miracle were constant, if it were capable of being repeated at our will or at the command of Messieurs the *savants,* like natural facts, it would be confounded with them, it would constitute a law which one could no longer distinguish from the laws of nature, it would lose with its physiognomy its whole reason for being. Either God does not declare himself by any sign, or he gives a manifest sign of himself. In the former case there is no miracle. In the latter, the miracle is essentially transitory, and so divine a brightness that it subdues with a flash.

Again:—

> He who refuses to appear before scientific juries makes no difficulty in presenting himself before these grand popular assizes. He reveals himself to humility, while he hides himself from pride.

And again:—

> M. Renan may well speak of democracy, the enfranchisement of the poor and the lowly. His doctrine tends simply to shut and double-bolt heaven in the face of the people, and to confide the key to hands which would never open it.

But M. Renan's great difficulty in receiving the miracles, the reviewer says, is his pantheism.

Next comes the question of the personality of Jesus. And here the reviewer exposes the flimsiness of M. Renan's attempt to reconstruct the idea of the divine man, and concludes that he is neither historian nor philosopher, but poet; he accordingly advises him to change the title of his book, and call it a romantic autobiography, and ends with a mock salutation of the new "son of the nebulous Armorica, scion of the Celtic bards"!

Professor Freppel's "Critical Examination" begins with the remark, that, though we had no reason to expect anything solid in the way of science and logic from such a man as M. Renan, we had a right to demand that a serious subject should be treated seriously. Strauss, he says, was serious, at least. But M. Renan knew his public and knew himself. He has enough of the show of learning to dazzle the superficial; but to refer us for information on preliminary and essential points to works long ago refuted, is an insult to scholarship and sense. In fact, M. Renan was not fit to write the **Life of Jesus.**

The matter is then taken up under several heads. 1. The Gospels. Here the author's admission that they are *mostly* from the writers to whom they are ascribed, is handled with searching severity. "The poetic preoccupations of M. Renan do not permit him to form any exact idea of the first and second centuries." 2. The Gospel of St. John. Here the writer argues the absurdity of M. Renan's theory of the aged Evangelist's writing his Gospel from jealousy of Peter, who figured too largely in the other three, and the fallacy of his inference from the glimpses of Oriental philosophy in the fourth Gospel. 3. The Supernatural. Under this head a distinction is made between

> the *fact* of the miracle and its miraculous *character.* If the question is of the simple fact, the material fact, the fact which falls under the cognizance of the senses, a person from the people, or a man of the world, enjoying the use of his faculties and endowed with sound organs, is as competent to see and understand, as the first *savant* on earth. It is not necessary to be a physiologist, physicist, or chemist, to be able to certify that one born blind began to see at a given moment, that a paralytic set himself to walking, that a deaf-mute recovered hearing and speech. As to the question of knowing whether such cures produced by a word, or a gesture, pass the forces of nature, that may belong to the sphere of science, if you will; but the fact in itself is within reach of everybody, and requires, in order to be observed and faithfully reported, neither a strong dose of erudition nor a long habit of scientific research.

Indeed, says the reviewer, even upon the question of the character of the fact, plain men would be no worse judges than scientific men, and might be better, because they would have no theory to blind them. He then ridicules at great length the demand for a scientific commission on miracles, and finally examines the author's way of disposing of the relation of Jesus to the popular mind in this matter of miracles; and this brings him to—4. The Person of Jesus Christ. "To exalt Jesus Christ in order to deceive one class, to degrade Jesus Christ in order to encourage another class,—behold the idea of the work." The reviewer proceeds to show that the insincerity ascribed to Jesus leaves him no longer even a *good man.* 5. Christianity. Here M. Renan is charged with not studying carefully the antecedents of our religion, the circumstances of its birth, or its doctrines and

institutions. 6. The Church. Here the idea is combated, that religion is a matter of pure sentiment, and is independent of form or formula. And the review ends with holy horror at the attempt to destroy faith in the virginity of Mary and the divinity of Christ.

Appended to the review is a severe letter to one of M. Renan's panegyrists in the *Revue des Deux Mondes,* who contends that he has not gone far enough, but ought to have said at once that *no part of the Gospels is written by companions of Jesus.*

The essay entitled "Criticism and Tactics" lays down the laws of the critical art, and means to show that M. Renan disregards them. "Self-constituted critic of the man-God, he knows little of man, and of God nothing." But the first chapter, though it opens in a very scientific style, soon passes into personal declamation; for it makes the three points,—1. True criticism implies a knowledge of its subject; 2. It supposes a *criterion*; 3. M. Renan had a special reason for keeping silence, namely, his antecedents. The second chapter begins the *exposé* of the "Processes of Modern Antichristianity" with strictures on the coolness of the free-thinkers in their classification of men as choice spirits and vulgar spirits, and ends with these words: "You are the *élite,* we are the vulgar. Say it less, and show it more." In the third chapter, entitled "Precautions against the Approaches of the Truth," is exposed M. Renan's system of keeping out of sight all that his adversaries have written. The fourth chapter is entitled "Disloyal Reticences." This relates to M. Renan's partial or perverted presentments of the history of Jesus, his blinking out of sight what would incommode his theory, and referring in a general way to texts which, if cited in full, would make against him. Chapter V. is headed, "Masking one's Colors under a Neutral Flag," which means, in its application to M. Renan, undermining Christian faith while professedly laboring only as a historian. Chapter VI. is on the "Perfidies of Language." "Every page," says the critic, speaking of M. Renan's style, "is a Bengal light: myriads of sparks, no hearth." He has many beautiful and holy words, but his meaning is evil. Chapter VII. treats of "Audacious Assertions." M. Renan assumes that history can take no cognizance of miracles. He attacks the authority of Jerome. He falsifies the Gospel records. Chapter VIII. "The Unbounded Extension of Conjecture." Chapter IX. is on *La Nuance,* that is to say, the insensible gradation by which right and wrong are alleged to run into each other. Chapter X. discusses the attributing to Jesus pious frauds or philanthropic impostures.

In conclusion, the reviewer comforts himself with the conviction that M. Renan's book will help the cause of truth. "Since the publication of this book, M. Didot, they say, has sold more New Testaments than for fifteen years before."

He summons the faithful to the defence of reason and revelation, and finally proposes the establishment of an "Academy of Catholic Science," with branches in the principal cities of France, with a general Review, and at the capital a library specially adapted to the preservation and diffusion of the Catholic faith. The review should "pitilessly reject feeble or inaccurate publications."

Of all the answers to M. Renan's book which we have seen, the one named last in our list, by the Abbé Michon, interests us most; not by any special strength of argument, but by the candor and kindliness of its tone, and by the fact that the writer takes an independent ground between the ultramontane party of "religious absolutism" and the sceptics. There is something touching in his appeal to M. Renan. He says in substance: You know our hands are tied in the Roman Catholic Church, so that we cannot furnish at present a full and fair explanation of these difficult subjects: you take an unfair advantage, when, with all the beauty and brilliancy of your style, you set forth difficulties which we feel as much as you, but which it should be your work, gentlemen of science, to come, and in a frank, friendly way invite us to help dispose of, if they can be disposed of; for, in regard to many of them, you yourself do not relieve the reader; you demolish, but do not build up. You cannot think to satisfy your age, your subject, or yourself, when you give us for the truth on the origins of Christianity, a bucolic romance. "Science imposes an obligation, Monsieur Renan." (*Science oblige, M. Renan.*) "Have you believed that the *Life of Jesus* would be taken for the work of a *savant?* Perhaps." "To construct an edifice, you must have materials. The question was difficult, nay, terrible," which you had to meet. "We know that you do not believe in the Christ-God; but we do not know why *we* ought not to believe in him. The member of the Institute has given us his judgment; the grave motives of his judgment remain as yet unknown to us." "Your conscience will reproach you with having knowingly risked deceiving the multitude, who are led only by imagination, in making them believe that you have scientific demonstration of what rests only on your personal affirmation." "I have a right to be severe in the examination of your proofs; and these proofs,—I do not wish them to be such as content the female readers of romances, but such as serious men who have long labored in the field of metaphysics, those mathematics of the spirit, demand of a man who has a name, and who belongs to the first learned body in Europe."

One cannot close an examination of these pamphlets, with their mixture of justice and injustice, without having awakened in him by both a keen regret that a man of M. Renan's accomplishments and ability should have laid himself open so recklessly to such assaults, and at the same time have afforded the advocates of ancient errors a fresh plea for holding fast to their old superstitions, by the loose, vacillating nature of the faith or feeling which he would substitute for them. It is, indeed, a disappointment, to find that M. Renan's book thus serves to confirm the erroneous views of the life and teachings of Jesus which have so long obscured the truth. But what else could follow from an attempt to construct an idea of Jesus, and leave out all respect for these wondrous works he himself refers to as God's works,—respect for them, we say, not merely as miracles, but as good, honest works, wrought in good faith and simplicity of heart? The pagan sentimentality of the dedication, in which the author associates the memory of his departed sister with that of the women who used in the ancient mysteries to mingle their tears in the sacred waters of the land of Adonis, preludes the gravest fault in the spirit of the book,—the want of a true manliness and godliness, of a high principle, in short, in his imaginary Jesus, to balance and connect the sentimental element, and to save the name of that just man from being made to cover the most unaccountable kind of pious and philanthropic fraud that history has related or fiction feigned.

In the first part of this article, the question was asked, whether what we had known of M. Renan's doing and writing *before* his *Life of Jesus* would make us think him the man to do justice to such a subject; and now we have to say, that something which he has written *since* that work came out gives us a glimpse of a state of mind which may well have been very unpropitious in some important respects, not before alluded to, for a biographer of Him who brought to light the immortal life of man.

The *Revue des Deux Mondes* for October 15th, 1863, opens with a letter written by M. Renan from the seaside. Contemplating the immensity of the universe, he begins by confessing his old preference for natural science over those historical and critical studies in which he had been so much engaged; then ascending in thought from human history to geology, thence to astronomy, from that still higher to chemistry (the science of atomic combinations), and finally to dynamics (the realm and period of pure forces); pausing there on the border of the unknown region of spirit, and returning on his track, downward and onward, he anticipates the day when the process of development which has been going on in nature will be complete, and when, "although *we* shall for myriads of years have been dust, and the particles which composed our material being shall have been disengaged and passed through incalculable transformations, *we* shall *revive* in the form of that world which we shall have contributed to make." And then, too, God will come to a complete recognition and consciousness of himself. Just as in the Hindoo theology an inert and unconscious godhead, Brahm, reaches conscious and creative activity in Brahma; so God, who "knows himself better in the plant than in the rock, . . . in Buddha than in Socrates, in Christ than in Buddha," will (M. Renan deprecates the inference, but it seems to us logical) become complete, being until then infinite in the sense of *unfinished,* like truth, according to Schiller, which "always is a-being, never is."

But our chief concern is with M. Renan's idea of *human* personality, and on this point the following significant words are to be specially noted: "Consciousness is in fact, so far as we are concerned, a resultant; now the resultant disappears with the organism whence it proceeds; the effect vanishes with the cause; the brain being decomposed, consciousness must then disappear. . . . The place which man occupies in God, the opinion which absolute justice has of him, the rank that he holds in the only true world, namely, the world according to God,—in a word, his part in the general consciousness,—that is his veritable being." "It is in God that man is immortal."

Does not M. Renan reveal here a Straussian, a Hegelian creed,—in fact, almost repeating Strauss's melancholy parody, that the faith in a personal immortality is the last enemy that shall be destroyed? Do not the vague and shifting words in which he seems to endeavor at once to convey and to conceal his real meaning, justify us in attributing to him such a disbelief in conscious personal immortality as singularly disqualifies a man for expounding the life of one who, like Jesus, made the truth of individual immortality the chief ground of consolation and warning to men as moral beings, even if it does not explain in some measure, by the want of respect for human personality, the capricious manner in which M. Renan deals with the elements that compose his ideal Jesus?

Here we close our discussion of M. Renan's views; but we cannot yet leave the subject without recurring for a few moments to the question, whether the work which M. Renan has attempted needs to be done at all. On this point we have a word or two more to say.

There are two ways of writing the **Life of Jesus**: the one is simply to ascertain and arrange the facts of his external history; the other is, then to go on and so interpret and explain those facts as to make it seen and felt what manner of man he was in spirit and purpose; for in these, after all, is a man's true life. Now, a **Life of Jesus** of *this* kind seems to us still, at this day, eminently needed. We want, first, to have a conviction founded on internal and external evidence that Jesus is the name of a real man, and not of a fictitious one; then, that he is an honest man in heart and a sound one in mind,—one who, instead of being carried away by popular passion, calmly resists it and rules himself,—in short, one who can be *believed* (as well as believed *on* or *in*), respected, and trusted; and then, when we once

really have Jesus as a genuine and good man, we are prepared to receive him for what he is more. Then we are prepared to judge soberly of the meaning and value of what he says of himself, and of what others have said of him. Then we are prepared to take a more intelligent view than we could otherwise have done of his miraculous works as well as words, and, in short, to appreciate his true relation at once to God and to man. And then, too, the life of Jesus will be brought into such a light that it can be seen to be the *Gospel of today.* We shall have him both as an Example and a Teacher. He will be in the midst of us a presence and a power; for we shall feel that his times are essentially our times, and our trials essentially his. He will be our Leader and our Legislator, and thus, by once really believing in him as a man, we shall have him as a Messiah. What thoughtful person does not see and feel how sorely this is needed,—does not see and feel how much the pernicious sophistries, the political and moral wrongs of this professedly civilized and Christianized era, are aggravated by the want of sound convictions touching the relation of Jesus to us? It is anything but a mere piece of scholarly amusement, then, it is of vital importance to bring back to this age the living Christ. The dispute between the disciples of an historical and those of a spiritual Christ is wholly unnecessary and misleading. The historical Jesus once made real to the souls of men, becomes the spiritual Jesus,—then for the first time we have the real point and power of his example.

Before this can be, however, there must be a better idea than the present orthodox and popular notions constitute, of the whole subject of the connection between human nature and the Divine, as well as the relation of God to the material world. There must be a more clear and settled understanding of the meaning of inspiration. Until we get that, our belief in the miraculous Messiah and his miraculous life will continue to be what it has hitherto been with such a vast proportion of men,—a barren wonder.

Note

1. [Ernest Renan,] *La Chaire d'Hébreu,* p. 12.

***Blackwood's Edinburgh Magazine* (review date October 1864)**

SOURCE: *"The Life of Jesus." Blackwood's Edinburgh Magazine* 96, no. 588 (October 1864): 417-31.

[*In the following review, the critic condemns the skeptical tone of* The Life of Jesus.]

It is a reproach frequently addressed to the Church, that she is more disposed to utter fulminations against the heretics who assail her, than to reply with sound reason and argument to their attacks. People say that the clergy are as ready as ever to denounce, and, when the occasion serves, to persecute, but that they are very slow to do manful battle for their faith, and meet their antagonists with their own opinions. Such a reproach has a specially severe meaning in an age so generally tolerant and reasonable, entertaining so large an amount of amiable, devout, and intelligent heretics, and feeling itself so capable of calm discussion upon every subject under the sun. Toleration has indeed become so universal that we have not only ceased to persecute, but have to a great extent ceased to understand the conditions under which persecution is possible; and people have even been known to assert that the 'Essays and Reviews,' and indeed Dr Colenso himself, instead of being condemned, should have been answered. This idea, however, like most effusions of popular sentiment, contains, along with a little truth, a great deal of injustice. When theology was treated scientifically, and the assailants of Christianity were men who had the grace to wait a response, and to accept in good faith the *rôle* of Deist, Atheist, or Sceptic, it was practicable enough to prepare replies to all their arguments, and Christian apologists were not wanting; but the matter has entirely changed since those days, in England at least. The utterances of sceptical opinion, which may be considered most dangerous, are at present about as unanswerable as a popular novel. In saying so we do not mean to imply any sneer at the popular qualities which make such a work as M. Rénan's *Vie de Jésus* attractive to the ordinary reader. There is no reason why a book should be less worthy of consideration or thought because it is so written as to be always pleasant to read. The impossibility of serious reply to such a production arises from a perfectly different cause. It is because of its ephemeral and momentary nature that it is next to impossible for the defenders of Christianity to reply specially to such an attack. Unless, indeed, we could secure a previous understanding with the intending assailant, and so have due entry into the lists along with him in all the stately politeness of chivalry, it is difficult to see what the Christian champion can do. What his adversary has prepared and elaborated by the toil of years, by travels and researches which demand leisure, he must either reply to flying, putting not only himself but his argument under the most serious disadvantages—or he must be content to record only his denial and disapproval of it, in face of a generation which, at the height of its admiration, has already half forgotten what its enthusiasm was about. A few months ago the work of which we speak was discussed everywhere. Last summer we found it in its primitive shape, an imposing volume, in the chief bookseller's shop of a little Scotch country town, where French literature seldom penetrates. In spring, straying vaguely into Detken's, in Naples, in search of the English traveller's chief solace, the novels of the Tauchnitz series, we found not only that popular body of lit-

erature, but even the multitudinous volumes of Dumas and his disciples, lost and buried under a locust flood of little volumes in yellow paper, the cheap edition of the *Vie de Jésus.* The book had thrust itself into all kinds of editions in the meanwhile, and had ranged freely between and beyond the antipodal regions of the High Street, Kennaquhair, and the Palazzo Reale. A book of such universal prevalence would seem, at first sight, the work of all others which it was the Church's duty to answer. And it is very possible that at the present moment conscientious "apologists" are labouring hard after the airy footsteps of M. Rénan, and making a solid response at their leisure to his production. But in the mean time the whirligig Time has brought about its revenges. The tide has turned. The "wind of doctrine" has swept over Christendom and disappeared. The shelves that once groaned under his various-sized octavos have now forgotten Rénan. Care and research are necessary today to find a single copy of the book which a little while ago lay as thick as autumn leaves. Under such circumstances, what is the Christian critic to do? So far as it is possible to reply by a rapid magazine article or flying *feuilleton,* he has a chance of following on the traces of his agile opponent, but there are many people who object to such weapons of religious defence. To meet the highly-polished and cunningly-prepared arrow thus delivered flying, by the heavy artillery which requires both time and space for its evolutions, is manifestly impossible; for the sparkling projectile has flown into oblivion and darkness long before the great guns can be got in order, and the world does but pause to ask what it is all about when the tardy broadside rings into all the echoes. To be sure, it is a very good thing that such assaults upon the common faith should be ephemeral as well as periodical; but it is at the same time rather a hard case for the Christian teacher who has addressed himself to their serious consideration.

Such being the case, the most effectual, and indeed almost the only way to meet an assault such as we have described, is one which has finally produced the little volume entitled, 'The Christ of the Gospels and the Christ of Modern Criticism,'[1] an admirable though brief exposition at once of M. Rénan's books, and of the historical and philosophical as well as Christian principles which negative its conclusions. Principal Tulloch's Lectures have already fulfilled the primary and immediate purpose for which they were in no respect after date, and, having done so, come as fitly as modestly to the public, not so much in refutation of the brilliant Frenchman's idyll, as in calm remonstrance and protest against the principles at once of historical inquiry and moral criticism, which have produced this last and newest exposition of the ideas of the nineteenth century. Religious declamation or pious horror would be out of place from a chair in which theology has to be treated as a science, and where to prove all things is as necessary as to hold fast that which is true. Nor is it, fortunately, the custom nowadays to impute motives, or set down, as in more primitive times, a religious speculatist as naturally an impious man. Principal Tulloch himself is one of the chief leaders of religious thought in Scotland, and is neither afraid of speculation, nor disposed to confine it within artificial limits. On the contrary, he considers it a necessary instrument in the Church, destined to weed and winnow the superfluous matter which attaches itself to every real substance of truth; and it is, accordingly, without any undue heat or prejudice that he looks at M. Rénan, whose real qualities of scholarship he acknowledges without hesitation, and against whose honesty he makes no suggestion. The faults he alleges against the book are of a more radical quality. To call it blasphemous would have been easy. The critic, in the present case, goes much farther, and calls it unphilosophical. He finds fault with its principles, not only in a religious but in an intellectual point of view. He describes it as at once theoretical and dogmatic, rejecting the Catholic belief with the bland elevation of superior intelligence, yet claiming from its readers a faith in its own assumption, which no Pope has yet been able to extort from the unwilling world. As even popular oblivion cannot make the *Vie de Jésus* otherwise than interesting to everybody who is disposed to consider the subject it treats as the most important subject of discussion in the world, it may be worth while to sketch briefly the nature of M. Rénan's book. It is a new biography of the Founder of Christianity, treated according to the popular method of modern biography; and the writer is a scholar of acknowledged eminence, learned in all the intricacies of Asiatic literature, and professing to enter with a perfectly candid and unbiassed mind upon the consideration of those singular phenomena which attended the origin of the Christian religion. Such a man, one might say at the first glance, was a very fit historian of an era so momentous; but there are a few drawbacks to set against his qualifications for the office. The first and most important of these is, that though M. Rénan is not at all prejudiced against the great Author of Christianity, but, on the contrary, displays everywhere a great and even patronising partiality towards the wonderful Being whose life he relates, he sets out with an established theory concerning the world and its management, which from the first settles arbitrarily the most important questions involved. In the world, as it appears to M. Rénan, there are no complications except such as can be disposed of scientifically. He makes up his mind before he begins, that no supernatural power of whatsoever description has any hand in the matter. Like those humble descendants of the mummers of old who still linger about Scotland, the French savant has to send some one before him with a broom to sweep the stage clear for his drama; and it is with an apparent ignorance of any other reasonable theory of existence that he draws up the curtain, and discloses to his audience the clean and tidy platform upon which humanity has to

work out its history—a world, to wit, out of which, by a careless exercise of will, he has cleared everything divine and mysterious, leaving only Man and Law to fight out the oft-repeated battle through innumerable ages. Such a clean sweep at the beginning simplifies matters, though, at the same time, it eliminates the true soul of philosophy from the argument which follows, making it rather a laborious arrangement of facts to fit a theory, than an impartial examination of the actual for the demonstration of the true. Along with this, it is, however, plain that the acute and keen intelligence of the biographer has been struck to a wonderful degree by the character which he has set himself to portray. But for a little affectionate contempt for the extreme simplicity of the Galilean peasant which restores his balance of superiority as a historian, the philosopher would become an enthusiast; and even with that saving clause he lingers over the picture he is making with a kind of half-adoration. To account for the influence exercised by a man of humble station and uncultivated powers, not only over his own generation but over centuries of distant time and worlds of alien people, does indeed require that everything that is most noble and perfect in mind and spirit should at least be allowed to the individual who has occupied so singular a place in the world. M. Rénan accordingly depicts the Author of our religion in the warmest and brightest colours. So far from attempting to lessen the beauty of His character, he sets it forth, as we have said, with graceful enthusiasm, elaborating many a charming vignette by the way of that fair Eastern landscape, which he concludes to have imparted so much of its reflective calm and pastoral beauty to the soul of the young Nazarene. He describes to us, in very full detail, what Jesus knew and did not know, and the processes of thought and growth of ideas in His mind. He touches lightly, with a tender regret, on those unfortunate moments in which, beguiled by the wiles of his friends and the necessities of the time, this wonderful Reformer permitted Himself to be seduced into thaumaturgical performances and pretences of miracle. By these means,—by the beauty of Christ's character, and even, for M. Rénan is bold, of His person—by the enthusiasm of His followers, and the ingenuity of His disciples, and the mingled wants and credulity of the age,—the new biographer of Jesus of Nazareth does his best to account for Christianity. We do not at present pause to notice the still more profound difficulties he plunges himself into—difficulties much darker and uglier than those which he gets clear of by ignoring any sort of divine agency in the matter. We do but state the conditions under which he works, and the nature of the production thus evolved. He depicts to us a world busy and full, teeming with unintelligible creatures, each of them a profound secret to his neighbours, most of them unspeakably mysterious to themselves—all running their heads from time to time against the dead walls of law and order, which encompass their blind existence, yet by times addressing wistful looks towards a sky which, to the poetic souls among them, looks to have something behind its unfathomable depths. If any one ever made it, that unknown Being has retired behind His cloudy curtains, and left it to its own devices. But then amid the crowd there arises a Man, who not only marks Himself everlastingly upon the broad canvass, but affects the lives and fills the thoughts of myriads of people hundreds of years after, people more enlightened in many particulars than Himself—all this without any sort of influence in the matter except the ordinary laws of human influence—the power of natural greatness, genius, and truth. This is the picture M. Rénan draws, without, perhaps, quite perceiving all its difficulties; and indeed it is no light task for any historian to account for a wonderful and continuous religious movement in a world left all by itself to its own devices, without the possibility of any interference on the part of God.

It is this assumption, to start with, against which Dr Tulloch opens his protest. He complains that, while M. Rénan professes to enter upon the consideration of his subject with a mind entirely impartial and unbiassed by theory, it is in reality upon a foregone conclusion that he bases his entire argument. "The Gospels are partly legendary, because they are full of miracles;" such is the primary statement of the historian who proposes to interpret anew the life of Christ—a life wholly miraculous, according to Christian conception. To reject a certain miracle, or even all miracles, as insufficiently proved, is a different thing from the rejection of every miraculous possibility in the world, which is the conclusion with which M. Rénan sets out. The real meaning of this conception of the universe is ably set forth by Principal Tulloch in the following passage:—

> Here there can be no doubt of M. Rénan's philosophical sentiments, and as little doubt of the manner in which he applies them to history. It is his evident principle, as it is that of the whole school to which he belongs, to ignore the reality of any spiritual or divine government of the world. The order of the universe is fixed in certain laws, which exclude all personal intervention, and remain unchanging for ever. It is the business of science to discover these laws; it is the function of the historian to recognise their operation, and to interpret by them the whole course of past phenomena; for it admits of no question, that they are the same laws which we now see operating round us, which have been without deviation operating from the beginning. There is and can be no room, therefore, in history for miracle. There is no room even for God, save as the poetic or philosophic ideal of an inflexible system of law. This is Positivism in its general conception—the startling creed of a widely-prevailing philosophy. Not only Christianity, but Theism, is held to be a philosophical mistake. The world has not advanced, nay, has retrograded, from the days of the great schools of Greek science. It is the spirit of Lucretius, the recognition of his *inexorabile Fatum*, which is the highest point of

wisdom, and to which the world must return, as the spring of its highest progress, and the consummation of all knowledge. It is somewhat hard for the Christian apologist to be thus continually dragged from the fair field of historical evidence to a discussion of the ultimate principles of all truth. And yet it is a very instructive fact, that every school of unbelief is now driven to this resource. It makes its chief attack upon Christianity from behind general principles, not merely inimical to the Church and the supernatural foundation upon which it rests, but inimical to all religion—inimical, in fact, to all spiritual philosophy and every noble creative art and product of civilisation which has its root in the spiritual life of man—the sphere in which man is allied to a higher divine life than the mere nature around him which he can see and handle. For this is the real question involved in Positivism. It is not, as writers like M. Rénan ingeniously put it, a question between law and caprice, order and arbitrariness, in the government of the world. There is no Christian thinker who believes that the government of the world is otherwise than by general laws. The universe of nature is conceived by all reflective minds as a great order or *cosmos,* and the course of history, apparently irregular as it has been, as a consistent development in the great system of things. The Theist recognises the principle of *order* quite as plainly as the Positivist; but what he does not admit is the merely material character of this order. He maintains, on the contrary, that order is everywhere the direct expression of a living Divine will, which rules in and by the order. He acknowledges, equally with the Positivist, that the material facts or phenomena in the midst of which he lives are capable of classification into general laws, continually subsisting, and of which they may be regarded as the issue or manifestation; but he does not allow that these material phenomena or their laws exhaust the realities of being. On the contrary, he holds that the highest being of man is not contained in them, but is a part of, and is closely allied to, a higher order of being, transcending and embracing the other. Every higher activity of our nature presupposes and springs from this higher order of being. Religion has no meaning apart from it. Philosophy, as it has been conceived by all the highest minds of the human race—by a Socrates or a Pascal, or even by a Pythagoras or a Kant—has no basis without it. Art of every kind, poetry, painting, sculpture, imply and appeal to it, and, save for the inspiration they draw from thence, would be merely the toys of an idle and frivolous luxury. Civilisation in its legislative and judicial institutes, and in all the more characteristic and elevating forms of its manifestations, rests upon it, grows with its growth, and decays with its corruption. That man is something more than matter, that there is a divine spirit in him, and a divine spirit above him, in whom alone he lives, and that this divine order of being is higher than the mere material order, and may for wise and beneficent purposes supersede and traverse this lower order; that, in short, there is a living Supreme Will directly governing all things, and communing with and controlling the will of man—an Almighty and Personal hand, which none can stay from working,—such a faith is indeed eminently Christian. But it also lies more or less obscurely at the root of every form of religion, and every conception of man as a being capable of rational and moral progress. And this is what Positivism, if not in all cases expressly, yet in its essential character implicitly denies; for it acknowledges nothing higher than nature, and the system of laws into which nature may be resolved.

Such a philosophy, if philosophy it can be called, necessarily excludes all idea of miracles. It rejects the miraculous from history because it has already rejected God from the world. Let it pretend as it may not to impose theory upon history, it does so in the most obvious and sweeping manner. For why are miracles incredible? Not because they have been examined and found to be devoid of credit, but because the world proceeds by general laws, and not by personal agency. Deny this latter fact, and of course no miracle can have ever happened—for a miracle in its very idea presupposes personal agency. But admit the reality of Divine Intelligence and Will governing and acting in every manifestation of nature and of history, and it is impossible to exclude the idea of miracle, or at once set it aside.

Principal Tulloch follows up this statement of the entire basis of the question by entering into M. Rénan's special argument in respect to the miracles of the New Testament, which is in its way a skilful and specious piece of writing, with all that apparent candour and abstract air of justice which is so captivating to an inexperienced reader. "No miracle," he says, "has ever been performed before an assembly of men capable of verifying the miraculous character of a fact;" and he proceeds to state the circumstances under which it might be possible to convince himself, or any other person similarly enlightened, of a miraculous event. "Were a worker of miracles to present himself in these days," he says, "with pretensions sufficiently serious to be discussed, and to announce himself, we shall suppose, as capable of raising the dead, what should we do? We should appoint a commission composed of physiologists, physicians, chemists, and persons trained in historical criticism. This commission would choose a dead body; would assure themselves that it was in reality a dead body; would select a room for the experiment, and arrange an entire system of precautions necessary to place the result beyond doubt. If under such conditions the raising of the dead was effected, a probability nearly equal to certainty would be obtained. However, as an experiment must be always capable of repetition, as those who have once done a thing must be able to do it again, and there can be no question of easy or difficult in regard to miracles, the miracle-worker would be invited to reproduce the miraculous fact in other circumstances upon other dead bodies in another company." To this singular proposal, in which the strength and weakness of M. Rénan's mode of argument is very remarkably shown, Dr Tulloch replies by a very lucid and striking description of the difference between historical and scientific facts:

M. Rénan has here fallen into so plain a confusion as to confound a fact of experience, a profound historical incident, with a scientific conclusion. Facts of incident and contingency—and all historical facts, miraculous or otherwise, are of this class—belong to a sphere of their own, different from the scientific, and rest on their own characteristic and appropriate proof. Whether anything has happened or not is a question of contingency to be settled by the evidence of those who profess to have seen the thing happen. Did they really see it? were they truly cognisant of it? And were they capable of judging, not by scientific tests, but by the ordinary exercise of their senses and their judgment, whether what they saw was a reality, and not an illusion? Are they honest men, and have they no inducement to say that the thing happened if it did not happen? Such is the nature of historical evidence. Scientific evidence is of a different character; the evidence not of personal testimony but of continual demonstration. Scientific facts, unlike facts of mere contingency or incident, are truths of nature, which, once discovered, admit of repeated verification, because they rest on the constitution of things—the existing laws of the material universe: they are equally true at all times, therefore, and their proof can be demonstratively exhibited at one time as well as another. In the case of such facts personal evidence is of no consequence. No amount of such evidence, apart from scientific experiment and demonstration, could establish, for example, the law of gravitation, or the law of equilibrium of fluids. You or I may believe these scientific truths, because of Newton's statements on the one hand or Pascal's statements on the other; but any number of such statements does not form the appropriate evidence of such truths. They rest, on the contrary, on the evidence of direct observation and experiment, capable of constant repetition, and of being exhibited in formulæ of the utmost exactness and certainty. M. Rénan asks with triumph, 'Who does not know that no miracle has ever been performed under the conditions laid down by him?' May we not ask with a more justly-founded confidence, Who does not see that a miracle performed under such conditions would be no miracle at all? So soon as you can reduce any fact within scientific laws and conditions, it necessarily ceases to bear the character of a miracle. It is the very idea of miracle that it transcends these laws and conditions; that it is an incident or occurrence appearing within the sphere of human experience, but incapable of being resolved by the ordinary laws which govern this experience. If it can be so resolved, it loses all pretension to be miraculous, or even marvellous. If the case supposed by M. Rénan could really occur, the conclusions which he draws from it are not those which would really follow. The true inference would be, not that miraculous powers had been intrusted to certain persons, but that raising the dead was a natural or scientific process, and not an exhibition of miraculous or supernatural power at all. How could it be, if capable of spontaneous repetition in the manner suggested? for is not this capacity of repetition just the characteristic of a scientific fact? Is not the process described the very process by which some new truth or law of science is discovered and verified? A miracle, on the other hand, implies as its essential idea a special and extraordinary exercise of divine power which, from its very nature, it is absurd to suppose repeated with a view to verification. It pleased God Almighty, let us suppose, with a view to man's good and the demonstration of His own glory, to interpose in human affairs, arresting the ordinary action of the laws of nature, as in the case of immediate recovery from sickness or restoring the dead to life again. The operation of the natural forces which make up the course of human experience, and which only subsist at any moment, because God who appointed them continues them, is temporarily set aside for some wise end, so that the Original Will—of whom alone all these forces are, and whose power alone they express—is made bare, stands forth, as it were, in direct demonstration and authority. This is the Christian idea of a miracle—the will of God in direct and extraordinary exercise. This is the nature of the fact which M. Rénan insists upon calling together an assembly of scientific persons to settle. Is this the hand of God? They are to determine the question by experiment, and by an application of scientific tests. If the hand of God raises a dead man to life, it must repeat the process under a more rigorous and vigilant scientific scrutiny before the scientific notables can determine whether the thing has been really done or not. It is surely needless to add, that no miracle has hitherto been performed under such conditions, for the conditions entirely divest the supposed act of all divine character—nay, of all moral import.

Dr Tulloch does not conclude this clear and striking discrimination without an example. He takes from the Gospel the simple narrative of one of those resuscitations to which M. Rénan refers. It is the story of the widow's son:—

> Our Lord in the course of His journeys went into the city of Nain, and as He went ('and many of His disciples and much people went with Him'), He met a funeral procession, with the dead body of a young man carried on an open bier, according to the custom of the East, and his weeping mother following the bier 'And when the Lord saw her, He had compassion on her, and said unto her, Weep not. And He came and touched the bier: and they that bare him stood still. And He said, Young man, I say unto thee, Arise. And he that was dead sat up, and began to speak. And He delivered him to his mother. And there came a fear on all: and they glorified God, saying, That a great prophet is risen up among us; and, That God hath visited His people.' Think of this scene, a touching and memorable incident, one among many, though few so striking, in the life of our Lord; then recall for contrast M. Rénan's laboratory and assembly of scientific commissioners prepared to investigate the alleged resuscitation of a dead body, carefully selected and scientifically scrutinised. The contrasted facts are of an entirely different order, and the issue contemplated in the one case is quite distinct from the issue alleged in the other.

This, it appears to us, is meeting the question in its fullest and clearest signification with a quiet force, which is infinitely more powerful than any heat of indignation. There is, however, besides this ably-indicated difference, a certain peculiarity in the story of the evangelist, which in this case neither M. Rénan nor his critic take note of. It is the entire simplicity and the spontaneous—what one might call accidental—character of the whole transaction. No thought of proving anything,

even His own divine mission, appears in the words or in the act of the merciful visitor, whose compassionate heart was suddenly touched by the mother's tears. Of all the miracles of the New Testament, it is perhaps the one most entirely unconnected with conscious purpose and intention. The divine traveller stands before us, giving out of His liberality, as a human traveller, benevolent and sympathetic, might have given tears or alms to the desolate woman. *He* had the higher gift in His power, and He bestowed it out of the pity of His heart. He does not turn round to say, "Believe in me since I have raised this man from the dead," but goes silent upon His way, one may well believe, with sad thoughts of that infinite sea of human suffering, of which he had dried up one bitter drop, but with which the broader balance of nature and necessity forbade Him to interfere more largely. The miracle came out from Him like rays from the sun, or like, what is a better image, kindness and consolation from a good man, spontaneously, with no purpose beyond. And if one were but to take the narration simply, without the need of proving anything by it, it would not be difficult to perceive in most of the miracles of the Redeemer, not only this spontaneous, unprepared character, but along with it a wonderful sadness, as if the very solace He gave made Him but mourn the more over the awful margin of anguish which it did not consist with the purposes of Providence that He should relieve. What other meaning could be in those otherwise unnecessary tears which He wept over the grave He was about to open? It is unquestionable that the miracles are referred to both by Himself and His disciples as proofs of His mission; but yet it is only in a very few instances that He seems to have propounded them with this secondary end in view. Otherwise the story reads in most cases as if it had been a certain relaxation of divine self-control, a certain human susceptibility bursting into the composure of Godhead, which constrained Him to touch and heal—accompanied always by that divine melancholy, the grief of God over that grief of man which in the maintenance of His own larger order and universal system it was not meet to cure.

Such an idea is, however, so far from the thoughts of M. Rénan, that it does not seem for a moment to occur to him that there are still a great many people in Christendom who believe unfeignedly that Jesus of Nazareth was the Son of God as much as the Son of Mary; not a man of wonderful genius and high originality, but actually a Divine person. He does not recognise the possible existence of such an idea, but addresses himself as calmly to the narrative of that young life in Galilee, of the influences that went to the formation of so beautiful a character, and the circumstances which combined to beguile it from its natural *rôle* of tender reform and pious contemplation, into the more tragical Messianic character, as if it was agreed that all rational persons were of his way of thinking, and any other conception of the story impossible. In this satisfied and unpolemical mood the biographer proceeds to his picture, drawing it, as we have said, tenderly, and lingering upon the beautiful outline with patronising but genuine admiration. M. Rénan himself is much better educated, and more thoroughly informed than the noble young enthusiast whom he contemplates in the valleys of Galilee—and he is not unconscious of his advantages; but, nevertheless, he is aware that the figure he portrays is one unparalleled in the world. It is this, apart from all theories, which is the chief feature in his book—its argument in respect to miracles, and its criticism of the Gospels, are matters important enough to be treated in detail; but the grand peculiarity of the work is its full and clear confession of the personal sublimity and singularity of Christ. That excellence without parallel, that unequalled purity and moral grandeur, are *not* legendary. M. Rénan has heart and power to perceive that the human imagination is incapable of so magnificent an invention; and so far from desiring to detract from the glory of the figure which it his ambition to portray, his evident desire and intention is to add to it, and record more distinctly, according to his own ideas, its wonderful elevation and majesty. In so doing, it is impossible not to feel that he has served the cause which he means to injure. As it is, however, not only the French philosopher but the Christian critic whom we have at present before us, we prefer to give Principal Tulloch's conclusions on this subject rather than our own. In an eloquent passage he thus sets forth, in the first place, the profound importance to Christianity of this unparalleled character of Christ:—

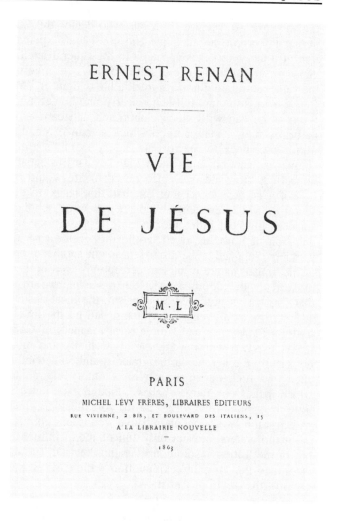

ERNEST RENAN

VIE

DE JÉSUS

M · L

PARIS

MICHEL LÉVY FRÈRES, LIBRAIRES ÉDITEURS
RUE VIVIENNE, 2 BIS, ET BOULEVARD DES ITALIENS, 15
A LA LIBRAIRIE NOUVELLE

1863

Title page for the 1863 first edition of Ernest Renan's Vie de Jésus.

There is no religion whose interest centres in the person and character of its founder in the same degree as Christianity. Christ is Christianity. In Him are all its truths, all its motives, all its glory summed up. In this respect it differs entirely from Mohammedanism or Buddhism, or any other religion which has largely influenced the world. They rest upon many influences. Christianity rests, above all, on Christ. It is the spiritual beauty and perfection of His character which has given it the hold it has upon the intelligence of the most intelligent nations of the world—which has given it the sway it has over the most spiritual and exalted souls that have ever lived in the world. . . . Christianity has been the highest spring of human civilisation; its most preserving strength. Why so? Because it has given to humanity a spiritual ideal—a perfect religious conception—which has been the light of the world. There has been no visible growth in this ideal, and no decay in it. It burst upon the world with a sudden illumination, perfect as it now is. It grew up *occulto velut arbor arvo*—a 'root out of a dry ground.' In the lapse of ages it has suffered no change, no diminution. Christian creeds have imperfectly defined, Christian institutions imperfectly represented it. Some Christian heroisms have even feebly imitated it. But nowhere has there been any advance beyond it. It remains the Light of the World, as it declared itself to be eighteen centuries ago. Whatever has suffered change, or seems like to suffer

change—whatever revision may await systems or ceremonies, modes of Christian thought or Christian government—this ideal remains lustrous with the same radiance—'the same yesterday, to-day, and for ever'—an example of all love and nobleness—of all grace and all true grandeur; inexhaustible in its spiritual fulness, incapable of improvement in its spiritual proportions. Art and life alike—the responsive intellectual and the responsive moral ideal in us—have found in it, and continue to find in it, a perennial fountain of inspiration: they catch some newer and higher and more celestial aspect of it; they reach perhaps, with the deepening thoughtfulness of increasing ages, some truer comprehension of it; but the manifoldness of its excellence exceeds their imitative grasp. It still towers above them, sympathetic at every point to the touch of human aspiration, but outreaching the highest possibility of human endeavour.

Such a wonderful existence, he proceeds to show, must have had a fit cause and origin; and it is perfectly consistent and intelligible to the Christian who recognises "the only begotten of the Father, full of grace and truth," in this most marvellous and unparalleled Man. "It is but fair, however, to require from one who denies this supernatural origin, an adequate and consistent explanation of a fact which has appeared to the general intelligence as well as to the eye of faith, so clearly to involve the supernatural, and to be unintelligible without it." M. Rénan admits the fact fully and clearly, and he accounts for it as he can with much elaboration and care—for naturally it is a matter upon which a man of candid mind, kept back by inexorable theory from the only simple explanation, must have found it hard to satisfy himself. A thousand dead men raised to life would be less of a miracle to account for than this Jesus, to the secret of whose existence even great Semitic scholarship can give but little clue; indeed, to pause upon the question of miracles at all, while this greatest of all wonders remained to be discussed, is but another proof of the limited nature of human perceptions even in their most acute development. M. Rénan's explanation is, that Christ was produced by Judaism, the most austere and narrow of all religious systems, and by the lovely pastoral landscapes and simple rural manners of Galilee—these two working together, but chiefly and most powerfully the last, upon the gracious and tender influence of which he enlarges with a dainty eloquence which makes one fain to believe, though experience is little in favour of the idea, that the soft hills and green pastures, the sweet shadow of olive woods and glimmer of inland waters, are not only full of moral influence, but of the loftiest inspiration. It is thus that Dr Tulloch examines the singular explanation which M. Rénan gives of the origin of Christ:—

> Jesus, according to M. Rénan, was the natural offspring of Judaism. He was the incarnation of its moral genius and its Messianic dreams—nothing more. Nature, the teaching of the synagogue, and the enthusiasm of the populace, made Him what He was. Could such a character spring out of such influences, and be produced from such sources? It appears to us wholly impossible. We may allow even so much for the sweet natural genius and the charming susceptibility of Jesus, but the result is still incredible; for let genius be of the most transcendent sort, it must yet connect itself by definite links with its age and time. The most admirable and unique human genius is found to stand in close intellectual and moral relation with its contemporaries. Its growth is understood from what they were, and the influences, direct or indirect, which they exercised upon it. There is in all cases, if not an entirely clear, yet an intelligible affinity between the highest genius and the tendencies in the midst of which it arose. This connection is entirely wanting in the case of Jesus. M. Rénan, indeed, talks of moral maxims that were rife in the synagogues, and kindred teachers, such as Hillel and Gamaliel. But his constant affirmations on this subject rest on no evidence, and receive no countenance even from his own detailed descriptions. The whole picture of Judaism which he draws is opposed to them. He keeps repeating statements about the moral teaching of the synagogue—statements, let it be remembered, confessedly founded on sources not in existence till two centuries after the Christian era—but he cannot point to

any corresponding features in the actual Judaism of the time. The features which this Judaism presented are sufficiently well known. Phariseeism and Sadduceeism represented its two predominant tendencies; and what they were, especially how utterly immoral they were, no one has better shown than our author. The former had lost the very idea of morality—had obscured and perverted its most obvious and fundamental obligations. A superstitious formalism, consecrating the most frivolous external observances, was its only principle, and baneful and malicious fanaticism its only passion. The Sadducees were without any pretence of spiritual feeling—materialists by profession, ambitious of power, wealth, pleasure, but without a particle of serious thought or sentiment. With both these great parties Christ had confessedly no relations except those of hostility. It is even a subject of congratulation to M. Rénan, that his hero, in the progress of His moral development, was so far removed from them in the quiet village of Galilee. . . . But when we look for any evidence of moral culture in the north any more than in the south—in Galilee any more than in Jerusalem—M. Rénan gives us nothing but picturesque description and dogmatic appeal to the Talmud. He has nowhere indicated, nowhere even explained, the marked contrast which, according to him, existed between the Judaism of Galilee and of Jerusalem. And for such a contrast there is not the slightest historical foundation. The spirit of the north was of a more free, simple, and natural character. The tendencies of Judaism had not then developed into the same hardened opposition. All that was characteristic in Judaism necessarily reached its most prominent expression in the capital. But withal, the Judaism of the north and of the south was substantially the same. . . . The disciples were Galileans. They were, one and all, members of the northern synagogues, and may be taken, from the mere fact of their association with Christ, as above the average examples of the religious and moral spirit which characterised the synagogues. Do they then show, apart from the direct influence and instruction of their Master, any lofty spiritual tendency, any characteristics of spiritual wisdom? Could St Peter, or even St John, before the day of Pentecost, when they accompanied our Lord on His Galilean journeys, be conceived as giving utterance to any such sermon as that on the Mount? . . . If the religious feeling of Galilee had been so much higher than the religious feeling of Jerusalem, would we not have had in the Gospels abundant traces of the fact? If such maxims as compose the Sermon on the Mount had been a common moral currency in the Galilean synagogues, could we not have found some evidence of this in the disciples of our Lord as well as in our Lord Himself? In short, M. Rénan's elaborate contrast, and the inferences he founds upon it, have, as we have said, no historical foundation. . . . The Christ of the Gospels, then, is unintelligible on M. Rénan's principles. There is really no foundation for the character which he has drawn. The origin of Christianity cannot be explained even by the most favourable concurrence of natural causes in Galilee eighteen centuries ago. Nature may do much for a responsive soul; but even its most glorious combinations have in themselves no creative effect. Sweet genius and a charming spiritual susceptibility may constitute an attractive character, and even rise to a height of powerful and commanding influence in dealing with current spiritual influences. . . . This is the obvious secret of such characters as those of St Francis of Assisi and others. Marvellous as their career and the power which they exercised may be, we understand them readily, because we see the conditions out of which they sprang. But these conditions we nowhere see in the case of Jesus. Let nature and genius have all the effect that can be ascribed to them, they have nowhere produced such a character; they have in no case—not even in one memorable case which will occur to most minds, that of Socrates—approximated to the production of such a character. No mere human influences have ever germinated into such a consummate expression of wisdom and love, of grace and truth. The loftiest human model still stands, with its strange mixture of loftiness and lowness, of Divine light and human darkness, of righteousness of aim and error of practice, at an infinite distance. Nor was this model, be it remembered, the production of Jewish soil and of an effete age.

We have quoted so largely in order to give a fair idea of the grave and searching yet gentle examination which M. Rénan's popular book has here met with. The point is, to our own thinking, of all others the one only and utterly vital point for Christianity. Christ *is* Christianity, as Principal Tulloch well says. If it was in the power of any assault to dim that spotless image, there would then be occasion in earnest to tremble for our faith, with all its divine consolations—consolations for which neither sceptic nor philosopher has any substitute to offer. Perhaps there is nothing which more clearly shows the wonderful pre-eminence of the portrait of the Gospels, than to contrast it not only with the ideal characters which from time to time Genius has produced, but even with the reproductions through the hands of lesser artists of that picture which came fresh out of the tender memory of John and Matthew, and their brother evangelists. From the Jesus of a popular sermon to the Son of God in Milton's majestic epic, almost every man who has touched the subject has thrown an involuntary cloud over the original portrait; and in respect to Art, the failure has been yet more striking. Here and there a gleam of divine significance has stolen into the face of the child-Saviour, as depicted by the greatest of painters; but we have never seen a picture which expressed divinity in the maturity of manhood, or would lead an uninstructed mind to the idea that the greatest of beings was there represented. It is the poise of the suspended figure, the reality of an attitude which is neither flying nor standing, which touches the spectator even before so famous a canvass as that of the 'Transfiguration;' it is not any divine effulgence in the image of the Redeemer; and still less is there any sentiment of Godhead in the muscular Christ of Michel Angelo. The only pictures of Him in which we remember to have felt a kind of shadow of the Divine, are those of the early Byzantine Christ, large and severe and pathetic, in which primitive art, struggling in chains of palpable difficulty, has yet set an expression of ineffable tenderness and

sorrow and awful simplicity, which, to our own thinking, is the most impressive yet attained by art, unless, indeed, we were to except Mr Holman Hunt's wonderful 'Light of the World,' under the eyes of which one would scarcely dare to think an ill thought.

If, however, we were to accept M. Rénan's account of the Gospels as books which grew into their present proportions under the hands of an innumerable quantity of authors, each man adding to his scanty MS. any incident or utterance that struck him specially, the wonder would be more and more increased; for of all modes of producing a picture full of such divine unity, this is about the last which could be supposed successful. At the same time, the account he gives of the Gospels is, in our judgment, a very important part of M. Rénan's book. It is one which perhaps his peculiar scholarship makes him more capable of treating thoroughly; and though we feel Principal Tulloch's explanation of his theory in respect to the Gospels of Matthew and Mark to be quite satisfactory, there is a little haste and imperfection in the lecture which discusses this point. M. Rénan dwells very strongly upon the difference between the earlier Gospels and that of John, which is indeed a very interesting distinction, and one which, apart from the learned and inaccessible discussions of scientific theology, the ordinary public would be more likely to find interest and instruction in than in many sermons. How far this characteristic distinction may have arisen from a difference of audience we do not undertake to decide; but an intelligent reader will perceive that in various specified cases the audience mentioned in the Gospel of John is of an altogether different character from the rustic crowds of Matthew. There is, in the first place, Nicodemus, with whom the Master treated in private of high and difficult matters, which it would have been utterly impracticable to discuss on the mountain or the shore of the lake, in presence of a fluctuating and ignorant multitude; and, towards the end of the Gospel, it is with the intimate circle of His immediate disciples, gathered round Him in awe, and dismay, and painful half-comprehension, like people at a deathbed, that the Saviour talks—speaking to them things which they understood "afterwards," as the record itself pathetically says. Such an auditory was little likely to be addressed in the broader general discourses with which the ministry of Christ began. To deliver to them, under such circumstances, another Sermon on the Mount, would have been a proceeding entirely false to that human nature which was ever surpassed but never contradicted by Jesus of Nazareth; and what is unquestionably true of the discussions which begin, and of the wonderful and affecting intercourse which closes this Gospel, has also, so far as we are able to judge, every appearance of being applicable to the intervening portions. It is not the outdoor crowd which can do nothing but listen, but the groups in the porches of the synagogues, on the steps of the Temple, curious and hostile, laying traps for the speaker, whom we perceive dimly through John's narrative; and the distinction is natural enough, and easy to understand. But the question is one which demands larger space and fuller treatment. It is to John we owe the narrative, unequalled in human literature, of these last communings with His chosen friends, which are to most Christian souls the most profoundly affecting part of the history of Christ. His is the story of that last mortal meal, where, as yet unassailed and uncondemned, the Redeemer sat among His followers with the prescience of death in His eyes, addressing to them those counsels and those promises of which it was hard for them to see the occasion; while they, alarmed and dismayed and awe-stricken, asked bewildered questions, and knew not what they said. The other day we went with reverence to see the remains of the great picture in which this subject has been represented by one of the greatest of painters, and which, to our eyes, looked more impressive under its film of decay and partial destruction than had it been as fresh and perfect as at first. But John is unspeakably a greater artist than Leonardo. With him there is no conventional grouping—no arbitrary attitudes. The awe and perplexity of the sad group, the explanations they seek in each other's eyes, the baffling veil of incapacity which bewilders their human comprehension of the Divine Sufferer, and makes even sympathy and love fall short in the effort, are such as no imagination ever gave form to. The difference between the painter and the evangelist, reminds us of a still greater difference in the comparison of Christ with Socrates, which is so much in favour with critics. Nothing could be more striking than the contrast between the last act of our Lord's life and the scene in the Athenian prison, where the philosopher accepts his doom while discussing general principles with his friends, and receives death with a certain indifference which is not even destitute of humour, treating his judges and executioners with a sober and tolerant contempt which is altogether human, and has not a spark of divinity in it. They have done their worst, poor creatures as they are; and now let us talk of more interesting matters. Such is the sentiment of the scene in which one of the very greatest of merely human personages is the chief actor, and which is told by lips no less skilful than those of Plato. So far as literary power goes, the evangelist had little chance with the philosopher; and it would be hard to explain, even by M. Rénan's learned commission of "physiologists, physicians, chemists, and persons trained in historical criticism," how the simple apostle has so infinitely transcended the great Italian and the greater Greek. Such a miracle is harder to account for than even restoration from the dead.

This is not a place to enter into any discussion of that which we, in common with all Christians, regard as the most awful event ever consummated in this world; but we cannot refrain from making one final extract from Dr Tulloch's valuable little book, in which he sets forth, with what seems to us a fine originality as well as unquestionable force and eloquence, one remarkable point of difference between the death of Christ and those of all the human martyrs and victims of popular ignorance or rage, with which the sceptical critic would fain confound it:—

> The modern theory of Christ's character by those who deny His divinity, is that of a great religious hero and martyr; one who died to vindicate human liberty and the right of spiritual intelligence against the oppression of priestcraft, and the servilities of a godless material power. This is so far the view of our author. In the closing period of His career Christ is to him something of such a hero and martyr. But he is conscious also how imperfectly such a character fits Christ, and especially the Christ of the Passion. . . . And what a story is that! What a picture of infinite mysterious sorrow—of shadow deeper than all other shadow that has ever lain on our earth! as Jesus withdrew from His disciples about a stone's cast, and fell on His face and prayed, saying, 'Father, if it be possible let this cup pass from me.' . . . But is this the characteristic spirit of the hero and martyr? Do we feel, as we read the story of the Passion, that we are contemplating merely the struggles of a great human soul? Is that agony and bloody sweat, that cry of impassioned mystery, that weakness and shrinking as from death, and, finally, that horror of great darkness as He hung upon the cross, and felt that God had forsaken Him—is all this of the nature of heroic martyrdom? Is it not something entirely different from the steadfast rejoicing willingness of a Paul—'I am ready to be offered, and the time of my departure is at hand;' from the blind headlong rapture of an Ignatius, 'Suffer me to be the food of wild beasts—do not intercede for me. Fire and the cross, the assaults of wild beasts, the tearing of my limbs, the breaking of my bones, the grinding of my whole body—I welcome them all'? Assuredly it is. As we stand in spirit by the side of the sleeping disciples and watch their suffering Lord; as we hear Him cry from the cross, 'My God, my God, why hast Thou forsaken me?' we feel we are entering into the communion of a deeper and more mysterious sorrow than the world has ever known—a sorrow which is not weakness—a sorrow in which no notes of mere martyr-triumph mingle, which no gleam of rejoicing heroism illumines, but which becomes bright with an awful meaning, then, and only then, when we recognise in it the reality of a Divine Sacrifice for the sins of the world, the offering of Him who, 'though He knew no sin, was made sin for us, that we might be made the righteousness of God in Him.'

It is difficult to go on after a conclusion so solemn; but we may permit ourselves to say, by way of winding up, that the alarm which is created in the Church by the appearance and sudden popularity of such a work as that of M. Rénan, is, though perhaps natural enough, an unreasonable panic. It is not only its ephemeral character which makes the impression produced unimportant; it is a much deeper and more radical incapacity. The school of thinkers to which M. Rénan belongs, and to which also belong some very eminent minds among ourselves, is entirely destructive in a religious point of view. It has nothing whatever to substitute for the hopes and consolations it takes from us. But there are a few, and only a very few, minds in this world which are so self-contained and self-sufficing as to be able to do without these consolations and hopes. To many of us life is so hard that it is the most we can do "to use," as says the special poet of our generation, "a little patience ere we die"—to most, some little light upon the darkness of the hereafter, some possibility of a life more worth living than this, is a primitive necessity of existence. The multitude have never been affected by the winds of doctrine which blow about the higher altitudes of intellect; and by the multitude we mean, not the poor, but the broad, general mass of common people—people of natural sympathies, warm affections, and active lives, who can no more spend their time in discussion than in any other unprofitable pastime. Let the *savants* take care of themselves. We cannot tell what may be the case in France among the poor, to whom M. Rénan, with an adroit adaptation which agrees but poorly with the dignity of his philosophy, has sent his book wrapped in a flattering preface; but notwithstanding chance infections, which may ruffle the composure of here and there a parish priest, any general effect in England is impossible. Christianity itself does not undertake to satisfy all the questions of the wistful spirit, but there is nothing else which makes any response at all out of the awful darkness in which, one time or other, every living soul loses some precious thing. The intellectual classes are, as we have said, limited in number, and presumably able to take care of themselves; and to persons consciously self-sufficing our argument may not seem a lofty one. But we are persuaded it is true. Mere scepticism attempting only to deprive us of our hopes will never reach the popular heart. "Consider the horizon," says M. Rénan, addressing the poor; "there rise the tints of the dawn, deliverance by means of resignation, labour, liberality, reciprocal support—deliverance by means of science, which, penetrating the laws of humanity, and more and more subduing matter, will found the dignity and the true liberty of all men. Let us prepare, each by doing his duty, this paradise of the future." Such a paradise does not accord with English imaginations; but even were it attained—had science done her best, sanitary and otherwise, and "reciprocal support" been realised in its highest ideal, the most intimate and profound of human miseries would still remain to be somehow provided for. People would still die, and hearts still break, and even the much-contemned priest would convey more consolation than M. Rénan. In England we are rather fond of taking fright upon this subject, and conceiving danger to the religion of the people where no danger exists. *That* is founded upon more imperative necessities, and wants that go deeper down. It is good that the Church should meet frankly and boldly all her assailants; but she may at the same

time take comfort in reflecting that the vast mass of her members are human creatures, and that no amount of eloquence is likely to convince them, instead of bread, to accept a stone.

Note

1. 'Lectures on M. Rénan's "Vie de Jésus."' By John Tulloch, D.D., Principal of the College of St Mary, in the University of St Andrews. Macmillan: 1864.

John Tulloch (lecture date 1864)

SOURCE: Tulloch, John. "General Remarks; Positivism and the Supernatural."[1] In *The Christ of the Gospels and the Christ of Modern Criticism: Lectures on M. Renan's 'Vie de Jésus,'* pp. 1-31. London: Macmillan and Co., 1864.

[*In the following lecture, Tulloch argues against the philosophical positivism that underpins Renan's position against miracles.*]

The publication of M. Renan's **Vie de Jésus** marks a crisis in the present course of philosophical and religious opinion. This is its chief significance. The book itself has been judged very differently, from different points of view—denied all merit by some—loudly applauded by others; but the grave import of its appearance, and of its immediate wide-spread circulation throughout Europe, cannot be questioned by any. It has caused a greater shock in Christendom than any work since Dr. Strauss's *Leben Jesu,* while the attractiveness of its form and style has already given it a reputation and an influence far more extensive than its more elaborate German predecessor. In England, and throughout the Continent, it is a common topic of conversation. It is heard of amidst all the excitements of political, and of military struggle; in the halls of Oxford, in the *salons* of Paris, in the churches of Italy, in the counting-houses of the Levant. While we write, it is the subject of solemn "reparation" services in all Catholic countries, and the Archbishop of Smyrna, Apostolic Vicar of Asia Minor, has just published a "Pastoral" to his Clergy, in vindication of the Faith against its daring statements. It is indispensable that students in divinity should know something of such a work, or rather—for no student can be kept ignorant of it—that they should be able to say something regarding it, not merely by way of deprecation and condemnation, but of intelligent appreciation and reply.

Like its German predecessor, the **Vie de Jésus** marks the spring-tide of an advancing wave of thought inimical to Christianity. As the former was the result of Hegelian speculation, and of the crisis reached by rationalistic criticism, the natural consummation of the anti-

Christian activity of the German intellect through many years; so the work of M. Renan is the result, and, it may be hoped, the consummation, of the course of materialistic thought—known as Positivism—which since then has been active, not only in France, but in England, Germany, and elsewhere, and of an historical criticism divorced from all faith and true reverence. So far there is a remarkable analogy between the works. They are the respective types of a definite mode of anti-Christian thought.

In other respects they do not present much resemblance. The *Vie de Jésus* is a more dangerous, but, so to speak, a less formidable book. It is more dangerous, because it addresses a far wider class of readers; it is designed to influence the young and the multitudes of educated and half-educated minds in our day, who are impelled by the atmosphere of inquiry surrounding them, to investigate such a subject as the origin of Christianity, but who have neither the resources nor the leisure to investigate it thoroughly. It is less formidable, because less solid, and apparently less earnest. In these qualities the German work is greatly superior. In the language of German theology the *Leben Jesu* was acknowledged to be a strictly scientific treatise, addressed to theologians and mainly aiming at their enlightenment and advance. With comparatively few attractions of manner and style, it is throughout grave, philosophical, and vigorously polemical, presenting an array of argument and learning far more imposing than the light and rapid pages of the present work.

But the chief difference in the influence of the two works, will be found to arise from the different modes of thought which they represent, and to which they appeal. Neither Hegelian philosophy, nor rationalistic criticism in its successive developments, strangely exciting as they were in Germany, created much excitement beyond Germany. The former has remained to this day an esoteric system, unknown save to a limited circle of speculative students; it is said to have been abandoned or idly regarded by Dr. Strauss himself in after years. Positivism, within the last quarter of a century, has become an active, and even fashionable mode of thought, and nowhere more so than amongst certain literary and intellectual circles in England. So far as it is a philosophy, it is adapted to the common understanding, and falls in fitly with the scientific and social tendencies of the time; while it has received a noted impulse from certain living writers of great ability.

But Positivism is, characteristically, not so much a definite philosophy, as a method of philosophising,—a way of thinking about science, life, and religion. And this way of thinking largely affects many who know little or nothing of M. Comte's particular opinions, or who may not even have heard of M. Comte himself. There is no one who knows anything of current literature, either French or English, who does not know that the influence of Positivism has in this manner extended widely, and prepared, as it were, for the reception of a work like M. Renan's, which should apply its principles and modes of reasoning to the Gospels and the Life of Jesus.

This state of intellectual preparation, combined with the genuine literary merits of the *Vie de Jésus,* is sufficient to account for its extraordinary circulation, and the remarkable interest which it has excited everywhere. There were waiting, so to speak, for such a book, many minds stored with vague novelties as to the growth of religious and social constitutions, and the general development of civilization, such as Positivism suggests, and groping in that dim perplexity of spiritual inquiry which is so common in our time. A volume which professes to account for the origin of Christianity, and to explain the appearance of Jesus on ordinary historical principles, within a few hundred pages, written in a charmingly facile style, and with an apparent depth of thoughtfulness and sentiment, could not fail to secure hosts of readers, and to excite universal attention.

Some critics, we observe, have turned the extremely popular character of the work into a reproach against it. They allege that a book of such a character places itself beyond the pale of grave theological discussion; that it is more a romance than anything else, and scarcely deserves serious refutation. Even Dr. Ewald, of Göttingen, who would be supposed by many in England to be a fellow-worker with M. Renan, is reported to have denounced the volume as conceived and written in a spirit unworthy of theological science. But whether such a reproach be deserving or not, we cannot help thinking that it is an unhappy device of Christian theology to despise and overlook any book, evidently influential, on such a ground. It would seem as if in certain quarters the old antagonism between Christianity and literature in its more attractive forms, still lingers. There are good people who seem to imagine, that a book cannot be at once very pleasant and very valuable. Dulness has its prescriptive rights; and a certain heaviness of thought and style is supposed to be peculiarly suitable in theological discussion. Gravity certainly always becomes such discussion. But even if the *Vie de Jésus* should appear to us lacking in appropriate gravity, it would be absurd to satisfy ourselves with neglecting and disparaging it merely on this account; for it is its very literary attractiveness, its clear beauty and fluency of style, its confident gaiety and piquancy of argument, the ease, lightness, and rapidity with which it moves along through all the difficulties of its subject,—the imaginative brilliance which lights up its descriptive sketches, and the glow of sentimental enthusiasm which is but seldom wanting in its moral discussions, which give to it its peculiar influence, and make it at once so seductive and so dangerous to many minds.

Nor, we confess, much as we shall find occasion to condemn M. Renan's tone, do we see any reason to doubt, upon the whole, his honesty of intention in this, or in any other of his works, which are mostly devoted to Biblical or religious subjects. In all of these works he seems animated by a spirit of inquiry, which, if tinged by a pervading materialism, and something of the careless, sensuous ethics of his country, is yet, in its way, thoughtful and sincere. He is deeply interested in the historical origin and development of religious opinions; and to the investigation of such topics he has brought the resources of a rare, comprehensive, and living learning. Of this latter point there can be no question, whatever we may think of the application he has made of his learning in the present case, particularly of those extravagant pretensions, as to the Talmud, by which he has sought to cover the weakness of his position, and to impose upon himself and others. His scholarly acquisitions he has further improved and vivified by residence in the East, and intelligent personal contact with Eastern manners and institutions; while to his other qualifications he adds that fine turn for generalization, so characteristic of the critical and historical intellect of France, and which gives to all its productions a rare charm for educated readers.

There is really no point of view, therefore, in which M. Renan can be conceived a weak or contemptible opponent, or in which his volume does not demand and require the awakened attention of the Christian theologian. In this conviction these lectures have originated, and as they have been written in some degree to satisfy the writer's own mind, as well as discharge a formal duty, they may be found helpful to guide and inform the minds of others.

I.

M. Renan's book first demands our attention in its philosophical aspect. It is the expression, we have said, of a prevailing philosophical tendency. Its fundamental and controlling conception takes its rise in a system of thought very marked at the present time. This fact is apparent on the face of the volume. The author not only does not conceal, but throughout the introduction and early chapters, parades, the great Positivist idea *of an unchanging material Law governing all things, the world of history, as well as the world of matter.* And in certain passages he expressly appeals to this idea as the necessarily guiding principle of all historical investigation,—and of the investigation of the origin of Christianity, no less than other historical problems,—in the very same manner as Strauss appealed to certain Hegelian conceptions, and sought to bring Christianity within their conditions. He tells us, as a matter of course, in one of his earliest pages,[2] that the "Gospels are partly legendary," for the reason that "they are full of miracles." Any miraculous relation is to him incompat-

ible with historical veracity. It is enough to stamp a record as so far fictitious or legendary, that it acknowledges the reality of the supernatural, or incloses any professed miraculous occurrences. And this, he contends, is not to impose any preconception or theory upon history, but simply to insist upon the critical observation and analysis of facts. "It is not in the name of this or that philosophy," he says,[3] "but it is in the name of a constant experience that we banish miracle from history. We do not say that 'miracle is impossible,' but merely that no miracle has been hitherto proved." "None of the miracles with which ancient histories are filled, have happened under scientific conditions. Uniform observation teaches us that they only happen in times and countries where people are prepared to believe them."

We shall afterwards have occasion to consider what he says on the special subject of "scientific conditions," applied to a miracle, and to examine the value of his supposed tests or conditions. In the meantime we wish to fix attention upon the general principles of his philosophy, rather than their particular application. He would have us to understand, from the above statement, that he, and the school to which he belongs, are free from theoretic bias in the interpretation of historical facts. But this is just what it is impossible to concede to them. *They are theorists,* and of a most extreme character, in their views of history, and their explanation of some of its most characteristic phenomena. M. Renan may pretend not to affirm the impossibility of miracles— merely to judge them from a critical and historical point of view; but such an affirmation is in the face of the whole spirit and scope of his book. It is contradicted almost in the very breath in which he utters it. For why should recitals of miracles be necessarily legendary,[4] if miracle be not held to be *à priori* impossible? On what ground, otherwise, are the Gospels at once pronounced to be partly legendary? For observe, this is said antecedent to all examination of the Gospel miracles, or their appropriate evidence. "No miracle has been hitherto proved!" Is not this to beg the whole question in a spirit of arbitrary theory? For what but such a theory can cover an affirmation of such sweeping generality.

But we are not left to mere inference for M. Renan's theoretic views on this subject. In another and very striking passage—striking both in itself and in its connexion—he enunciates them with the utmost plainness.[5] The passage is found in the chapter on the "Education of Jesus"—a chapter singular in its vague, bold, and unauthorized surmises. He describes the rustic simplicity in the midst of which Jesus passed His youth in Galilee, as a quiet villager, loving the country, and having no taste for the artifices and pomps of contemporary greatness. Of the imperial world surrounding Him, the youthful Son of Mary had evidently no just conception. The earth seemed to Him divided into kingdoms that made war one with another. The "Roman peace," the "Roman power," were to Him merely vague conceptions. The name of "Cæsar" alone had reached His ear. The imposing architectural works of the Herods in Galilee and its neighbourhood He regarded with displeasure. All He loved was the sweet Galilean country, with its artless villages, its clusters of lowly cottages, and gardens, and wine-presses hewn out of the rock, its wells, tombs, fig-trees, and olive-trees. "He remained always near to nature. The court of kings was to Him only a place where people lived arrayed in fine clothing." And while the youthful Jesus was thus ignorant of the contemporary events and circumstances of His time, He knew still less of its philosophy and science. The great idea of Greek science, the basis of all philosophy, was unknown to Him—the idea, namely, that the government of the world is by universal laws, and not by capricious deities. "Nearly a century before Him"—and we now translate directly from M. Renan—"Lucretius had expounded, in an admirable manner, the principle of the inflexibility of the laws of nature. The negation of miracle, the idea that all proceeds in the world by laws in which the personal intervention of superior beings has no part, were truths held in common by the great schools of every country which had received Greek science. Probably even Babylon and Persia were not strangers to them. But Jesus knew nothing of this progress. Although born in an epoch in which the principle of positive science was already proclaimed, He lived in the full consciousness of the supernatural. Never, perhaps, had the Jews been more possessed with a craving after the marvellous. . . . In this respect Jesus differed nothing from His compatriots. He believed in the existence of the Devil, whom He regarded as a sort of evil genius; He imagined that nervous maladies were the result of demon-possession. The marvellous was not exceptional to Him; it was the normal condition of His life. A man ignorant of physical law, and who believes that he can by prayer change the course of the weather, and arrest disease, and even death itself, finds nothing extraordinary in a miracle. The whole course of things is to him the result of the free volitions of Deity." Such a man was Jesus. Such was the intellectual state of Jesus.

Here there can be no doubt of M. Renan's philosophical sentiments, and as little doubt of the manner in which he applies them to history. It is his evident principle, as it is that of the whole school to which he belongs, to ignore the reality of any spiritual or Divine government of the world. The order of the universe is fixed in certain laws, which exclude all personal intervention, and remain unchanging for ever. It is the business of science to discover these laws; it is the function of the historian to recognise their operation, and to interpret by them the whole course of past phenomena; for it admits of no question that they are the same laws which we now see operating around us, which have been, without deviation, operating from the beginning.

There is, and can be, no room, therefore, in history for miracle. There is no room even for God, save as the poetic or philosophic ideal of an inflexible system of law. This is Positivism in its general conception—the startling creed of a widely prevailing philosophy. Not only Christianity, but Theism is held to be a philosophical mistake. The world has not advanced—nay, has retrograded from the days of the great schools of Greek science. It is the spirit of Lucretius, the recognition of his "inexorabile Fatum," which is the highest point of wisdom, and to which the world must return as the spring of its higher progress and the consummation of all knowledge.

It is somewhat hard for the Christian apologist, to be thus continually dragged from the fair field of historical evidence, to a discussion of the ultimate principles of all truth. And yet it is a very instructive fact, that every school of unbelief is now driven to this resource. It makes its chief attack upon Christianity from behind general principles, not merely inimical to the Church, and the supernatural foundation upon which it rests, but inimical to all religion; inimical, in fact, to all spiritual philosophy, and every noble creative art and product of civilization which has its root in the spiritual life of man—the sphere in which man is allied to a higher divine life than the mere nature around him, which he can see and handle. For this is the real question involved in Positivism. It is not, as writers like M. Renan ingeniously put it, a question between law and caprice, order and arbitrariness in the government of the world. There is no Christian thinker who believes that the government of the world is otherwise than by general laws. The universe of nature is conceived by all reflective minds as a great order or *cosmos,* and the course of history, apparently irregular as it has been, as a consistent development in the great system of things. The Theist recognises the principle of *order* quite as plainly as the Positivist; but what he does not admit, is, *the merely material character of this order.* He maintains on the contrary that order is everywhere the direct expression of a living Divine will, which rules in and by the order. He acknowledges, equally with the Positivist, that the material facts or phenomena in the midst of which he lives are capable of classification into general laws, continually subsisting, and of which they may be regarded as the issue or manifestation; but he does not allow that these material phenomena, or their laws, exhaust the realities of being. On the contrary, he holds that the highest being of man is not contained in them, but is a part of, and is closely allied to, a higher order of being, transcending and embracing the other. Every higher activity of our nature presupposes and springs from this higher order of being. Religion has no meaning apart from it. Philosophy, as it has been conceived by all the highest minds of the human race—by a Socrates or a Pascal, or even by a Pythagoras, or a Kant, has no basis without it. Art of every kind, poetry, painting, and sculpture, imply, and appeal to it; and, save for the inspiration they draw from thence, would be merely the toys of an idle and frivolous luxury. Civilization, in its legislative and judicial institutes, and in all the more characteristic and elevating forms of its manifestations, rests upon it, grows with its growth, and decays with its corruption. That man is something more than matter, that there is a Divine Spirit in him, and a Divine Spirit above him, in Whom alone he lives; and that this Divine order of Being is higher than the mere material order, and may for wise and beneficent purposes supersede and traverse this lower order; that, in short, there is a living Supreme Will, directly governing all things, and communing with, and controlling the will of man; an Almighty and Personal Hand, which "none can stay from working"—such a faith is indeed eminently Christian. But it also lies, more or less obscurely, at the root of every form of religion, and every conception of man as a being capable of rational and moral progress. And this is what Positivism, if not in all cases expressly, yet in its essential character implicitly, denies; for it acknowledges nothing higher than Nature, and the system of laws into which Nature may be resolved.

Such a Philosophy—if Philosophy it can be called—necessarily excludes all idea of miracles. It ejects the miraculous from history because it has already ejected God from the world. Let it pretend as it may not to impose theory upon history, it does so in the most obvious and sweeping manner. For why are miracles incredible?—not because they have been examined and found to be devoid of credit—but because the world proceeds by general laws and not by personal agency. Deny this latter fact, and of course no miracle can have ever happened—for a miracle in its very idea presupposes personal agency. But admit the reality of a Divine Intelligence and Will governing and acting in every manifestation of nature and of history, and it is impossible to exclude the idea of miracle, or at once set it aside. For if there be a Divine Intelligence and Will moving all things, and moving man, of which man is a sharer, how may they not manifest themselves directly to man? What is there then inconceivable, still less improbable, in the supernatural? Is not the Divine, or supernatural, the reality, the substance, of which Nature, the material, is only the shadow? And may not miracle, in its true conception, as brought before us in the life of Christ, and origin of Christianity, take its right place in the development of the world's history, as a direct manifestation of the Divine for human good; as the stretching forth of the Almighty hand, not by way of interference, still less of disturbance, but for the purpose of urging forward in a more powerful and consistent manner the wheels of the world's progress. *May not miracle be a fact of this kind?* We do not meantime take higher ground, and it is not necessary to take higher ground to upset the pretensions of our author's Philosophy. Surely we are entitled to this modest surmise! For how imper-

fect and dim after all must be our conceptions of the highest order,—how little can we be entitled to erect our little generalizations into exhaustive and universal canons! What poor judges must we be of the possible or impossible in the realm of God! We do not dare to assign bounds to the possibilities of history, or to apply our theories without reserve to the ways of God. All this Positivism does in its essential principles. Is it not enough to say of any philosophy, that it denies God and dishonours man? Taking away from the former all personality and freedom of action—from the latter all soul, all life beyond nature: degrading the one into a blind fate, the other into mere matter.

Whatever may be the rights of such a philosophy, it cannot have any claim to stand at the door of history, and to determine for us its laws, and the character of its facts. For let it be borne in mind that M. Renan does not offer a single word in vindication, or even in formal exposition of a theory by which he at once shuts out the miraculous from history, and God from the world which He has made. He does not profess to argue in its behalf; he simply announces it as the ultimate philosophy. The Gospels are partly legendary, because they are in part records of miraculous occurrences. The pretensions of a pseudo-philosophy cannot go further. We are at least entitled to hold our own position against such an insolent demand to surrender. Surely it is not the Christian apologist who is here the dogmatist. He believes in God, it is true, but he does not venture to accept the Christian miracles without inquiry and evidence. M. Renan at once rejects them without inquiry, because he has no faith in a living God, and no faith in the Divine government of the world.

Notes

1. The references are, throughout, to the fifth French edition.

2. Introduction, p. xv.

3. Ib. pp. 1. li.

4. Introduction, p. 1.

5. Pp. 30-43.

William G. Hutchison (essay date 1897)

SOURCE: Hutchison, William G. Introduction to *Renan's Life of Jesus,* translated by William G. Hutchison, pp. ix-xxxii. London: Walter Scott, 1897.

[*In the following essay, Hutchison examines the early criticism of* The Life of Jesus *as well as the sources Renan used to write his biography.*]

The year 1860 marked an important point in the life of Ernest Renan. Having acquired, by years of hard work and unremitting study, a European reputation as man of letters and as a writer of authority on the Semitic languages and Oriental archæology, he was commissioned by the Imperial government to proceed to Syria and undertake an expedition in quest of ancient Phœnician monuments, sites, and inscriptions. For this welcome opportunity of coming face to face with the land whose peoples, languages, and traditions had been of life-long and absorbing interest to him, Renan was probably indebted to his friend Prince Napoleon ("Plon Plon"), and, in a still greater degree, to a remarkable woman, Madame Cornu, to whose influence with Napoleon III. were due important improvements in higher education and the promotion of scientific and archæological research by the state. Renan's Phœnician expedition was perhaps the most notable of the scientific missions undertaken at the national cost.

Renan reached Beyrout in October. He was accompanied by his wife and his sister Henriette; and the latter remained with him after Madame Renan's enforced return to France. She was his constant companion and assistant; but he went home alone. At Byblos brother and sister were simultaneously stricken with fever, and Renan awoke from a long interval of unconsciousness to find that Henriette was dead. This bereavement was the great sorrow of a happy life. Like Madame Cornu, Henriette had been a silent benefactor, a good genius of whom the world knew little but of whom her brother knew much. From his short biographical sketch—originally printed for private circulation—and from the volume of correspondence recently published, one may learn how deeply he was indebted to her tender and unselfish solicitude, to her unfailing love, and to her unswerving intellectual honesty. As is related in the exquisitely phrased dedication to the present volume, the *Life of Jesus* had been begun, carried on, and, in its first form, completed during Renan's stay in Palestine, in the midst of the scenes in which the tragic story it relates had taken place. How clearly the essential features of the Syrian landscape impressed themselves on the historian, and with what subtle charm he rendered those impressions, one may judge from the praise that has been bestowed on his descriptions by later travellers.

But, while the *Life of Jesus* was in a high degree inspired by Renan's sojourn in the East, there can be no doubt that it would have been written had the author never left France. In a sense his whole previous life had formed a preparation for his task of chronicling the beginnings of Christianity, and all his studies had been subsidiary to the historical treatment cf what, in his view, was the most significant cycle of events in history. In an essay, first published about ten years before his visit to the East, he had submitted some previous historians of Jesus to a critical examination, the most interesting feature of which is the section devoted to Strauss, whose first *Life of Jesus* had appeared in 1835.

Despite his high appreciation of the German writer, Renan's view of Jesus as an actual person, the events of whose career were rather nuclei of legendary tradition than pure myths, and his characteristically French distrust of metaphysical theory, somewhat qualify his praise of the *Leben Jesu*.

It was only after careful revision that Renan's own book was given to the world. Considering the effusive emotion that not infrequently characterises the work, even in its final form, one may feel some gratitude for the fact that Renan, according to his own account, spent a year in toning down the exuberance of his first draft.[1] On its publication in 1863 it was soon apparent that the *Life of Jesus* was to be one of the most hotly discussed books of the century. By a very large public it was welcomed with undiscriminating applause. As Sainte-Beuve acutely remarked, we find in modern society a considerable number of persons, not believers, and yet at the same time neither decidedly nor systematically sceptical. Having, like Renan himself, a very full appreciation of the luxury of religious emotion, they are too deeply impressed with vague notions of the omnipotence of science, and, more or less unconsciously, have absorbed the modern spirit too much to be enticed back to the ancient ways. To this large body of readers, somewhat nebulous in their opinions, and disinclined to justify them in self-examination, Renan appealed with great success. It was pleasing for them to find that they had been Christians *sans le savoir,* and Christians without the difficulties and intellectual self-surrender of less easily satisfied souls. That the excessive praise of such readers as these should be balanced by a no less excessive depreciation on the part of the orthodox, and that the latter should turn and attempt to rend the new apostle to the Laodiceans, was but natural. Archbishops, Jesuits, priests, theological professors, and dissenting ministers joined eagerly in a heresy hunt of unprecedented dimensions, the heavens were darkened with a multitude of pamphlets, and reviews, and controversial treatises; pulpits rang with indignant denunciations; Renan's private character was picturesquely defamed; and an anonymous but pious lady, with the best intentions in the world, commenced the monthly despatch to him of a letter containing the brief warning, "There is a hell!"

That biography is one of the least facile of arts, that its really great and successful examples can be counted on the fingers, is almost platitude. The difficulties of adequately analysing one of our fellows, of reaching the secrets of his inmost nature, of satisfactorily accounting for his often inconsistent actions and ideas, are such as to make the path of the biographer one of great difficulty. While the novelist has only to obey his own æsthetic conscience and avoid any decided breach of probability, the writer of biography must necessarily come into conflict with those whose conceptions of his subject are already formed, and as diverse from his own as they well can be. And when that subject happens to be a man of a different age, of a different race, the materials for whose life are at once scanty and in great part untrustworthy, it is easy to see that the pitfalls and risk of error incidental to all biography are increased tenfold. All these difficulties Renan had in his work, and, over and above, he had the special difficulty of dealing with a subject in which everybody takes an interest, of which everybody has a theory, of which many people have a theory that in their minds is a certainty to be defended with passionate zeal, and with every available weapon.

It was perhaps only to be expected that orthodox critics of the last category should disregard their Master's aphorism about casting the first stone, and charge Renan with the terrible offence of having an *à priori* theory of his subject. Why it was unfair for him to have his own theory of Jesus, and how indeed he could have avoided forming one, are matters too deep for me to fathom. Dean Farrar, and for that matter, the author of the fourth Gospel, have never, so far as I know, been accused of unfairness on the ground that they had a firm belief in the divinity of Jesus before commencing their respective biographies. Interest in a subject is surely essential to its adequate treatment, and interest implies the formation of opinions.

But the champions of religious dogmas, whatever the particular creed held by them, have never looked with favour on the formation of opinions other than their own. *Sois mon frère ou je vous tue,* is a phrase that might come very appropriately from the lips of religious fanatics, whether Mohammedan zealots putting captive towns to the sword, or the officers of the Inquisition chastening heretics and freethinkers with a foretaste of hell fire. Of course nobody thought of putting Renan on the rack or tying him to the stake; but the doctrine that error—for which read deviation from orthodox theory—is a sin, coloured every reply to his book that came from the orthodox forces. However the leaders of these forces might differ among themselves, they were agreed that Christianity stands or falls by miracles and the supernatural, that any one who does not admit the divinity of Jesus is not qualified to write about him, and that, if he does write, his work is valueless, or rather, pernicious. In fairness it should be added that zealots at the opposite pole of thought, agreeing with their opponents that the existence of Christianity depends on the miraculous, attacked Renan with great warmth, on the ground that he unduly glorified the subject of his biography.[2] The sceptical friend whom Sainte-Beuve introduces into his critique of the *Life of Jesus* is very severe on what he regards as unnecessary concessions on the part of the author. Renan, he says, re-

sembles Charles II. telling General Monk to be anything he likes except king; all titles, all honours, all glories are to be ascribed to Jesus so long as he is not called God.[3]

For freethinkers who have grown conservative in their disbelief all assertion of the positive value, the enduring truth immanent in Christianity must be more or less galling; and passage from a Christianity relying on miracles and metaphysical theories about vicarious sacrifice, incarnation, and the Council of the Trinity to a Christianity relying on everyday human experience, must also be painful to those who think these miracles and theories essential to their faith. To Renan, however, such an assertion and such a passage seemed necessary, and credit for having done his best in the matter may at least be accorded him, however much his work may be attacked as regards execution and detail. Of the principal orthodox controversial works directed against the *Vie de Jésus,* I do not think it unfair to say that in them all the greater part of the adverse criticism, except such as might proceed equally well from an agnostic, is based on the assumption that, Jesus being God, Renan had no right to give him the same biographical treatment as he would have given to Socrates or Mohammed. In other words, he was wrong in weighing probabilities, in examining evidence, using that which seemed valuable and rejecting that which seemed valueless, or, in short, in using any of the comparative methods employed in writing secular history. To take some obvious instances, he had no right to assume that unusual events, alleged to have taken place in uncritical times when people were too little acquainted with nature to distinguish between it and super-nature, and not observed to recur in times when they can be scientifically tested, are unworthy of full credence; he had no right to point out the falsification by reality of the belief cherished by Jesus, or his reporters, of the imminent coming of the Messiah to judge and reign over the earth;[4] he had no right to remark on the obvious differences between the synoptic Jesus and the Jesus of the fourth Gospel, or to base his conception of the Master on the no less obvious fact that, historically, the former Jesus is much the more possible.

But the *Life of Jesus* was not primarily intended as a work of religious edification, though indeed I once heard an "anti-infidel" lecturer in Hyde Park call it one of his favourite books; it was an attempt at a historical view of the life and work "of a wonderful spirit, far above the heads of his reporters, still farther above the head of our popular theology, which has added its own misunderstanding of the reporters to the reporters' misunderstanding of Jesus."[5] In other words, Renan considered it essential to his purpose not to conceive of his authorities as supernaturally inspired works—which, as his orthodox critics usually forget, remains to be proved—but as books full of contradictions, myths, and naïve ignorance, in which the truth is only to be found by a process of sifting. "Criticism," as he remarked, "knows of no infallible texts; its first principle is to admit the possibility of error in the text which it studies."[6] It need scarcely be added that, while every serious student has long admitted this as an axiom for general historical investigation, it is only recently, and with considerable reluctance, that the principle has been partially adopted by orthodox writers dealing with religious history. To approach the critical consideration of an historical work there is then but one legitimate method—to inquire first, What are its authorities? and secondly, What use has been made of these authorities? Let us briefly consider these two questions in relation to the present work.

Renan's chief authorities may be classed under five heads: (1) The works of Philo, (2) those of Josephus, (3) the so-called Apocryphal books of the Old Testament, (4) the Talmud, and (5) the Gospels and other New Testament writings. Of course, besides these principal sources of information, there were innumerable others. Renan's encyclopædic reading, and his faculty for collecting and systematising his knowledge, make his pages bristle with references and citations. It was remarked of Hume that his History of England would have been more accurate but for his occasional necessity of imagining his facts, from the difficulty of navigating his portly person to the other end of the sofa where the means of verification lay. However much one may ascribe to Renan's imagination, his industry in collecting and utilising evidence from every quarter cannot be gainsaid. It will be well to give a brief outline of his views on the writings stated above.

The study of Philo permits one to judge of the ideas that were active in the world immediately before the birth of Jesus and during his lifetime. Although Philo lived in a Judaistic centre altogether removed from that of Jesus, and though there is no probability of his ever having even heard of him, there are curious parallelisms between the teachings of the Alexandrian doctor and those of the peasant of Nazareth. Similar parallelisms are also to be noted, it is true, with the recorded *Logia* of Hillel and other Jewish teachers anterior to Jesus.[7] The works of Josephus, the Old Testament apocryphal writings (such as the book of Enoch, the Assumption of Moses, the Jewish portion of the Sibylline Poems, and the book of Daniel[8]) and the Talmud, are of like service in giving a picture of contemporary thought and history and of the motive forces influencing them. Renan believes the notice of Jesus in the history of Josephus to be, in the main, authentic, although probably retouched by the Christians, who regarded his work as an essential document in their history and—probably in the second century—circulated an edition of it, corrected in accordance with their own ideas. The possible connection of the author of Luke and the Acts with Jo-

sephus I shall remark on later. In the Talmud (the compilation of which, Renan thinks, extended from about 200 to 500 A.D.) innumerable and important details of the Gospels find a commentary. Jewish theology and Christian theology having followed two parallel paths, the history of one cannot be understood without reference to the other.

The New Testament writings were naturally the main foundation for the *Life of Jesus,* and the author's use of them one of the principal points of attack by orthodox critics, the latter's grievance being his separation of what he regarded as historical from what he considered legendary and of the nature of *Aberglaube.* It was of course in the Synoptics, especially in Mark and Matthew, that he found most trustworthy material for the making of his history. But neither in Matthew nor in Mark in their present form do we have the original Gospels attributed to these writers. The first records of Jesus must of course have been oral. It was only when eye-witnesses were beginning to disappear, and when the idea of a closely approaching heavenly kingdom seemed to recede farther and farther into the future, that adherents sought to give floating reminiscence of their Master a durable form, and to write down the sayings and anecdotes that were in danger of being forgotten. And with these authentic reports of the sayings and doings of Jesus, it requires no great knowledge of human nature to believe, many others of an apocryphal kind must have been mingled. The members of the early Church, on special occasions or when confronted by special difficulties, must often have pondered what Jesus would have had to say about the matter. Considering that there was no settled New Testament canon, and that the material now forming this canon was then in a fluid state, it is easy to see how such hypothetical utterances, by passing from mouth to mouth, might ultimately be accepted as authentic. The first written Gospel was that known as the Gospel of the Hebrews, which was extant among the Judaistic Christians of Syria, until their destruction in the fifth century; and it somewhat resembled the Gospel of Matthew, though the latter was a perfectly distinct work. Mark indeed, a short biography dealing mainly with the acts of Jesus, was the first synoptic Gospel to be written, and the author of Matthew used both it and the Hebrew Gospel in the composition of his work, which is distinctively a report of the *Logia* or sayings of Jesus.[9] Neither of these Gospels could remain absolutely fixed. Even in the second century oral tradition was preferred, and, no doubt, those who possessed copies of one of the books were in the habit of adding details which might reach them from other sources, and of combining and amplifying narratives.

The Gospel of Luke is of a nature different from the more or less fragmentary Gospels of Mark and Matthew. "It is the work of a man who selects, prunes,

combines." In other words, it is a professedly complete history founded on previous documents. Renan does not think it probable that Luke, whom he holds to be the author of the Acts, knew the Gospel of Matthew, but he assimilated the whole of Mark, while about a third part of his book is to be found in neither the first nor the second Synoptic but comes from other sources. Luke's Gospel, in contrast to the more exclusive spirit of Peter, James, and the Judaistic Christians, is the Gospel of universal brotherhood and forgiveness of sins, and would appear to be the work of a disciple of Paul, a partisan for the admission of Gentiles, publicans, sinners, and heretics into the Christian community, an exponent of the wider view of the Master's teaching as applicable to all men in all lands.[10] Renan, who does not attach the same historical value to Luke as to Mark and Matthew, dates it from Rome about the end of the first century, and he attributes the many analogies between it and the history of Josephus to the authors' contemporary residence in that city. An even more direct connection between the two writers is maintained by Holtzmann and other German critics, proceeding on the generally recognised assumption that Luke was not a Jew but a Gentile Christian, from which they postulate that he got his knowledge of Jewish history from Josephus, whose works were largely circulated in Rome at the time.

However difficult the problem of the dates and connection of the Synoptics might be, and whatever careful discrimination was required in order to settle even tentatively the historical value that could be reasonably attached to them, the Gospel known as that of John presented difficulties of a still more serious nature, difficulties which Renan recognised by completely changing his views regarding the fourth Gospel in the thirteenth edition of the *Life of Jesus,* and devoting many pages to a discussion and defence of his new position. The theories, which have been, and are, held of the authenticity of the Gospel in question may be conveniently divided into four classes. In the first place we have the ordinary orthodox view, which requires no comment, that the fourth Gospel was written by John, son of Zebedee, that the facts recounted in it actually occurred, and that the discourses it attributes to Jesus were really uttered by him. Secondly, there is the theory, adopted by Renan in the earlier editions of his book, that the fourth Gospel is substantially the work of the apostle John, although it may have been edited and retouched by his disciples, that the events related are direct traditions, but that the discourses are frequently free compositions, only expressing the way in which the author conceived of the mind of Jesus. This comparatively moderate theory, held by Reuss, Ewald, and others, is in strong contrast to the more thoroughgoing scepticism of Baur, Strauss, Réville, and the Tübingen school generally, who maintained the absolute untrustworthiness of the fourth Gospel, and the impossibility

of regarding its relation of either events or discourses as historical. In short, we have before us a work of imagination, partly allegorical, in which the author's intention is not to give a plain biographical narrative, but to disseminate his own views of Jesus.

Renan's instinctive dislike to taking extreme or negative views, or at least to enunciating them distinctly, led him finally to a position midway between the theory originally held by him and the last-mentioned hypothesis. He regarded the fourth Gospel as not being the work of John, but as having been attributed to him by its author, one of his disciples writing about the year 100. The discourses are, he thought, entirely fictitious, or at least only represent the teaching of Jesus as Plato's Dialogues represent that of Socrates, but the narrative portions include valuable traditions, in part derived directly from John. Considering that Renan devotes more than a hundred closely printed pages to justifying and amplifying the theory which I have just epitomised, it is obviously impossible for me to deal adequately with the matter in the limits of a short introduction. I can only give therefore the briefest outline of his reasons for abandoning his first and more conservative conception, and for not adopting that of Tübingen.

To determine the approximate date of a literary work, it is admittedly necessary to take external evidence by finding when it was first mentioned or quoted. It is in the present instance significant that neither Polycarp, who was one of John's most devoted disciples, nor Papias, who must have had intercourse with some of John's followers and was ever eager for any scraps of tradition he could collect, says a word of a written Gospel by John, while Justin, even if he knew the work, does not connect it with the author of the Apocalypse. Moreover, in the pseudo-Clementine Homilies, in Marcion, and in the apocryphal Gospels, there is no indication of the fourth Gospel being given the same canonical authority as those of the Synoptics. On the other hand, it must have been written not later than 100, before full canonicity had been acquired by the synoptic Gospels, since otherwise it would have scarcely diverged so far from them; and it must have won its own place in the canon towards the close of the second century, for it played an important part in a theological controversy concerning the Passover at Laodicea about 170, and Theophilus of Antioch (about 180) positively asserts it to be from the pen of John. This stamp of authenticity, moreover, argues the existence of the book (probably as an edifying though uncanonical work) for some time preceding; such honour would scarcely have been accorded to a recent narrative.

What is to be gleaned from internal evidence? The author, whoever he was, attempts to pose as John, as an eye-witness of the events recorded, and throughout is manifest his desire to show that apostle in the best light,

to exhibit him as taking a leading rôle, as being "the disciple whom Jesus loved." In accordance with the wish to make the narrative appear the relation of an actual observer, there is much apparent exactitude of detail on many small points,[11] and in these Renan sees traditions proceeding directly from John. But of course the chief characteristic of the book is its discourses—discourses in which the exact position of the supernatural Jesus is stated with a metaphysical subtlety which in no way harmonises with the *Logia* of the Synoptics, or indeed with what one might naturally expect from a poor peasant belonging to a race which had, up to that time, exhibited no taste for abstract speculation, but which is entirely consistent with the intellectual state of Asia Minor at the time at which Renan supposes the Gospel to have been written. It is also to be noted that parables and exorcisms of demons, both frequent in the Synoptics, are entirely wanting. What argues moreover against the idea that this metaphysical treatise on the *Logos* could have been written by a Jewish fisherman, "an apostle of the circumcision," is that the author speaks of the Jews, their ceremonies and festivals, from an outsider's point of view, and almost disdainfully.[12] From these arguments which I have briefly summarised, Renan concludes that the fourth Gospel is not one of the earlier Christian books, and that it has not the same value to the historian as those attributed to Matthew, Mark, and Luke. Between the two conceptions implied in this contrast choice must be made: "If Jesus spoke as Matthew represents him, he could not have spoken as John represents him."[13]

Into an examination of Renan's exegetical theories I do not propose to enter. Such an examination would occupy a great many pages, and, after all, would only appeal to specialists. But one does not require to be a specialist in order to form an opinion of Renan's treatment of his subject, and of the general lines of the work as history and as literature. Its merits as a piece of literature are indeed very great. That supremely beautiful instrument for prose, the French language, has seldom been handled with higher distinction or with more consummate mastery than in certain passages of the **Life of Jesus,** passages of haunting beauty, which nevertheless are not of the nature of "purple patches," but have the quality of being integral and inevitable parts of the work in its totality. He had indeed subject-matter which was, in many respects, of great beauty morally and æsthetically, and it naturally inspired one of such extreme sensitivity to moral and æsthetic beauty. But he had the defects of his qualities in full measure. A friendly critic phrased the matter very neatly. "It must be confessed," said Réville, "that on the whole his Jesus appeals less to conscience than to the æsthetic sense." That in him legitimate and honest sentiment was but too ready to turn to sentimentalism, that occasionally he seems to feel for the mere pleasure of feeling, and betrays himself with such false and jangled notes as the sentimen-

talist is doomed to strike, is only too evident. Far too often the mingled nobility and sweetness of his utterance is apt to lose the former element and become almost nauseously saccharine in intensity. It is like passing from the Good Friday music in *Parsifal* to the treacly mysticism of the *Stabat Mater*. *Facilis descensus*—once let Renan begin to lose himself in clouds of universal benevolence and nebulous religiosity, and he perseveres in the downward course until the end of a chapter brings him back to his subject. This tendency of his art to over-reach itself and defeat its own object is manifest, not only in the style, but in the whole plan and character of the book. It begins with pastoral comedy and ends with tragedy. Obviously the antithesis is intended, but not less obviously the insistence with which it is urged makes it forced, unreal, almost theatrical. This is particularly characteristic of the earlier chapters of the book. Jesus is a sort of theological troubadour, the disciples a band of "happy children," amiable enthusiasts whose innocent doubts are gently but triumphantly crushed with a smile or a look, their life a delectable combination of idyllic vagrancy and *fêtes champêtres*. Orthodox conceptions of the founder and the beginnings of Christianity have assuredly been often grotesque and unreal in all conscience, but it has been reserved for a professedly serious student of history to put on record this Gospel in Dresden china, this picnic Christianity. Nor is the organic unity present which should make it possible for this *charmant docteur* with his *douceur extraordinaire* to be identified with the *sombre géant* of later days. I concede that the antithesis was actually existent, that Jesus on Calvary was very different from Jesus on the shore of Genesareth, and I have the fullest appreciation for Renan's treatment of the closing scenes of his tragedy, but I entirely fail to see that the former and latter Jesus as he presents them are consistent one with the other.

From the same source proceeds his frequent laxity in the use of certain words and phrases. To turn a sentence, to elaborate a peroration, he permits himself a latitude of expression which, in cold blood, he would probably have softened down, if not repudiated. To take the most cogent instance, he certainly lays himself open to the cross fire of both orthodox and heterodox critics by his indiscriminate and irresponsible employment of the words "God" and "Father," which might provoke a direct query as to whether he believed in a God or not, and, if not, why he constantly seemed to assume God's existence. One is sometimes persuaded of the truth of the saying that language was given to man to conceal thought. I am not forgetful that every man is entitled to his own definition of God; Spinoza was fond of repeating that "the love of God" was man's *summum bonum,* and, by the phrase "love of God," expressing a passionate zeal in the quest of scientific truth. Yet, to say the least of it, such diverse definitions are somewhat bewildering to the plain man. And, as the plain man in his

thousands was among Renan's readers, such equivocal usages of speech were scarcely commendable.

The mention of Spinoza's name at this point may recall another aspect of that thinker's work, of interest in the present case—his naturalistic explanations of some Old Testament miracles,—the Red Sea retreating before a strong wind, the Shunamite's son revived by the natural heat of Elisha's body, and so forth. Ingenious attempts of this kind were not altogether to Renan's taste, but he has not much better to offer: his treatment of miracles throughout is neither adequate nor satisfactory. In a manner scarcely worthy of a true critic, he makes no attempt to conceal his distaste for the whole matter, and, while he is too honest to minimise the importance of alleged supernatural occurrences giving an initial impetus to the new religion, he insists on their mere trickery and fraud in terms that betray his anxiety to point out that Jesus had far rather have worked no miracles at all, that he only worked them because it was expected of him to do so, because, had he not chosen to be a thaumaturgist, he would have had no success. This idea of Jesus deliberately making his choice in the matter and reluctantly conceding to popular opinion, seems to me as grotesque as Renan's sweeping condemnation of thaumaturgists,[14] in which order must necessarily be included Charcot, Heidenhain, and every modern physician who employs hypnotic suggestion as a therapeutic agent. If by such means disease *can* be successfully treated, why should they not be used? I think it was of Napoleon that an opposing general complained, that he won his victories only by a culpable disregard of the laws of strategy.

Nor are Renan's views embodied in a comprehensive and consistent whole; several miracles he does not mention at all, such as the incident of the Gadarene swine, that of the feeding of the multitude, and that of Jesus walking on the sea. On the production of wine from water at Cana he only bestows a passing reference without comment. In the majority of cases he adopts the well-known expedient of looking the difficulty boldly in the face, and passing on.[15] He does not seem to have a sufficiently full appreciation of the value of suggestion in the large number of pathological states due to neurotic causes. This of course may be explained by the fact that the subject has in great measure been investigated since the publication of his book. A valuable commentary on the Gospel miracles might be compiled, I imagine, from the clinical records of the Salpetrière. Such a commentary would probably show a very substantial basis of truth for the great majority of the healing miracles recorded of Jesus.

These miracles indeed may well be considered separately from those which are evidently of a mythical nature. In classifying or discussing occurrences of this kind, the first thing is to settle what we mean by a miracle. The orthodox person who asserts belief in miracles as infractions of the laws of nature—that glib phrase for observed sequences of phenomena—and the sceptic who denies them in a like manner, are equally exponents of a fallacy. Those who see in nature limitless possibilities, who believe that nature is all-inclusive and all-sufficing, who recognise that our science throws but a tiny flicker of light into the darkness around us, cannot accept the phrase "infraction of nature" as being other than meaningless. "The day-fly has better grounds for calling a thunder-storm supernatural than has man, with his experience of an infinitesimal fraction of duration, to say that the most astonishing event that can be imagined is beyond the scope of natural causes."[16] Renan, if I read him aright, has a tendency to imagine that the last word is said in the matter, that science can only speak negatively, that there is no hope of fresh light being cast. But those who see in experimental psychology a science, new indeed, but still a science, can scarcely endorse his verdict. To take a crucial instance: is the hypothesis that an apparition of the Master appeared to the disciples after his death so utterly absurd, that Renan can afford to dismiss the point in half a page of rhetorical questions and unctuous platitudes about the disciples' devotion and the divine power of woman's love?

But, reversing the procedure of the prophet who was called to give curses and disappointed his employer by bestowing blessings, I am confining myself to merely negative criticism, when the occasion manifestly requires some assertion of the positive value of the work which follows. This positive value, I imagine, mainly resides in its subjective aspect, in its character as an account of the immensely important movement of a long past age by one of the most interesting and sensitive intellects of our own century. This subjective quality is of course so apparent on every page, that it is generally the first point of attack for those who engage in the adverse criticism of the book. Renan indeed is a good instance of the egoistic historian, the narrator who is rather lyrical than dramatic; the Jesus with whom he presents us is a Renanised Jesus—a Jesus who is gentle, ironical, at times almost gay—a Jesus, in short, who in many features resembles M. Ernest Renan. But what would we have? A biography of Jesus suited to every one's taste is out of the question; apart from necessary diversities of view, the materials are too scanty and too thickly encrusted with legend, for adequately historical treatment to be possible. *"So redt' ich wenn ich Christus wär"*—"Had I been Christ I should have spoken so:"—the words might come from any one attempting such a treatment, a treatment which must less resemble history in its strict sense than the historical novel or play. Gaps, it is true, exist in all history, and the palm is to him who can best use his imagination in filling them up. But the history of the founder of Christianity consists mainly of gaps, and the personal equation being so important a feature in Renan's literary labours, we need feel neither surprised nor indignant that his ingenious attempts at filling up these gaps should partake so greatly of the character of a personal revelation.

Not only indeed have we a personal revelation in the **Life of Jesus,** we have a revelation of the time-spirit. I have already pointed out how aptly it fitted the intellectual and emotional temperament of a certain large number of persons; but, in no small measure, it had a wider bearing and represented a general tendency. To use a modern cant phrase, it appeared at a psychological moment. The somewhat barren deism of the eighteenth century, having fulfilled its purpose, had become a creed—or lack of creed—outworn. The deistic writers were fast fading into the limbo of oblivion. They had not written in vain so far as influence went, but if their influence remained, their books were forgotten. It is only Voltaire's wit, and his flashes of humorous common sense, that attract even the limited amount of attention from readers that his "philosophical works" now receive. Diderot, of course, was so much more than a destructive critic and facile writer, that, if anything, his reputation has a tendency to grow. But Holbach and his circle—Mirabaud, Fréret, Dumarsis, and the rest, have gone the way to dusty death.

Renan was not indeed the first French writer of this century to recognise the change which German exegesis had made in the problem. Reuss, Réville, and Scherer possess a European reputation as biblical critics, and all three were active before the publication of the **Life of Jesus**; while the foundation of the *Révue Germanique* had also had a deep influence on the formation of intellectual opinion in France. But Renan was the first to draw the attention of a wider public than that of *savants* and men of letters; and there can be little doubt that his success was mainly due to those of his characteristics—his insistent idealism, his almost devotional unction, and, it must be confessed, his frequent sentimentalism—in which he most widely diverged from the sceptics of the previous century.

These sceptics, who were fond of the discussion, if not the practice of ethics, seemed scarcely to realise that the world was not to be regenerated by rational codes of morals and ideals of justice alone. As Renan points out with great force, two elements contributed to the success of Christianity, a miraculous element and a moral element. The former gave the necessary initial impetus, the latter made the movement endure. In addition to these two powerful causes was the greatest cause of all,—the assertion by Jesus of love as the principle that should underlie the whole conduct of life. The Greek and Roman philosophers had made justice this underlying principle. But justice is an abstraction not to be understood by the people, or always by the philosophers themselves. Every one, on the other hand, can un-

derstand the love which Jesus taught as the greatest of all commandments, and, while he may see in it a counsel of perfection, can recognise aspiration towards that perfection as an essential feature in human progress.

Notes

1. [Ernest Renan,] *Souvenirs d'Enfance et de Jeunesse,* p. 355.

2. See, for example, *Opinion des déistes rationalistes sur la Vie de Jésus selon M. Renan,* par P. Larroque, Paris, 1863, a work which amply justifies the saying of the Goncourts, that when incredulity becomes a faith it is more unreasonable than religion.

3. Sainte-Beuve, *Nouveaux Lundis,* tom. vi.

4. The extremely significant sayings reported in Matt. x. 23, Luke xxi. 32, and Luke ix. 27, should be noted. See also 1 Cor. vii. 29; Philipp. iv. 5; 1 Peter iv. 7; 1 John ii. 18; James v. 8, 9; 1 Thess. iv. 16, 17.

5. Matthew Arnold, *Literature and Dogma,* p. 119.

6. *Vie de Jésus*: Préface de la 13me édition, p. 5.

7. See pp. 23 and 285. I hardly think, however, that Renan lays sufficient stress on the points of contact between the Hindu religions and Christian doctrine. Without taking Schopenhauer's extreme view, that an agreement is brought about in the most essential matters between Old Testament doctrines and the Indian religions, and that everything which is true in Christianity is to be found in Brahmanism and Buddhism—a view which obviously implies the satisfaction of "jesting Pilate's" demand for a definition of truth—there can be no doubt that resemblances exist, resemblances which extend to form as well as to idea. Thus the saying of Jesus, "The kingdom of heaven is within you," and his comparison with a grain of mustard seed may be placed beside, "This Self of mine in the heart within is smaller than a grain of rice, or a grain of mustard seed, or a grain of millet, or a grain of millet's kernel; this Self of mine, in the heart within, is greater than the earth, greater than the air, greater than heaven, greater than these worlds" (*Chhandogya Upanishad,* iii. 14, 3).

8. Some of Renan's reasons for classing the book of Daniel with the apocryphal writings may be briefly summarised. The character of the two languages in which it is written, the use of Greek words, the definite and dated account of events extending almost to the time of Antiochus Epiphanes, the incorrect details of Babylon, the apocalyptic character of the visions, and the place of the book in the Hebrew canon outside the series of the Prophets,

lead him to think that the work was a fruit of the great religious exaltation caused among the Jews by the persecution of Antiochus.

9. Papias, bishop of Hierapolis (in the first half of the second century), draws this distinction; he speaks of an anecdotic narrative written by Mark from reminiscences derived from the apostle Peter, and of a collection of sayings made by Matthew.

10. Note, for instance, that in Luke seventy disciples are sent out by Jesus, in the other Gospels only twelve.

11. See, for example, John ii. 6; iv. 52; v. 5; vi. 9, 19; xxi. 11.

12. See, for example, John ii. 6, 13; vi. 4; x. 31, 33; xviii. 36; xix. 31, 38, 42.

13. Renan's Introduction, p. 69.

14. See p. 163.

15. An exception must be made in the case of the Lazarus miracle. Here Renan, abandoning his more plausible hypothesis of premature burial, and following the somewhat far-fetched theory of Strauss and Baur, complacently pronounces the whole affair a pious fiction.

16. T. H. Huxley, *Life of Hume,* p. 132.

Lewis Freeman Mott (essay date 1921)

SOURCE: Mott, Lewis Freeman. "Syria; Henriette Renan; Professor of Hebrew; 'Life of Jesus.'" In *Ernest Renan,* pp. 207-41. New York: D. Appleton and Company, 1921.

[*In the following excerpt, Mott praises the intellectual courage and literary imagination of* The Life of Jesus.]

[The] greatest scandal to Renan's opponents was the publication of the *Life of Jesus* on June 24, 1863. Though certainly not so intended, it seemed like a gage of defiance designed to insult and irritate. That Renan had such a work in hand was no secret. Taine, who saw much of him at Chalifer, writes:

> He read me a long piece of his *Life of Jesus.* He constructs this life delicately but arbitrarily; the documents are too much altered, too uncertain. For the period of Nazareth, he puts together all the gentle and agreeable ideas of Jesus, removes all the gloomy ones, and makes a charming mystical pastoral. Then, in another chapter, he gathers every threat, every bitterness, and attaches these to the journey to Jerusalem. In vain Berthelot and I told him that this is putting a romance in place of a legend; that, by a mixture of hypotheses, he spoils those

parts that are certain; that the clerical party will triumph and pierce him in the weak spot, etc. He will hear nothing, see nothing but his idea, tells us that we are not artists, that a simply positive and dogmatic treatise would not reproduce the life that Jesus lived and must be made to live again, that he does not care if people howl, etc., etc. Lack of prudence and caution.[1]

Hints had even come to the general public. Sainte-Beuve had heard the substance of the work and let the readers of the *Constitutionnel* into his confidence in 1862, and on the verge of publication, in reviewing Dupanloup's *Avertissement à la jeunesse et aux pères de famille sur les attaques dirigées contre la religion par quelques écrivains de nos jours,* an attack on Littré, Maury, Renan, and Taine, Bersot suggests that, instead of paying any attention to these charges, Maury had better continue to busy himself with erudition, Taine with his *History of English Literature,* Littré with his dictionary, and Renan with the correction of the proofs of his *Life of Jesus.*[2] Even a distinguished foreigner like Senior noted (May 1) the substance of several long conversations held during the previous ten days with Renan on the subject of his unpublished, though already printed work, *Histoire critique des origines du Christianisme.*[3]

The advance notice in the *Débats* was written by the sturdy, but liberal-minded Jansenist, de Sacy,[4] and perhaps no fairer estimate of the work has been published. Out of the four Gospels and his own conjectures, Renan constructs, for this first volume of his *Origins of Christianity,* a sort of fifth Gospel, from which, to de Sacy's regret, miracles are absent. It is the "fruit of long labor and great inward agitations." The writer "seeks to conciliate the most exalted mysticism with the most hardy skepticism, the rigor of historical method with a transcendental imagination." The book is full of interest; the things have been actually seen, but de Sacy prefers the simplicity of the old Evangelists. "I believe in the Gospels of Matthew, Mark, Luke, and John; I do not believe in the Gospel of M. Renan." The remainder of the notice consists of an argument for liberty of criticism.[5]

The review in the *Débats* (August 28, 1863) was written by Bersot, who undertook the ticklish task unwillingly and against the advice of friends. He was not, indeed, a specialist in biblical studies. Thus the greater part of the article is taken up with a discussion of eighteenth-century skepticism as contrasted with the modern critical method. He imagines how the book might have been otherwise done, is surprised at the idea of a trick in the Raising of Lazarus, and realizes that the portrayal of Jesus as a delicate, charming young man, will wound, though not purposely. Jesus always hangs between science and art, and Renan, much in the manner of Ary Scheffer, has painted his picture. To this Renan privately answers, when thanking Bersot for his review:[6] "I assure you that I wrote the book with a sentiment far superior to petty vanity. . . . I do not believe that this way of trying to reconstruct the original physiognomies of the past is so arbitrary as you seem to believe. I have not seen the personage; I have not seen his photograph; but we have a multitude of descriptive details about him. To try to group these into something living is not as arbitrary as the entirely ideal procedure of Raphael or Titian."

The Catholic party greeted the book with howls of rage and with calumnies for which Renan thought he had a right to bring legal action for slander.[7] The most innocent of these tales was that Rothschild had subsidized him with a million francs. The most virulent of the printed libels was a pamphlet, *Renan en famille,*[8] a series of pretended letters between Renan and a supposed Sister Ursule, introduced, with the obvious intention of inflicting as much pain as possible, by a letter from the spirit of Henriette, in which she is made to say: "Blot out my name at once from that book, which is as badly written and heavy as it is abominable, and from that preface with its grotesque pretentiousness and its pitiable French." It is reported that the guests in a hotel at Dinard threatened to leave if Renan were allowed to remain there, and certainly a local newspaper published some malignant verses, beginning, "Breton, no! Jew sprung from the blood of Judas Iscariot, what have you come here for?" Even Jasmin published an offensive poem[9] in which "he left his sphere and forced his rustic pipe."[10] And the feeling did not soon abate. Taine tells with great glee the story of a young mistress of Plon-Plon, who complained bitterly that, on the trip to Norway in 1870, she had to sit at table with such an impious renegade.[11] Renan remained also a popular subject of caricatures, none of which seem to have been very brilliant.

Such was not, of course, the attitude of opponents of elevated sentiments, though their hostility was just as bitter. Cousin called the book an atheistical work.[12] Dupanloup and Gratry, among many, wrote opposition Lives of Jesus. The Empress with strange moderation said to Mme. Cornu: "It will do no harm to those who believe in Christ; and to those who do not it will do good."[13] She appreciated Renan's purpose. "No, indeed," he wrote to Sainte-Beuve,[14] "I have not wished to separate from the old trunk a single soul that was not ripe." What, on the other hand, the representative pious Catholic felt is perhaps best expressed in a letter written to Bersot by Montalembert (June 16, 1863?): "It must be easy for you to fancy what a Christian has to suffer in reading the *Life of Jesus.* Imagine what you yourself would feel if your father were treated publicly as a *charming impostor.* Just imagine that Jesus Christ is for us more than a father, that he is our God, that all our

hopes and all our consolations are based upon his divine personality, and then ask yourself if there could be for our hearts a more deadly wound than that here given."[15]

Renan seems, on the whole, to have been strangely obtuse to the offensiveness of his book to believers. He sent copies with an affectionate dedication to former comrades of Saint-Sulpice, some of them already bishops.[16] He was, indeed, so engrossed in his own idea that he could not sympathize with the opposite view, and seems to have felt the same naïve surprise at the rumpus over his *Life of Jesus* as he felt at the Abbé Cognat's refusal in early years to continue their discussions of Christianity.[17] In spite of all warnings, he went directly ahead, convinced that what he was doing was what needed to be done.

Meanwhile the book sold by the thousands, and during the latter half of '63, Paris talked of nothing else.[18] Renan did not utter a word in reply to attacks, a policy he had learned from the wise de Sacy. To a certain extent he had become insensible to abuse. "By character," he writes Bersot,[19] "I am entirely indifferent to such things; I do not believe they impede the progress of sane ideas. As for my book, it goes the better, and I might suspect my publisher of inspiring such opposition. Each edition of 5,000 is exhausted in eight or ten days and a letter from Lévy just received tells me that in this last period, the sale, far from slowing up, even goes faster. I say this without vanity, for it does not prove the book either good or bad. But it does prove that the means employed to smother it are not very efficacious." By November 60,000 copies had been sold, and translations had appeared in Dutch, German and Italian. The popularity of the most celebrated novels had, as Sainte-Beuve remarks, been surpassed.

Constructive criticism was furnished by Scherer in the *Temps*[20] and by Havet in the *Revue des deux Mondes* (August 1).[21] Another excellent criticism was that of Albert Réville.[22] After disposing of the dogmatic critics, including deists, Catholics and Protestants, Réville gives his own views, concluding that, on the whole, Renan has lessened rather than enlarged Jesus. The two main objections are Renan's confidence in the Fourth Gospel and his treatment of the Raising of Lazarus, which puts Jesus in the position of at least consenting to a pious fraud.[23] Both of these points Renan modified in the thirteenth, which was the first revised, edition, the Lazarus story being there regarded as a result of popular confusion, and the fourth Gospel being treated not as emanating from St. John, but as still containing incidents transmitted from an eyewitness of the crucifixion.

So far as the year 1863 is concerned, the whole matter is summed up in Sainte-Beuve's masterly *Lundi* of September 7.[24] Writing for the *Constitutionnel* and wishing to keep on good terms with the government, Sainte-Beuve was not, as he confesses to Renan,[25] entirely free, yet such restraint as he felt hindered him surprisingly little in conveying his liberalism and his sympathy.[26] Showing utter contempt for the corsairs of literature, who interrupt a scandalous tale to defend the divinity of Christ, he treats real opponents with a sort of respectful irony. These are personified in three objecting friends, a Catholic, a free-thinker and a political opportunist, who call on him under the pretext of asking his opinion, but really to express their own, which is "what is generally done when one goes to ask an opinion." "Feeble and foolhardy," "surrender and concession," "dangerous agitation," such are the three judgments, summing up, minus the abuse, the attitude of the unfriendly press and public. Sainte-Beuve himself appreciates thoroughly, though with some few delicately expressed reserves, the artistic qualities of the book. Renan is not content to destroy, he builds, for he knows that nothing is destroyed until something is put in its place. The *Life,* addressed to the public, has reached its address. It is a narrative, not of absolute fact, but probable and plausible, "not very far from the truth." Renan, "to be historian and story-teller from this new point of view, had to begin by being above all a diviner,[27] a poet drawing inspiration from the spirit of times and places, a painter able to read the lines of the horizon, the least vestiges left on the slopes of the hills, and skilled in evoking the genius of the region and the landscape. He has thus succeeded in producing a work of art even more than a history, and this presupposes on the part of the author a union, till now almost unique, of superior qualities, reflective, delicate and brilliant."[28]

But what Sainte-Beuve chiefly praises is Renan's courage. It is true the author did not have to flee Paris, as Rousseau had done a hundred years before, but he had drawn upon himself a strife with "a notable and little amiable portion of humanity for the rest of his life," enough to intimidate one of less firmness. "Those of us who have the honor of M. Renan's acquaintance know that he has strength enough to face the situation. He will show neither irritation, nor bad temper; he will remain calm and patient, even serene; he will retain his quiet smile; he will preserve his loftiness by never answering. He will vigorously pursue his work, his exposition henceforth more solid, more historical and scientific; no cries or clamors will cause him to deviate a single instant from his aim."[29]

Such words seem bold enough, yet Sainte-Beuve wrote personally to Renan: "You have won for us the right of discussion on this matter, hitherto forbidden to all. The dignity of your language and of your thoughts has forced the defenses,"[30] and again, at a later date, when thanking for an article on *Port-Royal:* "I place my intellectual honor in having my name associated with yours in this reform which is to be undertaken at the present period of the century. I have come too late and am about to finish. You are in full career, and you can long endure and fight. Your approval gives me the illusion that on some points my thought is entwined with yours."[31] Whatever may be the final judgment on the *Life of Jesus,* it was a resounding and ultimately triumphant blow for intellectual liberty in France.

Renan's conception is, without question, imaginative, but is controlled by experience and learning. He does not doubt; he affirms positively that Jesus was entirely human and that the miracles never took place. Neither materialistic nor mystical, he is reverent, enthusiastic, original and individual. His own experiences in the East give an extraordinary life to his pictures of ancient times. "You could not believe," he wrote Berthelot (November 9, 1860), "how many things in the past are explained when one has seen all this." A new sentiment enveloped biblical scenes and personages. With *Le Génie du christianisme,* Chateaubriand had swept the great mass of half indifferent readers into orthodoxy; but now his direct influence was spent, and this same mass was aroused and moved with a totally different result by the *Life of Jesus.* What was particularly irritating to the clergy was the fact that the child wonder of Tréguier, who had been expected to charm the worldly into the church by his genius, was, instead, leading people into paths that they considered the paths of perdition. And all the world was reading and discussing the abominable book. The leaders sharpened their knives for the victim. Renan lost his professorship in the Collège de France, but he became one of the most celebrated men of the world. Henceforth, not a word he uttered was spoken unheard.

Far from believing that he was doing harm, Renan proceeded to publish (March 4, 1864) a cheap edition for the poor, "the true disciples of Jesus," so that they too might come to love the Master as he himself loved him, not as God, but as a man overflowing with the divine spirit. "The sweetness of this unequaled idyll" would be a consolation and a support to those who had to bear heavy burdens.[32] He indeed believed in his work. It was to be an antidote to brutal skepticism and arid indifference. As he says in his dedication to the pure soul of his sister Henriette, "If at times you feared for it the narrow judgment of the frivolous, you were yet always persuaded that truly religious souls would in the end find it good."

Renan read all the serious criticisms of his work. No insult or calumny prevented him from profiting by what was urged. "As to those," he says, "who need to think in the interest of their belief, that I am ignorant, light-headed, or a man of bad faith, I shall not pretend to change their idea. If such an opinion is necessary to the repose of any pious persons, I should feel a real scruple about disabusing their minds." The thirteenth edition

(1867)[33] is carefully revised; though the changes are not so extensive as would appear from the differences in pagination, which are largely a matter of typesetting. A preface and appendix are added, there are slight ameliorations of style, and many important modifications and additions to the notes. The Lazarus story, in particular, is so altered as to remove any suspicion of connivance in trickery on the part of Jesus,[34] and the Gospel of John is no longer treated as being the direct work of the Apostle.[35] No evidence that was produced was, however, strong enough to convince Renan that the fourth Gospel did not contain fragments that emanated from an eyewitness of the crucifixion. This thirteenth edition is the final form of the *Life of Jesus,* and, whatever the various schools may think of it, it is still a living book.[36]

Notes

1. Taine, *Vie et correspondance,* vol. iii, p. 245.

2. *Débats,* April 27, 1863. Dupanloup's pamphlet consisted of a collection of citations from articles and books by the four writers. Bersot objects that to present such passages out of their context is unfair and that the appearance of the tract on the eve of the vote on Littré's candidacy for the Academy was an act of bad faith and against liberty of conscience. The following passage is quoted: "I will strip their works and tear away all their disguises. I wish to place them under the necessity of either denying my charges by affirming that they believe in God, the soul, immortality and religion, or of accepting publicly the title of atheists and materialists from which they shrink." (P. 9.) Dupanloup had been a member of the Academy since 1854. This time he was successful in defeating Littré, and in 1871, when Littré was finally elected, he resigned from the Academy, though his resignation could not be accepted and no successor was chosen till after his death in 1878. He did not live to see his two other abominations, Renan and Taine, take their academic seats.

3. N. W. Senior, *Conversations with Distinguished Persons during the Second Empire.*

4. Lévy feared that the edition might be seized by the government. Renan therefore requested de Sacy, Sainte-Beuve, and other liberal journalists to say that in their opinion such things had a right to be printed. See letter to Bersot August 28, 1863.

5. *Débats,* June 24, 1863, the date of publication.

6. August 28, 1863; *Bersot et ses amis,* p. 188.

7. Anti- and pro-Renan biographies were written. Carfort and Bazonge, *Biographie de Ernest Renan,* Paris, 1863, a pamphlet of about a hundred pages, dated December 10, 1863; E. Le Peltier, *Vie de E. Renan,* Paris, 1864, a pamphlet of thirty-one pages, dated October 10, 1863. Referring to the preceding brochure, Peltier says that, having learned that two fanatics in Brittany were falsifying Renan's biography, he had hastened to write his defense first. Neither is of any value.

8. By Ch. de Bussy, Paris, 1866.

9. *Lou poèto del puple à mossu Renan,* Agen, Août, 1864.

10. Sainte-Beuve, *Nouveaux Lundis,* vol. x, p. 170.

11. Letter of August 31, 1870.

12. Letter to Bersot, August 14, 1863.

13. Grant Duff, p. 70. Such opposition Lives, written to counteract the effect of Renan's, were apparently addressed exclusively to the French public. I cannot find that they have been translated. The continued popularity of Renan's work contradicts the Abbé Freppel's prediction in his *Examen critique* that "no one would talk of Renan's book in three or four months."

14. *Nouveaux Lundis,* vol. vi, p. 15, note.

15. *Bersot et ses amis,* p. 19.

16. Jules Simon, *Quatre Portraits.*

17. Renan's letters to Cognat and Cognat's account in *Renan hier et aujourd'hui.*

18. In his account of Renan's reception at the Academy, G. Valbert tells the anecdote of a lady who, after having devoured the *Life of Jesus,* said with a sigh: "I am so disappointed that it does not end in a marriage." *Revue des deux Mondes,* April 15, 1879, p. 941. As there are other similar anecdotes, e. g. of the English lady who wondered how the story would turn out—it is obvious that they are all apocryphal, a mere method of implying romance.

19. August 28, 1863; *Bersot et ses amis,* p. 189.

20. Scherer *Mélanges d'histoire religieuse.*

21. Havet's article, "L'Évangile et l'Histoire," gives a laudatory account of Renan's book with a few reflections, and then proceeds to the objections, which may be summed up in the general statement "that his criticism in detail is not always sufficiently firm and severe. M. Renan knows all that can be known, and no one has anything to teach him . . . he voluntarily refuses to follow his own criticism to the end."

22. *La Vie de Jésus de M. Renan,* 1864, a reprint from the *Revue germanique et française.*

23. These are also among the main objections of the Strassburg school, as set forth by Colani, *Examen de la vie de Jésus de Renan,* 1864.

24. *Nouveaux Lundis,* vi, p. 1 et seq. Sainte-Beuve also republished from the *Constitutionnel* his note recommending the book on the day of publication.

25. Letter of September 19, *Nouvelle Correspondance,* p. 183.

26. Sainte-Beuve was a valuable asset to the *Constitutionnel.* His name is signed to his articles in type as heavy as the titles, a distinction accorded to no other contributor.

27. In an essay on Ampère, Sainte-Beuve says, "In M. Ampère you always find one who divines beneath him who knows."

28. Pp. 16, 17.

29. Page 20.

30. September 19, 1863, *Nouvelle Correspondance,* p. 185.

31. November 17, 1867; *ibid.,* p. 246.

32. This edition, the title of which is simply *Jesus* (*Jésus* par Ernest Renan, 1864, in-18, xii and 262 pp.), was sold for one franc 25 centimes. A notice, followed by the introductory essay, was published in the *Débats* for March 2. Here Renan omits his Introduction, all of Chapter I except the first paragraph, Chapters xvi, xix, xxvi, and xxvii, together with other scattered passages, particularly that about Lazarus and much of the last chapter, in fact, everything that might give rise to misunderstandings.

33. This edition is announced in the *Débats,* September 1, by Bersot, who notes the important changes and quotes the preface, almost four columns of the newspaper.

34. Ed. 1863, pp. 359-364; ed. 1867, pp. 372-375. The criticism of this narrative cannot be understood by those who have read only the revised edition.

35. In the text, for example, "John, who claims to have seen" becomes "The fourth evangelist, who here introduces the Apostle John as an eyewitness."

36. An illustrated edition with a new preface—published in the *Débats,* February 21—was brought out in 1870. For critical remarks on the *Life of Jesus,* see the chapter on *The Origins of Christianity.*

John Haynes Holmes (essay date 1927)

SOURCE: Holmes, John Haynes. Introduction to *The Life of Jesus,* by Ernest Renan, pp. 15-23. New York: The Modern Library, 1955.

[*In the following essay, originally published in 1927, Holmes argues that* The Life of Jesus *was one of the most important and revolutionary books written in the nineteenth century and that the work remains a classic because of Renan's scholarly breadth and literary clarity.*]

"Ernest Renan's *Vie de Jésus,*" said the late Joseph Henry Allen, famous scholar and church historian, "is the one great literary monument of a century of New Testament criticism." This tribute to the immortal Frenchman's masterpiece was paid in 1895, just thirty-two years after its publication in 1863. Now that another thirty-two years have passed away, the tribute is seen to be inadequate. Renan's *Life of Jesus* is something more than a great monument of New Testament criticism. As we look back upon the nineteenth century as a definite period of history, we see that this book was one of the world-shaking books of a world-shaking epoch. It ranks with Darwin's *Origin of Species* and Marx's *Das Kapital* as a work which changed forever the currents of the world's thought and life.

In its own day, the *Life of Jesus* was a sensation of the first order. It brought down upon its author's devoted head such a whirlwind of rage and calumny as few men have ever endured, and fewer still survived. "Jew sprung from the blood of Judas Iscariot" was by no means the worst of the insults he received. The loss of his professorship in the Collège de France was only one of the penalties he suffered. "At the same time, and by the same token," says Renan's most recent biographer, Dr. Lewis Freeman Mott, "he became one of the most celebrated men of the world. Henceforth not a word he uttered was spoken unheard."

From the first hour of its publication, the *Life of Jesus* sold like a Waverly Novel. Its success was "immediate and immense," unprecedented for a scholarly work on a religious subject. Like Macauley's *History of England,* it lay on every library table, and was the subject of universal discussion. New editions of 5,000 copies each were exhausted in eight or ten days. Two months after the book's appearance, Renan writes his friend, Bersot, that "in this last period, the sale, far from slowing up, even goes faster." By November, five months after its initial publication, eleven editions, 60,000 copies, had been exhausted. Already there were German, Italian and Dutch translations of the book, and an English translation was on the way. A new and still wider circulation was opened up in March, 1864, when Renan published, under the simple title, *Jesus,* a cheap edition for the poor—"the true disciples of Jesus," as he called them. Offered at one franc 25 centimes the copy, this edition enjoyed an enormous sale. In 1876, the work was thoroughly revised, and incorporated in the author's *Origines du Christianisme* as Volume I of a series which was completed in 1881 by Volume VII on the reign of Marcus Aurelius.

Since this date, innumerable editions of the *Life* have appeared in France and other countries. The furor, of course, has long since died away. The book is today only one of a great host of biographies of the Nazarene, many of which have superceded it in scholarship, as others have surpassed it in radical opinion. But two full generations after its original appearance, Renan's volume is read more widely than any of its successors, and stands as the one sure standard by what these others are judged. Whatever the errors and inadequacies revealed by later extensions of knowledge, and "whatever the various schools may think of it," says Dr. Mott, "it is still a living book." The passing of time, that is today, has only served to establish Renan's *Life of Jesus* as the classic work upon the subject.

In recalling this amazing chapter of literary history, it may be well to consider some of the influences which were at work in the making of such a record.

(1)

Conspicuous is the fact that Renan's book was the first *biography* of Jesus, in the modern historical and literary sense of that word. From the time of Paul, down through all the centuries of Christian history, Jesus was regarded as the Messiah, the Son of God, the Divine Redeemer—that is, as a being apart, not in history but above history. All the writing about him, therefore, was theological, not scientific. The Christ was exalted that men might praise him, not studied and interpreted that men might know him. He was a revelation, like the Bible, to be accepted on penalty of outlawry in this world and damnation in the next. Not till Strauss wrote his stupendous *Leben Jesus,* was the spell upon the Nazarene broken. But the German studied the documents rather than the person, and presented not a man but a myth.

To Renan was left the opportunity and the task of writing about Jesus as a figure of history, and thus of producing a biography in the form and spirit of Voltaire's biography of Charles XII, or Southey's biography of Nelson. Renan set to work, in other words, to study and describe the Nazarene in exactly the same way in which he would have set to work to study and describe any other famous leader of humanity. He treated Jesus as other biographers had treated other great and famous men. Jesus, to him, was not divine, but human; he was not a being without time and place, but a Jew, born in Palestine, in the reign of Augustus. The Gospels were not scriptures, but documents, historical sources; "If the Gospels are like other books," wrote Renan, in the Preface to the thirteenth edition of the *Life,* "I am right in treating them in the same manner as the student of Greek, Arabian, or Hindu lore treats its legendary documents which he studies. Criticism knows no infallible texts; its first principle is to admit the possibility of er-

ror in the text which it examines." In the same way, Renan discarded every last vestige of the miraculous; "miracles," he wrote, "are things which never happen," and therefore, things which Jesus never did.

The result of such an attitude, now ordinary enough, but in the middle of the last century extraordinary beyond words to describe, was a life of Jesus which was human, natural, strictly critical, throughout. In this sense, it was something strange, unprecedented. When this book came out with its simple, yet devastating statement, "Jésus naguit á Nazareth, petite ville de Galilée. . . . Il sortit des rangs du peuple. Son père, Joseph, et sa mère, Marie, etaient des gens de mediocre condition" (Jesus was born at Nazareth, a small town of Galilee. . . . He sprang from the ranks of the people. His father, Joseph, and his mother, Mary, were of humble station), the world simply gasped in astonishment and horror. In two sentences there disappeared the lovely Bethlehem story, the dogma of the Virgin Birth, the whole theology of the incarnation and the atonement. And the remainder of the book kept pace with its beginning! Here was the story of a Jewish young man who lived, preached, suffered, made mistakes as well as performed brave deeds, said foolish as well as wise things, did no wonders beyond the wonders of the valiant soul, and at last died, was buried, and remained in the grave. This was a story never written before. It discovered a new phenomenon—the Jesus of History! And it shook the world like an earthquake.

(2)

It is this fact which explains the sensation created by Renan's book. But the sensation is only part of the story. What stirred the public with excitement and the church with anger, stirred as well the amazement and admiration of students. For here was a work of profound learning, a production worthy of one of the half-dozen greatest scholars of the nineteenth century.

It is not always remembered how supreme a figure was Renan among the scholars of his time—among the scholars, indeed, of all time. Master of a brilliant style, his achievements in the field of literature have tended to obscure, if not to hide altogether, his imperishable achievements in the field of learning. The great historian, Mommsen, saw the point when he declared, with some heat, that Renan was a true scholar, "in spite of the beauty of his style"! Certainly, Renan's life was a triumphant record of scholarly labors.

Abandoning the priesthood at the age of twenty-two, he pursued his studies at the University, the School of Oriental Languages, and the Collège de France, and in four years attracted marked attention by winning prizes, contributing extensively to periodicals, and publishing his first book, *Avenir de la Science* (*The Future of Science*). In 1849, he was sent by the Ministry of Education, and under instructions from the Academy of Inscriptions and Belles-Lettres, on a mission to investigate the libraries of Italy and report on their manuscript collections, particularly the Syrian and Arabic. On his return in 1851, he received an appointment as *attaché* in the department of manuscripts at the Bibliothéque Nationale, began writing for the *Revue des deu Mondes,* took his degree of Docteur-és-lettres, and was elected to the Council of the Societé Asiatique. The next few years were crowded with exhaustive studies, and voluminous writings in magazines both lay and learned. In 1856 he was elected to the Academy of Inscription and Belles-Lettres. In 1859 appeared his *Essais de morale et de critique,* and a translation of the Book of Job. In 1860, after publishing a translation of the Song of Songs, he accepted a mission to excavate Phoenician remains in Syria, under the inspiration of which he wrote the first draft of his *Life of Jesus* at Ghazir. On his return to Paris he was appointed professor of Hebrew, Chaldean and Syrian languages in the Collège de France by imperial decree dated January 11, 1862, an honor which he was destined to lose the following year when his *Life of Jesus* was published. After a second oriental trip in 1864-65, there followed years of exhausting work, first, on his *Origins of Christianity,* and secondly, on his *History of the People of Israel,* two of the supreme productions of nineteenth century scholarship. Master of many languages, ancient and modern, erudite in the lore of ages and places, expert in the technique of investigation and interpretation, imbued with the ideal as well as the methods of modern science, a man simple, sincere, courageous, "a saint, even if judged by the teachings of the Galilean Lake," Renan ranks, alike in spirit and in achievement, with men like Darwin and Pasteur as one of the immortals.

It was learning of this profound and extensive type which Renan brought to the writing of his *Life of Jesus.* More than any other man who has ever written upon the subject, with the possible exception of Nathaniel Schmidt, he was master of all the varied and complex material of language, history, tradition, *locale,* which went into the making of his work. The *Life* has often been condemned as imaginative. So it is—a masterpiece of the creative imagination! "If in writing the life of Jesus," said Renan, in his famous Preface, "one should confine himself to setting forth those matters which are certain, he must limit himself to a few lines . . . the texts give no certainty . . . we must strive to divine what they conceal, without being ever quite certain of having found it." But such imagination is the imagination of the archeologist who constructs a city from broken stones, of the paleontologist who conceives an extinct animal from scattered bones and teeth. Whatever conjecture entered into Renan's work was

backed by a wealth of learning controlled by a fearless and faithful mind. It is this which gives to the *Life of Jesus* an authority which has endured unshaken to this day.

(3)

But not yet have we explained the popularity of the book. This rested neither upon the sensational character of its conclusions, nor upon the authoritative nature of its learning, but upon its rare artistic qualities. We have spoken of Renan's literary style. This was unparalleled in the France of the nineteenth century for beauty, as the style of Voltaire was unparalleled in the France of the eighteenth century for clarity. The French are nearly always good writers; their greatest authors are the master stylists of the world; and of these Ernest Renan stands among the first. Put every other virtue aside, and his *Life of Jesus* is immortal simply as a piece of literature. If its conclusions were discredited, and its scholarship outgrown, we should still read it, as we read the *Republic* of Plato, for its perfection as a work of art. The loveliness of the Palestinian countryside, seen with Renan's own eyes and painted in upon the canvas with a brush of extraordinary skill—the color and bustle of the scene in Israel where Jesus lived—the ineffable charm of the brave young man who called his disciples and proclaimed the Kingdom—the pathos and passion of his experiences among his people—the unforgettable scenes of the last journey and the last week—these, as Renan presents them, are an eternal part of the literature of the world. They are among the things which man will not let die. The *Life,* be it said, does not rest alone upon such pages, as its main contribution is certainly not to be found in them. But these are what caught and held the multitude of readers who seized the volume when it came from the press, and it is what makes it now, when its pioneering work is done, a supremely "living book." Today, as not yesterday, we can get our information elsewhere, and get it more fully and accurately. But nowhere else can we read the immortal story in such magic phrases as those with which it has been clothed by Renan. Like a painting of Raphael, it must endure forever in the wonder and affection of mankind.

Sainte-Beuve, leading critic of his day, recognized and acclaimed this fact. Pointing out that the *Life,* addressed to the public, had reached its address, he said, "To be historian and story teller from this new point of view, (Renan) had to begin by being above all a diviner, a poet drawing inspiration from the spirit of times and places, and painter able to read the lines of the horizon, the least vestiges left on the slopes of the hills, and skilled in evoking the genius of the region and the landscape. He has thus succeeded in producing a work of art even more than a history, and this presupposes on the part of the author a union, till now almost unique, of superior qualities, reflective, delicate, and brilliant."

It is this combination of qualities which makes Renan's *Life of Jesus* the most famous and enduring work upon the subject ever written. If we were to estimate its supreme contribution to mankind, it would be its effect in clearing the way for a scientific and historical approach to the study of the Nazarene and of Christianity. Strauss undoubtedly broke the ground here, but Renan as undoubtedly drove the plough and planted the first seed. "You won for us," said Sainte-Beuve, "the right of discussion in this matter, hitherto forbidden." Since the publication of the *Life,* the study of New Testament times has been on a new basis, of fact instead of fiction, of truth instead of tradition. This whole field, hitherto set apart as a field of magic and miracle, has been reclaimed to history and the normal life of man. The multiplying biographies of Jesus, never so numerous nor so free as in our time, are as so many memorials to the master. And his own work, as this latest edition so eloquently certifies, still reigns among them!

M. J. Lagrange (essay date 1928)

SOURCE: Lagrange, M. J. "Antecedent Leanings, Negative Prejudice, and Positive Aspiration." In *Christ and Renan: A Commentary on Ernest Renan's "The Life of Jesus,"* translated by Maisie Ward, pp. 5-17. London: Sheed & Ward, 1928.

[*In the following essay, Lagrange criticizes the theological and historical arguments of* The Life of Jesus, *concentrating on how Renan's work differs from nineteenth-century German biblical exegesis.*]

From the very first, and in explaining his method, Renan is determined to distinguish himself from the German schools. And, in fact, the *Life of Jesus* was only discussed in Germany during the nineteenth century by theologians. The eighteenth century had seen the Orientalist, Reimarus, rejected by the theologians as a deist. Certainly these theologians did not resemble ours. They were emancipated enough to write "the gospel according to Hegel."

But they did remain more or less attached to Protestant Evangelicalism, and, anxious not to break with the gospels, they were content to eliminate whatever seemed to them intolerable to the modern world. Bruno Bauer had broken a lance with all Christian tradition, but he was still dogmatic, with the dogmatism of hate. Renan would not hear of dogma of whatever kind.

"The theologian is an interested party because of his dogma. Reduce this dogma as far as you will, it still remains for the artist and the critic a weight insupport-able. . . . Let us announce boldly: critical studies relating to the origins of Christianity will only say their last word when they are cultivated in a purely laic and secular spirit, after the methods of the Hellenists, the students of Arabic and Sanscrit, who, strangers to all theology, think neither of edifying nor of scandalising, neither of defending dogmas nor of overthrowing them."[1]

We sincerely wish that non-Christians *would* approach the origins of Christianity in this spirit, provided only that they are also prepared to accept the supernatural if the evidence is strong enough. But Renan was far removed from this impartiality: "To write the history of a religion it is necessary, firstly, to have believed it (otherwise we should not be able to understand how it has charmed and satisfied the human conscience[2]); in the second place to believe it no longer in an absolute manner, for absolute faith is incompatible with sincere history."[3]

Notice first the degree of discernment he awards himself as a former seminarist; yet observe also that even complete antecedent negation gives no guarantee of impartiality. Often as Renan has changed his opinions, there is one point on which he has never changed. He, too, has a *Credo* to which he has held unswervingly— the denial of the supernatural. And by the supernatural he does not only mean miracles, prophecies, and sacraments, but even the existence of a God distinct from the world. He rejected atheism as being bad taste, deism as too narrow a conception, and if he believed that a superior mind should not rank itself with the pantheists it was because he wished to retain the use of the word "God" as a "Category of the Ideal."

Moreover, these discussions on deism and pantheism serve only "little minds." "Were the men who have best comprehended God—Sakya-Mouni, Plato, St. Paul, St. Francis d'Assisi, and St. Augustine (at some periods of his fluctuating life)—deists or pantheists? Such a question has no meaning."[4] But if he thought it worthy of himself to float above these questions in which the "little minds" of Spinosa and Hegel exhausted themselves (for these men did count for him although he would have rejected Descartes and Bossuet, Pascal and St. Thomas Aquinas) Renan did set forth in a purely Oriental form his conviction of how God came to be. "Humanity makes divinity as the spider spins its web."[5]

When then, rejecting "individual supernatural facts," he claims to maintain "the supernatural in general," he is simply yielding to the prepossession for keeping Catholic words but using them with a purely Hegelian meaning. He remarked of Feuerbach that he was not an atheist, but rather a religious man, or that if he were an atheist it was after the German fashion, "devoutly and with unction."[6]

Later on he laughed at himself, and at this unction, but at first he did not laugh; he believed he had a mission, and he had no tenderness for the Catholicism he had abandoned. He believed the Church irrevocably lost. "The temples of Jesus, truly present, will crumble; the tabernacles believed to contain his flesh and blood will be shattered. Already the roof is open to the daylight, and the rain of heaven wets the face of the kneeling believer."[7]

Was Renan then in the frame of mind of a historian who thinks "neither of defending dogmas nor of upsetting them"? On the contrary, all his philosophical remarks witness to a lofty assurance, an absolute conviction. God, being at the term of human activity, how could He have intervened in the course of history? His mind was so thoroughly secularised that it necessarily assumed the denial of Christian dogma. He retained only the equivocal use of the *word* "God"—an old word, a little heavy, perhaps, but which has on its side "a long prescriptive right; to suppress it would be to throw humanity out of its track, and to separate oneself in speech from the simple beings who adore so well after their fashion."[8]

Language then does not express thought—at any rate when God is mentioned. It was necessary to remind the reader of these sayings, before reading this *Life of Jesus,* where sincerity is paraded so prominently, the conscience of the man of to-day distinguished from that of the Oriental, or even, we are forced to say, the sincerity of Jesus distinguished from that of His critical historian. Renan's reproach to Lamennais must also be weighed—that he "did not understand the irony of a certain sort of respect."[9]

Sceptics, advanced free thinkers, but men who do stop short somewhere, have pointed this out exactly like Catholic apologists. "It may be a little overdoing it," writes M. Séailles in the same ironic and measured style, "to attribute motives to a God who does not exist. Renan misuses mythology; he creates beings out of words."[10] Mgr. Dupanloup had said more simply, "He speaks like you, but does not think like you."[11]

On this point every one agrees—Renan first excluded God from history and then spoke of Him as if He existed. What did the word religion mean for him?

About this, too, he was definite enough. God being "The Category of the Ideal," religion was that part of the ideal to which souls offer sacrifice. For him this was science, for others whatever they loved best. Towards the end of his life he described this religion in a brutal formula, in words unworthy of his grey hairs. "The means of salvation are not the same for all. For one it is virtue; for another passion for truth; for another love of art; for others curiosity, ambition, travel, luxury, women, wealth; in a lower stage morphine and alcohol; the most dangerous mistake in social morality is the systematic suppression of pleasure."[12]

Must we say that this was simply lifting his mask and revealing what had always been at the bottom of his mind? Was his determination to speak as others spoke without thinking as they thought merely hypocrisy? Surely not, for a mere hypocrite would have gone straight forward for the priesthood without a shudder, like Paul de Gondi, the future Cardinal de Retz. Whence then the posture into which he forced himself, of calling himself religious, Christian even, and true disciple of Jesus?

Was it that at the bottom of his soul the religious sentiment persisted, the remains of tenderness towards the God who had been the joy of his youth? Yet, this God did not exist!

On leaving the seminary Renan became what he always remained, a convinced devotee of science. Science was to him his particular Category of the Ideal. If he tinged it with religiosity was it merely that he might not turn towards gross scepticism? It may well be. It always disgusted this acute and subtle nature to ally himself with the group of free-thinkers who went the further length of emptying their glasses in honour of Béranger's god of good fellows. But he might have stood alone.

Nor was his religious affectation a form of diplomatic prudence, necessary at a time when those in power listened to the voice of the bishops,—for he faced the storm and bore with dignity the imperial disfavour.

He must then have been in mind undecided enough to rest satisfied with vague ideas, but in character firm enough never to disclaim what had been his thought. He certainly knew how much he changed, but he stuck fast to a certain basis, and, having reduced his ideal to nothing but a vague love of truth, he could claim to have always been faithful to it. Why did he always keep the words—God, religion, and even in that last epicurean baseness the expression "to win salvation," except to avoid having disowned his original position?

And for the same reason he clung to his official admiration for Jesus. The lower he got on the slope which brought the former philosopher of the ideal down to the encourager of a debauchery which Epicurus would have rejected, the deeper and more horrifying became the gulf between his wanton toasts and his former gravity. When he began, and even when he was writing the *Life of Jesus* Renan still believed in the pure religion of the Ideal, and he attributed its origin to Jesus Christ.

It was assuredly a strange state of mind, an enigma for Frenchmen, and only to be explained by his attachment to German theology from the moment he left the seminary. He was careful to let us know that his faith was destroyed by historical criticism, not by philosophy. In company with more than one Catholic writer, M. Séailles refuses to believe this.

"The truth is," he writes, "that in 1843, at the end of his stay at Issy, when he knew neither Hebrew nor German, and had read neither Gesenius nor Ewald, he found in his reason alone a dangerous enemy to his faith."[13] In fact, one might readily say with M. Cognat, that "Hebrew is even more innocent than woman of his intellectual emancipation"[14]. But Renan was able to read in French the *Life of Jesus,* by Strauss, for Littré had just translated it.

Without disparagement of his marvellous talent, it may be said that Renan had not a philosophical mind. His impertinent claim to have mastered problems over which great geniuses exhaust themselves, is in fact an admission of incompetence. Philosophical objections affected him. But he viewed them in a fashion which tried to reconcile them with religion, giving up, indeed, the definite faith of Christians, but without abjuring Jesus Christ. The morality of Kant re-assures him, but Kant does not save Christ for him, and he still clings to keeping Christ. "I have been studying Germany, and I felt as though entering into a temple. Everything I found there was pure, exalted, moral, beautiful and touching. Oh my soul, we have found a treasure, the continuation of Jesus Christ. Their goodness overwhelms me: how sweet and strong they are! I think Christ will come to us from there. This vision of a new spirit seems to me an event similar to the birth of Christianity. . . . France seems to me more and more a country utterly empty of all share in the great work of the renewal of life in the human race. . . . Jesus Christ is nowhere to be found there."[15] This new life was, without doubt, that Hegelian conception to which Strauss had dedicated Christ as a type of God's union with man.

Renan, leaving the seminary definitely because he had lost his faith, was about to enter the world with a new faith, which allowed him still to speak of God and of religion, and to call himself a Christian. It is not mere pleasantry when he states "that the world will be eternally religious and that christianity, in a broad sense, is the last word in religion."[16]

By this remains of religious sentiment (of a very modern kind), almost as much as by his sweeping denial of the supernatural, he failed in the *rôle* he claimed of an impartial historian. Liberal Protestantism, Renan said, was incapable of writing the *Life of Jesus* because it still contained too much dogma. But he did not realise that he, too, had a dogma, the dogma of pure religion, without altars, without priests, without observances—not that religion preached by the deists, but that which might have been conceived by a Hegelian absorbed in developing and "organising God."

This is indeed a thesis—the thesis of the *Life of Jesus.* "'Christianity' has thus become almost a synonym of 'religion.' All that is done outside of this great and good Christian tradition is barren. Jesus gave religion to humanity as Socrates gave it philosophy. . . . Jesus founded the absolute religion, excluding nothing, and determining nothing unless it be the spirit [*sentiment*]."[17] "Whatever revolution takes place will not prevent us attaching ourselves in religion to the grand intellectual and moral line at the head of which shines the name of Jesus. In this sense we are Christians."[18] He repeats this constantly, without troubling to change his formulæ greatly. "A pure worship, a religion without priests and external observances, resting entirely on the feelings of the heart, on the imitation of God, on the direct relation of the conscience with the heavenly Father, was the result of these principles."[19] "It has been by the power of a religion free from all external forms that Christianity has attracted elevated minds."[20] "He founded the pure worship of all ages, of all lands, that which all elevated souls will practise until the end of time."[21] "It was a pure religion, without forms, or temple, or priest; it was the world's moral judgment delegated to the conscience of the just and the arm of the people."[22]

Clearly it is almost a monomania, and surely a sort of dogma—the positive complement of his denial of the supernatural. It would be strange if this dogma, which has to be proved, as it has not been revealed, had not affected the impartiality of the historian. As a matter of fact, Renan does not insist greatly on the positive side of his views. His formula, as we have seen, is supremely negative—the exclusion of external worship and of priesthood. He was inspired by the Hegelian idea of becoming—an idea as old as Heraclitus. The possibility of bringing contradictions into harmony suited his humour. But he had not resolutely accepted the identity of contradictions in the Idea which existed before the facts. Nor had he assented to the practical results according to Hegel, who had given a massive solidity to the Idea in the shape of the Prussian state. Renan's Idea was intangible, incorporeal, up in the air to such an extent that religion itself had to be robbed of all external support. All this means that his pure religion was also individualistic, and it was as such that it was understood and enjoyed in France. Who among us Frenchmen is seriously concerned in co-operating in the formation and organisation of the divine? But we still remembered the natural religion of Voltaire, and Renan lent a charm to this dry and unpoetic creed. In his own way he harmonised Voltaire and Rousseau. His rigid exclusion of the supernatural, of mystery, and of miracle satisfied the all too genuine French inclination for clear-cut ideas even if they lack height and depth; his moral sentiment satisfied the heart. Unhappily Renan from this time onwards was far below Rousseau in his sincere respect for the "holiness" of the Gospel. "Holiness" is not the atmosphere of the *Life of Jesus.* Such as he was, the ideal of the book was *his* ideal, and was that which he offered to the age he lived in. He loudly proclaimed the hope (and he was still sincere) of saving thereby whatever in religion is absolute and eternal—or rather whatever is of relative use now and in future . . . anyhow for the simple. This design is somewhat analogous to that of liberal Protestantism: it is only one degree lower in the amount of Christianity it contains. But it is only a question of degree. Resolved to reject the supernatural, and to look upon Jesus as the founder of "his" religion, he risked misunderstanding or even wilfully distorting the past. Renan was not the impartial historian that he claimed to be. Not to omit a shading off, which in his case would be serious, we must add to this the fact that his unbending principle was always varied by flights of fancy. But there remained always that aversion from the supernatural which was for this Breton the granite foundation of all thought. But he managed to escape from that systematic mentality that exposes many a German building, erected strictly according to rule, to a complete crash. History abhors contradictory assertions as much as philosophy, but the historian who knows how to measure his strength is modest in his assertions, and very often refuses to assert anything. As for Renan, he looked on contradictions as alternative ways of reaching truth. He carried this too far, but we shall have to note that his tact as a historian often saved him from sacrificing views which a more rigid mind must have excluded to safeguard the unity of his work.

Notes

1. p. x, French edition.

2. p. 31. The scruple is touching. But Mgr. Dupanloup recognised another note when he observed "It was again in reference to the unfortunate Lamennais that M. Renan wrote that those who come forth from the sanctuary and make war on *the dogma that they have served* have, in the blows that they strike, *a sure hand that the layman can never attain, a special note of coolness and assurance . . . the audacity of an intimate. Avertissement à la Jeunesse,* etc., p. 110, quoting *Essais,* p. 141, 2.

3. p. 31.

4. p. 69.

5. *Job* XL. Or less poetically "The universal work of all living things being to make a perfect God . . . reason . . . will one day undertake the supervision of this great work, and after organising humanity, will organise God." (*L'Avenir de Science,* p. 37).

6. *Liberté de Penser,* vol. VI, p. 347.

7. *Liberté de Penser,* Vol. III, p. 470.

8. *Etudes,* p. 419.

9. *Essais,* p. 187.

10. *Ernest Renan,* p. 282, note 2.

11. *Advertissement,* p. 15.

12. *Feuilles détachées,* p. 382.

13. *Ernest Renan,* p. 17.

14. Quoted by M. Séailles, op. cit. p. 17.

15. *Souvenirs,* p. 385.

16. *Questions Contemporaines,* p. 337.

17. *Life of Jesus,* pp. 236-7.

18. *Life of Jesus,* p. 237.

19. p. 73.

20. p. 86.

21. p. 140.

22. p. 162.

John T. Noonan (essay date 1949)

SOURCE: Noonan, John T. "Renan's *The Life of Jesus*: A Re-examination." *The Catholic Biblical Quarterly* 11 (1949): 26-39.

[*In the following essay, Noonan argues that* The Life of Jesus *is a deeply flawed work expressing many of the prejudices of nineteenth-century religious skepticism.*]

> They admit certainly a real and historical Jesus, but their historical Jesus is not a Messiah or a prophet or a Jew. They do not know what He wanted; they understand neither His life nor His death. Their Jesus is, in His own way, an eon, an impalpable, intangible being. Pure history does not know any such being.
>
> (Ernest Renan on the Protestant Liberals)[1]

> Why have we not laughed from the beginning at any rationalist or rationalizing **'Life of Jesus'**? Because neither the author nor the public were really emancipated from the magic of Christian faith.
>
> (George Santayana)[2]

> And devils went out from many, crying out and saying: Thou art the Son of God.
>
> (Luke 4:41)

* * *

The earliest rationalizers of the supernatural in Christ's works approached Him to ask, "Do we not say well that thou art a Samaritan, and hast a devil?" (John 8:40). The approach of obstinate unbelief to Jesus in the next 2,000 years was to take shape as varied as the prejudices and mythologies of the ages and the countries wherein the Faith was preached; but this short saying contains the essentials of its protest. There is evident, first of all, the confidence with which the rationalizers' hypothesis is set forth, the self-congratulation of the non-believer at having found at last the real key to Jesus' strange power. Secondly, there is emphasis on but a partial aspect of Jesus' works; and even that partial aspect is misrepresented. Here, the Jews ignore the beauty of His moral teaching, and concentrate only on His supernatural activities, representing them, of course, as diabolical. The whole God-man, Christ in His integrity, is not considered. The interrogators, proud of their discernment, then propound their explanation: an explanation which consists only in an appeal to the popular mind of the age. They attempt no direct refutation of the truth of Jesus' works or sayings; but they insinuate, first, that He is an alien to their civilization, and, secondly, that a plausible alternative explanation of His power can be constructed. The appeal is not, fundamentally, to reason, but to current preconceptions that would decide the case before examining it.

We are inclined today—Gentiles or Christians—to look with amused superiority at the hopeless inadequacy of these astute Jews' explanation; and we are inclined to dismiss with a kind of laughing charity the later slanders of Celsus and Porphyry and Trypho, and to confess candid amazement that reputable Roman jurists could have believed that Christianity was a perverted cannibalism. These, too, were all rationalizations, cast in the mold of the age's prejudices, of the supernatural power of Christianity. The attack on Jesus in the nineteenth century was, perhaps, less crude; and with a greater knowledge of Christian teaching, it could, perhaps, be subtler. But does its appeal to the preconceptions and prejudices of its age, its refusal to explore the facts directly, its partial dwelling on only one side of Jesus' life, differ essentially from the fatuous explanation of the Pharisees? Today is Renan's *Life of Jesus* invested with any more historical dignity than, say, Diocletian's apocryphal *Acts of Pilate*?[3]

Renan's work is, however, a classic—the literary masterpiece of nineteenth century religious liberalism; and as such, it offers itself as a fruitful source of instruction in the spirit of its age. Further, just as the observable laws of disintegration in every Christian heresy, in their repeated pattern of decay, set against the orderly maturing of the dogma of the Church, offer a strong negative motive of credibility—so too the inadequacy of every rationalist drawing of Christ but brings into more marked relief the integrity and the accuracy of the Catholic presentation of Jesus. That the non-believer must distort the texts, suppress the facts, and, above all, appeal not to evidence, but to the popular superstitions of his time is all clear testimony that the integrity of truth is present only in the Faith. A re-examination of Renan, can, then, still have value; an appraisal of his portrait of Jesus may exhibit immutable moral laws at work; and observation of the principles, methods and results of unbelief may become a negative means of demonstrating the seamless wholeness of truth.

To investigate once more this creative work of propaganda is not, therefore, to attempt the superfluous task of refuting it. That gentle and subtle distillation of scholarly acid, Père Lagrange's *Christ et Renan,* is, of course, the direct antidote to Renan; and, indirectly, the mere accumulation of eighty more years of biblical criticism have brought about Renan's total rejection on any scientific level. The falsehood has been dissected; our interest lies in restoring its anatomy, to understand its composition and the reasons for its nineteenth century growth.

Lagrange has brilliantly analyzed the combination of irresponsible aestheticism and doctrinal Hegelianism which mark Renan's work.[4] These ingredients are the personal contribution of Renan. But it is, perhaps, unfair to our distinguished author to consider his work either as an unscrupulous aesthetic *tour de force,* deluding, in its basic scepticism, even the writer's pious rationalist friends, or as an Hegelian exercise in dialectic, multiplying conflicts to produce a higher synthesis. Such mere personal predilections would not have produced the classic of a great age's mythology.

Contradictions, indeed, abound in the **Life of Jesus,** but it is important for us to understand that they were not created wantonly by Renan. They were rather, produced by the facts themselves when they were bent to fit a nineteenth century pattern. It is this larger pattern—the work, not of Renan alone, but of a generation's state of mind—that we must investigate.

In the pattern of the approach of unbelief to Christ there are at least two principles which are timeless. One has already been indicated—the necessity of accepting only part of the evidence, of then re-creating Christ in the shape of the age's prejudices, and leaving as a result only an eon, an intangible, impalpable being. The second timeless principle is an unexpected testifying, almost forcefully extorted by the facts, to Christ's uniqueness. The devils of Palestine were the first to give witness of this character, hating Christ, yet wonderfully attracted to the recognition of His divinity. A profound ambivalence reveals itself, and the unbeliever in the presence of the facts discloses unwillingly by his own lips that he is confronted by the Sign of Contradiction. The polarity of Christ, exhibited in His first meetings with the Jews, is demonstrated again in His examination by the more sophisticated incredulity of Renan's generation.

These two elements, the prejudiced re-shaping of Christ and a sense of His polarity, are, so to speak, constants, familiar in the approach of unbelief in every country and every century. The third principle which governs the larger framework of Renan's book is the special contribution of the nineteenth century. It fuses the two constants into the special nineteenth century mold and produces the nineteenth century's synthetic Christ. It is the nineteenth century dogma of rationalism. Every event in the cosmos, Renan argues, has a cause, but only a natural cause; and the human reason is capable of exploring these causes completely. Santayana rightly emphasizes the dependence of this dogma on the "magic of the Christian faith"; and in fact, Renan's *Life* was built on a strong residue of Christian tradition. Essentially, rationalism was an inheritance of the scholastic demonstration of the universality and intelligibility of causality and the scholastic proofs of the order and benevolence of nature. Rationalism, however, arbitrarily and unreasonably, limited the scholastic principle to the natural order alone and, denying a First of Final Cause, cut the principles from any rational context. Causality, benevolence, order, then, fell from the status of rationally demonstrated truths to rationalist matters of faith. But in their limited and perverted form they were, paradoxically, preserved by the Christian faith which rationalism denied. Every rationalist certitude, in effect, was supported "magically" by the Christian theistic confidences, ingrained in the intellect of Europe by centuries of faith, which the age of rationalism accepted uncritically as its own. Divorced from a theistic frame of reference, however, the fundamental Christian notions now naturalistically conceived, became mere dogma, in the pejorative sense of dogma—the assertion and test of popular orthodoxy, unsupported by intelligible proof, yet hallowed as immutable. Still, even rationalistic assumption, by retaining some idea of the order of nature, had its advantages and kept the reason from complete anarchy. Its enormous influence on Renan cannot be overestimated: it held him to a goal of finding a reasonable explanation for all the Gospel events; it bound him to accept only a naturalistic explanation as reasonable.

To estimate properly the weight of nineteenth orthodoxy on Renan it is fruitful, perhaps, to compare the *Life of Jesus* with a twentieth century work, Santayana's *The Idea of Christ in the Gospels*. Santayana, like Renan, is at once an aesthetic and an atheist. But unlike him he has no concern for nineteenth century prejudices. More logical, then, having denied God, he also denies causality completely. "Existence," he declares, "is necessarily unintelligible. Just as logically anything may happen, so the fact that anything in particular happens is irrational. It may be part of a sequence often repeated; but the fact that such a sequence ever occurs or occurs often remains an utterly arbitrary and inexplicable fact." In a chaotic world, there is no order, causality, or reason. At the same time, Santayana is freed from the limitations of a narrow rationalism, and he faces all the facts of the Gospels in their entirety. He does not, of course, end his scrutiny of the facts in be-

lief, for he has denied such *preambula fidei* as causality and God. Still, he is not compelled to falsify the facts to fit a pattern: he is unembarrassed at recognizing miracles. The painful evasion, the truncated quotations, the curious special pleadings of Renan are unknown to him.

When we have seen this freer honesty of Santayana, we can then realize how profoundly Renan's less candid methods have been determined by a narrower creed. They represent his earnest effort to make his account of Christ meet the demands of his age. Every event in the Gospels must be reasonably and naturally accounted for. Renan does not shrink from the task. He would not have been content with the simple-minded singleness of explanation of later eschatologists or the school of contemporary religions. He tries to face all, or at least most, of the aspects of Christ. The intellectual dishonesties and inconsistencies that appear most glaringly in him of all the rationalists are, indeed, only pathetic testimonies to the conscientious ardor with which he upheld the popular dogma of his age.

If the nineteenth century's credulity, then, sets up the framework in which Renan paints, it may now be well to consider some points of this painting in detail—not, it is to be repeated, by way of refutation—but simply to understand how the framework forces the artist to conform. We may note in particular in this detail the partial presentation of the facts, the unwilling fluctuation towards recognition of Christ, and the rigid obedience to the popular dogma of naturalism. The naturalist articles of faith are the popular credo with which the book begins. Renan avows candidly that it is disbelief in the supernatural which motivates his book.[5] But this candor is modified by cleverness, when Renan asserts this assumption, not in the name of any philosophy, "but in the name of universal experience." History, he asserts, records no miracles.[6] His reasoning, put baldly, runs as follows: miracles, the mundane intervention of the supernatural, are not possible in the Gospels because they are impossible everywhere; they are impossible everywhere, because they are possible nowhere. Historical testimony to miracles is, by its very nature, unworthy of consideration: "a supernatural account always implies credulity or imposture."[7] Contrast for a moment Santayana's more honest account correcting this stubborn obscurantism: "Historical evidence, impartially collected, is far from supporting the assumption that miracles are impossible; and logically, it is untenable."[8] Renan qualifies his dogmatic assumption with the following two-edged thrust: "Observation, which has never once been falsified, teaches us that miracles never happen but in times and countries in which they are believed, and before persons disposed to believe them."[9] This, as a valid objection, is perhaps as reasonable as remarking that battles never occur except in times and countries at war and between armies ready to fight them.

As Santayana more justly observes of the relation between faith and miracles, "The efficacy of prayer has itself regular conditions and degrees. Faith seems to be chief of these"; and he adds that faith is not be to confused with illusion.[10]

Renan, indeed, lays down his own terms for acknowledging a miracle and flatly asserts that they have never been met. His conditions are: (1) that a scientific commission have full power to choose the setting of the announced miracle and full authority to investigate all details concerning it; and (2) that the miracle be repeated. Yet in his own day, he could have pursued his tests at Lourdes, if a priori conceptions had not first decided him that he would be testing the non-existent. It may not be uncharitable to assume that if he had investigated and had seen the miraculous, he would have echoed Zola, "I will not believe, if all the sick at Lourdes rise from their beds."[11] Our Lord Himself has analyzed this "hardness of heart": "If they hear not Moses and the prophets, neither will they believe if one rise again from the dead" (Luke 16:31); an honest moral disposition is indispensable to a recognition of the supernatural.

In general, facing the factual Gospel testimonies, Renan dismisses the miracles lightly as delusions; but in the case of Lazarus, he does not scruple to charge pure fraud on the part of Lazarus' family,[12] and his handling of the evidence here is instructive in his fidelity to nineteenth century orthodoxy. His reconstruction of the case involves a simple denial or suppression of the only texts on which any story could be based at all. He ignores: (1) the flat statement that Lazarus had been buried for four days (John 11:17); (2) that Jesus had predicted his death (John 11:13); (3) that Mary and Martha are completely griefstricken and have no hope now in Jesus' aid (John 11:23-33); (4) that Jesus is surrounded by a number of sceptical Jews who are eager to see his power refuted (John 11:37); and (5) that Martha explicitly protests that Lazarus "is decaying", with an implied reference to the unpleasant smell of the corpse (John 11:39). Of course, John may have been an unmitigated liar, but it is absurd to accept the reality of the framework and then deny the heart of the story. Renan is, of course, placed in an embarrassing position here by his admission that the contemporary and hostile eyewitness belief in a miraculous resurrection "contributed sensibly to Jesus' death."[13] It was, according to Renan, "a publicly notorious" event that the leaders of Jewish orthodoxy could not afford to leave unnoticed.

Renan's explanations here seemed even to him so feeble that in the thirteenth edition of his *Life of Jesus* he was prompted to bolster them by a new idea that the Apostles misinterpreted Jesus' parable of Lazarus the beggar and that that was the ultimate basis of the Lazarus legend. This rationalization obviously has still less in common with the facts.

A corollary of nineteenth century dogma on miracles was a fixed distrust of those who were witnesses of them. The a priori rejection of the supernatural leads thus to an arbitrary treatment of the sources. At first, Renan hesitates for a moment and commits the literary absurdity of contending that "the most beautiful thing in the world [the Gospels] has proceeded from a purely popular elaboration";[14] but then contradicting himself, with better taste, he maintains carefully that the Gospels are substantially historical, that they are the work of eyewitnesses or the friends of eyewitnesses, that they present the character of their hero "with a great degree of truthfulness."[15] At the same time, he contends that the Gospels' authors are gullible and enthusiastic inventors.[16] He declares that they were "men of feeble intelligence," for "they believed in apparitions and spirits."[17] It is a strange logic which accepts as at least substantially accurate the report of Jesus' sayings, and rejects as fictional the account of his deeds. Apocryphal sayings, attributed to great personages at some historic moment, are far commoner in history than a complete set of apocryphal deeds. There is much sense and science in textual criticism on textual grounds; but the rejection of a saying or incident simply because it contradicts a priori assumptions would destroy the science of history. Renan accepts the reliability of his authorities on his own fiat alone, and only where he chooses; he denies them the reality of the very motive which impelled them to write, their knowledge of the signs and wonders of Christ.

Renan compares the Evangelists to four old soldiers of Napoleon who in 1850 or 1860 compose four biographies of him.[18] Let us follow him in this comparison. The central events of Napoleon's career, the "sign" of his military genius, the heart of his appeal to military men are his battles; and, provided that we were convinced that these four hypothetical chroniclers had really known and served a great emperor—quite apart from the external corroboration of other histories—we would rightly be charged with obstinate blindness if we denied that Napoleon had fought a single battle. What, then, we might ask, inspired his chroniclers to write? Why was he beloved by them? Surely his military epigrams alone did not form the basis of his reputation. Is Renan any less absurd—at least once he has accepted the eye witness authenticity of his documents—in denying Christ's miracles? The miracles are the very soul of the Gospels, the proof, in the Evangelists' minds, of Christ's authority. Moreover, the fact of the miracles and their extraordinary effect is as fully corroborated by the external testimony of the existence and growth of the worship of Christ as a deity in the heart of Yahwist Judaea as the fact of Napoleon's battles is corroborated by the independent testimony of their political consequences.

Renan's doctrinaire distrust of the Gospels as legendary is yet more strangely marked by his treatment of the Apocrypha. The Apocrypha, his good sense recognizes, are "insipid and puerile";[19] but he does not attempt to explain the obvious superiority of the canonical Gospels, which, in his eyes, are equally puerile fancies. Only a real difference in veracity could, of course, afford the explanation, and Renan will not openly face the difficulty. He later contrasts the "grotesqueness" of Jesus' childhood with Luke's account of His teaching in the Temple.[20] But he offers no comment on how Luke's "fiction" avoids the gross blunders of the other.

Renan's final attempt to support his picture of the "feeble intelligence" of the Evangelists is the contention that "the documents are in flagrant contradiction with each other."[21] But this bold assertion is made here without reference and is subsequently supported only by entirely arbitrary deductions. Christian commentators from the beginning have, of course, appreciated the variety of approach in the Gospels. Papias (*circa* 90 A.D.) is, I believe, the first biblical critic to note this.

Renan's position on his sources, as well as on the miracles, is, then, at once arbitrary and unreasonable. His popular distortions here, however, merely lay the groundwork for the treatment of Jesus Himself; for Jesus Himself, not the miracles or Evangelists alone, has always been the real stumbling block of disbelief. The ancient mythologies and early heresies consisted in travesties of Christ's divinity. Modern mythology has consisted in parodies of His humanity. Of these parodies, Renan's is one of the more distinguished. In the image of the nineteenth century humanist, the man of sweetness and light, Renan fashions his portrait of Jesus.

Jesus, according to nineteenth century taste, was a man "of infinite sweetness, vague poetry, and universal charm."[22] He was "the most charming rabbi of them all."[23] His discourses were adapted to the "cheerful imaginations of the Galileans."[24] It was "the charm of his speech" which captivated their "simple minds." "His preaching was gentle and pleasing."[25] Renan admits that this picture of "idealism and poesy" is true only of the early Jesus; on his third visit to Jerusalem, as Renan inimitably expresses it, "the cheerful moralist" becomes "a gloomy giant."[26] Let us explore, then, only the accuracy of Renan's portrait of Jesus in Galilee. It is in Galilee, in the Sermon on the Mount, that this young man of "amiable character" declares that at the last judgement He will say to the wicked, "I will profess unto them I never knew you; depart from me, you that work iniquity." (Mt. 8:23). Here too, Jesus announces "Every tree that bringeth not forth good fruit shall be cut down and shall be cast into the fire." (Mt. 7:19). Again it is in Galilee that Jesus proclaims to these simple Jews "fascinated" by his "extraordinary sweetness", that "many shall come from the east and the west and shall sit down with Abraham and Isaac and Jacob in the kingdom of heaven. But the children of the kingdom shall be cast out into the exterior darkness; there shall be weeping and gnashing of teeth." (Mt. 8:11, 12). It is in Galilee, sending out his twelve Apostles, that this cheerful dreamer declares of those who do not receive his messengers, "It shall be more tolerable for the land of Sodom and Gomorrah in the day of judgement, than for that city." (Mt. 10:15). Here too the young moralist strangely attacks his "kindly and simple" audiences, "Woe to thee, Corozain, woe to thee, Bethsaida, for if in Tyre and Sidon had been wrought the miracles that have been wrought in you, they had long ago done penance in sackcloth and ashes. But I say unto you, it shall be more tolerable for Tyre and Sidon in the day of Judgement than for you. And thou Capharnaum, shalt thou be exalted up to heaven? Thou shalt go down even unto hell." (Mt. 11:21-23). Are these sentiments calculated to appeal to the "cheerful imagination" of the inhabitants of the doomed towns? At least it is clear that they cheered no nineteenth century heart. Again, in Galilee, according to the contemporary testimony, it is not Jesus' "sweet and penetrating influence" that attracts the crowd: they admire him not for his meekness, but for his vigor: "For he was teaching them as one having power, not as the Scribes and Pharisees." (Mt. 7:29). The actions of "the most charming rabbi of them all" do not "exhale sweetness" to his Galileen spectators. Rather, "there came fear upon all, and they talked among themselves saying, 'What word is this for with authority and power He commandeth the unclean spirits and they go out.'" (Luke 4:34)

Renan, in fine, has falsified the historical Jesus here beyond recognition; for he has only dared to face one aspect of the truth. Renan's Jesus is not the founder of the "final religion," but the gossamer creation of the founder of French dilettantism. Like Renan and Oscar Wilde, he is simply a man of "exquisite feeling."

Renan climaxes his myth of the heroic dilettante with a picture of Jesus' religion carefully sketched in accordance with the most cultivated nineteenth century taste. Comte or Matthew Arnold might have been proud to have been its inventors. Jesus' religion rested, Renan asserts, on the feelings of the human heart.[27] It was without priests "and without dogma." "Nothing", in short, "could be less priestly than Jesus' attitude."[28] It is, perhaps, surprising to find a sophisticated critic like Renan falling into the naive Protestant error of seeking Jesus' theological manual in the pages of the Gospel narratives. It is less astonishing to discover that Renan's sole positive evidence that Jesus founded a religion of "pure spirit" rests on the manipulation of the truncated text of John 4:21-23. John 4:22 states the distasteful historical fact that salvation in this pure religion comes from the Jews. Renan, without any textual authority whatsoever, on purely his a priori assumption, cheerfully dismisses the verse as "interpolation."[29]

In the centuries-old ways of unbelief, then, Renan has been forced to consider only parts of the evidence, and supported by this partial evidence he has made a parody of Christ and Christ's religion to suit his contemporary prejudices. But he is too painfully aware of other facts to rest quite content with his partial synthesis. Further, he cannot evade the strange polarity of Christ. He frankly recognizes that "among the sons of men, there is none born who is greater than Jesus."[30] He grants willingly that the morality of the Gospels is "the highest creation of the human conscience",[31] and that this morality is "an absolutely new idea" which owes its origin to Jesus alone.[32] He contends, "that which in others would be an insupportable pride must not in Him, Jesus, be regarded as a presumption."[33] He considers it a maxim that "Love is not enkindled except of an object worthy of it," and infers Christ's greatness from the love that He inspired.[34] Again, noting that "Christianity was impressed with an original character which will never be effaced," he ascribes the imposition of this ineffacable character to Jesus alone.[35] He scouts the idea that the disciples created Jesus: "He was, rather, in everything superior to his disciples . . . St. Paul himself bears no comparison with Jesus."[36] Finally, he indignantly repudiates the possibility that Jesus may have been insane: "It has not yet been given to insanity to influence the progress of humanity."[37] But, rather, Jesus is "at the summit of human greatness. He established the final religion."[38] "All history is incomprehensible without Jesus."[39]

Here, perhaps, we might ponder the discerning remarks of Santayana, "A Lucifer might believe in the existence of a divine Christ without deigning to imitate Him";[40] and we might recall how the devils of Palestine confessed their God against their will. (Luke 4:41)

If Renan coupled a readiness to believe in miracles with this open homage to Jesus' religious spirit, he could not but believe Jesus to be divine. In these constant and reiterated admissions of Jesus' moral supremacy as absolutely without parallel, he is "not far from the kingdom of God." But he quickly draws back from entering, and, facing the urgency of the facts again, he is found to contradict the testimony of his moral sense rather than allow himself to abandon his nineteenth century mythology.

Accordingly, these sweeping tributes to Jesus' greatness are found to come to very little in any particular case treated by Renan when he finds Jesus' actions distasteful or disturbing to his assumptions. Jesus, unlike Renan, believed in miracles. The greatest of mankind was, then, guilty of what Renan calls "a beautiful er-ror—which was one day the means of showing his deficiencies in the eyes of the physicist and the chemist."[41] But if Renan is right in his conclusion, is "beautiful" the right adjective to apply to the delusion? Is it not, on Renan's basis, the source of an ugly credulity which has gripped Christian people from Peter to the present?

As Jesus not only believes in miracles, but professes to perform them, Renan's disapproval deepens. He cherishes the thought that Jesus "had the reputation of thaumaturgus imposed on him."[42] But he is finally driven to declare openly, "Acts which would not be considered as acts of illusion or folly held a large place in the life of Jesus."[43] Jesus, indeed, was so much the dupe of his age and his own self-confidence as "to think that he performed miracles."[44] In short, this "genius" who founded "the final religion" was, at least much of the time, signally deluded about the very religious powers he professed to hold. Such delusion might reasonably appear dangerous rather than lovely, and ultimately Renan, too, concludes that many of the recommendations of this deluded teacher "contain the germs of a true fanaticism."[45] Is this judgement reached inexorably by Renan's own rationalistic logic, to be reconciled with his tribute to Jesus' "perfect idealism as the highest rule of the virtuous life"?[46] Does the contradiction lie with Renan or Jesus?

A deluded fanatic is hardly an authority on morals, and in direct contradiction to his paean on Jesus' religious teaching, Renan reluctantly concludes that, because of Jesus, "a fatal germ of theocracy was introduced into the world."[47] And again, Renan, on his rationalist basis, cannot but be irritated by Jesus' promise of immortality to Mary Magdalene, and so is driven to see in it only an act of prideful self-exaltation.[48] Renan sitting as the moral judge of his self-confessed master of morality is not, perhaps, a happy self-portrait.

To this point, Renan has touched only on the obvious fanatical and theocratic implications of Jesus' teachings, and on what he calls gracefully, "the less inviting aspects"—Jesus' delusions as to his personal power. But he goes further in his rationalization of Christ to explain that at times indeed Jesus was irrational. He became "possessed of a singular taste for persecution and torment."[49] He was "carried away by this fearful progression of enthusiasm." "Sometimes one would have said his reason was distorted."[50] When Jesus went up to Jerusalem for the last time, "he was no longer himself." "His natural gentleness seems to have abandoned him; he was sometimes harsh and capricious."[51] In support of this thesis of Jesus' mental deterioration in Jerusalem, Renan brings in incidents as indubitably laid in Galilee, as Mark 9:18, as unmistakably early in Jesus' career as Mark 3:5, and as plainly contradictory to Renan's claims as Luke 8:45.[52] To regard the last incident—which occurs, anyway, in the Galilee days—as an example of harsh caprice is simply malicious absurdity. Reference is here made, also to Luke 9:41, another early incident; and Renan's statement of the disciples' growing fear of Jesus is supported by Mark 4:40, the very early miracle of the calming of the Sea of Galilee, and by Mark 5:15, the similarly early incident with the demoniacs and the pigs. The charge that "his disciples at times thought him to be mad" made again by Renan in a context that implies this to be a late phenomenon,[53] is supported by a single reference, Mark 3:21, which describes in fact, the belief of some of Jesus' *relatives*, not that of his disciples, that "he was possessed," in the early days of the Galilee preaching. Wilful misrepresentation cannot go much further.

Finally, Renan asserts that Jesus believed that He was "the universal reformer"[54] and announced that He would come in triumph to judge the world.[55] Renan dismisses these pretensions with a word: "His idea of the Son of God became disturbed and exaggerated."[56] Yet, as even Renan concedes, Jesus' idea of His omnipotence and union with the Father was not an evolved idea, but the basis of His whole life: "The first thought of Jesus, a thought so deeply rooted in him, that it had probably no beginning, was that he was the Son of God, the friend of his Father . . . in his paroxysm of heroic will be believed himself all-powerful."[57] Such thinking, unless supported by supernatural facts, might be safely diagnosed as lunacy. Renan observes dryly that Jesus' "excessively imaginative nature carried him incessantly beyond the bounds of human nature."[58] May we infer, more succinctly, he was simply mad? Renan never dares to trouble rationalist piety with this direct, and on his ground, logical conclusion. His hesitations are more subtle. Genius and lunacy are indistinguishable, he argues, and inspiration is the same as madness.[59] "The most beautiful things in the world are done in a state of fever."[60] So, too, even truth and falsehood do not exist, for they are inextricably mixed: "Everything great," Renan declares, "rests on a legend." Here Renan is close to the paradox of Santayana that human life itself is irrational: that the greatest of men should be preeminently irrational is then no surprise. That Renan does not proceed to this desperate conclusion, to which he is driven by the facts, not by his wishes, is a tribute to the strength of nineteenth century orthodoxy. Rationalism would not yet recognize that it ended in irrationality. That it logically ended there, if the conclusions were drawn, even in the work of a careful rationalist like Renan, affords a profound negative corroboration of Catholic scholarship. Here in the concrete sphere of biblical criticism, as well as in the abstract ranges of philosophy, denial of the supernatural leads to denial of the rational.

Eighty years later, the honey of Renan's style has somewhat cloyed. Nor can we, after two great wars, be expected to respond very quickly to the sentimental optimism of sweetness and light. The spirit of the **Life of Jesus,** meant to match another age's prejudices, has fled from it, and we contemplate today only the work's dry and creaking contrivances, once so subtly animated with malice. We see only the lifeless components of the masterpiece of religious liberalism: the dependence on a crude and narrow faith in naturalism, the inability to avoid a fitful testimony to Christ's supremacy, the half-conscious distortions, the half-unconscious suppressions, the fundamental necessity to destroy the Christ of history and to replace Him by a mythical humanist. An analysis of Renan's art of propaganda reveals to us old elements grouped in a new pattern. The anatomy of his dead work is for us now an important specimen in biblical criticism of the methods and results of those who have said in their hearts, "There is no God."

Notes

1. Cited in G. Ricciotti, *The Life of Christ* (Milwaukee: Bruce, 1944), p. 192.

2. G. Santayana, *The Idea of Christ in the Gospels* (New York: 1946), p. 5.

3. See Eusebius, *The Ecclesiastical History,* trans. Lake and Oulton (New York: Putnam, 1926), Vol. II, p. 343.

4. See M. J. Lagrange, O.P., *Christ and Renan* (London: Sheed and Ward, 1928), pp. 12-17.

5. Ernest Renan, *The Life of Jesus* (New York: Random House, 1927). P. 33.

6. Renan, *op. cit.,* p. 59.

7. *Ibid.,* p. 60.

8. Santayana, *op. cit.,* p. 77.

9. Renan, *op. cit.,* p. 59.

10. Santayana, *op. cit.,* p. 82.

11. See the interesting account, by a critic angrily hostile to Lourdes, of Zola's reaction to the cure of Marie Lemarchand of a tubercular lupus. "Zola's only comment was that the subject of hysterically-produced symptoms was not sufficiently known." (E. Saunders, *Lourdes*; London: 1940, p. 254.)

It is perhaps revealing also to listen to Zola himself. "I will admit that I came across some instances of real cures. Many cases of nervous disorders have undoubtedly been cured, and there have also been other cures, which may perhaps be attributed to errors of diagnosis on the part of doctors who attended the patients cured. These cures are based on the ignorance of the medical profession." (E. Zola, *Lourdes*; Chatto and Windus, London, 1903, pp. 8-9.) In short, when the expert testimony contradicts one's assumptions, one is free to deny the competency of the experts.

Miss Saunders own attitude to Lourdes is also instructive in the ways of unbelief. "The curing of an odd disease here and there, even *an organic disease in its last stages,* is not miraculous," she remarks, lightly assuming the point in dispute. Then she falls back on Santayana's explanation that, after all, everything is absurd. "The truth is that if certain inexplicable cures are called miraculous, the sudden contradiction of the malady might be called miraculous as well." (Saunders, *op. cit.,* p. 284.)

For competent medical testimony to the naturally inexplicable phenomena at Lourdes, see A. Guarner, *De l'instanéité des Guèrisons de Lourdes* (Paris: 1939); D. W. Walleyn, *Het Lourdesmirakel* (Bruges: 1939); A. Carrel, *Man The Unknown* (Harper Bros., New York), especially pp. 148-150.

12. Renan, *op. cit.,* p. 323.

13. *Ibid.,* p. 324.

14. *Ibid.,* p. 38.

15. *Ibid.,* pp. 49, 50, 55.

16. *Ibid.,* p. 54.

17. *Ibid.,* p. 184.

18. *Ibid.,* p. 132.

19. *Ibid.,*

20. *Ibid.,*

21. *Ibid.,* p. 58.

22. *Ibid.,* p. 120.

23. *Ibid.,* p. 133.

24. *Ibid.,* p. 166.

25. *Ibid.,* p. 186.

26. *Ibid.,* p. 125-126.

27. *Ibid.,* p. 129.

28. *Ibid.,* pp. 129, 132.

29. *Ibid.,* p. 234.

30. *Ibid.,* p. 251.

31. *Ibid.,* p. 128.

32. *Ibid.,* p. 132.

33. *Ibid.,* p. 236.

34. *Ibid.,* p. 385.

35. *Ibid.,* p. 376.

36. *Ibid.,* pp. 386-387.

37. *Ibid.,* p. 386.

38. *Ibid.,* p. 383.

39. *Ibid.,* p. 65.

40. Santayana, *op. cit.,* p. 174.

41. Renan, *op. cit.,* p. 97.

42. *Ibid.,* p. 255.

43. *Ibid.,* p. 256.

44. *Ibid.,* p. 251.

45. *Ibid.,* p. 298.

46. *Ibid.,* p. 383.

47. *Ibid.,* p. 290.

48. *Ibid.,* p. 331.

49. *Ibid.,* p. 292.

50. *Ibid.,* p. 293.

51. *Ibid.,* p. 293.

52. *Ibid.,* p. 293

53. *Ibid.,* p. 293.

54. *Ibid.,* pp. 151-152.

55. *Ibid.,* p. 161.

56. *Ibid.,* p. 294.

57. *Ibid.,* pp. 151-152.

58. *Ibid.,* p. 293.

59. *Ibid.,* p. 389.

60. *Ibid.,* p. 389.

Harold W. Wardman (essay date 1964)

SOURCE: Wardman, Harold W. "1860-1863: The Middle East and the 'Vie de Jésus.'" In *Ernest Renan: A Critical Biography,* pp. 72-90. London: The Athlone Press, 1964.

[*In the following excerpt, Wardman places* The Life of Jesus *in a tradition of nineteenth-century romantic humanism and focuses on Renan's depiction of Jesus as a historical figure on whom the myth of Christianity was constructed.*]

Though not his best historical work, the *Vie de Jésus* is too important a landmark in his life and in nineteenth century French literature to merit merely a passing attention. There can be no denying the importance of a work, whatever its actual worth, which spoke to the condition of so many Frenchmen and Europeans. Its place lies in that part of the romantic movement stemming from Chateaubriand and Madame de Staël which laid stress on the aesthetic and emotional aspect of Christianity. The way for it had doubtless also been prepared by the individualistic, unorthodox and yet near-Christian expression of religion in French romantic poetry. And when one thinks of romanticism in its broadest sense, social, philosophical and historical, as well as aesthetic, the first half of the nineteenth century so bristles with heresies—utopias, apocalypses and palingeneses—as to make the eighteenth century look tame by comparison. But even if it was only a portent among many others, the *Vie de Jésus* was certainly one of those which provoked the most impressive emotional release.

As to the Church, it had recognised the value of Chateaubriand's *Le Génie du Christianisme* as an apologia, while officially condemning it, and encouraged the rhetorical interpretation of Christianity by Lacordaire during the thirties. By countenancing the dilution of religion in its own interests, it was thus partly responsible for the fact that by 1863 there was a public receptive to the message of the *Vie de Jésus.* Renan's danger to the Church of course lay in the fact that he diluted Christianity in the interests of the devil's party and did so by starting from a downright rejection of the supernatural.

In the *Vie de Jésus* romantic sensibility is allied with a scholarship far superior, in spite of its weaknesses, to that of a Christian apologist like Chateaubriand. It is in fact a product of that refinement of religious feeling which Renan defended in his essays and critical studies of the fifties. But what was defensible in theory did not in this case always lead to artistically satisfactory creation. In the earlier part of the work Jesus has been refined to the point of being a figure of pastoral too far removed from contact with the real world. It is difficult to believe on any grounds that Jesus was 'charming'. It becomes more difficult to believe when one remembers that Renan was interpreting the Gospels with a view to 'harmonising' them. In other words, the literary qualities which earned the work its success when it appeared make it difficult to read today. Moreover, in spite of the scholarly control brought to bear on the texts this *Life* is undeniably an idealised portrait of Renan himself. For that reason on the other hand it is of interest to his biographer, and can be read for what it reveals of the mind and sensibility of a representative nineteenth century Frenchman, of wide culture, essentially sophisticated in his approach to religion, and yet uncritical enough to project himself on to his subject.

Yet Renan does not only appear in the work as the charming preacher of a lakeside idyll; he also portrays himself in more fanatical guise as the Jesus who suffered crucifixion. But he could not do this without at the same time presenting a historical reconstruction of a religion in the making, and it is here that he showed no small degree of insight and originality. His aim was to give a conjectural account of Jesus' life and the origins of Christianity, so he had no intention of making a contribution to the quest for the historical Jesus. His intention was to say not what really happened, but what might have happened. A romantic even in his scholarship, he even went so far as to say that if he were offered a 'definitive analysis' of the life of Jesus he would find it unacceptable, its clarity being proof of its inadequacy. This apparently perverse opinion illustrates his preference for obscurity in religion and in the history of religious origins. He was, in other words, drawn to the origins of religion because they were obscure, just as he preferred to think of God as mysteriously remote rather than clearly present in the world.

As to his attitude to his sources, his aim can be said to have been to interpret a mainly legendary tradition and there seems, incidentally, no reason why this should not be described as historical. For him, as in general for the so-called 'mythological' school of exegetists, the Gospels were legends with some basis in history.[1] They were not eye-witness accounts of the events which they narrated, but redactions of a popular, oral tradition. They were legends, in particular, because they contained miracles. Renan does not for that reason reject them as unhistorical, but he does not believe that they are truthful in the sense of giving reliable information about the supernatural. Legends then are unhistorical because they are not factual records. They are historical in so far as they lend themselves to explanation and interpretation on the assumption that miracles are due to the popular imagination either inventing a supernatural event when nothing occurred or else transforming an actual event.

According to the view under discussion, legends do give information about the religious consciousness of those who created them. 'Not the world, not objective existence and happenings are the scene of myth and religion, nor do religious tales pretend to be giving information on that score. What else is historical criticism of these Biblical stories doing if not following through to the end Schelling's thought that the active subject of mythology is to be sought in human consciousness itself and not somewhere outside it?'[2] One recognises here, with certain differences, Renan's conception of religion in *L'Avenir de la Science* and confirmed for him by his visit to Rome.

This did in fact involve him in certain difficulties relating to the question whether Jesus was a legendary creation or a person who really existed. It is sufficient here to remark that by 1863 he had convinced himself that Jesus had existed and exercised an irresistible moral fascination on his disciples. It therefore became necessary for him to show how the life of an existent being was caught up into a process of legendary invention about him.

For him, Jesus was not all 'sweetness and light' as he was for Matthew Arnold. He shows how in the face of opposition from the incredulous Jesus was forced to become a thaumaturge and even led to practise deception (a notion which profoundly shocked Catholics at the time, notably Montalembert) because of the obstinacy of the sceptical or the naïvety of the credulous who would not have believed in him had he not worked miracles. In accordance with one of Renan's favourite maxims, Jesus had to sully the purity of his ideal in order to succeed in his mission.

The same exigency explains the apocalyptical and messianic side of his teaching. His messianic legend grew up around him during his lifetime and he was powerless against it, even if, we are assured, he had wanted to keep himself free from what the popular imagination required of him. It was the product of a 'wholly spontaneous conspiration', a legendary transformation deriving from the Jewish prophetic books and years of Jewish national frustration. He was the sort of person the popular imagination saw sitting at God's right hand on the Day of Judgment. He was, in short, a religious leader trying to bring about a moral revolution through the people; all great changes, Renan asserts, are brought about through the people, but whoever leads them has to fall in with their 'illusions'. The crucifixion is the culmination of this pressure from the people in the sense that it forces Jesus into the role of a God who wills his own sacrifice. His death is thus described in Nietzschean terms as a heroically self-transcending act and an expression of the will to power over intractable human material. He had struggled with reality in the name of the ideal; the tension involved in this became intolerable and could only be broken by his death. But if he died a heroic death he died none the less a dupe of his own illusory belief that his death would usher in the Kingdom of Heaven. (Renan is, however, too discreet to say this openly.)

Thus the divine victim ascends into Heaven where the human imagination has placed him and so achieves immortality by living on in the mind of the race. He achieves it, in Renan's opinion, without the taint of egoism which makes ordinary mortals, including himself on his own admission, hope for a reward beyond the grave. Thus Jesus set him an example of selfless devotion to the cause of mankind.

The kingdom which he did found was the kingdom of the soul, without rites, temples or priests, where, Renan asserts, is to be found what is vainly sought for on earth, spiritual perfection and saintliness, complete detachment from the defilement of the world, 'freedom, in short, which society excludes as an impossibility, and which can only be enjoyed to the full within the mind'. What one misses here is any suggestion that Jesus preached a religion of love. Renan even goes so far as to impute to him the disdain which he himself felt towards the world, or as he calls it, 'cette grande doctrine du dédain transcendant'. This tendency in him had already been noticed by Schérer in 1859 who connected it with an intellectual dandyism and used of it the word 'dilettantisme' destined to be applied so indiscriminately to Renan in the latter part of his life.

Sainte-Beuve had also noted his fear of the banal. 'Not even M. Royer-Collard', he had written, 'was more anxious to belong to an élite and to share his thoughts with a select number than M. Renan is by instinct.'[3] That 'transcendental disdain' should be compatible with worshipping Jesus in spirit and truth certainly requires one to make radical alterations to one's notions of what Jesus stood for!

The commandment that Jesus should be so worshipped was, he maintains, applicable to a world which endures and not to one on the point of coming to an end. At the same time, he points out that this doctrine of the inner kingdom would not have established itself if Jesus had not sought death in the illusory belief that it would bring in the apocalyptic kingdom. Messianism then was the dynamic which ensured the permanence of the creed which Renan tried to put into practice himself. It is clear from this that he was not just a liberal historian who denied the messianic side of Jesus' teaching any value. He even admits that he himself takes refuge in the hope that the apocalypse will eventually come true in order to make up for the dissatisfaction which he feels over the actual world. The same wish-fulfilment has been seen to be present in his letter on the history of the cosmos to Berthelot in 1863.

In writing the *Vie de Jésus,* then, he was bearing witness on behalf of a religious humanism against the Scribes and Pharisees of the Catholic Church. Christianity for him had value because it manifested what was divine in human nature. The birth of Christianity was a sort of collective travail of the popular mind from which was delivered the person of the Messiah. Jesus was divine in the sense that he brought out the urge to god-making latent in human nature and because he was the finest expression of the divine which it could conceive. In so far then as Renan projected himself into the person of Jesus he imagined what it was like to be a god in the imperfect world of men and in so doing, reluctant though he was to admit it, he involved himself in the religious life of his time.

The central message of the work then is both coherent and convincing. One is persuaded that this is how Christianity might have come into being, not only because one knows that mass movements makes gods of those who lead them, but because Jesus the charismatic leader and victim of a collective myth is a tragic and compelling figure.

Notes

1. He was however far from being a slavish disciple of German scholars, which was how his Catholic critics tended to regard him. See e.g. the article previously referred to, 'Les Historiens critiques de Jésus', and the introductions to the volumes of the *Origines.*

2. E. Cassirer, *The Problem of Knowledge,* New Haven, 1950, p. 304.

3. *Nouveaux Lundis,* 5e éd., 1875, vol. 2, p. 415.

Richard M. Chadbourne (essay date 1968)

SOURCE: Chadbourne, Richard M. "Comedy of History." In *Ernest Renan,* pp. 65-84. New York: Twayne Publishers, 1968.

[*In the following excerpt, Chadbourne discusses Renan's biographical and historical treatment of Jesus, concentrating on the author's groundbreaking effort to recreate a modern and believable image of Jesus as man.*]

I THE GALILEAN REALITY

The first paragraph of Chapter One of *Vie de Jésus* ("The Place of Jesus in World History") states three ideas that will govern the entire *Origines du christianisme*: first, the "revolution" of Christianity is "the principal event in the history of the world"; second, this revolution required almost a thousand years to be achieved, that is, seven centuries to emerge from its Jewish antecedents and almost three centuries to establish itself as a "new religion"; and third, its immediate origins date from the reigns of Augustus and Tiberius, its founder being "a superior person" (*une personne supérieure*).

For the historical fact supporting this third idea Renan relies on the Synoptic Gospels and, to a lesser extent, on the Fourth Gospel.[1] Much less of a skeptic in this respect than Strauss or the liberal French Protestant exegetes, he believes that the Gospels have some historical validity; his narrative is based on an attempt to disengage history from legend in these sources. Under the heading of "legend" he classifies all the "miracles," on the a priori ground that the "miracle," understood as the specific intervention of a superhuman power in the operation of nature, is an impossibility. Jesus is "miraculous" only in the sense that he is governed by a fresh and powerful religious instinct, a primitive psychology with laws of its own, befitting the "childhood of humanity" and lost to modern men in a reflective and analytical age. But strangely different though his nature may be from ours, he remains bound by nature; he is a *miracle psychologique.*[2]

Traditional Catholic "lives" of Jesus had tended to be long on dogma and apologetics, and short on history. In fact, to term them "lives" at all may be a misnomer: the Protestant religious historian, Maurice Goguel, calls Renan's "the first *Vie de Jésus* to appear in a Catholic country."[3] Renan's Jesus is rooted in his race, his country, and his time, very much like the Racine or Byron of Taine's literary criticism; the difference lies in his degree of greatness and influence. He is a Jew, the perfect fruit of a long race of Jewish prophets, but his vision of goodness is shaped by the gentle pastoral beauty of the Galilean landscape, in contrast with the harsh landscape of Jerusalem. Galilee and Jerusalem are the positive and negative poles of this biography. The *Vie de Jésus,* unique in this way among all the books of the Judeo-Christian cycle, is cast as a pure idyll or pastoral. Serenity and joyousness, even gaiety, prevail. The sadness and suffering of Holy Week come as a kind of surprise, jarring with all that precedes. It has been said that Renan's Jesus has the flaw of being a mirror of Renan, and there is some truth in the charge. Yet in a number of important respects there is sharp dissimilarity between the historian and his subject, most strikingly in the fact that Jesus, unlike his historian, is not a learned man (*un savant*). To have ascribed to Jesus the limited knowledge, indeed the errors, of his age was perhaps Renan's most audacious stroke.[4]

The greatness of Jesus, for Renan, lies in his having given perfect, definitive expression to the age-old Hebrew dream of a universal religion of the spirit, without rites, doctrine, or external forms. He is the supreme *ébionite,* or believer in the brotherhood and moral equality of all men, including the poor and the lowly. Politically conservative (a feature his disciples will perpetuate), he is, in his preaching against the rich and respectable, socially revolutionary, in fact anarchistic. But above all—these are the epithets that recur most often—he is gentle (*doux*), delightful (*délicieux*), charming (*charmant, ravissant*). Renan has been ridiculed for his excessive use, if not abuse, of the adjective *charmant* applied to the Saviour. However, his use of this word is less absurd if we recall the full force of its etymological meaning, most probably the sense in which he intended it, namely, "enchanting," "bewitching," characterized by magic power over others. A modern historian might be inclined to say "charismatic."[5]

II DEIFICATION

The life of Jesus ends, for Renan, with his death on the cross. But this event merely gives further impetus to a process already begun during his lifetime: his deification. Renan had attempted to explain the "miracles" of Jesus as pious inventions of his disciples, or thaumaturgical acts exaggerated out of all proportion. In a manner consistent with this interpretation, he considers the greatest "miracle" attributed to Jesus—his own resurrection—as a legend arising from the understandable enthusiasm of his disciples (initially, from the "hysteria" of Mary Magdalene), who could not accept his mortality, who must, out of their love for him, "do violence to reality." Jesus, he claims, did not believe he was God, but allowed his disciples so to believe.

The transformation of a great religious leader into a God is, for Renan, a recurring pattern of religious history, having almost the force of a law. His pages on the psychology behind the creation of such divine legends are, of course, vital to his argument. The terms he uses ("pious fraud," etc.) are really inadequate, for they still suggest, despite all his careful qualifications, trickery or deceit—the very Voltairian argument he is in fact rejecting. But, although his vocabulary may fail him here, Renan's intentions are clear: the error and proneness to illusion he ascribes to Jesus' disciples are part of that "primitive psychology" for which *L'Avenir de la science* and the earlier philological works have already prepared us, a concrete application of his theory, by now familiar to us, of "humanity's childhood." Falsification of reality on the part of these sublime idealists becomes a kind of creative ignorance, an "illness" raised to the level where "the words healthy and ill are completely relative"—a generous interpretation to which, one need hardly add, Voltaire would not have subscribed.[6]

No life of Christ will ever satisfy everyone. Subjective feeling comes into play in this field, at least for those raised in Judeo-Christian traditions, with a power that it never has, say, when one judges a history of transportation or a history of the sonnet. For all those readers who find Renan's *Vie de Jésus* superficial, distasteful, or shocking, if not blasphemous, there will be as many who find it moving and its portion of truth substantial. The author himself, as he states in his final chapter, firmly believed that his critical approach, by "humanizing" Jesus, restored to him a greater dignity. It seems unfair to dismiss this opening volume of his historical cycle, as many have done, as merely a "novel" or a "poem." Once allowance has been made for the paucity and fragility of the historical sources available and for the probably insuperable difficulties involved in what Albert Schweitzer calls "the quest for the historical Jesus," Renan is essentially attempting in this work no more and no less than what any good historian attempts: to create an image of the past in which he can believe. And Renan can accept a Jesus who is "divine" only in the sense that he brought humanity closer than ever before to the "concept of the divine." The true flaw of his *Vie de Jésus* is not that it is "unhistorical" but that it is partial and one-sided. One wonders, above all, how such a gentle dreamer managed to end up on Calvary.

Notes

1. For Renan's position on the Fourth Gospel, see *Préface,* 13th edition, *Vie de Jésus* (IV, 19-21), and Appendix to same edition, "On the Use Which It Is Appropriate to Make of the Fourth Gospel in Writing the Life of Jesus." Renan retracts his belief that John authored this Gospel but continues to claim some historical value for its narrative portions.

2. Renan had already outlined this concept while still at Saint-Sulpice, in his "Essai psychologique sur Jésus-Christ" (May 1845), first published by Jean Pommier in *Revue de Paris,* Sept. 15, 1920. See also, "Les Historiens critiques de Jésus," *Etudes d'histoire religieuse.*

3. *The Life of Jesus* (trans. Olive Wyon, 1933), p. 50. Goguel is severe in his judgment of the work, but admits that Renan did achieve one thing: "He brought forward the problem of the life of Jesus in such a way that henceforward it was impossible to withdraw it from this leading position" (p. 52).

4. An interesting feature of Ch. III ("Education de Jésus"), in light of the discovery of the Dead Sea Scrolls, is Renan's belief that the Essenians represented a movement parallel to that of Jesus, but with no influence upon him (IV, 106-107). In *The Scrolls from the Dead Sea,* (1955), Ch. V, "What Would Renan Have Said?", Edmund Wilson reports his interview with A. Dupont-Sommer, professor of Hebrew at the Sorbonne and present director of the *Corpus Inscriptionum Semiticarum* founded by Renan, and a scholar "conscious of carrying on what may be called the Renanian tradition" (p. 100).

5. Erwin Goodenough, in *The Church in the Roman Empire* (1931), p. 13, speaks of Jesus' "powerful personal magnetism."

6. *Vie de Jésus,* IV, 367: "Which of us, pygmies that we are, could do what has been accomplished by the foolish Saint Francis of Assisi, the hysterical Saint Theresa of Avila? . . . *Les mots de sain et de malade sont tout relatifs.*"

Selected Bibliography

PRIMARY SOURCES

Original Editions

(PLACE OF PUBLICATION IS PARIS)

Etudes d'histoire religieuse. Michel Lévy, 1857.

Vie de Jésus. Michel Lévy, 1863. First vol. of *Origines.* Revised edition (13th), 1864. Abridged or popular edition, 1864.

Daniel L. Pals (excerpt date 1982)

SOURCE: Pals, Daniel L. "The Earlier Tradition in Britain: Lives from the Reformation to the 1860s." In *The Victorian "Lives" of Jesus,* pp. 19-58. San Antonio: Trinity University Press, 1982.

[In the following excerpt, Pals describes the importance of The Life of Jesus, *arguing that its immense popularity was due as much to Renan's imaginative literary style as the scandal his book's arguments provoked.]*

[Ernest Renan's celebrated *Vie de Jesus*] appeared in France in the middle of 1863, scored an astounding popular success, was translated immediately into the neighboring languages, and came out in Britain before the end of the year. The *Vie* was unquestionably a work of literary genius. Its sentimental charm and imaginative effects captivated the reading public, if not the scholarly community, of Europe. It passed swiftly through countless editions and new printings, earned its author celebrity status, and became beyond its age a literary classic, a book that, in the words of Stephen Neill, "will have readers until the world's end."[1] The author, Joseph Ernest Renan, was an Orientalist at the College de France who once intended to be a priest but lost his faith by reading German critical theology.[2] He was one of those rare men whose natural gifts included both the aptitude for patient, tedious scholarly investigation and the ability to put the results of his study into lucid, elegant, expressive prose. A biography of Christ aimed at the masses was the perfect showcase for such talents, and Renan applied them brilliantly to produce his alluring and unsettling book.

A sceptic and elitist, Renan held aloof from conventional beliefs and dismissed out of hand the traditional supernaturalist view of the scriptures. Like [David Friedrich] Strauss he believed that miracles did not occur; he felt the New Testament evangelists were not exempt from error, confusion, and the limitations of the age in which they lived. If they were inspired, this was only in the sense that the breath of genius has fallen on other human writers both before and after them. Thus, although it was certainly not errorless, the gospel record was in a real measure historical. Unlike Strauss, who [in his life of Jesus] reduced the substrate of fact in the gospels to a bare minimum, Renan believed the historian could recover a good deal of authentic data on the life of Christ. One could detect the basic thread of his ministry, his personal and religious motives, something of his travels and confrontations, and certainly the rare spiritual impact he made on those he met.

Jesus of Nazareth was born to poor parents who, despite the legends later associated with them, had no connection with the royal line of David. As a boy he was raised in the idyllic province of Galilee in the North, a region whose natural beauties contributed much to his disposition. He knew little of the Greeks and Romans, of Jewish sects, or the world outside his native province, though he had studied the Old Testament, especially the Psalms and the book of Daniel, and was acquainted with the maxims of the rabbi Hillel. His temperament was religious. Conscious of a close relation to God, he began as a young man to move about Galilee preaching a simple message of piety and love. He taught that men must understand God as Father and treat others as they would themselves. He spoke often of charity, and of the Galilean landscape, whose every hill and flower seemed to him a revelation of God's design. Men were moved by such words coming from the lips of a young, gentle, winning teacher. Jesus acquired a band of devoted followers.

But shortly he fell under the influence of John the Baptist—a more ascetic teacher who preached a message of judgment, repentance, and imminent world catastrophe. John drew Jesus into the steaming world of Jewish politico-religious passions. Although he at first sought to combine his gentler ideas with John's, Jesus' thinking came gradually to be dominated by the new and harsher conceptions. He meditated on the apocalypse. He began to think of himself as Judaism's long-awaited Messiah, the Son of God who at his final coming would signal the destruction of the present world and the advent of a new one. He came to Jerusalem with these ideas and was not well received, a turn of events which left him disillusioned with Jewish tradition and convinced that the law must be abolished. He then began to entertain the idea of self-sacrifice: the Messiah must be a suffering servant who by his death might bring about the sudden convulsion of the world and the end of days. Almost in spite of himself, Jesus was becoming a fanatic. He encouraged the credulous to believe he worked miracles, and he bitterly attacked the traditions of temple and law. When at length he came again to Jerusalem, his doom was imminent. The rulers had decided it better that he die than that the masses succumb to his delusions. During Passover week they had him seized by night in his favorite garden and carried off to a secret trial. Condemned to death for blasphemy, he was brought to the Roman governor who, alarmed by the crowd and the fanatical hatreds Jesus aroused, allowed him to be executed. He was crucified outside the city, a martyr to the fabrications of his own restless, ever more fanatical mind. His pathetic cry, "My God, my God, why hast thou forsaken me?," fell from the cross unanswered, a sad witness to the fate of a gentle teacher betrayed by the cruelty of men and his own overexcited dreams.

Such were the life and death of Christ. As for the resurrection and rise of Christianity, Renan left these for another work, though not without hinting at the explanation to come.

> Let us say, however, that the vivid imagination of Mary Magdalen played in this circumstance an essential part. Divine power of love! Sacred moments, in which the illusion of an impassioned woman gave to the world a deity risen from the grave![3]

It was Jesus' immediate followers—the women and disciples—who, refusing to accept his death, began to proclaim the supernatural Christ and the dogmas that built the Christian church.

The discussion of Renan's continental impact may be left to others.[4] Even before the English translation appeared, the British press began printing reviews, extended serial assessments, and brief appraisals. Virtually without exception, they were negative, ranging from outrage and invective to serious, heavy-handed refutation and amused sarcasm. As with Strauss, it seemed to be the denial of miracle that offended most. "Like its German predecessor," wrote John Tulloch, one of the more impartial critics,

> the "*Vie de Jesus*" marks the spring-tide of an advancing wave of thought inimical to Christianity. As the former was the result of Hegelian speculation, and of the crisis reached by rationalistic criticism, the natural consummation of the anti-Christian activity of the German intellect through many years; so the work of M. Renan is the result, and, it may be hoped, the consummation, of the course of materialistic thought—known as Positivism—which since then has been active, not only in France, but in England, Germany, and elsewhere, and of an historical criticism divorced from all faith and true reverence.[5]

Wrote another, "It is his principles which are incompatible with belief, in the ordinary sense of the word. It is the premises which are responsible for the conclusion . . . The *first* is a remarkable specimen of pure scientific dogmatism, viz. *that there neither is, nor can be, any such thing as a miracle.*"[6]

Though Renan was less sceptical than Strauss, he still did not hesitate to consign much in the gospels to the shadowy realm of legend, or to argue that the synoptics "long remained in a pliant condition" and grew up by a slow process of accumulation and revision of sayings and events.[7] To this the critic in *Blackwood's Magazine* retorted that "of all modes of producing a picture full of such divine unity, this is about the last which could be supposed successful."[8]

Renan also took a peculiar view of the gospel of John, contending that its sequence of events was accurate while its discourses placed in the mouth of Jesus were fictitious. This was a weak position, which succeeded in producing a rare instance of agreement between the Catholic *Dublin Review* and the rationalist *Westminster,* both of which attacked it as inconsistent and highly improbable.[9] Most repugnant of all, however, was Renan's suggestion that Jesus deceived men into believing he did miracles, then became victim of his own deceptions. The Methodist *London Quarterly,* a strident voice of orthodoxy, was incensed:

> The moral contradictions of this imaginary life are the most palpable and confounding . . . In the *Vie de Jesus* we find, however glozed over by fine words, duplicity, popular tact, self-seeking, higher than imperial ambition, moral weakness and cowardice in adopting opinions and conniving at practices which revolted him, falsehood, nefarious sorcery, rage in disappointment, ferocious invective at his enemies, the convulsions of insanity, and a wild clutch at death as the release from his desperate entanglements.[10]

Comments like this might be adduced from nearly the entire spectrum of religious opinion in Britain. "I trust that the sense of truth and reality . . . will reject the dream of one who pretended to establish a kingdom of God, who cheated men into the belief of it by exhibitions of imaginary power," wrote F. D. Maurice in *Macmillan's Magazine.*[11] "Infantile, ridiculous, ignorant, and off-hand" were the adjectives of the *Literary Churchman.*[12] R. W. Church, Richard Holt Hutton, and H. P. Liddon may be cited as only a few leaders of opinion who expressed similar, if less graphic, disapproval.[13]

There is, incidentally, a revealing side effect to be noted here. In its curious, negative way the menace of the new critical tradition as it first appeared on the British scene uncovered a certain underlying unity among religious factions which had been quarreling fiercely and publicly for decades. The infidelities of Strauss and Renan could be observed drawing various parties of British Christianity into a rather tight circle of defense around the dogmatic articles all regarded as the core of Christian belief. Protestant and Catholic, Church and dissent, High Church and Low, Ritualists and their opponents all seemed agreed that a traditional supernaturalist Christianity was crucial. Though there came to be some spokesmen for it, particularly in the mid-century Broad Church, a wholly naturalistic, liberal Christianity which stressed ethics and the moral teaching of Jesus never got the footing it acquired in Germany. Nor did it produce a Ritschl or Harnack. Instead, leaders from all the existing parties joined hands to attack the new criticism. Church and Liddon were High Churchmen, influenced by the Oxford movement; Tulloch was a Scottish Presbyterian; Maurice a mystical Broad Churchman; the *London Quarterly* spoke for conservative Methodism; the *Dublin Review* for literate Catholicism. Yet all came together in their opposition to the proposals of infidel critics. All held strongly to the inspiration of scripture, belief in miracles, the deity of Christ, the vicarious atonement, resurrection, and eternal life.[14]

Over against this conventional orthodoxy Britain had of course always had its intellectual rebels. There was the coterie of London rationalists whose roots went back to Deism and Tom Paine. As in the case of Hennell, the religious establishment did not feel greatly threatened by this group, particularly since the Evangelical and Oxford revivals of religion early in the century. Since the days of Joseph Butler, orthodoxy had produced apologists equal to the task. Even without such, the churches' entrenched position in the social order allowed them to argue from silence and ignore the gad-flies. But the present circumstance was different; native rationalism was acquiring formidable foreign allies whose arguments drew their strength from the new historical science. Hence the urge to join arms against the foreign critics. It would be false to say that Strauss and Renan realigned the parties of British Christianity, but their threat did awaken a sense of shared tradition and disclosed a bond that, however temporarily, transcended disagreements over ritualism, legal disabilities, and even the age-old problem of popery.

The chief complaints against Renan focused upon his critical assumptions, which seemed arbitrary and unconvincing. While some of the attacks merely vented basic ideological differences, others disclosed the real problems with the book. There certainly was truth in G. K. Chesterton's verdict, uttered much later, that the *Vie* "discredits supernatural stories that have some foundation, simply by telling natural stories that have no foundation."[15] Serious New Testament scholars in France and Germany were unimpressed by the *Vie,* whatever its popular success.[16] Schweitzer's criticisms in the *Quest* bordered on ridicule.[17]

The narrative of the *Vie,* however, was more difficult to fault. There was something so striking, so vivid and imaginative in its execution that even the most embittered critics were forced into grudging compliments. There was in the first place Renan's elegant style, which even a fierce opponent like Liddon conceded to be the *Vie*'s "one and only excellence."[18] Even in translation its fluid grace was apparent, as in this passage on Jesus' early ministry:

> Every one believed that at any moment the kingdom so much desired might appear. . . . No one, during the course of this magic apparition, measured time any more than we measure a dream. Duration was suspended; a week was as an age. But, whether it filled years or months, the dream was so beautiful that humanity has lived upon it ever since, and it is still our consolation to inhale its diluted fragrance. Never did so much joy expand the heart of man. For one moment, in the most vigorous effort she ever made to rise above the world, humanity forgot the leaden weight which

fastens her to earth, and the sorrows of the life below. Happy he who could see with his own eyes this divine unfolding, and share, though but for a day, this unexampled vision.[19]

Imagery of this sort seldom wears well; to contemporary ears it seems slightly excessive and overdrawn. In its day, however, it had appeal, particularly when applied to a subject like the life of Christ, which had so often endured the dry prose of the harmonist.

More important, what Renan conveyed through this language was precisely that sense of romance and Oriental realism which writers like Lant Carpenter and Milman had been hinting at decades earlier. Most of the *Vie de Jesus* had been written in 1860-61, while Renan and his sisters traveled in Palestine with a party exploring ancient Phoenicia. In the Introduction he recorded the powerful effect of this landscape upon his thinking:

> I have traversed, in every sense of the term, the Gospel region; I have visited Jerusalem, Hebron, and Samaria; scarcely any important locality in the history of Jesus has escaped me. All this history, which seems at a distance to float in the clouds of an unreal world, took thus a form, a solidity, which astonished me. The striking agreement of the texts and the places, the marvellous harmony of the Gospel idea with the country which served it as a framework, were to me a revelation. Before my eyes I had a fifth Gospel, torn but still legible; and from that time, through the narratives of Matthew and Mark, I saw, instead of an abstract being who might be said never to have existed, an admirable human figure living and moving.[20]

As much as anything, it was this "fifth gospel," this aspect of ancient time and place, of Jewish customs and character and social life which added fresh color and a novel look to Renan's work. To be sure, he achieved some of this effect by artifice, as when he gave biblical characters Hebrew names rather than their customary Western Christian equivalents. As the *Dublin Review's* critic shrewdly observed,

> A good half of the effect of M. Renan's book would be destroyed if he were made to use the common established names for persons and things. We have heard before of the Children of Israel, with their Law and their Prophets; but we bow down with awe before the Beni-Israel, the Thora, and the Nabis. Annas and Caiaphas, Judas Iscariot, Bartholemew, Joseph of Arimathea—we have known them from our childhood: but they have quite a new look as Hanan and Kaiapha, Judas of Kerioth, Nathanael Bar-Tolmai, and Joseph of Haramathaim.[21]

Still, the peculiar texture of the *Vie* arose from more than clever verbalisms. Renan was suitably equipped for his task. He was a Hebraist, well-grounded in Talmudic learning, and intimately acquainted with the social and physical landscape of ancient Judaism. His success throughout Europe was no accident.

More precisely, what were the effects of the *Vie* in Britain? They were several—and significant. First, there was the impact of its style. Since the gospel story is as old as Christendom, it faces the perennial hazard of becoming stale through familiarity. Sermons, moral exhortations, pious meditations must return with numbing frequency to the same incidents, the same discourses, the same miracles, the same narrative of passion and death. With Renan the story passed to a hand with the novelist's touch, a writer whose sketches of character and scenes had a living quality. For all the controversy it aroused, Strauss's Life was obscure and unread; it made its mark, like many German books, by reputation. Renan's book was different. It could be read, and it was very interesting. If it was scandalous, so much the better; people seemed to read it both because of the outrageous views and in spite of them. After the *Vie*, it may be said, a fresh, attractive, novelistic style comes to be a virtual prerequisite for a successful Life of Christ.

Second, Renan had mastered the art of what we may call historical romance. His evocations of the ancient scenes drawn from visits to the Holy Land did indeed function as a fifth gospel, for readers as well as the author. Granted that some of this effect was achieved by such contrivances as the strange spelling of proper names. For readers it was nonetheless a pleasing experience to gain from the *Vie* the distinct "feeling" for ancient Galilee that one got from Walter Scott for medieval Rotherwood forest, or from Carlyle for Paris under the Reign of Terror. Just how "religious" this romantic sentiment was is perhaps open to question. Yet there was little doubt that it seemed to further religious ends. Richard Holt Hutton of the *Spectator* confessed the paradox of the book: "I have never read a professedly sceptical book that tended more powerfully to strengthen the faith it struggles to supplant."[22] Renan's graphic style and historical romance had cleared a path for the kind of Life that transcended dry debates of the harmonists and the conventional style of the devotionists. Future writers could not ignore his work and still hope to succeed.

The *Vie* also taught a negative lesson, however. No matter how good the historical and stylistic innovations, no Life could be truly successful if it were wedded to such unequivocal anti-Christian scepticism. Success achieved on these terms could only be the success of scandal. The writer of Britain's definitive Life needed an orthodox voice.

Notes

1. Neill, Stephen. *The Interpretation of the New Testament, 1861-1961.* Oxford: Oxford University Press, 1964. p. 193.

2. Schweitzer, Albert. *The Quest for the Historical Jesus.* Trans. W. Montgomery. London: A. and C. Black 1910, 1922. p. 180.

3. Ernest Renan, *Life of Jesus,* tr. and rev. from the twenty-third ed. (Boston: Little, Brown, and Co., 1917) 402. The *Vie* was the first volume of a projected series on the "Origines du Christianisme"; it was in the second volume, "Les Apôtres," that Renan traced the rise of the dogmatic Christ of Paul and the apostles. For the sake of brevity, references to specific passages of the *Vie* have been omitted from the summary of its narrative.

4. A brief discussion of Renan's impact on the continent may be found in Maurice Goguel, *The Life of Jesus,* tr. Olive Wyon (1932; New York: Macmillan, 1944) 50-53; p. 53 n. 3 provides a list of some of the numerous responses to Renan in France and Germany.

5. John Tulloch, *The Christ of the Gospels and the Christ of Modern Criticism: Lectures on M. Renan's "Vie de Jesus"* (London: Macmillan and Co., 1864) 3-4.

6. "Renan's *Life of Jesus,*" *Edinburgh Review* 119 (April 1864) 578.

7. Renan, Introduction to the *Life of Jesus,* 44: "That the Gospels are in part legendary is quite evident, inasmuch as they are full of miracles and of the supernatural."

8. "The Life of Jesus," *Blackwood's Edinburgh Magazine* 96 (October 1864) 428.

9. "Renan's 'Vie de Jesus,'" *Dublin Review,* n.s. 2 (April 1864) 406-10; "Contemporary Literature: Theology and Philosophy," *Westminster Review,* n. s. 24 (October 1863) 540.

10. "Renan's Life of Jesus," *London Quarterly Review* 22 (April 1864) 296.

11. F. D. Maurice, "Christmas Thoughts on Renan's Vie de Jesus," *Macmillan's Magazine* 9 (January 1864) 196.

12. "Ernest Renan," *The Literary Churchman and Critical Record of Current Literature,* 1 October 1863. This was the second in a series of chapter by chapter reviews of the *Vie de Jesus* which ran into 1864. The *Literary Churchman* also gave extensive coverage to French replies to Renan.

13. Church reviewed the *Vie de Jesus* unfavorably in the *Guardian,* 9 September 1863; his essay is reprinted in R. W. Church, *Occasional Papers,* 2 vols. (London: Macmillan and Co., 1897) 190-204; Hutton's review, "M. Renan's 'Christ,'" appeared in the *Spectator* and is reprinted in Richard Holt Hutton, *Theological Essays,* 3d ed. rev. (London: Macmillan & Co., 1888). Liddon had severe words for Renan in a note on "Lives of our Lord" appended to the published version of his

Bampton Lectures for 1866; see H. P. Liddon, *The Divinity of Our Lord and Savior Jesus Christ,* 7th ed. (London: Rivingtons, 1875) 506-7. A register of pamphlets and book-length replies may be found in the *Brit. Mus. Catalogue,* s.v. "Renan, Joseph Ernest."

14. Tulloch was somewhat of an exception since he did not hold as keenly to traditional doctrines, and he grew more open to new views as time passed. See chapter three (p. 113 below) on his support for the Theological Translation Fund.

15. G. K. Chesterton, *Orthodoxy* (1908; Garden City, New York: Image Books, 1959) 43.

16. Goguel, *Life of Jesus,* 50-53, records the disillusionment of Eduard Reuss and the Strasbourg scholars when they opened the *Vie.*

17. Pp. 180-92.

18. Liddon, *Divinity of Our Lord,* 506.

19. Renan, *Life of Jesus,* 218-19.

20. Ibid., 72.

21. "Renan's Vie de Jesus," 396. The author, according to the *Wellesley Index to Victorian Periodicals,* ed. Walter Houghton, 2 vols. (Toronto: University of Toronto Press, 1966, 1972), s.v. "Dublin Review," was Father Henry James Coleridge, S. J., who was later to contribute much to British Catholic literature on the life of Christ.

22. "M. Renan's 'Christ,'" 306-7.

Elisabeth Hurth (essay date 1992)

SOURCE: Hurth, Elisabeth. "The 'Uses' of the 'Literary' Jesus: Ernest Rénan's *Life of Jesus* in New England." *ESQ* 38, no. 4 (1992): 315-37.

[*In the following essay, Hurth argues that although* The Life of Jesus *inspired much discussion and even imitation in nineteenth-century New England, the work's central position rejecting the divinity of Jesus was usually dismissed.*]

"There are two ways of writing the Life of Jesus," the *North American Review* observed in 1864. "The one is simply to ascertain and arrange the facts of his external history; the other is, then to go on and so interpret and explain those facts as to make it seen and felt what manner of man he was in spirit and purpose." A "life" of this latter kind seemed to the *Review* "still . . . eminently needed." It was necessary to have "first, . . . a conviction founded on internal and external evidence that Jesus is the name of a real man, and not of a ficti-

tious one; then, . . . to appreciate his true relation at once to God and to man. And then, too," it was believed, "the life of Jesus [would] be brought into such a light that it [could] be seen to be the *Gospel of to-day.*"[1] This step of transmuting the teaching of the historical Jesus into "the Gospel of to-day" was first undertaken in nineteenth-century literary adaptations of the life of Jesus. Here the authors transposed his life from the confines of exegesis and dogmatics to the domain of literature, to the fictional world of adventure, entertainment and pseudohistory. This mode of adaptation grew after 1850 into remarkably popular ways of demonstrating the contemporary relevance of the history of Jesus and reached a climax with Charles M. Sheldon's *In His Steps* (1897), which owed its extraordinary popularity once again to the express departure from the dry prose of the exegete.

The application of literary techniques to the life of Jesus spanned a broad spectrum. There were variations of martyr fiction, such as William Ware's *Probus* (1835) and Eliza B. Lee's *Parthenia; or, The last days of Paganism* (1858); dramatizations of the experience of Jesus' early followers, such as Florence M. Kingsley's *Titus, a Comrade of the Cross* (1895), *Stephen, a Soldier of the Cross* (1896), and *Paul, a Herald of the Cross* (1897); versions of historical romance, such as Ware's *Julian; or, Scenes in Judea* (1841), Maria T. Richard's *Life in Judea* (1855), and Joseph Holt Ingraham's *The Prince of the House of David* (1855); and adaptations in the form of realist novels, such as Harriet Beecher Stowe's *Footsteps of the Master* (1877) and Elizabeth Stuart Phelps's *The Story of Jesus Christ* (1898).[2] The transformation of the life of Jesus into entertaining fiction subverted critical exegesis and complex theological doctrines. In the fictional "lives" of Stowe, Phelps, and Ingraham, exegetical techniques were clearly subordinated to the requirements of narrative effect and dramatic force. Displacing theological doctrine by secularizing the religious bestseller, these literary adaptations offered a way of reading the biblical narratives without the burden of using a complex exegetical apparatus and of establishing confidence in the availability of the historical Jesus.

American audiences became acutely aware of this point when they were confronted in 1863 with Ernest Rénan's translation of the life of Jesus into fiction, a translation undertaken from the viewpoint of the literary artist rather than the historical critic. Rénan "humanized" the life of Jesus, combining criticism with fiction and investing the historical figure with the glamour of romance and "oriental" realism. Rénan thus conveyed a sense of the Palestinian landscape which he had experienced first hand. "All this history," he observed, "which at a distance seems to float in the clouds of an unreal world, . . . took a form, a solidity, which [revealed] . . . the striking agreement of the texts with the places, the marvellous harmony of the Gospel ideal with the country which served it as a framework." This "fifth Gospel, torn, but still legible," followed the pattern of sentimental history and was designed to leave an aesthetic impression. Jesus "returned, then, into his beloved Galilee," Rénan wrote of his "hero," "and found again his heavenly Father in the midst of the green hills and the clear fountains—and among the crowds of women and children, who, with joyous soul and the song of angels in their hearts, awaited the salvation of Israel."[3] Shying away from theological controversy and exegesis, Rénan thus popularized the historico-critical interests of Leben-Jesu researchers like H. E. G. Paulus and David Friedrich Strauss. Though in this respect his "life" appeared regressive and deficient, it found a ready market.[4] While the critical tradition of Strauss remained esoteric and unpopular among American audiences, the reliance on sentimental history contributed to Rénan's success as a bestselling religious author. Yet the story of the American reception of Rénan's life of Jesus also embodies a negative lesson. However vivid and entertaining his portrait of an amiable young "visionary," the transposition of the life of Jesus into the realm of fiction was only deemed acceptable by American reviewers if it avoided anti-Christian skepticism and if it fed into the cause of a precritical evidentialism affirming the historicity of the Jesus figure.

1

Rénan's attempt to sever history from theology and divest the life of Jesus of traditional dogma was not new for New England audiences. The breakup of the supernatural rationalist framework had already come to a high point with the publication of Strauss's *Leben Jesu* in 1835. The discussions of Strauss's work by Charles Hodge, "Strauss' Life of Jesus" (1837), Theodor Parker, "D. F. Strauss's Das Leben Jesu" (1840), Horatio B. Hackett, "Critique on Strauss's Life of Jesus" (1844), and Stephen G. Bulfinch, "Strauss's Life of Jesus:— The Mythic Theory" (1845), indicate that the entry of the *Leben Jesu* on the New England theological landscape directly involved the crucial issue of the historicity of Jesus. What in fact ignited these denunciations of Strauss was not his Hegelian conclusion but the alarming assertion that, since the gospel accounts were impregnated with mythical elements, next to nothing could be known about the historical Jesus.[5] At the core of Strauss's Hegelianism was the contradiction of positing one person as both human and divine. At this juncture, Hegelianism provided the "key to the whole of Christology" by excluding the possibility that a single individual could be the complete embodiment of God-man unity.[6] As Bulfinch, Hackett, and Parker acutely realized, Strauss, in denying that the divine idea of God-man unity could be identified with a particular historical individual or event, parted company with contemporary tradition not only in exegesis but also in

philosophy. On the exegetical front, Strauss left his American audiences with a Christianity desupernaturalized and stripped of miracles. On the philosophical front, he arrived at a Christianity depersonalized and anonymous, reducing Jesus to nothing more than a gifted genius whom legend had gradually deified. In this account, the Christian faith could be explained without reference to the Jesus of history. Strauss's "life" in this way firmly stayed on the side of the negative critique: it did not arrive at an "historical core," nor did it in fact set out to inquire after one.

Against an apologetic mode of appropriation which sought to embrace the findings of the new historical criticism without sacrificing the framework of evidentialism, Strauss's "speculative" approach "had a bad name." With thinkers like Andrews Norton, Octavius Brooks Frothingham's history of Unitarianism judged that Strauss was a "man of straw" who relinquished all claims to the "genuineness" and historical factuality of the gospel tradition.[7] Rénan's historical romance of Palestine, by contrast, at first sight seemed to be sharply set apart from the critical tradition of Leben-Jesu researchers like Strauss. Rénan's portrayal of the historical Jesus invested the narrative of his life with an immediacy and dramatic force which readers were accustomed to associate with secular romances. This literary portrait did not produce a "theoretical Christ," as Strauss had, with the "attributes of the hegelian Christ," but rather "the historical Christ, who bore the name of Jesus."[8] Under this premise the *Life of Jesus* presented a figure not of dogma and doctrine but of psychology, a "gentle," "delightful" preacher of a lakeside idyll who spread amidst the picturesque Galilean countryside a "religion de l'humanité."[9] "As often happens in very elevated natures," Rénan observed of his "great man," "tenderness of the heart was transformed in him into an infinite sweetness, a vague poetry, and a universal charm." This "poetic" approach to history posited "a form, a solidity," in scriptural history which affirmed, "in place of an abstract being, whose existence might have been doubted, . . . an admirable human figure," a man "living and moving" (47, 23). Rénan thus attested that the synoptics contained a history of the ministry of Jesus which permitted the reconstruction of authentic data and not merely of the attributes of "symbol" and "myth."

But in this reconstruction the traditional supernatural view of the Scriptures had no place. Rénan's rationalistic and pragmatic conception reduced the miracles of Jesus to pious inventions or thaumaturgical acts misinterpreted by his disciples in their religious enthusiasm. For Rénan, the miracles were in most cases frauds staged by Jesus himself. Rénan's Jesus portrait in this context traced the fall of an idealistic moralist who claimed the title of the "Son of God" for his mission and corrupted his pristine character in a futile effort to validate his divine mission in front of unbelieving crowds. In Jerusalem, Jesus entrapped and lost himself, Rénan supposed: Jesus became a "victim" of the fabrications of his own fanaticism. The "simple" teacher was entrapped by a mechanism which projected a messianic mission into his "divine nature," a mechanism which finally forced Jesus into the role of a God who sacrifices himself.[10]

Rénan's assertions stood in direct antagonism to supernaturalist studies in the older tradition of harmonies and devotional lives of Jesus—studies like Lant Carpenter's *Apostolical Harmony of the Gospels,* which offered American audiences a remarkably popular attempt to rehabilitate evidentialist premises by means of narrative realism. Carpenter's introductory dissertations on the Palestinian background of Jesus' time sought to "afford a distinct and vivid conception of scenery in which the heart must ever feel a holy interest."[11] As in the case of Rénan, a distinctly literary sensibility translated the life of Jesus into the terms of the discussion about evidences for or against factual claims, yielding an ally against disintegrating historical skepticism in the manner of Strauss. But in contrast to Rénan, Carpenter led his readers out on the side of orthodoxy with express appeals to miracles and clear assertions of Christ's divinity.

For Unitarian reviewers like William Henry Furness, the historical Jesus still carried the imprints of the dogmatic Christ of faith. Therefore, "language" failed Furness "in the attempt to describe the energy, the divine life, which appears in the character of Jesus, when he is contemplated as endowed with supernatural gifts."[12] This affirmation of the difficulty, if not impossibility, of an adequate Jesus portrait derived from a staunch adherence to supernaturalist premises of which Unitarian reviewers found no adequate literary and critical representation in Rénan. Judged against these premises, Rénan's "life" was insufficient and unacceptable. It was, reviewers charged, "a prime and fatal flaw in the very corner-stone of a theory of the life of Jesus, to begin with eliminating the supernatural element." "To bring back to this age the living Christ" required bringing into play both "historical" and "supernatural element[s]."[13] In this alignment of the two elements, the supernatural rationalist stance with its skepticism about the possibility of penetrating the psychology of Jesus acutely resurfaced. Unitarian reviewers firmly believed "in a peculiar influence exercised by God over his Son from the first miraculous inception of his being" and therefore did not "know . . . how to form from the development of other minds any theory of spiritual growth applicable."[14] This reassertion of supernaturalism precluded a biographical, developmental approach to the life of Jesus. All attempts to subject this pristine figure to "aesthetic" or "poetic" refinements in the manner of Rénan were therefore judged to be utterly deficient.

Ernest Renan, 1823-92.

Unitarian audiences, then, preferred works which aligned the "character" of Jesus with "a practical and pious" "motive" and did not, "like Rénan, invade or depreciate the moral character of Jesus" or merely produce "a free, imaginative construction."[15] These intentions, the *Christian Examiner* judged, emerged in studies in which the renditions of biblical history went hand in hand with authentic observations in "philology" and "archaeology." Robert Tornbull's *Christ in History* (1830), Harriet Martineau's *Traditions of Palestine* (1830), and above all Hackett's *Illustrations of Scripture; suggested by a tour through the Holy Land* (1855) were applauded as "invaluable" because they used "actual observation" and "original" illustrations to reconstruct Jesus' "character."[16] While Rénan's descriptive sketches dismissed out of hand the orthodox Christ, Hackett confirmed the factual truth of the biblical record and bolstered the evidence supplied by miracle and prophecy.

Those reviewers of Rénan who were committed to the transcendentalists' insistence on the divinity of man and the naturalness of miracles had other preferences. It was not Rénan's emphasis on the gradual corruption of Jesus' "character" that this camp singled out, but rather the view of him as a "great" and "inspired" man.

Rénan's historical romance of Palestine framed religious history in terms of the romantic theory of "genius" as determined by individual personalities. This application of the fictional convention of the "hero" to the life of Jesus assigned to him a place among the great men of history in a manner reminiscent of Emerson's notion of the "representative man." Thus Emerson stressed after his encounter with the *Vie de Jésus* that "when [he] wrote 'Representative Men,' [he] felt that Jesus was the 'Rep. Man' whom [he] ought to sketch: but the task required great gifts—steadiest insight & perfect temper; else, the consciousness of want of sympathy in the audience would make one petulant or sore, in spite of himself."[17] Emerson, then, found in Rénan a conception of Jesus as a poetic symbol validating the "new school's" premise that not Jesus alone but every spirit in human form was a divine. Rénan in this way seemed to concur with the intentions of a movement whose "mission" was "to spiritualize the too hard and literal Christianity that is common and make the religion of Jesus a true and more sanctifying principle to many souls."[18]

For Emerson, Christ was the poet whose task was to be "sayer" and "namer." Like Christ, the poet is "representative" and "stands among partial men for the complete man." The "office" of both is "to show . . . that God is, not was; that He speaketh, not spake." Otherwise, "the true Christianity,—a faith like Christ's in the infinitude of man,—is lost."[19] In this position, the poetic rendering of the person of Jesus went hand in hand with a denial of the historic faith of Unitarianism. On the ground of biblical fiction, however, the fictional adaptation of the historical Jesus was tied to the task of reassurance. Neither the transcendentalist nor the Unitarian reviewers of Rénan were prepared to follow the recurrent attempts of Leben-Jesu researchers like Strauss to deny the historicity of the Christ-event. The scope of responses to Rénan may have been broad enough to include the transhistorical intuitionism of Emerson, yet the underlying consensus was that "without some history of Christ, there could have been no belief in Christ, and no proper Christianity."[20] Rénan thus did not trigger in American thought a substantial reordering of theological discourse and religious experience as did Strauss and Hegel. Critical statements on Rénan's work were still very much consistent with evidentialism and revealed a common ground between the transcendentalist gospel and Unitarian Christianity centering around the historicity of the life of Jesus.

When it came to the "literary" approach of Rénan's historical romance, critics like Charles Timothy Brooks were therefore prepared to admire "M. Rénan's devotion to his 'hero'" and to "acknowledge . . . the charm of the narrative in which [he] has reproduced the events of Christ's marvellous passage across the scene of human life."[21] This reproduction was unanimously held to be far superior to Strauss's. Rénan seemed to Brooks, "equally with Strauss, to build up a Christ of his own out of the wreck of the actual history." But while Strauss substituted "for the historical Jesus an abstraction, M. Renan [supplied] one who [was] intensely flesh and blood and soul and spirit."[22]

The reference to Jesus as a "real person" seemed to validate the traditional historical "evidences" of Christianity which the Unitarian tradition championed. While Strauss left only "threads of historical truth," Rénan admitted "the four canonical Gospels as authentic," tracing them "almost wholly [to] the work of the authors to whom they are attributed."[23] Rénan's reassurances about the gospel sources thus appeared to serve above all else the cause of precritical evidentialism, contributing to a new awareness of the potential of fiction to address problems generated by historical and biblical criticism. The historical Jesus emerged as more "real" when seen against the literary portrayal of the Galilean setting. To summon the historical Jesus into the world of fiction was in this respect to safeguard his historicity and to retrieve him from the skepticism and uncertainty triggered by Strauss's historical criticism.

2

What gave the Unitarian and transcendentalist responses to Rénan coherence was a remarkable optimism about the availability and knowability of the historical Jesus. At a time when New England audiences were increasingly alert to recurrent assertions by Leben-Jesu researchers about the nonhistoricity of the Jesus figure, Rénan provided a "charming" portrait which seemed to affirm that historical knowledge and faith correlated perfectly. For another group of critics Rénan's "life" became the testing ground for a very different point centering around the equation of historic incarnation with a broad humanism. The divine uniqueness and "greatness" of Jesus were tenets no longer unanimously adhered to by the so-called "Free Religionists," left-wing Unitarians of the 1870s and 1880s who were acutely aware of "the inevitable surrender of orthodoxy" and who set out in turn to construct their "liberal movement in theology" upon experiential grounds.[24] Free Religionists denied "that Jesus was the founder of a church; or author either of a religion; of authority in belief, or ethics; or authority in faith."[25] Committed to humanistic convictions, liberal Unitarians from the 1870s onward were skeptical of all "speculative" Christology; "what we need," declared Frothingham, chief exponent of the Free Religionists, "is . . . not some new theory about Jesus, but some new appreciation of the manhood that belongs to every man."[26]

For the left-wing Unitarians gathered in the Free Religion movement, the indwelling of God in humanity was primary; and it was not reserved for the historic Christ only but rather belonged to all humankind. Moreover, Free Religion designated "a system of belief and method of life which grows up in the human mind, independently of any such historic source, preceding only from the soul itself."[27] It was therefore deemed imperative to "emancipate [Christ], as it were, from the limits of race, and to bring the spirit that he was . . . into vital relations with human thought and life."[28] The historic Christ, then, was no elevated divinity, nor a redeemer or savior, but rather a symbol of "humanity."[29]

Rénan's life of Jesus directly played into this interpretation. Appropriating Rénan's terms, Frothingham thus confirmed that indwelling divinity was not limited to the historical Jesus but rather incarnate in the entire human race. Here the "dogmatic" opposition between the Jesus of history and the Christ of faith, running as a recurrent theme through Rénan's study, was fully absorbed. With Rénan, Frothingham was convinced that

> by carrying over to the historical Jesus the impressions that theology had formed of him, and reading his life by the light of pure speculation, . . . men . . . construct a very plausible argument, which crumbles to pieces on the first intelligent perusal of the New Testament. The Christ of the Christian theology is not the Jesus of the Gospels, but a purely ideal person, a conception, an imagination, an intellectual vision, a splendid spiritual dream.[30]

On this basis Frothingham was prepared to acknowledge the biographical-literary approach of Rénan's life of Jesus. Frothingham found "here truly a Life of Jesus of Nazareth, . . . a real human life, with human cares and recreations, helps and hinderances, prudences and mistakes, victories and overthrows."[31]

Yet the reluctance to subject the figure of Jesus to the terms of psychological "development" was also prevalent among Free Religionists who appreciated the uses of Rénan's "literary" Jesus. With Rénan, the history of Jesus turned into "a romance," "pervaded with an atmosphere of natural, simple, pastoral joyousness." Rénan's Jesus was, Frothingham found, "a child of Nature," "a splendid idealist" and "visionary," "a believer in his Utopia, an unconscious and informal, but a true and sincere brother of the Essenes."[32] By contrast, in Frothingham's own version of the history of Jesus, The Cradle of the Christ, "no account [was] given of Jesus, and no account made of him." But "the omission," he explained, "has been intentional. The purpose . . . is to give the history of an idea, not the history of a person, to trace the development of a thought, not the influence of a life."[33] This was not to question the authenticity and historical reliability of the biblical accounts but rather to assert that the historic Christ was "pure spirit" and present everywhere. A fixation in time and place, whether literary or historico-critical, was therefore not possible.

This point coincides with Frothingham's reluctance to approach Rénan as a biblical exegete. Frothingham's position was not primarily critical or exegetical and produced no exegetical scrutiny of Rénan's interpretation. For Frothingham, a purely historical criticism "occupied with the task of establishing the genuineness and authenticity of the writings, . . . explaining texts in accordance with the preconceived theory of a divine origin, vindicating doubtful passages against the objections of skeptics," was insufficient. He judged that this type of criticism falsely "insisted on the necessity of a historical foundation for [Jesus'] character."[34] The biblical record served for Frothingham more as a spiritual guide to life; it did not present the source of theology but rather a source for the moral and ethical ideals of a broad humanism.

This reading went hand in hand with an apologetic stance: suspicious of any detachment of biblical revelation from historical-cultural contexts and skeptical of any references to the mythological, Frothingham was more inclined to replace critical exegesis with a basic loyalty to the historicity and integrity of the person of Jesus. On this count, his position aligned with Furness's Remarks on Rénan's Life of Jesus. Both Furness and Frothingham objected "on grounds higher than critical . . . to [Rénan's] interpretation." Rénan offered "a theory utterly fatal to the moral character of the 'colossal' man he [celebrated], thus sacrificing the moral greatness of Jesus to a perverse sense of historical truth."[35] Furness and Frothingham, in contrast, sought a life of Jesus "written from a spiritual point of view," a "life" in which both psychological causation pertaining to a human figure and doctrinal "attributes of the Christ of our theologians" receded behind "a way of dwelling on each event in the life of [the] Saviour till it [became] a quickening influence in our own hearts."[36]

In these statements it is evident that Frothingham's "Free Religion," commonly regarded by historians of American Protestantism as a "radical" front against Unitarian theology, actually harbored a moderately conservative approach which shied away from Rénan's stripping of the supernatural Christ and his "psychological interpretation" of staged miracles. Frothingham's Cradle of the Christ thus joined forces with those critics who judged that "the most spiritual apprehension of [Jesus] was the truest."[37] Therefore Rénan's "treatment of the materials before him [was] arbitrary and capricious," Frothingham held. Moreover, Rénan was simply "forgetting the place that Jesus holds in the estimation of the world; forgetting the effects he has wrought on the souls, hearts, lives of men." Rénan "imputes to [Jesus]," Frothingham charged, "the weaknesses of ordinary humanity, judges him by the rules he would apply to ordinary men, condemns or praises him, . . . as if he were an unknown actor in the medley of ordinary history."[38] From Rénan, then, Frothingham took the emphasis on the intuitions of the soul, on an "absolute religion" liberated from historical integuments, but the marks of Rénan's anti-Christian skepticism—the explanation of the miracles as pious inventions of the disciples or thaumaturgical acts, and the portrait of a great moralist assuming the title "Son of God" and regressing into an involuntary impostor—he rejected with critical weapons recalling the characteristic ring of Norton's charges against the "modern school" of "infidelity."[39]

3

Rénan's historical romance with its graphic style created a climate favorable to the departure from the dry prose of the life of Jesus harmonies. Edward E. Hale had already deplored in 1858 "the quiet coolness . . . with which . . . critics pass by the changes in the course of the Saviour's life, without any attempt to suggest cause and effect, motive or plan, or indeed any of the evidences of organic life running through the whole."[40] For the "systematic" reconstruction of the "character" of Jesus, historical and stylistic innovations were needed, and on this count American exegetes were prepared to accept more creative renditions in the form of fictional adaptations of the historical Jesus. But this shift to the realm of fiction and social theology was closely tied up with the task of establishing the traditional Christ. Thus H. G. Spaulding observed in the *Christian Examiner* in 1867: "Hitherto we have denied that the teachings of Jesus could have either rind or husk; and, transferring our ideal Christ to the pages of the evangelists, have made sad havoc with truth and nature by our violent theories of accommodation and substitution. A *constructive criticism* of the gospel records is the field of labor which now invites the Christian scholar."[41] On the ground of biblical fiction, this "constructive criticism" expressly precluded Rénan's anti-Christian skepticism. The fictional adaptation of the historical Jesus primarily had to reassure. Fiction here did not represent "a random form of literature, a mere vehicle of amusement," but rather one of the most effective "vehicles" for the perpetuation of evidentialist apologetics, a perpetuation in which the fictional pretense of authenticity and verisimilitude was of one piece with the doctrinal reassertion of the historical reliability of the life of Jesus narratives. In a literary context, "the character of the Saviour himself [was thus] everywhere allowed to stand out in its original, simple truth [and] majesty."[42]

That Rénan's *Life of Jesus* launched this use of the Jesus narrative is confirmed by several literary lives of Jesus which were consciously modelled after its example, the most important New England representations being Stowe's *Footsteps of the Master* and Phelps's *Story of Jesus Christ*. Rénan's pastoral and romantic portrait suggested to these authors that for a life of Jesus no genre affiliation seemed to fit except a literary one. "This book is not theology or criticism nor is it biography," Phelps observed of her life of Jesus. "It is neither history, controversy, nor a sermon. . . . It is a narrative."[43] Stowe felt free to insert poetry into episodes of Jesus' ministry and judged that there was "something wonderfully poetic in the simple history given by the different evangelists of the resurrection of our Lord." "It is like a calm, serene, dewy morning," she reflected, "after a night of thunder and tempest."[44] Phelps's *Story of Jesus Christ* characterized the "luxuriant vegetation of Nazareth" in a pastoral manner similarly reminiscent of the "charming" nature portraits in Rénan's "life": "The green that is half gold melted over the hillsides, and ran riot in the valley. Flowers were at a high tone. The red lamps of the pomegranates were burning freely. Fruit gardens touched in rich, metallic colors to the landscape; gold of apricot, with pale, silver leaves, purple of grape, and yellow-green of fig, passed each in its time."[45]

Beyond the pastoral influence, Phelps's and Stowe's interest in the psychological development of Jesus as a literary "character" echoed Rénan's appropriation of the realist novel. Rénan's "sketch" of the "purely human side of [Jesus'] character," the *Christian Examiner* observed, set out "to show how a gifted and enthusiastic Jewish peasant of the most exquisite temperament and moral genius, under the influence of the stimulating climate and more stimulating traditions of Judea, dreamed himself into a prophet."[46] Similarly, Phelps and Stowe not only presented external descriptions but also glimpses into the inner consciousness of Jesus. But their depiction of the developing Messianic consciousness did not present "a soul half-deluded and half-deluding," nor did they abrogate Jesus' status as "Mediator."[47] Phelps's and Stowe's novelistic adaptations were committed to orthodoxy; both "lives" presented the divine, saving Christ of faith, the "Mediator, both divine and human," "the generous Saviour and Giver," "the citadel" to which "the defenders" of Christianity could "retreat." In a time of "fighting about the outworks of Christianity," Stowe reiterated, "it is time to retreat to the citadel; and that citadel is Christ."[48] To adapt the life of Jesus to literature in this context primarily implied a defense of the soundness of this "citadel."

Hence neither Phelps nor Stowe had any use for theological controversy or vexing exegetical issues. Phelps was anxious to emphasize that she was "not unaware of the differences among New Testament critics," of the conflict between "the intellectual mode and Christian scholarship." Yet she did not allow the "vast controversy" over the life of Jesus Christ to enter into her "personal interpretation." "The life of Christ," Phelps was convinced, "was lived to inspire, not to confuse," and could serve as a source of inspiration quite apart from theological doctrines.[49] Therefore it did not matter to her "whether the star of Bethlehem was a meteor or a miracle, . . . whether Jesus was born in one year or the next, in this month or that." It was, moreover, of no consequence "whether he was baptized in Jordan River or Jordan region. . . . [And] whether Jesus revisited Nazareth once or twice [was] a point not worth two pages of controversy." For both Phelps and Stowe, the "sacred romance" of Jesus' life simply was not to be "torn and mangled" by critical "biographies . . . crowded with . . . erudition" and "tenacious of detail."[50]

The argument itself here was geared to a literary sensibility. In a concerted effort to present a Jesus figure cleansed from theology and exegesis, it sought to minimize theological controversy by sacrificing doctrine to aesthetic impression and sentimental history. Literary adaptations thus offered a figure whom readers "could understand without simultaneously accepting stories which they could no longer understand."[51] This marked a new stage in the complex relation of faith to historical revelation, one in which the life of Jesus was increasingly reconstructed along nonsupernaturalist lines. To summon Jesus into the world of literary novelization thus was to cut him off from the realm of metaphysics and theological doctrine and to tie him to an immanent kingdom of God which "did not seek to put the marvelous on exhibition" but rather asked for personal evangelism.[52]

For this conception of Jesus as primarily moral and spiritual rather than metaphysical and doctrinal, Rénan's "life" remained exemplary, not only because it offered a "living and moving" human being, but more importantly, because it also asserted that one could recover sufficient materials from the Gospels to construct such a portrait. Unlike Rénan's work, however, the narratives of Stowe and Phelps show them struggling with several incompatibilities between the literary claims of fiction and the theological claims of the life of Jesus, incompatibilities figuring as side issues in a much larger debate about the status and potentialities of prose fiction.[53] Against the background of a poetics hostile to fiction, Stowe and Phelps seemed reluctant to offer minute descriptions of Jesus' physical person independent of the scriptural texts. Stowe's novelistic "life" thus reiterated that Jesus and his words should be recorded "without paraphrase, diminution, or addition." The testimony of Scripture was sacrosanct and not to be superseded by creative adaptations. The "footsteps of the Master" were only to be traced in "the dear old book which we call the Bible."[54]

Therefore the "sacred romance" of Jesus' history was not to be regarded as mere "fiction." Phelps and Stowe repeatedly drew back to the time-honored device of claiming that their fictional discourses did in fact record

the truth, including in their novels declarations varying from authorial intrusions to designations of the narrative as "history."[55] Significantly, in these disclaimers, problems of authenticity and verisimilitude coincided with the evidentialist issue of the historicity and verifiability of the historical Jesus. Biblical fiction on the life of Jesus in this way approached the historicity of the Jesus of Nazareth in terms like those applied to the verisimilitude of fiction. To endow the fictional world with historical credibility was thus also to assert that the life of Jesus met general historiographic rules of verification.

Like Rénan's life of Jesus, Phelps's and Stowe's adaptations were prepared to unite literary and biblical interpretation in incipient form and to apply literary categories to the Jesus narratives. Phelps stressed the "simplicity, directness, force [and] persuasiveness" of such treatments.[56] But this transplanting of literary terms immediately issued into statements on the facticity of Jesus' existence and the historicity of his deeds. The body of literary criticism on realist narrative thus could not take hold in the literary renditions of the history of Jesus produced by American practitioners of the historical Jesus quest.

Predominant claims of verisimilitude also created a climate in which those difficulties of historical reconstruction that interested Rénan played no significant role. Crucial results of the historico-critical analysis which Rénan had followed were not assimilated. Suggestions for solving the synoptic problem went unnoticed, as did explorations into redaction criticism undertaken by the Tübingen school under Ferdinand Christian Baur. In their use of scriptural sources, the American advocates of biblical fiction on the life of Jesus entertained no doubts about the substantial reliability of the texts. Questions of critical exegesis and historico-critical method were immediately dissolved into questions of authenticity and credibility.

American practitioners were aware that Rénan's study challenged the presumption that historical research could legitimize faith. They were also aware of Rénan's point that revelation occurred in an historical process subject to later idealization. But none of these considerations could undermine what Furness persistently called "the historical truth" concerning Jesus.[57] "Take the extremest criticism even," the Unitarian Brooke Herford invited his readers,

> suppose that not one of the four Gospels was actually written by those immediate followers of Christ whose names they bear; that it was some generations before the story of Jesus was thus written down at all. This does not affect the main facts. It does not affect the historic reality of that great figure which left such an impress on those around that even for so long, though unrecorded, it kept itself in mind so clearly and distinctly.[58]

Against this background, Rénan's "literary" life of Jesus with its "deformed" character and the accompanying skepticism about scriptural claims of supernaturalism had limited impact against a common front that harmonized faith with history by using literature to bolster biblical evidentialist claims.

Notes

1. [Charles Timothy Brooks], "Rénan's *Life of Jesus,*" *North American Review* 98 (1864): 232.

2. For an analysis of these novels in the context of the historical Jesus quest, see Elisabeth Hurth, *In His Name: Comparative Studies in the Quest for the Historical Jesus* (Frankfurt/M.: Peter Lang, 1989), 180ff., on which the present discussion is based. See also the useful analysis of biblical fiction in David S. Reynolds, *Faith in Fiction: The Emergence of Religious Literature in America* (Cambridge: Harvard Univ. Press, 1981).

3. Ernest Rénan, *The Life of Jesus* (London: Trübner and Co., 1863; London: Watts and Co., 1904), 23, 46. All further references to this reprint of the first English edition of the *Vie de Jésus* are cited parenthetically.

4. See Brooks's assessment in his "Rénan's *Life of Jesus,*" 196-98, and Octavius Brooks Frothingham's in "Rénan's Life of Jesus," *Christian Examiner* 75 (1863): 320-21.

5. See, for example, [Stephen G. Bulfinch], "Strauss's *Life of Jesus*:—The Mythic Theory," *Christian Examiner* 39 (1845): 156.

6. Translated from David Friedrich Strauss, *Das Leben Jesu, kritisch bearbeitet* (*The life of Jesus, critically examined*), 2 vols. (Tübingen: C. F. Osiander, 1835-36), 2:734.

7. Octavius Brooks Frothingham, *Boston Unitarianism, 1820-1850: A Study of the Life and Works of Nathaniel Langdon Frothingham* (New York and London: G. P. Putnam's Sons, Knickerbocker Press, 1890), 70-71.

8. Ernest Rénan, *Studies of Religious History and Criticism,* authorized translation from the original French by Octavius Brooks Frothingham (New York: Carleton, 1864), 185.

9. Ernest Rénan, *Histoire des origines du christianisme* (*History of the origins of Christianity*), vol. 1 (Berlin: J. Springer, 1863), 159. The *Vie de Jésus* was the first volume of a projected series on the "origines du christianisme."

10. Translated from Rénan, *Histoire des origines,* 269.

11. Lant Carpenter, *An Apostolical Harmony of the Gospels,* 2nd ed. (London: Longman, 1838), v.

12. [William Henry Furness], "The Character of Christ, the Interpretation of Christianity; with an Exposition of the Circumstances of his Resurrection," *Christian Examiner* 15 (1834): 289.

13. Brooks, "Rénan's *Life of Jesus,*" 203, 233.

14. [John H. Morison], "Neander's *Life of Christ,*" *Christian Examiner* 46 (1849): 76.

15. [Joseph Henry Allen], "Review of Current Literature," *Christian Examiner* 82 (1867): 105, 107; "Review of Current Literature," *Christian Examiner* 78 (1865): 444.

16. [A. P. Peabody], "Strauss and the Mythic Theory," *North American Review* 91 (1860): 148.

17. *The Journals and Miscellaneous Notebooks of Ralph Waldo Emerson,* ed. William H. Gilman and Ralph H. Orth et al., 16 vols. (Cambridge: Harvard Univ. Press, Belknap Press, 1960-82), 15:224.

18. [Cyrus Augustus Bartol], review of *Theodore; or, The Skeptic's Conversion,* by De Wette, tr. James F. Clarke, vol. 10 of *Specimens of Foreign Literature, Christian Examiner* 31 (1842): 372.

19. *The Collected Works of Ralph Waldo Emerson,* ed. Alfred R. Ferguson and Joseph Slater et al., 4 vols. to date (Cambridge: Harvard Univ. Press, Belknap Press, 1971-), 3:5, 4; 1:89.

20. [F. W. P. Greenwood], "Historical Christianity," *Christian Examiner* 28 (1840): 166.

21. Brooks, "Rénan's *Life of Jesus,*" 206, 212.

22. Brooks, "Rénan's *Life of Jesus,*" 214.

23. William Henry Furness, *Remarks on Rénan's Life of Jesus* (Philadelphia, 1865), 21; Brooks, "Rénan's Life of Jesus," 211.

24. [Minot J. Savage], "The Inevitable Surrender of Orthodoxy," *North American Review* 148 (1889): 711-26; cf. Joseph Henry Allen, *Our Liberal Movement in Theology* (Boston: American Unitarian Association, 1882), 171-72.

25. James Freeman Clarke, *Steps of Belief* (Boston: American Associations, 1880), 139-40.

26. Octavius Brooks Frothingham, *Radical Work* (New York: D. G. Francis, 1868), 16.

27. Clarke, *Steps of Belief,* 141.

28. Octavius Brooks Frothingham, *The Birth of the Spirit Christ: A Sermon,* preached in New York, 28 December 1862, and distributed as a Christmas offering at the First Unitarian Church of Philadelphia on Christmas Day, 1885 (reprinted through

the kindness of a member of the Church in Philadelphia, 1885), 10.

29. Cf. Octavius Brooks Frothingham, *The Religion of
Humanity* (New York: Asak Butts, 1873), 88-90.

30. Frothingham, *Religion of Humanity,* 89.

31. [Octavius Brooks Frothingham], "Rénan's *Life of
Jesus,*" *Christian Examiner* 75 (1863): 320.

32. Frothingham, "Rénan's *Life of Jesus,*" 321, 322,
323, 324, 327.

33. Octavius Brooks Frothingham, *The Cradle of the
Christ: A Study in Primitive Christianity* (New
York: G. P. Putnam's Sons, 1877), 184.

34. Frothingham, *Cradle of the Christ,* 3, ix.

35. Frothingham, "Rénan's *Life of Jesus,*" 338; *Cradle
of the Christ,* 130.

36. Frothingham, "Rénan's *Life of Jesus,*" 334; *Religion of Humanity,* 87; Morison, "Neander's *Life of
Christ,*" 86-87.

37. Frothingham, *Cradle of the Christ,* 188.

38. Frothingham, "Rénan's *Life of Jesus,*" 333.

39. Andrews Norton, *A Discourse on the Latest Form
of Infidelity* (1839), in *The Transcendentalists: An
Anthology,* ed. Perry Miller (Cambridge: Harvard
Univ. Press, 1950), 210.

40. [Edward Everett Hale], "The Logical Order of the
Gospel Narratives," *Christian Examiner* 65
(1858): 208, 209.

41. H. G. Spaulding, "Jesus as Prophet and Messiah,"
Christian Examiner 83 (1867): 98.

42. [A. P. Peabody], "Philosophy of Fiction," *Christian Examiner* 32 (1842): 4; [Alvan Lamson],
"Notices of Recent Publications," *Christian Examiner* 37 (1844): 123.

43. Elizabeth Stuart Phelps, introductory note to *The
Story of Jesus Christ* (Boston and New York:
Houghton, Mifflin and Co., 1898), i.

44. Harriet Beecher Stowe, *Footsteps of the Master*
(New York: J. B. Ford, 1877), 283.

45. Phelps, *Story of Jesus Christ,* 6.

46. [Henry Whitney Bellows], review of *Ecce Homo:
A Survey of the Life and Work of Jesus Christ,*
Christian Examiner 81 (1866): 114-15.

47. Bellows, review of *Ecce Homo,* 114.

48. Stowe, *Footsteps,* 87, 13, 9.

49. Phelps, *Story of Jesus Christ,* viii, x, 3.

50. Phelps, *Story of Jesus Christ,* viii-x, 411; Stowe,
Footsteps, 283.

51. Owen Chadwick, *The Secularization of the European Mind in the Nineteenth Century* (Cambridge:
Cambridge Univ. Press, 1975), 223.

52. Stowe, *Footsteps,* 1, 143; cf. 148.

53. See also G. Harrison Orians, "Censure of Fiction
in American Romances and Magazines, 1789-
1810," *PMLA* 52 (1937): 195-214; Walter F.
Greiner, *Studien zur Entstehung der englischen
Romantheorie an der Wende zum 18. Jahrhundert*
(*Studies in the rise of the poetics of the English
novel at the turn of the 18th century*) (Tübingen:
Max Niemeyer, 1969), 168-71; and Irène Simon,
"Early Theories of Prose Fiction: Congreve and
Fielding," in *Imagined Worlds: Essays on Some
English Novels and Novelists in Honour of John
Butt,* ed. Maynard Mack and Ian Gregor (London:
Methuen and Co., 1968), 21-23.

54. Stowe, *Footsteps,* 10, 137, 26.

55. For a similar example, see Rev. J. H. Ingraham,
dedication to *The Pillar of Fire; or, Israel in Bond-
age* (New York: Pudney and Russell, 1859).

56. Phelps, *Story of Jesus Christ,* 168-69.

57. See, for example, Furness, *Remarks on Rénan's
Life,* 20-22.

58. Brooke Herford, "Jesus Christ," in *Unitarian Affirmations: Seven Discourses Given in Washington*
(Boston: American Unitarian Association, 1879),
77, 78.

Terence R. Wright (essay date summer 1994)

SOURCE: Wright, Terence R. "The Letter and the
Spirit: Deconstructing Renan's *Life of Jesus* and the Assumption of Modernity." *Religion and Literature* 26,
no. 2 (summer 1994): 55-71.

[*In the following essay, Wright examines* The Life of
Jesus *in postmodern terms, concluding that part of what
makes the work timeless is Renan's own awareness that
all evaluation of Jesus' life and teaching, including his
own, is conditioned by the age in which it is written.*]

To rewrite the life of Jesus from a rational historical
perspective is clearly central to the project of modernity, which is normally portrayed as sweeping away all
superstition and replacing it with an alternative scientific and emancipatory narrative. Postmodernity, initially defined (by Lyotard at least) as the abandonment
of such metanarratives, is now seen rather as "a weak-

ening of the metaphysical and rationalist pretensions of modernity" which does not so much abandon as probe, modify and complicate such stories of liberation and progress:

> Postmodernity cannot be a simple *rejection* of modernity; rather it involves a different modulation of its themes and categories, a greater proliferation of its language-games.
>
> (Laclau 329-30)

The boundary between modernity and postmodernity, in other words, is less clear than was first thought. We still need to retell the life of Jesus in our own words for our own time but we are less confident about our liberal rationalist assumptions, more self-critical and less dismissive of different perspectives.

This modulation of modernist assumptions is nowhere more evident than in the work of Ernest Renan, whose *Vie de Jésus* caused such a stir when it appeared in 1863 (Chadwick 219-22). Part of the work's success was its scandalous quality, which caused it to be taken up by the anticlerical faction in France and to be put on the Index. In Britain, as Daniel Pals has shown, the response was almost uniformly negative, uniting orthodox believers in defence of *English Common Sense Versus Foreign Fallacies* (the title of a pamphlet by du Boulay). He had already caused a furor in France by referring to Jesus as "cet homme incomparable" in his inaugural lecture as Professor of Hebrew at the College de France in 1862 (Reardon, *Liberalism* 295). He was to anger the orthodox even more in his later writing by referring to Jesus as divine in a manner that fell short of what they meant by the term, a clear illustration of his suspect, over-literary slipperiness. Nevertheless, the *Vie de Jésus* was recognized as "one of the events of the century" (296), "by far the greatest of all the imaginative lives of Jesus" (Neill 193).

Renan's reputation now, of course, is much diminished, partly as a result of Said's exposure of his ethnocentric and antisemitic tendencies as an Orientalist in two senses, one who wrote about the Orient and to do so invented a discourse which imposed his own western preconceptions upon the east. Renan is perceived as a bad modernist, someone who aimed at the characteristic goal of modernity, a unified, scientific narrative of the origins of Christianity, but who failed. Said quotes some of the many passages in *L'Avenir de la Science* which equate philology with modernity in a story of rationalism, criticism and liberalism driving out superstition in the name of science (Said 132-33). There is, of course, some truth in this portrait but it is partial (in both senses): Said selects only a part of Renan's writing in order to tell his own story. What he omits is the recognition on Renan's own part as "a man of letters," a title Said himself awards him, of the limitations of moder-

nity, the impossibility of telling the whole story of *The Origins of Christianity* even in seven volumes of which the *Vie de Jésus* was only the first.

These contradictions in Renan have been the occasion of much modernist ridicule, for instance that of Irving Babbitt: "no one knew better than Renan how to gild positivism with religiosity and throw around the operations of the scientific intellect a vague aroma of the infinite" (Reardon, *Religion* 237-38). In 1975 Bernard Reardon complained of the "curious amalgam of rationalism and romanticizing piety" in the *Vie de Jésus*. But by 1985 Reardon had come to recognize the extent to which Renan deliberately embraced contradiction, unlike the rationalists of the previous century who, intent on fixing and defining everything, had ignored whatever could not be fitted into their systems, "the infinite, the developing, . . . the spontaneous in all its forms" (Renan, *Oeuvres* 2: 1102; qtd. in Reardon, *Religion* 237-38). Reardon points to Renan's embracing of the dialogue form as part of this reaction against the coherence and unity demanded by modernity, enabling him to "look at a question from several different angles and finally turn away from any definite answer" (245). Renan's "constitutional ambivalence," torn between a commitment to science and a recognition of its limitations, led him to appreciate the flexibility of literary forms of religious expression. As he wrote in a letter of 1859,

> I am religious in a very real sense; but I do not believe that the formularies of rational religion themselves escape criticism. That is why art and poetry, which do not enclose their object in dogmatic propositions, give me far more satisfaction.
>
> (Reardon, "Renan" 201-02)

It is this other voice, which could be labelled postmodern in its hesitation to make grand claims for rational and scientific explanation, that I want to bring out more clearly in Renan.

This "postmodern" Renan appears most obviously at the end of *L'Avenir de la Science,* bidding an emotional farewell to the God of his youth whose voice he could no longer hear: "Farewell; although Thou hast deceived me, I love Thee still!" (Renan, *Future* 459-60). He can be heard in "Prayer on the Acropolis" burying the dead gods in their purple shroud before dwelling on the "nameless abyss" for which we are all destined: "Thou art the only true God, O Abyss!" (*Recollections* 60-61). This Renan anticipates the post-Christian predicament: "We are living on the shadow of a shadow. What will they live on after us?" (Heinegg 136). In recognizing the impossibility of covering over the abyss, or replacing his lost Catholicism with a liberal humanist alternative, Renan embraces contradiction, as when he addresses Christ on the cross at the climax of the *Vie de Jésus,* "Banner of our contradictions, thou wilt be the sign around which will be fought the fiercest battles [*Drapeau de nos contradictions, tu seras le signe autour duquel se livrera la plus ardente bataille*]" (*Life* 227; *Vie* 440-41).

The postmodern thinker I want to employ in dialogue with Renan is not Bataille, however, but Derrida, who invokes battles as fierce now in the name of English common sense as Renan then and who occupies a similar space on the borders of literature, philosophy and religion. Derrida quotes Bataille's onslaught on Hegel, a typically "modern" man in his blindness to the sacred, in *Writing and Difference.* The notion of sacrifice developed by Bataille serves to undermine too crudely rationalistic an understanding of modernity. It is Derrida's exploration of the opposition between the letter and the spirit that interests me most, however, related as it is to other oppositions between the body and the soul, outside and inside, literal and metaphorical, and writing and speech. I will briefly outline the way Derrida deconstructs these oppositions, central as they are to modern, western thought, before returning to Renan to notice them operating in the *Vie de Jésus.* To this extent I could be said to be deconstructing Renan but it is more accurate to say that Renan deconstructs himself. He is clearly aware both of these oppositions and of their inadequacy. The borderlines between these oppositions are constantly infringed as Renan both attempts an authoritative "modern" interpretation of Jesus and signals the impossibility of the attempt.

The opposition between the letter and the spirit is crucial in much of Derrida's work. As he says in *Of Grammatology,*

> writing, the letter, the sensible inscription, has always been considered by Western tradition as the body and matter external to the spirit, to breath, to speech, and to the logos.
>
> (35)

Part One of *Of Grammatology,* entitled "Writing before the Letter," traces through Western thought from Plato through Rousseau to Lévi-Strauss and Saussure a compulsion to degrade writing as inferior to speech, which they see as involving the direct, unmediated communication of mind or spirit. As the body causes the soul to sin, they argue, writing represents a fall from ideal communication. But, as Derrida shows by analyzing ambiguous or contradictory passages in each of these writers, it is a necessary and to some extent a fortunate fall. There is no communication that does not rely upon previously established differences that constitute writing before the letter. The attempt to get back to an original stable and unchanging truth, to re-present it without difference, to convey its essential spirit without mediating material form, is doomed to failure.

Other works by Derrida such as *Glas* and *Of Spirit* follow this privileging of spirit over matter in the work of Hegel and Heidegger. Hegel's concept of *Geist,* of history as the realization of spirit, of matter being sublated, *aufgehoben,* at once affirmed and denied, taken up into the spirit, is crucial here, as is his denigration of the Jewish contribution to religious advance. Hegel's early life of Jesus and his *Spirit of Christianity and Its Fate* contrast Christian freedom of spirit with Jewish enslavement to the law. Derrida quotes Hegel complaining of Jewish materialism and ugliness, altogether "lacking" the "spirit of beauty (*Geist der Schönheit*)" (Derrida, *Glas* 39a). The word *Geist* as Derrida shows in excruciating detail in *Of Spirit* (*De l'esprit*), has a checkered history in Heidegger as well. For a period, including the Rectorship Address, Heidegger returned to using the term but his 1953 essay on Trakl avoided even *geistig* as caught up in opposition to the material (*Stofflichen*), impossible to use without being sucked into the Platonic-Christian tradition (Derrida, *Spirit* 95-96).

Writing and Difference also discusses the spirit and the letter at great length, calling writing "the anguish of the hebraic *ruah*" (breath or spirit), faced like Jeremiah with the command to record divine inspiration and the doubt whether such engraving preserves or betrays revelation (9). Derrida relates this to similar problems with pneuma and spiritus. Writing on Levinas in "Violence and Metaphysics," an essay which refers to Renan's claim that respiration is the etymological origin of the word Being (139), Derrida asks, "how could Hebraism belittle the letter," given the place it gives to the Bible? He quotes Levinas to the effect that "the spirit is free in the letter" and "To love the Torah more than God" is "protection against the madness of a direct contact with the Sacred" (102). This essay ends by dwelling on the "historical *coupling* of Judaism and Hellenism," a difference within which we modern westerners live, a difference which cannot be reconciled, erased or reduced to Hegelian logic but belongs to the "unthinkable, unsayable, transcendence of the other" (153). It is characteristic of postmodernity not to impose one way of looking at things upon others but to be open to alterity, to eastern as well as western insights.

A later essay in the same volume, "La Parole Soufflée," plays on the "oversignification which overburdens" the word *soufflé* (breath or inspiration), quoting Artaud's attempt "to forbid that his speech be spirited away [*soufflé*] from his body" or "*inspired* by an *other* voice." Derrida insists that language can never be owned or fully appropriated. The letter is always "purloined" or "stolen," which amounts to acknowledging the autonomy of the signifier as the letter's historicity" (175-79). We are enmeshed, in other words, in linguistic, literary and religious codes and practices which resist our control and exceed our "meaning-to-say." There is, of course, an ongoing debate with Lacan here over whether the letter always arrives at its destination, as Lacan claims, or whether, as Derrida illustrates at great length in *The Post Card,* there is always an excess of meaning (*poste restante*) which remains on top of what was intended, a potential to generate fresh meaning which is the condition of possibility of literature.

Derrida turns to a disciple of Renan's, Anatole France, in *Margins of Philosophy,* in order to deconstruct the opposition between literal and metaphorical, to resist the Hegelian attempt to suppress metaphor as acceptable for primitive orientals but not for advanced western philosophers. France has one of the characters in a dialogue complain about philosophers who attempt to erase the metaphorical dimension of language and succeed in producing only "White Mythology," the title of this essay, an anaemic form of language. Such metaphysicians are likened to knife-grinders who efface all inscriptions on their coins and then claim that they have gained in value, having "nothing either English, German or French about them" but being "freed from all time and space," have become of "inestimable value" (Derrida, *Margins* 210). It is, of course, the material specificity of the coin, as of the letter, that gives it its value at a particular place and time.

Renan, to return at last to the mid-nineteenth century, is faced with a similar dilemma: how to apply the modern western critical spirit to ancient eastern religious texts such as the gospels without destroying their material specificity, how to resist Hegel's spiritualizing sublation of matter into spirit, of concrete image (*Vorstellung*) into philosophical concept (*Begriff*). His 1849 review of Strauss's *Leben Jesu* insists on the need to combine critical acumen with respect for the "noble characters and elevated symbols" of religious traditions (Renan, *Studies* 95, 108), expressing reservations about Strauss's application of the philosophy of Hegel to the gospels. Renan anticipates some aspects of Derrida's critique of Hegel in *Glas,* both of them resenting Hegel's disregard of historical specificity, all sublated into the spiritual (Derrida, *Glas* 30a-31a). Just as Derrida complains of Hegel's preference for "the speculative good friday that was formerly historic" (96a), so Renan calls Hegel's christology simply "the abstract thesis of the philosopher," a translation of the principle of sublation (*aufheben*) by which the material is caught up in the spiritual, "the man-God" enjoying through his death "only the suppression of his alienation, . . . an elevation and a return to God." This "Hegelian Christ," Renan fears, is too distant from "the historic Christ, he who bore the name of Jesus" (Renan, *Studies* 111-12).

Renan proceeds to paraphrase the passage in Strauss in which he argues that Christ was not a unique representation of the unity of human and divine. To quote George Eliot's translation (rather than an English trans-

lation of Renan's paraphrase of the French translation of the original German):

> is not the idea of the unity of the divine and human natures a real one in a far higher sense, when I regard the whole race of mankind as its realization, than when I single out one man as such a realization? is not an incarnation of God from eternity, a truer one than an incarnation limited to a particular point of time. . . . Humanity is the union of the two natures—God become man, the infinite manifesting itself in the finite, and the finite spirit remembering its infinitude; it is the child of the visible Mother and the invisible Father, Nature and spirit.
>
> (Strauss 780; Renan, *Studies* 112)

Notice here the phallocentric opposition between the visible Mother Nature and the invisible Father Spirit, repeated so often in the history of modernity, which equates rationality and progress with masculinity, developing out of and beyond the merely material and maternal (Culler 59). Renan identifies the problem here in Strauss as in Hegel as the dominance of spirit, which "brings matter into subjection more and more" (*Studies* 112).

For Renan, Strauss like his countryman Hegel lacks "the sentiment of history and facts, . . . of myths and symbols . . . as far as he is concerned, the primitive events of Christianity have passed out of real existence and out of nature" (114). Focussing as he does on the growth of legends and myths *about* Jesus, Strauss fails convincingly to explain how the disciples could come to believe that Jesus was the Messiah after the apparent failure of the cross. Renan here is not altogether fair to Strauss, who has quite a long and to my mind moving passage in which he discusses precisely this point, "the psychological necessity of solving the contradiction between the ultimate fate of Jesus" and their earlier faith in him as triumphant Messiah, which they did by re-reading the prophets and discovering there the notion of a suffering servant (Strauss 742). But it is true that Strauss plays down the role of Jesus, whose charismatic personality for Renan provides the answer to this problem, an answer which he insists that a French historian, less obsessed with "abstract speculation," would have come nearer to suggesting (119). Renan accepts that there is a considerable amount of legendary material in the gospels but insists that the essential character of the historical Jesus shines through them. His main difference from Strauss lies in his awareness that the concrete images of the gospels, even if they are not all historically accurate, cannot satisfactorily be subsumed in abstract concepts. In supposedly advancing from the letter to the spirit, Strauss lost the endearing and essential specificity of the gospels.

Renan's own *Life of Jesus,* however, also appears at times to suppress the letter in the interests of the spirit. Jesus, like Socrates, scorns writing and opposes the law, rejecting all outward forms, religious or political, in favor of an inward morality which lifts the soul above the temptations of the body. The introduction to the *Vie de Jésus* celebrates the early period of Christianity before the gospel texts were "defined and fixed dogmatically," when Christians preserved in their hearts the image of their lord: "The spirit was everything; the letter was nothing [*L'esprit était tout; la lettre n'était rien*]" (*Life* 10; *Vie* lvi). But Renan appears to value the material specificity of the synoptics, finding "the spirit of Jesus" much better represented in their "profoundly Hebraistic idiom" than in the Johannine discourses, with their "desire to prove a thesis," their "obscure Gnosticism" and "distorted metaphysics" (*Life* 15). It does not bother Renan that some of these details are not true to the letter" since they capture "the very spirit of Jesus," like an imaginatively restored vase in which some of the pieces may not be original (25, 29). The impression produced by the whole story is what counts. Already Renan is brought into contradiction, both valuing and undermining the specificity of the gospel narratives.

The story that Renan tells of Jesus involves a similar opposition between the spirit and matter, a prolonged and not always triumphant spiritual battle against material corruption. His idealistic Jesus is happiest at the very outset of his career, gallivanting with friends among the Galilean hills, before becoming embroiled in the religious and political controversies of his time. Renan describes how an "infinite charm was exhaled from his person" at this time, gathering around him a loose collection of followers who were not yet "disciples." Renan waxes lyrical on the young Jesus' beautiful voice and "amiable character, accompanied doubtless by one of those lovely faces [*une de ces figures ravissantes*] which sometimes appear in the Jewish race" (*Life* 71; *Vie* 84). It was this kind of effusion which gave Renan a bad name in Britain but it is important that he stresses the physical nature of Jesus' charm, the tangibility of the spirit which he exhales. The root-metaphor of breath will become even more important in Renan's treatment of the resurrection and descent of the Holy Spirit.

The religion of the charming young Jesus, Renan repeatedly insists, was entirely inward: "A pure worship, a religion without priests and external observances, resting entirely on the feelings of the heart" (73). He had no need to "affect any external signs of asceticism" or to produce books; as with other rabbis of the period, "everything was done by conversations" (75). This inwardness was briefly threatened by the influence of John the Baptist and his "external rites and ceremonies" (86) but his imprisonment left Jesus free to teach "the great doctrine of transcendent disdain [*dédain transcendent*], the true doctrine of liberty of souls" (*Life* 88; *Vie* 123). Jesus also, according to Renan, resisted the temptation to become a political agitator. Renan sees Jesus

as radically unworldly, "subversive" in annihilating rather than appropriating riches and power (91-92).

Renan's Jesus, the Galilean carpenter preaching to an audience of fishermen and peasants by the Lake of Tiberias, was altogether too gentle and otherworldly a figure for many of Renan's readers, especially Schweitzer, who ridiculed the characteristically "French lyricism" and "sentimentality" behind his "gentle Jesus" and "beautiful Mary," not to mention the "blue skies, seas of waving corn, distant mountains, gleaming lilies" and long-lashed mules (Schweitzer 181-82). Renan's Jesus does possess an anachronistically romantic disposition, "breathing nature and the perfume of the fields. He loved the flowers, and took from them his most charming lessons" (*Life* 109). Women and children "adored him" (121), hence the charge of alienating them from their families. Lest Renan's approach be thought too sentimental and unscholarly, it is worth saying that all these claims are supported by footnote references to biblical and other texts, footnotes omitted from the Everyman English translation. Renan insists that the essential inwardness of Jesus' original teaching, its rejection of all external wealth, remains at the heart of Christianity in spite of centuries of corruption and subservience to the rich and powerful: "the mark of origin is ever preserved [*on garde toujours la marque de ses origines*]" (*Life* 117; *Vie* 190). Renan's confident generalization here covers over precisely what is at issue: the nature of the original "mark" of Christianity and the possibility of its accurate "external" representation.

This particular binary opposition between inward and outward dominates Renan's account of Jesus' fatal encounter with defenders of the Jewish Law. For the inwardness of Jesus' teaching soon brings him into conflict with the religious leaders of Jerusalem, "a city of pedantry, acrimony, disputes, hatreds, and littleness of mind," dominated by the Pharisees and their devotion to the letter of the Law (*Life* 128). The Galileans are looked down on as unlettered in every sense, untouched by culture and speaking a "corrupt dialect" which "confounded the different aspirations of letters" (129). It is at this point in Renan's narrative that Jesus decides to make a complete break with "the narrow, hard, and uncharitable Law." In Renan's provocative terms, "Jesus was no longer a Jew" but an advocate of "the religion of humanity" (135). Jesus, to whom "the idea is all; the body . . . nothing" (144), appears almost to have escaped the material condition of ordinary mortals: "Intoxicated with infinite love, he forgot the heavy chain which holds the spirit captive" (145).

Not, however, for long. The second half of the *Vie de Jésus* takes on an increasingly tragic tone as the pure spirit of Jesus becomes embroiled in matters political and religious. Renan tries to explain how Jesus could allow his disciples to believe him capable of miracles, external signs of power whose temptation he had earlier resisted. For Renan as for Strauss, it is axiomatic that miracles do not happen, that modern science will always in principle be able to explain them. Renan points to "the need Jesus had of obtaining credence, and the enthusiasm of his disciples," which made exorbitant demands upon him (147). In a passage which was to cause great offence, Renan implies without ever explicitly stating that Jesus deceived his disciples by allowing them to believe him possessed of supernatural powers and was carried away by his own and their enthusiasm into thinking of himself as the Messiah. Renan explains,

> To the deeply earnest races of the West, conviction means sincerity to one's self. But sincerity to one's self has not much meaning to Oriental peoples, little accustomed to the subtleties of a critical spirit. Honesty and imposture are words which, in our rigid consciences, are opposed as two irreconcilable terms. In the East they are connected by numberless subtle links and windings. The authors of the Apocryphal books (of Daniel and of Enoch, for instance), men highly exalted, in order to aid their cause, committed, without a shadow of scruple, an act which we should term a fraud. Literal truth [*la verité matérielle*] has little value to the Oriental; he sees all through the medium of his ideas, his interests, and his passions [*il voit tout à travers ses préjugés, ses intérêts, ses passions*].
>
> (*Life* 147; *Vie* 263)

It is easy to cry "Orientalism" at this point and to read Renan, as Eleanor Shaffer does, as saying that Jesus was a Wily Oriental Gentleman who could not be trusted (Shaffer 200). But Renan is attempting here to deconstruct western as much as eastern assumptions or prejudices, "our rigid consciences" as much as their excitability. There is a similar passage in *The Gospels,* volume 5 of *The Origins of Christianity,* in which he tries to deconstruct the western opposition between truth and fiction as similarly over-rigid for the reading of eastern texts:

> The word "truth" has not the same significance for the Oriental as for ourselves. The Oriental tells with a bewitching candour and with the accent of a witness, a crowd of things which he has not seen and about which he is by no means certain. The fantastic tales of the Exodus from Egypt, which are told in Jewish families during the Feast of the Passover, deceive nobody, yet none the less they enchant those who listen to them. . . . It is the especial quality of the Oriental *agada* to touch most profoundly those who best know how fictitious it is. It is its triumph to have created such a masterpiece that all the world is deceived by it, and for want of knowing laws of this kind the credulous West has accepted as infallible truth the recital of facts which no human eye has ever seen.
>
> (Renan, *Oeuvres* 5: 104-05)

In this passage it is clearer that the "credulous West," ignorant of the literary conventions of ancient eastern literature, bears the brunt of Renan's criticism. Else-

where he discusses the "grand duality" within Judaism itself between the letter and the spirit, the Law and the Prophets, *halaka* and *agada,* Jerusalem and Galilee (*Oeuvres* 3: 32). For the *agadist,* "The spirit is everything; the letter is of no importance" (5: 47). The point is not to read literally that which was written with creative imagination though true to the spirit of Jesus.

That Renan's own creative narrative of the life of Jesus is a tragic tale of the corruption of spiritual truth by material conditions becomes even more evident in chapter 16 on "Miracles," in which Renan reminds us "that every idea loses something of its purity as soon as it aspires to realize itself" (150). He finds it "impossible, among the miraculous narratives so tediously enumerated in the Gospels," to distinguish between those falsely attributed to Jesus and "those in which he consented to play an active part." Miracles of healing Renan finds morally more acceptable since they were designed to alleviate suffering rather than to impress followers and could now probably be explained in terms of modern medicine. Details such as the application of saliva and "other offensive circumstances . . . savoring of jugglery" can probably be attributed to the disciples (151). Renan perceives Jesus as remaining truer to himself when stressing the inwardness of the kingdom, the liberty of the soul and its "separation from matter" than when indulging "his hope of a vain apocalypse, and of a second coming in great triumph upon the clouds of heaven." Renan is at his most arrogantly modern in offering to "pardon" Jesus for any "dream" which gave him strength to face his coming trials (161-62).

In exploring "The Institutions of Jesus" in chapter 18 Renan returns to his insistence that modern western minds need to abandon their habitual assumptions, to recognize "how remote from the thought of Jesus was the idea of a religious book containing a code and articles of faith," all of which were "contrary to the spirit of the infant sect" (169). Similarly Jesus believed in the informal "union of love" rather than an official Church, which for Renan was a later development. "Neither was there any theology or creed," Renan insists. Only later in the development of Christian theology, according to Renan, were concepts such as that of the Holy Spirit or Paraclete developed, the latter being a Greek word which "it is very doubtful whether Jesus used." He may have talked of "a baptism by fire and by the spirit" but "To Jesus this Holy Spirit was identical with the breath ever emanating from God the Father [*Ce Saint-Esprit, pour Jésus, n'était pas distinct de l'inspiration émanant de Dieu le Père d'une façon continue*]" (*Life* 168; *Vie* 310). Notice how the English translation resolves the ambiguity of the French *inspiration,* both literal breath and metaphorical inspiration. Only later did this spirit acquire an essential character, an *ousia,* a being, when people came to believe "that Jesus had promised the disciples to send them after his death, as a substitute for himself, a Spirit who should teach them all things" (168).

The development of the Lord's Supper from an act of memorial to a metaphysical sacrament provides Renan with another example of the way in which Jesus' vivid metaphorical language was "afterwards taken in a very literal sense [*pris avec une littéralité effrénée*]," a wild or unbridled literalness (**Life** 171; **Vie** 316). Jesus, Renan explains, was "very ideal in his conceptions and very concrete in their expression [*tres-materialiste dans les conceptions et très-matérialiste dans l'expression*]," so that in order to convey "the thought that . . . he was the life of the truly faithful, he said to his disciples, "I am your food," a phrase which, in figurative style (*tournée en style figure*), became "My flesh is your bread, my blood your drink." Renan insists that the symbolic re-enactment of this scene by the disciples after Jesus' death was a "wholly spiritual idea of the presence of souls" in which "the body counted for nothing" (317-18). He ends this chapter by emphasizing the untranslatability of Jesus' understanding of the eucharist into modern western terms:

> It is impossible to translate into our own essentially determinate language, in which a rigorous distinction between the actual and the metaphorical must always be observed, habits of style the essential character of which is to attribute to metaphor, or rather the idea it represents, a complete reality.

(172)

The French term rendered "actual" here is "sens propre," that concept so vilified by Derrida. Like Derrida too Renan recognizes the western tendency to subsume the signifier in an essential and unchanging signified. Derrida's *Glas* has a long section analyzing the figurative language of the Last Supper, the material specificity of which is "spiritualized" out of existence by Hegel, for whom the Eucharist becomes a matter of pure feeling and "the objects vanish as objects" (65a-70a). Renan too could be said to be attempting to deconstruct the western distinction between literal and metaphorical but in insisting that Jesus's "concepts" were spiritual, only his expression "concrete" (*matérialiste*), Renan demonstrates his own embeddedness in modern western modes of thought. He betrays too modernist a confidence in knowing not only what Jesus actually said but what he thought.

To return to the narrative, as Renan himself does after this digression, Jesus, under the pressure of persecution and opposition within Jerusalem, changes in character. His otherworldliness takes on a "harsh gloomy" hue, the "cheerful moralist" changing into a "somber giant" (175). His condemnation of opponents grows fiercer; he

begins to court persecution and even death as part of his mission. He appears "disturbed," suffering "great mental anguish and agitation." The disciples think him "mad," his enemies "possessed" (178). The spirit of gentleness and tolerance is replaced with rage and anger. Renan paints a vivid picture of the "Last Week of Jesus" (chapter 23) in which this generally "joyous and serene" soul is filled with "deep melancholy," with terror, doubt and exhaustion (205). Death itself comes as a release, a final triumph of the spirit over matter and a tactical mistake on the part of his enemies, who would have done better to let him exhaust "himself in a desperate struggle with the impossible" (200).

Renan, of course, leaves Jesus in the tomb; for him there is no resurrection, simply the victory of the "Divine power of love" over the harsh reality of death. On discovering the empty tomb Mary Magdalen is credited with beginning the rumor that Christ was risen, a belief "quickly spread among the disciples. Love caused it to find ready credence everywhere" (230). Tantalizingly, Renan leaves the story there, promising to return to the subject where it belongs, not in the life of Jesus but in the history of the early church:

> For the historian, the life of Jesus finishes with his last sigh [*son dernier soupir*]. But such was the impression [*la trace*] he had left in the hearts of his disciples and of a few devoted women that during some weeks more it was as if he were living and consoling them.
>
> (**Life** 230; **Vie** 449)

The disciples, according to Renan, make the mistake of erecting this "trace" of memory into a living spirit, an essence, a divine being.

Renan develops his explanation of the resurrection in more detail at the beginning of the second volume of **The History of the Origins of Christianity,** entitled **The Apostles.** Here he admits that his reconstruction of these events can only be a matter of "probability" because of the "incoherency" and "contradictions" in the sources (4). Again, Mary Magdalen plays the key role, for it is she, having reported the taking away of the body, who returns to the tomb to experience the visionary and intangible presence of Jesus. To Mary, "Queen and patroness of idealists," more than anyone else belongs this "miracle of love" since her experience of the risen Christ became the type of all subsequent resurrection experiences (6). As at La Salette in 1846, a comparison Renan makes explicit (22), and at Lourdes in 1858, where similarly impressionable young women claim to have seen the Blessed Virgin, "it is the characteristic of such states of soul . . . to be contagious" (9). Soon the disciples were reporting similar experiences. Renan reminds us that "the degree of intellectual culture" they possessed was not high (10). Cleopas and his friend on the Emmaus road fail to notice their companion slipping away and convince themselves it was Jesus. Renan paints a vivid picture of the disciples in the Upper Room feeling "a slight breath of wind passed over the face of the assembly" and hearing sounds which they interpret as the word *schalom* or "peace": "It was impossible to doubt; Jesus was present; he was there, in the assembly. It was his dear voice; everyone recognized it." Since Jesus had promised to be with them as often as they gathered in his name, it now became "an accepted fact" that he had appeared before them and breathed upon them the holy spirit" (12).

This is Renan at his most readable, the novelist imaginatively recreating what might have happened. He soon dons his more confident scientific hat to complain of the way "credulity became a hideous emulation and a kind of out-bidding one another" in claims to have experienced the risen Lord (15). The disciples' return to Galilee is seen to have revived their beautiful memories of the young Jesus, providing an ideal setting for the indulgence of their "grand and melancholy dreams" (19). The historical question to which Renan admits he has no definite answer is what happened to the body. He accepts that the same disciples who experienced the resurrection cannot have spirited it away; he does not accuse them of conscious fraud. Among the many other possibilities he turns once again to Mary Magdalen and the passionate nature of "the women of the East," their "want of education, and the peculiar shade of their sincerity," a nice example of Renan's Orientalism at its most rampant. But he finally draws "a veil over these mysteries," accepting that "the material incident" which "induced belief in the resurrection" is less important than the love which was its "real" cause (23-24).

All the resurrection experiences are felt in tangible material form. The disciples feel the risen Jesus in the tangible form of breath or wind, as if Jesus had physically "breathed on them out of his own mouth" (28), just as Mary Magdalen "pretended" that "mysterious breath" that she had felt "was the actual breath of Jesus himself." Again, Renan claims to know the real inward meaning of these experiences: "These simple consciences referred, as usual, to some exterior cause the exquisite sentiments which were being created in them" (33). Elijah too had experienced God "in the form of a gentle wind, . . . a slight rustling noise" and Isaiah as "a certain rustling at the doors." Such "hallucinations" were by no means new "among persons so nervous and so excited" (33). And this is how Renan explains the experience of Pentecost, which he sets during a ferocious thunderstorm with violent winds and "prodigious sheets of lightning" giving rise to the belief that tongues of fire had settled upon them (34-35). These primitive Orientals get carried away, having no means of distinguishing between inward and outward, feeling and fact.

So it is that Renan the modernist explains "scientifically," in terms acceptable to modern western thought, the "events" of the life and death of Jesus, his resurrection and the descent of the Holy Spirit. His claim throughout is to have escaped from the literal understanding characteristic of naive believers to the true spiritual meaning. And yet, as we have seen, Renan repeatedly warns us against imposing our modern western understanding of the opposition between truth and fiction, literal and metaphorical, upon the products of ancient eastern imaginations. And, of course, his own reconstruction of these events is itself the work of a vivid imagination. This contradiction is apparent in Renan's ambivalence towards writing, letters in the sense of literature, in particular the gospels. Renan constantly reminds us that Jesus himself never resorted to writing; his teaching was "so little dogmatic that he never thought of writing it or causing it to be written" (Renan, *Life* 235).

In recounting the development of written gospels in the fifth volume of *The Origins of Christianity* Renan calls the process of recording the sayings of Jesus onto parchment a decline from the heady days of inspiration by the loving memory of Jesus. The Galilean disciples "would have laughed" at the very idea. Hence the paradox of the early church not valuing the texts which were to become the cornerstone of the faith (Renan, *Origins* 49). Again and again Renan rhapsodizes over the beauties of the gospels, which capture the spirit of Jesus though often fictitious in detail (53). He calls Matthew "a fairy palace constructed wholly of luminous stones" (104), and "the most important book that has ever been written" (112). He particularly enjoys the fact that the "habitual reading of the world is a book where the priest is always in fault, where respectable people are always hypocrites, where the lay authorities are always scoundrels, and where all the rich are damned" (112). He goes into raptures over the more respectable Luke, "the most literary of the gospels, . . . the most beautiful book there is," imagining "the pleasure that the author must have had in writing it" (148). Writing, in other words, turns out not to be so unimportant after all and in writing the *Vie de Jésus* Renan could be said to be attempting to emulate Luke's original pleasure. He admits that it takes not only "ability" and "boldness" but also a certain "naiveté to translate the Gospel into the style of his time" (53).

Not many critics have accused Renan of naiveté. And yet he seems to recognize here the limitations of the modernist project, the need to preserve the letter of the gospels, their material literary form, as well as reinterpret their spirit. Each writing of the life of Jesus, ancient and modern, is culture-specific. Any reading of the gospels involves a dialogue between two very different cultures, that of the time of writing and that of the time of reading. No one can avoid the challenge of interpretation they offer, nor should anyone claim that his or her interpretation fixes their meaning. Renan's awareness of the limitations of modernity, his occasional rebellion against the oppositions between letter and spirit, truth and fiction, speech and writing, inward and outward, literal and metaphorical, oppositions on which his modernist project is founded, I would argue, both brings him into self-contradiction and rescues him from the confines of his age. As he writes in the final chapter of the *Vie de Jésus,* in a passage which anticipates many postmodern beliefs,

> The religion of Jesus is not limited. The Church has its epochs and its phases; it has shut itself up in creeds which are, or will be, temporary; but Jesus has founded the absolute religion, excluding nothing, and determining nothing unless it be the spirit. His creeds are not fixed dogmas, but images susceptible of indefinite interpretations.

Renan recognizes, in other words, that his own interpretation of the essential "spirit" of Jesus is not the final word, does not exhaust the potential of the letter, does not represent its final destination.

Works Cited

Chadbourne, Richard M. *Ernest Renan.* New York: Twayne, 1968.

Chadwick Owen. *The Secularization of the European Mind in the Nineteenth Century.* Cambridge: Cambridge UP, 1975.

Charlton, D. G. *Positivist Thought in France During the Second Empire 1852-1870.* Oxford: Oxford UP, 1959.

Culler, Jonathan. *On Deconstruction.* London: Routledge, 1983.

Derrida, Jacques. *Glas.* Trans. John P. Leavey Jr. and Richard Rand. Lincoln and London: U of Nebraska P, 1986.

———. *Margins of Philosophy.* Trans. Alan Bass. Brighton: Harvester, 1982.

———. *Of Grammatology.* Trans. Gayatri Spivak. Baltimore and London: Johns Hopkins UP, 1976.

———. *Of Spirit: Heidegger and the Question.* Trans. Geoffrey Bennington and Rachel Bowlby. Chicago and London: U of Chicago P, 1989.

———. *The Post Card: From Socrates to Freud and Beyond.* Trans. Alan Bass. Chicago and London: U of Chicago P, 1987.

———. *Writing and Difference.* Trans. Alan Bass. Chicago and London: U of Chicago P, 1978.

du Boulay, John. *English Common Sense versus Foreign Fallacies in Questions of Religion.* London, 1864.

Heinegg, Peter. "Hebrew or Hellene?: Religious Ambivalence in Renan." *Texas Quarterly* 18 (1975): 120-36.

Laclau, Ernesto. "Politics and the Limits of Modernity." *Postmodernism: A Reader.* Ed Thomas Docherty. Hemel Hempstead: Harvester Wheatsheaf, 1993.

Neill, Stephen. *The Interpretation of the New Testament 1861-1961.* Oxford: Oxford UP, 1964.

Pals, Daniel L. *The Victorian "Lives" of Jesus.* San Antonio: Trinity UP, 1982.

Reardon, Bernard. *Liberalism and Tradition: Aspects of Catholic Thought in Nineteenth-Century France.* Cambridge: Cambridge UP, 1975.

———. *Religion in the Age of Romanticism.* Cambridge: Cambridge UP, 1985.

———. "Ernest Renan and the Religion of Science." *The Critical Spirit and the Will to Believe.* Ed. David Jasper and T. R. Wright. Basingstoke and London: Macmillan, 1988.

Renan, Ernest. *The Future of Science.* Trans. Albert Vandam and C. B. Pitman, London: Chapman and Hall, 1891.

———. *The History of the Origins of Christianity.* 7 vols. London: Mathieson, n.d.

———. *The Life of Jesus.* London: J. M. Dent, 1927.

———. *Oeuvres Completes.* 10 vols. Paris: Calmann-Levy, 1947-61.

———. *Recollections of My Youth.* Trans. C. B. Pitman. London: Chapman and Hall, 1892.

———. *Studies of Religious History.* London: Heinemann, 1893.

———. *Vie de Jésus.* Paris: Calmann-Levy, n.d.

Said, Edward. *Orientalism.* Harmondsworth: Penguin, 1978, 1985.

Schweitzer, Albert. *The Quest for the Historical Jesus.* Trans. W. Montgomery. London: A. and C. Black, 1910, 1922.

Shaffer, E. S. *"Kubla Khan" and The Fall of Jerusalem.* Cambridge: Cambridge UP, 1975.

Strauss, David Friedrich. *The Life of Jesus Critically Examined.* Trans. George Eliot. London: SCM Press, 1846, 1973.

Wardman, H. W. *Ernest Renan: A Critical Biography.* London: Athlone P, 1964.

David C. J. Lee (essay date 1996)

SOURCE: Lee, David C. J. "Fiction Christ." In *Ernest Renan: In the Shadow of Faith,* pp. 187-206. London: Duckworth, 1996.

[In the following excerpt, Lee asserts that Renan structured Vie de Jésus *in accordance with the conventions of the novel genre.]*

L'humanité . . . veut un Dieu-homme. Elle se satis-
fera.

Drames philosophiques, Oeuvres complètes III, 559.

There can scarcely be a sense in which *Vie de Jésus* does not mark a crossroads. The book's publication in June 1863 led to Renan's first serious encounter with international celebrity. Of all his works it perhaps represents his one authentic brush with immortality. If so, its appearance was timely, for in the February before *Vie de Jésus* came off the presses, its author reached the age of forty, that frontier of reassessment and recollection induced by first intimations of life's finitude. Indeed, researching his subject in Syria in 1861, Renan had, as he recalls, 'been touched by death's wing' (IV, 12). His sister, to whose memory he dedicates his book, had been its victim and when he left her body behind near Byblus, he also left there something of his youth. In one respect the high point of Renan's intellectual and artistic development, *Vie de Jésus* is in another the protest of his middle age against the prospect of extinction. When Renan, in a recollection of Horace, added the single word 'Exegi' to his finished manuscript,[1] he was perhaps saying nothing less. It was time to set his life in enduring bronze.

The critical path that leads Renan to his biography of 1863 and even to regarding it as the keystone of his entire life's edifice is already signposted by his *Essai psychologique sur Jésus Christ* of 1845. From the moment of his first anxieties at Saint-Sulpice over his faith and calling, it is as though each new phase in his career and writing becomes an act of remembrance and dedication to the Christ he has forsaken. Renan's subsequent dualist theories of language, race, knowledge itself, suppose a central term modelled on the cultural hinge which in his mind and memory Jesus represents. His sense of personal dissatisfaction and the irony in which it is progressively cloaked seem constantly to refer him to the same missing archetype. Now, almost twenty years after invoking Wiseman's theory of extraordinary natural laws to explain the supernova of Jesus' appearance on earth, the former seminarist is drawn to begin the major academic project of his maturity, the *Histoire des origines du christianisme* and its Semitic sequel, at its historic and historical mid-point, to reopen the book of his own and humanity's past, at its central page. The haunting dream sequence in the *Cahiers de jeunesse,* so reminiscent of Jean Paul Richter, in which Renan envisages a face-to-face encounter with Jesus, is in this respect as symptomatic as it is prophetic. 'Who would I have', he reflects, 'were you to elude me even after eighteen hundred years?' (IX, 244). Renan's readiness in his later biography to regard Jesus as a flesh and blood character rather than a mythical entity in the manner of Strauss may initially be seen as a response to this deep-seated need. Jesus is a ghost from the past but also a lost friend and an intimate real-

ity.[2] If it has become commonplace to claim that there is much autobiography in Renan's portrait of 1863,[3] it is because his profoundest longings were reflected back to him in that divine mirror. Renan's Jesus, suggests Laudyce Rétat in a subtle and complex observation, is an embodiment of Renan's own relationship with Jesus.[4]

But that of his world, too. What is true of Renan individually may also be held true of his century. *Vie de Jésus* stands at the fulcrum of nineteenth-century thought and art and reflects the age's innermost divisions. The traumas experienced by Richter, Nerval or Vigny in contemplating a mortal and comfortless Christ, the secular alternatives to Christian teaching promised by science or socialism, the attentions of Christologists such as Bauer or Strauss, collectively bear witness to the same combination of anxiety and fascination at a time of general religious decline, intellectual uncertainty and political unrest. The cult of infancy that starts with Rousseau, the regret for the psychological integrity of time lost which ends with Proust, seem always to derive their inspiration from the child of Nazareth as do those nineteenth-century voyages of wonder and exploration which eventually inspire an entire Europe to spread corrupting hands across the uncolonised globe. The common ground is the temptation afforded by unsullied soil or unsullied spirit to the divided and decadent, by the secret that seemed to have evaded a tired and introspective continent but which, it was felt, still lay buried in some uncomplicated region of mind or world. When Renan travelled to ancient Phoenicia in 1860, he was undertaking an academic but also a ritual journey to civilisation's birthplace and the presumed heart of its modern malaise. In a different form, the same thought is expressed in the introduction to the first edition of *Vie de Jésus,* which Renan concludes with the reflection that an understanding of religious history is only possible for a former believer like himself (IV, 83): where his *Vie de Jésus* can be considered the epitome of nineteenth-century consciousness is in its being the book of an age still capable of recalling its Christian origins with sympathy and nostalgia, even as it was persuaded to renounce them as childish fantasies.

As the example of Proust most comprehensively demonstrates, the conflicting demands of this age find a convergence in that form of literature whose rise to prominence coincides most nearly with that of the post-Revolutionary world order, prose fiction. To Balzac's definition of the novel as 'un carrefour de problèmes', might be added the reflection that the genre itself marks a crossroads for modern, secular man.[5] For the novel's development is at once consistent with the emergence of the new middle class, its liberal and democratic drive, and with the lack that such drive creates—with the need, that is, sensed by this same class for those forms of security and coherence previously associated with political order and religious conviction. Novels tell of meaning, pattern, structure, of that 'sense of an ending' of which Frank Kermode writes, at the same time as of a world where experience has begun to show endings to be unpredictable and the meaning of life to be obscure. Proust's quest for maternal protection through the medium of his own narrative here coincides with Sartre's description of the nineteenth-century novel as a source of reassurance for the *bourgeoisie* and subsequently with Barthes' recognition that the novel serves to provide a contingent world with the image of a lost essence.[6] With the novel we are entering the world of self-administered illusion, of the hunger for significance in a climate of doubt and change, for the strength of something akin to faith in a meaningful life in a period of religious scepticism. Standing indeed on the same symbolic axis as Christ himself, the novel is an ironic substitute for His message to fallen mankind of recoverable innocence, value, mediation. Were a single book to succeed in registering and exploring the many facets that are combined in such a function—spiritual, philosophical, artistic—its centrality could hardly be mistaken, and it is at this point of meeting that we again encounter Renan's *Vie de Jésus*.

Colin Smith's persuasive account of what is termed the 'fictionalist element' in Renan's thought provides an initial frame of reference. Smith returns us to certain thought systems of the nineteenth century as precursors of what Hans Vaihinger would later systematise into the principle of 'as if', and shows that Renan was himself disposed, by temperament as much as intellectual influence, to acknowledge that a degree of consciously sustained falsehood, the need to think and act as if what could be proven false were true, is necessary to the moral and emotional well-being of mankind. 'God is subjective but we must act *as if* he possessed objective reality; Jesus was a mortal man but we may profitably think of him *as if* he were God incarnate and rose from the dead.'[7] As early as the *Cahiers de jeunesse* and again in *L'Avenir de la science,* Renan entertains the prospect of the emptiness of abstract thought reduced to its ultimate terms. Existence requires the cosmetic 'boursouflure' of discursiveness, approximation, symbolic content, if it is to be preserved from the A = A of analytic stalemate: 'Things obtain their value from what humanity sees in them, from the sentiments it has attached to them, from the symbols it has derived from them' (III, 879). Persuaded by his experience in Rome in 1849 that such symbolism is centred in religious faith and worship, Renan's conclusion becomes the prediction of Antistius in *Le Prêtre de Nemi* of 1885: 'Humanity desires a God who is both finite and infinite, real and ideal; it adores the ideal; but it needs the ideal to be personified; it wants a God-man; it will have one' (III, 559). This appreciation on the part of the author of *Vie de Jésus* of the human craving for a symbol of value is, of course, consistent with his own loss of faith, but it may be added that he is objectively justified in

sensing that valuelessness is a secular state and the fiction of value a secular need. The ultimate fiction may thus be regarded as a need to abjure the secular, and its ultimate form, at least in secularised Christian societies, is a fiction of Christ.

Professor Smith is not concerned with reconciling the 'as if' principle in Renan with literary fiction as it is also being discussed here, although his recognition that 'for Renan religion is largely an aesthetic affair', invites that reconciliation in the form taken by Renan's *Vie de Jésus* from 1863. Many commentators have been quick to recognise in his book characteristics which seem more nearly those of the novel than a work of exacting historical or biblical scholarship[8] but few have been prepared to examine *Vie de Jésus* in this light, much less acknowledge these affinities as a vital part of its function and importance. But if *Vie de Jésus* may also be read as an instance of literary fiction, its form and its subject propose a challenging integration. In Renan's own terms, a fiction Christ is required by a world unable to conceive its traditional symbol of transcendent value as a fiction. In the language of the age of the novel, *Vie de Jésus* affords a society setting aside the Christian story of the divine Christ of truth, the substitute of 'the great coherent lie'.[9]

In one respect, of course, such an integration is by no means unique to Renan. The emergence of the early Christian novel, typified in Victorian England by Newman's *Callista,* Kingsley's *Hypatia* or Wiseman's *Fabiola,* in France by Chateaubriand's early contribution to the genre, *Les Martyrs,* assuredly has much to tell us about Renan's most celebrated undertaking. In making, indeed, the observation that Renan's Life was the first of its kind written for the Catholic world,[10] Schweitzer underlines the degree to which nineteenth-century Europe as a whole, Protestant as well as Catholic, had, in the course of secularisation, become sensitive to Christianity in a new way. Renan's book may have its intellectual origins in the work of German Protestant theology, but the latter's contribution to Christology had been neglected in the popular imagination for the very reasons that made Renan's reworking of it such a success: the inclination of the Victorian reader to endow Christianity with sentiment and romance. What smacks to Schweitzer of the Catholic in Renan—his feeling for the lyricism of the Gospel story, its aesthetic charm, plasticity, even sensuality—is precisely what offered satisfaction to an age disposed as a whole to preserve the religious in the association of pious feelings with literary pleasure.

We must be prepared in Renan's case, however, to distinguish between the satisfaction of such feelings and their ironic exploitation. The former seminarist knew and understood the Catholic mind and its tastes well enough to be able to cultivate them, but he might more readily have subscribed to Carlyle's sentiments writing in *Past and Present* of his age's hypocritical sensibilities: 'You touch the focal-centre of all our disease, of our frightful nosology of diseases, when you lay your hand on this. There is no religion; there is no God; man has lost his soul, and vainly seeks antiseptic salt' (*Collected Works,* 1870-1, XIII, 172). 'We mostly read badly', contributes the author of *Vie de Jésus* himself, introducing his translation of Ecclesiastes of 1882, 'when we read on our knees' (VII, 555).

The equivalent work to *Vie de Jésus* from an earlier period in Renan's career and in the development of his century is *L'Avenir de la science,* in that it still enshrines the Revolutionary belief in the achievement of social and intellectual progress through the human will and acts of human intervention. The equivalent Romantic Christology is that of the influential Strauss, for whom Christ is no more but no less than a noble symbol of man's pursuit of transcendence. Conceived in the mode of Hegel, both works posit active engagement with traditional Christianity and its translation into a modern idiom via the medium of myth. In Strauss' *Leben* as for Renan evoking the 'great moral teacher' of 1848, Jesus is revisited only to the extent of serving as a model of the human spirit triumphant. If Renan, fifteen years later, chooses on the other hand to invest the Christian story with the opaqueness of what he now terms 'legend', it is in response to that change of values in contemporary French society and thought inaugurated by the Second Empire which invites human history to be deemed impenetrable and human nature itself subject to drives other than that of the questing intellect. The new relationship is again that revealed by Renan's earlier *Averroès et l'averroïsme* with respect to history or perhaps Fromentin's Dominique before the mystery of Madeleine: what was optimistically held to be the province of mankind in development is now restored to the obscurity of its own laws and nature.

But the ironical undertow already discerned beneath this transfer is always present and Sainte-Beuve perhaps sensed the true character of *Vie de Jésus* when he said that it reminded him of the transformation undergone by the one-time brigands who became the Knights of Malta: 'C'est d'un effet singulier à première vue' (*Nouveaux lundis,* 7 September 1863, 1866, VI, 23). The transposition of history into art noted by Renan in his essay on Augustin Thierry of 1857 is the most symptomatic indicator of this process as much as it is anticipated by his revisions of stance and style in 'Les Historiens critiques de Jésus'. Art in its formal plasticity is the residual mode of the historian in his tactical surrender to the other: time, nature, or ignorance. Thus conceived, the Christ of history stands apart from the analytic intelligence, while his erstwhile critic or adversary becomes his ironically respectful advocate. In its most developed form, this ironical historical art is then at one

with the novel. As an impression is to an academic painting or the noun to the active verb, the novel is the historian's place of atemporal retreat and concealment. Ultimately Renan's book concerns the new age's own taste for religious artefacts and religious sentiments; his Christian novel is an ironic rejoinder to Christian novels, his Christ of fiction a badge of convenience worn for a world beset by fiction.

* * *

The use of fiction as a vehicle for the exploration of the mentality which brought fiction into being is, of course, a strategy associated with Renan's novelist contemporary, Gustave Flaubert. Men of the same generation and of similar dispositions and temperaments, both seem to have concentrated the energies of their intellectual maturities on an enquiry into the psychology of fiction and its relevance to modern societies. Both writers sense that the cult of the fictional is related to their generation's loss of intellectual and moral integrity in its surrender under the Second Empire to political despotism, materialism and feminised values, and both typify the response of the beleaguered intelligentsia of the age in their ironic flirtation with its own tastes. If Renan adds a dimension which in Flaubert, explicitly at least, is lacking, it is from his perspective as a historian that the fictionalist tendencies of the time are most clearly manifest in the contamination of historical truth and, as a historian of religion, that any enquiry into such tendencies must always return us to the foundations of Western religion and the interpretation accorded to the life of Christ. Whereas Flaubert eschewed 'les beaux sujets' in his disdain for the triviality and mediocrity of his age, his own analysis thus led Renan to what is arguably the greatest subject of all. What is mediocre in Renan's eyes is not the man, but the minds that have nailed him to fiction's cross.

Flaubert's two modern novels of the Second Empire period, *Madame Bovary* and *L'Education sentimentale,* highlight the misunderstanding and mismanagement of life induced by fiction's influence. As Emma Bovary fails to find in real marriage, motherhood, adultery, the satisfaction that she has been led to expect from them by clandestine reading of pulp romance at her convent, so Frédéric in *L'Education sentimentale* experiences what Cortland terms 'the collision of dream and reality',[11] as a result of the fiction he entertains of his love for Madame Arnoux. Life to each is a disappointment because it fails to resemble the image received from literary fiction; what Flaubert conceives to be 'sentimental' about the generation he depicts in his great novel of 1869 being its inclination to invest reality with fictional feelings and fictional meanings.

The internal contradiction that has then not escaped the novelist's commentators, is that the instrument employed to portray such attitudes is the very one that is seen as its cause; the behaviour of the characters is echoed in the form in which that behaviour is recounted, generalising it as a condition in which writer and reader as much as protagonist are embroiled, and creating the conditions for authorial irony. Through the self-conscious replication of subject in form, clarity of transcendent meaning is blocked by the immanence of the text in a parody of the cloying immanentism of the age. The 'book about nothing' to which Flaubert aspired as the pinnacle of his artistic ambition, constantly recoils upon itself, burying its own head in the folds of endless circularity.

Ambivalence and irony of this kind are, of course, already present in Renan's *Etudes d'histoire religieuse* and *Essais de morale et de critique* of the 1850s as in his earlier experiment in fiction, *Patrice*. What he terms 'tact' in his essay on the Académie Française from 1859 is as faithful a summary as any of Flaubert's address to his sentimental world. Where *Vie de Jésus* nonetheless marks a development from these earlier 'essays' and 'studies' not only concerns the book's subject, but is of the same order which separates an artist's sketch from a fully-fledged painting, or a statement of literary methodology from its comprehensive application. Renan, we are reminded by Mary Darmesteter,[12] drafted *Vie de Jésus* in Palestine in the space of a few months, away from Western reference books and libraries, and the fluency and autonomy of this genesis is retained in the finished work. With *Vie de Jésus* we are dealing with the thing itself, the vertiginous masterpiece, whose ironic concentricity approaches Flaubert's own ideal.

> I have managed to endow all this with a sense of organic development, something entirely absent from the Gospels. As a consequence, I trust that my readers will be met by living beings and not those pale, lifeless phantoms: Jesus, Mary, Peter, etc . . . turned into abstractions and reduced to types.
>
> As with the vibrations of a sound plate, I have attempted to produce the bow stroke which arranges the sand grains in natural waves.
>
> (E. Renan and M. Berthelot, *Correspondance, 1847-1892,* 12 September 1861, p. 284)

Renan writing here from Beirut in 1861 to his chemist friend Berthelot begins to give an indication of where this affinity lies. For what is at issue here concerns the uncertain boundary and ironic interplay between history and imaginative art.

Art in some form can never be said to be wholly absent from historiography, in that all writing entails the literary skills of formal organisation, communication, persuasion. The historian may even feel justified, in pursuance of his legitimate goal of recreating the general character of an epoch or the personality of a given individual, in borrowing the techniques of dramatist or novelist to round out individual lives into psychologically coherent entities on the basis of established models of human development. It is thus that Renan, writing in the fifth chapter of *Vie de Jésus,* can explain his approach to his own central character:

> . . . the development of character is everywhere the same; and there is no doubt that the growth of so powerful an individuality as that of Jesus obeyed very rigorous laws.
>
> (IV, 131[13])

The exploitation by generations of novelists of 'faits divers' culled from journalism as a starting point for fictional intrigue is another such point of contact between the two domains whose aims of social understanding, psychological or political analysis, constantly mesh with one another. When Balzac wrote of being at once 'secretary to his age' and the student of its 'secret laws', he was saying as much: the historian and the novelist are familiar bedfellows in their concern to record and investigate the government of individuals and societies.

As Lukács in his study of the historical novel suggests, however, what distinguishes Balzac's age from that of Flaubert is the breakdown following the Revolution of 1848 of the belief that the historical past could be distinguished from the present and thereby usefully contribute to an understanding of it, and it is at this point that the erstwhile historian finds renewed common cause with the novelist in the purely anecdotal exploration of history.[14] Renan's rejection in his letter to Berthelot of a taxonomic approach to the inhabitants of the Biblical past in favour of what he terms 'living beings', is indicative of a shift away from the ideal of historical knowledge and historical perspective towards a view of these beings as mere constituents of an imagined present. In the same way, his insistence on the importance of 'organic development', achieved by the aesthetic coherence of his own writing, points to the abandonment of any truly historical register for what amounts to a form of literary naturalism. Where indeed *Vie de Jésus* may begin to be conceived as a kind of novel is in an ideological context, involving the replacement of the historical transcendence of the previous age by perceptions of society and the individual founded on the model of organic nature, whose own 'rigorous laws' render history irrelevant and reduce to Flaubertian 'nothingness' the historian's endeavours.

Darwin's *Origin of Species* was published in French in 1862[15] and, in October 1863, a few months after the appearance of his own best-selling work, Renan gave to the *Journal des débats* his 'open' letter to Berthelot, 'Les Sciences de la nature et les sciences historiques'. In it he expresses regret at not having taken a career in natural science, and concedes that history should recognise its minor place in the grander design of evolution: 'The entire destiny of planet earth is thereby explainable even if as yet unexplained' (I, 639). Where Renan's earlier version of the historical process, as instanced by the appeal of Wiseman's theory of natural cataclysm or his own seismic vision in *L'Avenir de la science,* still allows for the exceptional as an explanation of historical causality, this revised one admits only to the unbroken chain of organic constancy: 'the relentless action of ordinary causes' (I, 637). By the same token, his previous vision of the historical sciences as the avenue to man's true understanding of himself and his destiny now has to be placed against a conception of the historian deprived of his primary status in the intellectual hierarchy; 'In fine, what goes by the name of history is the history of the last hour, as though, in trying to understand the history of France, we were confined to knowing what happened in the last ten years' (I, 644). It is a view which will lead him to write in his later *Souvenirs* of history as a 'little conjectural science' (II, 852) and the irony of these words from the pen of an historian is inseparable from the subordination of history to art highlighted by *Vie de Jésus.*

What Renan's book owes to this new understanding of historical time and historical causation initially concerns the perceived limits of scientific knowledge that derive from it, and the perception of human behaviour and human societies which these epistemological limitations reflect. The celebrated discussion of the miraculous in the 1867 preface to *Vie de Jésus,* perhaps represents the best example of what is now authentically Positivist in his own thinking: miracles cannot be refuted a priori; they simply lie outside the province which knowledge, in its present state, permits itself to explore. Equally, the explanation given by Renan of the personality and development of Jesus sits well on a view of the individual, however unusual, as always subject to what, in his public exchange with Berthelot, he terms 'ordinary causes'. For in contrast to the Jesus of the *Essai psychologique* from his last months at Saint-Sulpice, the hero of *Vie de Jésus* emerges as the wholly natural product of his Galilean homeland and tribal roots, just as his subsequent formation is shown to be the result of contemporary political and social circumstances. If Renan required any corroboration for this determinist mechanism, he could also have found it in the work of his friend and countryman, Taine, whose *Histoire de la littérature anglaise* appeared in the same year as *Vie de Jésus,* including its preface containing the much-quoted trilogical formula of environmental causation by 'la race, le milieu, le moment'.

Not least, Renan's readiness to depict in Jesus a very fallible mortal who is flattered by his followers into living out his dramatic role, seems destined to underline the conformity of the individual to other normalising pressures: in a manner fit to recall the collectivism of Zola or the faceless puppets of Maupassant's social analysis, it is the group or the crowd who now determine the conduct of the man. The hero of *Vie de Jésus* is doubtless far removed from the cynically exploitive Duroy of Maupassant's *Bel-Ami* of 1885, but he shares something of the same capacity for flexing to the social breeze. In this respect the quality of 'charm' to which Renan repeatedly draws attention in his hero is less a personal charisma, more a kind of absolute compliance with the world around him.

Here it becomes pertinent to make an initial incursion into the subject of Renan's chosen title. For the omission of the definite article—'*Vie de Jésus*', not 'La Vie de Jésus' as it is commonly mis-styled—itself suggests an emphasis on the generic rather than the particular, the organic rather than the individualist. A comparable response seems to have led Maupassant again to give that most universal of all titles 'Une Vie' to his first novel as though no life was distinct from any other. To apply to the life and the events whose uniqueness is the basis of all Christian teaching, if not the entire culture of the West, what, in these terms, is 'vie' is to aim indeed at calculated symmetry: what is mortality most mediocre on one side is the name of all aspirations to individuality and transcendence on the other.

And this, of course, is the crux of the matter at once for the Christian facing the challenge of Renan's book and for the historian-artist who created it. For Renan here disturbs a Schopenhauerian spectre by which his novelist contemporaries were also haunted: the illusion attending the *principium individuationis*. Frédéric Moreau begins the great journey to nowhere that is Flaubert's *L'Education sentimentale* with the thought that 'the happiness which his nobility of soul deserved was slow in coming' (tr. Baldick); the meteoric rise to social stardom of Georges Duroy is matched, conversely, only by the nullity and facticity of his own personality. In the same way, the obscuring of individuality serves to render arbitrary the historian's attempts to explain historical development in heroic terms. Shorn of their uniqueness, 'normalised' by the supposed constancy of natural law, earlier events and even the greatest of individuals are subsumed within a past where meaning is cloaked beneath the anonymity of 'life'. 'The abstract contempt for "external" history', observes Lukács of the nature-based outlook of the Second-Empire, 'gives historical events a grey, everyday character, reduces them to a simple level of spontaneity.'[16] 'The living tradition', writes Renan exemplifying the point in his later study of the Gospels, 'was the great reservoir from which all drew their water. Hence the explanation of this apparently surprising fact, that the texts which subsequently became the most important part of Christianity came into being obscurely and confusedly . . .' (V, 51). Transcendent history's sun is now organic nature's sunflower, inclining before the light that is bestowed on it:

the mystery of a process which gave rise spontaneously to legend, image, popular illusion.

One aspect of *Vie de Jésus* to which this new conception of history gives rise was noted by Taine himself when he detected a connection between Renan's methods of scholarship and writing and those of contemporary painting; '. . . he does not proceed from one precise truth to another, he gropes about, he feels his way. He has *impressions*. That word says it all' (Taine, *Vie et correspondance,* II, 3rd ed., 1908, 242). Writing then himself in the 1867 preface to *Vie de Jésus,* Renan confirms what is suggested here: 'I wanted to create a picture in which the colours were blended as they are in nature, which would resemble mankind, that is to say noble and childish at the same time' (IV, 33). 'All great things', he explains later, 'are done through the people; we can lead the people only by adapting ourselves to its ideas' (IV, 242). As with a painting by Manet, *a fortiori* Monet, the fate of the historian is to be condemned to depict a world from which the intellectual and historical is missing. The corresponding characteristic to that accorded by Renan to his 'charming' but fraudulent hero belongs now with *Vie de Jésus* itself: the book's fundamental nature and source of its irony lies in its reflecting a picture-book world without depth of understanding, in its being a self-conscious mirror of what other people think they see.

It is, however, Renan's sense, developed in his subsequent study of the Gospels, that the spread of Christianity was itself an artistic rather than historical phenomenon that ultimately determines the nature of his own book in the context of the impossibility of disengagement from organic time: 'It was the Gospel that won over hearts, that delightful mixture of poetry and moral sense, that account suspended between dream and reality in a paradise where time goes unmeasured. There is surely a degree of literary wonderment in all this' (V, 94). The scientific insouciance, furthermore, that he detects in the Gospels—'imprecise chronology, casual transitions, careless of reality' (V, 93)—will become that of his own writing. 'The overall effect is of an enchanted palace, built entirely of brilliant stones. An exquisite vagueness . . . leads the narrative to hover as in a dream between earth and sky' (V, 153). Wardman is rightly sensitive to this correspondence between Renan's biography and its Christian models,[17] but so is the author of *Vie de Jésus* himself: 'There will always be lives of Jesus. What is more, the Life of Jesus will always enjoy great success when the writer has the necessary skill, boldness and innocence to translate the Gospels into the style of his times' (V, 94). As Renan's choice of title may also be held to convey, there is at the heart of *Vie de Jésus* and central to its entire character an alternative sense of the generic applicable to a story on which humanity has imposed an indelible literary stereotype.

But there is a final twist to this intricate spiral and one which suggests the true relationship between Renan's Jesus and Renan himself. For, in contrast to his noble moralist from the opening paragraph of *L'Avenir de la science,* Renan now conceives Jesus' own personality as being governed by an artist's mentality and timing in the face of the disturbing enigma of life. Jesus himself is 'ce grand maître en ironie' (IV, 294), 'embracing at the same time various orders of truths' (IV, 265), 'at once very ideal in his conceptions and very concrete in their expression' (IV, 274). This artist Christ is himself also an ironist and a fictionalist, responding to his world as his biographers of old responded to him by living his life to its demanded, fictional conclusion: it is at the bidding of humanity's need for his story rather than history that he had to live as he did: 'So closely was he identified with his idea, that his idea became him, absorbed him, turned his biography into what it had to be. There was in him what theologians call "communication of idioms". There is the same communication between the first and penultimate book of this history' (V, 157). Renan is writing here of his own *Vie de Jésus* and his own study of the Gospels, *Les Evangiles.* Perhaps he already sensed that the final irony of this pattern of circular 'communication' lay in his own achievement thereby of a form of ironic immortality.

* * *

Renan's introduction to *Vie de Jésus* of 1863 and his preface to the thirteenth edition of 1867 are valuable as signposts to this ironic interior. Forming two separate 'introductions', each originally conceived in different circumstances to meet different needs,[18] they become englobed in the modern version of the finished work as though offering separate avenues to it. Alfaric is certainly justified in suggesting that Renan's earlier introduction 'falsifies the perspective' of the text itself,[19] but any such falsification has perhaps to be viewed in the light of a work constructed from many such approximations and whose artistic aim, as defined by Renan himself, is 'the making of a true whole out of parts which are only half true' (IV, 30). The reversal of the chronological order of writing in the order of reading itself contributes to the intervalency of the two texts which together assume the character of self-conscious self-repudiation.

Significantly, indeed, the 1863 introduction to *Vie de Jésus* posits a rational history available to the rationalist historian. It is here that Renan presents himself as the erstwhile believer standing respectfully but necessarily apart from events and values from another age and another mentality: 'The most beautiful thing in the world has thus proceeded from an obscure and purely popular elaboration' (IV, 55). It remains possible, however, to reconstruct this past using modern analytical tools and modern analogies, and Strauss in particular is singled out for his fault in this respect 'of taking up . . . the historical ground too little' (IV, 44). Confronting the classic problem of the authority of the four Gospels as records of the life and teachings of Christ, 'we will inquire only', writes Renan, 'in what degree the data furnished by the Gospels may be employed in a history formed according to rational principles' (IV, 50).

Since they are, in part at least, concerned with the miraculous and the supernatural they must, to some degree, be considered legendary but retain their value as 'des biographies légendaires', for which a modern analogy might be sought in the account given by a group of former Napoleonic soldiers of their great leader: 'It is clear that their narratives would contain numerous errors and great discordances. One of them would place Wagram before Marengo; another would write without hesitation that Napoleon drove the government of Robespierre from the Tuileries; a third would omit expeditions of the highest importance' (IV, 74). On the other hand, 'the character of the hero', 'the impression he made around him', would be likely to emerge with clarity and truthfulness.

His own *Vie de Jésus* will thus apply the same logic in search of 'the very soul of history'. Such an endeavour involves the recognition that any great life is 'an organic whole' demanding an imaginative response on the part of the historian which has its counterpart in the 'tact' and 'taste' of art: 'In histories such as this, the great test that we have got the truth is to have succeeded in combining the texts in such a manner that they shall constitute a logical, probable narrative, harmonious throughout' (IV, 81). Classical verisimilitude and 'bienséance', together with a classical sense of unity, are here invoked to serve the cause of classic historiography.

The world depicted by Renan in his 1867 preface and the historian's role in confronting it are, however, of a very different stamp. Where one invites a reading of *Vie de Jésus* as a work of cautious scholarship supported by tasteful conjecture, the other presents rational scholarship as a travesty of history and the ironic disposition of the artist as the sole source of communion with a past of discord, folly and madness. Where one conceives the Gospel 'legends' as understandable and decipherable, the other compares them to the superstitious belief in ghosts and monsters. Where one presents Jesus as a glamorous hero to be treated with respect and adulation, the other depicts him as an appealing but fraudulent witchdoctor. Where one distances itself from his teaching in a gesture of gratitude and respect, the other identifies his dark beliefs alive in all human nature.

Refusing in this case to be drawn into any form of active controversy—'that would have meant speaking of myself, something I never do' (IV, 14)—Renan initiates

a complementary discussion of the value to be attached to sacred writing which is also implicitly a discussion of the value of *all* writing: 'Every rule of criticism assumes that the document which is the subject of study has only relative value, that such a document may be mistaken, that it may be corrected by a better document' (IV, 17). What to the sceptic may be a falsehood, to the believer may be a truth; evidence of a single miracle would turn his own text into 'un tissu d'erreurs' (IV, 15). His own introduction to the edition of 1863 has been 'retouched and completed' (IV, 21), particularly where it deals with the controversial Fourth Gospel. We are in a realm where nothing written is ever what it seems or may have seemed but of 'delicate approximations' (IV, 15). 'Because a thing is written down', observes Renan majestically, 'it does not follow that it has to be true' (IV, 17).

The master of this shifting world is then truly the artist rather than the historian, 'art holding the key to the most intimate laws of truth' (IV, 19). Without it, a life of Jesus would be confined to a series of disconnected banalities, the meagrest of 'faits divers': 'He existed. He was from Nazareth in Galilee. He was a magnetic preacher and his sayings left a profound mark on the memories of his disciples. His two principal followers were Peter and John, the sons of Zebedee. He aroused the hatred of the orthodox Jews who contrived to have him put to death by Pontius Pilate, then procurator of Judea. He was crucified outside the city gate. It was afterwards believed that he rose from the dead' (IV, 25). Beyond this 'le doute est permis', and answers can only be formulated in the shape of questions. Earlier Protestant scholars, reflects Renan, have clumsily confined themselves to the 'incidents' of Jesus' life through want of any appreciation of 'la théorie de la vie spirituelle' (IV, 29). The epithet has, of course, two distinct meanings in French: in engaging with the spiritual we are engaging the ironic mind and understanding.

This is also the message which underlies Renan's reflections towards the end of his preface, on the nature of the society in which Jesus lived and the kind of character he must have been. To the ironic symmetries of art corresponds history's ironic purpose: 'The world is a comedy at once infernal and divine, a strange round led by a genial dancemaster, in which good and evil, ugliness and beauty file past in their assigned stations, with a view to the fulfilment of an unknown purpose. History is not history if it does not alternately charm and revolt us, sadden and console us as we read it' (IV, 30-1). *A fortiori*, humanity's religious origins are the arena for this historical comedy, for with them we enter 'a world of women, children, passionate and deranged mentalities', in which it is impossible to separate fraud from honesty, calculation from innocence, as much as it is inappropriate to evaluate it as we might choose: 'Ne faisons pas le passé à notre image' (IV, 32).

Jesus himself is, finally, to be viewed as part of this web of ignorance and imperfection, for he was its 'charmer', a magician who succeeded in satisfying its tastes and needs rather than a scholar, a moralist or a saint. History is a record of great deeds achieved by 'consciences troubles' and there is no great founder who has not ended his career by 'desperate measures' whatever the innocence of his original goals: 'I had to make my hero handsome and charming (for, without any doubt he was); and this in spite of actions which, in our day, would be viewed in an unfavourable light' (IV, 34). 'If the picture had been without a shadow, this would have been the proof that it was false' (IV, 33). We are, concludes Renan, dealing with human nature as the entomologist would observe the transformations of a chrysalis into a butterfly without prejudice or passion. But this analogy is significant in another way. Free and pure spirit he may seem but, like the butterfly, the historian is merely his more primitive self in another guise. The religious that marks humanity's pupal phase is stamped indelibly on all our futures: 'Est Deus in nobis. . . .' (IV, 39).

Whether or not it is appropriate to regard Renan's introduction and preface as integral to *Vie de Jésus,* assumes at this point less importance than the awareness that together they represent the attitudes of mind from which the biography itself takes its being. Read chronologically, the book's twin introductions tell of the retreat of the academic mind into the ironic and ludic as the result of the ideological shifts which characterise the period of Renan's maturity, whether they are those of history itself, society or politics. Judged inappropriate by Lagrange,[20] Renan's comparison in his 1863 introduction between the legends surrounding Jesus and those which sprang up in Napoleon's armies, plainly points at a contrast with the empire of falsehood and hysteria ushered in half a century later by a politically 'charming fraud'. Inescapably, too, there is in this juxtaposition of values an account of psychosexual transfer from male- to female-centred values, the Apollonian to the Dionysian, and with it the withdrawal of the critical spirit, the intellect and the will behind the ironical mask imposed on it by the instinctual, the bodily and popular. In this regard, the introduction of 1863 is to Renan's later preface what *L'Avenir de la science* is to *Vie de Jésus*: where there was once critical and historical distance, there is now only the irony latent in pure parody. Most significantly, however, this exchange anticipates the life of Jesus himself as told by Renan. For *Vie de Jésus* is itself the story of noble masculinity lost, of illusions becoming the norm, of fiction being imposed upon the historically pure and of history's death at the hands of the fanatical multitude.

* * *

His new faith has not destroyed the old one and has taken away nothing of its poetry. He loves two things

at once. The observer delights in this untroubled struggle. What a charming state of being, without being anything in particular.

(V, 159-60)

Writing here in **Les Evangiles** on the qualities of St Matthew's Gospel, Renan perhaps comes nearest to defining the nature of his own. For what we have termed the 'fictional' in *Vie de Jésus* is less an obvious presence, more a state of absence, the result of the weighing of intellectual and sentimental allegiances against one another to neutralise their monopoly on consciousness and preserve their value only as part of an artistic structure. 'The true novel form', says Cortland again of Flaubert, 'is the amorphous state of the uncommitted mind.'[21] There is nothing here of the calculated dialectics of Renan's later **Dialogues philosophiques** but something close to a suspension of time and self experienced by a reader immersed in a novel; sensing always its factitiousness, but lulled into compliance with it. The novel is also that which charms to deceive. This is Renan's subject but also his method of approach to it. His book is at once an investigation and a demonstration of what it investigates: the power of the plausible and spiritually satisfying to engage and progressively lay hold of the imagination.

Evidence of the presence of such a progression begins with what have frequently been identified as two contrasting atmospheres or moods in *Vie de Jésus.* Developing his account of Renan's method, Taine detected a tendency on the part of his friend to divide his Life of Jesus into complementary phases: 'He gathers all the gentle and pleasant thoughts of Jesus together in the Nazareth period and leaves out the sad ones, creating a lovely, mystical pastoral. Then, in another chapter, he introduces all the threats and all the bitterness, which he relates to the journey to Jerusalem' (*Vie et correspondance,* II, 245). Renan indeed writes of Jesus' early years in Galilee as being lived 'amid enchanting scenes', radiant with birds and blossoms to the point where 'the whole history of infant Christianity has become in this manner a delightful pastoral' (IV, 127), while the picture he paints of Jerusalem is that of 'un monde odieux', enveloped in an arid wasteland (IV, 214-15).

As Taine himself reveals through his use in the same context of a vocabulary more suited to the plastic arts, this structure is in one respect a reflection of the self-conscious plasticity of *Vie de Jésus,* its internal rhymes and symmetries. There are no historical or even biblical grounds for dividing the career of Christ in this way any more than for Renan's unhesitating claim that Jesus had brothers and sisters (IV, 100), or that he began his teaching before meeting John the Baptist (IV, 150). Like a painting or a novel, the book's first call is on the requirements of the artefact: the historical events and characters are servants to the form. In another, however, the polar structure of *Vie de Jésus* serves, like its two introductions, to replicate the overall journey represented by the narrative as clarity and enlightenment give way to a kind of intellectual darkness, simplicity and integrity to irony and illusion.

For at the beginning of *Vie de Jésus,* the character that emerges from the bountiful Galilean landscape is himself of spontaneous stature and generosity: 'une personne supérieure' (IV, 85), 'l'homme incomparable' (IV, 96). A son of the people but different by his elevated mind and spirit, Jesus has 'a profound idea of the familiar relations of man with God, and an exaggerated belief in the power of man' (IV, 111). Attractive in appearance, strong of character 'he did not preach his opinions; he preached himself' (IV, 133), his personal sense of his unique relationship with God his Father being translated into a single, simple idea: 'A pure worship, a religion without priests and external observances, resting entirely on the feelings of the heart, on the imitation of God . . .' (IV, 139). What Renan regards as the first of a series of key doctrines, each associated with a different phase in Jesus' life, is born in this personality entirely at one with himself and his world in 'the kingdom of God'.

The presumed death of Joseph his father and Jesus' encounter with John the Baptist, however, induce an initial change in him, for he finds himself the subject of an exclusively maternal love and then befriending a young male companion. Imagined by Renan to be a man of Jesus' own age, John is an ally but also an influence and a rival: 'Jesus thought himself obliged to do like John' (IV, 152). The adoption of the practice of baptism, of fasting and ascetic isolation in the desert are the first indications of surrender to the popular imagination, just as his ideas now assume a popular, revolutionary colour. The kingdom of God is now 'a refuge for souls in the midst of the empire of brute force' (IV, 161). 'The "world" is in this manner the enemy of God and his saints; but God will awaken and avenge his saints. The day is at hand, for the abomination is at its height. The reign of goodness will have its turn' (IV, 158). Inspired by this 'millenarism', a growing group of disciples begin to identify Jesus as the Messiah and he in turn is inspired by their convictions: 'the more people believed in him, the more he believed in himself' (IV, 172). His days at Capernaum and on the shores of the Lake of Tiberias are the focus of the 'delicate communism' of the beatitudes, of his identification with the poor and the meek of the 'continual feast' (IV, 203), already distinct from the ascetic society of John, of weddings, hospitality, conviviality.

It is with Jesus' first real contact with Jerusalem around the year 31 that Renan, however, associates the completion of this progressive change in his hero's persona and conception of his mission. Once in the capital city, 'the little Galilean community were here far from being at home' (IV, 213). Jesus himself 'was lost in the crowd' (IV, 217). A stranger to the Temple and its ways 'the charming teacher who forgave everyone, provided they loved him, could find little sympathy in this sanctuary of vain disputes and obsolete sacrifices' (IV, 220). Confronted by the hostility of the Jews, Jesus now comes to see himself as the enemy of Judaism and to associate with unorthodox 'Hellenes' (IV, 227). As opinion contrives to identify in him the true 'son of David', it conflates with his own sense of messianic mission to create the living legend of his birth at Bethlehem, of a stable and a star: 'Nothing great has been established which does not rest on a legend. The only culprit in such cases is humanity, willing to be deceived' (IV, 242).

Chapter XVI of *Vie de Jésus,* concerning miracles, belongs to this context of increasing social pressures on the will and individuality of Jesus. Since miracles were held to be evidence of divinity, 'Jesus was, therefore, obliged to choose between two alternatives—either to renounce his mission or to become a thaumaturgist' (IV, 244). Uncomprehending of any distinction between the world of the natural and the supernatural, he accedes to acts which have encouraged belief in him over the centuries. 'Socrates and Pascal', remarks Renan, 'had their delusions', and, in an echo of the latter: 'human frailties only engender frailty; great things have ever great causes in man's nature, though often evolved amid trivialities which to shallow minds veil their grandeur' (IV, 251).

Pascalian doubleness and 'finesse d'esprit' now indeed become central to Jesus' own character and teaching with respect to the kingdom of God, the one persona able to satisfy society's needs for a message of consolation, the other to live out its own loftier ideals. 'C'est parce qu'elle était à double face que sa pensée a été féconde' (IV, 260). Jesus thus emerges as the 'incomparable artist', the great ironist capable by a kind of 'exalted divination' of embracing 'divers ordres de vérités': 'The phrase, "kingdom of God", expresses also, very happily, the want which the soul experiences of a supplementary destiny, of a compensation for the present life' (IV, 264).

This ambivalent and ironical message, however, also serves as a trigger to a kind of self-assessment on the part of Renan's hero. Increasingly misanthropic and introverted like some wasted and benighted star whose energies are concentrated within itself, the 'sombre giant' (IV, 280) of his final years rediscovers self-esteem and personal integrity with this bifurcation of his mission:

> He might still have avoided death; but he would not. Love for his work sustained him. He was willing to

drink the cup to the dregs. Henceforth we behold Jesus entirely himself; his character unclouded.

(IV, 321-2)

But as he himself sinks into history there to rest in peace in 'profoundly united to his Father' (IV, 349), which was his first and only ideal, the world itself is fashioning his teaching and his image to its own other ends.

For his credulous disciples, every act of the master is now redolent with symbolism. An insignificant meal becomes 'par une illusion inévitable' (IV, 326), one of the central memories of Western consciousness; a phrase blurted out by a dying and disillusioned man an awesome message to a waiting world; a chance discovery by a woman of the people of an empty tomb the ultimate miracle to bear his name to eternity:

> What had taken place? In treating of the history of the Apostles we shall have to examine this point, and to make inquiry into the origin of the legends relative to the resurrection. For the historian, the life of Jesus finishes with his last sigh. But such was the impression he had left in the hearts of his disciples and of a few devoted women that during some weeks more it was as if he were living and consoling them. Had his body been taken away, or did enthusiasm, always credulous, create afterwards the group of narratives by which it was sought to establish faith in the resurrection? In the absence of opposing documents, this can never be ascertained. Let us say, however, that the strong imagination of Mary Magdalene played an important part in this circumstance. Divine power of love! Sacred moments in which the passion of one possessed gave to the world a resuscitated God!

(IV, 356)

All the elements that go to form this celebrated sequence, its associations with the feminine, the Tainean notion of 'hallucination', the power of 'impression', 'in the absence of opposing documents', point to it as a reflection on the process of polarisation that has occurred in the course of Jesus' own story, and of which *Vie de Jésus* itself is the testimony. As the historical Jesus withdraws from life into final solitude and death, the fictitious which he has briefly courted rushes in full flood to fill the vacant space. And so too for the historian of Jesus that his biographer might have been. What Renan indeed seems to have envisaged as he nears the conclusion of his own artistic 'mission', is a total correspondence between all its constituent elements, to the extent that the story of Jesus has become his story recounted by and for Mary, making the reader of a potential 'Vie de Jésus' the reader of its hallucinatory and hallucinating alternate. Illusion is inevitable when the soul of history vacates the world, leaving behind an empty tomb.

This is ironical writing of a high order, based in part on what an early commentator described as the 'zigzags' of Renan's style[22]—a technical term from psychology like 'hallucinée', used in conjunction with 'divine', 'sacred', 'God'—in part on the domination of interrogatives or other expressions of conjecture; most formidably, however, on the underlying implication that no clear historical nor spiritual message can escape from the rings of psychological and social exigency under which it is concealed. Appropriately, the first sentence of *Vie de Jésus* refers the reader to 'the great event in the history of the world', its last word is the name of Jesus himself; for with Jesus and because of Jesus we must always stand somewhere on the axis formed by fact and fidelity, in the strange half-light, that is, that *Vie de Jésus* has itself created for us.

* * *

The remarkable result was a book that was read by everyone and satisfied no one. The official Church was outraged by Renan's deceiver-Christ, the more so as it sensed the danger in the beguiling envelope. Historical criticism was dismayed by Renan's concessions to piety and sentiment. Even those who, temperamentally, might have been in tune with him, declared themselves baffled by what they saw as a sleight of hand. He was too much a sceptic and not enough of one at the same time.[23]

In itself, the contributing thought was not new, nor was Renan's purpose to alter minds. He had added nothing of substance to the debate on the historical Jesus, nor to his own position with respect to Christian belief. *Vie de Jésus* reveals clearly enough this position to be what it always was: that of the high-minded idealist of *L'Avenir de la science* disposed to countenance the existence of a supreme being and to behave as its servant, while he yet remained scornful of attempts to formalise this attachment into a codified creed or set of tangible symbols. Equally, he appreciated the nature of more humble forms of belief sufficiently to recognise that they were beyond his influence or interference. 'A single, supreme and unapproachable God', he had written in his *Etudes d'histoire religieuse,* 'is evidently too austere a dogma for certain eras and certain countries' (VII, 226). It was not in any attempt to promote a rationalised or diluted belief that Renan wrote *Vie de Jésus.* This was more, though, than calculated disinterestedness. The power lay in the compelling yet disturbing nature of the art, in that which all could recognise as appealing but with which none could feel secure.

It is when viewed in this light that *Vie de Jésus* changes sense and changes subject to the point where what is superficially accessory to it becomes its authentic essence. The vehicle of ironic narrative employed by Renan is a reminder to all strands and levels of opinion that transcendent meaning is a mask we place upon reality as readily and as arbitrarily as those humble fishermen long ago. His Life of Jesus like their master as it depicts him has the invitingly empty quality of being all things to all men. If 'nothing happens' as is often claimed in Flaubert's *L'Education sentimentale,* nothing happens in *Vie de Jésus* and for the same reasons: the self-nullifying ironic is the expression of the social and psychological disorientation renewed as well as resisted in modern, secular man. Renan, who wrote no study of the novel, seems nevertheless to have sensed like his great novelist contemporary that literary fiction as no other genre held the key to this new unfulfilled state of being, both in the sense of being its symptom and the illusory location of its cure. Poised as it is in the ironic space between truth and make-believe, the novel is at once a reminder of that space and an artificial bridge across it, parading incoherence as coherence, division as unity. To read it as to write it becomes an act consistent with the post-Christian human condition, a palm-strewn journey to a cross of print and cardboard. Michelet was right, in connection with *Vie de Jésus,* to speak of 'the flaccid and sickly tendencies of the novel, serving the cause of *homo duplex*' (*Journal,* ed. Claude Digeon, III, 168). What he failed to see was that all Renan's cruel and gentle message was there. Either there exists a living Christ of truth, or there is the 'flag of our contradictions' (IV, 351) flying over a novel eternally entitled *Vie de Jésus.*

As to Renan's authentically historical message, he reserved that for the remainder of his account of what he terms the 'origins' of Christianity, which *Vie de Jésus* already reveals to involve a paradoxical journey away from the true religion of mind and heart. The brief life of that religion was a moment when Jesus stood alone among the Galilean hills addressing his unseen Father, its evolution its necessary decadence. Born to live out that simple relationship, Jesus himself found the world more disposed to put its faith in a shadow. Renan was about to extend that message and to discover at the pinnacle of this faith of such frail foundation a Roman emperor teaching himself and the world to die.

Notes

1. Prosper Alfaric, *Les Manuscrits de la 'Vie de Jésus' d'Ernest Renan,* Les Belles-Lettres, 1939, p. 319. Horace, *Odes,* III, xxx, 1: 'Exegi monumentum aere perennius'—'I seek a monument of everlasting bronze'.

2. Cf. the preceding paragraph from the same page of the *Cahiers de jeunesse* (*OC* IX, 244), where Renan regrets ever having given the impression of being a follower of Strauss: 'O Jésus, non, aurais-je pu te renier? Oh! mon coeur en est navré. Il me faut que tu aies vécu, et vécu dans l'idéal qu'on [nous] a laissé de toi. Cet idéal qui me ravit, ah!, si ce n'était qu'un type! Non, il me faut, pour t'aimer, que tu aies été mon semblable, ayant comme moi un coeur de chair.'

3. Alfaric, *op. cit.,* p. lxiii: 'Ce n'est plus un villageois galiléen du début de notre ère que nous avons ici; c'est un Français du XIXe siècle, en qui la culture du temps a pris sa forme la plus haute et la plus affinée, c'est Renan avec toute la richesse et la séduction personnelle.' But in the same vein, see also Gabriel Séailles, *Ernest Renan: essai de biographie psychologique,* Perrin, 1895, p. 137: 'Renan ne sait pas assez s'oublier lui-même, il a voulu que Jésus lui renvoyât sa propre image et il s'est surtout complu à cette image'; and Mary James Darmesteter, *La Vie d'Ernest Renan,* Calmann-Lévy, 1898, p. 173: 'Toutefois le livre demeure moins une reconstruction scientifique que le reflet d'un certain idéal moral que l'auteur portait en lui'.

4. Rétat, *Religion et imagination religieuse: leurs formes et leurs rapports dans l'oeuvre d'Ernest Renan,* p. 287.

5. See the interesting review by Thomas R. Edwards: 'People in Trouble', *New York Review of Books,* XIX, (20 July 1972), 20-2. Presenting a group of contemporary novels, Edwards makes the observation that 'the novel from its beginning has dwelt upon the secular life, men and women making do in a realm God hasn't visited for quite a while. Here people are on their own, they have careers instead of vocations, stories don't always predict their own endings, meaning is not found in events but gets attached to them more or less provisionally. . . . Living in a world whose mysteries may be meaningless, secular man is necessarily man in trouble . . .' (p. 20).

6. Frank Kermode, *The Sense of an Ending: Studies in the Theory of Fiction,* Oxford University Press, 1967. Sartre, *Qu'est-ce que la littérature?,* Gallimard, 1948, p. 169. Barthes, *Le Degré zéro de l'écriture,* Seuil, 1953, p. 51.

7. Colin Smith, 'The Fictionalist Element in Renan's Thought', *French Studies,* IX (1955), 30.

8. Renan's friends were the first to view with suspicion the similarities they detected between *Vie de Jésus* and a work of fiction and they were soon followed by a host of others. Taine recalls joining Berthelot in admonishing Renan in this regard when he read them part of his manuscript in August 1862: 'En vain Berthelot et moi nous lui disons que c'est mettre le roman à la place de la légende' (*Vie et correspondance,* Hachette, II (3rd ed., 1908), 245). Michelet was inspired by his reading of *Vie de Jésus* a year later to thoughts of 'combattre le roman par l'histoire' (*Journal,* ed. Claude Digeon, Gallimard, III (1976), 168). P. Larroque, identifying himself as a 'déiste rationaliste', concluded: 'M. Renan vient de construire un roman qui a obtenu un succès de vogue. Mais un roman, quelque plein d'intérêt qu'il

puisse être, c'est trop peu quand avait été annoncée une oeuvre de science sérieuse' (*La Vie de Jésus selon M. Renan,* Dentu, 1863, p. 4). The Tübingen school of criticism founded in the tradition of Bauer and Strauss had similar misgivings as Theodor Keim demonstrated in a series of articles for the Augsburg *Allgemeine Zeitung* of September 1863: 'Nur bleibt gerade hier die Frage offen: wahr oder wahrscheinlich? Geschichte oder Phantasie, ein Roman, wie ihn das Land etwa weckt oder die Zeit gern liest?' (15 Sept. 1863, p. 4278). Meanwhile, official Catholic opinion at home remained merciless in its treatment of this feature of Renan's book. See, for example, J.-T. Loyson, *Une prétendue Vie de Jésus; ou M. Ernest Renan, historien, philosophe et poëte,* 3rd ed., Douniol, 1863, p. 71: 'Quel délicieux roman!'; or Alphonse Gratry, *Les Sophistes et la critique,* Douniol/Lecoffre, 1864, p. 169: 'Rien de commun avec l'histoire! . . . C'est donc un roman historique? Non, c'est un roman non historique: ce jugement émane de l'Institut.' A scholarly modern critic, Alfaric, allows for the book's appeal 'en dépit de son caractère fictif' (*op. cit.,* p. lxiii) and Chadbourne speaks in the same vein of *Vie de Jésus* as 'a best-selling fictional work far inferior to other books of his Christian and Judaic history in historical value and even interest' ('Renan, or the contemptuous approach to literature', *Yale French Studies,* II (1949), 96). Georges Sorel, *Le Système historique de Renan* (G. Jacques, 1905-6), Slatkine Reprints, 1971, argues from the more positive viewpoint that all modern history has its roots in the novel before concluding that: 'Renan se trouvait dans des conditions singulièrement favorables à la composition d'un roman et, en effet, la *Vie de Jésus* fut un roman' (p. 34).

9. Nelly Cormeau, *Physiologie du roman,* Nizet, 1966, p. 22.

10. Albert Schweitzer, *The Quest of the Historical Jesus,* 2nd English ed., A. and C. Black Ltd., 1926, p. 181ff.

11. Peter Cortland, *The Sentimental Education. An Examination of Flaubert's Education Sentimentale,* Mouton and Co., 1967, p. 105.

12. Darmesteter, *op. cit.,* pp. 172-3. It was in May 1860 that Renan was invited by Napoleon III to undertake the mission of archaeological exploration to Lebanon and Palestine which would eventually lead to the publication of *Vie de Jésus.* He arrived in Beirut, accompanied by his sister, on 29 October 1860 and returned to France almost exactly a year later on 24 October 1861. Following a series of expeditions into Palestine during the spring of 1861, he appears to have begun drafting *Vie de Jésus* in July and by mid-September is able to announce in a letter to Berthelot the near completion of his 'gros morceau en portefeuille' (E. Renan and M. Berthelot, *Correspondance, 1847-1892,* p. 284). Henriette's death on 24 September thus came as her brother neared the end of his project, interrupting it and leaving Renan to complete final work on what is sometimes known as 'the first Vie de Jésus' in Paris during the autumn. Subsequently Renan undertook a revision of his entire manuscript before its publication on 24 June 1863. See also Alfaric, *op. cit.,* pp. xvi-xxvii; Pommier, *Renan d'après des documents inédits,* ch. VII; not least Renan's own account of his Phoenician expedition: *La Mission de Phénicie,* Impr. impériale, 1864-74.

13. Translations of this and other quotations in this chapter from the Introduction and text of *Vie de Jésus* are taken from the Everyman Library edition, Dent, 1927, which reprints the first anonymous English translation published by Trübner in December, 1863. Translations of Renan's 1867 Preface are my own.

14. Georg Lukács, *The Historical Novel,* tr. H. and S. Mitchell, Merlin, 1962, ch. III.

15. *De l'Origine des espèces,* tr. Clémence-Auguste Royer, Guillaumin, 1862. The original English edition appeared in 1859.

16. Lukács, *op. cit,* p. 211.

17. Harold W. Wardman, *Renan: historien philosophe,* C.D.U./SEDES, 1979, p. 21: 'Il n'en reste pas moins que Jésus, tel que le dépeint sa *Vie de Jésus,* garde l'empreinte des impressions esthétiques et religieuses qu'a suscitées en lui sa propre éducation religieuse et sa lecture des Evangiles.'

18. Chiefly, of course, those imposed by public and professional incomprehension following the initial publication of *Vie de Jésus.* Closely contemporary with the second volume of the *Origines, Les Apôtres,* the 1867 preface to *Vie de Jésus* represents a concession to those aspects of human behaviour and human history on which Renan reflects in the introduction to his later volume: 'Calomnies, contresens, falsifications des idées et des textes, raisonnements triomphants sur des choses que l'adversaire n'a pas dites, cris de victoire sur des erreurs qu'il n'a pas commises, rien ne paraît déloyal à celui qui croit tenir en main les intérêts de la vérité absolue. J'aurais fort ignoré l'histoire si je ne m'étais attendu à tout cela' (*OC* IV, 462) See also below, ch. VII, note 16.

19. Alfaric, *op. cit,* p. lxii: '[L'Introduction] a fait prendre pour un travail de science pure ce qui ne voulait être d'abord, ce qui n'était vraiment qu'une oeuvre d'art.'

20. P. M.-J. Lagrange, *La Vie de Jésus d'après Renan*, Lecoffre, 1923, p. 63: 'Tout est faux dans ce parallèle.'

21. Cortland, *op. cit.*, p. 10.

22. Keim, *art. cit.* 15 September 1863, p. 4278.

23. George Sand, writing to Prince Jérôme Napoleon in November 1863, summed up something of this bewilderment and its causes: 'Il y a des traits de lumière vive dans l'ouvrage, qui empêchent un esprit attentif de s'égarer. Mais il y a trop d'efforts charmants et puérils pour endormir la clairvoyance des esprit prévenus, et pour sauver d'une main ce qu'il détruit de l'autre. Cela tient, non pas comme on l'a beaucoup dit, à un reflet de l'éducation du séminaire, dont ce mâle talent n'aurait pas su se débarrasser,—je ne crois pas cela—mais à un engouement d'artiste pour son sujet' (*Correspondance*, ed. G. Lubin, Garnier, XVIII (1984), 124-5). Cf. Jean Guitton, *Oeuvres complètes: critique religieuse*, p. 494: 'Ce qui étonne en lisant Renan n'est pas qu'il soit sceptique, c'est qu'il ne le soit pas davantage; c'est que, niant l'essence, il retiene tant d'accidents; que vidant le témoignage de sa partie nucléaire, il ait tant de sympathie pour les enveloppes.'

Select Bibliography

WORKS BY RENAN

Renan, Ernest. *Mission de Phénicie dirigée par M. Ernest Renan*, Paris, Imprimerie impériale, 1864-74.

STUDIES WHOLLY OR PARTLY DEVOTED TO RENAN

Darmesteter (Mary James), *La Vie d'Ernest Renan*, Paris, Calmann-Lévy, 1898.

Keim (Theodor), 'Das Leben Jesu von Renan', *Allgemeine Zeitung*, Augsburg, 15 Sept. 1863, pp. 4277-9; 16 Sept. 1863, pp. 4293-4; 17 Sept. 1863, pp. 4309-11.

Pommier (Jean), *Renan d'après des documents inédits*, Paris, Perrin, 1923.

Rétat (Laudyce), *Religion et imagination religieuse: leurs formes et leurs rapports dans l'oeuvre d'Ernest Renan*, Paris, Klincksieck, 1977.

TWENTIETH-CENTURY SOURCES, STUDIES OF RELATED MOVEMENTS AND AUTHORS

Cortland (Peter), *The Sentimental Education: An Examination of Flaubert's Education Sentimentale*, The Hague, Mouton and Co., 1967.

FURTHER READING

Criticism

Gaigalas, Vytas V. "The Church Bells Toll Against the 'Antichrist' (1863)." In *Ernest Renan and His French Catholic Critics*, pp. 33-60. North Quincy, Mass.: The Christopher Publishing House, 1972.

> Describes how the French Catholic clergy responded to the publication of *The Life of Jesus*.

"Renan's "Vie de Jésus." *The Dublin Review* (April 1864): 386-489.

> Argues that *The Life of Jesus* is a detestable attack on Christian faith in the divinity of Jesus.

Schaff, Rev. Dr. *The Romance of M. Renan and the Christ of the Gospels: Three Essays*, New York: Carlton & Lanahan, 1868, 239 p.

> Refutes the main arguments of *The Life of Jesus*, a work here described as "poison."

Taylor, Isaac. "The Present Position of the Argument Concerning Christianity: Ernest Rénan." In *The Restoration of Belief*, pp. 360-83. New York: Macmillan and Co., 1864.

> Argues that *The Life of Jesus* is full of contradictions and factual misrepresentations and that Renan fails to understand the message of Jesus and the gospel writers.

Tulloch, John. *Lectures on M. Renan's 'Vie de Jésus.'* London: Macmillan and Co., 1864, 220 p.

> Refutes Renan's arguments, critical method, and biographical portrait of Jesus.

How to Use This Index

The main references

> **Calvino, Italo**
> 1923-1985 .... **CLC 5, 8, 11, 22, 33, 39,**
> **73; SSC 3, 48**

list all author entries in the following Gale Literary Criticism series:

AAL = *Asian American Literature*
BG = *The Beat Generation: A Gale Critical Companion*
BLC = *Black Literature Criticism*
BLCS = *Black Literature Criticism Supplement*
CLC = *Contemporary Literary Criticism*
CLR = *Children's Literature Review*
CMLC = *Classical and Medieval Literature Criticism*
DC = *Drama Criticism*
HLC = *Hispanic Literature Criticism*
HLCS = *Hispanic Literature Criticism Supplement*
HR = *Harlem Renaissance: A Gale Critical Companion*
LC = *Literature Criticism from 1400 to 1800*
NCLC = *Nineteenth-Century Literature Criticism*
NNAL = *Native North American Literature*
PC = *Poetry Criticism*
SSC = *Short Story Criticism*
TCLC = *Twentieth-Century Literary Criticism*
WLC = *World Literature Criticism, 1500 to the Present*
WLCS = *World Literature Criticism Supplement*

The cross-references

> See also CA 85-88, 116; CANR 23, 61;
> DAM NOV; DLB 196; EW 13; MTCW 1, 2;
> RGSF 2; RGWL 2; SFW 4; SSFS 12

list all author entries in the following Gale biographical and literary sources:

AAYA = *Authors & Artists for Young Adults*
AFAW = *African American Writers*
AFW = *African Writers*
AITN = *Authors in the News*
AMW = *American Writers*
AMWR = *American Writers Retrospective Supplement*
AMWS = *American Writers Supplement*
ANW = *American Nature Writers*
AW = *Ancient Writers*
BEST = *Bestsellers*
BPFB = *Beacham's Encyclopedia of Popular Fiction: Biography and Resources*
BRW = *British Writers*
BRWS = *British Writers Supplement*
BW = *Black Writers*
BYA = *Beacham's Guide to Literature for Young Adults*
CA = *Contemporary Authors*
CAAS = *Contemporary Authors Autobiography Series*
CABS = *Contemporary Authors Bibliographical Series*
CAD = *Contemporary American Dramatists*
CANR = *Contemporary Authors New Revision Series*
CAP = *Contemporary Authors Permanent Series*
CBD = *Contemporary British Dramatists*
CCA = *Contemporary Canadian Authors*
CD = *Contemporary Dramatists*
CDALB = *Concise Dictionary of American Literary Biography*
CDALBS = *Concise Dictionary of American Literary Biography Supplement*
CDBLB = *Concise Dictionary of British Literary Biography*

CMW = *St. James Guide to Crime & Mystery Writers*
CN = *Contemporary Novelists*
CP = *Contemporary Poets*
CPW = *Contemporary Popular Writers*
CSW = *Contemporary Southern Writers*
CWD = *Contemporary Women Dramatists*
CWP = *Contemporary Women Poets*
CWRI = *St. James Guide to Children's Writers*
CWW = *Contemporary World Writers*
DA = *DISCovering Authors*
DA3 = *DISCovering Authors 3.0*
DAB = *DISCovering Authors: British Edition*
DAC = *DISCovering Authors: Canadian Edition*
DAM = *DISCovering Authors: Modules*
   DRAM: Dramatists Module; MST: Most-studied Authors Module;
   MULT: Multicultural Authors Module; NOV: Novelists Module;
   POET: Poets Module; POP: Popular Fiction and Genre Authors Module
DFS = *Drama for Students*
DLB = *Dictionary of Literary Biography*
DLBD = *Dictionary of Literary Biography Documentary Series*
DLBY = *Dictionary of Literary Biography Yearbook*
DNFS = *Literature of Developing Nations for Students*
EFS = *Epics for Students*
EXPN = *Exploring Novels*
EXPP = *Exploring Poetry*
EXPS = *Exploring Short Stories*
EW = *European Writers*
FANT = *St. James Guide to Fantasy Writers*
FW = *Feminist Writers*
GFL = *Guide to French Literature,* Beginnings to 1789, 1798 to the Present
GLL = *Gay and Lesbian Literature*
HGG = *St. James Guide to Horror, Ghost & Gothic Writers*
HW = *Hispanic Writers*
IDFW = *International Dictionary of Films and Filmmakers: Writers and Production Artists*
IDTP = *International Dictionary of Theatre: Playwrights*
LAIT = *Literature and Its Times*
LAW = *Latin American Writers*
JRDA = *Junior DISCovering Authors*
MAICYA = *Major Authors and Illustrators for Children and Young Adults*
MAICYAS = *Major Authors and Illustrators for Children and Young Adults Supplement*
MAWW = *Modern American Women Writers*
MJW = *Modern Japanese Writers*
MTCW = *Major 20th-Century Writers*
NCFS = *Nonfiction Classics for Students*
NFS = *Novels for Students*
PAB = *Poets: American and British*
PFS = *Poetry for Students*
RGAL = *Reference Guide to American Literature*
RGEL = *Reference Guide to English Literature*
RGSF = *Reference Guide to Short Fiction*
RGWL = *Reference Guide to World Literature*
RHW = *Twentieth-Century Romance and Historical Writers*
SAAS = *Something about the Author Autobiography Series*
SATA = *Something about the Author*
SFW = *St. James Guide to Science Fiction Writers*
SSFS = *Short Stories for Students*
TCWW = *Twentieth-Century Western Writers*
WLIT = *World Literature and Its Times*
WP = *World Poets*
YABC = *Yesterday's Authors of Books for Children*
YAW = *St. James Guide to Young Adult Writers*

Literary Criticism Series
Cumulative Author Index

al-Hariri, al-Qasim ibn 'Ali Abu Muhammad al-Basri 1054-1122 .... **CMLC 63**
See also RGWL 3

Ali, Ahmed 1908-1998 .... **CLC 69**
See also CA 25-28R; CANR 15, 34; EWL 3

Ali, Tariq 1943- .... **CLC 173**
See also CA 25-28R; CANR 10, 99

Alighieri, Dante
See Dante

Allan, John B.
See Westlake, Donald E(dwin)

Allan, Sidney
See Hartmann, Sadakichi

Allan, Sydney
See Hartmann, Sadakichi

Allard, Janet .... **CLC 59**

Allen, Edward 1948- .... **CLC 59**

Allen, Fred 1894-1956 .... **TCLC 87**

Allen, Paula Gunn 1939- ..... **CLC 84; NNAL**
See also AMWS 4; CA 112; 143; CANR 63, 130; CWP; DA3; DAM MULT; DLB 175; FW; MTCW 1; RGAL 4

Allen, Roland
See Ayckbourn, Alan

Allen, Sarah A.
See Hopkins, Pauline Elizabeth

Allen, Sidney H.
See Hartmann, Sadakichi

Allen, Woody 1935- .... **CLC 16, 52, 195**
See also AAYA 10, 51; CA 33-36R; CANR 27, 38, 63, 128; DAM POP; DLB 44; MTCW 1

Allende, Isabel 1942- ... **CLC 39, 57, 97, 170; HLC 1; SSC 65; WLCS**
See also AAYA 18; CA 125; 130; CANR 51, 74, 129; CDWLB 3; CLR 99; CWW 2; DA3; DAM MULT, NOV; DLB 145; DNFS 1; EWL 3; FW; HW 1, 2; INT CA-130; LAIT 5; LAWS 1; LMFS 2; MTCW 1, 2; NCFS 1; NFS 6, 18; RGSF 2; RGWL 3; SSFS 11, 16; WLIT 1

Alleyn, Ellen
See Rossetti, Christina (Georgina)

Alleyne, Carla D. .... **CLC 65**

Allingham, Margery (Louise) 1904-1966 .... **CLC 19**
See also CA 5-8R; 25-28R; CANR 4, 58; CMW 4; DLB 77; MSW; MTCW 1, 2

Allingham, William 1824-1889 ...... **NCLC 25**
See also DLB 35; RGEL 2

Allison, Dorothy E. 1949- .... **CLC 78, 153**
See also AAYA 53; CA 140; CANR 66, 107; CSW; DA3; FW; MTCW 1; NFS 11; RGAL 4

Alloula, Malek .... **CLC 65**

Allston, Washington 1779-1843 ...... **NCLC 2**
See also DLB 1, 235

Almedingen, E. M. .... **CLC 12**
See Almedingen, Martha Edith von
See also SATA 3

Almedingen, Martha Edith von 1898-1971
See Almedingen, E. M.
See also CA 1-4R; CANR 1

Almodovar, Pedro 1949(?)- .... **CLC 114; HLCS 1**
See also CA 133; CANR 72; HW 2

Almqvist, Carl Jonas Love 1793-1866 .... **NCLC 42**

al-Mutanabbi, Ahmad ibn al-Husayn Abu al-Tayyib al-Jufi al-Kindi 915-965 .... **CMLC 66**
See also RGWL 3

Alonso, Damaso 1898-1990 .... **CLC 14**
See also CA 110; 131; 130; CANR 72; DLB 108; EWL 3; HW 1, 2

Alov
See Gogol, Nikolai (Vasilyevich)

al'Sadaawi, Nawal
See El Saadawi, Nawal
See also FW

Al Siddik
See Rolfe, Frederick (William Serafino Austin Lewis Mary)
See also GLL 1; RGEL 2

Alta 1942- .... **CLC 19**
See also CA 57-60

Alter, Robert B(ernard) 1935- .... **CLC 34**
See also CA 49-52; CANR 1, 47, 100

Alther, Lisa 1944- .... **CLC 7, 41**
See also BPFB 1; CA 65-68; CAAS 30; CANR 12, 30, 51; CN 7; CSW; GLL 2; MTCW 1

Althusser, L.
See Althusser, Louis

Althusser, Louis 1918-1990 .... **CLC 106**
See also CA 131; 132; CANR 102; DLB 242

Altman, Robert 1925- .... **CLC 16, 116**
See also CA 73-76; CANR 43

Alurista .... **HLCS 1**
See Urista (Heredia), Alberto (Baltazar)
See also DLB 82; LLW 1

Alvarez, A(lfred) 1929- .... **CLC 5, 13**
See also CA 1-4R; CANR 3, 33, 63, 101; CN 7; CP 7; DLB 14, 40

Alvarez, Alejandro Rodriguez 1903-1965
See Casona, Alejandro
See also CA 131; 93-96; HW 1

Alvarez, Julia 1950- .... **CLC 93; HLCS 1**
See also AAYA 25; AMWS 7; CA 147; CANR 69, 101, 133; DA3; DLB 282; LATS 1:2; LLW 1; MTCW 1; NFS 5, 9; SATA 129; WLIT 1

Alvaro, Corrado 1896-1956 .... **TCLC 60**
See also CA 163; DLB 264; EWL 3

Amado, Jorge 1912-2001 ... **CLC 13, 40, 106; HLC 1**
See also CA 77-80; 201; CANR 35, 74; CWW 2; DAM MULT, NOV; DLB 113; EWL 3; HW 2; LAW; LAWS 1; MTCW 1, 2; RGWL 2, 3; TWA; WLIT 1

Ambler, Eric 1909-1998 .... **CLC 4, 6, 9**
See also BRWS 4; CA 9-12R; 171; CANR 7, 38, 74; CMW 4; CN 7; DLB 77; MSW; MTCW 1, 2; TEA

Ambrose, Stephen E(dward) 1936-2002 .... **CLC 145**
See also AAYA 44; CA 1-4R; 209; CANR 3, 43, 57, 83, 105; NCFS 2; SATA 40, 138

Amichai, Yehuda 1924-2000 .. **CLC 9, 22, 57, 116; PC 38**
See also CA 85-88; 189; CANR 46, 60, 99, 132; CWW 2; EWL 3; MTCW 1

Amichai, Yehudah
See Amichai, Yehuda

Amiel, Henri Frederic 1821-1881 .... **NCLC 4**
See also DLB 217

Amis, Kingsley (William) 1922-1995 ...... **CLC 1, 2, 3, 5, 8, 13, 40, 44, 129**
See also AITN 2; BPFB 1; BRWS 2; CA 9-12R; 150; CANR 8, 28, 54; CDBLB 1945-1960; CN 7; CP 7; DA; DA3; DAB; DAC; DAM MST, NOV; DLB 15, 27, 100, 139; DLBY 1996; EWL 3; HGG; INT CANR-8; MTCW 1, 2; RGEL 2; RGSF 2; SFW 4

Amis, Martin (Louis) 1949- .... **CLC 4, 9, 38, 62, 101**
See also BEST 90:3; BRWS 4; CA 65-68; CANR 8, 27, 54, 73, 95, 132; CN 7; DA3; DLB 14, 194; EWL 3; INT CANR-27; MTCW 1

Ammianus Marcellinus c. 330-c. 395 .... **CMLC 60**
See also AW 2; DLB 211

Ammons, A(rchie) R(andolph) 1926-2001 ...... **CLC 2, 3, 5, 8, 9, 25, 57, 108; PC 16**
See also AITN 1; AMWS 7; CA 9-12R; 193; CANR 6, 36, 51, 73, 107; CP 7; CSW; DAM POET; DLB 5, 165; EWL 3; MTCW 1, 2; PFS 19; RGAL 4

Amo, Tauraatua i
See Adams, Henry (Brooks)

Amory, Thomas 1691(?)-1788 .... **LC 48**
See also DLB 39

Anand, Mulk Raj 1905- .... **CLC 23, 93**
See also CA 65-68; CANR 32, 64; CN 7; DAM NOV; EWL 3; MTCW 1, 2; RGSF 2

Anatol
See Schnitzler, Arthur

Anaximander c. 611B.C.-c. 546B.C. .... **CMLC 22**

Anaya, Rudolfo A(lfonso) 1937- ...... **CLC 23, 148; HLC 1**
See also AAYA 20; BYA 13; CA 45-48; CAAS 4; CANR 1, 32, 51, 124; CN 7; DAM MULT, NOV; DLB 82, 206, 278; HW 1; LAIT 4; LLW 1; MTCW 1, 2; NFS 12; RGAL 4; RGSF 2; WLIT 1

Andersen, Hans Christian 1805-1875 .... **NCLC 7, 79; SSC 6, 56; WLC**
See also AAYA 57; CLR 6; DA; DA3; DAB; DAC; DAM MST, POP; EW 6; MAICYA 1, 2; RGSF 2; RGWL 2, 3; SATA 100; TWA; WCH; YABC 1

Anderson, C. Farley
See Mencken, H(enry) L(ouis); Nathan, George Jean

Anderson, Jessica (Margaret) Queale 1916- .... **CLC 37**
See also CA 9-12R; CANR 4, 62; CN 7

Anderson, Jon (Victor) 1940- .... **CLC 9**
See also CA 25-28R; CANR 20; DAM POET

Anderson, Lindsay (Gordon) 1923-1994 .... **CLC 20**
See also CA 125; 128; 146; CANR 77

Anderson, Maxwell 1888-1959 .... **TCLC 2, 144**
See also CA 105; 152; DAM DRAM; DFS 16, 20; DLB 7, 228; MTCW 2; RGAL 4

Anderson, Poul (William) 1926-2001 .... **CLC 15**
See also AAYA 5, 34; BPFB 1; BYA 6, 8, 9; CA 1-4R; 181; 199; CAAE 181; CAAS 2; CANR 2, 15, 34, 64, 110; CLR 58; DLB 8; FANT; INT CANR-15; MTCW 1, 2; SATA 90; SATA-Brief 39; SATA-Essay 106; SCFW 2; SFW 4; SUFW 1, 2

Anderson, Robert (Woodruff) 1917- .... **CLC 23**
See also AITN 1; CA 21-24R; CANR 32; DAM DRAM; DLB 7; LAIT 5

Anderson, Roberta Joan
See Mitchell, Joni

Anderson, Sherwood 1876-1941 .. **SSC 1, 46; TCLC 1, 10, 24, 123; WLC**
See also AAYA 30; AMW; AMWC 2; BPFB 1; CA 104; 121; CANR 61; CDALB 1917-1929; DA; DA3; DAB; DAC; DAM MST, NOV; DLB 4, 9, 86; DLBD 1; EWL 3; EXPS; GLL 2; MTCW 1, 2; NFS 4; RGAL 4; RGSF 2; SSFS 4, 10, 11; TUS

Andier, Pierre
See Desnos, Robert

Andouard
See Giraudoux, Jean(-Hippolyte)

Armah, Ayi Kwei 1939- . **BLC 1; CLC 5, 33, 136**
See also AFW; BW 1; CA 61-64; CANR 21, 64; CDWLB 3; CN 7; DAM MULT, POET; DLB 117; EWL 3; MTCW 1; WLIT 2

Armatrading, Joan 1950- .... **CLC 17**
See also CA 114; 186

Armitage, Frank
See Carpenter, John (Howard)

Armstrong, Jeannette (C.) 1948- .... **NNAL**
See also CA 149; CCA 1; CN 7; DAC; SATA 102

Arnette, Robert
See Silverberg, Robert

Arnim, Achim von (Ludwig Joachim von Arnim) 1781-1831 ..... **NCLC 5; SSC 29**
See also DLB 90

Arnim, Bettina von 1785-1859 ...... **NCLC 38, 123**
See also DLB 90; RGWL 2, 3

Arnold, Matthew 1822-1888 ..... **NCLC 6, 29, 89, 126; PC 5; WLC**
See also BRW 5; CDBLB 1832-1890; DA; DAB; DAC; DAM MST, POET; DLB 32, 57; EXPP; PAB; PFS 2; TEA; WP

Arnold, Thomas 1795-1842 .... **NCLC 18**
See also DLB 55

Arnow, Harriette (Louisa) Simpson 1908-1986 .... **CLC 2, 7, 18**
See also BPFB 1; CA 9-12R; 118; CANR 14; DLB 6; FW; MTCW 1, 2; RHW; SATA 42; SATA-Obit 47

Arouet, Francois-Marie
See Voltaire

Arp, Hans
See Arp, Jean

Arp, Jean 1887-1966 .... **CLC 5; TCLC 115**
See also CA 81-84; 25-28R; CANR 42, 77; EW 10

Arrabal
See Arrabal, Fernando

Arrabal, Fernando 1932- ... **CLC 2, 9, 18, 58**
See Arrabal (Teran), Fernando
See also CA 9-12R; CANR 15; EWL 3; LMFS 2

Arrabal (Teran), Fernando 1932-
See Arrabal, Fernando
See also CWW 2

Arreola, Juan Jose 1918-2001 .... **CLC 147; HLC 1; SSC 38**
See also CA 113; 131; 200; CANR 81; CWW 2; DAM MULT; DLB 113; DNFS 2; EWL 3; HW 1, 2; LAW; RGSF 2

Arrian c. 89(?)-c. 155(?) .... **CMLC 43**
See also DLB 176

Arrick, Fran .... **CLC 30**
See Gaberman, Judie Angell
See also BYA 6

Arrley, Richmond
See Delany, Samuel R(ay), Jr.

Artaud, Antonin (Marie Joseph) 1896-1948 .... **DC 14; TCLC 3, 36**
See also CA 104; 149; DA3; DAM DRAM; DLB 258; EW 11; EWL 3; GFL 1789 to the Present; MTCW 1; RGWL 2, 3

Arthur, Ruth M(abel) 1905-1979 ..... **CLC 12**
See also CA 9-12R; 85-88; CANR 4; CWRI 5; SATA 7, 26

Artsybashev, Mikhail (Petrovich) 1878-1927 .... **TCLC 31**
See also CA 170; DLB 295

Arundel, Honor (Morfydd) 1919-1973 .... **CLC 17**
See also CA 21-22; 41-44R; CAP 2; CLR 35; CWRI 5; SATA 4; SATA-Obit 24

Arzner, Dorothy 1900-1979 .... **CLC 98**

Asch, Sholem 1880-1957 .... **TCLC 3**
See also CA 105; EWL 3; GLL 2

Ascham, Roger 1516(?)-1568 .... **LC 101**
See also DLB 236

Ash, Shalom
See Asch, Sholem

Ashbery, John (Lawrence) 1927- .. **CLC 2, 3, 4, 6, 9, 13, 15, 25, 41, 77, 125; PC 26**
See Berry, Jonas
See also AMWS 3; CA 5-8R; CANR 9, 37, 66, 102, 132; CP 7; DA3; DAM POET; DLB 5, 165; DLBY 1981; EWL 3; INT CANR-9; MTCW 1, 2; PAB; PFS 11; RGAL 4; WP

Ashdown, Clifford
See Freeman, R(ichard) Austin

Ashe, Gordon
See Creasey, John

Ashton-Warner, Sylvia (Constance) 1908-1984 .... **CLC 19**
See also CA 69-72; 112; CANR 29; MTCW 1, 2

Asimov, Isaac 1920-1992 ..... **CLC 1, 3, 9, 19, 26, 76, 92**
See also AAYA 13; BEST 90:2; BPFB 1; BYA 4, 6, 7, 9; CA 1-4R; 137; CANR 2, 19, 36, 60, 125; CLR 12, 79; CMW 4; CPW; DA3; DAM POP; DLB 8; DLBY 1992; INT CANR-19; JRDA; LAIT 5; LMFS 2; MAICYA 1, 2; MTCW 1, 2; RGAL 4; SATA 1, 26, 74; SCFW 2; SFW 4; SSFS 17; TUS; YAW

Askew, Anne 1521(?)-1546 .... **LC 81**
See also DLB 136

Assis, Joaquim Maria Machado de
See Machado de Assis, Joaquim Maria

Astell, Mary 1666-1731 .... **LC 68**
See also DLB 252; FW

Astley, Thea (Beatrice May) 1925- .. **CLC 41**
See also CA 65-68; CANR 11, 43, 78; CN 7; DLB 289; EWL 3

Astley, William 1855-1911
See Warung, Price

Aston, James
See White, T(erence) H(anbury)

Asturias, Miguel Angel 1899-1974 .... **CLC 3, 8, 13; HLC 1**
See also CA 25-28; 49-52; CANR 32; CAP 2; CDWLB 3; DA3; DAM MULT, NOV; DLB 113, 290; EWL 3; HW 1; LAW; LMFS 2; MTCW 1, 2; RGWL 2, 3; WLIT 1

Atares, Carlos Saura
See Saura (Atares), Carlos

Athanasius c. 295-c. 373 .... **CMLC 48**

Atheling, William
See Pound, Ezra (Weston Loomis)

Atheling, William, Jr.
See Blish, James (Benjamin)

Atherton, Gertrude (Franklin Horn) 1857-1948 .... **TCLC 2**
See also CA 104; 155; DLB 9, 78, 186; HGG; RGAL 4; SUFW 1; TCWW 2

Atherton, Lucius
See Masters, Edgar Lee

Atkins, Jack
See Harris, Mark

Atkinson, Kate 1951- .... **CLC 99**
See also CA 166; CANR 101; DLB 267

Attaway, William (Alexander) 1911-1986 .... **BLC 1; CLC 92**
See also BW 2, 3; CA 143; CANR 82; DAM MULT; DLB 76

Atticus
See Fleming, Ian (Lancaster); Wilson, (Thomas) Woodrow

Atwood, Margaret (Eleanor) 1939- ... **CLC 2, 3, 4, 8, 13, 15, 25, 44, 84, 135; PC 8; SSC 2, 46; WLC**
See also AAYA 12, 47; AMWS 13; BEST 89:2; BPFB 1; CA 49-52; CANR 3, 24, 33, 59, 95, 133; CN 7; CP 7; CPW; CWP; DA; DA3; DAB; DAC; DAM MST, NOV, POET; DLB 53, 251; EWL 3; EXPN; FW; INT CANR-24; LAIT 5; MTCW 1, 2; NFS 4, 12, 13, 14, 19; PFS 7; RGSF 2; SATA 50; SSFS 3, 13; TWA; WWE 1; YAW

Aubigny, Pierre d'
See Mencken, H(enry) L(ouis)

Aubin, Penelope 1685-1731(?) .... **LC 9**
See also DLB 39

Auchincloss, Louis (Stanton) 1917- .. **CLC 4, 6, 9, 18, 45; SSC 22**
See also AMWS 4; CA 1-4R; CANR 6, 29, 55, 87, 130; CN 7; DAM NOV; DLB 2, 244; DLBY 1980; EWL 3; INT CANR-29; MTCW 1; RGAL 4

Auden, W(ystan) H(ugh) 1907-1973 . **CLC 1, 2, 3, 4, 6, 9, 11, 14, 43, 123; PC 1; WLC**
See also AAYA 18; AMWS 2; BRW 7; BRWR 1; CA 9-12R; 45-48; CANR 5, 61, 105; CDBLB 1914-1945; DA; DA3; DAB; DAC; DAM DRAM, MST, POET; DLB 10, 20; EWL 3; EXPP; MTCW 1, 2; PAB; PFS 1, 3, 4, 10; TUS; WP

Audiberti, Jacques 1899-1965 .... **CLC 38**
See also CA 25-28R; DAM DRAM; EWL 3

Audubon, John James 1785-1851 . **NCLC 47**
See also ANW; DLB 248

Auel, Jean M(arie) 1936- .... **CLC 31, 107**
See also AAYA 7, 51; BEST 90:4; BPFB 1; CA 103; CANR 21, 64, 115; CPW; DA3; DAM POP; INT CANR-21; NFS 11; RHW; SATA 91

Auerbach, Erich 1892-1957 .... **TCLC 43**
See also CA 118; 155; EWL 3

Augier, Emile 1820-1889 .... **NCLC 31**
See also DLB 192; GFL 1789 to the Present

August, John
See De Voto, Bernard (Augustine)

Augustine, St. 354-430 .... **CMLC 6; WLCS**
See also DA; DA3; DAB; DAC; DAM MST; DLB 115; EW 1; RGWL 2, 3

Aunt Belinda
See Braddon, Mary Elizabeth

Aunt Weedy
See Alcott, Louisa May

Aurelius
See Bourne, Randolph S(illiman)

Aurelius, Marcus 121-180 .... **CMLC 45**
See Marcus Aurelius
See also RGWL 2, 3

Aurobindo, Sri
See Ghose, Aurabinda

Aurobindo Ghose
See Ghose, Aurabinda

Austen, Jane 1775-1817 ...... **NCLC 1, 13, 19, 33, 51, 81, 95, 119; WLC**
See also AAYA 19; BRW 4; BRWC 1; BRWR 2; BYA 3; CDBLB 1789-1832; DA; DA3; DAB; DAC; DAM MST, NOV; DLB 116; EXPN; LAIT 2; LATS 1:1; LMFS 1; NFS 1, 14, 18, 20; TEA; WLIT 3; WYAS 1

Auster, Paul 1947- .... **CLC 47, 131**
See also AMWS 12; CA 69-72; CANR 23, 52, 75, 129; CMW 4; CN 7; DA3; DLB 227; MTCW 1; SUFW 2

Austin, Frank
See Faust, Frederick (Schiller)
See also TCWW 2

MULT, POET, POP; DFS 3, 11, 16; DLB 5, 7, 16, 38; DLBD 8; EWL 3; MTCW 1, 2; PFS 9; RGAL 4; TUS; WP

Baratynsky, Evgenii Abramovich 1800-1844 .... **NCLC 103**
See also DLB 205

Barbauld, Anna Laetitia 1743-1825 .... **NCLC 50**
See also DLB 107, 109, 142, 158; RGEL 2

Barbellion, W. N. P. .... **TCLC 24**
See Cummings, Bruce F(rederick)

Barber, Benjamin R. 1939- .... **CLC 141**
See also CA 29-32R; CANR 12, 32, 64, 119

Barbera, Jack (Vincent) 1945- .... **CLC 44**
See also CA 110; CANR 45

Barbey d'Aurevilly, Jules-Amedee 1808-1889 .... **NCLC 1; SSC 17**
See also DLB 119; GFL 1789 to the Present

Barbour, John c. 1316-1395 .... **CMLC 33**
See also DLB 146

Barbusse, Henri 1873-1935 .... **TCLC 5**
See also CA 105; 154; DLB 65; EWL 3; RGWL 2, 3

Barclay, Bill
See Moorcock, Michael (John)

Barclay, William Ewert
See Moorcock, Michael (John)

Barea, Arturo 1897-1957 .... **TCLC 14**
See also CA 111; 201

Barfoot, Joan 1946- .... **CLC 18**
See also CA 105

Barham, Richard Harris 1788-1845 .... **NCLC 77**
See also DLB 159

Baring, Maurice 1874-1945 .... **TCLC 8**
See also CA 105; 168; DLB 34; HGG

Baring-Gould, Sabine 1834-1924 ... **TCLC 88**
See also DLB 156, 190

Barker, Clive 1952- .... **CLC 52; SSC 53**
See also AAYA 10, 54; BEST 90:3; BPFB 1; CA 121; 129; CANR 71, 111, 133; CPW; DA3; DAM POP; DLB 261; HGG; INT CA-129; MTCW 1, 2; SUFW 2

Barker, George Granville 1913-1991 .... **CLC 8, 48**
See also CA 9-12R; 135; CANR 7, 38; DAM POET; DLB 20; EWL 3; MTCW 1

Barker, Harley Granville
See Granville-Barker, Harley
See also DLB 10

Barker, Howard 1946- .... **CLC 37**
See also CA 102; CBD; CD 5; DLB 13, 233

Barker, Jane 1652-1732 .... **LC 42, 82**
See also DLB 39, 131

Barker, Pat(ricia) 1943- ...... **CLC 32, 94, 146**
See also BRWS 4; CA 117; 122; CANR 50, 101; CN 7; DLB 271; INT CA-122

Barlach, Ernst (Heinrich) 1870-1938 .... **TCLC 84**
See also CA 178; DLB 56, 118; EWL 3

Barlow, Joel 1754-1812 .... **NCLC 23**
See also AMWS 2; DLB 37; RGAL 4

Barnard, Mary (Ethel) 1909- .... **CLC 48**
See also CA 21-22; CAP 2

Barnes, Djuna 1892-1982 .... **CLC 3, 4, 8, 11, 29, 127; SSC 3**
See Steptoe, Lydia
See also AMWS 3; CA 9-12R; 107; CAD; CANR 16, 55; CWD; DLB 4, 9, 45; EWL 3; GLL 1; MTCW 1, 2; RGAL 4; TUS

Barnes, Jim 1933- .... **NNAL**
See also CA 108, 175; CAAE 175; CAAS 28; DLB 175

Barnes, Julian (Patrick) 1946- . **CLC 42, 141**
See also BRWS 4; CA 102; CANR 19, 54, 115; CN 7; DAB; DLB 194; DLBY 1993; EWL 3; MTCW 1

Barnes, Peter 1931-2004 .... **CLC 5, 56**
See also CA 65-68; CAAS 12; CANR 33, 34, 64, 113; CBD; CD 5; DFS 6; DLB 13, 233; MTCW 1

Barnes, William 1801-1886 .... **NCLC 75**
See also DLB 32

Baroja (y Nessi), Pio 1872-1956 .... **HLC 1; TCLC 8**
See also CA 104; EW 9

Baron, David
See Pinter, Harold

Baron Corvo
See Rolfe, Frederick (William Serafino Austin Lewis Mary)

Barondess, Sue K(aufman) 1926-1977 .... **CLC 8**
See Kaufman, Sue
See also CA 1-4R; 69-72; CANR 1

Baron de Teive
See Pessoa, Fernando (Antonio Nogueira)

Baroness Von S.
See Zangwill, Israel

Barres, (Auguste-)Maurice 1862-1923 .... **TCLC 47**
See also CA 164; DLB 123; GFL 1789 to the Present

Barreto, Afonso Henrique de Lima
See Lima Barreto, Afonso Henrique de

Barrett, Andrea 1954- .... **CLC 150**
See also CA 156; CANR 92

Barrett, Michele .... **CLC 65**

Barrett, (Roger) Syd 1946- .... **CLC 35**

Barrett, William (Christopher) 1913-1992 .... **CLC 27**
See also CA 13-16R; 139; CANR 11, 67; INT CANR-11

Barrie, J(ames) M(atthew) 1860-1937 .... **TCLC 2**
See also BRWS 3; BYA 4, 5; CA 104; 136; CANR 77; CDBLB 1890-1914; CLR 16; CWRI 5; DA3; DAB; DAM DRAM; DFS 7; DLB 10, 141, 156; EWL 3; FANT; MAICYA 1, 2; MTCW 1; SATA 100; SUFW; WCH; WLIT 4; YABC 1

Barrington, Michael
See Moorcock, Michael (John)

Barrol, Grady
See Bograd, Larry

Barry, Mike
See Malzberg, Barry N(athaniel)

Barry, Philip 1896-1949 .... **TCLC 11**
See also CA 109; 199; DFS 9; DLB 7, 228; RGAL 4

Bart, Andre Schwarz
See Schwarz-Bart, Andre

Barth, John (Simmons) 1930- ... **CLC 1, 2, 3, 5, 7, 9, 10, 14, 27, 51, 89; SSC 10**
See also AITN 1, 2; AMW; BPFB 1; CA 1-4R; CABS 1; CANR 5, 23, 49, 64, 113; CN 7; DAM NOV; DLB 2, 227; EWL 3; FANT; MTCW 1; RGAL 4; RGSF 2; RHW; SSFS 6; TUS

Barthelme, Donald 1931-1989 ... **CLC 1, 2, 3, 5, 6, 8, 13, 23, 46, 59, 115; SSC 2, 55**
See also AMWS 4; BPFB 1; CA 21-24R; 129; CANR 20, 58; DA3; DAM NOV; DLB 2, 234; DLBY 1980, 1989; EWL 3; FANT; LMFS 2; MTCW 1, 2; RGAL 4; RGSF 2; SATA 7; SATA-Obit 62; SSFS 17

Barthelme, Frederick 1943- ...... **CLC 36, 117**
See also AMWS 11; CA 114; 122; CANR 77; CN 7; CSW; DLB 244; DLBY 1985; EWL 3; INT CA-122

Barthes, Roland (Gerard) 1915-1980 .... **CLC 24, 83; TCLC 135**
See also CA 130; 97-100; CANR 66; DLB 296; EW 13; EWL 3; GFL 1789 to the Present; MTCW 1, 2; TWA

Bartram, William 1739-1823 .... **NCLC 145**
See also ANW; DLB 37

Barzun, Jacques (Martin) 1907- ..... **CLC 51, 145**
See also CA 61-64; CANR 22, 95

Bashevis, Isaac
See Singer, Isaac Bashevis

Bashkirtseff, Marie 1859-1884 .... **NCLC 27**

Basho, Matsuo
See Matsuo Basho
See also PFS 18; RGWL 2, 3; WP

Basil of Caesaria c. 330-379 .... **CMLC 35**

Basket, Raney
See Edgerton, Clyde (Carlyle)

Bass, Kingsley B., Jr.
See Bullins, Ed

Bass, Rick 1958- .... **CLC 79, 143; SSC 60**
See also ANW; CA 126; CANR 53, 93; CSW; DLB 212, 275

Bassani, Giorgio 1916-2000 .... **CLC 9**
See also CA 65-68; 190; CANR 33; CWW 2; DLB 128, 177, 299; EWL 3; MTCW 1; RGWL 2, 3

Bastian, Ann .... **CLC 70**

Bastos, Augusto (Antonio) Roa
See Roa Bastos, Augusto (Antonio)

Bataille, Georges 1897-1962 .... **CLC 29; TCLC 155**
See also CA 101; 89-92; EWL 3

Bates, H(erbert) E(rnest) 1905-1974 .... **CLC 46; SSC 10**
See also CA 93-96; 45-48; CANR 34; DA3; DAB; DAM POP; DLB 162, 191; EWL 3; EXPS; MTCW 1, 2; RGSF 2; SSFS 7

Bauchart
See Camus, Albert

Baudelaire, Charles 1821-1867 . **NCLC 6, 29, 55; PC 1; SSC 18; WLC**
See also DA; DA3; DAB; DAC; DAM MST, POET; DLB 217; EW 7; GFL 1789 to the Present; LMFS 2; PFS 21; RGWL 2, 3; TWA

Baudouin, Marcel
See Peguy, Charles (Pierre)

Baudouin, Pierre
See Peguy, Charles (Pierre)

Baudrillard, Jean 1929- .... **CLC 60**
See also DLB 296

Baum, L(yman) Frank 1856-1919 .. **TCLC 7, 132**
See also AAYA 46; BYA 16; CA 108; 133; CLR 15; CWRI 5; DLB 22; FANT; JRDA; MAICYA 1, 2; MTCW 1, 2; NFS 13; RGAL 4; SATA 18, 100; WCH

Baum, Louis F.
See Baum, L(yman) Frank

Baumbach, Jonathan 1933- .... **CLC 6, 23**
See also CA 13-16R; CAAS 5; CANR 12, 66; CN 7; DLBY 1980; INT CANR-12; MTCW 1

Bausch, Richard (Carl) 1945- .... **CLC 51**
See also AMWS 7; CA 101; CAAS 14; CANR 43, 61, 87; CSW; DLB 130

Baxter, Charles (Morley) 1947- . **CLC 45, 78**
See also CA 57-60; CANR 40, 64, 104, 133; CPW; DAM POP; DLB 130; MTCW 2

Baxter, George Owen
See Faust, Frederick (Schiller)

Baxter, James K(eir) 1926-1972 .... **CLC 14**
See also CA 77-80; EWL 3

Baxter, John
See Hunt, E(verette) Howard, (Jr.)

Bayer, Sylvia
See Glassco, John

Baynton, Barbara 1857-1929 .... **TCLC 57**
See also DLB 230; RGSF 2

Beagle, Peter S(oyer) 1939- .... **CLC 7, 104**
See also AAYA 47; BPFB 1; BYA 9, 10, 16; CA 9-12R; CANR 4, 51, 73, 110; DA3; DLBY 1980; FANT; INT CANR-4; MTCW 1; SATA 60, 130; SUFW 1, 2; YAW
Bean, Normal
See Burroughs, Edgar Rice
Beard, Charles A(ustin)
1874-1948 .... **TCLC 15**
See also CA 115; 189; DLB 17; SATA 18
Beardsley, Aubrey 1872-1898 .... **NCLC 6**
Beattie, Ann 1947- ..... **CLC 8, 13, 18, 40, 63, 146; SSC 11**
See also AMWS 5; BEST 90:2; BPFB 1; CA 81-84; CANR 53, 73, 128; CN 7; CPW; DA3; DAM NOV, POP; DLB 218, 278; DLBY 1982; EWL 3; MTCW 1, 2; RGAL 4; RGSF 2; SSFS 9; TUS
Beattie, James 1735-1803 .... **NCLC 25**
See also DLB 109
Beauchamp, Kathleen Mansfield 1888-1923
See Mansfield, Katherine
See also CA 104; 134; DA; DA3; DAC; DAM MST; MTCW 2; TEA
Beaumarchais, Pierre-Augustin Caron de
1732-1799 .... **DC 4; LC 61**
See also DAM DRAM; DFS 14, 16; EW 4; GFL Beginnings to 1789; RGWL 2, 3
Beaumont, Francis 1584(?)-1616 .. **DC 6; LC 33**
See also BRW 2; CDBLB Before 1660; DLB 58; TEA
Beauvoir, Simone (Lucie Ernestine Marie Bertrand) de 1908-1986 .... **CLC 1, 2, 4, 8, 14, 31, 44, 50, 71, 124; SSC 35; WLC**
See also BPFB 1; CA 9-12R; 118; CANR 28, 61; DA; DA3; DAB; DAC; DAM MST, NOV; DLB 72; DLBY 1986; EW 12; EWL 3; FW; GFL 1789 to the Present; LMFS 2; MTCW 1, 2; RGSF 2; RGWL 2, 3; TWA
Becker, Carl (Lotus) 1873-1945 ..... **TCLC 63**
See also CA 157; DLB 17
Becker, Jurek 1937-1997 .... **CLC 7, 19**
See also CA 85-88; 157; CANR 60, 117; CWW 2; DLB 75, 299; EWL 3
Becker, Walter 1950- .... **CLC 26**
Beckett, Samuel (Barclay)
1906-1989 .. **CLC 1, 2, 3, 4, 6, 9, 10, 11, 14, 18, 29, 57, 59, 83; DC 22; SSC 16, 74; TCLC 145; WLC**
See also BRWC 2; BRWR 1; BRWS 1; CA 5-8R; 130; CANR 33, 61; CBD; CDBLB 1945-1960; DA; DA3; DAB; DAC; DAM DRAM, MST, NOV; DFS 2, 7, 18; DLB 13, 15, 233; DLBY 1990; EWL 3; GFL 1789 to the Present; LATS 1:2; LMFS 2; MTCW 1, 2; RGSF 2; RGWL 2, 3; SSFS 15; TEA; WLIT 4
Beckford, William 1760-1844 .... **NCLC 16**
See also BRW 3; DLB 39, 213; HGG; LMFS 1; SUFW
Beckham, Barry (Earl) 1944- .... **BLC 1**
See also BW 1; CA 29-32R; CANR 26, 62; CN 7; DAM MULT; DLB 33
Beckman, Gunnel 1910- .... **CLC 26**
See also CA 33-36R; CANR 15, 114; CLR 25; MAICYA 1, 2; SAAS 9; SATA 6
Becque, Henri 1837-1899 .... **DC 21; NCLC 3**
See also DLB 192; GFL 1789 to the Present
Becquer, Gustavo Adolfo
1836-1870 .... **HLCS 1; NCLC 106**
See also DAM MULT
Beddoes, Thomas Lovell 1803-1849 .. **DC 15; NCLC 3**
See also DLB 96
Bede c. 673-735 .... **CMLC 20**
See also DLB 146; TEA

Bedford, Denton R. 1907-(?) .... **NNAL**
Bedford, Donald F.
See Fearing, Kenneth (Flexner)
Beecher, Catharine Esther
1800-1878 .... **NCLC 30**
See also DLB 1, 243
Beecher, John 1904-1980 .... **CLC 6**
See also AITN 1; CA 5-8R; 105; CANR 8
Beer, Johann 1655-1700 .... **LC 5**
See also DLB 168
Beer, Patricia 1924- .... **CLC 58**
See also CA 61-64; 183; CANR 13, 46; CP 7; CWP; DLB 40; FW
Beerbohm, Max
See Beerbohm, (Henry) Max(imilian)
Beerbohm, (Henry) Max(imilian)
1872-1956 .... **TCLC 1, 24**
See also BRWS 2; CA 104; 154; CANR 79; DLB 34, 100; FANT
Beer-Hofmann, Richard
1866-1945 .... **TCLC 60**
See also CA 160; DLB 81
Beg, Shemus
See Stephens, James
Begiebing, Robert J(ohn) 1946- .... **CLC 70**
See also CA 122; CANR 40, 88
Begley, Louis 1933- .... **CLC 197**
See also CA 140; CANR 98; DLB 299
Behan, Brendan (Francis)
1923-1964 .... **CLC 1, 8, 11, 15, 79**
See also BRWS 2; CA 73-76; CANR 33, 121; CBD; CDBLB 1945-1960; DAM DRAM; DFS 7; DLB 13, 233; EWL 3; MTCW 1, 2
Behn, Aphra 1640(?)-1689 .. **DC 4; LC 1, 30, 42; PC 13; WLC**
See also BRWS 3; DA; DA3; DAB; DAC; DAM DRAM, MST, NOV, POET; DFS 16; DLB 39, 80, 131; FW; TEA; WLIT 3
Behrman, S(amuel) N(athaniel)
1893-1973 .... **CLC 40**
See also CA 13-16; 45-48; CAD; CAP 1; DLB 7, 44; IDFW 3; RGAL 4
Belasco, David 1853-1931 .... **TCLC 3**
See also CA 104; 168; DLB 7; RGAL 4
Belcheva, Elisaveta Lyubomirova
1893-1991 .... **CLC 10**
See also Bagryana, Elisaveta
Beldone, Phil "Cheech"
See Ellison, Harlan (Jay)
Beleno
See Azuela, Mariano
Belinski, Vissarion Grigoryevich
1811-1848 .... **NCLC 5**
See also DLB 198
Belitt, Ben 1911- .... **CLC 22**
See also CA 13-16R; CAAS 4; CANR 7, 77; CP 7; DLB 5
Bell, Gertrude (Margaret Lowthian)
1868-1926 .... **TCLC 67**
See also CA 167; CANR 110; DLB 174
Bell, J. Freeman
See Zangwill, Israel
Bell, James Madison 1826-1902 .... **BLC 1; TCLC 43**
See also BW 1; CA 122; 124; DAM MULT; DLB 50
Bell, Madison Smartt 1957- ...... **CLC 41, 102**
See also AMWS 10; BPFB 1; CA 111, 183; CAAE 183; CANR 28, 54, 73; CN 7; CSW; DLB 218, 278; MTCW 1
Bell, Marvin (Hartley) 1937- .... **CLC 8, 31**
See also CA 21-24R; CAAS 14; CANR 59, 102; CP 7; DAM POET; DLB 5; MTCW 1
Bell, W. L. D.
See Mencken, H(enry) L(ouis)
Bellamy, Atwood C.
See Mencken, H(enry) L(ouis)

Bellamy, Edward 1850-1898 ..... **NCLC 4, 86, 147**
See also DLB 12; NFS 15; RGAL 4; SFW 4
Belli, Gioconda 1949- .... **HLCS 1**
See also CA 152; CWW 2; DLB 290; EWL 3; RGWL 3
Bellin, Edward J.
See Kuttner, Henry
Bello, Andres 1781-1865 .... **NCLC 131**
See also LAW
Belloc, (Joseph) Hilaire (Pierre Sebastien Rene Swanton) 1870-1953 .... **PC 24; TCLC 7, 18**
See also CA 106; 152; CWRI 5; DAM POET; DLB 19, 100, 141, 174; EWL 3; MTCW 1; SATA 112; WCH; YABC 1
Belloc, Joseph Peter Rene Hilaire
See Belloc, (Joseph) Hilaire (Pierre Sebastien Rene Swanton)
Belloc, Joseph Pierre Hilaire
See Belloc, (Joseph) Hilaire (Pierre Sebastien Rene Swanton)
Belloc, M. A.
See Lowndes, Marie Adelaide (Belloc)
Belloc-Lowndes, Mrs.
See Lowndes, Marie Adelaide (Belloc)
Bellow, Saul 1915- . **CLC 1, 2, 3, 6, 8, 10, 13, 15, 25, 33, 34, 63, 79, 190; SSC 14; WLC**
See also AITN 2; AMW; AMWC 2; AMWR 2; BEST 89:3; BPFB 1; CA 5-8R; CABS 1; CANR 29, 53, 95, 132; CDALB 1941-1968; CN 7; DA; DA3; DAB; DAC; DAM MST, NOV, POP; DLB 2, 28, 299; DLBD 3; DLBY 1982; EWL 3; MTCW 1, 2; NFS 4, 14; RGAL 4; RGSF 2; SSFS 12; TUS
Belser, Reimond Karel Maria de 1929-
See Ruyslinck, Ward
See also CA 152
Bely, Andrey .... **PC 11; TCLC 7**
See Bugayev, Boris Nikolayevich
See also DLB 295; EW 9; EWL 3; MTCW 1
Belyi, Andrei
See Bugayev, Boris Nikolayevich
See also RGWL 2, 3
Bembo, Pietro 1470-1547 .... **LC 79**
See also RGWL 2, 3
Benary, Margot
See Benary-Isbert, Margot
Benary-Isbert, Margot 1889-1979 .... **CLC 12**
See also CA 5-8R; 89-92; CANR 4, 72; CLR 12; MAICYA 1, 2; SATA 2; SATA-Obit 21
Benavente (y Martinez), Jacinto
1866-1954 .... **HLCS 1; TCLC 3**
See also CA 106; 131; CANR 81; DAM DRAM, MULT; EWL 3; GLL 2; HW 1, 2; MTCW 1, 2
Benchley, Peter (Bradford) 1940- .. **CLC 4, 8**
See also AAYA 14; AITN 2; BPFB 1; CA 17-20R; CANR 12, 35, 66, 115; CPW; DAM NOV, POP; HGG; MTCW 1, 2; SATA 3, 89
Benchley, Robert (Charles)
1889-1945 .... **TCLC 1, 55**
See also CA 105; 153; DLB 11; RGAL 4
Benda, Julien 1867-1956 .... **TCLC 60**
See also CA 120; 154; GFL 1789 to the Present
Benedict, Ruth (Fulton)
1887-1948 .... **TCLC 60**
See also CA 158; DLB 246
Benedikt, Michael 1935- .... **CLC 4, 14**
See also CA 13-16R; CANR 7; CP 7; DLB 5

Betti, Ugo 1892-1953 .... **TCLC 5**
See also CA 104; 155; EWL 3; RGWL 2, 3

Betts, Doris (Waugh) 1932- ..... **CLC 3, 6, 28;**
SSC 45
See also CA 13-16R; CANR 9, 66, 77; CN 7; CSW; DLB 218; DLBY 1982; INT CANR-9; RGAL 4

Bevan, Alistair
See Roberts, Keith (John Kingston)

Bey, Pilaff
See Douglas, (George) Norman

Bialik, Chaim Nachman
1873-1934 .... **TCLC 25**
See also CA 170; EWL 3

Bickerstaff, Isaac
See Swift, Jonathan

Bidart, Frank 1939- .... **CLC 33**
See also CA 140; CANR 106; CP 7

Bienek, Horst 1930- .... **CLC 7, 11**
See also CA 73-76; DLB 75

Bierce, Ambrose (Gwinett)
1842-1914(?) ..... **SSC 9, 72; TCLC 1, 7,**
44; WLC
See also AAYA 55; AMW; BYA 11; CA 104; 139; CANR 78; CDALB 1865-1917; DA; DA3; DAC; DAM MST; DLB 11, 12, 23, 71, 74, 186; EWL 3; EXPS; HGG; LAIT 2; RGAL 4; RGSF 2; SSFS 9; SUFW 1

Biggers, Earl Derr 1884-1933 .... **TCLC 65**
See also CA 108; 153; DLB 306

Billiken, Bud
See Motley, Willard (Francis)

Billings, Josh
See Shaw, Henry Wheeler

Billington, (Lady) Rachel (Mary)
1942- .... **CLC 43**
See also AITN 2; CA 33-36R; CANR 44; CN 7

Binchy, Maeve 1940- .... **CLC 153**
See also BEST 90:1; BPFB 1; CA 127; 134; CANR 50, 96; CN 7; CPW; DA3; DAM POP; INT CA-134; MTCW 1; RHW

Binyon, T(imothy) J(ohn) 1936- .... **CLC 34**
See also CA 111; CANR 28

Bion 335B.C.-245B.C. .... **CMLC 39**

Bioy Casares, Adolfo 1914-1999 ... **CLC 4, 8,**
13, 88; HLC 1; SSC 17
See Casares, Adolfo Bioy; Miranda, Javier; Sacastru, Martin
See also CA 29-32R; 177; CANR 19, 43, 66; CWW 2; DAM MULT; DLB 113; EWL 3; HW 1, 2; LAW; MTCW 1, 2

Birch, Allison .... **CLC 65**

Bird, Cordwainer
See Ellison, Harlan (Jay)

Bird, Robert Montgomery
1806-1854 .... **NCLC 1**
See also DLB 202; RGAL 4

Birkerts, Sven 1951- .... **CLC 116**
See also CA 128; 133, 176; CAAE 176; CAAS 29; INT CA-133

Birney, (Alfred) Earle 1904-1995 .. **CLC 1, 4,**
6, 11; PC 52
See also CA 1-4R; CANR 5, 20; CP 7; DAC; DAM MST, POET; DLB 88; MTCW 1; PFS 8; RGEL 2

Biruni, al 973-1048(?) .... **CMLC 28**

Bishop, Elizabeth 1911-1979 ..... **CLC 1, 4, 9,**
13, 15, 32; PC 3, 34; TCLC 121
See also AMWR 2; AMWS 1; CA 5-8R; 89-92; CABS 2; CANR 26, 61, 108; CDALB 1968-1988; DA; DA3; DAC; DAM MST, POET; DLB 5, 169; EWL 3; GLL 2; MAWW; MTCW 1, 2; PAB; PFS 6, 12; RGAL 4; SATA-Obit 24; TUS; WP

Bishop, John 1935- .... **CLC 10**
See also CA 105

Bishop, John Peale 1892-1944 ..... **TCLC 103**
See also CA 107; 155; DLB 4, 9, 45; RGAL 4

Bissett, Bill 1939- .... **CLC 18; PC 14**
See also CA 69-72; CAAS 19; CANR 15; CCA 1; CP 7; DLB 53; MTCW 1

Bissoondath, Neil (Devindra)
1955- .... **CLC 120**
See also CA 136; CANR 123; CN 7; DAC

Bitov, Andrei (Georgievich) 1937- ... **CLC 57**
See also CA 142; DLB 302

Biyidi, Alexandre 1932-
See Beti, Mongo
See also BW 1, 3; CA 114; 124; CANR 81; DA3; MTCW 1, 2

Bjarme, Brynjolf
See Ibsen, Henrik (Johan)

Bjoernson, Bjoernstjerne (Martinius)
1832-1910 .... **TCLC 7, 37**
See also CA 104

Black, Robert
See Holdstock, Robert P.

Blackburn, Paul 1926-1971 .... **CLC 9, 43**
See also BG 2; CA 81-84; 33-36R; CANR 34; DLB 16; DLBY 1981

Black Elk 1863-1950 .... **NNAL; TCLC 33**
See also CA 144; DAM MULT; MTCW 1; WP

Black Hawk 1767-1838 .... **NNAL**

Black Hobart
See Sanders, (James) Ed(ward)

Blacklin, Malcolm
See Chambers, Aidan

Blackmore, R(ichard) D(oddridge)
1825-1900 .... **TCLC 27**
See also CA 120; DLB 18; RGEL 2

Blackmur, R(ichard) P(almer)
1904-1965 .... **CLC 2, 24**
See also AMWS 2; CA 11-12; 25-28R; CANR 71; CAP 1; DLB 63; EWL 3

Black Tarantula
See Acker, Kathy

Blackwood, Algernon (Henry)
1869-1951 .... **TCLC 5**
See also CA 105; 150; DLB 153, 156, 178; HGG; SUFW 1

Blackwood, Caroline 1931-1996 .... **CLC 6, 9,**
100
See also BRWS 9; CA 85-88; 151; CANR 32, 61, 65; CN 7; DLB 14, 207; HGG; MTCW 1

Blade, Alexander
See Hamilton, Edmond; Silverberg, Robert

Blaga, Lucian 1895-1961 .... **CLC 75**
See also CA 157; DLB 220; EWL 3

Blair, Eric (Arthur) 1903-1950 .... **TCLC 123**
See Orwell, George
See also CA 104; 132; DA; DA3; DAB; DAC; DAM MST, NOV; MTCW 1, 2; SATA 29

Blair, Hugh 1718-1800 .... **NCLC 75**

Blais, Marie-Claire 1939- .... **CLC 2, 4, 6, 13,**
22
See also CA 21-24R; CAAS 4; CANR 38, 75, 93; CWW 2; DAC; DAM MST; DLB 53; EWL 3; FW; MTCW 1, 2; TWA

Blaise, Clark 1940- .... **CLC 29**
See also AITN 2; CA 53-56; CAAS 3; CANR 5, 66, 106; CN 7; DLB 53; RGSF 2

Blake, Fairley
See De Voto, Bernard (Augustine)

Blake, Nicholas
See Day Lewis, C(ecil)
See also DLB 77; MSW

Blake, Sterling
See Benford, Gregory (Albert)

Blake, William 1757-1827 . **NCLC 13, 37, 57,**
127; PC 12; WLC
See also AAYA 47; BRW 3; BRWR 1; CD-BLB 1789-1832; CLR 52; DA; DA3; DAB; DAC; DAM MST, POET; DLB 93, 163; EXPP; LATS 1:1; LMFS 1; MAICYA 1, 2; PAB; PFS 2, 12; SATA 30; TEA; WCH; WLIT 3; WP

Blanchot, Maurice 1907-2003 .... **CLC 135**
See also CA 117; 144; 213; DLB 72, 296; EWL 3

Blasco Ibanez, Vicente 1867-1928 . **TCLC 12**
See also BPFB 1; CA 110; 131; CANR 81; DA3; DAM NOV; EW 8; EWL 3; HW 1, 2; MTCW 1

Blatty, William Peter 1928- .... **CLC 2**
See also CA 5-8R; CANR 9, 124; DAM POP; HGG

Bleeck, Oliver
See Thomas, Ross (Elmore)

Blessing, Lee 1949- .... **CLC 54**
See also CAD; CD 5

Blight, Rose
See Greer, Germaine

Blish, James (Benjamin) 1921-1975 . **CLC 14**
See also BPFB 1; CA 1-4R; 57-60; CANR 3; DLB 8; MTCW 1; SATA 66; SCFW 2; SFW 4

Bliss, Frederick
See Card, Orson Scott

Bliss, Reginald
See Wells, H(erbert) G(eorge)

Blixen, Karen (Christentze Dinesen)
1885-1962
See Dinesen, Isak
See also CA 25-28; CANR 22, 50; CAP 2; DA3; DLB 214; LMFS 1; MTCW 1, 2; SATA 44; SSFS 20

Bloch, Robert (Albert) 1917-1994 .... **CLC 33**
See also AAYA 29; CA 5-8R, 179; 146; CAAE 179; CAAS 20; CANR 5, 78; DA3; DLB 44; HGG; INT CANR-5; MTCW 1; SATA 12; SATA-Obit 82; SFW 4; SUFW 1, 2

Blok, Alexander (Alexandrovich)
1880-1921 .... **PC 21; TCLC 5**
See also CA 104; 183; DLB 295; EW 9; EWL 3; LMFS 2; RGWL 2, 3

Blom, Jan
See Breytenbach, Breyten

Bloom, Harold 1930- .... **CLC 24, 103**
See also CA 13-16R; CANR 39, 75, 92, 133; DLB 67; EWL 3; MTCW 1; RGAL 4

Bloomfield, Aurelius
See Bourne, Randolph S(illiman)

Bloomfield, Robert 1766-1823 ..... **NCLC 145**
See also DLB 93

Blount, Roy (Alton), Jr. 1941- .... **CLC 38**
See also CA 53-56; CANR 10, 28, 61, 125; CSW; INT CANR-28; MTCW 1, 2

Blowsnake, Sam 1875-(?) .... **NNAL**

Bloy, Leon 1846-1917 .... **TCLC 22**
See also CA 121; 183; DLB 123; GFL 1789 to the Present

Blue Cloud, Peter (Aroniawenrate)
1933- .... **NNAL**
See also CA 117; CANR 40; DAM MULT

Bluggage, Oranthy
See Alcott, Louisa May

Blume, Judy (Sussman) 1938- .... **CLC 12, 30**
See also AAYA 3, 26; BYA 1, 8, 12; CA 29-32R; CANR 13, 37, 66, 124; CLR 2, 15, 69; CPW; DA3; DAM NOV, POP; DLB 52; JRDA; MAICYA 1, 2; MAICYAS 1; MTCW 1, 2; SATA 2, 31, 79, 142; WYA; YAW

Blunden, Edmund (Charles)
1896-1974 .... **CLC 2, 56**
See also BRW 6; CA 17-18; 45-48; CANR
54; CAP 2; DLB 20, 100, 155; MTCW 1;
PAB

Bly, Robert (Elwood) 1926- .... **CLC 1, 2, 5, 10, 15, 38, 128; PC 39**
See also AMWS 4; CA 5-8R; CANR 41,
73, 125; CP 7; DA3; DAM POET; DLB
5; EWL 3; MTCW 1, 2; PFS 6, 17; RGAL
4

Boas, Franz 1858-1942 .... **TCLC 56**
See also CA 115; 181

Bobette
See Simenon, Georges (Jacques Christian)

Boccaccio, Giovanni 1313-1375 ... **CMLC 13, 57; SSC 10**
See also EW 2; RGSF 2; RGWL 2, 3; TWA

Bochco, Steven 1943- .... **CLC 35**
See also AAYA 11; CA 124; 138

Bode, Sigmund
See O'Doherty, Brian

Bodel, Jean 1167(?)-1210 .... **CMLC 28**

Bodenheim, Maxwell 1892-1954 .... **TCLC 44**
See also CA 110; 187; DLB 9, 45; RGAL 4

Bodenheimer, Maxwell
See Bodenheim, Maxwell

Bodker, Cecil 1927-
See Bodker, Cecil

Bodker, Cecil 1927- .... **CLC 21**
See also CA 73-76; CANR 13, 44, 111;
CLR 23; MAICYA 1, 2; SATA 14, 133

Boell, Heinrich (Theodor)
1917-1985 ..... **CLC 2, 3, 6, 9, 11, 15, 27, 32, 72; SSC 23; WLC**
See Boll, Heinrich
See also CA 21-24R; 116; CANR 24; DA;
DA3; DAB; DAC; DAM MST, NOV;
DLB 69; DLBY 1985; MTCW 1, 2; SSFS
20; TWA

Boerne, Alfred
See Doeblin, Alfred

Boethius c. 480-c. 524 .... **CMLC 15**
See also DLB 115; RGWL 2, 3

Boff, Leonardo (Genezio Darci)
1938- .... **CLC 70; HLC 1**
See also CA 150; DAM MULT; HW 2

Bogan, Louise 1897-1970 .... **CLC 4, 39, 46, 93; PC 12**
See also AMWS 3; CA 73-76; 25-28R;
CANR 33, 82; DAM POET; DLB 45, 169;
EWL 3; MAWW; MTCW 1, 2; PFS 21;
RGAL 4

Bogarde, Dirk
See Van Den Bogarde, Derek Jules Gaspard
Ulric Niven
See also DLB 14

Bogosian, Eric 1953- .... **CLC 45, 141**
See also CA 138; CAD; CANR 102; CD 5

Bograd, Larry 1953- .... **CLC 35**
See also CA 93-96; CANR 57; SAAS 21;
SATA 33, 89; WYA

Boiardo, Matteo Maria 1441-1494 .... **LC 6**

Boileau-Despreaux, Nicolas 1636-1711 . **LC 3**
See also DLB 268; EW 3; GFL Beginnings
to 1789; RGWL 2, 3

Boissard, Maurice
See Leautaud, Paul

Bojer, Johan 1872-1959 .... **TCLC 64**
See also CA 189; EWL 3

Bok, Edward W(illiam)
1863-1930 .... **TCLC 101**
See also CA 217; DLB 91; DLBD 16

Boker, George Henry 1823-1890 . **NCLC 125**
See also RGAL 4

Boland, Eavan (Aisling) 1944- .. **CLC 40, 67, 113; PC 58**
See also BRWS 5; CA 143, 207; CAAE
207; CANR 61; CP 7; CWP; DAM POET;
DLB 40; FW; MTCW 2; PFS 12

Boll, Heinrich
See Boell, Heinrich (Theodor)
See also BPFB 1; CDWLB 2; EW 13; EWL
3; RGSF 2; RGWL 2, 3

Bolt, Lee
See Faust, Frederick (Schiller)

Bolt, Robert (Oxton) 1924-1995 .... **CLC 14**
See also CA 17-20R; 147; CANR 35, 67;
CBD; DAM DRAM; DFS 2; DLB 13,
233; EWL 3; LAIT 1; MTCW 1

Bombal, Maria Luisa 1910-1980 .... **HLCS 1; SSC 37**
See also CA 127; CANR 72; EWL 3; HW
1; LAW; RGSF 2

Bombet, Louis-Alexandre-Cesar
See Stendhal

Bomkauf
See Kaufman, Bob (Garnell)

Bonaventura .... **NCLC 35**
See also DLB 90

Bond, Edward 1934- .... **CLC 4, 6, 13, 23**
See also AAYA 50; BRWS 1; CA 25-28R;
CANR 38, 67, 106; CBD; CD 5; DAM
DRAM; DFS 3, 8; DLB 13; EWL 3;
MTCW 1

Bonham, Frank 1914-1989 .... **CLC 12**
See also AAYA 1; BYA 1, 3; CA 9-12R;
CANR 4, 36; JRDA; MAICYA 1, 2;
SAAS 3; SATA 1, 49; SATA-Obit 62;
TCWW 2; YAW

Bonnefoy, Yves 1923- . **CLC 9, 15, 58; PC 58**
See also CA 85-88; CANR 33, 75, 97;
CWW 2; DAM MST, POET; DLB 258;
EWL 3; GFL 1789 to the Present; MTCW
1, 2

Bonner, Marita .... **HR 2**
See Occomy, Marita (Odette) Bonner

Bonnin, Gertrude 1876-1938 .... **NNAL**
See Zitkala-Sa
See also CA 150; DAM MULT

Bontemps, Arna(ud Wendell)
1902-1973 ..... **BLC 1; CLC 1, 18; HR 2**
See also BW 1; CA 1-4R; 41-44R; CANR
4, 35; CLR 6; CWRI 5; DA3; DAM
MULT, NOV, POET; DLB 48, 51; JRDA;
MAICYA 1, 2; MTCW 1, 2; SATA 2, 44;
SATA-Obit 24; WCH; WP

Boot, William
See Stoppard, Tom

Booth, Martin 1944-2004 .... **CLC 13**
See also CA 93-96; 188; 223; CAAE 188;
CAAS 2; CANR 92

Booth, Philip 1925- .... **CLC 23**
See also CA 5-8R; CANR 5, 88; CP 7;
DLBY 1982

Booth, Wayne C(layson) 1921- .... **CLC 24**
See also CA 1-4R; CAAS 5; CANR 3, 43,
117; DLB 67

Borchert, Wolfgang 1921-1947 .... **TCLC 5**
See also CA 104; 188; DLB 69, 124; EWL
3

Borel, Petrus 1809-1859 .... **NCLC 41**
See also DLB 119; GFL 1789 to the Present

Borges, Jorge Luis 1899-1986 ... **CLC 1, 2, 3, 4, 6, 8, 9, 10, 13, 19, 44, 48, 83; HLC 1; PC 22, 32; SSC 4, 41; TCLC 109; WLC**
See also AAYA 26; BPFB 1; CA 21-24R;
CANR 19, 33, 75, 105, 133; CDWLB 3;
DA; DA3; DAB; DAC; DAM MST,
MULT; DLB 113, 283; DLBY 1986;
DNFS 1, 2; EWL 3; HW 1, 2; LAW;
LMFS 2; MSW; MTCW 1, 2; RGSF 2;
RGWL 2, 3; SFW 4; SSFS 17; TWA;
WLIT 1

Borowski, Tadeusz 1922-1951 .... **SSC 48; TCLC 9**
See also CA 106; 154; CDWLB 4; DLB
215; EWL 3; RGSF 2; RGWL 3; SSFS
13

Borrow, George (Henry)
1803-1881 .... **NCLC 9**
See also DLB 21, 55, 166

Bosch (Gavino), Juan 1909-2001 ..... **HLCS 1**
See also CA 151; 204; DAM MST, MULT;
DLB 145; HW 1, 2

Bosman, Herman Charles
1905-1951 .... **TCLC 49**
See Malan, Herman
See also CA 160; DLB 225; RGSF 2

Bosschere, Jean de 1878(?)-1953 ... **TCLC 19**
See also CA 115; 186

Boswell, James 1740-1795 ... **LC 4, 50; WLC**
See also BRW 3; CDBLB 1660-1789; DA;
DAB; DAC; DAM MST; DLB 104, 142;
TEA; WLIT 3

Bottomley, Gordon 1874-1948 ..... **TCLC 107**
See also CA 120; 192; DLB 10

Bottoms, David 1949- .... **CLC 53**
See also CA 105; CANR 22; CSW; DLB
120; DLBY 1983

Boucicault, Dion 1820-1890 .... **NCLC 41**

Boucolon, Maryse
See Conde, Maryse

Bourget, Paul (Charles Joseph)
1852-1935 .... **TCLC 12**
See also CA 107; 196; DLB 123; GFL 1789
to the Present

Bourjaily, Vance (Nye) 1922- .... **CLC 8, 62**
See also CA 1-4R; CAAS 1; CANR 2, 72;
CN 7; DLB 2, 143

Bourne, Randolph S(illiman)
1886-1918 .... **TCLC 16**
See also AMW; CA 117; 155; DLB 63

Bova, Ben(jamin William) 1932- ...... **CLC 45**
See also AAYA 16; CA 5-8R; CAAS 18;
CANR 11, 56, 94, 111; CLR 3, 96; DLBY
1981; INT CANR-11; MAICYA 1, 2;
MTCW 1; SATA 6, 68, 133; SFW 4

Bowen, Elizabeth (Dorothea Cole)
1899-1973 . **CLC 1, 3, 6, 11, 15, 22, 118; SSC 3, 28, 66; TCLC 148**
See also BRWS 2; CA 17-18; 41-44R;
CANR 35, 105; CAP 2; CDBLB 1945-
1960; DA3; DAM NOV; DLB 15, 162;
EWL 3; EXPS; FW; HGG; MTCW 1, 2;
NFS 13; RGSF 2; SSFS 5; SUFW 1;
TEA; WLIT 4

Bowering, George 1935- .... **CLC 15, 47**
See also CA 21-24R; CAAS 16; CANR 10;
CP 7; DLB 53

Bowering, Marilyn R(uthe) 1949- .... **CLC 32**
See also CA 101; CANR 49; CP 7; CWP

Bowers, Edgar 1924-2000 .... **CLC 9**
See also CA 5-8R; 188; CANR 24; CP 7;
CSW; DLB 5

Bowers, Mrs. J. Milton 1842-1914
See Bierce, Ambrose (Gwinett)

Bowie, David .... **CLC 17**
See Jones, David Robert

Bowles, Jane (Sydney) 1917-1973 ..... **CLC 3, 68**
See Bowles, Jane Auer
See also CA 19-20; 41-44R; CAP 2

Bowles, Jane Auer
See Bowles, Jane (Sydney)
See also EWL 3

Bowles, Paul (Frederick) 1910-1999 . **CLC 1, 2, 19, 53; SSC 3**
See also AMWS 4; CA 1-4R; 186; CAAS
1; CANR 1, 19, 50, 75; CN 7; DA3; DLB
5, 6, 218; EWL 3; MTCW 1, 2; RGAL 4;
SSFS 17

Bowles, William Lisle 1762-1850 . **NCLC 103**
See also DLB 93

Box, Edgar
See Vidal, (Eugene Luther) Gore
See also GLL 1

Boyd, James 1888-1944 .... **TCLC 115**
See also CA 186; DLB 9; DLBD 16; RGAL
4; RHW

Boyd, Nancy
See Millay, Edna St. Vincent
See also GLL 1

Boyd, Thomas (Alexander)
1898-1935 .... **TCLC 111**
See also CA 111; 183; DLB 9; DLBD 16

Boyd, William 1952- .... **CLC 28, 53, 70**
See also CA 114; 120; CANR 51, 71, 131;
CN 7; DLB 231

Boyesen, Hjalmar Hjorth
1848-1895 .... **NCLC 135**
See also DLB 12, 71; DLBD 13; RGAL 4

Boyle, Kay 1902-1992 .... **CLC 1, 5, 19, 58,
121; SSC 5**
See also CA 13-16R; 140; CAAS 1; CANR
29, 61, 110; DLB 4, 9, 48, 86; DLBY
1993; EWL 3; MTCW 1, 2; RGAL 4;
RGSF 2; SSFS 10, 13, 14

Boyle, Mark
See Kienzle, William X(avier)

Boyle, Patrick 1905-1982 .... **CLC 19**
See also CA 127

Boyle, T. C.
See Boyle, T(homas) Coraghessan
See also AMWS 8

Boyle, T(homas) Coraghessan
1948- .... **CLC 36, 55, 90; SSC 16**
See Boyle, T. C.
See also AAYA 47; BEST 90:4; BPFB 1;
CA 120; CANR 44, 76, 89, 132; CN 7;
CPW; DA3; DAM POP; DLB 218, 278;
DLBY 1986; EWL 3; MTCW 2; SSFS 13,
19

Boz
See Dickens, Charles (John Huffam)

Brackenridge, Hugh Henry
1748-1816 .... **NCLC 7**
See also DLB 11, 37; RGAL 4

Bradbury, Edward P.
See Moorcock, Michael (John)
See also MTCW 2

Bradbury, Malcolm (Stanley)
1932-2000 .... **CLC 32, 61**
See also CA 1-4R; CANR 1, 33, 91, 98;
CN 7; DA3; DAM NOV; DLB 14, 207;
EWL 3; MTCW 1, 2

Bradbury, Ray (Douglas) 1920- .... **CLC 1, 3,
10, 15, 42, 98; SSC 29, 53; WLC**
See also AAYA 15; AITN 1, 2; AMWS 4;
BPFB 1; BYA 4, 5, 11; CA 1-4R; CANR
2, 30, 75, 125; CDALB 1968-1988; CN
7; CPW; DA; DA3; DAB; DAC; DAM
MST, NOV, POP; DLB 2, 8; EXPN;
EXPS; HGG; LAIT 3, 5; LATS 1:2;
LMFS 2; MTCW 1, 2; NFS 1; RGAL 4;
RGSF 2; SATA 11, 64, 123; SCFW 2;
SFW 4; SSFS 1, 20; SUFW 1, 2; TUS;
YAW

Braddon, Mary Elizabeth
1837-1915 .... **TCLC 111**
See also BRWS 8; CA 108; 179; CMW 4;
DLB 18, 70, 156; HGG

Bradfield, Scott (Michael) 1955- .... **SSC 65**
See also CA 147; CANR 90; HGG; SUFW
2

Bradford, Gamaliel 1863-1932 .... **TCLC 36**
See also CA 160; DLB 17

Bradford, William 1590-1657 .... **LC 64**
See also DLB 24, 30; RGAL 4

Bradley, David (Henry), Jr. 1950- .... **BLC 1;
CLC 23, 118**
See also BW 1, 3; CA 104; CANR 26, 81;
CN 7; DAM MULT; DLB 33

Bradley, John Ed(mund, Jr.) 1958- . **CLC 55**
See also CA 139; CANR 99; CN 7; CSW

Bradley, Marion Zimmer
1930-1999 .... **CLC 30**
See Chapman, Lee; Dexter, John; Gardner,
Miriam; Ives, Morgan; Rivers, Elfrida
See also AAYA 40; BPFB 1; CA 57-60; 185;
CAAS 10; CANR 7, 31, 51, 75, 107;
CPW; DA3; DAM POP; DLB 8; FANT;
FW; MTCW 1, 2; SATA 90, 139; SATA-
Obit 116; SFW 4; SUFW 2; YAW

Bradshaw, John 1933- .... **CLC 70**
See also CA 138; CANR 61

Bradstreet, Anne 1612(?)-1672 ...... **LC 4, 30;
PC 10**
See also AMWS 1; CDALB 1640-1865;
DA; DA3; DAC; DAM MST, POET; DLB
24; EXPP; FW; PFS 6; RGAL 4; TUS;
WP

Brady, Joan 1939- .... **CLC 86**
See also CA 141

Bragg, Melvyn 1939- .... **CLC 10**
See also BEST 89:3; CA 57-60; CANR 10,
48, 89; CN 7; DLB 14, 271; RHW

Brahe, Tycho 1546-1601 .... **LC 45**
See also DLB 300

Braine, John (Gerard) 1922-1986 . **CLC 1, 3,
41**
See also CA 1-4R; 120; CANR 1, 33; CD-
BLB 1945-1960; DLB 15; DLBY 1986;
EWL 3; MTCW 1

Braithwaite, William Stanley (Beaumont)
1878-1962 .... **BLC 1; HR 2; PC 52**
See also BW 1; CA 125; DAM MULT; DLB
50, 54

Bramah, Ernest 1868-1942 .... **TCLC 72**
See also CA 156; CMW 4; DLB 70; FANT

Brammer, William 1930(?)-1978 ...... **CLC 31**
See also CA 77-80

Brancati, Vitaliano 1907-1954 .... **TCLC 12**
See also CA 109; DLB 264; EWL 3

Brancato, Robin F(idler) 1936- .... **CLC 35**
See also AAYA 9; BYA 6; CA 69-72; CANR
11, 45; CLR 32; JRDA; MAICYA 2;
MAICYAS 1; SAAS 9; SATA 97; WYA;
YAW

Brand, Dionne 1953- .... **CLC 192**
See also BW 2; CA 143; CWP

Brand, Max
See Faust, Frederick (Schiller)
See also BPFB 1; TCWW 2

Brand, Millen 1906-1980 .... **CLC 7**
See also CA 21-24R; 97-100; CANR 72

Branden, Barbara .... **CLC 44**
See also CA 148

Brandes, Georg (Morris Cohen)
1842-1927 .... **TCLC 10**
See also CA 105; 189; DLB 300

Brandys, Kazimierz 1916-2000 .... **CLC 62**
See also EWL 3

Branley, Franklyn M(ansfield)
1915-2002 .... **CLC 21**
See also CA 33-36R; 207; CANR 14, 39;
CLR 13; MAICYA 1, 2; SAAS 16; SATA
4, 68, 136

Brant, Beth (E.) 1941- .... **NNAL**
See also CA 144; FW

Brathwaite, Edward Kamau
1930- .... **BLCS; CLC 11; PC 56**
See also BW 2, 3; CA 25-28R; CANR 11,
26, 47, 107; CDWLB 3; CP 7; DAM
POET; DLB 125; EWL 3

Brathwaite, Kamau
See Brathwaite, Edward Kamau

Brautigan, Richard (Gary)
1935-1984 .... **CLC 1, 3, 5, 9, 12, 34, 42;
TCLC 133**
See also BPFB 1; CA 53-56; 113; CANR
34; DA3; DAM NOV; DLB 2, 5, 206;
DLBY 1980, 1984; FANT; MTCW 1;
RGAL 4; SATA 56

Brave Bird, Mary .... **NNAL**
See Crow Dog, Mary (Ellen)

Braverman, Kate 1950- .... **CLC 67**
See also CA 89-92

Brecht, (Eugen) Bertolt (Friedrich)
1898-1956 ..... **DC 3; TCLC 1, 6, 13, 35;
WLC**
See also CA 104; 133; CANR 62; CDWLB
2; DA; DA3; DAB; DAC; DAM DRAM,
MST; DFS 4, 5, 9; DLB 56, 124; EW 11;
EWL 3; IDTP; MTCW 1, 2; RGWL 2, 3;
TWA

Brecht, Eugen Berthold Friedrich
See Brecht, (Eugen) Bertolt (Friedrich)

Bremer, Fredrika 1801-1865 .... **NCLC 11**
See also DLB 254

Brennan, Christopher John
1870-1932 .... **TCLC 17**
See also CA 117; 188; DLB 230; EWL 3

Brennan, Maeve 1917-1993 ... **CLC 5; TCLC
124**
See also CA 81-84; CANR 72, 100

Brent, Linda
See Jacobs, Harriet A(nn)

Brentano, Clemens (Maria)
1778-1842 .... **NCLC 1**
See also DLB 90; RGWL 2, 3

Brent of Bin Bin
See Franklin, (Stella Maria Sarah) Miles
(Lampe)

Brenton, Howard 1942- .... **CLC 31**
See also CA 69-72; CANR 33, 67; CBD;
CD 5; DLB 13; MTCW 1

Breslin, James 1930-
See Breslin, Jimmy
See also CA 73-76; CANR 31, 75; DAM
NOV; MTCW 1, 2

Breslin, Jimmy .... **CLC 4, 43**
See Breslin, James
See also AITN 1; DLB 185; MTCW 2

Bresson, Robert 1901(?)-1999 .... **CLC 16**
See also CA 110; 187; CANR 49

Breton, Andre 1896-1966 .. **CLC 2, 9, 15, 54;
PC 15**
See also CA 19-20; 25-28R; CANR 40, 60;
CAP 2; DLB 65, 258; EW 11; EWL 3;
GFL 1789 to the Present; LMFS 2;
MTCW 1, 2; RGWL 2, 3; TWA; WP

Breytenbach, Breyten 1939(?)- .. **CLC 23, 37,
126**
See also CA 113; 129; CANR 61, 122;
CWW 2; DAM POET; DLB 225; EWL 3

Bridgers, Sue Ellen 1942- .... **CLC 26**
See also AAYA 8, 49; BYA 7, 8; CA 65-68;
CANR 11, 36; CLR 18; DLB 52; JRDA;
MAICYA 1, 2; SAAS 1; SATA 22, 90;
SATA-Essay 109; WYA; YAW

Bridges, Robert (Seymour)
1844-1930 .... **PC 28; TCLC 1**
See also BRW 6; CA 104; 152; CDBLB
1890-1914; DAM POET; DLB 19, 98

Bridie, James .... **TCLC 3**
See Mavor, Osborne Henry
See also DLB 10; EWL 3

Brin, David 1950- .... **CLC 34**
See also AAYA 21; CA 102; CANR 24, 70,
125, 127; INT CANR-24; SATA 65;
SCFW 2; SFW 4

Bustos Domecq, H(onorio)
See Bioy Casares, Adolfo; Borges, Jorge
Luis

Butler, Octavia E(stelle) 1947- .. **BLCS; CLC
38, 121**
See also AAYA 18, 48; AFAW 2; AMWS
13; BPFB 1; BW 2, 3; CA 73-76; CANR
12, 24, 38, 73; CLR 65; CPW; DA3;
DAM MULT, POP; DLB 33; LATS 1:2;
MTCW 1, 2; NFS 8; SATA 84; SCFW 2;
SFW 4; SSFS 6; YAW

Butler, Robert Olen, (Jr.) 1945- ...... **CLC 81,
162**
See also AMWS 12; BPFB 1; CA 112;
CANR 66; CSW; DAM POP; DLB 173;
INT CA-112; MTCW 1; SSFS 11

Butler, Samuel 1612-1680 .... **LC 16, 43**
See also DLB 101, 126; RGEL 2

Butler, Samuel 1835-1902 .... **TCLC 1, 33;
WLC**
See also BRWS 2; CA 143; CDBLB 1890-
1914; DA; DA3; DAB; DAC; DAM MST,
NOV; DLB 18, 57, 174; RGEL 2; SFW 4;
TEA

Butler, Walter C.
See Faust, Frederick (Schiller)

Butor, Michel (Marie Francois)
1926- .... **CLC 1, 3, 8, 11, 15, 161**
See also CA 9-12R; CANR 33, 66; CWW
2; DLB 83; EW 13; EWL 3; GFL 1789 to
the Present; MTCW 1, 2

Butts, Mary 1890(?)-1937 .... **TCLC 77**
See also CA 148; DLB 240

Buxton, Ralph
See Silverstein, Alvin; Silverstein, Virginia
B(arbara Opshelor)

Buzo, Alex
See Buzo, Alexander (John)
See also DLB 289

Buzo, Alexander (John) 1944- .... **CLC 61**
See also CA 97-100; CANR 17, 39, 69; CD
5

Buzzati, Dino 1906-1972 .... **CLC 36**
See also CA 160; 33-36R; DLB 177; RGWL
2, 3; SFW 4

Byars, Betsy (Cromer) 1928- .... **CLC 35**
See also AAYA 19; BYA 3; CA 33-36R,
183; CAAE 183; CANR 18, 36, 57, 102;
CLR 1, 16, 72; DLB 52; INT CANR-18;
JRDA; MAICYA 1, 2; MAICYAS 1;
MTCW 1; SAAS 1; SATA 4, 46, 80;
SATA-Essay 108; WYA; YAW

Byatt, A(ntonia) S(usan Drabble)
1936- .... **CLC 19, 65, 136**
See also BPFB 1; BRWC 2; BRWS 4; CA
13-16R; CANR 13, 33, 50, 75, 96, 133;
DA3; DAM NOV, POP; DLB 14, 194;
EWL 3; MTCW 1, 2; RGSF 2; RHW;
TEA

Byrne, David 1952- .... **CLC 26**
See also CA 127

Byrne, John Keyes 1926-
See Leonard, Hugh
See also CA 102; CANR 78; INT CA-102

Byron, George Gordon (Noel)
1788-1824 ..... **DC 24; NCLC 2, 12, 109;
PC 16; WLC**
See also BRW 4; BRWC 2; CDBLB 1789-
1832; DA; DA3; DAB; DAC; DAM MST,
POET; DLB 96, 110; EXPP; LMFS 1;
PAB; PFS 1, 14; RGEL 2; TEA; WLIT 3;
WP

Byron, Robert 1905-1941 .... **TCLC 67**
See also CA 160; DLB 195

C. 3. 3.
See Wilde, Oscar (Fingal O'Flahertie Wills)

Caballero, Fernan 1796-1877 .... **NCLC 10**

Cabell, Branch
See Cabell, James Branch

Cabell, James Branch 1879-1958 .... **TCLC 6**
See also CA 105; 152; DLB 9, 78; FANT;
MTCW 1; RGAL 4; SUFW 1

Cabeza de Vaca, Alvar Nunez
1490-1557(?) .... **LC 61**

Cable, George Washington
1844-1925 .... **SSC 4; TCLC 4**
See also CA 104; 155; DLB 12, 74; DLBD
13; RGAL 4; TUS

Cabral de Melo Neto, Joao
1920-1999 .... **CLC 76**
See Melo Neto, Joao Cabral de
See also CA 151; DAM MULT; LAW;
LAWS 1

Cabrera Infante, G(uillermo) 1929- . **CLC 5,
25, 45, 120; HLC 1; SSC 39**
See also CA 85-88; CANR 29, 65, 110; CD-
WLB 3; CWW 2; DA3; DAM MULT;
DLB 113; EWL 3; HW 1, 2; LAW; LAWS
1; MTCW 1, 2; RGSF 2; WLIT 1

Cade, Toni
See Bambara, Toni Cade

Cadmus and Harmonia
See Buchan, John

Caedmon fl. 658-680 .... **CMLC 7**
See also DLB 146

Caeiro, Alberto
See Pessoa, Fernando (Antonio Nogueira)

Caesar, Julius .... **CMLC 47**
See Julius Caesar
See also AW 1; RGWL 2, 3

Cage, John (Milton, Jr.)
1912-1992 .... **CLC 41; PC 58**
See also CA 13-16R; 169; CANR 9, 78;
DLB 193; INT CANR-9

Cahan, Abraham 1860-1951 .... **TCLC 71**
See also CA 108; 154; DLB 9, 25, 28;
RGAL 4

Cain, G.
See Cabrera Infante, G(uillermo)

Cain, Guillermo
See Cabrera Infante, G(uillermo)

Cain, James M(allahan) 1892-1977 .. **CLC 3,
11, 28**
See also AITN 1; BPFB 1; CA 17-20R; 73-
76; CANR 8, 34, 61; CMW 4; DLB 226;
EWL 3; MSW; MTCW 1; RGAL 4

Caine, Hall 1853-1931 .... **TCLC 97**
See also RHW

Caine, Mark
See Raphael, Frederic (Michael)

Calasso, Roberto 1941- .... **CLC 81**
See also CA 143; CANR 89

Calderon de la Barca, Pedro
1600-1681 .... **DC 3; HLCS 1; LC 23**
See also EW 2; RGWL 2, 3; TWA

Caldwell, Erskine (Preston)
1903-1987 .... **CLC 1, 8, 14, 50, 60; SSC
19; TCLC 117**
See also AITN 1; AMW; BPFB 1; CA 1-4R;
121; CAAS 1; CANR 2, 33; DA3; DAM
NOV; DLB 9, 86; EWL 3; MTCW 1, 2;
RGAL 4; RGSF 2; TUS

Caldwell, (Janet Miriam) Taylor (Holland)
1900-1985 .... **CLC 2, 28, 39**
See also BPFB 1; CA 5-8R; 116; CANR 5;
DA3; DAM NOV, POP; DLBD 17; RHW

Calhoun, John Caldwell
1782-1850 .... **NCLC 15**
See also DLB 3, 248

Calisher, Hortense 1911- ..... **CLC 2, 4, 8, 38,
134; SSC 15**
See also CA 1-4R; CANR 1, 22, 117; CN
7; DA3; DAM NOV; DLB 2, 218; INT
CANR-22; MTCW 1, 2; RGAL 4; RGSF
2

Callaghan, Morley Edward
1903-1990 ..... **CLC 3, 14, 41, 65; TCLC
145**
See also CA 9-12R; 132; CANR 33, 73;
DAC; DAM MST; DLB 68; EWL 3;
MTCW 1, 2; RGEL 2; RGSF 2; SSFS 19

Callimachus c. 305B.C.-c.
240B.C. .... **CMLC 18**
See also AW 1; DLB 176; RGWL 2, 3

Calvin, Jean
See Calvin, John
See also GFL Beginnings to 1789

Calvin, John 1509-1564 .... **LC 37**
See Calvin, Jean

Calvino, Italo 1923-1985 .... **CLC 5, 8, 11, 22,
33, 39, 73; SSC 3, 48**
See also AAYA 58; CA 85-88; 116; CANR
23, 61, 132; DAM NOV; DLB 196; EW
13; EWL 3; MTCW 1, 2; RGSF 2; RGWL
2, 3; SFW 4; SSFS 12

Camara Laye
See Laye, Camara
See also EWL 3

Camden, William 1551-1623 .... **LC 77**
See also DLB 172

Cameron, Carey 1952- .... **CLC 59**
See also CA 135

Cameron, Peter 1959- .... **CLC 44**
See also AMWS 12; CA 125; CANR 50,
117; DLB 234; GLL 2

Camoens, Luis Vaz de 1524(?)-1580
See Camoes, Luis de
See also EW 2

Camoes, Luis de 1524(?)-1580 . **HLCS 1; LC
62; PC 31**
See Camoens, Luis Vaz de
See also DLB 287; RGWL 2, 3

Campana, Dino 1885-1932 .... **TCLC 20**
See also CA 117; DLB 114; EWL 3

Campanella, Tommaso 1568-1639 .... **LC 32**
See also RGWL 2, 3

Campbell, John W(ood, Jr.)
1910-1971 .... **CLC 32**
See also CA 21-22; 29-32R; CANR 34;
CAP 2; DLB 8; MTCW 1; SCFW; SFW 4

Campbell, Joseph 1904-1987 .... **CLC 69;
TCLC 140**
See also AAYA 3; BEST 89:2; CA 1-4R;
124; CANR 3, 28, 61, 107; DA3; MTCW
1, 2

Campbell, Maria 1940- .... **CLC 85; NNAL**
See also CA 102; CANR 54; CCA 1; DAC

Campbell, (John) Ramsey 1946- ..... **CLC 42;
SSC 19**
See also AAYA 51; CA 57-60; CANR 7,
102; DLB 261; HGG; INT CANR-7;
SUFW 1, 2

Campbell, (Ignatius) Roy (Dunnachie)
1901-1957 .... **TCLC 5**
See also AFW; CA 104; 155; DLB 20, 225;
EWL 3; MTCW 2; RGEL 2

Campbell, Thomas 1777-1844 .... **NCLC 19**
See also DLB 93, 144; RGEL 2

Campbell, Wilfred .... **TCLC 9**
See Campbell, William

Campbell, William 1858(?)-1918
See Campbell, Wilfred
See also CA 106; DLB 92

Campion, Jane 1954- .... **CLC 95**
See also AAYA 33; CA 138; CANR 87

Campion, Thomas 1567-1620 .... **LC 78**
See also CDBLB Before 1660; DAM POET;
DLB 58, 172; RGEL 2

Camus, Albert 1913-1960 ...... **CLC 1, 2, 4, 9,
11, 14, 32, 63, 69, 124; DC 2; SSC 9,
76; WLC**
See also AAYA 36; AFW; BPFB 1; CA 89-
92; CANR 131; DA; DA3; DAB; DAC;
DAM DRAM, MST, NOV; DLB 72; EW

Cassity, (Allen) Turner 1929- .... **CLC 6, 42**
See also CA 17-20R, 223; CAAE 223;
CAAS 8; CANR 11; CSW; DLB 105

Castaneda, Carlos (Cesar Aranha)
1931(?)-1998 .... **CLC 12, 119**
See also CA 25-28R; CANR 32, 66, 105;
DNFS 1; HW 1; MTCW 1

Castedo, Elena 1937- .... **CLC 65**
See also CA 132

Castedo-Ellerman, Elena
See Castedo, Elena

Castellanos, Rosario 1925-1974 .... **CLC 66;
HLC 1; SSC 39, 68**
See also CA 131; 53-56; CANR 58; CD-
WLB 3; DAM MULT; DLB 113, 290;
EWL 3; FW; HW 1; LAW; MTCW 1;
RGSF 2; RGWL 2, 3

Castelvetro, Lodovico 1505-1571 .... **LC 12**

Castiglione, Baldassare 1478-1529 ...... **LC 12**
See Castiglione, Baldesar
See also LMFS 1; RGWL 2, 3

Castiglione, Baldesar
See Castiglione, Baldassare
See also EW 2

Castillo, Ana (Hernandez Del)
1953- .... **CLC 151**
See also AAYA 42; CA 131; CANR 51, 86,
128; CWP; DLB 122, 227; DNFS 2; FW;
HW 1; LLW 1; PFS 21

Castle, Robert
See Hamilton, Edmond

Castro (Ruz), Fidel 1926(?)- .... **HLC 1**
See also CA 110; 129; CANR 81; DAM
MULT; HW 2

Castro, Guillen de 1569-1631 .... **LC 19**

Castro, Rosalia de 1837-1885 ... **NCLC 3, 78;
PC 41**
See also DAM MULT

Cather, Willa (Sibert) 1873-1947 . **SSC 2, 50;
TCLC 1, 11, 31, 99, 132, 152; WLC**
See also AAYA 24; AMW; AMWC 1;
AMWR 1; BPFB 1; CA 104; 128; CDALB
1865-1917; CLR 98; DA; DA3; DAB;
DAC; DAM MST, NOV; DLB 9, 54, 78,
256; DLBD 1; EWL 3; EXPN; EXPS;
LAIT 3; LATS 1:1; MAWW; MTCW 1,
2; NFS 2, 19; RGAL 4; RGSF 2; RHW;
SATA 30; SSFS 2, 7, 16; TCWW 2; TUS

Catherine II
See Catherine the Great
See also DLB 150

Catherine the Great 1729-1796 .... **LC 69**
See Catherine II

Cato, Marcus Porcius
234B.C.-149B.C. .... **CMLC 21**
See Cato the Elder

Cato, Marcus Porcius, the Elder
See Cato, Marcus Porcius

Cato the Elder
See Cato, Marcus Porcius
See also DLB 211

Catton, (Charles) Bruce 1899-1978 . **CLC 35**
See also AITN 1; CA 5-8R; 81-84; CANR
7, 74; DLB 17; SATA 2; SATA-Obit 24

Catullus c. 84B.C.-54B.C. .... **CMLC 18**
See also AW 2; CDWLB 1; DLB 211;
RGWL 2, 3

Cauldwell, Frank
See King, Francis (Henry)

Caunitz, William J. 1933-1996 .... **CLC 34**
See also BEST 89:3; CA 125; 130; 152;
CANR 73; INT CA-130

Causley, Charles (Stanley)
1917-2003 .... **CLC 7**
See also CA 9-12R; 223; CANR 5, 35, 94;
CLR 30; CWRI 5; DLB 27; MTCW 1;
SATA 3, 66; SATA-Obit 149

Caute, (John) David 1936- .... **CLC 29**
See also CA 1-4R; CAAS 4; CANR 1, 33,
64, 120; CBD; CD 5; CN 7; DAM NOV;
DLB 14, 231

Cavafy, C(onstantine) P(eter) .... **PC 36;
TCLC 2, 7**
See Kavafis, Konstantinos Petrou
See also CA 148; DA3; DAM POET; EW
8; EWL 3; MTCW 1; PFS 19; RGWL 2,
3; WP

Cavalcanti, Guido c. 1250-c.
1300 .... **CMLC 54**

Cavallo, Evelyn
See Spark, Muriel (Sarah)

Cavanna, Betty .... **CLC 12**
See Harrison, Elizabeth (Allen) Cavanna
See also JRDA; MAICYA 1; SAAS 4;
SATA 1, 30

Cavendish, Margaret Lucas
1623-1673 .... **LC 30**
See also DLB 131, 252, 281; RGEL 2

Caxton, William 1421(?)-1491(?) .... **LC 17**
See also DLB 170

Cayer, D. M.
See Duffy, Maureen

Cayrol, Jean 1911- .... **CLC 11**
See also CA 89-92; DLB 83; EWL 3

Cela (y Trulock), Camilo Jose
See Cela, Camilo Jose
See also CWW 2

Cela, Camilo Jose 1916-2002 .... **CLC 4, 13,
59, 122; HLC 1; SSC 71**
See Cela (y Trulock), Camilo Jose
See also BEST 90:2; CA 21-24R; 206;
CAAS 10; CANR 21, 32, 76; DAM
MULT; DLBY 1989; EW 13; EWL 3; HW
1; MTCW 1, 2; RGSF 2; RGWL 2, 3

Celan, Paul .... **CLC 10, 19, 53, 82; PC 10**
See Antschel, Paul
See also CDWLB 2; DLB 69; EWL 3;
RGWL 2, 3

Celine, Louis-Ferdinand .. **CLC 1, 3, 4, 7, 9,
15, 47, 124**
See Destouches, Louis-Ferdinand
See also DLB 72; EW 11; EWL 3; GFL
1789 to the Present; RGWL 2, 3

Cellini, Benvenuto 1500-1571 .... **LC 7**

Cendrars, Blaise .... **CLC 18, 106**
See Sauser-Hall, Frederic
See also DLB 258; EWL 3; GFL 1789 to
the Present; RGWL 2, 3; WP

Centlivre, Susanna 1669(?)-1723 .... **LC 65**
See also DLB 84; RGEL 2

Cernuda (y Bidon), Luis 1902-1963 . **CLC 54**
See also CA 131; 89-92; DAM POET; DLB
134; EWL 3; GLL 1; HW 1; RGWL 2, 3

Cervantes, Lorna Dee 1954- ..... **HLCS 1; PC
35**
See also CA 131; CANR 80; CWP; DLB
82; EXPP; HW 1; LLW 1

Cervantes (Saavedra), Miguel de
1547-1616 .... **HLCS; LC 6, 23, 93; SSC
12; WLC**
See also AAYA 56; BYA 1, 14; DA; DAB;
DAC; DAM MST, NOV; EW 2; LAIT 1;
LATS 1:1; LMFS 1; NFS 8; RGSF 2;
RGWL 2, 3; TWA

Cesaire, Aime (Fernand) 1913- .... **BLC 1;
CLC 19, 32, 112; DC 22; PC 25**
See also BW 2, 3; CA 65-68; CANR 24,
43, 81; CWW 2; DA3; DAM MULT,
POET; EWL 3; GFL 1789 to the Present;
MTCW 1, 2; WP

Chabon, Michael 1963- ... **CLC 55, 149; SSC
59**
See also AAYA 45; AMWS 11; CA 139;
CANR 57, 96, 127; DLB 278; SATA 145

Chabrol, Claude 1930- .... **CLC 16**
See also CA 110

Chairil Anwar
See Anwar, Chairil
See also EWL 3

Challans, Mary 1905-1983
See Renault, Mary
See also CA 81-84; 111; CANR 74; DA3;
MTCW 2; SATA 23; SATA-Obit 36; TEA

Challis, George
See Faust, Frederick (Schiller)
See also TCWW 2

Chambers, Aidan 1934- .... **CLC 35**
See also AAYA 27; CA 25-28R; CANR 12,
31, 58, 116; JRDA; MAICYA 1, 2; SAAS
12; SATA 1, 69, 108; WYA; YAW

Chambers, James 1948-
See Cliff, Jimmy
See also CA 124

Chambers, Jessie
See Lawrence, D(avid) H(erbert Richards)
See also GLL 1

Chambers, Robert W(illiam)
1865-1933 .... **TCLC 41**
See also CA 165; DLB 202; HGG; SATA
107; SUFW 1

Chambers, (David) Whittaker
1901-1961 .... **TCLC 129**
See also CA 89-92; DLB 303

Chamisso, Adelbert von
1781-1838 .... **NCLC 82**
See also DLB 90; RGWL 2, 3; SUFW 1

Chance, James T.
See Carpenter, John (Howard)

Chance, John T.
See Carpenter, John (Howard)

Chandler, Raymond (Thornton)
1888-1959 .... **SSC 23; TCLC 1, 7**
See also AAYA 25; AMWC 2; AMWS 4;
BPFB 1; CA 104; 129; CANR 60, 107;
CDALB 1929-1941; CMW 4; DA3; DLB
226, 253; DLBD 6; EWL 3; MSW;
MTCW 1, 2; NFS 17; RGAL 4; TUS

Chang, Diana 1934- .... **AAL**
See also CWP; EXPP

Chang, Eileen 1921-1995 .... **AAL; SSC 28**
See Chang Ai-Ling; Zhang Ailing
See also CA 166

Chang, Jung 1952- .... **CLC 71**
See also CA 142

Chang Ai-Ling
See Chang, Eileen
See also EWL 3

Channing, William Ellery
1780-1842 .... **NCLC 17**
See also DLB 1, 59, 235; RGAL 4

Chao, Patricia 1955- .... **CLC 119**
See also CA 163

Chaplin, Charles Spencer
1889-1977 .... **CLC 16**
See Chaplin, Charlie
See also CA 81-84; 73-76

Chaplin, Charlie
See Chaplin, Charles Spencer
See also DLB 44

Chapman, George 1559(?)-1634 . **DC 19; LC
22**
See also BRW 1; DAM DRAM; DLB 62,
121; LMFS 1; RGEL 2

Chapman, Graham 1941-1989 .... **CLC 21**
See Monty Python
See also CA 116; 129; CANR 35, 95

Chapman, John Jay 1862-1933 .... **TCLC 7**
See also CA 104; 191

Chapman, Lee
See Bradley, Marion Zimmer
See also GLL 1

Chapman, Walker
See Silverberg, Robert

Chappell, Fred (Davis) 1936- .... **CLC 40, 78, 162**
See also CA 5-8R, 198; CAAE 198; CAAS 4; CANR 8, 33, 67, 110; CN 7; CP 7; CSW; DLB 6, 105; HGG

Char, Rene(-Emile) 1907-1988 .... **CLC 9, 11, 14, 55; PC 56**
See also CA 13-16R; 124; CANR 32; DAM POET; DLB 258; EWL 3; GFL 1789 to the Present; MTCW 1, 2; RGWL 2, 3

Charby, Jay
See Ellison, Harlan (Jay)

Chardin, Pierre Teilhard de
See Teilhard de Chardin, (Marie Joseph) Pierre

Chariton fl. 1st cent. (?)- .... **CMLC 49**

Charlemagne 742-814 .... **CMLC 37**

Charles I 1600-1649 .... **LC 13**

Charriere, Isabelle de 1740-1805 .. **NCLC 66**

Chartier, Alain c. 1392-1430 .... **LC 94**
See also DLB 208

Chartier, Emile-Auguste
See Alain

Charyn, Jerome 1937- .... **CLC 5, 8, 18**
See also CA 5-8R; CAAS 1; CANR 7, 61, 101; CMW 4; CN 7; DLBY 1983; MTCW 1

Chase, Adam
See Marlowe, Stephen

Chase, Mary (Coyle) 1907-1981 .... **DC 1**
See also CA 77-80; 105; CAD; CWD; DFS 11; DLB 228; SATA 17; SATA-Obit 29

Chase, Mary Ellen 1887-1973 .... **CLC 2; TCLC 124**
See also CA 13-16; 41-44R; CAP 1; SATA 10

Chase, Nicholas
See Hyde, Anthony
See also CCA 1

Chateaubriand, Francois Rene de 1768-1848 .... **NCLC 3, 134**
See also DLB 119; EW 5; GFL 1789 to the Present; RGWL 2, 3; TWA

Chatterje, Sarat Chandra 1876-1936(?)
See Chatterji, Saratchandra
See also CA 109

Chatterji, Bankim Chandra 1838-1894 .... **NCLC 19**

Chatterji, Saratchandra .... **TCLC 13**
See Chatterje, Sarat Chandra
See also CA 186; EWL 3

Chatterton, Thomas 1752-1770 .... **LC 3, 54**
See also DAM POET; DLB 109; RGEL 2

Chatwin, (Charles) Bruce 1940-1989 .... **CLC 28, 57, 59**
See also AAYA 4; BEST 90:1; BRWS 4; CA 85-88; 127; CPW; DAM POP; DLB 194, 204; EWL 3

Chaucer, Daniel
See Ford, Ford Madox
See also RHW

Chaucer, Geoffrey 1340(?)-1400 .. **LC 17, 56; PC 19, 58; WLCS**
See also BRW 1; BRWC 1; BRWR 2; CD-BLB Before 1660; DA; DA3; DAB; DAC; DAM MST, POET; DLB 146; LAIT 1; PAB; PFS 14; RGEL 2; TEA; WLIT 3; WP

Chavez, Denise (Elia) 1948- .... **HLC 1**
See also CA 131; CANR 56, 81; DAM MULT; DLB 122; FW; HW 1, 2; LLW 1; MTCW 2

Chaviaras, Strates 1935-
See Haviaras, Stratis
See also CA 105

Chayefsky, Paddy .... **CLC 23**
See Chayefsky, Sidney
See also CAD; DLB 7, 44; DLBY 1981; RGAL 4

Chayefsky, Sidney 1923-1981
See Chayefsky, Paddy
See also CA 9-12R; 104; CANR 18; DAM DRAM

Chedid, Andree 1920- .... **CLC 47**
See also CA 145; CANR 95; EWL 3

Cheever, John 1912-1982 ..... **CLC 3, 7, 8, 11, 15, 25, 64; SSC 1, 38, 57; WLC**
See also AMWS 1; BPFB 1; CA 5-8R; 106; CABS 1; CANR 5, 27, 76; CDALB 1941-1968; CPW; DA; DA3; DAB; DAC; DAM MST, NOV, POP; DLB 2, 102, 227; DLBY 1980, 1982; EWL 3; EXPS; INT CANR-5; MTCW 1, 2; RGAL 4; RGSF 2; SSFS 2, 14; TUS

Cheever, Susan 1943- .... **CLC 18, 48**
See also CA 103; CANR 27, 51, 92; DLBY 1982; INT CANR-27

Chekhonte, Antosha
See Chekhov, Anton (Pavlovich)

Chekhov, Anton (Pavlovich) 1860-1904 ...... **DC 9; SSC 2, 28, 41, 51; TCLC 3, 10, 31, 55, 96; WLC**
See also BYA 14; CA 104; 124; DA; DA3; DAB; DAC; DAM DRAM, MST; DFS 1, 5, 10, 12; DLB 277; EW 7; EWL 3; EXPS; LAIT 3; LATS 1:1; RGSF 2; RGWL 2, 3; SATA 90; SSFS 5, 13, 14; TWA

Cheney, Lynne V. 1941- .... **CLC 70**
See also CA 89-92; CANR 58, 117; SATA 152

Chernyshevsky, Nikolai Gavrilovich
See Chernyshevsky, Nikolay Gavrilovich
See also DLB 238

Chernyshevsky, Nikolay Gavrilovich 1828-1889 .... **NCLC 1**
See Chernyshevsky, Nikolai Gavrilovich

Cherry, Carolyn Janice 1942-
See Cherryh, C. J.
See also CA 65-68; CANR 10

Cherryh, C. J. .... **CLC 35**
See Cherry, Carolyn Janice
See also AAYA 24; BPFB 1; DLBY 1980; FANT; SATA 93; SCFW 2; SFW 4; YAW

Chesnutt, Charles W(addell) 1858-1932 .... **BLC 1; SSC 7, 54; TCLC 5, 39**
See also AFAW 1, 2; BW 1, 3; CA 106; 125; CANR 76; DAM MULT; DLB 12, 50, 78; EWL 3; MTCW 1, 2; RGAL 4; RGSF 2; SSFS 11

Chester, Alfred 1929(?)-1971 .... **CLC 49**
See also CA 196; 33-36R; DLB 130

Chesterton, G(ilbert) K(eith) 1874-1936 . **PC 28; SSC 1, 46; TCLC 1, 6, 64**
See also AAYA 57; BRW 6; CA 104; 132; CANR 73, 131; CDBLB 1914-1945; CMW 4; DAM NOV, POET; DLB 10, 19, 34, 70, 98, 149, 178; EWL 3; FANT; MSW; MTCW 1, 2; RGEL 2; RGSF 2; SATA 27; SUFW 1

Chiang, Pin-chin 1904-1986
See Ding Ling
See also CA 118

Chief Joseph 1840-1904 .... **NNAL**
See also CA 152; DA3; DAM MULT

Chief Seattle 1786(?)-1866 .... **NNAL**
See also DA3; DAM MULT

Ch'ien, Chung-shu 1910-1998 .... **CLC 22**
See Qian Zhongshu
See also CA 130; CANR 73; MTCW 1, 2

Chikamatsu Monzaemon 1653-1724 ... **LC 66**
See also RGWL 2, 3

Child, L. Maria
See Child, Lydia Maria

Child, Lydia Maria 1802-1880 .. **NCLC 6, 73**
See also DLB 1, 74, 243; RGAL 4; SATA 67

Child, Mrs.
See Child, Lydia Maria

Child, Philip 1898-1978 .... **CLC 19, 68**
See also CA 13-14; CAP 1; DLB 68; RHW; SATA 47

Childers, (Robert) Erskine 1870-1922 .... **TCLC 65**
See also CA 113; 153; DLB 70

Childress, Alice 1920-1994 . **BLC 1; CLC 12, 15, 86, 96; DC 4; TCLC 116**
See also AAYA 8; BW 2, 3; BYA 2; CA 45-48; 146; CAD; CANR 3, 27, 50, 74; CLR 14; CWD; DA3; DAM DRAM, MULT, NOV; DFS 2, 8, 14; DLB 7, 38, 249; JRDA; LAIT 5; MAICYA 1, 2; MAIC-YAS 1; MTCW 1, 2; RGAL 4; SATA 7, 48, 81; TUS; WYA; YAW

Chin, Frank (Chew, Jr.) 1940- ...... **CLC 135; DC 7**
See also CA 33-36R; CANR 71; CD 5; DAM MULT; DLB 206; LAIT 5; RGAL 4

Chin, Marilyn (Mei Ling) 1955- .... **PC 40**
See also CA 129; CANR 70, 113; CWP

Chislett, (Margaret) Anne 1943- ...... **CLC 34**
See also CA 151

Chitty, Thomas Willes 1926- .... **CLC 11**
See Hinde, Thomas
See also CA 5-8R; CN 7

Chivers, Thomas Holley 1809-1858 .... **NCLC 49**
See also DLB 3, 248; RGAL 4

Choi, Susan 1969- .... **CLC 119**
See also CA 223

Chomette, Rene Lucien 1898-1981
See Clair, Rene
See also CA 103

Chomsky, (Avram) Noam 1928- ..... **CLC 132**
See also CA 17-20R; CANR 28, 62, 110, 132; DA3; DLB 246; MTCW 1, 2

Chona, Maria 1845(?)-1936 .... **NNAL**
See also CA 144

Chopin, Kate .... **SSC 8, 68; TCLC 127; WLCS**
See Chopin, Katherine
See also AAYA 33; AMWR 2; AMWS 1; BYA 11, 15; CDALB 1865-1917; DA; DAB; DLB 12, 78; EXPN; EXPS; FW; LAIT 3; MAWW; NFS 3; RGAL 4; RGSF 2; SSFS 17; TUS

Chopin, Katherine 1851-1904
See Chopin, Kate
See also CA 104; 122; DA3; DAC; DAM MST, NOV

Chretien de Troyes c. 12th cent. - . **CMLC 10**
See also DLB 208; EW 1; RGWL 2, 3; TWA

Christie
See Ichikawa, Kon

Christie, Agatha (Mary Clarissa) 1890-1976 .. **CLC 1, 6, 8, 12, 39, 48, 110**
See also AAYA 9; AITN 1, 2; BPFB 1; BRWS 2; CA 17-20R; 61-64; CANR 10, 37, 108; CBD; CDBLB 1914-1945; CMW 4; CPW; CWD; DA3; DAB; DAC; DAM NOV; DFS 2; DLB 13, 77, 245; MSW; MTCW 1, 2; NFS 8; RGEL 2; RHW; SATA 36; TEA; YAW

Christie, Philippa .... **CLC 21**
See Pearce, Philippa
See also BYA 5; CANR 109; CLR 9; DLB 161; MAICYA 1; SATA 1, 67, 129

Christine de Pizan 1365(?)-1431(?) .... **LC 9**
See also DLB 208; RGWL 2, 3

Chuang Tzu c. 369B.C.-c. 286B.C. .... **CMLC 57**

Chubb, Elmer
See Masters, Edgar Lee

Chulkov, Mikhail Dmitrievich
1743-1792 .... **LC 2**
See also DLB 150

Churchill, Caryl 1938- .... **CLC 31, 55, 157;
DC 5**
See Churchill, Chick
See also BRWS 4; CA 102; CANR 22, 46,
108; CBD; CWD; DFS 12, 16; DLB 13;
EWL 3; FW; MTCW 1; RGEL 2

Churchill, Charles 1731-1764 .... **LC 3**
See also DLB 109; RGEL 2

Churchill, Chick 1938-
See Churchill, Caryl
See also CD 5

Churchill, Sir Winston (Leonard Spencer)
1874-1965 .... **TCLC 113**
See also BRW 6; CA 97-100; CDBLB
1890-1914; DA3; DLB 100; DLBD 16;
LAIT 4; MTCW 1, 2

Chute, Carolyn 1947- .... **CLC 39**
See also CA 123

Ciardi, John (Anthony) 1916-1986 . **CLC 10,
40, 44, 129**
See also CA 5-8R; 118; CAAS 2; CANR 5,
33; CLR 19; CWRI 5; DAM POET; DLB
5; DLBY 1986; INT CANR-5; MAICYA
1, 2; MTCW 1, 2; RGAL 4; SAAS 26;
SATA 1, 65; SATA-Obit 46

Cibber, Colley 1671-1757 .... **LC 66**
See also DLB 84; RGEL 2

Cicero, Marcus Tullius
106B.C.-43B.C. .... **CMLC 3**
See also AW 1; CDWLB 1; DLB 211;
RGWL 2, 3

Cimino, Michael 1943- .... **CLC 16**
See also CA 105

Cioran, E(mil) M. 1911-1995 .... **CLC 64**
See also CA 25-28R; 149; CANR 91; DLB
220; EWL 3

Cisneros, Sandra 1954- .... **CLC 69, 118, 193;
HLC 1; PC 52; SSC 32, 72**
See also AAYA 9, 53; AMWS 7; CA 131;
CANR 64, 118; CWP; DA3; DAM MULT;
DLB 122, 152; EWL 3; EXPN; FW; HW
1, 2; LAIT 5; LATS 1:2; LLW 1; MAI-
CYA 2; MTCW 2; NFS 2; PFS 19; RGAL
4; RGSF 2; SSFS 3, 13; WLIT 1; YAW

Cixous, Helene 1937- .... **CLC 92**
See also CA 126; CANR 55, 123; CWW 2;
DLB 83, 242; EWL 3; FW; GLL 2;
MTCW 1, 2; TWA

Clair, Rene .... **CLC 20**
See Chomette, Rene Lucien

Clampitt, Amy 1920-1994 .... **CLC 32; PC 19**
See also AMWS 9; CA 110; 146; CANR
29, 79; DLB 105

Clancy, Thomas L., Jr. 1947-
See Clancy, Tom
See also CA 125; 131; CANR 62, 105;
DA3; INT CA-131; MTCW 1, 2

Clancy, Tom .... **CLC 45, 112**
See Clancy, Thomas L., Jr.
See also AAYA 9, 51; BEST 89:1, 90:1;
BPFB 1; BYA 10, 11; CANR 132; CMW
4; CPW; DAM NOV, POP; DLB 227

Clare, John 1793-1864 .. **NCLC 9, 86; PC 23**
See also DAB; DAM POET; DLB 55, 96;
RGEL 2

Clarin
See Alas (y Urena), Leopoldo (Enrique
Garcia)

Clark, Al C.
See Goines, Donald

Clark, (Robert) Brian 1932- .... **CLC 29**
See also CA 41-44R; CANR 67; CBD; CD
5

Clark, Curt
See Westlake, Donald E(dwin)

Clark, Eleanor 1913-1996 .... **CLC 5, 19**
See also CA 9-12R; 151; CANR 41; CN 7;
DLB 6

Clark, J. P.
See Clark Bekederemo, J(ohnson) P(epper)
See also CDWLB 3; DLB 117

Clark, John Pepper
See Clark Bekederemo, J(ohnson) P(epper)
See also AFW; CD 5; CP 7; RGEL 2

Clark, Kenneth (Mackenzie)
1903-1983 .... **TCLC 147**
See also CA 93-96; 109; CANR 36; MTCW
1, 2

Clark, M. R.
See Clark, Mavis Thorpe

Clark, Mavis Thorpe 1909-1999 ...... **CLC 12**
See also CA 57-60; CANR 8, 37, 107; CLR
30; CWRI 5; MAICYA 1, 2; SAAS 5;
SATA 8, 74

Clark, Walter Van Tilburg
1909-1971 .... **CLC 28**
See also CA 9-12R; 33-36R; CANR 63,
113; DLB 9, 206; LAIT 2; RGAL 4;
SATA 8

Clark Bekederemo, J(ohnson) P(epper)
1935- .... **BLC 1; CLC 38; DC 5**
See Clark, J. P.; Clark, John Pepper
See also BW 1; CA 65-68; CANR 16, 72;
DAM DRAM, MULT; DFS 13; EWL 3;
MTCW 1

Clarke, Arthur C(harles) 1917- .... **CLC 1, 4,
13, 18, 35, 136; SSC 3**
See also AAYA 4, 33; BPFB 1; BYA 13;
CA 1-4R; CANR 2, 28, 55, 74, 130; CN
7; CPW; DA3; DAM POP; DLB 261;
JRDA; LAIT 5; MAICYA 1, 2; MTCW 1,
2; SATA 13, 70, 115; SCFW; SFW 4;
SSFS 4, 18; YAW

Clarke, Austin 1896-1974 .... **CLC 6, 9**
See also CA 29-32; 49-52; CAP 2; DAM
POET; DLB 10, 20; EWL 3; RGEL 2

Clarke, Austin C(hesterfield) 1934- .. **BLC 1;
CLC 8, 53; SSC 45**
See also BW 1; CA 25-28R; CAAS 16;
CANR 14, 32, 68; CN 7; DAC; DAM
MULT; DLB 53, 125; DNFS 2; RGSF 2

Clarke, Gillian 1937- .... **CLC 61**
See also CA 106; CP 7; CWP; DLB 40

Clarke, Marcus (Andrew Hislop)
1846-1881 .... **NCLC 19**
See also DLB 230; RGEL 2; RGSF 2

Clarke, Shirley 1925-1997 .... **CLC 16**
See also CA 189

Clash, The
See Headon, (Nicky) Topper; Jones, Mick;
Simonon, Paul; Strummer, Joe

Claudel, Paul (Louis Charles Marie)
1868-1955 .... **TCLC 2, 10**
See also CA 104; 165; DLB 192, 258; EW
8; EWL 3; GFL 1789 to the Present;
RGWL 2, 3; TWA

Claudian 370(?)-404(?) .... **CMLC 46**
See also RGWL 2, 3

Claudius, Matthias 1740-1815 .... **NCLC 75**
See also DLB 97

Clavell, James (duMaresq)
1925-1994 .... **CLC 6, 25, 87**
See also BPFB 1; CA 25-28R; 146; CANR
26, 48; CPW; DA3; DAM NOV, POP;
MTCW 1, 2; NFS 10; RHW

Clayman, Gregory .... **CLC 65**

Cleaver, (Leroy) Eldridge
1935-1998 .... **BLC 1; CLC 30, 119**
See also BW 1, 3; CA 21-24R; 167; CANR
16, 75; DA3; DAM MULT; MTCW 2;
YAW

Cleese, John (Marwood) 1939- .... **CLC 21**
See Monty Python
See also CA 112; 116; CANR 35; MTCW 1

Cleishbotham, Jebediah
See Scott, Sir Walter

Cleland, John 1710-1789 .... **LC 2, 48**
See also DLB 39; RGEL 2

Clemens, Samuel Langhorne 1835-1910
See Twain, Mark
See also CA 104; 135; CDALB 1865-1917;
DA; DA3; DAB; DAC; DAM MST, NOV;
DLB 12, 23, 64, 74, 186, 189; JRDA;
LMFS 1; MAICYA 1, 2; NCFS 4; NFS
20; SATA 100; SSFS 16; YABC 2

Clement of Alexandria
150(?)-215(?) .... **CMLC 41**

Cleophil
See Congreve, William

Clerihew, E.
See Bentley, E(dmund) C(lerihew)

Clerk, N. W.
See Lewis, C(live) S(taples)

Cleveland, John 1613-1658 .... **LC 106**
See also DLB 126; RGEL 2

Cliff, Jimmy .... **CLC 21**
See Chambers, James
See also CA 193

Cliff, Michelle 1946- .... **BLCS; CLC 120**
See also BW 2; CA 116; CANR 39, 72; CD-
WLB 3; DLB 157; FW; GLL 2

Clifford, Lady Anne 1590-1676 .... **LC 76**
See also DLB 151

Clifton, (Thelma) Lucille 1936- .... **BLC 1;
CLC 19, 66, 162; PC 17**
See also AFAW 2; BW 2, 3; CA 49-52;
CANR 2, 24, 42, 76, 97; CLR 5; CP 7;
CSW; CWP; CWRI 5; DA3; DAM MULT,
POET; DLB 5, 41; EXPP; MAICYA 1, 2;
MTCW 1, 2; PFS 1, 14; SATA 20, 69,
128; WP

Clinton, Dirk
See Silverberg, Robert

Clough, Arthur Hugh 1819-1861 ... **NCLC 27**
See also BRW 5; DLB 32; RGEL 2

Clutha, Janet Paterson Frame 1924-2004
See Frame, Janet
See also CA 1-4R; 224; CANR 2, 36, 76;
MTCW 1, 2; SATA 119

Clyne, Terence
See Blatty, William Peter

Cobalt, Martin
See Mayne, William (James Carter)

Cobb, Irvin S(hrewsbury)
1876-1944 .... **TCLC 77**
See also CA 175; DLB 11, 25, 86

Cobbett, William 1763-1835 .... **NCLC 49**
See also DLB 43, 107, 158; RGEL 2

Coburn, D(onald) L(ee) 1938- .... **CLC 10**
See also CA 89-92

Cocteau, Jean (Maurice Eugene Clement)
1889-1963 ...... **CLC 1, 8, 15, 16, 43; DC
17; TCLC 119; WLC**
See also CA 25-28; CANR 40; CAP 2; DA;
DA3; DAB; DAC; DAM DRAM, MST,
NOV; DLB 65, 258; EW 10; EWL 3; GFL
1789 to the Present; MTCW 1, 2; RGWL
2, 3; TWA

Codrescu, Andrei 1946- .... **CLC 46, 121**
See also CA 33-36R; CAAS 19; CANR 13,
34, 53, 76, 125; DA3; DAM POET;
MTCW 2

Coe, Max
See Bourne, Randolph S(illiman)

Coe, Tucker
See Westlake, Donald E(dwin)

Coen, Ethan 1958- .... **CLC 108**
See also AAYA 54; CA 126; CANR 85

Coen, Joel 1955- .... **CLC 108**
See also AAYA 54; CA 126; CANR 119

The Coen Brothers
See Coen, Ethan; Coen, Joel

de Filippo, Eduardo 1900-1984 ... **TCLC 127**
See also CA 132; 114; EWL 3; MTCW 1; RGWL 2, 3

Defoe, Daniel 1660(?)-1731 .... **LC 1, 42, 108; WLC**
See also AAYA 27; BRW 3; BRWR 1; BYA 4; CDBLB 1660-1789; CLR 61; DA; DA3; DAB; DAC; DAM MST, NOV; DLB 39, 95, 101; JRDA; LAIT 1; LMFS 1; MAICYA 1, 2; NFS 9, 13; RGEL 2; SATA 22; TEA; WCH; WLIT 3

de Gourmont, Remy(-Marie-Charles)
See Gourmont, Remy(-Marie-Charles) de

de Gournay, Marie le Jars 1566-1645 ..... **LC 98**
See also FW

de Hartog, Jan 1914-2002 .... **CLC 19**
See also CA 1-4R; 210; CANR 1; DFS 12

de Hostos, E. M.
See Hostos (y Bonilla), Eugenio Maria de

de Hostos, Eugenio M.
See Hostos (y Bonilla), Eugenio Maria de

Deighton, Len .... **CLC 4, 7, 22, 46**
See Deighton, Leonard Cyril
See also AAYA 6; BEST 89:2; BPFB 1; CDBLB 1960 to Present; CMW 4; CN 7; CPW; DLB 87

Deighton, Leonard Cyril 1929-
See Deighton, Len
See also AAYA 57; CA 9-12R; CANR 19, 33, 68; DA3; DAM NOV, POP; MTCW 1, 2

Dekker, Thomas 1572(?)-1632 ..... **DC 12; LC 22**
See also CDBLB Before 1660; DAM DRAM; DLB 62, 172; LMFS 1; RGEL 2

de Laclos, Pierre Ambroise Franois
See Laclos, Pierre Ambroise Francois

Delacroix, (Ferdinand-Victor-)Eugene 1798-1863 .... **NCLC 133**
See also EW 5

Delafield, E. M. .... **TCLC 61**
See Dashwood, Edmee Elizabeth Monica de la Pasture
See also DLB 34; RHW

de la Mare, Walter (John) 1873-1956 . **SSC 14; TCLC 4, 53; WLC**
See also CA 163; CDBLB 1914-1945; CLR 23; CWRI 5; DA3; DAB; DAC; DAM MST, POET; DLB 19, 153, 162, 255, 284; EWL 3; EXPP; HGG; MAICYA 1, 2; MTCW 1; RGEL 2; RGSF 2; SATA 16; SUFW 1; TEA; WCH

de Lamartine, Alphonse (Marie Louis Prat)
See Lamartine, Alphonse (Marie Louis Prat) de

Delaney, Franey
See O'Hara, John (Henry)

Delaney, Shelagh 1939- .... **CLC 29**
See also CA 17-20R; CANR 30, 67; CBD; CD 5; CDBLB 1960 to Present; CWD; DAM DRAM; DFS 7; DLB 13; MTCW 1

Delany, Martin Robison 1812-1885 .... **NCLC 93**
See also DLB 50; RGAL 4

Delany, Mary (Granville Pendarves) 1700-1788 .... **LC 12**

Delany, Samuel R(ay), Jr. 1942- .... **BLC 1; CLC 8, 14, 38, 141**
See also AAYA 24; AFAW 2; BPFB 1; BW 2, 3; CA 81-84; CANR 27, 43, 115, 116; CN 7; DAM MULT; DLB 8, 33; FANT; MTCW 1, 2; RGAL 4; SATA 92; SCFW; SFW 4; SUFW 2

De la Ramee, Marie Louise (Ouida) 1839-1908
See Ouida
See also CA 204; SATA 20

de la Roche, Mazo 1879-1961 .... **CLC 14**
See also CA 85-88; CANR 30; DLB 68; RGEL 2; RHW; SATA 64

De La Salle, Innocent
See Hartmann, Sadakichi

de Laureamont, Comte
See Lautreamont

Delbanco, Nicholas (Franklin) 1942- .... **CLC 6, 13, 167**
See also CA 17-20R, 189; CAAE 189; CAAS 2; CANR 29, 55, 116; DLB 6, 234

del Castillo, Michel 1933- .... **CLC 38**
See also CA 109; CANR 77

Deledda, Grazia (Cosima) 1875(?)-1936 .... **TCLC 23**
See also CA 123; 205; DLB 264; EWL 3; RGWL 2, 3

Deleuze, Gilles 1925-1995 .... **TCLC 116**
See also DLB 296

Delgado, Abelardo (Lalo) B(arrientos) 1930-2004 .... **HLC 1**
See also CA 131; CAAS 15; CANR 90; DAM MST, MULT; DLB 82; HW 1, 2

Delibes, Miguel .... **CLC 8, 18**
See Delibes Setien, Miguel
See also EWL 3

Delibes Setien, Miguel 1920-
See Delibes, Miguel
See also CA 45-48; CANR 1, 32; CWW 2; HW 1; MTCW 1

DeLillo, Don 1936- ..... **CLC 8, 10, 13, 27, 39, 54, 76, 143**
See also AMWC 2; AMWS 6; BEST 89:1; BPFB 1; CA 81-84; CANR 21, 76, 92, 133; CN 7; CPW; DA3; DAM NOV, POP; DLB 6, 173; EWL 3; MTCW 1, 2; RGAL 4; TUS

de Lisser, H. G.
See De Lisser, H(erbert) G(eorge)
See also DLB 117

De Lisser, H(erbert) G(eorge) 1878-1944 .... **TCLC 12**
See de Lisser, H. G.
See also BW 2; CA 109; 152

Deloire, Pierre
See Peguy, Charles (Pierre)

Deloney, Thomas 1543(?)-1600 .... **LC 41**
See also DLB 167; RGEL 2

Deloria, Ella (Cara) 1889-1971(?) ..... **NNAL**
See also CA 152; DAM MULT; DLB 175

Deloria, Vine (Victor), Jr. 1933- ...... **CLC 21, 122; NNAL**
See also CA 53-56; CANR 5, 20, 48, 98; DAM MULT; DLB 175; MTCW 1; SATA 21

del Valle-Inclan, Ramon (Maria)
See Valle-Inclan, Ramon (Maria) del

Del Vecchio, John M(ichael) 1947- .. **CLC 29**
See also CA 110; DLBD 9

de Man, Paul (Adolph Michel) 1919-1983 .... **CLC 55**
See also CA 128; 111; CANR 61; DLB 67; MTCW 1, 2

DeMarinis, Rick 1934- .... **CLC 54**
See also CA 57-60, 184; CAAE 184; CAAS 24; CANR 9, 25, 50; DLB 218

de Maupassant, (Henri Rene Albert) Guy
See Maupassant, (Henri Rene Albert) Guy de

Dembry, R. Emmet
See Murfree, Mary Noailles

Demby, William 1922- .... **BLC 1; CLC 53**
See also BW 1, 3; CA 81-84; CANR 81; DAM MULT; DLB 33

de Menton, Francisco
See Chin, Frank (Chew, Jr.)

Demetrius of Phalerum c. 307B.C.- .... **CMLC 34**

Demijohn, Thom
See Disch, Thomas M(ichael)

De Mille, James 1833-1880 .... **NCLC 123**
See also DLB 99, 251

Deming, Richard 1915-1983
See Queen, Ellery
See also CA 9-12R; CANR 3, 94; SATA 24

Democritus c. 460B.C.-c. 370B.C. . **CMLC 47**

de Montaigne, Michel (Eyquem)
See Montaigne, Michel (Eyquem) de

de Montherlant, Henry (Milon)
See Montherlant, Henry (Milon) de

Demosthenes 384B.C.-322B.C. ...... **CMLC 13**
See also AW 1; DLB 176; RGWL 2, 3

de Musset, (Louis Charles) Alfred
See Musset, (Louis Charles) Alfred de

de Natale, Francine
See Malzberg, Barry N(athaniel)

de Navarre, Marguerite 1492-1549 ..... **LC 61**
See Marguerite d'Angouleme; Marguerite de Navarre

Denby, Edwin (Orr) 1903-1983 .... **CLC 48**
See also CA 138; 110

de Nerval, Gerard
See Nerval, Gerard de

Denham, John 1615-1669 .... **LC 73**
See also DLB 58, 126; RGEL 2

Denis, Julio
See Cortazar, Julio

Denmark, Harrison
See Zelazny, Roger (Joseph)

Dennis, John 1658-1734 .... **LC 11**
See also DLB 101; RGEL 2

Dennis, Nigel (Forbes) 1912-1989 ...... **CLC 8**
See also CA 25-28R; 129; DLB 13, 15, 233; EWL 3; MTCW 1

Dent, Lester 1904-1959 .... **TCLC 72**
See also CA 112; 161; CMW 4; DLB 306; SFW 4

De Palma, Brian (Russell) 1940- ...... **CLC 20**
See also CA 109

De Quincey, Thomas 1785-1859 ..... **NCLC 4, 87**
See also BRW 4; CDBLB 1789-1832; DLB 110, 144; RGEL 2

Deren, Eleanora 1908(?)-1961
See Deren, Maya
See also CA 192; 111

Deren, Maya .... **CLC 16, 102**
See Deren, Eleanora

Derleth, August (William) 1909-1971 .... **CLC 31**
See also BPFB 1; BYA 9, 10; CA 1-4R; 29-32R; CANR 4; CMW 4; DLB 9; DLBD 17; HGG; SATA 5; SUFW 1

Der Nister 1884-1950 .... **TCLC 56**
See Nister, Der

de Routisie, Albert
See Aragon, Louis

Derrida, Jacques 1930- .... **CLC 24, 87**
See also CA 124; 127; CANR 76, 98, 133; DLB 242; EWL 3; LMFS 2; MTCW 1; TWA

Derry Down Derry
See Lear, Edward

Dersonnes, Jacques
See Simenon, Georges (Jacques Christian)

Desai, Anita 1937- .... **CLC 19, 37, 97, 175**
See also BRWS 5; CA 81-84; CANR 33, 53, 95, 133; CN 7; CWRI 5; DA3; DAB; DAM NOV; DLB 271; DNFS 2; EWL 3; FW; MTCW 1, 2; SATA 63, 126

Desai, Kiran 1971- .... **CLC 119**
See also BYA 16; CA 171; CANR 127

de Saint-Luc, Jean
See Glassco, John

de Saint Roman, Arnaud
See Aragon, Louis

Desbordes-Valmore, Marceline
1786-1859 .... **NCLC 97**
See also DLB 217

Descartes, Rene 1596-1650 .... **LC 20, 35**
See also DLB 268; EW 3; GFL Beginnings
to 1789

Deschamps, Eustache 1340(?)-1404 .. **LC 103**
See also DLB 208

De Sica, Vittorio 1901(?)-1974 .... **CLC 20**
See also CA 117

Desnos, Robert 1900-1945 .... **TCLC 22**
See also CA 121; 151; CANR 107; DLB
258; EWL 3; LMFS 2

Destouches, Louis-Ferdinand
1894-1961 .... **CLC 9, 15**
See Celine, Louis-Ferdinand
See also CA 85-88; CANR 28; MTCW 1

de Tolignac, Gaston
See Griffith, D(avid Lewelyn) W(ark)

Deutsch, Babette 1895-1982 .... **CLC 18**
See also BYA 3; CA 1-4R; 108; CANR 4,
79; DLB 45; SATA 1; SATA-Obit 33

Devenant, William 1606-1649 .... **LC 13**

Devkota, Laxmiprasad 1909-1959 . **TCLC 23**
See also CA 123

De Voto, Bernard (Augustine)
1897-1955 .... **TCLC 29**
See also CA 113; 160; DLB 9, 256

De Vries, Peter 1910-1993 ..... **CLC 1, 2, 3, 7,
10, 28, 46**
See also CA 17-20R; 142; CANR 41; DAM
NOV; DLB 6; DLBY 1982; MTCW 1, 2

Dewey, John 1859-1952 .... **TCLC 95**
See also CA 114; 170; DLB 246, 270;
RGAL 4

Dexter, John
See Bradley, Marion Zimmer
See also GLL 1

Dexter, Martin
See Faust, Frederick (Schiller)
See also TCWW 2

Dexter, Pete 1943- .... **CLC 34, 55**
See also BEST 89:2; CA 127; 131; CANR
129; CPW; DAM POP; INT CA-131;
MTCW 1

Diamano, Silmang
See Senghor, Leopold Sedar

Diamond, Neil 1941- .... **CLC 30**
See also CA 108

Diaz del Castillo, Bernal
1496-1584 .... **HLCS 1; LC 31**
See also LAW

di Bassetto, Corno
See Shaw, George Bernard

Dick, Philip K(indred) 1928-1982 ... **CLC 10,
30, 72; SSC 57**
See also AAYA 24; BPFB 1; BYA 11; CA
49-52; 106; CANR 2, 16, 132; CPW;
DA3; DAM NOV, POP; DLB 8; MTCW
1, 2; NFS 5; SCFW; SFW 4

Dickens, Charles (John Huffam)
1812-1870 .... **NCLC 3, 8, 18, 26, 37, 50,
86, 105, 113; SSC 17, 49; WLC**
See also AAYA 23; BRW 5; BRWC 1, 2;
BYA 1, 2, 3, 13, 14; CDBLB 1832-1890;
CLR 95; CMW 4; DA; DA3; DAB; DAC;
DAM MST, NOV; DLB 21, 55, 70, 159,
166; EXPN; HGG; JRDA; LAIT 1, 2;
LATS 1:1; LMFS 1; MAICYA 1, 2; NFS
4, 5, 10, 14, 20; RGEL 2; RGSF 2; SATA
15; SUFW 1; TEA; WCH; WLIT 4; WYA

Dickey, James (Lafayette)
1923-1997 .... **CLC 1, 2, 4, 7, 10, 15, 47,
109; PC 40; TCLC 151**
See also AAYA 50; AITN 1, 2; AMWS 4;
BPFB 1; CA 9-12R; 156; CABS 2; CANR
10, 48, 61, 105; CDALB 1968-1988; CP
7; CPW; CSW; DA3; DAM NOV, POET,

POP; DLB 5, 193; DLBD 7; DLBY 1982,
1993, 1996, 1997, 1998; EWL 3; INT
CANR-10; MTCW 1, 2; NFS 9; PFS 6,
11; RGAL 4; TUS

Dickey, William 1928-1994 .... **CLC 3, 28**
See also CA 9-12R; 145; CANR 24, 79;
DLB 5

Dickinson, Charles 1951- .... **CLC 49**
See also CA 128

Dickinson, Emily (Elizabeth)
1830-1886 ... **NCLC 21, 77; PC 1; WLC**
See also AAYA 22; AMW; AMWR 1;
CDALB 1865-1917; DA; DA3; DAB;
DAC; DAM MST, POET; DLB 1, 243;
EXPP; MAWW; PAB; PFS 1, 2, 3, 4, 5,
6, 8, 10, 11, 13, 16; RGAL 4; SATA 29;
TUS; WP; WYA

Dickinson, Mrs. Herbert Ward
See Phelps, Elizabeth Stuart

Dickinson, Peter (Malcolm) 1927- .. **CLC 12,
35**
See also AAYA 9, 49; BYA 5; CA 41-44R;
CANR 31, 58, 88; CLR 29; CMW 4; DLB
87, 161, 276; JRDA; MAICYA 1, 2;
SATA 5, 62, 95, 150; SFW 4; WYA; YAW

Dickson, Carr
See Carr, John Dickson

Dickson, Carter
See Carr, John Dickson

Diderot, Denis 1713-1784 .... **LC 26**
See also EW 4; GFL Beginnings to 1789;
LMFS 1; RGWL 2, 3

Didion, Joan 1934- . **CLC 1, 3, 8, 14, 32, 129**
See also AITN 1; AMWS 4; CA 5-8R;
CANR 14, 52, 76, 125; CDALB 1968-
1988; CN 7; DA3; DAM NOV; DLB 2,
173, 185; DLBY 1981, 1986; EWL 3;
MAWW; MTCW 1, 2; NFS 3; RGAL 4;
TCWW 2; TUS

Dietrich, Robert
See Hunt, E(verette) Howard, (Jr.)

Difusa, Pati
See Almodovar, Pedro

Dillard, Annie 1945- .... **CLC 9, 60, 115**
See also AAYA 6, 43; AMWS 6; ANW; CA
49-52; CANR 3, 43, 62, 90, 125; DA3;
DAM NOV; DLB 275, 278; DLBY 1980;
LAIT 4, 5; MTCW 1, 2; NCFS 1; RGAL
4; SATA 10, 140; TUS

Dillard, R(ichard) H(enry) W(ilde)
1937- .... **CLC 5**
See also CA 21-24R; CAAS 7; CANR 10;
CP 7; CSW; DLB 5, 244

Dillon, Eilis 1920-1994 .... **CLC 17**
See also CA 9-12R, 182; 147; CAAE 182;
CAAS 3; CANR 4, 38, 78; CLR 26; MAI-
CYA 1, 2; MAICYAS 1; SATA 2, 74;
SATA-Essay 105; SATA-Obit 83; YAW

Dimont, Penelope
See Mortimer, Penelope (Ruth)

Dinesen, Isak ..... **CLC 10, 29, 95; SSC 7, 75**
See Blixen, Karen (Christentze Dinesen)
See also EW 10; EWL 3; EXPS; FW; HGG;
LAIT 3; MTCW 1; NCFS 2; NFS 9;
RGSF 2; RGWL 2, 3; SSFS 3, 6, 13;
WLIT 2

Ding Ling .... **CLC 68**
See Chiang, Pin-chin
See also RGWL 3

Diphusa, Patty
See Almodovar, Pedro

Disch, Thomas M(ichael) 1940- ... **CLC 7, 36**
See Disch, Tom
See also AAYA 17; BPFB 1; CA 21-24R;
CAAS 4; CANR 17, 36, 54, 89; CLR 18;
CP 7; DA3; DLB 8; HGG; MAICYA 1, 2;
MTCW 1, 2; SAAS 15; SATA 92; SCFW;
SFW 4; SUFW 2

Disch, Tom
See Disch, Thomas M(ichael)
See also DLB 282

d'Isly, Georges
See Simenon, Georges (Jacques Christian)

Disraeli, Benjamin 1804-1881 ... **NCLC 2, 39,
79**
See also BRW 4; DLB 21, 55; RGEL 2

Ditcum, Steve
See Crumb, R(obert)

Dixon, Paige
See Corcoran, Barbara (Asenath)

Dixon, Stephen 1936- .... **CLC 52; SSC 16**
See also AMWS 12; CA 89-92; CANR 17,
40, 54, 91; CN 7; DLB 130

Djebar, Assia 1936- .... **CLC 182**
See also CA 188; EWL 3; RGWL 3; WLIT
2

Doak, Annie
See Dillard, Annie

Dobell, Sydney Thompson
1824-1874 .... **NCLC 43**
See also DLB 32; RGEL 2

Doblin, Alfred .... **TCLC 13**
See Doeblin, Alfred
See also CDWLB 2; EWL 3; RGWL 2, 3

Dobroliubov, Nikolai Aleksandrovich
See Dobrolyubov, Nikolai Alexandrovich
See also DLB 277

Dobrolyubov, Nikolai Alexandrovich
1836-1861 .... **NCLC 5**
See Dobroliubov, Nikolai Aleksandrovich

Dobson, Austin 1840-1921 .... **TCLC 79**
See also DLB 35, 144

Dobyns, Stephen 1941- .... **CLC 37**
See also AMWS 13; CA 45-48; CANR 2,
18, 99; CMW 4; CP 7

Doctorow, E(dgar) L(aurence)
1931- .... **CLC 6, 11, 15, 18, 37, 44, 65,
113**
See also AAYA 22; AITN 2; AMWS 4;
BEST 89:3; BPFB 1; CA 45-48; CANR
2, 33, 51, 76, 97, 133; CDALB 1968-
1988; CN 7; CPW; DA3; DAM NOV,
POP; DLB 2, 28, 173; DLBY 1980; EWL
3; LAIT 3; MTCW 1, 2; NFS 6; RGAL 4;
RHW; TUS

Dodgson, Charles L(utwidge) 1832-1898
See Carroll, Lewis
See also CLR 2; DA; DA3; DAB; DAC;
DAM MST, NOV, POET; MAICYA 1, 2;
SATA 100; YABC 2

Dodsley, Robert 1703-1764 .... **LC 97**
See also DLB 95; RGEL 2

Dodson, Owen (Vincent) 1914-1983 .. **BLC 1;
CLC 79**
See also BW 1; CA 65-68; 110; CANR 24;
DAM MULT; DLB 76

Doeblin, Alfred 1878-1957 .... **TCLC 13**
See Doblin, Alfred
See also CA 110; 141; DLB 66

Doerr, Harriet 1910-2002 .... **CLC 34**
See also CA 117; 122; 213; CANR 47; INT
CA-122; LATS 1:2

Domecq, H(onorio Bustos)
See Bioy Casares, Adolfo

Domecq, H(onorio) Bustos
See Bioy Casares, Adolfo; Borges, Jorge
Luis

Domini, Rey
See Lorde, Audre (Geraldine)
See also GLL 1

Dominique
See Proust, (Valentin-Louis-George-Eugene)
Marcel

Don, A
See Stephen, Sir Leslie

Drummond de Andrade, Carlos
1902-1987 .... **CLC 18; TCLC 139**
See Andrade, Carlos Drummond de
See also CA 132; 123; LAW

Drummond of Hawthornden, William
1585-1649 .... **LC 83**
See also DLB 121, 213; RGEL 2

Drury, Allen (Stuart) 1918-1998 .... **CLC 37**
See also CA 57-60; 170; CANR 18, 52; CN
7; INT CANR-18

Dryden, John 1631-1700 ..... **DC 3; LC 3, 21;
PC 25; WLC**
See also BRW 2; CDBLB 1660-1789; DA;
DAB; DAC; DAM DRAM, MST, POET;
DLB 80, 101, 131; EXPP; IDTP; LMFS
1; RGEL 2; TEA; WLIT 3

du Bellay, Joachim 1524-1560 .... **LC 92**
See also GFL Beginnings to 1789; RGWL
2, 3

Duberman, Martin (Bauml) 1930- ..... **CLC 8**
See also CA 1-4R; CAD; CANR 2, 63; CD
5

Dubie, Norman (Evans) 1945- .... **CLC 36**
See also CA 69-72; CANR 12, 115; CP 7;
DLB 120; PFS 12

Du Bois, W(illiam) E(dward) B(urghardt)
1868-1963 ..... **BLC 1; CLC 1, 2, 13, 64,
96; HR 2; WLC**
See also AAYA 40; AFAW 1, 2; AMWC 1;
AMWS 2; BW 1, 3; CA 85-88; CANR
34, 82, 132; CDALB 1865-1917; DA;
DA3; DAC; DAM MST, MULT, NOV;
DLB 47, 50, 91, 246, 284; EWL 3; EXPP;
LAIT 2; LMFS 2; MTCW 1, 2; NCFS 1;
PFS 13; RGAL 4; SATA 42

Dubus, Andre 1936-1999 ..... **CLC 13, 36, 97;
SSC 15**
See also AMWS 7; CA 21-24R; 177; CANR
17; CN 7; CSW; DLB 130; INT CANR-
17; RGAL 4; SSFS 10

Duca Minimo
See D'Annunzio, Gabriele

Ducharme, Rejean 1941- .... **CLC 74**
See also CA 165; DLB 60

du Chatelet, Emilie 1706-1749 .... **LC 96**

Duchen, Claire .... **CLC 65**

Duclos, Charles Pinot- 1704-1772 .... **LC 1**
See also GFL Beginnings to 1789

Dudek, Louis 1918-2001 .... **CLC 11, 19**
See also CA 45-48; 215; CAAS 14; CANR
1; CP 7; DLB 88

Duerrenmatt, Friedrich 1921-1990 ... **CLC 1,
4, 8, 11, 15, 43, 102**
See Durrenmatt, Friedrich
See also CA 17-20R; CANR 33; CMW 4;
DAM DRAM; DLB 69, 124; MTCW 1, 2

Duffy, Bruce 1953(?)- .... **CLC 50**
See also CA 172

Duffy, Maureen 1933- .... **CLC 37**
See also CA 25-28R; CANR 33, 68; CBD;
CN 7; CP 7; CWD; CWP; DFS 15; DLB
14; FW; MTCW 1

Du Fu
See Tu Fu
See also RGWL 2, 3

Dugan, Alan 1923-2003 .... **CLC 2, 6**
See also CA 81-84; 220; CANR 119; CP 7;
DLB 5; PFS 10

du Gard, Roger Martin
See Martin du Gard, Roger

Duhamel, Georges 1884-1966 .... **CLC 8**
See also CA 81-84; 25-28R; CANR 35;
DLB 65; EWL 3; GFL 1789 to the
Present; MTCW 1

Dujardin, Edouard (Emile Louis)
1861-1949 .... **TCLC 13**
See also CA 109; DLB 123

Duke, Raoul
See Thompson, Hunter S(tockton)

Dulles, John Foster 1888-1959 .... **TCLC 72**
See also CA 115; 149

Dumas, Alexandre (pere)
1802-1870 .... **NCLC 11, 71; WLC**
See also AAYA 22; BYA 3; DA; DA3;
DAB; DAC; DAM MST, NOV; DLB 119,
192; EW 6; GFL 1789 to the Present;
LAIT 1, 2; NFS 14, 19; RGWL 2, 3;
SATA 18; TWA; WCH

Dumas, Alexandre (fils) 1824-1895 ...... **DC 1;
NCLC 9**
See also DLB 192; GFL 1789 to the Present;
RGWL 2, 3

Dumas, Claudine
See Malzberg, Barry N(athaniel)

Dumas, Henry L. 1934-1968 .... **CLC 6, 62**
See also BW 1; CA 85-88; DLB 41; RGAL
4

du Maurier, Daphne 1907-1989 .. **CLC 6, 11,
59; SSC 18**
See also AAYA 37; BPFB 1; BRWS 3; CA
5-8R; 128; CANR 6, 55; CMW 4; CPW;
DA3; DAB; DAC; DAM MST, POP;
DLB 191; HGG; LAIT 3; MSW; MTCW
1, 2; NFS 12; RGEL 2; RGSF 2; RHW;
SATA 27; SATA-Obit 60; SSFS 14, 16;
TEA

Du Maurier, George 1834-1896 ..... **NCLC 86**
See also DLB 153, 178; RGEL 2

Dunbar, Paul Laurence 1872-1906 ... **BLC 1;
PC 5; SSC 8; TCLC 2, 12; WLC**
See also AFAW 1, 2; AMWS 2; BW 1, 3;
CA 104; 124; CANR 79; CDALB 1865-
1917; DA; DA3; DAC; DAM MST,
MULT, POET; DLB 50, 54, 78; EXPP;
RGAL 4; SATA 34

Dunbar, William 1460(?)-1520(?) .... **LC 20**
See also BRWS 8; DLB 132, 146; RGEL 2

Dunbar-Nelson, Alice .... **HR 2**
See Nelson, Alice Ruth Moore Dunbar

Duncan, Dora Angela
See Duncan, Isadora

Duncan, Isadora 1877(?)-1927 .... **TCLC 68**
See also CA 118; 149

Duncan, Lois 1934- .... **CLC 26**
See also AAYA 4, 34; BYA 6, 8; CA 1-4R;
CANR 2, 23, 36, 111; CLR 29; JRDA;
MAICYA 1, 2; MAICYAS 1; SAAS 2;
SATA 1, 36, 75, 133, 141; SATA-Essay
141; WYA; YAW

Duncan, Robert (Edward)
1919-1988 .... **CLC 1, 2, 4, 7, 15, 41, 55;
PC 2**
See also BG 2; CA 9-12R; 124; CANR 28,
62; DAM POET; DLB 5, 16, 193; EWL
3; MTCW 1, 2; PFS 13; RGAL 4; WP

Duncan, Sara Jeannette
1861-1922 .... **TCLC 60**
See also CA 157; DLB 92

Dunlap, William 1766-1839 .... **NCLC 2**
See also DLB 30, 37, 59; RGAL 4

Dunn, Douglas (Eaglesham) 1942- .... **CLC 6,
40**
See also CA 45-48; CANR 2, 33, 126; CP
7; DLB 40; MTCW 1

Dunn, Katherine (Karen) 1945- .... **CLC 71**
See also CA 33-36R; CANR 72; HGG;
MTCW 1

Dunn, Stephen (Elliott) 1939- .... **CLC 36**
See also AMWS 11; CA 33-36R; CANR
12, 48, 53, 105; CP 7; DLB 105; PFS 21

Dunne, Finley Peter 1867-1936 ...... **TCLC 28**
See also CA 108; 178; DLB 11, 23; RGAL
4

Dunne, John Gregory 1932-2003 ..... **CLC 28**
See also CA 25-28R; 222; CANR 14, 50;
CN 7; DLBY 1980

Dunsany, Lord .... **TCLC 2, 59**
See Dunsany, Edward John Moreton Drax
Plunkett
See also DLB 77, 153, 156, 255; FANT;
IDTP; RGEL 2; SFW 4; SUFW 1

**Dunsany, Edward John Moreton Drax
Plunkett** 1878-1957
See Dunsany, Lord
See also CA 104; 148; DLB 10; MTCW 1

Duns Scotus, John 1266(?)-1308 ... **CMLC 59**
See also DLB 115

du Perry, Jean
See Simenon, Georges (Jacques Christian)

Durang, Christopher (Ferdinand)
1949- .... **CLC 27, 38**
See also CA 105; CAD; CANR 50, 76, 130;
CD 5; MTCW 1

Duras, Marguerite 1914-1996 . **CLC 3, 6, 11,
20, 34, 40, 68, 100; SSC 40**
See also BPFB 1; CA 25-28R; 151; CANR
50; CWW 2; DLB 83; EWL 3; GFL 1789
to the Present; IDFW 4; MTCW 1, 2;
RGWL 2, 3; TWA

Durban, (Rosa) Pam 1947- .... **CLC 39**
See also CA 123; CANR 98; CSW

Durcan, Paul 1944- .... **CLC 43, 70**
See also CA 134; CANR 123; CP 7; DAM
POET; EWL 3

Durfey, Thomas 1653-1723 .... **LC 94**
See also DLB 80; RGEL 2

Durkheim, Emile 1858-1917 .... **TCLC 55**

Durrell, Lawrence (George)
1912-1990 ..... **CLC 1, 4, 6, 8, 13, 27, 41**
See also BPFB 1; BRWS 1; CA 9-12R; 132;
CANR 40, 77; CDBLB 1945-1960; DAM
NOV; DLB 15, 27, 204; DLBY 1990;
EWL 3; MTCW 1, 2; RGEL 2; SFW 4;
TEA

Durrenmatt, Friedrich
See Duerrenmatt, Friedrich
See also CDWLB 2; EW 13; EWL 3;
RGWL 2, 3

Dutt, Michael Madhusudan
1824-1873 .... **NCLC 118**

Dutt, Toru 1856-1877 .... **NCLC 29**
See also DLB 240

Dwight, Timothy 1752-1817 .... **NCLC 13**
See also DLB 37; RGAL 4

Dworkin, Andrea 1946- .... **CLC 43, 123**
See also CA 77-80; CAAS 21; CANR 16,
39, 76, 96; FW; GLL 1; INT CANR-16;
MTCW 1, 2

Dwyer, Deanna
See Koontz, Dean R(ay)

Dwyer, K. R.
See Koontz, Dean R(ay)

Dybek, Stuart 1942- .... **CLC 114; SSC 55**
See also CA 97-100; CANR 39; DLB 130

Dye, Richard
See De Voto, Bernard (Augustine)

Dyer, Geoff 1958- .... **CLC 149**
See also CA 125; CANR 88

Dyer, George 1755-1841 .... **NCLC 129**
See also DLB 93

Dylan, Bob 1941- .... **CLC 3, 4, 6, 12, 77; PC
37**
See also CA 41-44R; CANR 108; CP 7;
DLB 16

Dyson, John 1943- .... **CLC 70**
See also CA 144

Dzyubin, Eduard Georgievich 1895-1934
See Bagritsky, Eduard
See also CA 170

E. V. L.
See Lucas, E(dward) V(errall)

Eagleton, Terence (Francis) 1943- .. **CLC 63,
132**
See also CA 57-60; CANR 7, 23, 68, 115;
DLB 242; LMFS 2; MTCW 1, 2

Elliott, Janice 1931-1995 .... **CLC 47**
See also CA 13-16R; CANR 8, 29, 84; CN 7; DLB 14; SATA 119

Elliott, Sumner Locke 1917-1991 ..... **CLC 38**
See also CA 5-8R; 134; CANR 2, 21; DLB 289

Elliott, William
See Bradbury, Ray (Douglas)

Ellis, A. E. .... **CLC 7**

Ellis, Alice Thomas .... **CLC 40**
See Haycraft, Anna (Margaret)
See also DLB 194; MTCW 1

Ellis, Bret Easton 1964- ...... **CLC 39, 71, 117**
See also AAYA 2, 43; CA 118; 123; CANR 51, 74, 126; CN 7; CPW; DA3; DAM POP; DLB 292; HGG; INT CA-123; MTCW 1; NFS 11

Ellis, (Henry) Havelock
1859-1939 .... **TCLC 14**
See also CA 109; 169; DLB 190

Ellis, Landon
See Ellison, Harlan (Jay)

Ellis, Trey 1962- .... **CLC 55**
See also CA 146; CANR 92

Ellison, Harlan (Jay) 1934- ... **CLC 1, 13, 42, 139; SSC 14**
See also AAYA 29; BPFB 1; BYA 14; CA 5-8R; CANR 5, 46, 115; CPW; DAM POP; DLB 8; HGG; INT CANR-5; MTCW 1, 2; SCFW 2; SFW 4; SSFS 13, 14, 15; SUFW 1, 2

Ellison, Ralph (Waldo) 1914-1994 .... **BLC 1; CLC 1, 3, 11, 54, 86, 114; SSC 26; WLC**
See also AAYA 19; AFAW 1, 2; AMWC 2; AMWR 2; AMWS 2; BPFB 1; BW 1, 3; BYA 2; CA 9-12R; 145; CANR 24, 53; CDALB 1941-1968; CSW; DA; DA3; DAB; DAC; DAM MST, MULT, NOV; DLB 2, 76, 227; DLBY 1994; EWL 3; EXPN; EXPS; LAIT 4; MTCW 1, 2; NCFS 3; NFS 2; RGAL 4; RGSF 2; SSFS 1, 11; YAW

Ellmann, Lucy (Elizabeth) 1956- ..... **CLC 61**
See also CA 128

Ellmann, Richard (David)
1918-1987 .... **CLC 50**
See also BEST 89:2; CA 1-4R; 122; CANR 2, 28, 61; DLB 103; DLBY 1987; MTCW 1, 2

Elman, Richard (Martin)
1934-1997 .... **CLC 19**
See also CA 17-20R; 163; CAAS 3; CANR 47

Elron
See Hubbard, L(afayette) Ron(ald)

El Saadawi, Nawal 1931- .... **CLC 196**
See al'Sadaawi, Nawal; Sa'adawi, al-Nawal; Saadawi, Nawal El; Sa'dawi, Nawal al-
See also CA 118; CAAS 11; CANR 44, 92

Eluard, Paul .... **PC 38; TCLC 7, 41**
See Grindel, Eugene
See also EWL 3; GFL 1789 to the Present; RGWL 2, 3

Elyot, Thomas 1490(?)-1546 .... **LC 11**
See also DLB 136; RGEL 2

Elytis, Odysseus 1911-1996 .... **CLC 15, 49, 100; PC 21**
See Alepoudelis, Odysseus
See also CA 102; 151; CANR 94; CWW 2; DAM POET; EW 13; EWL 3; MTCW 1, 2; RGWL 2, 3

Emecheta, (Florence Onye) Buchi
1944- .... **BLC 2; CLC 14, 48, 128**
See also AFW; BW 2, 3; CA 81-84; CANR 27, 81, 126; CDWLB 3; CN 7; CWRI 5; DA3; DAM MULT; DLB 117; EWL 3; FW; MTCW 1, 2; NFS 12, 14; SATA 66; WLIT 2

Emerson, Mary Moody
1774-1863 .... **NCLC 66**

Emerson, Ralph Waldo 1803-1882 . **NCLC 1, 38, 98; PC 18; WLC**
See also AMW; ANW; CDALB 1640-1865; DA; DA3; DAB; DAC; DAM MST, POET; DLB 1, 59, 73, 183, 223, 270; EXPP; LAIT 2; LMFS 1; NCFS 3; PFS 4, 17; RGAL 4; TUS; WP

Eminescu, Mihail 1850-1889 .. **NCLC 33, 131**

Empedocles 5th cent. B.C.- .... **CMLC 50**
See also DLB 176

Empson, William 1906-1984 ... **CLC 3, 8, 19, 33, 34**
See also BRWS 2; CA 17-20R; 112; CANR 31, 61; DLB 20; EWL 3; MTCW 1, 2; RGEL 2

Enchi, Fumiko (Ueda) 1905-1986 ..... **CLC 31**
See Enchi Fumiko
See also CA 129; 121; FW; MJW

Enchi Fumiko
See Enchi, Fumiko (Ueda)
See also DLB 182; EWL 3

Ende, Michael (Andreas Helmuth)
1929-1995 .... **CLC 31**
See also BYA 5; CA 118; 124; 149; CANR 36, 110; CLR 14; DLB 75; MAICYA 1, 2; MAICYAS 1; SATA 61, 130; SATA-Brief 42; SATA-Obit 86

Endo, Shusaku 1923-1996 ..... **CLC 7, 14, 19, 54, 99; SSC 48; TCLC 152**
See Endo Shusaku
See also CA 29-32R; 153; CANR 21, 54, 131; DA3; DAM NOV; MTCW 1, 2; RGSF 2; RGWL 2, 3

Endo Shusaku
See Endo, Shusaku
See also CWW 2; DLB 182; EWL 3

Engel, Marian 1933-1985 .... **CLC 36; TCLC 137**
See also CA 25-28R; CANR 12; DLB 53; FW; INT CANR-12

Engelhardt, Frederick
See Hubbard, L(afayette) Ron(ald)

Engels, Friedrich 1820-1895 .. **NCLC 85, 114**
See also DLB 129; LATS 1:1

Enright, D(ennis) J(oseph)
1920-2002 .... **CLC 4, 8, 31**
See also CA 1-4R; 211; CANR 1, 42, 83; CP 7; DLB 27; EWL 3; SATA 25; SATA-Obit 140

Enzensberger, Hans Magnus
1929- .... **CLC 43; PC 28**
See also CA 116; 119; CANR 103; CWW 2; EWL 3

Ephron, Nora 1941- .... **CLC 17, 31**
See also AAYA 35; AITN 2; CA 65-68; CANR 12, 39, 83

Epicurus 341B.C.-270B.C. .... **CMLC 21**
See also DLB 176

Epsilon
See Betjeman, John

Epstein, Daniel Mark 1948- .... **CLC 7**
See also CA 49-52; CANR 2, 53, 90

Epstein, Jacob 1956- .... **CLC 19**
See also CA 114

Epstein, Jean 1897-1953 .... **TCLC 92**

Epstein, Joseph 1937- .... **CLC 39**
See also CA 112; 119; CANR 50, 65, 117

Epstein, Leslie 1938- .... **CLC 27**
See also AMWS 12; CA 73-76, 215; CAAE 215; CAAS 12; CANR 23, 69; DLB 299

Equiano, Olaudah 1745(?)-1797 . **BLC 2; LC 16**
See also AFAW 1, 2; CDWLB 3; DAM MULT; DLB 37, 50; WLIT 2

Erasmus, Desiderius 1469(?)-1536 ..... **LC 16, 93**
See also DLB 136; EW 2; LMFS 1; RGWL 2, 3; TWA

Erdman, Paul E(mil) 1932- .... **CLC 25**
See also AITN 1; CA 61-64; CANR 13, 43, 84

Erdrich, Louise 1954- .... **CLC 39, 54, 120, 176; NNAL; PC 52**
See also AAYA 10, 47; AMWS 4; BEST 89:1; BPFB 1; CA 114; CANR 41, 62, 118; CDALBS; CN 7; CP 7; CPW; CWP; DA3; DAM MULT, NOV, POP; DLB 152, 175, 206; EWL 3; EXPP; LAIT 5; LATS 1:2; MTCW 1; NFS 5; PFS 14; RGAL 4; SATA 94, 141; SSFS 14; TCWW 2

Erenburg, Ilya (Grigoryevich)
See Ehrenburg, Ilya (Grigoryevich)

Erickson, Stephen Michael 1950-
See Erickson, Steve
See also CA 129; SFW 4

Erickson, Steve .... **CLC 64**
See Erickson, Stephen Michael
See also CANR 60, 68; SUFW 2

Erickson, Walter
See Fast, Howard (Melvin)

Ericson, Walter
See Fast, Howard (Melvin)

Eriksson, Buntel
See Bergman, (Ernst) Ingmar

Eriugena, John Scottus c.
810-877 .... **CMLC 65**
See also DLB 115

Ernaux, Annie 1940- .... **CLC 88, 184**
See also CA 147; CANR 93; NCFS 3, 5

Erskine, John 1879-1951 .... **TCLC 84**
See also CA 112; 159; DLB 9, 102; FANT

Eschenbach, Wolfram von
See Wolfram von Eschenbach
See also RGWL 3

Eseki, Bruno
See Mphahlele, Ezekiel

Esenin, Sergei (Alexandrovich)
1895-1925 .... **TCLC 4**
See Yesenin, Sergey
See also CA 104; RGWL 2, 3

Eshleman, Clayton 1935- .... **CLC 7**
See also CA 33-36R, 212; CAAE 212; CAAS 6; CANR 93; CP 7; DLB 5

Espriella, Don Manuel Alvarez
See Southey, Robert

Espriu, Salvador 1913-1985 .... **CLC 9**
See also CA 154; 115; DLB 134; EWL 3

Espronceda, Jose de 1808-1842 ..... **NCLC 39**

Esquivel, Laura 1951(?)- ... **CLC 141; HLCS 1**
See also AAYA 29; CA 143; CANR 68, 113; DA3; DNFS 2; LAIT 3; LMFS 2; MTCW 1; NFS 5; WLIT 1

Esse, James
See Stephens, James

Esterbrook, Tom
See Hubbard, L(afayette) Ron(ald)

Estleman, Loren D. 1952- .... **CLC 48**
See also AAYA 27; CA 85-88; CANR 27, 74; CMW 4; CPW; DA3; DAM NOV, POP; DLB 226; INT CANR-27; MTCW 1, 2

Etherege, Sir George 1636-1692 . **DC 23; LC 78**
See also BRW 2; DAM DRAM; DLB 80; PAB; RGEL 2

Euclid 306B.C.-283B.C. .... **CMLC 25**

Eugenides, Jeffrey 1960(?)- .... **CLC 81**
See also AAYA 51; CA 144; CANR 120

Euripides c. 484B.C.-406B.C. .... **CMLC 23, 51; DC 4; WLCS**
See also AW 1; CDWLB 1; DA; DA3; DAB; DAC; DAM DRAM, MST; DFS 1, 4, 6; DLB 176; LAIT 1; LMFS 1; RGWL 2, 3

Evan, Evin
See Faust, Frederick (Schiller)

Evans, Caradoc 1878-1945 ... **SSC 43; TCLC 85**
See also DLB 162

Evans, Evan
See Faust, Frederick (Schiller)
See also TCWW 2

Evans, Marian
See Eliot, George

Evans, Mary Ann
See Eliot, George
See also NFS 20

Evarts, Esther
See Benson, Sally

Everett, Percival
See Everett, Percival L.
See also CSW

Everett, Percival L. 1956- .... **CLC 57**
See Everett, Percival
See also BW 2; CA 129; CANR 94

Everson, R(onald) G(ilmour) 1903-1992 .... **CLC 27**
See also CA 17-20R; DLB 88

Everson, William (Oliver) 1912-1994 .... **CLC 1, 5, 14**
See also BG 2; CA 9-12R; 145; CANR 20; DLB 5, 16, 212; MTCW 1

Evtushenko, Evgenii Aleksandrovich
See Yevtushenko, Yevgeny (Alexandrovich)
See also CWW 2; RGWL 2, 3

Ewart, Gavin (Buchanan) 1916-1995 .... **CLC 13, 46**
See also BRWS 7; CA 89-92; 150; CANR 17, 46; CP 7; DLB 40; MTCW 1

Ewers, Hanns Heinz 1871-1943 ..... **TCLC 12**
See also CA 109; 149

Ewing, Frederick R.
See Sturgeon, Theodore (Hamilton)

Exley, Frederick (Earl) 1929-1992 .... **CLC 6, 11**
See also AITN 2; BPFB 1; CA 81-84; 138; CANR 117; DLB 143; DLBY 1981

Eynhardt, Guillermo
See Quiroga, Horacio (Sylvestre)

Ezekiel, Nissim (Moses) 1924-2004 .. **CLC 61**
See also CA 61-64; 223; CP 7; EWL 3

Ezekiel, Tish O'Dowd 1943- .... **CLC 34**
See also CA 129

Fadeev, Aleksandr Aleksandrovich
See Bulgya, Alexander Alexandrovich
See also DLB 272

Fadeev, Alexandr Alexandrovich
See Bulgya, Alexander Alexandrovich
See also EWL 3

Fadeyev, A.
See Bulgya, Alexander Alexandrovich

Fadeyev, Alexander .... **TCLC 53**
See Bulgya, Alexander Alexandrovich

Fagen, Donald 1948- .... **CLC 26**

Fainzilberg, Ilya Arnoldovich 1897-1937
See Ilf, Ilya
See also CA 120; 165

Fair, Ronald L. 1932- .... **CLC 18**
See also BW 1; CA 69-72; CANR 25; DLB 33

Fairbairn, Roger
See Carr, John Dickson

Fairbairns, Zoe (Ann) 1948- .... **CLC 32**
See also CA 103; CANR 21, 85; CN 7

Fairfield, Flora
See Alcott, Louisa May

Fairman, Paul W. 1916-1977
See Queen, Ellery
See also CA 114; SFW 4

Falco, Gian
See Papini, Giovanni

Falconer, James
See Kirkup, James

Falconer, Kenneth
See Kornbluth, C(yril) M.

Falkland, Samuel
See Heijermans, Herman

Fallaci, Oriana 1930- .... **CLC 11, 110**
See also CA 77-80; CANR 15, 58; FW; MTCW 1

Faludi, Susan 1959- .... **CLC 140**
See also CA 138; CANR 126; FW; MTCW 1; NCFS 3

Faludy, George 1913- .... **CLC 42**
See also CA 21-24R

Faludy, Gyoergy
See Faludy, George

Fanon, Frantz 1925-1961 .... **BLC 2; CLC 74**
See also BW 1; CA 116; 89-92; DAM MULT; DLB 296; LMFS 2; WLIT 2

Fanshawe, Ann 1625-1680 .... **LC 11**

Fante, John (Thomas) 1911-1983 .... **CLC 60; SSC 65**
See also AMWS 11; CA 69-72; 109; CANR 23, 104; DLB 130; DLBY 1983

Far, Sui Sin .... **SSC 62**
See Eaton, Edith Maude
See also SSFS 4

Farah, Nuruddin 1945- ...... **BLC 2; CLC 53, 137**
See also AFW; BW 2, 3; CA 106; CANR 81; CDWLB 3; CN 7; DAM MULT; DLB 125; EWL 3; WLIT 2

Fargue, Leon-Paul 1876(?)-1947 .... **TCLC 11**
See also CA 109; CANR 107; DLB 258; EWL 3

Farigoule, Louis
See Romains, Jules

Farina, Richard 1936(?)-1966 .... **CLC 9**
See also CA 81-84; 25-28R

Farley, Walter (Lorimer) 1915-1989 .... **CLC 17**
See also AAYA 58; BYA 14; CA 17-20R; CANR 8, 29, 84; DLB 22; JRDA; MAICYA 1, 2; SATA 2, 43, 132; YAW

Farmer, Philip Jose 1918- .... **CLC 1, 19**
See also AAYA 28; BPFB 1; CA 1-4R; CANR 4, 35, 111; DLB 8; MTCW 1; SATA 93; SCFW 2; SFW 4

Farquhar, George 1677-1707 .... **LC 21**
See also BRW 2; DAM DRAM; DLB 84; RGEL 2

Farrell, J(ames) G(ordon) 1935-1979 .... **CLC 6**
See also CA 73-76; 89-92; CANR 36; DLB 14, 271; MTCW 1; RGEL 2; RHW; WLIT 4

Farrell, James T(homas) 1904-1979 . **CLC 1, 4, 8, 11, 66; SSC 28**
See also AMW; BPFB 1; CA 5-8R; 89-92; CANR 9, 61; DLB 4, 9, 86; DLBD 2; EWL 3; MTCW 1, 2; RGAL 4

Farrell, Warren (Thomas) 1943- ...... **CLC 70**
See also CA 146; CANR 120

Farren, Richard J.
See Betjeman, John

Farren, Richard M.
See Betjeman, John

Fassbinder, Rainer Werner 1946-1982 .... **CLC 20**
See also CA 93-96; 106; CANR 31

Fast, Howard (Melvin) 1914-2003 .. **CLC 23, 131**
See also AAYA 16; BPFB 1; CA 1-4R, 181; 214; CAAE 181; CAAS 18; CANR 1, 33, 54, 75, 98; CMW 4; CN 7; CPW; DAM NOV; DLB 9; INT CANR-33; LATS 1:1; MTCW 1; RHW; SATA 7; SATA-Essay 107; TCWW 2; YAW

Faulcon, Robert
See Holdstock, Robert P.

Faulkner, William (Cuthbert) 1897-1962 .... **CLC 1, 3, 6, 8, 9, 11, 14, 18, 28, 52, 68; SSC 1, 35, 42; TCLC 141; WLC**
See also AAYA 7; AMW; AMWR 1; BPFB 1; BYA 5, 15; CA 81-84; CANR 33; CDALB 1929-1941; DA; DA3; DAB; DAC; DAM MST, NOV; DLB 9, 11, 44, 102; DLBD 2; DLBY 1986, 1997; EWL 3; EXPN; EXPS; LAIT 2; LATS 1:1; LMFS 2; MTCW 1, 2; NFS 4, 8, 13; RGAL 4; RGSF 2; SSFS 2, 5, 6, 12; TUS

Fauset, Jessie Redmon 1882(?)-1961 .. **BLC 2; CLC 19, 54; HR 2**
See also AFAW 2; BW 1; CA 109; CANR 83; DAM MULT; DLB 51; FW; LMFS 2; MAWW

Faust, Frederick (Schiller) 1892-1944(?) .... **TCLC 49**
See Austin, Frank; Brand, Max; Challis, George; Dawson, Peter; Dexter, Martin; Evans, Evan; Frederick, John; Frost, Frederick; Manning, David; Silver, Nicholas
See also CA 108; 152; DAM POP; DLB 256; TUS

Faust, Irvin 1924- .... **CLC 8**
See also CA 33-36R; CANR 28, 67; CN 7; DLB 2, 28, 218, 278; DLBY 1980

Faustino, Domingo 1811-1888 ...... **NCLC 123**

Fawkes, Guy
See Benchley, Robert (Charles)

Fearing, Kenneth (Flexner) 1902-1961 .... **CLC 51**
See also CA 93-96; CANR 59; CMW 4; DLB 9; RGAL 4

Fecamps, Elise
See Creasey, John

Federman, Raymond 1928- .... **CLC 6, 47**
See also CA 17-20R, 208; CAAE 208; CAAS 8; CANR 10, 43, 83, 108; CN 7; DLBY 1980

Federspiel, J(uerg) F. 1931- .... **CLC 42**
See also CA 146

Feiffer, Jules (Ralph) 1929- ...... **CLC 2, 8, 64**
See also AAYA 3; CA 17-20R; CAD; CANR 30, 59, 129; CD 5; DAM DRAM; DLB 7, 44; INT CANR-30; MTCW 1; SATA 8, 61, 111

Feige, Hermann Albert Otto Maximilian
See Traven, B.

Feinberg, David B. 1956-1994 .... **CLC 59**
See also CA 135; 147

Feinstein, Elaine 1930- .... **CLC 36**
See also CA 69-72; CAAS 1; CANR 31, 68, 121; CN 7; CP 7; CWP; DLB 14, 40; MTCW 1

Feke, Gilbert David .... **CLC 65**

Feldman, Irving (Mordecai) 1928- ..... **CLC 7**
See also CA 1-4R; CANR 1; CP 7; DLB 169

Felix-Tchicaya, Gerald
See Tchicaya, Gerald Felix

Fellini, Federico 1920-1993 .... **CLC 16, 85**
See also CA 65-68; 143; CANR 33

Felltham, Owen 1602(?)-1668 .... **LC 92**
See also DLB 126, 151

Felsen, Henry Gregor 1916-1995 ..... **CLC 17**
  See also CA 1-4R; 180; CANR 1; SAAS 2;
  SATA 1
Felski, Rita .... **CLC 65**
Fenno, Jack
  See Calisher, Hortense
Fenollosa, Ernest (Francisco)
  1853-1908 .... **TCLC 91**
Fenton, James Martin 1949- .... **CLC 32**
  See also CA 102; CANR 108; CP 7; DLB
  40; PFS 11
Ferber, Edna 1887-1968 .... **CLC 18, 93**
  See also AITN 1; CA 5-8R; 25-28R; CANR
  68, 105; DLB 9, 28, 86, 266; MTCW 1,
  2; RGAL 4; RHW; SATA 7; TCWW 2
Ferdowsi, Abu'l Qasem 940-1020 . **CMLC 43**
  See also RGWL 2, 3
Ferguson, Helen
  See Kavan, Anna
Ferguson, Niall 1964- .... **CLC 134**
  See also CA 190
Ferguson, Samuel 1810-1886 .... **NCLC 33**
  See also DLB 32; RGEL 2
Fergusson, Robert 1750-1774 .... **LC 29**
  See also DLB 109; RGEL 2
Ferling, Lawrence
  See Ferlinghetti, Lawrence (Monsanto)
Ferlinghetti, Lawrence (Monsanto)
  1919(?)- ..... **CLC 2, 6, 10, 27, 111; PC 1**
  See also CA 5-8R; CANR 3, 41, 73, 125;
  CDALB 1941-1968; CP 7; DA3; DAM
  POET; DLB 5, 16; MTCW 1, 2; RGAL 4;
  WP
Fern, Fanny
  See Parton, Sara Payson Willis
Fernandez, Vicente Garcia Huidobro
  See Huidobro Fernandez, Vicente Garcia
Fernandez-Armesto, Felipe .... **CLC 70**
Fernandez de Lizardi, Jose Joaquin
  See Lizardi, Jose Joaquin Fernandez de
Ferre, Rosario 1938- ...... **CLC 139; HLCS 1;**
  SSC 36
  See also CA 131; CANR 55, 81; CWW 2;
  DLB 145; EWL 3; HW 1, 2; LAWS 1;
  MTCW 1; WLIT 1
Ferrer, Gabriel (Francisco Victor) Miro
  See Miro (Ferrer), Gabriel (Francisco
  Victor)
Ferrier, Susan (Edmonstone)
  1782-1854 .... **NCLC 8**
  See also DLB 116; RGEL 2
Ferrigno, Robert 1948(?)- .... **CLC 65**
  See also CA 140; CANR 125
Ferron, Jacques 1921-1985 .... **CLC 94**
  See also CA 117; 129; CCA 1; DAC; DLB
  60; EWL 3
Feuchtwanger, Lion 1884-1958 .... **TCLC 3**
  See also CA 104; 187; DLB 66; EWL 3
Feuerbach, Ludwig 1804-1872 ..... **NCLC 139**
  See also DLB 133
Feuillet, Octave 1821-1890 .... **NCLC 45**
  See also DLB 192
Feydeau, Georges (Leon Jules Marie)
  1862-1921 .... **TCLC 22**
  See also CA 113; 152; CANR 84; DAM
  DRAM; DLB 192; EWL 3; GFL 1789 to
  the Present; RGWL 2, 3
Fichte, Johann Gottlieb
  1762-1814 .... **NCLC 62**
  See also DLB 90
Ficino, Marsilio 1433-1499 .... **LC 12**
  See also LMFS 1
Fiedeler, Hans
  See Doeblin, Alfred

Fiedler, Leslie A(aron) 1917-2003 ..... **CLC 4,**
  13, 24
  See also AMWS 13; CA 9-12R; 212; CANR
  7, 63; CN 7; DLB 28, 67; EWL 3; MTCW
  1, 2; RGAL 4; TUS
Field, Andrew 1938- .... **CLC 44**
  See also CA 97-100; CANR 25
Field, Eugene 1850-1895 .... **NCLC 3**
  See also DLB 23, 42, 140; DLBD 13; MAI-
  CYA 1, 2; RGAL 4; SATA 16
Field, Gans T.
  See Wellman, Manly Wade
Field, Michael 1915-1971 .... **TCLC 43**
  See also CA 29-32R
Field, Peter
  See Hobson, Laura Z(ametkin)
  See also TCWW 2
Fielding, Helen 1958- .... **CLC 146**
  See also CA 172; CANR 127; DLB 231
Fielding, Henry 1707-1754 .... **LC 1, 46, 85;**
  WLC
  See also BRW 3; BRWR 1; CDBLB 1660-
  1789; DA; DA3; DAB; DAC; DAM
  DRAM, MST, NOV; DLB 39, 84, 101;
  NFS 18; RGEL 2; TEA; WLIT 3
Fielding, Sarah 1710-1768 .... **LC 1, 44**
  See also DLB 39; RGEL 2; TEA
Fields, W. C. 1880-1946 .... **TCLC 80**
  See also DLB 44
Fierstein, Harvey (Forbes) 1954- ..... **CLC 33**
  See also CA 123; 129; CAD; CD 5; CPW;
  DA3; DAM DRAM, POP; DFS 6; DLB
  266; GLL
Figes, Eva 1932- .... **CLC 31**
  See also CA 53-56; CANR 4, 44, 83; CN 7;
  DLB 14, 271; FW
Filippo, Eduardo de
  See de Filippo, Eduardo
Finch, Anne 1661-1720 .... **LC 3; PC 21**
  See also BRWS 9; DLB 95
Finch, Robert (Duer Claydon)
  1900-1995 .... **CLC 18**
  See also CA 57-60; CANR 9, 24, 49; CP 7;
  DLB 88
Findley, Timothy (Irving Frederick)
  1930-2002 .... **CLC 27, 102**
  See also CA 25-28R; 206; CANR 12, 42,
  69, 109; CCA 1; CN 7; DAC; DAM MST;
  DLB 53; FANT; RHW
Fink, William
  See Mencken, H(enry) L(ouis)
Firbank, Louis 1942-
  See Reed, Lou
  See also CA 117
Firbank, (Arthur Annesley) Ronald
  1886-1926 .... **TCLC 1**
  See also BRWS 2; CA 104; 177; DLB 36;
  EWL 3; RGEL 2
Fish, Stanley
  See Fish, Stanley Eugene
Fish, Stanley E.
  See Fish, Stanley Eugene
Fish, Stanley Eugene 1938- .... **CLC 142**
  See also CA 112; 132; CANR 90; DLB 67
Fisher, Dorothy (Frances) Canfield
  1879-1958 .... **TCLC 87**
  See also CA 114; 136; CANR 80; CLR 71,;
  CWRI 5; DLB 9, 102, 284; MAICYA 1,
  2; YABC 1
Fisher, M(ary) F(rances) K(ennedy)
  1908-1992 .... **CLC 76, 87**
  See also CA 77-80; 138; CANR 44; MTCW
  1
Fisher, Roy 1930- .... **CLC 25**
  See also CA 81-84; CAAS 10; CANR 16;
  CP 7; DLB 40

Fisher, Rudolph 1897-1934 .... **BLC 2; HR 2;**
  SSC 25; TCLC 11
  See also BW 1, 3; CA 107; 124; CANR 80;
  DAM MULT; DLB 51, 102
Fisher, Vardis (Alvero) 1895-1968 .... **CLC 7;**
  TCLC 140
  See also CA 5-8R; 25-28R; CANR 68; DLB
  9, 206; RGAL 4; TCWW 2
Fiske, Tarleton
  See Bloch, Robert (Albert)
Fitch, Clarke
  See Sinclair, Upton (Beall)
Fitch, John IV
  See Cormier, Robert (Edmund)
Fitzgerald, Captain Hugh
  See Baum, L(yman) Frank
FitzGerald, Edward 1809-1883 .... **NCLC 9**
  See also BRW 4; DLB 32; RGEL 2
Fitzgerald, F(rancis) Scott (Key)
  1896-1940 ... **SSC 6, 31, 75; TCLC 1, 6,**
  14, 28, 55, 157; WLC
  See also AAYA 24; AITN 1; AMW; AMWC
  2; AMWR 1; BPFB 1; CA 110; 123;
  CDALB 1917-1929; DA; DA3; DAB;
  DAC; DAM MST, NOV; DLB 4, 9, 86,
  219, 273; DLBD 1, 15, 16; DLBY 1981,
  1996; EWL 3; EXPN; EXPS; LAIT 3;
  MTCW 1, 2; NFS 2, 19, 20; RGAL 4;
  RGSF 2; SSFS 4, 15; TUS
Fitzgerald, Penelope 1916-2000 . **CLC 19, 51,**
  61, 143
  See also BRWS 5; CA 85-88; 190; CAAS
  10; CANR 56, 86, 131; CN 7; DLB 14,
  194; EWL 3; MTCW 2
Fitzgerald, Robert (Stuart)
  1910-1985 .... **CLC 39**
  See also CA 1-4R; 114; CANR 1; DLBY
  1980
FitzGerald, Robert D(avid)
  1902-1987 .... **CLC 19**
  See also CA 17-20R; DLB 260; RGEL 2
Fitzgerald, Zelda (Sayre)
  1900-1948 .... **TCLC 52**
  See also AMWS 9; CA 117; 126; DLBY
  1984
Flanagan, Thomas (James Bonner)
  1923-2002 .... **CLC 25, 52**
  See also CA 108; 206; CANR 55; CN 7;
  DLBY 1980; INT CA-108; MTCW 1;
  RHW
Flaubert, Gustave 1821-1880 .... **NCLC 2, 10,**
  19, 62, 66, 135; SSC 11, 60; WLC
  See also DA; DA3; DAB; DAC; DAM
  MST, NOV; DLB 119, 301; EW 7; EXPS;
  GFL 1789 to the Present; LAIT 2; LMFS
  1; NFS 14; RGSF 2; RGWL 2, 3; SSFS
  6; TWA
Flavius Josephus
  See Josephus, Flavius
Flecker, Herman Elroy
  See Flecker, (Herman) James Elroy
Flecker, (Herman) James Elroy
  1884-1915 .... **TCLC 43**
  See also CA 109; 150; DLB 10, 19; RGEL
  2
Fleming, Ian (Lancaster) 1908-1964 . **CLC 3,**
  30
  See also AAYA 26; BPFB 1; CA 5-8R;
  CANR 59; CDBLB 1945-1960; CMW 4;
  CPW; DA3; DAM POP; DLB 87, 201;
  MSW; MTCW 1, 2; RGEL 2; SATA 9;
  TEA; YAW
Fleming, Thomas (James) 1927- ...... **CLC 37**
  See also CA 5-8R; CANR 10, 102; INT
  CANR-10; SATA 8
Fletcher, John 1579-1625 .... **DC 6; LC 33**
  See also BRW 2; CDBLB Before 1660;
  DLB 58; RGEL 2; TEA

Fraser, Antonia (Pakenham) 1932- . **CLC 32, 107**
See also AAYA 57; CA 85-88; CANR 44, 65, 119; CMW; DLB 276; MTCW 1, 2; SATA-Brief 32

Fraser, George MacDonald 1925- ...... **CLC 7**
See also AAYA 48; CA 45-48, 180; CAAE 180; CANR 2, 48, 74; MTCW 1; RHW

Fraser, Sylvia 1935- .... **CLC 64**
See also CA 45-48; CANR 1, 16, 60; CCA 1

Frayn, Michael 1933- . **CLC 3, 7, 31, 47, 176**
See also BRWC 2; BRWS 7; CA 5-8R; CANR 30, 69, 114, 133; CBD; CD 5; CN 7; DAM DRAM, NOV; DLB 13, 14, 194, 245; FANT; MTCW 1, 2; SFW 4

Fraze, Candida (Merrill) 1945- .... **CLC 50**
See also CA 126

Frazer, Andrew
See Marlowe, Stephen

Frazer, J(ames) G(eorge)
1854-1941 .... **TCLC 32**
See also BRWS 3; CA 118; NCFS 5

Frazer, Robert Caine
See Creasey, John

Frazer, Sir James George
See Frazer, J(ames) G(eorge)

Frazier, Charles 1950- .... **CLC 109**
See also AAYA 34; CA 161; CANR 126; CSW; DLB 292

Frazier, Ian 1951- .... **CLC 46**
See also CA 130; CANR 54, 93

Frederic, Harold 1856-1898 .... **NCLC 10**
See also AMW; DLB 12, 23; DLBD 13; RGAL 4

Frederick, John
See Faust, Frederick (Schiller)
See also TCWW 2

Frederick the Great 1712-1786 .... **LC 14**

Fredro, Aleksander 1793-1876 .... **NCLC 8**

Freeling, Nicolas 1927-2003 .... **CLC 38**
See also CA 49-52; 218; CAAS 12; CANR 1, 17, 50, 84; CN 7; DLB 87

Freeman, Douglas Southall
1886-1953 .... **TCLC 11**
See also CA 109; 195; DLB 17; DLBD 17

Freeman, Judith 1946- .... **CLC 55**
See also CA 148; CANR 120; DLB 256

Freeman, Mary E(leanor) Wilkins
1852-1930 .... **SSC 1, 47; TCLC 9**
See also CA 106; 177; DLB 12, 78, 221; EXPS; FW; HGG; MAWW; RGAL 4; RGSF 2; SSFS 4, 8; SUFW 1; TUS

Freeman, R(ichard) Austin
1862-1943 .... **TCLC 21**
See also CA 113; CANR 84; CMW 4; DLB 70

French, Albert 1943- .... **CLC 86**
See also BW 3; CA 167

French, Antonia
See Kureishi, Hanif

French, Marilyn 1929- .. **CLC 10, 18, 60, 177**
See also BPFB 1; CA 69-72; CANR 3, 31; CN 7; CPW; DAM DRAM, NOV, POP; FW; INT CANR-31; MTCW 1, 2

French, Paul
See Asimov, Isaac

Freneau, Philip Morin 1752-1832 .. **NCLC 1, 111**
See also AMWS 2; DLB 37, 43; RGAL 4

Freud, Sigmund 1856-1939 .... **TCLC 52**
See also CA 115; 133; CANR 69; DLB 296; EW 8; EWL 3; LATS 1:1; MTCW 1, 2; NCFS 3; TWA

Freytag, Gustav 1816-1895 .... **NCLC 109**
See also DLB 129

Friedan, Betty (Naomi) 1921- .... **CLC 74**
See also CA 65-68; CANR 18, 45, 74; DLB 246; FW; MTCW 1, 2; NCFS 5

Friedlander, Saul 1932- .... **CLC 90**
See also CA 117; 130; CANR 72

Friedman, B(ernard) H(arper)
1926- .... **CLC 7**
See also CA 1-4R; CANR 3, 48

Friedman, Bruce Jay 1930- .... **CLC 3, 5, 56**
See also CA 9-12R; CAD; CANR 25, 52, 101; CD 5; CN 7; DLB 2, 28, 244; INT CANR-25; SSFS 18

Friel, Brian 1929- .... **CLC 5, 42, 59, 115; DC 8; SSC 76**
See also BRWS 5; CA 21-24R; CANR 33, 69, 131; CBD; CD 5; DFS 11; DLB 13; EWL 3; MTCW 1; RGEL 2; TEA

Friis-Baastad, Babbis Ellinor
1921-1970 .... **CLC 12**
See also CA 17-20R; 134; SATA 7

Frisch, Max (Rudolf) 1911-1991 ... **CLC 3, 9, 14, 18, 32, 44; TCLC 121**
See also CA 85-88; 134; CANR 32, 74; CD-WLB 2; DAM DRAM, NOV; DLB 69, 124; EW 13; EWL 3; MTCW 1, 2; RGWL 2, 3

Fromentin, Eugene (Samuel Auguste)
1820-1876 .... **NCLC 10, 125**
See also DLB 123; GFL 1789 to the Present

Frost, Frederick
See Faust, Frederick (Schiller)
See also TCWW 2

Frost, Robert (Lee) 1874-1963 .. **CLC 1, 3, 4, 9, 10, 13, 15, 26, 34, 44; PC 1, 39; WLC**
See also AAYA 21; AMW; AMWR 1; CA 89-92; CANR 33; CDALB 1917-1929; CLR 67; DA; DA3; DAB; DAC; DAM MST, POET; DLB 54, 284; DLBD 7; EWL 3; EXPP; MTCW 1, 2; PAB; PFS 1, 2, 3, 4, 5, 6, 7, 10, 13; RGAL 4; SATA 14; TUS; WP; WYA

Froude, James Anthony
1818-1894 .... **NCLC 43**
See also DLB 18, 57, 144

Froy, Herald
See Waterhouse, Keith (Spencer)

Fry, Christopher 1907- .... **CLC 2, 10, 14**
See also BRWS 3; CA 17-20R; CAAS 23; CANR 9, 30, 74, 132; CBD; CD 5; CP 7; DAM DRAM; DLB 13; EWL 3; MTCW 1, 2; RGEL 2; SATA 66; TEA

Frye, (Herman) Northrop
1912-1991 .... **CLC 24, 70**
See also CA 5-8R; 133; CANR 8, 37; DLB 67, 68, 246; EWL 3; MTCW 1, 2; RGAL 4; TWA

Fuchs, Daniel 1909-1993 .... **CLC 8, 22**
See also CA 81-84; 142; CAAS 5; CANR 40; DLB 9, 26, 28; DLBY 1993

Fuchs, Daniel 1934- .... **CLC 34**
See also CA 37-40R; CANR 14, 48

Fuentes, Carlos 1928- .. **CLC 3, 8, 10, 13, 22, 41, 60, 113; HLC 1; SSC 24; WLC**
See also AAYA 4, 45; AITN 2; BPFB 1; CA 69-72; CANR 10, 32, 68, 104; CD-WLB 3; CWW 2; DA; DA3; DAB; DAC; DAM MST, MULT, NOV; DLB 113; DNFS 2; EWL 3; HW 1, 2; LAIT 3; LATS 1:2; LAW; LAWS 1; LMFS 2; MTCW 1, 2; NFS 8; RGSF 2; RGWL 2, 3; TWA; WLIT 1

Fuentes, Gregorio Lopez y
See Lopez y Fuentes, Gregorio

Fuertes, Gloria 1918-1998 .... **PC 27**
See also CA 178; 180; DLB 108; HW 2; SATA 115

Fugard, (Harold) Athol 1932- . **CLC 5, 9, 14, 25, 40, 80; DC 3**
See also AAYA 17; AFW; CA 85-88; CANR 32, 54, 118; CD 5; DAM DRAM; DFS 3, 6, 10; DLB 225; DNFS 1, 2; EWL 3; LATS 1:2; MTCW 1; RGEL 2; WLIT 2

Fugard, Sheila 1932- .... **CLC 48**
See also CA 125

Fukuyama, Francis 1952- .... **CLC 131**
See also CA 140; CANR 72, 125

Fuller, Charles (H.), (Jr.) 1939- .... **BLC 2; CLC 25; DC 1**
See also BW 2; CA 108; 112; CAD; CANR 87; CD 5; DAM DRAM, MULT; DFS 8; DLB 38, 266; EWL 3; INT CA-112; MTCW 1

Fuller, Henry Blake 1857-1929 .... **TCLC 103**
See also CA 108; 177; DLB 12; RGAL 4

Fuller, John (Leopold) 1937- .... **CLC 62**
See also CA 21-24R; CANR 9, 44; CP 7; DLB 40

Fuller, Margaret
See Ossoli, Sarah Margaret (Fuller)
See also AMWS 2; DLB 183, 223, 239

Fuller, Roy (Broadbent) 1912-1991 ... **CLC 4, 28**
See also BRWS 7; CA 5-8R; 135; CAAS 10; CANR 53, 83; CWRI 5; DLB 15, 20; EWL 3; RGEL 2; SATA 87

Fuller, Sarah Margaret
See Ossoli, Sarah Margaret (Fuller)

Fuller, Sarah Margaret
See Ossoli, Sarah Margaret (Fuller)
See also DLB 1, 59, 73

Fulton, Alice 1952- .... **CLC 52**
See also CA 116; CANR 57, 88; CP 7; CWP; DLB 193

Furphy, Joseph 1843-1912 .... **TCLC 25**
See Collins, Tom
See also CA 163; DLB 230; EWL 3; RGEL 2

Fuson, Robert H(enderson) 1927- .... **CLC 70**
See also CA 89-92; CANR 103

Fussell, Paul 1924- .... **CLC 74**
See also BEST 90:1; CA 17-20R; CANR 8, 21, 35, 69; INT CANR-21; MTCW 1, 2

Futabatei, Shimei 1864-1909 .... **TCLC 44**
See Futabatei Shimei
See also CA 162; MJW

Futabatei Shimei
See Futabatei, Shimei
See also DLB 180; EWL 3

Futrelle, Jacques 1875-1912 .... **TCLC 19**
See also CA 113; 155; CMW 4

Gaboriau, Emile 1835-1873 .... **NCLC 14**
See also CMW 4; MSW

Gadda, Carlo Emilio 1893-1973 ...... **CLC 11; TCLC 144**
See also CA 89-92; DLB 177; EWL 3

Gaddis, William 1922-1998 ... **CLC 1, 3, 6, 8, 10, 19, 43, 86**
See also AMWS 4; BPFB 1; CA 17-20R; 172; CANR 21, 48; CN 7; DLB 2, 278; EWL 3; MTCW 1, 2; RGAL 4

Gaelique, Moruen le
See Jacob, (Cyprien-)Max

Gage, Walter
See Inge, William (Motter)

Gaiman, Neil (Richard) 1960- .... **CLC 195**
See also AAYA 19, 42; CA 133; CANR 81, 129; DLB 261; HGG; SATA 85, 146; SFW 4; SUFW 2

Gaines, Ernest J(ames) 1933- .. **BLC 2; CLC 3, 11, 18, 86, 181; SSC 68**
See also AAYA 18; AFAW 1, 2; AITN 1; BPFB 2; BW 2, 3; BYA 6; CA 9-12R; CANR 6, 24, 42, 75, 126; CDALB 1968-1988; CLR 62; CN 7; CSW; DA3; DAM MULT; DLB 2, 33, 152; DLBY 1980; EWL 3; EXPN; LAIT 5; LATS 1:2; MTCW 1, 2; NFS 5, 7, 16; RGAL 4; RGSF 2; RHW; SATA 86; SSFS 5; YAW

Gaitskill, Mary (Lawrence) 1954- .... **CLC 69**
See also CA 128; CANR 61; DLB 244

Gladkov, Fedor Vasil'evich
See Gladkov, Fyodor (Vasilyevich)
See also DLB 272

Gladkov, Fyodor (Vasilyevich)
1883-1958 .... **TCLC 27**
See Gladkov, Fedor Vasil'evich
See also CA 170; EWL 3

Glancy, Diane 1941- .... **NNAL**
See also CA 136, 225; CAAE 225; CAAS
24; CANR 87; DLB 175

Glanville, Brian (Lester) 1931- .... **CLC 6**
See also CA 5-8R; CAAS 9; CANR 3, 70;
CN 7; DLB 15, 139; SATA 42

Glasgow, Ellen (Anderson Gholson)
1873-1945 .... **SSC 34; TCLC 2, 7**
See also AMW; CA 104; 164; DLB 9, 12;
MAWW; MTCW 2; RGAL 4; RHW;
SSFS 9; TUS

Glaspell, Susan 1882(?)-1948 ..... **DC 10; SSC
41; TCLC 55**
See also AMWS 3; CA 110; 154; DFS 8,
18; DLB 7, 9, 78, 228; MAWW; RGAL
4; SSFS 3; TCWW 2; TUS; YABC 2

Glassco, John 1909-1981 .... **CLC 9**
See also CA 13-16R; 102; CANR 15; DLB
68

Glasscock, Amnesia
See Steinbeck, John (Ernst)

Glasser, Ronald J. 1940(?)- .... **CLC 37**
See also CA 209

Glassman, Joyce
See Johnson, Joyce

Gleick, James (W.) 1954- .... **CLC 147**
See also CA 131; 137; CANR 97; INT CA-
137

Glendinning, Victoria 1937- .... **CLC 50**
See also CA 120; 127; CANR 59, 89; DLB
155

Glissant, Edouard (Mathieu)
1928- .... **CLC 10, 68**
See also CA 153; CANR 111; CWW 2;
DAM MULT; EWL 3; RGWL 3

Gloag, Julian 1930- .... **CLC 40**
See also AITN 1; CA 65-68; CANR 10, 70;
CN 7

Glowacki, Aleksander
See Prus, Boleslaw

Gluck, Louise (Elisabeth) 1943- .. **CLC 7, 22,
44, 81, 160; PC 16**
See also AMWS 5; CA 33-36R; CANR 40,
69, 108, 133; CP 7; CWP; DA3; DAM
POET; DLB 5; MTCW 2; PFS 5, 15;
RGAL 4

Glyn, Elinor 1864-1943 .... **TCLC 72**
See also DLB 153; RHW

Gobineau, Joseph-Arthur
1816-1882 .... **NCLC 17**
See also DLB 123; GFL 1789 to the Present

Godard, Jean-Luc 1930- .... **CLC 20**
See also CA 93-96

Godden, (Margaret) Rumer
1907-1998 .... **CLC 53**
See also AAYA 6; BPFB 2; BYA 2, 5; CA
5-8R; 172; CANR 4, 27, 36, 55, 80; CLR
20; CN 7; CWRI 5; DLB 161; MAICYA
1, 2; RHW; SAAS 12; SATA 3, 36; SATA-
Obit 109; TEA

Godoy Alcayaga, Lucila 1899-1957 .. **HLC 2;
PC 32; TCLC 2**
See Mistral, Gabriela
See also BW 2; CA 104; 131; CANR 81;
DAM MULT; DNFS 1; HW 1, 2; MTCW 1,
2

Godwin, Gail (Kathleen) 1937- ..... **CLC 5, 8,
22, 31, 69, 125**
See also BPFB 2; CA 29-32R; CANR 15,
43, 69, 132; CN 7; CPW; CSW; DA3;
DAM POP; DLB 6, 234; INT CANR-15;
MTCW 1, 2

Godwin, William 1756-1836 .. **NCLC 14, 130**
See also CDBLB 1789-1832; CMW 4; DLB
39, 104, 142, 158, 163, 262; HGG; RGEL
2

Goebbels, Josef
See Goebbels, (Paul) Joseph

Goebbels, (Paul) Joseph
1897-1945 .... **TCLC 68**
See also CA 115; 148

Goebbels, Joseph Paul
See Goebbels, (Paul) Joseph

Goethe, Johann Wolfgang von
1749-1832 .... **DC 20; NCLC 4, 22, 34,
90; PC 5; SSC 38; WLC**
See also CDWLB 2; DA; DA3; DAB;
DAC; DAM DRAM, MST, POET; DLB
94; EW 5; LATS 1; LMFS 1:1; RGWL 2,
3; TWA

Gogarty, Oliver St. John
1878-1957 .... **TCLC 15**
See also CA 109; 150; DLB 15, 19; RGEL
2

Gogol, Nikolai (Vasilyevich)
1809-1852 .... **DC 1; NCLC 5, 15, 31;
SSC 4, 29, 52; WLC**
See also DA; DAB; DAC; DAM DRAM,
MST; DFS 12; DLB 198; EW 6; EXPS;
RGSF 2; RGWL 2, 3; SSFS 7; TWA

Goines, Donald 1937(?)-1974 ... **BLC 2; CLC
80**
See also AITN 1; BW 1, 3; CA 124; 114;
CANR 82; CMW 4; DA3; DAM MULT;
POP; DLB 33

Gold, Herbert 1924- ... **CLC 4, 7, 14, 42, 152**
See also CA 9-12R; CANR 17, 45, 125; CN
7; DLB 2; DLBY 1981

Goldbarth, Albert 1948- .... **CLC 5, 38**
See also AMWS 12; CA 53-56; CANR 6,
40; CP 7; DLB 120

Goldberg, Anatol 1910-1982 .... **CLC 34**
See also CA 131; 117

Goldemberg, Isaac 1945- .... **CLC 52**
See also CA 69-72; CAAS 12; CANR 11,
32; EWL 3; HW 1; WLIT 1

Golding, Arthur 1536-1606 .... **LC 101**
See also DLB 136

Golding, William (Gerald)
1911-1993 ..... **CLC 1, 2, 3, 8, 10, 17, 27,
58, 81; WLC**
See also AAYA 5, 44; BPFB 2; BRWR 1;
BRWS 1; BYA 2; CA 5-8R; 141; CANR
13, 33, 54; CDBLB 1945-1960; CLR 94;
DA; DA3; DAB; DAC; DAM MST, NOV;
DLB 15, 100, 255; EWL 3; EXPN; HGG;
LAIT 4; MTCW 1, 2; NFS 2; RGEL 2;
RHW; SFW 4; TEA; WLIT 4; YAW

Goldman, Emma 1869-1940 .... **TCLC 13**
See also CA 110; 150; DLB 221; FW;
RGAL 4; TUS

Goldman, Francisco 1954- .... **CLC 76**
See also CA 162

Goldman, William (W.) 1931- ...... **CLC 1, 48**
See also BPFB 2; CA 9-12R; CANR 29,
69, 106; CN 7; DLB 44; FANT; IDFW 3,
4

Goldmann, Lucien 1913-1970 .... **CLC 24**
See also CA 25-28; CAP 2

Goldoni, Carlo 1707-1793 .... **LC 4**
See also DAM DRAM; EW 4; RGWL 2, 3

Goldsberry, Steven 1949- .... **CLC 34**
See also CA 131

Goldsmith, Oliver 1730-1774 .... **DC 8; LC 2,
48; WLC**
See also BRW 3; CDBLB 1660-1789; DA;
DAB; DAC; DAM DRAM, MST, NOV,
POET; DFS 1; DLB 39, 89, 104, 109, 142;
IDTP; RGEL 2; SATA 26; TEA; WLIT 3

Goldsmith, Peter
See Priestley, J(ohn) B(oynton)

Gombrowicz, Witold 1904-1969 .... **CLC 4, 7,
11, 49**
See also CA 19-20; 25-28R; CANR 105;
CAP 2; CDWLB 4; DAM DRAM; DLB
215; EW 12; EWL 3; RGWL 2, 3; TWA

Gomez de Avellaneda, Gertrudis
1814-1873 .... **NCLC 111**
See also LAW

Gomez de la Serna, Ramon
1888-1963 .... **CLC 9**
See also CA 153; 116; CANR 79; EWL 3;
HW 1, 2

Goncharov, Ivan Alexandrovich
1812-1891 .... **NCLC 1, 63**
See also DLB 238; EW 6; RGWL 2, 3

Goncourt, Edmond (Louis Antoine Huot) de
1822-1896 .... **NCLC 7**
See also DLB 123; EW 7; GFL 1789 to the
Present; RGWL 2, 3

Goncourt, Jules (Alfred Huot) de
1830-1870 .... **NCLC 7**
See also DLB 123; EW 7; GFL 1789 to the
Present; RGWL 2, 3

Gongora (y Argote), Luis de
1561-1627 .... **LC 72**
See also RGWL 2, 3

Gontier, Fernande 19(?)- .... **CLC 50**

Gonzalez Martinez, Enrique
See Gonzalez Martinez, Enrique
See also DLB 290

Gonzalez Martinez, Enrique
1871-1952 .... **TCLC 72**
See Gonzalez Martinez, Enrique
See also CA 166; CANR 81; EWL 3; HW
1, 2

Goodison, Lorna 1947- .... **PC 36**
See also CA 142; CANR 88; CP 7; CWP;
DLB 157; EWL 3

Goodman, Paul 1911-1972 ..... **CLC 1, 2, 4, 7**
See also CA 19-20; 37-40R; CAD; CANR
34; CAP 2; DLB 130, 246; MTCW 1;
RGAL 4

GoodWeather, Harley
See King, Thomas

Googe, Barnabe 1540-1594 .... **LC 94**
See also DLB 132; RGEL 2

Gordimer, Nadine 1923- ...... **CLC 3, 5, 7, 10,
18, 33, 51, 70, 123, 160, 161; SSC 17;
WLCS**
See also AAYA 39; AFW; BRWS 2; CA
5-8R; CANR 3, 28, 56, 88, 131; CN 7;
DA; DA3; DAB; DAC; DAM MST, NOV;
DLB 225; EWL 3; EXPS; INT CANR-28;
LATS 1:2; MTCW 1, 2; NFS 4; RGEL 2;
RGSF 2; SSFS 2, 14, 19; TWA; WLIT 2;
YAW

Gordon, Adam Lindsay
1833-1870 .... **NCLC 21**
See also DLB 230

Gordon, Caroline 1895-1981 . **CLC 6, 13, 29,
83; SSC 15**
See also AMW; CA 11-12; 103; CANR 36;
CAP 1; DLB 4, 9, 102; DLBD 17; DLBY
1981; EWL 3; MTCW 1, 2; RGAL 4;
RGSF 2

Gordon, Charles William 1860-1937
See Connor, Ralph
See also CA 109

Gordon, Mary (Catherine) 1949- .... **CLC 13,
22, 128; SSC 59**
See also AMWS 4; BPFB 2; CA 102;
CANR 44, 92; CN 7; DLB 6; DLBY
1981; FW; INT CA-102; MTCW 1

Gordon, N. J.
See Bosman, Herman Charles

Gordon, Sol 1923- .... **CLC 26**
See also CA 53-56; CANR 4; SATA 11

Hamilton, Clive
See Lewis, C(live) S(taples)

Hamilton, Edmond 1904-1977 .... **CLC 1**
See also CA 1-4R; CANR 3, 84; DLB 8; SATA 118; SFW 4

Hamilton, Eugene (Jacob) Lee
See Lee-Hamilton, Eugene (Jacob)

Hamilton, Franklin
See Silverberg, Robert

Hamilton, Gail
See Corcoran, Barbara (Asenath)

Hamilton, (Robert) Ian 1938-2001 . **CLC 191**
See also CA 106; 203; CANR 41, 67; CP 7; DLB 40, 155

Hamilton, Jane 1957- .... **CLC 179**
See also CA 147; CANR 85, 128

Hamilton, Mollie
See Kaye, M(ary) M(argaret)

Hamilton, (Anthony Walter) Patrick
1904-1962 .... **CLC 51**
See also CA 176; 113; DLB 10, 191

Hamilton, Virginia (Esther)
1936-2002 .... **CLC 26**
See also AAYA 2, 21; BW 2, 3; BYA 1, 2, 8; CA 25-28R; 206; CANR 20, 37, 73, 126; CLR 1, 11, 40; DAM MULT; DLB 33, 52; DLBY 01; INT CANR-20; JRDA; LAIT 5; MAICYA 1, 2; MAICYAS 1; MTCW 1, 2; SATA 4, 56, 79, 123; SATA-Obit 132; WYA; YAW

Hammett, (Samuel) Dashiell
1894-1961 .... **CLC 3, 5, 10, 19, 47; SSC 17**
See also AAYA 59; AITN 1; AMWS 4; BPFB 2; CA 81-84; CANR 42; CDALB 1929-1941; CMW 4; DA3; DLB 226, 280; DLBD 6; DLBY 1996; EWL 3; LAIT 3; MSW; MTCW 1, 2; RGAL 4; RGSF 2; TUS

Hammon, Jupiter 1720(?)-1800(?) .... **BLC 2; NCLC 5; PC 16**
See also DAM MULT, POET; DLB 31, 50

Hammond, Keith
See Kuttner, Henry

Hamner, Earl (Henry), Jr. 1923- ...... **CLC 12**
See also AITN 2; CA 73-76; DLB 6

Hampton, Christopher (James)
1946- .... **CLC 4**
See also CA 25-28R; CD 5; DLB 13; MTCW 1

Hamsun, Knut .... **TCLC 2, 14, 49, 151**
See Pedersen, Knut
See also DLB 297; EW 8; EWL 3; RGWL 2, 3

Handke, Peter 1942- .... **CLC 5, 8, 10, 15, 38, 134; DC 17**
See also CA 77-80; CANR 33, 75, 104, 133; CWW 2; DAM DRAM, NOV; DLB 85, 124; EWL 3; MTCW 1, 2; TWA

Handy, W(illiam) C(hristopher)
1873-1958 .... **TCLC 97**
See also BW 3; CA 121; 167

Hanley, James 1901-1985 ..... **CLC 3, 5, 8, 13**
See also CA 73-76; 117; CANR 36; CBD; DLB 191; EWL 3; MTCW 1; RGEL 2

Hannah, Barry 1942- .... **CLC 23, 38, 90**
See also BPFB 2; CA 108; 110; CANR 43, 68, 113; CN 7; CSW; DLB 6, 234; INT CA-110; MTCW 1; RGSF 2

Hannon, Ezra
See Hunter, Evan

Hansberry, Lorraine (Vivian)
1930-1965 ... **BLC 2; CLC 17, 62; DC 2**
See also AAYA 25; AFAW 1, 2; AMWS 4; BW 1, 3; CA 109; 25-28R; CABS 3; CAD; CANR 58; CDALB 1941-1968; CWD; DA; DA3; DAB; DAC; DAM DRAM, MST, MULT; DFS 2; DLB 7, 38; EWL 3; FW; LAIT 4; MTCW 1, 2; RGAL 4; TUS

Hansen, Joseph 1923- .... **CLC 38**
See Brock, Rose; Colton, James
See also BPFB 2; CA 29-32R; CAAS 17; CANR 16, 44, 66, 125; CMW 4; DLB 226; GLL 1; INT CANR-16

Hansen, Martin A(lfred)
1909-1955 .... **TCLC 32**
See also CA 167; DLB 214; EWL 3

Hansen and Philipson eds. .... **CLC 65**

Hanson, Kenneth O(stlin) 1922- .... **CLC 13**
See also CA 53-56; CANR 7

Hardwick, Elizabeth (Bruce) 1916- . **CLC 13**
See also AMWS 3; CA 5-8R; CANR 3, 32, 70, 100; CN 7; CSW; DA3; DAM NOV; DLB 6; MAWW; MTCW 1, 2

Hardy, Thomas 1840-1928 .... **PC 8; SSC 2, 60; TCLC 4, 10, 18, 32, 48, 53, 72, 143, 153; WLC**
See also BRW 6; BRWC 1, 2; BRWR 1; CA 104; 123; CDBLB 1890-1914; DA; DA3; DAB; DAC; DAM MST, NOV, POET; DLB 18, 19, 135, 284; EWL 3; EXPN; EXPP; LAIT 2; MTCW 1, 2; NFS 3, 11, 15, 19; PFS 3, 4, 18; RGEL 2; RGSF 2; TEA; WLIT 4

Hare, David 1947- .... **CLC 29, 58, 136**
See also BRWS 4; CA 97-100; CANR 39, 91; CBD; CD 5; DFS 4, 7, 16; DLB 13; MTCW 1; TEA

Harewood, John
See Van Druten, John (William)

Harford, Henry
See Hudson, W(illiam) H(enry)

Hargrave, Leonie
See Disch, Thomas M(ichael)

Hariri, Al- al-Qasim ibn 'Ali Abu Muhammad al-Basri
See al-Hariri, al-Qasim ibn 'Ali Abu Muhammad al-Basri

Harjo, Joy 1951- ..... **CLC 83; NNAL; PC 27**
See also AMWS 12; CA 114; CANR 35, 67, 91, 129; CP 7; CWP; DAM MULT; DLB 120, 175; EWL 3; MTCW 2; PFS 15; RGAL 4

Harlan, Louis R(udolph) 1922- .... **CLC 34**
See also CA 21-24R; CANR 25, 55, 80

Harling, Robert 1951(?)- .... **CLC 53**
See also CA 147

Harmon, William (Ruth) 1938- .... **CLC 38**
See also CA 33-36R; CANR 14, 32, 35; SATA 65

Harper, F. E. W.
See Harper, Frances Ellen Watkins

Harper, Frances E. W.
See Harper, Frances Ellen Watkins

Harper, Frances E. Watkins
See Harper, Frances Ellen Watkins

Harper, Frances Ellen
See Harper, Frances Ellen Watkins

Harper, Frances Ellen Watkins
1825-1911 ..... **BLC 2; PC 21; TCLC 14**
See also AFAW 1, 2; BW 1, 3; CA 111; 125; CANR 79; DAM MULT, POET; DLB 50, 221; MAWW; RGAL 4

Harper, Michael S(teven) 1938- ... **CLC 7, 22**
See also AFAW 2; BW 1; CA 33-36R, 224; CAAE 224; CANR 24, 108; CP 7; DLB 41; RGAL 4

Harper, Mrs. F. E. W.
See Harper, Frances Ellen Watkins

Harpur, Charles 1813-1868 .... **NCLC 114**
See also DLB 230; RGEL 2

Harris, Christie
See Harris, Christie (Lucy) Irwin

Harris, Christie (Lucy) Irwin
1907-2002 .... **CLC 12**
See also CA 5-8R; CANR 6, 83; CLR 47; DLB 88; JRDA; MAICYA 1, 2; SAAS 10; SATA 6, 74; SATA-Essay 116

Harris, Frank 1856-1931 .... **TCLC 24**
See also CA 109; 150; CANR 80; DLB 156, 197; RGEL 2

Harris, George Washington
1814-1869 .... **NCLC 23**
See also DLB 3, 11, 248; RGAL 4

Harris, Joel Chandler 1848-1908 ..... **SSC 19; TCLC 2**
See also CA 104; 137; CANR 80; CLR 49; DLB 11, 23, 42, 78, 91; LAIT 2; MAICYA 1, 2; RGSF 2; SATA 100; WCH; YABC 1

Harris, John (Wyndham Parkes Lucas) Beynon 1903-1969
See Wyndham, John
See also CA 102; 89-92; CANR 84; SATA 118; SFW 4

Harris, MacDonald .... **CLC 9**
See Heiney, Donald (William)

Harris, Mark 1922- .... **CLC 19**
See also CA 5-8R; CAAS 3; CANR 2, 55, 83; CN 7; DLB 2; DLBY 1980

Harris, Norman .... **CLC 65**

Harris, (Theodore) Wilson 1921- .... **CLC 25, 159**
See also BRWS 5; BW 2, 3; CA 65-68; CAAS 16; CANR 11, 27, 69, 114; CD-WLB 3; CN 7; CP 7; DLB 117; EWL 3; MTCW 1; RGEL 2

Harrison, Barbara Grizzuti
1934-2002 .... **CLC 144**
See also CA 77-80; 205; CANR 15, 48; INT CANR-15

Harrison, Elizabeth (Allen) Cavanna
1909-2001
See Cavanna, Betty
See also CA 9-12R; 200; CANR 6, 27, 85, 104, 121; MAICYA 2; SATA 142; YAW

Harrison, Harry (Max) 1925- .... **CLC 42**
See also CA 1-4R; CANR 5, 21, 84; DLB 8; SATA 4; SCFW 2; SFW 4

Harrison, James (Thomas) 1937- ...... **CLC 6, 14, 33, 66, 143; SSC 19**
See Harrison, Jim
See also CA 13-16R; CANR 8, 51, 79; CN 7; CP 7; DLBY 1982; INT CANR-8

Harrison, Jim
See Harrison, James (Thomas)
See also AMWS 8; RGAL 4; TCWW 2; TUS

Harrison, Kathryn 1961- .... **CLC 70, 151**
See also CA 144; CANR 68, 122

Harrison, Tony 1937- .... **CLC 43, 129**
See also BRWS 5; CA 65-68; CANR 44, 98; CBD; CD 5; CP 7; DLB 40, 245; MTCW 1; RGEL 2

Harriss, Will(ard Irvin) 1922- .... **CLC 34**
See also CA 111

Hart, Ellis
See Ellison, Harlan (Jay)

Hart, Josephine 1942(?)- .... **CLC 70**
See also CA 138; CANR 70; CPW; DAM POP

Hart, Moss 1904-1961 .... **CLC 66**
See also CA 109; 89-92; CANR 84; DAM DRAM; DFS 1; DLB 7, 266; RGAL 4

Harte, (Francis) Bret(t)
1836(?)-1902 ... **SSC 8, 59; TCLC 1, 25; WLC**
See also AMWS 2; CA 104; 140; CANR 80; CDALB 1865-1917; DA; DA3; DAC; DAM MST; DLB 12, 64, 74, 79, 186; EXPS; LAIT 2; RGAL 4; RGSF 2; SATA 26; SSFS 3; TUS

Hartley, L(eslie) P(oles) 1895-1972 ... **CLC 2, 22**
See also BRWS 7; CA 45-48; 37-40R; CANR 33; DLB 15, 139; EWL 3; HGG; MTCW 1, 2; RGEL 2; RGSF 2; SUFW 1

Hartman, Geoffrey H. 1929- .... **CLC 27**
See also CA 117; 125; CANR 79; DLB 67

Hartmann, Sadakichi 1869-1944 ... **TCLC 73**
See also CA 157; DLB 54

Hartmann von Aue c. 1170-c. 1210 .... **CMLC 15**
See also CDWLB 2; DLB 138; RGWL 2, 3

Hartog, Jan de
See de Hartog, Jan

Haruf, Kent 1943- .... **CLC 34**
See also AAYA 44; CA 149; CANR 91, 131

Harvey, Caroline
See Trollope, Joanna

Harvey, Gabriel 1550(?)-1631 .... **LC 88**
See also DLB 167, 213, 281

Harwood, Ronald 1934- .... **CLC 32**
See also CA 1-4R; CANR 4, 55; CBD; CD 5; DAM DRAM, MST; DLB 13

Hasegawa Tatsunosuke
See Futabatei, Shimei

Hasek, Jaroslav (Matej Frantisek)
1883-1923 .... **SSC 69; TCLC 4**
See also CA 104; 129; CDWLB 4; DLB 215; EW 9; EWL 3; MTCW 1, 2; RGSF 2; RGWL 2, 3

Hass, Robert 1941- ... **CLC 18, 39, 99; PC 16**
See also AMWS 6; CA 111; CANR 30, 50, 71; CP 7; DLB 105, 206; EWL 3; RGAL 4; SATA 94

Hastings, Hudson
See Kuttner, Henry

Hastings, Selina .... **CLC 44**

Hathorne, John 1641-1717 .... **LC 38**

Hatteras, Amelia
See Mencken, H(enry) L(ouis)

Hatteras, Owen .... **TCLC 18**
See Mencken, H(enry) L(ouis); Nathan, George Jean

Hauptmann, Gerhart (Johann Robert)
1862-1946 .... **SSC 37; TCLC 4**
See also CA 104; 153; CDWLB 2; DAM DRAM; DLB 66, 118; EW 8; EWL 3; RGSF 2; RGWL 2, 3; TWA

Havel, Vaclav 1936- ..... **CLC 25, 58, 65, 123; DC 6**
See also CA 104; CANR 36, 63, 124; CD-WLB 4; CWW 2; DA3; DAM DRAM; DFS 10; DLB 232; EWL 3; LMFS 2; MTCW 1, 2; RGWL 3

Haviaras, Stratis .... **CLC 33**
See Chaviaras, Strates

Hawes, Stephen 1475(?)-1529(?) .... **LC 17**
See also DLB 132; RGEL 2

Hawkes, John (Clendennin Burne, Jr.)
1925-1998 .. **CLC 1, 2, 3, 4, 7, 9, 14, 15, 27, 49**
See also BPFB 2; CA 1-4R; 167; CANR 2, 47, 64; CN 7; DLB 2, 7, 227; DLBY 1980, 1998; EWL 3; MTCW 1, 2; RGAL 4

Hawking, S. W.
See Hawking, Stephen W(illiam)

Hawking, Stephen W(illiam) 1942- . **CLC 63, 105**
See also AAYA 13; BEST 89:1; CA 126; 129; CANR 48, 115; CPW; DA3; MTCW 2

Hawkins, Anthony Hope
See Hope, Anthony

Hawthorne, Julian 1846-1934 .... **TCLC 25**
See also CA 165; HGG

Hawthorne, Nathaniel 1804-1864 ... **NCLC 2, 10, 17, 23, 39, 79, 95; SSC 3, 29, 39; WLC**
See also AAYA 18; AMW; AMWC 1; AMWR 1; BPFB 2; BYA 3; CDALB 1640-1865; DA; DA3; DAB; DAC; DAM MST, NOV; DLB 1, 74, 183, 223, 269; EXPN; EXPS; HGG; LAIT 1; NFS 1, 20; RGAL 4; RGSF 2; SSFS 1, 7, 11, 15; SUFW 1; TUS; WCH; YABC 2

Haxton, Josephine Ayres 1921-
See Douglas, Ellen
See also CA 115; CANR 41, 83

Hayaseca y Eizaguirre, Jorge
See Echegaray (y Eizaguirre), Jose (Maria Waldo)

Hayashi, Fumiko 1904-1951 .... **TCLC 27**
See Hayashi Fumiko
See also CA 161

Hayashi Fumiko
See Hayashi, Fumiko
See also DLB 180; EWL 3

Haycraft, Anna (Margaret) 1932-
See Ellis, Alice Thomas
See also CA 122; CANR 85, 90; MTCW 2

Hayden, Robert E(arl) 1913-1980 ..... **BLC 2; CLC 5, 9, 14, 37; PC 6**
See also AFAW 1, 2; AMWS 2; BW 1, 3; CA 69-72; 97-100; CABS 2; CANR 24, 75, 82; CDALB 1941-1968; DA; DAC; DAM MST, MULT, POET; DLB 5, 76; EWL 3; EXPP; MTCW 1, 2; PFS 1; RGAL 4; SATA 19; SATA-Obit 26; WP

Haydon, Benjamin Robert
1786-1846 .... **NCLC 146**
See also DLB 110

Hayek, F(riedrich) A(ugust von)
1899-1992 .... **TCLC 109**
See also CA 93-96; 137; CANR 20; MTCW 1, 2

Hayford, J(oseph) E(phraim) Casely
See Casely-Hayford, J(oseph) E(phraim)

Hayman, Ronald 1932- .... **CLC 44**
See also CA 25-28R; CANR 18, 50, 88; CD 5; DLB 155

Hayne, Paul Hamilton 1830-1886 . **NCLC 94**
See also DLB 3, 64, 79, 248; RGAL 4

Hays, Mary 1760-1843 .... **NCLC 114**
See also DLB 142, 158; RGEL 2

Haywood, Eliza (Fowler)
1693(?)-1756 .... **LC 1, 44**
See also DLB 39; RGEL 2

Hazlitt, William 1778-1830 ...... **NCLC 29, 82**
See also BRW 4; DLB 110, 158; RGEL 2; TEA

Hazzard, Shirley 1931- .... **CLC 18**
See also CA 9-12R; CANR 4, 70, 127; CN 7; DLB 289; DLBY 1982; MTCW 1

Head, Bessie 1937-1986 ...... **BLC 2; CLC 25, 67; SSC 52**
See also AFW; BW 2, 3; CA 29-32R; 119; CANR 25, 82; CDWLB 3; DA3; DAM MULT; DLB 117, 225; EWL 3; EXPS; FW; MTCW 1, 2; RGSF 2; SSFS 5, 13; WLIT 2; WWE 1

Headon, (Nicky) Topper 1956(?)- ..... **CLC 30**

Heaney, Seamus (Justin) 1939- ..... **CLC 5, 7, 14, 25, 37, 74, 91, 171; PC 18; WLCS**
See also BRWR 1; BRWS 2; CA 85-88; CANR 25, 48, 75, 91, 128; CDBLB 1960 to Present; CP 7; DA3; DAB; DAM POET; DLB 40; DLBY 1995; EWL 3; EXPP; MTCW 1, 2; PAB; PFS 2, 5, 8, 17; RGEL 2; TEA; WLIT 4

Hearn, (Patricio) Lafcadio (Tessima Carlos)
1850-1904 .... **TCLC 9**
See also CA 105; 166; DLB 12, 78, 189; HGG; RGAL 4

Hearne, Samuel 1745-1792 .... **LC 95**
See also DLB 99

Hearne, Vicki 1946-2001 .... **CLC 56**
See also CA 139; 201

Hearon, Shelby 1931- .... **CLC 63**
See also AITN 2; AMWS 8; CA 25-28R; CANR 18, 48, 103; CSW

Heat-Moon, William Least .... **CLC 29**
See Trogdon, William (Lewis)
See also AAYA 9

Hebbel, Friedrich 1813-1863 . **DC 21; NCLC 43**
See also CDWLB 2; DAM DRAM; DLB 129; EW 6; RGWL 2, 3

Hebert, Anne 1916-2000 .... **CLC 4, 13, 29**
See also CA 85-88; 187; CANR 69, 126; CCA 1; CWP; CWW 2; DA3; DAC; DAM MST, POET; DLB 68; EWL 3; GFL 1789 to the Present; MTCW 1, 2; PFS 20

Hecht, Anthony (Evan) 1923- ...... **CLC 8, 13, 19**
See also AMWS 10; CA 9-12R; CANR 6, 108; CP 7; DAM POET; DLB 5, 169; EWL 3; PFS 6; WP

Hecht, Ben 1894-1964 ..... **CLC 8; TCLC 101**
See also CA 85-88; DFS 9; DLB 7, 9, 25, 26, 28, 86; FANT; IDFW 3, 4; RGAL 4

Hedayat, Sadeq 1903-1951 .... **TCLC 21**
See also CA 120; EWL 3; RGSF 2

Hegel, Georg Wilhelm Friedrich
1770-1831 .... **NCLC 46**
See also DLB 90; TWA

Heidegger, Martin 1889-1976 .... **CLC 24**
See also CA 81-84; 65-68; CANR 34; DLB 296; MTCW 1, 2

Heidenstam, (Carl Gustaf) Verner von
1859-1940 .... **TCLC 5**
See also CA 104

Heidi Louise
See Erdrich, Louise

Heifner, Jack 1946- .... **CLC 11**
See also CA 105; CANR 47

Heijermans, Herman 1864-1924 .... **TCLC 24**
See also CA 123; EWL 3

Heilbrun, Carolyn G(old)
1926-2003 .... **CLC 25, 173**
See Cross, Amanda
See also CA 45-48; 220; CANR 1, 28, 58, 94; FW

Hein, Christoph 1944- .... **CLC 154**
See also CA 158; CANR 108; CDWLB 2; CWW 2; DLB 124

Heine, Heinrich 1797-1856 .... **NCLC 4, 54, 147; PC 25**
See also CDWLB 2; DLB 90; EW 5; RGWL 2, 3; TWA

Heinemann, Larry (Curtiss) 1944- .. **CLC 50**
See also CA 110; CAAS 21; CANR 31, 81; DLBD 9; INT CANR-31

Heiney, Donald (William) 1921-1993
See Harris, MacDonald
See also CA 1-4R; 142; CANR 3, 58; FANT

Heinlein, Robert A(nson) 1907-1988 . **CLC 1, 3, 8, 14, 26, 55; SSC 55**
See also AAYA 17; BPFB 2; BYA 4, 13; CA 1-4R; 125; CANR 1, 20, 53; CLR 75; CPW; DA3; DAM POP; DLB 8; EXPS; JRDA; LAIT 5; LMFS 2; MAICYA 1, 2; MTCW 1, 2; RGAL 4; SATA 9, 69; SATA-Obit 56; SCFW; SFW 4; SSFS 7; YAW

Helforth, John
See Doolittle, Hilda

Heliodorus fl. 3rd cent. - .... **CMLC 52**

Hellenhofferu, Vojtech Kapristian z
See Hasek, Jaroslav (Matej Frantisek)

Heller, Joseph 1923-1999 . **CLC 1, 3, 5, 8, 11, 36, 63; TCLC 131, 151; WLC**
See also AAYA 24; AITN 1; AMWS 4; BPFB 2; BYA 1; CA 5-8R; 187; CABS 1; CANR 8, 42, 66, 126; CN 7; CPW; DA;

DA3; DAB; DAC; DAM MST, NOV, POP; DLB 2, 28, 227; DLBY 1980, 2002; EWL 3; EXPN; INT CANR-8; LAIT 4; MTCW 1, 2; NFS 1; RGAL 4; TUS; YAW

Hellman, Lillian (Florence)
1906-1984 .. **CLC 2, 4, 8, 14, 18, 34, 44, 52; DC 1; TCLC 119**
See also AAYA 47; AITN 1, 2; AMWS 1; CA 13-16R; 112; CAD; CANR 33; CWD; DA3; DAM DRAM; DFS 1, 3, 14; DLB 7, 228; DLBY 1984; EWL 3; FW; LAIT 3; MAWW; MTCW 1, 2; RGAL 4; TUS

Helprin, Mark 1947- .... **CLC 7, 10, 22, 32**
See also CA 81-84; CANR 47, 64, 124; CDALBS; CPW; DA3; DAM NOV, POP; DLBY 1985; FANT; MTCW 1, 2; SUFW 2

Helvetius, Claude-Adrien 1715-1771 .. **LC 26**

Helyar, Jane Penelope Josephine 1933-
See Poole, Josephine
See also CA 21-24R; CANR 10, 26; CWRI 5; SATA 82, 138; SATA-Essay 138

Hemans, Felicia 1793-1835 ...... **NCLC 29, 71**
See also DLB 96; RGEL 2

Hemingway, Ernest (Miller)
1899-1961 .... **CLC 1, 3, 6, 8, 10, 13, 19, 30, 34, 39, 41, 44, 50, 61, 80; SSC 1, 25, 36, 40, 63; TCLC 115; WLC**
See also AAYA 19; AMW; AMWC 1; AMWR 1; BPFB 2; BYA 2, 3, 13, 15; CA 77-80; CANR 34; CDALB 1917-1929; DA; DA3; DAB; DAC; DAM MST, NOV, DLB 4, 9, 102, 210; DLBD 1, 15, 16; DLBY 1981, 1987, 1996, 1998; EWL 3; EXPN; EXPS; LAIT 3, 4; LATS 1:1; MTCW 1, 2; NFS 1, 5, 6, 14; RGAL 4; RGSF 2; SSFS 17; TUS; WYA

Hempel, Amy 1951- .... **CLC 39**
See also CA 118; 137; CANR 70; DA3; DLB 218; EXPS; MTCW 2; SSFS 2

Henderson, F. C.
See Mencken, H(enry) L(ouis)

Henderson, Sylvia
See Ashton-Warner, Sylvia (Constance)

Henderson, Zenna (Chlarson)
1917-1983 .... **SSC 29**
See also CA 1-4R; 133; CANR 1, 84; DLB 8; SATA 5; SFW 4

Henkin, Joshua .... **CLC 119**
See also CA 161

Henley, Beth .... **CLC 23; DC 6, 14**
See Henley, Elizabeth Becker
See also CABS 3; CAD; CD 5; CSW; CWD; DFS 2; DLBY 1986; FW

Henley, Elizabeth Becker 1952-
See Henley, Beth
See also CA 107; CANR 32, 73; DA3; DAM DRAM, MST; MTCW 1, 2

Henley, William Ernest 1849-1903 .. **TCLC 8**
See also CA 105; DLB 19; RGEL 2

Hennissart, Martha 1929-
See Lathen, Emma
See also CA 85-88; CANR 64

Henry VIII 1491-1547 .... **LC 10**
See also DLB 132

Henry, O. ..... **SSC 5, 49; TCLC 1, 19; WLC**
See Porter, William Sydney
See also AAYA 41; AMWS 2; EXPS; RGAL 4; RGSF 2; SSFS 2, 18

Henry, Patrick 1736-1799 .... **LC 25**
See also LAIT 1

Henryson, Robert 1430(?)-1506(?) ...... **LC 20**
See also BRWS 7; DLB 146; RGEL 2

Henschke, Alfred
See Klabund

Henson, Lance 1944- .... **NNAL**
See also CA 146; DLB 175

Hentoff, Nat(han Irving) 1925- .... **CLC 26**
See also AAYA 4, 42; BYA 6; CA 1-4R; CAAS 6; CANR 5, 25, 77, 114; CLR 1, 52; INT CANR-25; JRDA; MAICYA 1, 2; SATA 42, 69, 133; SATA-Brief 27; WYA; YAW

Heppenstall, (John) Rayner
1911-1981 .... **CLC 10**
See also CA 1-4R; 103; CANR 29; EWL 3

Heraclitus c. 540B.C.-c. 450B.C. ... **CMLC 22**
See also DLB 176

Herbert, Frank (Patrick)
1920-1986 .... **CLC 12, 23, 35, 44, 85**
See also AAYA 21; BPFB 2; BYA 4, 14; CA 53-56; 118; CANR 5, 43; CDALBS; CPW; DAM POP; DLB 8; INT CANR-5; LAIT 5; MTCW 1, 2; NFS 17; SATA 9, 37; SATA-Obit 47; SCFW 2; SFW 4; YAW

Herbert, George 1593-1633 ...... **LC 24; PC 4**
See also BRW 2; BRWR 2; CDBLB Before 1660; DAB; DAM POET; DLB 126; EXPP; RGEL 2; TEA; WP

Herbert, Zbigniew 1924-1998 ..... **CLC 9, 43; PC 50**
See also CA 89-92; 169; CANR 36, 74; CD-WLB 4; CWW 2; DAM POET; DLB 232; EWL 3; MTCW 1

Herbst, Josephine (Frey)
1897-1969 .... **CLC 34**
See also CA 5-8R; 25-28R; DLB 9

Herder, Johann Gottfried von
1744-1803 .... **NCLC 8**
See also DLB 97; EW 4; TWA

Heredia, Jose Maria 1803-1839 .... **HLCS 2**
See also LAW

Hergesheimer, Joseph 1880-1954 ... **TCLC 11**
See also CA 109; 194; DLB 102, 9; RGAL 4

Herlihy, James Leo 1927-1993 .... **CLC 6**
See also CA 1-4R; 143; CAD; CANR 2

Herman, William
See Bierce, Ambrose (Gwinett)

Hermogenes fl. c. 175- .... **CMLC 6**

Hernandez, Jose 1834-1886 .... **NCLC 17**
See also LAW; RGWL 2, 3; WLIT 1

Herodotus c. 484B.C.-c. 420B.C. .. **CMLC 17**
See also AW 1; CDWLB 1; DLB 176; RGWL 2, 3; TWA

Herrick, Robert 1591-1674 .... **LC 13; PC 9**
See also BRW 2; BRWC 2; DA; DAB; DAC; DAM MST, POP; DLB 126; EXPP; PFS 13; RGAL 4; RGEL 2; TEA; WP

Herring, Guilles
See Somerville, Edith Oenone

Herriot, James 1916-1995 .... **CLC 12**
See Wight, James Alfred
See also AAYA 1, 54; BPFB 2; CA 148; CANR 40; CLR 80; CPW; DAM POP; LAIT 3; MAICYA 2; MAICYAS 1; MTCW 2; SATA 86, 135; TEA; YAW

Herris, Violet
See Hunt, Violet

Herrmann, Dorothy 1941- .... **CLC 44**
See also CA 107

Herrmann, Taffy
See Herrmann, Dorothy

Hersey, John (Richard) 1914-1993 .... **CLC 1, 2, 7, 9, 40, 81, 97**
See also AAYA 29; BPFB 2; CA 17-20R; 140; CANR 33; CDALBS; CPW; DAM POP; DLB 6, 185, 278, 299; MTCW 1, 2; SATA 25; SATA-Obit 76; TUS

Herzen, Aleksandr Ivanovich
1812-1870 .... **NCLC 10, 61**
See Herzen, Alexander

Herzen, Alexander
See Herzen, Aleksandr Ivanovich
See also DLB 277

Herzl, Theodor 1860-1904 .... **TCLC 36**
See also CA 168

Herzog, Werner 1942- .... **CLC 16**
See also CA 89-92

Hesiod c. 8th cent. B.C.- .... **CMLC 5**
See also AW 1; DLB 176; RGWL 2, 3

Hesse, Hermann 1877-1962 ... **CLC 1, 2, 3, 6, 11, 17, 25, 69; SSC 9, 49; TCLC 148; WLC**
See also AAYA 43; BPFB 2; CA 17-18; CAP 2; CDWLB 2; DA; DA3; DAB; DAC; DAM MST, NOV; DLB 66; EW 9; EWL 3; EXPN; LAIT 1; MTCW 1, 2; NFS 6, 15; RGWL 2, 3; SATA 50; TWA

Hewes, Cady
See De Voto, Bernard (Augustine)

Heyen, William 1940- .... **CLC 13, 18**
See also CA 33-36R; 220; CAAE 220; CAAS 9; CANR 98; CP 7; DLB 5

Heyerdahl, Thor 1914-2002 .... **CLC 26**
See also CA 5-8R; 207; CANR 5, 22, 66, 73; LAIT 4; MTCW 1, 2; SATA 2, 52

Heym, Georg (Theodor Franz Arthur)
1887-1912 .... **TCLC 9**
See also CA 106; 181

Heym, Stefan 1913-2001 .... **CLC 41**
See also CA 9-12R; 203; CANR 4; CWW 2; DLB 69; EWL 3

Heyse, Paul (Johann Ludwig von)
1830-1914 .... **TCLC 8**
See also CA 104; 209; DLB 129

Heyward, (Edwin) DuBose
1885-1940 .... **HR 2; TCLC 59**
See also CA 108; 157; DLB 7, 9, 45, 249; SATA 21

Heywood, John 1497(?)-1580(?) .... **LC 65**
See also DLB 136; RGEL 2

Hibbert, Eleanor Alice Burford
1906-1993 .... **CLC 7**
See Holt, Victoria
See also BEST 90:4; CA 17-20R; 140; CANR 9, 28, 59; CMW 4; CPW; DAM POP; MTCW 2; RHW; SATA 2; SATA-Obit 74

Hichens, Robert (Smythe)
1864-1950 .... **TCLC 64**
See also CA 162; DLB 153; HGG; RHW; SUFW

Higgins, Aidan 1927- .... **SSC 68**
See also CA 9-12R; CANR 70, 115; CN 7; DLB 14

Higgins, George V(incent)
1939-1999 .... **CLC 4, 7, 10, 18**
See also BPFB 2; CA 77-80; 186; CAAS 5; CANR 17, 51, 89, 96; CMW 4; CN 7; DLB 2; DLBY 1981, 1998; INT CANR-17; MSW; MTCW 1

Higginson, Thomas Wentworth
1823-1911 .... **TCLC 36**
See also CA 162; DLB 1, 64, 243

Higgonet, Margaret ed. .... **CLC 65**

Highet, Helen
See MacInnes, Helen (Clark)

Highsmith, (Mary) Patricia
1921-1995 .... **CLC 2, 4, 14, 42, 102**
See Morgan, Claire
See also AAYA 48; BRWS 5; CA 1-4R; 147; CANR 1, 20, 48, 62, 108; CMW 4; CPW; DA3; DAM NOV, POP; DLB 306; MSW; MTCW 1, 2

Highwater, Jamake (Mamake)
1942(?)-2001 .... **CLC 12**
See also AAYA 7; BPFB 2; BYA 4; CA 65-68; 199; CAAS 7; CANR 10, 34, 84; CLR 17; CWRI 5; DLB 52; DLBY 1985; JRDA; MAICYA 1, 2; SATA 32, 69; SATA-Brief 30

Highway, Tomson 1951- ...... **CLC 92; NNAL**
See also CA 151; CANR 75; CCA 1; CD 5;
DAC; DAM MULT; DFS 2; MTCW 2

Hijuelos, Oscar 1951- .... **CLC 65; HLC 1**
See also AAYA 25; AMWS 8; BEST 90:1;
CA 123; CANR 50, 75, 125; CPW; DA3;
DAM MULT, POP; DLB 145; HW 1, 2;
LLW 1; MTCW 2; NFS 17; RGAL 4;
WLIT 1

Hikmet, Nazim 1902(?)-1963 .... **CLC 40**
See also CA 141; 93-96; EWL 3

Hildegard von Bingen 1098-1179 . **CMLC 20**
See also DLB 148

Hildesheimer, Wolfgang 1916-1991 .. **CLC 49**
See also CA 101; 135; DLB 69, 124; EWL
3

Hill, Geoffrey (William) 1932- ...... **CLC 5, 8,
18, 45**
See also BRWS 5; CA 81-84; CANR 21,
89; CDBLB 1960 to Present; CP 7; DAM
POET; DLB 40; EWL 3; MTCW 1; RGEL
2

Hill, George Roy 1921-2002 .... **CLC 26**
See also CA 110; 122; 213

Hill, John
See Koontz, Dean R(ay)

Hill, Susan (Elizabeth) 1942- ...... **CLC 4, 113**
See also CA 33-36R; CANR 29, 69, 129;
CN 7; DAB; DAM MST, NOV; DLB 14,
139; HGG; MTCW 1; RHW

Hillard, Asa G. III .... **CLC 70**

Hillerman, Tony 1925- .... **CLC 62, 170**
See also AAYA 40; BEST 89:1; BPFB 2;
CA 29-32R; CANR 21, 42, 65, 97; CMW
4; CPW; DA3; DAM POP; DLB 206, 306;
MSW; RGAL 4; SATA 6; TCWW 2; YAW

Hillesum, Etty 1914-1943 .... **TCLC 49**
See also CA 137

Hilliard, Noel (Harvey) 1929-1996 ... **CLC 15**
See also CA 9-12R; CANR 7, 69; CN 7

Hillis, Rick 1956- .... **CLC 66**
See also CA 134

Hilton, James 1900-1954 .... **TCLC 21**
See also CA 108; 169; DLB 34, 77; FANT;
SATA 34

Hilton, Walter (?)-1396 .... **CMLC 58**
See also DLB 146; RGEL 2

Himes, Chester (Bomar) 1909-1984 .. **BLC 2;
CLC 2, 4, 7, 18, 58, 108; TCLC 139**
See also AFAW 2; BPFB 2; BW 2; CA 25-
28R; 114; CANR 22, 89; CMW 4; DAM
MULT; DLB 2, 76, 143, 226; EWL 3;
MSW; MTCW 1, 2; RGAL 4

Hinde, Thomas .... **CLC 6, 11**
See Chitty, Thomas Willes
See also EWL 3

Hine, (William) Daryl 1936- .... **CLC 15**
See also CA 1-4R; CAAS 15; CANR 1, 20;
CP 7; DLB 60

Hinkson, Katharine Tynan
See Tynan, Katharine

Hinojosa(-Smith), Rolando (R.)
1929- .... **HLC 1**
See Hinojosa-Smith, Rolando
See also CA 131; CAAS 16; CANR 62;
DAM MULT; DLB 82; HW 1, 2; LLW 1;
MTCW 2; RGAL 4

Hinton, S(usan) E(loise) 1950- .. **CLC 30, 111**
See also AAYA 2, 33; BPFB 2; BYA 2, 3;
CA 81-84; CANR 32, 62, 92, 133;
CDALBS; CLR 3, 23; CPW; DA; DA3;
DAB; DAC; DAM MST, NOV; JRDA;
LAIT 5; MAICYA 1, 2; MTCW 1, 2; NFS
5, 9, 15, 16; SATA 19, 58, 115; WYA;
YAW

Hippius, Zinaida (Nikolaevna) .... **TCLC 9**
See Gippius, Zinaida (Nikolaevna)
See also DLB 295; EWL 3

Hiraoka, Kimitake 1925-1970
See Mishima, Yukio
See also CA 97-100; 29-32R; DA3; DAM
DRAM; GLL 1; MTCW 1, 2

Hirsch, E(ric) D(onald), Jr. 1928- .... **CLC 79**
See also CA 25-28R; CANR 27, 51; DLB
67; INT CANR-27; MTCW 1

Hirsch, Edward 1950- .... **CLC 31, 50**
See also CA 104; CANR 20, 42, 102; CP 7;
DLB 120

Hitchcock, Alfred (Joseph)
1899-1980 .... **CLC 16**
See also AAYA 22; CA 159; 97-100; SATA
27; SATA-Obit 24

Hitchens, Christopher (Eric)
1949- .... **CLC 157**
See also CA 152; CANR 89

Hitler, Adolf 1889-1945 .... **TCLC 53**
See also CA 117; 147

Hoagland, Edward 1932- .... **CLC 28**
See also ANW; CA 1-4R; CANR 2, 31, 57,
107; CN 7; DLB 6; SATA 51; TCWW 2

Hoban, Russell (Conwell) 1925- ... **CLC 7, 25**
See also BPFB 2; CA 5-8R; CANR 23, 37,
66, 114; CLR 3, 69; CN 7; CWRI 5; DAM
NOV; DLB 52; FANT; MAICYA 1, 2;
MTCW 1, 2; SATA 1, 40, 78, 136; SFW
4; SUFW 2

Hobbes, Thomas 1588-1679 .... **LC 36**
See also DLB 151, 252, 281; RGEL 2

Hobbs, Perry
See Blackmur, R(ichard) P(almer)

Hobson, Laura Z(ametkin)
1900-1986 .... **CLC 7, 25**
See Field, Peter
See also BPFB 2; CA 17-20R; 118; CANR
55; DLB 28; SATA 52

Hoccleve, Thomas c. 1368-c. 1437 ...... **LC 75**
See also DLB 146; RGEL 2

Hoch, Edward D(entinger) 1930-
See Queen, Ellery
See also CA 29-32R; CANR 11, 27, 51, 97;
CMW 4; DLB 306; SFW 4

Hochhuth, Rolf 1931- .... **CLC 4, 11, 18**
See also CA 5-8R; CANR 33, 75; CWW 2;
DAM DRAM; DLB 124; EWL 3; MTCW
1, 2

Hochman, Sandra 1936- .... **CLC 3, 8**
See also CA 5-8R; DLB 5

Hochwaelder, Fritz 1911-1986 .... **CLC 36**
See Hochwalder, Fritz
See also CA 29-32R; 120; CANR 42; DAM
DRAM; MTCW 1; RGWL 3

Hochwalder, Fritz
See Hochwaelder, Fritz
See also EWL 3; RGWL 2

Hocking, Mary (Eunice) 1921- .... **CLC 13**
See also CA 101; CANR 18, 40

Hodgins, Jack 1938- .... **CLC 23**
See also CA 93-96; CN 7; DLB 60

Hodgson, William Hope
1877(?)-1918 .... **TCLC 13**
See also CA 111; 164; CMW 4; DLB 70,
153, 156, 178; HGG; MTCW 2; SFW 4;
SUFW 1

Hoeg, Peter 1957- .... **CLC 95, 156**
See also CA 151; CANR 75; CMW 4; DA3;
DLB 214; EWL 3; MTCW 2; NFS 17;
RGWL 3; SSFS 18

Hoffman, Alice 1952- .... **CLC 51**
See also AAYA 37; AMWS 10; CA 77-80;
CANR 34, 66, 100; CN 7; CPW; DAM
NOV; DLB 292; MTCW 1, 2

Hoffman, Daniel (Gerard) 1923- . **CLC 6, 13,
23**
See also CA 1-4R; CANR 4; CP 7; DLB 5

Hoffman, Eva 1945- .... **CLC 182**
See also CA 132

Hoffman, Stanley 1944- .... **CLC 5**
See also CA 77-80

Hoffman, William 1925- .... **CLC 141**
See also CA 21-24R; CANR 9, 103; CSW;
DLB 234

Hoffman, William M(oses) 1939- ..... **CLC 40**
See Hoffman, William M.
See also CA 57-60; CANR 11, 71

Hoffmann, E(rnst) T(heodor) A(madeus)
1776-1822 .... **NCLC 2; SSC 13**
See also CDWLB 2; DLB 90; EW 5; RGSF
2; RGWL 2, 3; SATA 27; SUFW 1; WCH

Hofmann, Gert 1931- .... **CLC 54**
See also CA 128; EWL 3

Hofmannsthal, Hugo von 1874-1929 ... **DC 4;
TCLC 11**
See also CA 106; 153; CDWLB 2; DAM
DRAM; DFS 17; DLB 81, 118; EW 9;
EWL 3; RGWL 2, 3

Hogan, Linda 1947- ..... **CLC 73; NNAL; PC
35**
See also AMWS 4; ANW; BYA 12; CA 120,
226; CAAE 226; CANR 45, 73, 129;
CWP; DAM MULT; DLB 175; SATA
132; TCWW 2

Hogarth, Charles
See Creasey, John

Hogarth, Emmett
See Polonsky, Abraham (Lincoln)

Hogg, James 1770-1835 .... **NCLC 4, 109**
See also DLB 93, 116, 159; HGG; RGEL 2;
SUFW 1

Holbach, Paul Henri Thiry Baron
1723-1789 .... **LC 14**

Holberg, Ludvig 1684-1754 .... **LC 6**
See also DLB 300; RGWL 2, 3

Holcroft, Thomas 1745-1809 .... **NCLC 85**
See also DLB 39, 89, 158; RGEL 2

Holden, Ursula 1921- .... **CLC 18**
See also CA 101; CAAS 8; CANR 22

Holderlin, (Johann Christian) Friedrich
1770-1843 .... **NCLC 16; PC 4**
See also CDWLB 2; DLB 90; EW 5; RGWL
2, 3

Holdstock, Robert
See Holdstock, Robert P.

Holdstock, Robert P. 1948- .... **CLC 39**
See also CA 131; CANR 81; DLB 261;
FANT; HGG; SFW 4; SUFW 2

Holinshed, Raphael fl. 1580- .... **LC 69**
See also DLB 167; RGEL 2

Holland, Isabelle (Christian)
1920-2002 .... **CLC 21**
See also AAYA 11; CA 21-24R; 205; CAAE
181; CANR 10, 25, 47; CLR 57; CWRI
5; JRDA; LAIT 4; MAICYA 1, 2; SATA
8, 70; SATA-Essay 103; SATA-Obit 132;
WYA

Holland, Marcus
See Caldwell, (Janet Miriam) Taylor
(Holland)

Hollander, John 1929- .... **CLC 2, 5, 8, 14**
See also CA 1-4R; CANR 1, 52; CP 7; DLB
5; SATA 13

Hollander, Paul
See Silverberg, Robert

Holleran, Andrew 1943(?)- .... **CLC 38**
See Garber, Eric
See also CA 144; GLL 1

Holley, Marietta 1836(?)-1926 .... **TCLC 99**
See also CA 118; DLB 11

Hollinghurst, Alan 1954- .... **CLC 55, 91**
See also CA 114; CN 7; DLB 207; GLL 1

Hollis, Jim
See Summers, Hollis (Spurgeon, Jr.)

Holly, Buddy 1936-1959 .... **TCLC 65**
See also CA 213

Holmes, Gordon
See Shiel, M(atthew) P(hipps)

Hueffer, Ford Madox
See Ford, Ford Madox
Hughart, Barry 1934- .... **CLC 39**
See also CA 137; FANT; SFW 4; SUFW 2
Hughes, Colin
See Creasey, John
Hughes, David (John) 1930- .... **CLC 48**
See also CA 116; 129; CN 7; DLB 14
Hughes, Edward James
See Hughes, Ted
See also DA3; DAM MST, POET
Hughes, (James Mercer) Langston
1902-1967 ..... **BLC 2; CLC 1, 5, 10, 15,
35, 44, 108; DC 3; HR 2; PC 1, 53;
SSC 6; WLC**
See also AAYA 12; AFAW 1, 2; AMWR 1;
AMWS 1; BW 1, 3; CA 1-4R; 25-28R;
CANR 1, 34, 82; CDALB 1929-1941;
CLR 17; DA; DA3; DAB; DAC; DAM
DRAM, MST, MULT, POET; DFS 6, 18;
DLB 4, 7, 48, 51, 86, 228; EWL 3; EXPP;
EXPS; JRDA; LAIT 3; LMFS 2; MAI-
CYA 1, 2; MTCW 1, 2; PAB; PFS 1, 3, 6,
10, 15; RGAL 4; RGSF 2; SATA 4, 33;
SSFS 4, 7; TUS; WCH; WP; YAW
Hughes, Richard (Arthur Warren)
1900-1976 .... **CLC 1, 11**
See also CA 5-8R; 65-68; CANR 4; DAM
NOV; DLB 15, 161; EWL 3; MTCW 1;
RGEL 2; SATA 8; SATA-Obit 25
Hughes, Ted 1930-1998 . **CLC 2, 4, 9, 14, 37,
119; PC 7**
See Hughes, Edward James
See also BRWC 2; BRWR 2; BRWS 1; CA
1-4R; 171; CANR 1, 33, 66, 108; CLR 3;
CP 7; DAB; DAC; DLB 40, 161; EWL 3;
EXPP; MAICYA 1, 2; MTCW 1, 2; PAB;
PFS 4, 19; RGEL 2; SATA 49; SATA-
Brief 27; SATA-Obit 107; TEA; YAW
Hugo, Richard
See Huch, Ricarda (Octavia)
Hugo, Richard F(ranklin)
1923-1982 .... **CLC 6, 18, 32**
See also AMWS 6; CA 49-52; 108; CANR
3; DAM POET; DLB 5, 206; EWL 3; PFS
17; RGAL 4
Hugo, Victor (Marie) 1802-1885 .... **NCLC 3,
10, 21; PC 17; WLC**
See also AAYA 28; DA; DA3; DAB; DAC;
DAM DRAM, MST, NOV, POET; DLB
119, 192, 217; EFS 2; EW 6; EXPN; GFL
1789 to the Present; LAIT 1, 2; NFS 5,
20; RGWL 2, 3; SATA 47; TWA
Huidobro, Vicente
See Huidobro Fernandez, Vicente Garcia
See also DLB 283; EWL 3; LAW
Huidobro Fernandez, Vicente Garcia
1893-1948 .... **TCLC 31**
See Huidobro, Vicente
See also CA 131; HW 1
Hulme, Keri 1947- .... **CLC 39, 130**
See also CA 125; CANR 69; CN 7; CP 7;
CWP; EWL 3; FW; INT CA-125
Hulme, T(homas) E(rnest)
1883-1917 .... **TCLC 21**
See also BRWS 6; CA 117; 203; DLB 19
Humboldt, Wilhelm von
1767-1835 .... **NCLC 134**
See also DLB 90
Hume, David 1711-1776 .... **LC 7, 56**
See also BRWS 3; DLB 104, 252; LMFS 1;
TEA
Humphrey, William 1924-1997 .... **CLC 45**
See also AMWS 9; CA 77-80; 160; CANR
68; CN 7; CSW; DLB 6, 212, 234, 278;
TCWW 2
Humphreys, Emyr Owen 1919- .... **CLC 47**
See also CA 5-8R; CANR 3, 24; CN 7;
DLB 15

Humphreys, Josephine 1945- ..... **CLC 34, 57**
See also CA 121; 127; CANR 97; CSW;
DLB 292; INT CA-127
Huneker, James Gibbons
1860-1921 .... **TCLC 65**
See also CA 193; DLB 71; RGAL 4
Hungerford, Hesba Fay
See Brinsmead, H(esba) F(ay)
Hungerford, Pixie
See Brinsmead, H(esba) F(ay)
Hunt, E(verette) Howard, (Jr.)
1918- .... **CLC 3**
See also AITN 1; CA 45-48; CANR 2, 47,
103; CMW 4
Hunt, Francesca
See Holland, Isabelle (Christian)
Hunt, Howard
See Hunt, E(verette) Howard, (Jr.)
Hunt, Kyle
See Creasey, John
Hunt, (James Henry) Leigh
1784-1859 .... **NCLC 1, 70**
See also DAM POET; DLB 96, 110, 144;
RGEL 2; TEA
Hunt, Marsha 1946- .... **CLC 70**
See also BW 2, 3; CA 143; CANR 79
Hunt, Violet 1866(?)-1942 .... **TCLC 53**
See also CA 184; DLB 162, 197
Hunter, E. Waldo
See Sturgeon, Theodore (Hamilton)
Hunter, Evan 1926- .... **CLC 11, 31**
See McBain, Ed
See also AAYA 39; BPFB 2; CA 5-8R;
CANR 5, 38, 62, 97; CMW 4; CN 7;
CPW; DAM POP; DLB 306; DLBY 1982;
INT CANR-5; MSW; MTCW 1; SATA
25; SFW 4
Hunter, Kristin 1931-
See Lattany, Kristin (Elaine Eggleston)
Hunter
Hunter, Mary
See Austin, Mary (Hunter)
Hunter, Mollie 1922- .... **CLC 21**
See McIlwraith, Maureen Mollie Hunter
See also AAYA 13; BYA 6; CANR 37, 78;
CLR 25; DLB 161; JRDA; MAICYA 1,
2; SAAS 7; SATA 54, 106, 139; SATA-
Essay 139; WYA; YAW
Hunter, Robert (?)-1734 .... **LC 7**
Hurston, Zora Neale 1891-1960 .... **BLC 2;
CLC 7, 30, 61; DC 12; HR 2; SSC 4;
TCLC 121, 131; WLCS**
See also AAYA 15; AFAW 1, 2; AMWS 6;
BW 1, 3; BYA 12; CA 85-88; CANR 61;
CDALBS; DA; DA3; DAC; DAM MST,
MULT, NOV; DFS 6; DLB 51, 86; EWL
3; EXPN; EXPS; FW; LAIT 3; LATS 1:1;
LMFS 2; MAWW; MTCW 1, 2; NFS 3;
RGAL 4; RGSF 2; SSFS 1, 6, 11, 19;
TUS; YAW
Husserl, E. G.
See Husserl, Edmund (Gustav Albrecht)
Husserl, Edmund (Gustav Albrecht)
1859-1938 .... **TCLC 100**
See also CA 116; 133; DLB 296
Huston, John (Marcellus)
1906-1987 .... **CLC 20**
See also CA 73-76; 123; CANR 34; DLB
26
Hustvedt, Siri 1955- .... **CLC 76**
See also CA 137
Hutten, Ulrich von 1488-1523 .... **LC 16**
See also DLB 179
Huxley, Aldous (Leonard)
1894-1963 .... **CLC 1, 3, 4, 5, 8, 11, 18,
35, 79; SSC 39; WLC**
See also AAYA 11; BPFB 2; BRW 7; CA
85-88; CANR 44, 99; CDBLB 1914-1945;
DA; DA3; DAB; DAC; DAM MST, NOV;

DLB 36, 100, 162, 195, 255; EWL 3;
EXPN; LAIT 5; LMFS 2; MTCW 1, 2;
NFS 6; RGEL 2; SATA 63; SCFW 2;
SFW 4; TEA; YAW
Huxley, T(homas) H(enry)
1825-1895 .... **NCLC 67**
See also DLB 57; TEA
Huysmans, Joris-Karl 1848-1907 ... **TCLC 7,
69**
See also CA 104; 165; DLB 123; EW 7;
GFL 1789 to the Present; LMFS 2; RGWL
2, 3
Hwang, David Henry 1957- .... **CLC 55, 196;
DC 4, 23**
See also CA 127; 132; CAD; CANR 76,
124; CD 5; DA3; DAM DRAM; DFS 11,
18; DLB 212, 228; INT CA-132; MTCW
2; RGAL 4
Hyde, Anthony 1946- .... **CLC 42**
See Chase, Nicholas
See also CA 136; CCA 1
Hyde, Margaret O(ldroyd) 1917- ..... **CLC 21**
See also CA 1-4R; CANR 1, 36; CLR 23;
JRDA; MAICYA 1, 2; SAAS 8; SATA 1,
42, 76, 139
Hynes, James 1956(?)- .... **CLC 65**
See also CA 164; CANR 105
Hypatia c. 370-415 .... **CMLC 35**
Ian, Janis 1951- .... **CLC 21**
See also CA 105; 187
Ibanez, Vicente Blasco
See Blasco Ibanez, Vicente
Ibarbourou, Juana de 1895-1979 ..... **HLCS 2**
See also DLB 290; HW 1; LAW
Ibarguengoitia, Jorge 1928-1983 ..... **CLC 37;
TCLC 148**
See also CA 124; 113; EWL 3; HW 1
Ibn Battuta, Abu Abdalla
1304-1368(?) .... **CMLC 57**
See also WLIT 2
Ibn Hazm 994-1064 .... **CMLC 64**
Ibsen, Henrik (Johan) 1828-1906 .... **DC 2;
TCLC 2, 8, 16, 37, 52; WLC**
See also AAYA 46; CA 104; 141; DA; DA3;
DAB; DAC; DAM DRAM, MST; DFS 1,
6, 8, 10, 11, 15, 16; EW 7; LAIT 2; LATS
1:1; RGWL 2, 3
Ibuse, Masuji 1898-1993 .... **CLC 22**
See Ibuse Masuji
See also CA 127; 141; MJW; RGWL 3
Ibuse Masuji
See Ibuse, Masuji
See also CWW 2; DLB 180; EWL 3
Ichikawa, Kon 1915- .... **CLC 20**
See also CA 121
Ichiyo, Higuchi 1872-1896 .... **NCLC 49**
See also MJW
Idle, Eric 1943- .... **CLC 21**
See Monty Python
See also CA 116; CANR 35, 91
Idris, Yusuf 1927-1991 .... **SSC 74**
See also AFW; EWL 3; RGSF 2, 3; RGWL
3; WLIT 2
Ignatow, David 1914-1997 .... **CLC 4, 7, 14,
40; PC 34**
See also CA 9-12R; 162; CAAS 3; CANR
31, 57, 96; CP 7; DLB 5; EWL 3
Ignotus
See Strachey, (Giles) Lytton
Ihimaera, Witi (Tame) 1944- .... **CLC 46**
See also CA 77-80; CANR 130; CN 7;
RGSF 2; SATA 148
Ilf, Ilya .... **TCLC 21**
See Fainzilberg, Ilya Arnoldovich
See also EWL 3
Illyes, Gyula 1902-1983 .... **PC 16**
See also CA 114; 109; CDWLB 4; DLB
215; EWL 3; RGWL 2, 3

James, William 1842-1910 .... **TCLC 15, 32**
See also AMW; CA 109; 193; DLB 270, 284; NCFS 5; RGAL 4

Jameson, Anna 1794-1860 .... **NCLC 43**
See also DLB 99, 166

Jameson, Fredric (R.) 1934- .... **CLC 142**
See also CA 196; DLB 67; LMFS 2

Jami, Nur al-Din 'Abd al-Rahman
1414-1492 .... **LC 9**

Jammes, Francis 1868-1938 .... **TCLC 75**
See also CA 198; EWL 3; GFL 1789 to the Present

Jandl, Ernst 1925-2000 .... **CLC 34**
See also CA 200; EWL 3

Janowitz, Tama 1957- .... **CLC 43, 145**
See also CA 106; CANR 52, 89, 129; CN 7; CPW; DAM POP; DLB 292

Japrisot, Sebastien 1931- .... **CLC 90**
See Rossi, Jean-Baptiste
See also CMW 4; NFS 18

Jarrell, Randall 1914-1965 .... **CLC 1, 2, 6, 9, 13, 49; PC 41**
See also AMW; BYA 5; CA 5-8R; 25-28R; CABS 2; CANR 6, 34; CDALB 1941-1968; CLR 6; CWRI 5; DAM POET; DLB 48, 52; EWL 3; EXPP; MAICYA 1, 2; MTCW 1, 2; PAB; PFS 2; RGAL 4; SATA 7

Jarry, Alfred 1873-1907 .... **SSC 20; TCLC 2, 14, 147**
See also CA 104; 153; DA3; DAM DRAM; DFS 8; DLB 192, 258; EW 9; EWL 3; GFL 1789 to the Present; RGWL 2, 3; TWA

Jarvis, E. K.
See Ellison, Harlan (Jay)

Jawien, Andrzej
See John Paul II, Pope

Jaynes, Roderick
See Coen, Ethan

Jeake, Samuel, Jr.
See Aiken, Conrad (Potter)

Jean Paul 1763-1825 .... **NCLC 7**

Jefferies, (John) Richard
1848-1887 .... **NCLC 47**
See also DLB 98, 141; RGEL 2; SATA 16; SFW 4

Jeffers, (John) Robinson 1887-1962 .. **CLC 2, 3, 11, 15, 54; PC 17; WLC**
See also AMWS 2; CA 85-88; CANR 35; CDALB 1917-1929; DA; DA3; DAM MST, POET; DLB 45, 212; EWL 3; MTCW 1, 2; PAB; PFS 3, 4; RGAL 4

Jefferson, Janet
See Mencken, H(enry) L(ouis)

Jefferson, Thomas 1743-1826 .. **NCLC 11, 103**
See also AAYA 54; ANW; CDALB 1640-1865; DA3; DLB 31, 183; LAIT 1; RGAL 4

Jeffrey, Francis 1773-1850 .... **NCLC 33**
See Francis, Lord Jeffrey

Jelakowitch, Ivan
See Heijermans, Herman

Jelinek, Elfriede 1946- .... **CLC 169**
See also CA 154; DLB 85; FW

Jellicoe, (Patricia) Ann 1927- .... **CLC 27**
See also CA 85-88; CBD; CD 5; CWD; CWRI 5; DLB 13, 233; FW

Jelloun, Tahar ben 1944- .... **CLC 180**
See Ben Jelloun, Tahar
See also CA 162; CANR 100

Jemyma
See Holley, Marietta

Jen, Gish .... **AAL; CLC 70**
See Jen, Lillian
See also AMWC 2

Jen, Lillian 1956(?)-
See Jen, Gish
See also CA 135; CANR 89, 130

Jenkins, (John) Robin 1912- .... **CLC 52**
See also CA 1-4R; CANR 1; CN 7; DLB 14, 271

Jennings, Elizabeth (Joan)
1926-2001 .... **CLC 5, 14, 131**
See also BRWS 5; CA 61-64; 200; CAAS 5; CANR 8, 39, 66, 127; CP 7; CWP; DLB 27; EWL 3; MTCW 1; SATA 66

Jennings, Waylon 1937- .... **CLC 21**

Jensen, Johannes V(ilhelm)
1873-1950 .... **TCLC 41**
See also CA 170; DLB 214; EWL 3; RGWL 3

Jensen, Laura (Linnea) 1948- .... **CLC 37**
See also CA 103

Jerome, Saint 345-420 .... **CMLC 30**
See also RGWL 3

Jerome, Jerome K(lapka)
1859-1927 .... **TCLC 23**
See also CA 119; 177; DLB 10, 34, 135; RGEL 2

Jerrold, Douglas William
1803-1857 .... **NCLC 2**
See also DLB 158, 159; RGEL 2

Jewett, (Theodora) Sarah Orne
1849-1909 .... **SSC 6, 44; TCLC 1, 22**
See also AMW; AMWC 2; AMWR 2; CA 108; 127; CANR 71; DLB 12, 74, 221; EXPS; FW; MAWW; NFS 15; RGAL 4; RGSF 2; SATA 15; SSFS 4

Jewsbury, Geraldine (Endsor)
1812-1880 .... **NCLC 22**
See also DLB 21

Jhabvala, Ruth Prawer 1927- . **CLC 4, 8, 29, 94, 138**
See also BRWS 5; CA 1-4R; CANR 2, 29, 51, 74, 91, 128; CN 7; DAB; DAM NOV; DLB 139, 194; EWL 3; IDFW 3, 4; INT CANR-29; MTCW 1, 2; RGSF 2; RGWL 2; RHW; TEA

Jibran, Kahlil
See Gibran, Kahlil

Jibran, Khalil
See Gibran, Kahlil

Jiles, Paulette 1943- .... **CLC 13, 58**
See also CA 101; CANR 70, 124; CWP

Jimenez (Mantecon), Juan Ramon
1881-1958 .... **HLC 1; PC 7; TCLC 4**
See also CA 104; 131; CANR 74; DAM MULT, POET; DLB 134; EW 9; EWL 3; HW 1; MTCW 1, 2; RGWL 2, 3

Jimenez, Ramon
See Jimenez (Mantecon), Juan Ramon

Jimenez Mantecon, Juan
See Jimenez (Mantecon), Juan Ramon

Jin, Ha .... **CLC 109**
See Jin, Xuefei
See also CA 152; DLB 244, 292; SSFS 17

Jin, Xuefei 1956-
See Jin, Ha
See also CANR 91, 130; SSFS 17

Joel, Billy .... **CLC 26**
See Joel, William Martin

Joel, William Martin 1949-
See Joel, Billy
See also CA 108

John, Saint 10(?)-100 .... **CMLC 27, 63**

John of Salisbury c. 1115-1180 ..... **CMLC 63**

John of the Cross, St. 1542-1591 .... **LC 18**
See also RGWL 2, 3

John Paul II, Pope 1920- .... **CLC 128**
See also CA 106; 133

Johnson, B(ryan) S(tanley William)
1933-1973 .... **CLC 6, 9**
See also CA 9-12R; 53-56; CANR 9; DLB 14, 40; EWL 3; RGEL 2

Johnson, Benjamin F., of Boone
See Riley, James Whitcomb

Johnson, Charles (Richard) 1948- .... **BLC 2; CLC 7, 51, 65, 163**
See also AFAW 2; AMWS 6; BW 2, 3; CA 116; CAAS 18; CANR 42, 66, 82, 129; CN 7; DAM MULT; DLB 33, 278; MTCW 2; RGAL 4; SSFS 16

Johnson, Charles S(purgeon)
1893-1956 .... **HR 3**
See also BW 1, 3; CA 125; CANR 82; DLB 51, 91

Johnson, Denis 1949- . **CLC 52, 160; SSC 56**
See also CA 117; 121; CANR 71, 99; CN 7; DLB 120

Johnson, Diane 1934- .... **CLC 5, 13, 48**
See also BPFB 3; CA 41-44R; CANR 17, 40, 62, 95; CN 7; DLBY 1980; INT CANR-17; MTCW 1

Johnson, E. Pauline 1861-1913 .... **NNAL**
See also CA 150; DAC; DAM MULT; DLB 92, 175

Johnson, Eyvind (Olof Verner)
1900-1976 .... **CLC 14**
See also CA 73-76; 69-72; CANR 34, 101; DLB 259; EW 12; EWL 3

Johnson, Fenton 1888-1958 .... **BLC 2**
See also BW 1; CA 118; 124; DAM MULT; DLB 45, 50

Johnson, Georgia Douglas (Camp)
1880-1966 .... **HR 3**
See also BW 1; CA 125; DLB 51, 249; WP

Johnson, Helene 1907-1995 .... **HR 3**
See also CA 181; DLB 51; WP

Johnson, J. R.
See James, C(yril) L(ionel) R(obert)

Johnson, James Weldon 1871-1938 .. **BLC 2; HR 3; PC 24; TCLC 3, 19**
See also AFAW 1, 2; BW 1, 3; CA 104; 125; CANR 82; CDALB 1917-1929; CLR 32; DA3; DAM MULT, POET; DLB 51; EWL 3; EXPP; LMFS 2; MTCW 1, 2; PFS 1; RGAL 4; SATA 31; TUS

Johnson, Joyce 1935- .... **CLC 58**
See also BG 3; CA 125; 129; CANR 102

Johnson, Judith (Emlyn) 1936- ... **CLC 7, 15**
See Sherwin, Judith Johnson
See also CA 25-28R; 153; CANR 34

Johnson, Lionel (Pigot)
1867-1902 .... **TCLC 19**
See also CA 117; 209; DLB 19; RGEL 2

Johnson, Marguerite Annie
See Angelou, Maya

Johnson, Mel
See Malzberg, Barry N(athaniel)

Johnson, Pamela Hansford
1912-1981 .... **CLC 1, 7, 27**
See also CA 1-4R; 104; CANR 2, 28; DLB 15; MTCW 1, 2; RGEL 2

Johnson, Paul (Bede) 1928- .... **CLC 147**
See also BEST 89:4; CA 17-20R; CANR 34, 62, 100

Johnson, Robert .... **CLC 70**

Johnson, Robert 1911(?)-1938 .... **TCLC 69**
See also BW 3; CA 174

Johnson, Samuel 1709-1784 .... **LC 15, 52; WLC**
See also BRW 3; BRWR 1; CDBLB 1660-1789; DA; DAB; DAC; DAM MST; DLB 39, 95, 104, 142, 213; LMFS 1; RGEL 2; TEA

Johnson, Uwe 1934-1984 .. **CLC 5, 10, 15, 40**
See also CA 1-4R; 112; CANR 1, 39; CD-WLB 2; DLB 75; EWL 3; MTCW 1; RGWL 2, 3

Johnston, Basil H. 1929- .... **NNAL**
See also CA 69-72; CANR 11, 28, 66; DAC; DAM MULT; DLB 60

Johnston, George (Benson) 1913- .... **CLC 51**
See also CA 1-4R; CANR 5, 20; CP 7; DLB 88

Kanin, Garson 1912-1999 .... **CLC 22**
See also AITN 1; CA 5-8R; 177; CAD;
CANR 7, 78; DLB 7; IDFW 3, 4

Kaniuk, Yoram 1930- .... **CLC 19**
See also CA 134; DLB 299

Kant, Immanuel 1724-1804 ..... **NCLC 27, 67**
See also DLB 94

Kantor, MacKinlay 1904-1977 .... **CLC 7**
See also CA 61-64; 73-76; CANR 60, 63;
DLB 9, 102; MTCW 2; RHW; TCWW 2

Kanze Motokiyo
See Zeami

Kaplan, David Michael 1946- .... **CLC 50**
See also CA 187

Kaplan, James 1951- .... **CLC 59**
See also CA 135; CANR 121

Karadzic, Vuk Stefanovic
1787-1864 .... **NCLC 115**
See also CDWLB 4; DLB 147

Karageorge, Michael
See Anderson, Poul (William)

Karamzin, Nikolai Mikhailovich
1766-1826 .... **NCLC 3**
See also DLB 150; RGSF 2

Karapanou, Margarita 1946- .... **CLC 13**
See also CA 101

Karinthy, Frigyes 1887-1938 .... **TCLC 47**
See also CA 170; DLB 215; EWL 3

Karl, Frederick R(obert)
1927-2004 .... **CLC 34**
See also CA 5-8R; 226; CANR 3, 44

Karr, Mary 1955- .... **CLC 188**
See also AMWS 11; CA 151; CANR 100;
NCFS 5

Kastel, Warren
See Silverberg, Robert

Kataev, Evgeny Petrovich 1903-1942
See Petrov, Evgeny
See also CA 120

Kataphusin
See Ruskin, John

Katz, Steve 1935- .... **CLC 47**
See also CA 25-28R; CAAS 14, 64; CANR
12; CN 7; DLBY 1983

Kauffman, Janet 1945- .... **CLC 42**
See also CA 117; CANR 43, 84; DLB 218;
DLBY 1986

Kaufman, Bob (Garnell) 1925-1986 . **CLC 49**
See also BG 3; BW 1; CA 41-44R; 118;
CANR 22; DLB 16, 41

Kaufman, George S. 1889-1961 ...... **CLC 38;
DC 17**
See also CA 108; 93-96; DAM DRAM;
DFS 1, 10; DLB 7; INT CA-108; MTCW
2; RGAL 4; TUS

Kaufman, Sue .... **CLC 3, 8**
See Barondess, Sue K(aufman)

Kavafis, Konstantinos Petrou 1863-1933
See Cavafy, C(onstantine) P(eter)
See also CA 104

Kavan, Anna 1901-1968 .... **CLC 5, 13, 82**
See also BRWS 7; CA 5-8R; CANR 6, 57;
DLB 255; MTCW 1; RGEL 2; SFW 4

Kavanagh, Dan
See Barnes, Julian (Patrick)

Kavanagh, Julie 1952- .... **CLC 119**
See also CA 163

Kavanagh, Patrick (Joseph)
1904-1967 .... **CLC 22; PC 33**
See also BRWS 7; CA 123; 25-28R; DLB
15, 20; EWL 3; MTCW 1; RGEL 2

Kawabata, Yasunari 1899-1972 ..... **CLC 2, 5,
9, 18, 107; SSC 17**
See Kawabata Yasunari
See also CA 93-96; 33-36R; CANR 88;
DAM MULT; MJW; MTCW 2; RGSF 2;
RGWL 2, 3

Kawabata Yasunari
See Kawabata, Yasunari
See also DLB 180; EWL 3

Kaye, M(ary) M(argaret)
1908-2004 .... **CLC 28**
See also CA 89-92; 223; CANR 24, 60, 102;
MTCW 1, 2; RHW; SATA 62; SATA-Obit
152

Kaye, Mollie
See Kaye, M(ary) M(argaret)

Kaye-Smith, Sheila 1887-1956 .... **TCLC 20**
See also CA 118; 203; DLB 36

Kaymor, Patrice Maguilene
See Senghor, Leopold Sedar

Kazakov, Iurii Pavlovich
See Kazakov, Yuri Pavlovich
See also DLB 302

Kazakov, Yuri Pavlovich 1927-1982 . **SSC 43**
See also Kazakov, Iurii Pavlovich; Kazakov,
Yury
See also CA 5-8R; CANR 36; MTCW 1;
RGSF 2

Kazakov, Yury
See Kazakov, Yuri Pavlovich
See also EWL 3

Kazan, Elia 1909-2003 .... **CLC 6, 16, 63**
See also CA 21-24R; 220; CANR 32, 78

Kazantzakis, Nikos 1883(?)-1957 .... **TCLC 2,
5, 33**
See also BPFB 2; CA 105; 132; DA3; EW
9; EWL 3; MTCW 1, 2; RGWL 2, 3

Kazin, Alfred 1915-1998 ..... **CLC 34, 38, 119**
See also AMWS 8; CA 1-4R; CAAS 7;
CANR 1, 45, 79; DLB 67; EWL 3

Keane, Mary Nesta (Skrine) 1904-1996
See Keane, Molly
See also CA 108; 114; 151; CN 7; RHW

Keane, Molly .... **CLC 31**
See Keane, Mary Nesta (Skrine)
See also INT CA-114

Keates, Jonathan 1946(?)- .... **CLC 34**
See also CA 163; CANR 126

Keaton, Buster 1895-1966 .... **CLC 20**
See also CA 194

Keats, John 1795-1821 ...... **NCLC 8, 73, 121;
PC 1; WLC**
See also AAYA 58; BRW 4; BRWR 1; CD-
BLB 1789-1832; DA; DA3; DAB; DAC;
DAM MST, POET; DLB 96, 110; EXPP;
LMFS 1; PAB; PFS 1, 2, 3, 9, 17; RGEL
2; TEA; WLIT 3; WP

Keble, John 1792-1866 .... **NCLC 87**
See also DLB 32, 55; RGEL 2

Keene, Donald 1922- .... **CLC 34**
See also CA 1-4R; CANR 5, 119

Keillor, Garrison .... **CLC 40, 115**
See Keillor, Gary (Edward)
See also AAYA 2; BEST 89:3; BPFB 2;
DLBY 1987; EWL 3; SATA 58; TUS

Keillor, Gary (Edward) 1942-
See Keillor, Garrison
See also CA 111; 117; CANR 36, 59, 124;
CPW; DA3; DAM POP; MTCW 1, 2

Keith, Carlos
See Lewton, Val

Keith, Michael
See Hubbard, L(afayette) Ron(ald)

Keller, Gottfried 1819-1890 .... **NCLC 2; SSC
26**
See also CDWLB 2; DLB 129; EW; RGSF
2; RGWL 2, 3

Keller, Nora Okja 1965- .... **CLC 109**
See also CA 187

Kellerman, Jonathan 1949- .... **CLC 44**
See also AAYA 35; BEST 90:1; CA 106;
CANR 29, 51; CMW 4; CPW; DA3;
DAM POP; INT CANR-29

Kelley, William Melvin 1937- .... **CLC 22**
See also BW 1; CA 77-80; CANR 27, 83;
CN 7; DLB 33; EWL 3

Kellogg, Marjorie 1922- .... **CLC 2**
See also CA 81-84

Kellow, Kathleen
See Hibbert, Eleanor Alice Burford

Kelly, M(ilton) T(errence) 1947- ...... **CLC 55**
See also CA 97-100; CAAS 22; CANR 19,
43, 84; CN 7

Kelly, Robert 1935- .... **SSC 50**
See also CA 17-20R; CAAS 19; CANR 47;
CP 7; DLB 5, 130, 165

Kelman, James 1946- .... **CLC 58, 86**
See also BRWS 5; CA 148; CANR 85, 130;
CN 7; DLB 194; RGSF 2; WLIT 4

Kemal, Yasar
See Kemal, Yashar
See also CWW 2; EWL 3

Kemal, Yashar 1923(?)- .... **CLC 14, 29**
See also CA 89-92; CANR 44

Kemble, Fanny 1809-1893 .... **NCLC 18**
See also DLB 32

Kemelman, Harry 1908-1996 .... **CLC 2**
See also AITN 1; BPFB 2; CA 9-12R; 155;
CANR 6, 71; CMW 4; DLB 28

Kempe, Margery 1373(?)-1440(?) ... **LC 6, 56**
See also DLB 146; RGEL 2

Kempis, Thomas a 1380-1471 .... **LC 11**

Kendall, Henry 1839-1882 .... **NCLC 12**
See also DLB 230

Keneally, Thomas (Michael) 1935- ... **CLC 5,
8, 10, 14, 19, 27, 43, 117**
See also BRWS 4; CA 85-88; CANR 10,
50, 74, 130; CN 7; CPW; DA3; DAM
NOV; DLB 289, 299; EWL 3; MTCW 1,
2; NFS 17; RGEL 2; RHW

Kennedy, A(lison) L(ouise) 1965- ... **CLC 188**
See also CA 168, 213; CAAE 213; CANR
108; CD 5; CN 7; DLB 271; RGSF 2

Kennedy, Adrienne (Lita) 1931- .... **BLC 2;
CLC 66; DC 5**
See also AFAW 2; BW 2, 3; CA 103; CAAS
20; CABS 3; CANR 26, 53, 82; CD 5;
DAM MULT; DFS 9; DLB 38; FW

Kennedy, John Pendleton
1795-1870 .... **NCLC 2**
See also DLB 3, 248, 254; RGAL 4

Kennedy, Joseph Charles 1929-
See Kennedy, X. J.
See also CA 1-4R; 201; CAAE 201; CANR
4, 30, 40; CP 7; CWRI 5; MAICYA 2;
MAICYAS 1; SATA 14, 86, 130; SATA-
Essay 130

Kennedy, William 1928- ... **CLC 6, 28, 34, 53**
See also AAYA 1; AMWS 7; BPFB 2; CA
85-88; CANR 14, 31, 76; CN 7; DA3;
DAM NOV; DLB 143; DLBY 1985; EWL
3; INT CANR-31; MTCW 1, 2; SATA 57

Kennedy, X. J. .... **CLC 8, 42**
See Kennedy, Joseph Charles
See also CAAS 9; CLR 27; DLB 5; SAAS
22

Kenny, Maurice (Francis) 1929- ..... **CLC 87;
NNAL**
See also CA 144; CAAS 22; DAM MULT;
DLB 175

Kent, Kelvin
See Kuttner, Henry

Kenton, Maxwell
See Southern, Terry

Kenyon, Jane 1947-1995 .... **PC 57**
See also AMWS 7; CA 118; 148; CANR
44, 69; CP 7; CWP; DLB 120; PFS 9, 17;
RGAL 4

Kenyon, Robert O.
See Kuttner, Henry

Kepler, Johannes 1571-1630 .... **LC 45**

Krumwitz
See Crumb, R(obert)

Krutch, Joseph Wood 1893-1970 ..... **CLC 24**
See also ANW; CA 1-4R; 25-28R; CANR 4; DLB 63, 206, 275

Krutzch, Gus
See Eliot, T(homas) S(tearns)

Krylov, Ivan Andreevich
1768(?)-1844 .... **NCLC 1**
See also DLB 150

Kubin, Alfred (Leopold Isidor)
1877-1959 .... **TCLC 23**
See also CA 112; 149; CANR 104; DLB 81

Kubrick, Stanley 1928-1999 .... **CLC 16;**
TCLC 112
See also AAYA 30; CA 81-84; 177; CANR 33; DLB 26

Kumin, Maxine (Winokur) 1925- ..... **CLC 5,**
13, 28, 164; PC 15
See also AITN 2; AMWS 4; ANW; CA 1-4R; CAAS 8; CANR 1, 21, 69, 115; CP 7; CWP; DA3; DAM POET; DLB 5; EWL 3; EXPP; MTCW 1, 2; PAB; PFS 18; SATA 12

Kundera, Milan 1929- . **CLC 4, 9, 19, 32, 68,**
115, 135; SSC 24
See also AAYA 2; BPFB 2; CA 85-88; CANR 19, 52, 74; CDWLB 4; CWW 2; DA3; DAM NOV; DLB 232; EW 13; EWL 3; MTCW 1, 2; NFS 18; RGSF 2; RGWL 3; SSFS 10

Kunene, Mazisi (Raymond) 1930- ... **CLC 85**
See also BW 1, 3; CA 125; CANR 81; CP 7; DLB 117

Kung, Hans .... **CLC 130**
See Kung, Hans

Kung, Hans 1928-
See Kung, Hans
See also CA 53-56; CANR 66; MTCW 1, 2

Kunikida Doppo 1869(?)-1908
See Doppo, Kunikida
See also DLB 180; EWL 3

Kunitz, Stanley (Jasspon) 1905- .. **CLC 6, 11,**
14, 148; PC 19
See also AMWS 3; CA 41-44R; CANR 26, 57, 98; CP 7; DA3; DLB 48; INT CANR-26; MTCW 1, 2; PFS 11; RGAL 4

Kunze, Reiner 1933- .... **CLC 10**
See also CA 93-96; CWW 2; DLB 75; EWL 3

Kuprin, Aleksander Ivanovich
1870-1938 .... **TCLC 5**
See Kuprin, Aleksandr Ivanovich; Kuprin, Alexandr Ivanovich
See also CA 104; 182

Kuprin, Aleksandr Ivanovich
See Kuprin, Aleksander Ivanovich
See also DLB 295

Kuprin, Alexandr Ivanovich
See Kuprin, Aleksander Ivanovich
See also EWL 3

Kureishi, Hanif 1954(?)- .... **CLC 64, 135**
See also CA 139; CANR 113; CBD; CD 5; CN 7; DLB 194, 245; GLL 2; IDFW 4; WLIT 4; WWE 1

Kurosawa, Akira 1910-1998 ..... **CLC 16, 119**
See also AAYA 11; CA 101; 170; CANR 46; DAM MULT

Kushner, Tony 1956(?)- .... **CLC 81; DC 10**
See also AMWS 9; CA 144; CAD; CANR 74, 130; CD 5; DA3; DAM DRAM; DFS 5; DLB 228; EWL 3; GLL 1; LAIT 5; MTCW 2; RGAL 4

Kuttner, Henry 1915-1958 .... **TCLC 10**
See also CA 107; 157; DLB 8; FANT; SCFW 2; SFW 4

Kutty, Madhavi
See Das, Kamala

Kuzma, Greg 1944- .... **CLC 7**
See also CA 33-36R; CANR 70

Kuzmin, Mikhail (Alekseevich)
1872(?)-1936 .... **TCLC 40**
See also CA 170; DLB 295; EWL 3

Kyd, Thomas 1558-1594 .... **DC 3; LC 22**
See also BRW 1; DAM DRAM; DLB 62; IDTP; LMFS 1; RGEL 2; TEA; WLIT 3

Kyprianos, Iossif
See Samarakis, Antonis

L. S.
See Stephen, Sir Leslie

Laȝamon
See Layamon
See also DLB 146

Labrunie, Gerard
See Nerval, Gerard de

La Bruyere, Jean de 1645-1696 .... **LC 17**
See also DLB 268; EW 3; GFL Beginnings to 1789

Lacan, Jacques (Marie Emile)
1901-1981 .... **CLC 75**
See also CA 121; 104; DLB 296; EWL 3; TWA

Laclos, Pierre Ambroise Francois
1741-1803 .... **NCLC 4, 87**
See also EW 4; GFL Beginnings to 1789; RGWL 2, 3

Lacolere, Francois
See Aragon, Louis

La Colere, Francois
See Aragon, Louis

La Deshabilleuse
See Simenon, Georges (Jacques Christian)

Lady Gregory
See Gregory, Lady Isabella Augusta (Persse)

Lady of Quality, A
See Bagnold, Enid

La Fayette, Marie-(Madelaine Pioche de la
Vergne) 1634-1693 .... **LC 2**
See Lafayette, Marie-Madeleine
See also GFL Beginnings to 1789; RGWL 2, 3

Lafayette, Marie-Madeleine
See La Fayette, Marie-(Madelaine Pioche de la Vergne)
See also DLB 268

Lafayette, Rene
See Hubbard, L(afayette) Ron(ald)

La Flesche, Francis 1857(?)-1932 ...... **NNAL**
See also CA 144; CANR 83; DLB 175

La Fontaine, Jean de 1621-1695 .... **LC 50**
See also DLB 268; EW 3; GFL Beginnings to 1789; MAICYA 1, 2; RGWL 2, 3; SATA 18

Laforgue, Jules 1860-1887 . **NCLC 5, 53; PC**
14; SSC 20
See also DLB 217; EW 7; GFL 1789 to the Present; RGWL 2, 3

Lagerkvist, Paer (Fabian)
1891-1974 ..... **CLC 7, 10, 13, 54; TCLC**
144
See Lagerkvist, Par
See also CA 85-88; 49-52; DA3; DAM DRAM, NOV; MTCW 1, 2; TWA

Lagerkvist, Par .... **SSC 12**
See Lagerkvist, Paer (Fabian)
See also DLB 259; EW 10; EWL 3; MTCW 2; RGSF 2; RGWL 2, 3

Lagerloef, Selma (Ottiliana Lovisa)
1858-1940 .... **TCLC 4, 36**
See Lagerlof, Selma (Ottiliana Lovisa)
See also CA 108; MTCW 2; SATA 15

Lagerlof, Selma (Ottiliana Lovisa)
See Lagerloef, Selma (Ottiliana Lovisa)
See also CLR 7; SATA 15

La Guma, (Justin) Alex(ander)
1925-1985 . **BLCS; CLC 19; TCLC 140**
See also AFW; BW 1, 3; CA 49-52; 118; CANR 25, 81; CDWLB 3; DAM NOV; DLB 117, 225; EWL 3; MTCW 1, 2; WLIT 2; WWE 1

Laidlaw, A. K.
See Grieve, C(hristopher) M(urray)

Lainez, Manuel Mujica
See Mujica Lainez, Manuel
See also HW 1

Laing, R(onald) D(avid) 1927-1989 . **CLC 95**
See also CA 107; 129; CANR 34; MTCW 1

Laishley, Alex
See Booth, Martin

Lamartine, Alphonse (Marie Louis Prat) de
1790-1869 .... **NCLC 11; PC 16**
See also DAM POET; DLB 217; GFL 1789 to the Present; RGWL 2, 3

Lamb, Charles 1775-1834 ..... **NCLC 10, 113;**
WLC
See also BRW 4; CDBLB 1789-1832; DA; DAB; DAC; DAM MST; DLB 93, 107, 163; RGEL 2; SATA 17; TEA

Lamb, Lady Caroline 1785-1828 ... **NCLC 38**
See also DLB 116

Lamb, Mary Ann 1764-1847 .... **NCLC 125**
See also DLB 163; SATA 17

Lame Deer 1903(?)-1976 .... **NNAL**
See also CA 69-72

Lamming, George (William) 1927- ... **BLC 2;**
CLC 2, 4, 66, 144
See also BW 2, 3; CA 85-88; CANR 26, 76; CDWLB 3; CN 7; DAM MULT; DLB 125; EWL 3; MTCW 1, 2; NFS 15; RGEL 2

L'Amour, Louis (Dearborn)
1908-1988 .... **CLC 25, 55**
See Burns, Tex; Mayo, Jim
See also AAYA 16; AITN 2; BEST 89:2; BPFB 2; CA 1-4R; 125; CANR 3, 25, 40; CPW; DA3; DAM NOV, POP; DLB 206; DLBY 1980; MTCW 1, 2; RGAL 4

Lampedusa, Giuseppe (Tomasi) di
.... **TCLC 13**
See Tomasi di Lampedusa, Giuseppe
See also CA 164; EW 11; MTCW 2; RGWL 2, 3

Lampman, Archibald 1861-1899 ... **NCLC 25**
See also DLB 92; RGEL 2; TWA

Lancaster, Bruce 1896-1963 .... **CLC 36**
See also CA 9-10; CANR 70; CAP 1; SATA 9

Lanchester, John 1962- .... **CLC 99**
See also CA 194; DLB 267

Landau, Mark Alexandrovich
See Aldanov, Mark (Alexandrovich)

Landau-Aldanov, Mark Alexandrovich
See Aldanov, Mark (Alexandrovich)

Landis, Jerry
See Simon, Paul (Frederick)

Landis, John 1950- .... **CLC 26**
See also CA 112; 122; CANR 128

Landolfi, Tommaso 1908-1979 .... **CLC 11, 49**
See also CA 127; 117; DLB 177; EWL 3

Landon, Letitia Elizabeth
1802-1838 .... **NCLC 15**
See also DLB 96

Landor, Walter Savage
1775-1864 .... **NCLC 14**
See also BRW 4; DLB 93, 107; RGEL 2

Landwirth, Heinz 1927-
See Lind, Jakov
See also CA 9-12R; CANR 7

Lane, Patrick 1939- .... **CLC 25**
See also CA 97-100; CANR 54; CP 7; DAM POET; DLB 53; INT CA-97-100

Mackay, Mary 1855-1924
  See Corelli, Marie
  See also CA 118; 177; FANT; RHW
Mackay, Shena 1944- .... **CLC 195**
  See also CA 104; CANR 88; DLB 231
Mackenzie, Compton (Edward Montague)
  1883-1972 .... **CLC 18; TCLC 116**
  See also CA 21-22; 37-40R; CAP 2; DLB
  34, 100; RGEL 2
Mackenzie, Henry 1745-1831 .... **NCLC 41**
  See also DLB 39; RGEL 2
Mackey, Nathaniel (Ernest) 1947- .... **PC 49**
  See also CA 153; CANR 114; CP 7; DLB
  169
MacKinnon, Catharine A. 1946- .... **CLC 181**
  See also CA 128; 132; CANR 73; FW;
  MTCW 2
Mackintosh, Elizabeth 1896(?)-1952
  See Tey, Josephine
  See also CA 110; CMW 4
MacLaren, James
  See Grieve, C(hristopher) M(urray)
Mac Laverty, Bernard 1942- .... **CLC 31**
  See also CA 116; 118; CANR 43, 88; CN
  7; DLB 267; INT CA-118; RGSF 2
MacLean, Alistair (Stuart)
  1922(?)-1987 .... **CLC 3, 13, 50, 63**
  See also CA 57-60; 121; CANR 28, 61;
  CMW 4; CPW; DAM POP; DLB 276;
  MTCW 1; SATA 23; SATA-Obit 50;
  TCWW 2
Maclean, Norman (Fitzroy)
  1902-1990 .... **CLC 78; SSC 13**
  See also CA 102; 132; CANR 49; CPW;
  DAM POP; DLB 206; TCWW 2
MacLeish, Archibald 1892-1982 ... **CLC 3, 8,
  14, 68; PC 47**
  See also AMW; CA 9-12R; 106; CAD;
  CANR 33, 63; CDALBS; DAM POET;
  DFS 15; DLB 4, 7, 45; DLBY 1982; EWL
  3; EXPP; MTCW 1, 2; PAB; PFS 5;
  RGAL 4; TUS
MacLennan, (John) Hugh
  1907-1990 .... **CLC 2, 14, 92**
  See also CA 5-8R; 142; CANR 33; DAC;
  DAM MST; DLB 68; EWL 3; MTCW 1,
  2; RGEL 2; TWA
MacLeod, Alistair 1936- .... **CLC 56, 165**
  See also CA 123; CCA 1; DAC; DAM
  MST; DLB 60; MTCW 2; RGSF 2
Macleod, Fiona
  See Sharp, William
  See also RGEL 2; SUFW
MacNeice, (Frederick) Louis
  1907-1963 .... **CLC 1, 4, 10, 53**
  See also BRW 7; CA 85-88; CANR 61;
  DAB; DAM POET; DLB 10, 20; EWL 3;
  MTCW 1, 2; RGEL 2
MacNeill, Dand
  See Fraser, George MacDonald
Macpherson, James 1736-1796 .... **LC 29**
  See Ossian
  See also BRWS 8; DLB 109; RGEL 2
Macpherson, (Jean) Jay 1931- .... **CLC 14**
  See also CA 5-8R; CANR 90; CP 7; CWP;
  DLB 53
Macrobius fl. 430- .... **CMLC 48**
MacShane, Frank 1927-1999 .... **CLC 39**
  See also CA 9-12R; 186; CANR 3, 33; DLB
  111
Macumber, Mari
  See Sandoz, Mari(e Susette)
Madach, Imre 1823-1864 .... **NCLC 19**
Madden, (Jerry) David 1933- .... **CLC 5, 15**
  See also CA 1-4R; CAAS 3; CANR 4, 45;
  CN 7; CSW; DLB 6; MTCW 1
Maddern, Al(an)
  See Ellison, Harlan (Jay)

Madhubuti, Haki R. 1942- ... **BLC 2; CLC 6,
  73; PC 5**
  See Lee, Don L.
  See also BW 2, 3; CA 73-76; CANR 24,
  51, 73; CP 7; CSW; DAM MULT, POET;
  DLB 5, 41; DLBD 8; EWL 3; MTCW 2;
  RGAL 4
Madison, James 1751-1836 .... **NCLC 126**
  See also DLB 37
Maepenn, Hugh
  See Kuttner, Henry
Maepenn, K. H.
  See Kuttner, Henry
Maeterlinck, Maurice 1862-1949 ..... **TCLC 3**
  See also CA 104; 136; CANR 80; DAM
  DRAM; DLB 192; EW 8; EWL 3; GFL
  1789 to the Present; LMFS 2; RGWL 2,
  3; SATA 66; TWA
Maginn, William 1794-1842 .... **NCLC 8**
  See also DLB 110, 159
Mahapatra, Jayanta 1928- .... **CLC 33**
  See also CA 73-76; CAAS 9; CANR 15,
  33, 66, 87; CP 7; DAM MULT
Mahfouz, Naguib (Abdel Aziz Al-Sabilgi)
  1911(?)- .... **CLC 153; SSC 66**
  See Mahfuz, Najib (Abdel Aziz al-Sabilgi)
  See also AAYA 49; BEST 89:2; CA 128;
  CANR 55, 101; DA3; DAM NOV;
  MTCW 1, 2; RGWL 2; SSFS 9
Mahfuz, Najib (Abdel Aziz al-Sabilgi)
  .... **CLC 52, 55**
  See Mahfouz, Naguib (Abdel Aziz Al-
  Sabilgi)
  See also AFW; CWW 2; DLBY 1988; EWL
  3; RGSF 2; WLIT 2
Mahon, Derek 1941- .... **CLC 27; PC 60**
  See also BRWS 6; CA 113; 128; CANR 88;
  CP 7; DLB 40; EWL 3
Maiakovskii, Vladimir
  See Mayakovski, Vladimir (Vladimirovich)
  See also IDTP; RGWL 2, 3
Mailer, Norman (Kingsley) 1923- . **CLC 1, 2,
  3, 4, 5, 8, 11, 14, 28, 39, 74, 111**
  See also AAYA 31; AITN 2; AMW; AMWC
  2; AMWR 2; BPFB 2; CA 9-12R; CABS
  1; CANR 28, 74, 77, 130; CDALB 1968-
  1988; CN 7; CPW; DA; DA3; DAB;
  DAC; DAM MST, NOV, POP; DLB 2,
  16, 28, 185, 278; DLBD 3; DLBY 1980,
  1983; EWL 3; MTCW 1, 2; NFS 10;
  RGAL 4; TUS
Maillet, Antonine 1929- .... **CLC 54, 118**
  See also CA 115; 120; CANR 46, 74, 77;
  CCA 1; CWW 2; DAC; DLB 60; INT CA-
  120; MTCW 2
Mais, Roger 1905-1955 .... **TCLC 8**
  See also BW 1, 3; CA 105; 124; CANR 82;
  CDWLB 3; DLB 125; EWL 3; MTCW 1;
  RGEL 2
Maistre, Joseph 1753-1821 .... **NCLC 37**
  See also GFL 1789 to the Present
Maitland, Frederic William
  1850-1906 .... **TCLC 65**
Maitland, Sara (Louise) 1950- .... **CLC 49**
  See also CA 69-72; CANR 13, 59; DLB
  271; FW
Major, Clarence 1936- ..... **BLC 2; CLC 3, 19,
  48**
  See also AFAW 2; BW 2, 3; CA 21-24R;
  CAAS 6; CANR 13, 25, 53, 82; CN 7;
  CP 7; CSW; DAM MULT; DLB 33; EWL
  3; MSW
Major, Kevin (Gerald) 1949- .... **CLC 26**
  See also AAYA 16; CA 97-100; CANR 21,
  38, 112; CLR 11; DAC; DLB 60; INT
  CANR-21; JRDA; MAICYA 1, 2; MAIC-
  YAS 1; SATA 32, 82, 134; WYA; YAW
Maki, James
  See Ozu, Yasujiro

Malabaila, Damiano
  See Levi, Primo
Malamud, Bernard 1914-1986 .. **CLC 1, 2, 3,
  5, 8, 9, 11, 18, 27, 44, 78, 85; SSC 15;
  TCLC 129; WLC**
  See also AAYA 16; AMWS 1; BPFB 2;
  BYA 15; CA 5-8R; 118; CABS 1; CANR
  28, 62, 114; CDALB 1941-1968; CPW;
  DA; DA3; DAB; DAC; DAM MST, NOV,
  POP; DLB 2, 28, 152; DLBY 1980, 1986;
  EWL 3; EXPS; LAIT 4; LATS 1:1;
  MTCW 1, 2; NFS 4, 9; RGAL 4; RGSF
  2; SSFS 8, 13, 16; TUS
Malan, Herman
  See Bosman, Herman Charles; Bosman,
  Herman Charles
Malaparte, Curzio 1898-1957 .... **TCLC 52**
  See also DLB 264
Malcolm, Dan
  See Silverberg, Robert
Malcolm X .... **BLC 2; CLC 82, 117; WLCS**
  See Little, Malcolm
  See also LAIT 5; NCFS 3
Malherbe, Francois de 1555-1628 .... **LC 5**
  See also GFL Beginnings to 1789
Mallarme, Stephane 1842-1898 ...... **NCLC 4,
  41; PC 4**
  See also DAM POET; DLB 217; EW 7;
  GFL 1789 to the Present; LMFS 2; RGWL
  2, 3; TWA
Mallet-Joris, Francoise 1930- .... **CLC 11**
  See also CA 65-68; CANR 17; CWW 2;
  DLB 83; EWL 3; GFL 1789 to the Present
Malley, Ern
  See McAuley, James Phillip
Mallon, Thomas 1951- .... **CLC 172**
  See also CA 110; CANR 29, 57, 92
Mallowan, Agatha Christie
  See Christie, Agatha (Mary Clarissa)
Maloff, Saul 1922- .... **CLC 5**
  See also CA 33-36R
Malone, Louis
  See MacNeice, (Frederick) Louis
Malone, Michael (Christopher)
  1942- .... **CLC 43**
  See also CA 77-80; CANR 14, 32, 57, 114
Malory, Sir Thomas 1410(?)-1471(?) . **LC 11,
  88; WLCS**
  See also BRW 1; BRWR 2; CDBLB Before
  1660; DA; DAB; DAC; DAM MST; DLB
  146; EFS 2; RGEL 2; SATA 59; SATA-
  Brief 33; TEA; WLIT 3
Malouf, (George Joseph) David
  1934- .... **CLC 28, 86**
  See also CA 124; CANR 50, 76; CN 7; CP
  7; DLB 289; EWL 3; MTCW 2
Malraux, (Georges-)Andre
  1901-1976 .... **CLC 1, 4, 9, 13, 15, 57**
  See also BPFB 2; CA 21-22; 69-72; CANR
  34, 58; CAP 2; DA3; DAM NOV; DLB
  72; EW 12; EWL 3; GFL 1789 to the
  Present; MTCW 1, 2; RGWL 2, 3; TWA
Malthus, Thomas Robert
  1766-1834 .... **NCLC 145**
  See also DLB 107, 158; RGEL 2
Malzberg, Barry N(athaniel) 1939- ... **CLC 7**
  See also CA 61-64; CAAS 4; CANR 16;
  CMW 4; DLB 8; SFW 4
Mamet, David (Alan) 1947- .. **CLC 9, 15, 34,
  46, 91, 166; DC 4, 24**
  See also AAYA 3; CA 81-84; CABS 3;
  CANR 15, 41, 67, 72, 129; CD 5; DA3;
  DAM DRAM; DFS 2, 3, 6, 12, 15; DLB
  7; EWL 3; IDFW 4; MTCW 1, 2; RGAL
  4
Mamoulian, Rouben (Zachary)
  1897-1987 .... **CLC 16**
  See also CA 25-28R; 124; CANR 85

Mandelstam, Osip
See Mandelstam, Osip (Emilievich)
See also EW 10; EWL 3; RGWL 2, 3
Mandelstam, Osip (Emilievich)
1891(?)-1943(?) .... **PC 14; TCLC 2, 6**
See Mandelshtam, Osip
See also CA 104; 150; MTCW 2; TWA
Mander, (Mary) Jane 1877-1949 ... **TCLC 31**
See also CA 162; RGEL 2
Mandeville, Bernard 1670-1733 .... **LC 82**
See also DLB 101
Mandeville, Sir John fl. 1350- ...... **CMLC 19**
See also DLB 146
Mandiargues, Andre Pieyre de .... **CLC 41**
See Pieyre de Mandiargues, Andre
See also DLB 83
Mandrake, Ethel Belle
See Thurman, Wallace (Henry)
Mangan, James Clarence
1803-1849 .... **NCLC 27**
See also RGEL 2
Maniere, J.-E.
See Giraudoux, Jean(-Hippolyte)
Mankiewicz, Herman (Jacob)
1897-1953 .... **TCLC 85**
See also CA 120; 169; DLB 26; IDFW 3, 4
Manley, (Mary) Delariviere
1672(?)-1724 .... **LC 1, 42**
See also DLB 39, 80; RGEL 2
Mann, Abel
See Creasey, John
Mann, Emily 1952- .... **DC 7**
See also CA 130; CAD; CANR 55; CD 5;
CWD; DLB 266
Mann, (Luiz) Heinrich 1871-1950 ... **TCLC 9**
See also CA 106; 164, 181; DLB 66, 118;
EW 8; EWL 3; RGWL 2, 3
Mann, (Paul) Thomas 1875-1955 .... **SSC 5,
70; TCLC 2, 8, 14, 21, 35, 44, 60;
WLC**
See also BPFB 2; CA 104; 128; CANR 133;
CDWLB 2; DA; DA3; DAB; DAC; DAM
MST, NOV; DLB 66; EW 9; EWL 3; GLL
1; LATS 1:1; LMFS 1; MTCW 1, 2; NFS
17; RGSF 2; RGWL 2, 3; SSFS 4, 9;
TWA
Mannheim, Karl 1893-1947 .... **TCLC 65**
See also CA 204
Manning, David
See Faust, Frederick (Schiller)
See also TCWW 2
Manning, Frederic 1882-1935 .... **TCLC 25**
See also CA 124; 216; DLB 260
Manning, Olivia 1915-1980 .... **CLC 5, 19**
See also CA 5-8R; 101; CANR 29; EWL 3;
FW; MTCW 1; RGEL 2
Mano, D. Keith 1942- .... **CLC 2, 10**
See also CA 25-28R; CAAS 6; CANR 26,
57; DLB 6
Mansfield, Katherine . **SSC 9, 23, 38; TCLC
2, 8, 39; WLC**
See Beauchamp, Kathleen Mansfield
See also BPFB 2; BRW 7; DAB; DLB 162;
EWL 3; EXPS; FW; GLL 1; RGEL 2;
RGSF 2; SSFS 2, 8, 10, 11; WWE 1
Manso, Peter 1940- .... **CLC 39**
See also CA 29-32R; CANR 44
Mantecon, Juan Jimenez
See Jimenez (Mantecon), Juan Ramon
Mantel, Hilary (Mary) 1952- .... **CLC 144**
See also CA 125; CANR 54, 101; CN 7;
DLB 271; RHW
Manton, Peter
See Creasey, John
Man Without a Spleen, A
See Chekhov, Anton (Pavlovich)
Manzoni, Alessandro 1785-1873 ... **NCLC 29,
98**
See also EW 5; RGWL 2, 3; TWA

Map, Walter 1140-1209 .... **CMLC 32**
Mapu, Abraham (ben Jekutiel)
1808-1867 .... **NCLC 18**
Mara, Sally
See Queneau, Raymond
Maracle, Lee 1950- .... **NNAL**
See also CA 149
Marat, Jean Paul 1743-1793 .... **LC 10**
Marcel, Gabriel Honore 1889-1973 . **CLC 15**
See also CA 102; 45-48; EWL 3; MTCW 1,
2
March, William 1893-1954 .... **TCLC 96**
See also CA 216
Marchbanks, Samuel
See Davies, (William) Robertson
See also CCA 1
Marchi, Giacomo
See Bassani, Giorgio
Marcus Aurelius
See Aurelius, Marcus
See also AW 2
Marguerite
See de Navarre, Marguerite
Marguerite d'Angouleme
See de Navarre, Marguerite
See also GFL Beginnings to 1789
Marguerite de Navarre
See de Navarre, Marguerite
See also RGWL 2, 3
Margulies, Donald 1954- .... **CLC 76**
See also AAYA 57; CA 200; DFS 13; DLB
228
Marie de France c. 12th cent. - ..... **CMLC 8;
PC 22**
See also DLB 208; FW; RGWL 2, 3
Marie de l'Incarnation 1599-1672 ...... **LC 10**
Marier, Captain Victor
See Griffith, D(avid Lewelyn) W(ark)
Mariner, Scott
See Pohl, Frederik
Marinetti, Filippo Tommaso
1876-1944 .... **TCLC 10**
See also CA 107; DLB 114, 264; EW 9;
EWL 3
Marivaux, Pierre Carlet de Chamblain de
1688-1763 .... **DC 7; LC 4**
See also GFL Beginnings to 1789; RGWL
2, 3; TWA
Markandaya, Kamala .... **CLC 8, 38**
See Taylor, Kamala (Purnaiya)
See also BYA 13; CN 7; EWL 3
Markfield, Wallace 1926-2002 .... **CLC 8**
See also CA 69-72; 208; CAAS 3; CN 7;
DLB 2, 28; DLBY 2002
Markham, Edwin 1852-1940 .... **TCLC 47**
See also CA 160; DLB 54, 186; RGAL 4
Markham, Robert
See Amis, Kingsley (William)
Markoosie .... **NNAL**
See Patsauq, Markoosie
See also CLR 23; DAM MULT
Marks, J
See Highwater, Jamake (Mamake)
Marks, J.
See Highwater, Jamake (Mamake)
Marks-Highwater, J
See Highwater, Jamake (Mamake)
Marks-Highwater, J.
See Highwater, Jamake (Mamake)
Markson, David M(errill) 1927- .... **CLC 67**
See also CA 49-52; CANR 1, 91; CN 7
Marlatt, Daphne (Buckle) 1942- .... **CLC 168**
See also CA 25-28R; CANR 17, 39; CN 7;
CP 7; CWP; DLB 60; FW
Marley, Bob .... **CLC 17**
See Marley, Robert Nesta

Marley, Robert Nesta 1945-1981
See Marley, Bob
See also CA 107; 103
Marlowe, Christopher 1564-1593 . **DC 1; LC
22, 47; PC 57; WLC**
See also BRW 1; BRWR 1; CDBLB Before
1660; DA; DA3; DAB; DAC; DAM
DRAM, MST; DFS 1, 5, 13; DLB 62;
EXPP; LMFS 1; RGEL 2; TEA; WLIT 3
Marlowe, Stephen 1928- .... **CLC 70**
See Queen, Ellery
See also CA 13-16R; CANR 6, 55; CMW
4; SFW 4
Marmion, Shakerley 1603-1639 .... **LC 89**
See also DLB 58; RGEL 2
Marmontel, Jean-Francois 1723-1799 .. **LC 2**
Maron, Monika 1941- .... **CLC 165**
See also CA 201
Marquand, John P(hillips)
1893-1960 .... **CLC 2, 10**
See also AMW; BPFB 2; CA 85-88; CANR
73; CMW 4; DLB 9, 102; EWL 3; MTCW
2; RGAL 4
Marques, Rene 1919-1979 .. **CLC 96; HLC 2**
See also CA 97-100; 85-88; CANR 78;
DAM MULT; DLB 305; EWL 3; HW 1,
2; LAW; RGSF 2
Marquez, Gabriel (Jose) Garcia
See Garcia Marquez, Gabriel (Jose)
Marquis, Don(ald Robert Perry)
1878-1937 .... **TCLC 7**
See also CA 104; 166; DLB 11, 25; RGAL
4
Marquis de Sade
See Sade, Donatien Alphonse Francois
Marric, J. J.
See Creasey, John
See also MSW
Marryat, Frederick 1792-1848 .... **NCLC 3**
See also DLB 21, 163; RGEL 2; WCH
Marsden, James
See Creasey, John
Marsh, Edward 1872-1953 .... **TCLC 99**
Marsh, (Edith) Ngaio 1895-1982 .. **CLC 7, 53**
See also CA 9-12R; CANR 6, 58; CMW 4;
CPW; DAM POP; DLB 77; MSW;
MTCW 1, 2; RGEL 2; TEA
Marshall, Garry 1934- .... **CLC 17**
See also AAYA 3; CA 111; SATA 60
Marshall, Paule 1929- .. **BLC 3; CLC 27, 72;
SSC 3**
See also AFAW 1, 2; AMWS 11; BPFB 2;
BW 2, 3; CA 77-80; CANR 25, 73, 129;
CN 7; DA3; DAM MULT; DLB 33, 157,
227; EWL 3; LATS 1:2; MTCW 1, 2;
RGAL 4; SSFS 15
Marshallik
See Zangwill, Israel
Marsten, Richard
See Hunter, Evan
Marston, John 1576-1634 .... **LC 33**
See also BRW 2; DAM DRAM; DLB 58,
172; RGEL 2
Martel, Yann 1963- .... **CLC 192**
See also CA 146; CANR 114
Martha, Henry
See Harris, Mark
Marti, Jose
See Marti (y Perez), Jose (Julian)
See also DLB 290
Marti (y Perez), Jose (Julian)
1853-1895 .... **HLC 2; NCLC 63**
See Marti, Jose
See also DAM MULT; HW 2; LAW; RGWL
2, 3; WLIT 1
Martial c. 40-c. 104 .... **CMLC 35; PC 10**
See also AW 2; CDWLB 1; DLB 211;
RGWL 2, 3

Mayne, William (James Carter)
1928- .... **CLC 12**
See also AAYA 20; CA 9-12R; CANR 37,
80, 100; CLR 25; FANT; JRDA; MAI-
CYA 1, 2; MAICYAS 1; SAAS 11; SATA
6, 68, 122; SUFW 2; YAW

Mayo, Jim
See L'Amour, Louis (Dearborn)
See also TCWW 2

Maysles, Albert 1926- .... **CLC 16**
See also CA 29-32R

Maysles, David 1932-1987 .... **CLC 16**
See also CA 191

Mazer, Norma Fox 1931- .... **CLC 26**
See also AAYA 5, 36; BYA 1, 8; CA 69-72;
CANR 12, 32, 66, 129; CLR 23; JRDA;
MAICYA 1, 2; SAAS 1; SATA 24, 67,
105; WYA; YAW

Mazzini, Guiseppe 1805-1872 .... **NCLC 34**

McAlmon, Robert (Menzies)
1895-1956 .... **TCLC 97**
See also CA 107; 168; DLB 4, 45; DLBD
15; GLL 1

McAuley, James Phillip 1917-1976 .. **CLC 45**
See also CA 97-100; DLB 260; RGEL 2

McBain, Ed
See Hunter, Evan
See also MSW

McBrien, William (Augustine)
1930- .... **CLC 44**
See also CA 107; CANR 90

McCabe, Patrick 1955- .... **CLC 133**
See also BRWS 9; CA 130; CANR 50, 90;
CN 7; DLB 194

McCaffrey, Anne (Inez) 1926- .... **CLC 17**
See also AAYA 6, 34; AITN 2; BEST 89:2;
BPFB 2; BYA 5; CA 25-28R, 227; CAAE
227; CANR 15, 35, 55, 96; CLR 49;
CPW; DA3; DAM NOV, POP; DLB 8;
JRDA; MAICYA 1, 2; MTCW 1, 2; SAAS
11; SATA 8, 70, 116, 152; SATA-Essay
152; SFW 4; SUFW 2; WYA; YAW

McCall, Nathan 1955(?)- .... **CLC 86**
See also AAYA 59; BW 3; CA 146; CANR
88

McCann, Arthur
See Campbell, John W(ood, Jr.)

McCann, Edson
See Pohl, Frederik

McCarthy, Charles, Jr. 1933-
See McCarthy, Cormac
See also CANR 42, 69, 101; CN 7; CPW;
CSW; DA3; DAM POP; MTCW 2

McCarthy, Cormac .... **CLC 4, 57, 101**
See McCarthy, Charles, Jr.
See also AAYA 41; AMWS 8; BPFB 2; CA
13-16R; CANR 10; DLB 6, 143, 256;
EWL 3; LATS 1:2; TCWW 2

McCarthy, Mary (Therese)
1912-1989 .. **CLC 1, 3, 5, 14, 24, 39, 59;**
SSC 24
See also AMW; BPFB 2; CA 5-8R; 129;
CANR 16, 50, 64; DA3; DLB 2; DLBY
1981; EWL 3; FW; INT CANR-16;
MAWW; MTCW 1, 2; RGAL 4; TUS

McCartney, (James) Paul 1942- . **CLC 12, 35**
See also CA 146; CANR 111

McCauley, Stephen (D.) 1955- .... **CLC 50**
See also CA 141

McClaren, Peter .... **CLC 70**

McClure, Michael (Thomas) 1932- ... **CLC 6,**
10
See also BG 3; CA 21-24R; CAD; CANR
17, 46, 77, 131; CD 5; CP 7; DLB 16;
WP

McCorkle, Jill (Collins) 1958- .... **CLC 51**
See also CA 121; CANR 113; CSW; DLB
234; DLBY 1987

McCourt, Frank 1930- .... **CLC 109**
See also AMWS 12; CA 157; CANR 97;
NCFS 1

McCourt, James 1941- .... **CLC 5**
See also CA 57-60; CANR 98

McCourt, Malachy 1931- .... **CLC 119**
See also SATA 126

McCoy, Horace (Stanley)
1897-1955 .... **TCLC 28**
See also AMWS 13; CA 108; 155; CMW 4;
DLB 9

McCrae, John 1872-1918 .... **TCLC 12**
See also CA 109; DLB 92; PFS 5

McCreigh, James
See Pohl, Frederik

McCullers, (Lula) Carson (Smith)
1917-1967 .... **CLC 1, 4, 10, 12, 48, 100;**
SSC 9, 24; TCLC 155; WLC
See also AAYA 21; AMW; AMWC 2; BPFB
2; CA 5-8R; 25-28R; CABS 1, 3; CANR
18, 132; CDALB 1941-1968; DA; DA3;
DAB; DAC; DAM MST, NOV; DFS 5,
18; DLB 2, 7, 173, 228; EWL 3; EXPS;
FW; GLL 1; LAIT 3, 4; MAWW; MTCW
1, 2; NFS 6, 13; RGAL 4; RGSF 2; SATA
27; SSFS 5; TUS; YAW

McCulloch, John Tyler
See Burroughs, Edgar Rice

McCullough, Colleen 1938(?)- .. **CLC 27, 107**
See also AAYA 36; BPFB 2; CA 81-84;
CANR 17, 46, 67, 98; CPW; DA3; DAM
NOV, POP; MTCW 1, 2; RHW

McCunn, Ruthanne Lum 1946- .... **AAL**
See also CA 119; CANR 43, 96; LAIT 2;
SATA 63

McDermott, Alice 1953- .... **CLC 90**
See also CA 109; CANR 40, 90, 126; DLB
292

McElroy, Joseph 1930- .... **CLC 5, 47**
See also CA 17-20R; CN 7

McEwan, Ian (Russell) 1948- .... **CLC 13, 66,**
169
See also BEST 90:4; BRWS 4; CA 61-64;
CANR 14, 41, 69, 87, 132; CN 7; DAM
NOV; DLB 14, 194; HGG; MTCW 1, 2;
RGSF 2; SUFW 2; TEA

McFadden, David 1940- .... **CLC 48**
See also CA 104; CP 7; DLB 60; INT CA-
104

McFarland, Dennis 1950- .... **CLC 65**
See also CA 165; CANR 110

McGahern, John 1934- ... **CLC 5, 9, 48, 156;**
SSC 17
See also CA 17-20R; CANR 29, 68, 113;
CN 7; DLB 14, 231; MTCW 1

McGinley, Patrick (Anthony) 1937- . **CLC 41**
See also CA 120; 127; CANR 56; INT CA-
127

McGinley, Phyllis 1905-1978 .... **CLC 14**
See also CA 9-12R; 77-80; CANR 19;
CWRI 5; DLB 11, 48; PFS 9, 13; SATA
2, 44; SATA-Obit 24

McGinniss, Joe 1942- .... **CLC 32**
See also AITN 2; BEST 89:2; CA 25-28R;
CANR 26, 70; CPW; DLB 185; INT
CANR-26

McGivern, Maureen Daly
See Daly, Maureen

McGrath, Patrick 1950- .... **CLC 55**
See also CA 136; CANR 65; CN 7; DLB
231; HGG; SUFW 2

McGrath, Thomas (Matthew)
1916-1990 .... **CLC 28, 59**
See also AMWS 10; CA 9-12R; 132; CANR
6, 33, 95; DAM POET; MTCW 1; SATA
41; SATA-Obit 66

McGuane, Thomas (Francis III)
1939- .... **CLC 3, 7, 18, 45, 127**
See also AITN 2; BPFB 2; CA 49-52;
CANR 5, 24, 49, 94; CN 7; DLB 2, 212;
DLBY 1980; EWL 3; INT CANR-24;
MTCW 1; TCWW 2

McGuckian, Medbh 1950- .... **CLC 48, 174;**
PC 27
See also BRWS 5; CA 143; CP 7; CWP;
DAM POET; DLB 40

McHale, Tom 1942(?)-1982 .... **CLC 3, 5**
See also AITN 1; CA 77-80; 106

McIlvanney, William 1936- .... **CLC 42**
See also CA 25-28R; CANR 61; CMW 4;
DLB 14, 207

McIlwraith, Maureen Mollie Hunter
See Hunter, Mollie
See also SATA 2

McInerney, Jay 1955- .... **CLC 34, 112**
See also AAYA 18; BPFB 2; CA 116; 123;
CANR 45, 68, 116; CN 7; CPW; DA3;
DAM POP; DLB 292; INT CA-123;
MTCW 2

McIntyre, Vonda N(eel) 1948- .... **CLC 18**
See also CA 81-84; CANR 17, 34, 69;
MTCW 1; SFW 4; YAW

McKay, Claude .... **BLC 3; HR 3; PC 2;**
TCLC 7, 41; WLC
See McKay, Festus Claudius
See also AFAW 1, 2; AMWS 10; DAB;
DLB 4, 45, 51, 117; EWL 3; EXPP; GLL
2; LAIT 3; LMFS 2; PAB; PFS 4; RGAL
4; WP

McKay, Festus Claudius 1889-1948
See McKay, Claude
See also BW 1, 3; CA 104; 124; CANR 73;
DA; DAC; DAM MST, MULT, NOV,
POET; MTCW 1, 2; TUS

McKuen, Rod 1933- .... **CLC 1, 3**
See also AITN 1; CA 41-44R; CANR 40

McLoughlin, R. B.
See Mencken, H(enry) L(ouis)

McLuhan, (Herbert) Marshall
1911-1980 .... **CLC 37, 83**
See also CA 9-12R; 102; CANR 12, 34, 61;
DLB 88; INT CANR-12; MTCW 1, 2

McManus, Declan Patrick Aloysius
See Costello, Elvis

McMillan, Terry (L.) 1951- . **BLCS; CLC 50,**
61, 112
See also AAYA 21; AMWS 13; BPFB 2;
BW 2, 3; CA 140; CANR 60, 104, 131;
CPW; DA3; DAM MULT, NOV, POP;
MTCW 2; RGAL 4; YAW

McMurtry, Larry (Jeff) 1936- .. **CLC 2, 3, 7,**
11, 27, 44, 127
See also AAYA 15; AITN 2; AMWS 5;
BEST 89:2; BPFB 2; CA 5-8R; CANR
19, 43, 64, 103; CDALB 1968-1988; CN
7; CPW; CSW; DA3; DAM NOV, POP;
DLB 2, 143, 256; DLBY 1980, 1987;
EWL 3; MTCW 1, 2; RGAL 4; TCWW 2

McNally, T. M. 1961- .... **CLC 82**

McNally, Terrence 1939- .... **CLC 4, 7, 41, 91**
See also AMWS 13; CA 45-48; CAD;
CANR 2, 56, 116; CD 5; DA3; DAM
DRAM; DFS 16, 19; DLB 7, 249; EWL
3; GLL 1; MTCW 2

McNamer, Deirdre 1950- .... **CLC 70**

McNeal, Tom .... **CLC 119**

McNeile, Herman Cyril 1888-1937
See Sapper
See also CA 184; CMW 4; DLB 77

McNickle, (William) D'Arcy
1904-1977 .... **CLC 89; NNAL**
See also CA 9-12R; 85-88; CANR 5, 45;
DAM MULT; DLB 175, 212; RGAL 4;
SATA-Obit 22

Miles, Josephine (Louise)
1911-1985 .... **CLC 1, 2, 14, 34, 39**
See also CA 1-4R; 116; CANR 2, 55; DAM
POET; DLB 48

Militant
See Sandburg, Carl (August)

Mill, Harriet (Hardy) Taylor
1807-1858 .... **NCLC 102**
See also FW

Mill, John Stuart 1806-1873 .... **NCLC 11, 58**
See also CDBLB 1832-1890; DLB 55, 190,
262; FW 1; RGEL 2; TEA

Millar, Kenneth 1915-1983 .... **CLC 14**
See Macdonald, Ross
See also CA 9-12R; 110; CANR 16, 63,
107; CMW 4; CPW; DA3; DAM POP;
DLB 2, 226; DLBD 6; DLBY 1983;
MTCW 1, 2

Millay, E. Vincent
See Millay, Edna St. Vincent

Millay, Edna St. Vincent 1892-1950 .... **PC 6;
TCLC 4, 49; WLCS**
See Boyd, Nancy
See also AMW; CA 104; 130; CDALB
1917-1929; DA; DA3; DAB; DAC; DAM
MST, POET; DLB 45, 249; EWL 3;
EXPP; MAWW; MTCW 1, 2; PAB; PFS
3, 17; RGAL 4; TUS; WP

Miller, Arthur 1915- ...... **CLC 1, 2, 6, 10, 15,
26, 47, 78, 179; DC 1; WLC**
See also AAYA 15; AITN 1; AMW; AMWC
1; CA 1-4R; CABS 3; CAD; CANR 2,
30, 54, 76, 132; CD 5; CDALB 1941-
1968; DA; DA3; DAB; DAC; DAM
DRAM, MST; DFS 1, 3, 8; DLB 7, 266;
EWL 3; LAIT 1, 4; LATS 1:2; MTCW 1,
2; RGAL 4; TUS; WYAS 1

Miller, Henry (Valentine)
1891-1980 .... **CLC 1, 2, 4, 9, 14, 43, 84;
WLC**
See also AMW; BPFB 2; CA 9-12R; 97-
100; CANR 33, 64; CDALB 1929-1941;
DA; DA3; DAB; DAC; DAM MST, NOV;
DLB 4, 9; DLBY 1980; EWL 3; MTCW
1, 2; RGAL 4; TUS

Miller, Hugh 1802-1856 .... **NCLC 143**
See also DLB 190

Miller, Jason 1939(?)-2001 .... **CLC 2**
See also AITN 1; CA 73-76; 197; CAD;
CANR 130; DFS 12; DLB 7

Miller, Sue 1943- .... **CLC 44**
See also AMWS 12; BEST 90:3; CA 139;
CANR 59, 91, 128; DA3; DAM POP;
DLB 143

Miller, Walter M(ichael), Jr.)
1923-1996 .... **CLC 4, 30**
See also BPFB 2; CA 85-88; CANR 108;
DLB 8; SCFW 4

Millett, Kate 1934- .... **CLC 67**
See also AITN 1; CA 73-76; CANR 32, 53,
76, 110; DA3; DLB 246; FW; GLL 1;
MTCW 1, 2

Millhauser, Steven (Lewis) 1943- .... **CLC 21,
54, 109; SSC 57**
See also CA 110; 111; CANR 63, 114, 133;
CN 7; DA3; DLB 2; FANT; INT CA-111;
MTCW 2

Millin, Sarah Gertrude 1889-1968 ... **CLC 49**
See also CA 102; 93-96; DLB 225; EWL 3

Milne, A(lan) A(lexander)
1882-1956 .... **TCLC 6, 88**
See also BRWS 5; CA 104; 133; CLR 1,
26; CMW 4; CWRI 5; DA3; DAB; DAC;
DAM MST; DLB 10, 77, 100, 160; FANT;
MAICYA 1, 2; MTCW 1, 2; RGEL 2;
SATA 100; WCH; YABC 1

Milner, Ron(ald) 1938-2004 ..... **BLC 3; CLC
56**
See also AITN 1; BW 1; CA 73-76; CAD;
CANR 24, 81; CD 5; DAM MULT; DLB
38; MTCW 1

Milnes, Richard Monckton
1809-1885 .... **NCLC 61**
See also DLB 32, 184

Milosz, Czeslaw 1911- ...... **CLC 5, 11, 22, 31,
56, 82; PC 8; WLCS**
See also CA 81-84; CANR 23, 51, 91, 126;
CDWLB 4; CWW 2; DA3; DAM MST,
POET; DLB 215; EW 13; EWL 3; MTCW
1, 2; PFS 16; RGWL 2, 3

Milton, John 1608-1674 ..... **LC 9, 43, 92; PC
19, 29; WLC**
See also BRW 2; BRWR 2; CDBLB 1660-
1789; DA; DA3; DAB; DAC; DAM MST,
POET; DLB 131, 151, 281; EFS 1; EXPP;
LAIT 1; PAB; PFS 3, 17; RGEL 2; TEA;
WLIT 3; WP

Min, Anchee 1957- .... **CLC 86**
See also CA 146; CANR 94

Minehaha, Cornelius
See Wedekind, (Benjamin) Frank(lin)

Miner, Valerie 1947- .... **CLC 40**
See also CA 97-100; CANR 59; FW; GLL
2

Minimo, Duca
See D'Annunzio, Gabriele

Minot, Susan 1956- .... **CLC 44, 159**
See also AMWS 6; CA 134; CANR 118;
CN 7

Minus, Ed 1938- .... **CLC 39**
See also CA 185

Mirabai 1498(?)-1550(?) .... **PC 48**

Miranda, Javier
See Bioy Casares, Adolfo
See also CWW 2

Mirbeau, Octave 1848-1917 .... **TCLC 55**
See also CA 216; DLB 123, 192; GFL 1789
to the Present

Mirikitani, Janice 1942- .... **AAL**
See also CA 211; RGAL 4

Mirk, John (?)-c. 1414 .... **LC 105**
See also DLB 146

Miro (Ferrer), Gabriel (Francisco Victor)
1879-1930 .... **TCLC 5**
See also CA 104; 185; EWL 3

Misharin, Alexandr .... **CLC 59**

Mishima, Yukio ... **CLC 2, 4, 6, 9, 27; DC 1;
SSC 4**
See Hiraoka, Kimitake
See also AAYA 50; BPFB 2; GLL 1; MJW;
MTCW 2; RGSF 2; RGWL 2, 3; SSFS 5,
12

Mistral, Frederic 1830-1914 .... **TCLC 51**
See also CA 122; 213; GFL 1789 to the
Present

Mistral, Gabriela
See Godoy Alcayaga, Lucila
See also DLB 283; DNFS 1; EWL 3; LAW;
RGWL 2, 3; WP

Mistry, Rohinton 1952- ... **CLC 71, 196; SSC
73**
See also CA 141; CANR 86, 114; CCA 1;
CN 7; DAC; SSFS 6

Mitchell, Clyde
See Ellison, Harlan (Jay)

Mitchell, Emerson Blackhorse Barney
1945- .... **NNAL**
See also CA 45-48

Mitchell, James Leslie 1901-1935
See Gibbon, Lewis Grassic
See also CA 104; 188; DLB 15

Mitchell, Joni 1943- .... **CLC 12**
See also CA 112; CCA 1

Mitchell, Joseph (Quincy)
1908-1996 .... **CLC 98**
See also CA 77-80; 152; CANR 69; CN 7;
CSW; DLB 185; DLBY 1996

Mitchell, Margaret (Munnerlyn)
1900-1949 .... **TCLC 11**
See also AAYA 23; BPFB 2; BYA 1; CA
109; 125; CANR 55, 94; CDALBS; DA3;
DAM NOV, POP; DLB 9; LAIT 2;
MTCW 1, 2; NFS 9; RGAL 4; RHW;
TUS; WYAS 1; YAW

Mitchell, Peggy
See Mitchell, Margaret (Munnerlyn)

Mitchell, S(ilas) Weir 1829-1914 .... **TCLC 36**
See also CA 165; DLB 202; RGAL 4

Mitchell, W(illiam) O(rmond)
1914-1998 .... **CLC 25**
See also CA 77-80; 165; CANR 15, 43; CN
7; DAC; DAM MST; DLB 88

Mitchell, William (Lendrum)
1879-1936 .... **TCLC 81**
See also CA 213

Mitford, Mary Russell 1787-1855 ... **NCLC 4**
See also DLB 110, 116; RGEL 2

Mitford, Nancy 1904-1973 .... **CLC 44**
See also CA 9-12R; DLB 191; RGEL 2

Miyamoto, (Chujo) Yuriko
1899-1951 .... **TCLC 37**
See Miyamoto Yuriko
See also CA 170, 174

Miyamoto Yuriko
See Miyamoto, (Chujo) Yuriko
See also DLB 180

Miyazawa, Kenji 1896-1933 .... **TCLC 76**
See Miyazawa Kenji
See also CA 157; RGWL 3

Miyazawa Kenji
See Miyazawa, Kenji
See also EWL 3

Mizoguchi, Kenji 1898-1956 .... **TCLC 72**
See also CA 167

Mo, Timothy (Peter) 1950(?)- ... **CLC 46, 134**
See also CA 117; CANR 128; CN 7; DLB
194; MTCW 1; WLIT 4; WWE 1

Modarressi, Taghi (M.) 1931-1997 ... **CLC 44**
See also CA 121; 134; INT CA-134

Modiano, Patrick (Jean) 1945- .... **CLC 18**
See also CA 85-88; CANR 17, 40, 115;
CWW 2; DLB 83, 299; EWL 3

Mofolo, Thomas (Mokopu)
1875(?)-1948 .... **BLC 3; TCLC 22**
See also AFW; CA 121; 153; CANR 83;
DAM MULT; DLB 225; EWL 3; MTCW
2; WLIT 2

Mohr, Nicholasa 1938- .... **CLC 12; HLC 2**
See also AAYA 8, 46; CA 49-52; CANR 1,
32, 64; CLR 22; DAM MULT; DLB 145;
HW 1, 2; JRDA; LAIT 5; LLW 1; MAI-
CYA 2; MAICYAS 1; RGAL 4; SAAS 8;
SATA 8, 97; SATA-Essay 113; WYA;
YAW

Moi, Toril 1953- .... **CLC 172**
See also CA 154; CANR 102; FW

Mojtabai, A(nn) G(race) 1938- ..... **CLC 5, 9,
15, 29**
See also CA 85-88; CANR 88

Moliere 1622-1673 ..... **DC 13; LC 10, 28, 64;
WLC**
See also DA; DA3; DAB; DAC; DAM
DRAM, MST; DFS 13, 18, 20; DLB 268;
EW 3; GFL Beginnings to 1789; LATS
1:1; RGWL 2, 3; TWA

Molin, Charles
See Mayne, William (James Carter)

Molnar, Ferenc 1878-1952 .... **TCLC 20**
See also CA 109; 153; CANR 83; CDWLB
4; DAM DRAM; DLB 215; EWL 3;
RGWL 2, 3

Momaday, N(avarre) Scott 1934- ...... **CLC 2,
19, 85, 95, 160; NNAL; PC 25; WLCS**
See also AAYA 11; AMWS 4; ANW; BPFB
2; BYA 12; CA 25-28R; CANR 14, 34,
68; CDALBS; CN 7; CPW; DA; DA3;

Morrison, Chloe Anthony Wofford
See Morrison, Toni
Morrison, James Douglas 1943-1971
See Morrison, Jim
See also CA 73-76; CANR 40
Morrison, Jim .... **CLC 17**
See Morrison, James Douglas
Morrison, Toni 1931- ..... **BLC 3; CLC 4, 10, 22, 55, 81, 87, 173, 194**
See also AAYA 1, 22; AFAW 1, 2; AMWC 1; AMWS 3; BPFB 2; BW 2, 3; CA 29-32R; CANR 27, 42, 67, 113, 124; CDALB 1968-1988; CLR 99; CN 7; CPW; DA; DA3; DAB; DAC; DAM MST, MULT, NOV, POP; DLB 6, 33, 143; DLBY 1981; EWL 3; EXPN; FW; LAIT 2, 4; LATS 1:2; LMFS 2; MAWW; MTCW 1, 2; NFS 1, 6, 8, 14; RGAL 4; RHW; SATA 57, 144; SSFS 5; TUS; YAW
Morrison, Van 1945- .... **CLC 21**
See also CA 116; 168
Morrissy, Mary 1957- .... **CLC 99**
See also CA 205; DLB 267
Mortimer, John (Clifford) 1923- ..... **CLC 28, 43**
See also CA 13-16R; CANR 21, 69, 109; CD 5; CDBLB 1960 to Present; CMW 4; CN 7; CPW; DA3; DAM DRAM, POP; DLB 13, 245, 271; INT CANR-21; MSW; MTCW 1, 2; RGEL 2
Mortimer, Penelope (Ruth)
1918-1999 .... **CLC 5**
See also CA 57-60; 187; CANR 45, 88; CN 7
Mortimer, Sir John
See Mortimer, John (Clifford)
Morton, Anthony
See Creasey, John
Morton, Thomas 1579(?)-1647(?) .... **LC 72**
See also DLB 24; RGEL 2
Mosca, Gaetano 1858-1941 .... **TCLC 75**
Moses, Daniel David 1952- .... **NNAL**
See also CA 186
Mosher, Howard Frank 1943- .... **CLC 62**
See also CA 139; CANR 65, 115
Mosley, Nicholas 1923- .... **CLC 43, 70**
See also CA 69-72; CANR 41, 60, 108; CN 7; DLB 14, 207
Mosley, Walter 1952- .... **BLCS; CLC 97, 184**
See also AAYA 57; AMWS 13; BPFB 2; BW 2; CA 142; CANR 57, 92; CMW 4; CPW; DA3; DAM MULT, POP; DLB 306; MSW; MTCW 2
Moss, Howard 1922-1987 . **CLC 7, 14, 45, 50**
See also CA 1-4R; 123; CANR 1, 44; DAM POET; DLB 5
Mossgiel, Rab
See Burns, Robert
Motion, Andrew (Peter) 1952- .... **CLC 47**
See also BRWS 7; CA 146; CANR 90; CP 7; DLB 40
Motley, Willard (Francis)
1909-1965 .... **CLC 18**
See also BW 1; CA 117; 106; CANR 88; DLB 76, 143
Motoori, Norinaga 1730-1801 .... **NCLC 45**
Mott, Michael (Charles Alston)
1930- .... **CLC 15, 34**
See also CA 5-8R; CAAS 7; CANR 7, 29
Mountain Wolf Woman 1884-1960 . **CLC 92; NNAL**
See also CA 144; CANR 90
Moure, Erin 1955- .... **CLC 88**
See also CA 113; CP 7; CWP; DLB 60
Mourning Dove 1885(?)-1936 .... **NNAL**
See also CA 144; CANR 90; DAM MULT; DLB 175, 221

Mowat, Farley (McGill) 1921- .... **CLC 26**
See also AAYA 1, 50; BYA 2; CA 1-4R; CANR 4, 24, 42, 68, 108; CLR 20; CPW; DAC; DAM MST; DLB 68; INT CANR-24; JRDA; MAICYA 1, 2; MTCW 1, 2; SATA 3, 55; YAW
Mowatt, Anna Cora 1819-1870 ..... **NCLC 74**
See also RGAL 4
Moyers, Bill 1934- .... **CLC 74**
See also AITN 2; CA 61-64; CANR 31, 52
Mphahlele, Es'kia
See Mphahlele, Ezekiel
See also AFW; CDWLB 3; DLB 125, 225; RGSF 2; SSFS 11
Mphahlele, Ezekiel 1919- ... **BLC 3; CLC 25, 133**
See Mphahlele, Es'kia
See also BW 2, 3; CA 81-84; CANR 26, 76; CN 7; DA3; DAM MULT; EWL 3; MTCW 2; SATA 119
Mqhayi, S(amuel) E(dward) K(rune Loliwe) 1875-1945 .... **BLC 3; TCLC 25**
See also CA 153; CANR 87; DAM MULT
Mrozek, Slawomir 1930- .... **CLC 3, 13**
See also CA 13-16R; CAAS 10; CANR 29; CDWLB 4; CWW 2; DLB 232; EWL 3; MTCW 1
Mrs. Belloc-Lowndes
See Lowndes, Marie Adelaide (Belloc)
Mrs. Fairstar
See Horne, Richard Henry Hengist
M'Taggart, John M'Taggart Ellis
See McTaggart, John McTaggart Ellis
Mtwa, Percy (?)- .... **CLC 47**
Mueller, Lisel 1924- .... **CLC 13, 51; PC 33**
See also CA 93-96; CP 7; DLB 105; PFS 9, 13
Muggeridge, Malcolm (Thomas)
1903-1990 .... **TCLC 120**
See also AITN 1; CA 101; CANR 33, 63; MTCW 1, 2
Muhammad 570-632 .... **WLCS**
See also DA; DAB; DAC; DAM MST
Muir, Edwin 1887-1959 . **PC 49; TCLC 2, 87**
See Moore, Edward
See also BRWS 6; CA 104; 193; DLB 20, 100, 191; EWL 3; RGEL 2
Muir, John 1838-1914 .... **TCLC 28**
See also AMWS 9; ANW; CA 165; DLB 186, 275
Mujica Lainez, Manuel 1910-1984 ... **CLC 31**
See Lainez, Manuel Mujica
See also CA 81-84; 112; CANR 32; EWL 3; HW 1
Mukherjee, Bharati 1940- ..... **AAL; CLC 53, 115; SSC 38**
See also AAYA 46; BEST 89:2; CA 107; CANR 45, 72, 128; CN 7; DAM NOV; DLB 60, 218; DNFS 1, 2; EWL 3; FW; MTCW 1, 2; RGAL 4; RGSF 2; SSFS 7; TUS; WWE 1
Muldoon, Paul 1951- .... **CLC 32, 72, 166**
See also BRWS 4; CA 113; 129; CANR 52, 91; CP 7; DAM POET; DLB 40; INT CA-129; PFS 7
Mulisch, Harry (Kurt Victor)
1927- .... **CLC 42**
See also CA 9-12R; CANR 6, 26, 56, 110; CWW 2; DLB 299; EWL 3
Mull, Martin 1943- .... **CLC 17**
See also CA 105
Muller, Wilhelm .... **NCLC 73**
Mulock, Dinah Maria
See Craik, Dinah Maria (Mulock)
See also RGEL 2
Munday, Anthony 1560-1633 .... **LC 87**
See also DLB 62, 172; RGEL 2
Munford, Robert 1737(?)-1783 .... **LC 5**
See also DLB 31

Mungo, Raymond 1946- .... **CLC 72**
See also CA 49-52; CANR 2
Munro, Alice 1931- .... **CLC 6, 10, 19, 50, 95; SSC 3; WLCS**
See also AITN 2; BPFB 2; CA 33-36R; CANR 33, 53, 75, 114; CCA 1; CN 7; DA3; DAC; DAM MST, NOV; DLB 53; EWL 3; MTCW 1, 2; RGEL 2; RGSF 2; SATA 29; SSFS 5, 13, 19; WWE 1
Munro, H(ector) H(ugh) 1870-1916 .... **WLC**
See Saki
See also AAYA 56; CA 104; 130; CANR 104; CDBLB 1890-1914; DA; DA3; DAB; DAC; DAM MST, NOV; DLB 34, 162; EXPS; MTCW 1, 2; RGEL 2; SSFS 15
Murakami, Haruki 1949- .... **CLC 150**
See Murakami Haruki
See also CA 165; CANR 102; MJW; RGWL 3; SFW 4
Murakami Haruki
See Murakami, Haruki
See also CWW 2; DLB 182; EWL 3
Murasaki, Lady
See Murasaki Shikibu
Murasaki Shikibu 978(?)-1026(?) ... **CMLC 1**
See also EFS 2; LATS 1:1; RGWL 2, 3
Murdoch, (Jean) Iris 1919-1999 ... **CLC 1, 2, 3, 4, 6, 8, 11, 15, 22, 31, 51**
See also BRWS 1; CA 13-16R; 179; CANR 8, 43, 68, 103; CDBLB 1960 to Present; CN 7; CWD; DA3; DAB; DAC; DAM MST, NOV; DLB 14, 194, 233; EWL 3; INT CANR-8; MTCW 1, 2; NFS 18; RGEL 2; TEA; WLIT 4
Murfree, Mary Noailles 1850-1922 .. **SSC 22; TCLC 135**
See also CA 122; 176; DLB 12, 74; RGAL 4
Murnau, Friedrich Wilhelm
See Plumpe, Friedrich Wilhelm
Murphy, Richard 1927- .... **CLC 41**
See also BRWS 5; CA 29-32R; CP 7; DLB 40; EWL 3
Murphy, Sylvia 1937- .... **CLC 34**
See also CA 121
Murphy, Thomas (Bernard) 1935- ... **CLC 51**
See also CA 101
Murray, Albert L. 1916- .... **CLC 73**
See also BW 2; CA 49-52; CANR 26, 52, 78; CSW; DLB 38
Murray, James Augustus Henry
1837-1915 .... **TCLC 117**
Murray, Judith Sargent
1751-1820 .... **NCLC 63**
See also DLB 37, 200
Murray, Les(lie Allan) 1938- .... **CLC 40**
See also BRWS 7; CA 21-24R; CANR 11, 27, 56, 103; CP 7; DAM POET; DLB 289; DLBY 2001; EWL 3; RGEL 2
Murry, J. Middleton
See Murry, John Middleton
Murry, John Middleton
1889-1957 .... **TCLC 16**
See also CA 118; 217; DLB 149
Musgrave, Susan 1951- .... **CLC 13, 54**
See also CA 69-72; CANR 45, 84; CCA 1; CP 7; CWP
Musil, Robert (Edler von)
1880-1942 .... **SSC 18; TCLC 12, 68**
See also CA 109; CANR 55, 84; CDWLB 2; DLB 81, 124; EW 9; EWL 3; MTCW 2; RGSF 2; RGWL 2, 3
Muske, Carol .... **CLC 90**
See Muske-Dukes, Carol (Anne)
Muske-Dukes, Carol (Anne) 1945-
See Muske, Carol
See also CA 65-68; 203; CAAE 203; CANR 32, 70; CWP

Musset, (Louis Charles) Alfred de
1810-1857 .... **NCLC 7**
See also DLB 192, 217; EW 6; GFL 1789
to the Present; RGWL 2, 3; TWA

Mussolini, Benito (Amilcare Andrea)
1883-1945 .... **TCLC 96**
See also CA 116

Mutanabbi, Al-
See al-Mutanabbi, Ahmad ibn al-Husayn
Abu al-Tayyib al-Jufi al-Kindi

My Brother's Brother
See Chekhov, Anton (Pavlovich)

Myers, L(eopold) H(amilton)
1881-1944 .... **TCLC 59**
See also CA 157; DLB 15; EWL 3; RGEL
2

Myers, Walter Dean 1937- .. **BLC 3; CLC 35**
See also AAYA 4, 23; BW 2; BYA 6, 8, 11;
CA 33-36R; CANR 20, 42, 67, 108; CLR
4, 16, 35; DAM MULT, NOV; DLB 33;
INT CANR-20; JRDA; LAIT 5; MAICYA
1, 2; MAICYAS 1; MTCW 2; SAAS 2;
SATA 41, 71, 109; SATA-Brief 27; WYA;
YAW

Myers, Walter M.
See Myers, Walter Dean

Myles, Symon
See Follett, Ken(neth Martin)

Nabokov, Vladimir (Vladimirovich)
1899-1977 .... **CLC 1, 2, 3, 6, 8, 11, 15,
23, 44, 46, 64; SSC 11; TCLC 108;
WLC**
See also AAYA 45; AMW; AMWC 1;
AMWR 1; BPFB 2; CA 5-8R; 69-72;
CANR 20, 102; CDALB 1941-1968; DA;
DA3; DAB; DAC; DAM MST, NOV;
DLB 2, 244, 278; DLBD 3; DLBY 1980,
1991; EWL 3; EXPS; LATS 1:2; MTCW
1, 2; NCFS 4; NFS 9; RGAL 4; RGSF 2;
SSFS 6, 15; TUS

Naevius c. 265B.C.-201B.C. .... **CMLC 37**
See also DLB 211

Nagai, Kafu .... **TCLC 51**
See Nagai, Sokichi
See also DLB 180

Nagai, Sokichi 1879-1959
See Nagai, Kafu
See also CA 117

Nagy, Laszlo 1925-1978 .... **CLC 7**
See also CA 129; 112

Naidu, Sarojini 1879-1949 .... **TCLC 80**
See also EWL 3; RGEL 2

Naipaul, Shiva(dhar Srinivasa)
1945-1985 .... **CLC 32, 39; TCLC 153**
See also CA 110; 112; 116; CANR 33;
DA3; DAM NOV; DLB 157; DLBY 1985;
EWL 3; MTCW 1, 2

Naipaul, V(idiadhar) S(urajprasad)
1932- .... **CLC 4, 7, 9, 13, 18, 37, 105;
SSC 38**
See also BPFB 2; BRWS 1; CA 1-4R;
CANR 1, 33, 51, 91, 126; CDBLB 1960
to Present; CDWLB 3; CN 7; DA3; DAB;
DAC; DAM MST, NOV; DLB 125, 204,
207; DLBY 1985, 2001; EWL 3; LATS
1:2; MTCW 1, 2; RGEL 2; RGSF 2;
TWA; WLIT 4; WWE 1

Nakos, Lilika 1903(?)-1989 .... **CLC 29**

Napoleon
See Yamamoto, Hisaye

Narayan, R(asipuram) K(rishnaswami)
1906-2001 .. **CLC 7, 28, 47, 121; SSC 25**
See also BPFB 2; CA 81-84; 196; CANR
33, 61, 112; CN 7; DA3; DAM NOV;
DNFS 1; EWL 3; MTCW 1, 2; RGEL 2;
RGSF 2; SATA 62; SSFS 5; WWE 1

Nash, (Fredric) Ogden 1902-1971 . **CLC 23;
PC 21; TCLC 109**
See also CA 13-14; 29-32R; CANR 34, 61;
CAP 1; DAM POET; DLB 11; MAICYA
1, 2; MTCW 1, 2; RGAL 4; SATA 2, 46;
WP

Nashe, Thomas 1567-1601(?) .... **LC 41, 89**
See also DLB 167; RGEL 2

Nathan, Daniel
See Dannay, Frederic

Nathan, George Jean 1882-1958 .... **TCLC 18**
See Hatteras, Owen
See also CA 114; 169; DLB 137

Natsume, Kinnosuke
See Natsume, Soseki

Natsume, Soseki 1867-1916 .... **TCLC 2, 10**
See Natsume Soseki; Soseki
See also CA 104; 195; RGWL 2, 3; TWA

Natsume Soseki
See Natsume, Soseki
See also DLB 180; EWL 3

Natti, (Mary) Lee 1919-
See Kingman, Lee
See also CA 5-8R; CANR 2

Navarre, Marguerite de
See de Navarre, Marguerite

Naylor, Gloria 1950- ..... **BLC 3; CLC 28, 52,
156; WLCS**
See also AAYA 6, 39; AFAW 1, 2; AMWS
8; BW 2, 3; CA 107; CANR 27, 51, 74,
130; CN 7; CPW; DA; DA3; DAC; DAM
MST, MULT, NOV, POP; DLB 173; EWL
3; FW; MTCW 1, 2; NFS 4, 7; RGAL 4;
TUS

Neff, Debra .... **CLC 59**

Neihardt, John Gneisenau
1881-1973 .... **CLC 32**
See also CA 13-14; CANR 65; CAP 1; DLB
9, 54, 256; LAIT 2

Nekrasov, Nikolai Alekseevich
1821-1878 .... **NCLC 11**
See also DLB 277

Nelligan, Emile 1879-1941 .... **TCLC 14**
See also CA 114; 204; DLB 92; EWL 3

Nelson, Willie 1933- .... **CLC 17**
See also CA 107; CANR 114

Nemerov, Howard (Stanley)
1920-1991 .... **CLC 2, 6, 9, 36; PC 24;
TCLC 124**
See also AMW; CA 1-4R; 134; CABS 2;
CANR 1, 27, 53; DAM POET; DLB 5, 6;
DLBY 1983; EWL 3; INT CANR-27;
MTCW 1, 2; PFS 10, 14; RGAL 4

Neruda, Pablo 1904-1973 .. **CLC 1, 2, 5, 7, 9,
28, 62; HLC 2; PC 4; WLC**
See also CA 19-20; 45-48; CANR 131; CAP
2; DA; DA3; DAB; DAC; DAM MST,
MULT, POET; DLB 283; DNFS 2; EWL
3; HW 1; LAW; MTCW 1, 2; PFS 11;
RGWL 2, 3; TWA; WLIT 1; WP

Nerval, Gerard de 1808-1855 ... **NCLC 1, 67;
PC 13; SSC 18**
See also DLB 217; EW 6; GFL 1789 to the
Present; RGSF 2; RGWL 2, 3

Nervo, (Jose) Amado (Ruiz de)
1870-1919 .... **HLCS 2; TCLC 11**
See also CA 109; 131; DLB 290; EWL 3;
HW 1; LAW

Nesbit, Malcolm
See Chester, Alfred

Nessi, Pio Baroja y
See Baroja (y Nessi), Pio

Nestroy, Johann 1801-1862 .... **NCLC 42**
See also DLB 133; RGWL 2, 3

Netterville, Luke
See O'Grady, Standish (James)

Neufeld, John (Arthur) 1938- .... **CLC 17**
See also AAYA 11; CA 25-28R; CANR 11,
37, 56; CLR 52; MAICYA 1, 2; SAAS 3;
SATA 6, 81, 131; SATA-Essay 131; YAW

Neumann, Alfred 1895-1952 .... **TCLC 100**
See also CA 183; DLB 56

Neumann, Ferenc
See Molnar, Ferenc

Neville, Emily Cheney 1919- .... **CLC 12**
See also BYA 2; CA 5-8R; CANR 3, 37,
85; JRDA; MAICYA 1, 2; SAAS 2; SATA
1; YAW

Newbound, Bernard Slade 1930-
See Slade, Bernard
See also CA 81-84; CANR 49; CD 5; DAM
DRAM

Newby, P(ercy) H(oward)
1918-1997 .... **CLC 2, 13**
See also CA 5-8R; 161; CANR 32, 67; CN
7; DAM NOV; DLB 15; MTCW 1; RGEL
2

Newcastle
See Cavendish, Margaret Lucas

Newlove, Donald 1928- .... **CLC 6**
See also CA 29-32R; CANR 25

Newlove, John (Herbert) 1938- .... **CLC 14**
See also CA 21-24R; CANR 9, 25; CP 7

Newman, Charles 1938- .... **CLC 2, 8**
See also CA 21-24R; CANR 84; CN 7

Newman, Edwin (Harold) 1919- ...... **CLC 14**
See also AITN 1; CA 69-72; CANR 5

Newman, John Henry 1801-1890 . **NCLC 38,
99**
See also BRWS 7; DLB 18, 32, 55; RGEL
2

Newton, (Sir) Isaac 1642-1727 ...... **LC 35, 53**
See also DLB 252

Newton, Suzanne 1936- .... **CLC 35**
See also BYA 7; CA 41-44R; CANR 14;
JRDA; SATA 5, 77

New York Dept. of Ed. .... **CLC 70**

Nexo, Martin Andersen
1869-1954 .... **TCLC 43**
See also CA 202; DLB 214; EWL 3

Nezval, Vitezslav 1900-1958 .... **TCLC 44**
See also CA 123; CDWLB 4; DLB 215;
EWL 3

Ng, Fae Myenne 1957(?)- .... **CLC 81**
See also BYA 11; CA 146

Ngema, Mbongeni 1955- .... **CLC 57**
See also BW 2; CA 143; CANR 84; CD 5

Ngugi, James T(hiong'o) . **CLC 3, 7, 13, 182**
See Ngugi wa Thiong'o

Ngugi wa Thiong'o
See Ngugi wa Thiong'o
See also DLB 125; EWL 3

Ngugi wa Thiong'o 1938- ... **BLC 3; CLC 36,
182**
See Ngugi, James T(hiong'o); Ngugi wa
Thiong'o
See also AFW; BRWS 8; BW 2; CA 81-84;
CANR 27, 58; CDWLB 3; DAM MULT,
NOV; DNFS 2; MTCW 1, 2; RGEL 2;
WWE 1

Niatum, Duane 1938- .... **NNAL**
See also CA 41-44R; CANR 21, 45, 83;
DLB 175

Nichol, B(arrie) P(hillip) 1944-1988 . **CLC 18**
See also CA 53-56; DLB 53; SATA 66

Nicholas of Cusa 1401-1464 .... **LC 80**
See also DLB 115

Nichols, John (Treadwell) 1940- .... **CLC 38**
See also AMWS 13; CA 9-12R, 190; CAAE
190; CAAS 2; CANR 6, 70, 121; DLBY
1982; LATS 1:2; TCWW 2

Nichols, Leigh
See Koontz, Dean R(ay)

Nichols, Peter (Richard) 1927- .... **CLC 5, 36, 65**
See also CA 104; CANR 33, 86; CBD; CD 5; DLB 13, 245; MTCW 1

Nicholson, Linda ed. .... **CLC 65**

Ni Chuilleanain, Eilean 1942- .... **PC 34**
See also CA 126; CANR 53, 83; CP 7; CWP; DLB 40

Nicolas, F. R. E.
See Freeling, Nicolas

Niedecker, Lorine 1903-1970 ..... **CLC 10, 42; PC 42**
See also CA 25-28; CAP 2; DAM POET; DLB 48

Nietzsche, Friedrich (Wilhelm)
1844-1900 .... **TCLC 10, 18, 55**
See also CA 107; 121; CDWLB 2; DLB 129; EW 7; RGWL 2, 3; TWA

Nievo, Ippolito 1831-1861 .... **NCLC 22**

Nightingale, Anne Redmon 1943-
See Redmon, Anne
See also CA 103

Nightingale, Florence 1820-1910 ... **TCLC 85**
See also CA 188; DLB 166

Nijo Yoshimoto 1320-1388 .... **CMLC 49**
See also DLB 203

Nik. T. O.
See Annensky, Innokenty (Fyodorovich)

Nin, Anais 1903-1977 ..... **CLC 1, 4, 8, 11, 14, 60, 127; SSC 10**
See also AITN 2; AMWS 10; BPFB 2; CA 13-16R; 69-72; CANR 22, 53; DAM NOV, POP; DLB 2, 4, 152; EWL 3; GLL 2; MAWW; MTCW 1, 2; RGAL 4; RGSF 2

Nisbet, Robert A(lexander)
1913-1996 .... **TCLC 117**
See also CA 25-28R; 153; CANR 17; INT CANR-17

Nishida, Kitaro 1870-1945 .... **TCLC 83**

Nishiwaki, Junzaburo
See Nishiwaki, Junzaburo
See also CA 194

Nishiwaki, Junzaburo 1894-1982 .... **PC 15**
See Nishiwaki, Junzaburo; Nishiwaki Junzaburo
See also CA 194; 107; MJW; RGWL 3

Nishiwaki Junzaburo
See Nishiwaki, Junzaburo
See also EWL 3

Nissenson, Hugh 1933- .... **CLC 4, 9**
See also CA 17-20R; CANR 27, 108; CN 7; DLB 28

Nister, Der
See Der Nister
See also EWL 3

Niven, Larry .... **CLC 8**
See Niven, Laurence Van Cott
See also AAYA 27; BPFB 2; BYA 10; DLB 8; SCFW 2

Niven, Laurence Van Cott 1938-
See Niven, Larry
See also CA 21-24R, 207; CAAE 207; CAAS 12; CANR 14, 44, 66, 113; CPW; DAM POP; MTCW 1, 2; SATA 95; SFW 4

Nixon, Agnes Eckhardt 1927- .... **CLC 21**
See also CA 110

Nizan, Paul 1905-1940 .... **TCLC 40**
See also CA 161; DLB 72; EWL 3; GFL 1789 to the Present

Nkosi, Lewis 1936- .... **BLC 3; CLC 45**
See also BW 1, 3; CA 65-68; CANR 27, 81; CBD; CD 5; DAM MULT; DLB 157, 225; WWE 1

Nodier, (Jean) Charles (Emmanuel)
1780-1844 .... **NCLC 19**
See also DLB 119; GFL 1789 to the Present

Noguchi, Yone 1875-1947 .... **TCLC 80**

Nolan, Christopher 1965- .... **CLC 58**
See also CA 111; CANR 88

Noon, Jeff 1957- .... **CLC 91**
See also CA 148; CANR 83; DLB 267; SFW 4

Norden, Charles
See Durrell, Lawrence (George)

Nordhoff, Charles Bernard
1887-1947 .... **TCLC 23**
See also CA 108; 211; DLB 9; LAIT 1; RHW 1; SATA 23

Norfolk, Lawrence 1963- .... **CLC 76**
See also CA 144; CANR 85; CN 7; DLB 267

Norman, Marsha 1947- . **CLC 28, 186; DC 8**
See also CA 105; CABS 3; CAD; CANR 41, 131; CD 5; CSW; CWD; DAM DRAM; DFS 2; DLB 266; DLBY 1984; FW

Normyx
See Douglas, (George) Norman

Norris, (Benjamin) Frank(lin, Jr.)
1870-1902 .... **SSC 28; TCLC 24, 155**
See also AAYA 57; AMW; AMWC 2; BPFB 2; CA 110; 160; CDALB 1865-1917; DLB 12, 71, 186; LMFS 2; NFS 12; RGAL 4; TCWW 2; TUS

Norris, Leslie 1921- .... **CLC 14**
See also CA 11-12; CANR 14, 117; CAP 1; CP 7; DLB 27, 256

North, Andrew
See Norton, Andre

North, Anthony
See Koontz, Dean R(ay)

North, Captain George
See Stevenson, Robert Louis (Balfour)

North, Captain George
See Stevenson, Robert Louis (Balfour)

North, Milou
See Erdrich, Louise

Northrup, B. A.
See Hubbard, L(afayette) Ron(ald)

North Staffs
See Hulme, T(homas) E(rnest)

Northup, Solomon 1808-1863 ...... **NCLC 105**

Norton, Alice Mary
See Norton, Andre
See also MAICYA 1; SATA 1, 43

Norton, Andre 1912- .... **CLC 12**
See Norton, Alice Mary
See also AAYA 14; BPFB 2; BYA 4, 10, 12; CA 1-4R; CANR 68; CLR 50; DLB 8, 52; JRDA; MAICYA 2; MTCW 1; SATA 91; SUFW 1, 2; YAW

Norton, Caroline 1808-1877 .... **NCLC 47**
See also DLB 21, 159, 199

Norway, Nevil Shute 1899-1960
See Shute, Nevil
See also CA 102; 93-96; CANR 85; MTCW 2

Norwid, Cyprian Kamil
1821-1883 .... **NCLC 17**
See also RGWL 3

Nosille, Nabrah
See Ellison, Harlan (Jay)

Nossack, Hans Erich 1901-1978 .... **CLC 6**
See also CA 93-96; 85-88; DLB 69; EWL 3

Nostradamus 1503-1566 .... **LC 27**

Nosu, Chuji
See Ozu, Yasujiro

Notenburg, Eleanora (Genrikhovna) von
See Guro, Elena (Genrikhovna)

Nova, Craig 1945- .... **CLC 7, 31**
See also CA 45-48; CANR 2, 53, 127

Novak, Joseph
See Kosinski, Jerzy (Nikodem)

Novalis 1772-1801 .... **NCLC 13**
See also CDWLB 2; DLB 90; EW 5; RGWL 2, 3

Novick, Peter 1934- .... **CLC 164**
See also CA 188

Novis, Emile
See Weil, Simone (Adolphine)

Nowlan, Alden (Albert) 1933-1983 ... **CLC 15**
See also CA 9-12R; CANR 5; DAC; DAM MST; DLB 53; PFS 12

Noyes, Alfred 1880-1958 ...... **PC 27; TCLC 7**
See also CA 104; 188; DLB 20; EXPP; FANT; PFS 4; RGEL 2

Nugent, Richard Bruce 1906(?)-1987 ... **HR 3**
See also BW 1; CA 125; DLB 51; GLL 2

Nunn, Kem .... **CLC 34**
See also CA 159

Nwapa, Flora (Nwanzuruaha)
1931-1993 .... **BLCS; CLC 133**
See also BW 2; CA 143; CANR 83; CD-WLB 3; CWRI 5; DLB 125; EWL 3; WLIT 2

Nye, Robert 1939- .... **CLC 13, 42**
See also CA 33-36R; CANR 29, 67, 107; CN 7; CP 7; CWRI 5; DAM NOV; DLB 14, 271; FANT; HGG; MTCW 1; RHW; SATA 6

Nyro, Laura 1947-1997 .... **CLC 17**
See also CA 194

Oates, Joyce Carol 1938- .. **CLC 1, 2, 3, 6, 9, 11, 15, 19, 33, 52, 108, 134; SSC 6, 70; WLC**
See also AAYA 15, 52; AITN 1; AMWS 2; BEST 89:2; BPFB 2; BYA 11; CA 5-8R; CANR 25, 45, 74, 113, 129; CDALB 1968-1988; CN 7; CP 7; CPW; CWP; DA; DA3; DAB; DAC; DAM MST, NOV, POP; DLB 2, 5, 130; DLBY 1981; EWL 3; EXPS; FW; HGG; INT CANR-25; LAIT 4; MAWW; MTCW 1, 2; NFS 8; RGAL 4; RGSF 2; SSFS 17; SUFW 2; TUS

O'Brian, E. G.
See Clarke, Arthur C(harles)

O'Brian, Patrick 1914-2000 .... **CLC 152**
See also AAYA 55; CA 144; 187; CANR 74; CPW; MTCW 2; RHW

O'Brien, Darcy 1939-1998 .... **CLC 11**
See also CA 21-24R; 167; CANR 8, 59

O'Brien, Edna 1936- ..... **CLC 3, 5, 8, 13, 36, 65, 116; SSC 10**
See also BRWS 5; CA 1-4R; CANR 6, 41, 65, 102; CDBLB 1960 to Present; CN 7; DA3; DAM NOV; DLB 14, 231; EWL 3; FW; MTCW 1, 2; RGSF 2; WLIT 4

O'Brien, Fitz-James 1828-1862 ..... **NCLC 21**
See also DLB 74; RGAL 4; SUFW

O'Brien, Flann .... **CLC 1, 4, 5, 7, 10, 47**
See O Nuallain, Brian
See also BRWS 2; DLB 231; EWL 3; RGEL 2

O'Brien, Richard 1942- .... **CLC 17**
See also CA 124

O'Brien, (William) Tim(othy) 1946- . **CLC 7, 19, 40, 103; SSC 74**
See also AAYA 16; AMWS 5; CA 85-88; CANR 40, 58, 133; CDALBS; CN 7; CPW; DA3; DAM POP; DLB 152; DLBD 9; DLBY 1980; LATS 1:2; MTCW 2; RGAL 4; SSFS 5, 15

Obstfelder, Sigbjoern 1866-1900 .... **TCLC 23**
See also CA 123

O'Casey, Sean 1880-1964 .... **CLC 1, 5, 9, 11, 15, 88; DC 12; WLCS**
See also BRW 7; CA 89-92; CANR 62; CBD; CDBLB 1914-1945; DA3; DAB; DAC; DAM DRAM, MST; DFS 19; DLB 10; EWL 3; MTCW 1, 2; RGEL 2; TEA; WLIT 4

Pendennis, Arthur Esquir
See Thackeray, William Makepeace
Penn, William 1644-1718 .... **LC 25**
See also DLB 24
PEPECE
See Prado (Calvo), Pedro
Pepys, Samuel 1633-1703 ... **LC 11, 58; WLC**
See also BRW 2; CDBLB 1660-1789; DA;
DA3; DAB; DAC; DAM MST; DLB 101,
213; NCFS 4; RGEL 2; TEA; WLIT 3
Percy, Thomas 1729-1811 .... **NCLC 95**
See also DLB 104
Percy, Walker 1916-1990 .... **CLC 2, 3, 6, 8,**
14, 18, 47, 65
See also AMWS 3; BPFB 3; CA 1-4R; 131;
CANR 1, 23, 64; CPW; CSW; DA3;
DAM NOV, POP; DLB 2; DLBY 1980,
1990; EWL 3; MTCW 1, 2; RGAL 4;
TUS
Percy, William Alexander
1885-1942 .... **TCLC 84**
See also CA 163; MTCW 2
Perec, Georges 1936-1982 .... **CLC 56, 116**
See also CA 141; DLB 83, 299; EWL 3;
GFL 1789 to the Present; RGWL 3
Pereda (y Sanchez de Porrua), Jose Maria
de 1833-1906 .... **TCLC 16**
See also CA 117
Pereda y Porrua, Jose Maria de
See Pereda (y Sanchez de Porrua), Jose
Maria de
Peregoy, George Weems
See Mencken, H(enry) L(ouis)
Perelman, S(idney) J(oseph)
1904-1979 .. **CLC 3, 5, 9, 15, 23, 44, 49;**
SSC 32
See also AITN 1, 2; BPFB 3; CA 73-76;
89-92; CANR 18; DAM DRAM; DLB 11,
44; MTCW 1, 2; RGAL 4
Peret, Benjamin 1899-1959 .... **PC 33; TCLC**
20
See also CA 117; 186; GFL 1789 to the
Present
Peretz, Isaac Leib 1851(?)-1915
See Peretz, Isaac Loeb
See also CA 201
Peretz, Isaac Loeb 1851(?)-1915 ...... **SSC 26;**
TCLC 16
See Peretz, Isaac Leib
See also CA 109
Peretz, Yitzhok Leibush
See Peretz, Isaac Loeb
Perez Galdos, Benito 1843-1920 ..... **HLCS 2;**
TCLC 27
See Galdos, Benito Perez
See also CA 125; 153; EWL 3; HW 1;
RGWL 2, 3
Peri Rossi, Cristina 1941- .. **CLC 156; HLCS**
2
See also CA 131; CANR 59, 81; CWW 2;
DLB 145, 290; EWL 3; HW 1, 2
Perlata
See Peret, Benjamin
Perloff, Marjorie G(abrielle)
1931- .... **CLC 137**
See also CA 57-60; CANR 7, 22, 49, 104
Perrault, Charles 1628-1703 .... **LC 2, 56**
See also BYA 4; CLR 79; DLB 268; GFL
Beginnings to 1789; MAICYA 1, 2;
RGWL 2, 3; SATA 25; WCH
Perry, Anne 1938- .... **CLC 126**
See also CA 101; CANR 22, 50, 84; CMW
4; CN 7; CPW; DLB 276
Perry, Brighton
See Sherwood, Robert E(mmet)
Perse, St.-John
See Leger, (Marie-Rene Auguste) Alexis
Saint-Leger

Perse, Saint-John
See Leger, (Marie-Rene Auguste) Alexis
Saint-Leger
See also DLB 258; RGWL 3
Perutz, Leo(pold) 1882-1957 .... **TCLC 60**
See also CA 147; DLB 81
Peseenz, Tulio F.
See Lopez y Fuentes, Gregorio
Pesetsky, Bette 1932- .... **CLC 28**
See also CA 133; DLB 130
Peshkov, Alexei Maximovich 1868-1936
See Gorky, Maxim
See also CA 105; 141; CANR 83; DA;
DAC; DAM DRAM, MST, NOV; MTCW
2
Pessoa, Fernando (Antonio Nogueira)
1888-1935 ..... **HLC 2; PC 20; TCLC 27**
See also CA 125; 183; DAM MULT; DLB
287; EW 10; EWL 3; RGWL 2, 3; WP
Peterkin, Julia Mood 1880-1961 ...... **CLC 31**
See also CA 102; DLB 9
Peters, Joan K(aren) 1945- .... **CLC 39**
See also CA 158; CANR 109
Peters, Robert L(ouis) 1924- .... **CLC 7**
See also CA 13-16R; CAAS 8; CP 7; DLB
105
Petofi, Sandor 1823-1849 .... **NCLC 21**
See also RGWL 2, 3
Petrakis, Harry Mark 1923- .... **CLC 3**
See also CA 9-12R; CANR 4, 30, 85; CN 7
Petrarch 1304-1374 .... **CMLC 20; PC 8**
See also DA3; DAM POET; EW 2; LMFS
1; RGWL 2. 3
Petronius c. 20-66 .... **CMLC 34**
See also AW 2; CDWLB 1; DLB 211;
RGWL 2, 3
Petrov, Evgeny .... **TCLC 21**
See Kataev, Evgeny Petrovich
Petry, Ann (Lane) 1908-1997 .. **CLC 1, 7, 18;**
TCLC 112
See also AFAW 1, 2; BPFB 3; BW 1, 3;
BYA 2; CA 5-8R; 157; CAAS 6; CANR
4, 46; CLR 12; CN 7; DLB 76; EWL 3;
JRDA; LAIT 1; MAICYA 1, 2; MAIC-
YAS 1; MTCW 1; RGAL 4; SATA 5;
SATA-Obit 94; TUS
Petursson, Halligrimur 1614-1674 .... **LC 8**
Peychinovich
See Vazov, Ivan (Minchov)
Phaedrus c. 15B.C.-c. 50 .... **CMLC 25**
See also DLB 211
Phelps (Ward), Elizabeth Stuart
See Phelps, Elizabeth Stuart
See also FW
Phelps, Elizabeth Stuart
1844-1911 .... **TCLC 113**
See Phelps (Ward), Elizabeth Stuart
See also DLB 74
Philips, Katherine 1632-1664 . **LC 30; PC 40**
See also DLB 131; RGEL 2
Philipson, Morris H. 1926- .... **CLC 53**
See also CA 1-4R; CANR 4
Phillips, Caryl 1958- .... **BLCS; CLC 96**
See also BRWS 5; BW 2; CA 141; CANR
63, 104; CBD; CD 5; CN 7; DA3; DAM
MULT; DLB 157; EWL 3; MTCW 2;
WLIT 4; WWE 1
Phillips, David Graham
1867-1911 .... **TCLC 44**
See also CA 108; 176; DLB 9, 12, 303;
RGAL 4
Phillips, Jack
See Sandburg, Carl (August)
Phillips, Jayne Anne 1952- .... **CLC 15, 33,**
139; SSC 16
See also AAYA 57; BPFB 3; CA 101;
CANR 24, 50, 96; CN 7; CSW; DLBY
1980; INT CANR-24; MTCW 1, 2; RGAL
4; RGSF 2; SSFS 4

Phillips, Richard
See Dick, Philip K(indred)
Phillips, Robert (Schaeffer) 1938- ... **CLC 28**
See also CA 17-20R; CAAS 13; CANR 8;
DLB 105
Phillips, Ward
See Lovecraft, H(oward) P(hillips)
Philostratus, Flavius c. 179-c.
244 .... **CMLC 62**
Piccolo, Lucio 1901-1969 .... **CLC 13**
See also CA 97-100; DLB 114; EWL 3
Pickthall, Marjorie L(owry) C(hristie)
1883-1922 .... **TCLC 21**
See also CA 107; DLB 92
Pico della Mirandola, Giovanni
1463-1494 .... **LC 15**
See also LMFS 1
Piercy, Marge 1936- .... **CLC 3, 6, 14, 18, 27,**
62, 128; PC 29
See also BPFB 3; CA 21-24R; 187; CAAE
187; CAAS 1; CANR 13, 43, 66, 111; CN
7; CP 7; CWP; DLB 120, 227; EXPP;
FW; MTCW 1, 2; PFS 9; SFW 4
Piers, Robert
See Anthony, Piers
Pieyre de Mandiargues, Andre 1909-1991
See Mandiargues, Andre Pieyre de
See also CA 103; 136; CANR 22, 82; EWL
3; GFL 1789 to the Present .
Pilnyak, Boris 1894-1938 . **SSC 48; TCLC 23**
See Vogau, Boris Andreyevich
See also EWL 3
Pinchback, Eugene
See Toomer, Jean
Pincherle, Alberto 1907-1990 ...... **CLC 11, 18**
See Moravia, Alberto
See also CA 25-28R; 132; CANR 33, 63;
DAM NOV; MTCW 1
Pinckney, Darryl 1953- .... **CLC 76**
See also BW 2, 3; CA 143; CANR 79
Pindar 518(?)B.C.-438(?)B.C. .... **CMLC 12;**
PC 19
See also AW 1; CDWLB 1; DLB 176;
RGWL 2
Pineda, Cecile 1942- .... **CLC 39**
See also CA 118; DLB 209
Pinero, Arthur Wing 1855-1934 .... **TCLC 32**
See also CA 110; 153; DAM DRAM; DLB
10; RGEL 2
Pinero, Miguel (Antonio Gomez)
1946-1988 .... **CLC 4, 55**
See also CA 61-64; 125; CAD; CANR 29,
90; DLB 266; HW 1; LLW 1
Pinget, Robert 1919-1997 .... **CLC 7, 13, 37**
See also CA 85-88; 160; CWW 2; DLB 83;
EWL 3; GFL 1789 to the Present
Pink Floyd
See Barrett, (Roger) Syd; Gilmour, David;
Mason, Nick; Waters, Roger; Wright, Rick
Pinkney, Edward 1802-1828 .... **NCLC 31**
See also DLB 248
Pinkwater, Daniel
See Pinkwater, Daniel Manus
Pinkwater, Daniel Manus 1941- .... **CLC 35**
See also AAYA 1, 46; BYA 9; CA 29-32R;
CANR 12, 38, 89; CLR 4; CSW; FANT;
JRDA; MAICYA 1, 2; SAAS 3; SATA 8,
46, 76, 114; SFW 4; YAW
Pinkwater, Manus
See Pinkwater, Daniel Manus
Pinsky, Robert 1940- .... **CLC 9, 19, 38, 94,**
121; PC 27
See also AMWS 6; CA 29-32R; CAAS 4;
CANR 58, 97; CP 7; DA3; DAM POET;
DLBY 1982, 1998; MTCW 2; PFS 18;
RGAL 4
Pinta, Harold
See Pinter, Harold

Post, Melville Davisson
1869-1930 .... **TCLC 39**
See also CA 110; 202; CMW 4

Potok, Chaim 1929-2002 ... **CLC 2, 7, 14, 26, 112**
See also AAYA 15, 50; AITN 1, 2; BPFB 3;
BYA 1; CA 17-20R; 208; CANR 19, 35,
64, 98; CLR 92; CN 7; DA3; DAM NOV;
DLB 28, 152; EXPN; INT CANR-19;
LAIT 4; MTCW 1, 2; NFS 4; SATA 33,
106; SATA-Obit 134; TUS; YAW

Potok, Herbert Harold -2002
See Potok, Chaim

Potok, Herman Harold
See Potok, Chaim

Potter, Dennis (Christopher George)
1935-1994 .... **CLC 58, 86, 123**
See also CA 107; 145; CANR 33, 61; CBD;
DLB 233; MTCW 1

Pound, Ezra (Weston Loomis)
1885-1972 .. **CLC 1, 2, 3, 4, 5, 7, 10, 13, 18, 34, 48, 50, 112; PC 4; WLC**
See also AAYA 47; AMW; AMWR 1; CA
5-8R; 37-40R; CANR 40; CDALB 1917-
1929; DA; DA3; DAB; DAC; DAM MST,
POET; DLB 4, 45, 63; DLBD 15; EFS 2;
EWL 3; EXPP; LMFS 2; MTCW 1, 2;
PAB; PFS 2, 8, 16; RGAL 4; TUS; WP

Povod, Reinaldo 1959-1994 .... **CLC 44**
See also CA 136; 146; CANR 83

Powell, Adam Clayton, Jr.
1908-1972 .... **BLC 3; CLC 89**
See also BW 1, 3; CA 102; 33-36R; CANR
86; DAM MULT

Powell, Anthony (Dymoke)
1905-2000 .... **CLC 1, 3, 7, 9, 10, 31**
See also BRW 7; CA 1-4R; 189; CANR 1,
32, 62, 107; CDBLB 1945-1960; CN 7;
DLB 15; EWL 3; MTCW 1, 2; RGEL 2;
TEA

Powell, Dawn 1896(?)-1965 .... **CLC 66**
See also CA 5-8R; CANR 121; DLBY 1997

Powell, Padgett 1952- .... **CLC 34**
See also CA 126; CANR 63, 101; CSW;
DLB 234; DLBY 01

Powell, (Oval) Talmage 1920-2000
See Queen, Ellery
See also CA 5-8R; CANR 2, 80

Power, Susan 1961- .... **CLC 91**
See also BYA 14; CA 160; NFS 11

Powers, J(ames) F(arl) 1917-1999 ..... **CLC 1, 4, 8, 57; SSC 4**
See also CA 1-4R; 181; CANR 2, 61; CN
7; DLB 130; MTCW 1; RGAL 4; RGSF
2

Powers, John J(ames) 1945-
See Powers, John R.
See also CA 69-72

Powers, John R. .... **CLC 66**
See Powers, John J(ames)

Powers, Richard (S.) 1957- .... **CLC 93**
See also AMWS 9; BPFB 3; CA 148;
CANR 80; CN 7

Pownall, David 1938- .... **CLC 10**
See also CA 89-92, 180; CAAS 18; CANR
49, 101; CBD; CD 5; CN 7; DLB 14

Powys, John Cowper 1872-1963 ... **CLC 7, 9, 15, 46, 125**
See also CA 85-88; CANR 106; DLB 15,
255; EWL 3; FANT; MTCW 1, 2; RGEL
2; SUFW

Powys, T(heodore) F(rancis)
1875-1953 .... **TCLC 9**
See also BRWS 8; CA 106; 189; DLB 36,
162; EWL 3; FANT; RGEL 2; SUFW

Prado (Calvo), Pedro 1886-1952 ... **TCLC 75**
See also CA 131; DLB 283; HW 1; LAW

Prager, Emily 1952- .... **CLC 56**
See also CA 204

Pratchett, Terry 1948- .... **CLC 197**
See also AAYA 19, 54; BPFB 3; CA 143;
CANR 87, 126; CLR 64; CN 7; CPW;
CWRI 5; FANT; SATA 82, 139; SFW 4;
SUFW 2

Pratolini, Vasco 1913-1991 .... **TCLC 124**
See also CA 211; DLB 177; EWL 3; RGWL
2, 3

Pratt, E(dwin) J(ohn) 1883(?)-1964 . **CLC 19**
See also CA 141; 93-96; CANR 77; DAC;
DAM POET; DLB 92; EWL 3; RGEL 2;
TWA

Premchand .... **TCLC 21**
See Srivastava, Dhanpat Rai
See also EWL 3

Preseren, France 1800-1849 .... **NCLC 127**
See also CDWLB 4; DLB 147

Preussler, Otfried 1923- .... **CLC 17**
See also CA 77-80; SATA 24

Prevert, Jacques (Henri Marie)
1900-1977 .... **CLC 15**
See also CA 77-80; 69-72; CANR 29, 61;
DLB 258; EWL 3; GFL 1789 to the
Present; IDFW 3, 4; MTCW 1; RGWL 2,
3; SATA-Obit 30

Prevost, (Antoine Francois)
1697-1763 .... **LC 1**
See also EW 4; GFL Beginnings to 1789;
RGWL 2, 3

Price, (Edward) Reynolds 1933- ... **CLC 3, 6, 13, 43, 50, 63; SSC 22**
See also AMWS 6; CA 1-4R; CANR 1, 37,
57, 87, 128; CN 7; CSW; DAM NOV;
DLB 2, 218, 278; EWL 3; INT CANR-
37; NFS 18

Price, Richard 1949- .... **CLC 6, 12**
See also CA 49-52; CANR 3; DLBY 1981

Prichard, Katharine Susannah
1883-1969 .... **CLC 46**
See also CA 11-12; CANR 33; CAP 1; DLB
260; MTCW 1; RGEL 2; RGSF 2; SATA
66

Priestley, J(ohn) B(oynton)
1894-1984 .... **CLC 2, 5, 9, 34**
See also BRW 7; CA 9-12R; 113; CANR
33; CDBLB 1914-1945; DA3; DAM
DRAM, NOV; DLB 10, 34, 77, 100, 139;
DLBY 1984; EWL 3; MTCW 1, 2; RGEL
2; SFW 4

Prince 1958- .... **CLC 35**
See also CA 213

Prince, F(rank) T(empleton)
1912-2003 .... **CLC 22**
See also CA 101; 219; CANR 43, 79; CP 7;
DLB 20

Prince Kropotkin
See Kropotkin, Peter (Aleksieevich)

Prior, Matthew 1664-1721 .... **LC 4**
See also DLB 95; RGEL 2

Prishvin, Mikhail 1873-1954 .... **TCLC 75**
See Prishvin, Mikhail Mikhailovich

Prishvin, Mikhail Mikhailovich
See Prishvin, Mikhail
See also DLB 272; EWL 3

Pritchard, William H(arrison)
1932- .... **CLC 34**
See also CA 65-68; CANR 23, 95; DLB
111

Pritchett, V(ictor) S(awdon)
1900-1997 ... **CLC 5, 13, 15, 41; SSC 14**
See also BPFB 3; BRWS 3; CA 61-64; 157;
CANR 31, 63; CN 7; DA3; DAM NOV;
DLB 15, 139; EWL 3; MTCW 1, 2;
RGEL 2; RGSF 2; TEA

Private 19022
See Manning, Frederic

Probst, Mark 1925- .... **CLC 59**
See also CA 130

Prokosch, Frederic 1908-1989 ...... **CLC 4, 48**
See also CA 73-76; 128; CANR 82; DLB
48; MTCW 2

Propertius, Sextus c. 50B.C.-c.
16B.C. .... **CMLC 32**
See also AW 2; CDWLB 1; DLB 211;
RGWL 2, 3

Prophet, The
See Dreiser, Theodore (Herman Albert)

Prose, Francine 1947- .... **CLC 45**
See also CA 109; 112; CANR 46, 95, 132;
DLB 234; SATA 101, 149

Proudhon
See Cunha, Euclides (Rodrigues Pimenta)
da

Proulx, Annie
See Proulx, E(dna) Annie

Proulx, E(dna) Annie 1935- ...... **CLC 81, 158**
See also AMWS 7; BPFB 3; CA 145;
CANR 65, 110; CN 7; CPW 1; DA3;
DAM POP; MTCW 2; SSFS 18

Proust, (Valentin-Louis-George-Eugene)
Marcel 1871-1922 ..... **SSC 75; TCLC 7, 13, 33; WLC**
See also AAYA 58; BPFB 3; CA 104; 120;
CANR 110; DA; DA3; DAB; DAC; DAM
MST, NOV; DLB 65; EW 8; EWL 3; GFL
1789 to the Present; MTCW 1, 2; RGWL
2, 3; TWA

Prowler, Harley
See Masters, Edgar Lee

Prus, Boleslaw 1845-1912 .... **TCLC 48**
See also RGWL 2, 3

Pryor, Richard (Franklin Lenox Thomas)
1940- .... **CLC 26**
See also CA 122; 152

Przybyszewski, Stanislaw
1868-1927 .... **TCLC 36**
See also CA 160; DLB 66; EWL 3

Pteleon
See Grieve, C(hristopher) M(urray)
See also DAM POET

Puckett, Lute
See Masters, Edgar Lee

Puig, Manuel 1932-1990 .... **CLC 3, 5, 10, 28, 65, 133; HLC 2**
See also BPFB 3; CA 45-48; CANR 2, 32,
63; CDWLB 3; DA3; DAM MULT; DLB
113; DNFS 1; EWL 3; GLL 1; HW 1, 2;
LAW; MTCW 1, 2; RGWL 2, 3; TWA;
WLIT 1

Pulitzer, Joseph 1847-1911 .... **TCLC 76**
See also CA 114; DLB 23

Purchas, Samuel 1577(?)-1626 .... **LC 70**
See also DLB 151

Purdy, A(lfred) W(ellington)
1918-2000 .... **CLC 3, 6, 14, 50**
See also CA 81-84; 189; CAAS 17; CANR
42, 66; CP 7; DAC; DAM MST, POET;
DLB 88; PFS 5; RGEL 2

Purdy, James (Amos) 1923- .... **CLC 2, 4, 10, 28, 52**
See also AMWS 7; CA 33-36R; CAAS 1;
CANR 19, 51, 132; CN 7; DLB 2, 218;
EWL 3; INT CANR-19; MTCW 1; RGAL
4

Pure, Simon
See Swinnerton, Frank Arthur

Pushkin, Aleksandr Sergeevich
See Pushkin, Alexander (Sergeyevich)
See also DLB 205

Pushkin, Alexander (Sergeyevich)
1799-1837 .... **NCLC 3, 27, 83; PC 10; SSC 27, 55; WLC**
See Pushkin, Aleksandr Sergeevich
See also DA; DA3; DAB; DAC; DAM
DRAM, MST, POET; EW 5; EXPS; RGSF
2; RGWL 2, 3; SATA 61; SSFS 9; TWA

P'u Sung-ling 1640-1715 .... **LC 49; SSC 31**

Rao, Raja 1909- .... **CLC 25, 56**
  See also CA 73-76; CANR 51; CN 7; DAM
  NOV; EWL 3; MTCW 1, 2; RGEL 2;
  RGSF 2

Raphael, Frederic (Michael) 1931- ... **CLC 2, 14**
  See also CA 1-4R; CANR 1, 86; CN 7;
  DLB 14

Ratcliffe, James P.
  See Mencken, H(enry) L(ouis)

Rathbone, Julian 1935- .... **CLC 41**
  See also CA 101; CANR 34, 73

Rattigan, Terence (Mervyn)
  1911-1977 .... **CLC 7; DC 18**
  See also BRWS 7; CA 85-88; 73-76; CBD;
  CDBLB 1945-1960; DAM DRAM; DFS
  8; DLB 13; IDFW 3, 4; MTCW 1, 2;
  RGEL 2

Ratushinskaya, Irina 1954- .... **CLC 54**
  See also CA 129; CANR 68; CWW 2

Raven, Simon (Arthur Noel)
  1927-2001 .... **CLC 14**
  See also CA 81-84; 197; CANR 86; CN 7;
  DLB 271

Ravenna, Michael
  See Welty, Eudora (Alice)

Rawley, Callman 1903-2002
  See Rakosi, Carl
  See also CA 21-24R; CANR 12, 32, 91

Rawlings, Marjorie Kinnan
  1896-1953 .... **TCLC 4**
  See also AAYA 20; AMWS 10; ANW;
  BPFB 3; BYA 3; CA 104; 137; CANR 74;
  CLR 63; DLB 9, 22, 102; DLBD 17;
  JRDA; MAICYA 1, 2; MTCW 2; RGAL
  4; SATA 100; WCH; YABC 1; YAW

Ray, Satyajit 1921-1992 .... **CLC 16, 76**
  See also CA 114; 137; DAM MULT

Read, Herbert Edward 1893-1968 ..... **CLC 4**
  See also BRW 6; CA 85-88; 25-28R; DLB
  20, 149; EWL 3; PAB; RGEL 2

Read, Piers Paul 1941- .... **CLC 4, 10, 25**
  See also CA 21-24R; CANR 38, 86; CN 7;
  DLB 14; SATA 21

Reade, Charles 1814-1884 .... **NCLC 2, 74**
  See also DLB 21; RGEL 2

Reade, Hamish
  See Gray, Simon (James Holliday)

Reading, Peter 1946- .... **CLC 47**
  See also BRWS 8; CA 103; CANR 46, 96;
  CP 7; DLB 40

Reaney, James 1926- .... **CLC 13**
  See also CA 41-44R; CAAS 15; CANR 42;
  CD 5; CP 7; DAC; DAM MST; DLB 68;
  RGEL 2; SATA 43

Rebreanu, Liviu 1885-1944 .... **TCLC 28**
  See also CA 165; DLB 220; EWL 3

Rechy, John (Francisco) 1934- ...... **CLC 1, 7, 14, 18, 107; HLC 2**
  See also CA 5-8R, 195; CAAE 195; CAAS
  4; CANR 6, 32, 64; CN 7; DAM MULT;
  DLB 122, 278; DLBY 1982; HW 1, 2;
  INT CANR-6; LLW 1; RGAL 4

Redcam, Tom 1870-1933 .... **TCLC 25**

Reddin, Keith .... **CLC 67**
  See also CAD

Redgrove, Peter (William)
  1932-2003 .... **CLC 6, 41**
  See also BRWS 6; CA 1-4R; 217; CANR 3,
  39, 77; CP 7; DLB 40

Redmon, Anne .... **CLC 22**
  See Nightingale, Anne Redmon
  See also DLBY 1986

Reed, Eliot
  See Ambler, Eric

Reed, Ishmael 1938- ..... **BLC 3; CLC 2, 3, 5, 6, 13, 32, 60, 174**
  See also AFAW 1, 2; AMWS 10; BPFB 3;
  BW 2, 3; CA 21-24R; CANR 25, 48, 74,
  128; CN 7; CP 7; CSW; DA3; DAM
  MULT; DLB 2, 5, 33, 169, 227; DLBD 8;
  EWL 3; LMFS 2; MSW; MTCW 1, 2;
  PFS 6; RGAL 4; TCWW 2

Reed, John (Silas) 1887-1920 .... **TCLC 9**
  See also CA 106; 195; TUS

Reed, Lou .... **CLC 21**
  See Firbank, Louis

Reese, Lizette Woodworth 1856-1935 . **PC 29**
  See also CA 180; DLB 54

Reeve, Clara 1729-1807 .... **NCLC 19**
  See also DLB 39; RGEL 2

Reich, Wilhelm 1897-1957 .... **TCLC 57**
  See also CA 199

Reid, Christopher (John) 1949- .... **CLC 33**
  See also CA 140; CANR 89; CP 7; DLB
  40; EWL 3

Reid, Desmond
  See Moorcock, Michael (John)

Reid Banks, Lynne 1929-
  See Banks, Lynne Reid
  See also AAYA 49; CA 1-4R; CANR 6, 22,
  38, 87; CLR 24; CN 7; JRDA; MAICYA
  1, 2; SATA 22, 75, 111; YAW

Reilly, William K.
  See Creasey, John

Reiner, Max
  See Caldwell, (Janet Miriam) Taylor
  (Holland)

Reis, Ricardo
  See Pessoa, Fernando (Antonio Nogueira)

Reizenstein, Elmer Leopold
  See Rice, Elmer (Leopold)
  See also EWL 3

Remarque, Erich Maria 1898-1970 . **CLC 21**
  See also AAYA 27; BPFB 3; CA 77-80; 29-
  32R; CDWLB 2; DA; DA3; DAB; DAC;
  DAM MST, NOV; DLB 56; EWL 3;
  EXPN; LAIT 3; MTCW 1, 2; NFS 4;
  RGWL 2, 3

Remington, Frederic 1861-1909 ..... **TCLC 89**
  See also CA 108; 169; DLB 12, 186, 188;
  SATA 41

Remizov, A.
  See Remizov, Aleksei (Mikhailovich)

Remizov, A. M.
  See Remizov, Aleksei (Mikhailovich)

Remizov, Aleksei (Mikhailovich)
  1877-1957 .... **TCLC 27**
  See Remizov, Alexey Mikhaylovich
  See also CA 125; 133; DLB 295

Remizov, Alexey Mikhaylovich
  See Remizov, Aleksei (Mikhailovich)
  See also EWL 3

Renan, Joseph Ernest 1823-1892 . **NCLC 26, 145**
  See also GFL 1789 to the Present

Renard, Jules(-Pierre) 1864-1910 .. **TCLC 17**
  See also CA 117; 202; GFL 1789 to the
  Present

Renault, Mary .... **CLC 3, 11, 17**
  See Challans, Mary
  See also BPFB 3; BYA 2; DLBY 1983;
  EWL 3; GLL 1; LAIT 1; MTCW 2; RGEL
  2; RHW

Rendell, Ruth (Barbara) 1930- .. **CLC 28, 48**
  See Vine, Barbara
  See also BPFB 3; BRWS 9; CA 109; CANR
  32, 52, 74, 127; CN 7; CPW; DAM POP;
  DLB 87, 276; INT CANR-32; MSW;
  MTCW 1, 2

Renoir, Jean 1894-1979 .... **CLC 20**
  See also CA 129; 85-88

Resnais, Alain 1922- .... **CLC 16**

Revard, Carter (Curtis) 1931- .... **NNAL**
  See also CA 144; CANR 81; PFS 5

Reverdy, Pierre 1889-1960 .... **CLC 53**
  See also CA 97-100; 89-92; DLB 258; EWL
  3; GFL 1789 to the Present

Rexroth, Kenneth 1905-1982 .... **CLC 1, 2, 6, 11, 22, 49, 112; PC 20**
  See also BG 3; CA 5-8R; 107; CANR 14,
  34, 63; CDALB 1941-1968; DAM POET;
  DLB 16, 48, 165, 212; DLBY 1982; EWL
  3; INT CANR-14; MTCW 1, 2; RGAL 4

Reyes, Alfonso 1889-1959 .... **HLCS 2; TCLC 33**
  See also CA 131; EWL 3; HW 1; LAW

Reyes y Basoalto, Ricardo Eliecer Neftali
  See Neruda, Pablo

Reymont, Wladyslaw (Stanislaw)
  1868(?)-1925 .... **TCLC 5**
  See also CA 104; EWL 3

Reynolds, Jonathan 1942- .... **CLC 6, 38**
  See also CA 65-68; CANR 28

Reynolds, Joshua 1723-1792 .... **LC 15**
  See also DLB 104

Reynolds, Michael S(hane)
  1937-2000 .... **CLC 44**
  See also CA 65-68; 189; CANR 9, 89, 97

Reznikoff, Charles 1894-1976 .... **CLC 9**
  See also CA 33-36; 61-64; CAP 2; DLB 28,
  45; WP

Rezzori (d'Arezzo), Gregor von
  1914-1998 .... **CLC 25**
  See also CA 122; 136; 167

Rhine, Richard
  See Silverstein, Alvin; Silverstein, Virginia
  B(arbara Opshelor)

Rhodes, Eugene Manlove
  1869-1934 .... **TCLC 53**
  See also CA 198; DLB 256

R'hoone, Lord
  See Balzac, Honore de

Rhys, Jean 1894(?)-1979 ...... **CLC 2, 4, 6, 14, 19, 51, 124; SSC 21, 76**
  See also BRWS 2; CA 25-28R; 85-88;
  CANR 35, 62; CDBLB 1945-1960; CD-
  WLB 3; DA3; DAM NOV; DLB 36, 117,
  162; DNFS 2; EWL 3; LATS 1:1; MTCW
  1, 2; RGEL 2; RGSF 2; RHW; TEA;
  WWE 1

Ribeiro, Darcy 1922-1997 .... **CLC 34**
  See also CA 33-36R; 156; EWL 3

Ribeiro, Joao Ubaldo (Osorio Pimentel)
  1941- .... **CLC 10, 67**
  See also CA 81-84; CWW 2; EWL 3

Ribman, Ronald (Burt) 1932- .... **CLC 7**
  See also CA 21-24R; CAD; CANR 46, 80;
  CD 5

Ricci, Nino (Pio) 1959- .... **CLC 70**
  See also CA 137; CANR 130; CCA 1

Rice, Anne 1941- .... **CLC 41, 128**
  See Rampling, Anne
  See also AAYA 9, 53; AMWS 7; BEST
  89:2; BPFB 3; CA 65-68; CANR 12, 36,
  53, 74, 100, 133; CN 7; CPW; CSW;
  DA3; DAM POP; DLB 292; GLL 2;
  HGG; MTCW 2; SUFW 2; YAW

Rice, Elmer (Leopold) 1892-1967 ...... **CLC 7, 49**
  See Reizenstein, Elmer Leopold
  See also CA 21-22; 25-28R; CAP 2; DAM
  DRAM; DFS 12; DLB 4, 7; MTCW 1, 2;
  RGAL 4

Rice, Tim(othy Miles Bindon)
  1944- .... **CLC 21**
  See also CA 103; CANR 46; DFS 7

Rich, Adrienne (Cecile) 1929- ... **CLC 3, 6, 7, 11, 18, 36, 73, 76, 125; PC 5**
  See also AMWR 2; AMWS 1; CA 9-12R;
  CANR 20, 53, 74, 128; CDALBS; CP 7;
  CSW; CWP; DA3; DAM POET; DLB 5,
  67; EWL 3; EXPP; FW; MAWW; MTCW
  1, 2; PAB; PFS 15; RGAL 4; WP

Saint-Exupery, Antoine (Jean Baptiste Marie Roger) de 1900-1944 .... **TCLC 2, 56; WLC**
See also BPFB 3; BYA 3; CA 108; 132; CLR 10; DA3; DAM NOV; DLB 72; EW 12; EWL 3; GFL 1789 to the Present; LAIT 3; MAICYA 1, 2; MTCW 1, 2; RGWL 2, 3; SATA 20; TWA

St. John, David
See Hunt, E(verette) Howard, (Jr.)

St. John, J. Hector
See Crevecoeur, Michel Guillaume Jean de

Saint-John Perse
See Leger, (Marie-Rene Auguste) Alexis Saint-Leger
See also EW 10; EWL 3; GFL 1789 to the Present; RGWL 2

Saintsbury, George (Edward Bateman) 1845-1933 .... **TCLC 31**
See also CA 160; DLB 57, 149

Sait Faik .... **TCLC 23**
See Abasiyanik, Sait Faik

Saki .... **SSC 12; TCLC 3**
See Munro, H(ector) H(ugh)
See also BRWS 6; BYA 11; LAIT 2; MTCW 2; RGEL 2; SSFS 1; SUFW

Sala, George Augustus 1828-1895 . **NCLC 46**

Saladin 1138-1193 .... **CMLC 38**

Salama, Hannu 1936- .... **CLC 18**
See also EWL 3

Salamanca, J(ack) R(ichard) 1922- .. **CLC 4, 15**
See also CA 25-28R; 193; CAAE 193

Salas, Floyd Francis 1931- .... **HLC 2**
See also CA 119; CAAS 27; CANR 44, 75, 93; DAM MULT; DLB 82; HW 1, 2; MTCW 2

Sale, J. Kirkpatrick
See Sale, Kirkpatrick

Sale, Kirkpatrick 1937- .... **CLC 68**
See also CA 13-16R; CANR 10

Salinas, Luis Omar 1937- ... **CLC 90; HLC 2**
See also AMWS 13; CA 131; CANR 81; DAM MULT; DLB 82; HW 1, 2

Salinas (y Serrano), Pedro 1891(?)-1951 .... **TCLC 17**
See also CA 117; DLB 134; EWL 3

Salinger, J(erome) D(avid) 1919- .. **CLC 1, 3, 8, 12, 55, 56, 138; SSC 2, 28, 65; WLC**
See also AAYA 2, 36; AMW; AMWC 1; BPFB 3; CA 5-8R; CANR 39, 129; CDALB 1941-1968; CLR 18; CN 7; CPW 1; DA; DA3; DAB; DAC; DAM MST, NOV, POP; DLB 2, 102, 173; EWL 3; EXPN; LAIT 4; MAICYA 1, 2; MTCW 1, 2; NFS 1; RGAL 4; RGSF 2; SATA 67; SSFS 17; TUS; WYA; YAW

Salisbury, John
See Caute, (John) David

Sallust c. 86B.C.-35B.C. .... **CMLC 68**
See also AW 2; CDWLB 1; DLB 211; RGWL 2, 3

Salter, James 1925- .. **CLC 7, 52, 59; SSC 58**
See also AMWS 9; CA 73-76; CANR 107; DLB 130

Saltus, Edgar (Everton) 1855-1921 . **TCLC 8**
See also CA 105; DLB 202; RGAL 4

Saltykov, Mikhail Evgrafovich 1826-1889 .... **NCLC 16**
See also DLB 238:

Saltykov-Shchedrin, N.
See Saltykov, Mikhail Evgrafovich

Samarakis, Andonis
See Samarakis, Antonis
See also EWL 3

Samarakis, Antonis 1919-2003 .... **CLC 5**
See Samarakis, Andonis
See also CA 25-28R; 224; CAAS 16; CANR 36

Sanchez, Florencio 1875-1910 .... **TCLC 37**
See also CA 153; DLB 305; EWL 3; HW 1; LAW

Sanchez, Luis Rafael 1936- .... **CLC 23**
See also CA 128; DLB 305; EWL 3; HW 1; WLIT 1

Sanchez, Sonia 1934- .... **BLC 3; CLC 5, 116; PC 9**
See also BW 2, 3; CA 33-36R; CANR 24, 49, 74, 115; CLR 18; CP 7; CSW; CWP; DA3; DAM MULT; DLB 41; DLBD 8; EWL 3; MAICYA 1, 2; MTCW 1, 2; SATA 22, 136; WP

Sancho, Ignatius 1729-1780 .... **LC 84**

Sand, George 1804-1876 ..... **NCLC 2, 42, 57; WLC**
See also DA; DA3; DAB; DAC; DAM MST, NOV; DLB 119, 192; EW 6; FW; GFL 1789 to the Present; RGWL 2, 3; TWA

Sandburg, Carl (August) 1878-1967 . **CLC 1, 4, 10, 15, 35; PC 2, 41; WLC**
See also AAYA 24; AMW; BYA 1, 3; CA 5-8R; 25-28R; CANR 35; CDALB 1865-1917; CLR 67; DA; DA3; DAB; DAC; DAM MST, POET; DLB 17, 54, 284; EWL 3; EXPP; LAIT 2; MAICYA 1, 2; MTCW 1, 2; PAB; PFS 3, 6, 12; RGAL 4; SATA 8; TUS; WCH; WP; WYA

Sandburg, Charles
See Sandburg, Carl (August)

Sandburg, Charles A.
See Sandburg, Carl (August)

Sanders, (James) Ed(ward) 1939- .... **CLC 53**
See Sanders, Edward
See also BG 3; CA 13-16R; CAAS 21; CANR 13, 44, 78; CP 7; DAM POET; DLB 16, 244

Sanders, Edward
See Sanders, (James) Ed(ward)
See also DLB 244

Sanders, Lawrence 1920-1998 .... **CLC 41**
See also BEST 89:4; BPFB 3; CA 81-84; 165; CANR 33, 62; CMW 4; CPW; DA3; DAM POP; MTCW 1

Sanders, Noah
See Blount, Roy (Alton), Jr.

Sanders, Winston P.
See Anderson, Poul (William)

Sandoz, Mari(e Susette) 1900-1966 .. **CLC 28**
See also CA 1-4R; 25-28R; CANR 17, 64; DLB 9, 212; LAIT 2; MTCW 1, 2; SATA 5; TCWW 2

Sandys, George 1578-1644 .... **LC 80**
See also DLB 24, 121

Saner, Reg(inald Anthony) 1931- .... **CLC 9**
See also CA 65-68; CP 7

Sankara 788-820 .... **CMLC 32**

Sannazaro, Jacopo 1456(?)-1530 .... **LC 8**
See also RGWL 2, 3

Sansom, William 1912-1976 . **CLC 2, 6; SSC 21**
See also CA 5-8R; 65-68; CANR 42; DAM NOV; DLB 139; EWL 3; MTCW 1; RGEL 2; RGSF 2

Santayana, George 1863-1952 .... **TCLC 40**
See also AMW; CA 115; 194; DLB 54, 71, 246, 270; DLBD 13; EWL 3; RGAL 4; TUS

Santiago, Danny .... **CLC 33**
See James, Daniel (Lewis)
See also DLB 122

Santmyer, Helen Hooven 1895-1986 .... **CLC 33; TCLC 133**
See also CA 1-4R; 118; CANR 15, 33; DLBY 1984; MTCW 1; RHW

Santoka, Taneda 1882-1940 .... **TCLC 72**

Santos, Bienvenido N(uqui) 1911-1996 ... **AAL; CLC 22; TCLC 156**
See also CA 101; 151; CANR 19, 46; DAM MULT; EWL; RGAL 4; SSFS 19

Sapir, Edward 1884-1939 .... **TCLC 108**
See also CA 211; DLB 92

Sapper .... **TCLC 44**
See McNeile, Herman Cyril

Sapphire
See Sapphire, Brenda

Sapphire, Brenda 1950- .... **CLC 99**

Sappho fl. 6th cent. B.C.- ... **CMLC 3, 67; PC 5**
See also CDWLB 1; DA3; DAM POET; DLB 176; PFS 20; RGWL 2, 3; WP

Saramago, Jose 1922- .... **CLC 119; HLCS 1**
See also CA 153; CANR 96; CWW 2; DLB 287; EWL 3; LATS 1:2

Sarduy, Severo 1937-1993 .... **CLC 6, 97; HLCS 2**
See also CA 89-92; 142; CANR 58, 81; CWW 2; DLB 113; EWL 3; HW 1, 2; LAW

Sargeson, Frank 1903-1982 .... **CLC 31**
See also CA 25-28R; 106; CANR 38, 79; EWL 3; GLL 2; RGEL 2; RGSF 2; SSFS 20

Sarmiento, Domingo Faustino 1811-1888 .... **HLCS 2**
See also LAW; WLIT 1

Sarmiento, Felix Ruben Garcia
See Dario, Ruben

Saro-Wiwa, Ken(ule Beeson) 1941-1995 .... **CLC 114**
See also BW 2; CA 142; 150; CANR 60; DLB 157

Saroyan, William 1908-1981 ... **CLC 1, 8, 10, 29, 34, 56; SSC 21; TCLC 137; WLC**
See also CA 5-8R; 103; CAD; CANR 30; CDALBS; DA; DA3; DAB; DAC; DAM DRAM, MST, NOV; DFS 17; DLB 7, 9, 86; DLBY 1981; EWL 3; LAIT 4; MTCW 1, 2; RGAL 4; RGSF 2; SATA 23; SATA-Obit 24; SSFS 14; TUS

Sarraute, Nathalie 1900-1999 .... **CLC 1, 2, 4, 8, 10, 31, 80; TCLC 145**
See also BPFB 3; CA 9-12R; 187; CANR 23, 66; CWW 2; DLB 83; EW 12; EWL 3; GFL 1789 to the Present; MTCW 1, 2; RGWL 2, 3

Sarton, (Eleanor) May 1912-1995 ..... **CLC 4, 14, 49, 91; PC 39; TCLC 120**
See also AMWS 8; CA 1-4R; 149; CANR 1, 34, 55, 116; CN 7; CP 7; DAM POET; DLB 48; DLBY 1981; EWL 3; FW; INT CANR-34; MTCW 1, 2; RGAL 4; SATA 36; SATA-Obit 86; TUS

Sartre, Jean-Paul 1905-1980 . **CLC 1, 4, 7, 9, 13, 18, 24, 44, 50, 52; DC 3; SSC 32; WLC**
See also CA 9-12R; 97-100; CANR 21; DA; DA3; DAB; DAC; DAM DRAM, MST, NOV; DFS 5; DLB 72, 296; EW 12; EWL 3; GFL 1789 to the Present; LMFS 2; MTCW 1, 2; RGSF 2; RGWL 2, 3; SSFS 9; TWA

Sassoon, Siegfried (Lorraine) 1886-1967 .... **CLC 36, 130; PC 12**
See also BRW 6; CA 104; 25-28R; CANR 36; DAB; DAM MST, NOV, POET; DLB 20, 191; DLBD 18; EWL 3; MTCW 1, 2; PAB; RGEL 2; TEA

Satterfield, Charles
See Pohl, Frederik

Satyremont
See Peret, Benjamin

Saul, John (W. III) 1942- .... **CLC 46**
See also AAYA 10; BEST 90:4; CA 81-84; CANR 16, 40, 81; CPW; DAM NOV, POP; HGG; SATA 98

256, 275; EWL 3; EXPP; EXPS; LAIT 4;
MTCW 2; NFS 4; PFS 9, 16; RGAL 4;
RGSF 2; SSFS 4, 8, 10, 11

Sillanpaa, Frans Eemil 1888-1964 ... **CLC 19**
See also CA 129; 93-96; EWL 3; MTCW 1

Sillitoe, Alan 1928- .. **CLC 1, 3, 6, 10, 19, 57, 148**
See also AITN 1; BRWS 5; CA 9-12R, 191;
CAAE 191; CAAS 2; CANR 8, 26, 55;
CDBLB 1960 to Present; CN 7; DLB 14,
139; EWL 3; MTCW 1, 2; RGEL 2;
RGSF 2; SATA 61

Silone, Ignazio 1900-1978 .... **CLC 4**
See also CA 25-28; 81-84; CANR 34; CAP
2; DLB 264; EW 12; EWL 3; MTCW 1;
RGSF 2; RGWL 2, 3

Silone, Ignazione
See Silone, Ignazio

Silver, Joan Micklin 1935- .... **CLC 20**
See also CA 114; 121; INT CA-121

Silver, Nicholas
See Faust, Frederick (Schiller)
See also TCWW 2

Silverberg, Robert 1935- .... **CLC 7, 140**
See also AAYA 24; BPFB 3; BYA 7, 9; CA
1-4R, 186; CAAE 186; CAAS 3; CANR
1, 20, 36, 85; CLR 59; CN 7; CPW; DAM
POP; DLB 8; INT CANR-20; MAICYA
1, 2; MTCW 1, 2; SATA 13, 91; SATA-
Essay 104; SCFW 2; SFW 4; SUFW 2

Silverstein, Alvin 1933- .... **CLC 17**
See also CA 49-52; CANR 2; CLR 25;
JRDA; MAICYA 1, 2; SATA 8, 69, 124

Silverstein, Shel(don Allan)
1932-1999 .... **PC 49**
See also AAYA 40; BW 3; CA 107; 179;
CANR 47, 74, 81; CLR 5, 96; CWRI 5;
JRDA; MAICYA 1, 2; MTCW 2; SATA
33, 92; SATA-Brief 27; SATA-Obit 116

Silverstein, Virginia B(arbara Opshelor)
1937- .... **CLC 17**
See also CA 49-52; CANR 2; CLR 25;
JRDA; MAICYA 1, 2; SATA 8, 69, 124

Sim, Georges
See Simenon, Georges (Jacques Christian)

Simak, Clifford D(onald) 1904-1988 . **CLC 1, 55**
See also CA 1-4R; 125; CANR 1, 35; DLB
8; MTCW 1; SATA-Obit 56; SFW 4

Simenon, Georges (Jacques Christian)
1903-1989 .... **CLC 1, 2, 3, 8, 18, 47**
See also BPFB 3; CA 85-88; 129; CANR
35; CMW 4; DA3; DAM POP; DLB 72;
DLBY 1989; EW 12; EWL 3; GFL 1789
to the Present; MSW; MTCW 1, 2; RGWL
2, 3

Simic, Charles 1938- .... **CLC 6, 9, 22, 49, 68, 130**
See also AMWS 8; CA 29-32R; CAAS 4;
CANR 12, 33, 52, 61, 96; CP 7; DA3;
DAM POET; DLB 105; MTCW 2; PFS 7;
RGAL 4; WP

Simmel, Georg 1858-1918 .... **TCLC 64**
See also CA 157; DLB 296

Simmons, Charles (Paul) 1924- .... **CLC 57**
See also CA 89-92; INT CA-89-92

Simmons, Dan 1948- .... **CLC 44**
See also AAYA 16, 54; CA 138; CANR 53,
81, 126; CPW; DAM POP; HGG; SUFW
2

Simmons, James (Stewart Alexander)
1933- .... **CLC 43**
See also CA 105; CAAS 21; CP 7; DLB 40

Simms, William Gilmore
1806-1870 .... **NCLC 3**
See also DLB 3, 30, 59, 73, 248, 254;
RGAL 4

Simon, Carly 1945- .... **CLC 26**
See also CA 105

Simon, Claude (Eugene Henri)
1913-1984 .... **CLC 4, 9, 15, 39**
See also CA 89-92; CANR 33, 117; CWW
2; DAM NOV; DLB 83; EW 13; EWL 3;
GFL 1789 to the Present; MTCW 1

Simon, Myles
See Follett, Ken(neth Martin)

Simon, (Marvin) Neil 1927- ... **CLC 6, 11, 31, 39, 70; DC 14**
See also CA 32; AITN 1; AMWS 4; CA
21-24R; CANR 26, 54, 87, 126; CD 5;
DA3; DAM DRAM; DFS 2, 6, 12, 18;
DLB 7, 266; LAIT 4; MTCW 1, 2; RGAL
4; TUS

Simon, Paul (Frederick) 1941(?)- ..... **CLC 17**
See also CA 116; 153

Simonon, Paul 1956(?)- .... **CLC 30**

Simonson, Rick ed. .... **CLC 70**

Simpson, Harriette
See Arnow, Harriette (Louisa) Simpson

Simpson, Louis (Aston Marantz)
1923- .... **CLC 4, 7, 9, 32, 149**
See also AMWS 9; CA 1-4R; CAAS 4;
CANR 1, 61; CP 7; DAM POET; DLB 5;
MTCW 1, 2; PFS 7, 11, 14; RGAL 4

Simpson, Mona (Elizabeth) 1957- ... **CLC 44, 146**
See also CA 122; 135; CANR 68, 103; CN
7; EWL 3

Simpson, N(orman) F(rederick)
1919- .... **CLC 29**
See also CA 13-16R; CBD; DLB 13; RGEL
2

Sinclair, Andrew (Annandale) 1935- . **CLC 2, 14**
See also CA 9-12R; CAAS 5; CANR 14,
38, 91; CN 7; DLB 14; FANT; MTCW 1

Sinclair, Emil
See Hesse, Hermann

Sinclair, Iain 1943- .... **CLC 76**
See also CA 132; CANR 81; CP 7; HGG

Sinclair, Iain MacGregor
See Sinclair, Iain

Sinclair, Irene
See Griffith, D(avid Lewelyn) W(ark)

Sinclair, Mary Amelia St. Clair 1865(?)-1946
See Sinclair, May
See also CA 104; HGG; RHW

Sinclair, May .... **TCLC 3, 11**
See Sinclair, Mary Amelia St. Clair
See also CA 166; DLB 36, 135; EWL 3;
RGEL 2; SUFW

Sinclair, Roy
See Griffith, D(avid Lewelyn) W(ark)

Sinclair, Upton (Beall) 1878-1968 ..... **CLC 1, 11, 15, 63; WLC**
See also AMWS 5; BPFB 3; BYA 2; CA
5-8R; 25-28R; CANR 7; CDALB 1929-
1941; DA; DA3; DAB; DAC; DAM MST,
NOV; DLB 9; EWL 3; INT CANR-7;
LAIT 3; MTCW 1, 2; NFS 6; RGAL 4;
SATA 9; TUS; YAW

Singe, (Edmund) J(ohn) M(illington)
1871-1909 .... **WLC**

Singer, Isaac
See Singer, Isaac Bashevis

Singer, Isaac Bashevis 1904-1991 .. **CLC 1, 3, 6, 9, 11, 15, 23, 38, 69, 111; SSC 3, 53; WLC**
See also AAYA 32; AITN 1, 2; AMW;
AMWR 2; BPFB 3; BYA 1, 4; CA 1-4R;
134; CANR 1, 39, 106; CDALB 1941-
1968; CLR 1; CWRI 5; DA; DA3; DAB;
DAC; DAM MST, NOV; DLB 6, 28, 52,
278; DLBY 1991; EWL 3; EXPS; HGG;
JRDA; LAIT 3; MAICYA 1, 2; MTCW 1,
2; RGAL 4; RGSF 2; SATA 3, 27; SATA-
Obit 68; SSFS 2, 12, 16; TUS; TWA

Singer, Israel Joshua 1893-1944 .... **TCLC 33**
See also CA 169; EWL 3

Singh, Khushwant 1915- .... **CLC 11**
See also CA 9-12R; CAAS 9; CANR 6, 84;
CN 7; EWL 3; RGEL 2

Singleton, Ann
See Benedict, Ruth (Fulton)

Singleton, John 1968(?)- .... **CLC 156**
See also AAYA 50; BW 2, 3; CA 138;
CANR 67, 82; DAM MULT

Siniavskii, Andrei
See Sinyavsky, Andrei (Donatevich)
See also CWW 2

Sinjohn, John
See Galsworthy, John

Sinyavsky, Andrei (Donatevich)
1925-1997 .... **CLC 8**
See Siniavskii, Andrei; Sinyavsky, Andrey
Donatovich; Tertz, Abram
See also CA 85-88; 159

Sinyavsky, Andrey Donatovich
See Sinyavsky, Andrei (Donatevich)
See also EWL 3

Sirin, V.
See Nabokov, Vladimir (Vladimirovich)

Sissman, L(ouis) E(dward)
1928-1976 .... **CLC 9, 18**
See also CA 21-24R; 65-68; CANR 13;
DLB 5

Sisson, C(harles) H(ubert)
1914-2003 .... **CLC 8**
See also CA 1-4R; 220; CAAS 3; CANR 3,
48, 84; CP 7; DLB 27

Sitting Bull 1831(?)-1890 .... **NNAL**
See also DA3; DAM MULT

Sitwell, Dame Edith 1887-1964 ..... **CLC 2, 9, 67; PC 3**
See also BRW 7; CA 9-12R; CANR 35;
CDBLB 1945-1960; DAM POET; DLB
20; EWL 3; MTCW 1, 2; RGEL 2; TEA

Siwaarmill, H. P.
See Sharp, William

Sjoewall, Maj 1935- .... **CLC 7**
See Sjowall, Maj
See also CA 65-68; CANR 73

Sjowall, Maj
See Sjoewall, Maj
See also BPFB 3; CMW 4; MSW

Skelton, John 1460(?)-1529 ..... **LC 71; PC 25**
See also BRW 1; DLB 136; RGEL 2

Skelton, Robin 1925-1997 .... **CLC 13**
See Zuk, Georges
See also AITN 2; CA 5-8R; 160; CAAS 5;
CANR 28, 89; CCA 1; CP 7; DLB 27, 53

Skolimowski, Jerzy 1938- .... **CLC 20**
See also CA 128

Skram, Amalie (Bertha)
1847-1905 .... **TCLC 25**
See also CA 165

Skvorecky, Josef (Vaclav) 1924- ...... **CLC 15, 39, 69, 152**
See also CA 61-64; CAAS 1; CANR 10,
34, 63, 108; CDWLB 4; CWW 2; DA3;
DAC; DAM NOV; DLB 232; EWL 3;
MTCW 1, 2

Slade, Bernard .... **CLC 11, 46**
See Newbound, Bernard Slade
See also CAAS 9; CCA 1; DLB 53

Slaughter, Carolyn 1946- .... **CLC 56**
See also CA 85-88; CANR 85; CN 7

Slaughter, Frank G(ill) 1908-2001 ... **CLC 29**
See also AITN 2; CA 5-8R; 197; CANR 5,
85; INT CANR-5; RHW

Slavitt, David R(ytman) 1935- ..... **CLC 5, 14**
See also CA 21-24R; CAAS 3; CANR 41,
83; CP 7; DLB 5, 6

Slesinger, Tess 1905-1945 .... **TCLC 10**
See also CA 107; 199; DLB 102

Symonds, John Addington
1840-1893 .... NCLC 34
See also DLB 57, 144

Symons, Arthur 1865-1945 .... TCLC 11
See also CA 107; 189; DLB 19, 57, 149;
RGEL 2

Symons, Julian (Gustave)
1912-1994 .... CLC 2, 14, 32
See also CA 49-52; 147; CAAS 3; CANR
3, 33, 59; CMW 4; DLB 87, 155; DLBY
1992; MSW; MTCW 1

Synge, (Edmund) J(ohn) M(illington)
1871-1909 .... DC 2; TCLC 6, 37
See also BRW 6; BRWR 1; CA 104; 141;
CDBLB 1890-1914; DAM DRAM; DFS
18; DLB 10, 19; EWL 3; RGEL 2; TEA;
WLIT 4

Syruc, J.
See Milosz, Czeslaw

Szirtes, George 1948- .... CLC 46; PC 51
See also CA 109; CANR 27, 61, 117; CP 7

Szymborska, Wislawa 1923- ... CLC 99, 190;
PC 44
See also CA 154; CANR 91, 133; CDWLB
4; CWP; CWW 2; DA3; DLB 232; DLBY
1996; EWL 3; MTCW 2; PFS 15; RGWL
3

T. O., Nik
See Annensky, Innokenty (Fyodorovich)

Tabori, George 1914- .... CLC 19
See also CA 49-52; CANR 4, 69; CBD; CD
5; DLB 245

Tacitus c. 55-c. 117 .... CMLC 56
See also AW 2; CDWLB 1; DLB 211;
RGWL 2, 3

Tagore, Rabindranath 1861-1941 .... PC 8;
SSC 48; TCLC 3, 53
See also CA 104; 120; DA3; DAM DRAM,
POET; EWL 3; MTCW 1, 2; PFS 18;
RGEL 2; RGSF 2; RGWL 2, 3; TWA

Taine, Hippolyte Adolphe
1828-1893 .... NCLC 15
See also EW 7; GFL 1789 to the Present

Talayesva, Don C. 1890-(?) .... NNAL

Talese, Gay 1932- .... CLC 37
See also AITN 1; CA 1-4R; CANR 9, 58;
DLB 185; INT CANR-9; MTCW 1, 2

Tallent, Elizabeth (Ann) 1954- .... CLC 45
See also CA 117; CANR 72; DLB 130

Tallmountain, Mary 1918-1997 .... NNAL
See also CA 146; 161; DLB 193

Tally, Ted 1952- .... CLC 42
See also CA 120; 124; CAD; CANR 125;
CD 5; INT CA-124

Talvik, Heiti 1904-1947 .... TCLC 87
See also EWL 3

Tamayo y Baus, Manuel
1829-1898 .... NCLC 1

Tammsaare, A(nton) H(ansen)
1878-1940 .... TCLC 27
See also CA 164; CDWLB 4; DLB 220;
EWL 3

Tam'si, Tchicaya U
See Tchicaya, Gerald Felix

Tan, Amy (Ruth) 1952- . AAL; CLC 59, 120,
151
See also AAYA 9, 48; AMWS 10; BEST
89:3; BPFB 3; CA 136; CANR 54, 105,
132; CDALBS; CN 7; CPW 1; DA3;
DAM MULT, NOV, POP; DLB 173;
EXPN; FW; LAIT 3, 5; MTCW 2; NFS
1, 13, 16; RGAL 4; SATA 75; SSFS 9;
YAW

Tandem, Felix
See Spitteler, Carl (Friedrich Georg)

Tanizaki, Jun'ichiro 1886-1965 ... CLC 8, 14,
28; SSC 21
See Tanizaki Jun'ichiro
See also CA 93-96; 25-28R; MJW; MTCW
2; RGSF 2; RGWL 2

Tanizaki Jun'ichiro
See Tanizaki, Jun'ichiro
See also DLB 180; EWL 3

Tanner, William
See Amis, Kingsley (William)

Tao Lao
See Storni, Alfonsina

Tapahonso, Luci 1953- .... NNAL
See also CA 145; CANR 72, 127; DLB 175

Tarantino, Quentin (Jerome)
1963- .... CLC 125
See also AAYA 58; CA 171; CANR 125

Tarassoff, Lev
See Troyat, Henri

Tarbell, Ida M(inerva) 1857-1944 . TCLC 40
See also CA 122; 181; DLB 47

Tarkington, (Newton) Booth
1869-1946 .... TCLC 9
See also BPFB 3; BYA 3; CA 110; 143;
CWRI 5; DLB 9, 102; MTCW 2; RGAL
4; SATA 17

Tarkovskii, Andrei Arsen'evich
See Tarkovsky, Andrei (Arsenyevich)

Tarkovsky, Andrei (Arsenyevich)
1932-1986 .... CLC 75
See also CA 127

Tartt, Donna 1963- .... CLC 76
See also AAYA 56; CA 142

Tasso, Torquato 1544-1595 .... LC 5, 94
See also EFS 2; EW 2; RGWL 2, 3

Tate, (John Orley) Allen 1899-1979 .. CLC 2,
4, 6, 9, 11, 14, 24; PC 50
See also AMW; CA 5-8R; 85-88; CANR
32, 108; DLB 4, 45, 63; DLBD 17; EWL
3; MTCW 1, 2; RGAL 4; RHW

Tate, Ellalice
See Hibbert, Eleanor Alice Burford

Tate, James (Vincent) 1943- ..... CLC 2, 6, 25
See also CA 21-24R; CANR 29, 57, 114;
CP 7; DLB 5, 169; EWL 3; PFS 10, 15;
RGAL 4; WP

Tauler, Johannes c. 1300-1361 ...... CMLC 37
See also DLB 179; LMFS 1

Tavel, Ronald 1940- .... CLC 6
See also CA 21-24R; CAD; CANR 33; CD
5

Taviani, Paolo 1931- .... CLC 70
See also CA 153

Taylor, Bayard 1825-1878 .... NCLC 89
See also DLB 3, 189, 250, 254; RGAL 4

Taylor, C(ecil) P(hilip) 1929-1981 .... CLC 27
See also CA 25-28R; 105; CANR 47; CBD

Taylor, Edward 1642(?)-1729 .... LC 11
See also AMW; DA; DAB; DAC; DAM
MST, POET; DLB 24; EXPP; RGAL 4;
TUS

Taylor, Eleanor Ross 1920- .... CLC 5
See also CA 81-84; CANR 70

Taylor, Elizabeth 1932-1975 ..... CLC 2, 4, 29
See also CA 13-16R; CANR 9, 70; DLB
139; MTCW 1; RGEL 2; SATA 13

Taylor, Frederick Winslow
1856-1915 .... TCLC 76
See also CA 188

Taylor, Henry (Splawn) 1942- .... CLC 44
See also CA 33-36R; CAAS 7; CANR 31;
CP 7; DLB 5; PFS 10

Taylor, Kamala (Purnaiya) 1924-2004
See Markandaya, Kamala
See also CA 77-80; 227; NFS 13

Taylor, Mildred D(elois) 1943- .... CLC 21
See also AAYA 10, 47; BW 1; BYA 3, 8;
CA 85-88; CANR 25, 115; CLR 9, 59,
90; CSW; DLB 52; JRDA; LAIT 3; MAI-
CYA 1, 2; SAAS 5; SATA 135; WYA;
YAW

Taylor, Peter (Hillsman) 1917-1994 .. CLC 1,
4, 18, 37, 44, 50, 71; SSC 10
See also AMWS 5; BPFB 3; CA 13-16R;
147; CANR 9, 50; CSW; DLB 218, 278;
DLBY 1981, 1994; EWL 3; EXPS; INT
CANR-9; MTCW 1, 2; RGSF 2; SSFS 9;
TUS

Taylor, Robert Lewis 1912-1998 .... CLC 14
See also CA 1-4R; 170; CANR 3, 64; SATA
10

Tchekhov, Anton
See Chekhov, Anton (Pavlovich)

Tchicaya, Gerald Felix 1931-1988 .. CLC 101
See Tchicaya U Tam'si
See also CA 129; 125; CANR 81

Tchicaya U Tam'si
See Tchicaya, Gerald Felix
See also EWL 3

Teasdale, Sara 1884-1933 .... PC 31; TCLC 4
See also CA 104; 163; DLB 45; GLL 1;
PFS 14; RGAL 4; SATA 32; TUS

Tecumseh 1768-1813 .... NNAL
See also DAM MULT

Tegner, Esaias 1782-1846 .... NCLC 2

Teilhard de Chardin, (Marie Joseph) Pierre
1881-1955 .... TCLC 9
See also CA 105; 210; GFL 1789 to the
Present

Temple, Ann
See Mortimer, Penelope (Ruth)

Tennant, Emma (Christina) 1937- .. CLC 13,
52
See also BRWS 9; CA 65-68; CAAS 9;
CANR 10, 38, 59, 88; CN 7; DLB 14;
EWL 3; SFW 4

Tenneshaw, S. M.
See Silverberg, Robert

Tenney, Tabitha Gilman
1762-1837 .... NCLC 122
See also DLB 37, 200

Tennyson, Alfred 1809-1892 ... NCLC 30, 65,
115; PC 6; WLC
See also AAYA 50; BRW 4; CDBLB 1832-
1890; DA; DA3; DAB; DAC; DAM MST,
POET; DLB 32; EXPP; PAB; PFS 1, 2, 4,
11, 15, 19; RGEL 2; TEA; WLIT 4; WP

Teran, Lisa St. Aubin de .... CLC 36
See St. Aubin de Teran, Lisa

Terence c. 184B.C.-c. 159B.C. ...... CMLC 14;
DC 7
See also AW 1; CDWLB 1; DLB 211;
RGWL 2, 3; TWA

Teresa de Jesus, St. 1515-1582 .... LC 18

Terkel, Louis 1912-
See Terkel, Studs
See also CA 57-60; CANR 18, 45, 67, 132;
DA3; MTCW 1, 2

Terkel, Studs .... CLC 38
See Terkel, Louis
See also AAYA 32; AITN 1; MTCW 2; TUS

Terry, C. V.
See Slaughter, Frank G(ill)

Terry, Megan 1932- .... CLC 19; DC 13
See also CA 77-80; CABS 3; CAD; CANR
43; CD 5; CWD; DFS 18; DLB 7, 249;
GLL 2

Tertullian c. 155-c. 245 .... CMLC 29

Tertz, Abram
See Sinyavsky, Andrei (Donatevich)
See also RGSF 2

Tesich, Steve 1943(?)-1996 .... CLC 40, 69
See also CA 105; 152; CAD; DLBY 1983

Tesla, Nikola 1856-1943 .... TCLC 88

Teternikov, Fyodor Kuzmich 1863-1927
See Sologub, Fyodor
See also CA 104

Tevis, Walter 1928-1984 .... **CLC 42**
See also CA 113; SFW 4

Tey, Josephine .... **TCLC 14**
See Mackintosh, Elizabeth
See also DLB 77; MSW

Thackeray, William Makepeace
1811-1863 .... **NCLC 5, 14, 22, 43; WLC**
See also BRW 5; BRWC 2; CDBLB 1832-
1890; DA; DA3; DAB; DAC; DAM MST,
NOV; DLB 21, 55, 159, 163; NFS 13;
RGEL 2; SATA 23; TEA; WLIT 3

Thakura, Ravindranatha
See Tagore, Rabindranath

Thames, C. H.
See Marlowe, Stephen

Tharoor, Shashi 1956- .... **CLC 70**
See also CA 141; CANR 91; CN 7

Thelwell, Michael Miles 1939- .... **CLC 22**
See also BW 2; CA 101

Theobald, Lewis, Jr.
See Lovecraft, H(oward) P(hillips)

Theocritus c. 310B.C.- .... **CMLC 45**
See also AW 1; DLB 176; RGWL 2, 3

Theodorescu, Ion N. 1880-1967
See Arghezi, Tudor
See also CA 116

Theriault, Yves 1915-1983 .... **CLC 79**
See also CA 102; CCA 1; DAC; DAM
MST; DLB 88; EWL 3

Theroux, Alexander (Louis) 1939- .... **CLC 2,
25**
See also CA 85-88; CANR 20, 63; CN 7

Theroux, Paul (Edward) 1941- ..... **CLC 5, 8,
11, 15, 28, 46**
See also AAYA 28; AMWS 8; BEST 89:4;
BPFB 3; CA 33-36R; CANR 20, 45, 74,
133; CDALBS; CN 7; CPW 1; DA3;
DAM POP; DLB 2, 218; EWL 3; HGG;
MTCW 1, 2; RGAL 4; SATA 44, 109;
TUS

Thesen, Sharon 1946- .... **CLC 56**
See also CA 163; CANR 125; CP 7; CWP

Thespis fl. 6th cent. B.C.- .... **CMLC 51**
See also LMFS 1

Thevenin, Denis
See Duhamel, Georges

Thibault, Jacques Anatole Francois
1844-1924
See France, Anatole
See also CA 106; 127; DA3; DAM NOV;
MTCW 1, 2; TWA

Thiele, Colin (Milton) 1920- .... **CLC 17**
See also CA 29-32R; CANR 12, 28, 53,
105; CLR 27; DLB 289; MAICYA 1, 2;
SAAS 2; SATA 14, 72, 125; YAW

Thistlethwaite, Bel
See Wetherald, Agnes Ethelwyn

Thomas, Audrey (Callahan) 1935- .... **CLC 7,
13, 37, 107; SSC 20**
See also AITN 2; CA 21-24R; CAAS 19;
CANR 36, 58; CN 7; DLB 60; MTCW 1;
RGSF 2

Thomas, Augustus 1857-1934 .... **TCLC 97**

Thomas, D(onald) M(ichael) 1935- . **CLC 13,
22, 31, 132**
See also BPFB 3; BRWS 4; CA 61-64;
CAAS 11; CANR 17, 45, 75; CDBLB
1960 to Present; CN 7; CP 7; DA3; DLB
40, 207, 299; HGG; INT CANR-17;
MTCW 1, 2; SFW 4

Thomas, Dylan (Marlais) 1914-1953 .... **PC 2,
52; SSC 3, 44; TCLC 1, 8, 45, 105;
WLC**
See also AAYA 45; BRWS 1; CA 104; 120;
CANR 65; CDBLB 1945-1960; DA; DA3;
DAB; DAC; DAM DRAM, MST, POET;
DLB 13, 20, 139; EWL 3; EXPP; LAIT
3; MTCW 1, 2; PAB; PFS 1, 3, 8; RGEL
2; RGSF 2; SATA 60; TEA; WLIT 4; WP

Thomas, (Philip) Edward 1878-1917 . **PC 53;
TCLC 10**
See also BRW 6; BRWS 3; CA 106; 153;
DAM POET; DLB 19, 98, 156, 216; EWL
3; PAB; RGEL 2

Thomas, Joyce Carol 1938- .... **CLC 35**
See also AAYA 12, 54; BW 2, 3; CA 113;
116; CANR 48, 114; CLR 19; DLB 33;
INT CA-116; JRDA; MAICYA 1, 2;
MTCW 1, 2; SAAS 7; SATA 40, 78, 123,
137; SATA-Essay 137; WYA; YAW

Thomas, Lewis 1913-1993 .... **CLC 35**
See also ANW; CA 85-88; 143; CANR 38,
60; DLB 275; MTCW 1, 2

Thomas, M. Carey 1857-1935 .... **TCLC 89**
See also FW

Thomas, Paul
See Mann, (Paul) Thomas

Thomas, Piri 1928- .... **CLC 17; HLCS 2**
See also CA 73-76; HW 1; LLW 1

Thomas, R(onald) S(tuart)
1913-2000 .... **CLC 6, 13, 48**
See also CA 89-92; 189; CAAS 4; CANR
30; CDBLB 1960 to Present; CP 7; DAB;
DAM POET; DLB 27; EWL 3; MTCW 1;
RGEL 2

Thomas, Ross (Elmore) 1926-1995 .. **CLC 39**
See also CA 33-36R; 150; CANR 22, 63;
CMW 4

Thompson, Francis (Joseph)
1859-1907 .... **TCLC 4**
See also BRW 5; CA 104; 189; CDBLB
1890-1914; DLB 19; RGEL 2; TEA

Thompson, Francis Clegg
See Mencken, H(enry) L(ouis)

Thompson, Hunter S(tockton)
1937(?)- .... **CLC 9, 17, 40, 104**
See also AAYA 45; BEST 89:1; BPFB 3;
CA 17-20R; CANR 23, 46, 74, 77, 111,
133; CPW; CSW; DA3; DAM POP; DLB
185; MTCW 1, 2; TUS

Thompson, James Myers
See Thompson, Jim (Myers)

Thompson, Jim (Myers)
1906-1977(?) .... **CLC 69**
See also BPFB 3; CA 140; CMW 4; CPW;
DLB 226; MSW

Thompson, Judith .... **CLC 39**
See also CWD

Thomson, James 1700-1748 .... **LC 16, 29, 40**
See also BRWS 3; DAM POET; DLB 95;
RGEL 2

Thomson, James 1834-1882 .... **NCLC 18**
See also DAM POET; DLB 35; RGEL 2

Thoreau, Henry David 1817-1862 .. **NCLC 7,
21, 61, 138; PC 30; WLC**
See also AAYA 42; AMW; ANW; BYA 3;
CDALB 1640-1865; DA; DA3; DAB;
DAC; DAM MST; DLB 1, 183, 223, 270,
298; LAIT 2; LMFS 1; NCFS 3; RGAL
4; TUS

Thorndike, E. L.
See Thorndike, Edward L(ee)

Thorndike, Edward L(ee)
1874-1949 .... **TCLC 107**
See also CA 121

Thornton, Hall
See Silverberg, Robert

Thorpe, Adam 1956- .... **CLC 176**
See also CA 129; CANR 92; DLB 231

Thubron, Colin (Gerald Dryden)
1939- .... **CLC 163**
See also CA 25-28R; CANR 12, 29, 59, 95;
CN 7; DLB 204, 231

Thucydides c. 455B.C.-c. 395B.C. .. **CMLC 17**
See also AW 1; DLB 176; RGWL 2, 3

Thumboo, Edwin Nadason 1933- .... **PC 30**
See also CA 194

Thurber, James (Grover)
1894-1961 .. **CLC 5, 11, 25, 125; SSC 1,
47**
See also AAYA 56; AMWS 1; BPFB 3;
BYA 5; CA 73-76; CANR 17, 39; CDALB
1929-1941; CWRI 5; DA; DA3; DAB;
DAC; DAM DRAM, MST, NOV; DLB 4,
11, 22, 102; EWL 3; EXPS; FANT; LAIT
3; MAICYA 1, 2; MTCW 1, 2; RGAL 4;
RGSF 2; SATA 13; SSFS 1, 10, 19;
SUFW; TUS

Thurman, Wallace (Henry)
1902-1934 .... **BLC 3; HR 3; TCLC 6**
See also BW 1, 3; CA 104; 124; CANR 81;
DAM MULT; DLB 51

Tibullus c. 54B.C.-c. 18B.C. .... **CMLC 36**
See also AW 2; DLB 211; RGWL 2, 3

Ticheburn, Cheviot
See Ainsworth, William Harrison

Tieck, (Johann) Ludwig
1773-1853 .... **NCLC 5, 46; SSC 31**
See also CDWLB 2; DLB 90; EW 5; IDTP;
RGSF 2; RGWL 2, 3; SUFW

Tiger, Derry
See Ellison, Harlan (Jay)

Tilghman, Christopher 1946- .... **CLC 65**
See also CA 159; CSW; DLB 244

Tillich, Paul (Johannes)
1886-1965 .... **CLC 131**
See also CA 5-8R; 25-28R; CANR 33;
MTCW 1, 2

Tillinghast, Richard (Williford)
1940- .... **CLC 29**
See also CA 29-32R; CAAS 23; CANR 26,
51, 96; CP 7; CSW

Timrod, Henry 1828-1867 .... **NCLC 25**
See also DLB 3, 248; RGAL 4

Tindall, Gillian (Elizabeth) 1938- ...... **CLC 7**
See also CA 21-24R; CANR 11, 65, 107;
CN 7

Tiptree, James, Jr. .... **CLC 48, 50**
See Sheldon, Alice Hastings Bradley
See also DLB 8; SCFW 2; SFW 4

Tirone Smith, Mary-Ann 1944- .... **CLC 39**
See also CA 118; 136; CANR 113; SATA
143

Tirso de Molina 1580(?)-1648 .... **DC 13;
HLCS 2; LC 73**
See also RGWL 2, 3

Titmarsh, Michael Angelo
See Thackeray, William Makepeace

**Tocqueville, Alexis (Charles Henri Maurice
Clerel Comte) de** 1805-1859 .. **NCLC 7,
63**
See also EW 6; GFL 1789 to the Present;
TWA

Toer, Pramoedya Ananta 1925- ...... **CLC 186**
See also CA 197; RGWL 3

Toffler, Alvin 1928- .... **CLC 168**
See also CA 13-16R; CANR 15, 46, 67;
CPW; DAM POP; MTCW 1, 2

Toibin, Colm
See Toibin, Colm
See also DLB 271

Toibin, Colm 1955- .... **CLC 162**
See Toibin, Colm
See also CA 142; CANR 81

Tolkien, J(ohn) R(onald) R(euel)
1892-1973 .... **CLC 1, 2, 3, 8, 12, 38;
TCLC 137; WLC**
See also AAYA 10; AITN 1; BPFB 3;
BRWC 2; BRWS 2; CA 17-18; 45-48;
CANR 36; CAP 2; CDBLB 1914-1945;
CLR 56; CPW 1; CWRI 5; DA; DA3;
DAB; DAC; DAM MST, NOV, POP;
DLB 15, 160, 255; EFS 2; EWL 3; FANT;
JRDA; LAIT 1; LATS 1:2; LMFS 2;

Villaurrutia, Xavier 1903-1950 ...... **TCLC 80**
See also CA 192; EWL 3; HW 1; LAW

Villaverde, Cirilo 1812-1894 .... **NCLC 121**
See also LAW

Villehardouin, Geoffroi de
1150(?)-1218(?) .... **CMLC 38**

Villiers, George 1628-1687 .... **LC 107**
See also DLB 80; RGEL 2

Villiers de l'Isle Adam, Jean Marie Mathias Philippe Auguste 1838-1889 ... **NCLC 3; SSC 14**
See also DLB 123, 192; GFL 1789 to the Present; RGSF 2

Villon, Francois 1431-1463(?) . **LC 62; PC 13**
See also DLB 208; EW 2; RGWL 2, 3; TWA

Vine, Barbara .... **CLC 50**
See Rendell, Ruth (Barbara)
See also BEST 90:4

Vinge, Joan (Carol) D(ennison)
1948- .... **CLC 30; SSC 24**
See also AAYA 32; BPFB 3; CA 93-96; CANR 72; SATA 36, 113; SFW 4; YAW

Viola, Herman J(oseph) 1938- .... **CLC 70**
See also CA 61-64; CANR 8, 23, 48, 91; SATA 126

Violis, G.
See Simenon, Georges (Jacques Christian)

Viramontes, Helena Maria 1954- .... **HLCS 2**
See also CA 159; DLB 122; HW 2; LLW 1

Virgil
See Vergil
See also CDWLB 1; DLB 211; LAIT 1; RGWL 2, 3; WP

Visconti, Luchino 1906-1976 .... **CLC 16**
See also CA 81-84; 65-68; CANR 39

Vitry, Jacques de
See Jacques de Vitry

Vittorini, Elio 1908-1966 .... **CLC 6, 9, 14**
See also CA 133; 25-28R; DLB 264; EW 12; EWL 3; RGWL 2, 3

Vivekananda, Swami 1863-1902 .... **TCLC 88**

Vizenor, Gerald Robert 1934- .... **CLC 103; NNAL**
See also CA 13-16R, 205; CAAE 205; CAAS 22; CANR 5, 21, 44, 67; DAM MULT; DLB 175, 227; MTCW 2; TCWW 2

Vizinczey, Stephen 1933- .... **CLC 40**
See also CA 128; CCA 1; INT CA-128

Vliet, R(ussell) G(ordon)
1929-1984 .... **CLC 22**
See also CA 37-40R; 112; CANR 18

Vogau, Boris Andreyevich 1894-1938
See Pilnyak, Boris
See also CA 123; 218

Vogel, Paula A(nne) 1951- ... **CLC 76; DC 19**
See also CA 108; CAD; CANR 119; CD 5; CWD; DFS 14; RGAL 4

Voigt, Cynthia 1942- .... **CLC 30**
See also AAYA 3, 30; BYA 1, 3, 6, 7, 8; CA 106; CANR 18, 37, 40, 94; CLR 13, 48; INT CANR-18; JRDA; LAIT 5; MAICYA 1, 2; MAICYAS 1; SATA 48, 79, 116; SATA-Brief 33; WYA; YAW

Voigt, Ellen Bryant 1943- .... **CLC 54**
See also CA 69-72; CANR 11, 29, 55, 115; CP 7; CSW; CWP; DLB 120

Voinovich, Vladimir (Nikolaevich)
1932- .... **CLC 10, 49, 147**
See also CA 81-84; CAAS 12; CANR 33, 67; CWW 2; DLB 302; MTCW 1

Vollmann, William T. 1959- .... **CLC 89**
See also CA 134; CANR 67, 116; CPW; DA3; DAM NOV, POP; MTCW 2

Voloshinov, V. N.
See Bakhtin, Mikhail Mikhailovich

Voltaire 1694-1778 .... **LC 14, 79; SSC 12; WLC**
See also BYA 13; DA; DA3; DAB; DAC; DAM DRAM, MST; EW 4; GFL Beginnings to 1789; LATS 1:1; LMFS 1; NFS 7; RGWL 2, 3; TWA

von Aschendrof, Baron Ignatz
See Ford, Ford Madox

von Chamisso, Adelbert
See Chamisso, Adelbert von

von Daeniken, Erich 1935- .... **CLC 30**
See also AITN 1; CA 37-40R; CANR 17, 44

von Daniken, Erich
See von Daeniken, Erich

von Hartmann, Eduard
1842-1906 .... **TCLC 96**

von Hayek, Friedrich August
See Hayek, F(riedrich) A(ugust von)

von Heidenstam, (Carl Gustaf) Verner
See Heidenstam, (Carl Gustaf) Verner von

von Heyse, Paul (Johann Ludwig)
See Heyse, Paul (Johann Ludwig von)

von Hofmannsthal, Hugo
See Hofmannsthal, Hugo von

von Horvath, Odon
See von Horvath, Odon

von Horvath, Odon
See von Horvath, Odon

von Horvath, Odon 1901-1938 .... **TCLC 45**
See von Horvath, Oedoen
See also CA 118; 194; DLB 85, 124; RGWL 2, 3

von Horvath, Oedoen
See von Horvath, Odon
See also CA 184

von Kleist, Heinrich
See Kleist, Heinrich von

von Liliencron, (Friedrich Adolf Axel) Detlev
See Liliencron, (Friedrich Adolf Axel) Detlev von

Vonnegut, Kurt, Jr. 1922- . **CLC 1, 2, 3, 4, 5, 8, 12, 22, 40, 60, 111; SSC 8; WLC**
See also AAYA 6, 44; AITN 1; AMWS 2; BEST 90:4; BPFB 3; BYA 3, 14; CA 1-4R; CANR 1, 25, 49, 75, 92; CDALB 1968-1988; CN 7; CPW 1; DA; DA3; DAB; DAC; DAM MST, NOV, POP; DLB 2, 8, 152; DLBD 3; DLBY 1980; EWL 3; EXPN; EXPS; LAIT 4; LMFS 2; MTCW 1, 2; NFS 3; RGAL 4; SCFW; SFW 4; SSFS 5; TUS; YAW

Von Rachen, Kurt
See Hubbard, L(afayette) Ron(ald)

von Rezzori (d'Arezzo), Gregor
See Rezzori (d'Arezzo), Gregor von

von Sternberg, Josef
See Sternberg, Josef von

Vorster, Gordon 1924- .... **CLC 34**
See also CA 133

Vosce, Trudie
See Ozick, Cynthia

Voznesensky, Andrei (Andreievich)
1933- .... **CLC 1, 15, 57**
See Voznesensky, Andrey
See also CA 89-92; CANR 37; CWW 2; DAM POET; MTCW 1

Voznesensky, Andrey
See Voznesensky, Andrei (Andreievich)
See also EWL 3

Wace, Robert c. 1100-c. 1175 .... **CMLC 55**
See also DLB 146

Waddington, Miriam 1917-2004 .... **CLC 28**
See also CA 21-24R; 225; CANR 12, 30; CCA 1; CP 7; DLB 68

Wagman, Fredrica 1937- .... **CLC 7**
See also CA 97-100; INT CA-97-100

Wagner, Linda W.
See Wagner-Martin, Linda (C.)

Wagner, Linda Welshimer
See Wagner-Martin, Linda (C.)

Wagner, Richard 1813-1883 ..... **NCLC 9, 119**
See also DLB 129; EW 6

Wagner-Martin, Linda (C.) 1936- .... **CLC 50**
See also CA 159

Wagoner, David (Russell) 1926- .... **CLC 3, 5, 15; PC 33**
See also AMWS 9; CA 1-4R; CAAS 3; CANR 2, 71; CN 7; CP 7; DLB 5, 256; SATA 14; TCWW 2

Wah, Fred(erick James) 1939- .... **CLC 44**
See also CA 107; 141; CP 7; DLB 60

Wahloo, Per 1926-1975 .... **CLC 7**
See also BPFB 3; CA 61-64; CANR 73; CMW 4; MSW

Wahloo, Peter
See Wahloo, Per

Wain, John (Barrington) 1925-1994 . **CLC 2, 11, 15, 46**
See also CA 5-8R; 145; CAAS 4; CANR 23, 54; CDBLB 1960 to Present; DLB 15, 27, 139, 155; EWL 3; MTCW 1, 2

Wajda, Andrzej 1926- .... **CLC 16**
See also CA 102

Wakefield, Dan 1932- .... **CLC 7**
See also CA 21-24R, 211; CAAE 211; CAAS 7; CN 7

Wakefield, Herbert Russell
1888-1965 .... **TCLC 120**
See also CA 5-8R; CANR 77; HGG; SUFW

Wakoski, Diane 1937- ..... **CLC 2, 4, 7, 9, 11, 40; PC 15**
See also CA 13-16R, 216; CAAE 216; CAAS 1; CANR 9, 60, 106; CP 7; CWP; DAM POET; DLB 5; INT CANR-9; MTCW 2

Wakoski-Sherbell, Diane
See Wakoski, Diane

Walcott, Derek (Alton) 1930- ... **BLC 3; CLC 2, 4, 9, 14, 25, 42, 67, 76, 160; DC 7; PC 46**
See also BW 2; CA 89-92; CANR 26, 47, 75, 80, 130; CBD; CD 5; CDWLB 3; CP 7; DA3; DAB; DAC; DAM MST, MULT, POET; DLB 117; DLBY 1981; DNFS 1; EFS 1; EWL 3; LMFS 2; MTCW 1, 2; PFS 6; RGEL 2; TWA; WWE 1

Waldman, Anne (Lesley) 1945- .... **CLC 7**
See also BG 3; CA 37-40R; CAAS 17; CANR 34, 69, 116; CP 7; CWP; DLB 16

Waldo, E. Hunter
See Sturgeon, Theodore (Hamilton)

Waldo, Edward Hamilton
See Sturgeon, Theodore (Hamilton)

Walker, Alice (Malsenior) 1944- .... **BLC 3; CLC 5, 6, 9, 19, 27, 46, 58, 103, 167; PC 30; SSC 5; WLCS**
See also AAYA 3, 33; AFAW 1, 2; AMWS 3; BEST 89:4; BPFB 3; BW 2, 3; CA 37-40R; CANR 9, 27, 49, 66, 82, 131; CDALB 1968-1988; CN 7; CPW; CSW; DA; DA3; DAB; DAC; DAM MST, MULT, NOV, POET, POP; DLB 6, 33, 143; EWL 3; EXPN; EXPS; FW; INT CANR-27; LAIT 3; MAWW; MTCW 1, 2; NFS 5; RGAL 4; RGSF 2; SATA 31; SSFS 2, 11; TUS; YAW

Walker, David Harry 1911-1992 ...... **CLC 14**
See also CA 1-4R; 137; CANR 1; CWRI 5; SATA 8; SATA-Obit 71

Walker, Edward Joseph 1934-2004
See Walker, Ted
See also CA 21-24R; 226; CANR 12, 28, 53; CP 7

Walker, George F. 1947- .... **CLC 44, 61**
   See also CA 103; CANR 21, 43, 59; CD 5;
   DAB; DAC; DAM MST; DLB 60

Walker, Joseph A. 1935- .... **CLC 19**
   See also BW 1, 3; CA 89-92; CAD; CANR
   26; CD 5; DAM DRAM, MST; DFS 12;
   DLB 38

Walker, Margaret (Abigail)
   1915-1998 .... **BLC; CLC 1, 6; PC 20;**
   TCLC 129
   See also AFAW 1, 2; BW 2, 3; CA 73-76;
   172; CANR 26, 54, 76; CN 7; CP 7;
   CSW; DAM MULT; DLB 76, 152; EXPP;
   FW; MTCW 1, 2; RGAL 4; RHW

Walker, Ted .... **CLC 13**
   See Walker, Edward Joseph
   See also DLB 40

Wallace, David Foster 1962- ... **CLC 50, 114;**
   SSC 68
   See also AAYA 50; AMWS 10; CA 132;
   CANR 59, 133; DA3; MTCW 2

Wallace, Dexter
   See Masters, Edgar Lee

Wallace, (Richard Horatio) Edgar
   1875-1932 .... **TCLC 57**
   See also CA 115; 218; CMW 4; DLB 70;
   MSW; RGEL 2

Wallace, Irving 1916-1990 .... **CLC 7, 13**
   See also AITN 1; BPFB 3; CA 1-4R; 132;
   CAAS 1; CANR 1, 27; CPW; DAM NOV,
   POP; INT CANR-27; MTCW 1, 2

Wallant, Edward Lewis 1926-1962 ... **CLC 5,**
   10
   See also CA 1-4R; CANR 22; DLB 2, 28,
   143, 299; EWL 3; MTCW 1, 2; RGAL 4

Wallas, Graham 1858-1932 .... **TCLC 91**

Waller, Edmund 1606-1687 .... **LC 86**
   See also BRW 2; DAM POET; DLB 126;
   PAB; RGEL 2

Walley, Byron
   See Card, Orson Scott

Walpole, Horace 1717-1797 .... **LC 2, 49**
   See also BRW 3; DLB 39, 104, 213; HGG;
   LMFS 1; RGEL 2; SUFW 1; TEA

Walpole, Hugh (Seymour)
   1884-1941 .... **TCLC 5**
   See also CA 104; 165; DLB 34; HGG;
   MTCW 2; RGEL 2; RHW

Walrond, Eric (Derwent) 1898-1966 .... **HR 3**
   See also BW 1; CA 125; DLB 51

Walser, Martin 1927- .... **CLC 27, 183**
   See also CA 57-60; CANR 8, 46; CWW 2;
   DLB 75, 124; EWL 3

Walser, Robert 1878-1956 ..... **SSC 20; TCLC**
   18
   See also CA 118; 165; CANR 100; DLB
   66; EWL 3

Walsh, Gillian Paton
   See Paton Walsh, Gillian

Walsh, Jill Paton .... **CLC 35**
   See Paton Walsh, Gillian
   See also CLR 2, 65; WYA

Walter, Villiam Christian
   See Andersen, Hans Christian

Walters, Anna L(ee) 1946- .... **NNAL**
   See also CA 73-76

Walther von der Vogelweide c.
   1170-1228 .... **CMLC 56**

Walton, Izaak 1593-1683 .... **LC 72**
   See also BRW 2; CDBLB Before 1660;
   DLB 151, 213; RGEL 2

Wambaugh, Joseph (Aloysius), Jr.
   1937- .... **CLC 3, 18**
   See also AITN 1; BEST 89:3; BPFB 3; CA
   33-36R; CANR 42, 65, 115; CMW 4;
   CPW 1; DA3; DAM NOV, POP; DLB 6;
   DLBY 1983; MSW; MTCW 1, 2

Wang Wei 699(?)-761(?) .... **PC 18**
   See also TWA

Warburton, William 1698-1779 .... **LC 97**
   See also DLB 104

Ward, Arthur Henry Sarsfield 1883-1959
   See Rohmer, Sax
   See also CA 108; 173; CMW 4; HGG

Ward, Douglas Turner 1930- .... **CLC 19**
   See also BW 1; CA 81-84; CAD; CANR
   27; CD 5; DLB 7, 38

Ward, E. D.
   See Lucas, E(dward) V(errall)

Ward, Mrs. Humphry 1851-1920
   See Ward, Mary Augusta
   See also RGEL 2

Ward, Mary Augusta 1851-1920 ... **TCLC 55**
   See Ward, Mrs. Humphry
   See also DLB 18

Ward, Peter
   See Faust, Frederick (Schiller)

Warhol, Andy 1928(?)-1987 .... **CLC 20**
   See also AAYA 12; BEST 89:4; CA 89-92;
   121; CANR 34

Warner, Francis (Robert le Plastrier)
   1937- .... **CLC 14**
   See also CA 53-56; CANR 11

Warner, Marina 1946- .... **CLC 59**
   See also CA 65-68; CANR 21, 55, 118; CN
   7; DLB 194

Warner, Rex (Ernest) 1905-1986 ...... **CLC 45**
   See also CA 89-92; 119; DLB 15; RGEL 2;
   RHW

Warner, Susan (Bogert)
   1819-1885 .... **NCLC 31, 146**
   See also DLB 3, 42, 239, 250, 254

Warner, Sylvia (Constance) Ashton
   See Ashton-Warner, Sylvia (Constance)

Warner, Sylvia Townsend
   1893-1978 .. **CLC 7, 19; SSC 23; TCLC**
   131
   See also BRWS 7; CA 61-64; 77-80; CANR
   16, 60, 104; DLB 34, 139; EWL 3; FANT;
   FW; MTCW 1, 2; RGEL 2; RGSF 2;
   RHW

Warren, Mercy Otis 1728-1814 ..... **NCLC 13**
   See also DLB 31, 200; RGAL 4; TUS

Warren, Robert Penn 1905-1989 .. **CLC 1, 4,**
   6, 8, 10, 13, 18, 39, 53, 59; PC 37; SSC
   4, 58; WLC
   See also AITN 1; AMW; AMWC 2; BPFB
   3; BYA 1; CA 13-16R; 129; CANR 10,
   47; CDALB 1968-1988; DA; DA3; DAB;
   DAC; DAM MST, NOV, POET; DLB 2,
   48, 152; DLBY 1980, 1989; EWL 3; INT
   CANR-10; MTCW 1, 2; NFS 13; RGAL
   4; RGSF 2; RHW; SATA 46; SATA-Obit
   63; SSFS 8; TUS

Warrigal, Jack
   See Furphy, Joseph

Warshofsky, Isaac
   See Singer, Isaac Bashevis

Warton, Joseph 1722-1800 .... **NCLC 118**
   See also DLB 104, 109; RGEL 2

Warton, Thomas 1728-1790 .... **LC 15, 82**
   See also DAM POET; DLB 104, 109;
   RGEL 2

Waruk, Kona
   See Harris, (Theodore) Wilson

Warung, Price .... **TCLC 45**
   See Astley, William
   See also DLB 230; RGEL 2

Warwick, Jarvis
   See Garner, Hugh
   See also CCA 1

Washington, Alex
   See Harris, Mark

Washington, Booker T(aliaferro)
   1856-1915 .... **BLC 3; TCLC 10**
   See also BW 1; CA 114; 125; DA3; DAM
   MULT; LAIT 2; RGAL 4; SATA 28

Washington, George 1732-1799 .... **LC 25**
   See also DLB 31

Wassermann, (Karl) Jakob
   1873-1934 .... **TCLC 6**
   See also CA 104; 163; DLB 66; EWL 3

Wasserstein, Wendy 1950- ... **CLC 32, 59, 90,**
   183; DC 4
   See also CA 121; 129; CABS 3; CAD;
   CANR 53, 75, 128; CD 5; CWD; DA3;
   DAM DRAM; DFS 5, 17; DLB 228;
   EWL 3; FW; INT CA-129; MTCW 2;
   SATA 94

Waterhouse, Keith (Spencer) 1929- . **CLC 47**
   See also CA 5-8R; CANR 38, 67, 109;
   CBD; CN 7; DLB 13, 15; MTCW 1, 2

Waters, Frank (Joseph) 1902-1995 .. **CLC 88**
   See also CA 5-8R; 149; CAAS 13; CANR
   3, 18, 63, 121; DLB 212; DLBY 1986;
   RGAL 4; TCWW 2

Waters, Mary C. .... **CLC 70**

Waters, Roger 1944- .... **CLC 35**

Watkins, Frances Ellen
   See Harper, Frances Ellen Watkins

Watkins, Gerrold
   See Malzberg, Barry N(athaniel)

Watkins, Gloria Jean 1952(?)- .... **CLC 94**
   See also BW 2; CA 143; CANR 87, 126;
   DLB 246; MTCW 2; SATA 115

Watkins, Paul 1964- .... **CLC 55**
   See also CA 132; CANR 62, 98

Watkins, Vernon Phillips
   1906-1967 .... **CLC 43**
   See also CA 9-10; 25-28R; CAP 1; DLB
   20; EWL 3; RGEL 2

Watson, Irving S.
   See Mencken, H(enry) L(ouis)

Watson, John H.
   See Farmer, Philip Jose

Watson, Richard F.
   See Silverberg, Robert

Watts, Ephraim
   See Horne, Richard Henry Hengist

Watts, Isaac 1674-1748 .... **LC 98**
   See also DLB 95; RGEL 2; SATA 52

Waugh, Auberon (Alexander)
   1939-2001 .... **CLC 7**
   See also CA 45-48; 192; CANR 6, 22, 92;
   DLB 14, 194

Waugh, Evelyn (Arthur St. John)
   1903-1966 .. **CLC 1, 3, 8, 13, 19, 27, 44,**
   107; SSC 41; WLC
   See also BPFB 3; BRW 7; CA 85-88; 25-
   28R; CANR 22; CDBLB 1914-1945; DA;
   DA3; DAB; DAC; DAM MST, NOV,
   POP; DLB 15, 162, 195; EWL 3; MTCW
   1, 2; NFS 13, 17; RGEL 2; RGSF 2; TEA;
   WLIT 4

Waugh, Harriet 1944- .... **CLC 6**
   See also CA 85-88; CANR 22

Ways, C. R.
   See Blount, Roy (Alton), Jr.

Waystaff, Simon
   See Swift, Jonathan

Webb, Beatrice (Martha Potter)
   1858-1943 .... **TCLC 22**
   See also CA 117; 162; DLB 190; FW

Webb, Charles (Richard) 1939- .... **CLC 7**
   See also CA 25-28R; CANR 114

Webb, Frank J. .... **NCLC 143**
   See also DLB 50

Webb, James H(enry), Jr. 1946- ...... **CLC 22**
   See also CA 81-84

Webb, Mary Gladys (Meredith)
   1881-1927 .... **TCLC 24**
   See also CA 182; 123; DLB 34; FW

Webb, Mrs. Sidney
   See Webb, Beatrice (Martha Potter)

LATS 1:1; MAWW; MTCW 1, 2; NFS 5, 11, 15, 20; RGAL 4; RGSF 2; RHW; SSFS 6, 7; SUFW; TUS

Wharton, James
See Mencken, H(enry) L(ouis)

Wharton, William (a pseudonym) . CLC 18, 37
See also CA 93-96; DLBY 1980; INT CA-93-96

Wheatley (Peters), Phillis
1753(?)-1784 ... BLC 3; LC 3, 50; PC 3; WLC
See also AFAW 1, 2; CDALB 1640-1865; DA; DA3; DAC; DAM MST, MULT, POET; DLB 31, 50; EXPP; PFS 13; RGAL 4

Wheelock, John Hall 1886-1978 .... CLC 14
See also CA 13-16R; 77-80; CANR 14; DLB 45

Whim-Wham
See Curnow, (Thomas) Allen (Monro)

White, Babington
See Braddon, Mary Elizabeth

White, E(lwyn) B(rooks)
1899-1985 .... CLC 10, 34, 39
See also AITN 2; AMWS 1; CA 13-16R; 116; CANR 16, 37; CDALBS; CLR 1, 21; CPW; DA3; DAM POP; DLB 11, 22; EWL 3; FANT; MAICYA 1, 2; MTCW 1, 2; NCFS 5; RGAL 4; SATA 2, 29, 100; SATA-Obit 44; TUS

White, Edmund (Valentine III)
1940- .... CLC 27, 110
See also AAYA 7; CA 45-48; CANR 3, 19, 36, 62, 107, 133; CN 7; DA3; DAM POP; DLB 227; MTCW 1, 2

White, Hayden V. 1928- .... CLC 148
See also CA 128; DLB 246

White, Patrick (Victor Martindale)
1912-1990 ...... CLC 3, 4, 5, 7, 9, 18, 65, 69; SSC 39
See also BRWS 1; CA 81-84; 132; CANR 43; DLB 260; EWL 3; MTCW 1; RGEL 2; RGSF 2; RHW; TWA; WWE 1

White, Phyllis Dorothy James 1920-
See James, P. D.
See also CA 21-24R; CANR 17, 43, 65, 112; CMW 4; CN 7; CPW; DA3; DAM POP; MTCW 1, 2; TEA

White, T(erence) H(anbury)
1906-1964 .... CLC 30
See also AAYA 22; BPFB 3; BYA 4, 5; CA 73-76; CANR 37; DLB 160; FANT; JRDA; LAIT 1; MAICYA 1, 2; RGEL 2; SATA 12; SUFW 1; YAW

White, Terence de Vere 1912-1994 ... CLC 49
See also CA 49-52; 145; CANR 3

White, Walter
See White, Walter F(rancis)

White, Walter F(rancis) 1893-1955 ... BLC 3; HR 3; TCLC 15
See also BW 1; CA 115; 124; DAM MULT; DLB 51

White, William Hale 1831-1913
See Rutherford, Mark
See also CA 121; 189

Whitehead, Alfred North
1861-1947 .... TCLC 97
See also CA 117; 165; DLB 100, 262

Whitehead, E(dward) A(nthony)
1933- .... CLC 5
See also CA 65-68; CANR 58, 118; CBD; CD 5

Whitehead, Ted
See Whitehead, E(dward) A(nthony)

Whiteman, Roberta J. Hill 1947- ...... NNAL
See also CA 146

Whitemore, Hugh (John) 1936- .... CLC 37
See also CA 132; CANR 77; CBD; CD 5; INT CA-132

Whitman, Sarah Helen (Power)
1803-1878 .... NCLC 19
See also DLB 1, 243

Whitman, Walt(er) 1819-1892 .. NCLC 4, 31, 81; PC 3; WLC
See also AAYA 42; AMW; AMWR 1; CDALB 1640-1865; DA; DA3; DAB; DAC; DAM MST, POET; DLB 3, 64, 224, 250; EXPP; LAIT 2; LMFS 1; PAB; PFS 2, 3, 13; RGAL 4; SATA 20; TUS; WP; WYAS 1

Whitney, Phyllis A(yame) 1903- .... CLC 42
See also AAYA 36; AITN 2; BEST 90:3; CA 1-4R; CANR 3, 25, 38, 60; CLR 59; CMW 4; CPW; DA3; DAM POP; JRDA; MAICYA 1, 2; MTCW 2; RHW; SATA 1, 30; YAW

Whittemore, (Edward) Reed, Jr.
1919- .... CLC 4
See also CA 9-12R, 219; CAAE 219; CAAS 8; CANR 4, 119; CP 7; DLB 5

Whittier, John Greenleaf
1807-1892 .... NCLC 8, 59
See also AMWS 1; DLB 1, 243; RGAL 4

Whittlebot, Hernia
See Coward, Noel (Peirce)

Wicker, Thomas Grey 1926-
See Wicker, Tom
See also CA 65-68; CANR 21, 46

Wicker, Tom .... CLC 7
See Wicker, Thomas Grey

Wideman, John Edgar 1941- ... BLC 3; CLC 5, 34, 36, 67, 122; SSC 62
See also AFAW 1, 2; AMWS 10; BPFB 4; BW 2, 3; CA 85-88; CANR 14, 42, 67, 109; CN 7; DAM MULT; DLB 33, 143; MTCW 2; RGAL 4; RGSF 2; SSFS 6, 12

Wiebe, Rudy (Henry) 1934- .. CLC 6, 11, 14, 138
See also CA 37-40R; CANR 42, 67, 123; CN 7; DAC; DAM MST; DLB 60; RHW

Wieland, Christoph Martin
1733-1813 .... NCLC 17
See also DLB 97; EW 4; LMFS 1; RGWL 2, 3

Wiene, Robert 1881-1938 .... TCLC 56

Wieners, John 1934- .... CLC 7
See also BG 3; CA 13-16R; CP 7; DLB 16; WP

Wiesel, Elie(zer) 1928- .... CLC 3, 5, 11, 37, 165; WLCS
See also AAYA 7, 54; AITN 1; CA 5-8R; CAAS 4; CANR 8, 40, 65, 125; CDALBS; CWW 2; DA; DA3; DAB; DAC; DAM MST, NOV; DLB 83, 299; DLBY 1987; EWL 3; INT CANR-8; LAIT 4; MTCW 1, 2; NCFS 4; NFS 4; RGWL 3; SATA 56; YAW

Wiggins, Marianne 1947- .... CLC 57
See also BEST 89:3; CA 130; CANR 60

Wigglesworth, Michael 1631-1705 .... LC 106
See also DLB 24; RGAL 4

Wiggs, Susan .... CLC 70
See also CA 201

Wight, James Alfred 1916-1995
See Herriot, James
See also CA 77-80; SATA 55; SATA-Brief 44

Wilbur, Richard (Purdy) 1921- ..... CLC 3, 6, 9, 14, 53, 110; PC 51
See also AMWS 3; CA 1-4R; CABS 2; CANR 2, 29, 76, 93; CDALBS; CP 7; DA; DAB; DAC; DAM MST, POET; DLB 5, 169; EWL 3; EXPP; INT CANR-29; MTCW 1, 2; PAB; PFS 11, 12, 16; RGAL 4; SATA 9, 108; WP

Wild, Peter 1940- .... CLC 14
See also CA 37-40R; CP 7; DLB 5

Wilde, Oscar (Fingal O'Flahertie Wills)
1854(?)-1900 ..... DC 17; SSC 11; TCLC 1, 8, 23, 41; WLC
See also AAYA 49; BRW 5; BRWC 1, 2; BRWR 2; BYA 15; CA 104; 119; CANR 112; CDBLB 1890-1914; DA; DA3; DAB; DAC; DAM DRAM, MST, NOV; DFS 4, 8, 9; DLB 10, 19, 34, 57, 141, 156, 190; EXPS; FANT; LATS 1:1; NFS 20; RGEL 2; RGSF 2; SATA 24; SSFS 7; SUFW; TEA; WCH; WLIT 4

Wilder, Billy .... CLC 20
See Wilder, Samuel
See also DLB 26

Wilder, Samuel 1906-2002
See Wilder, Billy
See also CA 89-92; 205

Wilder, Stephen
See Marlowe, Stephen

Wilder, Thornton (Niven)
1897-1975 .. CLC 1, 5, 6, 10, 15, 35, 82; DC 1, 24; WLC
See also AAYA 29; AITN 2; AMW; CA 13-16R; 61-64; CAD; CANR 40, 132; CDALBS; DA; DA3; DAB; DAC; DAM DRAM, MST, NOV; DFS 1, 4, 16; DLB 4, 7, 9, 228; DLBY 1997; EWL 3; LAIT 3; MTCW 1, 2; RGAL 4; RHW; WYAS 1

Wilding, Michael 1942- ...... CLC 73; SSC 50
See also CA 104; CANR 24, 49, 106; CN 7; RGSF 2

Wiley, Richard 1944- .... CLC 44
See also CA 121; 129; CANR 71

Wilhelm, Kate .... CLC 7
See Wilhelm, Katie (Gertrude)
See also AAYA 20; BYA 16; CAAS 5; DLB 8; INT CANR-17; SCFW 2

Wilhelm, Katie (Gertrude) 1928-
See Wilhelm, Kate
See also CA 37-40R; CANR 17, 36, 60, 94; MTCW 1; SFW 4

Wilkins, Mary
See Freeman, Mary E(leanor) Wilkins

Willard, Nancy 1936- .... CLC 7, 37
See also BYA 5; CA 89-92; CANR 10, 39, 68, 107; CLR 5; CWP; CWRI 5; DLB 5, 52; FANT; MAICYA 1, 2; MTCW 1; SATA 37, 71, 127; SATA-Brief 30; SUFW 2

William of Malmesbury c. 1090B.C.-c. 1140B.C. .... CMLC 57

William of Ockham 1290-1349 ..... CMLC 32

Williams, Ben Ames 1889-1953 ..... TCLC 89
See also CA 183; DLB 102

Williams, C(harles) K(enneth)
1936- .... CLC 33, 56, 148
See also CA 37-40R; CAAS 26; CANR 57, 106; CP 7; DAM POET; DLB 5

Williams, Charles
See Collier, James Lincoln

Williams, Charles (Walter Stansby)
1886-1945 .... TCLC 1, 11
See also BRWS 9; CA 104; 163; DLB 100, 153, 255; FANT; RGEL 2; SUFW 1

Williams, Ella Gwendolen Rees
See Rhys, Jean

Williams, (George) Emlyn
1905-1987 .... CLC 15
See also CA 104; 123; CANR 36; DAM DRAM; DLB 10, 77; IDTP; MTCW 1

Williams, Hank 1923-1953 .... TCLC 81
See Williams, Hiram King

Williams, Helen Maria
1761-1827 .... NCLC 135
See also DLB 158

Williams, Hiram Hank
See Williams, Hank

Literary Criticism Series
Cumulative Topic Index

This index lists all topic entries in Gale's *Classical and Medieval Literature Criticism* (CMLC), *Contemporary Literary Criticism* (CLC), *Drama Criticism* (DC), *Literature Criticism from 1400 to 1800* (LC), *Nineteenth-Century Literature Criticism* (NCLC), *Short Story Criticism* (SSC), and *Twentieth-Century Literary Criticism* (TCLC). The index also lists topic entries in the Gale Critical Companion Collection, which includes the following publications: *The Beat Generation* (BG), and *Harlem Renaissance* (HR).

Topic Index

Topic Index

NCLC Cumulative Nationality Index

Schopenhauer, Arthur **51**
Schumann, Robert **143**
Storm, (Hans) Theodor (Woldsen) **1**
Tieck, (Johann) Ludwig **5, 46**
Varnhagen, Rahel **130**
Wagner, Richard **9, 119**
Wieland, Christoph Martin **17**

GREEK

Foscolo, Ugo **8, 97**
Solomos, Dionysios **15**

HUNGARIAN

Arany, Janos **34**
Madach, Imre **19**
Petofi, Sándor **21**

INDIAN

Chatterji, Bankim Chandra **19**
Dutt, Michael Madhusudan **118**
Dutt, Toru **29**

IRISH

Allingham, William **25**
Banim, John **13**
Banim, Michael **13**
Boucicault, Dion **41**
Carleton, William **3**
Croker, John Wilson **10**
Darley, George **2**
Edgeworth, Maria **1, 51**
Ferguson, Samuel **33**
Griffin, Gerald **7**
Jameson, Anna **43**
Le Fanu, Joseph Sheridan **9, 58**
Lever, Charles (James) **23**
Maginn, William **8**
Mangan, James Clarence **27**
Maturin, Charles Robert **6**
Merriman, Brian **70**
Moore, Thomas **6, 110**
Morgan, Lady **29**
O'Brien, Fitz-James **21**
Sheridan, Richard Brinsley **5, 91**

ITALIAN

Alfieri, Vittorio **101**
Collodi, Carlo **54**
Foscolo, Ugo **8, 97**
Gozzi, (Conte) Carlo **23**
Leopardi, Giacomo **22, 129**
Manzoni, Alessandro **29, 98**
Mazzini, Guiseppe **34**
Nievo, Ippolito **22**

JAPANESE

Akinari, Ueda **131**
Ichiyō, Higuchi **49**
Motoori, Norinaga **45**

LITHUANIAN

Mapu, Abraham (ben Jekutiel) **18**

MEXICAN

Lizardi, Jose Joaquin Fernandez de **30**
Najera, Manuel Gutierrez **133**

NORWEGIAN

Collett, (Jacobine) Camilla (Wergeland) **22**
Wergeland, Henrik Arnold **5**

POLISH

Fredro, Aleksander **8**
Krasicki, Ignacy **8**
Krasiński, Zygmunt **4**
Mickiewicz, Adam **3, 101**
Norwid, Cyprian Kamil **17**
Slowacki, Juliusz **15**

ROMANIAN

Eminescu, Mihail **33, 131**

RUSSIAN

Aksakov, Sergei Timofeyvich **2**
Bakunin, Mikhail (Alexandrovich) **25, 58**
Baratynsky, Evgenii Abramovich **103**
Bashkirtseff, Marie **27**
Belinski, Vissarion Grigoryevich **5**
Bestuzhev, Aleksandr Aleksandrovich **131**
Chernyshevsky, Nikolay Gavrilovich **1**
Dobrolyubov, Nikolai Alexandrovich **5**
Dostoevsky, Fedor Mikhailovich **2, 7, 21, 33, 43, 119**
Gogol, Nikolai (Vasilyevich) **5, 15, 31**
Goncharov, Ivan Alexandrovich **1, 63**
Granovsky, Timofei Nikolaevich **75**
Griboedov, Aleksandr Sergeevich **129**
Herzen, Aleksandr Ivanovich **10, 61**
Karamzin, Nikolai Mikhailovich **3**
Krylov, Ivan Andreevich **1**
Lermontov, Mikhail Yuryevich **5, 47, 126**
Leskov, Nikolai (Semyonovich) **25**
Nekrasov, Nikolai Alekseevich **11**
Ostrovsky, Alexander **30, 57**
Pavlova, Karolina Karlovna **138**
Pisarev, Dmitry Ivanovich **25**
Pushkin, Alexander (Sergeyevich) **3, 27, 83**
Saltykov, Mikhail Evgrafovich **16**
Smolenskin, Peretz **30**
Turgenev, Ivan **21, 37, 122**
Tyutchev, Fyodor **34**
Zhukovsky, Vasily (Andreevich) **35**

SCOTTISH

Baillie, Joanna **2**
Beattie, James **25**
Blair, Hugh **75**
Campbell, Thomas **19**
Carlyle, Thomas **22, 70**
Ferrier, Susan (Edmonstone) **8**
Galt, John **1, 110**
Hogg, James **4, 109**
Jeffrey, Francis **33**
Lockhart, John Gibson **6**
Mackenzie, Henry **41**
Miller, Hugh **143**
Oliphant, Margaret (Oliphant Wilson) **11, 61**
Scott, Walter **15, 69, 110**
Stevenson, Robert Louis (Balfour) **5, 14, 63**
Thomson, James **18**
Wilson, John **5**
Wright, Frances **74**

SERBIAN

Karadžić, Vuk Stefanović **115**

SLOVENIAN

Kopitar, Jernej **117**
Prešeren, Francè **127**

SPANISH

Alarcon, Pedro Antonio de **1**
Bécquer, Gustavo Adolfo **106**
Caballero, Fernan **10**
Castro, Rosalia de **3, 78**
Espronceda, Jose de **39**
Larra (y Sanchez de Castro), Mariano Jose de **17, 130**
Martínez de la Rosa, Francisco de Paula **102**
Tamayo y Baus, Manuel **1**
Zorrilla y Moral, Jose **6**

SWEDISH

Almqvist, Carl Jonas Love **42**
Bremer, Fredrika **11**
Stagnelius, Eric Johan **61**
Tegner, Esaias **2**

SWISS

Amiel, Henri Frederic **4**
Burckhardt, Jacob (Christoph) **49**
Charriere, Isabelle de **66**
Gotthelf, Jeremias **117**
Keller, Gottfried **2**
Lavater, Johann Kaspar **142**
Meyer, Conrad Ferdinand **81**
Wyss, Johann David Von **10**

UKRAINIAN

Shevchenko, Taras **54**

VENEZUELAN

Bello, Andrés **131**

NCLC-145 Title Index